OXFORD COMMENTARIES ON INTERNATIONAL LAW

General Editors: *Professor Philip Alston*, Professor of International Law at New York University, and *Vaughan Lowe QC*, Essex Court Chambers, London and Emeritus Fellow of All Souls College, Oxford.

The International Convention on the Elimination of All Forms of Racial Discrimination

The International Convention on the Elimination of All Forms of Racial Discrimination

A Commentary

PATRICK THORNBERRY

OXFORD
UNIVERSITY PRESS

OXFORD
UNIVERSITY PRESS

Great Clarendon Street, Oxford, OX2 6DP,
United Kingdom

Oxford University Press is a department of the University of Oxford.
It furthers the University's objective of excellence in research, scholarship,
and education by publishing worldwide. Oxford is a registered trade mark of
Oxford University Press in the UK and in certain other countries

First published 2016
First published in paperback 2018

Published in the United States of America by Oxford University Press
198 Madison Avenue, New York, NY 10016, United States of America

British Library Cataloguing in Publication Data
Data available

Library of Congress Cataloging in Publication Data
Data available

ISBN 978–0–19–926533–6 (Hbk.)
ISBN 978–0–19–882740–5 (Pbk.)

To Angela, for all her patience and understanding,
and to our daughters Francesca and Camilla

Acknowledgements

The author is grateful for the support and encouragement of family, friends, and colleagues in the preparation of this book over a number of years. In particular, the inspiration derived from working in the Committee on the Elimination of Racial Discrimination (CERD) from 2001–14 was crucial to completing the project, as well as the comments on issues and drafts from, in particular, CERD members Alexey Avtonomov, Francisco Calí Tzay, Anastasia Crickley, Régis de Gouttes, Ion Diaconu, Chris Maina Peter, Linos-Alexander Sicilianos, and Carlos Vázquez. At all times, the Committee has been assisted by an able Secretariat, including CERD Secretaries Mac Darrow, Nathalie Prouvez, Torsten Schackel, and Gabriella Habtom, to all of whom thanks is warmly extended. The author has also profited greatly from 'formal' or casual discussions with friends and colleagues, notably Margaret Bedggood, Mylène Bidault, Nazila Ghanea, David Keane, Monica Mookherjee, Andrew Shacknove, Francesca Thornberry, Annapurna Waughray, Alexandra Xanthaki, and others too numerous to mention but always appreciated. Discussions with students at Keele University and on the Oxford MSt in International Human Rights Law have been of tremendous assistance in developing ideas and clarifying concepts. The kind gift of the set of papers on the Convention from Michael Banton, former member and Chair of CERD, was indispensable to the completion of the work. The author also wishes to thank the editors at Oxford University Press for their generous encouragement and patience, especially John Louth, Merel Alstein, and, latterly, Emma Endean and Clare Jones.

Contents

Table of Cases

INTERNATIONAL

African Commission on Human and Peoples' Rights

Committee on the Elimination of Racial Discrimination (CERD)

Committee against Torture

European Commission on Human Rights

European Committee on Social Rights

European Court of Human Rights

European Court of Justice

ICCPR Human Rights Committee

Inter-American Commission on Human Rights

Inter-American Court of Human Rights

International Court of Justice

International Criminal Tribunal for Rwanda

Permanent Court of International Justice

NATIONAL

Australia

Botswana

Canada

India

Japan

South Africa

United Kingdom

United States

Table of Legislation

INTERNATIONAL INSTRUMENTS

NATIONAL LEGISLATION

Australia

Bosnia

Botswana

Cyprus

Denmark

France

Germany

Guyana

India

Ireland

List of Abbreviations

ACHR	American Convention on Human Rights
ACHPR	African Charter on Human and Peoples' Rights
BIOT	British Indian Ocean Territory
CAT	Convention against Torture
CEDAW	Convention on the Elimination of Discrimination against Women
CERD	Committee on the Elimination of Racial Discrimination
CESCR	Committee on Economic, Social and Cultural Rights
CMW	International Convention on the Protection of the Rights of All Migrant Workers and their Families
CPED	International Convention for the Protection of All Persons from Enforced Disappearance
CRPD	Convention on the Rights of Persons with Disabilities
CRC	Convention on the Rights of the Child
DRC	Democratic Republic of the Congo
DRC	Documentation and Research Centre
ECHR	European Convention on Human Rights
ECRI	European Commission against Racism and Intolerance
EMRIP	Expert Mechanism on the Rights of Indigenous Peoples
EW	early warning
FCNM	Framework Convention for the Protection of National Minorities
FGM	female genital mutilation
FPIC	free, prior and informed consent
GC	General comment
GR	General recommendation
ICC	International Criminal Court
ICCPR	International Covenant on Civil and Political Rights
ICERD	International Convention on the Elimination of All Forms of Racial Discrimination
ICESCR	International Covenant on Economic, Social and Cultural Rights
ICJ	International Court of Justice
IDP	Internally displaced persons
ILC	International Law Commission
ILO	International Labour Organization
KCAB	Korean Commercial Arbitration Board
LOIPR	List of issues prior to reporting procedure
NGO	Non-governmental organization
NHRCK	National Human Rights Commission of Korea
NHRI	National human rights institution
NTAA	Native Title Amendment Act
NTA	Native Title Act
OHCHR	Office of the United Nations High Commissioner for Human Rights
OPCAT	Optional Protocol to the Convention against Torture

OSCE	Organization for Security and Co-operation in Europe
POA	Programme of Action
RDA	Racial Discrimination Act
UA	Urgent action
UDHR	Universal Declaration of Human Rights
UN	United Nations
UNDM	United Nations Declaration on Minorities
UNDRIP	UN Declaration on the Rights of Indigenous Peoples
UNESCO	United Nations Educational, Scientific and Cultural Organization
UNHCR	United Nations High Commissioner for Refugees
UPR	Universal periodic review
VCLT	Vienna Convention on the Law of Treaties

1. Introduction

The adoption by the General Assembly of the United Nations of the International Convention on the Elimination of All Forms of Racial Discrimination (the Convention/ICERD) on 21 December 1965 represented a signal moment in international law and relations.[1] Building on a Declaration of two years earlier,[2] the Convention expanded upon key statements of principle in the Charter of the United Nations and the Universal Declaration of Human Rights (UDHR). The text, elaborated through a succession of UN bodies, consists of a title, preamble, and twenty-five articles, most of which are devoted to procedural and technical matters, and includes the articles that set up and elaborate the mandate of the Committee on the Elimination of Discrimination (CERD). The seven articles devoted to substantive aspects of racial discrimination commence with a definition of racial discrimination. The Convention, annexed to resolution 2106 A (XX) of the General Assembly, was adopted by 106 votes to none, with one abstention, later changed to an affirmative vote.[3] It was not a particularly difficult birth, nor was the gestation prolonged: its emergence from drafting into the light of day was swift by UN standards, propelled forwards by an extraordinary political momentum.

The Convention did not emerge *ex nihilo* but carried with it a weight of political, ideological, and institutional baggage. In the General Assembly, reaction to its adoption varied in tone and substance. In the adoption speeches, the summaries of the content and significance of the Convention reflected different sets of preoccupations: 'all parties were agreed that racial discrimination was an evil, but their ideas about the nature of that evil derived from different experiences and beliefs'.[4] For many delegates, colonialism was the great racial evil, and apartheid its twin. The stentorian language of Morozov, the representative of the USSR, made the point in unambiguous terms: 'Racism and racial discrimination are such shameful and odious products of imperialism and colonialism that all peoples and all decent human beings are resolutely demanding that they be ended.'[5] The association between racial discrimination and colonial systems was stressed by the General Assembly through a resolution adopted alongside the Convention,[6] which recalled the Colonial Declaration and the UN Special Committee on Decolonization,[7]

[1] Entered into force 4 January 1969.

[2] Declaration on the Elimination of All Forms of Racial Discrimination, adopted by the UN General Assembly on 20 November 1963 by resolution 1904 (XVIII).

[3] 21 December 1965, GAOR, twentieth session, 1406th plenary meeting, A/PV.1406, para. 60. Mexico abstained but changed its stance shortly afterwards to support for the Convention: GAOR, twentieth session, 1408th plenary meeting, A/PV.1408, para. 2.

[4] M. Banton, *International Action against Racial Discrimination* (Clarendon Press, 1996), p. 70.

[5] A/PV.1406, para. 113. He added that to the people of the Soviet Union, 'all questions connected with the elimination of racism and other forms of discrimination are a thing of the past—they are history' (*ibid.*, para.121).

[6] Resolution 2106 B (XX).

[7] The Declaration on the Granting of Independence to Colonial Countries and Peoples, contained in General Assembly resolution 1514 (XV), 14 December 1960 (the Colonial Declaration); The Special Committee on the Situation with regard to the Implementation of the Declaration on the Granting of Independence to Colonial Countries and Peoples, established by GA resolution 1654 (XVI), 27 November 1961 (the Special Committee on Decolonization, or the Committee of 24).

and recognized that close cooperation between the Special Committee and the Committee on the Elimination of Racial Discrimination (CERD) would facilitate the achievement of the aims of the Convention and the Colonial Declaration.[8]

Many Western or Western-aligned States, including colonial powers, preferred to dwell on forms of discrimination such as anti-Semitism and the shattering of world peace resulting from Nazi ideology. States within and without the colonial/anti-colonial polarity looked towards the UN Charter and the UDHR as signposts to a transcendent order of human rights that would supplant and eliminate racial discrimination. The representative of Italy (Bosco), judged the Convention 'a landmark' in the history of the United Nations and took a long view: the Convention was

> first and foremost a solemn affirmation of the will of the peoples...to do away once and for all with abominable doctrines and practices which for too many centuries, and until the present day, have been the cause of suffering and...distress. No one can fail to remember the millions of victims that racial hatred and anti-Semitism have made in our generation. No one can fail to be conscience-stricken and revolted by the policy of racial segregation...still rife today...The Universal Declaration of Human Rights has pointed the way for us.[9]

The representative of the United States (Willis) supported the Convention as a whole because of its 'constructive humanitarian objectives', being more than a 'lofty statement of ideals'.[10] Ospina of Colombia declared the Convention 'a resounding victory'.[11] Such sentiments were not inconsistent with the views of many delegates that racial discrimination was not practised 'at home' or was not a concept applicable to 'their' minorities or indigenous peoples, if any such were recognized.

Enormous geopolitical, legal, and social changes have occurred since that momentous day in 1965 when ICERD was formally adopted. The international human rights landscape was thinly populated and primarily 'universalist' in character. The principal general instruments contextualizing Convention practice included the UDHR, the Genocide Convention,[12] ILO Convention 111,[13] the UNESCO Convention against Discrimination in Education,[14] and the Declaration against Racial Discrimination; and at the regional level the European Convention on Human Rights and Fundamental Freedoms (ECHR),[15] and the American Declaration on the Rights and Duties of Man.[16] The Covenants and other 'core' UN human rights conventions had still to be adopted and further regional conventions were some distance away. Some normative 'differentiation' had developed in areas that would engage CERD over its lifespan: on the Political Rights

[8] Sixth preambular paragraph.

[9] A/PV.1406, paras. 109–10.

[10] *Ibid.*, para. 98.

[11] *Ibid.*, para. 78. This assessment went together with a critical judgement (*ibid.*, paras. 67–73) on the inclusion of 'dissemination of ideas based on racial superiority' in Article 4(a), a critique related to a rejected proposal by Argentina, Colombia, Ecuador, Panama, and Peru (A/L.480) to delete the dissemination offence.

[12] Convention on the Prevention and Punishment of the Crime of Genocide 1948.

[13] ILO Convention No 111 concerning Discrimination in Respect of Employment 1958.

[14] UNESCO Convention against Discrimination in Education 1960.

[15] European Convention for the Protection of Human Rights and Fundamental Freedoms 1950.

[16] Adopted by the Ninth International Conference of American States, Bogotá, 1948.

of Women,[17] refugees and stateless persons,[18] and slavery.[19] With regard to indigenous peoples, ILO Convention 107 on Indigenous and Tribal Populations stood as an imperfect representation of the rights of communities whose destiny was therein treated as uncertain,[20] while ethnic minority rights, omitted in name from the UN Charter and the UDHR, and from ICERD, were feared by many to threaten the national unity of post-colonial States. The spirit of the age favoured nation-building after the colonial trauma. As is evident from many speeches during the drafting of the Convention and following its adoption, its range of application was widely assumed to be the remaining colonial territories and South Africa; the equality of nations, national unity, and freedom from racial discrimination, were understood as mutually constitutive. The Convention is phrased in universalist language that does not single out threatened groups by name; it is also 'individualist' after the fashion of the UDHR, though 'group' nuances stemming from the subject-matter—race and ethnicity—make it a less than perfect simulacrum of individual rights.

Since 1965, 'universal' human rights have been further elaborated, applying to all regions and continents, while 'differentiated' rights of categories of persons and groups have also proliferated, spurred on by the intellectual fervour and activism of feminism and cognate movements in civil society, and by the persistent activism of self-defining groups such as indigenous peoples. The individual rights framework has been sustained, enriched, and challenged by the growth of collective rights, and projects of integration distinguished from projects of assimilation. Self-determination, a building block of the Convention, continues and flourishes in diverse forms. 'Official' apartheid has been dismantled. The mighty Western colonial systems have been reduced to almost nothing, though international hierarchies have not disappeared and assert themselves in changed geopolitical environments. People in movement represent an astonishing global phenomenon that contributes to new conformations of cultural and ethnic diversity. Corporations and other private actors condition the lives of a mass of human beings as governments retreat from formal discrimination, which increasingly assumes a 'private' face. The changes furnish contexts for the continuing work of the Committee on the Elimination of Racial Discrimination which, in common with sister human rights bodies, strives to implement the Convention as a meaningful contribution to the common good in conditions of rapid change in the understanding and reach of increasingly 'culturalized' and diversified human rights.[21]

While the drafters of the Convention may have envisaged straightforward applications of the non-discrimination norm, simplicity, as Makkonen has ruefully remarked,[22] is not

[17] Convention on the Political Rights of Women 1953.

[18] Convention relating to the Status of Refugees 1951; Convention relating to the Status of Stateless persons 1954; Convention on the Reduction of Statelessness 1961.

[19] Slavery Convention 1926; Supplementary Convention on the Abolition of Slavery, the Slave trade, and Institutions and practices Similar to Slavery 1957.

[20] Convention on the Protection and Integration of Indigenous and Tribal Populations 1957; the Convention dealt with 'populations' that were 'not yet integrated into the national community' rather than self-determining 'peoples'.

[21] F. Lenzerini, *The Culturalization of Human Rights Law* (Oxford University Press, 2014).

[22] T. Makkonen, *Equal in Fact, Unequal in Law: Racial and Ethnic Discrimination and the Legal Response Thereto in Europe* (Martinus Nijhoff, 2012), p.258: 'even the experts in this field are exhausted by the insurmountable amount of relevant materials'. Further, with regard to CERD's general recommendations, he observes, p. 257, that 'these documents tend to be couched in technical and open language, which means that

the hallmark of current practice. The passing of time since the 1960s has highlighted a range of questions that had not presented themselves, were not clearly perceived, or were dormant at the time of ICERD's drafting: hence the mantra that the Convention should be read as a 'living instrument'. The present work endeavours to trace a path through the thickets of interpretative practice, focusing largely on a critical evaluation of the work of CERD. Sections on the drafting of the Convention are presented systematically to illuminate concepts that surface in the text and, only secondarily, to counterpoint suggested interpretations, bearing in mind that the practical utilization of the *travaux préparatoires* has diminished over time. The illustrative materials scattered throughout the chapters purport to be significant and informative though certainly not exhaustive. Unreferenced observations of the author made on the basis of thirteen years as a member of CERD are made only rarely, lest they stamp the product as little more than 'a private masterpiece of doctored recollections'.[23] At the end of the journey through the Convention, it may be possible to decide whether the Convention is a 'landmark', a 'resounding victory', a 'lofty statement of ideals', or all of these or none, and whether it is 'fit for purpose' now and for the future.

these interpretative texts themselves need interpretation'; on this last point, see K. Popper, *The Open Society and its Enemies*, vol. 2 (5th edn, London: Routledge, 1966), pp. 10, 11, 16, 21.

[23] Thomas Kinsella, *Baggot Street Deserta* (Dolmen Press, 1958).

2. The Convention

Genesis and Background

While the definition of racial discrimination in the Convention reaches beyond 'race' to include discrimination on the grounds of colour, descent, and national or ethnic origin, the ideology of 'race' represented the major point of departure for the drafters of the Convention and warrants explanation, even if the intellectual force of, especially, its 'scientific' variant has dissipated in light of a century of critical theory. While anti-colonial sentiment does not infuse every element of a text that includes such a broad definition, it has left a significant mark on the Convention from the title and preamble onwards and buttressed the political will to lock the instrument into position. At the adoption of the Convention, Verret, the representative of Haiti, offered a rough-edged account of racial theorising and its brutalizing effects that included but reached beyond the colonial paradigm:

> Now, heaven be praised, we have produced a document of which the least that can be said is that it is reasonably reassuring. We applaud it, and . . . join in the chorus of authoritative voices of the nations assembled . . . to intone in all solemnity the hymn of reconciliation among the races which fantastic theories tend to divide, vaunting the supremacy of some peoples over others regarded as inferior and hence despised and held in servitude, if not indeed destined for utter annihilation. That was the judgement of Gobineau and his disciples and his theory of the inequality of human races . . . and a whole series of sorcerers' apprentices who came after them . . . we share the distaste felt by the majority of the peoples of the world for all forms of racial discrimination, no matter by what means they are called: anti-semitism, colonialism, nazism apartheid and all such. They are all of them as degrading as the minds that conceived them.[1]

Following Verret's perspective, the present chapter commences with a brief resumé of racial theory in its interface with colonialism, while recognizing that in international law and relations, theory was complemented by assertions of difference and hierarchy that rested on analogous but not identical grounds. The discrediting of racial theory through conceptual revision and legal standards is also discussed, even as those standards continue to 'recycle' the vocabulary of race in their efforts to confront it. The final section of the chapter reviews the landmark normative and institutional developments that led to the Convention. Subsequent chapters address the fate of racial theory in the text of the Convention and current arguments on the virtues or otherwise of including 'race' as a component of the legal regulation of discrimination.

A. Race: Sorcerers and Apprentices

Analytical accounts of race have tended to focus on extremes of racial theory in the nineteenth and twentieth centuries while noting that distinctions among peoples on the basis of observable differences were recognized in all known periods of civilization.

[1] A/PV.1406, paras. 79–87.

Commenting on ancient societies, Boxill and others reflect on Plato's speculation that some people are constructed of intrinsically inferior material, and Aristotle's theory of essences and natural kinds, and slaves by nature, theories that, while they did not lead to the invention of race, suggest that the sources of the idea 'may be deeper and less tractable than the contemporary consensus seems to suppose'.[2] Racial theory represents only one among many metaphors accounting for differences among human beings, and represents, according to Banton, a European idiom of defining otherness.[3] Much of the initial vocabulary links to Iberian languages[4] even if, as Sweet argues, a fully developed ideology of race was not articulated in fifteenth-century Iberia.[5] The widening of European horizons consequent upon the 'discovery' of the Americas had generated puzzlement and degrees of taxonomic fervour among academicians with regard to peoples unaccounted for by the Bible. *Inter alia*, the Biblical monogenist line,[6] important to religious belief, was challenged by the striking, unexpected evidence of human diversity.[7] Lawyer-theologians elaborated principles from a base of mediaeval scholasticism, Christocentric presumptions, natural law, and Papal authority,[8] and applied them to the relations between the Spaniards and the 'Indians'. Their arguments implicated the viability of collectives of peoples and nations, and the status and worth of individual human beings. The assessments of the European presence and behaviour in the Americas were intimately connected to their opinions about the 'quality' of the peoples under European domination. The Spanish discourses, evincing heady combinations of religious and political speech, nonetheless suggest themselves as *in pari materia* with the later racial and cognate classifications of humanity[9] and produced similar disempowering effects.

In the development of discourse over succeeding centuries to encompass a recognizably racial framework, there are many claimants to membership to Verret's illustrious company of sorcerers' apprentices.[10] The division by Blumenbach (1752–1840) of the human race

[2] B. Boxill, 'Introduction', in B. Boxill (ed.), *Race and Racism* (Oxford University Press, 2001), pp. 14–15 [henceforth *Race and Racism*].

[3] M. Banton, *International Action against Racial Discrimination* (Clarendon Press, 1996), pp. 76–82 [henceforth *International Action*].

[4] The great key words 'Mestizo, Mulatto, Negro, Indian and Caste originated in the Iberian peninsula, and from there they spread abroad, in common probably with the word "race" itself': L. Poliakov, *The Aryan Myth: A History of Racist and Nationalist Ideas in Europe*, cited in D. Keane, *Caste-Based Discrimination in International Human Rights Law* (Ashgate, 2007), p. 72 [henceforth *Caste-Based Discrimination*].

[5] J. Sweet, 'The Iberian Roots of American Racist Thought', *William and Mary Quarterly* 54/1 (1977), 143–66; with reference to the development of slavery in particular, Sweet, *ibid.*, 166, argues that Iberian racism was 'a necessary pre-condition' for this development.

[6] In Genesis, descent from a single pair; Adam and Eve. The later story of the flood led to racialization of the story of the children of Noah and the curse on the children of Ham: D. Keane, *Caste-Based Discrimination*, pp. 75–7.

[7] M. Banton, *Racial Theories* (Cambridge University Press, 1987), p. 7 [henceforth *Racial Theories*], recalls that Montaigne (1533–92) used the New World discoveries to pose questions on what were the real virtues of European life, finding no hierarchical distinctions of civilization and barbarity between Europeans and the Brazilians.

[8] Notably the 'Bulls of Donation' delivered by Pope Alexander VI in 1493 granting overseas territory to Spain and Portugal, leading to the demarcation in the Treaty of Tordesillas of 1494; the Bull *Inter Caetera* of 4 May 1493 expressed the Pope's desire that the 'barbarous nations' be subjugated and brought to the Christian religion: text at <http://www.nativeweb.org/pages/legal/indig-inter-caetera.html>. For recent reflection, see concluding observations on the Holy See, CERD/C/VAT/CO/16-23, paras 16–17.

[9] J. Comas, *Racial Myths* (UNESCO, 1951), p. 7.

[10] Keane, *Caste-Based Discrimination*, Chapter 2, lists many of them.

into five varieties—the Caucasian, the Mongolian, the Malayan, the Ethiopian, and the American—initiated a classificatory scheme that endured over time. Blumenbach held to the 'degenerative thesis' whereby the original pair of Adam and Eve were Caucasian, and differences among peoples came through environmental factors; he did not, however, believe that Africans were inferior to other human beings.[11] Banton highlights the importance of Cuvier (1769–1832) who, although believing in one human species, blurred distinctions between species and varieties (of the same species) through the employment of 'type'. This represented an important intellectual move in hardening group differentiation: 'types' endured over time and could 'outlive... language, history, religion, customs and recollections'.[12] Linked to his taxonomically flexible theory of human differentiation, Cuvier discerned an intellectual and cultural hierarchy that placed white people at the top and black people at the bottom.

Of Gobineau, a star performer among the 'sorcerers', the reference is to Comte Arthur de Gobineau, 'aristocrat, litterateur, and diplomat',[13] whose *Essai sur L'Inégalité des Races Humaines*, appeared in 1853.[14] Gobineau (1816–82) promoted the idea that human characteristics were determined by race and further developed the notion of permanent racial types: the black, the yellow, and the white, concluding that the black and yellow races were not progenitors of civilizations and that superior attributes were associated with Europeans. He elaborated the theory of the Aryan race, a term originally synonymous with linguistic Indo-European but which became in Gobineau's terms '*la race germanique*', the race that represented everything positive.[15] Gobineau was unsure about the common origin of the races but felt constrained by science and the Bible to stifle his doubts; in any case, regardless of common or multiple origins, human beings were split into distinctive component parts, and racial mixing broke natural barriers and produced degeneration.[16]

Robust advocacy of polygenism—the theory that human beings have multiple origins—is associated with Agassiz (1807–73), who believed that there was one human species but that races were the result of separate creations, and that the Adam and Eve narrative referred essentially to the 'White' race. The natural provinces of the animal world revealed analogous 'special provinces' of the races of men—races with different attributes—while he argued that polygenism did not undermine the spiritual commonality

[11] J.F. Blumenbach, *De Generis Humani Varietate Nativa* (Vandenhoek and Ruprecht, 1795). Demel argues that 'degeneration' in Blumenbach's work referred to environmental adaptation rather than 'degradation': R. Kowner and W. Demel (eds), *Race and Racism in Modern East Asia: Western and Eastern Constructions* (Brill, 2012), p. 68.

[12] Banton, *Racial Theories*, p. 41, citing J.C. Nott and G.R. Gliddon, *Types of Mankind, or Ethnological Researches* (1854); Banton, *ibid.*, p. 43, comments that race, 'used in the sense of a pure or permanent type underlying the diversities of modern populations... is still significant'.

[13] T. J. Le Melle, 'Race in International Relations', *International Studies Perspectives* 10/1 (2009), 77–83, at 79.

[14] Tome Premier, Paris, Librairie de Firmin Didot Frères, 1853, dedicated to George V, King of Hanover and Duke of Cumberland. The author is listed as Premier Secretaire de la Légation de France en Suisse, and Membre de la Société Asiatique de Paris.

[15] 'The Aryas, he contended, were no longer pure, but some of their miscegenated descendants still carried enough Aryan blood to claim the right to rule. These descendants were the aristocrats of the white nations... social superiority was to be determined in terms of whiteness': Le Melle, 'Race in International Relations', 79.

[16] Keane, *Caste-Based Discrimination*, pp. 92–5.

of all people.[17] Darwin on the other hand, in *The Descent of Man*,[18] argued against the 'scientific racism' and polygenism of Agassiz, asserting the common ancestry of human beings and that racial differences were superficial and without survival value. Further, the Darwinian vision of evolutionary change did not sit well with static notions of races that endured over time, though that did not prevent Spencer and others from pressing the evolution metaphor into service.

On the basis of the works of Gobineau and many others, 'scientific race theory' took race as the key to understanding variation amongst human beings, with the races manifested by distinct physical characteristics and cultural attributes[19] and arranged in a hierarchy of value and ability. The races were permanent and enduring and were the key to understanding intergroup relations. In the course of the development of theory, racial character was imperfectly distinguished from national character when the latter was subject to expression through racial as well as cultural metaphors; character that was 'predicated upon an intuitive sense of consanguinity'.[20] National character so defined contributed to the racialization of international relations.[21]

An account of subsequent race theory would thread a (convoluted) passage through 'Social Darwinism',[22] which, inspired in part by Herbert Spencer's (1820–1903) use of 'the survival of the fittest',[23] sought to apply a variant of evolutionary theory to competition among racial groups. Perry and colleagues comment that '[t]he loose application of Darwin's biological concepts to the social world, where they did not apply . . . buttressed imperialism, racism, nationalism and militarism . . . Social Darwinists insisted that nations and races were engaged in a struggle for survival in which only the fittest survive and deserve to survive . . . war was nature's way of eliminating the unfit.'[24] The element of unfitness attached in varying degrees to the non-white races and also to those suffering from mental disabilities or physical infirmity.

[17] <http://en.wikipedia.org/wiki/Louis_Agassiz>; E. Lurie, 'Louis Agassiz and the Races of Man', *Isis* 45/3 (1954), 227–42.

[18] Charles Darwin, *The Descent of Man, and Selection in Relation to Sex* (Princeton University Press, 1871, reprinted 1981), Chapter 7 'On the Races of Man', pp. 214–50.

[19] For a concise account see L. Outlaw, 'Towards a Critical Theory of Race', in Boxill, *Race and Racism*, pp. 58–82.

[20] W. Connor, 'A Nation is a Nation, is a State, is an Ethnic Group . . . ', in J. Hutchinson and A.D. Smith (eds.), *Nationalism* (Oxford University Press, 1994), pp. 36–46, p. 37; Connor adds that the 'word *nation* comes from the Latin and . . . clearly conveyed the idea of common blood ties. It was derived from the past participle of the verb *nasci*, meaning to be born . . . hence the Latin noun, *nationem*, connoting *breed* or *race*' (*ibid.*, p. 38).

[21] In proceedings before the Third Committee of the UN General Assembly in the drafting of the Convention, the representative of Mauritania observed: 'Not content with proclaiming the superiority of white men and condemning the mixing of blood, racists had even gone so far as to establish a hierarchy even within the white race. The Nazis and Fascists had invented Aryanism, which gave rise to such secondary forms as Teutonism, Anglo-Saxonism and Celtism. All such racist ideologies, however, must eventually meet the same fate': A/C.3/SR.1165, para. 23.

[22] G. Claeys, '"The Survival of the Fittest" and the Origins of Social Darwinism', *Journal of the History of Ideas* 61/2 (2000), 223–40.

[23] The association between Darwin and 'Social Darwinism' is tenuous, not least because Spencer published his evolutionary ideas about society before Darwin published his theory: Spencer's *Progress: Its Laws and Causes* was published by the Westminster Review in April 1857; C. Darwin, *On the Origin of Species* (John Murray, 1859).

[24] M. Perry, M. Chase, J. Jacob, M. Jacob, and T. Von Laue, *Western Civilization: Ideas, Politics, and Society*, vol. 2 (10th edn, Wadsworth Cengage, 2013), pp. 569–70.

Francis Galton's eugenics—those 'targeted interventions in the evolution of mankind' and for its betterment[25]—also came to fix on race and racial hygiene.[26] In 1905, the German physician Alfred Ploetz founded the Society for Race Hygiene which centred on the notion of an ideal 'Nordic Race'; the founding of the International Society for Race Hygiene followed in 1907.[27] Eugenics was one of the many ideas that fed into the heady stew of Nazi practice and theory, including the anti-Semitic writings of Houston Stewart Chamberlain who evoked the Aryan race at the head of which were the Teutonic peoples.[28] Chamberlain's writings influenced the chief theorist of Nazi race policy, Alfred Rosenberg.[29] Translated into legislation and practice,[30] Nazi theory emphasized racial purity, while developing purgative, eugenic programmes of euthanasia, sterilization, and genocide, against 'races' and on others who threatened the 'degeneration' of German stock.[31] Rosenberg posited race protection, breeding, and hygiene as unavoidable requirements of the new age, and laid out the parameters of the eugenics programme, railing against 'the insane principle of the equality and equal rights of all races and religions'.[32]

B. Race and Colonialism

The association between colonialism and racial discrimination strenuously asserted by many delegates in the drafting and adoption of the Convention is challenged by Banton who argues that racial discrimination 'was not a prime mover of colonial expansion but an outcome that varied in importance from place to place'.[33] Anghie, on the other hand, argues that race and culture were central to colonialism and to international law in general, which he regards as shaped from its outset by the notion of cultural difference and how to manage it.[34] The contribution of racial theory to legal justifications of colonial enterprises may be understood in the practical context of larger discourses of differentiation and hierarchy among peoples—discourses that did not necessarily employ 'race' though they tended to do so where 'scientific racism' was echoed in the 'science' of legal positivism.

[25] See the collection of essays in A. Bashford and P. Levine (eds), *The Oxford Handbook of the History of Eugenics* (Oxford University Press, 2010).

[26] S. Kühl (transl. L. Schofer), *For the Betterment of the Race: The Rise and Fall of the International Movement for Eugenics and Racial Hygiene* (Palgrave Macmillan, 2013), p. 12 [henceforth *For the Betterment of the Race*]; M. Turda, 'Race, Science, and Eugenics in the Twentieth Century', in Bashford and Levine (eds), *Oxford Handbook of the History of Eugenics*, pp. 62–79.

[27] Kühl, *For the Betterment of the Race*, pp. 14–15.

[28] *Die Grundlagen des neunzehnten Jahrhunderts: Foundations of the Nineteenth Century*, translation from German by J. Lees (John Lane, The Bodley Head, 1912).

[29] A. Rosenberg, *Der Mythus des zwanzigsten Jahrhunderts*, published in Munich 1930, translated as *The Myth of the Twentieth Century*, a volume following on from Stewart Chamberlain's *Foundations of the Nineteenth Century*.

[30] Notably the Nuremberg Race Laws of 1935: the Reich Citizenship Law, and the Law for the Protection of German Blood and German Honour, English translations at <http://www.ushmm.org/wlc/en/article.php?ModuleId=10007903>; J. Scales-Trent, 'Racial Purity Laws in the United States and Nazi Germany: The Targeting Process', *Human Rights Quarterly* 23/2 (2001), 260–307.

[31] Kühl, *For the Betterment of the Race*, Chapter 5; R.N. Proctor, *Racial Hygiene: Medicine under the Nazis* (Harvard University Press, 1988); J. Connelly, 'Nazis and Slavs: From Race Theory to Racist Practice', *Central European History* 32/1 (1999), 1–33.

[32] Cited by Keane, *Caste-Based Discrimination*, p. 103.

[33] Banton, *International Action*, p. 70.

[34] Under nineteenth-century international law, 'special doctrines and norms had to be devised for the purposes of defining, identifying and placing the uncivilized': A. Anghie, *Imperialism, Sovereignty and the Making of International Law* (Cambridge University Press, 2004), p. 36.

Obregón summarizes developments in international hierarchical discourse and practice over a period of centuries:

From the 16th century to the early 19th century, the concepts of civilized/uncivilized (and other pairs such as progressive/backward, cultured/barbarian, modern/primitive, white/black) which categorized and stratified peoples, nations or States were key to the language of informal European imperialism. In the late 19th century, the language of civilization transitioned to formal imperialism sustained by international law.[35]

Anghie highlights the work of Vitoria in setting the early parameters for the operation of cultural difference in international law. Vitoria (1483–1546)[36] reflected on the legality of Spanish conquest of the New World in a manner redolent of other debates regarding the acquisition of colonies. The fact that the Indians of the New World were infidels did not deprive them of *dominium*: they too could have legitimate rulers. Vitoria did not find full equality of rights under the *ius gentium* for natives and Spaniards: his legal conclusions were asymmetric, weighing the scales to favour the latter over the former.[37] In the course of his exposition of the application of Natural Law to the case of the Indians, Vitoria suggested that they were 'some kind of natural children, heirs to a state of true reason',[38] thereby introducing a motif—the native population as children—that reverberated through later centuries of conquest and oppression,[39] lending its style and shape to hierarchical international institutions such as the Mandates system of the twentieth-century League of Nations.

A particularly demeaning account of the newly 'discovered' Americans was presented by Sepúlveda (1489–1573) in his short dialogue entitled *Democrates Secundus*,[40] for whom the 'Indians' were 'persons of natural rudeness and inferiority', of limited understanding, fit to be classified as Aristotle's *servi a natura* (slaves by nature).[41] In a dramatic confrontation with Sepúlveda before the Council of the Indies,[42] the Dominican friar

[35] L. Obregón, 'The Civilized and the Uncivilized', in B. Fassbender and A. Peters (eds), *The Oxford Handbook of the History of International Law* (Oxford University Press, 2012), pp. 917–39, p. 937.

[36] For a succinct account of Vitoria, see A. Brett, 'Francisco de Vitoria (1483–1546) and Francisco Suárez (1548–1617)', *Oxford Handbook of the History of International Law*, pp. 1086–91.

[37] *Inter alia*, the recognition of the *dominium* of the Indians did not unduly impinge on the rights of the Spaniards who had, *inter alia*, *ius gentium* rights to trade and travel: 'Christians have a right to preach and declare the Gospel in barbarian lands . . . If the Spaniards have a right to travel and trade among the Indians, they can teach the truth to those willing to hear them, especially as regards matters pertaining to salvation and happiness': F de Vitoria, *De Indis et de Jure Belli Relectiones* (E. Nys (ed.), transl. J. Bate, The Carnegie Institute of Washington, 1917), p. 160. See also T. Todorov, *The Conquest of America: The Question of the Other* (Harper and Row, 1992), p. 150: 'We are accustomed to seeing Vitoria as a defender of the Indians, but if we question, not the subject's intentions, but the impact of his discourse, it is clear that his role is quite different: under cover of an international law based on reciprocity, he in reality supplies a legal basis to the wars of colonization.'

[38] A. Pagden, 'Dispossessing the Barbarian: the Language of Spanish Thomism and the Debate over the Property Rights of the American Indians', in A. Pagden (ed.), *The Languages of Political Theory in Early Modern Europe* (Cambridge University Press, 1990), p. 86.

[39] The legal institution thereby introduced became known as the Doctrine of Guardianship, which, in this case, demanded that 'Spain's governance of the Indians must be based on the principle of acting for their welfare and not merely that [the welfare] of Spain': J.B. Scott, *The Spanish Origin of International Law* (Clarendon Press, 1934), p. 78.

[40] Juan Ginés de Sepúlveda, *Democrates secundus sive de justis causis belli apud Indios*; A. Losada (ed.), *Democrates segundo, o de las justas causas de la guerra contra los indios* (2nd edn, Consejo Superior de Investigaciones Cientificas, Instituto Francisco de Vitoria, 1984).

[41] Sepúlveda is extensively discussed in L. Hanke, *Aristotle and the American Indians: A Study of Race Prejudice in the Modern World* (Hollis and Carter, 1959).

[42] The debate is vividly recounted by Hanke, *Aristotle and the American Indians, ibid.*

Bartolomé de las Casas (1484–1566) argued against Sepúlveda, denying the doctrine of natural slavery and arguing that the Indians were rational creatures capable of apprehending the Christian religion, which is suitable for all human beings.[43] Pagden asserts that Sepúlveda's dialogue constituted 'the most virulent and uncompromising argument for the inferiority of the American Indian ever written',[44] while Las Casas is claimed as a precursor of modern teaching on the rights of man.[45] Sepúlveda's stance has been subjected to further negative commentary but also to more positive evaluations through close readings of his works in context.[46]

The developing vocabulary of race, along with allied markers such as 'civilization', proved a stimulating accompaniment to further expansionist initiatives of European powers into Africa and Asia.[47] New perspectives distinguished the civilized peoples from the uncivilized in a more thoroughgoing manner than had been the case under the internally contested Spanish acquisition of territory in the Americas. Non-European nations were presented as unfit for membership of the family of nations, with international law increasingly presented as a European creation, an idea 'that was part of the ideology of colonialism'.[48] Justifications of exclusion from membership of the system of international law, and the acquisition of colonies, were facilitated alike by the intellectual constructs of an 'anthropologically informed positivism',[49] shot through with a vocabulary underpinned by the twin hierarchies of race and civilization. Hence Westlake:

> The inflow of the white race cannot be stopped, where there is land to cultivate, ore to be mined, commerce to be developed, sport to enjoy, curiosity to be satisfied . . . International law has to treat natives as uncivilized. It regulates, for the mutual benefit of civilized States, the claims that they make to sovereignty . . . and leaves the treatment of the natives to the conscience of the State to which sovereignty is awarded.[50]

Westlake supported the taking of possession of non-European countries against the will of their inhabitants, disapproving of treaties of cession by native rulers because they 'were not intelligent enough to understand the subject matter of such treaties'.[51] Lorimer's

[43] Protector de Indios, Las Casas achieved lasting fame as defender of indigenous rights, with Hanke's work contributing to very positive evaluations. For a more critical view, portraying Las Casas as primarily motivated by a concern to convert the Indians through a form of 'ecclesiastical imperialism' see D. Castro, *Another Face of Empire: Bartolomé De Las Casas, Indigenous Rights and Ecclesiastical Imperialism* (Duke University Press, 2007).

[44] A. Pagden, *The Fall of Natural Man: The American Indian and the Origins of Comparative Ethnology* (Cambridge University Press, 1982), p. 109.

[45] E. O'Gorman, 'Lewis Hanke on the Spanish Struggle for Justice in the Conquest of America', *Hispanic American Historical Review* 29/4 (1949), 563–71.

[46] B. Tierney, *The Idea of Natural Rights: Studies on Natural Rights, Natural Law, and Church Law, 1150–1625* (Eerdmans, 2001), Chapters XI and XII.

[47] C.H. Alexandrowicz, *The European–African Confrontation* (Sijthoff, 1973); see his comment summarizing historical developments, p. 6.

[48] A. Orakhelashvili, 'The Idea of European International Law', *European Journal of International Law* 17/2 (2006), 315–47, 325 [henceforth *European International Law*]; Orakhelashvili, *ibid*., 327 observes that the notion of European international law 'was an idea of the racial superiority of Europeans over non-Europeans, who were considered uncivilized and unable to understand international law . . . International law could be made and enforced only by those who were racially superior; those who were racially inferior could not take part in its development.'

[49] M. Craven, 'Colonialism and Domination', *Oxford Handbook of the History of International Law*, pp. 862–89, p. 887.

[50] J. Westlake, *Chapters on the Principles of International Law* (Cambridge University Press, 1894), pp. 142–3 [henceforth *Chapters*].

[51] Orakhelashvili, *European International Law*, 326.

concurring approach added duties to rights so that that colonization 'of barbarians and savages... are duties morally and jurally inevitable'.[52] International law according to Westlake was 'a tool for the supremacy of the interests of "peoples of European blood" over those of the inhabitants of the territories' they colonized.[53] Rights of colonial acquisition were discussed extensively by M.F. Lindley who discerned divisions among jurists on the issue of 'the acquisition of sovereignty over the territories of backward peoples': those who admitted sovereignty, those who qualified it by reference to the needs of the civilized State when the primitive peoples have too much land, and the views of Westlake and others who thought like him.[54]

Allowing for equivocal practice and fluctuating terminology, the language in which the issues are discussed is striking in its hierarchical, debilitating assumptions regarding the peoples who inhabited the territories. In practice, territory was acquired by a mixture of modes; the extent to which inhabited territories were treated as equivalent to empty territory is controversial.[55] Bull stated that it was clear 'that the Europeans did not put forward any general claim that African land was *territorium nullius*... but chose to recognise the existence of local communities with rights both of political independence and ownership, at least until the time came when they were strong enough to overthrow these communities'.[56] The attempts at Berlin African Conference of 1884–5 to lay down ground rules for the acquisition of African territory did not, however, establish clear rules regarding local consent,[57] while Article VI of the General Act gave further expression to the patronizing doctrine of guardianship or trust in providing that the European powers bound themselves to watch over the preservation of the native tribes to care for the improvement of the conditions of their moral and material well-being. The European powers also promised help in suppressing slavery and, in light of their part in promoting it, the slave trade.[58]

[52] J. Lorimer, *The Institutes of the Law of Nations, A Treatise of the Jural Relations of Separate Political Communities*, vol 2 (Blackwood and Sons, 1883), p. 28.

[53] Westlake, *Chapters*, p. 320.

[54] M.F. Lindley, *The Acquisition and Government of Backward Territory in International Law* (Negro Universities Press, reprinted from 1926), pp. 11–18.

[55] See the discussion by Fitzmaurice, 'Discovery, Conquest, and Occupation of Territory', *Oxford Handbook of the History of International Law*, pp. 840–61, pp. 856–60, distinguishing *territorium nullius* (territory devoid of sovereignty) from *terra nullius* (land where there was literally no one or inhabited by people) (p. 859) 'who counted as nothing'. With regard to Australia, see E. Scott, 'Taking Possession of Australia—the Doctrine of Terra Nullius (No-Man's Land), 26/1 *Journal and Proceedings, Royal Australian Historical Society* (1940), 1–19. The question of the application of *terra nullius* to Australia was the focal point of the twentieth-century judgment in *Mabo and Others v Queensland* (No. 2), High Court of Australia, [1992] HCA 23; 175 CLR 1 (3 June 1992): the doctrine was rejected and native title recognized. For contemporary polemics following the case, see Connor, *The Invention of Terra Nullius: Historical and Legal Fictions on the Foundation of Australia* (Macleay Press, 2005); response by, *inter alios*, A. Fitzmaurice, 'Evidence Tailored to Fit an Argument', <http://www.onlineopinion.com.au/view.asp?article=4269&page=3>.

[56] H. Bull, 'European States and African Political Communities', in H. Bull and A. Watson (eds), *The Expansion of International Society* (Clarendon Press, 1984), p. 111.

[57] Craven, 'Colonialism and Domination', *Oxford Handbook of the History of International Law*, pp. 80–1; A. Fitzmaurice, 'The Genealogy of Terra Nullius', *Australian Historical Studies* 129 (2007), 1–15.

[58] M. Hurst (ed.), *Key Treaties of the Great Powers 1814–1914*, vol 2 (David and Charles, 1972), pp. 885–6; the rubric for the cited paragraph of Article VI is 'Preservation and Improvement of Native Tribes; Slavery, and the Slave Trade'.

C. Race and the Slave Trade

The enormous growth of the slave trade itself connects with the hierarchical classification of human beings. In light of the claim that Europeans invented 'race' only after they had enslaved Africans in order to find a justification,[59] Boxill argues that race was invented primarily to explain human variety 'but it paved and eased the way to the European enslavement of Africans' and was among the background assumptions that enabled Europeans to rationalise their actions.[60] Thus, 'as the idea of race became widely accepted, it drew a veil between the races that clouded their understanding of each other and hardened their mutual alienation . . . the invention of the idea of race probably made it easier for Europeans to commit the crime of slavery'.[61] The phenomenon of slavery, including its severe forms such as chattel slavery, was an institution that reached back into the recesses of antiquity. Drescher and Finkelman contend that

> [t]he transition from universal acceptability . . . to limiting enslavement to certain religions, races, or ethnicities . . . reflects the transition from the ancient to the modern world . . . As Europe became Christian, only non-Europeans could be slaves. Expansion to Africa and the Americas allowed for enslavement based solely on race—first Africans and Indians, and by the 18th century, only Africans.[62]

The grounds of justification of slavery moved on from the basis of capture in war, or the heathen, barbarian, and infidel status of the slaves, towards a clearer racial basis as race theory moved on. Jefferson, reflecting on whether the savage and the slave could live civilized lives, advanced 'as a suspicion only, that the blacks . . . are inferior to the whites in the endowments both of body and of mind . . . This unfortunate difference of colour, and perhaps of faculty, is a powerful obstacle to the emancipation of these people.'[63] Trade in slaves was regarded as permissible under the law of nations until well into the nineteenth century, and the great luminaries of international law paid little attention to the phenomenon, in striking contrast to that paid to piracy and pirates as *hostes humani generis*.[64] The doctrine espoused among English, Dutch, and French jurists that slaves were free 'as soon as they reached the soil or breathed the air of their nations',[65] or that the trade violated natural law,[66] did not immediately translate into an international law remit for apprehension of the slavers.

Commencing with attacks on its transatlantic version, the eventual undermining of the slave trade through a combination of enlightened thinking, the economic self-interest of States in the vanguard of the anti-slavery movement, and the impassioned resistance of the slaves themselves, many of whom took their inspiration from the Haitian revolution,

[59] A view associated with E. Williams, *Capitalism and Slavery* (University of North Carolina Press, 1944).

[60] Boxill, 'Introduction', *Race and Racism*, p. 5.

[61] Boxill, *Race and Racism*, p. 23.

[62] S. Drescher and P. Finkelman, 'Slavery', *Oxford Handbook of the History of International Law*, pp. 890–916, p. 893.

[63] Notes on the State of Virginia, 1787, cited in I. Kramnick (ed.), *The Portable Enlightenment Reader* (Penguin Books, 1995), p. 668.

[64] Drescher and Finkelman, *Oxford Handbook of the History of International Law*, pp. 897–9.

[65] *Ibid.*, p. 895. See *Somerset v Stewart* (1772), 98 Eng. Rep. 499 (KB).

[66] In *The Antelope* (1825), 23 US 66, Chief Justice Marshall held that although contrary to the law of nature and in violation of American law, the slave trade was consistent with the law of nations; cf. the *Le Louis* (1817), 165 ER 1464.

came too late for the millions subjected to it over centuries and for their descendants.[67] The abolition of the slave trade bequeathed the concept of crimes against humanity to international law in recognition of the enormity of the crime visited upon masses of (mostly African) human beings.[68] The Haitian revolution offered a model of resistance to colonial power, coupled with a claim to have abolished slavery forever, and an inversion of vocabulary whereby the European was tainted as the 'barbarian' and 'Black' was proclaimed with pride.[69]

D. Race, Mandates, Minorities

Key developments in the first decades of the twentieth century, notably those associated with the League of Nations, contributed to emblematic changes in the range of States accepted as 'subjects' of international law, in the treatment of colonies, and in international legal discourse concerning individual and group rights. Changes introduced by the League such as the mandates, the treaties and declarations concerning minorities, the development of labour rights, and the abolition of the slave trade, coexisted with continuation and reaffirmation of nineteenth-century suppositions regarding national status and race.

'World opinion' regarding racial discrimination, as expressed through the dominant Western powers, presented itself vividly in reaction to Japan's proposal to include a racial equality clause in the Covenant of the League of Nations.[70] Treated by some as exemplifying 'new diplomacy', the post-First World War Paris Peace Conference gathered together a significant number of actors from outside the circle of Great Powers: in the excited phrases of W.E.B. Du Bois, '[n]ot simply England, Italy, and the Great Powers are there, but all the little nations . . . Not only groups, but races'.[71] Japanese opinion, highly sensitized by, *inter alia*, perceived slights against Japanese nationals in the immigration policies of Australia, Canada, and the US, invested hopes in the ability of the Paris Conference and the leadership of President Woodrow Wilson to address racial prejudice,

[67] For appraisals, see P. Manning, *Slavery and African Life: Occidental, Oriental, and African Slave Trades* (Cambridge University Press, 1990); H. Thomas, *The Slave Trade: The Story of the African Slave Trade 1440–1870* (Simon and Schuster, 1997). Materials on the trade from the NGO Anti-Slavery International's collection may be found at: <http://www.antislavery.org/english/resources/transatlantic_enslavement_resources.aspx>; including an eighteenth- and nineteenth-century collection at <http://www.recoveredhistories.org>.

[68] J.S. Martinez, *The Slave Trade and the Origins of International Human Rights Law* (Oxford University Press, 2012), pp. 114 ff; Martinez, *ibid.*, p. 115, attributes the first use of the term to Wheaton's treatise of 1842, *Enquiry into the Validity of the British Claim to a Right of Visitation and Search of American Vessels Suspected to be Engaged in the African Slave-Trade* (Lea and Blanchard, 1842). The Congress of Vienna 1815 declared the slave trade 'repugnant to the principles of humanity and universal morality'; instruments such as the Declaration Respecting the Abolition of the Slave trade 1822 and the Treaty for the Suppression of the African Slave-Trade 1841, were followed by the General Act of the Conference of Berlin 1885 to which was attached a Declaration which prohibited the trade in accordance with the principles of the law of nations; the General Act of the Brussels Conference Relating to the African Slave Trade 1890 cemented the abolition process: for references see J.A Fernandez, '*Hostes Humani Generis*: Pirates, Slavers, and Other Criminals' *Oxford Handbook of the History of International Law*, pp. 120–44, pp. 131–3.

[69] L. Obregón, 'The Civilized and the Uncivilized', *Oxford Handbook of the History of International Law*, pp. 917–39, at p. 923.

[70] P.G. Lauren, 'Human Rights in History: Diplomacy and Racial Equality at the Paris Peace Conference', *Diplomatic History* 2(3) (1978), 257–78 [henceforth 'Human Rights in History'].

[71] Lauren, 'Human Rights in History', 258.

demanding that the Japanese delegation 'should insist on the equal international treatment of all races . . . not only for Japan but for all the countries of Asia'.[72] Racial discrimination was understood not only as demeaning in itself but as a menace to world peace; hence, for all such reasons, 'inferiority must end'.[73] Japan submitted—and re-submitted[74]—a clause for inclusion in the Covenant of the League:

> The equality of nations being a basic principle of the League of Nations, the High Contracting Parties agree to accord as soon as possible to all alien nationals of States members of the League, equal and just treatment in every respect, making no distinction, either in law or in fact, on account of their race or nationality.[75]

The racial equality proposal was tagged on to a clause on the free exercise of religion, a draft of which (later revised) had been provided by President Wilson.[76] Unlike the formulation on religion, which applied to 'persons generally within the States' jurisdiction', and represented 'a new excursion into the realms of State sovereignty',[77] the reach of the proposal on racial equality was limited to alien nationals of States members of the League.[78] Despite intense diplomatic activity on the part of Japan, including assurances that it would not use the clause as a wedge to insert more immigrants into the US, the proposal was rejected, as was the proposal on religious freedom. A revised amendment by Japan for inclusion in the preamble of 'the principle of equality of nations and just treatment of their nationals' was also rejected on the ground that the principle of the equality of nations was already implicit in the League as an institution, so that it was not necessary to state it in the preamble; the revision had discarded any reference to 'race'.[79] In subsequent speeches at the League, Japan declared that its diplomacy had aimed at setting forth a guiding principle for future international relations and was not an encroachment on the internal affairs of nations.[80] McKean concludes on the episode:

> Despite President Wilson's insistence that the result was not a rejection of the principle of the equality of nations and peoples, it was regrettable that no provision on the question, or on religious or racial equality, was included in the Covenant. Positive recognition of the legal right to equality of treatment of races and religious groups had to wait another thirty years for the United Nations Charter and subsequent instruments.[81]

[72] Asahi, 11 December 1918, Lauren, *ibid.*, 260.

[73] Lauren, *ibid.*, 260.

[74] *Ibid.*, 265.

[75] *Ibid.*, 264.

[76] For versions of the 'religious article', see D.H. Miller, *The Drafting of the Covenant* vol. 2 (G.B. Putnam's Sons, 1928), p. 105, and *ibid.*, p. 307. Miller observed that the proposal by Japan 'had helped to make impossible any article on religious liberty': W.A. McKean, *Equality and Discrimination under International Law* (Clarendon Press, 1983), pp. 15–17 [henceforth *Equality and Discrimination*].

[77] McKean, *Equality and Discrimination*, 17.

[78] McKean observes, that 'The Japanese proposal, which had only sought equality of treatment of aliens with a State's own nationals, was not particularly radical since, in those countries where a State's treatment of its own nationals fell below the minimum standard, aliens would . . . be entitled to enjoy the international standard' *ibid.*, p. 17.

[79] The revised amendment garnered eleven out of seventeen votes at the League of Nations Commission, but President Wilson, chairing the session, insisted on unanimity before the amendment could pass. The Japanese proposal was supported by Brazil, France, Italy, China, Greece, Serbia, and Czechoslovakia. For an overview, see E.J. Dillon, *The Inside Story of the Peace Conference* (Harper and Bros., 1920), Chapter XVI.

[80] Lauren, 'Human Rights in History', 274.

[81] McKean, *Equality and Discrimination*, pp. 19–20.

It is evident that the notion of racial hierarchies was not uncongenial to statesmen of the post–First World War powers. It is also notable that the language of race informs the proposal by Japan and the discursive context in which the proposal was placed. The challenge presented by the proposal appeared less of one to the idea of race than to the notions of inferiority and superiority associated with it.

The League of Nations, despite the promises of Wilsonian rhetoric regarding self-determination, did not enshrine any such principle in the Covenant. Many groups claiming self-determination had to be satisfied with what the League offered in the field of minority rights. Colonial systems remained for the time being outside self-determination, the doctrine that would eventually sweep them aside in the era of the United Nations. Some territories detached from existing colonial systems were placed under the system of mandates rather than enjoying full emancipation. Article 22 of the Covenant of the League of Nations commenced by delineating the subjects of the Mandate system: to colonies and territories which, as a consequence of the late war had ceased to be under the sovereignty of the States which formerly governed them 'and are inhabited by peoples not yet able to stand by themselves under the strenuous conditions of the modern world', there should be applied the principle that 'the well-being and development of such peoples form a sacred trust of civilisation'; accordingly 'the tutelage of such peoples should be entrusted to advanced nations' and exercised by them as Mandatories of the League. This came with the rider that the mandate must differ according to the stage of development of the people including geographical situation, economic conditions, and similar circumstances. A distinctly hierarchical classification of territories was instituted to carry through the promise to the League, leading to the creation of A-, B-, and C-class mandates. While the system may have been welcomed as tempering the exercise of colonialism through the infusion of an international dimension, its value was also downplayed by critics as constituting in essence a modified projection of nineteenth century and earlier classifications and rankings,[82] while some have glimpsed the shade of De Gobineau in the ranking arrangements.[83]

In addition to the generalized proposals on racial equality and religious freedom, the question of minorities loomed large in the post-war efforts of reconstruction. The application of the principle of self-determination involved reduction in the Turkish dominions, the dismemberment of the Austro-Hungarian Empire, the creation of new States, and the addition of substantial territory to others.[84] The reconfigurations satisfied the aspirations of some nationalities but frustrated others. As with the issues of religious toleration and self-determination, President Wilson was active with regard to the case for

[82] A. Anghie, 'The Evolution of International Law: Colonial and Postcolonial Realities', *Third World Quarterly* 27.5 (2006), 739–53; also, A. Anghie, *Imperialism, Sovereignty and the Making of International Law* (Cambridge University Press, 2004), Chapter 3, 'Colonialism and the Birth of International Institutions: the Mandate System of the League of Nations', pp. 115–95.

[83] T.J. Le Melle, 'Race in International Relations', *International Studies Perspectives* 10 (2009), 77–83, 80.

[84] *Protection of Minorities* (United Nations, 1967) includes a list of the key instruments. For a general evaluation, see P. Thornberry, *International Law and the Rights of Minorities* (Clarendon Press, 1991), Chapter 3: 'The Protection of Minorities by the League of Nations', pp. 38–52, as well as works cited by the author [henceforth *Rights of Minorities*]; a more recent evaluation of the League system in light of later developments in human rights is undertaken in J. Castellino, 'The Protection of Minorities and Indigenous Peoples in International Law: A Comparative Temporal Analysis', *International Journal of Minority and Group Rights* 17/3 (2010), 393–422; see also H. Hannum, 'The Concept and Definition of Minorities', in M. Weller (ed.), *Universal Minority Rights* (Oxford University Press, 2007), pp. 56–73, esp. pp. 53–6.

the international protection of 'racial and religious minorities', in light of his expressed sentiment that '[n]othing, I venture to say, is more likely to disturb the peace of the world than the treatment which might . . . be meted out to . . . minorities.'[85] Wilson's clauses for inclusion in the Covenant were too strong for the assembled statesmen in suggesting the need for positive action on the part of States to achieve equal treatment and security for, both in law and in fact, minorities, and no discrimination either in law or in fact for religion. In the event, the protection of minorities was taken care of through a series of treaties and declarations principally affecting Eastern Europe that included general rights and specific protection for 'racial, religious or linguistic minorities'—the retention 'of 'racial' in the description of the protected groups is notable in light of the later preference for accounting for the rights of 'ethnic' minorities, and the inclusion of 'ethnic origin' among the prohibited grounds of discrimination in the International Convention on the Elimination of All Forms of Racial Discrimination (ICERD); the favoured contemporary discourse of ethnicity is not, however, free from demeaning hierarchical implications.[86]

Opinions of the Permanent Court of International Justice figure among the more remote conceptual building blocks of ICERD in distinguishing various forms of equality and discrimination,[87] notably the distinction between equality/discrimination in 'fact' and in 'law'. In *German Settlers in Poland*, the Court recognized the concepts of 'equality in fact as well as . . . legal equality in the sense of absence of discrimination in the words of the law'.[88] In *Polish Nationals in Danzig*, the court stated that the prohibition of discrimination 'in order to be effective, must ensure the absence of discrimination in fact as well as law'.[89] In *Minority Schools in Albania*,[90] the court took the view that fulfilling the objectives of the League's system to protect minorities required that nationals belonging to minorities be placed on a footing of 'perfect equality' with other nationals. The opinion stated that equality in law precluded discrimination of any kind, whereas equality in fact may involve the necessity of different treatment in order to attain a result that establishes an equilibrium between different situations.[91] Nuanced concepts of discrimination and equality are not always appreciated: in *Minority Schools*, a minority of the judges preferred a strict equality approach—'equal in measure'—to the flexible concept adopted by the majority.[92]

E. Comment

At a certain point in human history, Robert Knox's epiphany that 'race in human affairs is everything' expressed his view of much of the reality of art, science, literature,[93] even if its

[85] Thornberry, *Rights of Minorities*, 41.

[86] M. Shahabuddin, '"Ethnicity" in the International Law of Minority Protection: the Post-Cold War Context in Perspective', *Leiden Journal of International Law* 25 (2012), 885–907, 887–91.

[87] McKean, *Equality and Discrimination*, pp. 27–33; Thornberry, *Rights of Minorities*, chapter 3; E. W. Vierdag, *The Concept of Discrimination in International Law—With Special Reference to Human Rights* (Martinus Nijhoff, 1973); Vierdag, *ibid.*, pp. 48–54, finds that before the First World War, 'discrimination' was a term employed only in Anglo-American legal relations, making its way thenceforth into international law as well as usage in other legal systems.

[88] PCIJ Ser. B, No. 6, 24 (1923).

[89] [1932] PCIJ, Ser. A/B, No. 44, 28.

[90] [1935] PCIJ, Ser. A/B, No. 64.

[91] *Minority Schools in Albania*, 17–19.

[92] Dissenting opinion of Judges Hurst, Rostorowsky, and Negulesco, *Minority Schools in Albania*, 26.

[93] R. Knox, *Races of Men: A Philosophical Enquiry into the Influence of Race over the Destinies of Nations* (2nd edn, Henry Renshaw, 1862), Preface [henceforth *Races of Men*].

effects did not, in his view, necessarily favour European pretensions to dominance.[94] An intellectual reaction against the heady brew of racial theory developed steadily throughout the twentieth century, even as Nazi racial hygiene practice reached its apogee. Apart from the chaos of attempts at taxonomies of races, cultural anthropologists such as Boas and Benedict[95] and biologists such as Huxley and Hogben attacked the fundamentals of race theory.[96] The distinction between genotype and phenotype was also a crucial move in undermining the theory, suggesting that 'a confused biological determinism had established itself, conflating genes, physiognomy, and culture'.[97] Influential currents of opinion maintained that genetic differences between population groups did not translate into 'races', nor did they determine culture, customs, law, and the rest, while assertions of superiority and inferiority could never be properly classed as 'scientific'.[98] The notion of 'scientific racism' has largely passed into history.

On the institutional side, the unegalitarian nature of the international system was effectively sustained by the League arrangements, despite statements from the dominant powers that the treaties and declarations were not a badge of second-class citizenship of the international community.[99] Germany developed its racial practice and theory untrammelled by general obligations with regard to the League,[100] presenting itself in the external forum as a champion of the rights of minorities, a presentation that pre-dated the taking of power by the National Socialists.[101] The differentiation of status between States subject to the minorities regime and those exempted from it was less marked than in the hierarchical formalization of the Mandates. The difference between the two systems intimates the continuance of another hierarchy, that between 'Europe' and the rest, expressed in the continuation of vast systems of Empire that endured well into the era of the United Nations.

94 With regard to colonial domination, Knox's preface in *Races of Men* is pessimistic, arguing that his conclusions will disturb: 'the inordinate self-esteem of the Saxon will be especially shocked . . . nor will he listen to a theory which . . . proves to him that his race cannot domineer over the earth . . . cannot hold in permanence any portion of any continent but the one on which he *first* originated' (emphasis in the original).

95 From a vast oeuvre, see R. Benedict, *Race, Science and Politics* (Viking Press, 1940); F. Boas, *Race, Language and Culture* (University of Chicago Press, 1940); *Race and Democratic Society* (J.J. Augustin, 1945).

96 E. Barkan, *The Retreat of Scientific Racism* (Cambridge University Press, 1992). See also the excellent short summary of the critical developments in A. Rattansi, *Racism: A Very Short Introduction* (Oxford University Press, 2007), pp. 70–6 [henceforth *Racism*].

97 Rattansi, *Racism*, p. 72.

98 The contribution of UNESCO to the deconstruction of race is discussed briefly in Chapter 3.

99 Thornberry, *The Rights of Minorities*, 41.

100 Obligations regarding minorities were undertaken in the Treaty between Germany and Poland on Upper Silesia 1922: see *Rights of Minorities in Upper Silesia* (*Germany v Poland*), (1928) PCIJ Ser. A, no. 15.

101 C. Fink, 'Defender of Minorities: Germany in the League of Nations, 1926–1933', *Central European History* 5/4 (1972), 330–57; C. Raitz von Frentz, *A Lesson Forgotten: Minority Protection under the League of Nations—The Case of the German Minority in Poland 1920–1934* (LIT Verlag, 1999).

3. Towards the Convention

A. Development of Standards

The response of the international community to the eras of colonialism, the Holocaust, race theory and race practice, was complex and revolutionary, ultimately encompassing opening up the membership of the international community through the United Nations (UN) organization, the gradual undermining of colonialism and hierarchy among nations through adoption of the principle of self-determination, and the introduction of principles of human rights and non-discrimination. To the egalitarian recognition of the equality of peoples and nations, and the development of international human rights standards, the further undermining of the concept of race supplied a third and crucial element to the complex genealogy of the Convention.

Despite awareness of the international ramifications of Hitler's doctrines of racial superiority, neither the Atlantic Charter nor the Declaration of the United Nations of 1942 broached the question of race explicitly, though the former referred to the right of every people to choose their own government. However, the fourth principle of the Potsdam conference of 1945 stated that 'all Nazi laws which provided the basis of the Hitler regime or established discrimination grounded on race, creed or political opinion shall be abolished';[1] peace treaties with Axis powers provided similarly.[2] At the Dumbarton Oaks conference on the future world organization, China proposed for inclusion among the organization's fundamental principles that 'the principle of equality of all States and all races shall be upheld'.[3] The proposal did not appear in the draft charter which made only a fleeting reference to human rights 'buried deep within the draft'.[4] The San Francisco Conference struck a different note, with human rights and racial equality making their presence strongly felt from the outset. Opening speeches by India, Haiti, and Uruguay argued for the necessity to repudiate 'doctrines of racial division and discrimination'.[5] Echoes of the proposal on racial equality by Japan at the Versailles Conference haunted some delegations, including those of New Zealand and Australia, the latter concerned about potential threats to its 'White Australia' policy.[6]

The collective voice of the 'small nations' in favour of principles of human rights and non-discrimination eventually prevailed in the text of the UN Charter. The prohibition of racial discrimination found broad support among the non-European States including the States of the Americas, the Soviet Union (USSR), and, exceptionally among Europeans,

[1] J. Morsink, *The Universal Declaration of Human Rights: Origins, Drafting and Intent* (University of Pennsylvania Press, 1999), p. 102 [henceforth *The Universal Declaration*].

[2] *Ibid.*

[3] P.G. Lauren, 'First Principles of Racial Equality: History and Politics and Diplomacy of Human Rights Provisions in the United Nations Charter', *Human Rights Quarterly* 5 (1983), 1–26, at 10 [henceforth *First Principles*].

[4] Lauren, *First Principles*, 12.

[5] *Ibid.*, 15.

[6] *Ibid.*, 14.

France. Those States who feared its inclusion in the Charter were mollified to an extent by the protective presence of Article 2(7) of the Charter on domestic jurisdiction. In the event, the UN Charter does not elaborate on human rights and fundamental freedoms but refers to respect, realization, etc, of the rights 'without distinction as to race, sex, language, or religion' in Articles 1(3), 13(1), 55(c), and 76(c). According to one author, this 'short list of non-discrimination items is the only explicit way the UN Charter gives content to the idea of human rights'.[7] The non-discrimination element nonetheless prompted Chilean delegate Santa Cruz to assert before the General Assembly's Third Committee that 'the United Nations had been founded principally to combat discrimination in the world'.[8]

In light of the strictures on colonialism advanced by many delegates in the drafting of the Convention, self-determination stands as a further key element in the UN Charter. Articles 1(2) and 55 refer to the principle of self-determination, and a relationship is established between the concept of self-determination and the enjoyment of human rights. While the Charter did not enshrine a right of dependent peoples to independence, the combination of explicit references to self-determination and the chapters on non-self-governing (Chapter XI) and trust territories (Chapter XII) effectively 'ensured that the first fruits of self-determination fell to colonial territories in the Empires of the Western Powers through emergence as independent States'.[9] The anti-colonial vision of self-determination as emancipation from colonial rule culminated in General Assembly resolution 1514 (XV)—the 'Colonial Declaration' of 1960—which presented itself as an interpretation of the Charter. The Colonial Declaration is explicitly incorporated into the preamble and Article 15 of the International Convention on the Elimination of All Forms of Racial Discrimination (ICERD).[10]

The Charter did not follow the League of Nations in making express provision for minorities: no amendments favouring the protection of minorities were submitted at San Francisco. Concerns regarding the treatment of minorities were reflected in the post-war treaties of peace, in the setting up of the UN Sub-Commission on the Prevention of Discrimination and Protection of Minorities, and in the drafting of the Convention on the Prevention and Punishment of the Crime of Genocide, while General Assembly resolution 217C (III) declared that the United Nations could not 'remain indifferent 'to the fate of minorities. The momentum in favour of the non-discrimination paradigm was amplified by the United States and Latin American States, anxious not to universalize the League minority regime in case it might disturb policies of assimilation. The non-discrimination formula was attractive in developing a universalist vocabulary that remained vague on specifics when compared to the concrete commitments demanded by instruments on minority rights. The language of anti-discrimination also suited nations *in statu nascendi*: united polities were imagined as easier to build without

[7] Morsink, *The Universal Declaration*, p. 92.

[8] *Ibid.* For precision, it may be noted that the Charter refers to 'distinction', not 'discrimination', while the Universal Declaration of Human Rights (UDHR) employs both terms.

[9] P. Thornberry, 'The Democratic or Internal Aspect of Self-Determination with some Remarks on Federalism', in C. Tomuschat (ed.), *Modern Law of Self-Determination* (Martinus Nijhoff, 1993), pp. 101–38, p. 109.

[10] See discussion of self-determination in Chapters 5 and 13.

commitments to protecting the identities of sub-State groups.[11] The resistance to specific rights for minorities continued through the drafting of ICERD.[12]

B. The Universal Declaration of Human Rights

The UN Charter and the UDHR stimulated and contextualized later exercises elaborating the principle of non-discrimination on grounds listed in ICERD. 'Colour' was inserted into the grounds of discrimination in Article 2 of the UDHR, despite the absence of reference to it in the Charter. Delegates reasoned that since there was no scientific definition of race, then 'colour' should be added as a precautionary measure, tilting the text towards a general or 'folk'—as opposed to a 'scientific'—notion of race.[13] Issues in the debate on 'national origin' were effectively reprised in the drafting of ICERD. In the view of the Sub-Commission, 'national origin' was to be interpreted, not in the sense of citizenship but as evoking 'national characteristics'.[14] Analogously, the discussion of 'caste' and 'descent' in the *travaux* of ICERD is foreshadowed in (unsuccessful) proposals by India to include 'caste' among the grounds in the UDHR.[15] On 'hate speech', the UDHR, like ICERD, addresses 'incitement to . . . discrimination';[16] however, the UDHR refers only to protection from such incitement, which is not as such prohibited nor declared a crime. Elements of debates over Article 4 of ICERD appear in the speech of the USSR delegate:

> Freedom of the press and free speech could not serve as a pretext for propagating views which poisoned public opinion. Propaganda in favour of racial or national exclusiveness or superiority merely served as an ideological mask for imperialistic aggression. That was how German imperialists attempted to justify by racial considerations their plan for destruction and pillage in Europe and Asia.[17]

As with the UN Charter, the UDHR did not address the protection of minorities, raising questions as to the scope of the non-discrimination principle and whether and to what extent it could effectively subsume the protection of minorities under its broad umbrella.[18] At the United Nations, various bodies, including the Secretary-General and the Sub-Commission on the Prevention of Discrimination and Protection of Minorities, contributed to the intellectual reconstruction of discrimination and minority rights, exercising significant influence on the course of normative developments.[19] The Sub-Commission explained the prevention of discrimination as 'the prevention of any action

[11] P. Thornberry, *International Law and the Rights of Minorities* (Clarendon Press, 1991), Chapters 10, 11, and 12 [henceforth *Rights of Minorities*].

[12] The issue is discussed in the present work, especially in Chapters 6, 13, and 20.

[13] Morsink, *The Universal Declaration*, pp. 102–3.

[14] E/CN.4/Sub.2/SR.21, p. 5.

[15] Morsink, *The Universal Declaration*, p. 115.

[16] Article 7 of the UDHR provides: 'All are equal before the law and entitled without any discrimination to equal protection of the law. All are entitled to equal protection against any discrimination in violation of this Declaration and against any incitement to such discrimination.'

[17] AC.1/SR.7, p. 9, cited Morsink, *The Universal Declaration*, p. 70, discussion of 'hate speech', *ibid.*, pp. 69–72.

[18] Thornberry, *Rights of Minorities*, Chapters 29 ff.

[19] *The Main Types and Causes of Discrimination (Memorandum Submitted by the Secretary-General)* (United Nations 1949), Sales No 1949 XIV 3; *Definition and Classification of Minorities (Memorandum Submitted by the Secretary General)* (United Nations, 1950), Sales No 1950 XIV 3.

which denies to individuals or groups equality of treatment which they may wish', while the protection of minorities is 'the protection of non-dominant groups which, while wishing in general for equality of treatment with the majority, wish for a measure of differential treatment in order to preserve basic characteristics which they possess and which distinguish them from the majority of the population'.[20] The formulation in the memorandum of the UN Secretary-General regarded prevention of discrimination as 'the suppression or prevention of any conduct which denies or restricts a person's right to equality'. The protection of minorities on the other hand, although inspired by the principle of equality, required positive action whereby concrete service is rendered to the minority group.[21] In both cases, the protection of minorities was defined in positive terms and linked the preservation of the identity of minorities. The full potential of principles of equality and non-discrimination to generate forms of positive action would take time to establish itself in international practice.

C. Disenchanting Race

The work of the UN in the field of human rights also encompassed a fundamental critique of the concept of race. The United Nations Educational, Scientific and Cultural Organization (UNESCO) produced its Four Statements on the Race Question: the Statement on Race, 1950; Statement on the Nature of Race and Race Differences, 1951; Proposals on the Biological Aspects of Race, 1964; and the Statement on Race and Racial Prejudice, 1967 which was the basis of the UNESCO Declaration on Race and Racial Prejudice 1978.[22] The first three UNESCO statements played a role in the drafting of ICERD,[23] while all four have exercised influence on the practice of the Committee on the Elimination of Racial Discrimination (CERD).

The first Statement begins with resounding affirmation: 'Scientists have reached general agreement . . . that mankind is one: that all men belong to the same species', and, less resoundingly, they are also 'probably derived from the same common stock'.[24] Different 'populations' exhibit differing gene frequencies which are few compared to 'the vast numbers of genes common to all human beings'.[25] '"Race" therefore designates a population characterised by gene concentrations or physical characters that fluctuate over time.'[26] In view of 'serious errors' when race is used in popular parlance, 'it would be better when speaking of human races to drop the term "race" altogether and speak of ethnic groups'.[27] The Statement asserts further that '[f]or all practical social purposes, "race" is not so much a biological phenomenon as a social myth'.[28]

[20] E/CN.4/52, Section V (Sub-Commission, first session, 1947), pp. 13–14.

[21] *The Main Types and Causes of Discrimination*, paras 6 and 7.

[22] The statements were published together by UNESCO in 1969 as *Four Statements on the Race Question*, [henceforth *Four Statements*] together with two individual essays: by J. Herniaux, *Biological Aspects of the Race Question*; and M. Banton, *Social Aspects of the Race Question*.

[23] Discussed in D. Keane, *Caste-Based Discrimination in International Human Rights Law* (Ashgate, 2007), pp. 176–7 [henceforth *Caste-Based Discrimination*].

[24] *First Statement on Race*, para. 1.

[25] Para. 2.

[26] Para. 4.

[27] Para. 6.

[28] Para. 14.

Amidst criticism from biologists of the first Statement, UNESCO convened another group which drew up the 1951 Statement on the Nature of Race and Race Differences.[29] The second Statement sustained the chief conclusions of the first but with differences of emphasis, noting from the outset the 'unanimity in reaching the primary conclusion that there were no scientific grounds whatever for the racialist position regarding purity of race and the hierarchy of inferior and superior races' to which this leads.[30] Nonetheless, the 1951 Statement does not deny the existence of races, recording agreement that there were no differences in mental ability between different racial groups and that hybridization of races did not lead to disadvantageous results.[31] In contrast to the suggestion in the 1950 Statement to drop the term 'race' and substitute it with the word 'ethnic', the 1951 Statement displays no agreement on a substitute term. The Statement also clarified that '[n]ational, religious, geographical, linguistic and cultural groups do not necessarily coincide with racial groups... the cultural traits of such groups have no demonstrated connection with racial traits'.[32] The 1951 Statement is not free of its own kind of hierarchical classification, not on the character and abilities of 'races' but instead in distinguishing between non-literate and 'civilized' people.[33] This implicit ranking is redressed to an extent by the observation that inherited genetic differences are not a major factor 'in producing the differences between the cultures and cultural achievements of different peoples or groups'.[34]

The 1964 Proposals on the Biological Aspects of Race continue to portray the view that differences in human populations are primarily attributable to historical and environmental factors, and that cultural achievements are unrelated to the transmission of genetic endowments. Further, neither 'in the field of hereditary potentialities concerning... intelligence and the capacity for cultural development, nor in that of physical traits' is there any justification for the concept of 'inferior' and 'superior' races.[35] The 1964 Statement is notable for introducing the term 'racism' in its assertion that the 'biological data... stand in open contradiction to the tenets of racism'.[36]

UNESCO maintained its interest in race questions after the adoption of ICERD. The combative 1967 Statement on Race and Racial Prejudice elaborates on the theme of racism, a phenomenon that constitutes a 'particularly striking obstacle to the recognition of equal dignity for all, which continues to haunt the world',[37] while it lacks 'any scientific basis'.[38] The Statement is more reticent than its predecessors on 'races', observing that the term's usage is 'partly conventional and partly arbitrary and does not imply any hierarchy

[29] The explanatory introduction to the second Statement, which carries the name of the rapporteur L.C. Dunn, notes that 'it was chiefly sociologists who gave their opinions and framed' the First Statement, without the authority of the physical anthropologists and geneticists.

[30] 1951 Statement, Rapporteur's Introduction.

[31] *Ibid.*, Rapporteur's Introduction: 'The physical anthropologists and the man in the street both know that races exist; the former, from the scientifically recognisable and measurable congeries of traits which he uses in classifying the varieties of man; the latter from the immediate evidence of his senses when he sees an African, a European, an Asiatic and an American Indian together.'

[32] 1951 Statement, para. 3.

[33] Para. 5.

[34] Para. 6.

[35] 1964 Statement, para. 13.

[36] Para. 13.

[37] *Statement on Race and Racial Prejudice*, para. 1.

[38] Para. 3.

whatsoever', and, further, that racial divisions have limited scientific interest.[39] The 1967 Statement goes on to argue that race relations problems are social in origin rather than biological and, *inter alia*, that racism 'has not been a universal phenomenon'; reference is made to slavery, colonialism, and anti-Semitism as examples of racist practice.[40] Unlike the earlier Statements, the fourth Statement reflects on the causes of racial prejudice and strategies to combat it, including prevention by law and related means of racists from acting on their beliefs,[41] and utilization of 'agencies of enlightenment' including education.[42] The interplay of 'law' and 'education' continued through the drafting processes into the text of the Convention.

D. Racial Prejudice, Religious Intolerance

In resolution 1510 (XV) of 12 December 1960, the UN General Assembly, noting with gratification the consistent condemnation by the United Nations of 'the manifestations of racial and national hatred, religious intolerance and racial prejudice which still exist in the world',[43] and declaring itself 'alarmed by the fact that tendencies to racial and national hatred are still not sufficiently combated in many parts of the world by orienting youth in the spirit of the Charter of the United Nations',[44] called upon the governments of all States 'to take all necessary measures to prevent all manifestations of racial, religious and national hatred'.[45] Resolution 1510 also expressed the principle that the United Nations 'is duty bound to combat these manifestations, to establish the facts and causes of their origin, and to recommend resolute and effective measures which can be taken against them'.[46] The resolution was adopted following an outburst of anti-Semitic incidents, including 'the Swastika epidemic',[47] in various parts of the world in 1959 and 1960, incidents condemned by the Sub-Commission on Prevention of Discrimination and Protection of Minorities (the Sub-Commission)[48] as well as by its parent body, the Commission on Human Rights (the Commission).[49]

Resolution 3 (XII) of the Sub-Commission commenced with an expression of the deep concern of the Commission at manifestations of anti-Semitism and other similar forms of

[39] Para. 3(b).
[40] Para. 7.
[41] Paras 13 and 17.
[42] Paras 14 and 16.
[43] Resolution 1510 (XV), preambular para. 2.
[44] *Ibid.*, preambular para. 4.
[45] *Ibid*, para. 2.
[46] *Ibid.*, preambular para. 5.
[47] H.J. Ehrlich, 'The swastika epidemic of 1959–60: anti-Semitism and community characteristics', *Social Problems*, 9/3 (1962), 264–72; O. Cohen, 'The swastikas on the wall: a survey of reactions', *XIV.1 The Wiener Library Bulletin* (1960), 209–13. According to Epstein, 'This first wave, which came to be dubbed the "swastika epidemic" was observed in Western Europe, the United States, and Latin America. It started with the desecration of a synagogue in Cologne on December 25, 1959 by two young Germans who were promptly apprehended and severely punished. Some 685 incidents were recorded in Germany, and over 600 in the United States. All told, nearly 2,500 incidents were recorded in 400 localities throughout the world. Most of them occurred in January or February 1960, and consisted of cemetery and synagogue desecrations and graffiti. Cases of a graver character, such as assaults on Jews and arson were rare, but some were also reported. This wave, which erupted unexpectedly, was of a universal character': S. Epstein, 'Cyclical patterns in antisemitism: the dynamics of anti-Jewish violence in western countries since the 1950s', *2 Acta* (SICSA, 1993).
[48] E/CN.4/800, pp. 58–71.
[49] Resolution 6 (XVI).

racial and national hatred and religious and racial prejudices, reminiscent of 'the crimes and outrages committed by the Nazis prior to and during the Second World War'.[50] *Inter alia*, the resolution condemned the manifestations as violations of the UN Charter and the Universal Declaration of Human Rights and, in group-oriented language, 'as a violation of the human rights of the groups against which they are directed',[51] urging appropriate punitive action, initiation or intensification of 'programmes of education designed to eradicate the racialist views and the prejudice reflected in these manifestations', as well as data gathering and comments on the manifestations, actions taken against them, views on their causes, etc.[52] During the discussions on the draft, a proposal to replace 'anti-Semitism' by 'anti-Jewish' was made and withdrawn,[53] and a proposal to make specific reference to the Nuremberg International Tribunal was also not adopted.[54] In the course of data evaluation by the Sub-Commission in 1961, it was suggested that the General Assembly be encouraged to undertake preparation of an international convention to impose specific legal obligations to prohibit manifestations of racial and national hatreds,[55] perhaps, as Schwelb remarks, contemplating an instrument 'of far narrower scope than what eventually became the Convention of 1965'.[56]

In 1961, the Economic and Social Council presented a draft resolution on the problem of 'Manifestations of Racial Prejudice and National and Religious Intolerance' to the General Assembly,[57] referring, *inter alia*, to the education of public opinion with a view to the eradication of racial prejudice and national and religious intolerance. The resolution called on governments of all States 'to take all necessary steps to rescind discriminatory laws which have the effect of creating and perpetuating racial prejudice and national and religious intolerance' and to adopt legislation prohibiting such discrimination and take legislative or other appropriate measures to combat such prejudice and intolerance.[58] The resolution did not refer to the idea of an international declaration or convention on racial and religious discrimination, nor did it make specific reference to anti-Semitism.

The move towards instruments on racial and religious discrimination made further strides at the seventeenth session of the General Assembly in 1962 under the agenda item 'Manifestations of racial prejudice and national and religious intolerance'. In the general debate, the representative of Israel recalled fresh manifestations of anti-Semitism: in the past year, 'scarcely a week had passed without reports of bombs thrown at Jewish schools, Jewish business premises machine-gunned, synagogues set on fire, gatherings by organized gangs of hoodlums, swastikas and filthy slogans smeared on buildings and Jewish cemeteries desecrated . . . organized Nazi groups had recently become bolder in some countries'.[59] The intervention included an attack on 'cultural

[50] Resolution 3 (XII) A, preambular para. 1.

[51] Resolution 3 (XII) B, para. 1.

[52] E/CN.4/800, para. 194.

[53] *Ibid.*, para. 169 (Krishnaswami).

[54] *Ibid.*, paras 168, 171, 179, 186 (Mironova).

[55] E/CN.4/815, paras 176 and 185.

[56] E. Schwelb, 'The International Convention on the Elimination of All Forms of Racial Discrimination', *ICLQ* 15 (1966), 996–1068, 998 [henceforth *The International Convention*].

[57] Resolution 826 B (XXXII), 27 July 1961.

[58] *Ibid.*, para. 2.

[59] A/C.3/SR.1165, para. 11. The representative made specific reference to 'Rockwell' (George Lincoln Rockwell, founder of the American Nazi party) and also to Colin Jordan, to which the UK replied that 'the trouble had . . . arisen from the intense rage and fury of the British public at the preachings and activities of a

discrimination'[60] against Jews in an unnamed country which in turn provoked a series of interventions by representatives commenting unfavourably on the treatment of Palestinians by Israel.[61] A positive reception in the Third Committee of the General Assembly (the Third Committee) was accorded to a seminal speech by the representative of Mauritania introducing a resolution for a convention on the elimination of racial discrimination.[62] Commencing with the claim that that all discrimination 'sprang from the desire to dominate',[63] the representative elaborated on four 'myths': of pure blood; of colour, (groups 'were despised and ostracised because of the degree of pigmentation of their skin'); the 'Jewish myth' ('latter-day racists had been connected with the pseudo-scientific idea of a Jewish race'); and the myth of racial superiority. He urged an impartial and humanitarian spirit and a practical approach on the part of the United Nations to addressing the problems of discrimination.

In the course of discussions, some delegations expressed a preference for a declaration instead of a convention,[64] which they thought might be premature.[65] There was wide support for the preparation of a declaration on racial discrimination, followed by a convention.[66] Other delegations supported an instrument addressing religious as well as racial discrimination[67] while still others pointed to the necessary coexistence of educative measures to combat racial discrimination along with legislation,[68] reminding fellow delegates that racial prejudice 'would not disappear overnight'.[69] Thus, the representative of France argued that, while in some cases legislative measures were indispensable,

> [l]egislative steps alone, however, were not enough, for it was in the minds of men that racial prejudice and intolerance were born, and the law was not always able to change states of mind. It was necessary to teach . . . the origins of discrimination and intolerance so that those evils could be analysed and methods evolved of combating them . . . Education in the narrow sense was not sufficient . . . it should be aimed at instilling . . . civic feeling, mutual understanding and a sense of individual responsibility. It should be oriented towards democracy.[70]

small group of neo-fascists headed by Colin Jordan, a group which numbered less than 100 members in a total population of 55 million': A/C.3/SR.1165, para. 39.

[60] A/C.3/SR.1165, para. 12.

[61] This was despite the protest by the representative of Israel that 'he had been careful to avoid any reference to the unfortunate and tragic conflict between Israel and her Arab neighbours': A/C.3/SR.1165, paragraph 35; also A/C.3/SR.1168, para. 13.

[62] A/C.3/SR.1165, paras 18–27.

[63] A/C.3/SR.1165, para. 19. A representative of UNESCO intervened to state that 'real scientists had refuted the allegations of so-called scientific racism' adding references to recent work of UNESCO (*The Race Question in Modern Science* and *The Race Question in Modern Thought*), concluding that 'no branch of science could provide racism with the slightest argument on which to base its theories': A/C.3/SR.1168, para. 2.

[64] A/C.3/SR.1171, para. 2 (New Zealand).

[65] The representative of Saudi Arabia, supporting the formulation of principles for a declaration on the elimination of racial discrimination (A/C.3/SR.1166, para. 9), also argued that 'the notion of race had little to do with discrimination, which was based rather on prejudice, tradition and custom', *ibid.*, para. 7.

[66] Remarks of the representatives of Congo Brazzaville, A/C.3/SR.1167, paras 17 and 18; Greece, *ibid.*, para. 35.

[67] Proposal of Liberia, A/C.3/L.1012/Rev.1.

[68] The representative of Nepal commented that 'education and legislation were indivisible': A/C.3/SR.1169, para. 3.

[69] Representative of Chile, A/C.3/SR.1167, para. 24.

[70] A/C.3/SR.1167, paras 3–6. To similar effect, remarks of the representative of Romania, A/C.3/SR.1166, paras 17–21, who added, *ibid.*, para. 19, that 'Romania had permanently eliminated all forms of discrimination whether racial, national or religious'. The Philippines on the other hand recommended that 'governments

Prefiguring the content of ICERD, the representative of Czechoslovakia made the substantive proposal that a convention on racial discrimination

> should include a definition of racial hatred and discrimination that included all forms of preaching racial superiority or incitement to racial hatred; an obligation on the contracting States to prevent, within their territories, any manifestation of hatred based on race or colour; an obligation . . . to make the incitement or manifestation of racial hatred a criminal offence; and an obligation . . . to carry out, within a specified time-limit, all the legislative, administrative or other measures required for implementation of the convention.[71]

In the event, the Third Committee adopted separate resolutions on racial discrimination and religious discrimination.[72] Schwelb summarizes the position:

> The decision to separate the problem of 'religious intolerance' from that of 'racial discrimination' had been brought about by political undercurrents which had very little to do with the merits of the problem. The opposition to coverage of religious as well as racial discrimination had come from some of the Arab delegations; it reflected the Arab–Israeli conflict. In addition, many delegations, particularly those from Eastern Europe, did not consider questions of religion to be as important and urgent as questions of race. The decision to draft two separate sets of instruments on the two problems was a compromise solution; it was understood that the instruments relating to racial discrimination would receive priority.[73]

Some delegations also suggested 'technical reasons'[74] why instruments on racial discrimination should be prioritized. According to the United Arab Republic, racial discrimination 'was a relatively simple issue, but the same could not be said of religious discrimination'.[75] Some idea of the assumed technical complexity of addressing religious discrimination in a convention can be gleaned from remarks by the representative of the Byelorussian Soviet Socialist Republic (SSR) who referred to 'the persecution of atheists in certain countries', and, more approvingly, the adoption of measures 'against inhuman religious practices or cults which destroyed people morally or physically'.[76] A further compendious account of the difficulties of addressing religious discrimination was offered by the representative of Saudi Arabia in terms of the complexity of dealing with sceptics, atheists, and other philosophies and ideologies, the varied forms taken by religion, the different bases and structures of religions, their different character and rites, the problems caused by religious fanaticism, the dietetic practices of religions, etc, concluding that if 'it

should make an honest and searching self-examination to determine where they might have fallen short of perfection': A/C.3/SR.1167, para. 15.

[71] A/C.3/SR.1165, para. 49.

[72] The draft resolution, A/C.3/L.1006/Rev.6 and Add. 1, regarding the preparation of a draft declaration and a draft convention on the elimination of all forms of racial discrimination, was adopted unanimously, A/C.3/SR.1173, para. 17. The draft resolution on the preparation of a draft declaration and a draft convention on the elimination of all forms of religious intolerance, A/C.3/L.1016, as amended verbally, was adopted unanimously, A/C.3/SR.1173, para. 19.

[73] Schwelb, *The International Convention*, 999.

[74] Venezuela, A/C.3/SR.1173, para. 5: 'there would be great technical difficulties in drafting a convention that would be acceptable to all countries'. In similar vein, the representative of Argentina *ibid.*, para. 4: 'international action on the question of religious intolerance should be limited to a declaration, since the subject was not suited to an international convention'.

[75] A/C.3/SR.1173, para. 11.

[76] A/C.3/SR/1173, para. 27.

was decided to prepare a document on the elimination of religious discrimination, it could not be confined to the five or six leading religions of the world, but would have to take account of all existing religions, which was a technical impossibility'.[77] The representative of Iraq contextualized differences between racial and religious discrimination:

> racial discrimination was particularly odious because it denied the fact that all human beings, by virtue of belonging to the human race, shared a common humanity, had a right to common needs, aspirations, faults and virtues; therein lay the essential difference between that form of discrimination and intolerance based on religion. Religious discrimination was of an entirely different character, as was demonstrated by the fact that the goal of religious wars had been to induce peoples to adopt a particular religion irrespective of their colour or race.[78]

In debates there were also references to work on religious intolerance particularly in the Sub-Commission, interference with which would 'completely paralyse' its work.[79] The debates in the General Assembly evince a sense of strong political polarization in the indignant assertions and rebuttals of discriminatory practices. The tensions generated by conflict in the Middle East are also apparent, as are further tensions evident from interchanges between independent States and their former colonial 'masters'. One delegation described the debating atmosphere as 'tense',[80] a diplomatic understatement.

The General Assembly elaborated on 'manifestations of racial prejudice', with a notable focus on public education and rectification of the legal situation, in resolution 1779 (XVII).[81] At the same meeting, in resolution 1780 (XVII),[82] the Assembly requested the Economic and Social Council to ask the Commission on Human Rights to prepare a draft Declaration on the Elimination of All Forms of Racial Discrimination and a draft Convention on the same subject. The preamble to the resolution recited, *inter alia*, that the General Assembly was '[d]eeply disturbed by the manifestations of discrimination based on differences of race, colour and religion still in evidence throughout the world',[83] and that it was necessary to take 'all possible steps conducive to the final and total elimination of all such manifestations, which violate the Charter of the United Nations and the Universal Declaration of Human Rights'.[84] A similar set of expressed motivations prompted the Assembly to look forward to the preparation of a declaration and convention on religious intolerance in resolution 1781 (XVII). Resolutions 1780 and 1781 envisaged the submission of their respective draft declarations by the eighteenth session of the General Assembly and not later than the twentieth session in the case of the draft conventions.[85] Following resolutions 1780 and 1781, the UN drafting work on 'race' was effectively split off from work on 'religion', a decision with consequences for the work of the Committee on the Elimination of Racial Discrimination.

77 A/C.3/SR.1171, paras 13–17 in particular.
78 A/C.3/SR.1171, para. 19.
79 Saudi Arabia, A/C.3/SR.1171, para. 17.
80 Mali, A/C.3/SR.1171, para. 23.
81 7 December 1962.
82 7 December 1962.
83 Resolution 1780 (XVII), preambular para. 2.
84 *Ibid.*, para. 3.
85 Resolution 1781 (XVII) noted in preambular para. 5 that 'the Commission on Human Rights is preparing draft principles on freedom and non-discrimination in the matter of religious rights and practices'.

E. The Declaration on the Elimination of Racial Discrimination

On the 'racial' side, the Commission on Human Rights prepared a draft declaration[86] which was transmitted by the Economic and Social Council to the General Assembly[87] and proclaimed as the UN Declaration on the Elimination of All Forms of Racial Discrimination on 20 November 1963.[88] The Declaration is described by McKean as a 'preliminary reconnaissance' of the principle of non-discrimination, and, while it differs in marked respects from the eventual Convention, it introduces some key themes.[89] Individual provisions of the Declaration are set out in various chapters of the present work.

The preamble to the Declaration recalls UN Charter principles of dignity and equality of human beings and its promise of respect for human rights and fundamental freedoms for all without distinction as to race, sex, language, or religion;[90] succeeding paragraphs recall the grounds of non-discrimination in the Universal Declaration of Human Rights, particularly those of 'race, colour or national origin', as well as its equality provisions including 'equal protection against any discrimination and against any incitement to such discrimination'.[91] There are links with the anti-colonial movement in references to the condemnation of colonialism by the United Nations and to the Colonial Declaration of 1960. There follows a statement rebutting 'any doctrine of racial differentiation or superiority' as 'scientifically false, morally condemnable, socially unjust and dangerous'[92] and that there is no justification for racial discrimination either in theory or in practice. There is a nuance of difference between the formulation in the Declaration and its equivalent in ICERD which describes as scientifically false, etc 'any doctrine of superiority based on racial differentiation',[93] laying heavier emphasis on the rejection of claims or doctrines of racial 'superiority' compared to racial 'differentiation', whereas the Declaration is robust in rejecting both.[94]

The Declaration is hesitant on the ubiquity of racial discrimination, referring to its 'manifestations' 'in certain areas of the world', some of which are imposed by certain governments by means of legislative, administrative, or other measures, in the form, *inter alia*, of apartheid, segregation, and separation, as well as by the promotion and dissemination of doctrines of racial superiority and expansionism. The text identifies governmental policies of discrimination as violating human rights and tending to jeopardize friendly relations among peoples, cooperation between nations, and international peace and security. There is no definition of discrimination; instead, Article 1 compounds various sentiments expressed in the preamble:

> Discrimination between human beings on the ground of race, colour or ethnic origin is an offence to human dignity and shall be condemned as a denial of the principles of the Charter of the United Nations, as a violation of the human rights and fundamental freedoms proclaimed in the Universal

86 E/CN.4/846, para. 210, resolution 7 (XV), Annex.

87 Economic and Social Council resolution 958E (XXXVI).

88 Resolution 1904 (XVIII).

89 W.A. McKean, *Equality and Discrimination under International Law* (Clarendon Press, 1983), p. 154 [henceforth *Equality and Discrimination*].

90 Preambular para. 1.

91 Preambular paras 2 and 3.

92 Preambular para. 5.

93 ICERD, preambular para. 6.

94 Further discussion in Chapter 5. See also D. Keane, *Caste-Based Discrimination*.

Declaration of Human Rights, as an obstacle to friendly and peaceful relations among nations and as a fact capable of disturbing peace and security among peoples.[95]

In adopting the Declaration, the General Assembly emphasized the importance of the speedy preparation and adoption of an international convention on the elimination of all forms of racial discrimination, and requested the Economic and Social Council to mandate the Commission on Human Rights to give absolute priority to the preparation of the convention.[96]

F. From Declaration to Convention

The Sub-Commission took up the task ('the most important task of its existence')[97] of preparing the Convention at its sixteenth session in 1964, devoting a total of twenty-one plenary meetings to this.[98] The background documentation included the Declaration on the Elimination of Racial Discrimination, and a note from the Secretary-General of the United Nations outlining the history of the consideration of the question by that body.[99] In addition to various International Labour Organization (ILO) and UNESCO documents,[100] the note contained comments or proposals relating to a convention submitted by six governments.[101] The Sub-Commission also had before it a statement submitted by the International League for the Rights of Man.[102] Three key drafts emanated from Sub-Commission members,[103] referred to throughout the present work as the Abram, Calvocoressi, and Ivanov/Ketrzynski drafts.

The report of the Sub-Commission summarizes the general feeling that the convention should set out clearly and precisely the obligations of States and provide effective measures of implementation,[104] and also recalls the broad agreement among Sub-Commission members that the draft convention should be based primarily upon the Declaration on Racial Discrimination.[105] Capotorti, however, noted that there were opposing views on the subject: 'Some members considered, like Calvocoressi, that the convention could not embody all the elements of the Declaration. Others, on the contrary, considered that the convention should be fuller and more detailed',[106] and be capable of being signed,

[95] The 'switch' from the preambular recall of the Universal Declaration's prohibition of discrimination based on 'race, colour or national origin' to a reference to discrimination based on 'race, colour or ethnic origin' is notable: Article 2 of the Universal Declaration does not employ the term 'ethnic'.

[96] General Assembly resolution 1906 (XVIII).

[97] Comment by the Chairman, Santa Cruz, E/CN.4/Sub.2/SR.410, p. 6.

[98] Report of the sixteenth session of the Sub-Commission, E/CN.4/Sub.2/241. Discussions in the Sub-Commission are found in E/CN.4/Sub.2/SR.406–18, 420, 422–5, and 427–9.

[99] E/CN.4/Sub.2/234 and Add. 1.

[100] Convention Concerning Discrimination in Respect of Employment and Occupation (ILO Convention 111 of 1958), the UNESCO Convention against Discrimination in Education 1960, and the text of the Protocol of 1962 Instituting a Conciliation and Good Offices Commission, etc, to settle disputes arising from the Convention against Discrimination in Education.

[101] Czechoslovakia, Honduras, Madagascar, Nigeria, Trinidad and Tobago, and the United Kingdom, Annex IV to the Secretary-General's note.

[102] E/CN.4/Sub.2/NGO/36.

[103] The Abram draft, E/CN.4/Sub.2/L.308, and *ibid.*, Add.1/rev.1; and Add.1/rev.1/Corr.1; the Calvocoressi draft, E/CN.4/Sub.2/L.309; the Ivanov and Ketrzynski draft, E/CN.4/Sub.2/L.314: see Annex I of the Report of the sixteenth session of the Sub-Commission, E/CN.4/873.

[104] E/CN.4/873, para. 27.

[105] *Ibid.*, para. 28.

[106] E/CN.4/Sub.2/SR.408, p. 3.

ratified, and applied by the greatest possible number of countries.[107] Saario stressed that the draft should also be general in scope 'in order to remain valid for the longest possible time; care should therefore be taken not to mention phenomena limited to a particular area or to the present time'.[108] Ketrzynski argued that the work must be based on the present situation and that the members should not be asking themselves 'whether *apartheid* would still exist in twenty years' time'.[109]

The draft Convention as adopted by the Sub-Commission at its sixteenth session contained a preamble and nine substantive articles, plus an article X with three paragraphs on measures to give effect to the Convention.[110] By resolution 2 (XVI), the Sub-Commission also transmitted to the Commission a 'preliminary draft as an expression of the general views of the Sub-Commission on additional measures of implementation which will help to make the draft international convention . . . more effective'.[111] At the request of the Sub-Commission, the Secretary-General transmitted to the Commission the records containing the views expressed by Sub-Commission members on the draft convention. Further, the Secretary-General submitted to the Commission a working paper presenting alternative forms for final clauses, including those submitted by members of the Sub-Commission and taking into account provisions included in the texts of conventions prepared by the United Nations and its specialized agencies.[112]

The Commission prioritized the preparation of the draft, devoted its 775th to 810th meetings to the task of preparing the Convention,[113] utilizing a wide range of documentary input from the Sub-Commission, UN bodies and specialized agencies,[114] governments,[115] as well as written statements from non-governmental organizations (NGOs).[116] The Commission adopted the draft Convention[117] comprising a preamble and seven substantive articles (deleting Articles VIII and IX of the Sub-Commission's text) at its twentieth session, passing consideration of Article X to the General Assembly through the Economic and Social Council for lack of time.

[107] *Ibid.*

[108] E/CN.4/Sub.2/SR.408, p. 5. He later elaborated to observe that 'once an international convention was adopted it became an integral part of international law; it should therefore state rules which were of lasting value', *ibid.*, p. 7.

[109] E/CN.4/Sub.2/SR.408, p. 6.

[110] The draft Convention is reproduced as an Annex to Sub-Commission Resolution I (XVI): E/CN.4/873; E/CN.4/Sub.2/241, p. 44 (the resolution), pp. 45–50 (draft International Convention on the Elimination of All Forms of Racial Discrimination).

[111] E/CN.4/873, para. 123.

[112] E/CN.4/L.679.

[113] E/CN.4/SR.775–810.

[114] *Inter alia*, the Commission on Human Rights had before it the text of ILO Convention No 111 concerning discrimination in respect of employment and occupation, and the text of the UNESCO Convention against Discrimination in Education 1960, E/CN.43/Sub.2/234/Annex I and Annex II.

[115] Proposals and comments from the governments of Burma, Honduras, Madagascar, Nigeria, Trinidad and Tobago, Ukrainian SSR, the USSR, and the United Kingdom: E/CN.4/Sub.2/234/Annex IV. A working paper from the government of Czechoslovakia to the seventeenth session of the UN General Assembly was also made available to the Commission: E/CN.4/234/Add. 1–3.

[116] Including the Co-ordinating Board of Jewish Organizations (E/CN.4/NGO/115); the International League for the Rights of Man (E/CN.4/NGO/119); World Jewish Congress (E/CN.4/NGO/121); International Federation of Christian Trade Unions (E/CN.4/NGO/122); and the International Commission of Jurists (E/CN.4/NGO/123).

[117] At its twentieth session, ECOSOC official Records, thirty-seventh session, Supplement No 8 (E/3873), Chapter II, draft resolution I (XX).

The Council, in resolution 1015B (XXXVII),[118] transmitted the Commission articles to the General Assembly, as well as a number of documents not voted on by the Commission, including the proposal for an additional article on anti-Semitism submitted by the United States of America and the sub-amendment submitted by the Union of Soviet Socialist Republics (USSR) and discussions on these proposals,[119] Article X of the Sub-Commission's draft, and the preliminary draft on measures of implementation transmitted by the Sub-Commission was also transmitted, as well as the working paper by the Secretary-General on final clauses of the draft Convention.[120] The Third Committee of the General Assembly decided not to include any reference to specific forms of racial discrimination.[121] The Plenary of the General Assembly added a new Article 20 on reservations before adopting the Convention as a whole.[122]

G. Comment

Despite a steadily weakening intellectual base, the concept of race was drafted into a range of international instruments, ostensibly on the basis that to confront the phenomenon it was necessary to name it. It was also deemed necessary to attack its 'scientific' credibility in an international normative instrument that incorporates a surprising conflation of intellectual and practical regulation.

In the eyes of many delegates drafting the Convention, the most vivid international expression of racial discourse emerged from its employment in colonial expansion and in the justification of slavery.[123] While the generators of colonial enterprise are multiple, racial distinctions played their part together with cognate notions of hierarchy in facilitating the colonizing processes and making them more amenable to conscience. Imagining groups as approximating to sub-species of lesser intellect and moral worth is eminently capable of facilitating imperialist designs. The transcending of the colonial framework opened up the theatre of operations of the Convention to all States parties. The recognition of the ubiquity of racial discrimination has been painful for many, perhaps particularly for those who were the most prominent in anti-colonial struggles.

Minorities (and non-citizens) were not generously treated in the drafting process. Deleted Article VIII, discussed further in Chapter 7 in connection with non-citizens, proposed that nothing in the Convention was to be interpreted as implying any right to discriminate on any basis other than those listed in Article I, nor 'as implying a grant of equal political rights to nationals of a contracting State or a grant of political rights to distinct racial ethnic or national group as such',[124] to which latter element Matsch proposed to add 'in a contracting State where no such special rights have been or are

[118] 30 July 1964.

[119] A/6181, paras 4–12.

[120] E/CN.4/L.679.

[121] Greece and Hungary proposed a draft resolution (A/C.3/L.1244) that the Convention should not include reference to specific forms of racial discrimination; the proposal was adopted by 82 votes to 12, with 10 abstentions: A/6181, paras 7 and 9. The decision did not affect the already adopted article on segregation and apartheid.

[122] Article 20 was adopted by the Plenary of the General Assembly by 82 votes to 4, with 21 abstentions, A/PV.1406, para. 57.

[123] Discussed in Chapter 2.

[124] E/CN.4/Sub.2/L.340.

granted'.[125] Textual reformulations produced the following:[126] 'Nothing in the present Convention may be interpreted as implicitly recognizing or denying political or other rights to non-nationals nor to groups of persons of a common race, colour, ethnic or national origin which exist or may exist as distinct groups within a State party.'[127] Discussions in the Commission did not lead to agreement on substance. The position of nationals and non-nationals under the Convention thus fell to be determined by Article 1, while the question of special rights for groups, including questions of autonomy or self-determination, was not addressed as such.

However, apart from its preamble, the Convention focuses little on international relations but overwhelmingly on the 'internality' of racial discrimination, of which anti-Semitism, Nazism, and apartheid presented themselves as only the most disturbing examples. Other 'internalities' stemming from multicultural realities of States would gradually transform the implementation challenge. Changes in the contours of identity politics from visualizing the anti-colonial States as 'one people, one nation' towards a view of States as composed of sub-groups including ethnic minorities, indigenous peoples, and others, were destined to broaden the readings of the Convention. Splitting off racial from religious discrimination improved the governability of the Convention but at the cost of some incoherence vis-à-vis the intersection between religion and ethnicity, setting in place the puzzle of appraising, on grounds of race and ethnicity, discrimination against the enjoyment of religious freedoms. The race–religion relationship continues to fray the edges of the Convention.

The genealogy of the Convention is complex: it has many progenitors. The experts and delegates drafting the text absorbed influences and processed theories and practice in their own manner, leaving the marks of their reflections on the adopted instrument. They also instituted the Committee on the Elimination of Racial Discrimination, mandating it to take the standards towards their stated goal: the elimination of racial discrimination. The following chapter addresses the Committee and its functions which, equally with its receptive approach to developments in standards of human rights, has not positioned its procedures outside the currents of change.

[125] E/CN.4/Sub.2/L.341.

[126] Drafts by Cuevas Cancino, E/CN.4/Sub.2/L.347; and by Krishnaswami and Mudawi, E/CN.4/Sub.2/L.348.

[127] E/CN.4/874, para. 242.

4. The Convention and the Committee

A. Introduction

Following its title and extensive preamble, the Convention is divided into three parts: the substantive norms prohibiting racial discrimination (Articles 1–7), the analysis of which constitutes the main body of the present work; the Committee on the Elimination of Racial Discrimination (CERD) and its procedures (Articles 8–16); and final clauses relating to signature, ratification, and accession, reservations, denunciation, the role of the International Court of Justice, revision of the Convention, etc (Articles 17–25). This chapter focuses on fully functioning CERD procedures, with briefer reference to other procedures 'on the books' that have not engendered sufficient practice: the inter-State procedure, the non-functioning of which may be contrasted with the active engagement with the Convention by the International Court of Justice in *Georgia v Russian Federation*;[1] and the procedure under Article 15, which has seen its operative decolonization context progressively eroded. The discussion reflects on the principal developments since CERD became operational, while maintaining a primarily analytical focus. The legal and geopolitical changes that have occurred since the adoption of the Convention have marked its procedures as much as the substantive norms.[2]

177 States are parties to the Convention,[3] of which 57 have accepted the optional procedure for individual communications under Article 14.[4] The list of States parties ratifying, acceding, or succeeding to the Convention falls into patterns: for example, the dominant mode of signifying consent to be bound for post-USSR States is accession,

[1] *Application of the International Convention on the Elimination of All Forms of Racial Discrimination (Georgia v Russian Federation), Provisional Measures, ICJ Reports 2008, p. 353; Preliminary Objections, Judgment, ICJ Reports 2011, p. 70.* Article 22 is discussed further in Chapter 19 of the present work.

[2] While the present chapter does not proceed on an article-by-article basis, it broadly follows the style of the chapters on substantive norms in setting out a brief drafting history of the Committee and its procedures, followed by an account of current practice and concluding comments.

[3] Angola, Bhutan, Nauru, Palau, Sao Tome and Principe, and Singapore, have signed but not ratified the Convention: <https://treaties.un.org/pages/ViewDetails.aspx?src=TREATY&mtdsg_no=IV-2&chapter=4&lang=en>.

[4] Article 17 of the Convention opens it for signature 'by any State member of the United Nations or member of any of its specialized agencies, by any State party to the Statute of the International Court of Justice, and by any other State which has been invited by the General Assembly of the United Nations to become a party to this Convention'; Article 18 provides for accession to the Convention by States referred to in Article 17. In the drafting, Poland proposed that the Convention should be open for signature 'by all States': A/C.3/L.1272. The Polish amendment was defeated by 41 votes to 32, with 18 abstentions: A/6181, para. 177; for discussions, see A/C.3/SR/1358 and A/C.3/SR.1366. The representative of the US argued against the amendment, suggesting it would place a burden on the Secretary-General to decide what entities not members of the United Nations were States, and that many members of the United Nations 'would be unwilling to sign and ratify the Convention if by doing so they would have to enter into treaty relations with entities they did not recognize as States': A/C.3/SR.1366, para. 27. The formula in the Convention is termed 'the Vienna formula', deriving from Articles 81–83 of the Vienna Convention on the Law of Treaties; for brief discussion, see A. Aust, *Handbook of International Law* (2nd edn, Cambridge University Press, 2010), p. 62. Later conventions, such as CEDAW and the CRC, use the 'all States' formula. A number of States have made declarations to the effect that, in light of the principle of the sovereign equality of States, Articles 17 and 18 in themselves constitute a form of discrimination in preventing States outside the Vienna formula from making an effective contribution to the Convention.

while States of the former Yugoslavia are listed as parties through succession. At the time of writing, Palestine is the latest addition to the list of States parties.[5] CERD is now only one among core UN 'treaty bodies', themselves situated in a wider framework of 'mechanisms' complementing the panoply of standards.[6] In the field of racial discrimination, there is a range of further mechanisms at the UN level, including some developed following the Durban World Conference on Racism.[7] Related non-treaty mechanisms include the Special Rapporteur on Contemporary Forms of Racism, Racial Discrimination, Xenophobia and Related Intolerance;[8] the Working Group on the Effective Implementation of the Durban Declaration and Programme of Action;[9] the Working Group of Experts on persons of African Descent,[10] and the Independent Eminent Experts Group.[11] Within human rights mechanisms, treaty bodies occupy a distinctive space, with procedures replicated across a range of instruments, developed to different degrees according to the exigencies of the instrument in question. At the regional level, Article 15 of the Inter-American Convention against Racism, Racial Discrimination and Related Forms of Intolerance provides for the establishment of an Inter-American Committee for the Prevention and Elimination of Racism, Racial Discrimination, and All Forms of Discrimination and Intolerance.[12]

The UN treaty bodies have membership of experts varying in number from ten to twenty-three, while twenty-five experts of the Sub-Committee on the Prevention of Torture implement the Optional Protocol to the Convention against Torture (OPCAT). The members of treaty bodies are nominated and elected by States parties, the exception being the Committee on Economic, Social and Cultural Rights (CESCR), the membership of which is elected by the UN Economic and Social Council and is subject to regional distribution.[13] Members of treaty bodies are independent and not subject to government control; equally, they are not international civil servants employed by the United Nations.

A set of broadly similar procedures have been developed by the treaty bodies to assist States parties in the implementation of their obligations: the examination of State reports, processing of inter-State or individual communications, adoption of general comments known as general recommendations in the case of CERD and the Convention on the

[5] In April 2014, the Palestinian leadership signed accession letters for a range of international instruments, including the Convention and other UN core human rights treaties; the move is referred to in the press briefing for the UN Secretary-General: <http://www.un.org/News/briefings/docs/2014/db140410.doc.htm>.

[6] For an overview, see J. Connors and M. Schmidt, 'United Nations', in D. Moeckli, S. Shah, and S. Sivakumaran (eds), *International Human Rights Law* (2nd edn, Oxford University Press, 2014), 359–97, at 375–87 [henceforth *International Human Rights Law*]; also, *United Nations Reform: Measures and Proposals, Note by the Secretary-General*, A/66/860, 26 June 2012 [henceforth *United Nations Reform*].

[7] World Conference against Racism, Racial Discrimination, Xenophobia and Related Intolerance, 31 August to 8 September 2001, A/CONF.189/12. See also CERD GR 28 on the follow-up to the World Conference Against Racism.

[8] Established by Commission on Human Rights resolution 1993/20; see also resolution 1994/64, 9 February 1994.

[9] Commission on Human Rights resolution 2002/68, and Economic and Social Council decision 2002/270, 25 June 2002.

[10] Commission on Human Rights resolution 2002/68, 25 April 2002, and 2003/30, 25 April 2003.

[11] General Assembly resolution 56/266, 27 March 2002.

[12] <http://www.oas.org/en/sla/dil/docs/inter_american_treaties_A-68_racism.pdf>. Although it is not a treaty body, distinguished work in the field of anti-racism has been undertaken by the European Commission against Racism and Intolerance (ECRI): <http://www.coe.int/t/dghl/monitoring/ecri/default_en.asp>.

[13] Connors and Schmidt in *International Human Rights Law*, p. 376.

Elimination of All Forms of Discrimination Against Women (CEDAW), inquiry procedures, and in the case of CERD, an 'early warning and urgent action' procedure, a concept echoed in the Convention on the Rights of Persons with Disabilities (CRPD) and the International Convention for the Protection of All Persons from Enforced Disappearance (CPED).[14] Sundry 'follow-up' mechanisms to track the fate of the concluding observations and recommendations of various committees have been developed,[15] as well as for opinions on individual cases. Eight of the core UN human rights treaties—the International Covenant on Civil and Political Rights (ICCPR), the Convention against Torture (CAT), the International Convention on the Elimination of All Forms of Racial Discrimination (ICERD), CEDAW, the CRPD, CRC, CPED, and the International Covenant on Economic, Social and Cultural Rights (ICESCR)—have functioning individual communications procedures.[16] The procedures for inter-State claims that have been elaborated for ICERD, the ICCPR, ICESCR, CAT, CPED, Convention on Migrant Workers (CMW), and the Convention on the Rights of the Child (CRC), share the distinction of not having been tested in practice.

Treaty bodies are designated as committees, not courts of law, a distinction that has stimulated the growth of a body of commentary on the nature and extent of their 'authority' in decision-making and interpretation of their constituent treaties.[17] The regular *modus operandi* of the treaty bodies is decision by consensus, with dissents uncommon, though the procedure under the First Optional Protocol to the ICCPR has generated a significant number of dissenting opinions.[18] The growth of commonalities in the work of the treaty bodies is facilitated in part by servicing of their operations by the Secretariat of the United Nations.[19] Harmonization of their efforts is encouraged in, for example, reporting procedures, through the development of a system whereby States prepare a 'common core document' containing general background on the domestic framework for the implementation of human rights, and a 'treaty-specific document' that (ideally) responds in detail to the requirements of the treaty in question;[20] guidelines for 'common core' and 'treaty-specific' documents are referred to extensively in the present work. Reform of the system, currently surfacing as 'the treaty body strengthening process', has been on the agenda of the United Nations for decades.[21]

[14] *Other Activities of the Human Rights Treaty Bodies*, etc, HRI/MC/2013/3, 22 April 2013, p. 5. See also United Nations, *Handbook for Human Rights Treaty Body Members*, HR/PUB/15/2 (2015).

[15] *Ibid.*, pp. 3–5.

[16] The complaints procedure for the CMW is not yet in force: the CRC procedure entered into force in 2014.

[17] See, *inter alia*, the detailed appraisals of key issues regarding the status and authority of treaty body decisions in H. Keller and G. Ulfstein (eds), *UN Human Rights Treaty Bodies: Law and Legitimacy* (Cambridge University Press, 2012). [henceforth *UN Human Rights Treaty Bodies*].

[18] Until recently, it was accurate to state that no dissent had been recorded under the individual communications procedure under Article 14 of ICERD. A first such dissenting opinion—by CERD member Vázquez—was published in 2013 in *TBB-Turkish Union in Berlin/Brandenburg v Germany*, CERD/C/82/D/48/2010 (2013). A footnote to *Jama v Denmark*, CERD/C/75/D/41/2008 (2009), records the non-participation of CERD member Peter in the adoption of the Committee's opinion.

[19] *United Nations Reform*, pp. 16–17.

[20] The system of harmonized guidelines on reporting including a 'common core document' and a 'treaty-specific document' was introduced in 2006: HRI/MC/2006/3 and Corr.1; the background is briefly explained in *United Nations Reform*, p. 52.

[21] Reform/strengthening is comprehensively treated in S. Egan, 'Strengthening the United Nations Human Rights Treaty Body System', *Human Rights Law Review* 13.2 (2013), 209–43 [henceforth *Strengthening the Treaty Body System*].

B. *Travaux Préparatoires*

I. The Committee

The principal drafting burden regarding the measures of implementation fell to the Third Committee of the General Assembly, utilizing materials developed by the Sub-Commission on the Prevention of Discrimination and Protection of Minorities on the basis of proposals submitted by Sub-Commission member Ingles.[22] The Sub-Commission considered the first article of these proposed measures, and incorporated it in the draft convention as Article X.[23]

> 1. The States parties to this Convention undertake to submit a report on the legislative or other measures which they have adopted and which give effect to the provisions of this Convention, (a) within one year after the entry into force of the Convention for the State concerned and (b) thereafter every two years and whenever the Economic and Social Council so requests upon recommendation of the Commission on Human Rights and after consultation with the States parties. 2. All reports shall be submitted to the Secretary-General of the United Nations for consideration by the Economic and Social Council which may transmit them to the Commission on Human Rights or the specialized agency for information, study and, if necessary, general recommendation. 3. The States parties directly concerned may submit to the Economic and Social Council observations on any general recommendations that may be made in accordance with paragraph 2 of this article.[24]

The draft Article did not refer to a monitoring committee specific to the Convention. Resolution 2 (XVI) of the Sub-Commission annexed a preliminary but extensive draft of 'additional measures of implementation', the centrepiece of which was the proposal to institute a Good Offices and Conciliation Committee 'responsible for seeking the amicable settlement of disputes between States parties concerning the interpretation, application or fulfilment of the . . . Convention'.[25] The proposed eleven-member Committee, comprising 'persons of high moral standing and acknowledged impartiality', was to be elected by the UN General Assembly,[26] and could establish its own rules of procedure which were, however, subject to an initial 'vetting' by States parties.[27] It was envisaged that the Committee would make recommendations to the Economic and Social Council to request an opinion from the International Court of Justice 'on any legal question connected with a matter of which the Committee is seized'.[28]

The Commission on Human Rights decided not to examine the article because of lack of time, and instead adopted resolution 1 (XX), which recommended to the Economic and Social Council that it submit the text of Article X to the General Assembly together with the records of discussion in the Commission.[29] The relevant Commission records are sparse, consisting largely of comments on the importance of implementation in order, in

[22] E/CN.4/Sub.2/L.321.

[23] E/CN.4/873, para. 117.

[24] Resolution I (XVI), Draft International Convention on the Elimination of All Forms of Racial Discrimination, Annex, E/CN.4/Sub.2/241, pp. 45–50.

[25] Annex to resolution 2 (XVI), Article 1, E/CN.4/873, pp. 51–7.

[26] *Ibid.*, Article 2.

[27] Annex to resolution 2 (XVI), Article 9.

[28] *Ibid.*, Article 11.

[29] E/CN.4/874, paras 281–82; discussions in the Commission are summarized, *ibid.*, paras 284–8.

the words of one delegate, to make the Convention 'a truly effective instrument'.[30] The inclusion of measures of implementation in the Convention was broadly supported in order to distinguish the Convention from the Declaration on the Elimination of Racial Discrimination.[31] Some representatives resisted the idea of an expert committee in favour of a committee of States parties.[32]

In the Third Committee, proposals of The Philippines[33] incorporated the Sub-Commission's suggestion of a 'Good Offices and Conciliation Committee' of eleven members. A text designated Article VIII was proposed by Ghana, Mauritania, and The Philippines,[34] and later individuated into Article VIII—Article 8 of the Convention—and Article VIII (bis) (Article 9 of the Convention).[35] In the first of these drafts,[36] the 'Good Offices and Conciliation Committee' became merely a 'Committee' with eighteen 'experts' holding four-year terms, whose field of expertise was not specified. In the revised draft by the co-sponsors,[37] the 'Committee' acquired a personality, becoming the 'Committee on the Elimination of Racial Discrimination'.[38] Unsuccessful amendments included the proposal to ratchet up the level of expertise by requiring, as a condition of membership, 'acknowledged competence with regard to the problem of the elimination of racial discrimination and of the observance of human rights'.[39] Tanzania unsuccessfully proposed to rename the Committee 'the United Nations Committee on the Elimination of Racial Discrimination';[40] its proposal to transfer the burden of experts' expenses in the performance of Committee duties from the national State of the member to 'the regular budget of the United Nations' was also rejected.[41]

II. Convention Procedures

The text of Article VIII (bis) proposed to the Third Committee by Ghana, Mauritania, and The Philippines[42] is identical to the ultimately agreed version of Article 9 except for the final clause of paragraph 2, which in the draft referred to 'comments, if any, from the States parties concerned' as opposed to simply 'comments, if any, from States parties' in the final text; at the 1351st meeting the representative of the United Kingdom (UK) orally

[30] Representative of the Philippines, E/CN.4/SR.810, p. 7.
[31] E/CN.4/874, para. 285.
[32] *Ibid.*, para. 286.
[33] A/C.3/L.1221.
[34] A/C.3/L.1291.
[35] A/C.3/L.1293.
[36] A/C.3/L.1291.
[37] A/C.3/L.1293.
[38] *Ibid.*, para. 1.
[39] Uruguay, A/C.3/L.1296, rejected by 16 votes to 13, with 62 abstentions: A/6181, para. 110(a)(v).
[40] A/C.3/L.1295, rejected by 55 votes to 22, with 17 abstentions: A/6181, para. 110(a)(i).
[41] A/C.3/L.1295. The amendment was rejected by 39 votes to 32, with 22 abstentions: A/6181, para. 110(f)(i). Article 8(6) of the Convention provides that States parties 'shall be responsible for the expenses of the members of the Committee while they are in performance of Committee duties'. Regular requests to States parties are made by the Committee on the basis of amendments made by States parties in 1992, which would require the Secretary-General to provide the necessary facilities for the effective performance of the functions of the Committee, and that members of the Committee shall 'receive emoluments from United Nations resources on such terms and conditions as the General Assembly may decide'; the amendments will enter into force when accepted by a two-thirds majority of States parties. Although the changes were endorsed by the General Assembly in resolutions commencing with resolution 47/111, only 45 States parties have accepted them: <https://treaties.un.org/pages/ViewDetails.aspx?src=TREATY&mtdsg_no=IV-2-a&chapter=4&lang=en>.
[42] A/C.3/L.1293.

proposed to delete 'the' and 'concerned' from the proposed text.[43] An earlier suggestion by Ghana, Mauritania, and The Philippines regarding prior consultation with States parties before reporting to the General Assembly[44] does not appear in the later draft. The representative of Sudan proposed the deletion of 'suggestions and',[45] arguing against the prospect of a committee making specific proposals.[46] India also warned against placing States parties 'in the dock because of shortcomings in implementing the Convention'.[47] Tanzania on the other hand, unsuccessfully proposed the deletion of 'general' before 'recommendations'[48]—the representative had commented unfavourably on the restriction of the Committee's powers to suggestions and 'general' recommendations, arguing that 'the committee should have to examine specific questions and make precise recommendations'.[49]

The import of the amendments of Sudan and Tanzania was later recalled in the CERD progress report, *The First Twenty Years*,[50] according to which the Third Committee 'had before it two antithetical amendments... Under the first proposal,[51] the Committee would have been empowered to make "general recommendations" only; under the second,[52] it would have competence to make "suggestions" and "recommendations" without restrictions as to the generality or specificity of either.'[53] The report goes on to suggest that by retaining the word 'suggestions', the 'the authors of the Convention wanted to avoid language that might have inhibited the Committee from adopting "suggestions" relating to particular cases',[54] while by retaining 'general', 'the Third Committee appears to have intended that the competence of the Committee to "recommend" was to be exercised only in situations of general relevance'.[55] This does not answer the question as to what constitutes a situation of 'general relevance' for a recommendation, or what forms a 'suggestion' may take.

As regards the inter-State procedure, the draft of Article X (Article 11) proposed by Ghana, Mauritania, and The Philippines[56] differed from the final version only in limited respects. In paragraph 1 of the draft, the term 'complaint' was used, in contrast to 'communication' in the final version, while 'shall submit' was used in the draft and final versions. Paragraph 3 of the draft did not qualify the remedies to be exhausted as 'domestic', and omitted the principle in the final text referring to the situation where the application of remedies is unreasonably prolonged. Paragraph 5 of the draft is the same as the final version, except for the addition of 'Adequate notice of the date on which the matter will be considered shall be given to the States parties concerned.' Successful amendments to paragraph 1 included that of Mexico changing 'complaint' to

[43] The amendment was adopted by 25 votes to 18, with 44 abstentions: A/6181, para. 114(b)(iii).
[44] A/C.3/L.1291.
[45] A/6181,para. 113; the amendment was defeated by 68 votes to 2, with 19 abstentions, *ibid.*, para. 114(b)(i).
[46] A/C.3/SR.1352, para. 7.
[47] A/C.3/SR.1352, para. 14.
[48] Rejected by 58 votes to 4, with 27 abstentions.
[49] A/C.3/SR.1351, para. 37.
[50] *The First Twenty Years, Progress Report of the Committee on the Elimination of Racial Discrimination* (United Nations, 1991) [henceforth *The First Twenty Years*].
[51] Of Sudan.
[52] Of Tanzania.
[53] *The First Twenty Years*, para. 118.
[54] *Ibid.*, para. 119.
[55] *Ibid.*, para. 119.
[56] A/C.3/L.1291.

'communication'.[57] For paragraph 3, the proposal of Canada and Italy to qualify 'remedies' by 'domestic' was also accepted.[58]

The inclusion of 'domestic' before 'remedies' was strongly criticized by the representative of Tanzania on grounds that it 'represented a deliberate attempt to provide a State which had violated the Convention with unlimited opportunities for frustrating the true purpose of the instrument by continuing indefinitely to argue that all domestic remedies had not yet been exhausted'.[59] The question of the burden of proof that domestic remedies had been exhausted drew forth varying suggestions including that the burden fell on the receiving State;[60] on the complainant;[61] that only the State itself could decide whether domestic remedies had been exhausted;[62] and that it was ultimately up to the Committee which would have before it the report on measures adopted to give effect to the provisions of the Convention.[63] The requirement of adequate notice etc in paragraph 5 was rejected on the proposal of Austria.[64]

Draft Article XI (Article 12), proposed by Ghana, Mauritania, and The Philippines,[65] centring on the election, composition, and meetings of the Ad Hoc Conciliation Commission for inter-State disputes, was retained in substantially the same form through the drafting process, while paragraph 1 mainly reflects a proposal by Canada.[66] Paragraph 2 of the draft article (now Article 12(2)) was proposed by Tanzania,[67] while its suggestion to devolve the expenses of the Commission to the regular budget of the United Nations was rejected. An additional paragraph from Tanzania proposing that the recommendations of the Commission were to be made public 'but not necessarily the evidence received in camera by the Commission', was also rejected.[68] The three-State draft of Article XII (Article 13) regarding findings and recommendations of the Ad Hoc Commission, was processed in two stages;[69] the principal change was to replace a reference to communicating the report of the Commission and comments of the States parties concerned to the Secretary-General of the United Nations with the current text: communication to 'other States parties to this Convention'.[70]

The draft additional measures of implementation included in Sub-Commission resolution 2 (XVI) did not include provision for petitions from individuals. In the Commission on Human Rights, the representative of Austria commented that 'for States alone to be entitled to submit disputes relating to the Convention to the committee might lead to conflict between States and run counter to the Convention'.[71] Thus, 'it would be preferable to grant individuals a right of petition, subject to very strict rules of procedure

[57] A/6181, para. 120.
[58] *Ibid.*, para. 124.
[59] A/C.3/SR.1353, para. 44.
[60] Israel, *ibid.*, para. 32; Tanzania, para. 44.
[61] Senegal, A/C.3/SR.1353, para. 48.
[62] Trinidad and Tobago, *ibid.*, 38.
[63] Mauritania, *ibid.*, para. 55.
[64] The article as a whole was adopted by 83 votes to 0 with 2 abstentions: A/6181, para. 127.
[65] A/C.3/L.1291.
[66] A/C.3/L.1298.
[67] A/C.3/L.1299.
[68] Summary of voting in A/6181, para. 137.
[69] A/C.3/L.1291 and A/C.3/L.1301.
[70] A/6181, para. 142.
[71] E/CN.4/SR.810, p. 9.

designed to prevent abuses'.[72] The sentiment was echoed by a number of delegates in the Third Committee, one of which—The Netherlands—asserted that 'the right of individual petition was the most effective means of giving effect to human rights in general and the present convention in particular',[73] adding that:

> [i]n practical terms . . . complaints by one State against another . . . did not offer a sufficient guarantee of the safeguard of human rights. States were little inclined to occupy themselves with individual cases which did not affect them or their citizens . . . In other words, States would tend to formulate complaints only for political reasons. Moreover, if the individual's right of communication was not recognized and it was left to States to adopt the necessary measures of redress, aggrieved citizens might try to secure the assistance of foreign governments, which might create tension and conflict and . . . harm the cause of human rights and anti-discrimination.[74]

The documentation on measures of implementation included in the report of the twentieth session of the UN General Assembly included the basic papers prepared by The Philippines,[75] a twelve-country consortium of Latin American States,[76] and The Netherlands,[77] each of which incorporated suggestions relating to an individual communications procedure. All three documents referred in slightly varying terms to the possibility of communications emanating from individuals or groups of individuals, and from non-governmental organizations (NGOs), with or without reference to the requirement that the NGOs must have consultative status with the Economic and Social Council.[78] The paper of The Netherlands envisaged the possibility of 'victim' status for NGOs.[79] Later, revised texts do not deviate from the line of envisioning the petitions procedure applying to individuals and groups of individuals.[80]

In the Third Committee, paragraph 1 of the draft article XIII (Article 14)[81] provided for the competence of the Committee, following a declaration by a State party to that effect, 'to receive and consider communications from individuals or groups of individuals claiming to be victims of a violation by that State party of any of the rights set forth in this Convention'. A principal thrust of the three-Power proposal (Ghana, Mauritania, The Philippines) was for the institution of national committees 'composed of individuals independent of the government or other national body which shall be competent in the first instance to receive and consider petitions' from individuals or groups of individuals.[82] This body was envisaged as competent to seek redress 'in appropriate cases' from the State party, and would keep a register of complaints, certified copies of which were to be filed with the Secretary-General 'on the understanding that the contents shall not be publicly

[72] *Ibid.*, p. 10.
[73] A/C.3/SR.1355, para. 45.
[74] *Ibid.*, para. 46.
[75] A/C.3/L.1221.
[76] A/C.3/L.1268.
[77] A/C.3/L.1270.
[78] Thus, in the paper of the Philippines, A/C.3/L.1221, the Committee would be empowered to receive petitions addressed to the Secretary-General from 'any person or groups of individuals claiming to be the victim of a violation . . . or from any non-governmental organization in consultative status with the Economic and Social Council'.
[79] 'The Committee may receive petitions . . . from any person, non-governmental organization in consultative status . . . or group of persons claiming to be the victim of a violation' by the State party: A/C.3/L.1270.
[80] A/C.3/L.1291/Add.1; A/C.3/L.1303; A/C.3/L.1308; A/C.3/L.1315; and A/C.3/L.1308/Rev.1.
[81] A/C.3/L.1291/Add.1.
[82] A/C.3/L.1291/Add.1, article XIII, para. 2.

disclosed'.[83] The proposal precipitated the withdrawal of a text submitted by Saudi Arabia setting up the national committees as substitutes for an international mechanism.[84] Further refinements followed, largely relating to the role of the national committees.[85] The reference to this national institution was replaced by the phrase 'a body within its national legal order', adding the requirement that petitioners to such a body 'have exhausted other available local remedies'.[86] In case of a failure to obtain satisfaction from such a body within six months, the petitioner had the right to communicate the matter to the treaty body.[87] A successful amendment proposed by Lebanon as to who could petition added the qualifier 'within its jurisdiction' after 'groups of individuals'.[88]

A fourteen-Power amendment qualified earlier admissibility proposals on the exhaustion of domestic remedies to exclude such a requirement 'where the application of the remedies is unreasonably prolonged'.[89] Representatives made brief excursions into possible distinctions between 'petitions' and 'communications'; the softer term 'communication', according to one representative, being preferable in light of an envisaged procedure in which a committee 'would merely take cognizance of existing problems, without passing any judgements'.[90] Such a committee (and process) was stated to be 'in no way comparable' to the European Commission on Human Rights which could even, *inter alia*, refer a case to the European Court.[91] There was strongly expressed resistance to the possibility of petitions or communications emanating from non-nationals: 'the right of petition should be accorded only to the nationals of the State concerned';[92] no such restriction appears in the final text. According to the representative of Canada, the result of the drafting manoeuvres was that 'the article could not be more optional than it was'.[93] The stress on the 'optional' may, however, have facilitated the procedure's remaining within the body of the Convention. The arguably disproportionate amount of time spent in discussing the nature and role of the 'national body' may be read as an indirect product of the climate of doubt, hesitation, and expectation surrounding the birth of a new and potentially challenging international procedure. In relation to the proposal by Saudi Arabia to privilege the national petition system, Schwelb comments that 'by way of a political compromise the optional right of petitioning a national authority and . . . to communicate with an international authority were both included in the Convention'.[94]

Draft Article XIII (bis) (Article 15) establishes a relationship between the Convention and decolonization processes with regard to petitions from and reports on territories to

[83] *Ibid.*, para. 5.

[84] A/C.3/L.1297.

[85] The first revised text, contained in A/C.3/L.1308, was submitted at the 1362nd meeting of the Third Committee by a group of eleven States: A/6181, para. 148.

[86] A/C.3/L.1308, article XIII, para. 2.

[87] *Ibid.*, para. 4.

[88] A/C.3/L.1315.

[89] A/C.3/L.1308/Rev.1, now Article 14(7)(a).

[90] Comment by the representative of Italy, A/C.3/SR.1357, para. 30.

[91] *Ibid.*

[92] A/C.3/SR.1357, para. 45, the representative of Iraq.

[93] A/C.3/SR.1357, para. 9; the representative added that '[s]ince it left States free to recognize or not to recognize, by means of a declaration, the competence of the committee to receive petitions from their nationals, it should reassure those States which regarded the right of petition as inappropriate in the existing state of international relations.'

[94] E. Schwelb, 'The International Convention on the Elimination of All Forms of Racial Discrimination', *ICLQ* 15 (1966), 996–1068, 1043 [henceforth *The International Convention*].

which General Assembly resolution 1514 (XV) applies. An initial text proposed that the Committee could examine petitions 'from the inhabitants of non-independent Territories' regarding measures adopted by the Administering Authority to give effect to the Convention: the petitions would be examined in consultation with that Authority, and the Committee would cooperate with relevant bodies of the United Nations.[95] Reservations expressed by representatives on the Third Committee questioned whether the article was necessary to achieve the purposes of the Convention,[96] and on whether a hierarchy was being established where States with colonial responsibilities were regarded as second-class;[97] the representative of The Netherlands was among those who referred to the implication that the Convention might apply to States not parties to it.[98] The outline of the article was changed through a series of amendments. In the event, the 'UN bodies' stand as an intermediary layer between the Committee and, ultimately, the inhabitants of the non-self-governing and trust territories,[99] instead of in a direct relationship. The UK and Portugal voted against the article as a whole, while Australia, Belgium, Canada, France, the US, and Upper Volta abstained.[100]

A text of Article 16 proposed by Ghana, Mauritania, and The Philippines stated that the provisions of the Convention 'concerning the settlement of disputes or complaints' shall be applied 'without prejudice to existing constitutional or other binding provisions of agencies related to the United Nations' dealing with settlement of disputes or complaints in the field of discrimination, and shall not prevent... States parties... from having recourse to other procedures for settling a dispute'.[101] The proposal relates closely to the final text; 'existing constitutional or other binding provisions' was replaced by 'other procedures available for settling disputes, etc.' following a proposal by New Zealand;[102] 'available' was deleted on an oral proposal by Lebanon.[103]

C. Practice

I. The Committee

The Committee on the Elimination of Discrimination is composed,[104] according to Article 8(1), of 'eighteen experts of high moral standing and acknowledged impartiality

[95] A/C.3/L.1307. The reference to consultation with the Administering Authority was removed in later drafts: A/C.3/L.1307/Rev.2 and Rev.3.

[96] Representative of Nigeria, A/C.3/SR.1363, para. 41.

[97] Representative of the UK, *ibid.*, para. 37; Australia, A/C.3/SR.1364, para. 26; New Zealand, A/C.3/SR.1364, para. 27. The remarks of the UK were rejected by, *inter alia*, the representative of the UAR, A/C.3/SR.1364, para. 35.

[98] A/C.3/SR.1364, para. 6.

[99] The resulting arrangements were strongly defended by the representative of Lebanon, who observed that a petition system had been set up by the United Nations, and that 'to give a committee outside the Organization the powers mentioned' would only weaken the United Nations; the best solution would be 'to give the Committee established under the Convention the status of a body of experts and... the possibility of expressing its views and making recommendations to the different UN organs': A/C.3/SR.1368, para. 33.

[100] A/6181, para. 166 (g).

[101] A/C.3/L.1291 (Article XIII).

[102] A/C.3/L.1304.

[103] Oral proposal at the 1358th meeting. The article as a whole was adopted by 78 votes to none, with one abstention: A/6181, para. 171(c).

[104] There is no reference in the treaty to the broad purpose of the Committee, unlike for example the Committee on the Rights of the Child, charged under Article 43 of that Convention with 'examining the

elected by States from among their nationals, who shall serve in their personal capacity'. A special meeting of the States parties every two years elects nine members at a time. Meetings of the Committee have taken place in Geneva since 1986.[105] Members are required to be 'experts' but not necessarily 'experts on racial discrimination',[106] and the membership has often included persons with foreign policy and other 'official' connections. Commentators suggest that the early perception of the Convention as relating primarily to foreign rather than domestic affairs produced its effects on the composition of the Committee;[107] on the other hand, the presence of diplomats in a treaty body is not unique to CERD, which is situated in the upper-middle range for its complement of active and retired diplomats.[108] Successive Committees have had a mixed membership of diplomats, academics, graduates of NGO or activist sectors, and national human rights institutions, etc. No single profession dominates, or a geographical or cultural group: at different times in the life of the Committee, different regions have been over- or under-represented.[109]

General Recommendation (GR) 9 strongly recommends that States respect the status of Committee members as independent experts, expressing alarm at the tendency of 'representatives of States, organizations and groups' to put pressure on the membership, and recommending that States parties 'respect unreservedly' the status of Committee members. On taking office, members make a solemn declaration that they will perform duties and exercise powers as a member of the Committee 'honourably, faithfully, impartially and conscientiously'.[110] There is no formal rule of procedure requiring members to resile from proceedings when their own State is in dialogue with the

progress made by States parties in achieving the realization of the obligations undertaken'. The purposes of the Committee are, presumably, subsumed under the purposes and objectives of the Convention as a whole.

[105] M. Banton, *International Action against Racial Discrimination* (Clarendon Press, 1996), pp. 142–4 [henceforth *International Action*]. Article 10(4) of the Convention refers to meetings taking place at UN Headquarters, but following the establishment of the UN division of human rights in Geneva and the setting up of the Office of the High Commissioner on Human Rights, difficulties with costs have militated against holding sessions elsewhere. Over the life of the Committee, in addition to Geneva, sessions have been held in New York, Paris, and Vienna.

[106] Compare with treaty provisions on, for example, members of the Human Rights Committee who shall have 'recognized competence in the field of human rights': Article 28(2) of the ICCPR. Ulfstein observes that 'no professional requirements are listed in the CERD': 'Individual Complaints', in Keller and Ulfstein, *UN Human Rights Treaty Bodies*, pp. 73–115, p. 78. Banton, *International Action*, p. 309, comments that 'members generally can be considered as experts in racial discrimination only in respect of the knowledge they have built up in the course of examining State reports'.

[107] Van Boven remarks that the perception of the Convention as foreign policy produced a situation where 'many States parties . . . nominated active or retired diplomats, foreign ministry officials, former foreign ministers, and similar personalities to serve as members'; he questions whether such membership 'is fully consistent with the terms of Article 8', T. van Boven, 'Discrimination and Human Rights Law; Combating Racism', in S. Fredman (ed.), *Discrimination and Human Rights*: the Case of Racism (Oxford University Press, 2001), pp. 112–33 at p. 113 [henceforth *Discrimination and Human Rights*].

[108] *Background Information on Enhancing and Strengthening the Expertise and Independence of Treaty Body Members*, HRI/MC/2012/2, 18 April 2012, pp. 2–6. According to this information, 17 per cent of CERD membership falls under 'Diplomat/Government official', and 17 per cent under a second category of 'retired diplomat/Government official; the aggregate for all the comparable treaty bodies (including CERD) is 18.1 per cent for active diplomats and 6 per cent for retired diplomats, with the highest overall figure represented by the Committee on Migrant workers: 57 per cent of active diplomats/officials and 7 per cent in the 'retired' category.

[109] Over-representation of a particular region is not *ipso facto* contrary to the Convention: the syntax of Article 8 is that experts must be impartial, etc, while 'consideration is given' to the desideratum of equitable geographical distribution.

[110] Rule 14 of the Rules of Procedure, HRI/GEN/3/Rev.3, p. 69.

Committee,[111] although for Article 14 communications, a member should not take part in the examination of a communication if they have 'any personal interest in the case', or 'participated in any capacity in the making of any decision on the case'.[112] The Committee made only a brief response to the 'Addis Ababa Guidelines' on independence and impartiality of treaty body members[113] and, while reiterating its support for the principle of independence and impartiality of members in the exercise of their duties, has not explicitly adopted the guidelines.[114] In practice, members are discouraged from participating in discussions regarding their home State; the extent to which the policy of abstention is maintained correlates with the approach of the Chairman and the attitude of individual members.[115] The Committee has had a predominantly male membership, with a 'gender imbalance' slightly more marked than in treaty bodies as a whole,[116] though as a result of the elections of 2015, the Committee will have seven women members. CERD does not have a rule limiting the number of times a member may serve on the Committee.[117]

II. Reporting under Article 9

Article 9(1) of the Convention obliges each State party to submit an initial report on the application of the treaty within one year of the entry into force of the Convention for the State concerned, and 'thereafter every two years and whenever the Committee so requests'. Article 9 conditions the 'regular' periodic reporting and the 'early warning and urgent action' procedures. Early in its working life, the Committee issued a general recommendation which included the statement that States had an obligation to report 'whether or not racial discrimination exists in their respective territories',[118] which suggests that the notion of the potential ubiquity of racial discrimination had not been assimilated by all States parties.

The Committee's examination of State reports[119] remains the centrepiece of its work. Recent practice has been to examine periodic reports in two sessions per annum, along

[111] The situation contrasts with those in comparable UN treaty bodies, governed by procedural constraints with regard to reporting as well as communications and other procedures: HRI/MC/2012/2, pp. 6–12; for the Human Rights Committee, see A/53/40, Vol. 1, Annex III.

[112] Rule 89, HRI/GEN/3/Rev.3, p. 87.

[113] Addis Ababa Guidelines on the Independence and Impartiality of Members of Human Rights Treaty Bodies, A/67/222 (2012), adopted by the twenty-fourth Annual Meeting of Chairs of Treaty Bodies.

[114] The Committee took note of the guidelines, recalled GR 9, declared its strong support for 'the independence and impartiality of its members in all of its activities and practices' in accordance with the Convention, and expressed a belief that the guidelines 'can provide a basis for further discussions, as appropriate': A/68/18, Annex VIII B. 'Internalization' of the Addis Ababa Guidelines and other measures is among the issues and recommendations in *United Nations Reform*. Issues are reviewed in I. Truscan, *The Independence of UN Human Rights Treaty Body Members* (Geneva Academy, 2012), who notes, p. 3, that CERD is the only treaty body that has dedicated a general recommendation to the question of the independence of its members. At its August 2014 session, the Committee decided to institute a rapporteur for reprisals, to be appointed in 2015; see also the San José Guidelines against Intimidation or Reprisals, HRI/MC/2015/6.

[115] In the experience of the present author as a member of CERD (2001–14), most members of the Committee maintained a public silence in discussions concerning their 'home' State.

[116] HRI/MC/2012/2, pp. 2–6. The author became a member of CERD in 2001 when the Committee had three women members; before the membership profile resulting from elections in 2013 which produced four women members, no Committee since 2001 had more than two women members.

[117] *United Nations Reform*, pp. 74–80.

[118] GR 2. CERD Reports are formally submitted to the UN Secretary-General.

[119] The guidelines of the various treaty bodies relating to the part of State reports containing general information were consolidated into a single text, now found in a 'common core document' submitted by States

with a number of 'review countries', examined (or discussed) in the absence of a report.[120] The examination of reports places a heavy burden on the Committee, especially in view of the lack of any preparatory session; the Committee does not work in 'chambers' in order to expedite the handling of reports. To reduce the reporting burden on States parties, CERD accepts multiple reports in one document,[121] and other time-saving strategies.[122] The Convention's two-year periodicity is the shortest reporting cycle among the UN core human rights treaties.

The practice of appointing country rapporteurs began in 1988; the responsibility of the rapporteur is 'to prepare a thorough study and evaluation of each State report, to prepare a comprehensive list of questions to put to representatives of the reporting state and to lead the discussion in the Committee'.[123] The rapporteur system emerged through proposals from a working group of the Committee and sparked off a lively debate,[124] some members doubting whether the proposed system would bring the desired efficiency savings. There was concern that the diversity of expertise among CERD members would make it difficult for a particular rapporteur to cover the whole field raised in the report. Despite the initial hesitancy of members, the procedure has been thoroughly 'normalized'; the identity of country rapporteurs is currently in the public domain.

A feature of the CERD procedure until recently was that no list of questions was sent to the state party in advance of proceedings; the claimed advantage was that this practice allowed for 'a spontaneous, frank and wide-ranging discussion of issues'.[125] CERD subsequently moved to a list of issues approach, modifying this to a 'list of themes'.[126] The list of issues/questions approach had produced situations where the Committee was deluged by information supplied at a very late stage by reporting States, rendering it almost incapable of assimilation.[127] The examination of reports begins with an introduction by the representative of the reporting State, who is followed by the country rapporteur and other CERD members.[128] After the completion of questioning, the representative again takes the floor and is invited to engage in further dialogue with members; the country rapporteur then endeavours to summarize the main points discussed. At its August 2014 session, following a call by the General Assembly[129] and recommendations from the twenty-sixth meeting of Chairpersons,[130] the Committee

party to one or more international human rights instruments; this is complemented by treaty-specific guidelines: see p. 36 above. The current CERD-specific guidelines were adopted in 2007: CERD/C/2007/1.

120 The Committee is scheduled to hold three sessions in the period 2015–17: General Assembly resolution 68/268, 21 April 2014, paras 26–8.

121 A/45/18, para. 29.

122 In 2001, the Committee adopted the 'Bossuyt amendment' (named after the then rapporteur of the Committee), the effect of which is to skip one reporting cycle: A/56/18, para. 477.

123 CERD SR.827, paras 40 and 52–75.

124 CERD/C/SR.827, paras 52–79.

125 A/51/18, para. 596.

126 A/65/18, chapter XII, para. 85.

127 CERD has not yet given full consideration to the 'list of issues prior to reporting' procedure (LOIPR) adopted by the Human Rights Committee, the CAT and CMW to ensure a focused and concise examination of reports.

128 Initially, CERD hesitated to invite State delegations, with some Committee members objecting to 'cross-examination' of representatives: Banton, *International Action*, p. 109. Tomuschat observes that after two initial years reviewing reports, CERD concluded that 'such endeavours were largely futile if there was no one to listen', C. Tomuschat, *Human Rights: Between Idealism and Realism* (Oxford University Press, 2008), p. 175.

129 A/RES/68/268, 21 April 2014.

130 June 2014.

decided to adopt a 'simplified reporting procedure' through a gradual process, prioritizing reports that are more than ten years overdue.[131]

Prior to 1991, when the Committee began the practice of adopting collective 'concluding observations', members of the Committee expressed individual opinions that appeared in the summary records. Concluding observations of the Committee are currently structured into an 'introduction',[132] followed, where pertinent, by 'factors and difficulties impeding the implementation of the Convention' (war, natural disasters, poverty, etc),[133] 'positive aspects', and 'concerns and recommendations' taken together. In principle, the recommendations are confined to matters brought up in the Committee's dialogue with the State party, though there is some flexibility in this.[134] The 'customized' recommendations on specific issues are added to by a number of standard paragraphs—'other recommendations'—on matters that include ratification of related treaties, follow-up to the Durban Declaration and Programme of Action,[135] follow-up to concluding observations, paragraphs of particular importance, consultations with civil society, and the schedule for presentation of the next report. With some variation in vocabulary, the Committee encourages the dissemination of its observations 'in the official and commonly used languages, as appropriate', sometimes adding references to minority or indigenous languages.[136] The concluding observations are made public at the end of the CERD session.[137]

Following Article 9(2), the 'comments, if any, from States parties' on the observations are included in the Committee's annual report to the UN General Assembly. In practice, only a few States have chosen to offer these comments which may, however, touch on fundamental disagreements between the Committee and the State party. The practice of requesting that subsequent reports 'address all the points raised' in the concluding observations has stimulated responses by States which, along with their responses under follow-up, serve to enlarge the range of commentary on the Committee's conclusions and open them up to greater challenge. In practice, the Committee works by consensus in addressing State reports; in some instances 'consensus' is thin in that members dispute

[131] A/70/18, para. 56. For details of the simplified reporting procedure, see *United Nations Reform*, pp. 48–52.

[132] A particularly lengthy and critical 'introduction' appears in the 2012 concluding observations on Israel, where the Committee recalls that, notwithstanding the issues of security and stability in the region, the principles of the Convention apply to 'Israel proper' and the Occupied Palestinian Territories; in particular Israeli settlements on the Occupied Territory are declared to be illegal under international law and an obstacle to the enjoyment of human rights by the whole population: CERD/CISR/CO/14-16, paras 2, 3, and 4. Further on the Occupied Territories, see Chapter 8 on Article 2.

[133] The note by the Secretariat for the 26th meeting of Chairpersons—HRI/MC/2014/2, 'concluding observations', para. 31—suggests that CERD has eliminated this category, which, however, continues to be used in appropriate cases: recent observations on Cyprus, CERD/C/CYP/CO/17-22, para. 6, stand as one example; see also the extensive citation of factors regarding the situation of Iraq: CERD/C/IRQ/CO/15-21, para. 5.

[134] The dialogue with France in 2010 was a case in point, with members hesitating on the inclusion of references in the concluding observations to Roma 'collective repatriations' that took place shortly after the dialogue: the observations eventually made such a reference, CERD/C/FRA/CO/17-19, para. 14.

[135] The follow-up to Durban paragraph may elicit resistant comment from States who were not entirely enamoured of the Durban 'process'.

[136] Further discussion in Chapters 8 and 17 of the present work.

[137] At its August 2014 meeting, the Committee decided to adopt the framework for concluding observations recommended by the 26th annual meeting of Chairpersons in June 2014; the pattern largely follows the present scheme, but omits the 'factors and difficulties' element.

particular recommendations but agree 'not to disturb the consensus' and decline to press for a vote.[138]

Reminders may be sent by the Secretary-General to States parties from which reports are overdue, according to which, if a report is not received by a specified time, the Committee will review the implementation of the Convention in the absence of a report. Initially, the procedure for review was limited and cautious and based 'upon the last reports submitted by the State party concerned and their consideration by the Committee'.[139] The reason for the initial caution was the provision in Article 9.2. that the Committee's 'suggestions and general recommendations' shall be 'based on the examination of the *reports and information received from the States parties*',[140] one implication of which could be to require the presentation of an initial report before any 'review'. An imaginative move was made by the Committee in 1996 in deciding that 'in view of the absence of an initial report, the Committee shall consider as an initial report all information submitted by the State party to other organs of the United Nations or, in the absence of such material, reports and information prepared by organs of the United Nations'.[141] Review outcomes have included a set of concluding observations in standard form and even 'provisional concluding observations'.[142]

III. Follow-up to Concluding Observations

The Committee added a 'follow-up procedure' to check implementation of its recommendations, supplementing Rule 65 of its rules of procedure: a coordinator and an alternate were appointed by the Committee at its sixty-fifth session in 2004. Terms of reference set out in the Committee's annual report to the General Assembly for 2005 amplify the meagre statement of responsibilities in the Rules of Procedure.[143] The modus operandi of the 'coordinator on follow-up' includes cooperation with the respective country rapporteur. The coordinator is responsible for monitoring respect for deadlines for receipt of information set by the Committee and for sending reminders on such to the State party. In conjunction with the country rapporteur, the coordinator endeavours to analyse information received from the State party, take up with the State party the issues of further information, and make recommendations to the Committee in relation to information received or not received. The terms envisage a progress report by the coordinator to the Committee and the adoption of formal recommendations, if any.

The annual report to the General Assembly includes a chapter on follow-up to concluding observations. Three or four specific paragraphs in the concluding observations constitute the normal basis for requesting follow-up responses. In selecting paragraphs, attention focuses on which paragraphs are specific enough to permit substantive responses

[138] This observation stems from the author's experience as a member of the Committee.
[139] A/46/18, para. 27.
[140] Emphasis added.
[141] A/51/18, para. 608; see also L. Valencia Rodriguez, 'The International Convention on the Elimination of All Forms of Racial Discrimination', in *Manual on Human Rights Reporting* (United Nations, 1997), p. 299.
[142] A/59/18, paras 434–58.
[143] A/60/18, Annex IV. Guidelines are set out in A/61/18, Annex VI, which envisage, *inter alia*, wide dissemination by States parties of the Committee's concluding observations, cooperation with national human rights institutions and NGOs, and the development of national action plans; meetings with States parties are also suggested as possibilities. In practice the procedure operates through written submissions and responses thereto.

after one year. These typically include such requests as reporting on the progress of a bill through the legislature or in the setting up of a national human rights institution; generalized or large-scale recommendations are not appropriate for this procedure. Most of the responses from States parties address issues of fact and may challenge the Committee's appreciation of the situations concerned. Information from States parties under the procedure may nonetheless stimulate Committee requests for further, clarifying explanations. Following a slow start, States have gradually become more responsive to the follow-up procedure, though absent or delayed responses are not uncommon.[144]

IV. Early Warning and Urgent Action

The Committee has developed an early warning and urgent action procedure (EW/UA) to address patterns of oppression which may lead to greater violence[145] or slide towards genocide,[146] adopting a working paper on preventive and reactive measures in 1993.[147] Further context for the move included the reports of the UN Secretary-General, *An Agenda for Peace*,[148] and the report to the General Assembly for 1992.[149] As summarized in subsequent annual reports of the Committee, efforts to prevent serious violations would include early-warning measures and urgent procedures. The distinction between the types of measures in the working paper was explained by one of its promoters as 'a distinction between early-warning measures for preventing structural problems from escalating into conflicts and urgent action measures for situations requiring the immediate attention of the Committee'.[150] The Working Paper envisaged the addressees for expressions of concern and recommendations, in addition to the State party concerned, to include the special rapporteur on contemporary forms of racism, other human rights bodies dealing with the question, and the Secretary-General, 'along with a recommendation that the matter be brought to the attention of the Security Council'.[151]

CERD adopted new early warning and urgent action guidelines in 2007.[152] The guidelines recall the 2004 'Stockholm' speech of the Secretary-General on prevention of genocide and refer to persistent patterns of racial discrimination 'in some cases with genocidal dimensions'.[153] Most situations addressed by the guidelines fall short of genocide, and the 'indicators' for triggering the procedure include the important qualification that, since such indicators 'may be present in situations not requiring immediate

[144] The author bases these evaluations on information supplied by the Secretariat during the author's term as follow-up rapporteur of the Committee. Additional to follow-up requests, concluding observations also identify recommendations 'of particular importance', on which detailed information on concrete measures taken is expected in the next periodic report.

[145] At its sixty-fifth session, the Committee established a working group on early warning and urgent action procedures, A/59/18, Annex XII.

[146] The Committee held a thematic discussion on prevention of genocide at its 66th session in 2005: CERD/C/SR.1683–84. A 'Declaration on the Prevention of Genocide' was adopted at the same session. At its sixty-seventh session, CERD adopted a follow-up to the Declaration on 'indicators of patterns of systematic and massive racial discrimination', in order, *inter alia*, 'to assess the existence of factors known to be important components of situations leading to conflict and genocide': A/60/18, para. 20.

[147] A/48/18, para. 18 and Annex III.

[148] A/47/277-S/24111, in particular paras 15, 18, 20, and 23.

[149] A/47/1. See also the Committee's letter to the Secretary-General, A/48/18, Annex VI.

[150] De Gouttes, CERD/C/SR.974/Add.1, para. 5.

[151] *Working Paper*, para. 10.

[152] A/62/18, Annex III, Guidelines for the Early Warning and Urgent Action Procedure.

[153] *Ibid.*, para. 7.

attention to prevent and limit serious violations of the Convention, the Committee shall assess their significance in light of the gravity and scale of the situation'.[154] Subject to the 'gravity and scale' criterion, the list of indicators[155] is broadly similar to that of 1993. References to encroachment 'on the traditional lands of indigenous peoples or forced removal of these peoples from their lands', and 'polluting or hazardous activities that reflect a pattern of racial discrimination with substantial harm to specific groups' strike new notes. The list of potential addressees is expanded and varied in the 2007 text to include the Human Rights Council, the Special Adviser on the Prevention of Genocide, and regional intergovernmental organizations and human rights mechanisms.[156] The bulk of situations brought under the procedures are dealt with by letters sent by the Chairman to the State party concerned; other, ostensibly more serious cases may be the subject of a Committee 'decision', or a 'statement', published in full in the annual report to the General Assembly.[157]

There has been a gradual change in the profile of cases dealt with under the procedure,[158] which was initially focused to a significant extent on the fallout from conflicts in the former Yugoslavia and Central Africa; events regarding Israel, and the situation regarding Native Title in Australia, have also been prominent.[159] Many (most) current cases refer to indigenous peoples. Applying the 'gravity and scale' criterion, it may be argued that threats that might not disturb a larger group can result in potentially irremediable cultural and material losses for many indigenous societies, particularly those of smaller scale.[160] The Committee has also addressed issues regarding the Roma, generalized ethnic violence as well as violence or discrimination against foreigners and refugees, and it tends to comment on a conflict wherever it senses the presence of an 'ethnic' element. The statement regarding violent conflict in Libya referred to the impact on 'non-citizens, migrant populations, migrant workers, refugees and persons belonging to other minority groups',[161] together, in the perception of the Committee, constituting the ethnic dimension to engage the Convention.

[154] *Ibid.*, para. 12.

[155] The indicators are set out in para. 12 of the revised guidelines.

[156] At its seventy-seventh session in 2010, the Committee sent letters to the Council of Europe and the European Union expressing deep concern regarding the resurgence of racism against Roma in several European States, including mass expulsions: A/65/18, p. 10.

[157] As example, the Committee published one decision and three statements under the procedure in 2011: Decision 1 (78) on Côte D'Ivoire; Statements on the situation in Libya, the situation in the Syrian Arab Republic, and on Dale Farm (UK). By 2012, the Committee had adopted some 40 decisions under the procedure since its inception in the 1990s, the coverage of which included major conflict areas in Africa, the Middle East, and the Former Yugoslavia. The Committee adopted a 'resolution' in the case of Burundi: A/51/18, p. 13.

[158] The history of the procedure taken as a whole reveals that the concerns of the Committee have been widely distributed across a varied range of groups and situations.

[159] I. Diaconu, *Racial Discrimination* (Eleven International Publishing, 2011), pp. 349 ff. [henceforth *Racial Discrimination*]. For an account of the Committee's activities regarding native title in Australia, see P. Thornberry, *Indigenous Peoples and Human Rights* (Manchester University Press, 2002), pp. 218–23.

[160] For example, all cases bar two in Chapter II of the annual report for 2012/13 (A/68/18) refer to indigenous peoples—in Cameroon, Costa Rica, Ethiopia, Guyana, India, Nepal, Peru, The Philippines, Suriname, the United Republic of Tanzania, and the US: the two 'exceptions' are letters regarding military bases in Okinawa and Roma in Slovakia. Notable 'decisions' concerning indigenous peoples include Decision 1(66) of 2005 on the New Zealand Foreshore and Seabed Act, A/60/16, ch. II; and Decision 1(68) regarding the Western Shoshone in the USA, A/61/18, ch. II.

[161] A/66/18, pp. 7–8.

Knowledge of this procedure has steadily grown amongst NGOs and community groups. The procedure does not depend on a State having submitted a report and is typically initiated by an NGO/community organization, though the Committee (or a member) may also engage the procedure *ex proprio motu*.[162] The procedure functions under Article 9(1)(b) of the Convention, which refers to a Committee power to request a report at any time. States may sense that the procedure is a loose cannon and challenge its application as well as the substance of the claim,[163] especially where they have not accepted the individual communications procedure under Article 14. Unlike the latter, early warning does not employ formal admissibility criteria such as exhaustion of domestic remedies. Available early warning/urgent action information, summarized by the Secretariat, is processed by a working group, the conclusions of which are presented to the plenary for discussion and ratification. In many cases, the Committee's concerns or admonitions stimulate a dialogue with the State party concerned. In some instances the procedure merges with follow-up or may taper off to a request that information be included in the next periodic report of the State party.

V. Sources of Information

Unlike the CRC[164] and the CMW,[165] ICERD does not expressly envisage a role for NGOs, referring only to information received from States parties as the basis for examination of State party reports by the Committee. In its early operation, CERD experienced difficulties in how to treat information provided by NGOs or media reports, and 'the debate about permissible sources continued intermittently for twenty years'.[166] Matters came to a head in 1991 when the Committee decided that members, in addition to information from State reports, 'must have access, as independent experts, to all other available sources of information, governmental and non-governmental'.[167] The use of a variety of sources of information appears squarely within the Convention in that the

[162] Para. 13 of the 2007 Guidelines refers to information available to engage the procedure emanating from 'inter alia, United Nations agencies and human rights bodies, special procedures... regional human rights mechanisms, and national human rights institutions and non-governmental organizations'. The list is not exhaustive in not even referring to the potential role of members of CERD. Except as respondents to Committee's enquiries, States parties are notably absent from the list of information providers, though there is nothing to rule out the use of information on other parties to the Convention indirectly provided by States working through the listed channels. However, in the light of the relationship of the procedure to Article 9, and the existence of the inter-State procedure in Articles 11–13, it would be inappropriate for a State to engage directly with the Committee under early warning/urgent action vis-à-vis the conduct of another State party.

[163] Israel took particularly strong objection to Decision 2 (63) regarding Israel's amendment to the Citizenship and Entry into Israel Law of July 2003, expressing that it was 'surprised and shocked by such a decision', which had referred to the negative effect of the law on family reunification and marriage: A/58/18, ch. II (CERD decision), *ibid.*, Annex VII (reaction of Israel and the CERD response); *inter alia*, Israel claimed that the early warning approach represented an attempt to pre-empt and undermine the normal reporting process, a claim denied by the Committee.

[164] Article 45(a).

[165] Article 74(4).

[166] Banton, *International Action*, p. 103. Describing the situation as it existed by 1980, Lerner notes simply that the Committee was 'prevented from taking advantage of information supplied by non-governmental organizations', *International Convention*, p. 119; for early discussion, see A/8718, paras 27–33, cited by Lerner, *ibid.*

[167] Decision 1 (XL), A/46/18, Annex VII B.

'examination' of reports in Article 9 strongly suggests that the information they contain should be tested against external reference points, otherwise the 'examination' would be drained of significance. However, while NGOs furnish indispensable services to the Committee, their information is subject in principle to appraisal and evaluation by members on a similar basis to other information.[168] In addition to the submission by NGOs of written material to the Committee, including shadow/alternative reports, the briefing of Committee members by NGOs through informal lunchtime meetings has become part of the regular *modus operandi*. In 2011, CERD added a further practice of hearing submissions at the beginning of the week from NGOs on States reporting in that week.[169]

The efforts of civil society and national and international NGOs are vital to Committee work since its research capacity is limited and *in situ* visits to reporting States are not a part of its regular practice.[170] NGOs contribute best when their submissions are researched and referenced in a verifiable manner, when they track assertions in the State report, and consolidate their submissions in a limited number of documents. Overwhelming the Committee with documentation may result in useful points vanishing into the ether. Recent experience, including lobbying of the Committee, suggests that national and international NGOs are becoming more attuned to CERD processes and its mandate and that the dialogue with the Committee may be an event of national significance. The maintenance of web pages by the Secretariat has improved the visibility of CERD (and other treaty bodies) to civil society and the development of webcasting promises the same. The Committee has recognized the contribution of accredited national human rights institutions (NHRIs), recommending that States parties establish them,[171] and it has developed modalities for their accommodation in reporting and other procedures.[172]

Information presented to the Committee currently encompasses reports emanating from various bodies, including UN agencies, special procedures, and the universal periodic review (UPR) process. Sources from regional bodies may also appear though the emphasis is placed on United Nations materials. Written reports are supplemented by *in personam* appearances of special rapporteurs, UN independent experts, etc, while the International Labour Organization (ILO) and the United Nations High Commissioner for Refugees (UNHCR) engage the Committee on a regular basis.[173] Country rapporteurs are presented by the Secretariat with the most extensive 'package' of materials for their State review; all members of the Committee are at liberty to peruse such information.

[168] CERD has no explicit rule on confidentiality of NGO information—compare the practice of other treaty bodies in HRI/MC/2006/4, para. 96. However, if an NGO requests confidentiality for its submissions to CERD, such requests will be honoured.

[169] A/65/18, Chapter XII, para. 87.

[170] Following initial hesitations on the part of some CERD members, the 'country presentations' prepared by the Secretariat may include NGO material.

[171] GR 17, A/48/18, Chapter VIII B; A/62/18, Annex IX, Rule 40 (2).

[172] 'CERD provided NHRIs . . . present with the opportunity to make an oral presentation in the plenary on the second day of the consideration of the State party's report. NHRI representatives were seated separately from representatives of NGOs, with a sign clearly identifying them': HRI/MC/2006/4, para. 94.

[173] The standard organizational chapter of the annual report refers to cooperation with the ILO, the UNHCR, UNESCO, the special procedures of the Human Rights Council, and regional human rights mechanisms; the 2014 version is contained in A/69/18, ch. I. E.

VI. General Recommendations

By March 2015, thirty-five general recommendations had been adopted by the Committee, dealing with obligations of States parties under specific articles or principles of the convention,[174] aspects and modalities of discrimination,[175] fields of concern for the principle of non-discrimination,[176] institutions to address racial discrimination,[177] particular human groups or categories,[178] as well as a general recommendation on the right to self-determination,[179] and follow-up to the Durban World Conference,[180] and the Durban Review Conference.[181] Some initial recommendations were prompted by the reluctance of States to admit the existence of racial discrimination on their territories.[182] Other recommendations are prompted (in part) by reservations made to the Convention,[183] the situation in particular States or groups of States, the prevalence of certain patterns of discrimination, and the vulnerable situation of specific communities.

The general recommendations of the Committee vary considerably in length and style with a marked tendency in later recommendations towards increased word count. General recommendations may base themselves more or less exclusively on the provisions of the Convention, recalling the preamble as well as the operative articles;[184] the *travaux préparatoires* have also been drawn upon.[185] Many later general recommendations recall earlier ones, providing continuity and consistency of approach to enhance authority; concluding observations may be recalled in a similar process.[186] GR 32 on special measures is contextualized as being based on 'the Committee's extensive repertoire of practice referring to special measures . . . practice includes the concluding observations on the reports of States parties . . . communications under Article 14 and earlier general recommendations', listing GR 8 (on Article 1), GR 27 (on the Roma), and GR 29 (discrimination based on descent).[187] Recommendations may also be offered as clarifications of Convention concepts.[188]

[174] For example, GR 7 and GR 15 on Article 4; GR 8 on Article 1, paras 1 and 4; GR 9 on Article 8, para. 1, GR 4 on Article 1, GR 16 on Article 9, GR 19 on Article 3, GR 20 on Article 5, GR 24 on Article 1, GR 26 on Article 6, and GR 32 on special measures.

[175] GR 25 on gender-related dimensions of racial discrimination.

[176] GR 31 on racial discrimination in the field of criminal justice.

[177] GR 17 on the establishment of national institutions to facilitate the implementation of the Convention, and GR 18 on the establishment of an international tribunal to prosecute crimes against humanity.

[178] GR 23 on indigenous peoples; GR 27 on the Roma; GR 22 on refugees and displaced persons; GR 29 on descent; GR 11 and GR 30 on non-citizens; GR 34 on people of African descent.

[179] GR 31.

[180] GR 28 on 'Follow-up to the World Conference Against Racism, Racial Discrimination, Xenophobia and Related Intolerance'.

[181] GR 33.

[182] See, for example, GR 2 and GR 5.

[183] In response to reservations made against Article 4 in order to protect freedom of expression, the Committee is resolute in its view that 'the prohibition of the dissemination of all ideas based upon racial superiority or hatred is compatible with the right to freedom of opinion and expression': GR 15; see also GR 35, para. 23.

[184] For recall of the preamble, see GR 3; GR 20, para. 1; GR 32, para. 5; GR 35, para. 5.

[185] GR 32, para. 20; GR 35, para. 10.

[186] The Committee's consistent approach is referred to in GR 29, preamble, and GR 23, para. 1; GR 27, preamble, refers to the concluding observations of the Committee.

[187] Para. 2. See also para. 3 of GR 35.

[188] GR 30, preamble.

Developments elsewhere in international law generally[189] and in human rights in particular may be cited specifically, and in other cases have clearly influenced the drafting of the text; background conditions relating to ethnic conflicts,[190] the threat of organized violence, or the resurgence of authoritarian ideologies have also been cited as justifying the adoption of a recommendation.[191] GR 23 on indigenous peoples echoes language used in the (then) UN draft declaration on indigenous peoples and ILO Convention No. 169;[192] GR 27 on the Roma is at once influenced by debates elsewhere and contributes to such debates, while prospectively acting as a catalyst to further action; GR 32 on special measures was influenced by, *inter alia*, GR 25 of CEDAW;[193] GR 35 on racist hate speech was spurred on in part by the emergence of General Comment 34 of the Human Rights Committee on freedoms of opinion and expression. Some general recommendations explicitly articulate the Committee's approach to the interpretation of the Convention, employing the metaphor of 'guidance'—hence GR 32 describes its purpose as 'to provide, in the light of the Committee's experience, practical guidance on the meaning of special measures under the Convention in order to assist States parties in the discharge of their obligations... Such guidance may be regarded as consolidating the wealth of Committee recommendations for States parties.'[194] According to one reading, the Committee is competent to interpret the Convention insofar as it is required for the performance of its functions: 'Such an interpretation *per se* is not binding on States parties, but it affects their reporting obligations and their internal and external behaviour.'[195]

The development of a general recommendation is largely a matter of individual initiative to persuade colleagues to approve and refine the proposal collectively. The general recommendations on the Roma, descent/caste, non-citizens, special measures, discrimination against people of African descent, and combating racist hate speech, followed from open 'thematic discussions';[196] it has not been CERD practice to call for public comments on draft recommendations. The general recommendations have endeavoured to elaborate and clarify many Convention provisions; some issues suggested as appropriate for a general recommendation have not seen the light of day.[197] The utilization of the general recommendations is interstitial: the Committee will expect States parties to conform to patterns set out in the recommendations and will question State representatives in the light of the accumulated guidance in the recommendations.

[189] GR 11 on non-citizens, para. 3, and GR 30, para. 2, reach out to principles of international law; GR 21, paras 2 and 3 refer to self-determination; GR 18 refers to international tribunals to prosecute crimes against humanity.

[190] GR 22 on Article 5 and refugees, preamble.

[191] GR 15, para. 1.

[192] P. Thornberry, 'Confronting Racial Discrimination: A CERD Perspective', *HRLR* 5 (2005), 239–69, 260–62 [henceforth '*Confronting Racial Discrimination*'].

[193] In addition to ICERD sources, GR 32 recites in para. 3 that its drafting has also taken account of the work of the Sub-Commission on the Promotion and Protection of Human Rights and GR 25 of CEDAW on temporary special measures.

[194] Para. 4.

[195] Valencia Rodriguez, in *Manual on Human Rights Reporting* (Geneva: United Nations, 1997), HR/PUB/91/1/Rev.1, p. 300 (citing an unnamed author); Banton, *International Action*, p. 104.

[196] Thematic discussions open the Committee to contributions from UN human rights bodies, NGOs, etc; general debates are for the Committee itself.

[197] A general recommendation on the relationship between racial discrimination and discrimination on the ground of religion would, in all likelihood, have followed from a thematic discussion envisaged in 2007, A/62/18, para. 538; no such discussion took place.

The Committee has travelled some distance since some members stated with confidence that it had no mandate to interpret the Convention;[198] it has, however, been reticent in arrogating authority in this respect.[199]

VII. The Inter-State Dispute Procedure: Articles 11–13

The inter-State dispute procedure set out in Articles 11–13 of the Convention which, unlike the communications procedure under Article 14, is not optional, has not been tested in practice; correspondingly, the provisions of the Convention are elaborated only to a minor extent by the rules of procedure.[200] The procedure involves reference to the Committee under Article 11 of a claim by one State party that another State party 'is not giving effect to the provisions of the Convention', and, if the matter is 'not adjusted to the satisfaction of both parties', a second reference to the Committee may follow subject to the application of the non-exhaustion of domestic remedies rule 'in conformity with the generally recognized principles of international law'. Article 12 envisages the appointment by the CERD Chairman, with the unanimous consent of the parties to the dispute, of an Ad Hoc Conciliation Commission 'comprising five persons who may or may not be members of the Committee' with its own Chairman and rules of procedure.[201] Article 13 outlines the concluding stages of the procedure: a report to the CERD Chairman 'containing such recommendations as it may think proper for the amicable solution of the dispute'; the disputants then inform the CERD Chairman whether or not they accept the Commission's recommendations, with all other parties to the Convention being informed in due course.

In light of the reality of its general non-invocation, and unlike the under-functioning procedure under Article 15, no chapter of the annual report is devoted to the inter-State dispute system. Banton refers to a flurry of discussion around the sixth periodic report of Syria as to whether an Article 11 notification had been received.[202] A suggestion was made that if a State party made an allegation against another State even without specifically citing the procedure, the Committee could treat this as a communication under Article 11; this was overruled by the Chairman in the face of, *inter alia*, an express denial by the alleging State that it was invoking Article 11. Banton nonetheless refers to a series of 'disguised interstate disputes' which have punctuated the life of the Committee involving such as Cyprus, Panama, and the United States (US), and a cluster of States with regard to Israel;[203] sundry other disguised disputes may arise when a part of the territory of a reporting State is controlled by elements assumed to be supported by another State. GR 16 on Article 9 nonetheless reminds States parties that Article 11 'is the only procedural

[198] Banton, *International Action*, pp 102–4, 126, and 158–60 cites (p. 126) the opinion of the UN office on Legal Affairs that 'the right to give authoritative interpretations of the Convention . . . rested . . . in the first instance, with CERD itself, as the body responsible for monitoring compliance with the Convention, and ultimately with the States parties': A/C.3/40/SR. 46. The present author, in his capacity as a member of CERD, nonetheless noted sentiments expressed by members during the drafting of GR 32 (2009) that it was for States to interpret the Convention and not the Committee.

[199] For illuminating discussions of general comments (recommendations) and interpretation by treaty bodies, see the collection of essays in H. Keller and G. Ulfstein, *UN Human Rights Treaty Bodies*.

[200] HRI/GEN/3/Rev.3, rules 69–79.

[201] Rule 72 envisages consultations with the States parties to the dispute with regard to the composition of the Commission.

[202] Banton, *International Action*, p. 128; A/33/18, paras 169–73.

[203] Banton, *ibid.*, pp. 108–12.

means available' to States for drawing to the attention of the Committee when they consider that some other State is not giving effect to the provisions of the Convention.[204]

VIII. The (Optional) Communications Procedure: Article 14

The hesitations of representatives in the drafting of the Convention regarding the innovative nature of then Article 14 procedure will be recalled. The fears of the representative of Upper Volta in the drafting of the Convention that if a communications procedure were included, 'the proposed committee might be swamped by thousands of petitions which it would be unable to handle effectively',[205] has not been borne out. Of the fifty-seven countries which have made the optional declaration under Article 14, communications have emanated from fewer than a quarter of such States parties, while the Committee adopted its opinion on only a fifty-sixth communication in 2015.[206] Typically, the Committee handles only a small number of cases annually. Recommendations by the Committee urging States parties to accept the procedure have had limited effect.

Communications are in practice submitted to the Secretariat of the Office of the High Commissioner for Human Rights and registered with the petitions team. A model complaint form facilitates the complainant, who is expected to provide basic information regarding identity,[207] the State concerned, the Convention articles alleged to be violated, the steps taken to exhaust domestic remedies, or in the words of the model complaint form, 'to obtain redress within the State concerned'.[208] If the information presented is incomplete, further particulars may be requested before the complaint is registered.[209] A decision to register a case may be made pending the receipt of further information.[210] Except in the case of duly verified exceptional circumstances, the communication must be submitted within six months 'after all available domestic remedies have been exhausted, including, where applicable, those included in paragraph 2 of article 14'.[211]

The author of the communication is invited to state whether they are submitting on their own behalf as alleged victims of discrimination or on another's behalf. In the latter case, the complainant should present the authorization from the person concerned or, if he/she is not authorized, explain the nature of the relationship to the alleged victim and why the author considers it appropriate to bring the case on their behalf.[212] The normal procedure in cases where an author represents a victim is for the author to present a power

[204] The Human Rights Committee has similarly encouraged States parties to utilize the (optional) inter-State procedure set out in Articles 41–3 of the ICCPR: Human Rights Committee General Comment 31, *The Nature of the General Legal Obligation Imposed on States Parties to the Covenant*, para. 2: HRI/GEN/1/Rev.9 (Vol. I), pp. 243–7, para. 2.

[205] A/C.3/SR.1363, para. 13.

[206] *V.S. v Slovakia*, CERD/C/88/D/56/2014 (2015).

[207] Article 14(6)(a) and Rule 91.a provide that the Committee shall not receive anonymous communications.

[208] The generalities regarding necessary information to process the complaint are included in rule 84. Bayefsky observes that the UN 'does not provide legal aid or financial assistance to authors, nor does CERD require that States parties provide legal aid where an individual wishes to submit a communication', and advises authors to determine whether or not their own legal system provides the possibility of legal aid: <http://www.bayefsky.com/complain/28_cerd.php>.

[209] Questions asked by the petitions team may incidentally assist authors in clarifying the legal basis of the case, but the responsibility presenting as clear a case as possible rests with the author.

[210] Rule 84.4.

[211] Rule 91(f).

[212] Rule 91(b).

of attorney from the victim to act on their behalf;[213] where the victim is detained or has disappeared they may be represented without such a power.

The Secretary-General may request clarification in relation to a communication of the 'extent to which the same matter is being examined under another procedure of international investigation or settlement';[214] the rule relates to information and is not included in the 'conditions for admissibility of communications'.[215] Among the States parties declaring acceptance of the procedure, a number have included in their declarations a reservation that 'this procedure applies only insofar as the Committee has established that the same matter is not being examined, or has not been examined by another international body of investigation or settlement'.[216] Occasionally, a State party questions admissibility because a similar case had been filed with another body. In *Koptova v Slovakia*, the Committee responded to a claim by the State party that a similar case had been filed with the European Court of Human Rights, noting that the author of the communication was not the petitioner before the European Court and that, even if she had been, 'neither the Convention nor the rules of procedure prevented the Committee from examining a case that was also being considered by another international body'.[217]

It may also be noted that, regarding recourse to procedures outside the Convention, Article 16 provides that the provisions of the Convention concerning the settlement of disputes or complaints 'shall be applied without prejudice to other procedures for settling disputes or complaints in the field of discrimination' laid down in instruments and conventions of the United Nations and its specialized agencies, 'and shall not prevent the States parties from having recourse to other procedures for settling a dispute in accordance with general or special international agreements in force between them'. As noted earlier, the article originated from a proposal by Ghana, Mauritania, and The Philippines and was little discussed. While the phrasing of the article relating to procedures for 'the settlement of disputes or complaints' within the Convention is clearly adequate to cover individual as well as inter-State complaints, the second part of the sentence refers only to 'the States parties . . . having recourse' to procedures outside the Convention and is silent on recourse for individuals or groups of persons. Lerner, following Schwelb, suggests that the article be given a liberal interpretation, so that 'if States parties would prefer to have recourse to other procedures in force between them, the Convention would not be an obstacle to this'.[218] The same would apply to individuals who prefer to seek remedies other than those in the Convention.[219]

[213] The author in such cases does not have to be a lawyer but simply a person authorized under the power of attorney.

[214] Rule 84.

[215] Rule 91. Compare Article 5(2)(a) of the Optional protocol to the ICCPR, discussed in S. Joseph and M. Castan, *The International Covenant on Civil and Political Rights: Cases, Materials and Commentary* (3rd edn, Oxford University Press, 2013), Chapter 5 'Consideration under Another International Procedure' [henceforth *The ICCPR*].

[216] This formula is employed in the declaration of Andorra and is repeated with minor variations in language by 17 other States parties. In some cases, the reference is to other cases being 'considered' rather than 'examined'. The formula is explicitly described as a 'reservation' in the declaration of Norway.

[217] *Koptova v Slovakia*, CERD/C/57/D/13/1998 (2000), para. 6.3.

[218] N. Lerner, *The U.N. Convention on the Elimination of All Forms of Racial Discrimination*, p. 90. References in the present work to the volume by Lerner are to the 1980 edition; citations of the 2015 reprint revised by the author are specifically indicated.

[219] With reference to the ECHR as an example of 'other procedures', Schwelb comments: 'Although Article 16 . . . does not say so expressly, it cannot have been the intention of the General Assembly and of the States

The rules of procedure for Article 14 envisage the establishment of a pre-sessional working group of the Committee.[220] In practice: the Committee addresses the communications in full session with interpretation provided. Meetings to examine communications are closed,[221] though they can be open to the public in cases of general issues relating to the procedure should the Committee so decide.[222] The Committee is mandated to 'decide as soon as possible whether as communication is admissible',[223] and can request additional written information or clarifications.[224] If admissibility is disputed on the ground of non-exhaustion of domestic remedies, the State party is required to give details 'of the effective remedies available to the alleged victim in the particular circumstances of the case';[225] decisions on inadmissibility can be reviewed.[226] Interim measures may be recommended by the Committee 'to avoid possible irreparable damage to the person or persons who claim to be victim(s) of the alleged violations'.[227] The formulation of the views of the Committee is expressed as the formulation of an 'opinion',[228] a term that is not used in Article 14, which refers instead to 'suggestions and recommendations'. In practice, if an individual member wishes to present an individual opinion, the member will be required to draft the opinion without the assistance of the Secretariat.

A complex of admissibility issues arose in *Dragan Durmic v Serbia and Montenegro*[229] where in light of a series of 'tests' by a law centre of discrimination against Roma in public places in Serbia, individuals of Roma origin had been refused entry to a discotheque, while non-Roma individuals were admitted. Regarding time limits for bringing a claim,[230] the Committee recalled that communications must be submitted to it, except in the case of duly verified exceptional circumstances, within six months after all available domestic remedies have been exhausted. It observed that the courts of Serbia and Montenegro had not yet considered the matter and therefore the six-month rule had not yet begun to run.[231] The discotheque incident took place before the optional declaration under Article 14, leading to an objection regarding admissibility *ratione temporis*, in response to which the Committee noted that the violations were ongoing and had continued since the date of the incident and after the State party's declaration under Article 14, thus the claim was admissible. Regarding remedies unduly prolonged, the Committee observed that the

parties to affect the rights of the individual arising from ... the European Convention': Schwelb, *The International Convention*, p. 1048. The rules of procedure for inter-State claims are silent on Article 16 situations.

220 Rule 86.

221 Rule 88.

222 Rule 88.

223 Rule 86.1.

224 In addition to the domestic remedies' condition, Rule 91 requires the Committee to ascertain that 'the communication is compatible with the provisions of the Convention', and it 'is not an abuse of the right to submit a communication'.

225 Rule 92.7.

226 Rule 93.2. A decision that a communication is admissible may also be revoked: rule 94.6.

227 Rule 94.3.

228 Rule 95.

229 CERD/C/68/D/29/2003 (2006).

230 Rule 91(f).

231 *Dragan Durmic*, para. 6.1. On the State party's claim that the petitioner violated Article 14, para. 4, of the Convention, by publicly disseminating the contents of his petition, the Committee took the view that the obligation to refrain from publishing information on individual petitions, prior to examination by the Committee, applied only to the Secretary General of the United Nations, specifically, acting through the Secretariat, and not to the parties to the petition who remain at liberty to publish any information at their disposal relating to a petition: paras 6.2 and 6.3.

petitioner had sought to have his claims of violations of the Convention by the State party adjudicated for over four-and-a-half years, since the incident in February 2000, and the State party itself had conceded that the prospect of an early review was unlikely. Accordingly remedies were unduly prolonged and their 'non-exhaustion' did not bar the applicant.[232]

The remedies must be potentially effective to justify the duty to exhaust them.[233] A line of cases makes the point that in many cases of alleged discrimination, civil remedies may not be appropriate in cases involving criminal offences in that the former lead only to compensation and not to criminal conviction;[234] in light of the public nature of crime, private prosecutions may also be inappropriate.[235]

On the other hand, 'mere doubts' about the effectiveness of remedies do not absolve a complainant from pursuing them.[236] Domestic remedies must be exhausted by the petitioners 'and not by other organizations or individuals'.[237]

Article 14(1) refers to the Committee's competence to receive and consider communications from 'individuals or groups of individuals' within its jurisdiction claiming to be victims. The provision has exercised the committee in a number of cases, particularly with regard to 'groups of individuals'.[238] In *POEM and FASM v Denmark*, the question of capacity to bring a claim was addressed, the petitioners contending that Article 14 does not prevent NGOs from submitting claims: POEM and FASM were NGOs which represented a group of people and can thus bring claims under Article 14. They also contended that Article 14 should be interpreted along the lines of the European Convention on Human Rights which expressly provides for the right of NGOs to apply to the Court.[239] CERD did not comment, but noted only that the case in Denmark had not been brought by the organizations but by the Documentation and Research Centre (DRC). CERD therefore said that 'domestic remedies have to be exhausted by the petitioners themselves and not by other organizations or individuals', thus the communication was declared inadmissible.[240]

In *Documentation and Advisory Centre on Racial Discrimination v Denmark*[241] the Centre claimed victim status under Article 14. The case concerned an advertisement for a 'Danish foreman' for a construction project in Latvia; this was objected to by the Centre,

[232] Also *B.M.S. v Australia*, CERD/C/54/D/8/1996 (1999), para. 6.2; *Z.U.B.S. v Australia*, CERD/C/55/D/6/1995 (2000), para. 6.4.

[233] *L.R. et al. v Slovakia*, CERD/C/66/D/31/2003 (2005), para. 6.1. citing in support its own jurisprudence in *Lacko v Slovakia*, CERD/C/59/D/11/1998 (2002), and cases before the Human Rights Committee, *R.T. v France*, CCPR/C/35/D/262/1987 (1989), and *Kaaber v Iceland*, CCPR/C/58/D/674/1995 (1996); para. 6.2, citing *Koptova v Slovakia*, paras 2.9 and 6.4.

[234] *Habassi v Denmark*, CERD/C/54/D/10/1997 (2000), para. 6.1; *Lacko v Slovakia*, para. 6.3; *Sefic v Denmark*, CERD/C/66/D/32/2003 (2005), para. 6.2; *Gelle v Denmark*, CERD/C/68/D/34/2004 (2006), para. 6.6.

[235] *Gelle v Denmark*, para. 6.5; *Adan v Denmark*, CERD/C/77/D/43/2008 (2010), para. 6.3.

[236] *D.S. v Sweden*, CERD/C/59/D/21/2001 (2001), para. 6.4. Further discussion in Chapter 16 on Article 6.

[237] *POEM and FASM v Denmark*, CERD/C/62/D/22/2002 (2003), para. 6.3. See further the commentary on Article 6.

[238] Romania qualifies its acceptance of the communications procedure on the ground that Article 14 does not confer competence on the Committee to receive the communications of 'persons invoking the existence and infringement of collective rights'.

[239] Paras 5.2 and 5.3.

[240] Para. 6.3.

[241] CERD/C/63/D/28/2003 (2003).

claiming it discriminated on the grounds of national or ethnic origin. The communication was submitted by the Centre represented by its head of the board of trustees. The complaint alleged that although she did not herself apply for the job, 'she should be considered a victim of the discriminatory advertisement, since it would have been futile for her to apply for the post'. Moreover, the petitioner itself—the Centre—should be recognized as having status of victim since it represented a large group of persons of non-Danish origin discriminated against by the job advertisement. The Centre pleaded in support of victim status its specific mandate on racial discrimination, the ethnic composition of its board of trustees, and its record in protecting victims, so that 'it should be considered as a victim or as representing an unspecified number of unidentified victims'.[242] The Committee concluded that it did

> not exclude the possibility that a group of persons representing . . . the interests of a racial or ethnic group may submit an individual communication, provided that it is able to prove that it has been an alleged victim of a violation . . . or that one of its members has been a victim, and if it is able . . . to provide due authorization to this effect.[243]

It was noted that no member of the board of trustees had applied for the job, while the petitioner had not argued that any of the members of the board, or another identifiable person whom the petitioner would be authorized to represent, had a genuine interest in, or showed the necessary qualifications for, the vacancy.[244] It did not automatically follow that persons not directly and personally affected by discrimination may claim to be a victim: 'Any other conclusion would open the door for popular actions (*actio popularis*) against the relevant legislation of States parties.'[245]

In the *Jewish Community of Oslo et al. v Norway*[246] three organizations and a number of individuals complained to the Committee following the acquittal of a pro-Nazi speaker on charges under the Norwegian Penal Code. The authors claimed they were victims because of the general inability of Norwegian law to protect them from dissemination of anti-Semitic and racist propaganda, and because of their membership of a particular group of potential victims facing an imminent risk of racial discrimination.[247] The Committee agreed with the authors' submissions, considering that, in the circumstances, they had established that they belong to a category of potential victims.[248] Additionally, the Committee took the view that it:

> did not consider the fact that three of the authors are organizations posed any problem to admissibility . . . Article 14 . . . refers specifically to the Committee's competence to receive complaints from 'groups of individuals' . . . to interpret this . . . to require that each individual within the group be an individual victim of an alleged violation, would be to render meaningless the reference to 'groups of individuals' . . . bearing in mind the nature of the organizations' activities and the classes of person they represent,[249] they too satisfied the 'victim' requirement in Article 14.[250]

[242] Para. 5.3.
[243] Para. 6.4.
[244] Para. 6.5.
[245] Para. 6.6; also *A.S. v Russian Federation*, CERD/C/79/D/45/2009 (2012), para. 7.2.
[246] CERD/C/67/D/30/2003 (2005).
[247] *Jewish Community*, para. 7.3.
[248] *Ibid.*, para. 7.3.
[249] The three organizations were the Jewish Community of Oslo, the Jewish Community of Trondheim, and the Norwegian Antiracist Centre.
[250] *Jewish Community*, para. 7.4. The point in *Jewish Communities* on 'groups of individuals' was cited by the Committee in *Zentralrat Deutscher Sinti und Roma et al. v Germany*, CERD/C/72/D/38/2006 (2008), para.7.2.

The petition from the organization in *TBB-Turkish Union v Germany* was admitted by the Committee which found victim status in light of (a) the organization's activities and aims in furtherance of equality and non-discrimination, (b) the group of individuals it represents 'namely persons of Turkish heritage in Berlin and Brandenburg', and (c) that it had been directly affected by the impugned speech critical of Turks in Germany. The Committee therefore considered that 'the fact that the petitioner is a legal entity is not an obstacle to admissibility'.[251]

The question of 'potential victims' also arose in *Koptova v Slovakia*, a case concerning local authority resolutions banning particular Romany families from settling in a district. The author of the communication, a Roma, could, in the view of the Committee, be considered a victim 'since she belonged to a group of the population directly targeted by the resolutions in question'.[252] It was stated that, although the wording of the Municipal Council resolutions referred explicitly to members of Roma communities previously domiciled in the concerned municipalities, 'the context in which they were adopted clearly indicates that other Romas would have been equally prohibited from settling'.[253] The author, who had not entered the municipality since the anti-Roma resolutions had been adopted, said this was in part because she feared that they could be enforced against her.[254] The issue of potential victims was also taken up in *Jewish Communities*, where the Committee aligned itself with the views of the Human Rights Committee and the European Court of Human Rights.[255]

From its earliest Article 14 decisions,[256] the Committee has made 'suggestions and recommendations' even in cases where no violation was found.[257] In *Z.U.B.S v Australia* where, following the finding that the Convention had not been violated, it was suggested that 'the State party simplify the procedures to deal with complaints of racial discrimination, in particular those in which more than one recourse measure is available, and avoid any delay in the consideration of such complaints'.[258] In *Hagan v Australia*, another case of non-violation, the recommendation was to remove a racially offensive sign and inform the Committee of the action taken.[259]

[251] Para. 11.3. Under the optional Protocol to ICCPR, while victims must be individuals, there is 'no objection to a group of individuals, who claim to be similarly affected, collectively to submit a communication about alleged violation of their rights': *Ominayak (On Behalf of Lubicon Lake Band) v Canada*, Communication CCPR/C/38/D/167/1984 (1990), para. 32.1; see also *Diergaardt and Ors v Namibia*, CCPR/C/69/D/760/1997 (2000); *Howard v Canada*, CCPR/C/84/D/879/1999 (2005). Corporations and associations can submit claims on their own behalf under the European Convention on Human Rights: *Sunday Times v UK*, ECtHR, App. No. 6538/74 (1977), freedom of expression of a media organization; *Refah Partisi (Welfare Party) and ors v Turkey*, App. Nos 41340-44/98 (2003), dissolution of a political party. This facility is not available to petitioners under the ICCPR; NGOs have no standing to submit claims, though they can assist authors of communications: *Hertzberg and ors v Finland*, CCPR/C/15/D/61/1979 (1982), Joseph and Castan, *The ICCPR*, pp. 75–6.

[252] *Koptova v Slovakia*, CERD/C/57/D/13/1998 (2000), para. 6.5.

[253] *Ibid.*, para. 10.1.

[254] *Ibid.*, para. 3.2.

[255] Jewish Community, para. 7.3. See also *Murat Er v Denmark*, CERD/C/71/D/D/40/2007 (2007), paras 6.2 and 6.3.

[256] *Yilmaz-Dogan v The Netherlands*, CERD/C/36/D/1/1984 (1988), para. 10.

[257] Further, even in cases deemed inadmissible, the Committee has been tempted to develop its position through *obiter dicta* on the interpretation of the Convention: *Kenneth Moylan v Australia*, CERD/C/83/D/47/2010 (2013), para. 6.2.

[258] Para. 11.

[259] CERD/C/62/D/26/2002 (2002), para. 8.

IX. Follow-up to Communications

CERD is a relative latecomer to an explicitly formulated follow-up communications to its Article 14 opinions along the lines of that established by the Human Rights Committee in 1990.[260] In 1993, *L.K. v The Netherlands* requested information on 'follow-up' to an Article 14 decision in the next periodic report of the State party,[261] in application of rule 95.5 of the rules of procedure.[262] At its sixty-sixth session, CERD requested the Secretariat to prepare a paper on the modalities of follow-up to the procedure under Article 14. The request was made in the context of the discussion in *L.R. v Slovakia*[263] where, having found violations of several articles of the Convention, the Committee stated that it wished to receive, within ninety days, information from the government of the Slovakia about the measures to be taken to give effect to the Committee's Opinion. In 2005, at its sixty-seventh session, the Committee decided, '[i]n light of the positive experiences of other treaty bodies'[264] to add two new paragraphs to the rules of procedure.[265] The *L.R.* formula, with minor variations, has been used in subsequent cases. The first rapporteur on follow-up to communications was appointed in 2006[266] and the first report, reflecting all cases in which the Committee found violations or made suggestions and recommendations in the absence of a violation, was included in the annual report of the Committee.[267] The exercise in tabulation, updated versions of which are included in subsequent annual reports, indicates whether follow-up replies are considered satisfactory 'in that they display the willingness of the State party to implement the . . . recommendations', or unsatisfactory 'because they do not address . . . the recommendations at all or only relate to certain aspects'.[268] Follow-up assessments may be challenged by States parties, sometimes vigorously.[269]

X. Petitions from Inhabitants of Trust and non-Self-Governing Territories: Article 15

Article 15 in its final form aspires to the eventual disappearance of colonialism—'pending the achievement of the objectives' of the Colonial Declaration—which also suggests a lessening in importance over time of the Article 15 procedure itself: this has proved to be

260 A/45/40, Vol. II, Annex XI (1990). See also rules 101 and 103 of the Committee's rules of procedure.

261 Communication No. 4/1991, decision of 16 March 1993, para. 7.

262 'The State party concerned shall be invited to inform the Committee in due course of the action it takes in conformity with the Committee's suggestions and recommendations.'

263 Communication No. 31/2003, A/60/18, Annex III A.

264 A/61/18, para. 485.

265 A/60/18, Annex IV. II. 'The Committee may designate one or several Special Rapporteurs for follow-up on Opinions adopted by the Committee under Article 14, paragraph 7 of the Convention, for the purpose of ascertaining the measures taken by States parties in the light of the Committee's suggestions and recommendations': Rule 95.6; rule 95.7, 'The Special Rapporteur(s) may establish such contacts and take such action as appropriate for the proper discharge of the follow-up mandate. The special rapporteur(s) will make such recommendations for further action by the Committee as may be necessary; he/she (they) will report to the Committee on follow-up activities as required, and the Committee shall include information on follow-up activities in its annual report.'

266 Committee member Sicilianos.

267 A/61/18, Annex V.

268 A/61/18, para. 488.

269 See follow-up discussion of *Dawas and Shawva v Denmark*, CERD/C/80/D/46/2009 (2012), in A/68/18, Annex IV, pp. 160–5.

the case.[270] The reporting procedure under the Article 9 procedure has been immeasurably more successful in eliciting information from all States parties with dependent territories than the special procedure of Article 15. The essence of the envisaged procedure is that the Committee will receive copies of petitions from the inhabitants of non-self-governing and trust territories and all other territories to which the Colonial Declaration applies to the relevant bodies of the United Nations, as well as reports on measures applied by the administering powers,[271] in both cases on matters 'directly related to the principles and objectives' of the Convention, and will express opinions and make recommendations thereon. A summary of petitions and reports, along with the opinions and recommendations of the Committee, is included in the annual report.[272] The article does not limit the reach of the provision to States parties to the Convention; on the other hand, 'the Authorities furnishing the information to the United Nations bodies . . . are not all under legally binding obligations to adopt the anti-discrimination measures envisaged in the Convention or report on them'.[273]

The relevant chapter in the report has, however, become formulaic, reciting that it is difficult for the Committee to fulfil its obligations under the article comprehensively owing to the fact that reports of UN bodies 'contain only scant information relating to the principles and objectives of the Convention'; this is despite requests from the very first session of the Committee attempting to elicit information. The recognition of difficulties with the procedure may be followed by noting significant ethnic diversity in the territories concerned that warrants close watch on incidents and trends which reflect racial discrimination and greater efforts to raise awareness of the Convention.[274] The recitals conclude with reminders to States parties administering the territories to include details on the implementation of the Convention in such territories in their periodic reports, a stance that appears to confirm the marginalization of Article 15. Diaconu refers to the lack of response to repeated requests from CERD to the UN Secretary-General for an explanation of the non-use of the Article 15 procedure by UN bodies.[275]

Committee practice encourages the inclusion in reports under Article 9 of the Convention of information on non-self-governing and other territories under the jurisdiction of States parties,[276] especially in light of the virtual non-functioning of the special procedure under Article 15.

[270] Para. 1 of Article 15 is, according to one authority, 'intended to eliminate the doubts of those who alleged that this article could be interpreted as a way of agreeing to the perpetuation of colonialism': Lerner, *The U.N. Convention on the Elimination of Racial Discrimination*, p. 87.

[271] It is unclear from the syntax of para. 2(b) whether the envisaged reports emanate from the UN bodies or from the administering States.

[272] The first session of the Committee issued a statement of its responsibilities with regard to Article 15 in which it noted, *inter alia*, that it was not authorized to receive petitions directly or otherwise except through the organs referred to in Article 15(2); on the other hand, it was proposed to examine this principle in strict conformity with its mandate while guarding against depriving petitioners or the competent bodies of the United Nations of the opportunity to have petitions considered by an appropriate international body.

[273] *The First Twenty Years*, p. 43.

[274] The CERD annual report for 2012–13, A68/18, chapter VIII, refers to working papers prepared by the Secretariat for the Special Committee and the Trusteeship Council on sixteen territories, listed in CERD/C/81/3; a figure unchanged in recent years.

[275] *Racial Discrimination*, pp. 341 and 344.

[276] 'States parties which are administering Non-Self-Governing Territories or otherwise exercising jurisdiction over territories are requested to include, or to continue to include in their reports . . . pursuant to Article 9 . . . relevant information on the implementation of the Convention in all territories under their jurisdiction': A53/18, para. 439 (c).

Under Article 9, issues concerning dependent territories of administering powers have been raised, prompting the Committee to request information on ethnic composition, on how the Convention is applied, on the progress of legislation against racial discrimination, and on including respect for human rights in constitutional arrangements while having due regard to local culture and customs.[277] Failure to provide information on the application of the Convention opens the State party to censure by the Committee.[278]

D. Comment

The drafting of the Convention generated lively argument on the proposed supervisory mechanism, concentrated principally in the Third Committee of the General Assembly, where discussions were preceded by an illuminating exchange of general views. The representatives of The Philippines and Ghana introduced and explained the basic structure of reports, inter-State claims, petitions, and a dispute settlement mechanism envisioned for 'the first major international agreement on human rights to emerge from the United Nations, and the first to be preceded by a declaration'.[279] Ghana explained that without implementation clauses, 'the draft Convention could be but a declaration, which would contribute nothing new to the world',[280] to which the UK added that 'agreement on principles was not enough. States were . . . obliged to go further, under the preamble and in Articles 55 and 56 of the Charter.'[281] The Committee that eventually became the Committee on the Elimination of Racial Discrimination emerged from proposals that largely reflect its present shape,[282] a result that was not without alternatives in light of preferences for 'a special organ composed of States parties',[283] or an enhanced role for national committees which 'would submit to the Secretary-General certified copies of their registries',[284] or screen petitions before forwarding to an international committee.[285] Of the implementation mechanisms, the reporting procedure was the least controversial,[286] perhaps because it did not appear particularly threatening to States' interests; the inter-State procedure was discussed at a length that appears inordinate in light of its (hitherto) non-activation by the Committee;[287] the petitions

[277] Examples in Diaconu, *Racial Discrimination*, pp. 341–4.

[278] Concluding observations on The Netherlands, CERD/C/NLD/CO/18, para. 15, requesting complete information on the implementation of the Convention 'in all territories of the State party'.

[279] Remarks of the representative of The Philippines, A/C.3/SR.1344, para. 30—general introductory statement in paras 14–35; Ghana, *ibid.*, paras 36–45.

[280] Ghana, *ibid.*, para. 38.

[281] A/C.3/SR.1344, para. 53; 'special international guarantees designed to prevent abuses and possible violations of the principles of the Convention' were absolutely vital: Representative of Italy, *ibid.*, para. 58.

[282] For example in the texts proposed by Ghana, A/C.3/L.1274/Rev.1; and Mauritania and The Philippines, A/C.3/L.1291.

[283] Remarks of the representative of the USSR, A/C3/SR.1344, para. 73.

[284] Proposal of Saudi Arabia, *ibid.*, para. 76.

[285] A/C.3/L.1274/Rev.1, Article XII.

[286] But 'of only limited value, since reports submitted by States tended to paint too rosy a picture': representative of The Netherlands, A/C.3/SR.1344, para. 63.

[287] The proposed inter-State complaints mechanism was criticized by Tanzania in light of State sovereignty: A/C.3/SR.1345, paras 40–1; the representative did not see how complaints regarding human rights could be

procedure appeared alarming to some delegates,[288] but 'valuable and effective' to others.[289]

The drafting demonstrates 'the importance which each State attached to its national sovereignty',[290] which inhibited some from supporting the (not entirely novel) concept of an international body with the potential to criticize States, even if not designated as a court.[291] Introducing the consolidated draft that replaced the individual drafts by Ghana, Mauritania, and The Philippines,[292] the representative of Ghana explained that the clauses were to be based on generally accepted principles of international law and should not violate State sovereignty. While accession to any treaty entailed a partial loss of sovereignty and natural rights that sometimes went beyond national boundaries, the right of petition 'should not be internationalized so as to undermine the sovereignty of States', and 'disputes should be settled in a spirit of mutual understanding'.[293] The drafters of the Convention were able to draw upon only a limited number of examples of supervision systems, notably those of the ILO and the *United Nations Educational, Scientific and Cultural Organization* (UNESCO),[294] a feature that highlights the pioneering quality of the Convention mechanisms.

Half a century following the adoption of the Convention, the existence of a multiplicity of supervision systems is an outstanding feature of the international human rights landscape. Treaty bodies and allied mechanisms at UN and regional levels are standard, accepted fixtures in the legal firmament, even if their output is not always wholeheartedly welcomed by States. While sovereignty considerations may have diminished force, the operation of human rights at the UN is characterized more by the accumulation of persuasive quasi-judicial and reporting procedures rather than formal court processes, despite occasional ruminations on setting up a world court on human rights. The complex of mechanisms has nonetheless been pivotal in the development of an expansive network of standards that contributes to the formation of customary law even if specific decision-making procedures do not possess a legally 'binding' quality. In addition to the growth of justiciable procedures, there has also been a shift in reporting mechanisms from a listening mode to active monitoring, while the body of 'interpretative' general comments (recommendations) constantly increases. In the case of treaty bodies, decades of reflection have

settled by conciliation. On the same issue, India, A/C.3/SR.1346, para. 21, questioned whether a non-judicial committee could exercise judicial functions.

288 Iraq, A/C.3/SR.1347, para. 7, asserting that acceptance of the implementation proposals, with particular reference to the right of petition, 'would be to embark on a very dangerous adventure'.

289 The Netherlands, A/C.3/SR.1344, para. 64, with reference to 'petitions from individuals, groups, and non-governmental organizations'. Similarly, Canada, A/C.3/SR.1345, para. 11, argued for the necessity for groups and individuals within a State to 'have access to competent decision-makers outside the State... non-national authorities should be vested with the authority to judge the treatment which a State meted out to its nationals'.

290 Ivory Coast, A/C.3/SR.1345, para. 4. For France, on the other hand, *ibid.*, para. 17, 'the act of ratification itself was an exercise in sovereignty'.

291 According to Malaysia, *ibid.*, para. 38, 'both the Philippines and Ghanaian drafts contained clauses which would allow interference by one State Party in the affairs of another. Such provisions were morally wrong and contrary to... the United Nations Charter... in the field of racial discrimination, they could scarcely be invoked unless a State employed spies throughout the territory of another State in order to detect alleged violations.'

292 A/C.3/L.21291, replacing A/C.3/L.1274/Rev.1, A/C.3/L.1289, and A/C.3/L.1221, respectively.

293 A/C.3/SR.1349, para. 29.

294 A representative of the ILO outlined its supervision system at length: A/C.3/SR.1349, paras 14–27.

focused on improvements in their overall efficiency through coordination and convergence of monitoring approaches,[295] and even the merger of committees into a 'unified standing body';[296] current UN activity focuses on 'strengthening' rather than merging the monitoring systems of individual treaties.[297]

In light of the geopolitical changes referred to earlier, the tension between conceptions of sovereignty and internationalized procedures colours the proceedings of the Committee more faintly than before. The Committee initially adopted cautious approaches to the interpretation of the mechanisms. As new States consolidated their sovereignty and a post-Cold War ambiance emboldened the Committee, sterner stances on the implementation of the Convention were gradually embraced. The 'suggestions and general recommendations' in the Convention have mutated into focused and lengthy concluding observations with an increasingly sharp critical edge. Critiques of implementation by States parties can be more robust than the drafters of the Convention might have appreciated, even when the language of 'violation' is avoided and 'constructive dialogue' preferred.[298]

Despite the ethic of cooperation between State parties and the treaty body, critical reactions from sovereign States are not uncommon. The facility granted in Article 9(2) for States parties to comment on the 'suggestions and general recommendations' of the Committee has been capably used. The comments have ranged from mild disagreement on points of detail to suggestions that the Committee has exceeded its mandate through over-generous interpretation of standards, trespassing on the sovereign prerogatives of States. In some instances, States have complained that the concluding observations do not faithfully reflect the dialogue with the Committee.[299] The performance of the Committee has also drawn allegations of having 'integrated political bias' against certain States or groups of States.[300] The 'charge' was vigorously rejected by the Committee in a set of published comments dedicated to vindicating the Committee's approach to the 'principles of objectivity, equality and fairness to States'. The comments recall that Committee members bring expertise to the Committee in the light of their particular background and experience, the result of which is 'a dynamic pluralism', the 'checks and balances' of which

[295] Bearing in mind that 'the treaty system is a *de facto* one that was in fact never designed to be a system'; the shared characteristics of the treaty bodies 'in terms of their nature, functions and powers, together with the steadily increasing, occasionally overlapping and sometimes contradictory demands placed on the States parties, have led to them . . . being conceptualized as a system, in need of reform as a comprehensive whole': Egan, *Strengthening the Treaty Body System*, 211.

[296] *Concept Paper on the High Commissioner's Proposal for a Unified Standing Treaty Body*, HRI/MC/2006/1, 22 March 2006.

[297] *United Nations Reform*, includes the report of the High Commissioner on Human Rights on strengthening the human rights treaty bodies; previous initiatives are summarized, *ibid.*, p. 28; see also Egan, *Strengthening the Treaty Body System*, 210–14. The response of CERD to the report is reproduced in: <http://www2.ohchr.org/english/>, 31 August 2012.

[298] Sundry theories of international competence that may have assisted treaty bodies in the development of competences include that of inherent powers, or powers by necessary implication, a concept traceable to the Advisory Opinion of the ICJ in the *Reparations Case* of 1949: discussion by Keller and Grover in Keller and Ulfstein, *UN Human Rights Treaty Bodies*, pp. 127–8.

[299] See, for example, comments by Latvia, A/58/18, Annex VII.

[300] In evaluating the work of the Human Rights Committee, Buergenthal suggested that the growth of its prestige was due in part to the perception on the Cold War period that 'CERD, with its jurisdiction over racial discrimination, offered the Soviet Union and its allies as well as many non-aligned third world nations a propaganda tool to be used against the West': T. Buergenthal, 'The UN Human Rights Committee', *Max Planck Yearbook of the United Nations*, 5 (2001), 341–98, 342.

minimize the risk of bias.[301] It is evident from this and other episodes recounted in the present work that the perceived integrity and objectivity of treaty bodies is a primary qualification and justification for their existence.

The review procedure represented a move towards improving compliance with obligations under Article 9, while the early warning and urgent action procedure has made imaginative use of the facility in Article 9(1)(b) to request a report and further information outside the standard of two-year period. While there is a degree of overlap between early warning/urgent action and communications under Article 14, the Committee has, in taking the view the Convention permits both approaches, underlined their different objectives and methodologies. The reference to 'further information' in Article 9(1)(b) may be interpreted to embrace further information stemming from the periodic reports—hence the follow-up procedure—as well as further information after the initial early warning/urgent action engagement with the State party. The early warning/urgent action procedure does not employ an admissibility arm equivalent to that in Article 14. Such a formal requirement would sit awkwardly with the facility for an individual Committee member to raise an issue; in practice the Committee relies on the good sense of its working group to act as a screening device for potentially incompatible applications.

The early warning/urgent action procedure strengthens the protective armoury of the Convention and elaborates its collective dimension in a wide range of contexts: the engagement of the procedure with the rights of indigenous groups is a notable feature of current practice. Critical voices, including among Committee membership, have suggested that, in developing an apparent pre-eminent concern with indigenous peoples, the procedure has deviated from its original purpose of addressing large-scale threats or rights violations; informal proposals have been made to institute a sub-committee or working group on indigenous issues. However, most members accept that the procedure represents a valuable addition to the mechanisms operated by the Committee as one open to all groups whose situations fall to be considered under the 2007 criteria. The early warning procedure stands as a justifiable application of monitoring possibilities under Article 9.

Large-scale threats of human rights violations continue to be addressed by the Committee under various procedural arms in addition to early warning, including the 'standard' reporting procedure under Article 9. The reporting procedure reflects on the situation in the whole of the State party, addressing the evidence of discrimination, the range of protagonists, the experience of victims, the legal framework *in toto*, and the response of the authorities—including the legal and social reaction to discrimination, and the action plans and anti-discrimination strategies. In their network of recommendations, concluding observations encapsulate the past, present and possible futures of key populations groups,

[301] The response also recalled that 'the human rights treaty body system is dedicated to an objective examination by independent experts of the fulfilment of obligations undertaken by States in the field of human rights'; further, with regard to concluding observations under Article 9, they 'should be understood not as the outcome of a judicial process but as a step in the ongoing dialogue between the Committee and the States parties'; and Committee responses, whether in the reporting or early warning procedure, 'must necessarily adapt to the circumstances before it'. The Committee referred to GR 9 of 1990, which included the observation that 'respect for the independence of the experts is essential to secure full observance of human rights and fundamental freedoms': *Comments of the Committee on a Report on the United Nations Treaty System* (2001), A/56/18, Annex VI.

the bellwethers of racial discrimination. Filigreed, smaller-scale instances of discrimination generally fall to be addressed under Article 14.

On the Article 14 procedure, the understanding of the phrase 'groups of individuals... claiming to be victims' for the purpose of submitting communications, has developed incrementally. In practice the phrase 'groups of individuals' has been evoked principally in the context of petitioning by anti-racist organizations, usually anti-discrimination advocacy organizations in their home countries.[302] The status of a petitioner as a legal entity is not an obstacle to admissibility.[303] The victim requirement for an organization may be satisfied on the basis of its activities and aims and the groups of individuals it represents, and the organization can be treated formally as a victim even if each individual member of such an organization does not count as a victim.[304] For Article 14 purposes, the Committee has not sharply distinguished discrimination against the organization *qua* organization and discrimination against the organization's racial or ethnic 'constituency', but has tended to synthesize the two in a common appreciation of victim status. The Committee tends to reiterate points regarding the activities, aims, and nature of an organization as dispositive of questions as to 'representativity',[305] which may in turn be challenged by States parties.[306] The addition of 'groups of individuals' has not opened out the communications procedure to the full flow of group concerns that characterizes procedures under Article 9 or, presumptively, Articles 11–13;[307] Article 14 practice has produced only a modest amplification of the collective dimension of the Convention, though the importance of the practice should not be underestimated, considering that in cases of racial discrimination, an individual victim may stand as a symbolic 'representative' of all other members of a racial/ethnic group.

'Victims' for the purposes of Article 14 also include potential victims from an affected community, a feature that also resonates with the sense that racial discrimination against individuals indirectly targets groups. The 'victim' perspective for Article 14 has been maintained by the Committee, and *actio popularis* deflected, despite occasional pleas such as that by counsel for the petitioner in *Koptova*, who argued, in relation to resolutions barring Roma persons from a municipality, that the Committee ought to have jurisdiction to consider claims 'relevant to the general or public interest, even in exceptional cases where the victim requirement has not been satisfied... the promulgation and maintenance in force of resolutions banning an entire ethnic minority from residing or entering an

[302] In *Jewish Community of Oslo*, the petitioners argued, para. 5.2, that 'groups of individuals', 'whatever its outer limits may be, clearly covers entities that organize individuals for a specific, common purpose, such as congregations and membership organizations'.

[303] *TBB-Turkish Union*, paras 11.2–11.4.

[304] *TBB-Turkish Union*, paras 11.3, 11.4.

[305] In *TBB-Turkish Union*, the petitioning organization itself claimed authority to represent the victim demographic group—persons of Turkish heritage in Berlin and Brandenburg—as its 'most visible and attentively heard voice': para. 7.1.

[306] Critical remarks by the respondent State party in *TBB-Turkish Union*, paras 4.3 and 6.1. In the case of acting for another person, the UN Model Complaint Form requests specific authorization, or an explanation of the nature of the relationship with that other person and why it is considered appropriate to act on their behalf.

[307] See the succinct discussion of CERD group claims in G. Pentassuglia, *Minority Groups and Judicial Discourse in International Law: A Comparative Perspective* (Martinus Nijhoff, 2009), pp. 157–8. In the jurisprudence of the Human Rights Committee, Pentassuglia suggests, p. 157, that in the absence of specific community authorization, 'a mandate... may be inferred from the author's status within the community or other factors'.

entire municipality is precisely the kind of case that should satisfy a "general interest" rule'.[308] Issues of general interest are part of the regular diet of dialogues under Article 9.

The Committee has engaged in heart-searching as to why the communication procedure has not attracted more attention in States parties that accept the Article 14 option, and why only one-third of States parties (approximately) have opted in. Part of the answer may lie in the unpalatability of a finding of racial discrimination,[309] especially but not limited to States that were prominent in the anti-colonial and anti-apartheid struggles, the embers of which still burn. Other aspects limiting the appeal of Article 14 include the availability of alternative international procedures, the weakness of civil society in many States parties, and continued misunderstandings as to the nature and scope of racial discrimination, still deemed irrelevant by some States parties as a contributor to social tensions on home soil.[310] It is arguable that addressing racial discrimination as a large-scale social phenomenon is better served by the holistic, dialogic approaches associated with other Convention procedures, compared to a judgmental procedure of limited scope such as Article 14, hemmed in by procedural constraints. On the other hand, Article 14 practice is responsive to the plight of named victims, clarifies interpretative minutiae, and lends a sharper edge to the deliberations of the Committee.

Current Committee practice involves recurrent citations of general recommendations. The CESCR has defined the purpose of issuing general comments as (a) to make the experience gained so far through the examination of States parties' reports available for the benefit of all States parties, in order to assist and promote their further implementation of the Covenant; (b) to draw the attention of the States parties to insufficiencies disclosed by a large number of reports; (c) to suggest improvements in the reporting procedures; and (d) to stimulate the activities of the States parties, international organizations, and the specialized agencies concerned in achieving progressively and effectively the full realization of the rights recognized in the Covenant.[311] As with other treaty bodies, the general recommendations of CERD have moved from clarifications of procedure towards analyses of substantive norms and the application of rights and obligations to sundry categories of persons and groups. Only some of the basic concepts in the Convention have been subjected to analysis. Notable absences include the concept of 'race' itself, the relationship between non-discrimination and minority rights, the jurisdictional, territorial reach of the Convention, the notion of anti-racist education—remedied to a limited degree by GR

[308] Para. 5.4. The Committee did not comment on the submission, but was content to describe the author as a victim because she belonged to a targeted group (para. 6.5), any member of which would have been barred from residence (para. 10.1).

[309] Khaitan distinguishes between 'lay' meanings of discrimination and discrimination in law—for laypersons, 'discrimination entails some fault. In law, the actor may not be at fault': T. Khaitan, *A Theory of Discrimination Law* (Oxford University Press, 2015), p. 2. This distinction may carry validity in disputes concerning the application of domestic civil law (though hardly into criminal law), but it does not easily translate into international law and is not perhaps intended to do so. The reactions of States to many findings of CERD under Article 14 and Article 9, including the early warning system, suggest that findings of racial discrimination are perceived as assigning blame to States parties and are not 'morally' neutral.

[310] In a submission that transcends the ICERD context, the UK states that it 'remains to be convinced of the added practical value to people in the United Kingdom of rights of individual petition under the Convention. The United Kingdom has strong and effective laws on racial discrimination under which individuals may seek remedies in the courts or tribunals . . . by contrast, the treaty monitoring committees are not courts . . . cannot award damages or produce a legal ruling on the meaning of law': CERD/C/GBR/21-23, para. 272.

[311] E/2000/22, para. 51.

35—and the application of the principle of free, prior and informed consent in the case of indigenous peoples.

Although its general recommendations draw upon the work of sister treaty bodies, CERD has not taken the step of drafting a recommendation in conjunction with another treaty body, as has been done, for example, by CEDAW and CRC.[312] Areas such as control of extraterritorial corporate activity and education appear eminently suitable for a joint general recommendation/comment with CESCR, and the intersection of race and gender with CEDAW. The joint CEDAW/CRC recommendation stimulated a process of reflection on common normative elements in the two conventions, a process that appears particularly appropriate for ICERD, given the exiguous accounts of rights in Article 5 and the practice of drawing upon other human rights instruments to flesh out its contents. Joint interpretations could also improve the consistency of signalling to governments on human rights actions to be taken.

As noted, not all Committee procedures have proceeded in step. The inter-State procedure is currently moribund but susceptible to activation. The focus of Articles 11–13 is different from Article 22 in that the Committee procedure is directed to claims that a State party is not giving effect to the Convention, while Article 22 is ostensibly directed to broader legal issues of interpretation and application; on the other hand, both are dispute- and decision-centred, so that the choice of the disputants may turn on the difference between engaging a judicial body, the International Court of Justice (ICJ), and engaging a committee of experts, CERD. The limited activation of the procedure under Article 15, on the other hand, stems from important changes in the legal and political framework since the 1960s. The Committee has also been hamstrung in its treatment of reservations. Here, the principal constraint stems from the text of the Convention, which hands over the responsibility of deciding on compatibility to an improbable two-thirds assembly of States parties, the dimensions of which constantly increase with the number of States joining the Convention. CERD has expressed its disapproval of individual reservations on numerous occasions, with persuasive rather than dispositive effect.[313]

CERD's information base has improved considerably since the activation of its mandate. Productive symbiosis with the cluster of mechanisms on race, indigenous, refugee and minority, and gender issues under the category of 'special procedures' is a feature of the life of the Committee. The flow of information from UN sources—including the UPR—and regional sources and civil society has served to sharpen perceptions of racial discrimination from a multiplicity of angles. The test of the procedural infrastructure and information base is the extent to which it assists in the furtherance of the aims and objectives of the Convention. Normative development and imagination and adaptation to the objects and purposes of the Convention flourish best under procedures carried through with integrity, intelligence, serious human rights commitment, on the basis of positions and actions clearly justifiable in the light of the mandate. CERD has innovated in its procedures and sought to justify its innovations within the terms of the Convention. Fuller consideration of the extent to which the Committee has effectively furthered the objectives of the Convention is best deferred until the results of its labours are accounted for and evaluated—the principal burden of the chapters that follow.

[312] Joint General Recommendation 31 of CEDAW and General Comment 18 of the CRC on harmful practices, CEDAW/C/GC/31/CRC/C/GC/18 (2014).

[313] See Chapter 18.

5. Title and Preamble

International Convention on the Elimination of All Forms of Racial Discrimination

The States Parties to this Convention,

Considering that the Charter of the United Nations is based on the principles of the dignity and equality inherent in all human beings, and that all Member States have pledged themselves to take joint and separate action, in co-operation with the Organization, for the achievement of one of the purposes of the United Nations which is to promote and encourage universal respect for and observance of human rights and fundamental freedoms for all, without distinction as to race, sex, language or religion,

Considering that the Universal Declaration of Human Rights proclaims that all human beings are born free and equal in dignity and rights and that everyone is entitled to all the rights and freedoms set out therein, without distinction of any kind, in particular as to race, colour or national origin,

Considering that all human beings are equal before the law and are entitled to equal protection of the law against any discrimination and against any incitement to discrimination,

Considering that the United Nations has condemned colonialism and all practices of segregation and discrimination associated therewith, in whatever form and wherever they exist, and that the Declaration on the Granting of Independence to Colonial Countries and Peoples of 14 December 1960 (General Assembly resolution 1514 (XV)) has affirmed and solemnly proclaimed the necessity of bringing them to a speedy and unconditional end,

Considering that the United Nations Declaration on the Elimination of All Forms of Racial Discrimination of 20 November 1963 (General Assembly resolution 1904 (XVIII)) solemnly affirms the necessity of speedily eliminating racial discrimination throughout the world in all its forms and manifestations and of securing understanding of and respect for the dignity of the human person,

Convinced that any doctrine of superiority based on racial differentiation is scientifically false, morally condemnable, socially unjust and dangerous, and that there is no justification for racial discrimination, in theory or in practice, anywhere,

Reaffirming that discrimination between human beings on the grounds of race, colour or ethnic origin is an obstacle to friendly and peaceful relations among nations and is capable of disturbing peace and security among peoples and the harmony of persons living side by side even within one and the same State,

Convinced that the existence of racial barriers is repugnant to the ideals of any human society,

Alarmed by manifestations of racial discrimination still in evidence in some areas of the world and by governmental policies based on racial superiority or hatred, such as policies of apartheid, segregation or separation,

Resolved to adopt all necessary measures for speedily eliminating racial discrimination in all its forms and manifestations, and to prevent and combat racist doctrines and practices in order to promote understanding between races and to build an international community free from all forms of racial segregation and racial discrimination,

Bearing in mind the Convention concerning Discrimination in respect of Employment and Occupation adopted by the International Labour Organization in 1958, and the Convention against Discrimination in Education adopted by the United Nations Educational, Scientific and Cultural Organization in 1960,

Desiring to implement the principles embodied in the United Nations Declaration on the Elimination of All Forms of Racial Discrimination and to secure the earliest adoption of practical measures to that end,

Have agreed as follows:

A. Introduction

The preamble comprises twelve paragraphs and is considerably longer than the preambles to the UN Declaration of Human Rights (UDHR), the International Covenant on Economic, Social and Cultural Rights (ICESCR), and the International Covenant on Civil and Political Rights (ICCPR), though shorter than the International Convention on the Elimination of All Forms of Racial Discrimination's (ICERD) companion instrument on discrimination, the Convention on the Elimination of All Forms of Discrimination against Women (CEDAW).[1] Preambles are generally employed in the realm of interpretation of treaties or declarations and other 'soft law' emanations, and do not, with rare exceptions, have binding force.[2] While there is no separate provision on preambles in the Vienna Convention on the Law of Treaties, the general rule of interpretation expressed in Article 31 provides that a treaty shall be interpreted in good faith in accordance with the ordinary meaning to be given to the terms of the treaty in their context and in light of their object and purpose, with the text of the treaty defined to include its preamble and annexes.[3] In the drafting of the Convention, the representative of Poland in the Commission on Human Rights commented:

> If most conventions and Covenants contained a preamble, it was because the preamble was an important and even indispensable element. In the text before the Commission, the preamble was the legal and substantive basis of the Convention. As a legal basis, it referred to the legal documents which were binding on the various United Nations bodies; as a substantive basis, it sets forth the historical circumstances which had led to the adoption of the Convention. In addition to being a sort of *ratio legis* of the instrument which it preceded, the preamble was an important factor in its interpretation.[4]

According to one author, preambles do not stipulate rights or obligations, rather 'they are narratives that seek to establish legitimacy with regard to the origins and purposes of a piece of legislation, to outline the processes that led to the enactment of the legislation, and to better communicate these rationales to the document's multiple audiences'.[5] The

[1] The UDHR has eight substantive preambular paragraphs; the ICESCR and the ICCPR have five substantive paragraphs each, while CEDAW has 15. Of the core UN human rights treaties, the CRPD has the longest preamble, running to 25 paragraphs. As the representative of Canada remarked in discussions on the draft preamble of ICERD, it was 'its strength and not its length' that was important: A/C.3/SR.1301, para. 9.

[2] H. Pazarci, '1969 Vienna Convention, Preamble', in O. Korten and P. Klein (eds), *The Vienna Convention on the Law of Treaties: A Commentary* (Oxford University Press, 2011), p. 6, notes 29, 30, and 31.

[3] Vienna Convention on the Law of Treaties 1969.

[4] E/CN.4/SR.777, p. 9. See also the comment by the representative of Denmark, E/CN.4/SR.779, p. 4.

[5] T.H. Malloy, 'Title and preamble', in M. Weller (ed.), *The Rights of Minorities in Europe* (Oxford University Press, 2005), pp. 49–72, at p. 56.

author's references to narratives, legitimacy, origins, purposes, and rationales resonate with the substance and structure of the preamble to ICERD. The narrative and process elements of the preamble are complemented by substantive doctrinal assertions regarding science, morality, and the fundamentals of racial discrimination, supplemented by statements on the impact of discrimination on international affairs. The preamble amplifies and adds nuance to the anti-colonial and anti-apartheid narratives that dominated the drafting of the Convention, while projecting the optimistic possibility of an international community free from racial discrimination, an optimism amplified by the title of the Convention.

As an interpretative tool, the preamble to ICERD is potentially important, especially in light of the absence of guidance elsewhere in the Convention on sources of interpretation to be utilized. The Convention contains nothing equivalent to Article 29 of the American Convention on Human Rights (ACHR),[6] or Articles 60 and 61 of the African Charter on Human and Peoples' Rights (ACHPR).[7] Specific references by the Committee on the Elimination of Racial Discrimination (CERD) to the preamble are, however, unusual, though its contents may be subsumed under recommendations regarding 'the objectives and purposes' of the Convention, and, subject to the further comments in the present chapter on the concepts in the preamble, may work subliminally through the regular interpretative practice of the Committee.

B. *Travaux Préparatoires*

I. Title of the Convention

The title of the Convention on the Elimination of All Forms of Racial Discrimination, prefigured in General Assembly resolution 1780 (XVII) and the Declaration suggests ambition in declaring its objective as the 'elimination' of 'all forms' of racial discrimination. According to Banton, the Convention 'is founded upon the lie that racial discrimination, as defined in ICERD... can be eliminated. There is no question that it can be reduced, and maybe if it was defined in some other way could be eliminated', but to aim for the elimination of the conduct defined in Article 1.1 is another matter.[8] Economy of truth notwithstanding, a convention on the *reduction* of racial discrimination would hardly generate the same zeal and commitment as a convention dedicated to its *elimination*.[9] It is not abundantly clear from the *travaux* how the experts and delegates involved in the drafting, who perceived racial discrimination as necessitating an enduring instrument to combat it, reflected on the fit between the title and the elusiveness of the target.

[6] Article 29 ACHR states that no provision of the Convention shall be interpreted as 'precluding other rights or guarantees that are inherent in the human personality or derived from representative democracy as a form of government' or as excluding or limiting the effect that the American Declaration of the Rights and Duties of Man 'and other international acts of the same nature may have'.

[7] The Commission 'shall draw inspiration from international law on human and peoples' rights', references to the UN Charter and the UDHR, 'African instruments on human and peoples' rights' and others follow; Article 61 adapts Article 38 of the Statute of the ICJ, and includes references, *inter alia*, 'African practices consistent with international norms on human and peoples' rights'. Further on the interpretation of the ICERD, see Chapter 20.

[8] M. Banton, *International Action against Racial Discrimination* (Clarendon Press, 1996), p. 50 [henceforth *International Action*].

[9] Present author's emphasis.

The assertions that discrimination was related to colonial systems and specific 'isms' provides a partial explanation for the laxity of the title and the alarm expressed in the preamble at manifestations of discrimination 'in some areas of the world'. On the other hand, the refusal to name the 'isms'[10]—apart from apartheid, colonialism, and racism—'racist doctrines and practices' in the preamble, suggests awareness that the Convention would not be forever tied to specific locations and manifestations, as does the suggestion by Kuwait to designate the Convention as a 'universal' rather than an 'international' instrument.[11]

As regards the 'forms' of discrimination, the Third Committee decided not to hold a general debate on the Convention as a whole. The summary records are complicated by the decision at its 1311th meeting to adopt the proposal by Greece and Hungary 'not to include in the draft International Convention . . . any reference to specific forms of racial discrimination'.[12] This was despite an earlier decision to include references to segregation and apartheid in Article 3 of the Convention, an inconsistency that troubled some delegates. The reference to a specific form of racial discrimination in Article 3 was defended by Ghana on the ground that the South African government's claim that apartheid was not racial discrimination 'made it essential that the unanimous opinion to the contrary be clearly stated in the Convention'.[13] Nigeria averred that apartheid differed from other forms of racial discrimination 'in that it was the official policy of a State member of the United Nations'.[14] Arguments over naming anti-Semitism, Nazism, Fascism, etc, permeate the summary records, stimulating a raft of amendments subsequently 'overruled' by the decision of the Third Committee.[15] The proposals implicated the preamble but also Articles 3 and 4. 'Isms' or practices proposed for the text but eventually not adopted included 'nazist practices' and 'nazist and other similar practices',[16] anti-Semitism,[17] the compendious 'anti-Semitism, Zionism, nazism, neo-nazism and all other forms of the policy and ideology of colonialism, national and race hatred and exclusiveness',[18] and 'dissemination of racial, fascist, nazi or other ideas'.[19] The difficulty for many delegates in such lists was summarized by the representative of Saudi Arabia who, while stating awareness of the horrors of Nazism, argued that 'there were countless "isms" which would have to be enumerated if any one was'.[20] Thus, 'while the greatest

[10] '[T]hat class of untried social theories which are known by the name of isms': J.R. Lowell, *Political Essays* (Houghton, Mifflin, 1888, reprint Forgotten Books, 2013), pp. 138–9; also R. Williams, *Keywords* (Fontana Press, 1988), pp. 173–4; M. Quinion, *Ologies and Isms: A Dictionary of Word Beginnings and Endings* (Oxford University Press, 2005).

[11] A/C.3/SR.1301, para. 71.

[12] A/C.3/L.1244; A/6181, para. 7. The amendment was adopted on a roll call vote by 82 votes to 12, with 10 abstentions. Australia, Austria, Belgium, Bolivia, Brazil, Canada, Israel, Luxembourg, the Netherlands, the UK, the US, and Uruguay voted against the resolution; China, Costa Rica, Dominican Republic, Finland, France, Haiti, Italy, Ivory Coast, Mexico, and Venezuela abstained.

[13] A/C.3/SR.1313, para. 10. Further discussion of anti-Semitism in Chapter 10 (Article 3).

[14] A/C.3/SR.1313, para. 18; also the discussion of Article 3 in Chapter 10.

[15] A/6181, para. 10 lists the amendments naming forms of racial discrimination which were not pressed to a vote.

[16] Amendment with revisions by Poland, A/C.3/L.1210.

[17] 'States parties condemn anti-Semitism and shall take action as appropriate for its speedy eradication in the territories subject to their jurisdiction': Proposal by Brazil and the USA, A/C.3/L.1211.

[18] Amendment by the USSR to the text proposed by Brazil and the USA, A/C.3/L.1231 and Corr. 1.

[19] Czechoslovakia, A/C.3/L.1220. See also the list proposed by Jordan: 'fascist, colonial, tribal, Zionist and other similar practices', A/C.3/SR.1301, para. 79.

[20] A/C.3/SR.1300, para. 6.

recent affliction of Europe had been nazism, for the rest of the world it had no doubt been colonialism . . . in addition, Arabs had suffered from a certain "ism", yet no delegation had asked that it should be mentioned'.[21] He also queried the meaning of 'anti-Semitism, bearing in mind that 95 percent of persons of Semitic origin were Arabs', and that if this was intended as referring to Jews, then this was more appropriately styled as religious, not racial intolerance.[22] He argued that '[o]nly confusion could result from mixing ethnology and religion'.[23] In response, the representative of Israel pointed out that '[t]he Jewish people knew exactly what anti-Semitism was, for it had too long been its victim, whether for racial, religious or other reasons; to those who had suffered from racial discrimination, qualifiers were not important.'[24]

Those supporting the inclusion of textual references to their unfavourite 'isms' tended to argue that some scourges were more grievous than others,[25] that the United Nations had been founded to combat this or that evil practice,[26] and that manifestations of certain evils were ongoing.[27] Those opposed to such references pointed out that all forms of racial discrimination were to be combated[28] so that any enumeration would necessarily be incomplete,[29] and that the Convention should be future-oriented and not wholly dominated by the recent past,[30] a contention articulated by, *inter alios*, the representative of Kuwait who argued that an instrument 'which should be general in scope and addressed to posterity should not be limited in time and space, as reference to an episodic and circumscribed form of racial discrimination would necessarily make it'.[31] The representative of Malawi thought it 'not impossible that another form of discrimination, perhaps even more dangerous than those of the past, might appear somewhere in the world after the Convention had been approved'.[32]

II. The Preamble

The drafts of the preamble differed considerably in substance and length. As context for the convention, the Abram draft made reference to the Declaration on the Elimination of Racial Discrimination, the Universal Declaration of Human Rights, Convention No. 111 of the International Labour Organization, and the United Nations Educational, Scientific and Cultural Organization (UNESCO) Convention against Discrimination in

[21] *Ibid.*

[22] *Ibid.*, paras 7 and 8. See also the concurring remarks of the representative of Hungary re anti-Semitism as religious intolerance, A/C.3/SR.1301, para. 22.

[23] A/C.3/SR.1300, para. 8.

[24] A/C.3/SR.1301, para. 38.

[25] Re Nazism, the representative of Yugoslavia 'could not understand why a reference to something which had caused the extermination of millions of human beings and against which many States represented in the Committee had fought valiantly . . . should be deleted. It was useful to recall . . . experiences of the recent past, especially since such practices persisted in various parts of the world . . . many countries were still threatened by neo-Nazi organizations': A/C.3/SR.1300, para. 20.

[26] Czechoslovakia on Nazism, A/C.3/SR.1301, para. 19.

[27] 'Nazism was not merely an aberration of the past; it was a scourge which continued to ravage the world': Israel, A/C.3/SR.1301, para. 36.

[28] Remarks of the representative of Cameroon, A/C.3/SR.1300, para. 26; Mauritania, A/C.3/SR.1301, para. 23; Afghanistan, *ibid.*, para. 25; India, *ibid.*, para. 27; France, *ibid*, para. 40; Senegal, *ibid.*, para. 64;

[29] Lebanon, A/C.3/SR.1301, para. 51.

[30] 'Anti-Semitism was probably not the most odious practice at the present time': representative of Hungary, A/C.3/SR.1301, para. 22.

[31] *Ibid.*, para. 71.

[32] *Ibid.*, para. 81.

Education.[33] The Calvocoressi text was briefer, recalling Article 55 of the United Nations Charter and that the contracting states were acting in pursuance of resolution 1904 (XVIII).[34] Introducing a reference to the Colonial Declaration of 1960, Ketrzynski explained that there was 'a relation of cause and effect between the phenomenon of colonialism . . . and the continued existence of racial discrimination. The only weapon left to colonialism today was the idea of racial superiority.'[35] Abram, on the other hand, argued that 'not all forms of discrimination derived from colonialism',[36] a position supported by Bouquin who denied that the elimination of all forms of racial discrimination 'could be reduced to the abolition of colonialism'.[37] A text submitted by Calvocoressi and Capotorti subsumed the references to key texts in the initial drafts, including the reference to the Colonial Declaration, adding that the elimination of racial discrimination was a major contribution to international peace and security, jeopardized by, *inter alia*, 'governmental policies based on racial superiority or hatred, such as . . . *apartheid*, segregation or separation'.[38]

There was substantial comment in the Sub-Commission on the question of racial differentiation and superiority. The Ivanov/Ketrzynski text envisaged the convention as 'proceeding from' the Declaration on Racial Discrimination, emphasizing in particular its 'proclamation' that 'any doctrine of racial differentiation or superiority is scientifically false, morally condemnable, socially unjust and dangerous, and that there is no justification for racial discrimination in theory or in practice'.[39] Abram argued that it

> was inaccurate to maintain that doctrines of racial differentiation were scientifically false. On the contrary, the whole purpose of the effort to eliminate racial discrimination was to protect the differences between races apparent to any observer; those differences were indeed among the beauties and glories of the human race.[40]

He later proposed to alter in part the wording of the Sub-Commission's working group's draft preamble to read:[41] '*Convinced* that any doctrine of superiority based on racial differentiation is scientifically false',[42] adding that, in his view, 'the doctrine of racial superiority was the root cause of racial discrimination'.[43] This was objected to by Ketrzynski who argued that racism was not based merely on the doctrine of superiority, but 'frequently found its justification precisely in the differences between individuals or groups'; in Ketrzynski's view, Abram's position would 'support the argument that there was no discrimination so long as all racial groups enjoyed "separate, but equal" treatment'.[44] Abram received support,[45] notably from Bouquin, who argued that the Sub-

33 E/CN.4/Sub.2/L.308.
34 E/CN.4/Sub.2/L.309.
35 E/CN.4./Sub.2/SR.409, pp. 6–8 at p. 6.
36 E/CN.4/Sub.2/SR.410, p. 7.
37 E/CN.4/Sub.2/SR.409, p. 12.
38 E/CN.4/Sub.2/L.313.
39 E/CN.4/Sub.2/L.314, taken from the fifth preambular paragraph of the Declaration.
40 E/CN.4/Sub.2/SR.410, p. 11.
41 E/CN.4/Sub.2/L.317.
42 E/CN.4/Sub.2/SR.413, p. 5.
43 *Ibid.*
44 *Ibid.*
45 E/CN.4/Sub.2/SR.413, pp. 6–7 at p. 7.

Commission should stress the falsity and repugnance of ideas of racial superiority, since it was difficult to deny the existence of racial differentiation:

According to the UNESCO publication *The Race Concept*, a group of physical anthropologists and geneticists . . . had concluded, not that there were no differences between races, but that 'genetic differences are of little significance in determining the social and cultural differences between different groups of men' . . . UNESCO had noted that the declaration adopted by the group had stressed the purely physical nature of differences between races and . . . that racial differences implied neither superiority not inferiority. Just as in the case of discrimination based on sex, the real point was, not that differences existed, but that absolute equality should be ensured.[46]

The Abram proposal was eventually rejected in the face of opposition,[47] particularly from the Chairman, Santa Cruz, who recalled that UNESCO specialists had concluded 'that the concept of race commonly held was scientifically false and that there were no basic differences in capacity, aptitude or ability between racial or ethnic groups'.[48] He later elaborated:

The wording of the original text was based directly on the conclusions of a UNESCO group of experts, indicating that, while biological differences between the various races existed, they were not great enough to affect the moral life and relationships between human beings, or the domain of social or political organization. It followed from these conclusions that all doctrines based on racial differentiation, whether a doctrine proclaiming the superiority of one race over another, such as nazism, or a doctrine based solely on the notion of difference, such as *apartheid*, were equally pernicious.[49]

The lengthy preamble presented to the Commission on Human Rights[50] read as follows:

Considering

1. That the Charter of the United Nations is based on the principle of the dignity and equality inherent in all human beings and imposes on all Members of the United nations the obligations to ensure, promote and encourage universal respect for and observance of human rights and fundamental freedoms for all without distinction as to race, sex, language or religion,
2. That the . . . [UDHR] . . . proclaims that all human beings are born free and equal in dignity and rights and that everyone is entitled to all the rights and freedoms set out in the Declaration, without distinction of any kind,
3. That . . . [the Colonial Declaration] . . . condemned colonialism and all practices of segregation and discrimination connected with it and proclaimed the necessity of bringing them, as well as colonialism in all its forms, to a speedy and unconditional end,
4. That . . . [the Declaration against Racial Discrimination] . . . solemnly affirmed the necessity of speedily eliminating racial discrimination throughout the world in all its forms and manifestations,
5. *Convinced* that any doctrine based on racial differentiation or superiority is scientifically false, morally condemnable, socially unjust and dangerous, and that there is no justification for racial discrimination in theory or in practice anywhere,

[46] E/CN.4/Sub.2/SR.413, p. 7. Bouquin reminded the Sub-Commission of ongoing work on the race question by UNESCO, suggesting that the question of race 'was thus not as simple as some members of the Sub-Commission seemed to think': E/CN.4/Sub.2/SR/414, p. 4.

[47] The Abram amendment was first adopted, E/CN.4/Sub.2/SR.413, p. 10, but was rejected at the next meeting, E/CN.4/Sub.2/SR.414, p. 2.

[48] E/CN.4/Sub.2/SR.413, p. 6.

[49] E/CN.4/Sub.2/SR.414, pp. 3–4.

[50] E/CN.4/874, Report on the twentieth session of the Commission on Human Rights, para. 25.

6. *Reaffirming* that discrimination between human beings on the grounds of race, colour or ethnic origin is an obstacle to friendly and peaceful relations among nations and is a fact capable of disturbing peace and security among peoples as did the evil racial doctrines and practices of nazism in the past,
7. *Concerned* by manifestations of racial discrimination still in evidence in some areas of the world and by governmental policies based on racial superiority or hatred, such as policies of apartheid, segregation or separation, and desiring therefore to adopt further measures in order to eliminate racial discrimination in all its forms and manifestations as soon as possible,
8. *Bearing in mind* the Convention on Discrimination in Respect of Employment and Occupation adopted by ILO in 1958, and the Convention against Discrimination in Education adopted by UNESCO in 1960,
9. *Desiring* to implement the principles in the [UN Declaration against Racial Discrimination] . . . and to secure the earliest adoption by Contracting States of practical measures to that end,

Have agreed as follows . . .

The formulation in the opening paragraph of the Sub-Commission's draft—that the UN Charter *imposes* human rights obligations on all members of the United Nations—was too strong for some delegations at the Commission;[51] the amendments proposed by Lebanon and The Philippines, joined by India, were designed to avoid reproducing the idea that the Charter imposed obligations regarding human rights.[52] Those favouring mention of Charter obligations preferred to retain the Sub-Commission's text with its statement of an obligation to 'ensure' universal respect for human rights and fundamental freedoms.[53] The second draft paragraph was amended on a proposal by Lebanon to add 'in particular as to race, colour or national origin' at the end,[54] despite objections that 'national origin' was open to varying interpretations and that the issue was better dealt with under Article 1.[55] Discussion on the paragraph of the Sub-Commission draft concerning the Colonial Declaration revolved in part around the 'forms' colonialism might take, hence an amendment by the United States (US) was criticized because it deleted the Sub-Commission's reference to 'colonialism in all its forms, wherever it exists', and recalled only the affirmation in the Declaration that 'an end must be put to

[51] Preambular paragraph 1 'gave an erroneous interpretation of the Charter. If the obligation to ensure, promote and encourage universal respect for an observance of human rights and fundamental freedoms already existed for member States, then it would be superfluous to draft human rights covenants': remarks of the representative of the United Kingdom, E/CN.4/SR.775, p. 11. According to the representative of The Philippines, 'varying interpretations were possible of the extent of obligations assumed by members under the Charter': E/CN.4/SR.776, p. 4.

[52] The amendment of the Lebanon (E/CN.4/L.682) referred instead to 'international co-operation in promoting and encouraging respect' for human rights, and 'joint and separate action' in co-operation with the United Nations; that of The Philippines (E/CN.4/L.683) also referred to 'joint and separate action' and to promotion of human rights. The joint Lebanon/Philippines amendment (E/CN.4/L.686) again referred to 'joint and separate action' and to the purposes of the UN to 'promote universal respect for and observance of' human rights', etc. This was revised in the Lebanon/Philippines/India joint amendment (E/CN.4/L.686/Rev.1) to add 'and encourage' after 'promote'.

[53] Summary of discussions in E/CN.4/874, paras 43–7. See, for example, remarks of the representative of the USSR, E/CN.4/SR.776, pp. 5–8, supporting the 'strong' interpretation of the Charter, and remarks of the Ukrainian SSR, E/CN.4/SR.777, p. 8, to similar effect: for Member States, 'to take measures to ensure respect for human rights was to implement the Charter; the actions of States on the international plane could not be separated from their actions on the national plane'. The revised amendment of Lebanon, The Philippines, and India was adopted by 16 votes to none, with 5 abstentions: E/CN.4/874, para. 61.

[54] Adopted by 17 votes to none, with 3 abstentions: E/CN.4/874, para. 62.

[55] Observation of the United Kingdom, E/CN.4/SR.781, p. 10. See Chapter 6 on Article 1.

colonialism and all practices of segregation and discrimination associated therewith'.[56] The amendment by the US was not pressed to a vote,[57] and the Commission adopted a revised amendment submitted by The Philippines which recalled the condemnation by the United Nations of 'colonialism and all practices of discrimination associated therewith, in whatever form and wherever they exist',[58] so that the notion of forms of colonialism was retained.

There was a significant shift away from the Sub-Commission's text in relation to paragraph 5 which condemned, etc, 'any doctrine based on racial differentiation or superiority', towards an acceptance of the formula proposed by Lebanon condemning doctrines of 'superiority based on racial differentiation'.[59] The Commission was influenced by the intervention of a representative of UNESCO[60] who noted that the text in Spanish contradicted the English and French texts in that the former condemned the notion of superiority based on racial differentiation whereas the English and French texts condemned notions of racial superiority or differentiation as scientifically false, etc. The representative preferred the version in Spanish and found ambiguity in the use of the term 'differentiation' in English and French texts. If it implied that racial differences were scientifically false, it was inaccurate; if it meant 'separate but equal', 'that was in no way a scientific matter'.[61]

Discussion of paragraph 6 of the Sub-Commission draft centred on the request by the representative of France to vote separately on the inclusion of the words 'of nazism',[62] the lengthier discussion in the Commission tracking that in the Sub-Commission. Those supporting the retention of the reference argued that Nazism was the most striking historical instance of a racial evil, had led to the Second World War, and was resurgent in some countries.[63] In response, it was pointed out that Nazism had not been individuated as an evil in the Declaration on Racial Discrimination nor in the Universal Declaration of Human Rights or the UN Charter; in the event, 'of nazism' was deleted by the Commission.[64] A substantive proposal by Italy looked towards the building of a world society free from discrimination; while 'world society' had been used in the Declaration on Racial Discrimination,[65] a consensus formed in support of the concept of an

[56] E/CN.4/L.684. The amendment was strongly criticized by the USSR: E/CN.4/SR.780, pp. 4–5.

[57] E/CN.4/874, para. 63.

[58] E/CN.4/L.683/Rev.1, adopted by 19 votes to none, with 2 abstentions: E/CN.4/874, para. 63. The formula was endorsed by, *inter alios*, the representative of India who argued that to 'speak of colonialism in all its forms amounted to implicitly including racism, which was a manifestation of colonialism': E/CN.4/SR.779, p. 10.

[59] E/CN.4/L.683, para. 3. The amendment was adopted unanimously: E/CN.4/874, para. 65.

[60] Lebanon stated that its proposal for change 'was directly attributable' to the UNESCO intervention: E/CN.4/SR.777, p. 5; India stated agreement with the UNESCO representative: E/CN.4/SR.778, p. 4.

[61] E/CN.4/SR.775, pp. 8–9.

[62] E/CN.4/874, paras 54–6.

[63] E/CN.4/874, para. 56. The reference to Nazism was supported by, *inter alios*, the USSR, Costa Rica, Chile, and Poland. In response France stated that there was 'no precedent for referring specifically to Nazism in a document of the kind being considered... He... wished to see the reference deleted purely for reasons of form, and not for reasons of substance': E/CN.4/SR.782, p. 6. Ecuador abstained in the vote on Nazism, not because the country was not outraged by Nazism 'but because if the reference had been retained the paragraph would imply that the doctrines and practices of Nazism were the only instance of racism which had in the past disturbed peace and security among peoples. Such a statement was historically inaccurate': E/CN.4/SR.782, p. 5.

[64] By a narrow vote of 8 to 6, with 5 abstentions: E/CN.4/874, para. 66.

[65] Preambular para. 11 of the Declaration.

'international community' in the draft Convention.[66] The revised paragraph was adopted because it also retained the important notion of the 'speedy elimination' of racial discrimination.[67]

A preamble of ten paragraphs was presented to the Third Committee.

The States Parties to this Convention,

Considering that the Charter of the United Nations is based on the principle of the dignity and equality inherent in all human beings, and that all member States have pledged themselves to take joint and separate action, in co-operation with the Organization, for the achievement of one of the purposes of the United Nations which is to promote and encourage universal respect for and observance of human rights and fundamental freedoms for all, without distinction as to race, sex, language or religion,

Considering that the Universal Declaration of Human Rights proclaims that all human beings are born free and equal in dignity and rights and that everyone is entitled to all the rights and freedoms . . . therein, without distinction of any kind, in particular as to race, colour or national origin,

Considering that the United Nations has condemned colonialism and all practices of segregation associated therewith, in whatever form and wherever they exist, and that the . . . [Colonial Declaration] . . . has affirmed and solemnly proclaimed the necessity of bringing them to a speedy and unconditional end,

Considering that . . . [the United Nations Declaration against racial discrimination] . . . solemnly affirms the necessity of speedily eliminating racial discrimination throughout the world in all its forms and manifestations,

Convinced that any doctrine of superiority based on racial differentiation is scientifically false, morally condemnable, socially unjust and dangerous, and that there is no justification for racial discrimination, in theory or in practice, anywhere,

Reaffirming that discrimination between human beings on the grounds of race, colour or ethnic origin is an obstacle to friendly and peaceful relations among nations and is capable of disturbing peace and security among peoples as evil racial doctrines and practices have done in the past,

Concerned by manifestations of racial discrimination still in evidence in some areas of the world and by governmental policies based on racial superiority or hatred, such as policies of *apartheid*, segregation or separation,

Resolved to adopt all necessary measures for speedily eliminating racial discrimination in all its forms and manifestations and to prevent and combat racist doctrines and practices in order to build an international community free from all forms of racial segregation and racial discrimination,

Bearing in mind the [ILO] Convention concerning Discrimination in respect of Employment and Occupation . . . and the [UNESCO] Convention against Discrimination in Education . . .

Desiring to implement the principles in the [UN Declaration against Discrimination] . . . and to secure the earliest adoption of practical measures to that end,

Have agreed as follows:

[66] The jointly sponsored paragraph (E/CN.4/874, para. 42) read: '*resolved* to adopt all necessary measures for eliminating speedily racial discrimination in all its forms and manifestations and to prevent and combat racist doctrines and practices in order to build an international community free from all forms of racial segregation and racial discrimination'.

[67] E/CN.4/874, paras 58 and 67; adoption was by 17 votes to none, with 4 abstentions.

New paragraphs were proposed by Romania,[68] and by Brazil, Colombia, and Senegal.[69] The Romanian proposal added, after the second paragraph, the consideration that 'all human beings are equal before the law and are entitled to equal protection of the law against any discrimination and against any incitement to discrimination'. The representative explained that it was important that everyone should be protected from discrimination by the State 'because any effort to eliminate racial discrimination depended on the measures taken by States . . . to protect the equal rights of their citizens'.[70] Brazil, Colombia, and Senegal proposed to add after the sixth paragraph: '*Convinced* that the existence of racial barriers is repugnant to the ideals of any civilized society', but in view of objections to the use of 'civilized'[71] it was orally revised to substitute 'human' for 'civilized'.[72] In response to questioning on the meaning of 'racial barriers', the representative of Senegal explained that such barriers existed 'wherever communities were separated from each other on the basis of racial criteria, as was the case in South Africa . . . the idea of racial barriers was as specific as that of geographical or customs barriers'.[73] Austria objected to the reference, 'which might be understood to refer to barriers between national and ethnic groups within one country . . . The wording . . . was not in harmony with the fundamental rights of national and ethnic minorities, which would be protected by the . . . Convention as a whole.'[74]

C. Practice

The first two preambular paragraphs introduce the human rights background pertaining to the UN Charter and the UDHR and recall the pledge in Article 56 of the Charter to implement the purposes of Article 55. The first paragraph restates the non-discrimination formula of the Charter—'race, sex, language or religion'—while the second highlights 'race, colour or national origin' from among the grounds of discrimination in Article 2 of the UDHR. Fundamental concepts of dignity and equality are extracted from both instruments and from the Declaration against Racial Discrimination.[75] Dignity is not

[68] A/C.3/L.1219, as revised on the proposal of the UK, A/C.3/L.1230. This amendment was adopted unanimously: A/6181, para. 27.

[69] A/C.3/L.1217.

[70] A/C.3/SR.1300, para. 13. She added (*ibid.*) that it was 'only States, in the exercise of their sovereignty, that could really put an end to racial discrimination'.

[71] For example, the representative of India objected that 'it could be interpreted that racial discrimination was permissible in a society which interested Powers might dub as uncivilized': A/C.3/SR.1301, para. 28.

[72] A/6181, paras 22–3. The racial barriers paragraph was adopted by 79 votes to none, with one abstention: A/6181, para. 27; a second 'racial barriers' amendment by these States, as orally revised, was withdrawn at the 1302nd meeting: A/6181, para. 25.

[73] A/C.3/SR.1301, para. 62. The representative understood 'civilized society' to mean 'any normative society guided by an ethical outlook whose fundamental general principles were laid down in the Universal Declaration of Human Rights; its opposite was savage society, which was dominated by the idea of might is right': A/C.3/SR.1301, para. 63.

[74] A/C.3/SR.1302, para. 5.

[75] The Preamble to CEDAW makes three references to dignity, while the CRC contains eight, and the CRPD nine references; the ICCPR refers to dignity in the Preamble and in Article 10 in connection with reference to persons deprived of liberty; the CESCR includes dignity in its Preamble and with reference to education. The IACHR and the ACHPR make repeated references to dignity throughout, with the latter instrument linking dignity to the aspirations of the peoples collectively as well as the individual right to respect of 'the dignity inherent in a human being' (Article 5). With regard to minorities and indigenous peoples, the United Nations Declaration on Minorities (UNDM) refers to dignity in its Preamble; the UNDRIP focuses

referred to in the operative articles of the Convention, unlike the Declaration against Racial Discrimination, which bluntly describes racial discrimination as 'an offence to human dignity'.[76] The preamble's recall of dignity on a par with equality among the fundamental bases of the contemporary human rights system underscores its significance among underlying rationales for the prohibition of racial discrimination,[77] leading to the statement in CERD GR 32 on special measures that the Convention is 'based on' the principles of the dignity and equality of all human beings.[78]

In practice, CERD has made limited but varied use of 'dignity'.[79] The term appears in general recommendations besides GR 32, including but not limited to group-specific recommendations. Thus, GR 13 refers to dignity in connection with the duties of law enforcement officials, enjoined to 'respect as well as protect human dignity',[80] while GR 31 links it to sensitivity to victims of discrimination in the criminal process.[81] GR 21 on self-determination refers to the right of persons belonging to ethnic groups 'to lead lives of dignity';[82] GR 22 on refugees and displaced persons recalls the UN Charter and UDHR references to dignity, and GR 23 on indigenous peoples calls on States parties to ensure that members of indigenous peoples are free and equal in dignity and rights. A substantive point is made in GR 29—on discrimination based on descent—regarding measures to replace stereotyped and demeaning images of descent-based groups with images, etc, 'which convey the message of the inherent dignity of all human beings and their equality of human rights'.[83]

References to dignity in cases under Article 14 appear in statements by petitioners:[84] issues such as gross disparagement of group dignity,[85] the humiliation and loss of dignity from being refused access to public spaces,[86] as well as the conceptualization of dignity in

little on dignity in express terms, though many of its concepts may be deemed to imply dignity in terms of inherent worth and also status: Article 15 refers to the 'dignity and diversity' of indigenous cultures, traditions, etc. Further references in C. McCrudden, 'Human Dignity and Judicial Interpretation of Human Rights', *European Journal of International Law* 19 (2008), 655–724 [henceforth 'Human Dignity and Judicial Interpretation'].

[76] Art. 1.

[77] 'Dignity' appears alongside equal rights in the Preamble to the UN Charter 'the dignity and worth of the human person'; the UDHR repeats the phrase in its preamble, also referring therein to 'inherent dignity', while Article 1 includes the famous line that '[a]ll human beings are born equal in dignity and rights', see also Articles 22 and 23.

[78] Para. 6.

[79] For general treatments, see P.G. Carozza, 'Human Dignity', in D. Shelton (ed.), *The Oxford Handbook of International Human Rights Law* (Oxford University Press, 2013), pp. 345–59 [henceforth *Human Dignity*]; and 'Human Dignity and Judicial Interpretation of Human Rights: A Reply', *European Journal of International Law* 19 (2008), 931–44 [henceforth *Human Dignity and Judicial Interpretation of Human Rights*]; G. Kateb, *Human Dignity* (Harvard University Press, 2011); D. Kretzmer and E. Klein (eds), *The Concept of Human Dignity in Human Rights Discourse* (Brill/Nijhoff, 2002); C. McCrudden, 'Human Dignity and Judicial Interpretation'; M. Rosen, *Dignity: its History and Meaning* (Harvard University Press, 2012); a succinct critique of the uses of 'dignity' in the field of discrimination and equality is presented in A. McColgan, *Discrimination, Equality and the Law* (Hart Publishing, 2014), esp. pp. 23–33 [henceforth *Discrimination*].

[80] Para. 2.

[81] Para. 19.

[82] Paras 5.

[83] Para. VV.

[84] In *L.R. v Slovakia*, CERD/C/66/D/31/2003, para. 5.5, the petitioners cited the European Commission on Human Rights in the *East African Asians* case to the effect that 'immigration admission denied on the basis of colour and race . . . constituted an affront to human dignity'.

[85] *Jewish Community of Oslo and ors v Norway*, CERD/C/67/D/30/2003, (2005), paras 8.2 and 9.5.

[86] *Durmic v Serbia and Montenegro*, CERD/C/68/D/29/2003 (2006) para. 2.3.

domestic law,[87] have all been adverted to. The matter is put simply in some cases: racial discrimination is an assault on human dignity.[88] The Committee has tended not to refer to dignity in its opinions under Article 14, preferring to cite the operative articles of the Convention.[89] By contrast with the communications procedure, the Committee has been more forthright with its recommendations under Article 9. Explicit references to dignity have appeared in connection with, *inter alia*, allegations of forced evictions,[90] media racism,[91] return of displaced persons,[92] training of law enforcement officials,[93] and a comprehensive programme to address the human rights situation of stateless persons.[94]

Most of the evocations of dignity by the Committee refer to the dignity of persons or individuals but collective dimensions are also in evidence and may be deduced from particular contexts through association with indigenous peoples, cultures, etc.[95] In a rare explanatory statement, individual and group dimensions of dignity and equality appear together in CERD GR 35 on combating racist hate speech, defining such speech as 'a form of other-directed speech which rejects the core human rights principles of human dignity and equality, and seeks to degrade the standing of individuals and groups in the estimation of society'.[96] A sense that collective dignity is being invoked in substance if not in name may be gleaned from scattered references to demeaning or stereotyping portrayals of peoples, suggesting the lack of respect associated with attacks on dignity.[97] Beyond the curt statement in GR 35, the Committee has not offered a general definition or conceptualization of 'dignity'.

The third paragraph of the preamble, lifted almost verbatim from Article 7 of the UDHR, mediated by the preamble to the Declaration against Racial Discrimination,

[87] Citing an *amicus curiae* brief by the German Institute for Human Rights, the petitioner in *TBB-Turkish Union in Berlin/Brandenburg v Germany*, CERD/C/82/D/48/2010 (2013), paras 8.2, 8.3, recalled the jurisprudence of the Federal Constitutional Court to the effect that the notion of human dignity 'prohibits making a person the mere object of the State or subjecting the person to treatment which fundamentally calls into question his/her quality as a human being. Assaults on human dignity include . . . degradation, stigmatization or social exclusion and other forms of conduct that deny the affected person's right to respect as a human being . . . Racist ideas are characterized by their calling into question the individuality of human beings and thus also their human dignity.'

[88] *L.A. v Slovakia*, CERD/C/85/D/49/2011 (2014), para. 2.5. The communication involved persons of Roma ethnicity refused access to a discotheque. For the purposes of Slovak law on financial compensation for discrimination, it was necessary to prove a real and grave diminution of human dignity, which the petitioners asserted was the case (paras 2.5 and 3.3.) but was denied by the State party (para. 4.4.). The Committee did not comment on the rival applications of 'dignity' to the events in question.

[89] The reference to dignity in the Committee's statement of opinion, para. 12.2 of *TBB-Turkish Union*, merely recalls the German Criminal Code.

[90] Concluding observations on the UK, CERD/C/GBR/CO/18-20, para. 28; on Serbia, CERD.C/SRB/CO/1, para. 14.

[91] Concluding observations on Argentina, CERD/C/65/CO/1, para. 15.

[92] Concluding observations on the Russian Federation, CERD/C/62/CO/7, para. 18.

[93] Concluding observations on Portugal, CERD/C/65/CO/6, para. 10; and Spain, CERD/C/64/CO/6, para. 11.

[94] Concluding observations on Kuwait, CERD/C/KWT/CO/15-20, para. 17.

[95] For association between dignity and culture and religion, see *Christian Education South Africa v Minister of Education* (2000), 4 SA 757 (CC).

[96] Para. 10.

[97] CERD/C/PER/CO/14-17, para. 19: stereotyped and demeaning portrayals of indigenous peoples and Afro-Peruvian communities; CERD/C/GTM/CO/12-13, para. 17: stereotyped, disparaging characterizations of indigenous peoples in Guatemala; CERD/C/IRN/CO/18-19, para. 10: stereotyped and demeaning portrayals of Azeri 'peoples and communities' in the media in Iran. See also CESCR General Comment No. 21, the Right to Take Part in Cultural Life, E/C.12/GC/21, para. 40 (2009).

recalls equality before the law and the wider concept of equal protection of the law. Unlike 'dignity', notions of equality have been subsumed into the text of the Convention in varied formulations, though 'equal protection of the law' does not appear as such in the operative text, unlike 'equality before the law'. The concept of equality has been extensively pored over by the Committee, and the preambular references to the broader concept of 'equal protection of the law' appear to have influenced its thinking: hence, GR 32 on special measures asserts that:

> [t]he principle of equality underpinned by the Convention combines formal equality before the law with equal protection of the law, with substantive or *de facto* equality in the enjoyment and exercise of human rights as the aim to be achieved by the faithful implementation of its principles.[98]

As in the UDHR, the preamble refers to protection against incitement to discrimination as a human rights entitlement. The incitement narrative is further developed in Article 4 of the Convention, which mandates that such protection be declared an offence punishable by law. The placing of incitement among fundamental principles in the preamble accords with the severity of the Article 4 provisions and the treatment of this article by CERD as a crucial element in the fight against racial discrimination.

The fourth paragraph of the preamble forges a link between the fight against discrimination, colonialism, and segregation. The reference to General Assembly resolution 1514(XV)—the 'Colonial Declaration'—explicitly links the Convention with decolonization processes, suggesting, as did many in the drafting process, that racial discrimination was fundamental to colonization, perceived at the time as a paradigmatically Western project. The Colonial Declaration devotes itself to the rights of peoples to be free and builds on the general human rights and non-discrimination language in the Charter of the United Nations: *inter alia*, the subjection of peoples to alien subjugation, etc, is stated to be 'a denial of fundamental human rights'.[99] The preamble to the Convention echoes the general anti-colonial stance prevalent at the United Nations in its reference to 'colonialism and all practices of segregation and discrimination' associated with it, while the reference to bringing colonialism and these practices to a speedy and unconditional end recalls the preamble to the Colonial Declaration. The reciprocity of reference to colonialism in the Convention and the Colonial Declaration, together with the implied reference to apartheid, is played out principally in Article 3 of the Convention, which addresses segregation and apartheid, and in Article 15, the largely moribund procedure for examining petitions from territories to which General Assembly resolution 1514(XV) applies.[100]

Despite the intimacy of connection between the Colonial Declaration and the Convention, the Committee's General Recommendation on the right of self-determination (GR 21 of 1996) makes no reference to the Declaration, referring only to the UN Charter, the Covenants on Human Rights, and the UN Declaration on the Rights of Persons belonging to Minorities. The Recommendation also cites General Assembly resolution 2625(XXV)—the 'Friendly Relations Declaration'[101]—which is more flexible as regards

[98] Para. 6.

[99] Colonial Declaration, Article 1.

[100] Discussed in Chapter 4.

[101] Extensive references to the Declaration are made in C. Tomuschat (ed.), *Modern Law of Self-Determination* (1993) [henceforth *Modern Law*].

outcomes of self-determination exercises than the independence-focused Colonial Declaration in referring to forms of self-determination other than independence, such as free association with an independent State, 'integration', and any other political status 'freely determined by a people'. Two 'aspects' of self-determination are distinguished in the Recommendation:

> The right to self-determination of peoples has an internal aspect, that is to say, the rights of all peoples to pursue freely their economic, social and cultural development without outside interference. In that respect there exists a link with the right of every citizen to take part in the conduct of affairs at any level... In consequence, Governments are to represent the whole population without distinction as to race, colour, descent or national or ethnic origin. The external aspect of self-determination implies that all peoples have the right to determine freely their political status and their place in the international community based upon the principle of equal rights and exemplified by the liberation of peoples from colonialism.[102]

With regard to territorial integrity, GR 21 co-opts the formula in the Friendly Relations Declaration:

> None of the Committee's actions shall be construed as authorizing or encouraging any action which would dismember or impair, totally or in part, the territorial integrity or political unity of sovereign and independent States conducting themselves in accordance with the principle of equal rights and self-determination of peoples and possessing a government representing the whole people belonging to the territory, without distinction as to race, creed or colour.[103]

The paragraph adds that 'international law has not recognised a general right of peoples unilaterally to declare secession from a State'.[104]

The distinction between two 'aspects' of self-determination was not made in the Colonial Declaration but is one that reflects further developments in the understanding and practice of self-determination, which has expanded to include post-colonial contexts, and to a human rights phase linked to incorporation in the Covenants, supplementing the original decolonization focus.[105] The recommendation stresses the link between self-determination and the enjoyment of human rights in the context of which attention is also drawn to the UN Declaration on the Rights of Persons Belonging to Minorities (UNDM). In the Committee, and bearing in mind that there are 177 independent States parties to ICERD, the application of self-determination has moved on to address groups within States, notably the treatment of indigenous peoples. While specific use of self-determination language as applied to particular groups remains rare,[106] CERD has endorsed the UN Declaration on the Rights of Indigenous Peoples (UNDRIP), Article

[102] Para. 4.

[103] Para. 6. The annual report of CERD to the General Assembly (A/51/16), paragraphs General Recommendations 20, 21, and 22 together so that para. 1 of GR 21 is rendered as para. 6: footnotes in the present work separate the paragraphs into three sets.

[104] Para. 6, where it is stated that this restriction 'does not, however exclude the possibility of arrangements reached by free agreement of all parties concerned'.

[105] See, among many contributions, A. Cassese, *Self-Determination of Peoples* (Cambridge University Press, 1995); A. Cobban, *The Nation-State and National Self-Determination* (Fontana, 1969); K. Knop, *Diversity and Self-Determination in International Law* (Cambridge University Press, 2002); collection of essays in Tomuschat, *Modern Law*.

[106] For examples, see, in the case of Finland, the reference to 'the Sámi people's rights, recognized in the United Nations Declaration on the Rights of Indigenous Peoples, to self-determination': CERD/C/FIN/CO/20-22, para. 12; and, less clearly, in the case of Vietnam, CERD/C/VNM/CO/10-14, para. 12.

3 of which (adapting the language of Article 1 of the Covenants) states simply that indigenous peoples 'have the right to self-determination. By virtue of that right they freely determine their political status and freely pursue their economic, social and cultural development';[107] to which Article 4 adds that indigenous peoples 'in exercising their right to self-determination, have the right to autonomy or self-government in matters relating to their internal and local affairs, as well as ways and means for financing their autonomous functions'.

Even if not expressly listed among the rights to be protected by the Convention, respect for self-determination counts among the fundamental values of the Convention expressed through the preamble. Because the Convention characteristically directs itself to the treatment of groups within States, it is not inherently surprising that CERD activity fixes on what are described as the internal dimensions of self-determination, when the Committee finds it useful to invoke the right. The reading of secession in GR 21 is cautious but not out of line with subsequent international developments,[108] though any purported 'guarantee' of territorial integrity in the Friendly Relations Declaration is fringed with ambiguity.[109]

The fifth and twelfth paragraphs refer to the Declaration on the Elimination of All Forms of Racial Discrimination, while Article 7 of the Convention envisages propagating its purposes and principles. The manner of inclusion of the Declaration in the Convention's preamble and operative text suggests that its significance is more than historical; that its principles are structured into the Convention and may be called upon to resolve interpretative doubts in the latter. On the other hand, the greater specificity of the Convention, coupled with the constant evocation of its rules and principles in the work of CERD, has made such resort a less than compelling interpretative strategy; it is also the case that many formulae in the Declaration were rejected by the drafters of the

[107] For a fuller analysis of the right of self-determination under the Declaration, see H. Quane, 'The UN Declaration on the Rights of Indigenous Peoples: New Directions for Self-Determination and Participation Rights', in S. Allen and A. Xanthaki (eds), *Reflections on* the *UN Declaration on the Rights of Indigenous Peoples* (Hart Publishing, 2011), pp. 259–87.

[108] See Supreme Court of Canada, *Quebec Secession reference*, [1998] 2 S.C.R. 217, esp. paras 111–38. The secession issue remains controversial; the ICJ avoided confronting it directly in the *Advisory Opinion on Accordance with International Law of the Unilateral Declaration of Independence in Respect of Kosovo*, ICJ Advisory Opinion, 22 July 2010, ICJ reports, paras 82–4, where the majority noted, *inter alia*, that while 'the international law on self-determination' conferred upon 'part of the population of an existing State the right to separate from that State' this is a matter 'on which radically different views were expressed'; in consequence it was not necessary to resolve that question. The Opinion of the International Court of Justice emerged following the issuance of a declaration of independence from Serbia. A number of States recognized Kosovo, while others, including Serbia and the USSR, argued that the declaration of independence was contrary to international law. In the African context, see *Gunme v Cameroon*, No. 266/2003 ACHPR Annual Activity Report (2008–09), where the African Commission on Human Rights stated, para. 190, that it was obligated to uphold the territorial integrity of States and could not 'envisage, condone or encourage secession but that self-determination could be accomplished by autonomy within a sovereign State'. The Commission also raised the issue of so-called remedial secession where massive violations of human rights may call into question the territorial integrity of States, a proposition that may be derived from some (contested) readings of the Declaration on Friendly Relations. For general commentary, see D. Shelton, Self-Determination in Regional Human Rights Law: From Kosovo to Cameroon', *AJIL* 105 (2011), 60–81; P. Thornberry, 'The Democratic or Internal Aspect of Self-Determination with some Remarks on Federalism', in Tomuschat, *Modern Law,* pp. 101–38 [henceforth 'The Democratic or Internal Aspect of Self-Determination']; R. Wilde, 'Self-Determination, Secession and Dispute Settlement after the Kosovo Advisory Opinion', *Leiden Journal of International Law* 24 (2011), 149–54.

[109] Thornberry, 'The Democratic or Internal Aspect of Self-Determination' 101–38. For further reflections on forms of self-determination in light of the provisions of the ICERD, see Chapter 13.

Convention. The Declaration is perhaps best understood as a repository of general principle, underlining the commitment of the United Nations as a whole to the elimination of racial discrimination, and as further embedding the fundamental anti-discrimination standard.

The sixth paragraph of the preamble includes a deliberate, subtle but important departure from its equivalent (preambular paragraph 5) in the Declaration. What is condemned and epistemologically undermined in the Convention is 'any doctrine of superiority *based on* racial differentiation', and not, as in the Declaration, 'any doctrine of racial differentiation *or* superiority'.[110] If racial theory propounds that 'races' may be differentiated one from another and that some races are superior or inferior to others, the Convention focuses on inferiority/superiority as the 'villain of the piece'. Keane suggests that 'the Convention in its preamble tacitly supports the concept of the existence of separate races',[111] and that CERD should repudiate the notion of race.[112] The issue has returned to trouble CERD in connection with the reluctance of some States parties to the Convention to retain 'race' in their anti-discrimination legislation.[113] The paragraph is unusual among international human rights treaties in claiming that doctrines of racial superiority are, *inter alia*, 'scientifically false', as well as being morally condemnable, unjust, and dangerous; the Declaration makes the same judgement on science, morality, and danger, while further undermining doctrines of racial superiority by relegating them to the lowly status of a 'prejudice'.[114] The preamble takes its tone from the work of UNESCO, where the contributing experts were agreed that notions of the purity and hierarchy of races were without scientific foundation, though differences between the 1950 and 1951 Statements were apparent on the usefulness of 'race'.

The seventh paragraph, an adaptation of paragraph 9 of the preamble of the Declaration and its Article 1, sets racial discrimination into the context of international relations and relations among peoples in the same state, underlining its force as an obstacle to peaceful and friendly relations and 'harmony'. The international relations theme is taken up in the promotion by Article 7 of positive messages to further understanding and friendship among nations. The potentially disruptive force of racial discrimination is the underlying theme of the inter-State complaints procedure set out in Articles 11, 12, and 13. The recognition of an international element to racial discrimination not explicitly limited to colonial situations represented a further significant step in the erosion of the notion of human rights as a 'domestic' matter. In practice, while there has been some outreach into the wider field of inter-State relations, the Committee's focus remains that of monitoring the treatment of individuals and groups within States and recommending measures to ameliorate situations. The bounded character of CERD's concerns has been challenged when faced with situations of international conflict,[115] including cases of

[110] Emphasis added.

[111] D. Keane, *Caste-Based Discrimination in International Human Rights Law* (Ashgate, 2007), p. 177 [henceforth *Caste-Based Discrimination*]. He adds, p. 176, that this 'departure from the position expressed by the signatories to the Declaration is similar to the difference between the first and second UNESCO statements on race, the second of which refused to deny the existence of... race in line with its predecessor, ... condemning only the notion of racial superiority'.

[112] Keane, *Caste-Based Discrimination,* p. 178.

[113] The issue is further discussed in Chapter 6.

[114] Preambular paragraph 9 of the Declaration.

[115] I. Diaconu, *Racial Discrimination* (Eleven International Publishing, 2011), pp. 191–4; D. Weissbrodt, 'The Approach of the Committee on the Elimination of Racial Discrimination to Interpreting and Applying

occupation of territory and evidence of extraterritorial activity by governments and corporations.[116]

The paradigmatic 'racial barriers' referred to in the eighth paragraph were those erected in pursuance of State-authorized segregation policies, along with their physical or geographical concomitants in terms of public services, lands, territory, etc. The major target was South Africa; segregation policies in the US and elsewhere represented another point of departure. 'Barriers', though not always 'racial barriers', continue to be referred to by CERD and include administrative and legal barriers,[117] practical barriers to employment,[118] barriers to development,[119] barriers to be redressed by dialogue and integration projects,[120] economic, social, and geographic barriers in access to basic services,[121] and language barriers.[122] Beyond the express strictures on segregation and apartheid in Article 3, the metaphor has proved appropriate in addressing structural discrimination such as 'possible barriers to naturalization that may exist for long-term or permanent residents of African descent'.[123]

As noted in the discussion of the *travaux*, Austria was concerned that the concept of inadmissible 'barriers' might trouble the Austrian system of minority rights, or potentially other systems, such as they existed in the 1960s.[124] The drafting of the Convention did not attest to a great deal of empathy towards the rights of minorities. The exigencies of decolonization and nation-building were still in the ascendant and no significant corpus of instruments on the rights of minorities had been developed, although Article 27 of the ICCPR would be launched in the year following the adoption of ICERD. 1966 was also the year in which Judge Tanaka, in a dissenting opinion in the International Court of Justice, disentangled segregation and apartheid from the rights of minorities as expressed in the minorities treaties under the League of Nations:

> In the case of the minorities treaties the norm of non-discrimination as a reverse side of the notion of equality before the law prohibits a State to exclude members of a minority group from participating in rights, interests and opportunities which a majority population group can enjoy. On the other hand, a minority group shall be guaranteed the exercise of their own religious and education activities. This guarantee is conferred on members of a minority group, for, the purpose of protection of their interests and not from the motive of discrimination itself... The spirit of the minorities treaties, therefore, is not negative and prohibitive, but positive and permissive... in these cases it is possible that the different treatment in certain aspects is reasonably required by the differences in religion, language, education, custom, etc., not by reason of race or colour.[125]

International Humanitarian Law', *Minnesota Journal of International Law* 19 (2010), 327–62 [henceforth *The Approach of the Committee to Humanitarian Law*].

116 See Chapters 8 and 10.

117 Concluding observations on Norway, CERD/C/NOR/CO/18, para. 11.

118 Concluding observations on Canada, CERD/C/CAN/CO/19-20, para. 19.

119 Concluding observations on the Dominican Republic, CERD/C/DOM/CO/13-14, para. 9.

120 Concluding observations on Serbia, CERD/C/SRB/CO/1, para. 17.

121 Concluding observations on Costa Rica, CERD/C/CRI/CO/18, para. 12.

122 Concluding observations on Mauritius, CERD/C/MUS/CO/15-19, para. 20; on Vietnam, CERD/C/VNM/CO/10-14, para. 9.

123 GR 34, para. 47.

124 For a general view, see *Protection of Minorities: Special Protective Measures of an International Character for Ethnic, Religious and Linguistic Groups* (United Nations, 1967), Sales No. 67.XIV.3.

125 Dissenting opinion, *South West Africa Cases (second phase)*, 1966, extracted in I. Brownlie, *Basic Documents on Human Rights* (3rd edn, Clarendon Press, 1992), pp. 568–98, at pp. 590–1 [henceforth *Basic Documents*].

The 'rehabilitation' of minority rights in international law through Article 27 of the ICCPR,[126] the UN Declaration on the Rights of Persons Belonging to Minorities,[127] and many other instruments, follows the general lines intimated by Judge Tanaka.[128] Minority rights do not constitute the 'racial barriers' referred to in ICERD but clarify the corpus of human rights to be protected from discrimination, intersecting with the non-discrimination principle through currents of mutual influence.

The ninth paragraph expresses fears—alarm, even—at manifestations of racial discrimination and at government policies of a specific nature; the paragraph also intimates an ethic of anti-discrimination as the polar opposite of 'segregation and separation'.[129] The reference to discrimination 'in some areas of the world' reflects assertions in the drafting process of the limited remit of the Convention as well as the judgements that such may not be the case. Any limitation on the scope of the Convention's concerns implied in the paragraph should be set against paragraph 5 with its recall of the necessity expressed in the Declaration of eliminating racial discrimination 'throughout the world'.[130] Paragraph 9 may therefore be judged as a protest and call to action against contemporary manifestations that does not rule out other manifestations; a similar interpretation may be placed upon the Declaration. The reference to 'governmental policies' is tied to the need to address the manifestations of racial discrimination with urgency, and should not be read as implying that only governments generate racial discrimination;[131] the operative articles of the Convention, notably Article 2, make it abundantly clear that the States must address discrimination generated by private parties.

Regarding the triplet of apartheid, segregation, and separation, the link was also asserted in the Declaration (along with the couplet 'segregation and discrimination') and retained for the Convention through the successive drafting stages. The inclusion of 'separation' echoes the pleadings in the South West Africa cases, where the applicants asserted the existence of a customary norm of non-discrimination or non-separation.[132] The International Convention on the Suppression and Punishment of the Crime of Apartheid prefers to couple 'discrimination and segregation', while defining apartheid to include measures designed to divide populations along racial lines and 'the creation of separate reserves and ghettos'.[133] The concepts of apartheid and segregation made their way into Article 3 of the Convention unaccompanied by 'separation'. CERD GR 3 (on relations with racist regimes in southern Africa) refers to apartheid, segregation, and discrimination; 'separation' is not mentioned. The Committee has, however, been

[126] 'In those States in which ethnic, religious or linguistic minorities exist, persons belonging to such minorities shall not be denied the right, in community with the other members of their group, to enjoy their own culture, to profess and practise their own religion, or to use their own language.'

[127] Adopted by General Assembly resolution 47/135, 18 December 1992.

[128] P. Thornberry, *International Law and the Rights of Minorities* (Clarendon Press, 1991) gives a general view of the period; for a succinct update, se R. McCorquodale, 'Group Rights', in D. Moeckli, S. Shah, and S. Sivakumaran (eds), *International Human Rights Law* (2nd edn, Oxford University Press, 2014), 333–55.

[129] The equivalent paragraph 8 in the preamble of the Declaration included references to 'apartheid, segregation and separation', as well as to 'doctrines of racial superiority and expansionism' in certain areas; Article 5 of the Declaration demanded the putting an end, without delay, to 'public policies of racial segregation and especially policies of apartheid, as well as all forms of racial discrimination and separation resulting from such policies'.

[130] Preamble of the Declaration, para. 11.1.

[131] See commentary in the present work on Articles 1 and 2.

[132] Judge Tanaka in Brownlie, *Basic Documents*, pp. 574, 576.

[133] Adopted by General Assembly resolution 3068 (XXVIII), 30 November 1973.

engaged by issues such as separation of families, of offenders from their communities,[134] and by claims regarding 'separate sectors' and 'separation of communities' in areas such housing and education,[135] as well as sundry forms of segregation.[136] The developments suggest that the Convention and wider international law are better represented by the norm of 'anti-segregation' rather than 'non-separation', a formula that runs the risk of cutting across established group-related rights in the field of education and elsewhere.[137]

The complex tenth paragraph echoes paragraph 5 in its sense of urgency directed towards the 'speedy' elimination of racial discrimination and complements paragraph 4, which applies the same resolve to colonialism. The three paragraphs cumulatively suggest that the 'speed' metaphor is appropriate because of the politically confined nature of discrimination and apartheid (and colonialism). The paragraphs confining racist phenomena should, however, be set against intimations in the preamble that the racial manifestations addressed by the Convention are global and not system-specific, such as paragraph 5, 'eliminating racial discrimination throughout the world', and paragraph 6, no justification for racial discrimination 'anywhere', as well as the recall of instruments such as the UDHR. The paragraph offers a vision of an international community transformed by the elimination of racial discrimination and racialized speech, built on a platform of inter-racial understandings. The reasons for the replacement of the Declaration's 'world society' by the Convention's 'international community' are not entirely clear, though the latter phrase presents a less monolithic vision, attuned to the reality of multiple sovereignties.[138] The phraseology of 'understanding between races' coheres with the (accepting?) mention of 'racial differentiation' in paragraph 6 and other elements in the Convention susceptible to the criticism that the Convention tends to naturalize the existence of distinct races of human beings.[139] The paragraph is cited by GR 3,[140] the Committee taking the view that the building of an international community free from racial segregation and discrimination should be pursued at the international level and not merely nationally.[141]

Further 'international solidarity' elements in practice include GR 18 on the establishment of an international tribunal to prosecute crimes against humanity; sundry comments on cooperation with international tribunals,[142] as well as the Committee's Early Warning and Urgent Action procedure in general; the Declaration on the Prevention of Genocide,

[134] Concluding observations on Canada, CERD/C/CAN/CO/18, para. 18.

[135] Concluding observations on Israel, CERD/C/ISR/CO/13, para. 22; CERD/C/ISR/CO/14-16, paras 24 and 27, and response of Israel to the latter set of concluding observations, A/68/18, Annex VII. See also CERD/C/SR.2131 and SR.2132 for extensive discussion of issues.

[136] See commentary in the present work on Article 3 of ICERD.

[137] See, in addition to the instruments on minorities and indigenous peoples referred to extensively in the present work, Articles 2 and 5 of the UNESCO Convention against Discrimination in Education 1960, UNTS, Vol. 429, p. 93.

[138] D. Armstrong, 'Law, Justice and the Idea of a World Society', *International Affairs* 75, 3 (1999), 547–61; C. Brown (2001), 'World Society and the English School: an "International Society" Perspective on World Society', London: LSE Research online, available at: <http://eprints.lse.ac.uk/archive/00000743>; B. Buzan, *From International to World Society? English School Theory and the Social Structure of Globalization* (Cambridge University Press, 2004).

[139] See commentary in the present work on Article 1.

[140] Para. 2.

[141] The notion of understanding among nations and racial/ethnic groups reaches into Article 7, discussed in Chapter 17.

[142] Concluding observations on Kenya, CERD/C/KEN/CO/1-4, para. 15; Serbia, CERD/C/SRB/CO/1, para. 22.

which finds it 'imperative to stimulate stronger ties and interaction between the global and local levels' across a range of human rights and security institutions;[143] the stream of recommendations to ratify cognate international human rights instruments, and the Committee's practical liaison with other UN and regional bodies in carrying out its regular work.

The paragraph includes a reference to 'racist' doctrines and practices.[144] Taking historical race narratives into account, and the drafting of the Convention, racism suggests, *ex facie*, attitudes and practices close to the tenets of racial theory, with the corollary that the closer the statement or act to 'hard' biological conceptions of race, the more 'racist' they are. On the other hand, notions of cultural racism have gained considerable currency, reading the concept of racial discrimination to cover the habits and practices of groups, culturally oriented or 'difference' racism.[145] Cultural racism is, according to some commentators, older than biological racism:[146] Anghie's reading of international law as engaged from the beginning with cultural difference will be recalled.[147] While there is no definition of racism in the Convention, the translation of its definition of racial discrimination into the vocabulary of racism demonstrates its significant concern with the 'cultural' or 'difference' variety of racism, bearing in mind that 'race' is only one element in the definition, and in light of the 'culturalization' of so many aspects of Convention practice.[148] The application of the Convention has made a signal contribution to the understanding of cultural/difference racism, an almost inevitable consequence of the wide definition employed in Article 1.

Some contemporary readings of racism recall elements from the Convention: hence the European Commission against Racism and Intolerance (ECRI) defines racism as 'the belief that a ground such as race, colour, language, religion, nationality or national or ethnic origin justifies contempt for a person or a group of persons, or the notion of superiority of a person or a group of persons'.[149] This account of racism stresses belief rather than action grounded upon such a belief. While the definition of racism in the Inter-American Convention against Racism is also theory-oriented, it also addresses potential consequences of racism:

> Racism consists of any theory, doctrine, ideology, or sets of ideas that assert a causal link between the phenotypic or genotypic characteristics of individuals or groups and their intellectual, cultural, and personality traits, including the false concept of racial superiority. Racism leads to racial inequalities, and to the idea that discriminatory relations between groups are morally and scientifically justified.

[143] A/60/18, ch. VIII. On cooperation with international criminal tribunals and related matters, see D. Weissbrodt, *The Approach of the Committee to Humanitarian Law*.

[144] 'Racist activities' are referred to in Article 4(a).

[145] According to Makkonen, both variants of racism 'serve the same higher level function: they are essentially and primarily ways to justify group supremacy': T. Makkonen, *Equal in Law, Unequal in Fact: Racial and Ethnic Discrimination and the Legal Response Thereto in Europe* (Martinus Nijhoff Publishers, 2012), p. 59. For a maximalist view of racism as a pervasive phenomenon, see D. Petrova, 'Racial Discrimination and the Rights of Minority Cultures', in S. Fredman (ed.), *Discrimination and Human Rights: The Case of Racism* (Oxford University Press, 2001), pp. 45–76.

[146] T. Modood, '"Difference" Cultural Racism and Anti-Racism', in B. Boxill (ed.), *Race and Racism* (Oxford University Press, 2001), pp. 238–56.

[147] A. Anghie, *Imperialism, Sovereignty and the Making of International Law* (Cambridge University Press, 2004), discussed in Chapters 2 and 3.

[148] F. Lenzerini, *The Culturalization of Human Rights Law* (Oxford University Press, 2014).

[149] GR 7, para. 1.

The Committee has not essayed a stand-alone definition of racism, though 'racism' and 'racist' are frequently employed by CERD in such areas as racist motivation in crime, racist offences, racist hate crimes, racism, and xenophobia, etc. A stream of paragraphs in CERD concluding observations endorsing the Durban Conference on Racism, etc, necessarily introduce 'racism' to the Committee's vocabulary, as do endorsements of the Additional Protocol to the Council of Europe's Convention on Cybercrime which addresses, *inter alia*, 'racist' acts committed through computer systems.[150] Regarding racist hate speech, CERD GR 35 is cautious on the use of 'racism', tying the proscription of 'racist hate speech' to the forms of speech disfavoured or proscribed by Article 4 of the Convention (incitement, dissemination of ideas of racial or ethnic superiority) in order to avoid situations where vague allegations of 'racist hate speech' may be made in order to stifle free speech, using the Convention as justification.

The eleventh (penultimate) paragraph refers to two treaties in force at the time of the adoption of ICERD, the first of which—International Labour Organization (ILO) Convention 111 on Discrimination in Employment and Occupation—incorporates a definition of discrimination, aspects of which resurface in Article 1 of ICERD, and the UNESCO Convention against Discrimination in Education.[151]

The Committee refers to these treaties on a regular basis, recommending that States parties adhere to them as treaties with provisions that have a direct relevance to communities that may be the subject of racial discrimination.[152] The preamble recites that ICERD was drafted 'bearing in mind' the two named Conventions, a statement that carries the suggestion that their content is broadly congruent with the provisions of ICERD. The policy of recommending sister treaties that echo the concerns of ICERD has moved forward steadily in CERD practice, currently through the inclusion of 'standard paragraphs' in concluding observations. The range of such recommendations implicates a wide, unbounded network of treaties and declarations deemed to contribute to furthering the objects and purposes of the Convention Compatibility with ICERD tends to be assumed even as details of language and concept show subtle departures from its text.

D. Comment

The preamble is a complex amalgam of historical recall, elaboration of the legal context from which the Convention emerged, protest at the immorality, injustice, repugnancy, and 'unscientific' nature of racial discrimination, a vision of an international community unscarred by racial discrimination, and, along with the title, a degree of optimism as to how this vision might be realized. Title and preamble reflect the fundamental values and aspirations of the Convention and the wider United Nations in an international system that was advancing towards a post-colonial phase while colonial vestiges remained, and apartheid appeared solidly ensconced in its heartlands. The fact that (Western) colonialism and

[150] ETS No. 189 (2003).

[151] Their definitions of racial discrimination are recalled in the commentary on Article 1 of the Convention.

[152] For recommendations on the UNESCO Convention, see concluding observations on Cameroon, CERD/C/CMR/CO/15-18, para. 22; Estonia, CERD/C/EST/CO/8-9, para. 21; Japan, CERD/C/JPN/CO/3-6, para. 22. For recommendations regarding the ILO Convention, Japan, CERD/C/JPN/CO/3-6, para. 27; Monaco, CERD/C/MCO/CO/6, para. 12.

apartheid have passed into history does not deprive the title and preamble of their power to guide and inspire. The Convention is presented in the preamble as a logical and necessary extension of human rights developments at the United Nations. Enduring elements complement the immediate focus on evils to be speedily eliminated. Interpretative practice does not generally focus on the preamble, though its guidance function may be presumed even if citations are rare and its utilization is unstated and subliminal.

As with other elements in the Convention, the text of the preamble was not achieved without struggle. The continuing ambiguities with regard to 'race' were not fully resolved in the preamble, and a degree of universalist myopia prevailed in the discussions of minorities, obfuscating the question of who the likely victims of racial discrimination would turn out to be. While the anti-colonial paradigm dominated the drafting, title and preamble intimate that the struggle against discrimination was likely to be global and not system-specific. The realistic refusal to name the 'isms'—anti-Semitism, Nazism, Fascism, *et al.*—suggested that racial discrimination could over time change its forms and was likely to do so; the Preamble to the Inter-American Convention on Racism takes this suggestion to a conclusion in explicitly recognizing that 'the phenomenon of racism has a dynamic capacity for renewal that enables it to assume new forms whereby it spreads and expresses itself politically, socially, culturally, and linguistically'.[153] The retention of the reference to apartheid in the Convention appears to cut against this perception, but the international struggle against it was in full flow so that refusal to name it might have appeared as a dereliction of duty: apartheid was an active State policy and represented a deliberate challenge to the United Nations human rights system writ large. The naming of apartheid also ties in with the nuance in the drafting that racial discrimination was then principally understood as an issue of State policy rather than stemming from the acts of private persons.

In the preamble, the elimination of racial discrimination is related to the respect for the dignity of the human person and the promise of equality;[154] ICERD thus takes its place among the canon of 'dignitarian' international human rights instruments. Ideas of dignity as inherent in human beings, of indignity as a descriptor of the degraded conditions of life endured by many groups,[155] of dignity as demanding equal status, respect, and concern on the basis of a common humanity, or linked to diversity and autonomy, are represented in the archives of the Committee. The diverse situations where dignity is employed by the Committee do not suggest a term of fixed meaning though the 'impact and the point of view of affected persons' figures significantly in specifying appropriate applications,[156] as do the connections between culture, identity, and dignity. As noted, the Committee has not developed a general position on the uses of dignity, nor clarity on its evaluative, as opposed to its evocative use any more evident from judicial practice and academic

[153] Makkonen, *Equal in Law, Unequal in Fact*, pp. 57–72.

[154] 'The natural equality of all human beings with respect to their dignity implies an absolute rejection of discrimination, which would be an offence to the fundamental rights of the person': Periodic Report of the Holy See, CERD/C/VAT/116-23, para. 44.

[155] With regard to indigenous peoples, compare *Yakye Axa v Paraguay*, IACtHR, Ser C No. 125, 17 June 2005, where the Court found an obligation on the part of Paraguay to adopt positive measures to enable the group to lead a dignified life in light of delays in recognizing the community's leadership and legal status an claims to land.

[156] E. Grant, 'Dignity and Equality', *Human Rights Law Review* 7 (2007), 299–399, 318–19, cited in McColgan, *Discrimination*, p. 32.

literature.[157] Appraisals of the use of dignity in national contexts, particularly with reference to Germany and South Africa,[158] have referred to 'paradoxes' in its application,[159] regarding its absolute or qualified nature, justiciability, negotiability, cosmopolitanism and/or cultural embeddedness, individual and collective aspects, paradoxes which the Committee, with its largely rhetorical approach and abundance of textual referents to equality and discrimination, has not been called upon to resolve.[160]

It may nonetheless be argued that dignity can be employed in evaluative mode when other interpretative codes suggest an intuitively unpalatable result flowing from a discrimination analysis. In the words of one writer, equality based on dignity 'must enhance rather than diminish the status of individuals',[161] and 'dignity should be regarded as one facet of a multi-dimensional notion of equality'.[162] Irrespective of any potential subsuming of dignity into equality, the expressions of dignity in the Convention may plausibly be used in an analogous manner, in opposition to the inappropriate use of equality in processes of 'levelling down' the enjoyment of rights, as well as lending weight and expansiveness to the interpretation of the equality and anti-discrimination norms,[163] including the collective dimensions so important in CERD practice. In the general practice of international human rights bodies, racial discrimination and violence have been paradigmatically described as assaults on human dignity.[164] Such a description may

[157] D Feldman, 'Human Dignity as a Legal Value: Parts I and II', *Public Law* 1999, 682–702 at 685, refers to the 'perplexing capacity of dignity to pull in several directions'.

[158] Carozza—*Human Dignity*, p. 347—observes that 'much of the development of the idea of human dignity in international human rights law in attributable to its widespread and more thickly developed status as a constitutional principle in a wide variety of constitutional systems, starting with the Irish Constitution of 1937', citing S. Moyn, 'The Secret History of Constitutional Dignity' (2012) available at: <http://papers.ssrn.com/sol3/papers.cfm?abstract_id=2159248>.

[159] H. Botha, 'Human Dignity: Constitutional Right, Absolute Ideal, or Contested value?', in M. Jovanović and I. Krstić (eds), *Human Rights Today: 60 Years of the Universal Declaration* (Eleven International Publishing, 2010), pp. 195–210. Article 1 of the German Basic Law provides that human dignity shall be inviolable, on which Botha comments (p. 198) that dignity 'belongs, alongside democracy, federalism and the social State, to an unalterable core of constitutional values and principles'. Section 10 of the South African Constitution provides that '[e]veryone has inherent dignity and the right to have their dignity respected and protected'; section 39 provides that dignity should guide the interpretation of constitutional rights.

[160] See, for example, the case of *Wackenheim v France*, where the Human Rights Committee in finding no violation of Article 26, endorsed a perspective on dignity that differed from that of the author of the Communication, who was the subject of 'dwarf-tossing' spectacles banned by the State: CCPR/C/75/D/854/1999 (2002); see also the decision of the South African Constitutional Court in *President of the Republic of South Africa v Hugo* (CCT 11/96) [1997] ZACC 4, cited in S. Fredman, *Discrimination Law* (2nd edn, Oxford University Press, 2011), p. 23 [henceforth *Discrimination Law*].

[161] Fredman, *Discrimination Law*, p. 21.

[162] *Ibid.*, p. 25.

[163] Carozza, *Human Dignity*.

[164] *Cyprus v Turkey*, App. No. 25781/94, ECHR 2001-IV, para. 306, discrimination based on race 'might, in certain circumstances, constitute an affront to human dignity'; *Nachova v Bulgaria*, App. No. 43577/98; App. No. 43579/98, ECHR 2005-VII, para. 145, racial violence is a 'particular affront to human dignity'. The language in the foregoing cases reflects the influence of the former European Commission on Human Rights in its recalling that, 'as generally recognized, a special importance should be attached to discrimination based on race... publicly to single out a group... for differential treatment on the basis of race might, in special circumstances, constitute a special form of affront to human dignity... [and] ... might therefore be capable of constituting degrading treatment': *East African Asians v the UK*, App. Nos 4403/70 *et al.*, Report of the European Commission on Human Rights, 14 December 1973, para. 207. The tentative language in such cases suggests that specific appraisals of circumstances are crucial in drawing legal conclusions as to whether dignity has been impaired. The uses of dignity under the European Convention on Human Rights belie the fact that it is a rare exception among international instruments in not including a reference to dignity.

be extended more widely to racial denigration and hierarchical theories of human value along with their historical implications that some racial/ethnic groups occupied lower rungs on the 'ladder of civilization' than others. In the history of international law, conceptions of dignity have often been thoroughly 'racialized'.

Discrimination, as accounted for in the preamble, pertains not only to race but to colour, national origin, and ethnic origin; the references to 'origin' comfortably accommodate the later addition of 'descent' to Article 1. Racial discrimination is seen to disturb the peace among nations and, paradigmatically, peace within nations. The approach to social policy set out in the preamble may be described as broadly 'integrationist'. While integration should be distinguished from assimilation, the negativity associated with minority rights in the drafting process suggested that assimilation was not then an uncongenial project, particularly for newly emerged States. CERD practice has gradually moved away from assimilationist assumptions, and the interpretation of 'segregation and separation' has opened out to embrace currents of thought on multi-ethnicity and the complex, multicultural nature of States that had little appeal to the legislators of the 1960s.[165] Nonetheless, preambular references to 'peace and security among peoples' and 'the harmony of persons living side by side' within States suggest that the objective of the Convention is to liberate, and that its objects and purposes will not be achieved through the destruction of personality of individuals and the collectives which they inhabit or are taken to represent. In this sense, the Convention stands alongside the Convention against Genocide and all conventions and declarations that insist on the rights of individuals and communities against those who would destroy them.

The pull exerted by the anti-colonial vision of self-determination set forth in the preamble has weakened over decades of CERD practice: the Committee's developed account of self-determination takes it considerably beyond the parameters of the Colonial Declaration though must be deemed to include them.[166] The range of groups and situations implicated in Committee work in the twenty-first century might well have surprised the drafters of the Convention, even if some attempted to peer over the boundaries of meaning and practice to unglimpsed 'forms' of discrimination. The Committee is aware of change, often describing the Convention as 'a living instrument',[167] as have other human rights bodies.[168] The suggestion is that one must be alive to 'the circumstances of contemporary society',[169] and signifies that interpretation is unfinished business, now and always.[170]

[165] See Chapter 10 on Article 3 of the Convention.

[166] See Chapter 14 on Article 5 of the Convention, Civil and Political Rights.

[167] *Hagan v Australia*, CERD/C/62/D/26/2002 (2003), para. 7.3. Bjorge attributes the coining of the phrase 'living instrument' to a report by Sørensen in 1975, three years before its adoption by the European Court of Human Rights: E. Bjorge, *The Evolutionary Interpretation of Treaties* (Oxford University Press, 2014), p. 12.

[168] See, *inter alia*, the Views of the Human Rights Committee in *Judge v Canada*, CCPR/C/78/D/829/1998 (2002), para. 10.3; Inter-American Court of Human Rights, *The Mayagna (Sumo) Awas Tingni Community v Nicaragua*, IACtHR Ser. C No. 79 [2001], para. 146; the living instrument concept suffuses the decision of African Commission on Human and Peoples' Rights in *Centre for Minority Rights Development (Kenya) and Minority Rights Group International on Behalf of Endorois Welfare Council* Comm 276/2003 (2009), discussion in G. Pentassuglia, 'Towards a Jurisprudential Articulation of Indigenous Land Rights', *EJIL* 22 (2011), 165–202; see also European Court of Human Rights, *Tyrer v the UK* App. No. 5856/72 (1978).

[169] *Hagan*, para. 7.3.

[170] Further discussion in Chapter 20.

While Committee practice revolves primarily around the operative articles of the Convention, the preamble should in principle, in light of the guidance it potentially offers to the objects and purposes of the Convention, assist in inclining the assessment of a disputed norm one way or another, even if it cannot be fully determinative. In the business of interpretation, the question of how much assistance is or can be derived from the preamble is best answered through the consideration of practice over time. The historical and contextual elements stand, as does the evaluation of the fundamentally unacceptable and damaging nature of racial discrimination and racist doctrines, and the concept of the Convention as a legal cutting edge to human rights standards developed since the UN Charter. The ideal of inter-racial harmony continues to inspire. The universalized description of non-discrimination set up in the preamble is enriched rather than depleted by the growth of differentiated bodies of human rights applying to groups and categories of person, even if the potential of the Convention to embrace this normative transformation was underdeveloped at the moment of its adoption.

6. Article 1

Definition of Racial Discrimination

The present chapter focuses on the definition of racial discrimination in paragraph 1 of Article 1. The limitations on the reach of the definition in paragraphs 2 and 3 are considered in the chapter immediately following; Article 1(4) is discussed together with paragraph 2 of Article 2 in Chapter 9 on special measures. The text of Article 1(1) is as follows:

> In this Convention, the term 'racial discrimination' shall mean any distinction, exclusion, restriction or preference based on race, colour, descent, or national or ethnic origin which has the purpose or effect of nullifying or impairing the recognition, enjoyment or exercise, on an equal footing, of human rights and fundamental freedoms in the political, economic, social, cultural or any other field of public life.

A. Introduction

Equality and non-discrimination are intrinsic to the architecture of human rights law, hence the statement in Article 1 of the Universal Declaration of Human Rights (UDHR): 'All human beings are born free and equal in dignity and rights.' The principles of equality, and non-distinction on the grounds of 'birth, nationality, language, race or religion',[1] figured in the minorities system of the League, in addition to the specific clauses on positive minority protection. In the era of the United Nations, the focus on universal human rights initially resulted in a significant atrophy of 'positive' elements, reflecting tendencies to treat equality and non-discrimination as promoting simple uniformity of treatment. According to Capotorti, 'the concept of equality and non-discrimination implies a formal guarantee of uniform treatment for all individuals—who must be ensured the enjoyment of the same rights and accept the same obligations'.[2] Nuanced concepts of equality and discrimination pre- and post-date Capotorti's statement[3] in protean guises such as formal and substantive equality; equality before (or under) the law and equal protection of the law; equality of results; *de jure* and *de facto* equality and their analogues in the prohibitions of discrimination: direct and indirect discrimination; structural discrimination; positive action, affirmative action, etc.[4]

[1] Article 2 of the Polish Minorities Treaty 1919; see also Article 7 on equality before the law: P. Thornberry, *International Law and the Rights of Minorities* (Clarendon Press, 1991), Appendix 1.

[2] F. Capotorti, *Study on the Rights of Persons belonging to Ethnic, Religious and Linguistic Minorities* (United Nations publication, Sales No. E.91.XIV.2), para. 241.

[3] In the minority rights regime of the League of Nations, see the Advisory opinions of the Permanent Court of International Justice in *Questions Relating to Settlers of German Origin in Poland*, PCIJ Ser. B, No. 6 (1923); *Minority Schools in Albania*, [1935] PCIJ, Ser. A/B, No. 64, comment on equality concepts in Chapter 2.

[4] A general view is provided in W. Vandenhole, *Non-Discrimination and Equality in the View of the UN Human Rights Treaty Bodies* (Intersentia, 2005).

The Charter of the United Nations and the UDHR incorporate basic equality and non-discrimination principles.[5] The UDHR expands the Charter 'grounds' of prohibited distinctions: 'race, sex, language, or religion', to 'race, colour, sex, language, religion, political or other opinion, national or social origin, property, birth or other status',[6] as well as providing for equality before the law and equal protection of the law.[7] Following the model of the Charter and the UDHR, virtually all general human rights instruments contain an equality or a non-discrimination clause,[8] or both.[9] The International Covenant on Civil and Political Rights (ICCPR), for example, includes a prohibition of discrimination,[10] a provision on the equal rights of men and women,[11] and a broad-based equality provision in Article 26 that demands 'equal and effective protection against discrimination on any ground such as race, colour, sex, language, religion, political or other opinion, national or social origin, property, birth or other status'; the provision on discrimination in Article 2(1) is limited to the rights 'recognized' in the Covenant, while the guarantee in Article 26 applies to human rights in general.[12] Grounds of discrimination appear in both 'open' and 'closed' lists, the former characterized by the inclusion of 'such as' before a list of grounds,[13] the latter confining discrimination to a single element such as 'sex' in the Convention on the Elimination of All Forms of Discrimination against Women (CEDAW), or 'disability' in the Convention on the Rights of Persons with Disabilities (CRPD),[14] or a list of grounds as in Article 1 of the International Convention on the Elimination of All Forms of Racial Discrimination (ICERD); lists are also capable of extension through including a prohibition of discrimination based on 'other status' additional to named grounds.[15]

The inclusion of equality and non-discrimination clauses also characterizes regional human rights instruments, including the African Charter on Human and Peoples' Rights,[16]

[5] In addition to the recital of prohibited grounds of discrimination in the sphere of human rights and fundamental freedoms, the preamble to the Charter pursues the equality theme in referring to 'the equal rights of men and women and of nations large and small', while operative articles recall 'the principle of equal rights and self-determination of peoples', Article 1(2), and 'the principle of the sovereign equality' of all Members of the United Nations, Article 2(1); equality principles are thus asserted to govern the relationships among sovereign States, peoples, and individuals.

[6] Article 2.

[7] Article 7.

[8] For a succinct list, see D. Moeckli, S. Shah, and S. Sivakumaran, *International Human Rights Law* (2nd edn, Oxford University Press, 2014), pp. 160–4 [henceforth *International Human Rights Law*].

[9] Exceptions in the UN system include the Convention against Torture and Other Cruel, Inhuman or Degrading Treatment and the International Convention on the Protection of All Persons from Enforced Disappearance. The SIM Human Rights database, canvassing human rights instruments of the African Union, the Council of Europe, the Organization of American States, and the United Nations (accessed 6 November 2013) finds 168 references to 'discrimination', 71 to 'equality', and 108 to 'equal'.

[10] Article 2(1).

[11] Article 3.

[12] *Broeks v The Netherlands*, CCPR/C/29/D/172/1984 (1987); General Comment 18, HRI/GEN/1/Rev.9, 195, para. 12. For a list of 'rights' not independently guaranteed in the ICCPR but addressed by the Human Rights Committee, see S. Joseph, J. Schultz, and M. Castan, *The International Covenant on Civil and Political Rights* (2nd edn, Oxford University Press, 2004), pp. 686–7.

[13] The phrase is found in both Article 2(1) and Article 26 of the ICCPR.

[14] Additionally, the preamble to the CRPD refers to multiple or aggravated forms of discrimination based on 'race, colour, sex, language, religion, political or other opinion, national, ethnic, indigenous or social origin, property, birth, age or other status'.

[15] Including Article 2(2) ICESCR, Article 2(1) ICCPR.

[16] Articles 2, 3, 18, and 28.

the American Convention on Human Rights,[17] the Arab Charter on Human Rights,[18] the European Convention on Human Rights,[19] and its Protocol 12,[20] as well as finding inclusion in specialized instruments on, for example, the rights of minorities[21] and indigenous peoples.[22] The longest list of 'grounds' or 'conditions' of prohibited discrimination appears in the Inter-American Convention against All Forms of Discrimination and Intolerance[23] which lists twenty-two, along with 'any other condition';[24] the Convention's scope on the protected rights is also broad, extending to discrimination against 'one or more human rights and fundamental freedoms enshrined in the international instruments applicable to the States parties'.[25]

Definitions of discrimination are thinner on the ground than statements of principle. Article 1(1) of the International Labour Organization (ILO) Discrimination (Employment and Occupation) Convention 1958 (ILO Convention 111)[26] defined discrimination for the purposes of that Convention as:

(a) Any distinction, exclusion or preference made on the basis of race, colour, sex, religion, political opinion, national extraction or social origin, which has the effect of nullifying or impairing equality of opportunity or treatment in employment or occupation;
(b) Such other distinction, exclusion or preference which has the effect of nullifying or impairing equality of opportunity or treatment . . . as may be determined by the Member concerned after consultation with representative employers' and workers' organizations . . .[27]

The range of grounds, the employment and the occupation context, and the omission of 'purpose' distinguish this definition from that of ICERD, but the broad affinity between the two conventions is obvious, not least in breaking down 'discrimination' into three sub-terms: 'distinction, exclusion or preference', and the emphasis on the *effects* of discrimination.[28] The same applies to the UNESCO Convention against Discrimination

[17] In addition to a 'standard' non-discrimination clause in Article 1 with a list of grounds, Article 24 provides that '[a]ll persons are equal before the law. Consequently, they are entitled, without discrimination, to equal protection of the law.'

[18] Articles 11 and 12.

[19] Article 14 of the ECHR.

[20] Whereas Article 14 of the ECHR applies only in the context of the rights contained in the Convention, Protocol 12 includes a non-discrimination guarantee that is not so limited and applies to 'any right set forth by law'. The European Court of Human Rights has interpreted Article 14 as not requiring an independent violation of another right before the non-discrimination provision is engaged: it is sufficient that the case is 'within the ambit' of another right, *Rasmussen v Denmark*, App. No. 8777/79 (1984).

[21] UN Declaration on the Rights of Persons belonging to National or Ethnic, Religious and Linguistic Minorities, Articles 2, 3, and 4.

[22] The preamble and Articles 3, 4, 20, and 24 of ILO Convention 169 on the Rights of Indigenous and Tribal Peoples; the preamble, and Articles 2, 8, 9, 14, 15, 16, 17, 21, 22, 24, and 46 of the UN Declaration on the Rights of Indigenous Peoples.

[23] Article 1(1), OEA/Ser. P AG/RES. 2805 (XLIII-O/13) 5 June 2013.

[24] 'Discrimination may be based on: nationality; age; sex; sexual orientation; gender identity and expression; language; religion; cultural identity; political opinions or opinions of any kind; social origin; socio-economic status; educational level; migrant, refugee, repatriate, stateless or internally displaced status; disability; genetic trait; mental or physical health condition, including infectious-contagious condition and debilitating psychological condition; or any other condition': Article 1(1).

[25] *Ibid.*

[26] 362 UNTS 31.

[27] See also para. 2 of Article 1: 'Any distinction [etc.] in respect of a particular job based on the inherent requirements thereof shall not be deemed to be discrimination.'

[28] Present author's emphasis. Compare the distinctions/effects critique of the ICERD definition in T. Meron, 'The Meaning and Reach of the International Convention on the Elimination of All Forms of Racial Discrimination', *AJIL* 79 (1985), 283–318, at 291 [henceforth *Meaning and Reach*].

in Education,[29] Article 1, paragraph 1 of which reads (in part) that 'the term "discrimination" includes any distinction, exclusion, limitation or preference which, being based on race, colour, sex, language, religion, political or other opinion, national or social origin, economic condition or birth, has the purpose or effect of nullifying or impairing equality of treatment in education'. This definition introduces the notion of 'purpose' into the argument and expands three sub-terms to four by adding 'limitation'. Later definitions build on the above and the example of ICERD. CEDAW defines discrimination against women along the lines of ICERD, but without listing 'preference' among the forms of discrimination, and without the limitation to 'public life'.[30] Article 2 of the CRPD similarly defines discrimination in its field of application, without limitation to 'public life', and introduces the notion of 'reasonable accommodation'.[31]

Even without benefit of a definition of discrimination in their constituent instruments, the concepts of equality and discrimination have been elaborated in the work of treaty monitoring bodies. The Human Rights Committee's General Comment (GC) 18[32] and GC 20 of the Committee on Economic, Social and Cultural Rights (CESCR)[33] set forth a complex matrix of concepts drawing on general developments in human rights practice. CESCR GC 20 employs the 'distinction, exclusion, restriction or preference' and the 'intention or effect' formulae, while differentiating between 'formal', 'substantive', 'direct', and 'indirect' discrimination; the term 'systemic discrimination' is also referred to, and discrimination is said to include 'incitement to discrimination and harassment'. Differential treatment on prohibited grounds is treated as discriminatory unless the justification for the differentiation is reasonable and objective.[34]

Among the grounds of discrimination in general instruments, 'race' is a standard inclusion.[35] Apart from ICERD, ethnicity or ethnic origin is infrequently listed as a ground of discrimination,[36] though it appears more consistently in instruments or specific provisions on minority rights,[37] including Article 27 of the ICCPR, and Article 30 of the Convention on the Rights of the Child (CRC),[38] as well as throughout the United Nations Declaration on Minorities (UNDM). The Framework Convention for the Protection of

[29] 1960.

[30] Article 1 of CEDAW. See below on the Inter-American Convention against Racism, etc.

[31] Article 2. 'Reasonable accommodation' is defined as 'necessary and appropriate modification and adjustments not imposing a disproportionate or undue burden, where needed in a particular case, to ensure to persons with disabilities the enjoyment or exercise on an equal basis with others of all human rights and fundamental freedoms'. See also Article 5.

[32] HRI/GEN/1/Rev.9 (Vol. I), pp. 195–8, para. 7.

[33] E/C.12/GC/20 (2009).

[34] *Ibid.*, para. 13. 'Reasonable and objective' is further broken down into concepts of legitimacy, compatibility with the Covenant, and proportionality between means and ends.

[35] The SIM human rights database logs thirty-eight references to 'race' in instruments of the UN, the African Union, the Council of Europe, and the OAS.

[36] Article 2 of the CRC refers to discrimination on the grounds, *inter alia*, of 'national, ethnic or social origin'.

[37] 'Ethnic' or 'ethnicity' is not referred to in the UDHR, nor in Articles 2 and 26 of the ICCPR on discrimination and equality; Article 2(2) of the ICESCR also omits the term. Among the regional instruments, the compendious Inter-American Convention against Intolerance and Discrimination omits 'ethnic', though any resulting gap will presumably be covered by its references to 'language' and 'cultural identity'. The European Convention on Human Rights (Article 14) forbids discrimination on any ground 'such as sex, race, colour, language, religion, political or other opinion, national or social origin, association with a national minority, property, birth or other status': again 'ethnicity' will be covered by a multiplicity of terms, including 'association with a national minority'.

[38] And in Article 29 on education.

National Minorities (FCNM), in addition to prohibiting discrimination (Article 4) 'based on belonging to a national minority', also seeks to protect (Article 5) 'persons who may be subject to threats or acts of discrimination, hostility or violence as a result of their ethnic, cultural, linguistic or religious identity'. The UNDRIP asserts the falsity of doctrines of superiority, based on, *inter alia*, 'ethnic or cultural differences' in its preamble, while Article 8 refers to mechanisms of prevention and redress for 'propaganda designed to promote or incite racial or ethnic discrimination' directed against indigenous peoples.

With regard to the definition of racial discrimination specifically, the Declaration on the Elimination of All Forms of Racial Discrimination does not include a specific definition; McKean nonetheless concludes that references in its preamble to the UN Charter and the UDHR show that discrimination means 'the denial of equality of dignity and rights before the law'.[39] Article 1(1) of the Inter-American Convention against Racism, Racial Discrimination, and Related Forms of Intolerance defines racial discrimination as 'any distinction, exclusion, restriction or preference, in any area of public or private life, the purpose or effect of which is to nullify or curtail the equal recognition, enjoyment or exercise of one or more human rights and fundamental freedoms enshrined in the international instruments applicable to the States parties'.[40] Further, racial discrimination 'may be based on race, colour, lineage, or national or ethnic origin'; equality is addressed separately by Article 2 which provides that every human being 'is equal under the law and has a right to equal protection against racism, racial discrimination, and related forms of intolerance in any sphere of life, public or private'. The Convention also explains indirect discrimination, multiple or aggravated discrimination, racism, special measures, and intolerance.[41]

B. *Travaux Préparatoires*

The Abram text of Article 1 defined racial discrimination for the purpose of the Convention as including 'any distinction, exclusion or preference made on the basis of race, colour, or ethnic origin, and in the case of States composed of different nationalities or persons of different national origin, discrimination based on such differences'.[42] Calvocoressi added 'limitation' to 'distinction, exclusion', etc.[43] The Abram reference to 'States composed of different nationalities' was the subject of a proposed amendment by Krishnaswami[44] but was retained in the sub-Commission's final draft. The Ivanov/Ketrzynski draft defined racial discrimination as 'any differentiation, ban on access, exclusion, preference or limitation based on race, colour, national or ethnic origin', supplying the important rider that the differentiation, etc, had 'the purpose or effect of nullifying or impairing equality in granting or practising human rights and fundamental freedoms in [the] political, economic, social, cultural, or any other field of public life'.[45] Racial discrimination was also declared as an 'offence to human dignity', and, *inter alia*, a

39 W.A. McKean, *Equality and Discrimination under International Law* (Clarendon Press, 1983), p. 153 [henceforth *Equality and Discrimination*].
40 Article 1(1), OEA/Ser.P.AG/RES.2805 (XLIII-O/13) 5 June 2013: see chapter 15.
41 Article 1, paras 2–6.
42 E/CN.4/Sub.2/L.308.
43 E/CN.4/Sub.2/L.309.
44 E/CN.4/Sub.2/L.310, para. 4.
45 E/CN.4/Sub.2/L.314.

denial of the rules of international law and the principles of the Charter of the United Nations. This did not survive into the final Sub-Commission text,[46] though the 'purpose or effect' aspect of discrimination did survive.

Regarding the 'grounds' of discrimination, Capotorti took a consistent stance against the inclusion of 'nationality' or 'national origin';[47] other experts also had difficulties with these terms.[48] On 'national origin', Santa Cruz explained that the concept had been used in the Universal Declaration of Human Rights and 'represented a new concept introduced because certain countries were currently practising discrimination against national groups which were not necessarily ethnic groups'.[49] In a wide-ranging comment on ethnic and allied forms of discrimination, Abram explained the importance of the reference in his text to 'ethnic origin':

> Ethnic discrimination might well be directed towards obliterating the social and cultural differences which defined and gave life and significance to a particular ethnic group . . . Ethnic differences were absolutely dependent for survival on language, schools, publications and other cultural institutions often regarded as characteristic of a nationality. However well-treated in other respects a member of an ethnic group may be, if he were cut off from his tradition and culture, he would be the victim of discrimination and the right of his group to survive would be jeopardized.[50]

Regarding 'race', Saario took the view that although, 'as UNESCO had shown, there was no such thing as "race", the term . . . would have to be used in the . . . convention . . . "race", "colour" and "ethnic origin" all meant much the same thing'.[51] Abram considered that it was inaccurate to maintain that doctrines of racial differentiation were scientifically false.[52] In the event, a working group draft defined racial discrimination as:

> any distinction, exclusion, restriction or preference based on race, colour, national or ethnic origin (and in the case of States composed of different nationalities discrimination based on such difference) which has the purpose or effect of nullifying or impairing the recognition, enjoyment or exercise of human rights and freedoms in political, economic, social, cultural or any other field of public life set forth *inter alia* in the Universal Declaration of Human Rights.[53]

In discussions prompted by Ingles,[54] the phrase 'on an equal footing', suggested by Ketryzinski and supported by Ivanov,[55] was accepted for insertion after 'exercise': the reference in the Ivanov/Ketrzynski text to nullifying or impairing 'equality in granting or

[46] The language of 'peaceful and friendly relations' appears in the preamble to the Convention; see also Article 7.

[47] E/CN.4/SR.411, pp. 5–6. Saario, *ibid.*, rather optimistically stated that 'everyone understood what was meant by the term "national origin"'.

[48] Calvocoressi preferred 'nationality' to 'national origin'; Cuevas Cancino and Santa Cruz preferred 'national origin' to 'nationality': E/CN.4/Sub.2/SR.411, pp. 9–10.

[49] E/CN.4/Sub.2/SR/410, p. 9. For an account of the introduction of the term into the UDHR, see J. Morsink, *The Universal Declaration of Human Rights: Origins, Drafting and Intent* (University of Pennsylvania Press, 1999), pp. 103–5 [henceforth *The Universal Declaration*].

[50] E/CN.4/Sub.2/SR.411, p. 5.

[51] E/CN.4/Sub.2/SR.411, p. 6.

[52] E/CN.4/Sub.2/SR.410, p. 11.

[53] E/CN.4/Sub.2/L.319.

[54] E/CN.4/Sub.2/SR.414, p. 7. In discussions, Capotorti stated that 'all the experts were agreed on mentioning the concept of equality of rights' in Article 1, E/CN.4/Sub.2/SR.414, p. 9. Not all were so convinced: for Santa Cruz, *ibid.*, the additional reference to equality appeared superfluous, since condemnation of discrimination 'necessarily included' condemnation of inequality.

[55] E/CN.4/Sub.2/SR.414, p. 8.

practising human rights',[56] transmuted in a later text into 'equality of treatment or opportunity',[57] had been omitted from the working group draft.[58] A proposal included in an intervention by the representative of Israel to provide additional guarantees of the collective rights of nationalities and ethnic groups and communities was not accepted by the Sub-Commission.[59]

Before the Commission on Human Rights, there was early objection from Ecuador to dealing with 'the question of national minorities', which was 'very controversial . . . and would undoubtedly give rise to difficulties'.[60] A complex amendment to the second part of the Sub-Commission's text by the United Kingdom (UK) was withdrawn in favour of a Lebanese proposal to end the paragraph at 'public life'.[61] The UK objected to the *inter alia* formula as introducing an element of vagueness into the paragraph,[62] though some representatives defended the phrasing since it would refer to a broader range of instruments, including national constitutions and laws, beyond the Universal Declaration.[63] The reference to the Universal Declaration, together with 'inter alia' was deleted; in the result, according to Schwelb, 'the Convention as adopted is not restricted to rights set forth in the Universal Declaration',[64] but extends to other, unspecified rights. The phrase in parenthesis in the Sub-Commission's text was deleted,[65] partly because it might, in the view of some representatives, have given rise to ambiguous interpretations and created problems for multinational states or states encouraging immigration.[66] In the Commission on Human Rights, the advisability of including 'national or' was challenged on the basis that, while it had been recognized in the Universal Declaration, it would be confusing in a convention on racial discrimination; additionally, it had not been included in the Declaration on Racial Discrimination.[67] The words 'national or' in paragraph 1 were retained by ten votes to nine, with one abstention.

The Third Committee examined the following text of article 1, paragraph 1:

> In this Convention the term 'racial discrimination' shall mean any distinction, exclusion, restriction or preference based on race, colour, [national] or ethnic origin which has the purpose or effect of nullifying or impairing the recognition, enjoyment or exercise, on an equal footing, of human rights and fundamental freedoms in the political, economic, social, cultural or any other field of public life. [In this paragraph the expression 'national origin' does not cover the status of any person as a citizen of a given State.]

[56] E/CN.4/Sub.2/L.314.

[57] Calvocoressi/Capotorti text, E/CN.4/Sub.2/L.318.

[58] E/CN.4/Sub.2/L.319.

[59] E/CN.4/Sub.2/SR.416, p. 8: 'The spiritual heritage and the cultural values of a group of persons of a particular ethnic origin are entitled to legal protection as such. No discrimination shall be permitted against them and other spiritual heritages and cultural values on the sole ground that they are those of persons of a particular race, colour or ethnic origin.'

[60] E/CN.4/SR.783, p. 10.

[61] E/CN.4/L.689 (amendment of the United Kingdom), recalled in the Report of the Commission on its Twentieth Session, E/CN.4/874, paras 74 and 75.

[62] E/CN.4/SR.784, p. 7.

[63] For statements supporting the retention of '*inter alia*' see interventions by the USSR, E/CN.4/SR.784, p. 8; India, *ibid.*; Ecuador, E/CN.4/SR.784, p. 9; and Canada, E/CN.4/SR./784, p. 10.

[64] E. Schwelb, 'The International Convention on the Elimination of All Forms of Racial Discrimination', *ICLQ* 15 (1966), 996–1068, at 1004 [henceforth *The International Convention*]: see chapter 15.

[65] By 14 votes to 2, with 1 abstention: E/CN.4/874, para. 94.

[66] E/CN.4/874, para. 86. See, for example, remarks of the representatives of Canada, E/CN.4/SR.784, p. 10; United Kingdom, E/CN.4/SR.786, p. 4,

[67] E/CN.4/874, para. 85.

A complex series of amendments included proposals[68] for the restoration of the Sub-Commission's phrase in parenthesis relating to different nationalities, and their phraseology of '*inter alia* in the Universal Declaration of Human Rights'.[69] A new paragraph 2 was proposed, making it clear that 'national origin' did not mean nationality or citizenship, so that the Convention would therefore 'not be applicable to distinctions, exclusions, restrictions or preferences based on differences of nationality or citizenship'.[70] This was withdrawn in favour of a text sponsored by nine States that became the final text of Article 1, paragraphs 1, 2, and 3, wherein national origin was retained among the grounds of discrimination and restrictive conditions inserted with regard to non-citizens.[71]

A number of attempts were made to explain 'national origin'. Defending the retention of the term, the representative of Poland referred to a situation in which a politically organized nation had been included within a different State but 'continued to exist as a nation in the social and cultural senses even though it had no government of its own'; members of such a nation within a State might thus be discriminated against, 'not as members of a particular race or as individuals, but as members of a nation which existed in its former political form'.[72] The summary records recall the following explanation from the representative of the United States (US):

> National origin differed from nationality in that national origin related to the past—the previous nationality or geographical region of the individual or of his ancestors—while nationality related to present status. The use of the former term . . . would make it clear that persons were protected against discrimination regardless of where they or their ancestors had come from. National origin differed from citizenship in that it related to non-citizens as well as citizens . . . the laws of her country concerning racial discrimination applied to both. National origin was narrower in scope than ethnic origin; the latter was associated with racial and cultural characteristics and inclusion of a reference to it would not necessarily cover the case of persons residing in foreign countries where their national origins were not respected.[73]

The representative of Senegal, supporting the retention of 'national origin', explained the difficulty for some delegations of including it, namely that they 'feared that its use would confer on aliens living in a State equality of rights in areas, political or other, which under the laws of the State were reserved exclusively to nationals'. It would, however, 'offer protection to persons of foreign birth who had become nationals of their country of residence . . . as well as foreign minorities within a State which might also be subjected to persecution'.[74] For a number of delegations, even if they did not all press their objections to a negative vote, the term 'national' denoted legal nationality or citizenship rather than ethnicity—issues of 'nationality', according to the representative of Cameroon, were different from racial discrimination where a person suffered from a situation 'for which he was in no way responsible, since he had not chosen his colour, race or origin . . . nationality,

[68] A/6181, Report of the Third Committee of the General Assembly, 18 December 1965, paras 30–37.

[69] Proposed by Brazil, A/C.3/L.1209. See also a similar multi-State amendment, A/C.3/L.1226 and Corr. 1, A/6181, para. 35.

[70] Amendment of France and the United States, A/C.3/L.1212, the amendment was later withdrawn: A/6181, para. 37.

[71] A/C.3/L.1238. The sponsoring States were Ghana, India, Kuwait, Lebanon, Mauritius, Morocco, Nigeria, Poland, and Senegal.

[72] A/C.3/SR.1304, para. 5.

[73] A/C.3/SR.1304, para. 23.

[74] A/C.3/SR.1304, para. 16.

on the other hand, did not imply that element of non-responsibility which made racial discrimination particularly odious'.[75] Jamaica argued that nationality was distinct from race and 'could itself be made the subject of a declaration'.[76] Notwithstanding the critical voices, the placing of 'national origin' among the prohibited grounds of discrimination in the Universal Declaration of Human Rights encouraged delegations to support its retention.[77]

'Descent' was not included as a ground of discrimination by the Sub-Commission or the Commission[78] but was suggested by India in the Third Committee.[79] The insertion was approved without much debate—the drafting record does not clarify relevant distinctions, though it appears that 'descent' was intended to cover confusions over 'national origin'.[80] Referring to the complex explanation given by the representative of the US regarding 'national origin', the representative of Ghana stated that it seemed to him to be adequately represented by 'descent' and 'place of origin' in the Indian proposal.[81]

The issue of 'public life' did not greatly trouble the drafters of the Convention, though the question of the reach of the Convention in other aspects concerned some Western governments. Hence the representative of Australia commented (in the context of draft Article 4) that Australia could not be expected to pass a special law criminalizing every person who utters a remark capable of being interpreted as advocating racial discrimination because 'to do so might well make martyrs out of people whose objectionable ideas would otherwise be rejected by reasoned argument, or more probably by ridicule'.[82] The text of Article 1 as a whole was adopted by eighty-nine votes to none, with eight abstentions.[83]

C. Practice

I. Reservations and Guidelines

The reservation by the US includes reference to Article 1:

> the Constitution and laws of the United States establish extensive protections against discrimination, reaching significant areas of non-governmental activity. Individual privacy and freedom from governmental interference in private conduct, however, are also recognized as among the fundamental values . . . The United States understands that the identification of the rights protected under

[75] A/C.3/SR.1305, para. 9.

[76] *Ibid.*, para. 26.

[77] Remarks by the representative of the United Arab Republic, A/C.3/SR.1305, para. 44; Lebanon, A/C.3/SR.1307, para. 1.

[78] While neither 'descent' nor 'caste' are referred to in the UDHR, India had suggested 'caste' as a replacement for 'birth' in Article 2, but did not insist on the proposal: Morsink, *The Universal Declaration*, p. 115. The Convention's reference to 'descent' is not unique in the canon of human rights: among instruments discussed in the present work, ILO Convention 169 on Indigenous and Tribal Peoples, Article 1(1)(b) covers indigenous status on the grounds, *inter alia*, of '*descent* from the populations which inhabited the country, or a geographical region to which the country belongs, at the time of conquest or colonization'. (emphasis added)

[79] A/C.3/L.1216. The key interventions of India were made in meetings 1299 and 1306 of the Third Committee of the General Assembly.

[80] According to the representative of India, A/C.3/SR.1299, para. 29, the amendment 'was intended to meet the objections raised by many delegations to the words "national origin"'.

[81] A/C.3/SR.1306, para. 12.

[82] A/C.3/SR.1306, para. 5. See also the remarks on freedom of speech in the Third Committee by the UK, SR.1315, paras 1–3; The Netherlands, SR.1316, paras 3–4; Ireland, SR.1318, para. 56.

[83] A/6181, para. 41.

the Convention by reference in article 1 to fields of 'public life' reflects a similar distinction between spheres of public conduct that are customarily the subject of governmental regulation, and spheres of private conduct that are not. To the extent, however, that the Convention calls for a broader regulation of private conduct, the United States does not accept any obligation under this Convention to enact legislation or take other measures . . . with respect to private conduct except as mandated by the Constitution and laws of the United States.[84]

The Guidelines of the Committee on the Elimination of Racial Discrimination (CERD-specific guidelines)[85] for Article 1 request basic information on whether the domestic law definition encompasses all the grounds in the Convention, on 'whether direct as well as indirect forms of discrimination' are included, and on the States Parties' understanding of 'public life'. The terms of the definition are not elaborated further. The common core document[86] and the CERD-specific Guidelines are more elaborate regarding demographic data. The first requests States to provide 'accurate information about the main demographic and ethnic characteristics of the country and its population', taking into account a list of indicators set out in an appendix.[87] A section on non-discrimination and equality does not make further reference to ethnicity but asks for information on 'specific vulnerable groups in the population', and on persons belonging to 'the most disadvantaged' groups.[88]

The CERD-specific guidelines explain further that the 'ethnic characteristics of the population, including those resulting from a mixing of cultures, are of particular importance to the Convention',[89] and that demographic indicators, if not provided in the core document, should be included in the CERD document, which includes the following advice:

Many States consider that, when conducting a census, they should not draw attention to factors like race, lest this reinforce divisions they wish to overcome or affect rules concerning the protection of personal data. If progress in eliminating discrimination based on race, colour, descent, or national or ethnic origin . . . is to be monitored, some indication is needed in the CERD-specific document of the number of persons who could be treated less favourably on the basis of these characteristics. States that do not collect information on these characteristics in their censuses are therefore requested to provide information on mother tongues, languages commonly spoken, or other indicators of ethnic diversity, together with any information about race, colour, descent, or national or ethnic origins derived from social surveys. In the absence of quantitative information, a qualitative description of the ethnic characteristics of the population should be supplied. States are advised to develop appropriate methodologies for the collection of relevant information.[90]

Information is also requested on which groups are to be considered to be national or ethnic minorities or indigenous peoples in the State party, as well as recommending the identification of descent-based communities, non-citizens, and internally displaced persons.[91]

[84] <http://treaties.un.org/Pages/ViewDetails.aspx?src=TREATY&mtdsg_no=IV-2&chapter=4&lang=en>.
[85] CERD/C/2007/1.
[86] For further explanation of reporting documentation, see Chapter 4 of the present work.
[87] HRI/GEN/2/Rev.5, chapter I, Appendix 3, *ibid.*, p. 23, requests information from reporting States on, *inter alia*, population distribution 'by mother tongue, religion and ethnicity, in rural and urban areas'. Information, 'disaggregated by sex, age, and main population groups', is requested throughout the Appendix.
[88] *ibid.*, paras 50–8.
[89] CERD/C/2007/1, para. 10.
[90] *Ibid.*, p. 3, para. 11.
[91] *Ibid.*, p. 3, para. 12.

II. Data

Demographics and related issues have been taken up in a sequence of general recommendations, commencing with General Recommendation (GR) 2. When some States parties describe their societies in terms of ethnic etc homogeneity, and even where this claim is part of State ideology, CERD nonetheless presses for relevant data.[92] Less drastic claims admitting the existence of some groups but not others, or describing them in a manner that may obscure their ethnic identity, are also subject to interrogatories.[93] The Committee is equally sceptical of contentions that, although there is ethnic diversity, there is no practice of discrimination in the State party;[94] claims that matters of individual privacy or sundry legal obstacles prevent the collection of ethnic data do not prevent the Committee from pressing its points. While noting the explanations by Germany regarding legislative provisions 'preventing the State party from identifying ethnic groups in a census' or otherwise drawing a distinction between citizens on the grounds of ethnic or linguistic origin, the Committee went on to make its usual points on the need for data to be provided.[95] Inadequacies in data collection methodologies are highlighted in many CERD comments, as well as discrepancies between figures provided in the State reports and those provided by other sources (usually non-governmental organizations (NGOs)). This last issue has arisen with some regularity in statistical offerings for populations of Roma,[96] though it is not confined to their situation.[97]

The data should be 'disaggregated' according to categories that regularly include ethnic composition, ethnic or national origin or nationality, sex or gender, and language.[98] Data disaggregated by caste, religion,[99] and occupational sector,[100] urban and rural areas,[101] may also be requested for specific cases. Data requests are made in general terms or in relation to particular articles under the Convention—hate speech, access to employment, political participation, etc.

III. Recognition

Discrimination under the Convention is not as such predicated on minority or indigenous status but extends more widely, as befits the 'universalist' inspiration behind the drafting project. Minorities and indigenous peoples have nonetheless gained important specifications of their individual and collective human rights since the adoption of the Convention

[92] Concluding observations on France, CERD/C/FRA/CO/17-19, para. 12.

[93] Concluding observations on Greece, CERD/C/GRC/CO/16-19, para. 9; and on Turkey, CERD/C/TUR/CO/3, para. 12.

[94] Concluding observations on The Philippines, CERD/C/PHL/CO/20, para. 13. The similar claim to the absence of discrimination by public authorities made by the Dominican Republic was dismissed, CERD/C/DOM/CO/12, para. 8, on the ground that 'no government is capable of knowing how each public official performs his or her functions'.

[95] CERD/C/DEU/CO/18, para. 14.

[96] Examples include Czech Republic, CERD/CZE/CO/7, para. 7, and Slovakia, CERD/C/SVK/CO/6-8, para. 7.

[97] Concluding observations on El Salvador combine a note on 'significant discrepancies' in ethnic statistics with a recommendation to improve census methodology, CERD/C/SLV/CO/14-15, para. 12.

[98] On disaggregation by gender, see GR 25, para. 6.

[99] Data on caste and religion were requested from Nepal, CERD/C/304/Add.107, para. 9.

[100] Uzbekistan, CERD/C/UZB/CO/5, para. 10.

[101] India, CERD/C/IND/CO/19, para. 9, data disaggregated by caste, tribe, gender, state/district, and rural/urban; Laos, CERD/C/LAO/CO/16-18, para. 19.

through instruments referred to throughout the present work, and the data called for by CERD may provide supporting evidence of ethnic complexity. In GR 24 on Article 1, the Committee applied the basic non-discrimination criterion to recognition, critiquing States 'that decide at their own discretion which groups constitute ethnic groups or indigenous peoples'.[102] The recommendation insists that certain criteria 'should be uniformly applied to all groups, in particular the number of persons concerned, and their being of a race, language or culture different from the majority or from other groups within the population'.[103] Despite a degree of ambiguity in the Committee's formulation stemming from the use of 'uniformly', the recommendation does not represent a plea for uniformity of treatment of groups irrespective of circumstances but advances an argument for consistency in applying recognition criteria in light of the fact that 'there is an international standard concerning the specific rights of people belonging to such groups', in addition to the broader standards on equal rights and non-discrimination.[104] Bearing in mind the present extensive use by the Committee of 'minority', it may be noted that the term was removed from GR 24 on Article 1 during the drafting process and does not appear in the final version, which focuses on national or ethnic groups and indigenous peoples.[105] The post-war sensitivity to 'minority rights' as superseded by 'non-discrimination' may have asserted itself in this instance, even if the recommendation recycles general understandings of 'minority', without recalling the name.

With regard to the receipt of variable information regarding 'the ways in which individuals are identified as being members of a particular racial or ethnic group or groups', GR 8 opts for the principle of self-identification 'if no justification exists to the contrary'.[106] Like ILO 169, the recommendation does not treat self-identification as an absolute or final criterion. In the case of indigenous peoples, the criteria set out in ILO Convention 169, including historical continuity, territorial connection, and distinct social, economic, cultural, and political institutions, are relevant in addition to self-identification, regarded as 'a fundamental criterion for determining the groups to which the provisions of this Convention apply', though not the only criterion—a qualification going back to the time of the League of Nations also places emphasis on 'objective factors'.[107] Standard approaches to such factors stem from understandings of minority and indigenous peoples expressed in international instruments and critical literature. While there is no 'official' definition of minorities in major international instruments including the UNDM,[108] definitions abound

[102] Para. 3.

[103] GR 24, para. 2.

[104] *Ibid.*, para. 3.

[105] Comment in CERD/C/SR.1363/Add.1, paras 14 and 15. In its drafting phase, the general recommendation was referred to as a 'general recommendation on demographic information', CERD/C/SR.1371, paras 18–22.

[106] A/45/18, Annex VII 1. Further discussion in Chapter 9. Compare *Sandra Lovelace v Canada*, where the Human Rights Committee stated with regard to the facts of the case that persons who are born and brought up on a reserve 'who have kept ties with their community and wish to maintain these ties must normally be considered as belonging to that minority': CCR/C/13/D/24/1977 (1981), para. 14.

[107] According to the Permanent Court of International Justice, 'the question whether a person does or does not belong to a racial, linguistic or religious minority . . . is a question of fact and not solely one of intention': *Rights of Minorities in Upper Silesia (Minority Schools)* [1927] PCIJ Ser. A No 15, p. 32.

[108] See, however, the proposal for an Additional Protocol to the European Convention for the Protection of Human Rights and Fundamental Freedoms, Parliamentary Assembly of the Council of Europe, Recommendation 1201 (1993).

among the commentariat,[109] and practical determinations are required of States. In the case of indigenous peoples, while the UNDRIP eschews definition in favour of a broad reading of self-determination, ILO Convention 169 provides a 'statement of coverage' of that instrument which, if not an *a priori* or universally applicable 'definition', serves some of the purposes of such.[110]

While the Committee's formulation of the self-identification principle explicitly addresses individuals, recommendations also affirm its applicability to groups. In the case of Botswana, where the State party expressed reluctance to recognize indigenous peoples on its territory, the Committee invited it 'to review its policy regarding indigenous peoples and, to that end, take into consideration the way in which the groups concerned perceive and define themselves'.[111] To Ukraine, in relation to a community 'of Ukrainian citizens, who consider themselves to be Ruthenians' the Committee recommended 'respect the right of persons and peoples to self-identification'.[112] The recognition and self-identification concepts applied by the Committee extend to 'naming names'—self-designation—on the basis that groups have a right to the dignity of their name as opposed to other names, possibly pejorative, imposed by those outside the group.[113] Hence the practice of requesting information on the acceptance by group members of particular group designations.

De minimis, States should, according to the Committee, recognize ethnic groups when the evidence of ethnicity adequately presents itself. In the case of Ireland, the Committee expressed concern at the State party's position on the Travellers—not recognized as an ethnic group—and encouraged concrete work towards such recognition, bearing in mind that recognition had important implications under the Convention.[114] With regard to ethnic or national minorities, Italy was urged to recognize Roma on an equal footing with 'historical' minorities;[115] Ecuador was subject to a similar recommendation.[116] Comments were made to Ukraine regarding the absence of official recognition of the

[109] The best known is probably that articulated by Capotorti, who defined a minority as: 'a[] group numerically inferior to the rest of the population of a State, in a non-dominant position, whose members—being nationals of the State—possess ethnic, religious or linguistic characteristics differing from those of the rest of the population and show, if only implicitly, a sense of solidarity, directed towards preserving their culture, traditions, religion or language': F. Capotorti, *Study on the Rights of Persons belonging to Ethnic, Religious and Linguistic Minorities*, E/CN.4/Sub.2/384/Rev.1 (1979), para. 568. In a voluminous literature, see H. Hannum, 'The Concept and Definition of Minorities', in M. Weller (ed.), *Universal Minority Rights* (Oxford University Press, 2007), pp. 49–73; G. Pentassuglia, *Defining 'Minority' in International Law: A Critical Appraisal* (2nd edn, Juridica Lapponica, 2000). See also the listing of studies, etc, in the note by the UN Secretary-General, E/CN.4/Sub.2/1984/31.

[110] See Article 1 of the Convention, and discussion and sources cited in P. Thornberry, *Indigenous Peoples and Human Rights* (Manchester University Press, 2002), esp. pp. 33–60; J.J. Corntassel, 'Who is Indigenous? Peoplehood and Ethnonationalist Approaches to Rearticulating Indigenous Identity', in C. Erni (ed.), *The Concept of Indigenous Peoples in Asia* (IWGIA, 2008), pp. 51–74.

[111] CERD/C/BWA/CO/116, para. 9.

[112] CERD/C/UKR/CO/19-21, para. 19.

[113] GR 27, para. 3, recommends that States 'respect the wishes of Roma as to the designation they want to be given'; the Committee is cautious regarding exonyms.

[114] CERD/C/IRL/CO/2, para. 20; see also CERD/C/IRL/CO/3-4, para. 12. Irish Travellers have been so recognized in England: *O'Leary v Punch Retail*, Westminster County Court (29 August 2000); in the case of Northern Ireland, Irish Travellers are included under the Race Relations (Northern Ireland) Order 1997.

[115] CERD/C/ITA/CO/15, para. 12; CERD/C/ITA/CO/16-18, para. 3.

[116] CERD/C/ECU/CO/19, para. 11, a guarantee to the Roma of free association for peaceful purposes was regarded by the Committee as insufficient; legal recognition of the Roma people as an ethnic minority was urged; see also CERD/C/ECU/CO/20-22, para. 13.

Ruthenian minority, despite their distinct minority characteristics.[117] The recognition of indigenous peoples gains enhanced force from the principle of self-determination expressed in the UNDRIP, an instrument endorsed by the Committee. The Committee has insisted that if a group falls under a particular designation such as 'indigenous people', and there is a demand to be recognized as such, then they should be so recognized.[118] In the case of Laos, the Committee recommended that the State party 'recognize the rights of persons belonging to minorities and indigenous peoples as set out in international law, regardless of the name given to such groups in domestic law'.[119] In its recommendation to Denmark regarding recognition of 'the Thule Tribe' of Greenland, the Committee proposed that concrete measures be taken 'to ensure that the status of the Thule tribe reflects established international norms on indigenous peoples' identification'.[120] CERD's approach extends to support for demands by groups for recognition in State constitutions.[121] The Committee has congratulated States parties when recognition in line with international standards is forthcoming.[122]

The Committee's observations on recognition are largely directed towards determinations made by States in their assessments of demographic data, regarded by the Committee as required in order to concretize anti-discrimination programmes including special measures.[123]

For individuals, self-identification discourages the State from assigning them to categories in a deterministic manner that would subvert the objects and purposes of the Convention. Criticisms of the scope of self-definition have been articulated by groups, concerned by what they see as its undue extension to individuals who have little or no

[117] CERD/C/UKR/CO/18, para. 20; a later recommendation was made in the context of an objective 'to recognize all minorities which claim to exist in the State party': CERD/C/UKR/CO/19-21, para. 19.

[118] Concluding observations on Denmark, CERD/C/DNK/CO/18-19, para. 17: 'The Committee reiterates that, pursuant to its general recommendation No. 8 (1990) and other United Nations instruments, the State party is urged to pay particular attention to self-identification as a critical factor in the identification and conceptualization of a people as indigenous'; see also concluding observations on Laos, CERD/C/LAO/CO/15, para. 17.

[119] CERD/C/LAO/CO/15, para. 17.

[120] CERD/C/DNK/18-19, para. 17; CERD/C/DNK/CO/20-21, para. 21.In the particular case, regarding the Uummannaq or Thule tribe, international standards are not univocal: the ILO Tripartite Committee noted that the members of the group shared the same conditions as the rest of the people of Greenland—'conditions which do not distinguish the people of the Uummannaq community from other Greenlanders, but which do distinguish Greenlanders as a group from the inhabitants of Denmark and the Faroe Islands': Governing Body, 280th session, March 2001, Representation under Article 24 of the ILO Constitution, Denmark, GB.280/18/5, cited in *Indigenous and Tribal Peoples' Rights in Practice: A Guide to ILO Convention 169* (International Labour Organization, 2009), p. 13. See also EctHR, *Hinqitaq 53 and ors v Denmark*, App. No. 18584/04 (2006), discussed in T. Koivurova, 'Jurisprudence of the European Court of Human Rights Regarding Indigenous Peoples: Retrospect and Prospect', *IJMGR* 18 (2011), 1–37, 22–4.

[121] Notable examples include Australia, CERD/C/AUS/CO/15-17, para. 15, and Chile, where the Committee urged the State party, *inter alia*, to prioritize 'recognizing the rights of indigenous peoples in the Constitution as a first step towards arriving at a consensus-based settlement of their claims': CERD/C/CHL/CO/18-19, para. 12; also CERD/C/CHL/CO/15-18, para. 16. In the case of Ethiopia, the Committee noted with appreciation the recognition of minority groups in the Constitution: CERD/C/ETH/CO/6-7, para. 9.

[122] Concluding observations on Japan, CERD/C/JPN/CO/3-6, para 5. The scene had previously been set in Japan by the Sapporo District Court in *Kayano et al. v Hokkaido Expropriation Committee*, 27 March 1997, *ILM* 38, 397, where the Court recognized the minority status of the Ainu while calling, in light of international standards for increased protection as an indigenous group. For the formal recognition in 2008 of the Ainu as indigenous, see: <http://www.japantimes.co.jp/news/2008/06/07/national/diet-officially-declares-ainu-indigenous/#.VdH6mH2aKSp>.

[123] Discussed in Chapter 9.

evident connection with the group in question.[124] For collectives, self-identification challenges State prerogatives to deflect the application of established rights. Challenges to the Committee's position have been forthcoming. Turkey stated that it 'did not adhere to the "self-identification" approach advocating the granting of minority status on the basis of the purely subjective perceptions or feelings of its members. Every State had the sovereign right to decide which groups of citizens it viewed as constituting minorities'.[125] The Committee in turn reiterated the relevance of GR 8, also expressing concern at the application of restrictive criteria to determine the existence of ethnic groups.[126]

IV. Discrimination

'Discrimination' is a term that may be used in positive, neutral, or negative senses. The Latin *discriminare* means simply 'to distinguish between',[127] and there is a positive sense in referring to 'a person of discrimination': one who displays a fineness or subtlety of judgement in intellectual or material matters. While international instruments vary in their use of 'distinction' and 'discrimination',[128] ICERD incorporates 'distinction' into the concept of racial discrimination. The definition of discrimination in ICERD and elsewhere in international human rights is essentially negative: unjust or unfair discrimination against a person or group/category of persons.[129] Accordingly, GR 32 treats 'positive discrimination' as an oxymoron.[130] The injustice or detriment associated with discrimination is calibrated in terms of 'nullifying or impairing' the recognition, etc, 'on an equal footing' of human rights.

In order to find discrimination that affects individuals or groups under Article 1, it needs to be established that individuals or groups are subject to distinctions, etc. 'based on' race, colour, etc. 'Based on' sits well with intentional discrimination in signifying motivations or reasons for action, but less well with discrimination in effect or indirect discrimination; the reformulation of 'based on' to 'on the grounds of' in GR 14 softens the discrepancy only a little. Makkonen contends that the recognition of indirect discrimination in *L.R. v Slovakia* implies the rejection of the approach according to which discrimination 'must be linked to acts which . . . single out . . . members of a particular group'.[131] In other circumstances, when categorization as indirect discrimination was avoided, the Committee has insisted that groups should be 'singled out' in order to engage the prohibitions in the

[124] See discussion regarding the Sámi of Finland in Chapter 9 on special measures.

[125] CERD/C/SR.1915, para. 5. The Turkish view was the subject of comment from members of the Committee. In the view of Diaconu, CERD/C/SR/1915, para. 32, 'the State party was not obliged to officially recognize the country's different ethnic groups as national minorities', but recognition should proceed based on objective criteria, etc; see also remarks of Prosper, *ibid*, para. 43. See also CERD/C/TUR/CO/4-6, paras. 13 and 14, expressing the view that Turkey is not precluded from recognizing minorities not specified in the Treaty of Lausanne 1923. CERD questions distinctions between recognized and unrecognized groups in order to reveal whether they conceal discriminatory practice.

[126] CERD/C/TUR/CO/3, para. 12.

[127] *Concise Oxford English Dictionary* (11th edn, Oxford University Press 2004), p. 410.

[128] The SIM database lists 26 references to 'distinction', and 168 to 'discrimination': <http://sim.law.uu.nl/SIM/Library/HRinstruments.nsf/%28organization%29/$Searchform?SearchViews>.

[129] 'The word 'discriminate' taken alone is now commonly used in the pejorative sense of an unfair, unreasonable, unjustifiable or arbitrary distinction': McKean, *Equality and Discrimination*, p. 10.

[130] This is the sense of GR 32, para. 12. See discussion in Chapter 9.

[131] T. Makkonen, *Equal in Fact, Unequal in Law* (Martinus Nijhoff, 2012), p.133 [henceforth *Equal in Fact, Unequal in Law*].

Convention,[132] a narrow approach to the 'targeting' of groups. The Committee's general understanding of discrimination is summarized in GR 32:

On the core notion of discrimination, general recommendation No. 30 (2004) of the Committee observed that differential treatment will 'constitute discrimination if the criteria for such differentiation, judged in the light of the objectives and purposes of the Convention, are not applied pursuant to a legitimate aim, and are not proportional to the achievement of this aim' (para. 4). As a logical corollary of this principle, General Recommendation No. 14 (1993) observes that 'differentiation of treatment will not constitute discrimination if the criteria for such differentiation, judged against the objectives and purposes of the Convention, are legitimate' (para. 2). The term 'non-discrimination' does not signify the necessity of uniform treatment when there are significant differences in situation between one person or group and another, or, in other words, if there is an objective and reasonable justification for differential treatment. To treat in an equal manner persons or groups whose situations are objectively different will constitute discrimination in effect, as will the unequal treatment of persons whose situations are objectively the same. The Committee has also observed that the application of the principle of non-discrimination requires that the characteristics of groups be taken into consideration.[133]

A separation should be made between 'differentiation' *simpliciter*, and (unfair) discrimination: the prevention of discrimination and the right to equality do not require identical treatment without regard to circumstances;[134] the nuanced understanding of equality since the time of the League of Nations has already been referred to here. The edifices of minority and indigenous rights and other categories of rights in international law rest upon nuances in the understanding of equality.[135] Objective and reasonable justifications for differential treatment may arise from appraisals of factual circumstances or by operation of law—the latter is evidenced by the acceptance under ICERD of rights applicable to members of specific groups or categories.[136] As an example of the former, in *Sefic v Denmark* the Committee decided that a requirement to speak Danish in order to purchase car

[132] In a case of abusive references to Muslims, 'no specific national or ethnic groups were directly targeted', and as with general references to foreigners, general references to Muslims 'do not single out a particular group of persons, contrary to Article 1 of the Convention': *P.S.N. v Denmark*, CERD/C/71/D/36/2006 (2007), paras 6.2 and 6.4.

[133] Para. 8.

[134] 'The prohibition of discrimination does not require identical treatment; in other words, not every differentiation amounts to a prohibited discrimination', K. Henrard, 'The Protection of Minorities through the Equality Provisions in the UN Human Rights Treaties: The UN Treaty Bodies', *IJMGR* 14 (2007), 141–80, 149.

[135] 'But the principle of non-discrimination is not inconsistent with the recognition that particularly vulnerable categories of people may need to be singled out for protection . . . and more specific norms have been developed to complement the general norms . . . mong these categories are workers, refugees, women, prisoners and other detainees, indigenous peoples, children, disabled persons, and migrant workers': H. Hannum, 'The Concept and Definition of Minorities' in M. Weller (ed.), *Universal Minority Rights* (Oxford University Press, 2007), pp. 49–73, p. 50. With regard to an objection by Suriname that the land claims by indigenous and Afro-descendant peoples were effectively discriminatory, the Inter-American Court of Human Rights recalled the 'well-established principle of international law that unequal treatment towards persons in unequal situations does not necessarily amount to impermissible discrimination . . . In the context of . . . indigenous and tribal peoples, this Court has already stated that that special measures are necessary in order to ensure their survival in accordance with their traditions and customs': *Saramaka People v Suriname*, IACtHR Ser. C No. 172 (2007), para. 103.

[136] In GR 31 on racial discrimination in the criminal justice system, para. 27 recommends that, prior to trial, States parties may give preference to non-judicial or parajudicial procedures for dealing with offences 'taking into account the cultural or customary background of the perpetrator, especially in the case of persons belonging to indigenous peoples'; in such cases, States are also advised, *ibid.*, para. 36, to give preference to alternatives to imprisonment' in light of ILO Convention 169 on Indigenous and Tribal Peoples.

insurance was reasonable in the circumstances. CERD considered that the reasons advanced by the company concerned, 'including the ability to communicate with the customer, the lack of resources of a small company to employ persons speaking different languages, and the fact that it is a company operating primarily through telephone contact', were reasonable and objective grounds for the requirement.[137] In *L.G v Korea*, with regard to the mandatory testing of foreigners—except ethnic Koreans—for drugs and HIV/AIDS, the Committee noted that the policy did not 'appear to be justified on public health grounds or any other ground'.[138] Differentiation may also be legitimated through the operation of a specific treaty or legal regime such as the European Union.[139]

Lerner reads the *travaux* to the effect that the four categories of discriminatory action—'distinction, exclusion, restriction and preference'—were intended to cover all types of acts based on racial motivations,[140] which suggests that they should not be interpreted restrictively. 'Distinctions' between national and ethnic minorities are referred to above; social, educational, and other forms of 'exclusion' have attracted Committee comment,[141] and support has been expressed for 'inclusion'.[142] An archival search for 'restriction' turns up instances of governmental restrictions on NGOs but also restrictions on non-citizens in the labour market,[143] on freedom of movement,[144] and caste restrictions.[145] As regards 'preferences', GR 32 generalizes that discrimination 'is constituted not simply by an unjustifiable "distinction, exclusion or restriction" but also by an unjustifiable "preference", making it especially important that States parties distinguish "special measures" from prohibited "preferences"'.[146]

The application of legal preferences was discussed in *D.F. v Australia*, a case concerning changes in Australian legislation affecting, *inter alia*, eligibility for certain social security payments. The petitioner, a New Zealand citizen resident in Australia, lost special status on account of legislative amendments to rules that previously favoured New Zealand citizens and was required to apply for a permanent residence visa to access certain social security benefits. In rejecting the claim of racial discrimination, Australia argued that whereas New Zealand citizens had previously received preferential treatment, the withdrawal of such advantages could not constitute discrimination, as it merely placed New

137 CERD/C/66/D/32/2003 (2005), para. 7.2.

138 CERD/C/86/D/51/2012 (2015), para. 7.4, discussed further in Chapter 7.

139 The European Court of Human Rights justified a difference in treatment as regards deportation for crime between EU citizens and others by referring to the European (EU) legal order, considering that 'such preferential treatment is based on an objective and reasonable justification, given that the Member States of the European Union form a special legal order, which has, in addition, established its own citizenship': *C. v Belgium*, App. No. 35/1995/541/627 (1996), para. 38; see also Human Rights Committee, *Shergill v Canada*, on the effects of reciprocal international social security agreements, CCPR/C/94/D/1506/2006 (2008). However, the mere existence of international agreements in such cases does not necessarily dispose of an issue of discrimination: *Karakurt v Austria*, CCPR/C/74/D/965/2000 (2002).

140 N. Lerner, *Group Rights and Discrimination in International Law* (Martinus Nijhoff, 1991), pp. 48–9.

141 Colombia, CERD/C/COL/CO/14, para. 18, on Afro-Colombians and indigenous peoples; Estonia, CERD/C/EST/CO/8-9, para. 17, widespread exclusion of Roma. Concluding observations on Nigeria link together 'social exclusion, segregation and mistreatment' with regard to allegations regarding the Osu: CERD/C/NGA/CO/18, para. 15.

142 GR 27, para. 17: see discussion in chapter 10.

143 Regarding Latvia, CERD/C/63/CO/8, para. 15.

144 Israel, CERD/C/ISR/CO/13, para. 34.

145 Nepal, CERD/C/64/CO/5, para. 12. See also GR 29, para. (a) and *passim*; GR 20, para. 2.

146 Para. 7. See, for example, concluding observations on Fiji, CERD/C/62/CO/3, para. 26; Bosnia and Herzegovina, CERD/C/BIH/CO/6, para. 11; and Israel, CERD/C/ISR/CO/13, para. 17.

Zealand citizens 'on an equal footing with people of other nationalities'[147]—an argument criticized by the petitioner as one of 'equality by deprivation'.[148] In finding no discrimination on the ground of national origin, the Committee observed that the distinction which had been made in favour of New Zealand citizens no longer applied: the changed provisions 'did not result in the operation of a distinction, but rather in the removal of such a distinction which had placed the petitioner and all New Zealand citizens in a more favourable position compared to other non-citizens'.[149]

Discrimination under Article 1 is expressed in terms of its *purpose or effect*, and CERD has been critical of jurisdictions that insist that claims of discrimination must be accompanied by evidence of intention.[150] The Committee continues to refer to 'purpose or effect' in its recommendations to States parties.[151] In order to determine whether there is discrimination in effect, GR 14 states that the Committee 'will look to see whether [an] action has an unjustifiable disparate impact upon a group' distinguished by race, colour, etc.[152] Citations of 'disparate impact' include observations on the impact of mandatory sentencing of aboriginals in Australia,[153] the disparate impact of natural disasters on low-income African-Americans,[154] and of felon disenfranchisement laws on persons belonging to minorities in the US.[155]

While continuing to employ the terms 'intention' and 'effect', a parallel terminology of *direct and indirect discrimination* has emerged in practice. In *L.R. v. Slovakia*, it was recalled that 'the definition of racial discrimination . . . expressly extends beyond measures which are explicitly discriminatory to encompass measures that are not discriminatory at face value but are discriminatory in fact and effect, that is, if they amount to indirect discrimination'.[156] Here, discrimination in effect is taken as equivalent to indirect discrimination, and discrimination in fact equated with discrimination in effect. Concluding observations on the US appear to erase distinctions between indirect and *de facto* discrimination, together deemed to occur 'where an apparently neutral provision, criterion or practice would put persons of a particular racial, ethnic or national origin at a disadvantage compared with other persons'.[157] In CERD practice, the essence of *de facto discrimination* (discrimination in fact) is the existence of discrimination in practice; analogously, *de facto* equality refers to equality in the enjoyment of human rights in practice. Committee statements on *de facto* discrimination suggest that the obligations under the Convention reach down into the social matrix, subject to the limitation to 'public life'. References to *de facto* discrimination have been particularly common in the context of immigration,[158] descent-based communities,[159] and Roma.[160]

[147] CERD/C/72/D/39/2006, (2008), para. 4.2.
[148] Para. 5.2.
[149] Para. 7.1.
[150] Concluding observations on the USA, CERD/C/USA/CO/6, para. 35; CERD/C/USA/CO/7-9, para. 5.
[151] For example in the post-9/11 statement on responses to terrorism, A/57/18, Chapter XI. C.
[152] GR 14, para. 2.
[153] CERD/C/AUS/CO/14, para. 20.
[154] CERD/C/USA/CO/6, para. 31.
[155] *Ibid.*, para. 27.
[156] CERD/C/66/D/31/2003, para. 10.4.
[157] CERD/C/USA/CO/6, para. 10.
[158] Concluding observations on Portugal, CERD/C/65/CO/7, para. 11.
[159] Concluding observations on Yemen, CERD/C/YEM/CO/16, para. 15.
[160] Among many examples, see concluding observations on Serbia, CERD/SRB/CO/1, para. 15. The Roma situations are frequently described as amounting to *de facto segregation*.

The amalgamation of terms has been the subject of comment. Frostell distinguishes between the purpose–effect axis and the direct–indirect axis, commenting that 'direct and indirect discrimination . . . might occur both in the presence and in the absence of a discriminatory purpose'.[161] De Schutter distinguishes between indirect discrimination: 'instances of conscious discrimination which hide behind the use of apparently neutral criteria', and 'disparate effect discrimination', rules/practices which 'although not calculated to produce such effect, impose a specific disadvantage on certain groups, or have a disproportionate impact' on them.[162] Irrespective of the provenance of the terminology,[163] the use of direct and indirect discrimination is strongly embedded in current human rights practice.[164] Definitions of these concepts in the human rights canon exhibit broad similarities with each other,[165] even if the terminology employed may wash over the distinctions appraised by De Schutter.[166]

CERD has not advanced a stand-alone definition of 'direct' and 'indirect' discrimination. Both terms appear as a heading in CERD's GR 32 on special measures but the explanation offered is couched in terms of 'purposive or intentional discrimination and discrimination in effect', suggesting that CERD has not drawn clean lines between the two pairings.[167] In assessing whether indirect discrimination is operative 'in fact and

[161] K. Frostell, 'Gender Difference and the Non-Discrimination Principle in the CCPR and the CEDAW', in L. Hannikainen and E. Nykanen (eds), *New Trends in Discrimination Law; International Perspectives* (Turku Law School, 1999), pp. 29–57, at p. 51. See also K. Henrard, Non-Discrimination and Full and Effective Equality', in M. Weller (ed.), *Universal Minority Rights* (Oxford University Press, 2007), pp. 75–147, at p. 113 and citations therein; D. Moeckli, 'Equality and non-Discrimination' in D. Moeckli, S. Shah, and S. Sivakumaran (eds), *International Human Rights Law*, p. 166.

[162] O. De Schutter, *International Human Rights Law* (Cambridge University Press, 2010), pp. 625–6 [*International Human Rights Law*].

[163] Vandenhole cites Frostell for the statement that the use of 'direct' and 'indirect' discrimination stems from the European Community legal order, *Non-Discrimination and Equality*, p. 35, n. 149; for early expression of the principle, see *Sotgiu v Deutsche Bundespost*, Case 152/73 (12 February 1974), para. 31. In international law, the case of *Minority Schools in Albania* [1935] PCIJ, Ser. A/B, No. 64 expresses essential elements of indirect or 'effects' discrimination. More general treatments of discrimination law, if not specifically international law, may trace the development of disparate impact jurisprudence to the US Supreme Court case of *Griggs v Duke Power* (1971) 401 U.S. 424: S. Fredman, *Discrimination Law* (2nd edn, Clarendon Press, 2011), pp. 177–80. See recently *Texas Department of Housing and Community Affairs v The Inclusive Communities Project, Inc. et al.*, Case No 13/1371, US Court of Appeal for the Fifth Circuit, 25 June 2015. In the case law of the ECHR, see *D.H. v Czech Republic*, App No 57325/00 (2007), para. 184.

[164] The Committee on Economic, Social and Cultural Rights defines terms as follows (E/C.12/GC/20, para. 10): '(a) *Direct Discrimination* occurs when an individual is treated less favourably than another person in a similar situation for a reason related to a prohibited ground . . . Direct discrimination also includes detrimental acts or omissions on the basis of prohibited grounds where there is no comparable similar situation (e.g. the case of a woman who is pregnant); (b) *Indirect discrimination* refers to laws, policies or practices which appear neutral at face value, but have a disproportionate impact on the exercise of . . . rights as distinguished by prohibited grounds of discrimination.' For a critique of the CESCR formulation, see De Schutter, *International Human Rights Law*, p. 640. The Human Rights Committee has explicitly acknowledged indirect discrimination in a number of cases, while General Comment 18 prefers the 'purpose or effect' formula: *Althammer v Austria*, CCPR/C/78/D/998/2001 (2003); *Simunek et al. v Czech Republic*, CCPR/C/54/D/516/1992 (1995); *Diergaardt v Namibia*, CCPR/C/69/D/760/1997 (2000).

[165] In *D.H. v Czech Republic*, the Grand Chamber observed (para. 184) that 'a difference in treatment may take the form of disproportionately prejudicial effects of a general policy or measure which, although couched in neutral terms, discriminates against a group'. General Policy Recommendation No. 7 (2002) of the European Commission against Racism and Intolerance (ECRI) on national legislation to combat racism and racial discrimination offers a general view: <http://www.coe.int/dhgl/monitoring/ecri/activities/GPR/EN/Rec>.

[166] Compare the definition of indirect discrimination in the Inter-American Convention against Racism, Article 1(2), discussed in the conclusion to the present chapter.

[167] GR 32, para. 7.

effect', CERD stated that it 'must take account of the particular context and circumstances . . . as by definition indirect discrimination can only be demonstrated circumstantially'.[168] While the Committee has not provided States parties with elaborate guidance on the evidence to demonstrate the presence of indirect—or structural—discrimination, general group-based data are regularly called for,[169] as well as scrutiny of the overall circumstances of particularly vulnerable groups,[170] or in relation to specific policies.[171]

In its exploration of the facets of racial discrimination, the Committee has highlighted *structural discrimination* or *structural inequalities*, notably regarding the situations of Afro-descendants and indigenous peoples in the Americas.[172] The position regarding Afro-descendants is summarized in GR 34, adopted in 2011:

> Racism and structural discrimination against people of African descent, rooted in the infamous regime of slavery, are evident in the situations of inequality affecting them and reflected, *inter alia*, in the following domains: their grouping, together with indigenous peoples, among the poorest of the poor; their low rate of participation and representation in political and institutional decision-making processes; additional difficulties they face in access to and completion and quality of education, which results in the transmission of poverty from generation to generation; inequality in access to the labour market; limited social recognition and valuation of their ethnic and cultural diversity; and a disproportionate presence in prison populations.[173]
>
> The Committee observes that overcoming the structural discrimination that affects people of African descent calls for the urgent adoption of special measures (affirmative action) . . . [174]

This extract highlights a multitude of epiphenomenal effects and takes the Committee close to a formal analysis of structural discrimination. The use of the term by the Committee frequently relates to discrimination as a product of historical processes that have marginalized populations from the institutions of the State and the enjoyment of basic rights.[175] The larger story in many cases, notably that of indigenous peoples, is that structures of State and society were crafted around models that offered little sense of

[168] *L.R. v Slovakia*, CERD/C/66/D/31/2003 (2005), para. 10.4.

[169] Concluding observations on Armenia, CERD/C/ARM/CO/5-6, para. 12.

[170] Concluding observations on The Netherlands, CERD/C/NLD/18, para. 6.

[171] Concluding observations on the Czech Republic, CERD/C/CZE/CO/7, para. 16, where CERD recommended a review of the 'methodological tools used to determine the cases in which children are to be enrolled in special schools so as to avoid indirect discrimination against Roma children on the basis of their cultural identity'.

[172] For example concluding observations on Colombia, CERD/C/COL/CO/14, para. 18; Peru, CERD/C/PER/CO/14-17, para. 10; Uruguay, CERD/C/URY/CO/16-20, paras 10–12, and the Bolivarian Republic of Venezuela, CERD/C/VEN/CO/18, para. 17. In the case of Uruguay, the Committee recommended (para. 12) vis-à-vis persons of African descent that the State party pursue 'efforts to introduce the ethno-racial dimension in all governmental plans, programmes and strategies relevant to the objective of combating and reversing structural discrimination; to allocate specific and sufficient budgets to them; and evaluate them periodically in order to improve their qualitative and quantitative results for the persons targeted'.

[173] CERD/C/GC/34, para. 6.

[174] *Ibid.*, para. 7. The term 'institutional discrimination' has, by contrast with structural discrimination, rarely been taken up: see concluding observations on Rwanda, CERD/C/304/Add.97, para. 6.

[175] Young, in a reformulation of discrimination as oppression, defining oppression as 'structural', the causes of which 'are embedded in unquestioned norms, habits and symbols, in the assumptions underlying institutional rules and the collective consequences following from those rules', referring also to 'often unconscious assumptions and reactions of well-meaning people in ordinary interactions . . . cultural stereotypes, and structural features of bureaucratic hierarchies': I.M. Young, *Justice and the Politics of Difference* (Princeton University Press, 1990), p. 41, cited in Bamforth *et al. Discrimination Law: Theory and Context*, p. 225.

ownership or participation on the part of non-dominant populations; indigenous peoples may regard the development of compensatory legal and constitutional practice in this respect as an aspect of 'belated State-building'.[176] Structural discrimination is also seen to impact on non-citizen, immigrant populations.[177] As a descriptor, 'structural' has been preferred by the Committee to 'systemic', the latter being used more commonly to refer to 'systemic inadequacies' in social programmes.[178] 'Institutional discrimination', focusing on results of the actions of 'institutions' as opposed to broader 'structures', is not part of CERD's regular repertoire.[179] The cultural and economic embeddedness of discriminatory 'structures' in many States suggest that the measures required to address such discrimination within a State will require the deployment of the full resources of the Convention.

V. Grounds of Discrimination

1. Race and colour

Whereas the use of the term 'grounds' (of discrimination) is commonplace, Article 1 refers to discrimination 'based on' race, colour, etc. 'Grounds' of discrimination are, however, referred to in the preamble to the Convention, and GR 14 states the Committee's opinion that 'the words "based on" do not bear any meaning different from "on the grounds of" in preambular paragraph 7'.[180] The list of grounds in Article 1 is expressed as limited.

While the Committee is critical of racist epithets,[181] 'race as such has seldom been explicitly mentioned as a prohibited ground',[182] and where it is referred to, is usually placed in a list along with other grounds, together constituting 'racial discrimination'. The Committee has set itself against notions of 'pure blood' and 'mixed blood', concerned by the idea of racial superiority that such terminology may entail.[183] Concern was also expressed regarding language appearing in the report of the Dominican Republic referring to the 'racial purity' and 'genetic characteristics' of different ethnic groups.[184] In contrast

[176] E.I.A. Daes, *Discrimination against Indigenous Peoples: Explanatory Note concerning the Draft Declaration on the Rights of Indigenous Peoples*, E/CN.4/Sub.2/1993/26/Add. 1, 19, para. 26.

[177] Concluding observations on Belgium, CERD/C/BEL/CO/16-19, para. 15, which also includes a reference to 'ethnic stratification'.

[178] 'Systemic' discrimination is understood by the Committee on Economic, Social and Cultural Rights as 'legal rules, policies, practices or predominant cultural attitudes in either the public or the private sector which create relative disadvantages for some groups, and privileges' for others: CESCR GC 20, para. 12, a definition of that is close to the present work's account of 'structural' discrimination.

[179] C. McCrudden, 'Institutional Discrimination', *Oxford Journal of Legal Studies* 2 (1982), 303–67; M. Bell, *Racism and Equality in the European Union* (Oxford University Press, 2008), p. 12 [henceforth *Racism and Equality*].

[180] GR 14, para. 1; also para. 11 of GR 35 on Combating Racist Hate Speech.

[181] *Hagan v Australia*, CERD/C/62/D/26/2002 (2003).

[182] W. Vandenhole, *Non-Discrimination and Equality in the View of the UN Human Rights Treaty Bodies* (Intersentia, 2005), p. 90 [henceforth *Non-Discrimination and Equality*], the comment predates recent lively discussions on 'race' referred to in the present chapter.

[183] Concluding observations on Republic of Korea, CERD/C/KOR/CO/14, para. 12. This followed a response by the State party to Committee questions, CERD/C/SR.1834, para. 11: inclusion in the State report 'had been intended to highlight the existence of significant social problems that the government wished to eradicate, rather than to condone notions of racial superiority'.

[184] CERD/C/DOM/CO/12, para. 8. The resulting critique by the Committee, *ibid.*, was mild: the use of such terms 'could lead to an erroneous interpretation of the State party's policies'. The subsequent report of the State party (2012) does not shed much light on the controversy; the language employed, 'while it could rightly be considered equivocal' is 'in no way or circumstance' the expression of a discriminatory policy': CERD/C/DOM/13-14, para. 205.

to its response to biological expressions of 'race', no equivalent expression of discomfort was advanced by the Committee in response to the statement by Cuba interpreting race as a social construct:

The naturalistic biological aspect of race, which reduces the human person to a number of specific features, is of little ideological or functional use when it comes to placing individuals in categories in order to establish a social record of the phenomenon . . . all the racial classifications are to some degree arbitrary and vary considerably depending on the taxonomic principle on which they are built . . . the classifications with which people act and function in concrete contexts do not always coincide fully with the classifications which may result from the application of a given 'scientific' criterion. The notion of race is thus taken to be a social construct.[185]

Notwithstanding sensitivities as to concept and language, CERD insists that national legislation should address all the grounds of discrimination in Article 1, including race. Norway explained the absence of 'race' from its Anti-Discrimination Act:

the Government has supported the view that the concept of race should not be used . . . The reason for this is that the concept of race is based on biological, hereditary characteristics, grounded in theories that have no justifiable scientific basis or content. Moreover, the concept has strong negative connotations . . . The Government therefore sees no need to use the term 'race' in the text of the statute.[186]

In response, the Committee expressed concern that the Act did not specifically cover discrimination on the ground of race and recommended that discrimination on this ground be adequately covered in existing legislation.[187] The following report of Norway included the further response:

In the Anti-Discrimination Act, legislators wished to avoid using the term 'race' in the text of the statute, although it is used in international rules. It was pointed out that one important measure to combat racism is to eliminate the idea that people can be divided into different races. It was emphasised that discrimination based on perceptions of a person's race must be regarded as discrimination based on ethnicity within the meaning of the Anti-Discrimination Act.[188]

The Committee maintained its position in concluding observations of 2011 and 2015.[189] Similarly in the case of Germany, the Committee noted the absence of a definition of racial discrimination because of historical sensitivities as to the use of racial terminology in the law, and suggested to the State party that adopting the terminology of the Convention offered more complete legal cover than any alternatives.[190] In the case of Sweden, the concern was that the deletion of 'race' might 'lead to difficulties with the qualification and processing of complaints, hindering the access to justice' for victims. The Committee did

[185] CERD/C/CUB/14-18, paras 2–5, at para. 5.

[186] CERD/C/497/Add. 1, para. 10.

[187] CERD/C/NOR/CO/18 para. 15.

[188] CERD/C/NOR/19-20, para. 11.

[189] CERD/C/NOR/CO/19-20, para. 8; CERD/C/NOR/CO/21-22, para. 9. For discussions pertaining to the latter, see CERD/C/SR.2373 and 2374.

[190] CERD/C/DEU/CO/18, para. 15: 'While noting the State party's reservations with regard to the use of the term "race", the Committee is concerned that the State party's strong focus on xenophobia, anti-Semitism and right-wing extremism may lead to the neglect of other forms of racial discrimination . . . in this respect, the Committee also regrets the absence of a definition of racial discrimination in the State party's domestic legislation.'

not explicitly call for the reinstatement of 'race', preferring to request that Sweden disseminate information as to what constituted racial discrimination under Swedish law.[191]

As with race, CERD expresses a preference that discrimination on the ground of colour be prohibited in domestic legislation. Norway was thus enjoined to include the Article 1 grounds of racial discrimination in its Anti-Discrimination Act,[192] while the inclusion by Moldova of 'skin colour' as a ground of discrimination in a draft labour law was welcomed by the Committee.[193] Colour-based discrimination is occasionally singled out by CERD as the essential ground in a particular case.[194] The Committee itself has referred to 'black' people and communities in a wide range of countries,[195] and generally follows the terminology used in State reports unless there is evidence that the communities in question object to it.[196]

2. *Descent*

The opposition of some States, notably India, to applying the ground of 'descent' to the caste system played its part in stimulating explanations by the Committee of its approach to 'descent'. The *Concise Oxford English Dictionary* offers a definition of descent as (apart from descending from a height or descending on a person in order to rob!) referring to 'a person's origin or nationality' and 'transmission by inheritance'[197] A thesaurus offers related words such as ancestry, extraction, family tree, genealogy, heredity, lineage, origin, and parentage.[198] A Secretariat paper for CERD's thematic discussion of descent-based discrimination in 2002 observed that 'descent'

> generally means the fact of 'descending' or being descended from an ancestor or ancestral stock. It is also equivalent to 'lineage, race, stock'. In legal terminology, this term signifies 'transmission of property, title, or quality, by inheritance'. The term descent implies inheriting from one generation to another characteristics that are evaluated in society in a positive or negative way, that is the status determined by birth.[199]

The proliferation of synonyms suggests overlap with other terms in Article 1, especially where they include 'origin',[200] a feature of Article 1 that reinforces Diaconu's assertion that 'the definition was composed by adding as many concepts as possible, in order to avoid any *lacunae*'.[201] 'Descent' is potentially the widest basis for the prohibition of discrimination.

[191] CERD/C/SWE/CO/19-21, para. 6.

[192] CERD/C/NOR/CO/19-20, para. 8; CERD/C/NOR/CO/21-22, paras 9 and 10.

[193] CERD/C/MDA/CO/8-9, para. 13.

[194] Concluding observations of 2013 on the Dominican Republic, CERD/C/DOM/CO/13-14, contain multiple references—paras 7, 8, 9, 14, 15, 16, and 17—to discrimination against 'dark-skinned' persons of African descent, including an expression of concern regarding the ambiguous requirement of a '*buena presencia*' (good appearance) to obtain a skilled job.

[195] See, for example, concluding observations on Ecuador, CERD/C/ECU/CO/19, para. 10; Morocco, A/65/18, p. 93, para. 19; and Switzerland, CERD/C/CHE/CO/6, para. 17.

[196] For a complex of arguments regarding 'fair-skinned aboriginal people' under question as not being 'genuinely' aboriginal, see Federal Court of Australia, *Eatock v Bolt* [2011] FCA 1103.

[197] *Concise Oxford English Dictionary*, p. 387.

[198] *The New Collins Dictionary and Thesaurus* (Collins, 1987), p. 265.

[199] CERD/C/61/Misc.13, para. 6.

[200] See above on discussions in the *travaux* on confusions over 'national origin'.

[201] I. Diaconu, *The definitions of racial discrimination*, background paper for the World Conference against Racism, E/CN.4/1999/WG.1/BP.10 (1999), para. 17.

The Committee's major statement on descent-based discrimination was made in 2002 as GR 29 'on article 1, paragraph 1 of the Convention (Descent)';[202] the recommendation emerged after an extensive Committee discussion preceded by an afternoon of interventions by governments, UN experts, and NGOs.[203] GR 29 was adopted in the year following the Durban conference; the absence of reference to caste in the final document of the conference[204] is compensated for by its inclusion in GR 29. The preamble to GR 29 confirms 'the consistent view of the Committee that the term "descent" in Article 1, paragraph 1 . . . does not solely refer to "race" and has a meaning and application which complement the other prohibited grounds of discrimination', and strongly reaffirms 'that discrimination based on descent includes discrimination against members of communities based on forms of social stratification such as caste and analogous systems of inherited status' which nullify or impair their equal enjoyment of human rights. The text of the recommendation does not offer a complete definition of 'descent-based discrimination',[205] but encourages governments to adopt measures, including taking steps

> to identify those descent-based communities under their jurisdiction who suffer from discrimination, especially on the basis of caste and analogous systems of inherited status, and whose existence may be recognized on the basis of various factors, including some or all of the following: inability or restricted ability to alter inherited status; socially enforced restrictions on marriage outside the community; private and public segregation, including in housing and education, access to public spaces, places of worship and public sources of food and water; limitation of freedom to renounce inherited occupations of degrading or hazardous work; subjection to debt bondage; subjection to dehumanizing discourses referring to pollution or untouchability; and generalized lack of respect for their human dignity and equality.

The emphasis is on discrimination against individuals locked in to a system from which they aspire to escape and which they find degrading, a system which involves 'a total lack of social mobility, for the status of an individual was determined by birth or social origin and could never change, regardless of personal merit'.[206] The description of this form of discrimination consists in a series of indicators or a 'cluster concept', in that no single element is a perfect indicator of the existence of such discrimination, but cumulatively they work together to assist governments to uncover the presence of descent-based discriminatory structures.

The preamble to the recommendation constructs a link between narrower conceptions of descent-based discrimination circulating around caste, and wider meanings by referring

[202] A/57/18, chapter XI. F. For general work at the United Nations, see Report of the Special Rapporteurs, Yokota and Chung, on discrimination based on work and descent: A/HRC/11/CRP.3, 18 May 2009, to which is annexed the *Draft Principles and Guidelines for the Effective Elimination of Discrimination Based on Work and Descent*.

[203] The thematic discussion took place on 9 August, CERD/C/SR.1531. There are no summary records for the proceedings on the previous day, on which twenty-three separate interventions (including five from African groups) were made by NGOs, one of which was a joint statement of thirty-two international NGOs; as well as interventions from four members of the Sub-Commission, and two governments, India and Nepal. A summary of the whole of the thematic discussion was made by the International Movement against all forms of Discrimination and Racism (IMADR). See also CERD/C/SR.1545, SR.1546 and SR.1547 for discussion of the draft general recommendation.

[204] The diplomacy of the government of India prevailed over determined efforts by Dalit groups in particular to insert a specific provision in the Durban Declaration and Programme of Action.

[205] CERD member Thornberry, CERD/CD/SR.1545, para. 43; Sicilianos, *ibid.*, para. 45.

[206] Remarks of CERD member de Gouttes, CERD/C/SR.1531, para. 40.

to persons of Asian and African descent, and indigenous and other forms of descent. The conception of descent-based discrimination in the recommendation is wider than caste, but includes it: the point is made in the preamble, and was individually endorsed by members of the Committee.[207] The language of invitation to States to recognize the operation of descent-based discrimination on their territory is further underlined by the preamble, which commends the efforts of those States which have taken measures against it: the overall tone of the recommendation is hortatory as much as critical.

The massive contestation of caste systems by Dalits and others, and the overwhelming evidence of caste oppression caught the attention of CERD members, while arguments in defence of the system under scrutiny were not overborne by the evidence presented to the Committee.[208] The recommendation incorporates a severe critique of a particular form of social and religious organization, even if the direct emphasis is on discrimination rather than the cultural system per se. The question of cultural intrusion may have troubled some members of the Committee but was addressed in the light of the evidence presented. If the question was whether the Committee was interfering in an unwarranted manner into historical, cultural, or religious systems, it might equally be asked whose culture was involved, and who spoke for that culture. The sense of belonging and meaning provided by a caste/descent group was greatly weakened when individuals and groups contested bother their 'membership' and the validity of their condition.[209] Some members of the Committee were less troubled by the possibility of intrusion and would have gone further than the recommendation.[210]

Discrimination based on descent has been addressed by the Committee in a variety of contexts including caste-based discrimination and discrimination based on African and, to a lesser extent, Asian descent, discussed below. Banton recalls the early case of Somalia,[211] where despite the reservations of the country rapporteur as to the applicability of the Convention,[212] and uncertainty among members as to how to characterize the conflict within the State,[213] the Committee 'expressed concern about the tragic circumstances prevailing in Somalia, which include conflicts based on descent'.[214] The descent frame has been considered appropriate to address forms of stratification in a widening range of

[207] See remarks of CERD member Pillai, CERD/C/SR.1531, paras 4–10; also Aboul-Nasr, *ibid.*, paras 2–3; Thornberry, *ibid.*, para. 13; Lindgren Alves, *ibid.*, para. 29; Yutzis, *ibid.*, para. 36; Diaconu, *ibid.*, para. 45.

[208] See generally, C. Bob, ' "Dalit Rights are Human Rights": Caste Discrimination, International Activism, and the Construction of a New Human Rights Issue', *HRQ* 29 (2007), 167–93; A. Waughray, 'Caste Discrimination and Minority Rights: the Case of India's Dalits', *IJMGR* 17 (2010), 327–53.

[209] Thornberry, CERD/C/SR.1531, para. 12.

[210] CERD member Lindgren Alves proposed an amendment to the draft GR whereby the Committee would state its understanding that 'caste systems are totally contrary to the International Convention on the Elimination of All Forms of Racial Discrimination', CERD/C/SR.1545, paras 49 and 78. This was immediately rejected by Thiam, *ibid.*, para. 79, who argued that 'it did not adequately reflect the reality of the African caste system'.

[211] Banton, *International Action*, p. 151.

[212] CERD/C/SR.948, para. 58 (Aboul-Nasr).

[213] De Gouttes, *ibid.*, para. 64, believed that 'an ethnic element' was involved; Ferrero Costa, *ibid.*, para. 65, discerned 'an ethnic, even a tribal aspect to the conflict'.

[214] CERD/C/SR.949, para. 5. Divisions among groups in Somalia are sometimes described as based on a clan system; sources also refer to occupational and caste-based stratification of groups in a patron-client relationship with 'noble clans'. On the general conflict situation, see S. Samatar, *Somalia: A Nation in Turmoil* (Minority Rights Group, 1995); on caste relationships, see A. Stevens, *Discrimination based on Descent in Africa*, paper presented to the 2002 CERD thematic discussion on descent-based discrimination for the International Dalit Solidarity Network, pp. 5–6 (on file with author).

States. Questions of caste and analogous systems of social stratification have been raised by State reports including those of Bahrain,[215] Bangladesh,[216] Burkina Faso,[217] Chad,[218] Ethiopia, India, Japan,[219] Mali,[220] Madagascar,[221] Mauritania,[222] Nepal,[223] Nigeria,[224] Senegal,[225] Suriname,[226] the UK,[227] and Yemen.[228]

The views of the Committee on descent-based have been contested by States parties, notably India and Japan. In the examination of the report of India in 1996, CERD affirmed that descent 'does not solely refer to "race"',[229] concluding that the situation of India's Scheduled Castes and Scheduled Tribes fell within the purview of the Convention. India disagreed, arguing that '"race" in India is distinct from "caste"',[230] while nevertheless

[215] CERD/C/BHR/CO/7, para. 16: the descent reference to Shia groups in Bahrain does not stand out in that the grounds distinguishing them are multiple and stated to include 'tribal or national origin, descent, culture or language'.

[216] CERD/C/304/Add.118, para. 11.

[217] CERD/C/BFA/CO/12-19, para. 8, referring to a caste system 'in certain ethnic groups', for which the committee recommended, among other measures, 'special legislation'.

[218] CERD/C/TCD/CO/15, para. 15; CERD/C/TCD/CO/16-18, para. 12.

[219] CERD/C/304/Add.114, para. 8 explaining the Committee's view of the relevance of descent-based discrimination in the case of the Burakumin community; the issue was taken up again in discussions of subsequent reports of Japan to the Committee, CERD/C/JPN/CO/3-6, para. 8; CERD/C/JPN/CO/7-9, para. 22.

[220] CERD/C/61/CO/7, para. 16.

[221] CERD/C/65/CO/4, para. 17.

[222] CERD/C/65/CO/5, para. 15. The recommendations to Madagascar and Mauritania expressed the Committee's concern over discrimination against descendants of slaves.

[223] CERD/C/304/Add.107, para. 11: 'The Committee remains concerned at the existence of caste-based discrimination and the denial which this system imposes on some segments of the population of the enjoyment of the rights contained in the Convention.'

[224] CERD/C/NGA/CO/18, para. 15, referring to 'members of the Osu and other similar communities'.

[225] CERD/C/61/CO/9, para. 11; CERD/C/SEN/CO/16-18, para. 13.

[226] CERD/C/SUR/CO/13-15, paras. 15 and 16.

[227] CERD/C/63/CO/11, para. 25; CERD/C/GBR/CO/18-20, para. 30, where CERD recommended that the responsible government Ministry invoke the Equality Act to 'provide for "caste to be an aspect of race" in order to provide remedies to victims of this form of discrimination'. A. Waughray, 'Caste Discrimination: A Twenty-First Century Challenge for UK Discrimination Law', *Modern Law Review* 72 (2009), 182–219; A Waughray, 'Capturing Caste in Law: Caste Discrimination and the Equality Act 2010', *Human Rights Law Review* 14 (2014), 359–79; M. Dhanda, A. Waughray, D. Mosse, and D. Keane, *Caste in Britain: Socio-Legal Review*, Equality and Human Rights Commission Research Report 91 (2014). See also *Chandhok and Another v Tirkey*, UKEAT/0190/14/KN, 2 December 2014, where, in a claim amended to include caste discrimination, a UK Employment Appeal Tribunal, following citation of, *inter alia*, the provisions of ICERD, refused to strike out the claim, finding that, although 'caste' was not an autonomous concept in the UK Equality Act, the facts surrounding the case suggested that 'ethnic origins' in the Act had a 'wide and flexible ambit' (including characteristics determined by 'descent'), so that caste could come within it. The case was returned to the Employment Tribunal in July 2015—at the time of writing, the judgment is reserved.

[228] CERD/C/YEM/CO/16, para. 15, focusing on 'descent-based, culturally distinct communities, among others, the Al-Akhdam'. The observations on the complexity of the population and to classes within it are contested in the later report of Yemen, CERD/C/YEM/17-18, paras 20–21.

[229] CERD/C/304/Add.13, para. 14. The position was forcefully expressed by many individual members of the Committee: 'If "descent" was the equivalent of "race", it would not have been necessary to include both concepts in the Convention' (Wolfrum, CERD/C/SR.1161, para. 20); 'The Committee's conceptions of "race" and "descent" clearly differed from those of the Government of India' (Van Boven, CERD/C/SR.1162, para.14); 'The fact that castes and tribes were based on descent brought them strictly within the Convention' (Chigovera, *ibid.*, para. 22). See also remarks of Aboul-Nasr, SR.1162, para. 27; de Gouttes, SR.1161, para. 32; Rechetov, SR.1161, para. 11.

[230] Consolidated tenth to fourteenth periodic reports of India, CERD/C/299/Add.3, para. 7: 'both castes and tribes are systems based on "descent" . . . It is obvious, however, that the use of the term "descent" in the Convention clearly refers to "race" . . . the policies of the Indian Government relating to Scheduled Castes and Scheduled Tribes do not come under the purview of Article 1 of the Convention.' See also CERD/C/SR.1161, para. 4; CERD/C/SR.1162, para. 36.

indicating its willingness to provide information on these groups.[231] The position of India in this respect was maintained throughout its dialogue with CERD in 2007,[232] where the delegation recalled that the Committee

> was familiar with India's position on the caste issue . . . as an issue outside the purview of the definition of racial discrimination . . . The Indian Constitution directly addressed the issue of caste through clearly guaranteed rights and affirmative action, which aimed to ensure that disadvantaged castes were brought into mainstream society. The Constitution drew a distinction between caste, race and descent, considering them as separate concepts.[233]

Another delegate said that 'his government had no doubt that the ordinary meaning of the term "racial discrimination" did not include caste. It was firmly accepted that the Indian caste system was not racial in origin. Caste was an institution unique to India'.[234] Further, regarding the drafting of the Convention, the delegate stated that the government's 'primary concern during that time related to the use of the term "national origin" . . . the proposal to include the term "descent" had been based on concerns regarding discriminatory treatment against Indians in their own land while under colonial rule, and to persons of Indian descent in countries where they had settled in large numbers'.[235] It was also asserted that caste 'could not be considered as descent, which signified genealogically demonstrable characteristics'.[236] In the event, the Committee reiterated its unchanged position on the meaning of Article 1, reaffirming that discrimination based on caste is fully covered.[237] India maintained its views with equal firmness.[238]

In the case of Japan, the Committee similarly observed that '"descent" has its own meaning and is not to be confused with race or national or ethnic or national origin', recommending the State to ensure the protection of the rights 'of all groups, including the Burakumin community'.[239] Japan stated that it did not share the Committee's interpretation of 'descent',[240] while going on to outline measures taken 'with the aim of resolving

[231] Preliminary comments of the government of India on the concluding observations adopted by [CERD] on the tenth to fourteenth periodic reports of India presented during the forty-ninth session of the Committee, A/51/18, p.128, para. 3(a). One of the representatives of India offered a nuanced view in stating that, CERD/C/SR.1163, para. 3, the 'notion of "race" was not entirely foreign to that of "caste"; but . . . racial differences were secondary to cultural ones . . . race had never really been determinant for caste'. CERD/C/SR.1163, para. 3; also para. 4, *ibid.*

[232] CERD/C/SR.1796 and 1797.

[233] CERD/C/SR.1796, para. 3.

[234] *Ibid.*, para. 7.

[235] *Ibid.*, para. 8.

[236] *Ibid.*, para. 13.

[237] CERD/C/IND/CO/19, para. 8.

[238] A62/18, Annex X, Comments of States parties on the Concluding Observations adopted by the Committee.

[239] Concluding Observations on Japan, CERD/C/304/Add.114, para. 8. A number of submissions highlighted the plight of Burakumin, a community historically identified with work in certain 'unclean' trades. See E.A. Su-lan Reber, 'Buraku Mondai in Japan: historical and modern perspectives and directions for the future' *Harvard Human Rights Journal* 12 (1999), 299 ff; M. Kurokawa, 'Markers of the 'Invisible Race', in Y. Takezawa (ed.), *Racial Representations in Asia* (Kyoto University Press and Trans-Pacific Press, 2011), pp. 32–52 [henceforth *Racial Representations*]. In the 2010 dialogue with Japan, CERD member de Gouttes, CERD/C/SR.1987, para. 47, cited stakeholder submissions regarding Buraku under the UPR process that described them as 'descendants of outcast communities in the feudal era, whose occupations had been deemed to be "tainted" with death or ritual impurity. Although the Burakumin had been liberated when the feudal caste system had been abolished in 1871, their long history of taboos and myths had left a continuous legacy of social exclusion.'

[240] A/56/18, Annex VII. A, para. 2.

the problem of discrimination against the Burakumin'.[241] In later dialogues with Japan, there is little evidence of convergence between the position of Japan and that of the Committee on 'descent', the delegation of Japan observing, *inter alia*, that there were no physical features distinguishing Burakumin from other Japanese.[242] CERD has reiterated its position, stating that it was encouraged by steps taken by Japan 'in the spirit of the Convention' to eliminate discrimination against Burakumin.[243]

Building upon the numerous references in the 2001 Durban Declaration to 'Africans and people of African descent',[244] and a smaller number of references to 'Asians and people of Asian descent',[245] the Programme of Action (POA) devoted a chapter to the former category. The POA made recommendations in areas such as participation in 'all political, economic, social and cultural aspects of society and in the advancement and economic development of their countries',[246] on additional investment and capacity-building,[247] on affirmative action or positive action initiatives,[248] on access to education,[249] on public service,[250] the justice system,[251] and on 'religious prejudice and intolerance'.[252] Regarding an issue more commonly associated with indigenous peoples, the POA urged States 'to resolve problems of ownership of ancestral lands inhabited for generations by people of African descent and to promote the productive utilization of land and the comprehensive development of these communities, respecting their culture and their specific forms of decision-making'.[253]

Following General Assembly resolution 64/169 proclaiming 2011 as the International Year for People of African Descent, the Committee held a thematic discussion on discrimination against people of African descent in March 2011 and drafted GR 34 on 'racial discrimination against people of African descent' at its seventy-ninth session in 2011. The recommendation does not attempt a definition of such descendants but states simply that people of African descent 'are those referred to as such by [the Durban documentation] and who identify themselves as people of African descent'.[254] In addition to the general human rights, specific rights are picked out including rights to land, cultural

[241] *Ibid.*, para. 3.

[242] CERD/C/SR.1988, paras 39 and 45.

[243] CERD/C/JPN/CO/3-6, para. 8. Japan continues to maintain the view that the Burakumin are not included under 'descent', a matter of regret to the Committee: CERD/C/JPN/CO/7-9, para. 22. For a reflection on historical treatment of Burakumin as a 'race' see Y. Takezawa, 'Towards a New Approach to Race and Racial Representations: Perspectives from Asia', Takezawa (ed.), *Racial Representations in Asia*, pp. 7–19.

[244] Paras 32–35. Paragraph 33 also refers to the African diaspora.

[245] Paras 36–38. Further paragraphs—13 and 103—link together 'Africans and people of African descent', 'Asians and people of Asian descent' and indigenous peoples.

[246] POA, para. 4.

[247] *Ibid.*, paras 5–6.

[248] *Ibid.*, para. 5.

[249] *Ibid.*, para. 10.

[250] *Ibid.*, para. 11.

[251] *Ibid.*, para. 12.

[252] *Ibid.*, para. 14.

[253] *Ibid.*, para. 13. The groups and situations intimated here exist in a number of Latin American States: see, for example, R. Price (ed.), *Maroon Societies: Rebel Slave communities in the Americas* (Anchor Books, 1973); for a particular case, see E.-R. Kambel and F. MacKay, *The Rights of Indigenous Peoples and Maroons in Suriname* (IWGIA, 1999). More general treatments of African descent in the Americas include G.R. Andrews, *Afro-Latin America 1800–2000* (Oxford University Press, 2004); Minority Rights Group, *No Longer Invisible: Afro-Latin Americans Today* (Minority Rights Group, 1995).

[254] GR 34, para. 1.

identity, protection of traditional knowledge, and prior consultation in decisions.[255] As noted, the recommendation emphasizes structural discrimination rooted in the infamous regime of slavery. The remit of the recommendation is global, though the imprint of the situation in the Americas looms large in the references to the slave trade, and the emphasis on property and land rights.

3. National or Ethnic Origin

The fundamental ambiguity in 'national origin' and 'nationality' is that the terms refer not only to legal nationality or citizenship but also to a concept of community in a spectrum that includes ethnicity: 'national origin' and overlapping terms are discussed further in the next chapter. Schwelb reads the *travaux* to the effect that there was 'no clear agreement whether the term "national origin" was to be understood in the politico-legal or in the ethnographical sense'.[256] Schwelb concludes his review of the terminology with the statement that '[f]or the practical purposes of the interpretation of the Convention . . . the three terms "descent", "national origin" and "ethnic origin" among them cover distinctions both on the ground of *present or previous nationality* in the ethnographical sense and on the ground of *previous* nationality on the "politico-legal" sense of citizenship'.[257] Sharp distinctions along such lines may be blurred making it difficult to visualize to which facet of identity is being adverted.

Where national origin is referred to in appraising discrimination, it is most frequently coupled with 'ethnic origin', suggesting that its primary register of meaning is ethnicity and not legal citizenship.[258] Ethnic origin is often used generically but may be expressly linked to ethnic minorities or indigenous peoples in phrases such as 'minority ethnic origin';[259] it has also been used in connection with refugees, asylum-seekers, and other

[255] *Ibid.*, para. 4.

[256] Schwelb, *The International Convention*, 1006–7.

[257] Schwelb, *The International Convention*, 1007 (emphasis in the original). However, as noted in the present chapter, the Committee has sought to carve out a specific niche for discrimination based on 'descent', at least in the limited context of caste or caste-like systems. Diaconu disagrees with Schwelb's analysis of 'national origin' insofar as it suggests coverage of discrimination on the ground of a previous (legal) nationality: I. Diaconu, *Racial Discrimination* (Eleven International Publishing, 2011), p. 70.

[258] According to Lord Fraser of Tullybelton in the UK House of Lords: 'For a group to constitute an ethnic group . . . it must, in my opinion, regard itself, and be regarded by others, as a distinct community by virtue of certain characteristics. Some of these . . . are essential; others are not essential but one or more of them . . . will help to distinguish the group from the surrounding community. The conditions which appear to me to be essential are these: (1) a long shared history, of which the group is conscious as distinguishing it from other groups, and the memory of which it keeps alive; (2) a cultural tradition of its own, including family and social customs and manners, often but not necessarily associated with religious observance. In addition to those two essential characteristics the following characteristics are, in my opinion, relevant: (3) either a common geographical origin, or descent from a small number of common ancestors; (4) a common language, not necessarily peculiar to the group; (5) a common literature peculiar to the group; (6) a common religion different from that of neighbouring groups or from the general community surrounding it; (7) being a minority . . .within a larger community': *Mandla v Dowell-Lee* [1983] 2 AC 548 (HL). As a definition, this is too demanding by international standards, especially in relation to elements 3 to 7, but also in respect of element 1, bearing in mind arguments as to the meaning of 'minority', which, according to the Human Rights Committee in General Comment 23, does not depend on being 'long-established'. The account may be more acceptable as a perfectionist conceptualisation where, as with CERD's account of descent-based discrimination, individual elements cumulatively identify the group in question but the issue of what constitutes 'indispensable' elements remains open.

[259] Moldova, CERD/C/MDA/CO/15, para. 21.

non-citizens.[260] 'National or ethnic origin' often function as a yoked pair of workhorses, employed whenever issues of colour ('visible minorities') are not the most prominent markers of discrimination. In practice, 'ethnic origin' is easily transmuted into 'ethnic minorities' and 'indigenous peoples', to the extent that discrimination against these communities may be treated as independent grounds in themselves.

4. *Intersections*

The term 'intersectionality' stems from feminist jurisprudence, notably the work of Kimberlé Crenshaw who introduced the term to preparatory sessions of the Durban World Conference of 2001.[261] Gender[262] supplies the most commonly appraised element for the axes of discrimination that intersect with the named grounds in Article 1(1). GR 25 recognizes that racial discrimination 'does not always affect women and men equally or in the same way',[263] and that 'certain forms of racial discrimination may be directed towards women specifically because of their gender', and may have consequences that affect primarily or only women such as 'sexual violence committed against women members of particular racial or ethnic groups in detention or during armed conflict; the forced sterilization of indigenous women; abuse of women workers in the informal sector or domestic workers . . . by their employers'.[264] There is a self-critical element in the recognition of the need for a more systematic Committee approach to evaluating and monitoring discrimination against women and to developing a more sharply focused methodology by giving particular consideration to '(a) the form and manifestation of racial discrimination; the circumstances in which racial discrimination occurs; (c) the consequences of racial discrimination; and (d) the availability and accessibility of remedies and complaint mechanisms for racial discrimination'.[265] Otto commends the approach of the Committee in opening the way 'to a deeper understanding of the structural dimensions of the intersection of race and gender discrimination and how they work together to intensify women's inequality'.[266]

While the scope of the recommendation is broad enough to address the human rights of men as well as women,[267] the text is focused on oppressive circumstances faced by

[260] In *L.G. v Korea*, the distinction between foreign English teachers who were ethnically Korean and those of non-Korean background was treated as one based on ethnic origin, CERD/C/86/D/51/2012 (2015), para. 7.4, discussion in Chapter 7.

[261] K.W. Crenshaw, 'Gender-related aspects of race discrimination', background paper for the Expert Meeting on Gender and Racial Discrimination, 21–24 November 2000, Zagreb, Croatia, EM/GRD/2000/W.P.1. Intersectional discrimination is understood, in for example, the case of black women, as reaching beyond the addition of two sources of discrimination, but as creating a 'qualitatively different, or synergistic' form of discrimination, so that 'the disadvantage experienced by black women is not the same as that experienced by white women or black men': Fredman, *Discrimination Law*, p. 140. *Inter alia*, the concept presents a case of heightened vulnerability of groups. Attempts to address intersectional discrimination at the level of domestic law have had mixed success, with some jurisdictions demanding that the discrimination be classified as either one 'ground' or another: see *De Graffenreid v General Motors* 413 F Supp142 (USA), with *Hassam v Jacobs NO and Others*, South Africa, cited in Fredman, *Discrimination Law*, p. 143; L'Heureux-Dube J, in *Egan v Canada* [1995], 2 SCR 513, p. 533.

[262] Or based on sex, concluding observations on Ecuador, CERD/C/ECU/CO/19, para. 13.

[263] GR 25, para. 1.

[264] *Ibid*., para. 2. The interrelationship between the rights of women, and racism, racial discrimination, etc, is set out in para. 10 of the preamble to CEDAW.

[265] *Ibid*., para. 5.

[266] D. Otto, 'Women's Rights', in Moeckli *et al*., *International Human Rights Law*, p. 329.

[267] According to Committee member January-Bardill, speaking at the drafting phase of the recommendation, CERD/C/SR.1391, para. 29, 'it was important . . . to think about gender as not being restricted to issues

women. Otto supplements her commendation of the recommendation in adding that while the language of gender 'potentially enables the relational quality of the gender stereotypes, which usually privileges men and disadvantages women, to be acknowledged', the potential remains inchoate in the general recommendation.[268] Gender dimensions are prominent in other general recommendations including GR 29 on descent-based discrimination,[269] and GR 30 on discrimination against non-citizens.[270] In cases of gender/race-based discrimination, the Committee's preferred metaphor is 'double discrimination', though usage is not consistent. In the case of Portugal, the Committee concluded that the State party had the obligation to guarantee the right of everyone to equality in the enjoyment of human rights 'without discrimination on *the basis of gender*, race, colour or national or ethnic origin', explicitly adding gender to the list of grounds.[271]

For discrimination based on religion in conjunction with the grounds in the Convention, the Committee has generally preferred to employ 'intersectionality' instead of double/multiple discrimination.[272] Addressing the situation of groups whose identity is partly constructed in terms of religion has proved awkward for the Committee, notwithstanding the inclusion of freedom of thought, conscience and religion among the protected rights in Article 5. The Committee did not carry through the promise, referred to in its 2007 report to the UN General Assembly, of holding a thematic discussion to clarify its understanding of the relationship between racial and religious discrimination.[273] States parties have occasionally been critical, suggesting that CERD has strayed beyond its mandate when concluding observations address the situation of a particular religious group.[274] Practice remains ad hoc, and, besides the metaphor of intersectionality,[275] CERD employs compound terms such as 'ethno-religious' to bring discrimination more clearly within the purview of the Convention,[276] while in other cases, references have been made simply to, for example, discrimination against 'Muslims'.[277] The comparative liberality of references to religion

involving women . . . gender-related dimensions of racial discrimination could . . . be a useful tool . . . in examining why black men, who were subjected to immense racial discrimination, were the subject of criminalization. That was as much a gender issue as rape.'

[268] Otto, in Moeckli *et al.*, *International Human Rights Law*, p. 330; Otto, p. 329, also notes that the few examples of intersectional discrimination provided are concerned with violence against women, which is the case with GR 25 but does not represent the scope of current CERD practice on intersectionality addressed in the present work; see further Chapters 13, 14, and 15, Article 5.

[269] 'Multiple discrimination against women members of descent-based communities', A/57/18, chapter XI. F, section 2.

[270] The recommendation refers to 'multiple discrimination faced by non-citizens, in particular concerning the children and spouses of non-citizen workers', A/59/18, chapter VIII, para. 8.

[271] CERD/C/PRT/CO/12-14, para. 18 (present author's emphasis); see also Iraq, CERD/C/IRQ/CO/15-21, para. 16.

[272] Reporting guidelines for Article 5(d)(vii) explicitly refer to the term.

[273] A/62/18, para. 538.

[274] Comments by the Islamic Republic of Iran on the concluding observations of the Committee, A/58/18, Annex VII.

[275] The usage has become almost standard: see, for example, concluding observations of 2011 in relation to Ireland, CERD/C/CO/34, para. 26; Serbia, CERD/SRB/CO/1, para. 18; and Yemen, CERD/C/YEM/CO/17-18, para. 18, Yemen maintains a reservation to the Article 5(d)(vii) on freedom of thought, conscience, and religion.

[276] Georgia, CERD/C/GEO/CO/3/Add.1, para. 18; Nigeria, CERD/C/NGA/CO/18, para. 14; Tanzania, CERD/C/TZA/CO/16, para. 20. See also para. 6 of GR 35.

[277] CERD/C/ITA/CO/16–18, para. 19.

in concluding observations contrasts with a narrower approach in the communications procedure under Article 14.[278]

VI. Nullifying or Impairing . . . Human Rights and Fundamental Freedoms

Language on nullifying or impairing was present in the *travaux* from the Ivanov/Ketryzinski draft onwards. The pairing of terms appears to open up the prospectus of discrimination, which need not be aimed at or have only nullifying effect on the 'recognition, enjoyment or exercise' of rights and freedoms but only impair them, presumably to some meaningful degree. The notion of impairment brings to mind decisions of the Human Rights Committee on indigenous rights and freedoms whereby not every interference amounts to a breach;[279] on the other hand, Meron speculates whether the making of racial distinctions per se constitutes racial discrimination under ICERD, without the need to demonstrate human rights effects.[280]

The Convention is an 'open' convention in that the prohibition of racial discrimination is not confined to discrimination in relation to a circumscribed list of rights and freedoms—the long list of protected and guaranteed rights in Article 5 is prefaced by the word 'notably'. The wide scope of the definition is confirmed by the *travaux*. Textual anomalies such as the absence of any reference to civil rights in Article 1 (they are included in Article 5) do not appear to have greatly troubled CERD.[281] Practice does not confine the scope of the Convention to any particular class or classes of rights. GR 32 states simply that the list of human rights to which the principle of non-discrimination applies 'is not closed and extends to any field of human rights regulated by the public authorities' in the State party.[282]

The wide sweep of rights covered by the non-discrimination principle is particularly important in relation to bodies of 'ethnic' and related rights that were less developed, or undeveloped, when the Convention was adopted; elaboration of the gender dimensions of racial discrimination has also involved comprehension of the principles of the CEDAW and related standards.[283] According to GR 32, the interpretation of the Convention as a 'living instrument' makes it imperative to read the Convention in a context-sensitive manner, context that includes 'the range of universal human right standards on the principle of non-discrimination and special measures'. The reference to 'universal' does not diminish the ambit of rights to be considered in applying the Convention: minority and indigenous rights and other category rights also apply 'universally'—wherever minorities, indigenous peoples, and other groups are present. The Committee has addressed a full complement of collective rights in its endorsement of the principles of ILO Convention 169 on Indigenous and Tribal Peoples and the UN Declaration on the Rights of Indigenous Peoples, up to and including self-determination.

[278] See Chapter 11 on Article 4.

[279] *Länsman v Finland*, CCPR/C/49/D/511/1992 (1993), para. 9; *Länsman et al. v Finland*, CCPR/C/58/D/671/1995 (1996), para. 10.

[280] Meron, *Meaning and Reach*, 291.

[281] Schwelb, *The International Convention*, 1005, observes that the *travaux* do not make it clear why civil rights were omitted or whether the omission was intentional, and suggests that it may have been an oversight in drafting, the definition having been drafted before the operative provisions had been worked out.

[282] Para. 9: see also Chapter 15.

[283] For a reflection on the background to GR 25, see *Gender Dimensions of Racial Discrimination* (Office of the UN High Commissioner for Human Rights, 2001), pp. 19–22.

VII. On an Equal Footing

In the drafting of the Convention, the phrase 'on an equal footing' was selected without much discussion, replacing a simple reference to 'equality' and a more complex suggestion on 'equality of treatment or opportunity'. References to equality are scattered throughout the text of the Convention, complementing the reference in Article1(1). The preamble refers to the 'dignity and equality' inherent in human beings, who are born 'free and equal' in dignity; equality before the law and equal protection of the law are also mentioned. Article 2(2) describes special measures as designed to guarantee 'the full and equal' enjoyment of human rights and fundamental freedoms, and warns that the measures should not extend to 'the maintenance of unequal or separate rights' after their objectives have been achieved. Article 5 refers to 'equality before the law', 'universal and equal suffrage', 'equal access to public service', 'equal pay for equal work', and 'equal participation in cultural activities'. Meron summarizes the combination of equality references in the Convention as indicating that the Convention 'promotes racial equality, not merely colour-neutral values' and not merely *de jure* but also *de facto* equality.[284] Makkonen reads 'equal footing' to supply the comparative element at the heart of discrimination, emphasizing that what is at stake is not identical treatment but equal treatment which allows for a measure of differential treatment.[285]

GR 14 on Article 1(1) refers to non-discrimination, together with equality before the law and equal protection of the law, as a basic principle in the protection of human rights: 'on an equal footing' is not referred to. GR 32 on special measures includes the banner headline that the objective of the measures is to advance 'effective equality', making the general statement that the concept of equality reflected in the Convention combines formal equality before the law with equal protection of the law, while *de facto* equality in the enjoyment and exercise of human rights is the aim to be achieved by the implementation of its principles.[286] The combination of phrases on equality in GR 32 implies that the Convention is concerned with objectives and outcomes as well as processes. The conclusion is fortified by the reference in Article 1 to 'the recognition, enjoyment or exercise' of human rights, phrasing that implies a commitment to substantive equality beyond the static legal geometry of formal equality.

The attention paid by CERD to the broader formulations of equality has meant that 'on an equal footing' is not overused in practice.[287] GR 32 nonetheless asserts that the principle of enjoyment of human rights on an equal footing 'is integral to the Convention's prohibition of discrimination'.[288] In *L.R. v Slovakia*, in a passage with appears to refer to Article 1, the concept was rephrased as 'on an equal basis'.[289] As applied in concluding observations, the phrase 'on an equal footing' has been drawn upon in sundry connections, including the importance of a good environment to ensure access to education and employment 'on an equal footing';[290] in recommendations to coordinate

[284] Meron, *Meaning and Reach*, 288.
[285] Makkonen, *Equal in Law, Unequal in Fact*, p. 131.
[286] Para. 6; see also Chapter 5.
[287] The precise phrase appears to be rarely used in international instruments—a search of the SIM human rights database found a reference in Article 13.4 of the European Social Charter.
[288] GR 32, para. 7.
[289] Para. 10.7.
[290] CERD/C/LTU/CO/3, para. 21.

federal and provincial programmes to ensure that rights in the Convention are enjoyed 'on an equal footing' throughout the territory of the State party;[291] and—part of the regular repertoire of CERD—to ensure that women can transmit nationality to spouses and children 'on an equal footing' with men.[292] While the interpretation of 'equal footing' is coloured by equality standards throughout the Convention, the phrase is not incompatible with the more expansive notions, in that the achievement of an equality platform strongly suggests positive action on the part of State authorities.

VIII. Any Other Field of Public Life

Article 1 defines discrimination in relation to the 'political, economic, social, cultural or any other field of public life'. According to Banton, the reference to public life was inserted to remove from the scope of the Convention discrimination within private relations.[293] Banton recalls a discussion where the Committee 'appeared to agree' that the effect of the phrase 'was to define the political, economic, social and cultural fields of life as fields of public life and to say that, if any other similar fields were ever recognized, they too would come within the scope of the definition'.[294]

The reference to public life does not sit well with some provisions of the Convention.[295] 'Field' is used in the Convention to define the scope of a provision, without being tagged to 'public life': Article 2(2) refers to special measures in the social, economic, cultural, and other fields; Article 7 addresses the fields of teaching, education, culture, and information. 'Field' and 'public life' are absent from Article 5, which focuses on rights. As used in Article 1(1), the fields of public life are referred to in broad terms so that, according to Diaconu, 'all spheres of public life' are effectively covered by the definition:[296] If an area of discrimination is not caught by one of the named 'fields' it is presumably caught by the reference to 'any other field'. CEDAW employs 'field' in analogous terms, referring to the advancement of women in 'all fields' and particularly in the political, economic, and cultural fields.[297] Fields of activity referred to in international instruments cover a spectrum that includes 'administration of justice' and 'fields relevant to the treatment of persons deprived on their liberty';[298] 'social welfare, financial matters, family law and property rights';[299] 'science, arts and culture', and many others. The use of 'field' in human rights instruments to signify broad institutional and discursive spaces suggests that 'field of public life' should not be viewed narrowly. While the reference to 'public life' suggests a realm of 'private life' which the Convention does not touch, Article 5 protects a wide range of rights from discrimination and is not ostensibly confined to public life.[300]

[291] CERD/C/CAN/CO/19-20, para. 9.
[292] CERD/C/KWT/CO/15-20, para. 18.
[293] Banton, *International Action*, p. 195.
[294] Banton, *International Action*, p. 195.
[295] Schwelb, *The International Convention*, 1004–05.
[296] Diaconu, *Racial Discrimination* (Eleven International Publishing, 2011), p. 32.
[297] Article 3 of CEDAW, see also the preamble.
[298] Optional Protocol to the CAT, Article 5(2).
[299] CPED, Article 24.6.
[300] Including, according to Schwelb, *The International Convention*, 1005–6, 'the right to marriage and choice of spouse, the right to inherit, the right to freedom of thought and conscience as distinct from freedom of expression'.

The *travaux* do not shed much light on the matter, though the sensitivities of some governments regarding the reach of the Convention will be recalled. A proposed general recommendation on public life was discussed by the Committee in 1993, eliciting views in favour of expanding the scope of the Convention towards private conduct, as well as more cautious approaches.[301] Members of the Committee were considerably exercised in the debate by the privatization of public life, and even the 'privatization of apartheid',[302] through exemptions of private bodies from anti-discrimination legislation. A majority agreed that the Convention was not confined to public life in any narrow sense, particularly taking Article 5 into account, and, even if Article 1 had been designed to limit the scope of the Convention, the Committee 'did not necessarily have to maintain that restricted scope'.[303] The failure to adopt a specific recommendation on public and private life has not inhibited the Committee from pronouncing on the issue. The body of CERD general recommendations on public and private life suggest that an expansive reading of Article 1(1) has become commonplace—'public life' was not even mentioned in an explanation of the paragraph in GR 14 on article 1(1).

D. Comment

The Committee has referred to a responsibility to ensure coherence in the interpretation of a constituent instrument not notable for this particular virtue.[304] The search for coherence has focused on the definition of racial discrimination as it has on the *modus operandi* of the Committee and the normative details of the text. Interpretative movement over time is paralleled by movement outwards in geographical space to underscore the potential ubiquity of racial discrimination. The interpretative practice of the Committee on Article 1 has been less 'literal' than all but recent practice on Article 4, and includes innovative terminology on forms of discrimination not specifically accounted for in Article 1.[305]

Partly in response to State denials of racial discrimination, requests for data permeate the CERD archive.[306] The evaluation of certain forms of discrimination—effects or indirect discrimination and, *a fortiori*, structural or institutional discrimination—makes particularly strong demands on the provision of data. CERD's standard line is that effective national policies to implement the Convention are impossible without an adequate database.[307] In the face of advocacy by self-defining groups and multiple

[301] CERD/C/SR.969, paras 19–44.

[302] Comment by Banton, CERD/C/SR.969, para. 21.

[303] Wolfrum, *ibid.*, para. 35. van Boven, *ibid.*, paras 26–7, had noted that the intention in the drafting 'had been to preserve the right to invite or not to invite a certain person into one's home . . . or to allow private clubs to choose their own members . . . However, the concept of "public life" had been interpreted quite widely even during the drafting of the Convention [and] was becoming broader and broader.' See also Diaconu, *ibid.*, para. 29 for a broad view of the scope of the Convention.

[304] *Jewish Community of Oslo v Norway*, CERD/C/67/D/30/2003 (2005), para. 10.3—the observation referred to Article 4 but may be extended to the Convention as a whole.

[305] The Inter-American Convention on Racism, etc, makes explicit reference to forms of discrimination distilled over years of CERD practice, referring in its preamble to 'combating racial discrimination in all its individual, structural, and institutional manifestations'.

[306] States may still be in denial, or even 'firm denial' of the existence of racial discrimination: concluding observations on the Dominican Republic, CERD/C/DOM/CO/13-14, para. 7.

[307] 'No progress can be made in elimination of any problem can be made if there is widespread denial about the existence of that problem': Makkonen, *Equal in Fact, Unequal in Law*, p. 279.

other factors in group recognition, the data questions reflect an ideology of assumed population diversity and ride roughshod over claims of ethnic homogeneity or a local absence of racial discrimination. In cases where levels of racism are apparently low, a standard Committee response is that anti-discrimination measures are needed in order to forestall its emergence. Intimations that the elaboration of data categories stimulates processes of ethnogenesis, or divides nations, have been given short shrift. The determined approach of the Committee in this respect may not adequately account for the variety of situations under review, bearing in mind that categorizations construct as well as respond to situations. It is also the case that racially focused discrimination weighs less heavily on some societies than on others. Banton recalls that equality concepts should be applied, *mutatis mutandis*, to States as well as persons and groups: equality does not require identical treatment, and 'it is necessary to recognize that some States face much greater challenges than others with respect to racial discrimination'.[308]

While practice does not prioritize particular data-collection methodologies, CERD has commented on census deficiencies, suggesting additional or better questions.[309] The task is to find quantitative and qualitative approaches that respect principles of consent, anonymity, and privacy and, when ethnic questions are constitutionally forbidden, to search for creative means of presenting an accurate demographic picture. Data collection based on the voluntary principle and self-ascription is distinguishable from the imposition of categorizations: compulsory registration of ethnicity or religion in public documents such as identity cards and passports is objectionable.[310] Bell notes that, in some cases, data carry the risk of reinforcing negative stereotypes; if crime statistics show an over-representation of ethnic groups in the criminal justice system, this may reinforce prejudices about a 'supposed criminal proclivity'[311] and lead to under-reporting when individuals decline to identify their ethnic affiliation—he cites the Roma as a case in point.[312] The problem of 'naming names' is adverted to in GR 35 on racist hate speech: 'Media should avoid referring unnecessarily to race, ethnicity, religion and other group characteristics in a manner that may promote intolerance.'[313]

The flexibility of the basic notion of 'discrimination' is a given in CERD practice—geared to unfair or unjust distinctions based on defined grounds; the concept does not demand uniform treatment irrespective of circumstances. Prominent markers referred to in GR 32 for appraising the permissibility of distinctions include the 'objectives and purposes of the Convention', their 'legitimate aim', 'proportionality', and whether there is any 'objective and reasonable justification' for differentiation.[314] Further, 'the principle of non-discrimination requires that the cultural characteristics of groups be taken into

308 Banton, *International Action*, p. 316.

309 As examples, Guatemala was recommended to 'continue to upgrade the methodology' to be used in a forthcoming census, CERD/C/GTM/CO/12-13, para. 6; Mauritania was recommended to carry out a more precise census, not limited to linguistic factors, CERD/C/65/CO/5, para. 9; Romania was recommended to improve its data collection methods, CERD/C/ROU/CO/16-19, para. 8.

310 In the application of such principles in Northern Ireland, self-definition may have functioned in tension with the data demands of equality legislation: De Schutter, *International Human Rights Law*, pp. 678–80.

311 M. Bell, *Racism and Equality*, p. 39.

312 *Ibid.*

313 GR 35, para. 40. See also para. 3 of GR 27 with regard to the Roma.

314 See also *Advisory Opinion of the Inter-American Court of Human Rights on Proposed Amendments to the Naturalization Provisions of the Constitution of Costa Rica*, IACtHR Ser. A No. 4 (1984), para. 57.

consideration'[315] in order to avoid discrimination through or in association with policies of integration or development,[316] or nation-building.[317] By extension, failure to treat differently persons whose situations are significantly different is inconsistent with the Convention: the corollary concept of an 'obligation to differentiate' also resonates with practice.[318] CERD has not unpacked all markers of acceptable differentiation, nor integrated them into a schematic model of review after the fashion of the European Court of Human Rights,[319] or analogous to that outlined by scholars such as Henrard,[320] though elements of such review surface naturally in various contexts, even in the absence of a rigid scheme. Judgements on the permissibility of distinctions are not rendered in terms of 'justifying' discrimination but in assessments as to whether or not discrimination has occurred in the first place.[321] Terms such as 'fair', 'positive', or 'arbitrary' discrimination have been greeted with puzzlement mixed with doubts as to their conformity with the Convention.[322] National usage may be at odds with Convention practice in that CERD treats discrimination as a legal conclusion on a human rights-denying practice, untrammelled by mollifying adjectives.

Assessing the presence of discrimination in the wider human rights framework implies that differentiation on the basis of, for example, minority or indigenous status is legitimate.

315 Para. 8.

316 Concluding observations on Namibia, CERD/C/NAM/CO/12, para. 24; Honduras, CERD/C/HND/CO/1-5, para. 7, where the Committee expressed a preference for 'identity-based development programmes'.

317 CERD/C/BWA/CO/16, para. 9, where the Committee linked this principle to the reluctance of the State party to recognize the existence of indigenous peoples on its territory.

318 The principle expressed by the European Court of Human Rights in *Thlimmenos v Greece* may be recalled: 'the right... not to be discriminated against in the enjoyment of... rights... is violated when States treat differently persons in analogous situations without providing an objective and reasonable justification... The right not to be discriminated against... is also violated when States without an objective and reasonable justification fail to treat differently persons whose situations are significantly different': App No 34369/97, European Court of Human Rights, Judgment of the Grand Chamber, 6 April 2000, para. 44. See also the *Belgian Linguistics Case*, 1 YBECHR 832, para. 44. See also information submitted to CERD by Thailand, referring to a draft bill on discrimination (gender and sexual orientation), defining discrimination in part as 'an action or failure to act to differentiate among': CERD/C/THA/CO/1-3/Add.1, para. 4.

319 'The Court reiterates that a difference in treatment is discriminatory if "it has no reasonable and objective justification", that is, if it does not pursue a "legitimate aim" or if there is not a reasonable relationship of proportionality between the means employed and the aim sought to be realised': *D.H. and Others v Czech Republic*, para. 196; see also, *ibid.*, para. 175. Among other authorities, see *Larkos v Cyprus*, App No 29515/95, 30 EHRR 597, para. 29.

320 K. Henrard, 'Non-Discrimination and Full and Effective Equality', in M. Weller (ed.), *Universal Minority Rights* (Oxford University Press, 2007), pp. 75–147, pp. 89–90 [henceforth *Non-Discrimination and Full and Effective Equality*]; the scheme asks (1) whether there is a differentiation that merits a justification test, or in other words is there a prima facie case of discrimination; (2) whether the differential treatment amounts to a prohibited discrimination or not: (1) is designated the review hurdle, and (2) the justification phase.

321 The Inter-American Convention on Racism, while not elucidating direct discrimination, refers to the possibility of justifying indirect discrimination, where a 'provision, criterion or practice has some reasonable and legitimate justification under international human rights law', a formulation that opens out the Convention to other sources of principle. While referring to 'unjustifiable disparate impact', the Committee has not elaborated a dichotomous regime of justifications for intentional/effects, direct/indirect discrimination, though in principle justification possibilities are wider for the latter pairings in light of the fact that they may result from policies and practices with benign motivations. See also the helpful discussion: 'Justifying direct discrimination?' in Fredman, *Discrimination Law*, pp. 196–202.

322 See remarks of Aboul-Nasr, Sicilianos, and Thornberry in discussions on the report of South Africa: CERD/C/SR.1367, paras 14, 25, and 27; regarding 'fair' discrimination, Aboul-Nasr (para. 14) asked: 'Surely discrimination could never be fair, whatever form it took?' regarding Chilean legislation on 'arbitrary discrimination', see CERD/C/CHL/CO/19-21, para. 9.

Even in this case, the non-discrimination principle has a role in appraising the treatment accorded to some groups compared with others, and the corresponding detriments. The Committee has interrogated distinctions made in domestic legislation between 'national minorities' and 'ethnic groups'.[323] Such patterns of distinction may be particularly complex in view of the widespread adoption of the term 'national minority' by European international instruments and domestic law. In the case of Austria, concern was expressed regarding the distinction between autochthonous minorities and other minority groups, as well as differentiation on the basis of historical settlement areas—distinctions that might lead to 'unjustified differential treatment'.[324] The categorization by a State of groups as autochthonous or national minorities has been accepted by the Committee as a legitimate exercise of sovereignty, but may raise concerns that distinctions between the rights recognised for some groups and not others are exaggerated and potentially discriminatory.

Because of the inclusion of 'discrimination in effect' in Article 1(1), the Committee has not been required to struggle to accommodate extended meanings in its interpretative practice: 'indirect' discrimination flows naturally from the 'purpose or effect' provision in the definition.[325] Equally, the Committee has taken the Convention to support 'positive action' as flowing from the reading of discrimination as linked to real world circumstances of individuals and groups, from insistence on the effective implementation in practice of obligations, including the action-oriented demands made by Article 2(1)(d), the express provisions on special measures, and the obligation to criminalize certain forms of conduct in Article 4.

Regarding the grounds of discrimination, CERD has also not been compelled to theorize the conceptual matrix that holds them together, whether as immutable or innate characteristics, characteristics over which there is no choice or control, marginalization, relative disadvantage, historical disadvantage, etc. While the grounds may present a logic in terms of characteristics, choice, marginalization, and oppression, they are better understood as a foreseeable product of the history and context of the Convention project—despite lengthy arguments over inclusions and exclusions, the emergence of a core of closely related grounds was a predictable consequence of the drafting process. The list of individual grounds suggests the overlapping or *pari materia* nature of the elements in Article 1(1) and their rough equality of importance. There has been little effort to distinguish between the different grounds in Article 1 to judge whether some are more amenable to 'differentiation' than others, nor to postulate a 'hierarchy' among them.[326] The definition refers to action 'based on' prohibited grounds: it does not descend into detail on how to assess the processes of deliberation of perpetrators, or the causes of action, though it has made clear that race/ethnicity need not be their sole ground. In practice it appears to be enough that the 'ground' makes a significant or not negligible contribution

[323] Examples include observations on Lithuania, CERD/C/LTU/CO/3, para. 9; and Slovenia, CERD/C/62/CO/9, para. 7.

[324] CERD/C/AUT/CO/17, para. 10.

[325] While the pairing of 'purpose or effect' suggests an obvious contrast, discrimination in 'effect' taken alone, as in ILO Convention 111, could logically include purposive and non-purposive action.

[326] The formulation of a hierarchy of standards of review from 'rationality review' to 'strict scrutiny' has not governed the implementation of the Convention: the diverse grounds are subsumed under 'racial discrimination'; De Schutter, *International Human Rights Law*, pp. 611–12, offers a succinct discussion of issues.

to the prohibited action, bearing in mind that discriminatory actions may result from a complex of factors, not all of which are legally relevant.[327]

Among the grounds, 'race' has given rise to practical difficulties with States parties and is potentially a poisoned chalice. In a broad reading of the *travaux*, Keane comments on 'the near unquestioning acceptance of the term by the delegates who drafted ICERD at all levels'.[328] The opportunity to side-step the race question provided by the configuration of the definition means that the Committee has not devoted much attention to unpacking race. The notion of a 'ground' as referring to reasons for discrimination does not commit to acceptance of the reality of imagined 'races', existing in the minds of those who discriminate.[329] Taken all together, the elements of ICERD do not, however, provide the strongest basis for such a repudiation. The preamble refers to 'racial barriers', and to 'understanding between races'; Articles 1(4) and 2(2) refer to rights 'for different racial groups'; Article 2(1) refers to promoting understanding 'among all races' and restates opposition to 'racial barriers'; while Article 7 refers to promoting friendship 'among . . . racial . . . groups'. References to race throughout the Convention should not necessarily be taken as an endorsement of a theory of separate human races. The text ranges itself against those who believe in races, or act as if they entertained such a belief. While the Convention is explicitly directed against 'racial superiority' rather than 'racial differentiation', its thoroughgoing condemnation of racist doctrines serves to discredit the notion of race itself.

Norway's 'disclaimer' regarding the use of 'race', discussed earlier, is echoed elsewhere. CESCR GC 20 states that the 'use of the term "race" in the Covenant or the present General Comment does not imply the acceptance of theories which attempt to determine the existence of separate human races'.[330] EU Directive 2000/43 forbidding discrimination on the grounds of 'racial or ethnic origin', the preamble to which declares that the European Union rejects theories which attempt to determine the existence of separate human races, so that the use of the term 'racial origin' in the Directive 'does not imply an acceptance of such theories'.[331] As to whether CERD should present a similar disclaimer, avoiding mention of race is not guaranteed to lighten the task of combating racist activity. CERD has been principally concerned by the legal and practical lacunae potentially caused by omitting race from domestic legislation and substituting it with references to ethnicity, where racial perceptions are addressed only indirectly, or by focusing on

[327] Arguments are characteristically put forward in cases of 'direct' discrimination. In UK law, *see R. v Birmingham City Council ex parte Equal opportunities Commission* [1989] AC 1155 (House of Lords); *James v Eastleigh BC* [1990] 2 AC 751 (House of Lords)—the 'but for' test; *R (on the application* of *E) v Governing Body of JFS and the Admissions Appeal Panel of JFS* [2009] UKSC 15.

[328] *Caste-Based Discrimination in International Law*, p. 178.

[329] See comments on discrimination on account of 'actual or perceived ethnicity' in *Timishev v Russia*, [2007] 44 EHRR 37, para. 56.

[330] Para. 19.

[331] Council Directive (EC) 2000/43 implementing the principle of equal treatment between persons irrespective of racial or ethnic origin [2000] OJ L180/22. The European Parliament decided in 1996 that the term 'race' 'should . . . be avoided in all official texts': resolution on the communication from the omission on racism, xenophobia and anti-Semitism, cited in Bell, *Racism and Equality*, p. 13, n. 50. GR 7 of the European Commission against Racism and Intolerance (ECRI) includes a footnote 1 to the effect that ECRI rejects theories based on the existence of different races but uses the term 'in order to ensure that those who are generally and erroneously perceived as belonging to "another race" are not excluded' from legislative protection: <http://www.coe.int/t/dghl/monitoring/ecri/activities/GPR/EN/Recommendation_N7/Recommendation_7_en.asp>.

'extremism' which may or may not signify a racial/ethnic content. The treatment of race as a social construct rather than a biological substratum does not appreciably weaken its power to generate discrimination.[332]

Recommendations to incorporate into domestic law all the grounds of discrimination in Article 1(1) apply also to 'colour'. While discrimination on the ground of colour is to be legislated against, the Committee has criticized the use of the term 'visible minorities' in legislation, on the ground that it could imply that 'whiteness' is the standard of 'normality' in the State concerned.[333] Albinism is a troubling contemporary issue that challenges the scope of 'colour' discrimination, and descent-based discrimination. While in this case 'colour' is not a proxy for race/ethnicity, people living with albinism, and suffering from stigma, social exclusion, and discrimination face 'a similar experience to . . . vulnerable racial minorities' because of their different skin colour.[334]

The listing of national and ethnic origin among the grounds has, despite the ambiguities attaching to 'national', facilitated the shift in focus from race and colour to ethnicity, and ethnic minorities in particular—Vandenhole observes that CERD treats discrimination against minorities as a specific theme, 'regardless of which prohibited grounds are involved'.[335] Nonetheless, the substantive Convention basis for this ethnicization of discrimination is extensive: 'ethnic origin' is referred to in the preamble and Articles 1, 4, and 5, while Article 7 refers to 'ethnical groups', to which it may be recalled that the dominant application of 'national origin' in the Convention relates to ethnicity rather than citizenship. In light of the practical emphasis on self-identification, the focus on ethnicity need not imply a reification of cultures, and works against cultural determinism, where persons are assigned membership irrespective of their consent.[336] As noted earlier,[337] translated into the vocabulary of racism, ICERD is significantly and even predominantly concerned with cultural or difference racism: 'racial discrimination' subsumes and transcends 'race'.

GR 29 endeavours to give shape to 'descent' as a ground of discrimination. The *travaux* refer to the claim that descent was intended to cover uncertainties over 'national origin'—a proposition restated by India in opposing the application of ICERD to caste-based discrimination. While this suggests a connection between 'nationality' in the ethnic/cultural sense and descent, this does not rule out a distinct space for 'descent' among the

[332] According to CERD member Kut in discussing a report of Sweden, CERD/C/SR.2251, para. 6: 'Although the concept of race was a social construct, that was precisely why it should form part of the legal framework to combat racism.'

[333] Concluding observations on Canada, CERD/CAN/CO/18, para. 13; CERD/C/SR.1790, para. 50 (Thornberry). The term is used on the nineteenth and twentieth report of Canada in relation to South Asians, Chinese, and Blacks: CERD/C/CAN/19-20, para. 22, and explained and defended, *ibid.*, in paras 41–43.

[334] UN Independent Expert on Minority issues, cited in *Persons with Albinism, Report of the Office of the High Commissioner for Human Rights*, A/HRC/24/57, 12 September 2013, para. 81. Other paragraphs of the report reflect on the relationship between albinism and disability (para. 78), and persons with albinism as a distinct group requiring specific attention (para. 83). See also African Commission on Human and Peoples' Rights, *Resolution on the Prevention of Attacks and Discrimination against Persons with Albinism*, 5 November 2013: <http://www.achpr.org/sessions/54th/resolutions/263/>. In March 2015, the Human Rights Council appointed an independent expert on the enjoyment of human rights by persons with albinism: A/HRC/RES/28/6.

[335] Vandenhole, *Non-Discrimination and Equality*, p. 95.

[336] In this last respect, CERD aligns the Convention with the principle of non-compulsion expressed in Article 3 of the UNDM and the Council of Europe's Framework Convention on the Protection of National Minorities, respectively.

[337] Chapter 5.

grounds. The formulation adopted by the Committee in GR 29 on descent-based discrimination includes the notion of inheritance, which places 'descent' in line with other grounds. The caste examples offered by India in the drafting of the Convention under the rubric of 'special measures' do not save caste from the application of the Convention: it is an unsustainable reading of ICERD that such groups are covered by provisions on special measures but are not within the definition in Article 1(1). The problem of caste in ICERD illustrates the more general problem of including the incorrigible variety of local institutions under a cosmopolitan rubric in the face of claims by States parties that cultures, institutions, or countries are 'unique'. In some cases, CERD has linked 'caste' with the situation of certain ethnic groups;[338] this should not be taken as a lack of confidence in the usefulness of the criterion of 'descent' but as recognizing a reality that the incidence of caste/descent-based discrimination may be local or intra-communal as well as national.

The listing of grounds in Article 1(1) has not unduly inhibited the discovery of fresh permutations of racial discrimination, bearing in mind the varying degrees of racialization of physical and cultural characteristics in contemporary societies.[339] Questions of minority and indigenous languages have been extensively addressed by the Committee, particularly in connection with Articles 5 and 7. The accounting of language as an independent ground of discrimination may be described as flowing from the ground of ethnic origin,[340] while gender has effectively been added to the list of grounds in a crystallization of the 'intersection' metaphor.[341] Among possible intersections, disability and sexual orientation have engaged the attention of the Committee only to a minor extent, a situation that is liable to change.[342] The intersectionality concept is objected to by the Holy See, highlighting in particular its use in relation to gender.[343]

[338] Concluding observations on Burkina Faso, CERD/C/BFA/CO/12-19, para. 8; Ethiopia, CERD/C/ETH/CO/7-16, para. 15.

[339] Bell, *Racism and Equality*, p. 9.

[340] In concluding observations on Mauritius, CERD recommended, in accordance with the Convention, adding language as a protected ground under the equal opportunities act: CERD/C/MUS/CO/15-19, para. 10.

[341] The Committee has insisted that race/ethnicity need not be the 'sole' ground of discrimination, and that municipal law provisions that insist it should be in order to engage the legislation are incorrect: Concluding observations on Austria, CERD/C/60/CO/1, para. 9. This opens out the concept to accommodate discrimination based simultaneously on a number of factors. In such cases, the author reads Committee sentiment to the effect that the race/ethnic element must be a 'substantial' or 'significant' contributor to the discrimination experienced. Compare the view of ECRI: for racism to have taken place, 'it is not necessary that one or more of the grounds . . . should constitute the only factor or the determining factor . . . it suffices that these grounds are among the factors leading to contempt or the notion of superiority': Explanatory Memorandum to *General Policy Recommendation No. 7 on National Legislation to Combat Racism and Racial Discrimination* (13 December 2002), para. 7.

[342] With regard to sexual orientation, see concluding observations on the Czech Republic, CERD/C/CZE/CO/7, para. 18; on LGBTI issues, concluding observations on Germany, CERD/C/DEU/CO/19-22, para. 16; The Netherlands, CERD/C/NLD/CO/19-21, para. 34, recommendation to take measures regarding LGBTI persons among asylum-seekers. Issues regarding disability have tended to emerge in connection with so-called special schools for children with mental disabilities to which Roma children are assigned rather than in terms of an intersection with race/ethnicity to create a new subject of discrimination: see for example concluding observations on Slovakia, CERD/C/SVK/CO/6-8, para. 16. Cf. Para. 57 of the Durban Programme of Action regarding the situation of persons with disabilities who are also subjected to racism, etc.

[343] Specific objection is taken to para. 7 of GR 32, which refers to intersectionality on grounds of gender and religion, and ostensibly *in toto* to GR 25 on gender dimensions of racial discrimination: 'the terms "gender" and intersectionality" are not found in the Convention . . . Moreover, the topic of women is addressed in a separate and distinct international instrument . . . the Convention on the Elimination of All Forms of Discrimination

In light of the drafting history of the Convention and occasional objections from States parties, the race/religion crossover has been cautiously treated. While the Committee refers to the intersectionality of racial/ethnic and religious discrimination, the metaphor does not always work well, in that, in many instances, ethnicity and religion cannot be differentiated with any certainty and are, on the contrary, effectively 'fused'. The Committee has used the uncomfortable term 'ethno-religious' to describe some such instances, though many indigenous groups exhibit similar characteristics, even if the term 'ethno-religious' is not applied to them. In other instances, there may be different perceptions as to the respective 'weight' of cultural and religious factors in constituting identity.[344] The structure of the Convention mandates the Committee to appraise evidence of discrimination against freedom of thought conscience and religion on ethnic/racial grounds—an inherently complex exercise capable of generating conceptual bewilderment.[345]

Discussions on the limitation to 'public life' in the definition have elicited a range of commentary. Makkonen suggests that 'public life' might 'simply convey the idea that whenever a country provides for a particular right, then that right comes within the purview of "public life" for that particular country'.[346] Ruggie comments that it is unclear 'how much the mention of "public life" in article 1 limits the scope of application of the Convention . . . references to public life have practically disappeared in opinions on communications and concluding observations, confirming the expansion of the Convention's reach and application'.[347] He suggests that, in practice, 'priority is given to acts of a public nature or acts that take place in the public sphere, and to private actors that perform a public role',[348] while noting also that the Committee has stressed that the public sphere is, indeed, the central focus of the Convention',[349] a comment that echoes views expressed in the communication procedure under Article 14.[350]

With regard to the public and private realms, discussions do not always distinguish two overlapping aspects: State responsibility for private actors with a public role, and the extent of permissible intervention in family and interpersonal relations. On the first issue, key provisions of the Convention address the activities of private actors, including Article 2 explicitly, Article 3 as interpreted by the Committee regarding segregation,[351] Article 4 on hate speech and racist organizations, and Article 5. The Convention holds States

against Women': CERD/C/VAT/16-23 (4 September 2014), para. 5. The results of the examination by the Committee of the report of the Holy See are discussed in Chapter 20.

344 See Chapters 11 and 13.

345 See Chapter 13.

346 T. Makkonen, *Equal in Law, Unequal in Fact*, p. 141.

347 Special Representative of the Secretary-General on Human Rights and Transnational Corporations and Other Business Enterprises, *Mapping State obligations for corporate acts: An examination of the UN Human Rights treaty system*, Report No. 1, International Convention on the Elimination of All Forms of Racial Discrimination, 18 December 2006, para. 12: <http://www.business-humanrights.org/Documents/State-Obligations-Corporate-Acts-CERD-18-Dec-2006.pdf>. Some recent concluding observations appear to bear out Ruggie's perceptions: Algeria, CERD/C/DZA/CO/15-19, para. 11, recommendation for a definition of discrimination 'that applies to all areas of public and private life'; Uzbekistan, CERD/C/UZB/CO/6-7, para. 7 (recommendation for a definition of discrimination 'covering all fields of public and private life').

348 *Ibid.*, para. 93.

349 *Ibid.*, para. 94.

350 See *Gelle v Denmark*, CERD/C/68/D/34/2004 (2006), para. 6.5, and *Quereshi v Denmark*, CERD/C/66/D/33/2003 (2005), para. 6.3, for remarks on the public arena as the central focus of the Convention.

351 Segregation 'which can also arise without any initiative or direct involvement by the public authorities': GR 19, para. 4, discussed in Chapter 10.

responsible for discriminatory activities carried out by 'any persons, group and organization'.[352] Beyond this template, rights to privacy and family life presumptively limit the reach of the Convention and the obligation of the State to regulate private conduct, so that legitimate questions may be asked about the desirability of carrying the principle of racial non-discrimination into the interstices of interpersonal or family relations.[353] The interrogation of endogamous cultural relations and traditions where the Committee has insisted on its application raises analogous questions, especially in light of the principle of self-determination.[354] Practice does, however, delve further into some areas of social relations compared with others.[355] If the central case of CEDAW is the effective promotion of social transformation down to the level of interpersonal relations, and that of ICERD the recognition of multiple groups within States and the regulation of the space they occupy, this has not ruled out 'intrusion' into cultural space to safeguard the rights of women. GR 25 on gender-related dimensions of racial discrimination of racial discrimination includes reference to (paragraph 2) 'discrimination against women in private spheres of life'. The Convention does not, however, delineate the private from the public with any degree of precision, and Henrard appears substantially correct in suggesting that it 'does not impose such positive obligation to prevent and eradicate private discrimination in a comprehensive way that would reach every interaction between private persons'.[356] In sum, practice under the Convention addresses 'private actors' more substantially than it does 'private life'.

[352] Article 2(1)(d).

[353] See the comment on *Nahlik v Austria*, CCPR/C/57/D/608/1995 (1996), para. 8.2 of which refers to discrimination in the 'quasi-public sphere', in Joseph *et al.*, *The International Covenant on Civil and Political Rights*, p. 734: 'Whilst the Covenant requires regulation of private sector discrimination in "quasi-public" arenas such as employment, housing, or access to publicly available goods and services, it may not require regulation within the "totally private" or personal sphere, such as the home or within the family or other private relationships... how could a State meaningfully regulate instances of parental disapproval over the race of a child's spouse?... the totally private sphere is perhaps best addressed by educational measures, rather than by coercive laws.' See also the Explanatory report to Protocol 12 of the European Convention on Human Rights, para. 26: States parties may not, under the pretext of protecting from discrimination, commit disproportionate interferences with the right to respect for private or family life'. De Schutter, *International Human Rights Law*, p. 614, distinguishes between 'interactions between private individuals in the context of market relationships, where non-discrimination law may intervene, and interactions in the "sphere of intimacy" of private and family life, where it should not'.

[354] The Human Rights Committee narrowed the gap between ethnicity and family life in *Hopu and Bessert v France*, CCPR/C/60/D/549/1993/Rev.1 (1997), where the construction of a hotel complex in Tahiti that threatened to destroy ancestral burial grounds was treated as a violation of the rights of the authors of the communication to family and privacy—their relationship to ancestors was considered an essential element in their identity. A dissenting opinion by Committee members Kretzmer and Buergenthal, joined by others, criticized the blurring of the line between family, privacy, and ethnicity, insisting, *inter alia*, that 'family' however extended 'does not include all members of one's ethnic or cultural group'.

[355] For comment on the gendered nature of the public/private divide, see S. Mullally, 'The UN, Minority Rights and Gender Equality: Setting Limits to Collective Claims', *IJMGR* 14 (2007), 263–83.

[356] Henrard, 'Non-Discrimination and Full and Effective Equality', p. 143.

7. Article 1, Paragraphs 2 and 3

Discrimination and Non-Citizens

2. This Convention shall not apply to distinctions, exclusions, restrictions or preferences made by a State Party to this Convention between citizens and non-citizens.

3. Nothing in this Convention may be interpreted as affecting in any way the legal provisions of States Parties concerning nationality, citizenship or naturalization, provided that such provisions do not discriminate against any particular nationality.

A. Introduction

The definition of discrimination in the International Convention on the Elimination of All Forms of Racial Discrimination (ICERD) appears to be significantly narrowed by the above paragraphs which, like Article 1(1), apply to the Convention as a whole. The potential limitation of the scope of the Convention as a consequence of Article 1(2) is particularly striking. The entitlements of 'everyone' or 'all persons' to enjoy human rights are set out in the core human rights texts from the Universal Declaration of Human Rights (UDHR) onwards. Taken at face value, the language of the two paragraphs appears to undermine the universalist ambition of the text, the progenitors of which include the UDHR. The 'non-citizens' in Article 1(2) will in most migration cases possess the citizenship of a State other than the State party whose conduct is under scrutiny by the Committee; in other cases the 'non-citizens' will be so in the sense of statelessness or 'undetermined citizenship'.[1]

In general terms and as befitting the character of human rights as rights decoupled from the possession of citizenship, Weissbrodt reminds us that the 'architecture of international human rights law is built on the premise that all persons, by virtue of their essential humanity, should equally enjoy all human rights'.[2] The principle that human rights apply to all, irrespective of citizenship, is emphasized by the Human Rights Committee in an observation that reflects the ethics of human rights more generally:

> In general, the rights set forth in the Covenant apply to everyone, irrespective of reciprocity, and irrespective of his or her nationality or statelessness ... Thus, the general rule is that each one of the rights of the Covenant must be guaranteed without discrimination between citizens and aliens. Aliens receive the benefit of the general requirement of non-discrimination in respect of the rights ... in the Covenant.[3]

[1] For use of the phrase, see concluding observations on Estonia, CERD/C/EST/CO/8-9, para. 15. For analogous indeterminacies, including the problem of 'the erased', see concluding observations on Slovenia, CERD/C/62/CO/9, para. 13, CERD/C/SVN/CO/7, para. 13; CERD/C/SVN/CO/8-11, paras 12 and 13.

[2] D. Weissbrodt, *The Human Rights of Non-Citizens* (Oxford University Press, 2008), p. 34.

[3] Human Rights Committee General Comment (GC) 15, *The Position of Aliens under the Covenant*, paras 1 and 2.

The universality of the human rights canon does not necessarily supply adequate detail or signpost practical solutions to a host of problems affecting non-citizens. A sizeable corpus of standards is clustered around sundry categories of non-citizen, including stateless persons,[4] asylum seekers and refugees,[5] migrants,[6] and trafficked persons,[7] while the Declaration on the Human Rights of Individuals who are Not Nationals of the Country in Which They Live is the general UN instrument in this field.[8] The range and scope of international instruments on the non-citizen categories suggests that, in addition to practical human rights handicaps based on legal status, non-citizens are likely to experience oppression resulting from racist and xenophobic attitudes and practices. Following the references to xenophobia in the Vienna Declaration and Programme of Action,[9] the Durban Declaration of 2001 recognizes that xenophobia against non-nationals, particularly migrants, refugees, and asylum-seekers, constituted one of the main sources of contemporary racism;[10] the Outcome Document of 2009 urges States to combat the persistence of xenophobic attitudes towards and negative stereotyping of non-citizens.[11] The oppressive realities behind the Durban statements are well recognized in the Committee on the Elimination of Racial Discrimination (CERD) practice, motivating it to adopt two general recommendations (GRs) on non-citizens: GR 11 in 1993,[12] and GR 30 in 2004,[13] in addition to GR 22 on Article 5 and Refugees, opinions under Article 14 and copious individual decisions and recommendations.

The rights of citizens and non-citizens are not expressed as fully congruent in the major international human rights instruments. The International Covenant on Civil and Political Rights (ICCPR) recognizes distinctions between citizens and non-citizens with respect to political rights,[14] freedom of movement,[15] and expulsion.[16] The limited exception to the non-discrimination provisions in Article 2(3) of the International Covenant-on Economic, Social and Cultural Rights (ICESCR) with regard to economic

[4] Convention relating to the Status of Stateless Persons 1954; Convention on the Reduction of Statelessness 1961. Chapter 4 of Weissbrodt, *The Human Rights of Non-Citizens*, canvasses a wide range of instruments relevant to statelessness.

[5] Notably the 1951 Convention relating to the Status of Refugees: see *infra* on GR 22.

[6] The CMW.

[7] Weissbrodt, *The Human Rights of Non-Citizens*, Chapter 9, 'Trafficked Persons'.

[8] Adopted by General Assembly resolution 40/144, 13 December 1985, the preamble to which recites general provisions on equality and, *inter alia*, recognizes 'that the protection of human rights and fundamental freedoms provided for in international instruments should also be ensured for individuals who are not nationals of the country in which they live'.

[9] A/CONF.157/23, paras 15 and 30 in the first chapter; paras 19–24 of the second.

[10] Para. 16, the particular recital is recalled in the preamble to CERD GR 30.

[11] Para. 76.

[12] A/48/18, Annex VIII B.

[13] A/59/18, chapter VIII.

[14] Article 25, rights to participate in public affairs, to vote and hold office, and to have access to public service.

[15] Article 12.

[16] Article 13, applying only to aliens. The general rule of application to all persons is set out in detail in GC 15 of the Human Rights Committee, *The Position of Aliens under the Covenant*, HRI/GEN/1/Rev.9 (Vol. I), pp. 189–91. GC 31, *The Nature of the General Legal Obligation Imposed on States parties to the Covenant*, *ibid.*, pp. 243–7, provides that 'the enjoyment of Covenant rights is not limited to citizens of States parties but must also be available to all individuals, regardless of nationality or statelessness, such as asylum-seekers, refugees, migrant workers and other persons, who may find themselves in the territory or subject to the jurisdiction of the State party. This principle also applies to those within the power or effective control of the forces of a State party acting outside its territory': for reflection on extraterritoriality in the context of ICERD, see the commentary on Article 2 in the present work.

rights may also be borne in mind,[17] even if there is no agreed account of what rights should be listed as 'economic'.[18] Distinctions between citizens and non-citizens in the enjoyment of human rights, and distinctions among non-citizens, may, therefore, be contemplated in particular circumstances. In this perspective, the human rights canon is a *lex imperfecta*, incompletely emancipated from associations with nationality and citizenship. The possession of nationality thereby assumes greater importance than it ought to as a facilitator of equitable treatment. In view of the links between lack of citizenship status and racism, it is appropriate that the International Convention on the Elimination of All Forms of Racial Discrimination (ICERD) lists the right to nationality as among the rights benefiting from the equal treatment and non-discrimination guarantees of Article 5.[19]

B. *Travaux Préparatoires*

The Sub-Commission's draft Convention included an article—VIII—relating to the interpretation of the Convention; the first version, submitted by Calvocoressi and Capotorti, included the provision that nothing in the Convention 'shall be interpreted as implying a grant of equal political rights to nationals of a contracting State or a grant of political rights to a distinct racial, ethnic or national group as such'.[20] The minorities element was attached to a provision regarding non-citizens in a draft by Cuevas Cancino:

> Nothing in this Convention shall be interpreted as implying positive obligations . . . [for States parties] . . . to grant a specific political or social status to aliens in their territory. It shall not be interpreted as a grant of political rights to racial, ethnic or national groups as such, if such a grant might destroy, in whole or in part, the national unity or territorial integrity of a State party.[21]

After further drafts,[22] the Chairman proposed a new text:

> Nothing in the present Convention may be interpreted as implicitly recognizing or denying political rights or obligations to non-nationals nor to groups of persons of a common race, colour, ethnic or national origin which exist or may exist as distinct groups within a State party.[23]

In discussions, 'political rights' was expanded to 'political or other rights', and the reference to 'or obligations' was dropped.[24] The amended text was submitted to the Commission and

[17] 'Developing countries, with due regard to human rights and their national economy, may determine to what extent they would guarantee the economic rights recognized in the present covenant to non-nationals.' Para. 30 CESCR GC 20, which states that 'nationality should not bar access to Covenant rights . . . the . . . rights apply to everyone including non-nationals', stresses that this is without prejudice to Article 2(3). Weissbrodt comments on Article 2(3) that, as 'an exception to the rule of equality, article 2(3) must be narrowly construed, may be relied upon only be developing countries, and only with respect to economic rights. States may not draw distinctions between citizens and non-citizens as to social and cultural rights': Weissbrodt, *The Human Rights of Non-Citizens*, p. 49.

[18] Thus, with regard to the right to education, GC 11 of the CESCR, para. 2, observes that 'the right to education . . . has been variously classified as an economic, rights, a social right and a cultural right. It is all of these'.

[19] Article 5(d)(iii).

[20] E/CN.4/Sub.2/L.340.

[21] E/CN.4/Sub.2/L.347.

[22] Including a text by Krishnaswami and Mudawi, E/CN.4/Sub.2./L.348.

[23] E/CN.4/Sub.2/L.349.

[24] E/CN.4/873, para. 109; voting is recalled, *ibid.*, para. 111.

discussed in a series of meetings.[25] Following suggestions for amendments, the representatives of France, India, and The Philippines proposed to replace the Sub-Commission's text by the following:

Nothing in the present Convention may be interpreted as affecting in any way the distinction between nationals and non-nationals of a State, as recognized by international law, in the enjoyment of political or other rights, or as amending provisions governing the exercise of political or other rights by naturalized persons; nor does anything in this Convention impose a duty to grant special political or other rights to any groups of persons because of race, colour or ethnic origin.[26]

In the event, India and The Philippines withdrew their sponsorship of the proposal; France stated that it would be willing to withdraw the amendment if the Commission reverted to the consideration of 'national origin' and deleted that reference from Article 1.[27] In complex discussions, the US proposed the deletion of the reference to 'international law', 'since no rule of international law specifically covered the question of the distinction between nationals and non-nationals concerning political and particularly other rights'.[28] The representative of the USSR argued that the draft article was a reservation clause, though it was not customary to reserve against matters that were not dealt with in the text;[29] he noted, however, that it 'was fully accepted that differences of status should exist between the nationals and the non-nationals of a State'.[30] The rather confused debate in the Commission was in part the result of continuing disagreements over the meaning and place of 'national origin' in Article 1. The proposed 'interpretative' Article VIII was deleted at the 808th meeting on the proposal of Austria.[31]

The inconclusive discussions of 'national origin' in the *travaux* allow comparatively little room for precise comment on the position of non-citizens in the emerging ICERD framework. The issues of citizenship were not clarified until the nine-power draft of Article 1 that emerged in the Third Committee shortly before adoption.[32] In themselves, the discussions of national origin as a ground of discrimination were strongly influenced by concerns on the part of many States about an undue opening out of the provisions against discrimination. According to India, the purpose of the draft Convention was 'to eliminate all forms of racial discrimination which might exist between the inhabitants of a given

[25] The article was considered at the 802nd to 804th meetings, and the 808th and 809th meetings of the Commission,

[26] E/CN.4/L.715. The phrase 'as recognized by international law' was subsequently deleted by the sponsors.

[27] E/CN.4/874, para. 255. In the view of France, its representative observed that Article VIII owed its existence to the inclusion of 'national origin', which the Commission was obliged to clarify: 'it was generally agreed that the case of non-nationals was one to which the Convention did not apply': E/CN.4/SR.803, p. 4; see also Denmark and the UK: E/CN.4/SR.804, pp. 10 and 8, respectively. In relation to naturalized persons, the representative of France recalled that 'France had laws and regulations which temporarily limited the political rights of naturalized persons, e.g. the right to vote. Naturalized persons . . . were often not very familiar with French politics [and] much less interested in political rights than in economic, social and cultural rights, at least during the first few years after their naturalization': E/CN.4/SR.802, p. 12.

[28] E/CN.4/SR.804, p. 5. According to the representative of Turkey, international law 'had not yet succeeded in defining the political, civil, economic, social and cultural rights listed in Article V' (Article 5): E/CN.4/SR.804, p. 7.

[29] E/CN.4/SR.804, p. 6; on the second element in the draft, the representative observed that, though it did not impose a duty to grant special political rights or the right to self-determination, it might give the impression that it wished to set aside or even prevent the exercise of the right of peoples to self-determination.

[30] E/CN.4/SR.804, p. 7.

[31] E/CN.4/874, para. 256.

[32] A/C.3/L.1238.

State; no delegation had suggested that the rights guaranteed and the duties imposed should be extended to aliens'.[33] According to the representative of Uganda, it was natural that a country which had just become independent should wish to give its own nationals the key posts in the economy hitherto largely held by nationals of the metropolitan country or other developed countries.[34] The latter statement hints at the residual fears of countries newly liberated from colonialism, anxious to consolidate their Statehood through, *inter alia*, building a strong apparatus of national governance and developing a local intelligentsia for key sectors of the economy. In the event, the ostensibly ungenerous Article 1(2) was adopted with little specific discussion of its terms.

With regard to 1(3), the term 'nationality' is used twice: in relation to the provisions of the States parties on nationality, citizenship, and naturalization, and on the principle that these should not discriminate against a particular nationality, raising the question as to whether the term is being used in the same sense in both cases. If the first use may be regarded as clear in referring to legal citizenship and related matters, the second is less so, bearing in mind the ambiguity of 'national' and 'nationality', and the fact that the Convention addresses various grounds of discrimination, one of which is 'national origin'. The view that 'nationality' shifts its meaning in 1(3) from the legal concept to a concept closer to ethnicity was expressed by the representative of the UK in the Third Committee who observed, following the voting on the article, that 'nationality' 'was obviously interpreted in different ways in different countries; her delegation understood the word "nationality" as used at the end of the new text . . . to mean persons of a particular national origin'.[35] The representative of Canada explained that he had voted in favour of 1(3) 'because the text adopted made it clear that individuals could have a nationality on the basis of race as well as citizenship'.[36] Schwelb suggests that paragraph 3 of Article 1 was inserted by the Third Committee because it 'appears, to a certain extent at least, to be a saving clause for maintaining disabilities of naturalized persons', recalling a range of constitutional provisions whereby offices of State are reserved to nationals by birth.[37]

C. Practice

I. Reservations and Declarations

Reservations in almost identical terms are extant for Monaco and Switzerland to Article 2 of the Convention which nonetheless relate to Article 1: the States parties reserve the right to apply their legal provisions the right to concerning the admission of foreigners. In the

[33] A/C.3/SR.1304, para. 19. See also the discussions on Article V (final Article 5) where India proposed to delete the words 'the right of everyone' because 'it did not make the distinction between citizens and non-citizens which any State might legitimately wish to make'. The representative noted that Article 1 made such a distinction which was why the delegation proposed there should be a reference to it in Article 5: A/C.3/SR.1308, para. 58; the amendment was withdrawn in light of the non-citizens clause in Article 1(2): A/C.3/SR.1309, para. 2.

[34] A/C.2/SR.1305, para. 30.

[35] A/C.3/SR.1307, para. 24, the text referred to is A/C.3/L.1238.

[36] A/C.3/SR.1307, para. 28.

[37] E. Schwelb, 'The International Convention on the Elimination of All Forms of Racial Discrimination', *ICLQ* 15 (1966), 996–1068, 1010–11 [henceforth 'The International Convention'].

case of the UK, distinctions made under immigration acts are expressed as being in relation to 1(1) 'or any other provision of the Convention'.[38]

II. Guidelines and General Recommendations

The CERD-specific guidelines on Article 1 are relatively brief on non-citizens, requesting information on 'the extent to which domestic law provides for differential treatment based on citizenship or immigration', taking into account Article 1(2) and (3), and GR 30.[39] However, the guidelines for Article 5 on information by relevant groups of potential victims of racial discrimination requests information on, *inter alios*, refugees and displaced persons, in light of GR 22 on Article 5, and on non-citizens, including immigrants, refugees, asylum-seekers, and stateless persons, in light of GR 30.[40]

At first glance, paragraphs 2 and 3 of Article 1 limit the applicability of the definition in Article 1(1) to the detriment of a potentially massive constituency. With regard to Article 1(2), Diaconu notes that, taken literally, the provision 'would have compelled the Committee to avoid any discussion on the situation of stateless populations or those of a foreign citizenship living on the territories of the States [parties]'.[41] This restrictive general stipulation is supplemented by paragraph 3 on access to citizenship which, while exempting legal provisions 'concerning nationality, citizenship or naturalization' from Convention control, provided that there is no discrimination 'against any particular nationality', is less evidently sweeping than 1(2) and at least reiterates the principle of non-discrimination in its limited field.[42] On the other hand, the 'literal reading' of 1(2) may not be as exclusionary as it superficially appears.

As noted, the double use of 'nationality' in 1(3) was the subject of comment in drafting the Convention, and subsequent commentators differ in their appreciation of the term. Schwelb reads the 'no discrimination against a particular nationality' as implying nationality in the 'politico-legal' sense, 'if for no other reason than because it ought not to be lightly assumed that within one sentence the same term is given two different meanings';[43] whereas its first use in the paragraph links with legal processes and concepts and not with nationality in an 'ethnic' sense.[44] Lerner, on the other hand, states that the second reference to 'nationality' is equivalent to 'national origin';[45] Diaconu takes the view that 'nationality' means citizenship in the first sense and national origin in the second.[46]

The paired paragraphs 2 and 3 of Article 1 stand in contrast to more open approaches to non-citizens found in other 'core' UN human rights treaties, even where nationality is

38 <https://treaties.un.org/pages/ViewDetails.aspx?src=TREATY&mtdsg_no=IV-2&chapter=4&lang=en>.
39 CERD/C/2007/1, p. 5.
40 *Ibid.*, p. 12.
41 I. Diaconu, *Racial Discrimination* (Eleven International Publishing, 2011), p. 152.
42 For an application of this principle in another context, see *Ponomaryovi v Bulgaria*, EctHR, App. No. 5335/05 (2011).
43 Schwelb, 'The International Convention', 1009; see also W.A. McKean, *Equality and Discrimination under International Law* (Clarendon Press, 1983), p. 157.
44 Schwelb, *ibid.*, 1009, refers to the 'historico-biological' understanding of nationality, substituted here by 'ethnic'; he also takes the view (1010) that 1(3) was 'to a certain extent at least... a savings clause for maintaining disabilities of naturalized persons'.
45 N. Lerner, *The UN Convention on the Elimination of All Forms of Racial Discrimination* (Sijthoff and Noordhoff, 1980), p. 30.
46 Diaconu, *Racial Discrimination*, p. 166.

not an expressly prohibited ground of discrimination. The relevance of the wider framework of human rights standards is intimated by CERD in paragraph 3 of GR 11 and paragraph 2 of GR 30, both of which imply that the restriction of rights in 1(2) and 1(3) is exceptional and should be construed narrowly. Article 1(3) may be read as 'qualifying' 1(2): as an exception to the exception that reinstates, within its frame, the non-discrimination principle as applicable among non-citizens when it concerns a particular nationality.

The general direction of the CERD approach has been to shrink progressively any lacuna in human rights protection represented by 1(2) and (3). In GR 11, the Committee affirmed that 1(2) and (3) did not exempt States parties from reporting on non-citizens: on the contrary, they were to 'report fully upon legislation on foreigners and its implementation'.[47] Paragraph 3 of the recommendation supplies a key interpretative move, which is carried on, *mutatis mutandis*, into the Committee's archive in general:

> The Committee... affirms that article 1, paragraph 2, must not be interpreted to detract in any way from the rights and freedoms recognised and enunciated in other instruments, especially the Universal Declaration of Human Rights, the International Covenant on Economic, Social and Cultural Rights and the International Covenant on Civil and Political Rights.

The listing, in support of an interpretative principle, of 'different categories' of instrument—a declaration and two conventions—has elicited critical comment,[48] though the inclusion of the International Bill of Rights in a non-exhaustive list of international human right standards is not unreasonable as a pointer to the broader acceptance of principles of international law.[49] While ICERD does not include a specific clause to ensure that it should not be interpreted to detract from other international standards,[50] GR 11 suggests that such a principle is at work in the practice of the Committee. An outstanding feature of CERD methodology in general is that a heterogeneous assembly of human rights instruments and principles is brought within the interpretative frame of the Committee, particularly with regard to the elaboration of rights under Article 5, but not confined to such.[51]

The more ambitious GR 30, adopted in 2004, builds upon a further decade of CERD practice, as well as the Durban Declaration and Programme of Action. Section I on the responsibilities of States reiterates the message of GR 11 in asserting that Article 1(2) 'must be construed so as to avoid undermining the basic prohibition of discrimination' and so should not detract from the principles of the International Bill of Rights.[52] The recommendation also highlights the generalist equality and non-discrimination provisions

[47] GR 11, para. 2.

[48] M. O'Flaherty, 'Substantive Provisions of the International Convention on the Elimination of All Forms of Racial Discrimination', in S. Pritchard (ed.), *Indigenous Peoples, the United Nations and Human Rights* (Zed Books and The Federation Press, 1998), pp. 162–83, at p. 168. The Committee has drawn heavily on other instruments on human rights, particularly in concluding observations on States reports: see the general discussion in Chapters 15 and 20.

[49] For a reflection on the consequences for States parties to ICERD of ratifying the Covenants, see T. Buergenthal, 'Implementing the UN Racial Convention', *Texas International Law Journal* 12 (1977), 187–221, 211.

[50] Examples of clauses include Article 5(2) of the ICCPR and the ICESCR; Articles 23 of CEDAW; 41 of the CRC, and 4(4) of the CRPD. In the field of minority rights, see Article 22 of the FCNM; for indigenous peoples, see Article 35 of ILO Convention 169. Non-treaty clauses include Articles 43 and 45 of the UNDRIP.

[51] See Chapters 15 and 20 in particular.

[52] Para. 2. GR 30 replaced GR 11.

of Article 5 as a counterweight to Article 1(2). The Committee might also have drawn upon the provisions of Article 6—remedies applicable to 'everyone' within the jurisdiction—and the similar provision in Article 14; the broad language of Article 2 can also be called upon to widen the anti-discrimination prospectus. Article 5 is recalled 'in particular' in the final preambular paragraph as the principal basis for the recommendation, the operative part of which widens GR 11 in stating that Article 5

> incorporates the obligation of States parties to prohibit and eliminate racial discrimination in the enjoyment of civil, political, economic, social and cultural rights. Although some of these rights, such as the right to participate in elections, to vote and stand for election, may be confined to citizens, human rights are, in principle, to be enjoyed by all persons. States parties are under an obligation to guarantee equality between citizens and non-citizens in the enjoyment of these rights to the extent recognized under international law.[53]

The paragraph is followed by the reflection that:

> Under the Convention, differential treatment based on citizenship or immigration status will constitute discrimination if the criteria for such differentiation, judged in the light of the objectives and purposes of the Convention, are not applied pursuant to a legitimate aim, and are not proportional to the achievement of this aim. Differentiation within the scope of Article 1, paragraph 4 . . . is not considered discriminatory.[54]

The last-cited statement might appear to suggest that 'citizenship or immigration status' is a ground of discrimination in itself, which would represent an addition to the grounds expressly laid out in the Convention. In light of the reference to 'the objectives and purposes of the Convention', and to Article 1(4), the 'differential treatment' referred to is racial/ethnic differentiation, which will constitute racial discrimination according to the 'usual tests'. While distinctions according to citizenship/nationality may be drawn by States parties, they will be tested for inferences that they are racially based, or used as a 'pretext for racial discrimination',[55] in purpose or effect. This interpretation is reinforced by the numerous references in the recommendation to discrimination on the basis of race, colour, descent, or national or ethnic origin that do not list legal nationality or citizenship as a specific ground of discrimination, as well as by subsequent practice. GR 30 proceeds to recommend that legislation should be revised to guarantee effective enjoyment of the rights in Article 5.[56] The recommendation underpins the understanding of the grounds of racial discrimination that includes their extension to gender, religion, and other instances by the operation of 'intersectionality', or 'multiple discrimination'.

GR 30 asserts that States should 'refrain from applying different standards of treatment to female non-citizen spouses and male non-citizen spouses of citizens';[57] and indirect discrimination: immigration policies should not have the effect of discriminating,[58] and neither should measures taken in the fight against terrorism, while non-citizens should not be 'subjected to racial or ethnic profiling or stereotyping'.[59] Sections on protection for

[53] Para. 3.
[54] Para. 4 of GR 30.
[55] T. Meron, 'The Meaning and Reach of the International Convention on the Elimination of All Forms of Racial Discrimination' *AJIL* 79 (1985), 283–318, 311–12.
[56] Para. 7.
[57] Para. 8.
[58] Para. 9.
[59] Para. 10.

non-citizens against hate speech and racial violence,[60] on the administration of justice,[61] on expulsion and deportation of non-citizens,[62] and on economic, social, and cultural rights,[63] flesh out the implications of the Convention for non-citizens, further etiolating potential restrictions on their enjoyment of human rights.

Section IV of GR 30 is devoted to 'access to citizenship' and impacts primarily on Article 1(3). States are recommended to ensure that 'particular groups of non-citizens are not discriminated against with regard to access to citizenship or naturalization, and to pay attention to possible barriers to naturalization that may exist for long-term or permanent residents'.[64] It is further stated that deprivation of citizenship on racial, etc, grounds is a breach of the obligation to ensure non-discriminatory enjoyment of the right to nationality,[65] and that statelessness, in particular statelessness among children, is to be reduced. The section also asks States to take into consideration that 'in some cases, denial of citizenship for long-term or permanent residents could result in . . . violation of the Convention's . . . principles'.[66]

Elements of GR 30 are adapted by GR 34 under the rubric of 'access to citizenship': States parties should ensure that 'legislation regarding citizenship and naturalization does not discriminate against people of African Descent', and should pay attention to 'possible barriers to naturalization that may exist for long-term or permanent residents of African descent'.[67]

In the narrower field of refugees and displaced persons, GR 30 is complemented by GR 22, which also draws on Article 5 of ICERD, while taking as a point of reference—'the main source of the international system for the protection of refugees in general'[68]—the 1951 Convention and the 1967 Protocol relating to the status of refugees. In addition to restating general principles regarding equality and non-discrimination, the recommendation adapts language from the last-named instruments, emphasizing that:

(a) All such refugees and displaced persons have the right freely to return to their homes of origin under conditions of safety;
(b) States parties are obliged to ensure that the return of such refugees and displaced persons is voluntary and to observed the principle of non-refoulement and non-expulsion of refugees;
(c) All such refugees and displaced persons have, after their return to their homes of origin, the right to have restored to them property of which they were deprived in the course of the conflict and to be compensated appropriately for any such property that cannot be restored . . .
(d) All such refugees and displaced persons have, after their return to their homes of origin, the right to participate fully and equally in public affairs at all levels and to have equal access to public services and to receive rehabilitation assistance.[69]

[60] Section IV.
[61] Section V.
[62] Section VI.
[63] Section VII.
[64] Para. 13. Cf. the ILC Draft Articles on Nationality of Natural Persons in relation to the Succession of States with commentaries 1999: <http://legal.un.org/ilc/texts/instruments/english/commentaries/3_4_1999.pdf>, Article 5 of which provides that 'persons having their habitual residence in the territory affected by the succession of States are presumed to acquire the nationality of the successor State on the date of such succession also GA resolution 55/153, 12 December 2000. See comment in Diaconu, *Racial Discrimination*, pp. 166–9.
[65] Commentary in the present work on Article 5.
[66] *Ibid.*, Para. 15.
[67] GR 34, para. 47; and, *ibid.*, para. 49.
[68] Preamble.
[69] Para. 2.

While GR 22 has not been cited as extensively as GR 30, this may be on account of its more limited field; the Committee has been consistent in its concern for refugees, asylum-seekers, displaced persons, and other casualties of migration and conflict.[70] In the case of Georgia, CERD recommended that, in light of GR 22, the State party 'continue its efforts to improve the situation of IDPs ... in particular with regard to integration, decent durable conditions, and food. It urges the State party to regulate the situation of those IDPs who will not be able to return soon'.[71] GR 22 may be cited along with GR 30 in highly specific recommendations with regard to refugees and IDPs.[72]

GR 30 built on the Committee's track record under Articles 14 and 9 in particular, and functions as a reference point for later developments.[73] The general recommendation has been cited in fields such as access to citizenship,[74] barriers to naturalization,[75] detention conditions,[76] education,[77] employment practices,[78] freedom of expression and religion,[79] the justice system,[80] migration in general including its gender dimensions and in connection with migrant workers[81]—including domestic migrant workers,[82] refugees and asylum-seekers including the issue of non-refoulement,[83] standards of physical and mental health,[84] transmission of citizenship,[85] and many other matters.

III. Communications under Article 14

Non-citizens have figured in Article 14 cases from the beginning—*Yilmaz-Dogan v The Netherlands*[86]—the citizenship of petitioners has been treated as irrelevant to admissibility of the communication. Where a citizenship distinction appears pertinent, the distinction may be interrogated by the Committee to see whether other factors are at work. Illustrative cases include *Habassi v Denmark*,[87] where a Tunisian permanent resident in Denmark (married to a Danish citizen) was denied a loan by a Danish bank because he was not a Danish citizen. The Committee observed that he was denied the loan 'on the sole ground of his non-Danish nationality',[88] having been told that the restriction was necessary in order to ensure repayment of the loan. In the view of the Committee, nationality was not the most appropriate requirement when deciding on the will or

70 Further examples in Chapters 13 and 14.

71 CERD/C/GEO/CO/4-5, para. 20.

72 Concluding observations on Chad, CERD/C/TCD/CO/16-18, para. 15, see also para. 14; Kuwait, CERD/C/KWT/CO/15-20, para. 20.

73 There is a helpful list of Article 14 communications disaggregated by nationality in S. Berry, 'Bringing Muslim Minorities within the International Convention on the Elimination of All Forms of Racial Discrimination—Square Peg in a Round Hole?' *Human Rights Law Review* 11/3, 2011, 423–50, at 424.

74 UAR, CERD/C/ARE/CO/12-17, para. 17; Liechtenstein, CERD/C/LIE/CO/4.

75 Mozambique, CERD/C/MOZ/CO/12, para. 17.

76 Canada, CERD/C/CAN/CO/18, para. 18; Morocco, CERD/C/MAR/CO/17-18, para. 14.

77 Germany, CERD/C/DEU/CO/18, 2008, paras 22 and 23.

78 Italy, CERD/C/ITA/CO/15, para. 17.

79 Iran, CERD/C/IRN/CO/18-19, para. 15.

80 Norway, CERD/C/NOR/CO/18, para. 18.

81 Mexico, CERD/C/MEX/CO/15, para. 16.

82 China, CERD/C/CHN/CO/10-13, CERD/C/HKG/CO/13, CERD/C/MAC/CO/13, para. 30.

83 Lithuania, CERD/C/LTU/CO/3, para. 14; Yemen, CERD/C/YEM/CO/16, para. 14.

84 Dominican Republic, CERD/C/DOM/CO/12, para. 18.

85 UAE, CERD/C/ARE/CO/12-17, para. 17.

86 CERD/C/36/D/1/1984 (1988).

87 CERD/C/54/D/10/1997 (1999).

88 Para. 9.3.

capacity to repay a loan, as a citizen could avoid repayment by moving himself or his property abroad. Habassi had therefore suffered discrimination. The Committee found—under Article 2(d)—that it was 'appropriate to initiate a proper investigation into the real reasons behind the bank's loan policy vis à vis foreign residents, in order to ascertain whether or not criteria involving racial discrimination, *within the meaning of article 1 of the Convention* was being applied'.[89]

Objections to a communication based on an exclusionary reading of 1(2) may receive short shrift from the Committee. In *D.R. v Australia*[90] CERD treated the case as concerning national origin rather than nationality and held that unfavourable distinctions with regard to social security and education were not made on the basis of national origin and that it was 'not possible to reach the conclusion that the system works to the detriment of persons of a particular national origin'.[91] Australia asserted that the applicant's arguments were based on his nationality, a ground of discrimination outside the purview of the Convention, to which the Committee responded:

> The State party argues that the author's allegations do not fall... within the scope of the definition of racial discrimination... in article 1(1)... The State party noted that this definition does not recognise nationality as a ground of racial discrimination.... Taking into account general recommendation 30... and in particular the necessity to interpret article 1, paragraph 2, of the Convention in the light of article 5, the Committee does not consider that the communication as such is prima facie incompatible with the provisions of the Convention.[92]

In some instances, the Committee has treated Article 1(2) as a factor in its decision. In *Diop v France*[93] a Senegalese citizen applied for admission to the French Bar. According to the Court of Cassation, the applicant met all the criteria for admission to the French bar, except one: French nationality. The applicant alleged violation of a number of articles of ICERD including the right to work, as well as denial of equal treatment, adding points on detriment to his family life since he could practise in Senegal but had to leave his family in France. The State party argued that the refusal to allow him to practice was exclusively based on nationality, not because he was Senegalese but because he was not French, and that it was exercising its prerogatives under Article 1(2). Regarding the interpretation of a Franco-Senegalese Convention on Establishment relied upon by the petitioner, the Committee commented that it was not within its mandate 'to interpret or monitor the application of bilateral conventions concluded between States parties... unless it can be ascertained that the application of these conventions results is manifestly discriminatory or arbitrary treatment of individuals under the jurisdiction of States parties'.[94] Regarding the French/non-French distinction, the Committee concluded that this 'operates as a preference or distinction between citizens and non-citizens... the refusal to admit Mr Diop to the Bar was based on the fact that he was not of French nationality, not on any of the grounds... in article 1, paragraph 1'.[95] Further, the Committee observed that the author's allegation of discrimination related to a situation in which the right to

[89] Para. 9.3 (emphasis added).
[90] CERD/C/75/D/42/2008 (2009).
[91] Para. 7.2.
[92] Para. 6.3.
[93] CERD/C/38/D/2/1989 (1990).
[94] Merits, para. 6.3.
[95] *Ibid.*, para. 6.6.

practise law existed only for French nationals and not to a situation in which 'this right has been granted in principle and may be generally invoked'.[96] The case was analysed as non-discriminatory because of (a) a French-not French distinction, assisted by (b) a reading of the scope of human rights obligations bearing on the respondent State.

Quereshi v Denmark No. 2 provides an instance of a general principle that limits the application of the Convention to non-citizens, as it does to other groups. In that case, insulting and derogatory statements were made by various members of a political party against 'Mohammedans', 'foreigners', 'fifth columnists', etc, with prosecutions following in some cases. The decision focused on statements made by one speaker in relation to 'foreigners' following the complaint that the speaker had equated 'a group of people of an ethnic origin other than Danish'[97] with criminality. The State party argued that the language employed by the speaker was so diffuse that it did not signify a group within the meaning of the law and was therefore inappropriate for prosecution under Article 266 (b) of the Danish Criminal Code.[98] In finding no violation of the Convention, the Committee endorsed the position of the State party in that 'a general reference to foreigners does not at present single out a group of persons, contrary to article 1 of the Convention, on the basis of a specific race, ethnicity, colour, descent, or national or ethnic origin'.[99] *Quereshi* was drawn upon by the Committee in the later hate speech case of *P.S.N. v Denmark*,[100] where, by analogy with general references to 'foreigners', a general reference to 'Muslims' was deemed not specific enough to engage the prohibitions in the Convention.[101]

In *A.M.M. v Switzerland*[102] the petitioner, a Somali national, complained under Articles 1, 4, 5, 6, and 7 of the Convention regarding various privations in the fields of education, employment, health, and privacy associated the system of 'F' permit holders—a status of temporary admission and not permanent residence. With regard to Article 1(2), the Committee followed the State party in its view that the complaints of the petitioner were based 'solely on his status under the law on foreign nationals and not on his origin or his Somali nationality'.[103] The Committee elaborated that the challenged regulations did 'not apply only to Somali nationals or a specific group of individuals within the meaning of Article 1 . . . temporary admission is a legal status and no particular link with the individual and his or her personal situation, such as that required to demonstrate discrimination' was inherent in such legal status.[104] Accordingly, while the Committee was not convinced that the facts before it constituted racial discrimination,[105] it drew

[96] Para. 6.6.

[97] CERD/C/66/D/33/2003 (2005), para. 2.8.

[98] Para. 2.13. The State party, *ibid.*, Para. 4.7, contrasted the case of derogatory references to guest workers which had attracted prosecution because 'according to general understanding, that expression designated a person living in Denmark of South European, Asian or African origin . . . persons originating from specific countries'.

[99] *ibid.*, para. 7.3. The Committee did however call the attention of the State party—*ibid.*, para. 8—to the hateful nature of the comments concerning foreigners, and to GR 30 on discrimination against non-citizens.

[100] CERD/C/71/D/36/2006 (2007).

[101] Para. 6.4. The case is further discussed in Chapter 11.

[102] CERD/C/84/D/50/2012 (2014).

[103] Para. 8.4; for the view of the State party, see paras 4.4, 4.5, and 4.11. In para. 4.5, Switzerland cited a study commissioned by the Federal Commission against Racism to the effect that 'a group defined by residence status is not one of those protected by the prohibition on discrimination'.

[104] Para. 8.4.

[105] Para. 8.6. The Committee considered that the petitioner had not 'unequivocally established' the existence of discriminatory acts based on ethnic origin or Somali nationality, a high standard of proof for Article 14 proceedings that appears to approach the criminal law standard of 'beyond reasonable doubt'.

attention to GR 30 and the statement therein of the obligation to eliminate discrimination against non-citizens in relation to working conditions and work requirements.[106]

In *L.G. v Republic of Korea*[107] the petitioner, a national of New Zealand, claimed violation of her rights under various articles of the Convention, on account of the regime of tests prescribed by the Korean authorities for HIV/AIDS and illegal drugs. No equivalent tests were required for Korean teachers, nor for 'foreign native speaking teachers who are ethnically Koreans . . . and who are considered "overseas Koreans"'.[108] The petitioner underwent a series of tests in 2008. On being informed that in order to renew her teaching contract, she would have to undergo a new series of tests, the petitioner refused to take them: 'while she was willing to undergo any health check required from her fellow Korean teachers, she would not undertake the medical tests required only from foreigners'.[109] Her employer stated that, while the petitioner was free to refuse the tests, a refusal would mean the termination of the teaching contract. A complaint to the National Human Rights Commission of Korea (NHRCK) and a request for mediation before the Korean Commercial Arbitration Board (KCAB) brought no relief to the complainant. The Committee observed that 'the NHRCK declined to investigate the . . . complaint', while 'no assessment of the compliance of the contested testing policy with the Convention was made by KCAB or any other State party authority'.[110] In finding that the State party had failed to carry out an assessment as to whether racially discriminatory criteria were at the origin of the testing policy, the Committee concluded that the petitioner's rights under Articles 2(1)(c) and (d), and Article 6 of the Convention had been violated,[111] as had the petitioner's right to work.[112]

> The mandatory testing policy limited to foreign English teachers who are not ethnically Koreans, does not appear to be justified on public health grounds or any other ground, and is a breach of the right to work without distinction as to race, colour, national or ethnic origin, in violation of the State party's obligation to guarantee the right to work as enshrined in Article 5 . . . (e)(i) of the Convention.[113]

With implied reference to Article 1(2), the Committee observed that, in light of the exemptions for Koreans and ethnic Koreans, the testing was 'therefore not decided on the basis of distinction between citizens and non-citizens, but of ethnic origin'. In response to the claims that the testing regime was viewed as a means 'to check the values and morality' of foreign English teachers,[114] paragraph 12 of GR 30 was recalled for its recommendation that States parties 'take resolute action to counter any tendency to target, stigmatize, stereotype or profile, on the basis of race, colour, descent, or national or ethnic origin, members of "non-Citizen" population groups, especially by politicians'.[115]

[106] Para. 33 of GR 30.
[107] CERD/C/86/D/51/2012 (2015).
[108] Para. 2.2.
[109] Para. 2.7. Further, the petitioner noted that 'such tests were stemming from a governmental policy and were not even prescribed by law, and that they contributed to promote xenophobic beliefs that "foreigners do drugs", "have diseases" and are "sex offenders"'. The government denied (para. 2.8) that there was any discriminatory intent behind the tests, which 'were needed to identify the foreigners who are doing drugs and have HIV/AIDS'.
[110] Para. 7.3.
[111] Para. 7.3; para. 8.
[112] The issue of violation of Article 5(e)(iv)—right to health, etc—was not separately examined: para. 7.5.
[113] Para. 7.4.
[114] *Ibid.*
[115] *Ibid.*

IV. Concluding Observations

As regards the run of concluding observations relating to non-citizens, bearing in mind the limitations on non-citizen rights in human rights instruments such as the ICCPR, distinctions between citizens and non-citizens in the field of political participation have nonetheless attracted the attention of the Committee. In the case of the Czech Republic, the Committee noted 'that several distinctions made under domestic law between the rights of citizens and non-citizens may not be fully justified . . . in particular that European Union non-citizens, although they are entitled to vote and be elected at local elections, may not belong to a political party'.[116] In the case of Latvia, the Committee recognized 'that political rights can be legitimately limited to citizens. Nevertheless, noting that most non-citizens have been residing in Latvia for many years, if not for their whole lives', the Committee strongly recommended 'that the State party consider facilitating the integration process by making it possible for all non-citizens who are long-time permanent residents to participate in local elections'.[117] To Estonia, the Committee reiterated an earlier concluding observation in conspicuously gentle terms, recommending that 'the State party give due consideration to the possibility of allowing non-citizens to participate in political parties'.[118]

The structure of basic legislation frequently raises the concerns of the Committee. In light of the information that the equality provisions of the Italian Constitution did not include non-citizens, the State party was urged 'to endure that non-citizens enjoy equal protection and recognition before the law'; CERD drew attention 'to the importance of ensuring that legislative guarantees against racial discrimination regardless of their immigration status'.[119] In the case of Tajikistan, the Committee recalled GR 30 and the fact that 'States parties have the duty to ensure that legislative guarantees against racial discrimination apply to non-citizens regardless of their immigration status, and that the implementation of legislation does not have a discriminatory effect on non-citizens'.[120] Many cases refer to the principle of the guarantee of equal rights between citizens and non-citizens 'to the extent recognized under international law'.[121] Specific exemptions of non-citizens from anti-discrimination protection, or limitations on such protection, have been subject to criticism,[122] including where they involve the exercise of discretionary powers—hence the recommendation to the UK to 'remove the exceptions based on ethnic and national origin to the exercise of immigration functions as well as the discretionary powers granted to the UK Border Agency . . . to discriminate at border posts among those entering the territory of the State party'.[123]

A key to ameliorating the situation of non-citizens is to grant citizenship—part of the 'reserved domain' intimated by 1(3). Access to citizenship may present considerable problems for certain minorities, and it raises the question of whether a particular

[116] CERD/C/CZE/CO/7, para. 18.

[117] Latvia, CERD/C/63/CO/8, para. 12.

[118] CERD/C/EST/CO/7, para. 14.

[119] CERD/C/ITA/CO/16-18, para. 12.

[120] CERD/C/TJK/CO/6-8, para. 16, under the heading: 'Discriminatory law against non-citizens'.

[121] Examples concluding observations on the Former Yugoslav Republic of Macedonia, CERD/C/MKD/CO/7, para.10; United Arab Emirates, CERD/C/ARE/CO/12-17, para.11; the USA, CERD/C/USA/CO/6, para.24. See also on Moldova, CERD/C/MDA/CO/8-9, para. 9.

[122] Botswana, CERD/C/BWA/CO/16, para. 8.

[123] Concluding observations on the UK, CERD/C/GBR/CO/18-20, para. 16.

nationality or nationalities is disproportionately disadvantaged by legal arrangements for the acquisition of citizenship. In a number of instances, the disadvantaged group has been the Roma, a situation adverted to in GR 27 on Discrimination against Roma with reference to legislation on citizenship and naturalization.[124] In the case of Italy, the Committee recommended 'measures to facilitate access to citizenship for stateless Roma, Sinti and non-citizens who have lived in Italy for many years, and to... removed existing barriers'.[125] In the case of the Russian Federation, CERD recommended that the State party's action plan for Roma should include 'measures to facilitate their access to residence registration, citizenship, education', and adequate housing and other rights, in accordance with GR 27.[126] The denial of naturalization following requests by persons of South-East Asian origin who met the relevant legal requirements raised concern in the case of Cyprus.[127] In the case of naturalization of refugees by Turkmenistan, it was recommended that 'the same treatment be granted to refugees of Turkmen, Uzbek, or other ethnic origin', including refugees from Afghanistan.[128]

Impediments to naturalization encountered in practice invariably elicit comments from the Committee in terms of information about the legal process, overemphasis on language as part of an integration strategy for non-citizens, the need for positive measures to attract applications for citizenship, etc.[129] In the case of Croatia, persons of Roma, Bosniak, and Serb origin were specifically referred to in terms of access to citizenship.[130] In such cases, the spectre of statelessness is evoked in the comments of the Committee as an impermissible consequence of barriers to citizenship, regularly coupled with invitations to the States parties to accede to the relevant UN conventions to avoid that consequence.[131] CERD practice is not consistent with one apparent motivation behind 1(3)—to exempt distinctions between citizens by birth and naturalized citizens from categorization as discrimination. Concern has been expressed regarding distinctions between citizens by birth and naturalized citizens in relation to access to public office;[132] rules on family reunification that disadvantaged naturalized citizens of non-European Union origin;[133] and restrictions to the right of naturalized citizens to participate in elections, where the State party was urged 'to accord equal civil and political rights to all citizens irrespective of the mode of acquisition of citizenship'.[134] Comments pertinent to 1(3) frequently overlap with or are subsumed under those on Article 5(d).

[124] Para. 4.

[125] CERD/C/ITA/CO/16-18, para. 24.

[126] CERD/C/RUS/CO/20-22, para. 15.

[127] CERD/C/CYP/CO/17-22, para. 18; the Committee requested data on naturalization requests and decisions 'disaggregated by ethnic group, sex, length of residence in the State party, and any other relevant criteria'.

[128] CERD/C/TKM/CO/5, para. 18.

[129] *Inter alia*, concluding observations on Estonia, CERD/C/61/CO/4, para. 10, CERD/C/EST/CO/7, para. 15, CERD/C/EST/CO/10-11, paras 9, 10, 11; Latvia, CERD/C/63/CO/8, para. 14; Nigeria, CERD/C/NGA/CO/18, para. 21.

[130] CERD/C/HRV/CO/8, para. 17.

[131] In the case of Turkmenistan, the Committee recommended measures to ensure that 'the solution of issues related to citizenship did not increase the number of stateless persons who would thereby be deprived of human rights and freedoms in practice': CERD/C/TKM/CO/6-7, para. 18.

[132] Concluding observations on Qatar, CERD/C/60/CO/11, para. 12.

[133] Concluding observations on Belgium, CERD/C/BEL/CO/16-19, para. 17.

[134] Concluding observations on Thailand, CERD/C/THA/CO/1-3, para. 13.

D. Comment

Discourses of a xenophobic nature characterize some national responses to contemporary phenomena of populations in flux. CERD's concerns have primarily related to the non-citizen category.[135] Without attempting a definition of 'xenophobia', GR 30 counsels the taking of 'steps to address xenophobic attitudes and behaviour towards non-citizens'.[136] Committee perceptions of xenophobia also colour many sets of concluding observations,[137] notably in the field of hate speech, although the capacity of xenophobic attitudes and prejudices to generate racial discrimination across a wider spectrum of rights is clear.[138] The etymology of 'xenophobia' is well known: from the Greek ξένος (xenos), stranger or foreigner and φόβος (phobos), fear; the term commonly understood as signifying hatred or fear of foreigners or strangers, of their politics or culture. The wider meaning of xenophobia is generalized fear of 'the Other'—'heterophobia' or fear of strangers; a narrower meaning relates to foreigners. 'Xenophobia' does not appear on the face of the principal HR instruments and does not benefit from a general normative definition. Even if they do not specifically identify the phenomenon, international instruments visualize xenophobia as setting the scene for negative action against targeted groups and violence against them, including genocide, where xenophobia characteristically transmutes itself into a language of dehumanization of others, easing the consciences of killers.[139] CERD's endorsement of the Durban documentation does not differentiate among a range of aspects: in GR 33, the Committee recommended to the States parties to be mindful that their response to the current financial and economic crisis should not lead to a situation which would increase poverty and underdevelopment and, potentially, a rise in racism, racial discrimination, xenophobia, and related intolerance against foreigners, immigrants, indigenous peoples, persons belonging to minorities, and other particularly

[135] For helpful references to phenomena of xenophobia, see the report to the General Assembly of the Special Rapporteur on Contemporary Forms of Racism, Racial Discrimination, Xenophobia and Related Intolerance, A/49/677 (1994), who stresses its similarities to racism and comments on overlaps. Xenophobia is not the subject of a definitive interpretation in international human rights instruments, nor is 'heterophobia'.

[136] See Section III. See also GR 31, preamble, and paras 4, 5, 26, 31, and 37, 38, and 40.

[137] Searching for 'xenophobia' in databases is complicated, perhaps particularly in the case of CERD, by the copious references to the Durban documentation that appear in the practice.

[138] Among many and various examples, see concluding observations on Chile, CERD/C/CHL/CO/15-18, para. 18; Dominican Republic, CERD/C/DOM/CO/13-14, paras 9 and 15; France, CERD/C/FRA/CO/17-19, para. 10; Germany, CERD/C/DEU/CO/18, para. 15; Portugal, CERD/C/PRT/CO/12-14, para. 14; Russian Federation, CERD/C/RUS/CO/20-22, paras 11 and 12; South Africa, CERD/C/ZAF/CO/13, para. 27; Sweden, CERD/C/SWE/CO/19-21, para. 11.

[139] The accounts of xenophobia in the panoply of human rights instruments oscillate between wide and narrow views; where xenophobia is explicitly referred to, it may be imperfectly distinguished from and mentioned alongside racism as in Article 2 of the Additional Protocol to the Council of Europe Cybercrime Convention, paragraph 1 of which offers a broad reading of xenophobia. For the purposes of this Protocol: 'racist and xenophobic material' means any written material, any image or any other representation of ideas or theories, which advocates, promotes or incites hatred, discrimination or violence, against any individual or group of individuals, based on race, colour, descent or national or ethnic origin, as well as religion if used as a pretext for any of these factors'. Xenophobia is also flagged up specifically in the Durban documentation. The Durban Declaration and Programme of Action link xenophobia, racism, and related intolerance. While the separate concepts are rarely individuated therein, paragraph 16 of the Durban Declaration underlines the perceptions of the participating States: 'We recognize that xenophobia against non-nationals, particularly migrants, refugees and asylum-seekers, constitutes one of the main sources of contemporary racism and that human rights violations against members of such groups occur widely in the context of discriminatory, xenophobic and racist practices.'

vulnerable groups all over the world.[140] The primary focus of the Convention is on racial discrimination. CERD practice takes a view of xenophobia as implicating a range of groups, though the paradigm case of non-citizens—or, *de minimis*, persons of foreign origin, or 'visible minorities'—attracts the most frequent references. While xenophobia as such is not the subject of the Convention, intolerance, racism, racial discrimination, and xenophobia have been identified by the Committee as a combined attitudinal stream that requires effective combating by the State concerned.

The archive of CERD recommendations on non-citizens represents a formidable body of work—no Committee session passes without extensive reference to non-citizens in the dialogue with States parties and in the concluding observations. The area of non-citizens is also an area where CERD copiously and persistently refers to international conventions on refugees and asylum-seekers, on migrant workers, and on statelessness. The Committee almost inevitably recommends ratification of the convention or conventions that apply to this field when it finds that the instrument in question is absent from the State party's portfolio.[141] In addition to the proliferation of recommendations on specific aspects of the rights of non-citizens, the Committee continues to stress need for data as the necessary background to a national anti-discrimination policy, and to appraise the shape of the legislative framework in broad terms. Specific data on immigration in general, disaggregated by nationality, and on the impact of laws and policies on immigrants may be called for.[142] States parties may also be enjoined to provide statistics on the national origin of, for example, migrant workers or refugees,[143] and on the ethnic background to naturalization requests in order to ensure that no particular nationality is discriminated against contrary to Article 1(3).[144]

The grounds of discrimination in Article 1(1) of ICERD do not include nationality, the explicit listing of which among the grounds of discrimination is also comparatively rare in the core UN instruments.[145] Treaty bodies have nonetheless deliberated on discrimination against non-nationals in the absence of an express ground of nationality;[146] the burden of addressing discrimination in such cases has tended to fall on 'national origin' or 'other status'.[147] In light of the limited range of grounds in ICERD, the limitations in 1(2) and 1(3) raise difficult issues. Meron describes 1(2) as 'overly broad', and suggests that 'a more careful formulation, placing upon the State the burden of demonstrating that its discriminatory action was based exclusively upon alienage would have been preferable.

140 Para. 1 (f).

141 See Chapter 15.

142 Concluding observations on Malta, CERD/C/MLT/CO/15-20, paras 6 and 16; Moldova, CERD/C/MDA/CO/8-9, para. 8.

143 Examples include Qatar, CERD/C/60/CO/11, para. 21, and Saudi Arabia, CERD/C/62/CO/8, para. 20.

144 Concluding observations on Cyprus, CERD/C/CYP/CO/17-22, para. 18: the Committee had noted with concern that 'naturalization requests, including by persons of South-East Asian origin, whose situations sometimes meet the State party's legal requirements for naturalization eligibility have some times been denied'.

145 Articles 1 and 7 of the CMW include 'nationality' among prohibited grounds; see also CPED Article 13.7.

146 Under the ICCPR, see, *inter alia*, *Adam v Czech Republic*, CCPR/C/57/D/586/1994 (1996); *Borzov v Estonia*, CCPR//81/D/1136/2002 (2004); *Ibrahima Gueye and Others v France*, CCPR/C/35/D/196/1985 (1989); *Karakurt v Austria* CCPR/C/74/D/965/2000 (2002); *Sipin v Estonia*, CCPR/C/93/D/1423/2005 (2008); *Tsarjov v Estonia*, CCPR/C/91/D/1223/2003 (2007); nationality is not specifically mentioned in the ICCPR as a ground of discrimination.

147 Vandenhole, *Non-Discrimination and Equality*, chapter III, summary of 'nationality' as a ground at p. 185.

The use of the citizenship exception as a pretext for discrimination could thus have been deterred'.[148] McKean observes that it is unfortunate that 'the restrictions upon aliens were not made more selective', suggesting that restrictions on the universality of rights follow inevitably from the existence of sovereign States.[149]

The negativity expressed in the *travaux* regarding non-citizens may be recalled, including the sweeping proposal to exclude them from the purview of the Convention *tout court*. The gap between the assumptions of at least some participants active in the drafting of the Convention and current practice is notable.[150] As the *travaux* suggest, the restrictive approach to non-citizens was to some extent bound up with the necessity of strengthening the sovereignty of newly independent States and nascent problems of the nationalization of resources including personnel. In light of the history of international law, protection of aliens may also have evoked memories of domination by powerful States,[151] raising concerns analogous to those intimated regarding minorities, especially powerful minorities, as obstacles to national consolidation. Many States in the drafting process were silent regarding the extension of the Convention to non-citizens, while some envisaged the need for the further development of international law.[152]

In outcome, the Convention is less generous than its predecessor Declaration on the Elimination of Racial Discrimination which, while it does not treat nationality as a ground of discrimination, does not include a clause equivalent to 1(2), and expressly applies the non-discrimination principle to 'access to citizenship'.[153] Of the instruments referred to in the preamble to the Convention, International Labour Organization (ILO) Convention 111 does not include nationality as a ground, though the list of grounds is not closed;[154] the UNESCO Convention against Discrimination in Education incorporates, among the undertakings by States parties, to 'give foreign nationals resident within their territory the same access to education as that given to their own nationals'.[155] Among newer instruments, the Inter-American Convention against Racism, Racial Discrimination and Related Intolerance, reaches, as its broad title implies, beyond the citizen/non-citizen distinction and does not contain a clause equivalent to ICERD 1(2) or 1(3). While the grounds of discrimination—race, colour, lineage, or national or ethnic origin—echo those in ICERD, the preamble to the Inter-American Convention recites the consideration that 'the individual and collective experience of discrimination must be taken into account to combat segregation and marginalization based on race, ethnicity, or nationality, and to protect the life plan of those individuals and communities at risk of such segregation and marginalization'.

148 Meron, *Meaning and Reach*, 311–12.

149 McKean, *Equality and Discrimination under International Law*, p. 158.

150 Implicit confinement of rights to citizens is suggested in remarks by, *inter alios*, representatives of Zambia, A/C.3/SR.1299, para. 41; Romania, A/C.3/SR.1300, para. 11; Senegal, A/C.3/SR.1304, para. 16; Hungary, *ibid.*, para. 21; and Ceylon, A/C.3/SR.1306, para. 28.

151 For a brief recapitulation of the minimum standard in the treatment of aliens and related institutions, see R. Kolb, 'The Protection of the Individual in Times of War and Peace', *The Oxford Handbook of the History of International Law*, pp. 317–37.

152 According to the representative of Jamaica, discussion of national origin diverted attention away from discrimination based on race; the question of nationality 'was a separate one which could itself be made the subject of a declaration': A/C.3/SR.1305, para. 26.

153 Article 3. See however the references to political and citizenship rights 'in his country', Article 6.

154 Article 1(1)(a), subject to the potential extension in 1(1)(b).

155 Article 3(e).

The worth of the Convention would be reduced for large segments of humanity if 1(2) and 1(3) were given a broad reading, leaving human rights concerns snagged in the thickets of nationality and citizenship.[156] Vandenhole comments that the narrowing by the Committee of exceptions to discrimination was well advanced before the advent of GR 30.[157] In a systemic sense, the practice of the Committee, on non-citizens and more generally, reaches out to other human rights instruments in order to buttress an interpretation of the Convention that is as inclusive as the text can sustain. In terms intrinsic to the text, the technical point that exceptions to a principle should be construed narrowly is important: in functional terms, paragraph 2 of Article 1 is an exception to a wider principle. Further, the potentially restrictive provisions in 1(2) and 1(3) have been set against Article 5 (and other generalist provisions), with the latter generally treated as dominant. It may, however be argued that, in light of the ambiguity of 1(2), the Committee's approach, based on taking the Convention as a whole in a wider context, does not appreciably transcend a literal reading—the conclusion that distinctions formally based on citizenship that conceal racial distinctions are prohibited by 1(1) is warranted by the text. A reading of 1(2) that rules out from the Convention any concern with non-citizens could be classified in Vienna Convention on the Law of Treaties (VCLT) terms as a 'manifestly absurd or unreasonable' reading of ICERD,[158] and as not corresponding to its object and purpose. In light of the ambition expressed in the Convention to eliminate racial discrimination, and a human rights approach *pro homine* and *pro femina*, it is reasonable to prefer effective interpretations that protect the widest span of potential victims.

With regard to 1(3) and the repeated use of 'nationality', the *travaux* and subsequent practice support the view that 'nationality' in the second sense of a forbidden ground of discrimination means 'national origin' on a par with 'ethnic origin'. Even in this case, distinctions must apply to a particular nationality (or nationalities) to fall foul of the provision. The reference to discrimination against a particular nationality is in line with the stance of the Committee that a general reference to foreigners which does not single out a group or groups is insufficient to validate a charge of discrimination. In light of the application of this last principle in the standard repertoire of the Committee, the right to nationality protected by Article 5, and attendant questions around citizenship and naturalization, are not treated as appreciably diminished by Article 1(3). The paragraph essentially serves as a reminder that while there are State prerogatives in the fields referred to, such prerogatives are limited by international anti-discrimination standards.

As elsewhere in CERD practice, the approach taken by the Committee for communications under Article 14 is more narrowly defined than in the generality of concluding

[156] 'There are different groups of non-citizens, including permanent residents, migrants, refugees, asylum-seekers, victims of trafficking, foreign students, temporary visitors, other kinds of non-immigrants and stateless people. While each of these groups may have rights based on separate legal regimes, the problems faced by most, if not all, non-citizens are very similar. These common concerns affect approximately 175 million individuals worldwide – or 3 percent of the world's population': Office of the United Nations High Commissioner for Human Rights, *The Rights of Non-Citizens* (New York and Geneva, 2006), p. 5. Weissbrodt, *The Rights of Non-Citizens*, p. 1, cites, on the basis of UN sources, a figure of 191 million persons 'who currently reside in a country other than where they were born'.

[157] *Non-Discrimination and Equality*, pp. 91–92.

[158] According to Article 32 of the VCLT, recourse may be had to supplementary means of interpretation when the textual method in Article 31 leaves the meaning ambiguous or obscure, or (b) 'leads to a result which is manifestly absurd or unreasonable'.

observations. As with other areas of practice, the Committee's recommendations to individual States on non-citizens generally avoid the language of violations. The recommendations express concern for the negative consequences for non-citizens in terms of direct, indirect, and structural discrimination flowing from State policies in general, legal institutions and practices, and 'measures' capable of influencing public opinion. The State-directed recommendations are broader than opinions under Article 14, oriented more towards general policy, and are hortatory and interrogative. The examination of reports under Article 9 generates holistic appraisals of situations in States parties that subsume and transcend a mass of detail. In terms of focus, the overall approach of a State party to deal with racial discrimination may be deemed insufficiently attentive to 'immigrants and foreigners'.[159] In many instances, recommendations seek to ascertain whether there exists a xenophobic climate of opinion that bears down heavily on non-citizens generally or particular categories thereof.

Despite the apparent limitations placed by the text of the Convention on concern for non-citizens, there is little appreciable difference between their treatment and the treatment of other groups by the Committee as victims of discrimination.[160] Practice with respect to non-citizens encompasses all the rights listed or implied in the Convention. While an amendment to the Convention deleting the qualifications on the scope of discrimination would not have a significant practical effect, it is worthy of consideration, financial crises notwithstanding, for its symbolic value in taking the Convention forward from some of the limiting assumptions of the 1960s.

[159] Concluding observations on Portugal, CERD/C/PRT/CO/12-14, para. 13; see also, *ibid.*, paras 14, 125, 16, and 20.

[160] See Chapters 11, 13, 14, and 15.

8. Article 2

Obligations to Eliminate Racial Discrimination

The present chapter addresses Article 2(1). Along with Article 1(4), Article 2(2) is the subject of Chapter 9 on special measures.

1. States Parties condemn racial discrimination and undertake to pursue by all appropriate means and without delay a policy of eliminating racial discrimination in all its forms and promoting understanding among all races, and, to this end:

(a) Each State Party undertakes to engage in no act or practice of racial discrimination against persons, groups of persons or institutions and to ensure that all public authorities and public institutions, national and local, shall act in conformity with this obligation;
(b) Each State Party undertakes not to sponsor, defend or support racial discrimination by any persons or organizations;
(c) Each State Party shall take effective measures to review governmental, national and local policies, and to amend, rescind or nullify any laws and regulations which have the effect of creating or perpetuating racial discrimination wherever it exists;
(d) Each State Party shall prohibit and bring to an end, by all appropriate means, including legislation as required by circumstances, racial discrimination by any persons, group or organization;
(e) Each State Party undertakes to encourage, where appropriate, integrationist multiracial organizations and movements and other means of eliminating barriers between races, and to discourage anything which tends to strengthen racial division.

A. Introduction

Human rights instruments, after the model of the Universal Declaration of Human Rights (UDHR), characteristically combine statements of rights with statements of obligation in order to convert principle into practice: the language of obligation varies according to the nature of the instrument. Following the definition of racial discrimination in Article 1, the complex and action-oriented Article 2 sets out the Convention's broadest portfolio of State 'undertakings' or obligations—referred to in Article 5 as 'fundamental obligations'—on the basis of which racial discrimination is prohibited across a spectrum of human rights. The breadth and depth of the requirements of Article 2, coupled with the obligations set out elsewhere in the Convention, might leave an impression that the International Convention on the Elimination of All Forms of Racial Discrimination (ICERD) is principally concerned with obligations rather than rights. The Committee on the Elimination of Racial Discrimination (CERD) has, however, found, by necessary implication, a wider presence of rights in the Convention beyond their explicit listing in Article 5.[1]

[1] *Moylan v Australia*, CERD/C/83/D/47/2010 92013), para. 6.2, citing *Habassi v Denmark*, CERD/C/54/D/10/1997 (1999), para. 10, *Ahmad v Denmark*, CERD/C/56/D/16/1999 (2000), para. 8, and *Durmic v Serbia and Montenegro*, CERD/C/68/D/29/2003 (2006), para. 10.

Instruments focusing on the elimination of particular evils analogous to racial discrimination, such as the Convention against Torture (CAT) and the International Convention for the Protection of All Persons from Enforced Disappearance (CPED), are replete with references to obligations, as is ICERD's sister instrument on discrimination, the Convention on the Elimination of All Forms of Discrimination against Women (CEDAW).[2] Texts devoted principally to the enunciation of rights characteristically include a general obligations clause supplemented by more detailed prescriptions. States parties to the International Covenant on Civil and Political Rights (ICCPR) undertake 'to respect and to ensure' the rights,[3] and those to the International Covenant on Economic, Social and Cultural Rights (ICESCR) 'to take steps . . . with a view to achieving progressively the full realization of the rights' as well as to guarantee that they will be exercised without discrimination.[4] The Convention on the Rights of the Child (CRC) opts for the basic formula of 'to respect and ensure' the rights 'without discrimination of any kind',[5] and devotes a wide range of articles to elaborating on the basic obligation; 'respect and ensure' is also employed by the International Convention on the Protection of the Rights of All Migrant Workers and their Families (CMW),[6] while the 'general obligations' article in the Convention on the Rights of Persons with Disabilities (CRPD) employs the formula of 'to ensure and promote'[7] the full realization of convention rights, and makes provision for the specifics of economic and social rights. Among the regional instruments on human rights, the African Charter on Human and Peoples' Rights (ACHPR) obliges States to 'recognise' the rights and adopt measures to give effect to them;[8] the European Convention on Human Rights (ECHR) includes a general obligations Article, directing States to 'secure' the rights,[9] while the American Convention on Human Rights (ACHR) mandates 'respect' for rights.[10] Group-oriented human rights instruments also concern themselves with general obligations—the United Nations Declaration on Minorities (UNDM), for example, elaborates a platform of obligations in Article 4, while the UN Declaration on the Rights of Indigenous Peoples (UNDRIP) employs a characteristic mix of rights and obligations throughout the greater part of its text.[11]

The nature and scope of obligations under human rights instruments has been the subject of sustained analysis over decades, resulting in deconstructive typologies and characterizations. Landmark studies and scholarly proposals from human rights bodies and academics include those prepared by Eide[12] and Shue.[13] The latter referred to moving

[2] CEDAW GR 28 addresses 'the core obligations of States parties under Article 2', an article that shows affinities with Article 2 of ICERD: CEDAW/C/GC/28, 16 December 2010. CERD has not issued a comparable general recommendation that covers the full range of obligations under Article 2 ICERD.

[3] Article 2(1).

[4] Article 2(1).

[5] Article 2(1).

[6] Article 7.

[7] Article 4.

[8] Article 1.

[9] Article 1.

[10] Article 1.

[11] See in particular, Articles 8, 11, 12, 13, 14, 15, 16, 17, 19, 21, 22, 26, 27, 29, 30, 31, 32, 36, and 38.

[12] *The Right to Adequate Food as a Human Right*, Final Report of the UN Special Rapporteur on the Right to Food, A. Eide, E/CN.4/Sub.2/1987/23. For use by the Committee on Economic, Social and Cultural Rights, see for example GC 12, *The Right to Adequate Food*, E/C.12/1999/5.

[13] H. Shue, *Basic Rights, Subsistence, Affluence and U.S. Foreign Policy* (2nd edn, Princeton University Press, 1996).

beyond the simplistic assumption that for every right there was a single correlative duty, and categorized duties in the field of human rights as duties (a) to avoid depriving, (b) to protect from deprivation, and (c) to aid. Eide's typology of obligations to respect, protect, and fulfil human rights has become a standard point of reference for monitoring institutions, activists, and commentators. Roughly translated, the obligation to respect signifies the primarily negative principle that the State should refrain from interfering with the enjoyment of a right; the obligation to protect implies that States should actively shield right holders from the actions of third parties;[14] the obligation to fulfil requires to duty-bearer 'to adopt appropriate legislative, administrative and other measures towards the full realization of human rights'.[15] For this last aspect of obligation, sub-obligations to facilitate, to promote,[16] and to provide have been individuated.[17] The typology of obligations was developed principally in the context of economic, social, and cultural rights,[18] though claims are made for it to function as a template for the generality of human rights in that it supplies nuance and progression to the simple distinction between positive and negative action.[19]

[14] Thus, 'in principle, any violation of rights recognized by the Convention carried out by an act of public authority or by persons who use their position of authority is imputable to the State. However, this does not define all the circumstances in which a State is obligated to prevent, investigate and punish human rights violations, nor all the cases in which the State might be found responsible for an infringement of those rights. An illegal act which violates human rights and which is initially not directly imputable to a State (for example, because it is the act of a private person or because the person responsible has not been identified) can lead to international responsibility of the State, not because of the act itself, but because of the lack of due diligence to prevent the violation or to respond to it as required by the Convention': *Velásquez Rodríguez v Honduras*, (Merits), IACtHR Ser. C No. 4 (1988), para. 172.

[15] *Principles and Guidelines for a Human Rights Approach to Poverty Reduction Strategies* (Office of the UN High Commissioner for Human Rights, 2005), para. 48—the foreword by the High Commissioner recalls that the work 'builds upon several previous publications of the Office of the United Nations High Commissioner for Human Rights, *Draft Guidelines on a Human Rights Approach to Poverty Reduction Strategies* (2002) and *Human Rights and Poverty Reduction: A Conceptual Framework* (2004), drafted by Professors Hunt, Nowak, and Siddiq Osmani, and also draws on consultations with various stakeholders (including Member States, intergovernmental and non-governmental organizations)'. The obligation to fulfil entails provision of a remedy for victims of human rights violations: *Velásquez Rodríguez v Honduras*, para. 176; in the present work, see the discussion of remedies in the commentary on Article 6 of ICERD.

[16] 'At its most general, the obligation to fulfil is considered also to involve an obligation to promote human rights, which means that States should adopt policies that *promote* rights both domestically (for example, human rights education) and internationally': F. Mégret, 'Nature of Obligations', in D. Moeckli, S. Shah, and S. Sivakumaran (eds.), *International Human Rights Law* (2nd edn, Oxford University Press, 2014), p. 103 (emphasis in the original) [henceforth *International Human Rights Law*].

[17] See the summary by W. Vandenhole, *Non-Discrimination and Equality in the View of the UN Human Rights Treaty Bodies* (Intersentia, 2005), pp. 187–90 [henceforth *Non-Discrimination and Equality*].

[18] For an example of their employment, see GC 12 of the Committee on Economic, Social and Cultural Rights, The Right to Adequate Food, E/C.12/1999/5 (1999), paras 14–20.

[19] D. Shelton and A. Gould, 'Positive and Negative Obligations', in D. Shelton (ed.), *The Oxford Handbook of International Human Rights Law* (Oxford University Press, 2015), pp. 562–83 [henceforth 'Positive and Negative Obligations']. The web page of the Office of the UN High Commissioner for Human Rights offers the following information: 'International human rights law lays down obligations which States are bound to respect. By becoming parties to international treaties, States assume obligations and duties under international law to respect, to protect and to fulfil human rights. The obligation to respect means that States must refrain from interfering with or curtailing the enjoyment of human rights. The obligation to protect requires States to protect individuals and groups against human rights abuses. The obligation to fulfil means that States must take positive action to facilitate the enjoyment of basic human rights.' <http://www.ohchr.org/en/professionalinterest/Pages/InternationalLaw.aspx>.

'Respect', 'protect', and 'fulfil' appear in the regular discourse of the Committee, even if not framed as a tripartite typology.[20] 'Respect' appears in contexts such as ensuring respect for the ways of life of ethnic groups,[21] in relation to particular rights and freedoms,[22] or human rights more generally. 'Protect' appears in many contexts, notably in protection of vulnerable groups such as indigenous peoples in their livelihoods[23] and in other respects—citations of the protection provisions of GR 23 are much in evidence;[24] in relation to other oppressed populations or individuals;[25] in measures to protect the security of persons from violence,[26] from stereotyping,[27] or simply from racial discrimination.[28] In the context of special measures in Articles 1(4) and 2(2), 'protection' is concerned, according to GR 32, with 'violations of human rights emanating from any source, including discriminatory activities of private persons'.[29] 'Fulfil' tends to appear in the context of fulfilment of obligations specifically or generally.

B. *Travaux Préparatoires*

The initial Sub-Commission drafts of a general obligations paragraph showed considerable variation. The Abram draft made reference to 'persons, groups of persons or institutions' to be protected against discrimination on various 'grounds' (the ultimate destination of which was Article 1 of the Convention)—'race, colour, or ethnic origin, or where applicable, on the basis of "nationality" or national origin'.[30] States would also be obliged not to encourage or lend support 'through police action or otherwise' to discrimination by 'any group, institution or individual'.[31] 'Grounds' of discrimination—'race, colour or ethnic origin'—were also alluded to in the drafts of Calvocoressi[32] and Kertzynski—'race, colour or ethnic origin or, where applicable, on the basis of "nationality" or national origin'.[33] The Calvocoressi draft included the obligation 'to pursue a national policy designed to prevent discrimination within its territory',[34] as well as broaching the issue of criminal responsibility for racial violence.[35] Legislation for the

20 For a critique of the typology, see I.E. Koch, 'Dichotomies, Trichtomies or Waves of Duties?' *Human Rights Law Review* 5 (2005), 81–103. Vandenhole, *Equality and Discrimination*, pp. 187–287, applies the typology of obligations to ICERD as well as to related instruments. The present chapter follows the more open and Convention-specific approach adopted (so far) by CERD.

21 Concluding observations on Thailand, CERD/C/THA/CO/1-3, para. 16.

22 Concluding observations on Turkmenistan, CERD/C/TKM/CO/5, para. 17 (freedom of religion).

23 Concluding observations on Finland, CERD/C/FIN/CO/20-22, para. 13.

24 Concluding observations on Costa Rica, CERD/C/CRI/CO/18, para. 10; Guatemala, CERD/C/GTM/CO/11, para. 17; Venezuela, CERD/C/VEN/CO/18, para. 20.

25 Concluding observations on Slovenia, CERD/C/SVN/CO/6-7, para. 12 (political rights).

26 Concluding observations on Colombia, CERD/C/COL/CO/14, para. 14; Israel, CERD/C/ISR/CO/13, para. 37.

27 Concluding observations on, CERD/C/CAN/CO/18, para. 14 (stereotypes associated with terrorism).

28 Concluding observations on Ecuador, CERD/C/ECU/CO/20-22, para. 13.

29 GR 32, para. 23.

30 E/CN.4/Sub.2/L.308, Article 2, para. 1.

31 Discrimination by groups, institutions, or individuals was also adverted to in the Kertzynski draft, E/CN.4/Sub.2/L.323, Article 2, para. 2.

32 E/CN.4/Sub.2/L.309, Article 2, para. 3.

33 E/CN.4/Sub.2/L.323, Article 2 para. 1.

34 E/CN.4/Sub.2/L.309, Article 2, para. 2. The Ivanov/Ketrzynski draft, E/CN.4/Sub.2/L.314, Article 2, para. 1, and the Ketrzynski draft, E/CN.4/Sub.2/L.323, Article 2, para. 2, also included limiting references to territory.

35 E/CN.4/Sub.2/L.309, Article 2, para. 3.

speedy elimination of racial discrimination was expressly adverted to in the Kertzynski text.[36] The Calvocoressi/Capotorti text selected for discussion included the following elements for what became paragraph 1 of Article 2 of the Convention:[37]

1. Each Contracting State undertakes to pursue by all appropriate means a policy of eliminating racial discrimination in all its forms.
2. Each Contracting State shall rigorously abstain from any act or practice of racial discrimination and undertakes that all its legislative, executive, administrative and judicial organs, and also local authorities and public institutions of all kinds within its territory, shall act in conformity with this obligation. No contracting State shall encourage, advocate or support racial discrimination by any individual, group or private organization.
3. Each Contracting State shall rescind any laws and regulations which have the effect of creating or perpetuating racial discrimination.
4. Each Contracting State undertakes to adopt all necessary measures, including legislation if appropriate, to prohibit racial discrimination by any individual, group or private organization.

Following discussions, the phrase 'and without delay' was added by the authors after 'all appropriate means' in the first sentence of paragraph 1; 'to this end' was also added at the end of the sentence. In a reorganization of the text, sub-paragraphs 2, 3, and 4 were converted into (a), (b), and (c) of paragraph 1.[38] Key deletions were made from new sub-paragraph (a), including the words 'rigorously', 'legislative, executive, administrative and judicial',[39] and 'private'.[40] 'Public institutions' was retained as a phrase because, as explained by Capotorti, the words 'could cover any institutions not entirely dependent on the State, established by law for public purposes';[41] he also defended the inclusion of a reference to local authorities 'which in many countries were not part of the State machinery'.[42] Reference to 'individuals' was changed to 'persons': according to Capotorti, the change widened the scope of the text.[43] The words 'take effective measures to revise government policies' were added to new sub-paragraph (b) after 'each contracting State shall',[44] and the order of sub-paragraph (c) was changed, placing the prohibition of racial discrimination first. The reference to 'within its territory' was also dropped, with Ferguson offering the comment that deletion of 'within its territory' would 'have the advantage of

[36] States parties would undertake not to permit, etc. racial discrimination in its territory 'and, if necessary . . . make legislative provision for and . . . implement such measures as are required for the speedy elimination of all racial discrimination': E/CN.4/Sub.2/L.323, Article 2, para. 3.

[37] E/CN.4/Sub.2/L.324, this text did not include a paragraph on special measures.

[38] E/CN.4/873, para. 59.

[39] Capotorti commented that the State 'was . . . a complex which included all its organs': E/CN.4/Sub.2/SR.415, p. 5.

[40] 'Private' appears to have been dropped because, in the words of Ketrzynski, 'it might be interpreted in some States as restrictive': E/CN.4/Sub.2/SR.415, p. 7; see also the comments of Ingles, E/CN.4/Sub.2/SR.415, p. 8, and Capotorti, E/CN.4/Sub.2/SR. 415, pp. 9 and 10.

[41] E/CN.4/Sub.2/SR.415, p. 9. Capotorti expanded on examples, which included 'not only organs which depended directly on the central government, but also autonomous entities such as State railways, public power authorities and local institutions'; the paragraph 'was intended to cover all public activities': E/CN.4/Sub.2/SR.417, p. 4. Following Capotorti, Lerner reads the provision as covering such autonomous entities, which 'are always of a public nature': N. Lerner, *The International Convention on the Elimination of All Forms of Racial Discrimination* (Sijthoff and Noordhoff, 1980), p. 37 [henceforth *The International Convention*].

[42] E/CN.4/Sub.2.SR.415, p. 9.

[43] E/CN.4/Sub.2/SR.415, p. 10.

[44] The difference between 'rescind' and 'nullify' in the paragraph was explained by Ferguson in response to a question by Capotorti: according to Ferguson, 'in common law countries, only bodies which had the power to make laws could rescind them . . . Bodies such as courts, which did not have the power to make laws, were entitled to nullify them': E/CN.4/Sub.2/SR.416, p. 6.

implying that the responsibility of the State extended to all areas in which it exercised authority'.[45] Further amendments by Ivanov were not accepted by the Sub-Commission, including one which incorporated an explanation of the unacceptability of racial discrimination as 'an infringement of the rights and an offence to the dignity of the human person and a denial of the rules of international law and of the principles and objectives set forth in the United Nations documents mentioned in the preamble of the present Convention'.[46]

The Commission on Human Rights had before it the following text of Article 2(1):

> States parties to the present Convention condemn racial discrimination and undertake to pursue by all appropriate means and without delay a policy of eliminating racial discrimination in all its forms, and to this end:
>
> (a) Each State party undertakes to engage in no act or practice of racial discrimination, and to ensure that all public authorities and public institutions, national and local, shall act in conformity with this obligation. Each State party undertakes not to encourage, advocate or support racial discrimination by any person, group or organization;
> (b) Each State party shall take effective measures to revise governmental and other public policies, and to rescind or nullify any laws or regulations which have the effect of creating or perpetuating racial discrimination wherever it exists.
> (c) Each State party shall prohibit racial discrimination by any person, group or organization, and undertakes to adopt all necessary measures, including legislation, if appropriate.

In discussions, Lebanon proposed and gained acceptance for the deletion of the second sentence of paragraph 1(a),[47] 'since it was unthinkable that States parties would encourage, advocate or support racial discrimination'.[48] An Austrian amendment to add the words 'against persons, groups or organizations' after 'practice of racial discrimination' on the basis that in the matter of the fundamental obligations of States parties it was important to be clear and explicit,[49] was also adopted.[50]

A number of amendments to paragraph 1(b) were accepted without objection. Hence the word 'revise' was replaced by 'review' on the proposal of the United Kingdom (UK),[51] whose representative argued that 'revise' implied that all countries would have to change their policy, while 'review' would mean that 'all governments would be required to examine their laws with care and would therefore be in a better position to decide what changes they should make in those laws'.[52] There was some discussion on the phrase 'rescind or nullify' in sub-paragraph (b), based partly on the text of Article 4 of the Declaration on the Elimination of All Forms of Racial Discrimination which used only the term 'rescind'.[53] This led to the suggestion that 'nullify' be deleted, in case it merely

[45] E/CN.4/Sub.2/SR.416, p. 5.

[46] E/CN.4/Sub.2/L.327, E/CN.4/Sub.2/SR.416, p. 5. The amendment was rejected by 6 votes to 4 with 3 abstentions: E/CN.4/Sub.2/241, para. 66. See also further comments by Ivanov, E/CN.4/Sub.2/SR.417, p. 7.

[47] E/CN.4/L.691. The proposal was adopted by 15 votes to 1 with 1 abstention: E/CN.4/874, para. 128.

[48] E/CN.4/874, para. 116. The 'unthinkable' substance of the impugned sentence appears as Article 2(1)(b) of the final text.

[49] E/CN.4/L.687; E/CN.4/SR.787, p. 7, representative of Austria.

[50] E/CN.4/874, para. 127: voting was 12 to none, with 8 abstentions.

[51] E/CN.4/L.689.

[52] E/CN.4/874, para. 117; observations of the United Kingdom in E/CN.4/SR.789, p. 4.

[53] Comment by the representative of The Netherlands, E/CN.4/SR.789, p. 6.

duplicated 'rescind'.[54] 'Nullify' was, however, retained along with 'rescind' on the basis that they were both a means of attaining the same end,[55] and by retaining both, the Commission would 'be sure of taking into account the differences between legal systems'.[56] On a proposal by India, the two terms were added to by 'amend' before 'rescind or nullify'.[57]

Discussions on sub-paragraph (c) brought forth a substantive dispute on whether the elimination of racial discrimination must inevitably take time. The UK proposed to delete the reference to 'prohibition' and replace it with 'undertake all necessary measures, including legislation if appropriate',[58] to bring racial discrimination to an end. The UK argued that the chapeau of paragraph 1 suggested that the elimination of racial discrimination would take time and that this was contradicted by sub-paragraph (c) where prohibition implied an immediate undertaking, bearing in mind that the rest of sub-paragraph (c) did not imply immediate action.[59] The UK also felt that to eliminate racial discrimination, methods other than legislation would be required,[60] including education.[61] The proposal, eventually superseded by an oral Turkish amendment,[62] nevertheless evoked strong opposition:

> If a State party refused to prohibit racial discrimination and proposed instead a very vague undertaking to bring it to an end within an unspecified period of time, the purpose for which the Convention had been drafted would never be attained. The question was whether the State party should begin by prohibiting discrimination . . . The United Kingdom text was far more than an exercise in semantics. The only States likely to be pleased by its wording were those which had no desire to take firm measures but were ready to affix their signatures to the Convention because of the pressure of public opinion . . . The . . . text would prolong the struggle against discrimination indefinitely and would provide . . . loopholes by means of which compliance . . . could be evaded.[63]

Despite this, the Turkish text, while retaining the word 'prohibition' was read, on account of its use of the phrase 'all appropriate means', to allow a certain latitude to States.[64]

[54] Observation of the Chairman, the representative of Ecuador, E/CN.4/SR.789, p. 6.

[55] Observation by the representative of India, E/CN.4/SR.789, p. 6.

[56] Representative of Austria, E/CN.4/SR.789, p. 7.

[57] E/CN.4/874, paras 118 and 119: on the proposal by India, 'It was considered that the text should contain some provision . . . for the amending of existing laws and regulations which had the effect of creating or perpetuating racial discrimination wherever it existed': *ibid.*, para. 119; E/CN.4/SR.789, p. 5.

[58] E/CN.4/L.689, summarized in E/3873; E/CN.4/874, para. 120.

[59] E/CN.4/SR.787, p. 10 for part of the UK explanation.

[60] The representative of Canada wondered 'whether it was really necessary to bind States to prohibit racial discrimination. If the intention was to place upon States the obligation to abolish racial discrimination, the Convention should emphasize positive measures to that end': E/CN.4/SR.788, p. 5; see also remarks by the representative of France, *ibid.*, pp. 6–7.

[61] The UK also made the point that, in common law countries, racial discrimination was dealt with not by making it an offence but by the protection given to all under the law in the enjoyment of human rights and fundamental freedoms: E/CN.4/SR.788, pp. 4–5.

[62] 'Each State party shall prohibit and bring to an end by all appropriate means, including legislation if necessary, racial discrimination by any person, group or national organization.'

[63] Comments by the representative of the USSR, E/CN.4/SR.787, p. 11.

[64] The Turkish amendment was adopted unanimously: E/CN.4/874, para. 132. Various comments on the text are made in E/CN.4/SR.788, pp. 9–10. The representative of Costa Rica read the Turkish proposal as emphasizing 'that States were to prohibit racial discrimination "by all appropriate means", that was to say any means within the law, and it did not commit them to enact new legislation unless it was necessary': E/CN.4/SR.788, p. 9.

The text of Article 2(1) before the Third Committee read as follows:

States parties condemn racial discrimination and undertake to pursue by all appropriate means and without delay a policy of eliminating racial discrimination in all its forms, and, to this end:

(a) Each State party undertakes to engage in no act or practice of racial discrimination against persons, groups of persons or institutions, and to ensure that all public authorities and public institutions, national and local, shall act in conformity with this obligation;
(b) Each State party shall take effective measures to review governmental and other public policies, and to amend, rescind or nullify any laws and regulations which have the effect of creating or perpetuating racial discrimination wherever it exists;
(c) Each State party shall prohibit and bring to an end, by all appropriate means, including legislation if necessary, racial discrimination by any persons, group or national organization.

In the Third Committee the phrase 'and promoting understanding among all races' was successfully proposed by Brazil, Colombia, and Senegal as an addition to the chapeau after 'racial discrimination in all its forms'.[65] The final Article 2, paragraph 1(b) of the Convention owes its place to a multi-State amendment which superseded an amendment of Brazil,[66] and was viewed as adding to the reach of the Convention.[67] The Commission's sub-paragraph (b) (sub-paragraph (c) of the Convention) was amended to replace the words 'other public' by 'national and local' by virtue of the same multi-State amendment.[68] Sub-paragraph (c) of the Commission's text (sub-paragraph (d) of the Convention) was also amended to delete from 'group or national organization' the word 'national', a change that widens its scope.[69] In this sub-paragraph, the phrase 'if necessary' was replaced by 'as required by circumstances' on the initiative of Poland and Ghana.[70] The Polish representative, echoing similar points made before the Commission, objected to the wording of the sub-paragraph which

was open to the interpretation that the decision as to whether there was any need for legislation to put an end to racial discrimination rested solely with the State concerned, even in States where no such legislation existed. There was therefore no guarantee that racial discrimination would be

[65] A/C.3/L.1217. The amendment was adopted by 85 votes to none, with 7 abstentions: General Assembly Official Records, Twentieth Session, Annexes, Agenda item 58, Report of the Third Committee, A/6181, para. 55.

[66] The amendment 'Each State party undertakes not to sponsor, defend or support racial discrimination by any persons or organizations' (A/C.3/L.1226 and Corr. 1) replaced 'Each State party undertakes not to encourage, advocate or support racial discrimination by any persons or organizations' (A/C.3/L.1209), which conveys essentially the same message. The multi-party amendment was adopted by 47 votes to 2 with 39 abstentions: A/6181, para. 55.

[67] The logic of the new paragraph did not commend itself to the representative of Italy: 'the Italian delegation considered that, if States undertook to prohibit certain activities, it was pointless to invite them, at the same time, not to encourage those activities': A/C.3/SR.1308, para. 20.

[68] A/C.3/L.1226 and Corr. 1; the amendment was adopted by 56 votes to 2 with 34 abstentions: A/6181, *ibid.* The representative of the Netherlands intimated that 'other public policies' was wider that 'national and local' in that it 'sufficed to cover all the policies to which sub-para. 1(a) applied': A/C.3/SR.1308, para. 12. Austria abstained on the paragraph because, according to the representative, 'legislation having local application was not possible in her country': A/C.3/SR.1308, para. 35.

[69] Now sub-para. (d) of Article 2.1 of the Convention; this was the result of an oral suggestion by Italy at the 1308th meeting, revising the multi-State amendment A/C.3/L.1226 and Corr. 1, and was adopted by 81 votes to 1, with 11 abstentions: A/6181, para. 49.

[70] A/C.3/L.1210, amendment by Poland to replace 'if necessary' by 'in the absence thereof' was itself replaced on the oral suggestion of Ghana at the 1308th meeting: A/6181, para. 48; the representative of Ghana observed that some delegations regarded the Polish phrase as 'too peremptory': A/C.3/SR.1308, para. 3.

prohibited by law in all States ... the Convention should impose upon States parties the obligation to prohibit racial discrimination through their legislation if they had not yet done so.[71]

As it had in the Commission, the UK objected, arguing that racial discrimination might persist even after the adoption of legislation, and that the General Assembly 'should not attempt to dictate to States, particularly since the nature and size of the problem varied from country to country'.[72] The representative of Haiti introduced a motif which became important in the life of the Convention: explaining Haiti's abstention, the representative 'could not accept the imposition on States of an obligation to adopt legislation which was not necessary in cases where, as in Haiti, racial discrimination did not exist'.[73]

Sub-paragraph (e) of Article 2.1, which had not figured in the text prepared by the Commission, was introduced by Brazil, Colombia, and Senegal.[74] This was supported by Ecuador, among others, because it 'contained a positive idea, in contrast with the negative character of all the previous provisions ... [and] ... concerned measures calculated to promote integration ... in keeping with the traditions of Latin America, where all multi-racial societies were integrated'.[75] On the other hand, in an explanation of vote, the representative of Costa Rica considered that 'the word "discourage" had no legal validity and only weakened the text'.[76] In a similar vein, the UK considered that the paragraph was superfluous and that the weak verb 'discourage' contrasted (badly) with the 'vigorous nature' of the language of Article 2, paragraph 1.[77] Austria abstained in the vote on sub-paragraph (e) 'since the problem of racial barriers did not exist in Austria'.[78]

C. Practice

I. Reservations and Declarations

A small number of reservations relate specifically to Article 2: on 2(1), Monaco declares that 'it reserves the right to apply its own legal provisions concerning the admission of foreigners to the labour market of the Principality'.[79] The reservation by the US is the most extensive, relating essentially to obligations to address private conduct: 'the United States does not accept any obligation under this Convention to enact legislation or take other measures under paragraph 1 of Article 2, sub-paragraphs 1(c) and (d) of Article 2, Article 3, and Article 5 with respect to private conduct except as mandated by the Constitution and laws of the United States'. The Committee noted the reservation with concern and has,[80] *inter alia*, invited the US to 'consider withdrawing or narrowing the scope of its reservation to Article 2 of the Convention'.[81] Banton is less respectful,

[71] A/C.3/SR.1306, para. 18. This was clarified further by the representative of Poland to the effect that if 'such legislation already existed, there was no need for adoption of any new legislation': A/C.3/SR.1307, para. 33.

[72] A/C.3/SR.1307, para. 3.

[73] A/C.3/SR.1308, para. 31.

[74] A/C.3/L.1217 was adopted on a roll-call vote by 97 votes to none, with 4 abstentions: A/6181, para. 55.

[75] A/C.3/SR.1308, para. 18. For comments by the representative of Italy, see para. 19, *ibid.*

[76] A/C.3/SR.1308, para. 29.

[77] *Ibid.*, para. 30. See also the negative comments of Jamaica, *ibid.*, para. 37.

[78] A/C.3/SR.1308, para. 36.

[79] The Committee has recommended that Monaco withdraw the reservation in light of 'developments in its legislation': A/65/18, p. 86, para. 7. Switzerland maintains a similar reservation.

[80] A/56/18, para. 392.

[81] CERD/C/USA/CO/6, para. 11. The issue is recalled and expanded in the 2014 concluding observations of the Committee, wherein the State party is called upon to consider withdrawing or narrowing the reservation

reflecting that 'the reservations [by the USA] show no understanding of the Convention and what it is attempting to achieve'.[82]

II. Guidelines

The harmonized reporting guidelines request information for the common core document that impinges on Article 2. In addition to information on the legal framework for the protection of human rights at the national level, more focused information is requested 'on whether the principle of non-discrimination is included as a general binding principle' in domestic law,[83] and on 'steps taken to ensure that discrimination in all its forms and on all grounds is prevented and combated in practice'.[84] The CERD-specific guidelines do little more than to restate the provisions of Article 2 paragraph by paragraph;[85] the only novel note is the request for information on whether a national human rights institution (NHRI) or other appropriate bodies have been mandated with the task of combating racial discrimination.

III. Convention Obligations and Domestic Law

International law requires that States bring their domestic (national) law into line with their international obligations and that domestic provisions may not be invoked to defeat an international obligation.[86] Article 2, as the principal repository of general obligations to implement the Convention, is a useful starting point to consider the relationship between the Convention and the law of the State, bearing in mind Leary's observation that the efficacy of human rights treaties depends in essence on their translation into domestic law.[87] Discussion of the relationship between systems of law is often enmeshed in generalized theory. Approaches to the incorporation of international law into domestic legal orders are sometimes characterized in reductionist mode as monist or dualist—the former signifying automatic incorporation into domestic law with binding effects therein, the latter implying that specific legislative adjustments are required to give international law binding effects within national legal orders.[88] The theories are saturated with competing notions of the superiority of one system over another, which may serve to obscure the complex connections between the domestic and international spheres.[89] There is a fair degree of convergence across civil and common law jurisdictions with regard to the incorporation of customary international law—automatic incorporation at least in theory, although issues of consonance with established domestic law and status in

'and broaden the protection afforded by law against all discriminatory acts perpetrated by private individuals, groups or organizations': CERD/C/USA/CO/7-9, para. 5.

82 *International Action*, p. 247.

83 HRI/GEN/2/Rev.5, p. 14, para. 52.

84 *Ibid.*, p. 14, para. 53.

85 CERD/C/2007/1, pp. 5–6.

86 Article 27 of the Vienna Convention on the Law of Treaties. For applications by the International Court of Justice, see the *Lockerbie* case, ICJ reports 1992, pp. 3, 32; *Avena* (*Mexico v USA*), (Provisional Measures) ICJ reports 2004, p. 12, p. 65, cited in M.N. Shaw, *International Law* (6th edn, Cambridge University Press, 2008), p. 135 [henceforth *International Law*].

87 V. Leary, *International Labour Conventions and National Law* (Martinus Nijhoff Publishers, 1982), p. 1.

88 For a general treatment, with useful illustrations, see Shaw, *International Law*, chapter 4; for application to international human rights conventions, see A. Byrnes and C. Renshaw, 'Within the State', in Moeckli *et al.*, *International Human Rights Law*, Chapter 22, at pp. 460–5.

89 For a helpful general review of the range of approaches to international law taken by domestic legal systems, see D. Sloss, 'Domestic Application of Treaties', D. Hollis (ed.), *The Oxford Guide to Treaties* (Oxford University Press, 2014), pp. 367–95 [henceforth *Domestic Application*].

the legal hierarchy position its practical effect.[90] On the other hand, patterns of incorporation of international treaties vary widely. Committee discussions regularly refer to the variety of techniques of incorporating human rights treaties into the domestic realm. International law does not dictate a preference for one system of incorporation over another but requires that, whatever the mode, the standards of the Convention in question are adequately reflected in domestic practice.

In States where the prevailing practice is automatic incorporation through constitutional provision, CERD prefers that constitutions underline the primacy of international treaties over domestic law as clearly as possible,[91] and frequently recalls that incorporation in the constitution may not in itself be sufficient. Apart from the question of the 'non-self-executing' nature of—at least some—of the provisions in the Convention,[92] the constitution may not be drafted in terms adequate to capture the full range of grounds of discrimination or the rights in the Convention.[93] Constitutional review[94] or amendments may be urged upon the State,[95] as well as supplementary legislation to give full effect to the Constitution and remedy legal lacunae.[96] Requested legislation may be compendious, as with Panama, recommended to 'adopt legislation to make fully effective the provisions of the constitution relating to non-discrimination and expressly prohibiting discrimination based on grounds of race and to guarantee the availability of effective remedies to endure implementation of such legislation'.[97] A State party may be requested to clarify the relationship between the Convention and domestic law.[98]

In the case of 'dualist' systems, the Committee accepts that there is no obligation to incorporate the Convention as such into law but may express regret that this has not been done, an argument linked to the concern that, without such incorporation, the Convention may not be given full effect. Thus, CERD reiterated to the UK 'its continuing concern that the State party's courts may not give full effect to the provisions of the Convention unless it is expressly incorporated into its domestic law or the State party adopt necessary provisions in its legislation'; the UK was therefore requested to reconsider its position—non-incorporation as such—'so that the Convention can be more readily invoked in the domestic courts of the State party'.[99] In the case of Denmark, CERD suggested that the non-incorporation of international treaties resulted 'in reluctance by

[90] Shaw, *International Law*, Chapter 4 'International Law and Municipal Law'.

[91] Concluding observations on Morocco, CERD/C/MAR/17-18, para. 8, recommend that the State party 'incorporate provisions in its constitution on the primacy of international treaties over domestic law, in order to ensure broad application of this principle and enable litigants to invoke the relevant provisions of the constitution before the courts'.

[92] Article 4 of the Convention is the most frequently cited Article with reference to its non-self-executing nature, and thus of the need to legislate its requirements to make them effective in domestic law.

[93] 'The Committee is concerned that the definition of racial discrimination in . . . the Constitution of Japan, which prescribes the principles of equality and non-discrimination, does not include the grounds of national or ethnic origin, colour or descent and therefore does not fully meet the requirements of Article 1 of the Convention': concluding observations on Japan, CERD/C/JPN/CO/7-9, para. 7; see also concluding observations on Korea, CERD/C/KOR/CO/14, para. 10.

[94] Concluding observations on Nigeria, CERD/C/NGA/CO/18, para. 11.

[95] Concluding observations on Bosnia and Herzegovina, CERD/C/BIH/CO/6, para. 11.

[96] Concluding observations on Colombia, CERD/C/COL/CO/14, para. 13. The Committee has also called for the 'entrenchment' of constitutional provisions and that legislative acts against racial discrimination prevail over all other legislation: concluding observations on Australia, CERD/C/AUS/CO/15-17, para. 110.

[97] CERD/C/PAN/CO/15-20, para. 9.

[98] Concluding observations on Portugal, CERD/C/PRT/CO/12-14, para. 11.

[99] CERD/C/GBR/CO/18-20, para. 10.

lawyers and judges to invoke such treaties in Danish courts'; incorporation, it was argued, was necessary 'to ensure [the Convention's] direct application before Danish courts in order to afford all individuals its full protection'.[100] When incorporation of the Convention is a possible agenda, it should be, according to the Committee, at an appropriately high level, not lower than other, comparable human rights treaties.[101] When incorporation is a less probable State agenda, the Committee's preference is for legislation to be as comprehensive as possible.[102]

Preoccupations over the functioning of the Convention in domestic law were aptly summarized by CERD member de Gouttes:

> The debate on the contrast between countries with a monist legal system, in which international treaties and agreements took precedence over domestic legislation as soon as they had been approved, and those with a dualist legal system was perhaps not the most consequential. It was more important to know whether a duly ratified instrument was self-executing. Even in the case of a monist system, any ratified treaty had to be accompanied by internal legislation defining the sanctions and penalties incurred for any derogation from the obligations... indeed, since no human rights treaty provided for punishment in the event of non-compliance with its provisions, implementing regulations were absolutely necessary to ensure its application.[103]

The Committee has not been completely consistent with regard to the self-executing nature of the provisions of the Convention *in toto*, with statements recalling that 'the Convention is not self-executing'[104] standing alongside statements that 'many provisions of the Convention' are not self-executing.[105] The Committee has made clear its view that Article 4 is not self-executing but requires implementing legislation, a proposition cemented into GR 35 on combating racist hate speech: 'As Article 4 is not self-executing, States parties are required by its terms to adopt legislation to combat racist hate speech that falls within its scope'.[106] Criticism of the 'far-reaching reservations' of the US,[107] particularly with regard to Article 4 and the limitation as to private conduct, has not extended to specific criticism of its declaration that the provisions of the Convention are not self-executing, though in this case, the absence of contestation does not necessarily signify agreement with the view of the State party.[108]

IV. The Reach of the Convention

Unlike the ICCPR, which requires a State party to respect and endure civil and political rights 'to all individuals within its territory and subject to its jurisdiction',[109] there is no

[100] CERD/C/DNK/CO/18-19, para. 8; CERD/C/NK/O/20-21, para. 8.

[101] Concluding observations on Norway, CERD/C/NOR/CO/19-20, para. 7.

[102] 'The Committee urges the State party to review its legislation and take the most appropriate approach for incorporating the Convention's provisions into domestic law, either by adopting a comprehensive law against racial discrimination or amending existing laws': concluding observations on Laos, CERD/C/LAO/CO/16-18, para. 7.

[103] CERD/C/SR.1444, para. 37, discussing the initial and second periodic report of Japan.

[104] Concluding observations on Japan, CERD/C/304/Add.114, para. 20.

[105] Concluding observations on Armenia, CERD/C/ARM/CO/5-6, para. 8; The Philippines, CERD/C/PHL/CO/20, para. 14.

[106] GR 35, para. 13.

[107] CERD/C/304/Add.125, paras 12 and 13; CERD/C/USA/CO/6, para. 11.

[108] For a review of the position in US courts on self-executing treaties and related issues, see C. Vázquez, 'Treaties as Law of the Land: The Supremacy Clause and the Judicial Enforcement of Treaties', *Harvard Law Review* 122 (2008), 599–695; Sloss, *Domestic Application*, 387, describes the position in the US as 'analytically incoherent'.

[109] Article 2(1).

equivalent general clause limiting the application of ICERD to the jurisdiction or territory of States parties.[110] Only two substantive Articles—Article 3 on segregation and apartheid and Article 6 on remedies—include such references: to 'territories under [the] jurisdiction' of States parties in Article 3, while Article 6 obliges States parties to assure to 'everyone within their jurisdiction' effective protection and remedies. In the context of the individual communications procedure, Article 14 envisages communications from individuals or groups of individuals within the jurisdiction of the State party. Neither Article 2—the general repository of obligations—nor Article 5, the principal repository of rights, refers to territory or jurisdiction.[111]

The question of the application of international human rights instruments beyond the national territory to extraterritorial acts and omissions has become a prominent focus of interest in recent international human rights practice.[112] According to the Human Rights Committee, a State party must respect and ensure ICCPR rights to anyone within its 'power or effective control',[113] even if not situated within the territory of the State party, a principle that also applies to 'those within the power or effective control of the forces of a State party acting outside its territory'.[114] CEDAW takes the view that 'States primarily exercise territorial jurisdiction. The obligations of States parties apply, however to [those] within their territory or effective control even if not situated within the territory. States parties are responsible for all their actions affecting human rights, regardless of whether the affected persons are in their territory.'[115] Other human rights instruments have been interpreted to include an extraterritorial dimension to human rights obligations, even if

[110] The ICESCR is similarly devoid of a provision regarding territory or jurisdiction, though, analogously to Article 14 of ICERD, its Optional Protocol envisages communications from people under the jurisdiction of a State party. The ACHR—Article 1(1)—requires States parties to respect and ensure the rights of persons subject to their jurisdiction, without reference to a territorial condition; an analogous provision appears in Article 1 of the ECHR.

[111] 'Jurisdiction' is a term with multiple meanings in international law and the international law of human rights, ranging over the different bases for the legal exercise of jurisdiction over persons outside the State's territory—delimitation of sovereign competence—to the question of obligations incurred towards groups and individuals protected by ICERD but situated extra-territorially. For a review of the general position in international law, see Shaw, *International Law*, Chapter 12; for distinctions between the position in general international law and that in human rights, see M. Milanovic, 'From Compromise to Principle: Clarifying the Conception of Jurisdiction in Human Rights Treaties', *HRLR* 8 (2008), 411–48; also the presentation by the last author on <http://webtv.un.org/news-features/watch/marko-milanovic-on-the-extraterritorial-application-of-human-rights-treaties/3875099482001>.

[112] International human rights law highlights different concerns than international law more broadly, historically concerned with the 'protection of aliens'; for a short summary, see R. Kolb, 'The Protection of the Individual in Times of War and Peace', in B. Fassbender and A. Peters (eds), *The Oxford Handbook of the History of International Law*, Chapter 13.

[113] Lubell summarizes the point: 'The very object and purpose of the Covenant would be severely undermined if States could evade responsibility by relocating their abuse of individuals': N. Lubell, Extraterritorial *Use of Force against Non-State Actors* (Oxford University Press, 2010), p. 205.

[114] General Comment 31, para. 10. Cases are relatively sparse: see discussion by S. Joseph and A. Fletcher, 'Scope of Application', chapter 6 of Moeckli *et al.*, *International Human Rights Law*, pp. 119–39, pp. 133–4, who note the assertion by the Human Rights Committee of the responsibility of Israel for the Occupied Territories, and of the US for Guantanamo Bay—both situations have been addressed by CERD. The authors conclude, p. 133, that 'the ICCPR and the ACHR apply extraterritorially where an affected person is under the effective control of a State's agents, rather than only where an affected person is within territory that is effectively controlled by a State', while observing, p. 138, that ECHR practice may not be fully consonant with their position.

[115] CEDAW GR 28 on 'the Core Obligations of States parties under Article 2', CEDAW/C/GC/28 (2010), para. 12.

practice does not always display consistency.[116] In *Construction of a Wall in Palestinian Occupied Territory*, the International Court of Justice (ICJ) stated with respect to the ICCPR that '[w]hile the jurisdiction of States is primarily territorial, it may sometimes be exercised outside the national territory. Considering the object and purpose of the [ICCPR] it would seem natural that, even when such is the case, States parties to the Covenant should be bound to comply with its provisions.'[117] With regard to the ICESCR, the ICJ noted that it contained no provision as to its scope of application; it was, however, 'not to be excluded that it applies both to territories over which a party has sovereignty and to those over which that State exercises territorial jurisdiction'.[118]

In the case of ICERD, in *Georgia v the Russian Federation* the ICJ observed that

> there is no restriction of a general nature in CERD relating to its territorial application... neither Article 2 nor Article 5, alleged violations of which are invoked by Georgia, contain a specific territorial limitation... the Court consequently finds that these provisions of CERD generally appear to apply, like other provisions of instruments of that nature, to the actions of a State party when it acts beyond its territory.[119]

With regard to human rights treaties which do not contain a provision delimiting their territorial application, Sivakumaran interprets the cited paragraph as representing a 'presumption... that they have extraterritorial effect'.[120] For ICERD, the 'presumption' is given substance by the removal, in the drafting process, of any territorial restriction on the ambit of the Convention.[121] The comment in *Georgia v Russian Federation* on 'instruments of that nature' is apt to include instruments of a 'universal' nature such as ICERD and the Covenants, etc, unconstrained by notions of '*espace juridique*'.[122] In light

[116] Notable cases before the European Court of Human Rights include *Loizidou v Turkey*, App. No. 15318/89 (1996); Cyprus *v Turkey*, App. No. 25781/94 (2001); *Ilaşcu and Others v Moldova and Russia*, App. No. 48787/99 (2004); *Issa v Turkey*, App. No. 31821/96 (2004); *Al Skeini and Others v UK*, App. No. 55721/07 (2011). In the Inter-American system, see *Saldano v Argentina*, Inter-American Commission report No. 38/99.

[117] *Legal consequences of the Construction of a Wall in the Occupied Palestinian Territory*, ICJ Advisory Opinion, 9 July 2004, para. 109; the Court found that the constant practice of the Human Rights Committee is consistent with this view, a practice confirmed by the *travaux préparatoires* of the Covenant. The Court therefore concluded, para. 111, that the ICCPR 'is applicable in respect of acts done by a State in the exercise of its jurisdiction outside its own territory'.

[118] *Construction of a Wall*, para. 112. As with the Human Rights Committee under the ICCPR, the Court cited the position taken by the Committee on Economic, Social and Cultural Rights in support of its reasoning. The interpretation of the scope of jurisdiction in *Construction of a Wall* was recalled by the Court in *Armed Activities on the Territory of the Congo (Democratic Republic of Congo v Uganda)*, Judgment of 19 December 2005, ICJ Rep. 168, para. 216.

[119] *Case Concerning Application of the International Convention on the Elimination of All Forms of Racial Discrimination, Georgia v Russian Federation*, Request for Provisional Measures, International Court of Justice, 15 October 2008, para. 109. The preceding paragraph. recited the disagreement of the parties on the territorial scope of obligations under ICERD: Georgia claimed that Russia's obligations extended to 'acts and omissions attributable to Russia' which had their locus 'within Georgia's territory and in particular in Abkhazia and South Ossetia'; Russia on the other hand, claimed that the Convention could not be applied extraterritorially and, in particular, that Articles 2 and 5 could not 'govern a State's conduct outside its own borders'. See further discussion in Chapter 19.

[120] S. Sivakumaran, 'International Humanitarian Law', in Moeckli *et al.*, *International Human Rights Law*, pp. 480–95, p. 494.

[121] Comment by Sub-Commission member Ferguson on the deletion of a reference to territory, *supra*, n. 45. The issue of territory was not well-aired in the *travaux*.

[122] European Court of Human Rights, *Banković et al. v Belgium et al.*, App. No. 52207/99, Admissibility (2001), para. 80: 'the [ECHR] is a multi-lateral treaty operating... in an essentially regional context and notably in the legal space (espace juridique) of the Contracting States... The Convention was not designed to be applied throughout the world'. For a critique, see M. Milanović, *Extraterritorial Application of Human Rights*

of such a presumption, it is noteworthy that Turkey entered a reservation declaring that its ratification of the Convention related 'exclusively with regard to the national territory where the Constitution and the legal and administrative order of the Republic of Turkey are applied'.[123]

In CERD practice, assertions regarding the responsibility of State X beyond territorial boundaries have characteristically been linked to situations where another State party—Y—has lost effective control over parts of its territory to the forces of State X (foreign occupation) or a secessionist administration presumed to be under the control of State X.[124] In the case of Cyprus, the Committee took a view on the occupation of 37 per cent of the territory of Cyprus by Turkish forces and its consequences in causing 'the *de facto* separation of the various ethnic and religious communities', an artificial division that was 'an obstacle to peace and the enjoyment of human rights in the region', impeding 'the construction of a progressive anti-discrimination strategy for the island as a whole'.[125] In the case of Moldova, it was noted that the Transniestria region 'continued to be outside the effective control of the State party, which was therefore unable to monitor the application of the Convention in that part of its territory'.[126] In these and other cases, the Committee has expressed serious concerns about the malign influence of international and internal conflicts on the enjoyment of human rights, together with recommendations on steps necessary to solve the resulting problems, including calls for prosecution of those responsible for violence and compensation for victims.[127] Recommended steps have also included confidence-building measures by States parties and civil society.[128]

Treaties: Law, Principles, and Policy (Oxford University Press, 2011), p. 40, describing a confusion between legality and the operation of facts in *Banković* as a category error; also M. Happold, 'Banković v Belgium, and the Territorial Scope of the European Convention on Human Rights', *HRLR* 3 (2003), 77–90.

[123] In concluding observations, the Committee encouraged the State party to consider withdrawing its reservation and declarations 'including removal of the territorial limitation to the application of the Convention': CERD/C/TUR/CO/3, para. 8. Cyprus objects to the 'declaration deeming it to be a reservation: 'the Government of the Republic of Cyprus has examined the declaration made by the Government of the Republic of Turkey to the International Convention on the Elimination of all Forms of Racial Discrimination (New York, 7 March 1966) on 16 September 2002 in respect of the implementation of the provisions of the Convention only to the States Parties with which it has diplomatic relations.

In the view of the Government of the Republic of Cyprus, this declaration amounts to a reservation. This reservation creates uncertainty as to the States Parties in respect of which Turkey is undertaking the obligations in the Convention. The Government of the Republic of Cyprus therefore objects to the reservation made by the Government of the Republic of Turkey. This reservation or the objection to it shall not preclude the entry into force of the Convention between the Republic of Cyprus and the Republic of Turkey': <https://treaties.un.org/pages/ViewDetails.aspx?src=TREATY&mtdsg_no=IV-2&chapter=4&lang=en#EndDec>. Further on reservations to the Convention, see Chapter 18.

[124] Such situations are characteristically listed in concluding observations under 'factors and difficulties' in implementing the Convention: discussion in Chapter 4 of the present work. For early practice of the Committee with regard to the Panama Canal Zone, the Golan Heights, Cyprus, the West Bank of the River Jordan, and Sinai, see Lerner, *The International Convention*, Chapter 4.

[125] CERD/C/304/Add.124, para. 3. The issue of lack of control by the State party over all of its territory is a recurring theme in observations on Cyprus: CERD/C/CYP/CO/17-22, para. 6. For earlier observations on Cyprus, see L. Holmström (ed.), *Concluding Observations of the UN Committee on the Elimination of Racial Discrimination* (Kluwer Law International, 2002), pp. 171–7 [henceforth *Concluding Observations*].

[126] Moldova, CERD/C/MDA/CO/8-9, para. 3.

[127] Examples include Decision 1(76) on Nigeria, A/65/18, pp. 6–7; Decision 1(77) on Kyrgyzstan, *ibid.*, pp. 7–8; Decision 1(78) on Côte d'Ivoire, A/66/18, pp. 6–7; Concluding observations on Kenya, CERD/C/KEN/CO/1-4, para. 15. For an extensive list of conflict-related recommendations, see I. Diaconu, *Racial Discrimination* (Eleven International Publishing, 2011), pp. 191–4.

[128] In the case of Cyprus, the Committee requested information on 'intercommunal initiatives undertaken by the State party and by civil society to restore mutual confidence and improve relations between ethnic and/or

In some cases, the Committee has supplemented assertions as to lack of 'effective control' by suggesting that responsibility for implementation of the Convention in the contested area lies elsewhere than with the reporting State. In the case of Georgia, the Committee, following its standard recital that 'Abkhazia and South Ossetia continue to be outside the effective control of the State party, which made it therefore unable to implement the Convention in these territories',[129] added the following:

The Committee notes the State party's position that the obligation for implementing the Convention in South Ossetia and Abkhazia belongs to a neighbouring country which has effective control over those territories. The Committee notes that it has in the past taken the view that States that have effective control over a territory have the responsibility under international law and the spirit of the Convention for implementing the Convention.[130]

Ex facie, the Committee's comment to Georgia appears as a *lex imperfecta* in that the position of the State party (Georgia) is noted without drawing a specific legal conclusion, although the second sentence intimates a wider practice 'under international law and the spirit of the Convention'.[131] The usual CERD approach in Article 9 cases is to draw attention to the inability of reporting States to apply the Convention in cases of occupation or secession, and to stress the need to end the occupation or resolve the conflict. In cases with 'international' dimensions, and in the absence thus far of proceedings under Articles 11–13, broader comments by the Committee are restrained in light of the country-by-country focus of reporting under Article 9. Lack of 'control' or 'effective control' in such cases has been treated by international bodies as diminishing, though not eliminating, obligations to apply human rights conventions on the part of the State whose territory is compromised,[132] so that jurisdiction may appear as 'a relative concept, a matter of degree determining the scope of the obligations of the State concerned'.[133] This

religious communities as well as raise awareness through the impartial teaching of the history of Cyprus in schools and other State institutions': CERD/C/CYP/CO/17-22, para. 7.

[129] CERD/C/GEO/CO/4-5, para. 8.

[130] *Ibid.*, para. 9.

[131] The preceding sentence of the paragraph refers to Security Council resolution 1866 (2009) requesting the parties in conflict to facilitate the free movement of refugees and internally displaced persons (IDPs).

[132] In *Ilaşcu and others v Moldova*, the European Court of Human Rights interpreted the 'jurisdiction' of States parties over secessionist territories as implying not the absence of jurisdiction but its reduced scope, so that the State must still endeavour, 'with all the legal and diplomatic means available to it . . . to continue to guarantee the enjoyment of . . . rights and freedoms': App No. 48787/99 (2004), para. 333, also para. 331. See also *Catan and Others v Moldova and Russia*, App. Nos. 43370/04, 8252/05, and 18454/06, (2012). For a Critique of *Ilaşcu* and *Catan*, see comments by M. Milanovic, <http://www.ejiltalk.org/grand-chamber-judgment-in-catan-and-others>. For further comment on the implications of Ilaşcu following the take-over of Crimea but the Russian Federation, see T.D. Grant, 'Ukraine v Russian Federation in Light of Ilaşcu: Two Short Points', <http://www.ejiltalk.org/ukraine-v-russian-federation-in-light-of-ilascu-two-short-points>. Clarification of distinctions between jurisdiction and attribution is offered in O. De Schutter, *International Human Rights Law* (Cambridge University Press, 2010), pp. 147 ff. [henceforth *International human Rights Law*]. Commentators have summarized Ilaşcu as implying that 'just because a State does not have plenary jurisdiction does not mean that it has none': F. Hampson and N. Lubell, *Amicus Curiae Brief for Georgia v Russia (II)*, ECHR, <http://repository.essex.ac.uk/9689/1/hampson-lubell-georgia-russia-amicus-01062014.pdf>.

[133] De Schutter, *ibid.*, p. 134. The point made by Besson may also be borne in mind: 'Without jurisdiction, there are no human rights applicable and hence no duties, and there can be no acts or omissions that would violate those duties that can be attributed to a State and *a fortiori* no potential responsibility of the State for violating those duties later on': S. Besson, 'The Extraterritoriality of the European Convention on Human Rights: Why Human Rights Depend on jurisdiction and what Jurisdiction Amounts to', <http://doc.rero.ch/record/32542/files/ExtraterritorialityECHR.pdf>.

approach is not at odds with the general tenor of CERD approaches to the resolution of conflicts.[134]

Interspersed with wider discussions of extraterritoriality, the issue of the applicability of international human rights law and international humanitarian law to specific situations has also been raised.[135] There has been a persistent line of disagreement between the Committee and Israel regarding the application of the Convention to territories under Israeli control,[136] with the Committee asserting applicability and the State party denying it. The detailed series of exchanges that took place in 2012 regarding the scope of application of the Convention are instructive, and included questions from Committee members as to why Israel denied applicability when the Occupied Territories were effectively under the control of the State party.[137] In response, the delegation of Israel noted that ICERD did not apply because no special declaration had been made extending it to the West Bank 'which lay outside Israeli national territory'; Palestinians did not exist in a state of legal limbo but were subject to the law of armed conflict.[138] Further, agreements had made the majority of Palestinians subject to Palestinian jurisdiction.[139] On the point of a special declaration, CERD member Diaconu asserted that the legal basis for jurisdiction was not a declaration 'but the fact that Israel occupied and controlled those territories. That was a generally accepted rule of international law'.[140] In response, the Israeli delegation stated that 'the understanding that all human rights conventions were territorially bound was connected to the use of . . . jurisdiction in the relevant provision of all such conventions . . . jurisdiction was commonly understood to be connected to . . .

[134] Responding to CERD's concluding observations of 2011, Georgia welcomed the acknowledgement 'that the third State that exercises effective control of Abkhazia . . . [etc.] . . . has a responsibility to observe and implement the Convention in these regions. Hence the Russian Federation bears responsibility for the respect, observance and implementation of the Convention in the occupied regions . . . Georgia . . . remains committed to report about undertaken efforts originating from its positive obligations vis-à-vis occupied regions of Georgia': A/66/18, Annex VIII. Co-opting the terminology of 'Occupied Territories', the 2014 periodic report of Georgia states that while Georgia 'fully undertakes the obligation to take all possible measures for implementing the provisions of the Convention . . . in light of its positive obligations under . . . human rights law, it contends that the primary responsibility . . . rests with the Russian Federation': CERD/C/GEO/6-8, para. 33. See generally, Diaconu, *Racial Discrimination*, pp. 191–4, 320–3.

[135] One commentator suggests that the reference in the Abram draft in the Sub-Commission, E/CN.4/Sub.2/L.308, Article 2, para. 2, referring to a prohibition on States lending support to racial discrimination 'through police action or otherwise', was dropped 'not because the delegates thought the use of force should not be covered, but because they did not want to include any language that could be limiting or confusing': C.G. Buys, 'Application of the International Convention on the Elimination of All Forms of Racial Discrimination', *AJIL* 103 (2009), 294–99, 297; the author cites the comments in E/CN/4/Sub.2/SR.419, p. 7, remarks of Mudawi.

[136] M. Banton, *International Action against Racial Discrimination* (Clarendon Press, 1996), pp. 128–30, and 300–3 [henceforth *International Action*]. See also Holmström (ed.), *Concluding Observations*, pp. 327–35. Early in its practice, CERD declared its competence to examine the manner in which Israel is fulfilling its obligations under the Convention 'with respect to everyone falling under the jurisdiction of Israel, including all persons living in the territories occupied by Israel': A/48/18, para. 83. In discussion of decisions by Israel on the inclusion of information on the Occupied Territories in its reports to CERD, concern was expressed by CERD members as to whether requesting such information could imply recognizing Israel's rights over such territories; other views were expressed that inclusion was necessitated by the de facto situation without regard to questions of legitimacy on the basis that 'the Convention was universal in scope and thus applied to every person who might be affected by the exercise of jurisdiction by a State party, whether that jurisdiction was legitimate or not': A/36/18, paras 108–9, 109. At the time no clear consensus emerged as to how the situation should be treated.

[137] Commenced by country rapporteur Kut, CERD/C/SR.2131, para. 18, followed by CERD members Diaconu, paras 23; de Gouttes, para. 35; Amir, para. 44; and Vázquez, para. 45.

[138] CERD/C/SR.2132, para. 4.

[139] *Ibid.*, para. 5, in any case, Israel did not have control of Gaza, responsibility for which lay with Hamas.

[140] *Ibid.*, para. 50.

sovereignty and by extension to . . . territoriality';[141] it was added that 'the law of armed conflict and international human rights law did not apply together in the present case',[142] despite a discernment of the 'profound connection between international human rights law and the law of armed conflict'.[143] In conclusion, the Committee took note of the willingness of the State party to discuss the situation in the West Bank and Gaza but regretted the absence of any such information in the State report. Further the Committee was 'deeply concerned at the position [of Israel] . . . that the Convention does not apply to all the territories under the State party's effective control', and recommended that it be applied to such territories.[144]

In the case of the US, discussions were interlinked with an assessment of the scope of Article 1(2) and the treatment of non-citizens. Hence the Committee regretted the position taken by the US 'the Convention is not applicable to the treatment of foreign detainees held as "enemy combatants", on the basis of the argument that the law of armed conflict is the exclusive *lex specialis* applicable', and that in any event, concern over the alleged unequal treatment of foreign detainees was not applicable in light of Article 1(2) of the Convention.[145] The Committee recalled GR 30 on non-citizens as well as its statement on measures to combat terrorism—which should not discriminate in purpose or effect on the grounds in Article 1; with regard to 'enemy combatants' the associated recommendation was for judicial review of the lawfulness and conditions of detention, and the right to remedy for human rights violations.

Pronouncements by the Committee on *lex specialis* are rare;[146] its approach to specific situations is evidence of the acceptance of the principle of the coexistence of international humanitarian law and international human rights law, especially in light of the prominence of the principle of non-discrimination, including on the grounds of race and nationality, in the Geneva Conventions.[147] The Committee has on occasions ventured to pronounce on the requirements of international humanitarian law, though the dominant approach is to translate the requirements of international humanitarian law into the human rights language of the Convention.[148] As Weissbrodt has demonstrated, the

141 CERD/C/SR.2132, para. 82.

142 *Ibid.*, para. 83.

143 *Ibid.*, para. 81.

144 CERD/C/ISR/CO/14-16, para. 10; see also, *ibid.*, paras 20 and 27. For similar arguments in relation to the ICCPR, see O. De Schutter, *International Human Rights Law*, p. 129.

145 CERD/C/USA/CO/6, para. 24.

146 *Lex specialis* (*lex specialis derogat generali*) has a double sense, the first of which is that the specific rule modifies the general rule to the extent of an inconsistency between them; the second is where the specific rule is an instance of the application of the more general but there is no inconsistency between them: Sivakumaran, 'International Humanitarian Law', in Moeckli *et al.*, *International Human Rights Law*, p. 489; authors have found the term unhelpful in that it 'was designed to deal with . . . a vertical relationship' and not 'the horizontal collision between two separate regimes': F. Hampson and N. Lubell, *Amicus Curiae Brief for Hassan v UK, ECHR*, para. 18 <http://repository.essex.ac.uk/9690/1/hampson-lubell-amicus-ecthr-oct-2013.pdf>. See also Chapter 18 with regard to the Committee's stance on reservations.

147 According to the ICRC, <https://www.icrc.org/eng/resources/documents/misc/57jqzq.htm>: 'The principle of non-discrimination underlies all international humanitarian law, which is a body of rules specifically intended to solve humanitarian problems arising directly from armed conflicts.' See in particular Art. 16, Geneva Convention III; Art. 13 Geneva Convention IV, and common Article 3; Art. 27, Geneva Convention IV; Additional Protocol I, Art. 75(1). The prohibition against 'adverse distinction' is considered by the ICRC to be part of customary international law.

148 In the case of Israel, the Committee stated that it regarded 'the Israeli settlements in the occupied territories as not only illegal under international law but also as obstacles to peace and to the enjoyment of human rights by the whole population': A/48/18, para. 87.

engagement of CERD with international humanitarian law has been persistent and wide-ranging through key CERD mechanisms, notably including the 'regular' reporting procedure, the archive of general recommendations, and the early warning and urgent action procedures.[149] With regard to CERD's concluding observations, Weissbrodt observes that

> [m]ention of international humanitarian norms or instruments generally come in the context of armed conflict, genocide or terrorism, and concentrate on refugees and displaced persons in attempts to ensure that these groups are protected during times of instability. CERD also places emphasis on cooperation with international tribunals, as they are a primary means by which the principles of the Race Convention can be enforced.[150]

CERD recommendations are characteristically made on the basis that the Convention norms should be applied in light of the 'root causes'[151] and ethnic/racial dimensions of a conflict situation, interpreted according to the grounds of discrimination in Article 1 and the 'forms' of discrimination developed under it. The prevalence of non-international, frequently ethnically based armed conflict highlights the appropriateness of applying universal norms of non-discrimination;[152] and, as the events surrounding *Georgia v the Russian Federation* conform, allegations of 'ethnic cleansing' are appropriate to take international conflicts within the non-discrimination frame. CERD also pays close attention to situations perceived as evolving into conflicts with ethnic dimensions.[153]

V. Chapeau: No Delay in Eliminating Racial Discrimination

The specific contribution of the chapeau is to lend a heightened sense of urgency to the Convention through the specific undertaking to pursue, 'by all appropriate means and without delay', a policy of eliminating racial discrimination and promoting understanding. The requirement of an anti-discrimination 'policy' is wide-ranging and in itself subsumes and intersects with the paragraphs and sub-paragraphs of the article. The language of the chapeau suggests legal guarantees and a range of measures including action plans and strategies, institutional mechanisms, indicators, benchmarks, and timelines for measurement and monitoring of the incidence and scale of discrimination in the society concerned, all dedicated to eliminating racial discrimination in practice 'in all its forms'; the last phrase is adequate to capture existing and developing forms of discrimination. The 'all appropriate means' provision was present in early drafts in the Sub-Commission; the addition of the 'no delay' clause in the Sub-Commission to tighten the obligation will also be recalled. Mahalic and Mahalic regard the phrase 'by all appropriate means' as a limitation clause,[154] however their suggestion that the formulation rules out 'inappropriate means', such as the use of force to secure an anti-discrimination policy, is

[149] D. Weissbrodt, 'The Approach of the Committee on the Elimination of Racial Discrimination to Interpreting and Applying International Humanitarian Law', *Minnesota Journal of International Law* 19 (2010), 327–62 [henceforth *The Approach of the Committee*].

[150] *Ibid.*, 349.

[151] Concluding observations on Kyrgyzstan, CERD/C/KGZS/CO/5-7, para. 5.

[152] As Weissbrodt observes, the Committee 'recognizes that armed conflicts represent serious obstacles to the implementation of the Race Convention and, further, that armed conflicts often stem from racially and ethnically motivated violence': *The Approach of the Committee*, p. 344.

[153] Comments to Sudan on the situation in Darfur, CERD/C/SDN/CO/12-16, para. 7.

[154] D. Mahalic and G. M. Mahalic, 'The Limitation Provisions of the International Convention on the Elimination of All Forms of Racial Discrimination' *HRQ* 9 (1987), 74–101, 85.

less of a limitation than a reminder to States that action to correct the injustice of discrimination against one group should not spill over into injustice against another: the means employed to pursue an anti-discrimination policy should not subvert their ends, judged according to the letter and spirit of the Convention. In a positive sense, the phrase 'all appropriate means' engages the full arsenal of measures available to the State to combat discrimination, described in GR 32 in the context of special measures as including 'the full span of legislative, executive, administrative, budgetary and regulatory instruments . . . as well as plans, policies, programmes and preferential regimes'.[155] Large-scale 'national strategies or plan[s] of action' are envisaged in GR 31 to eliminate structural discrimination; strategies should include, *inter alia*, 'specific objectives and actions as well as indicators against which progress can be measured'.[156]

The reference to speed of action is complemented by references elsewhere in the Convention. The relevant paragraphs in the preamble to speedily eliminating racial discrimination,[157] in Article 4 to 'immediate and positive measures', and in Article 7 to 'immediate and effective measures' reinforce the urgency of the message; the reference in 2(1) to a 'no delay' policy for 'promoting understanding' has its closest parallel in Article 7. Concluding observations are replete with references to action that is to be taken 'without delay'. Bearing in mind the generously broad concept of a 'policy' to eliminate racial discrimination,[158] references to accelerated action occur across a wide spectrum of issues. The passing or implementation of particular laws[159] or amending others may be recommended as a matter of urgency,[160] as well as the adoption of more general 'measures',[161] or putting mechanisms into place.[162] Urgency may also be regarded as intrinsic to the pursuit of investigations of complaints with due diligence.[163] Exhortations to speedy action may apply to general laws as well as those to benefit specific groups. In terms of Committee procedures, legislative and other processes that can be completed rapidly are likely to be singled out for accelerated reporting back under the Committee's 'follow-up procedure', while pressing, potentially serious issues of human rights of sufficient 'gravity and scale' are characteristically addressed under the Committee's 'early warning and urgent action procedure'. Urgent situations concerning indigenous communities have dominated the latter procedure in recent years, a situation to some extent paralleled in concluding observations on periodic reports.[164]

[155] GR 32, para. 13. See the fuller citation of this paragraph in Chapter 9.

[156] Para. 5.

[157] As well as its endorsement of the UN General Assembly's objective of speedily eliminating colonialism.

[158] Diaconu, *Racial Discrimination*, pp. 178–82, offers an extended reflection on 'types and forms of policies'.

[159] Recommendation to Paraguay to implement a languages act and provide a suitable budget therefor: CERD/C/PRY/CO/1-3, para. 19.

[160] Recommendation to Cuba to amend legislation on foreigners, CERD/C/CUB/14-18, para. 18.

[161] CERD/C/CAN/CO/18, para. 15, take necessary measures to amend the Indian Act in view of discriminatory effects on rights of aboriginal women and children.

[162] Recommendation to Kenya to mechanisms to implement constitutional provisions on political representation. CERD/C/KEN/CO/1-4, para. 20.

[163] Recommendation to Israel regarding expeditious investigations of racist complaints: CERD/C/ISR/CO/13, para. 30.

[164] Examples in 2011 include recommendations for urgent action to Bolivia, CERD/C/BOL/CO/17-20, para. 18; and Paraguay, CERD/C/PRY/CO/1-3, para. 17; in 2013, Chile, CERD/C/CHL/CO/19-21, para. 14. See the discussion in Chapter 4.

In relation to Article 2, the general interpretation offered by Australia that its obligations are 'of general principle and programmatic in character' may be borne in mind.[165] The claimed 'programmatic' element is *ex facie* irreconcilable with the explicit Article 2 requirement that an anti-discrimination policy must be pursued 'without delay'[166] and with the general characterization that, even in the case of avowedly programmatic rights, the elimination of discrimination in the enjoyment of such rights represents an obligation with immediate effect.[167] On the other hand, the immediacy required by Article 2 refers to the general notion of a policy to eliminate racial discrimination, important elements of which are clearly in place in the case of Australia, notably through specific discrimination legislation at federal and state levels.[168] The declaration entered by Australia with regard to Article 4(a) cuts across the grain of urgency in Article 2 as well as the explicit requirements of Article 4:

> The government of Australia . . . declares that Australia is not at present in a position specifically to treat as offences all the matters covered by Article 4(a) of the Convention. Acts of the kind there mentioned are punishable only to the extent provided by the existing criminal law dealing with such matters as the maintenance of public order, public mischief, assault, riot, criminal libel, conspiracy and attempts. It is the intention of the Australian Government, at the first suitable moment, to seek from Parliament legislation specifically implementing the terms of Article 4(a).

Unsurprisingly, the Committee has repeatedly called for the withdrawal of this reservation and for legislation to give full effect to Article 4;[169] the compatibility with the Convention of the Australian statement, characterized as a reservation also by the State party,[170] has not been tested under the Article 14 procedure. Characterization of statements as reservations effectively blocks any determination of compatibility by the Committee in light of two-thirds rule in Article 20(2); characterization as an interpretation on the other hand invites a comparison between the Committee's reading of the Convention and that of the State party.[171]

VI. Article 2(1)(a) No Discrimination by the State, Public Authorities, Public Institutions

Sub-paragraphs (a)–(c) distil the basic message that the State itself shall not discriminate, directly or indirectly. Statements in the *travaux* suggesting that discriminatory action by States was 'unthinkable' are best understood as relating to the view that State-sponsored racial discrimination was a colonial aberration and not the global phenomenon discerned

[165] *Hagan v Australia*, CERD/C/62/D/26/2002 (2003), para. 4.4.

[166] The similar wording of Article 2 of CEDAW draws the response from the CEDAW Committee that '[t]he words "without delay" make it clear that the obligation of States parties to pursue their policy by all appropriate means is of an immediate nature. This language is unqualified, and does not allow for any delayed or purposely chosen incremental implementation of the obligations that States assume': CEDAW GR 28 on Core Obligations under Article 2, para. 29.

[167] CESCR, General Comment No. 3, *The Nature of States Parties' Obligations (Art. 2, para. 1 of the Covenant)*, 14 December 1990, para. 1; paragraph 7 of CESCR General Comment No. 20 describes non-discrimination as 'an immediate and cross-cutting obligation'. For nuances regarding *de facto* and *de jure* discrimination, see B. Saul, D. Kinley, and J. Mowbray (eds.), *The International Covenant on Economic, Social and Political Rights: Commentary, Cases, and Materials* (Oxford University Press, 2014), pp. 203–5.

[168] Consult <https://www.humanrights.gov.au/guide-australias-anti-discrimination-laws>.

[169] CERD/C/AUS/CO/14, para. 12; CERD/C/AUS/CO/15-17, para. 17.

[170] *Hagan v Australia*, para. 4.7.

[171] See, for example, *T.K. v France*, CCPR/C/37/D/220/1987 (1989), dissenting opinion of Human Rights Committee member Higgins.

in Committee practice. 'Racial discrimination' in Article 2 must be assumed to carry its full meaning as discrimination in intention or effect as well as related forms identified in Committee practice. Article 2(1) addresses State-generated racial discrimination;[172] Article 4(c) refers to the impermissibility of promotion of discrimination or incitement thereto by public officials, authorities, or institutions;[173] Article 5 sets out a spectrum of rights that implicate State bodies particularly in the fields of justice, security, and political organization.

There is an overlap between 2(1)(a) and 2(1)(c) in that, if there are discriminatory policies, they must be reviewed, amended, rescinded, or nullified. State-generated discrimination may arise from specific legislation or specific or general policy. The CERD archive is replete with examples that range from relatively minor, filigreed instances of discrimination to severe forms of oppression as recognized in the early warning and urgent action procedure and further identified in the Committee indicators of mass violations of human rights.[174] Racial discrimination by organs of State, as a sub-set of the State's general obligation to eliminate racial discrimination *in toto*, remains among the Committee's principal concerns, not entirely eclipsed by the growing emphasis on responsibility for discrimination by private actors.

The State obligation not to discriminate reaches vertically through levels of governance and laterally to territories under State control. The explicit reference in 2(1)(a) to 'national and local' levels of State administration is noteworthy; the 'local' also figures in 2(1)(c) and 4(c). In light of the general principle of international law that internal law may not be invoked to defeat a charge of failure to perform a treaty, CERD has not been impressed by arguments that, for example, the government of a federation cannot compel component administrations to implement obligations under the Convention. This insistence on the responsibility of the State party to ensure that the Convention is implemented 'all the way down' through the levels of administration is made in the absence of a 'federal clause' in the Convention.[175] Such a clause was proposed during the drafting of the Convention but rejected in the Third Committee on the grounds,[176] *inter alia*, that a federal clause would have represented a weakening, and not a strengthening, of direct obligations to implement.[177]

[172] In *Hagan v Australia*, para. 4.5, the State party cited 'academic authority' to the effect that 2(1)(a) 'does not deal with private acts of discrimination': the citation was to Lerner, *The UN Convention on the Elimination of All Forms of Racial Discrimination*.

[173] For a summary of what count as organs of State in the practice of the Human Rights Committee, see D. McGoldrick, 'State Responsibility and the International Covenant on Civil and Political Rights', in M. Fitzmaurice and D. Sarooshi (eds), *Issues of State Responsibility before International Judicial Institutions* (Hart Publishing, 2004), 161–99.

[174] A/60/18, para. 20.

[175] 'Federal clauses' appear in a number of UN 'core' instruments and take the general form that the provisions of the convention 'shall apply to all parts of federal States without any limitations or exceptions'. Examples include Article 50 of the ICCPR, Article 28 of the ICESCR, Article 4 of the CRPD, and Article 41 of the CPED.

[176] The clause envisaged a distinction between Articles of the Convention under federal legislative jurisdiction and those under state (of the federation), cantonal, or provincial jurisdiction: in the latter case, the obligation expressed was 'to bring such Articles before the appropriate authorities with a favourable recommendation' (to implement): A/6181, para. 187. On the proposal of Poland, the clauses were rejected by 63 votes to 7, with 16 abstentions: *ibid.*, paras 188–89.

[177] Such a clause 'would substantially weaken the Convention as a whole by establishing inequality of obligations as between federal and unitary States. It would not be in conformity with international law, under which a federal State as a whole was regarded as a subject of international law': observations by the representative of Czechoslovakia, A/C.3/SR.1367, para. 6. According to the representative of the USA, *ibid.*, para. 8, 'such

Banton introduces the issue in relation to early reports of Canada;[178] it resurfaces in the Committee's conclusions on Canada, including those of 2007:

> The Committee, while welcoming the information that the Action Plan Against Racism: A Canada for All, together with other initiatives mentioned by the State party, will, *inter alia*, ensure the coordination of efforts of federal departments and provincial/territorial governments in the fight against racism, is concerned about remaining discrepancies in the level of implementation of the Convention among the provinces. The Committee underscores once again the responsibility of the Federal Government of Canada for the implementation of the Convention[179]

A similar exposition of CERD's position was made in 2008 in relation to Belgium in relation to discriminatory decrees of regional and local authorities. While noting that the State party has a federal structure, the Committee recalled that 'Belgium is a single State under international law and has the obligation to ensure the implementation of the provisions of the Convention throughout its territory'.[180] The insistence on full implementation is not confined to States with a federal structure, and it is clear from the text of 2(1)(a) that obligations implicate the actions of lower level or local authorities. The question of political and administrative divisions of States is addressed by paragraph 31 of GR 32 in the context of special measures, stating a broader principle:

> The internal structure of States parties, whether unitary, federal or decentralized, does not affect their responsibility under the Convention, when resorting to special measures, to secure their application throughout the territory of the State. In federal or decentralized States, the federal authority shall be responsible for designing a framework for the consistent application of special measures in all parts of the State where such measures are necessary.

GR 32 points to the need for consistent implementation of the Convention across the board, a Committee preference that regularly emerges in concluding observations. The emphasis in the above-cited paragraph on coordination is amplified in the case of the US through a recommendation to 'establish appropriate mechanisms to ensure a coordinated approach towards the implementation of the Convention at the federal, State and local levels'.[181] Mechanisms of coordination may be viewed as particularly pressing in heavily decentralized systems.[182] In the case of Italy, CERD expressed concern that 'the strongly decentralized system of Italy [might] lead to diversity of policies and decisions at the level of regions and provinces with regard to discrimination', and noted 'the need to adopt a global and comprehensive plan of action on human rights in view of the fragmented nature of measures on human rights taken by regional authorities'.[183] The last-cited

clauses tended to destroy the uniform application of international agreements by placing federal States in a special position'. The federal clause was vigorously advocated by Australia: A/C.3/SR.1367, paras 5 and 13.

[178] *International Action*, pp. 243–44.

[179] CERD/C/CAN/CO/18, para. 12. Coordination of federal and provincial mechanisms 'in order to remove discrepancies and disparities in the implementation of anti-racism legislation, policies, programmes and best practices' is urged in concluding observations of 2012: CERD/C/CAN/CO/19-20, para. 9.

[180] CERD/C/BEL/CO/15, para. 16; references to 'federal, regional and community levels' of governance are made in later concluding observations to Belgium in connection with structural discrimination, and Roma: CERD/C/BEL/CO/16-19, paras 15 and 18.

[181] CERD/C/USA/CO/6, para. 13.

[182] On devolution of powers potentially impeding the discharge of obligations, see concluding observations on France, CERD/C/FRA/CO/20-21, para. 4.

[183] CERD/C/ITA/CO/16-18, para. 27. Accordingly, the Committee recommended, *ibid.*, 'a mechanism for consultation and coordination with . . . local authorities'.

comment on Italy does not challenge the political and administrative organization of the State party. While the architecture of government is a sovereign prerogative, boundary/territorial manipulation can raise serious human rights concerns, including those connected with political participation, amounting in some cases to racial discrimination.[184] Particular systems of government have also been the subject of interrogation by the Committee for possible discriminatory effects.[185]

The reference to 'public authorities and public institutions' was the subject of analyses by CERD in *Anna Koptova v Slovakia*,[186] and *L.R. v Slovakia*.[187] The point for present purposes relates to the argument of the State party that municipal councils—alleged to have issued discriminatory resolutions targeting Roma—were not State bodies.[188] The Committee took the view, as articulated in *L.R.*, that 'the acts of municipal councils, including the adoption of public resolutions of legal character . . . amounted to acts of public authorities within the meaning of the Convention',[189] and that 'the racial discrimination in question is attributable to the State party'.[190] *L.R. v Slovakia* is also notable for the proposition that the obligation not to discriminate is not confined to the final steps in a process:

> In the Committee's view, it would be inconsistent with the purpose of the Convention, and elevate formalism over substance, to consider that the final step in the actual implementation of a particular human right . . . must occur in a non-discriminatory manner, while the necessary preliminary decision-making elements connected to that implementation were to be severed and be free from scrutiny . . . the Committee considers that the council resolutions in question, taking initially an important policy and practical step towards realization of the right to housing, followed by its revocation . . . taken together, do . . . amount to the impairment of the recognition or exercise on an equal basis of the human right to housing . . .[191]

In later concluding observations on Slovakia, the Committee noted with concern that the State party described 'the autonomy of local self-governing bodies as a major obstacle to achieving non-discrimination in access to social housing for the Roma community'.[192] The concern led to the recommendation that the State party 'take effective measures to implement the

[184] See M. Weller (ed.), *The Rights of Minorities in Europe* (Oxford University Press, 2005), particularly the comment by Jennifer Jackson-Preece on Article 16 of the Council of Europe Framework Convention for the Protection of National Minorities, *ibid.*, pp. 463–85.

[185] See comments by the Committee on the system of 'ethnic federalism' practised in Ethiopia, whereby the State party was requested to ensure that its operation served to protect all ethnic groups: CERD/C/ETH/CO/15, para. 16. Para. 15, *ibid.*, includes a related comment on diversity of court systems within the State party and a recommendation to ensure conformity with Article 2(1). For academic comment, see K. Tronvoll, 'Human Rights Violations in Federal Ethiopia: When Ethnic Identity is a Political Stigma', *IJMGR 15* (2008), 49–79, and G. Assefa, 'Human and Group Rights Issues in Ethiopia: a Reply to Kjetil Tronvoll', *IJMGR 16* (2009), 245–59.

[186] CERD/C/57/D/131998 (2000).

[187] CERD/C/66/D/31/2003 (2005). Article 2(1)(a) figures in other case but without notable illumination as to its meaning. Examples include *B.J. v Denmark*, CERD/C/56/D/17/1999 (2000). The claim under 2(1)(a) was contested by the State party (para. 4.3) because the facts involved discrimination by a private individual; the specifics of 2(1)(a) were not commented upon by the Committee.

[188] *Koptova*, para. 4.8; *L.R*, para. 2.3. Petitioners comments in *Koptova*, para. 5.18; petitioner's comments in *L.R.*, paras 5.1 and 5.3. Petitioners in both cases cited, *inter alia*, para. 4 of CERD's GR 15 on Article 4 (c), which stated that public authorities 'at all administrative levels, *including municipalities*' were bound by 4 (c) (present author's emphasis).

[189] *L.R. v Slovakia*, para. 6.3.

[190] *Ibid.*, para. 10.8.

[191] *Ibid.*, para. 10.7. For comment, see S. Joseph, 'The Right to Housing, Discrimination and the Roma in Slovakia', *HRLR 5* (2005), 347–49.

[192] CERD/C/SVK/CO/9-10, para. 16.

Convention and ensure that the principle of self-governance of local and regional bodies does not hamper its human rights obligations to promote economic, social and cultural rights of disadvantaged or discrimination groups, as per the Convention'.[193]

Discussions in the *travaux* clarified that 'public institutions' is wider than 'public authorities'. In *Hagan v Australia*, the State party claimed that the sports trust which owned the stadium which exhibited an offensive racial sign was 'a private body rather than a public authority or government agent', the acts of which therefore fell outside 2(1)(a) which did 'not deal with private acts of discrimination'.[194] This was contested by the petitioner, who pointed out that the trustees were appointed and could be removed by a minister and that their function was 'to manage land for public (community) purposes' and that the trust was 'therefore a public authority or institution for Convention purposes'.[195] The Committee did not comment on the Article 2 point in its reference to 'displaying a public sign considered to be racially offensive'.[196] In light of the general understanding of 'public institutions' in the drafting of Article 2, the more open interpretation of the sub-paragraph coheres better with the letter and spirit of the Convention.

VII. Article 2(1)(b) Not to Sponsor, Defend or Support Racial Discrimination by any Persons or Organizations

The trope of negative statements of obligation in Article 2 continues in Article 2(1)(b), which shifts the emphasis from discrimination by organs of State and 'public institutions' towards discrimination by actors backed by the State, though an expanded reading of 'public institutions' in 2(1)(a) suggests an overlap between the two sub-paragraphs. Non-State actors, or 'private' persons or organizations are not explicitly identified as the focus of the text: the reluctance of the drafters to qualify persons or organizations by 'private' will be recalled.[197] Lerner discerns a 'gradual system of undertakings' in Article 2, moving from negative statements in the first two sub-paragraphs to explicit statements of positive action;[198] 2(1)(b) in his view, 'simply intends to prevent persons or organizations engaged in racial discrimination getting the official support of the State'.[199] The provision complements the other reference to persons and organizations in Article 2, and the proscription of racist organizations in Article 4(b). The negative phraseology does not rule out an active stance by the State vis-à-vis the fulfilment of its obligation: in terms of the typology of obligations referred to above, Ruggie lists 2(1)(b) and 2(1)(d) as aspects of 'the obligation to protect'.[200]

[193] *Ibid.*

[194] Para. 4.5.

[195] Para. 5.4.

[196] Para. 8.

[197] The commentary on the International Law Commission's Draft Articles on State Responsibility for Internationally Wrongful Acts notes that 'the general rule is that the only conduct attributed to the State at the international level is that of its organs of government or of others who have acted under the direction, instigation or control of those organs, i.e. as agents of the State': <http://legal.un.org/legislativeseries/documents/Book25/Book25_part1_ch2.pdf>, commentary on chapter II, para. 2. CEDAW GR 28, para. 13, recalls the due diligence obligation on States parties to prevent discrimination by private actors, adding that the acts of some private actors may be attributed to the State under general international law.

[198] *The International Convention*, p. 37.

[199] *Ibid.*

[200] *Mapping State Obligations for Corporate Acts: An Examination of the UN Human Rights Treaty System, Report No. 1 International Convention on the Elimination of All Forms of Racial Discrimination*, 18 December 2006, p. 4.

Regarding the verbs in the sub-paragraph, 'sponsor' overlaps with 'support' and may be understood in terms of contribution to costs, taking responsibility for the acts of another, or generalized support for a person or organization.[201] 'Support' is wider and may include assistance, encouragement, or approval as well as financial support; in a related sense it may include 'endure' or 'tolerate'.[202] 'Defend' has an altogether more active significance, and, when too active, may be a good candidate to engage proscriptions such as those in Article 4. Regarding the potential application of 2(1)(b), Lerner's examples are those of 'an official publishing house that prints a racist book, or a local government that gives financial support to a school engaging in racial discrimination'.[203] Meron comments that 'support' may (arguably) encompass 'not only the extension of benefits as a positive action but also the failure to impose obligations that are required of other persons or organizations', instancing the granting of tax-exempt benefits to a private organization that discriminates on account of race.[204] In view of the extensive interpenetration and blurring of boundaries between public and private activities in modern States, including the financial nexus, the sub-paragraph potentially opens up a broad prospectus. The sub-paragraph is under-litigated in Article 14 cases. Along with 2(1)(a), the citation of 2(1)(b) was dismissed as irrelevant by the State party in *B.J. v Denmark*,[205] because that case did not involve State-promoted discrimination. In *Hagan v Australia*, the State party simply denied that the establishment of the sports ground trust in question, its continued existence, or its response to the claim by Hagan, engaged the sub-paragraph in any manner, a claim that was not commented upon by the Committee.[206]

2(1)(b) is relevant in principle to discrimination in any field covered by the Convention: activities of individuals as well as collective action are caught by the provision, and the term 'persons' includes legal persons such as corporations as well as natural persons. Cases include organizations close to the apparatus of governance as well as those removed from it. Egregious cases of State support for organizations in close proximity to governance would include, *inter alia*, private militias supported by the State, and funding for political parties. In concluding observations on the Russian Federation, CERD expressed concerned at information that Cossack organizations had engaged in acts of violence against ethnic groups, were used by local authorities to carry out enforcement operations, and enjoyed State funding. The Committee recommended that the State party ensure that no support would be provided 'to organizations that promote racial discrimination', and that Cossack paramilitary units be prevented from carrying out law enforcement functions against ethnic groups.[207] The Committee interrogated the Cossack question in later observations, concerned by information 'that voluntary "Cossack patrols" began to appear in 2012 . . . to carry out law enforcement functions alongside the police'.[208] Belgium was

[201] *Concise Oxford English Dictionary* (11th edn, Oxford University Press, 2004), pp. 1394–5.
[202] *Ibid.*, p. 1448.
[203] *Ibid.*
[204] T. Meron, *The Meaning and Reach of the International Convention on the Elimination of All Forms of Racial Discrimination*, *AJIL* 79 (1985), 283–318, 295.
[205] Para. 4.3.
[206] Para. 4.5.
[207] CERD/C/62/CO/7, para. 16.
[208] CERD/C/RUS/CO/20-22, para. 14.

requested to provide information on a law of 1998 on withdrawing financial support to political parties that incite racism or racial hostility.[209]

Corporations, whether acting territorially or extraterritorially,[210] have increasingly been drawn into the orbit of Article 2, notably in connection with despoliation of indigenous lands and territories, including sacred sites. The Committee is critical of arrangements for resource exploitation such as permissions for tourism developments, or concessions and licences for mining and logging operations, granted without the free, prior, and informed consent of the indigenous peoples concerned.[211] GR 23 summarized the seriousness of situations where 'indigenous peoples have been, and are still being, discriminated against and deprived of their human rights . . . and in particular that they have lost their land and resources to colonists, commercial companies and State enterprises'.[212] The concluding observations of the Committee provide examples of many cases involving indigenous peoples, which are, as noted, accorded a prominent place in the Committee's early warning procedure. In some instances, State bodies are implicated—Article 2(1)(a)—while many cases concern the activities of private corporations enjoying sundry forms of state support and approval. Notable early warning 'decisions' of the Committee include Decision 1(68) regarding the Western Shoshone,[213] and a series regarding resource exploitation in Suriname.[214] Letters of concern at the activities of corporations are more numerous than decisions: instructive illustrations of the Committee's approach include communications to Canada (2008 and 2009); France (2009); Niger (2009 and 2010); Papua New Guinea (2011); Peru (2010); The Philippines (2007–12); and Tanzania (2009–13).[215] The Committee may link its censuring of corporate activity to 2(1)(d) rather than 2(1)(b) without the implication that such activity is sponsored, defended, or supported by the State.

VIII. Article 2(1)(c) Review Policy, Amend, Rescind, Nullify Discriminatory Laws and Regulations

Continuing the logic of Article 2, instances of State-based and State-supported discrimination referred to in the first two sub-paragraphs require modifications of existing law and policy. The accumulation of verbs suggests an obligation to mount a holistic assault on defective legal structures and institutions. The *travaux* evidence some difficulties with terminology including the claimed redundancy of 'nullify' following 'rescind'; both were retained in order to satisfy the variety of concepts among legal systems. The injunctions to act are arranged more or less sequentially in that before action is taken, the policy architecture (including laws that express that policy) should be 'reviewed', followed by necessary amendments to laws and regulations, including their rescission. Lerner cites the *travaux* for the view that 'nullify' is equivalent to 'suppress entirely', which may add

[209] CERD/C/60/CO/2, para. 14.

[210] See remarks on extraterritorial activities of corporations in the present chapter.

[211] In some cases, the concerns have related to the activities of non-indigenous individuals who trespass on indigenous territories, rather than corporations: see for example the series of letter sent to Brazil regarding the Raposa Serra do Sol: <http://www2.ohchr.org/english/bodies/cerd/early-warning.htm>.

[212] GR 23, para. 3.

[213] A/61/18, pp. 7–10.

[214] Decision 1(67), A/60/18, pp. 9–10; 1(69), A/61/18, pp. 10–11.

[215] Individual letters may be found on the Committee's web page: <http://www2.ohchr.org/english/bodies/cerd/early-warning.htm>.

something to 'rescind'.[216] 'Nullify' may also have a stronger aftermath in terms of eliminating the lingering after-effects of misdirected or misapplied legislation.

Recommendations to review, amend, or rescind discriminatory legislation are common practice. The scope of a 'review' of legislation can extend from reviewing a specific law, including a constitutional provision,[217] to a general law or 'legal regime' such as a land regime,[218] review of legal remedies,[219] review of policies,[220] or review of 'positions' such as the position taken by a State party that a law against racial discrimination was not necessary.[221] Recommendations to 'amend' may come together with a recommendation to review,[222] or may stand alone, and, as with review, range from recommendations to amend specific pieces of legislation or adopt new legislation, to wholesale amendment of 'domestic laws, regulations or practices',[223] or harmonizing amendments of 'legislation on land, water, mining and other sectors' so that it does not conflict with other legislation on indigenous peoples.[224]

Bearing in mind the overlap between amendment and rescission, specific recommendations to abrogate or rescind laws or policies are uncommon—in the early warning/urgent action decision regarding the Western Shoshone, the US was urged to rescind trespass and collection notices, etc, inflicted on the Shoshone for using their ancestral lands.[225] 'Nullify' is more likely referred in data searches to with reference to the definition of discrimination in Article 1 rather than Article 2, though the challenge, referred to above, of remedying the after-effects of a formerly discriminatory legal system or laws is strongly felt in CERD practice, notably through recommendations to apply wide-ranging measures, such as those to address 'the legacy of apartheid' in the case of South Africa.[226] In the case of Serbia, 2(1)(c) was employed to cover existing structural discrimination, in that certain groups continued to be subject to exclusion and discrimination in employment, education, and participation in public affairs. Unspecific measures were recommended to address structural discrimination and the engagement of minorities with the public sphere.[227]

In *Hagan v Australia*, the author invoked, *inter alia*, 2(1)(c), stating that, under this provision, States parties have an obligation 'to amend laws having the effect of perpetuating racial discrimination . . . the use of words such as the offending term in a very public way provides the term with formal sanction or approval. Words convey ideas and power, and influence thoughts and beliefs. They may perpetuate racism.'[228] Australia replied regarding its Racial Discrimination Act that the fact that Hagan's claim under the Act was unsuccessful, 'did not detract from the effectiveness of that legislation', nor did it suggest

[216] Lerner, *The International Convention*, p. 37.
[217] Zambia, CERD/C/ZMB/CO/16, para. 12.
[218] Lao People's Democratic Republic, CERD/C/LAO/16-18, para. 16, review of the land regime was recommended with a view to recognizing the cultural aspect of land as an integral part of the identity of some ethnic groups.
[219] Estonia, CERD/C/EST/8-9, para. 18.
[220] Botswana, CERD/C/BWA/CO/16, para. 9.
[221] Korea, CERD/C/KOR/15-16, para. 6.
[222] Concluding observations on Jordan, CERD/C/JOR/CO/13-17, para. 11.
[223] Indonesia, CERD/C/IDN/CO/3, para. 16.
[224] Chile, CERD/C/CHL/CO/15-18, para. 23.
[225] CERD/C/USA/DEC/1 (2006), para. 10.
[226] Concluding observations on South Africa, CERD/C/ZAF/CO/3, para. 13.
[227] CERD/C/SRB/CO/1, para. 17.
[228] Para. 3.3.

that the Act created or perpetuated racial discrimination.[229] The Committee, while not finding a violation of the Convention, nonetheless recommended that 'the State party take the necessary measures to secure the removal of the offending term from the sign in question',[230] which suggests that, while 2(1)(c) was not deemed to be violated, measures in line with the spirit of the paragraph could and should have been taken.[231]

IX. Article 2(1)(d) Prohibit and Bring to an End, by all Appropriate Means Including Legislation as Required by Circumstances, Racial Discrimination by any Persons, Group, or Organization

This provision ranks as one of the key obligations in the Convention, described by Schwelb as 'the most important and far-reaching of all the substantive provisions'.[232] Over decades, CERD has built up a profile of an idealized architecture of laws and supporting institutions to give substance to the obligation in Article 2(1)(d), while making it abundantly clear that legislation is always 'appropriate' to combat racial discrimination—as Banton notes, 'for an action to be discriminatory in law, there must first be a law'.[233] Analogously, Mahalic and Mahalic contend that no State is exempt from the need to legislate.[234] Banton offers an overview of the paragraph, which

> is unqualified in its requirement that a State party bring to an end racial discrimination; it is not limited to the State sector or to governmental action or to the enactment of laws, but makes the State responsible for bringing to an end racial discrimination throughout the society.[235]

Progress in adopting and implementing legislation on racial discrimination is inevitably welcomed by the Committee. Strengthening existing legislation also draws favourable comment, as does the consolidation of institutional support for the anti-discrimination standards. The Committee's clear preference is for specific legislation against racial discrimination, while it is not contrary to the Convention to supplement this with laws against defamatory statements which cover racist statements even if they do not specifically target racism.[236] In light of the absence of legislation, Committee records are replete with recommendations urging the merits of a 'comprehensive law' or 'comprehensive legislation' against racial discrimination,[237] including a 'comprehensive' or clear definition thereof.[238] Preferences for a comprehensive approach extend to legislation to implement

[229] Para. 4.6.

[230] Para. 8.

[231] In *L.R. v Slovakia*, (para. 3.2) the petitioner alleged violation of, *inter alia*, 2(1)(c), but this was not the subject of comment from the Committee, which based its finding on Articles 2(1)(a), 5, and 6.

[232] At 1017.

[233] M. Banton, *Discrimination* (Open University Press, 1994), p. 6.

[234] P. 85; see comments, supra, p. 166.

[235] M. Banton, *International Action*, p. 199.

[236] *Sadic v Denmark*, para. 6.3.

[237] Concluding observations on Japan recommended 'a specific and comprehensive law' and 'specific and comprehensive legislation' against racial discrimination: CERD/C/JPN/CO/7-9, para. 8. While the divergence in terminology may represent a distinction without a difference, the 'law' formulation suggests a civil law codification approach, whereas 'legislation' offers a more open approach that would leave the details of legal design to the State party.

[238] Concluding observations on Fiji, CERD/C/FJI/CO/18-20, para. 9; Japan, CERD/C/JPN/CO/7-9, para. 7; Russian Federation, CERD/C/RUS/CO/19, para. 7.

particular articles of the Convention such as Article 4.[239] The shape of legislation envisaged by the Committee is set out in concluding observations:

The Committee urges the State party to accelerate the adoption of a comprehensive anti-discrimination act to stipulate, *inter alia*, the definition of direct and indirect as well as *de facto* and *de jure* discrimination, together with structural discrimination, liability for natural and legal persons extending to both public authorities and private persons, remedies to victims of racial discrimination and the institutional mechanisms necessary to guarantee the implementation of the provisions of the Act in a holistic manner.[240]

In addition to specific forms of legislation, the Committee frequently urges the inclusion in criminal codes of racial motivation as a general aggravating factor in sentencing,[241] a stance generalized in GR 31, encouraging States parties 'to incorporate a provision in their criminal legislation to the effect that committing offences for racial reasons generally constitutes an aggravating circumstance'.[242] CERD has criticized and recommended the amendment of legislation that makes the racial motivation element subject to a proviso that it must be the only motivation behind the offence.[243]

CERD has been particularly strong on the important role played by criminal law in anti-discrimination legislation, a preference not confined to the hate speech area.[244] Legislation to prevent racial discrimination should, however, reach beyond criminal law and include civil and administrative law. On proving discrimination in civil cases, recommendations are regularly made to 'reverse',[245] 'share',[246] or 'shift'[247] the burden of proof to respondents once plaintiffs have made out a prima facie case of discrimination. The requirement is occasionally detailed[248] and coupled with an explanation of why the change on burden of proof is warranted.[249] In the case of Cyprus, the limitation to certain defined areas of the principle of 'sharing' the burden of proof in

[239] Concluding observations on Croatia, CERD/C/HRV/CO/8, para. 12; on Tajikistan, CERD/C/TJK/CO/6-8, para. 10. Para. 9 of GR 35 on combating racist hate speech refers to the need for 'comprehensive legislation against racial discrimination, including civil and administrative law as well as criminal law'.

[240] Concluding observations on Ukraine, CERD/C/UKR/19-21, para. 5.

[241] Examples include concluding observations on Mauritius, CERD/C/MUS/CO/15-19, para. 11; Venezuela, CERD/C/VEN/CO/19-21, para. 14.

[242] Para. 4(a).

[243] 'The Committee is concerned that the provision on aggravating circumstances is used when a racist motivation appears to be the only motivation but not when there are mixed motives', a concern that led to a recommendation to establish that 'an offence with racist motivation constitutes an aggravating circumstance, including in cases where there are mixed motives': concluding observations on Italy, CERD/C/ITA/CO/16-18, para. 16.

[244] See Chapter 11. Concluding observations on this point in A/68/18 (2012 and 2013) include Algeria, CERD/C/DZA/CO/15-19, para. 12; Dominican Republic, CERD/C/DOM/CO/13-14, para. 11; Korea, CERD/C/KOR/CO/15-16, para. 8; Liechtenstein, CERD/C/LIE/CO/4-6, para. 9 (mainly re Article 4); Tajikistan, CERD/C/TJK/CO/6-8, para. 10; and Thailand, CERD/C/THA/CO/1-3, para. 9.

[245] Concluding observations on Morocco, MAR/CO/17-18, para. 18.

[246] Concluding observations on Moldova, CERD/C/MDA/CO/8-9, para. 9.

[247] Concluding observations on Iceland, CERD/C/ISL/CO/19-20, para. 15.

[248] In concluding observations on Australia, the State party was invited to address the issue of burden of proof 'so that once an alleged victim has established a prima facie case that he or she has been a victim of such discrimination, it shall be for the respondent to provide evidence of an objective and reasonable justification for differential treatment': CERD/C/AUS/CO/14, para. 15.

[249] The perceived difficulty may simply be that of substantiating claims of racial discrimination: concluding observations on Armenia, CERD/C/ARM/CO/5-6, para. 9.

civil cases drew forth the recommendation that the principle be applied 'to all civil law cases of racial discrimination'.[250]

In cases of defective or incomplete legislation, States may be urged to amend relevant legal codes and establish a broader range of liability.[251] The preference, in the interests of clarification, predictability, and accessibility, for a comprehensive legal framework goes in tandem with a preference for an integrated framework rather than a scattergun approach to laws,[252] and, *a fortiori*, a preference for a straightforward incorporation of the Convention into domestic law, as noted earlier. In this respect, the remarks made to the UK and Denmark regarding the non-incorporation of ICERD will be recalled; the critical comments focus on the perceived or asserted effects flowing from lack of a 'comprehensive' approach to legislation or lack of explicit incorporation. It may be argued, however, that pressing such points towards an expression of preference for a defined legal architecture would not do justice to the variety of national legal styles, in particular to the looser structures of common law systems.

Measured against the legislative patterns recommended, deficiencies in the existing legal framework attract critical attention, especially if important areas (as perceived by the Committee) are omitted;[253] recommendations to review and amend the legislation may follow. In light of the 'bring to an end' (racial discrimination) element in Article 2(1)(d), the implementation—and disparities in implementation[254]—and not merely the design of legal regimes, is apt to generate critical comment.[255] CERD is particularly attentive to the role of the courts—the pre-eminent 'supporting institutions'—in the implementation of anti-discrimination standards. Concerns have been expressed about such matters as the independence and impartiality of judges,[256] the possibilities of invoking the Convention in domestic courts,[257] the possibilities of addressing courts in the mother tongue of minorities,[258] and the representation[259]—including support for local legislation on proportionate representation[260]—of ethnic minorities and other groups in the judiciary and police.

The obligation to address racial discrimination 'by all appropriate means' in Article 2(1)(d) suggests strategies that reach beyond specific anti-discrimination legislation and its implementation. Strategies may be recommended in broad and unspecific terms, such as national plans of action, or focused on campaigns of education and awareness-raising. In virtue of the importance of the Durban World Conference as, *inter alia*, a repository of principle and action in the discrimination field, the Committee has arrived at a (more or less) standard formula, recommending that States parties give effect to the Durban Declaration and Programme of Action of 2001, taking into account the Durban Review

[250] CERD/C/CYP/CO/17-22, para. 9.

[251] Concluding observations on Turkmenistan, CERD/C/TKM/CO/6-7, para. 23.

[252] Concluding observations on Austria, CERD/C/AUT/CO/17, para. 12.

[253] In the case of Latvia, the provisions examined by the Committee did 'not fully cover civil, political, social, cultural and other fields of public life', as required by the Convention: CERD/C/63/CO/7, para. 8.

[254] Concluding observations on Austria, CERD/C/AUT/CO/17, para. 11.

[255] Concluding observations on Greece, CERD/C/GRC/CO/16-19, para. 10.

[256] Examples include Cambodia, CERD/C/KHM/CO/8-13, para. 13; Uzbekistan, CERD/C/UZB/CO/5, para. 12.

[257] CERD/C/DNK/CO/18-19, para. 8.

[258] CERD/C/ROU/CO/16-19, para. 19.

[259] Croatia, CERD/C/HRV/CO/8, para. 16; Lithuania, CERD/C/LTU/CO/4-5, para. 14.

[260] Moldova, CERD/C/MDA/CO/8-9, para. 16.

Conference in 2009 when implementing the Convention in their domestic legal order, and requesting information on action plans and other measures to implement their provisions. Durban-related recommendations have also less ambitiously referred to taking into account or giving effect to 'relevant parts' of the Durban instruments.[261] In response to the refusal by Israel to 'acknowledge and abide' by the Durban framework, CERD urged a re-examination of this position 'taking into consideration the evident importance of that document for a large segment of humanity';[262] the US was reminded of the importance of the Durban process 'for the achievement of the goals of the Convention'.[263] The Committee regretted the refusal of the Czech Republic to develop a national action plan against racism in line with Durban and urged the development of a plan.[264] The Holy See has expressed its strong reservations regarding recommendations to implement the Durban framework.[265]

This sub-paragraph features strongly in the communications procedure in combination with other articles. In *Habassi v Denmark* (refusal of a bank loanon account of his non-Danish nationality) the Committee found a violation of 2(1)(d) in combination with Article 6 in the absence of a proper investigation into whether racially discriminatory criteria were being applied.[266] What 2(1)(d) requires was considered by the same State party in another case where prosecution of a doorman followed the refusal of entry to a discotheque of the author who was of Iranian origin: not only 'has the State party adopted law that criminalizes acts of racial discrimination such as that of which the applicant was a victim . . . but . . . authorities have enforced these criminal provisions in a specific case'.[267]

On similar principles, a violation of 2(1)(d) in conjunction with Articles 4 and 6 was found in *Gelle v Denmark*,[268] where a politician criticized plans to consult with, *inter alios*, a Danish-Somali association prior to legislation on female genital mutilation (FGM) equating Somalis, in the words of the petitioner, with paedophiles and rapists.[269] The State party claimed, in light of 2(1)(d) and Article 6, that their evaluation of the statements 'fully satisfied the requirement that an investigation must be carried out with due diligence and expedition and must be sufficient to determine whether or not an act of racial discrimination . . . [had] . . . taken place'.[270] The Committee disagreed on the facts while maintaining the principle that it was not enough to declare acts of racial discrimination punishable on paper, they must also be effectively implemented, a principle reflected in, *inter alia*, Article 2(1)(d), which was specifically cited.[271] In *Murat Er v Denmark*, the Committee distinguished between legislation and its interpretation in the Danish courts as applied to the petitioner, which was deemed compatible with the Convention,[272] and the lack of effective investigation into an allegedly racist act, which

261 Examples include Ethiopia, CERD/C/ETH/CO/15, para. 29; Pakistan, CERD/C/PAK/CO/20, para. 27.

262 CERD/C/ISR/CO/14-16, para. 31.

263 CERD/C/USA/CO/6, para. 39.

264 CERD/C/CZE/CO/8-9, para. 23.

265 CERD/C/VAT/16-23, para. 5, discussed in the concluding chapter of the present work.

266 Para. 9.3. The Committee found that the author had also been denied an effective remedy. See the more detailed discussion in Chapter 7. See comment by the State party in para. 7.4.

267 *B.J. v Denmark*, para. 4.3. No violation was found in this case.

268 *Gelle v Denmark*, CERD/C/68/D/34/2004 (2006).

269 *Ibid.*, para. 2.2.

270 *Ibid.*, para. 4.4.

271 *Gelle v Denmark*, para. 7.3. See also *Jama v Denmark*, para. 7.3, and discussion in chapter 16.

272 *Murat Er v Denmark*, CERD/C/71/D/40/2007 (2007), para. 7.2.

violated Article 2(1)(d).[273] Contestations of alleged violations of 2(1)(d) by States parties are usually couched in terms of the facts of the situation; in other cases a substantive interpretative point is made. In *Murat Er*, the State party argued that:

> Article 2(1)(d) is a policy statement and the obligation it contains is a general principle [which] does not impose concrete obligations . . . and, even less, specific requirements on the wording of a possible national statute on racial discrimination. On the contrary, State parties enjoy a significant margin of appreciation in this regard.[274]

In some cases, the requirements of the sub-paragraph have been impressed upon a State party despite a claim that 'no racial discrimination' on the part of public authorities had manifested itself.[275]

X. Persons, Group, or Organization . . .

The concerns of 2(1)(d) encompass non-State 'private' actors. While secondary rules of State responsibility address the actions of private persons in general terms for purposes of attribution,[276] provisions in human rights treaties and practice are more explicit. With regard to the American Convention on Human Rights, the Inter-American Court of Human Rights articulated a basic principle that illegal actions violating human rights that are not directly imputable to the State can nonetheless lead to international responsibility 'not because of the act itself, but because of the lack of due diligence to prevent the violation or to respond to it'.[277] As is evident from the cases cited in the present section and Chapter 6, CERD addresses situations concerning private bodies as a matter of course, having become more explicit over time on the targets of its concern.[278]

CERD GR 19 reminds us that segregation may arise as an 'unintended by-product of the actions of private persons'[279] and, according to GR 20, to the extent that 'private institutions influence the exercise of rights or the availability of opportunities, the State party must ensure that the result has neither the purpose nor the effect of creating or perpetuating racial discrimination'.[280] In similar vein, GR 25 recalls the different life experiences of women and men, 'in areas of both public and private life',[281] referring to 'abuse of women workers in the informal sector or domestic workers' and to 'discrimination

[273] *Ibid*., para. 7.4.

[274] *Ibid*., para. 4.6. In other circumstances, CERD has shown little appreciation for the doctrine of margin of appreciation expressed as such, the use of which by a State party 'in order to strike a balance between existing interests is limited by its obligations under the Convention': concluding observations on Australia, CERD/C/AUS/CO/14, para. 16. However, insofar as 'margin of appreciation' spills over into interpretation in context, see especially the present commentary on Article 4.

[275] Concluding observations on the Dominican Republic, CERD/C/DOM/CO/12, para. 8.

[276] In a case where private parties are acting in a governmental capacity, where they are directed or controlled by a State, or where their conduct is acknowledged or adopted by a State: *Draft Articles on the Responsibility of States for Internationally Wrongful Acts*, A/56/10 (2001), Articles 5, 8, and 11.

[277] *Velásquez-Rodríguez v Honduras*, IACtHR, Ser. C No. 4 (10988), para. 172; for a general discussion, see Shelton and Gould, 'Positive and Negative Obligations', 577–82.

[278] Diaconu notes that previous practice of CERD that used 'broad terms' such as labour market and employment, has been sharpened up to refer to companies and corporations, restaurants, clubs and agencies, etc: *Racial Discrimination*, pp. 35–6.

[279] A/50/18, Annex VII, para. 3.

[280] A/51/18, Annex VIII A, para. 5.

[281] Para. 1.

against women in private spheres of life'.[282] Discriminatory practices 'mainly by local authorities and private owners' in relation to housing are referred to in GR 27 on Roma,[283] while in relation to descent/caste groups, GR 29 refers, *inter alia*, to special measures to promote the employment of members of affected communities 'in the public and private sectors'; 'measures against public bodies, private companies and other associations that investigate the descent background of applicants for employment'; 'discriminatory practices of local authorities or private owners' in housing, etc; 'public or private education systems'; and 'discrimination by public or private bodies and any harassment of students from descent-based communities'.[284]

In the Article 14 communications procedure, the first finding of a violation of the Convention—*Yilmaz-Dogan v The Netherlands*—addressed the legal consequences flowing from the actions of a private employer.[285] Analogous private sector cases characterize the Article 14 archive as a whole, emanating from the actions of banks,[286] loan and insurance companies,[287] prevention by private persons of individuals wishing to settle into a neighbourhood,[288] discrimination in access to restaurants, clubs, and discotheques, etc.[289] In the reporting procedure, CERD requests information on racial discrimination legislation in force for the private sector and is critical of the absence of such legislation.[290] With regard to the US reservation on regulation of private conduct, the Committee in 2001 recommended legislation applicable to 'the largest possible sphere of private conduct which is discriminatory',[291] and in similar vein in 2008 recommended the State party to 'broaden the protection afforded by the law against discriminatory acts perpetrated by private individuals, groups or organizations'.[292] CERD has been critical of exempting 'private transactions' from discrimination legislation in housing and related market areas.[293]

In addition to obligations resulting from situations of conflict and occupation of territory, CERD has explored the issue of extraterritorial activities of corporate actors domiciled within the State, an issue that generates significant international interest, and a strong but not exclusive emphasis on economic, social, and cultural rights.[294] Based in part on an analysis of the work of treaty bodies, the Special representative of the Secretary-General developed a 'Protect, Respect and Remedy' framework that focuses on State obligations to regulate corporate actors working beyond State territorial confines rather

282 Para. 2.
283 GR 27, para. 31.
284 Paras jj, kk, mm, and tt. See also GR 30 on non-citizens, paras 32, 33, and 34.
285 CERD/C/36/D/1/1984 (1988).
286 *Habassi v Denmark*.
287 *Sefic v Denmark*, CERD/C/66/D/32/2003 (2005).
288 *L.K. v The Netherlands*, CERD/C/42/D/1991 (1993).
289 *Lacko v Slovakia*, CERD/C/59/D/11/1998 (2001); *B.J. v Denmark*; *Durmic v Serbia and Montenegro*.
290 Concluding observations on China, CERD/C/304/Add.122, para. 17; Fiji, CERD/C/FJI/CO/117, para. 15.
291 CERD/C/304/Add.125, para. 13.
292 CERD/C/USA/CO/6, para. 11.
293 Concluding observations on Finland, CERD/C/FIN/CO/20-22, para. 9.
294 CEDAW has stated that the obligation of States parties to establish legal protection of the rights of women extends to acts of national corporations operating extraterritorially: General Comment 28 on the Core Obligations of States Parties under Article 2 (2010), infra, p. 194.

than through norms directly constraining corporations.[295] The latter framework was endorsed by the Human Rights Council in 2011 as the Guiding Principles on Business and Human Rights.[296]

The commentary on Guiding Principle 2 on business and human rights observes that,[297] at present, 'States are not generally required to regulate the extraterritorial activities of businesses domiciled in their territory and/or jurisdiction. Nor are they generally prohibited from doing so', adding that within 'these parameters some human rights treaty bodies recommend that home States take steps to prevent abuse abroad by businesses enterprises within their jurisdiction'.[298] These observations do not draw hard legal conclusions with regard to treaty body practice, in particular whether the international law position they distil is one of permissions as opposed to obligations. States may be 'permitted' to establish extraterritorial jurisdiction under a number of grounds as a function of sovereignty, while extraterritorial obligations under human rights treaties generally stem from situations of *de facto* control.[299] Augenstein and Kinley carry through the 'control' relationship expressed in cases of territorial occupation to the regulation of corporate activities abroad, contending that

> the (non) regulation or control of corporate actors by the State establishes a relationship of *de facto* power between the State and the individual constitutive of extra-territorial human rights obligations. A State's *de jure* authority to exercise extra-territorial jurisdiction under public international law not only delimits the State's lawful competence to regulate and control business entities as perpetrators of extra-territorial human rights violations, but also constitutes a *de facto* relationship of power of the State over the individual that brings the individual under the State's human rights jurisdiction and triggers corresponding extra-territorial obligations.[300]

Of the UN treaty bodies, GR 28 of CEDAW states that the obligation of States parties to establish legal protection of the rights of women on an equal basis with men, 'and to take all appropriate measures to eliminate discrimination against women by any person, organization or enterprise, also extend to acts of national corporations operating extraterritorially'.[301] General comments of the CESCR articulate extraterritoriality principles with some consistency with regard to the activities 'abroad' of private actors including corporations that affect rights to health, water, and social security.[302] According to De

[295] *UN Draft Norms on the Responsibilities of Transnational Corporations and Other Business Enterprises with regard to Human Rights*, E/CN.4/Sub2/2003/12, 26 August 2003.

[296] A/HRC/17/31, 21 March 2011. There is a helpful summary and comment in *Frequently Asked Questions about the Guiding Principles on Business and Human Rights* (United Nations, 2014).

[297] *Guiding Principles on Business and Human Rights: Implementing the United Nations 'Protect, Respect and Remedy' Framework* (United Nations, 2011): 'States should set out clearly the expectation that all business enterprises domiciled in their territory and/or jurisdiction respect human rights throughout their operations.'

[298] *Ibid.*, pp. 3–4.

[299] See references, *supra*, in the present chapter.

[300] D. Augenstein and D. Kinley, 'When Human Rights "Responsibilities" become "Duties": the Extra-Territorial Obligations of States that Bind Corporations', *University of Sydney Law School, Legal Studies Research Paper* (September 2012), available at: <http://ssrn.com/abstract=2149921 1>; further references to this field, are detailed especially in footnote 4. See also R. McCorquodale and P. Simons, 'Responsibility beyond Borders: State responsibility for Extraterritorial violations by Corporations of International Human Rights Law', *Modern Law Review* 70(4) (2007, 598–625.

[301] CEDAW/C/2010/47/GC.2 (2010), para. 36.

[302] General Comment No. 14, The Right to the Highest Attainable Standard of Health (2000), paras 39; General Comment No. 15, The Right to Water (2003), para. 31; General Comment 19, The Right to Social Security (2008), para. 54.

Schutter, the position of the CESCR 'is supported by an emerging scholarship that the extra-territorial obligations under the ICESCR entail, at a minimum, that States parties should refrain from the adoption of measures that could negatively affect the enjoyment of such rights abroad, and that they should control the activities of private actors, particularly transnational corporations which they recognize as having their "nationality", in order to ensure that such corporations do not violate these rights, directly or indirectly, in foreign jurisdictions'.[303] On the other hand, the author cautions that, in the current state of international law a clear obligation on States to control private actors operating outside their national territory has not yet crystallized, and that 'this is the case even as regards those private actors having the nationality of the State concerned, and whose behaviour therefore a State may decisively influence and on whom it may impose certain obligations in conformity with international law'.[304]

As noted, the Committee's approach to extraterritorial obligations has emerged through a pattern of recommendations where the predominant focus has been the rights of indigenous peoples. CERD set the ball rolling in 2007 in concluding observations on Canada, expressing concern regarding reports 'of adverse effects of economic activities connected with the exploitation of natural resources in countries outside Canada by transnational corporations registered in Canada on the right to land, health, living environment and the way of life of indigenous peoples', and recommending 'appropriate legislative or administrative measures' to prevent such activities, and in particular to 'explore ways to hold transnational organizations registered in Canada accountable'.[305] Similar recommendations referring to corporations 'registered' in a State party have been made in connection with the reports of the USA[306] and the UK.[307] In the case of Australia the issue of a national legal framework was raised.[308] In the case of Norway, concern was expressed about 'the effects on indigenous peoples and other ethnic groups in territories outside Norway, including impact on their way of life and on the environment, of the activities by transnational corporations domiciled in the territory and/or under the jurisdiction of Norway'. The attendant recommendation was more elaborate than for Canada: Norway was invited 'to explore ways to hold transnational corporations domiciled in the territory and/or under the jurisdiction of Norway accountable for any adverse impacts on the rights of indigenous peoples and other ethnic groups, in conformity with the principles of social responsibility and the ethics code of corporations'.[309]

303 De Schutter, *International Human Rights Law*, p. 163, and citations therein.

304 *Ibid.*, pp. 162–3.

305 CERD/C/CAN/CO/18, para. 17. CERD returned to the issue in 2012, reiterating its concerns and recommendations, despite Canada's invocation of the merits of its Corporate Responsibility Strategy, CERD/C/CAN/CO/19-20, para. 14.

306 CERD/C/USA/CO/6, para. 30, responded to in CERD/C/USA/7-9, para. 177; also CERD/C/USA/CO/7-9, para. 10.

307 CERD/C/GBR/CO/18-20, para. 29.

308 The Committee regretted the absence of a legal framework regulating the obligations of 'Australian corporations' at home and overseas, and in addition to recommending appropriate legislative or administrative measures as per Canada, encouraged Australia to fulfil its commitments under the different international initiatives it supports to advance 'responsible corporate citizenship', CERD/C/AUS/CO/15-17, para. 13.

309 CERD/C/NOR/CO/19-20, para. 17; CERD/C/NOR/CO/21-22, paras 23 and 24.

XI. Article (1)(e) Encouragement of Integrationist Multiracial Organizations and Movements and other Means of Eliminating Barriers Between Races—Discouraging Anything that Leads to Racial Division

The sub-paragraph, was introduced by sponsors in the Third Committee of the GA as a 'positive' statement, while its 'racial barriers' aspect links with the condemnation of such in the preamble and the anti-segregation focus of Article 3. Reporting guidelines interpret 'integrationist multiracial organizations' as 'non-governmental organizations and institutions that combat racial discrimination and foster mutual understanding',[310] phrases linked to the anti-discrimination infrastructure required to fulfil obligations under Article 2 generally, as well as the hortatory language of Article 7 and the preamble. The issue makes a rare appearance in the procedure under Article 14 in *Hagan v Australia*,[311] where the State party referred to academic commentary to the effect that 1(e) was broadly and vaguely worded, leaving undefined what 'integrationist' movements are and what 'strengthens' racial division.[312]

Practice does not greatly illuminate the State party's implicit question. In the face of concerns over 'the lack of social movements that promote integrationist multiracial values', Barbados was requested to 'create an enabling environment' for such organizations',[313] while Iceland was recommended to ensure adequate finding and independence for non-governmental organizations (NGOs) combating racial discrimination.[314] It would seem that organizations combating racial discrimination are ipso facto regarded as examples of 2(1)(e) organizations, an understanding that reaches out to human rights NGOs and NHRIs, especially those that attempt to translate ICERD principles into action and disseminate them to a wider public. The banning of human rights centres is thus liable to generate critical remarks,[315] as is making registration of NGOs unduly burdensome, blunting their critical capacity and shrinking the space for civil society, a critique that reaches out to attacks on human right defenders; pro-tolerance NGOs—and other organizations under the rubric of Article 7—are clearly regarded as worthy of support.[316] The sub-paragraph has also been used to criticize the prevalence of political parties structured on ethnic lines, based on the premise that this had the potential to increase ethnic tension;[317] while the observations made were contextual, such parties were clearly not the 'integrationist multiracial organizations' envisaged in the sub-paragraph. The opposite end of the integrationist spectrum is represented by the racist organizations envisaged in Article 4(b). If 'integrationist' is given a narrow meaning, the range of organizations to be

310 CERD/C/2007/1, p. 5.

311 CERD/C/62/D/26/2002 (2003), para. 4.6.

312 The sole citation is to Lerner, *The UN Convention*, p. 38.

313 CERD/C/BRB/CO/16, para. 12.

314 CERD/C/ISL/CO/18, para. 10.

315 Concluding observations on Bahrain, CERD/C/BHR/CO/7, para. 13.

316 Concluding observations on the Russian Federation recommend that legislation be reviewed 'to ensure that non-governmental organizations working with ethnic minorities, indigenous peoples, non-citizens and other vulnerable groups who are subjected to discrimination are able to carry out their work effectively to promote and protect the rights . . . in the Convention without any undue interference or onerous obligations': CERD/C/RUS/20-22, para. 13. In general, see the *Declaration on the Right and Responsibility of Individuals, Groups and Organs of Society to Promote and Protect Universally recognized Human Rights and Fundamental Freedoms*, adopted by the General Assembly in Resolution 53/144, 9 December 1998.

317 Concluding observations on Ethiopia, CERD/C/ETH/CO/7-16, para. 13.

encouraged will be correspondingly narrow; if however, the term is understood as 'in support of the principles of the Convention' the field is wider. NGOs and community organizations that 'promote a culture of tolerance and ethnic diversity'[318] are clearly within the remit of the clause and are to be encouraged. Public bodies are included in the 2(1)(e) remit.[319] Organizations that advocate respect for caste, immigrant, indigenous, and minority rights within the purview of the Convention are equally entitled to be regarded as 'integrationist'.

D. Comment

Article 2 is the engine of the Convention, using language of a 'vigorous nature' to convert rights into a platform for practical action.[320] While the article is logically organized in progressing from obligations directed at the State and its bodies—public authorities and public institutions, legislation, and policy—towards regulating the actions of persons and groups, it is not a masterpiece of drafting; the *travaux* reveal degrees of confusion regarding the proliferation of terms and the overlapping of sub-paragraphs. The drafting was strongly influenced by the metaphors of immediate action and speed of response, illustrating the then dominant view that the swift elimination of racial discrimination was achievable if only the colonial systems could be swiftly demolished and apartheid consigned to history. The assertions of 'no discrimination here', allied with those on the 'unthinkable' notion of State-sponsored discrimination outside the customary circles of infamy, cemented the overall approach.

The *travaux*, as elsewhere, also reveal the minor key competing views that laws and prohibitions would not succeed without the assistance of education in combating racial discrimination, and that uniformity of approach and strict, unbending regulation were not appropriate to the Convention in light of the plurality of legal, political, and social arrangements in States, correlated with the complexities of their cultures, histories, and demographics. The overall approach in the Convention, however, is to combine legalistic with educational elements: both are indispensable to achieving the aims of the Convention, and both are integral to the Article 2(1)(d) requirement to prohibit and bring racial discrimination to an end 'by all appropriate means'. The specifics of legislation, including criminal law, are further refined in Article 4; education as a right is protected, and education in human rights including the principles of the Convention is mandated, by Articles 5 and 7 respectively, while GR 35 on combating racist hate speech recalls that legislation and education are complementary and that legal prohibitions of discrimination have educational functions.

The paragraphs of Article 2 add up to a demanding prospectus for States parties, culminating in the sweeping provisions of 2(1)(d). The expansion of the concept of racial discrimination through the adoption of concepts such as indirect, and even structural discrimination, widens the obligations prospectus further, as does the extended notion of a discriminatory 'act'.[321] A paper prepared by CERD for the Intergovernmental Working Group on the Durban Declaration and Programme of Action summarized the import of the article:

[318] Concluding observations on Serbia, CERD/C/SRB/CO/1, para. 13.
[319] Concluding observations on Moldova, CERD/C/MDA/CO/15, para. 11.
[320] Remarks of the delegate of the UK in the Third Committee.
[321] *L.R. v Slovakia*, paras 10.2, 10.6, 10.7.

Article 2 is a comprehensive provision addressing all aspects of States parties' obligation to pursue a policy of eliminating discrimination. Inter alia, it embraces the obligation to ensure that public authorities and institutions refrain from engaging in racial discrimination, to prohibit racial discrimination by any persons, group or organization and to take positive measures where necessary to guarantee to all racial groups the full and equal enjoyment of human rights and fundamental freedoms.[322]

The paper goes on to recall the importance of NHRIs for Article 2,[323] an example of the accretion in Committee practice of 'standard' recommended cases for the achievement of optimum effects in the implementation of the undertakings—an institutional superstructure largely replicated in recommendations regarding Article 6. The architecture of human rights institutions is ultimately a matter for the State. CERD has, however, developed positions on appropriate institutions to support the implementation of law and policy such as, in addition to the indispensable role of the courts, anti-racism bodies, ombudsmen, equality bodies, 'defenders of rights', specific protection bodies for indigenous peoples, etc. Aspects of the functioning of such bodies are of regular concern to the Committee in terms of their visibility, their range of functions, their objectivity and independence from political interference, the scope of their mandates, and the availability of resources for their effective functioning, Many of the concerns regarding the architecture of national human rights bodies are subsumed in references to the 'Paris Principles' relating to the status of national institutions for the promotion and protection of human rights.[324] Recommendations to establish an NHRI,[325] or expand existing institutional mandates to comply with the Paris Principles are standard, and include recommendations on independence and autonomy,[326] financing and staffing,[327] on the involvement of civil society in the process of establishment,[328] and on taking steps toward accreditation by the International Coordinating Committee of National Institutions for the Promotion and Protection of Human Rights;[329] responses by States parties to the downgrading of an NHRI by the International Coordinating Committee have also been sought.[330]

It is clear from the last-cited CERD summary that Article 2 reflects an integrated approach to the elimination of racial discrimination that incorporates negative and

[322] *Views of the Committee on the Elimination of Racial Discrimination on the Implementation of the Convention on the Elimination of All Forms of Racial Discrimination and its Effectiveness*, submitted under the rubric of 'complementary standards', E/CN.4/2004/WG.21/10/Add.1, 17 September 2004, p. 13.

[323] *Ibid.*, p. 14.

[324] *Principles Relating to the Status of National Institutions*, annexed to General Assembly resolution 48/134 of 20 December 1993. National human rights institutions (NHRIs) are 'State bodies with a constitutional and / or legal mandate to protect and promote human rights. They are part of the State apparatus and are funded by the State . . . They are at arm's length from the government': *National Human Rights Institutions: History, Principles, Roles and Responsibilities* (United Nations, 2010), p. 13. The OHCHR web page includes updated information and documentation the place of national human rights institutions in the United Nations system: <http://www.ohchr.org/en/countries/nhrimain.aspx>.

[325] Recent examples include Estonia, CERD/C/EST/CO/8-9 (2010); CERD/C/ITA/CO/16-18 (2012); Malta, CERD/C/MLT/CO/15-20 (2011).

[326] CERD/C/BIH/CO/7-8 (2010).

[327] Vietnam, CERD/C/VNM/CO/10-14 (2012).

[328] Concluding observations on Italy, CERD/C/ITA/CO/16-18, para. 13.

[329] Concluding observations on Estonia, CERD/C/EST/CO/8-9, para. 10.

[330] Concluding observations on Cameroon, CERD/C/CMR/15-18, para. 13.

positive elements. While practice may approximate to the tripartite typology of obligations—respect, protect, fulfil—CERD has not systematically structured this usage in the manner of the CESCR and other bodies,[331] preferring to work though the implications of Article 2 by tracking the detailed demands made upon States parties by the Convention. Whether Committee work would gain in precision by the adoption of a typology of obligations is an open question, bearing in mind the already significant elaboration of detail in Article 2; similarly, the '4A' elaboration for the enjoyment of rights adopted by the CESCR (availability, accessibility, acceptability, and adaptability)[332] has not been adopted by CERD. A working 'typology' adopted by the Committee, referring to the 'substantive obligations in the Convention to prevent, protect against and remedy discriminatory acts', has been put forward in opinions under Article 14.[333]

With regard to the incorporation of the Convention into domestic legal systems, the practice has not been overly concerned with the nuances of theory.[334] Rather, it has sought to ensure that the provisions of the Convention are reflected as fully as possible in domestic law and practice, whatever patterns or techniques of incorporation are adopted. The Committee questions States on the reach of the Convention into court practice—whether it can be invoked in judicial or analogous proceedings, and to what effect. Absence of or limited invocation of the Convention before domestic courts is treated as a matter of concern,[335] not assuaged by claims that racial discrimination is not a significant issue in the State party concerned. The information from States asserting the direct applicability of the Convention in domestic law may sit uneasily with an absence of relevant cases where it is invoked: *inter alia*, training of judges and law officers in the principles of the Convention and its direct applicability may be recommended to remedy the situation.[336] The Committee has sought clarification of information that the application of the Convention is judged on a case by case basis, 'taking into consideration the purpose, meaning and wording of the provisions concerned',[337] although an examination of whether particular provisions are or are not self-executing would seem in itself to be unremarkable and undeserving of criticism.[338] Regarding the level of incorporation, expressed concerns for the status of the Convention in domestic law when compared with that of other human rights instruments are noted above, concerns that appear amply

[331] Even the lengthy section XI on economic, social, and cultural rights in CERD's GR 34 on persons of African descent does not reproduce the threefold typology.

[332] See, *inter alia*, CESCR General Comment No. 13 on *The Right to Education (Article 13)*: HRI/GEN/1/Rev.9 (Vol. I), pp. 63–77. The 4A scheme is discussed further in Chapter 15 of the present work.

[333] *A.M.M v Switzerland*, CERD/C/84/D/50/2012 (2014), para. 8.2; also *L. R v Slovakia*, para. 10.2.

[334] Concluding observations on Tanzania refer to its 'dualist' legal system: CERD/C/TZA/CO/16, para. 11. 'Monist' is used in the 2012 concluding observations on Jordan: CERD/C/JOR/CO/13-17, para. 8.

[335] Concluding observations on Vietnam, CERD/C/VNM/CO/10-14, para. 8.

[336] Concluding observations on Lithuania, CERD/C/LTU/CO/3, para. 10, and Namibia. CERD/C/NAM/CO/12, para. 10.

[337] Concluding observations on Japan, CERD/C/304/Add.114, para. 9. The delegation of Japan explained the position in CERD/C/SR.1144, para. 5. For a general treatment of the issue, see Y. Iwasawa, *International Law, Human Rights, and Japanese Law* (Clarendon Press, 1998).

[338] See the helpful summary of principles by A. Byrnes and C. Renshaw in Moeckli *et al.*, *International Human Rights Law*, pp. 460–5, who point out, p. 462, that the intention of the drafters of the treaty and the nature of the treaty provision may be factors in deciding whether the treaty or a provision thereof is directly applicable.

justified in light of the links between the Convention and the Charter of the United Nations,[339] customary international law, and even peremptory norms.[340]

In whatever form it takes, whether through civil law codes or the more diffuse methods employed by the common law, incorporation is, in the view of the Committee, not simply a matter of words on paper but is to be confirmed by programmes of practical action—legislative aesthetics are not an adequate response to the demands of the Convention.[341] The canons of practicality and effectiveness are further satisfied through awareness-raising and training in the principles of the Convention, notably for legal professionals and public service personnel, the promotion of institutional dialogue on the rights and obligations therein, and the transmission of the conclusions of the Committee to civil society. In the last respect, CERD has adopted its own version of the 'vernacularization' of its guidance functions,[342] exhorting States to disseminate their reports and the concluding observations thereon not only in official or national languages but also in 'other commonly used languages'.[343] This is an important reference principle for a Convention that centres on collective as well as individual rights, which, *inter alia*, serves to facilitate the realization of the right of minorities and comparable groups to participate in decisions affecting them.

With regard to the vertical and horizontal reach of the Convention, CERD has been robust on the requirement to implement the Convention through layers of governance, an obligation which has also been applied to religious and customary courts. Ethiopia was requested by the Committee to 'ensure that public authorities and officials, including those at the level of religious and customary courts, act in conformity with Article 2(1)';[344] in the case of Mozambique, information was requested on measures adopted 'to ensure that the actions of traditional authorities, and customary laws, are in conformity with . . . the Convention'.[345] The reaching down to customary and other institutions will be affected by the interpretation of 'private life' and freedom of association in the Convention and how these concepts should be applied to voluntary associations and ethnicities. The question of the Convention's 'reach'—and the Committee's approach to

[339] 'To establish . . . and to enforce, distinctions, exclusions, restrictions and limitations exclusively based on grounds of race, colour, descent or national or ethnic origin which constitute a denial of fundamental human rights is a flagrant violation of the purposes and principles of the Charter', *Legal Consequences for States of the Continued Presence of South Africa in Namibia*, ICJ Advisory Opinion of 21 June, para. 131.

[340] The Committee's own estimate of this link is included in a statement of 2002 on racial discrimination an measures to combat terrorism, where it was recalled simply that 'the prohibition of racial discrimination is a peremptory norm of international law from which no derogation is permitted': A/57/18, ch. XI C, para. 4. For a critical view, see P. Thornberry, *International Law and the Rights of Minorities* (Clarendon Press, 1991), pp. 326–8.

[341] While reflecting on different methodologies of importing international standards into domestic law, CEDAW takes the view that the Convention on Discrimination against Women 'may receive enhanced protection in those States where the Convention is automatically or through specific incorporation part of the domestic legal order': CEDAW GR 28, para. 31.

[342] S.E. Merry 'Transnational Human Rights and Local Activism: Mapping the Middle', *American Anthropologist* 108 (2006), 38–51; P. Levitt and S.E. Merry, 'Vernacularization on the Ground: Local Uses of Global Women's Rights in Peru, China, India and the United States', *Global Networks* 9 (2009), 441–61: <http://www.peggylevitt.org/assets/venacularization.pdf>.

[343] Dissemination and related issues are further discussed in the present work in the commentary on Article 7.

[344] CERD/C/ETH/CO/15, para. 14.

[345] CERD/C/MOZ/CO/12, para. 13.

interventions—intersects with questions on the content and role of religious and customary laws, though the two issues are not completely congruent.[346]

As to the lateral application of the Convention, the 'control' or 'effective control' principle characterizing situations of dependency or occupation has referred principally to control over a territory rather than extraterritorial application through control of persons by agents of a State. Both aspects of control potentially fit within the ICERD frame: the above-cited reference in *Georgia v Russian Federation* refers simply and openly to 'actions' of a State party. Practice has not consolidated itself in the form of a dedicated general recommendation, nor has extraterritoriality been engaged in the communications procedure under Article 14. International practice does not furnish ready answers to the further question of the comprehensiveness of State obligations when extraterritorial jurisdiction is established in terms of the triumvirate to 'respect, protect and fulfil' human rights.[347] In the case of the 'personal' mode of jurisdiction—where individuals are under the control of agents of the State—there is authority for the view that obligations can be 'divided and tailored', a limitation that would not apply to cases of territorial control through a subordinate local administration or armed forces, where the full range of human rights is applicable under the Convention in question.[348] In any case, 'dividing and tailoring' with regard to applying a determinate, context-specific range of human rights, would remain subject to ICERD standards prohibiting racial discrimination. It may be noted that Articles 3 and 6 of the Convention, which include reference to territory and to jurisdiction, appear not to have been treated in any different manner from Article 2 and the Convention generally when it comes to extraterritorial application.

The control principle is also deemed to apply to colonial territories, and the Committee is eminently capable of opposing its own view on the applicability of the Convention to that of the State party. In regretting the stance of the UK that the Convention does not apply to the British Indian Ocean Territory (BIOT),[349] the State party was reminded that

[346] For a brief discussion, see P. Thornberry, 'The Committee on the Elimination of Racial Discrimination—Questions of Concept and Practice', in R.F. Jørgensen and K. Slavensky (eds), *Implementing Human Rights—Essays in Honour of Morten Kjaerum* (Danish Institute for Human Rights, 2007), 318–36. For a general treatment of customary law, see B. Tobin: *Indigenous Peoples, Customary Law and Human Rights: Why Living Law Matters* (Routledge, 2014). A (partly) critical view of the work of the Committee—and the views of the present author—is offered in M.K. Addo, 'Practice of United Nations Treaty Bodies in the Reconciliation of Cultural Diversity with Universal Respect for Human Rights', *HRQ* 32 (2010), 601–64.

[347] The non-binding *Maastricht Principles on the Extraterritorial Obligations of States in the Area of Economic, Social and Cultural Rights*, cited by Joseph and Fletcher in Moeckli *et al.*, *International Human Rights Law*, p. 136, appear to take a maximalist position, with Principle 3 asserting that all States 'have obligations to respect, protect and fulfil human rights, including civil, cultural, economic, political and social rights, both within their territories and extraterritorially'.

[348] European Court of Human Rights, *Al-Skeini and Others v the UK*, App. No. 55721/07 (2011), para. 137 on 'tailoring'; however, in the case of lawful or unlawful military action, when a State 'exercises control of an area outside . . . national territory', the controlling State 'has the responsibility . . . to secure, within the area under its control, the entire range of substantive rights' set out (in the ECHR), and will be liable for any violations: *ibid.*, para. 138. See discussion in S. Allen, *The Chagos Islanders and International Law* (Hart Publishing, 2014), pp. 56–8.

[349] The UK expressed its views to the Committee in Annex XI of its report examined by the Committee in 2011—CERD/C/GBR/18-20—arguing that ICERD did not apply because, *inter alia*, the territory had no permanent inhabitants and that members of the armed forces, officials and contractors spent only brief periods there. The Committee took the view that the Chagossians had a right to return to the Territory and regarded restrictions on the right to return as racially discriminatory. For detailed and helpful commentary on the overall dispute, see S. Allen, 'International Law and the Resettlement of the (Outer) Chagos Islands', *HRLR* 8(4) (2008), 683–702; and *The Chagos Islanders and International Law*.

it had 'an obligation to ensure that the Convention is applicable in all territories under its control', to which was added the recommendation that 'all discriminatory restrictions on Chagossians (Ilois) from entering Diego Garcia or other islands on the BIOT be withdrawn'.[350]

With regard to the Committee's stance on the extraterritorial activities of corporations, States have contested the Committee' hortatory recommendations. Canada expressed the view that 'obligations under the Convention did not extend beyond [Canada's] borders' and that 'primary responsibility for social and environmental issues rested with the foreign State in which Canadian multinationals operated'.[351] Norway stated simply that issues regarding the activities of Norwegian firms abroad 'were outside the Committee's purview'.[352] The UK explained that UK anti-discrimination legislation 'was not extended to British companies operating overseas. They [the companies] bore primary responsibility for their actions, and legal responsibility for any human rights abuses rested with the authorities in the States concerned'.[353]

It remains to be seen whether the exploration of extraterritorial regulation will in due course meet with more positive responses.[354] The Committee's stance derives from the assumption that States parties can and should exercise control over the actions of corporations registered in the State. Practice has not adequately clarified the conditions for the exercise of control, what forms of control are in question, and what are the triggering conditions for the principle to operate. Thus far, the focus has been on recommendations for the protection of indigenous peoples from grave damage to lives, territories, and resources where their local State appears unable or unwilling to offer an equivalent response. The Committee's *in statu nascendi* approach includes elements that await further determination and would benefit from a general recommendation or statement, perhaps in conjunction with a body such as the CESCR, to implement the position as treaty interpretation and contribute to the development of international customary law.

The fulfilment of the demands of Article 2 is necessarily differentiated in light of the rights and different circumstances of groups and individuals; the development of policy is subject to the general Convention principle that uniformity of response to different circumstances can be discriminatory in itself.[355] The necessity to work on the basis of accurate, disaggregated data, applies to the discharge of obligations as elsewhere in the application of the Convention. Article 2 focuses on the elaboration and structuring of State efforts to combat discrimination through the prism of obligations, and is a vehicle for assessing the adequacy of measures taken towards the objectives of the Convention. The article is noteworthy in the breadth of its ambition to bring racial discrimination to an end—2(1)(d)—throughout society. Makkonen asserts that the combination of

350 CERD/C/GBR/CO/18-20, para. 12.

351 CERD/SR.2142, para. 73.

352 CERD/C/SR.2062, para. 23.

353 CERD/C/SR.2113, para. 67.

354 'There are strong policy reasons for home States to set out clearly the expectation that businesses respect human rights abroad, especially where the State itself is involved in or supports those businesses. The reasons include ensuring predictability for business enterprises by providing coherent and consistent messages, and preserving the State's own reputation': *Guiding Principles on Business and Human Rights*, commentary on Principle 2:'States should set out clearly the expectation that all business enterprises domiciled in their territory and/or jurisdiction respect human rights throughout their operations.'

355 See commentary in the present work on Article 1.

conventions and declarations to be implemented by States and intergovernmental organizations

> creates a statist culture which emphasises the role of legislation, policy programmes and other centrally coordinated action, and sustains the utopia that governments can effectively prevent people from engaging in discrimination and thereby eliminate all forms of discrimination. Such statism may inadvertently or even openly discourage non-State action[356]

Whatever the intellectual coherence and practicality of the Convention's ultimate ambition to eliminate racial discrimination, its 'statism' is increasingly mitigated by the growing impact of a range of actors beyond the State, working to make a reality of international professions of human rights standards. The spectrum of obligations in Article 2 integrates with the whole Convention, the implementation of which is markedly less 'statist' than in the early years following its adoption. Civil society has made tremendous strides in working with the Convention in a wide range of countries, while articulations of group rights press upon the interpretation of the text. Article 2, and the Convention as a whole, should be interpreted as not discouraging civil society but as soliciting its collaboration. GR 32 on special measures recalls the desideratum of consultation with affected communities and their active participation in the design and implementation of 'measures'[357]—plans, policies, and programmes—a stipulation that is applicable, *mutatis mutandis*, across the spectrum of activity engaged by Article 2.

[356] T. Makkonen, *Equal in Law, Unequal in Fact* (Martinus Nijhoff, 2012), p. 272.
[357] Para. 18.

9. Special Measures under the Convention

Definitions and Obligations

Article 1(4)
Special measures taken for the sole purpose of securing adequate advancement of certain racial or ethnic groups or individuals requiring such protection as may be necessary in order to ensure such groups or individuals equal enjoyment or exercise of human rights and fundamental freedoms shall not be deemed racial discrimination, provided, however, that such measures do not, as a consequence, lead to the maintenance of separate rights for different racial groups and that they shall not be continued after the objectives for which they were taken have been achieved.

Article 2(2)
States parties shall, when the circumstances so warrant, take, in the social, economic, cultural and other fields, special and concrete measures to ensure the adequate development and protection of certain racial groups or individuals belonging to them, for the purpose of guaranteeing them the full and equal enjoyment of human rights and fundamental freedoms. These measures shall in no case entail as a consequence the maintenance of unequal or separate rights for different racial groups after the objectives for which they were taken have been achieved.

A. Introduction

Through its provisions on special measures, the Convention connects with contemporary discussions of 'affirmative action' and 'positive action', though the concepts underlying such terms vary with institutional context. This contemporary terminology, clustered around the notions of equality and non-discrimination, is not unique to the field of race/ethnic relations but pervades other areas of human rights discourse including gender, disability, and allied fields where forms of discrimination manifest themselves. A generalized definition of the area under discussion is offered by Bossuyt: 'Affirmative action is a coherent packet of measures, of a temporary character, aimed specifically at correcting the position of members of a target group in one or more aspects of their social life, in order to obtain effective equality.'[1] 'Affirmative action' in the Bossuyt sense is a broad term, and may include areas of action outside the strict scope of Articles 1(4) and 2(2) of the International Convention on the Elimination of All Forms of Racial Discrimination (ICERD); the same is true, *a fortiori*, of 'positive action'.[2] Bossuyt distinguishes forms of

[1] M. Bossuyt, *Final Report on the Concept and Practice of Affirmative Action*, E/CN.4/Sub.2/2002/21, para. 6 [henceforth *Affirmative Action*]. Bossuyt notes in para. 8 that 'past and present affirmative action programmes have been concerned with women, blacks, immigrants, poor people, disabled persons, veterans, indigenous peoples, other racial groups, specific minorities, etc'. For a succinct review, with emphasis on international standards, see M. Tomei, *Affirmative Action for Racial Equality: Features, Impact and Challenges* (International Labour Office, 2005).

[2] A wide range of strategies are canvassed under this term in N. Bamforth, M. Malik, and C. O'Cinneide (eds), *Discrimination Law: Theory and Context* (Sweet and Maxwell, 2008), Chapters 6 and 7. See the discussion of CERD General Recommendation 32 in the present chapter.

affirmative action that include 'affirmative mobilization or affirmative fairness' which may be no more than encouragement of minority job applicants or strict scrutiny to ascertain whether fair standards have been applied to members of minority groups in application for social goods[3] and 'affirmative preference',[4] the latter being 'the most controversial form of affirmative action'.[5] Issues regarding special measures or affirmative action—in both Bossuyt senses, but especially the second, 'harder' sense—run through international human rights standards. In the field of race relations, controversies have arisen in many States, with those in India,[6] South Africa,[7] and the US,[8] being perhaps the most widely known and followed; the contribution of India to the drafting of the special measures provisions in ICERD was particularly significant.[9] Where possible, the present chapter employs the term 'special measures' to individuate the ICERD meaning of this term from among a thicket of associations.[10]

Special measures are now widely referred to in instruments of international human rights.[11]

[3] 'Affirmative mobilization and affirmative fairness both entail measures dedicated to overcoming the social problems of a target group, but the measures do not themselves entail discrimination against people who are not members of that group': Bossuyt, *Affirmative Action*, para. 74.

[4] *Ibid.*, paras 71–80; Bossuyt, *ibid.*, para. 75, describes affirmative preference as situations where 'someone's gender or race will be taken into account in the granting or withholding of social goods'.

[5] *Ibid.*, para. 78.

[6] T.E. Weisskopf, *Affirmative Action in the US and India: A Comparative Perspective* (Routledge, 2004); J. Faundez, *Affirmative Action: International Perspectives* (ILO, 1994). A short account of affirmative action in India is provided in the nineteenth periodic report of India to CERD, CERD/C/IND/19, paras 26 and 27.

[7] C. Romany and J.-B. Chu, 'Affirmative action in international human rights law: lessons from the United States and South Africa', *36 Connecticut Law Review* (2004), 831–70; C. de la Vega, 'The special measures mandate of the International Convention on the Elimination of All Forms of Racial Discrimination: Lessons from the United States and South Africa', *University of San Francisco research paper No. 2009–08*, available at <http/ssrn.com/abstract=1317934>; K. Adams, 'The Politics of Redress: South Africa Style Affirmative Action', *Journal of Modern African Studies* 35 (1997), 231–49. See also S. Ngcobo, 'The meaning of Article 4(1) of the UN Convention on the Elimination of All Forms of Discrimination against Women: a South African Perspective', in I. Boerefijn, F. Coomans, J. Goldschmidt, R. Holtmaat, and R. Wolleswinkel, *Temporary Special Measures: Accelerating De facto Equality of Women under Article 4(1) of the UN Convention on the Elimination of All forms of Discrimination against Women* (Intersentia, 2003), pp. 181–202 [henceforth *Temporary Special Measures*].

[8] Leading cases in the US law include; *Regents of the University of California v Bakke*, 438 U.S. 265 (1978), *Fullilove v Klutznick*, 448 U.S. 448 (1980), *Wygant v Jackson Board of Education*, 476 U.S. 267 (1986), *United States v Paradise*, 480 U.S. 149 (1987), *United Steelworkers of America v Weber*, 443 U.S. 193 (1979), *Adarand Constructors, Inc. v Pena*, 515 U.S. 200 (1995), *Grutter v Bollinger*, 539 U.S. 306 (2003), *Gratz v Bollinger*, 539 U.S. 244 (2003); there is extensive reference to US case law in the sixth periodic report of the United States, CERD/C/USA/6, paras 126–34. See also CERD comment on *Schuette v Coalition to Defend Affirmative Action*, US Supreme Court, 22 April 2014, CERD/C/USA/CO/7-9, para. 7.

[9] For India's contributions on this subject to the drafting of other UN conventions, see W. A. McKean, *Equality and Discrimination under International Law* (Clarendon Press, 1983), pp. 146–47 [henceforth *Equality and Discrimination*]; M. Craven, *The International Covenant on Economic, Social and Cultural Rights* (Clarendon Press, 1998), pp. 184–90.

[10] A thicket of terms 'as politically controversial as they are linguistically indeterminate': A. McColgan, *Discrimination Law: Text, Cases and Materials* (2nd edn, Hart Publishing, 2005), p. 130. In similar vein, Bossuyt observes that 'Affirmative action is a term used frequently, but, unfortunately, not always with the same meaning': Bossuyt, *Affirmative Action*, para. 5; he adds, *ibid.*, para. 6, that 'it is a concept without a generally accepted legal definition'.

[11] Useful discussions in: W.A. McKean, *Equality and Discrimination*; Boerefijn et al., *Temporary Special Measures*; K. Henrard, 'Non-discrimination and Full and Effective Equality', in M. Weller (ed.), *Universal Minority Rights* (Oxford University Press, 2007); K. Henrard, 'The Protection of Minorities through the Equality Provisions in the UN Human Rights Treaties: the UN Treaty Bodies', *IJMGR* 14 (2007), 141–80; A. Morawa, 'The evolving human right to equality', *1 European Yearbook of Minority Issues* 2001/2, 157–205.

Among 'discrimination instruments', Article 5(1) of International Labour Organization (ILO) Convention 111[12] provides for 'special measures of protection or assistance' in a manner that appears broad enough to cover measures that are of a temporary nature as well as permanent special measures; the measures in Article 5 of the Convention are not described as mandatory. The Convention on the Elimination of All Forms of Discrimination against Women (CEDAW) also explicitly provides for special measures,[13] and the elaboration of General Recommendation (GR) 25 on 'temporary special measures'[14] was a strong influence on the drafting of General Recommendation (GR) 32 of the Committee on the Elimination of Racial Discrimination. Of the other 'core' UN human rights treaties, whilst only the Convention on Persons with Disabilities makes explicit reference to 'special measures',[15] the treaty bodies of other core human rights treaties refer to the concept in practice and have adopted general comments; in this respect, the practice of the Human Rights Committee[16] and CESCR[17] is fairly extensive. The concluding observations of the Committee on the Rights of the Child reveal a more insistent concern with 'special needs', 'special education', and 'special attention' than with 'special measures',[18] although General Comment (GC) 11 on the rights of indigenous children[19] applies the terminology of special measures to a variety of rights.[20]

Provisions on special measures appear in instruments relating to ICERD's primary reference groups including ILO Convention 169 on Indigenous and Tribal Peoples[21] and

[12] Similarly, para. 6 of Recommendation 111 concerning Discrimination in Respect of Employment and Occupation (1958) provides that the application of the policy of prevention of discrimination in employment and occupation should not adversely affect special measures 'to meet the particular requirements of persons who, for reasons such as sex, age, disablement, family responsibilities or social or cultural status are generally recognised to require special protection or assistance'.

[13] Articles 4(1) and 4(2).

[14] General Recommendation No. 25: Article 4, para. 1 of the Convention (temporary special measures), HRI/GEN/1/Rev.9 (Vol. II), p. 365.

[15] Article 5(4).

[16] HRC GC No. 18 (1989), *Non-Discrimination*, para. 10, HRI/GEN/1/Rev.9, Vol. I, pp. 195–98. See also the reference to affirmative action in GC 4 on *Equal Rights of Men and Women in the Enjoyment of Civil and Political Rights*, HRI/GEN/1/Rev.9, Vol. I, p. 175; the reference to positive measures in GC 28 on *The Equality of Rights between Men and Women*, para. 3, HRI/GEN/1/Rev.9, Vol. I, pp. 228–34; *Jacobs v Belgium*, CCPR/C/81/D/943/2000 (2004), para. 9.3; *Ballantyne, Davidson and McIntyre v Canada*, CCPR/C/47/D/359/1989, 385/1989/Rev. 1 (1993), para. 11.4. According to Henrard, whilst 'there is no explicit provision in the ICCPR [on special measures], the HRC clearly accepts the legitimacy of affirmative action, [and] even points to an obligation to adopt such measures': Henrard, *Non-Discrimination and Equality*, p. 131. On the other hand, Vandenhole finds a conservative approach in the Human Rights Committee compared with CERD, noting that the former body 'has limited itself to suggesting affirmative action with regard to women . . . and exceptionally also with regard to minorities (mainly Roma)': W. Vandenhole, *Non-Discrimination and Equality in the View of the UN Human Rights Treaty Bodies* (Intersentia, 2005), p. 223.

[17] CESCR/C GC 16, (2005), para. 15, HRI/GEN/1/Rev.9, Vol. I, pp. 113–23; see also, *ibid.*, para. 35; GC 5 (1994) on persons with disabilities, paras 9 and 118, HRI/GEN/1/Rev.9, Vol. I, pp. 17–27; GC 13 (1999) on the right to education, para. 32, HRI/GEN/1/Rev.9, Vol. I, pp. 63–77. Para. 9 of GC 20 on non-discrimination in economic, social, and cultural rights describes special measures as legitimate 'as long as they represent reasonable, objective and proportional means to redress de facto discrimination and are discontinued when substantive equality has been sustainably achieved'. The paragraph suggests that some 'special measures' may be permanent: 'interpretation services for linguistic minorities' is one example provided: E/C.12/GC/20 (2009).

[18] Search of <http://www.universalhumanrightsindex.org> of 'special measures' and 'Committee on the Rights of the Child'.

[19] CRC/C/GC/11 (2009).

[20] Paras 5, 13, 20, 21, 24, 25, 29, 34, 50, 60, 80, and 81.

[21] Article 4.

the UN Declaration on the Rights of Indigenous Peoples.[22] The measures under the ILO Convention are not expressed as time-limited.[23] Also close to ICERD's concerns, the UNESCO Declaration on Race and Racial Prejudice engages with the vocabulary of special measures in providing that they 'must be taken to ensure equality in dignity and rights for individuals and groups wherever necessary, while ensuring that they are not such as to appear racially discriminatory'.[24] The UN Declaration on the Rights of Persons belonging to Minorities refers broadly to 'measures' but not to special measures,[25] although the commentary on the Declaration links this provision with ICERD.[26] Analogously, Article 4(2) of the Council of Europe Framework Convention for the Protection of National Minorities on 'adequate measures'[27] is linked through commentary to an ICERD-resonant formula.[28]

Acceptance of special measures in key regional human rights instruments is patchy. Thus, while the African Charter on Human and Peoples Rights does not include a provision on special measures, the Protocol on the Rights of Women in Africa[29] includes provisions on 'affirmative action'[30] and 'positive action'.[31] Neither the American Declaration nor the Inter-American Convention on Human Rights contains a clause on special measures, while the Inter-American Convention against Racism, Racial Discrimination and Related Forms of Intolerance addresses special measures in a manner reminiscent of ICERD.[32] The European Convention on Human Rights does not have a provision on special measures, and European Court of Human Rights practice in this area is relatively

[22] Article 21(2).

[23] M. Oelz, *Comments by the ILO* for CERD Thematic Discussion on Special Measures, 4–5 August 2008, p. 3, noting that under ILO Convention 159, the measures may be temporary or permanent (on file with OHCHR Secretariat); see also *ILO Convention on Indigenous and Tribal Peoples, 1989: A Manual* (ILO, 2000), p. 14. See also ILO Convention 107 on Indigenous and Tribal Populations, 1957, Article 3 of which set out rather grudging parameters for special measures of protection of the populations concerned, warning that care was to be taken that the measures were 'not used as a means of prolonging or creating a state of segregation', and that they 'will be continued only so long as there is need for special protection and only to the extent that such protection is necessary'.

[24] Declaration on Race and Racial Prejudice, adopted and proclaimed by the General Conference of UNESCO, November 1978, Article 9(2).

[25] Article 4(1).

[26] *Commentary of the Working Group on Minorities to the UN Declaration on the Rights of Persons belonging to National or Ethnic, Religious and Linguistic Minorities*, E/CN.4/Sub.2/ASC.5/2005/2 (2005), para. 55; also para. 82.

[27] K. Myntti, 'The Prevention of Discrimination v. Protection of Minorities—with Particular Reference to "Special Measures"', *Baltic Yearbook of International Law*, 2 (2002), 199–226, 220–3; in the same volume, P. Thornberry, 'The Framework Convention on National Minorities: a Provisional Appraisal and a Memory of the Baltic States', 127–57, at 140–1.

[28] 'Such measures need to be adequate, that is in conformity with the proportionality principle, in order to avoid violation of the rights of others as well as discrimination against others. This principle requires, among other things, that such measures do not extend, in time or in scope, beyond what is necessary in order to achieve the aim of full and effective equality': *Explanatory Report on the Framework Convention*, para. 39.

[29] Adopted at the Second ordinary Session of the Assembly of the African Union, July 2003.

[30] In Article 9(1) on the field of political participation.

[31] Article 2(1)(d) details an obligation to take 'corrective and positive action in those areas where discrimination against women in law and in fact continues to exist'; see also Article 12(2) regarding education, and Article 9(1).

[32] Article 1(5) provides that '[s]pecial measures or affirmative action adopted for the purpose of ensuring equal enjoyment or exercise of one or more human rights and fundamental freedoms of groups requiring such protection shall not be deemed racial discrimination provided that such measures do not lead to the maintenance of separate rights for different groups and are not continued once their objectives have been achieved'.

undeveloped.[33] Preambular paragraph 4 of Protocol 12 to the European Convention[34] reaffirms that 'the provision of special measures does not prevent States parties from taking measures in order to promote effective full and equality, provided that there is an objective and reasonable justification for those measures',[35] a less than ringing endorsement of the measures in contemplation.

B. *Travaux Préparatoires*

I. Article 1(4)

McKean summarizes among 'several general principles' resulting from a raft of UN studies on discrimination, including the early studies, the principles that '[c]ertain distinctions are legitimate if they are special measures designed to achieve rather than to prevent equality in the enjoyment of rights', and that 'such special measures are only legitimate if they are temporary'.[36] The Declaration on Racial Discrimination includes a provision that relates to State obligations rather than definition. Article 2(3) of the Declaration provides that:

> Special concrete measures shall be taken in appropriate circumstances in order to secure adequate development or protection of individuals belonging to certain racial groups with the object of ensuring the full enjoyment by such individuals of human rights and fundamental freedoms. These measures shall in no circumstances have as a consequence the maintenance of unequal or separate rights for different racial groups.

Building upon this background, the notion of 'special concrete measures' under Article 1 of the Convention[37] was initially broached in discussions in the Sub-Commission on a text proposed by Calvocoressi and Capotorti, paragraph 3 of which read:

> A Contracting State may take special concrete measures in appropriate circumstances in order to secure adequate development or protection of individuals belonging to certain racial groups with the object of ensuring the full enjoyment by such individuals of human rights and fundamental freedoms. These measures shall in no circumstances have as a consequence the maintenance of unequal or separate rights for different racial groups.[38]

On this basis, a draft text[39] was prepared by a working group which contributed to the final version adopted by the Sub-Commission, with the significant change from 'should not be deemed racial discrimination' in the working group draft to 'shall not be deemed

[33] See comment on *Petrovic v Austria* (1989), and *Van Raalte v Netherlands* (1997) by Henrard, *Universal Minority Rights*, p. 135. For comment on positive action in the context of the European Union, see J. Swiebel, 'What could the European Union learn from the CEDAW Convention?', in Boerefijn *et al.*, *Temporary Special Measures*, 51–61; Bamforth *et al.*, *Discrimination Law: Theory and Context*, 401–13.

[34] Of 2000, in force 1 April 2005.

[35] The Explanatory Report to the protocol adds in para. 16 that 'the present Protocol does not impose any obligation to adopt such measures. Such a programmatic obligation would sit ill with the whole nature of the Convention and its control system which are based on the collective guarantee of individual rights which are formulated in terms sufficiently specific to be justiciable.'

[36] McKean, *Equality and Discrimination*, pp. 95–96.

[37] By contrast, a larger number of drafts in the Sub-Commission addressed the issue of special measures under Article 2, including drafts by Abram, E/CN.4/Sub.2/L.308; Ferguson, E/CN.4/Sub.2/L.326; and Mudawi, E/CN.4/Sub.2/L.328.

[38] E/CN.4/Sub.2/L.318; E/CN.4/873, para. 47.

[39] E/CN.4/Sub.2/L.319; E/CN.4/873, para. 48.

racial discrimination in the final version.[40] Thus, the final text included the following paragraph 2:

> Measures giving preference to certain racial groups for the sole purpose of securing adequate development or protection of individuals belonging to them shall not be deemed racial discrimination, provided however that such measures do not, as a consequence, lead to the maintenance of unequal or separate rights for different racial groups.[41]

The phrase 'special concrete measures' does not figure in the text, only 'measures', and, while the 'non-separation' aspect of the measures is referred to, the temporary nature of the measures is not explicitly stated; it was also unstated in the Declaration. The Sub-Commission's text also describes the measures as giving 'preference', which was not the case in the Declaration. Cuevas Cancino argued that the measures should not 'be abruptly discontinued. In some cases, they became part of national institutions, and a permanent means of securing rights which were in the interests of the country as a whole.'[42] Ingles, on the other hand, suggested that it would be well to stress the special nature of measures giving preference to certain racial groups 'either by making it clear that temporary measures were envisaged or by adding at the end of the paragraph the idea that they should be terminated when the need no longer arose'.[43] Krishnaswami agreed with Ingles, stating that 'obviously those measures would end automatically as soon as the groups in question had reached the same stage of development as the rest of society'.[44] This last remark suggests that the temporary nature of special measures was implicitly recognized in the Sub-Commission's text, and that the issue of abrupt termination of the measures is a serious point to be considered.

Article 1 of the Sub-Commission draft was considered by the Commission at its 783rd to 788th meetings in February 1964. In the course of discussions the simple reference to 'measures' in the Sub-Commission's text was replaced by 'special measures' on the suggestion of Lebanon[45] and this phrase informed other amendments.[46] Referring to a joint Lebanese–Polish proposal,[47] the representative of Lebanon stated that the sponsors understood special measures to mean 'certain measures adopted exclusively in respect of certain underprivileged groups and designed to place them on an equal footing with other groups',[48] noting also that they 'had abandoned the idea of preferential measures suggested by the Sub-Commission'.[49] Lebanon also insisted on the term 'racial groups' to make it clear that the Convention should protect groups as well as individuals.[50] Some delegates cautioned against paying undue attention to groups,[51] and it was suggested that the draft Convention should 'promote the rights and freedoms of all human beings

[40] Present author's emphasis. L.319 also omits the definite Article before 'maintenance' in the penultimate line of the paragraph.

[41] E/CN.4/873, pp. 45 ff, resolution 1 (XVI), Annex.

[42] E/CN.4/Sub.2/SR.411, p. 9.

[43] E/CN.4/Sub.2/SR.414, pp. 7–8.

[44] E/CN.4/Sub.2/SR.414, p. 8.

[45] E/CN.4/L.691.

[46] E/CN.4/874, paras 76–82.

[47] E/CN.4/L.694.

[48] E/CN.4/SR.785, p. 5.

[49] *Ibid.*

[50] E/CN.4/874, para. 87; E/CN.4/SR.784, p. 7.

[51] The representative of Italy argued that 'the measures in question were those adopted for the protection of individuals belonging to certain racial groups, and not of the groups as such': E/CN.4/SR.784, p. 9.

without distinction of any kind. The aim should not be to emphasize the distinctions between different racial groups but rather to ensure that persons belonging to such groups could be integrated into the community'.[52] Ecuador, however, argued that, in international law, 'the emphasis had shifted over the years from the individual . . . to the group. Thus, the protection of minorities was a problem of groups. In Latin America there was a large indigenous population, the members of which were more aware of their existence as members of a group than of their existence as individuals.'[53]

Sundry amendments were subsequently replaced by a text submitted by India which was adopted unanimously and in light of its harmonization with the text of Article 2(2):[54]

> Special measures taken for the sole purpose of securing adequate development or protection of certain under-developed racial groups or individuals belonging to them in order to ensure to them equal enjoyment or exercise of human rights and fundamental freedoms shall not be deemed racial discrimination provided however that such measures do not, as a consequence, lead to the maintenance of separate rights for different racial groups, and that they shall not be continued after the objectives for which they were taken have been achieved.[55]

There was strong insistence on the part of certain representatives that special measures should not be maintained indefinitely,[56] hence the addition of a new final clause to the Sub-Commission's draft making it clear that the measures were not to survive the achievement of the objectives for which they were taken. The drafting process also produced the phrase 'under-developed racial groups or individuals'[57] which was sustained despite objections that, *inter alia*, it contained 'some element of offence' and was in any case already implicit in the overall text.[58] To address the potentially stigmatizing aspect of using 'under developed', the representative of Costa Rica suggested the insertion of the words 'economic and social' between 'adequate' and 'development' to 'make it clear that such groups were regarded as economically and socially—not racially—under-developed'.[59]

The final text of Article 1 prepared by the Commission on Human Rights and submitted by the Economic and Social Council to the General Assembly incorporated the following second paragraph:

> Special measures taken for the sole purpose of securing adequate development or protection of certain under-developed racial groups or individuals belonging to them in order to ensure such groups or individuals equal enjoyment or exercise of human rights and fundamental freedoms shall

[52] E/CN.4/874, para. 87.

[53] E/CN.4/SR.784, p. 10.

[54] E/CN.4/874, paras 91 and 97.

[55] E/CN.4/L.697/Rev.1. *Inter alia*, India referred to the special protective measures under the Constitution of India taken 'to enable certain castes and tribes to rise to the level of the rest of the community': E/CN.4/SR.784, p. 8.

[56] The Netherlands observed that this point 'had not been made clear in the Sub-Commission's text': E/CN.4/SR.784, p. 9.

[57] E/CN.4/L.695, an amendment jointly sponsored by Italy, Lebanon, The Netherlands, and Poland; E/3973, para. 88.

[58] E/CN.4/874, para. 89.

[59] E/CN.4/SR.786, p. 7. The representative did not press the point, declaring himself satisfied with the text as it stood. The representative of Ecuador, *ibid.*, commented that 'political development was also important since . . . groups were sometimes deprived of the franchise because of illiteracy', adding that, while 'the term "under-developed" was in his view inoffensive, some expression such as "which have not attained their full development" might be substituted'.

not be deemed racial discrimination, provided, however, that such measures do not, as a consequence, lead to the maintenance of separate rights for different racial groups and that they shall not be continued after the objectives for which they were taken have been achieved.[60]

Discussions in the Third Committee of the General Assembly focused on a limited number of questions relating to the paragraph, including (defeated) proposals to delete it by the Democratic Republic of the Congo and the Ivory Coast.[61] The reasons for the proposed deletion differed: whereas the suggestion of the Democratic Republic of the Congo was made essentially to avoid overlap with Article 2, the representative of the Ivory Coast raised more fundamental issues, arguing that the principle incorporated in the draft paragraph

had often been invoked in the past to justify colonialism. Moreover, the principle still represented discrimination, even though the aims might be good and even though limits were set for the length of time such special measures would be in effect. The paragraph as a whole was unfortunate: it opened the door to all sorts of legal manoeuvring to justify various kinds of racial discrimination and it would favour the racists more than their victims.[62]

Deletion of the paragraph would, in the representative's view, 'avoid a situation in which the Committee would become the unwitting accomplice of those who might try to distort its good intentions'.[63]

With echoes of similar disquiet to that expressed in Commission discussions, an extensive exchange took place in the Third Committee on 'under-developed' as a descriptor of beneficiaries of special measures. The Committee adopted oral proposals of India and Ethiopia to replace 'development or protection of certain under-developed racial groups or individuals belonging to them' with the words 'advancement of certain racial or ethnic groups or individuals requiring such protection as may be necessary'.[64] Some representatives favoured the term 'underprivileged' rather than 'under-developed',[65] the representative of Zambia commenting that '[i]f some countries were under-developed, the reason was to be sought in colonialism or in policies such as Apartheid by which indigenous peoples were denied the vote'.[66] On the other hand, the representative of

[60] General Assembly Official Records, Twentieth Session, Annexes, Agenda item 58: Draft International Convention on the Elimination of All Forms of Racial Discrimination, Report of the Third Committee, A/6181, para. 29.

[61] A/C.3/SR.1305, para. 32, Democratic Republic of the Congo; A/C.3/SR.1306, para. 23, the Ivory Coast. The proposals were defeated by 52 votes to 14 with 20 abstentions: A/6181, paras 39 and 41.

[62] A/C.3/SR.1306, para. 23.

[63] *Ibid.*

[64] The proposal was adopted by 34 votes to 20 with 36 abstentions: A/6181, paras 40 and 41.

[65] An amendment of Mauritania, Nigeria, and Uganda (A/C.3/L/1225) proposing to replace 'under-developed' by 'underprivileged' was withdrawn on presentation of the oral amendments of Ethiopia and India. For further criticism of the term 'under-developed' see remarks in A/C.3/SR.1304 by the representatives of Nigeria, paras 12 and 25; Guinea, para. 27; Tanzania, para. 28; USSR, para. 28; the UK, para. 33, for whom both 'underprivileged' and under-developed' were open to objection, and Pakistan, para. 34; also remarks in A/C.3/SR.1305 by the representatives of Argentina, para. 5; Cameroon, para. 10; Greece, para. 12; United Arab Republic, para. 14; Sierra Leone, para. 16; Zambia, para. 18; Turkey, para. 24; Nigeria, para. 25; Ethiopia, para. 29; Yemen, para. 41; Sudan, para. 42; and in A/C.3/SR.1306, Ghana, para. 12; Ceylon, para. 28, as well as reiterations of position by the United Arab Republic and Nigeria, whose representative explained that the 'reason why so many delegations opposed the use of the term "under-developed" was not primarily that it was offensive to certain groups, but that it was not a suitable description of a human individual or group': A/C/3/SR.1306, para. 30.

[66] A/C.3/SR.1305, para. 18.

Guinea, supporting 'underprivileged', considered that the paragraph on special measures 'dealt with the vital question of protecting racial groups or individuals who were the victims of under-development. Such groups and individuals were to be found in all countries, not only in the developing world. It should be clearly understood, however, that it was not the individuals or groups but their condition that was under-developed.'[67] According to the representative of Tanzania, the term 'under-developed'

> was entirely inappropriate . . . In matters of economics and trade, the word had acquired a clear and valid meaning in the United Nations. But to transfer the word to human beings was unjustifiable and dangerous. It would open the Convention to insidious interpretations which would expose certain groups to the very treatment against which the Convention was supposed to protect them. Those who discriminated against others often chose to call them under-developed, in order to justify their own attitudes and actions . . . There was no question that the term 'under-developed', which could be legitimately applied to countries in an economic context, was not valid in connection with human beings. He strongly supported the use of the word 'underprivileged'. It suggested the very situation for which the Convention was most needed—the situation in which one group suffered disabilities at the hands of another, dominant group.[68]

The representatives of India, while making a successful alternative proposal, defended the use of 'under-developed' and gave examples of who might benefit from special measures, taking the opportunity to introduce issues pertaining to the caste system. According to one, 'to characterize the groups alluded to in Article 1, paragraph 2 . . . the Indian Constitution used the term "backward"'.[69] In a wide-ranging intervention going to the basis of the special measures principle, another representative of India supported 'under-developed': he 'failed to see how the word . . . could be considered a reflection on anyone's inherent qualities; it merely described those who through deprivation had been unable to develop their innate potentialities'.[70] On the inclusion of special measures, his explanation was that the paragraph

> had been included in the draft Convention in order to provide for special and temporary measures to help certain groups of people, including one in his country, who, though of the same racial stock and ethnic origin as their fellow citizens, had for centuries been relegated by the caste system to a miserable and downtrodden condition. While it was true that the members of that group had been underprivileged in the sense that they had been denied the rights and privileges enjoyed by others, they had also been under-developed, not because of any lack within themselves, but because they had . . . been denied those advantages that were essential for the full development of the human personality.[71]

On the achievement of its independence, India 'had given the members of that group complete equality before the law and had passed constitutional and legal enactments to do away with all social and legal barriers to their advancement. That had not been sufficient, however, and they had also been given special rights with a view to raising their educational, social and economic status.'[72] India, supported by Ethiopia, accordingly

[67] A/C.3/SR.1304, para. 26.
[68] *Ibid*., para. 27.
[69] A/C.3/SR.1305, para. 33.
[70] A/C.3/SR.1306, para. 24.
[71] A/C.3/SR.1306, para. 25.
[72] *Ibid*. On 'underprivileged', he added that the Indian Constitution had abolished all privileges and titles, and that special rights mentioned 'had not been privileges but measures of protection': A/C.3/SR.1306, para. 26. See also the statement in A/C.3/SR.1304, para. 20, where references was made to 'the "scheduled castes" to whom Article 1, para. 2, would apply'. The representative of Nigeria, who maintained consistent opposition to

proposed to replace 'development or protection of certain under-developed racial groups or individuals belonging to them' by 'advancement of certain racial or ethnic groups or individuals requiring such protection as may be necessary'.[73] The part of the amendment adding 'or ethnic' to 'racial' was not debated. Nigeria argued that the Indian proposal should not have focused on particular groups.[74] India asserted that 'article 1, paragraph 2, was a special temporary provision relating to a special group, and was not intended to refer to racial groups in general'.[75] On the text adopted, the representative of Nigeria, explaining a negative vote on what became Article 1.4, argued that the text was weak 'because it would leave it to the authorities which might be responsible for racial oppression to decide whether or not special measures were necessary'.[76]

Comment on the travaux

The *travaux* signpost many questions of interpretation mulled over in subsequent Committee practice. The drafting evidences slippage of terminology between 'measures' and 'special measures' and a degree of caution about the effect of admitting special measures to the framework of non-discrimination and equality. This caution extends to allowing too much freedom to governments to decide when measures were warranted. The *travaux* nonetheless clarify that special measures taken according to Convention principles shall not be regarded as discriminatory, and do not constitute a 'preference'. Issues around termination of measures were discussed at many levels, and while there was broad agreement that the measures should not be maintained indefinitely, the question of the 'cut-off point' is susceptible to further elaboration. Group and individual dimensions of the application of measures reveal tensions between approaches to the overall philosophy of the Convention. The discussions focused on the application of measures mainly on the economic and social fields; their relevance for the cultural field was less clearly expressed. The question of beneficiaries was addressed mostly in terms of an abstract argument as to how they should best be described (under-developed, underprivileged, etc) in a manner that does not infringe their human dignity. Apart from sporadic intimations that the measures could concern indigenous and tribal groups, there was little clarity as to who might benefit from special measures; the major exception being caste groups, concretely identified by India as primary beneficiaries. The claim by the representative of India that the special measures provisions should not be applied to racial groups in general did not attract significant comment and goes against the grain of much of the discussion approving the broad descriptor, 'racial or ethnic groups', as the potential beneficiaries.

II. Article 2(2)

The initial Abram draft for the Sub-Commission made reference to 'special concrete measures',[77] as did the substantially similar draft of Ketryznski.[78] The initial Calvocoressi

the word 'underprivileged', expressly disagreed with the interpretation of the paragraph by India, contending that a 'large proportion of the world's population was underprivileged, while no group of human beings could justifiably be called under-developed': A/C.3/SR.1304, para. 25.

[73] A/C.3/SR.1306, paras 27 and 34.
[74] A/C.3/SR.1306, para. 30.
[75] A/C.3/SR.1306, para. 33.
[76] A/C.3.SR.1307, para. 23.
[77] E/CN.4/Sub.2/L.308; E/CN.4/873, para. 52.
[78] E/CN.4/Sub.2/L.323; E/CN.4/873, para. 55.

and Capotorti draft[79] taken as the basis for discussion did not include such a paragraph. Calvocoressi explained that 'the paragraph on special measures should be permissive rather than mandatory and that the proper place for it was... in the preamble'.[80] The Sub-Commission also discussed the phrase 'in appropriate circumstances' and whether the words 'may take' or 'shall take' special measures should be used. Krishnaswami considered that 'the expression "in appropriate circumstances" allowed governments sufficient latitude in the field in question'.[81] Much was made in the discussions of the need to avoid a situation such as that in South Africa, hence the importance of stating the reasons for taking special measures, because 'otherwise... a government could continue to keep certain racial groups separate from the rest of society under the pretext of protecting them'.[82] A number of experts referred to 'backward' groups requiring development, a term objected to by Krishnaswami as placing a stigma upon such groups.[83] The final text submitted by the Sub-Commission, reflecting amendments by Mudawi,[84] was adopted by the Sub-Commission by six votes to four with four abstentions:

> States parties shall take special concrete measures in appropriate circumstances in order to secure adequate development or protection of individuals belonging to under-developed racial groups with the object of ensuring the full enjoyment by such individuals of human rights and fundamental freedoms. These measures shall in no circumstances have as a consequence the maintenance of unequal or separate rights for different racial groups.[85]

Mudawi explained that his text 'imposed an obligation upon States to take concrete measures. Of course, that obligation was not absolute: such measures were to be taken in appropriate circumstances, as defined by the State through its legislative or judicial organs.'[86] A representative of the Commission on the Status of Women stated, in a foretaste of arguments concerning 'intersectionality' of grounds of discrimination, that 'the provision favouring under-developed racial groups would have great significance for the women in such groups'.[87]

The Commission considered Article 2 of the draft Convention at its 786th to 789th meetings. Various amendments submitted were replaced by a joint amendment of Italy, The Netherlands, and Poland which proposed the following:

> States parties shall take special concrete measures in appropriate circumstances for the sole purpose of securing adequate development or protection of certain under-developed groups or individuals belonging to them in order to ensure to them equal enjoyment of human rights and fundamental freedoms, provided however that such measures do not, as a consequence, lead to the maintenance of separate rights for different racial groups, and that they shall not be continued after the objectives for which they were taken have been achieved.[88]

[79] E/CN.4/Sub.2/L.324; E/CN.4/873, para. 56.

[80] E/CN.4/Sub.2/SR.415, p. 4. Saario concurred, arguing that special measures 'should be the subject of an authorization rather than an obligation': E/CN.4/Sub.2/SR.415, p. 10.

[81] E/CN.4/Sub.2/SR.416, p. 12.

[82] Krishnaswami, E/CN.4/Sub.2/SR.416, p. 12.

[83] E/CN.4/Sub.2/SR.416, p. 13.

[84] E/CN.4/Sub.2/L.328.

[85] E/CN.4/Sub.2/241, p. 47. The Abram draft preferred 'individuals belonging to certain racial groups' to 'individuals belonging to under-developed racial groups' in the draft adopted by the Sub-Commission, as did the draft by Ketrzynski.

[86] E/CN.4/Sub.2/SR.417, p. 6.

[87] E/CN.4/Sub.2/SR.417, p. 7.

[88] E/CN.4/L.696.

The sponsors of this amendment later incorporated a suggestion of The Philippines to insert after 'enjoyment' the words 'or exercise'[89] and a suggestion from the UK to replace 'them' before the word 'equal' with 'such groups or individuals'.[90] The text as amended narrowed the scope for special measures by insisting they be taken for the sole purpose of securing adequate development or protection of the groups or individuals concerned. Another change from the Sub-Commission text is the replacement of the phrase 'full enjoyment' of human rights by 'equal enjoyment' in response to a concern expressed by Lebanon that insisting on 'full enjoyment' 'might create a new kind of inequality, since some countries might be too poor to implement certain provisions in the Universal Declaration for the entire population, and yet, under the Convention, they might be obliged to ensure that those provisions were fully applied to under-developed racial groups'.[91] The joint amendment above addresses this concern.[92] The various redrafts of the Sub-Commission's text took account of the differences in purpose between Article 1 and Article 2 of the Convention.[93] Paragraph 2 of Article 2, as amended, was adopted unanimously by the Commission.[94]

The Third Committee had before it the following text:

> States parties shall take special concrete measures in appropriate circumstances for the sole purpose of securing adequate development or protection of certain under-developed racial groups or individuals belonging to them in order to ensure to such groups or individuals equal enjoyment or exercise of human rights and fundamental freedoms, provided however, that such measures do not, as a consequence, lead to the maintenance of separate rights for different racial groups and that they shall not be continued after the objectives for which they have been taken have been achieved.

The changes made by the Third Committee stemmed in part from a proposed amendment by Bulgaria to include between the words 'take' and 'special' the words 'in the social, economic and other fields',[95] a proposal revised on the suggestion of The Netherlands to insert the word 'cultural' after 'economic'.[96] Other changes from the

89 E/CN.4/SR.787, p. 4.

90 E/3873; E/CN.4/874, para. 114; E/CN.4/SR.787, p. 4.

91 E/3873; E/CN.4/874, para. 124; E/CN.4/SR.787, p. 5, Lebanon. See the comment by Chile, *ibid.*, recalling the claim that 'in undertaking to grant full enjoyment of human rights to under-developed racial groups, States having only modest resources might have to discriminate against the rest of the population', to which the representative responded that in the case of preferential treatment accorded by some Latin American countries to indigenous populations, 'such practices were not racial discrimination . . . the apparently privileged treatment meted out to those groups was merely intended to ensure the integrated development of the population as a whole'.

92 The USSR preferred 'full enjoyment' to 'equal enjoyment' because, while appreciating the difficulties expressed by Lebanon, 'the convention should not be limited to the present circumstances of newly independent countries, but should also cover their future needs': E/CN.4.SR.786, p. 8. Austria also preferred 'full enjoyment' because, in certain cases, 'it was not enough for all groups to enjoy equal rights; the nature of the rights should be such as to ensure the adequate development of those groups': E/CN.4/SR.787, pp. 4–5.

93 See in particular the discussions on the relationship between the articles in E/CN.4/SR.786, pp. 4 ff.

94 E/CN.4/874, para. 134. On the proposal of The Philippines, a separate vote on the term 'under-developed'—it was decided to retain the term by 7 votes to 2, with 12 abstentions: E/CN.4/SR.787, p. 7.

95 A/C.3/L.1218.

96 The representative of The Netherlands took the view that the Bulgarian amendment should mention 'the educational and cultural fields in which the deficiencies were greatest': A/C.3/SR.1308,para. 14; the remarks were supported by the representative of the Lebanon, *ibid.*, para. 24. Conjoined to A/C.3/L.1226 and Corr. 1, as revised, the Bulgarian amendment was adopted by 76 votes to 1 with 15 abstentions: General Assembly Official Records, Twentieth Session, Annexes, Agenda item 58, Report of the Third Committee, A/6181, para. 55.

Commission's text were the replacement of the phrase 'in appropriate circumstances' by 'when the circumstances so warrant';[97] the elimination of the phrase 'under-developed'; the reinstatement of 'full enjoyment' of rights in the new portmanteau phrase 'full and equal enjoyment of human rights and fundamental freedoms' and the replacement of the reference to 'sole purpose' in the Commission's text with 'purpose'. As in the Commission on Human Rights there was overlap between the issues discussed in the Third Committee under the special measures provisions of Article 1 and those of Article 2. The representative of India explained the difference between the two related paragraphs, observing that Article 1 defined racial discrimination and the special measures paragraph therein

> made an exception for cases where some States had taken steps to redress the injustices done in the past to a certain section of the people, by providing for special measures to secure their advancement, and this bring about a levelling of the social order. Article II was of a mandatory nature. It called upon States which did not demonstrate the same goodwill to assist the less-favoured elements of their population in raising themselves to the level of the more developed groups. Article II gave States a certain amount of latitude, since it stated that the measures in question were to be taken 'when the circumstances warrant this'.[98]

The Third Committee chairman expressed himself in similar terms.[99]

Comment on the travaux

Understandings of Article 2(2) merge into the interpretation of Article 1(4), bearing in mind that the former introduces few novel elements. The permissive/mandatory argument regarding the measures is resolved in favour of treating them as mandatory. Nonetheless, it was understood that they offer governments a certain latitude on account of the phrase 'when the circumstances so warrant'. On one reading, the use of 'warrant' may, when compared to the phrase it replaced—'in appropriate circumstances'—narrow the latitude accorded to States as to when the measures are to be applied: 'appropriateness' may suggest a more open-ended and subjective judgement. On the other hand, 'when the circumstances so warrant' while it focuses attention on the circumstances rather than the judgement, tends to push back the occasions for the application of measures, especially if 'warrant' translates as 'to necessitate'.[100] There should be little difference in practice between the terms, bearing in mind that appreciation and judgement inevitably infuse both formulations. Discussions also evoked the spectre of the South African situation where differential or separate rights acted as a cover for domination by a minority: this partly explains the prominence accorded to the limitations on special measures in Article 1(4) and in Article 2(2). The replacement of the Commission's 'sole purpose'—retained in Article 1(4)—by 'purpose' is not fully explained in the *travaux*.

[97] A/C.3/L.1226 and Corr.1, amendment of Argentina, Bolivia, Brazil, Chile, Colombia, Costa Rica, Dominican Republic, Ecuador, El Salvador, Guatemala, Haiti, Honduras, Mexico, Panama, Peru, Uruguay, and Venezuela, as orally revised: A/6181, paras 53 and 54.

[98] A/C.3/SR.1308, para. 7.

[99] A/C.3/SR.1307, para. 16.

[100] 'Warrant' in English has the meaning here of to justify or necessitate. The French text—'*si les circonstances l'exigent*'—the verb '*exiger*' signifying to require, demand, or call for, is the more forceful.

C. Practice

I. Reservations and Declarations

No reservations focus explicitly on special measures, though broader reservations are apt to include them. CERD-specific reporting guidelines do not elaborate on the provisions for special measures. The guidelines for Article 1(4) reiterate the request in paragraph 52 of the 'harmonized guidelines' for information on whether the legal system of the State party allows or provides for special measures, defined as measures 'to secure the adequate advancement of groups and individuals protected under the Convention'.[101]

II. General Aspects

Special measures emanate from the basic definition of discrimination in Article 1 of the Convention, functioning as an integral aspect of this definition, especially in view of its inclusion of 'preferences' as a form of discrimination. In principle, the concept of special measures interrelates with all aspects of rights recognized in the Convention and requires distinguishing from the many general references to 'measures' therein, from the preamble onwards. Special measures also interrelate with the provisions on remedies in Article 6, since the notion of a 'measure' is broad enough accommodate remedial measures. Besides appraising the precise requirements of Articles 1(4) and 2(2), major interpretative questions concern the assigning of boundaries between the general measures required by the Convention in many fields and the specific measures permitted and mandated by these two paragraphs.

Special measures have rarely figured in cases under Article 14. In *Moylan v Australia*,[102] an aboriginal man claimed that because aboriginal life expectancy was lower than for non-Aboriginal Australian males, he was discriminated against in relation to eligibility for a State pension:[103] the Convention required equal enjoyment of human rights and not merely de jure equality. The claimant argued that the State party was in breach of the Convention by failing to take the special measures necessary to achieve substantive equality. Citing GR 32, the State party recalled the references to need and realistic appraisal of circumstances and argued that no specific form of special measures was required by the Convention,[104] and that in any case differentiated social security was not the appropriate mechanism to address long-standing indigenous disadvantage. In declaring the communication inadmissible, the Committee nonetheless referred to the 'alleged structural discrimination related to pension entitlements',[105] a condition that in other circumstances has prompted a recommendation to apply special measures.[106] In light of the limitations of the cases, the elaboration of the meaning of special measures has fallen to the reporting procedure, and to GR 32.

[101] CERD/C/2007/1, p. 5.

[102] CERD/C/83/D/47/2010 (2013). See also *D.S. v Sweden*, CERD/C/59/D/21/2001 (2001), where Article 2(2) is referred to as applicable but the issue is not further pursued in the body of the case.

[103] The applicant claimed a difference life expectancy of 17 years, a figure disputed by the State party which referred to estimates of the difference as being 11.5 years: *ibid.*, paras 2(2) and 4(3) respectively.

[104] Para. 4.9.

[105] Para. 6.6.

[106] Concluding observations on Belgium, CERD/C/BEL/CO/16-19, para. 15, where the structural discrimination was associated with 'ethnic stratification' in employment.

The most important elements in Committee practice have been subsumed into CERD GR 32 on the meaning and scope of special measures in ICERD.[107] The recommendation follows a decision at the seventy-first session to embark on the task of drafting such a recommendation,[108] and a thematic discussion which took place at the seventy-third session of CERD in August 2008.[109] The recommendation recites that the drafting decision was made 'in light of the difficulties observed in the understanding' of the concept[110] and that the basis for special measures is 'the principle that laws, policies and practices adopted and implemented in order to fulfil obligations under the Convention require supplementing, when circumstances warrant, by the adoption of temporary special measures designed to secure to disadvantaged groups the full and equal enjoyment of human rights and fundamental freedoms'.[111] The recommendation has since been cited as representing CERD's understanding of the concept of special measures.[112]

1. Measures

In addition to being referred to in connection with special measures, calls for 'measures' are made in the preamble to the Convention and in Articles 2, 4, and 7. In the particular context of special measures, GR 32 defines 'measures' as including 'the full span of legislative, executive, administrative, budgetary and regulatory instruments, at every level in the State apparatus, as well as plans, policies, programmes and preferential regimes in areas such as employment, housing, education, culture, and participation in public life for disfavoured groups, devised and implemented on the basis of such instruments'.[113] Further, States parties are recommended to include provisions on special measures in their legal and administrative systems, 'whether through general legislation or legislation directed to specific sectors . . . as well as through plans, programmes and other policy initiatives referred to above at national, regional and local levels'.[114] The recommendation also invites parties to provide information in their reports on, *inter alia*, 'the nature of the measures and how they promote the advancement, development and protection of groups and individuals concerned'.[115] Measures recommended in CERD practice have included legislation, administrative action, judicial action,[116] plans and national strategies to combat discrimination,[117] reservation of seats in parliaments and public services,[118] and

[107] The General Recommendation was adopted at the 75th session of the Committee in August 2009.

[108] A/62/18, para. 539.

[109] A/63/18, para. 556. The task of drafting the recommendation was entrusted to CERD members Sicilianos and the present author.

[110] Para. 1; the text of the recommendation may be found in A/64/18, Annex VIII.

[111] GR 32, para. 11.

[112] Examples include concluding observations on Australia, CERD/AUS/CO/15-17, para. 16; Bolivia, CERD/C/BOL/CO/17-20, para. 13; Finland, CERD/C/FIN/CO/20-22, para. 15; Japan, CERD/C/JPN/CO/3-6, para. 19; Lithuania, CERD/C/LTU/CO/4-5, para. 15; Kyrgyzstan, CERD/C/KGZ/CO/5-7, para. 9; Sweden, CERD/C/SWE/CO/19-21, para. 8.

[113] Para. 13.

[114] Para. 13.

[115] Para. 37.

[116] A compendious recommendation for a variety of such positive measures is included in a recommendation to El Salvador, CERD/C/SLV/CO/13, para. 9.

[117] Concluding observations on Bosnia and Herzegovina, CERD/C/BIH/CO/6, para. 15; on Guyana, CERD/C/GUY/CO/14, para. 11.

[118] Concluding observations on India, CERD/C/IND/CO/19, para. 17; on Moldova, CERD/C/MDA/CO/15, para. 16.

quotas.[119] The term 'quotas' is not used in the recommendation but its reference to 'preferential regimes' is broad enough to accommodate them when they follow the parameters of the recommendation as a whole.[120]

2. *Special Measures and Related Terms*

In addition to the 'special measures' and 'special and concrete measures' in the text of ICERD, the Committee has employed 'affirmative action', 'positive action', and affirmative measures', which, together with the specific language in the text, seem, in the view of one author, 'to have been used indiscriminately to denote the same'.[121] The strict Convention sense is almost invariably intimated by using 'special measures', special concrete measures'[122] or 'affirmative action', especially when coupled with phrases taken from Articles 1(4) or 2(2) such as 'adequate development or protection',[123] 'advancement',[124] perhaps adding a reference to 'vulnerability',[125] or through explicit recall of Articles 1(4) or 2(2). The phrase 'temporary special measures' seems not to be a part of CERD's regular discourse, though 'temporariness' may simply be intimated by recalling the limitation provisions of Articles 1(4) and 2(2). GR 32 rejects the use of the term 'positive discrimination' in international human rights law as a '*contradictio in terminis*';[126] this would apply, *a fortiori*, to describing special measures as 'reverse discrimination'.

GR 32 notes that special measures include what may be described 'in some countries'[127] as affirmative measures, affirmative action, or positive action in cases where they conform to the provisions of Articles 1(4) or 2(2), but without endorsing a full functional equivalence of terms. The recommendation also refers to the distinction between positive measures required generally under the Convention—positive action which does not necessitate differentiated treatment—and special measures in stating that the obligation to take special measures 'is distinct from the general positive obligation of States parties to the Convention to secure human rights and fundamental freedoms on a non-discriminatory basis'.[128] Thus, an evaluation of the reach of Convention obligations to take 'measures' is intimately connected to the question of whether the terminology of special measures is being appropriately employed, so that individuals and communities

[119] Concluding observations on Moldova, CERD/C/MDA/CO/15, para. 19 (quotas for Roma pupils in education); on the Russian Federation, CERD/C/RUS/CO/19, para. 20 quotas for indigenous peoples in public bodies).

[120] Concluding observations on Cameroon recommend concrete measures to strengthen the participation of minorities and indigenous peoples 'including through the establishment of quotas, in accordance with the Convention and the Committee's General Recommendation 32 (2009)': CERD/C/CMR/CO/19-21, para. 11. The statement may be correct in reading implications from the Convention regarding the establishment of quotas, though if it carries the suggestion that GR 32 explicitly accepted quotas, it is evidently incorrect.

[121] Vandenhole, *Equality and Non-Discrimination*, p. 208.

[122] GR 32 notes in para. 32 that CERD has generally employed 'special measures' and 'special and concrete measures' as synonymous.

[123] Concluding observations on Botswana, CERD/C/61/CO/2, para. 12.

[124] Concluding observations on Suriname, CERD/C/64/CO/9, para. 19.

[125] Such as recommending in the case of Norway, measures to ensure 'adequate development and protection of certain highly vulnerable indigenous groups': CERD/C/NOR/CO/18, para. 17.

[126] Para. 12.

[127] Para. 12.

[128] Para. 14. The ambiguities in 'positive action' are referred to in CEDAW's GR 25 which notes its wide use in Europe and in UN documents, while it is also used in international human rights law to describe positive State action—'the obligation of a State to initiate action versus a State's obligation to abstain from action'.

will not be short-changed by substitution of full obligations under ICERD by temporary measures.[129] *Inter alia*, the recommendation also insists that 'special measures should clearly benefit groups and individuals in their enjoyment of human rights', a question that may be contested by 'beneficiary' groups.[130] The accumulation of cautions suggests that not every domestic use of either 'special measures' or 'affirmative action' or 'positive action' will necessarily equate to special measures under the Convention. The recommendation 'encourages States parties to employ terminology that clearly demonstrates the relationship of their laws and practice' to the concepts in the Convention.[131] The assumption underlying the recommendation is that a careful reading of the recommendation will minimize confusion between the specific obligations to take special measures and 'positive' obligations stemming from other articles.

3. *Special Measures and Permanent Rights*

The Committee has distinguished between special measures and the permanent rights of individuals and communities. Reflection on this relationship emerged from discussion of the report of New Zealand in 2007.[132] Under 'special measures', the report included information on, *inter alia*, Maori fisheries, the Foreshore and Seabed Act, the Maori Land Act, Maori and Pasifika education, Maori language, etc.[133] The inclusion of these materials provoked a question by the country rapporteur in the 'list of issues' as to 'why the State party considers that historical treaty settlements constitute special measures for the adequate development and protection of Maori';[134] the question was followed up by the rapporteur and colleagues in oral discussions.[135] A Statement by the New Zealand Race Relations Commissioner supported the critique: the Commissioner 'made it clear that special measures should not be confused with the Government's treaty obligations, indigenous rights, or general social and economic measures tailored to particular ethnic groups'.[136] The response of the delegation suggested that, in light of comments by Committee members on the scope of special measures, the matter could be reconsidered and that it might be preferable to include such information.[137] The representative made it clear that treaty settlements were not considered temporary measures by the State party.[138] In its concluding observations, the Committee reiterated its concern on the confusion of categories, drawing attention 'to the distinction to be drawn between special and temporary measures for the advancement of ethnic groups on the one hand and permanent rights of indigenous peoples on the other hand'.[139] Members were mindful

[129] For a similar point made in connection with CEDAW, see E. Evatt, 'The practical relevance of Article 4 CEDAW with particular attention for Articles 11, 13 and 14', in Boerefijn *et al.*, *Temporary Special Measures*, pp. 45–50.

[130] Para. 33; see points below relating to Australia's Northern Territory Emergency Response Act (NTERA).

[131] Para. 12. See also para. 37, recommendations regarding the contents of State reports.

[132] Fifteenth, sixteenth, and seventeenth reports of New Zealand, submitted as one document, CERD/C/NZL/17, 18 July 2006.

[133] CERD/C/NZL/17, paras 51–172.

[134] Question 3 on the list of issues.

[135] CERD/C/SR.1821, paras 38 (Sicilianos, country rapporteur), 57 (Thornberry), and 60 (Kemal); CERD/C/SR.1822, para. 30 (Thornberry).

[136] Statement by Joris de Bres, Race relations Commissioner, New Zealand Human Rights Commission (on file with author); and CERD/C/SR.1822, para. 4.

[137] CERD/C/SR.1822, para. 21.

[138] *Ibid.*

[139] CERD/C/NZL/CO/17, 15 August 2007, para. 15.

that including historical settlements under special measures would lend a certain fragility to the acknowledged structures of the New Zealand state, a perception advanced by Maori groups in their submissions.[140]

Distinctions between special measures and permanent indigenous and minority rights were referred to by members in the thematic discussion held in August 2008;[141] opinions thereon have been consolidated in GR 32:

> Special measures should not be confused with specific rights pertaining to certain categories of person or community, such as, for example the rights of persons belonging to minorities . . . and the rights of indigenous peoples, including rights to lands traditionally occupied by them and rights of women to non-identical treatment with men . . . States parties should carefully observe distinctions between special measures and permanent human rights in their law and practice.[142]

Entitlement to the rights of minorities or indigenous peoples obviously does not 'bar' the application of special measures to these groups, hence the further statement in paragraph 12 of the recommendation that the 'distinction between special measures and permanent rights implies that those entitled to permanent rights may also enjoy the benefits of special measures'—a weakly phrased statement deserving stronger emphasis in line with contemporary understandings of categories of rights.[143] Thus, following its acknowledgement of various positive measures taken by Montenegro on behalf of the Roma community and recognition of Roma rights, CERD expressed its concern about their general situation, recommending that the State party 'should implement stronger special measures targeting the Roma community to enable them to have practical access to education, employment in the public administration, healthcare and social welfare in a non-discriminatory manner'.[144]

4. *Consultation and Participation*

The Committee tends to insist on a precondition of consultations as part of the *modus operandi* for the application of special measures, in some cases casting the consultation net widely. In one case, CERD recommended that 'the adoption of any affirmative action programme be preceded by consultations involving all ethnic communities'.[145] The term 'participation' is preferred in some cases to 'consultation',[146] and in other cases, stronger language has been employed, registering a concern regarding 'the existing perception that . . . programmes are imposed without consultation and active participation' of the

[140] Treaty Tribes Coalition, Aotearoa Indigenous Rights Trust, Maori Party, Te Whānau-a-Apanui, and Peace Movement Aotearoa.

[141] For some contributions, see CERD/C/SR.1885, paras 3 (Avtonomov), 8 (de Gouttes), and 16 (Murillo Martinez).

[142] GR 32, para. 15. It may be observed that CERD has not always fully expressed the distinctions between special measures and permanent rights: CERD/C/SLV/CO/13 para. 10 (recommendation to El Salvador to ratify ILO Convention 169 incorporating reference to Article 2(2) of the Convention).

[143] It may be observed in passing that the quoted sentence distinguishes between 'entitlement' to permanent rights and the 'benefits' of special measures, suggesting that special measures are to be understood as functioning in the domain of State obligations rather than personal or community rights (entitlements). References to 'entitlement' to special measures in the preliminary draft of the recommendation—CERD/C/75/Misc.7/CRP.1—do not appear in the adopted version.

[144] CERD/C/MNE/CO/1 (2009), para. 17.

[145] Concluding observations on Fiji, CERD/C/62/CO/3, para. 16.

[146] Concluding observations on Yemen, CERD/C/YEM/CO/16, para. 15, referring to 'participation of members of affected communities'.

communities concerned.[147] Consultation or participation, on this view, should be as genuine and transparent as possible.[148] The expressed preference for consultation or participation may also extend to assessment and review of adopted measures.[149] The insistence that special measures should not simply be imposed on groups without their input is treated succinctly in GR 32: 'States parties should ensure that special measures are designed and implemented with affected communities and the active participation of such communities.'[150] The envisaged consultations and participation are not confined to beneficiary communities, but to 'affected' communities.[151] Repeal of special measures may also be linked to consultations. In the case of Botswana, the repeal of Article 14(3)(c) of the Constitution restricting entry of outsiders into Bushmen areas 'to the extent that such restrictions are reasonably required for the protection or well-being of Bushmen', was justified by the State party on grounds of obsolescence due to relocations 'after a decade of consultations'.[152] The concluding observations of the Committee evinced doubts as to the nature of the consultations and their human rights impact.[153] The nature of required participation with regard to special measures mirrors the parameters of the participation rights envisaged in Article 5(c) and the Convention more generally.[154]

5. *Limitations*

CERD has repeatedly drawn the attention of States parties to the limits of special measures in terms of duration and avoiding situations of segregation. This was one issue among others in the case of 'special schools' in the Czech Republic. The Committee recalled that special measures are legitimate provided they 'do not lead, in purpose or in practice, to the segregation of communities'.[155] Similar messages have been conveyed to reporting States, notably (and logically) when the Committee judges that the measures may have been pushed too far so as to amount to preferences or even discrimination in reverse, including cases when the exigencies of the moment for the application of special measures have passed.[156] In GR 32 the point that the measures should not lead to the maintenance of 'separate rights' for different racial groups is glossed in paragraph 26 with reference to Article 1(4) through linking it to opposition to apartheid and practices of segregation while insisting that the 'notion of inadmissible "separate rights" must be distinguished from rights accepted and recognised by the international community to secure the existence and identity of groups such as minorities, indigenous peoples and

147 Concluding observations on Namibia, CERD/C/NAM/CO/12, para. 12.

148 In the case of Moldova, CERD requested that Roma action plans be made available to the public in order to ensure that 'non-governmental organizations, in particular Roma organizations, can participate effectively in the implementation and monitoring of the plan': CERD/C/MDA/CO/15, para. 12.

149 Concluding observations on New Zealand, CERD/C/NZL/CO/17, para. 16.

150 Para. 18.

151 An earlier draft had referred to consultation/participation and 'beneficiary communities': CERD/C/GC/32/CRP.1, para. 20.

152 CERD/C/SR.1749, para. 17.

153 'The Committee notes with concern the discrepancy between the information provided by the State party that the residents of the Central Kalahari Game reserve have been consulted and have agreed to their relocation outside the Reserve, and persistent allegations that residents were forcibly removed': concluding observations on Botswana, CERD/C/BWA/CO/16.

154 See discussion in Chapter 13.

155 Concluding observations on the Czech Republic, CERD/C/CZE/CO/7, para. 17.

156 For an example of the latter situation, see concluding observations on CERD/C/BIH/CO/6, para. 11, discussed in Chapter 13.

other categories ... whose rights are similarly accepted and recognised within the framework of universal human rights'.[157] This reinforces the distinction made elsewhere in the recommendation between special measures and permanent rights.

On the 'temporary' aspect of special measures, the recommendation avers that this limitation 'is essentially functional and goal-related: the measures should cease to be applied when the objectives for which they were employed—the equality goals—have been sustainably achieved'.[158] 'Sustainably' does not appear in the CERD text, but has been used in a related context by CESCR/C.[159] The express limitation provisions on special measures are thus regarded as essential conditions for legitimacy under the norm of non-discrimination. While the language of the recommendation captures the obligations of States parties rather than devising 'entitlements' to special measures,[160] there will be cases where long-term enjoyment of the measures may create expectations for continuation and a sense of entitlement. The recommendation treads delicately at this point, cautioning only that States parties 'should ... carefully determine whether negative human rights consequences would arise for beneficiary communities consequent upon an abrupt withdrawal of special measures, especially if such have been established for a lengthy period of time'.[161] A complex question at the intersection of discrimination, identification of beneficiaries, and termination of special measures was raised in connection with the report of India examined in 2007,[162] where the Committee noted with concern 'that Dalits who convert to Islam or to Christianity to escape caste discrimination reportedly lose their entitlement under affirmative action programmes, unlike converts who become Buddhists or Sikhs',[163] recommending to India that it 'restore the eligibility for affirmative action benefits of all members of scheduled castes and scheduled tribes having converted to another religion'.[164] The termination of measures was judged according to the same principles of equality and non-discrimination as those governing their adoption and application.

III. Article 1(4)

1. *Shall Not be Deemed Racial Discrimination*

The relationship between special measures and non-discrimination is often recalled by the Committee, for which the use of special measures 'is fully compatible with the letter and spirit of the Convention'.[165] Distinctions between special measures and unfair preferences are not always made with finesse. CERD GR 14 on Article 1, paragraph 1 of the Convention provides that 'a differentiation of treatment will not constitute discrimination if the criteria for such differentiation, judged against the objectives and purposes of the Convention are legitimate or fall within the scope of article 1, paragraph 4 of the

[157] On the 2(2) limitations, the Recommendation, para. 35, takes the position that they are 'in essence the same, *mutatis mutandis*, as those expressed in Article 1, para. 4'.

[158] Para. 27.

[159] CESCR/C GC No. 20 on non-discrimination, para. 9.

[160] In the recommendation, the reference to entitlements relates only to the enjoyment of permanent human rights and not to special measures.

[161] CERD GR 32, para. 35.

[162] CERD/C/IND/19, para. 21.

[163] CERD/C/IND/CO/19, para. 21.

[164] *Ibid.*

[165] Concluding observations on Botswana, CERD/C/BWA/CO/16, para. 12.

Convention'.[166] The wording should not be read to suggest that differentiation under Article 1(4) is not 'legitimate': the summary records include the observation by the promoter of the draft that the recommendation 'had nothing to do with . . . special measures . . . in article 1(4)' and the Committee could, if it wished, 'include a statement in the text to the effect that the recommendation was without prejudice to article 1(4)'.[167] On the phrase 'shall not be deemed racial discrimination', paragraph 20 of GR 32 robustly asserts that Article 1(4)

> makes it clear that special measures taken . . . under the terms of the Convention do not constitute discrimination, a clarification reinforced by the *travaux préparatoires* of the Convention which record the drafting change from 'should not be deemed racial discrimination' to 'shall not be deemed racial discrimination' . . . special measures are not an exception to . . . non-discrimination but are integral to its meaning and essential to the project of eliminating racial discrimination and advancing human dignity and effective equality.

Responses of governments may not always appreciate or accept subtleties of category and state in effect that special measures are discriminatory. Guyana responded in 2008 to concluding observations of CERD by describing the Amerindian Act of 2006, the mainstay of Guyana's legislative framework for indigenous peoples, as 'a special measure discriminating in favour of Amerindians and . . . a special measure within Article 1, paragraph 4 of the Convention'.[168] Further, while the Act was justifiable to protect Amerindians, 'it cannot give Amerindians rights to the detriment of others'.[169] The formulation of the argument, besides (erroneously) subsuming the ensemble of indigenous rights under special measures, suggests that, from some perspectives, 'special measures' may be incorrectly characterized as rights to the detriment of others.

2. *Sole Purpose*

Actions may have various motivations or purposes. Article 1(4) provides that special measures are to be taken for the 'sole purpose' of securing adequate advancement of groups and individuals concerned.[170] GR 32 provides that the 'sole purpose' reference 'limits the scope of acceptable motivations for special measures under the Convention'.[171] It also suggests that the motivation 'should be made apparent from the nature of the measures themselves, the arguments used by the authorities to justify the measures, and the instruments designed to put the measures into effect'.[172] This may be difficult to discern in cases where a complex series of measures is presented together as a special measures 'package'. Issues of purpose were raised under CERD's early warning procedure in reaction to Australia's Northern Territory National Emergency Response Act (NTERA). The Act was promulgated in response to a report of the Northern Territory government documenting cases of child abuse in indigenous communities in the

[166] A/48/18, ch VIII B.
[167] CERD/C/SR.981, para. 61, Committee member Wolfrum. No such statement is included.
[168] CERD/C/GUY/CO/14/Add.1, para. 2.
[169] *Ibid.*, para. 70.
[170] The concept of 'sole purpose' was explained in the context of Australian provisions on racial discrimination: 'What is necessary for characterization of legislative provisions as having been "taken" for "a sole purpose" is that they can be seen, in the factual context, to be really and not colourably or fancifully referable to and explicable by the sole purpose which is said to provide their character. They will not be properly so characterised unless their provisions are capable of being reasonably considered to be appropriate and adapted to achieving that purpose': per Deane J. in *Gerhardy v Brown* (1985), 159 CLR 70, p. 149.
[171] GR 32, para. 21.
[172] Para. 21.

Northern Territory.[173] The whole of the Act, with its mix of measures on sale and consumption of alcohol, banning of pornography, acquisition of leases over aboriginal land, exclusion of customary law in sentencing, application of a system of income management, etc, was deemed a 'special measure' under Australia's Racial Discrimination Act (RDA),[174] while at the same time the new measures were excluded from the operation of Part II of the RDA.[175] In its response to CERD, intimating a proposed redesign of the measures, the government of Australia appeared to sense that the scope of the package was too broad: the revised measures, it stated, would 'either be more clearly special measures or non-discriminatory and will not involve suspension of the RDA'.[176]

3. Adequate Advancement

'Adequate advancement' implies 'goal-directed programmes which have the objective of alleviating and remedying disparities in the enjoyment of human rights and fundamental freedoms affecting particular groups and individuals, protecting them from discrimination'.[177] Such disparities 'include but are not confined to persistent or structural disparities and *de facto* inequalities resulting from the circumstances of history', so that it is 'not necessary to prove "historic" discrimination in order to validate a programme of special measures: the emphasis should be placed on correcting present disparities and on preventing further imbalances from arising'.[178] The emphasis on present circumstances is important in that 'historic' discrimination, its causes and responsibilities therefore, may be hard to demonstrate unequivocally. Highlighting present circumstances is more in keeping with the Convention as a whole in engaging the current responsibilities of the State by focusing on present and potential future situations.

'Advancement' is a concept that, at its worst, would do little more than echo the 'civilising mission', but at its best is positive and humanitarian in inspiration.[179] 'Advancement' was instructively raised in the NTERA case. From the viewpoint of the Australian government, the measures were clearly beneficial to the communities concerned in line with the requirement that a measure 'must result in a benefit to some or all members of a class of people'.[180] Australian non-governmental organizations (NGOs) on the other hand argued that the 'advancement' criterion was not satisfied in that the measures were not culturally appropriate and did not respect a range of aboriginal rights.[181] In the text of Article 1(4), the 'advancement' is ostensibly not well coordinated with 'protection', which is a narrower notion, especially since, in international human rights law generally, 'protection' primarily refers to protection from the acts of private persons. However, GR 32 includes the observation that 'protection' 'signifies protection

[173] R. Wild and P. Anderson, *Ampe Akelyernemane Meke Mekarle: Little Children are Sacred* (Board of Inquiry into the Protection of Aboriginal Children from Sexual Abuse, 2007).

[174] Section 132(1) of the NTERA provides that: '[t]he provisions of this Act, and any acts done under or for the purposes of those provisions, are, for the purposes of the Racial Discrimination Act 1975, special measures.'

[175] *Ibid.*, Section 132(2).

[176] Interim response of the Australian government, 4 March 2009 (on file with the CERD Secretariat). See also concluding observations on Australia, CERD/C/AUS/CO/15-17, para. 16.

[177] Para. 22.

[178] Para. 22.

[179] Chapter 2 of the present work.

[180] *Future Directions for the Northern Territory Emergency Response*, Australian Government discussion paper, 21 May 2009, p. 7.

[181] Request for urgent action, submitted 28 January 2009 (on file with OHCHR Secretariat).

from violations of human rights emanating from any source, including discriminatory activities of private persons', adding that special measures 'may have preventive (of human rights violations) as well as corrective functions', a point that reinforces that in paragraph 22 on the present/future orientation of the special measures provisions. The understanding of 'advancement' was interrogated in the Australian case of *Gerhardy v Brown*:

> A special measure must have the sole purpose of advancement, but what is 'advancement'? To some extent, that is a matter of opinion formed with reference to the circumstances in which the measure is intended to operate. 'Advancement' is not necessarily what the person who takes the measure regards as a benefit for the beneficiaries . . . The wishes of the beneficiaries . . . are of great importance (perhaps essential) in determining whether a measure is taken for the purpose of securing their advancement. The dignity of the beneficiaries is impaired and they are not advanced by having an unwanted material benefit foisted upon them.[182]

To which may be added the key international standards of participation in decisions affecting communities and the right to self-determination for indigenous peoples.[183]

4. *Racial or Ethnic Groups or Individuals Requiring Protection*

In terms of the racial or ethnic groups regularly identified as requiring special measures, it may be gathered from the above examples (and through much of the present work) that CERD practice is replete with references to minority and indigenous groups, and that, among minorities, Roma figure prominently. CERD GR 27[184] makes extensive references to unqualified 'measures' but also to 'special measures' in the context of employment and participation in central and local governmental bodies.[185] Similarly, GR 29 on descent-based discrimination[186] makes a limited reference to 'special measures'[187] and 'special and concrete measures'[188] amongst an abundance of references to 'measures', 'strict measures', 'resolute measures', 'mechanisms', 'programmes', and 'projects'. In the ICERD section of the Manual on Human Rights reporting, it is advised that information gathered for reporting under other international instruments on rights of vulnerable groups should be consulted for its potential relevance under ICERD, adding that with regard to Article 1(4), 'those are in particular articles 27 of ICCPR,[189] 2(3) of ICESCR,[190] 4 (temporary special measures) and 14 of CEDAW,[191] and 22, 23, and 30 of the CRC'.[192] Special measures are adverted to in paragraph 4 of CERD GR 30 on

[182] Per Brennan J. in *Gerhardy v Brown* (1985), 159 CLR 70, 135. See also *Bropho v Western Australia* [2007] FCA 519, per Nicholson J; *Aurukun Shire Council v CEO Office of Liquor Gaming and Racing* [2010] QCA 27; Morton *v Queensland Police Service* [2010] QCA 160, citations from Australian Human rights Commission: <https://www.humanrights.gov.au/publications/guidelines-understanding-special-measures-racial-discrimination-act-1975-cth-2011>.

[183] Discussion in Chapter 13.

[184] A/55/18, Annex V. C.

[185] GR 27, paras 28, 29, and 41.

[186] A/57/18, chapter XI. F.

[187] Para. (f) envisages special measures 'in particular concerning access to public functions, employment and education'.

[188] In terms of political and representation rights: GR 29, para. (bb).

[189] Rights of minorities.

[190] Referring to economic rights and non-nationals.

[191] Article 14 is a complex article on rural women.

[192] *Manual on Human Rights Reporting* (United Nations, 1997), p. 274. The section on ICERD was authored by CERD member Luis Valencia Rodriguez. Article 22 of CRC concerns refugee children, Article 23 concerns the disabled child, and Article 30 addresses the rights of minority and indigenous children.

non-citizens but limited to a simple recall that '[d]ifferentiation within the scope of article 1, paragraph 4 of the Convention relating to special measures is not considered as discriminatory'. A clearer affirmation of application to non-citizens appears in recommendations on Austria where, following a reference to vulnerable groups 'such as ethnic minorities, immigrants and asylum-seekers', the Committee recommended 'that the State party consider adopting special measures in favour of *such groups*'.[193]

The criterion of vulnerability represents one way of envisaging the span of potential beneficiaries, in addition to more formal analyses.[194] GR 32 opts for the latter in recalling CERD GR 8 (on Article 1, paragraphs 1 and 4), GR 27 (Roma), and GR 29 (descent), and opts for the formula that 'the measures shall in principle be available to any group or person covered by article 1 of the Convention', with the practice of the Committee one of the interpretative pointers, thus opening out the potential beneficiaries of the measures to include the above as well as cases individuated under the concept of intersectionality. The recommendation notes the difference between the broad ambiguous 'racial or ethnic groups or individuals requiring . . . protection' in 1(4), and 'racial groups or individuals belonging to them' in 2(2), concluding that the span of 'potential beneficiaries or addressees of special measures should . . . be understood in light of the overall objective of the Convention as dedicated to the elimination of all forms of racial discrimination, with special measures as an essential tool . . . for the achievement of this objective'.[195]

IV. Article 2(2)

1. *'Shall' Take Special Measures*

The Committee has stressed the mandatory nature of the requirement to take special measures 'when the circumstances so warrant'. CERD's exchanges with the US have been of service in drawing out key issues. In its 2001 concluding observations on the US, the Committee commented:

> With regard to affirmative action, the Committee notes with concern the position taken by the State party that the provisions of the Convention permit, but do not require States parties to adopt affirmative action measures to ensure the adequate development and protection of certain racial, ethnic or national groups. The Committee emphasizes that the adoption of special measures by States parties when the circumstances so warrant, such as in the case of persistent disparities, is an obligation stemming from article 2, paragraph 2, of the Convention.[196]

The observation was made in response to a double affirmation by the US: that affirmative action measures need not be race-based, and that the question of when they should be taken was a matter of discretion for the State party.[197] In its fourth to sixth report examined in 2008, the US responded to the Committee's earlier comment that:

[193] CERD/C/AUT/CO/17, para. 21 (present author's emphasis).

[194] See Chapter 15.

[195] Paras 24 and 25.

[196] CERD/C/304/Add.125, para. 20.

[197] The relevant passage in the report of the US read: 'Together, Article 1 (4) and Article 2 (2) permit, but do not require, States parties to adopt race-based affirmative action programmes without violating the Convention. Deciding when such measures are in fact warranted is left to the discretion of each State party': CERD/C/351/Add.1, para. 249. In the course of discussions, CERD member Reshetov noted that 'the United States considered—wrongly—that adoption of . . . special measures was left to the discretion of each State party . . . in reality, the Convention required States parties to take measures of that kind': CERD/C/SR.1474, para. 31. Another Committee member, Britz, read the US statement to mean that 'the measures would be of a general

The United States acknowledges that article 2 (2) requires States parties to take special measures 'when circumstances so warrant' and . . . the United States has in place numerous such measures. The decision concerning when such measures are in fact warranted is left to the judgment and discretion of each State Party. The decision concerning what types of measures should be taken is also left to the judgment and discretion of each State Party, and the United States maintains its position that, consistent with the Convention, special measures taken for the sole purpose of securing adequate advancement of certain racial or ethnic groups or individuals requiring such protection may or may not in themselves be race-based. For example, a 'special measure' might address the development or protection of a racial group without the measure itself applying on the basis of race (e.g., a measure might be directed at the neediest members of society without expressly drawing racial distinctions).[198]

The point was repeated in discussions before the Committee, where the delegation elaborated that decisions on the application of measures under Article 2(2) of the Convention should be left to the appreciation of the State party 'and that such measures need not necessarily be based on race or ethnic affiliation'.[199] The US position was restated during the thematic discussion on special measures:

The United States acknowledges that article 2(2) requires States parties to take special measures 'when circumstances so warrant' . . . the decision concerning when such measures are in fact warranted is left to the judgment and discretion of each State party. The decision concerning what types of measures should be taken is also left to the judgment and discretion of each State party, and . . . special measures . . . may or may not in themselves be race-based. For example, a 'special measure' might address the development or protection of a racial group without the measure itself applying on the basis of race (e.g., a measure might be directed at the neediest members of society without expressly drawing racial distinctions).[200]

These statements include a triple affirmation: *when* a special measure is to be adopted is a matter of State discretion, the *type of measure* is also subject to discretion, and special measures can be based on *need and not necessarily race-based*. Two paragraphs in particular in GR 32 go some way to addressing US issues. Paragraph 30 is clear on 'the mandatory nature of the obligation' to take special measures, which is 'not weakened by the addition of the phrase "when the circumstances so warrant", a phrase which should be read as providing context for the application of the measures'. Paragraph 5 on the interpretation of the Convention adds that '[c]ontext-sensitive interpretation . . . includes taking into account the particular circumstances of States parties', adding that while the 'conscientious application of Convention principles will produce variations in outcome . . . such variations must be fully justifiable in light of the principles of the Convention'. The recommendation does not address the question of 'need' as a race/needs dichotomy after the fashion of the US and recommends simply that the measures 'should be designed and implemented on the basis of need, grounded in a realistic appraisal of the current situation of individuals and communities concerned'.[201]

nature not directed to particular groups': CERD/C/SR.1475, para. 17. The delegate of the US appeared to merge both issues in responding that 'Article 2 imposed no obligation on States parties to utilize particular race-conscious measures': CERD/C/SR.1476, para. 5.

198 CERD/C/USA 6, para. 127.

199 CERD/C/SR.1853, para. 17 (translation from French by the author); CERD/C/SR.1854, para. 1.

200 On file with the OHCHR Secretariat.

201 Para. 16. The Committee has subsequently recommended to the US that it takes GR 32 into account: CERD/C/USA/CO/7-9, para. 7.

The Committee's own readings of the circumstances that warrant the application of measures refer to vulnerability,[202] marginalization,[203] inequality or structural inequality,[204] entrenched racism,[205] disadvantage,[206] and indirect discrimination,[207] while the precise nature of the disadvantage varies from case to case and will influence the type of remedies suggested by the Committee. In some cases, the Committee has itself referred to historic discrimination.[208] In others, the emphasis is on how continuing or further discrimination is to be prevented and disparities or persistent disparities and inequalities eliminated;[209] the proactive element emphasized by CERD also figures in GR 32. A compendium recommendation to Fiji in 2003 urged that affirmative action measures should be 'necessary in a democratic society, respect the principle of fairness, and... grounded in a realistic appraisal of the situation of indigenous Fijians as well as other communities'.[210] Paragraph 16 of GR 32 phrases this requirement as one according to which the measures 'should be appropriate to the situation to be remedied, be legitimate, necessary in a democratic society, respect the principles of fairness and proportionality, and be temporary'. In all such cases, the *objective appraisal* of various kinds of disadvantage is emphasized as crucial.

Addressing the conditions for the application of special measures raises the question of supporting data. States are regularly invited to identify the specific needs of populations,[211] and the issue of supporting data figures strongly in GR 32.[212] Failure to take measures when situations warrant them is liable to be criticized by the Committee. In the case of Antigua and Barbuda, CERD asked why, when the constitution provided for special measures, no such measures had been adopted, and whether data-gathering was adequate to assess the need for the measures.[213] In the case of Suriname, the Committee regretted that no special measures for the advancement of the education and health of indigenous and tribal peoples 'on the grounds that there are no available data suggesting that they need special protection'.[214] As with the background conditions for special measures, so also CERD has emphasized the need for data in assessing how many persons have benefited from the application of special measures,[215] and on which to base decisions on when measures should be discontinued.

[202] Special measures are not automatically associated with every indigenous group: in complex demographic situations, some indigenous can be more vulnerable than others; see concluding observations on Norway, CERD/C/NOR/CO/18, para. 17 (the East Saami).

[203] Concluding observations on Botswana, CERD/C/61/CO/2, para. 12.

[204] Concluding observations on Brazil, CERD/C/64/CO/2, para. 12.

[205] Concluding observations on Guatemala, CERD/C/GTM/CO/11, para. 12.

[206] Concluding observations on Botswana, CERD/C/BWA/CO/16, para. 13.

[207] Concluding observations on Madagascar, CERD/C/65/CO/4, A/59/18, para. 16.

[208] Concluding observations on Guatemala, CERD/C/GTM/CO/11, para. 12.

[209] Concluding observations on the US, CERD/C/USA/CO/6, para. 15.

[210] CERD/C/62/CO/3, para.15

[211] For example, concluding observations on Botswana, CERD/C/61/CO/2, para. 12. For general reflections on data questions, see Chapter 6.

[212] Paras 17, 35, 37.

[213] CERD/C/ATG/9, para. 13.

[214] CERD/C/64/CO/9, para. 19.

[215] Concluding observations on Slovenia, CERD/C/62/CO/9, A/58/18, para. 10; information on the results of programmes has been requested from, *inter alios*, Fiji: CERD/C/62/CO/3, para. 18.

2. Racial Groups or Individuals Belonging to Them

The Committee has issued guidance on the complex question of who should be regarded as members of groups that enjoy the protection of the Convention. As previously observed,[216] GR 8, linked both to the definition of racial discrimination and to special measures, sets out principles for determining group membership: identification as a member 'of a particular racial or ethnic group or groups' shall, 'if no justification exists to the contrary, be based upon self-identification by the individual concerned'.[217] The reference to 'group or groups' in GR 8 was inserted in order not to exclude the possibility that an individual might belong to more than one group.[218] An earlier draft of the recommendation to the effect that such identification 'shall exclusively be based' on self-identification drew the immediate response that 'exclusively' was too restrictive and placed too much pressure upon States to adopt a specific approach to the organisation of censuses and other data collection methods.[219] The issue of persons claiming to belong to a minority with which they had no connection was also raised.[220]

The question of what kind of 'justifications' may be pitted against simple reliance on self-identification is not clearly answered by the recommendation. While self-identification is the primary starting point, membership questions are paradigmatically negotiated through principled argument involving 'objective' cultural factors, community acceptance, and the objectives of recognition. In concluding observations on Finland, the State party was urged by the Committee to give greater weight to self-identification in relation to membership of the Sámi indigenous people.[221] In response, and in light of rulings by the Supreme Administrative Court of Finland on Sámi identity, the Sámi Council requested a revision of the recommendation in order to avoid endorsement of an 'absurd' Court ruling that 'allows a large part of the Finnish population' to claim Sámi status.[222] In the event, CERD recommended that Finland take more account of the UNDRIP, including its principle of self-determination, in its judgements regarding Sámi identity.[223] The later recommendation from the Committee rebalanced the previous conclusions in light of the fresh information provided. Group membership is addressed

[216] See Chapter 6.

[217] A/45/18, Annex VII. 1. In *Gunme v Cameroon*, the African Commission on Human and Peoples' Rights held that the people of Southern Cameroon qualify as such 'because they manifest numerous characteristics and affinities, which include a common history, linguistic tradition, territorial connection, and political outlook. More importantly *they identify themselves as a people with a separate and distinct identity*. Identity is an innate characteristic within a people. It is up to other external people to recognise such existence, but not to deny it': *Kevin Mgwanga Gunme et al. v Cameroon*, ACHPR, Comm. No. 266/2003, 27 May 2009, at para. 179; cited In J. Dugard and J. Reynolds, 'Apartheid, International Law, and the Occupied Palestinian Territory', *EJIL* 24 (2013), 867–913, 888 (emphasis added).

[218] CERD/C/SR.883, para. 57 (Banton).

[219] *Ibid.*, para. 59 (Banton).

[220] *Ibid.*, para. 62 (Song Shuhua).

[221] CERD/C/FIN/CO/19, para. 13.

[222] Observations by the Saami Council on Finland's twentieth, twenty-first, and twenty-second periodic reports to CERD, 13 August 2012, p. 5 (on file with CERD Secretariat). *Inter alia*, the Council cited the present author, 'Integrating the UN Declaration on the Rights of Indigenous Peoples into CERD Practice', in S. Allen and A. Xanthaki (eds), *Reflections on the UN Declaration on the Rights of Indigenous Peoples* (Hart Publishing, 2011), pp. 61–91, p. 83; Article 33.1 of the UNDRIP was also cited to buttress the Council's reminder that indigenous peoples have the right to determine their own identity or membership in accordance with their customs and traditions.

[223] CERD/C/FIN/CO/20-22, para. 13.

in GR 32 under its commentary on Article 2(2): beneficiaries of special measures 'may be groups or individuals belonging to such groups. The advancement and protection of communities through special measures is a legitimate objective to be pursued in tandem with respect for the rights and interests of individuals.'[224]

The general recommendation is robust on the advancement and protection of communities, if more tentative on the individual claim to membership than GR 8 in softening 'shall' (be based on self-identification) to a 'should'.

3. Adequate Development and Protection/Fields of Operation

The phrase contrasts with 'adequate advancement' in Article 1(4) and is treated cursorily in paragraph 33 of GR 32 to the effect that, special measures 'should clearly benefit groups in their enjoyment of human rights' and that, in all cases, 'it is clear that the reference to limitations of "development" relates only to the situation or condition in which groups or individuals find themselves and is not a reflection of any individual or group characteristic'. The paragraph adds the point that, in principle, 'special measures can reach into all fields of human rights deprivation, including deprivation of the enjoyment of any human rights expressly or impliedly protected by article 5 of the Convention'. Committee practice is replete with reference to areas where special measures should operate to enhance human rights. The measures have been recommended for, *inter alia*, representation in the military and the police,[225] in political systems,[226] the public service,[227] and the media;[228] for education, including reduction of achievement gaps,[229] employment, and housing;[230] to preserve heritage;[231] for the alleviation of poverty;[232] and to enhance freedom of movement and rights to participation.[233] Issues of representation and participation figure strongly in the corpus of recommendations.

D. Comment

The consolidation and clarification of practice in GR 32 does not address every nuance in the Convention's paragraphs on special measures,[234] including the use of 'special measures' in 1(4), and 'special and concrete measures' in 2(2), 'racial or ethnic groups' 1(4), and 'racial groups' 2(2)), 'adequate advancement' 1(4), and 'adequate development' 2(2). GR 32 states that these 'nuances of difference . . . do not disturb their essential unity of concept and purpose'.[235] Some of the differences appear to be linked to the function of the two paragraphs, so that 'special measures' as part of a definition becomes 'special and concrete measures' when it comes to their targeted application; in the Declaration, in the

[224] CERD GR 32, para. 34.
[225] Concluding observations on Ethiopia, CERD/C/ETH/CO/15, para. 25.
[226] Concluding observations on Ireland, CERD/C/IRL/CO/2, A/60/18, para. 22; concluding observations on Mongolia, CERD/C/MNG/CO/18, para. 15.
[227] Concluding observations on Nigeria, CERD/C/NGA/CO/18, para. 18.
[228] Concluding observations on Nepal, CERD/C/64/CO/5, para. 21.
[229] Concluding observations on Fiji, CERD/C/FJI/CO/17, para. 17.
[230] Concluding observations on Yemen, CERD/C/YEM/CO/16, para. 15.
[231] Concluding observations on Ukraine, CERD/C/UKR/CO/18, para. 18 (Ukraine).
[232] Concluding observations on Fiji, CERD/C/62/CO/3, para. 16.
[233] Concluding observations on South Africa, CERD/C/ZAF/CO/3, para. 19.
[234] T. Makkonen, *Equal in Law, Unequal in Fact* (Martinus Nijhoff, 2012), p. 143, fn. 128.
[235] Para. 29.

absence of a definition paragraph, the inclusion of 'special concrete measures' was linked to a paragraph resembling 2(2). In the drafting of 1(4), the reference to concrete measures disappeared at the Sub-Commission stage, whereas it was maintained through the stages of the drafting of 2(2). 'Racial groups' were referred to in early drafts of 1(4) and extended to 'racial or ethnic groups' on a proposal by India and Ethiopia: the *travaux* do not elucidate the reasons for the change, the latitude of which cannot be faulted in light of the non-racial examples of candidates for special measures offered by India. On 'advancement' and 'development', the difference between a definition and an obligation to take measures appears once more to have coloured the drafting, with India making a crucial intervention suggesting that the defined 'advancement' in 1(4) be translated into a duty in 2(2) to raise populations to the level of development of others.[236] The conditions for the termination of special measures are expressed differently between 1(4) and 2(2) with the former suggesting two conditions limiting special measures and the latter combining them into one. Despite this nuance, GR 32 suggests that the concept in 1(4) be applied, *mutatis mutandis*, to 2(2).[237] The drafting record shows awareness of duplication between 1(4) and 2(2) in this and other instances,[238] though the Committee has not been deflected by any such considerations from its robust endorsement of special measures and its treatment of the paragraphs as stating unified and not conflicting principles.

GR 32 refers to the autonomous meaning of special measures in the Convention, distinguishing this autonomous meaning from the variable usage in domestic legal systems of 'affirmative action' and related terms. A first draft of the recommendation referring to a functional equivalence between the use of affirmative action and the Convention's stance on special measures was softened in the drafting to respect the possibility that domestic usage may not conform to the requirements of the Convention as elaborated in the recommendation and CERD practice.[239] States parties are required to interrogate the specific requirements of the Convention before drawing the conclusion that their practice conforms to its requirements, regardless of the terminology adopted: terminology does not prevail over substance.

The concept is also linked in the recommendation to the world of contemporary human rights standards and the recommendation contributes to those standards.[240] The ICERD provisions emerge as an elaborated and refined version of the provision in the Declaration on Racial Discrimination, differing principally in greater emphasis placed on group protection.[241] In treaty law, the ICERD provisions have the closest affinity with

[236] A/C.3/SR. 1308, para. 7.

[237] Para. 35.

[238] See, for example, remarks of the representative of the United Arab Republic, A/C.3/SR.1306, para. 29.

[239] CERD/C/GC/32/CRP.1, para. 14.

[240] GR 32, along with other materials, is taken as primary evidence of 'contemporary understanding' of standards on racial discrimination and special measures' in extensive citations by Gageler J in the Australian case of *Maloney v The Queen* [2013] HCA 28 (June 2013), paras 288–328. The appellant, a member of an indigenous community, challenged the categorization of a prohibition of alcohol in a defined geographical area as a 'special measure', citing GR 32 as evidence of a changed international understanding. The appeal was dismissed by the High Court. In delivering their opinions, other judges, *inter alia*, doubted the Committee's interpretation of consultation with affected communities as necessarily flowing from the text of Articles 1(4) and 2(2), though French CJ accepted as a matter of common sense that prior consultation with an affected community and its substantial acceptance of a proposed measure as likely to be essential to the practical implementation of a measure, *ibid.*, para. 25. Kiefel J, *ibid.*, para. 176, appeared to assume (erroneously) that CERD recommendations 'had altered the text of the Convention'.

[241] D. Keane, *Caste-Based Discrimination in International Human Rights Law* (Ashgate, 2007), pp. 185–6.

CEDAW; affinity with other core texts is less clear if only on the basis that ICERD and CEDAW provide explicit definitions of special measures, though it is also true that nuances of difference exist on such issues as the duration of special measures and the relationship between grounds-based and needs-based measures. Differences of detail influence the boldness with which treaty bodies and other mechanisms approach the issue: treaty bases incorporate differentiated and less differentiated notions of equality and sustainability that determine the particular expressions of the concept. It is clear, however, that despite differences of register, the consolidation of CERD practice in GR 32 draws upon a range of instruments and bodies in differentiating between special measures and permanent rights, in the focus on consultations with communities, and in intimating the range of beneficiaries of special measures. As with the Committee's approach to the definition of racial discrimination, the description of the measures in paragraph 16 of the general recommendation—they should be 'legitimate, necessary in a democratic society, respect the principles of fairness and proportionality, and be temporary'—connects with other human rights vocabularies, global and regional, while suggesting a certain strictness in the conditions for their adoption.

The first of the two paragraphs on special measures expressly liberate the concept from homogenizing or mechanical applications of equality and non-discrimination,[242] a structural connection to be understood in light of the statement in GR 32 describing 'substantive or *de facto* equality in the enjoyment and exercise of human rights as the aim to be achieved'[243] by the faithful implementation of Convention principles. The express inclusion of special measures in the Convention also contributes to distinguishing this form of positive action from unjustifiable 'preferences'.[244] While the accumulation of cautions in the text of both paragraphs—duration, no separate rights, sole purpose—evinces a sense of the 'exceptional' nature of the concept, particularly as conceived in the drafting, practice has invested heavily in its description as a 'clarification' of Convention principles and as 'integral' to the meaning of non-discrimination.[245]

Special measures are also understood as key contributors to the overall Convention project of fighting racial discrimination. They may operate in any field of human rights deprivation including the rights listed or intimated in Article 5.[246] This generic linkage gives rise to the problem of identifying conceptual boundaries between the general obligations of States under a span of Convention articles and the particular obligation to take special measures. The issue is part of a broader puzzle of identifying lines between respecting obligations and rights of a permanent nature, and obligations to take situation-based and temporary action, boundaries that are signalled but not sharply demarcated in CERD practice. The boundary question is essentially one of interpretation. In terms of a victim-centred approach to the fulfilment of standards, it is submitted that the better strategy, if a choice must be made, would be to cramp the scope of the 'temporary' provisions in favour of more generous interpretation of the 'enduring' rights and obligations. In the analogous case of CEDAW, Evatt cautions against treating measures as

[242] The clearest demonstration of Committee thinking on the meaning of equality appears in para. 8 of GR 32.
[243] Para. 6.
[244] Para. 7; see also Chapter 6.
[245] Para. 20.
[246] Para. 33.

temporary special measures 'when they may be important, necessary, appropriate or long term measures for implementation of the Convention'.[247]

As defined in ICERD, special measures are group as well as individual-centred. This aspect, together with CERD insistence on consultation over special measures programmes and respect for community rights developed outside its walls, goes some way to remedy what Boyle and Baldaccini see as the lack of safeguards in the Convention against assimilationist policies particularly in promoting 'adequate development' of groups;[248] in light of the development of CERD practice and the onward growth of international standards, this last comment now appears dated. Committee practice has been careful to avoid language in its account of 'advancement' that would infringe the anti-hierarchical stance of the Convention, and insists on the equal dignity and value of all cultures. No specific guidance on the resolution of group–individual rights conflicts appears in GR 32: a conundrum on the scope of liberal rights appears in its consultation paragraph wherein, as observed, the 'affected communities' whose consultation and participation in the programme of special measures is sought, are not confined to direct beneficiary communities. This leaves unresolved the question of how aggressively an affirmative action programme dedicated to social uplift can be pursued in light of potential impacts on individual rights and the rights of other communities, though the Committee, as with its approach to freedom of speech and the proscription of racist hate speech,[249] does not view special measures as a zero-sum game and has criticized States parties for taking that view.

The strenuous assertion by the Committee of the mandatory nature of special measures when the circumstances warrant is another notable feature of practice, as is the vision of the measures as covering the whole gamut of human rights, and not simply economic and social rights. Equally, the insistence on the limits of special measures is designed to prevent them collapsing into a kind of reverse discrimination. This suggests the need for careful scrutiny of arrangements that may be presented under the rubric of special measures but which display instead the attributes of non-egalitarian 'privilege'. Scrutiny is also required of ostensibly hierarchical approaches to forcing measures over the heads of non-consenting populations, on the basis of States or other parties 'knowing better than' the populations concerned as to what is good for them. In spite of the Committee's conceptual accounting, 'hard cases' will continue to present themselves requiring fine-tuning in light of principle. The 'circumstances that warrant' special measures will be many and various. The Committee has not gone as far as to convert special measures into rights, though it could be argued that if there is a right to equal treatment, why not a right to all aspects of such treatment that are integral to the project of achieving equality? On the other hand, in light of the ethical balance of the Convention and the controversial nature of special measures, it may be more appropriate to continue to interpret special measures as obligations rather than rights and interpret such obligations in a manner that does not obscure or diminish the scope of the positive, action-requiring elements of other Convention provisions.

[247] In Boerefijn, *Temporary Special Measures*, p. 49.

[248] K. Boyle and A. Baldaccini, 'A critical evaluation of international human rights approaches to racism', in S. Fredman (ed.), *Discrimination and Human Rights: The Case of Racism* (Oxford University Press, 2001), pp. 135–91, at p. 158.

[249] Chapter 11 of the present work.

10. Article 3

Segregation and Apartheid

States parties particularly condemn racial segregation and apartheid and undertake to prevent, prohibit and eradicate all practices of this nature in territories under their jurisdiction.

A. Introduction

Article 3 is the shortest of the normative Articles in the Convention. The drafts of the article generated only a modicum of controversy, making its passage to adoption relatively smooth compared to most of the other non-procedural Articles: Article 7 was also relatively uncontroversial. Historical examples of State-enforced racial segregation,[1] besides that of South Africa, include Jewish segregation in England, Germany, other European countries, the Russian Empire, and the Middle East,[2] as well as segregation of Roma/Gypsies;[3] segregation in such cases typically figured as only one element in complex patterns and practices of racial oppression. The system of 'Jim Crow' laws[4] in the United States in the post-Civil War reconstruction period, and the *Plessy v Ferguson*[5] doctrine of 'separate but equal' facilities,[6] also feature in the history of segregation. The ultimately successful efforts of the US civil rights movement to abolish segregationist laws included the notable Civil Rights Act 1964,[7] incorporating titles such as 'desegregation of public facilities',[8] and 'desegregation of public education',[9] provided timely inspiration for the drafters of the Convention.[10] Practices of segregation were and are not confined to any

[1] 'Racial Segregation': <http://en.wikipedia.org/wiki/Racial_segregation>.

[2] C. Roth and J. Wigoder (eds), *The New Standard Jewish Encyclopaedia* (W. H. Allen, revised edition 1970).

[3] I. Pogány, *The Roma Café: Human Rights and the Plight of the Romani People* (Pluto Press, 2004); A. Fraser, The Gypsies (Blackwell, 1995); H. O'Nions, *Minority Rights Protection in International Law: The Roma of Europe* (Ashgate, 2012); C. Tavani, *Collective Rights and the Cultural Identity of the Roma: A Case Study of Italy* (Martinus Nijhoff, 2012).

[4] M.J. Klarman, *From Jim Crow to Civil Rights: the Supreme Court and the Struggle for Racial Equality* (Oxford University Press, 2004); L.F. Litwack, *Trouble in Mind: Black Southerners in the Age of Jim Crow* (Vintage Books, 1999). The term is associated with 'Jump Jim Crow', a song and dance routine performed by blacked-up white actor T.D. Rice.

[5] 163 U.S. 537 (1896).

[6] See the concluding section of the present chapter for further discussion.

[7] Introduced in its preamble as an Act '[t]o enforce the constitutional right to vote, to confer jurisdiction upon the district courts of the United States to provide injunctive relief against discrimination in public accommodations, to authorize the Attorney General to institute suits to protect constitutional rights in public facilities and public education, to extend the Commission on Civil Rights, to prevent discrimination in federally assisted programs, to establish a Commission on Equal Employment Opportunity, and for other purposes.'

[8] Title III.

[9] Title IV.

[10] In the sphere of education, 'desegregation' is defined in section 401 as 'the assignment of students to public schools and within such schools without regard to their race, colour, religion, or national origin, but "desegregation" shall not mean the assignment of students to public schools in order to overcome racial imbalance'.

particular form of society or group of States. Severe forms of segregation are also implicated in caste and analogous systems of social stratification.[11]

The references to apartheid in the preamble and Article 3 constitute an exception to the absence of named 'isms'—particular forms of racial discrimination—in the Convention as a whole.[12] The 'evil twins' in the article—segregation and apartheid—were not debated to the same extent through the *travaux*: the system of apartheid—'separateness'—claimed a significantly greater share of attention.[13] As observed elsewhere in the present work, the international reaction to apartheid in South Africa constituted an essential basis for the emergence of the Convention.[14] The formal institution of the apartheid system in South Africa after the elections of 1948 and the victory of the National Party had been preceded by a broad spectrum of segregationist legislation in the nineteenth and twentieth centuries.[15] Pass laws, disenfranchisement measures, laws providing for residential segregation, laws banning land sales to Indians, laws designed to force black South Africans into 'locations', etc, were features of the South African legal landscape before 1948.[16] Formalized racial classification—including a system of identity cards specifying racial group—was introduced in 1950;[17] race determined place of residence under the Group Areas Act of the same year.[18] Racially mixed marriages were forbidden in 1949,[19] and sexual relations between persons of different races were criminalized by the Immorality Acts.[20] Provisions to segregate education, employment, and the use of public amenities followed. In the political sphere, the policy of 'separate development' along racial lines resulted in a system of 'homelands' or 'Bantustans' for black South Africans;[21] 'coloured' voters suffered various acts of disenfranchisement.[22]

[11] GR 29 on descent-based discrimination, section 3.

[12] Discussed in Chapter 5 of the present work.

[13] For general treatments, see N.L. Clark and W.H. Worger, *South Africa: the Rise and Fall of Apartheid* (Pearson Education, 2004); A. Guelke, *Rethinking the Rise and Fall of Apartheid: South Africa and World Politics* (Palgrave Macmillan, 2005).

[14] 'Revulsion from *apartheid* was possibly the main motive force behind the adoption in 1965 of ICERD': M. Banton, *International Action against Racial Discrimination* (Clarendon Press, 1996), p. 28 [henceforth *International Action*]. India has taken up this theme to bolster its claim that caste discrimination was not within the contemplation of the drafters of the Convention: comments of India on the 2007 concluding observations of CERD, A/62/18, Annex X.

[15] 'South Africa under Apartheid': <http://en.wikipedia.org/wiki/South_Africa_under_apartheid>.

[16] T.R.H. Davenport and C. Saunders, *South Africa: A Modern History* (5th edn. Macmillan Press Ltd, 2000).

[17] Population Registration Act 1950, Act No. 30 of 1950, an 'Act to make provision for the compilation of a Register of the Population of the Union; for the issue of Identity Cards to persons whose names are included in the Register'; the Act was repealed by a statute of 1991.

[18] Act No. 41 of 1950.

[19] Prohibition of Mixed Marriages Act, No. 55 of 1949, 'to prohibit marriages between Europeans and non-Europeans', amended in 1968, repealed in 1985.

[20] The Immorality Act of 1927 prohibited sexual relations between 'Europeans' and 'Natives', and was amended in 1950 to prohibit sexual relations between 'Europeans' and 'non-Europeans'; a second Immorality Act of 1957 (subsequently named the Sexual Offences Act 1957) continued the prohibitions. The Acts were repealed in 1985 by the Immorality and Prohibition of Mixed Marriages Amendment Act.

[21] Promotion of Bantu Self-Government Act, No. 46 of 1959; Bantu Homelands Citizenship Act, No. 26 of 1970.

[22] The population was classified into four groups: Black, White, Indian, and Coloured. The 'coloured' group included persons of mixed descent that include persons of Bantu, Khoisan, Malay, and European ancestry.

Under persistent international pressure from within and without the United Nations,[23] as well as resistance from within South Africa, the regime that sustained the apartheid system was gradually undermined.[24] Following the release from prison of future President of South Africa Nelson Mandela in 1990, the planks in the apartheid system were ripped out in negotiations from that time until 1993. Elections in 1994 were the first to be held on the basis of universal suffrage. South Africa, an original member of the United Nations, resumed its seat at the United Nations in 1994. In response to the presentation in 2006 of the first report of South Africa under the Convention, the concluding observations of the Committee on the Elimination of Racial Discrimination (CERD) recorded 'the profound significance . . . the emotional overtones, of commencing this constructive dialogue with South Africa, in terms of the Convention whose genesis was strongly influenced by the cruel, inhuman and degrading effects of apartheid in that country'.[25]

I. Segregation and Apartheid

1. Segregation

'Segregation' is a term in common usage, meaning to 'set apart from the rest or each other', or to 'separate along racial, sexual, or religious lines', and may be defined in active or passive senses, 'the action of segregating or the state of being segregated'.[26] Practice also distinguishes *de jure* from *de facto* segregation. In the field of international human rights, 'segregation' crops up in a variety of contexts, though there is a paucity of express reference in the leading instruments on human rights. The term is employed in the Convention on the Rights of Persons with Disabilities (CRPD), Article 19 of which refers to preventing 'isolation or segregation from the community', while Article 23 refers to ensuring the prevention of segregation of children with disabilities in family life. Some of the usage in international instruments relates to discrimination whereas other instances—such as Article 10 of the International Covenant on Civil and Political Rights (ICCPR), referring to segregation of convicted persons from accused, and juveniles from adults—may not as such be correlated with discrimination.

At the level of the United Nations, multiple references to invidious, discriminatory forms of segregation have been made by treaty bodies, including statements on the rights of women with regard to occupational segregation, educational segregation, and analogous matters;[27] in the context of the rights of persons with disabilities,[28] and many other

[23] The preamble to UN General Assembly resolution 395 (V) on the Treatment of People of Indian Origin in the Union of South Africa, 2 December 1950, declared that a policy of racial segregation (apartheid) 'is necessarily based on doctrines of racial discrimination'; much subsequent UN activity vis-à-vis South Africa was based on this premise.

[24] A basic chronology of events in the relationship between South Africa and the United Nations is set out in <http://www.un.org/en/events/mandeladay/apartheid.shtml>.

[25] CERD/C/ZAF/CO/3, para. 2. The Committee also expressed its satisfaction, *ibid.*, para. 6, with 'the peaceful transition from apartheid' and the adoption of the Constitution in 1996 (in force 4 February 1997) with its Bill of Rights enshrining the values of human dignity, equality and non-racism'.

[26] *Concise Oxford English Dictionary* (11th edn, Oxford University Press, 2004), p. 1303.

[27] CEDAW has been particularly concerned with segregation questions, and has engaged the issue in GR 13 on 'Equal remuneration for Work of Equal Value' and through a considerable number of concluding observations to States parties: search for 'CEDAW' under keyword 'segregation', in <http://www.universalhumanrightsindex.org>. See also, among many possible further references, the Beijing Declaration of the Fourth World Conference on Women, A/CONF.177/20/Add.1 (1995), para. 24.

[28] GC 5 of the CESCR—'rights of persons with disabilities'—E/C.12/GC/5.

areas. In General Comment (GC) 20, the Committee on Economic, Social and Cultural Rights addresses 'systemic discrimination' and segregation under the general grounds of discrimination under Article 2 of the International Covenant on Economic, Social and Cultural Rights (ICESCR).[29] The regular subsumption of segregation under 'discrimination' partly accounts for the limited visibility of the former, including visibility as a search term in human rights databases. 'Integration', a generally approved policy stance under the Convention and a common antonym to segregation, makes a stronger showing in searches through the express references to it in a variety of international human rights instruments.[30]

Even as regards specifically racial/ethnic segregation, express references are not prolific. Besides the Declaration and Convention on Racial Discrimination, the leading point of reference is the UNESCO Declaration on Race and Racial Prejudice 1978, which broaches segregation and apartheid both separately and together in its preamble, and in Articles 1, 4, 6, and 10. Article 1(2) refers to apartheid as 'the extreme form of racism' and likens it in Article 4 to genocide as a crime against humanity,[31] whereas segregation, distinguished from apartheid, is stated, along with discrimination, to constitute a crime 'against the conscience and dignity of mankind'.[32] The Declaration defines neither 'segregation' nor 'apartheid' and in the latter case makes no reference to South Africa. The UNESCO Declaration against Discrimination in Education includes under the rubric of 'discrimination', 'establishing or maintaining separate educational systems or institutions for persons or groups of persons', a provision declared to be subject to Article 2, which provides that certain situations shall not be deemed to constitute discrimination, including:

> [t]he establishment or maintenance, for religious or linguistic reasons, of separate educational systems or institutions offering an education which is in keeping with the wishes of the pupil's parents or . . . guardians, if participation in such systems or attendance at such institutions is optional and if the education provided conforms to such standards as may be laid down or approved by the competent authorities, in particular for education of the same level.

The provision is complemented by Article 4(c), which provides a qualified right of members of national minorities 'to carry on their own educational activities, including the maintenance of schools and, depending on the educational policy of each State, the use or the teaching of their own language'.[33] Separation as such is not therefore equivalent to impermissible 'segregation'.[34]

General treaty body practice, along with practice of the UN special procedures, notably that of the Special Rapporteur on Contemporary Forms of Racism, the Independent

[29] GC 20 of the CESCR, E/C.12/GC/20, para. 39.

[30] Multiple references thereto are found in the CRPD, Articles 42–45, and the Optional Protocol to this convention, Articles 10–13; in the CRC, Article 23; the CMW, Article 45; and in regional instruments such as the Protocol to the ACHPR on the Rights of Women, Article 6; the African Charter on the Rights and Welfare of the Child, Articles 13, 17 and 30; the preamble and Article 15 of the European Social Charter. The SIM human rights database lists 22 such references.

[31] Article 4(2).

[32] Article 4(3).

[33] The right is not to be exercised in a manner which prevents the members of minorities from understanding the culture and language of the community as a whole and from participating in its activities, or which prejudices national sovereignty; standards in such schools should also not be lower than the general standard. The provisions as a whole reflect a strong integrationist perspective.

[34] See Chapter 5 of the present work.

Expert on Minorities,[35] and the Special Rapporteur on Education,[36] is replete with references to racial/ethnic segregation in health, education, and other fields of activity; caste or descent-based segregation also figures strongly in the archive.[37] The Special rapporteur on Racism has, *inter alia*, made observations on phenomena of 're-segregation', particularly in the fields of housing and education,[38] which suggests that segregation practices are not static but are capable of mutating and developing, a characteristic that enlarges the scope of the necessary vigilance on the part of the State to combat segregationist phenomena.

Taking only the example of educational segregation, issues have surfaced before sundry UN bodies, including treaty bodies, special procedures, and the universal periodic review (UPR), on segregated classes or schools, notably as regards Roma.[39] Essentially similar concerns with regard to educational segregation of Roma appear in the practice of regional bodies, particularly the European Court of Human Rights and other European bodies; the European Commission against Racism and Intolerance (ECRI) recommends that national legislation should define segregation among the forms of discrimination.[40] High-profile cases concerned with Roma educational segregation before the European Court of Human Rights include *D.H. and Others v Czech Republic*,[41] *Ŏrsŭs v Croatia*,[42] and *Horváth and Kiss v Hungary*.[43]

2. *Apartheid*

Apartheid is the second element in Article 3. By the time the Convention was being drafted, South Africa had been on the agenda of the United Nations since 1946.[44] On 22 June 1946, nine months after the coming into force of the UN Charter, India drew the

[35] The Independent Expert commented with respect to Hungary that 'the free-choice system for parents and the ability of schools to freely select or exclude students has been an engine to generate segregation', A/HRC/4/9/Add.2 (2007), para. 95. The elements on which this analysis is based are set out in paras 61–72 under the heading of 'segregation in education'.

[36] Samples include comments to the government of Bosnia and Herzegovina on the system of 'two schools under one roof', A/HRC/8/10/Add.4 (2008), paras 104 and 106. The Special Rapporteur includes 'segregation and assimilation practices' equally under the rubric of 'discrimination': *ibid.*, para. 109.

[37] Human Rights Watch, *Broken People: Caste Violence against India's 'Untouchables'* (Human Rights Watch, 1999); K. Nakano, M.J. Yutzis and R. Onoyama (eds), *Descent-Based Discrimination* (IMADR, 2004). For a comprehensive account of the treatment of segregation and other forms of caste discrimination by the UN human rights bodies, see International Dalit Solidarity Network, *Caste Discrimination and Human Rights* (9th edition, November 2014), <http://www.idsn.org/fileadmin/user_folder/pdf/New_files/UN/UNcompilation.pdf>. See also Chapter 6 on 'descent'.

[38] Mission to the USA, A/HRC/11/36/Add.3 (2009), paras 91 and 97.

[39] Information from <http://www.universalhumanrightsindex.org> using 'Segregation. Roma' as the search term.

[40] ECRI General Policy Recommendation No. 7: Key Elements of National Legislation against Racism and Racial Discrimination, para. 6. Paragraph 16 of the Explanatory Memorandum to the recommendation elaborates that '[s]egregation is the act by which a (natural or legal) person separates other persons on the basis of one of the enumerated grounds without an objective and reasonable justification, in conformity with the . . . definition of discrimination. As a result, the voluntary act of separating oneself from other persons on the basis of one of the enumerated grounds does not constitute segregation.' The basic definition of discrimination referred to is set out in para. 1 of the recommendation <http://www.coe.int/t/dghl/monitoring/ecri/activities/gpr/en/recommendation_n7/Recommendation_7_en.asp>.

[41] App. No. 57325/00 (2007).

[42] App. No. 15766/03 (2010).

[43] App. No. 11146/11 (2013).

[44] *The United Nations and Apartheid, 1948–1994* (UN Department of Public Information, 1995) provides a detailed chronology of landmarks in the UN response to *apartheid*.

attention of the General Assembly to the treatment of people of Indian origin in South Africa, requesting that the matter be placed on the agenda of the General Assembly. The principal issue provoking India to act was the passing of the Asiatic Land Tenure and Indian Representation Act, with its discriminatory measures against Indians.[45] In resolution 44(I), the General Assembly declared that South Africa's actions should be 'in conformity with ... international obligations under the agreements concluded between the two Governments [India and South Africa] and the relevant provisions of the Charter'.[46] The two governments were requested to report to the next session of the General Assembly on the measures that had been adopted to deal with the problem. Issues were not resolved between the two governments. In a subsequent session, the General Assembly declared that 'a policy of racial segregation (apartheid) is necessarily based on racial discrimination'.[47] The Indian initiative was broadened in 1952 to one that implicated the apartheid system as a whole, a system that became one of the period-defining preoccupations of the United Nations.

By 1954, the UN General Assembly had decided that 'apartheid constitutes a grave threat to the peaceful relations between ethnic groups in the world'.[48] Insofar as Article 2(7) of the UN Charter served to inhibit international action on the part of some States against the South African regime on grounds of 'domestic jurisdiction', UN action became more assertive following the Sharpeville massacre on 21 March 1960, a date later to be commemorated as the International Day for the Elimination of Racial Discrimination.[49] UN General Assembly resolution 1761 of November 1962 condemned the apartheid policies of South Africa as a violation of the UN Charter and a threat to international peace and security, called upon States to break off diplomatic relations and cease trading with South Africa, and established the UN Special Committee against Apartheid,[50] the mandate of which was terminated only in 1994 after South Africa resumed its UN seat.[51] The General Assembly labelled apartheid as a crime against humanity in 1966,[52] a label later endorsed by the Security Council[53] and the Convention on the Suppression and Punishment of the Crime of Apartheid (the Apartheid Convention),[54] the preamble to which recalls Article 3 of the International Convention on the Elimination of All Forms of Racial Discrimination (ICERD).

[45] Act No. 28 of 1946, renamed the Asian Land Tenure Act sought, *inter alia*, to confine Asian ownership and occupation of land to defined areas.

[46] GA resolution 44 (I), 8 December 1946.

[47] GA resolution 395 (V), 1950.

[48] Banton, *International Action*, p. 26.

[49] Proclaimed by General Assembly resolution 2142(XXI), 26 October 1966.

[50] The former name of the Committee was 'The Special Committee on the Policies of Apartheid of the Republic of South Africa'. This was shortened in 1971 to 'Special Committee on Apartheid', revised in 1974 to 'Special Committee against Apartheid': <http://www.aluka.org>.

[51] A succinct review of developments is set out in R. Schifter, 'Human Rights at the United Nations: The South Africa Precedent', *American University Journal of International Law and Policy* 8 (1993), 361–72.

[52] Resolution 2202(XXI), 16 December 1966.

[53] Resolution 556, 23 October 1984.

[54] Opened for signature under General Assembly resolution 3068 (XXVIII) of 30 November 1973. The resolution was adopted by 91 votes in favour and 26 abstentions. Portugal, South Africa, the United Kingdom, and the United States voted against the resolution. The opposition of the United States was expressed in terms of the redundancy of the Convention which was 'not necessary in view of the broad, all-inclusive provisions' of the ICERD: cited in I. Brownlie (ed.), *Basic Documents in Human Rights* (3rd edn, Clarendon Press, 1992), p. 162. 109 States have become parties to the Convention, but major Western States, including France, Germany, the Scandinavian States and Finland, Italy, Spain, the UK, and the USA remain outside; the State of

Article I of the Apartheid Convention declares apartheid to be an international crime; Article II provides that, for the purpose of the Convention,

the term 'the crime of apartheid' which shall include similar policies and practices of racial segregation and discrimination as practised in southern Africa, shall apply to the following inhuman acts committed for the purpose of establishing and maintaining domination by one racial group of persons over any other racial group of persons and systematically oppressing them.

The 'inhuman acts' criminalized in the Apartheid Convention carry over resonances from the Convention on the Prevention and Punishment of the Crime of Genocide—the references to murder, deliberate imposition of living conditions designed to cause physical destruction in whole or in part, etc. The Apartheid Convention also adds such infringements of rights as arbitrary arrests, denial of participation rights and development, labour exploitation, persecution of opponents of apartheid, as well as any measures, including legislative measures

designed to divide the population along racial lines by the creation of separate reserves and ghettos for the members of a racial group or groups, the prohibition of mixed marriages among members of various racial groups, the expropriation of landed property belonging to a racial group or groups or to members thereof.[55]

International criminal responsibility is stated to apply, 'irrespective of the motive involved', to individuals, members of organizations and institutions, and to representatives of the State, 'whether residing in the territory of the State in which the acts are perpetrated or in some other State',[56] who 'commit, participate in, directly incite or conspire to commit the crime'; directly abetting, encouraging, or cooperating in the commission of the crime of apartheid is also criminalized.[57] While the primary reference is to South Africa, the Convention is capable of wider application: parties undertake to adopt the necessary measures 'to suppress as well as to prevent any encouragement of the crime of apartheid and *similar segregationist policies or their manifestations* and to punish persons guilty of that crime'.[58]

The 1977 Additional Protocol I to the Geneva Conventions of 1949 recognizes apartheid as a grave breach of the Protocol without limiting its application to any particular State.[59] Article 7 of the Rome Statute of the International Criminal Court includes 'the crime of apartheid' as a crime against humanity, defining it as 'inhuman acts of a character similar to those referred to in paragraph 1,[60] committed in the context of an

Palestine has become a party to the Convention: <https://treaties.un.org/Pages/ ViewDetails.aspx?src=UNTSONLINE&tabid=2&mtdsg_no=IV-7&chapter=4&lang=en#Participants>.

[55] Article II (d).

[56] Article III.

[57] *Ibid.* Consideration was given in 1980 to the establishment of a special international criminal court to try those accused of apartheid, but no such court was established: commentary by Dugard, <http://legal.un.org/avl/ha/cspca/cspca.html>.

[58] Article IV (a). Present author's emphasis. Article IV (b) includes undertakings to adopt measures to 'prosecute, bring to trial and punish' the guilty persons 'whether or not such persons reside in the territory of the State in which the acts are committed or are nationals of that State or of some other State or are stateless persons'.

[59] Article 85(4)(c).

[60] Para. 1 of Article 7 lists the crimes against humanity including murder, extermination, deportation, etc, 'when committed as part of a widespread or systematic attack directed against any civilian population, with knowledge of the attack'.

institutionalized regime of systematic oppression and domination by one racial group over any other racial group or groups and committed with the intention of maintaining that regime'. Dugard writes that it 'may be concluded that the Apartheid Convention is dead as far as the original cause for its creation—apartheid in South Africa—is concerned, but that it lives on as a species of crime against humanity, under both customary international law and the Rome Statute of the International Criminal Court'.[61]

Apartheid was given a less dramatic definition in the International Convention against Apartheid in Sports, without specific recall of its criminal nature:[62]

> The expression 'apartheid' shall mean a system of institutionalized racial segregation and discrimination for the purpose of establishing and maintaining domination by one racial group of persons over another racial group of persons and systematically oppressing them, such as that pursued by South Africa, and 'apartheid in sports' shall mean the application of the policies and practices of such a system in sports activities, whether organized on a professional or an amateur basis.[63]

On the other hand, the preamble to the Apartheid in Sports Convention interrelates its provisions with those of the Apartheid Convention in providing that, in line with the latter, participation in sports exchanges with teams selected on the basis of apartheid, 'directly abets and encourages the commission of the crime of apartheid'.

International action for the elimination of apartheid was a staple item of the first two international decades against racism and racial discrimination, wherein apartheid was also condemned in a succession of international conferences. The First and Second World Conferences against Racism and Racial Discrimination were dominated by the question of apartheid—'the extreme form of institutionalized racism'[64]—under the 'racist regimes in Southern Africa',[65] with questions regarding Israel and the Palestinians emerging as a second principal motif. In the post-apartheid era, the Durban Declaration recalls that apartheid constitutes a crime against humanity and is a major source and manifestation of racism, racial discrimination, xenophobia and related intolerance, affirming that acts of apartheid, 'wherever and whenever they occurred . . . must be condemned and their recurrence prevented'.[66] The Durban Conference, according to the preamble to its Declaration and Programme of Action, drew inspiration from, *inter alia*, 'the heroic struggle of the people of South Africa against the institutionalized system of *apartheid*'. Apartheid recedes into the background in the final document of the Durban Review Conference of 2009, which includes, however, the poignant recall that 'slavery and the slave trade, including the transatlantic slave trade, apartheid, colonialism and genocide must never be forgotten'.[67]

[61] J. Dugard, Commentary on the Convention against Apartheid, UN Audiovisual Library of International Law, <http://untreaty.un.org/cod/avl/ha/cspca/cspca.html>.

[62] Adopted by General Assembly resolution 40/64, 10 December 1985.

[63] Article 1(a).

[64] Declaration of the First World Conference against Racism, para. 4.

[65] The phrase, with variations thereon, recurs in the documents of the two World Conferences. The Declaration(s) and Programme(s) of action of the first two World Conferences against Racism and Racial Discrimination in 1978 and 1983 are reproduced in UN Doc. E/CN.4/1999/WG.1/BP.1, 9 March 1999, part of a compilation prepared by the UN Secretariat for the (Durban, 2001)) World Conference against Racism, Racial Discrimination, Xenophobia and Related Intolerance.

[66] Durban Declaration, para. 15.

[67] Para. 62. Explicit reference to apartheid does not figure on the mandate of the Special Rapporteur on Racism under Human Rights Council 7/34, whereas it did in the initial mandate under Commission on Human Rights Resolution 1993/20. The latest mandate incorporates references to the Durban documentation.

B. *Travaux Préparatoires*

The Declaration on the Elimination of Racial Discrimination invests heavily in condemning apartheid and segregation. The preamble associates practices of segregation with colonialism, and expresses alarm at manifestations of racial discrimination imposed by governments 'in the form, *inter alia*, of apartheid, segregation and separation'. Article 5 declares that an end shall be put without delay 'to governmental and other public policies of racial segregation and especially policies of apartheid, as well as all forms of racial discrimination and separation resulting from such policies.' Phrases from the Declaration are taken up in the preamble to the Convention and find their way into Article 3. While the targets of the Declaration are ultimately wider than apartheid and (Western) colonialism, the pinpointing of these two systems as primary sources of racial discrimination is explicit.

In the drafting of the Convention, a text providing for the ending of racial segregation and especially apartheid was proposed in the Sub-Commission by Abram:[68]

> Each State party shall put an end without delay to governmental and other public policies of racial segregation and especially policies of apartheid, as well as all forms of racial discrimination and separation resulting from such policies.

A working group text was subsequently prepared[69] and then orally amended to the following: 'States parties particularly condemn racial segregation and apartheid and undertake to prevent, prohibit and eradicate, in territories subject to their jurisdiction, all practices of this nature.'[70] The phrase 'in territories subject to their jurisdiction' was suggested by Abram,[71] to which Calvocoressi replied that 'since apartheid could be interpreted as applying exclusively to the situation in South Africa, . . . Mr. Abram's amendment would help to make it clear that States were not being obligated to act in any areas which were not subject to their jurisdiction'.[72]

The text was discussed in the Commission at its 789th and 790th meetings. Two oral amendments were submitted, the first of which, by the United States, was to replace 'racial segregation and apartheid' by 'racial segregation, apartheid and anti-Semitism'.[73] The USSR proposed a sub-amendment to that of the US, adding 'nazism' after 'apartheid', and the words 'and other expressions of hatred based on doctrines of racial superiority' after 'anti-Semitism'.[74] The discussions, echoed elsewhere in the drafting process, evinced strong disagreement as to which were the most general, localized, permanent, enduring, or temporary manifestations of racial discrimination. The representative of The Netherlands opposed the reference to apartheid because it was 'only a temporary phenomenon and it was practised in only one State'.[75]

While anti-Semitism was widely condemned by representatives, the question of whether it should be included in a lexicon of base forms of discrimination for Article 3 purposes drew forth contradictory suggestions as to which forms of racial discrimination

[68] E/CN.4/Sub.2/L.308, Article III, para. 2.
[69] E/CN.4/Sub.2/L.338.
[70] E/CN.4/Sub.2/241, para. 71. The draft article was adopted unanimously: *ibid.*, para. 72.
[71] E/CN.4/Sub.2/SR.425, p. 3.
[72] E/CN.4/Sub.2/SR.425, p. 3.
[73] E/3873; E/CN.4/874, para. 138.
[74] *Ibid.*, para. 139.
[75] E/CN.4/SR.789, p. 11.

were closest in category (*ejusdem generis*) to apartheid. In the view of the representative of the US, anti-Semitism 'was an evil which should be mentioned side by side with apartheid and which was far from having disappeared after the Second World War'.[76] A substantial statement by a representative of the Agudas Israel World Organization that included a peroration on anti-Semitism in Germany, argued for the inclusion of a reference to anti-Semitism on the basis that, although it 'could possibly be said that anti-Semitism was included in the general condemnation of all racial discrimination',[77] it took many forms, some of which could easily escape legal formulae.[78] Additionally,

> the Jewish people were entitled to expect that, less than thirty years after the adoption of the Nuremberg laws, and less than five years after a new wave of neo-nazi propaganda, there would be an open and unambiguous condemnation of anti-Semitism in an international convention. Justice demanded that the evils of anti-Semitism should be considered no less important than those of apartheid.[79]

Contrary arguments were put forward by the USSR: comparing apartheid and anti-Semitism, the representative stated that the former was 'a general form of racial discrimination, which might be applied at any period and against any race. The latter was merely one manifestation of racial discrimination in a particular case.'[80] A possible (improbable?) consequence of including a reference to anti-Semitism was dramatized by the representative of the United Kingdom who observed that the draft article 'condemned not only racial segregation and apartheid, but also all practices of that nature', and, if anti-Semitism were included, it would be far from clear what prevention of the practice might involve: 'Would it then follow that States should . . . prohibit the publication of such works as those of Nietzsche and Schopenhauer?'[81]

Opinion against including a reference to anti-Semitism in Article 3 was based ostensibly on the sense that it did not easily 'fit' with segregation and apartheid, perceived as closely interrelated. Hence, according to the representative of Ecuador, the draft article dealt 'not with racial discrimination in general, but with segregation. The mention of apartheid was justified because the word . . . meant separation. Anti-Semitism, on the other hand, should be condemned in connection with discrimination in general'.[82] The representative of the USSR argued that anti-Semitism was a manifestation of discrimination against one particular race, whereas apartheid might be applied at any person and against any race.[83] The US amendment to Article 3 on anti-Semitism was withdrawn at the 790th meeting of the Commission.[84]

The phrase 'in territories subject to their jurisdiction' was the subject of discussion in light of critical remarks by the representative of the USSR regarding past attempts by

76 *Ibid.*, p. 10.

77 E/CN.4/SR.789, p. 9.

78 Including 'ethnological anti-Semitism' (Wilhelm Marr), 'metaphysical anti-Semitism' (Schopenhauer), and 'ethical anti-Semitism' (Nietzsche)—the last-named 'had probably been the spiritual father of the Nazi conception of the *Herrenvolk*': E/CN.4/SR.789, pp. 9–10.

79 E/CN.4/SR.789, pp. 8–10.

80 *Ibid.*, p. 12.

81 *Ibid.*, p. 11.

82 E/CN.4/SR.789,p. 10. He later added, *ibid.*, p. 12, that anti-Semitism was a form of discrimnation in general and not of segregation.

83 E/CN.4/SR.789, p. 12.

84 E/CN.4/874, para. 142.

colonial powers to expand their 'jurisdiction' beyond their own territory to include lands seized by them.[85] However, others argued that, as long as colonial and non-self-governing territories existed, 'the powers responsible for administering them were obligated to eliminate racial segregation and discrimination, and, in particular, apartheid in those territories',[86] and that 'signatories of the Convention assumed responsibility under Article III for eliminating racial discrimination there [the non-self-governing territory] as well as in the metropolitan country'.[87]

The text before the Third Committee read as follows:

States parties particularly condemn racial segregation and *apartheid* and undertake to prevent, prohibit and eradicate all practices of this nature in territories subject to their jurisdiction.[88]

Only one amendment was submitted to replace the expression 'subject to' by 'under' their jurisdiction.[89] Article III, as modified by the amendment, was unanimously adopted by the Committee.[90] Discussion was limited mainly to questions of language in translation, with a preference expressed by the representatives of France and Morocco for the replacement of '*placés sous*' by '*relevant de*';[91] according to the representative of Morocco, the term '*placés sous*' 'called to mind a trusteeship arrangement'.[92] At the time of the drafting of the Convention, arguments regarding extraterritorial application of the Convention had not taken their current form.[93] The 'outreach' elements under discussion related to colonial situations and are suffused with references to 'non-self-governing territories', 'administering powers', 'decolonization', etc. The remarks of the USSR suggest a fear that, in colonial situations, the asserted responsibilities of colonial powers would not easily detach themselves from assertions of rights.

The representative of Nigeria in the Third Committee later returned to the apartheid issue in discussing the forms of racial discrimination:

It had been claimed that the reference to apartheid in Article 3 . . . justified explicit references to other forms of racial discrimination. But apartheid was not only racial discrimination of the most violent kind; it differed from other forms in that it was the official policy of a State Member of the United Nations. The South African government had never denied the existence of that flagrant form of racial discrimination . . . its nature and consequences were no longer a matter of controversy. Since no other country had instituted that form of racial discrimination, the reference to apartheid was directed exclusively to the Government of South Africa.[94]

This and other remarks reveal an inconsistency as to whether the reference to apartheid in Article 3 was exclusive to South Africa or had wider significance. Schwelb recalls that

[85] E/CN.4/SR.790, p. 4: he added that colonial powers had no sovereign rights over such territories 'and the convention should not appear to grant them'.

[86] Remarks of the representative of Lebanon, E/CN.4/SR.790, p, 5.

[87] Remarks of the representative of Ecuador, E/CN.4/SR.790, p. 5. The representative of Dahomey, *ibid*., observed that there had been numerous precedents for a colonial power undertaking to extend the application of a Convention to territories under its jurisdiction; he could not understand why the reference to territories subject to the jurisdiction of the States parties 'should alarm the USSR representative'.

[88] A/6181, para. 57.

[89] A/C.3/L.1226 and Corr. 1.

[90] A/6181, para. 59.

[91] A/C.3/SR.1308, paras 43 and 44.

[92] *Ibid*., para. 44.

[93] See Chapter 8 on Article 2 of ICERD.

[94] A/C.3/SR.1313, para. 18.

South Africa 'did not participate in the debate or in any of the roll-call votes relating to the Convention in committee or in plenary'.[95] Article 3 was adopted unanimously by the Third Committee.[96] The drafting of Article 3 was completed three days before the vote to exclude references to specific forms of racial discrimination.[97]

C. Practice

I. Reservations and Declarations

As might be expected from the association in Article 3 between the crime of apartheid and the concept of segregation, and in light of their international history, reservations to Article 3 have tended to be fragmentary and indirect, limited and cautious.[98] The reservations by Fiji regarding the school system,[99] which implicated, *inter alia*, Article 3, were withdrawn in 2012. The US reservation with regard to private conduct specifically recalls Article 3 though segregation is not its focal point: the reservation is based on the broader distinction in the Convention between private and public life. The reservation by Turkey confining obligations to the 'national territory where the Constitution and the legal and administrative order of the Republic of Turkey are applied', and the Committee's invitation to withdraw it, were discussed earlier in this work in connection with Article 2;[100] the reservation is not directed to any specific article but applies to the Convention as a whole.

II. Guidelines

Reporting guidelines for Article 3 are reasonably extensive and include recall of general recommendations (GRs);[101] the immediately previous guidelines were short.[102] The present guidelines elaborate the point made in GR 19 that, while the reference to apartheid may have been directed exclusively to South Africa, the anti-segregation norm applies to all countries. Therefore information is requested on segregation practices 'in territories under the jurisdiction of the reporting State', in particular 'in cities where residential patterns may result from multiple discrimination based on low income and race, colour, descent or national or ethnic origin'.[103] Information on monitoring of trends that can give rise to 'racial segregation and ghettoization' is also requested,[104] as well as on measures to avoid as much as possible the segregation of groups and individuals protected

[95] E. Schwelb, *The International Convention on the Elimination of All Forms of Racial Discrimination*, *ICLQ* 15 (1966), 996–1068, 1021.

[96] At its 1308th meeting, A/6181, para. 59.

[97] A/6181, para. 7; A/C.3/SR.1312 and 1313.

[98] <https://treaties.un.org/pages/ViewDetails.aspx?src=TREATY&mtdsg_no=IV-2&chapter=4&lang=en>.

[99] The Committee noted that the reservation was inherited from colonial times and invited Fiji to withdraw it: A/58/18, para. 81; also A63/18, para. 164.

[100] Chapter 8. In concluding observations on the initial report of Turkey, CERD encouraged the State party to consider withdrawing the reservation and declarations, 'including removal of the territorial limitation to the Application of the Convention': A64/18, p. 97, para. 8. See the further discussion of reservations in Chapter 18.

[101] CERD/C/2007/1.

[102] HRI/GEN/2/Rev.4, p. 56. A footnote to the earlier guidelines (p. 53) recalls their revision in 2000 that, *inter alia*, eliminated the request for information on the status of relations with the racist regimes of southern Africa.

[103] Para. 1.

[104] Para. 2.

under the Convention—Roma, descent-based communities, and non-citizens are specifically mentioned—particularly in the areas of education and housing.[105]

III. Particularly Condemn

The Declaration on the Elimination of Racial Discrimination comprehensively condemned 'colonialism and all practices of segregation and discrimination associated therewith',[106] and found that 'any doctrine of racial differentiation or superiority' to be 'morally condemnable',[107] and condemned racial discrimination in general terms.[108] Article 3 of the Convention takes on these sentiments and adds heightened language to the condemnations elsewhere in the text, including the fourth preambular paragraph on 'colonialism and all practices of segregation and discrimination associated therewith', and its moral condemnation of racial theory in paragraph 6. Article 2(1) recites that 'States parties condemn racial discrimination', and Article 4 commences with a similar condemnation of 'all propaganda and all organizations which are based on ideas or theories of superiority', etc. It may be supposed that the targeting of segregation and apartheid draws attention to their special heinousness in the eyes of the drafters, in line with the long-term and severe condemnation by the international community of the international crime of apartheid. The severe language of the Convention suggests that States parties apply heightened scrutiny to manifestations of the conduct stigmatized by Article 3 in its public and private manifestations, and take effective action against it. The 'condemnations' also have an ethnical resonance in identifying impermissible practices in stark terms.

IV. Segregation

As observed, practice regarding racial 'segregation' has not always been evident, in part because the phenomenon has often been subsumed under other Articles of the Convention; further obfuscation derives from the close relationship between segregation and apartheid, phenomena that are not generally disentangled in concluding observations. Partly on account of the amount of attention devoted by the Committee to apartheid, it took time before a clear Committee statement emerged to give weight to the reference to segregation, beginning with the obligation to report on it. Banton observes that in CERD's treatment of reports by States parties, before the examination of the reports of Sweden and Germany in 1989, Article 3 was regarded as exclusively directed to apartheid.[109] In Committee proceedings, Banton, as a member of the Committee, referred to the obligation to report on situations such as residential segregation of foreign workers and to monitor them in case they resulted in racial discrimination. In examining the German report, he observed that in the Federal Republic

> there were residential and other concentrations of foreign workers that in any statistical analysis would fit the pattern of separation on segregation—even self-segregation . . . That form of segregation was certainly not imposed by the authorities . . . but Article 3 of the Convention nevertheless required the State party to report on it.[110]

[105] Para. 3.
[106] Fourth paragraph of the preamble. See the more detailed discussions of the Declaration in Chapters 3 and 5.
[107] Fifth paragraph of the preamble.
[108] Article 1.
[109] Banton, *International Action*, pp. 200–02.
[110] CERD/C/SR.844, para. 62.

Members of CERD took different views on the scope of the phrase 'practices of this nature' with regard to segregation. In committee, Banton summarized their positions:

> The Committee was divided on the scope to be given to Article 3 . . . under which States parties condemned segregation and apartheid and undertook to eradicate practices of that 'nature'. For some, who subscribed to a narrow interpretation, practices of that 'nature' meant cases where segregation was applied by the State, so that States would not be required to report on other forms of segregation such as residential segregation. For others, who advocated a broader interpretation, segregation took many forms ranging from the kind wholly conceived and practised by the State itself to the kind exemplified by certain religious communities that practised self-segregation.[111]

It is tolerably clear from this last statement that the apartheid model had continued to exert a tidal pull on the interpretation of segregation through its association with State policy. The early interpretation of Article 3 as being essentially concerned with apartheid has not however been sustained by the Committee; the accompanying proposition that segregation must be State-sponsored or 'apartheid-like' has also not been sustained. GR 19,[112] adopted in 1995—the year after South Africa resumed its seat at the UN—addresses both issues and attempts to highlight a discrete conceptual space for the concept of segregation. Commending the adoption of the recommendation, Committee members commented on the importance of States parties moving away from an exclusive concern with apartheid in their reporting on Article 3, bearing in mind the evidence of practices of segregation or analogous forms of discrimination in many countries.[113] Following GR 19, the reading of Article 3 as having the widest ambit is reflected in the standard practice of CERD.

The recommendation strongly emphasizes the importance of the reference to segregation in Article 3, recalling that, while the reference to apartheid therein may have been directed exclusively to South Africa, 'the article as adopted prohibits all forms of racial segregation in all countries'.[114] Paragraph 2 of the recommendation contextualizes the effects of history in recalling the obligation of States parties to rectify current situations of segregation: 'the obligation to eradicate practices of this nature includes the obligation to eradicate the consequences of such practices undertaken or tolerated by previous governments in the State or imposed by forces outside the State'.[115] Paragraph 3 shifts the

[111] CERD/C/SR.850, para. 46.

[112] A/50/18, Annex VII.

[113] CERD/C/SR.1125, paras 92–97, comments by CERD members van Boven, Wolfrum, Yutzis, Ahmadu, Shahi, and Sherifis. Yutzis, *ibid.*, para. 94, remarked on the adoption of GR 19 that South African apartheid could no longer be regarded as the model of racism, bearing in mind the subsequent development of numerous other forms.

[114] GR 19, para. 1. See also the evident concern expressed by members of the Committee regarding the term 'positive segregation', along with 'positive discrimination' in discussing a report by the Former Yugoslav Republic of Macedonia: CERD/C/SR.2365, paras 23, 24, 26, and 31; CERD/C/SR/2366, para. 44; and the concluding observations of the Committee, CERD/C/MKD/CO/8-10, paras 16 and 17, which expressed concern regarding the 'self-segregation' of Roma students. In response, the delegation of the State party stated—CERD/C/SR.2366, para. 50—that 'there was positive discrimination, but no positive segregation in the education system'. For further (critical) comments on 'positive discrimination;' see Chapters 6 and 9 of the present work.

[115] Post-apartheid South Africa was itself a recipient of an expression of concern by the Committee regarding the de facto segregation 'that persists as a legacy of apartheid in spite of the measures the State party has adopted to put an end to this situation, especially regarding the ownership of property, access to finance, and social services such as health, education and housing': CERD/C/ZAF/CO/3, para. 13.

emphasis from direct State-induced segregation towards its indirect and privately produced manifestations:

> The Committee observes that while conditions of complete or partial racial segregation may in some countries have been created by governmental policies, a condition of partial segregation may also arise as an unintended by-product of the actions of private persons. In many cities residential patterns are influenced by group differences in income, which are sometimes combined with differences of race, colour, descent and national or ethnic origin, so that inhabitants can be stigmatized and individuals suffer a form of discrimination in which racial grounds are mixed with other grounds.

The concluding paragraph reinforces the point by affirming that 'a condition of racial segregation can also arise without any initiative or direct involvement by the public authorities', inviting States parties 'to monitor all trends which can give rise to racial segregation, to work for the eradication of any negative consequences that ensue, and to describe any such action in their periodic reports'.

The reference to racial segregation in Article 3 also prompts the question as to whether 'racial' is to be understood narrowly as implicating only the first of the five listed grounds in Article 1 ('race') or in terms of all five (or the four listed grounds in Article 5), plus the 'intersections'. It is tolerably clear that in GR 19 'racial segregation' is understood as implicating all five grounds in Article 1 of the Convention, an impression strengthened by subsequent practice. GR 29 on descent-based discrimination[116] is notable regarding 'racial' segregation in clearly extending the concept to include caste and analogous communities, focusing on segregation of these communities in housing, education, and employment. The account of segregation in GR 29 cuts deep in that the existence of segregation is built into the cluster of criteria for recognizing the existence of descent-based communities. The statement on identifying the communities refers to 'private and public segregation, including in housing and education, access to public spaces, places of worship and public sources of food and water'.[117] Section 3 of GR 29 is devoted to elaborating principles regarding segregation, recommending action to

> (n) Monitor and report on trends which give rise to the segregation of descent-based communities and work for the eradication of the negative consequences resulting from such segregation;
> (o) Undertake to prevent, prohibit and eliminate practices of segregation directed against members of descent-based communities including in housing, education and employment;
> (p) Secure for everyone the right of access on an equal and non-discriminatory basis to any place or service intended for use by the general public;
> (q) Take steps to promote mixed communities in which members of affected communities are integrated with other elements of society and ensure that services to such settlements are accessible on an equal basis for all.

This proposals for action suggest appropriate policies generated by Article 3 in light of the Convention as a whole: monitoring of trends, working towards the elimination of segregation, securing access to public services, and promotion of integration. Issues have

[116] A/57/18, Chapter XI. F.
[117] Para. (a).

been followed up with respect to, for example, India,[118] Nigeria,[119] and Nepal.[120] Segregation of non-citizens is regarded as forbidden by the Convention and is addressed in GR 30 with regard to education and housing as well as in individual concluding observations.[121]

Perhaps the most consistently applied body of practice regarding segregation emerges from the Committee's response to questions regarding the Roma in a range of countries. Practice suggesting segregation of Roma has developed across the spectrum of human rights. Three emblematic areas are: access to places open to the public; education; and housing and residence. In the communications procedure, on the basis of allegations by petitioners that highlighted Article 3, opportunities to elaborate the concept of segregation have presented themselves but have not generally been taken up by the Committee. Identification of Article 3 concerns has been more forthcoming in the reporting procedure under Article 9, though even here, concluding observations have not consistently specified the articles of the Convention deemed to be applicable to the conduct in question.

Article 3 has been invoked by Roma petitioners in Article 14 cases, functioning as part of the background narrative when the Committee's findings are based on other articles. Communications relating to access to spaces open to the public—*Lacko v Slovakia*,[122] *Durmic v Serbia and Montenegro*,[123] and *L.A. v Slovakia*,[124] all of which have a strong component of segregation, are discussed under Article 5(f).[125] In *Koptova v Slovakia*,[126] resolutions of a local authority forbade—to permanent effect—Roma families from entering or settling in a village. In a complex claim, the provisions of Article 3 were invoked to the effect that they 'publicly and formally' referred to the author and other persons 'by their assumed racial/ethnic identity', singled them out for special treatment and thus expressly endorsed 'racial segregation and apartheid'.[127] In finding a violation of Article 5(d)(i) of the Convention, the Committee again made no comment on the claim under Article 3. Other cases raising Article 3 questions include *Z.U.B.S. v Australia*, where the State party rejected a claim of segregation arising from the author's complaint of segregation from English-speaking personnel in a works trip and a training course. The State party responded to this by stating simply that 'there was no system of racial segregation in Australia'.[128] In *D.S. v Sweden*, the complainant alleged discrimination on the basis of national origin and included Article 3 among the grounds of claim. No

[118] CERD/C/IND/CO/19, para. 13, wherein, concerning the Dalits, the State party is advised, *inter alia*, 'to take effective measures against segregation in public schools and residential segregation'.

[119] CERD/C/NGA/CO/18, para. 15, with reference to allegations of 'social exclusion, segregation and mistreatment' of the Osu and similar communities, despite the formal abolition on work and descent-based discrimination by the 1958 Osu Abolition Law.

[120] CERD/C/64/CO/5, para. 12, where the Committee expressed its concern about 'information on the existence of segregated residential areas for Dalits, social exclusion of inter-caste couples, restriction to certain types of employment, and denial of access to public spaces, places of worship and public sources of food and water'.

[121] Paras 31 and 32. For instances, see also concluding observations on Japan, CERD/C/304/Add.114, para. 15; Switzerland, CERD/C/60/CO/14, para. 9; France, CERD/FRA/CO/16, para. 12, explicitly citing GR 30; Ireland, CERD/C/IRL/CO/2, para. 13; Antigua and Barbuda, CERD/C/ATG/CO/9, para. 15.

[122] CERD/C/59/D/11/1998 (2001).

[123] CERD/C/68/D/29/2003 (2006); further discussion in Chapter 4.

[124] CERD/C/85/D/49/2011 (2014).

[125] Chapter 14.

[126] CERD/C/57/D/13/1998 (2000).

[127] Para. 3.1.

[128] CERD/C/55/D/6/1995 (1999), para. 4.4.

further elaboration by the petitioner or the Committee followed and the claim was declared inadmissible for non-exhaustion of domestic remedies.[129]

In the Committee's general statement on discrimination against the Roma—GR 27—segregation is referred to particularly with regard to housing and education. Paragraph 18 of GR 27 refers to preventing and avoiding as much as possible

> the segregation of Roma students, while keeping open the possibility for bilingual or mother-tongue tuition; to this end, to endeavour to raise the quality of education in all schools and the level of achievement in schools by the minority community, to recruit school personnel from among members of Roma communities and to promote intercultural education.

Paragraph 30 recommends the development and implementation of 'policies and projects aimed at avoiding segregation of Roma communities in housing' and the involvement of 'Roma communities and associations as partners together with other persons in housing project construction, rehabilitation and maintenance'. Paragraph 31 refers, *inter alia* and without specific recall of 'segregation', to the practice of placing Roma in camps outside populated areas, isolated and without access to health care and other facilities. The meaning of the foregoing paragraph is illuminated by paragraph 32 calling on States parties to offer camping places for nomadic Roma or travellers, equipped with all necessary facilities. The recommendation adds to the understanding of the wrong of segregation in implying that it is not the mere fact of separation that constitutes the segregation but the stigma associated with deliberate, other-directed placements, dissociated from choices made by the targeted group. Paragraph 33 on equal access for Roma to health care and social security services suggests that lack of such access is also an element in the concept of segregation outlined in the general recommendation. In these contiguous paragraphs we may sense the overlap between segregation and general discrimination, an impression fortified by a reading of the recommendation as a whole.

In the context of a broader span of concerns expressed by the Committee regarding segregation in education, including systems of 'two schools under one roof',[130] court decisions limiting the ability to address de facto segregation,[131] etc, concern over segregation of Roma pupils has generated a stream of recommendations, some expressed in forceful language. In the case of Poland, in 2003 the Committee, while noting the efforts of the State party to meet the educational needs of Roma pupils, expressed concern that 'in some cases these efforts have led to segregated classes having a lower standard of education than the Polish counterparts'.[132] Accordingly, the Committee recommended that 'new programmes integrate Roma children into mainstream schools as far as possible... and... recruit more teachers and teaching assistants from the Roma minority'.[133] In its 2009 dialogue with Poland, CERD welcomed the introduction of Roma teaching assistants and the gradual phasing out of separate education, while noting the high dropout rate of Roma pupils and the disadvantages resulting from lack of facility in the Polish language among Roma children. In this case, the suggested remedies included improved access to mainstream education and increased availability of bilingual education.[134]

[129] CERD/C/53/D/9/1997 (1998).
[130] Bosnia and Herzegovina, CERD/C/BIH/CO/7-8 (2010), para. 11.
[131] USA, CERD/C/USA/CO/6, para. 17.
[132] CERD/C/62/CO/6, para. 12.
[133] *Ibid.*
[134] CERD/C/POL/CO/19, para. 5.

Within the framework of the Committee's antipathy towards separate education provisions for Roma pupils, concern reaches an apogee of sorts over the placement of Roma pupils in 'special schools' or 'special classes' for children with mental disabilities, the selfsame issue that has exercised, *inter alios*, the European Court of Human Rights. In the case of the Czech Republic, following an expression of the Committee's deep concern regarding educational segregation, recommendations included, in the context of putting an end to such practices, a 'review of the methodological tools used to determine the cases in which children are to be enrolled in special schools so as to avoid indirect discrimination against Roma children on the basis of their cultural identity'.[135] Methodology and criteria for placements were also to the fore in conclusions on the Russian Federation that recommended careful review of such, coupled with a reminder of the importance of integration of ethnic minority children into the general education system.[136] Recommendations regarding the situation in Slovakia are also extensive, demanding an end to segregation practices, looking towards assessment of placements in special schools with a view to removing therefrom those pupils without mental disability, proposing a review of admission criteria, and an action plan for desegregation. The Committee also stressed links between educational segregation and discrimination in housing and employment.[137] In the recommendations to Slovakia, as a guide to appropriate policy, CERD adopted a paragraph of the recommendations of the UN Forum on Minority Issues on 'Minorities and the Right to Education' that synthesize a range of current provisions including the UNESCO Convention against Discrimination in Education:[138]

> State or local policies or practices that, *de jure* or *de facto*, result in separate classes or schools for minority pupils, or schools or classes with grossly disproportionately high numbers of minority pupils, on a discriminatory basis, are prohibited... In particular, the misuse of psychological or learning ability tests for enrolment of children in primary schools must be subjected to close scrutiny with respect to their potential to engender discriminatory outcomes. The creation and development of classes and schools providing education in minority languages should not be considered impermissible segregation, if the assignment to such classes and schools is of a voluntary nature. However, where separate educational institutions are established for minorities for linguistic, religious or cultural reasons, no barriers should be erected to prevent members of minority groups from studying at general educational institutions, should they or their families so wish.[139]

Later CERD recommendations continue the segregation theme under the general rubric of 'continued de facto segregation in the education system', with reference to 'the practice of Roma only schools or classes'.[140] The State party was recommended to take all necessary measures to eradicate segregation of Roma children in the school system, 'ensure that they enjoy equal opportunities to access to quality education'; as well as providing

> [f]or ways and means to eliminate overrepresentation of Roma students in specialized classes by addressing the root causes of the practice and... integrate them into mainstream education...

[135] CERD/C/CZE/CO/7, para. 17.

[136] CERD/C/RUS/CO/19, para. 27; compare Estonia, CERD/C/EST/CO/8-9, para. 17.

[137] CERD/C/SVK/CO/6-8, para. 16.

[138] *Ibid.*

[139] A/HRC/10/11/Add.1, para. 27.

[140] CERD expressed concern at information that Roma children were 'dramatically over-represented in special classes and special schools for children with intellectual disability': CERD/C/SVK/CO/9-10, para. 11.

increase human and financial resources for the education of Roma, in addition to organizing training on Roma rights for teachers and social personnel.[141]

As regards residential segregation, cases involving Roma have been in the forefront of the Committee's reflections, even if the leading CERD case on housing, *L.R. v Slovakia*, does not specifically address Article 3.[142] Critical descriptions nonetheless abound in the practice of the Committee of such as the isolation of Roma communities 'in ghetto-like neighbourhoods',[143] placing Roma in camps outside populated areas that are isolated and without access to health-care facilities,[144] of de facto segregation and forced evictions or expulsions,[145] and of grim housing conditions in segregated neighbourhoods.[146] The concerns extend to such policies as the construction of housing units to be occupied predominantly by Roma; in the view of the Committee, a policy that might be acceptable in the short term but was likely to perpetuate segregation in the long term.[147] Preferred remedies and approaches include—besides the elimination of bad practices, greater clarity of legal regulation in the sphere of housing and compliance with law,[148] and research into overall situations,[149] the involvement of Roma communities as partners in housing projects,[150] projects conducive to the facilitation of social inclusion,[151] close attention to the work of housing agencies,[152] and provision of alternative housing whenever forced evictions take place.[153] The Roma cases stand out as heightened cases of segregation in particular fields.

The Committee has also expressed concern for segregation in general contexts without specifying particular ethnic or other groups. Article 3 was cited by the Committee in the context of the system of ethnic federalism in Ethiopia as potentially leading to ethnic tensions.[154] Following the terms of GR 19, recommendations to monitor all tendencies that give rise to segregation have been issued on many occasions, as have recommendations to take appropriate legislative and other action. De facto segregation is currently of as much concern to CERD as policy-driven forms of segregation.[155] As with other aspects of discrimination, the Committee has not been impressed by claims that there is no need to take action in relation to Article 3 because racial discrimination is claimed by a State party to be unknown in its territory.[156]

[141] *Ibid.*

[142] CERD/C/66/D/31/2003 (2005). The petitioner instead chose to argue the case on Articles 2, 4, 5, and 6, with the Committee's disposition of the case resting on Article 2, 5, and 6. With regard to the housing element, the case is more fully discussed in Chapter 14; see also Chapter 8.

[143] Concluding observations on Slovakia, CERD/C/65/CO/7, para. 10.

[144] Concluding observations on Italy, CERD/C/ITA/CO/15, para. 14.

[145] Many references including in concluding observations on the Czech Republic, CERD/C/CZE/CO/7, para. 16; on Slovakia, CERD/C/SVK/CO/6-8, para. 17.

[146] Slovakia, *ibid.*

[147] Concluding observations on the Czech Republic, CERD/C/63/CO/4, para. 13.

[148] Concluding observations on the Czech Republic, CERD/C/CZE/CO/7, para. 16.

[149] Concluding observations on Estonia, CERD/C/EST/CO/8-9, para. 17.

[150] Concluding observations on Italy, CERD/C/ITA/CO/15, para. 14.

[151] *Ibid.*

[152] Concluding observations on Germany, CERD/C/DEU/CO/18, para. 17.

[153] Concluding observations on the Russian Federation, Russia, CERD/C/RUS/CO/19, para. 26.

[154] CERD/C/ETH/CO/15, para. 16.

[155] Among many possible examples, see references to socially based segregation issues intimated in concluding observations on Barbados, CERD/C/BRB/CO/16, para. 13.

[156] Concluding observations on Qatar, CERD/C/60/CO/11, para. 8.

V. Apartheid

It has been noted earlier that, in the earlier stages of CERD's work, State reports regarding Article 3 focused exclusively on apartheid, to the exclusion of consideration of how the other elements in the Article might be addressed. This approach stems in part from early CERD recommendations, etc, regarding relations between States parties and South Africa. GR 3—'concerning reporting by States parties'[157]—influenced the manner in which States parties reported on their implementation of Article 3. The resolution links domestic/internal action under the article with required action at the international level, expressing the view 'that measures adopted on the national level to give effect to the provisions of the Convention are interrelated with measures taken on the international level to encourage respect everywhere for the principles of the Convention'. The recommendation, adopted in 1972, cites UN General Assembly resolution 2784 (XXVI) which called upon 'all the trading partners of South Africa to abstain from any action that constitutes an encouragement to the continued violation of the principles and objectives [of ICERD] by South Africa and the illegal regime in Southern Rhodesia'.[158] Accordingly, the Committee welcomed 'the inclusion in the reports submitted under Article 9 . . . by any State party which chooses to do so, of information regarding the status of its diplomatic, economic and other relations with the racist regimes in southern Africa'. Decision 2(XI) of 1975[159] followed up the general recommendation, declaring forcefully that '[a]ll policies, practices or relations which have the effect of supporting, sustaining or encouraging racist regimes are irreconcilable with the commitment to the cause of the elimination of racial discrimination' inherent in becoming a party to ICERD.[160] States parties should therefore reconsider any such relations.[161]

The Committee, according to a Chairman's statement of 1985, had 'co-ordinated and sustained activities' to combat the terrible scourge of apartheid,[162] with, as recalled by Banton, members insisting that 'action against apartheid had to be one of their highest priorities'.[163] This was despite doubts about the propriety of requesting information from States parties concerning their political relations with the South African regime. Questions to the representatives of Belgium on relations with South Africa from Committee members in 1979 highlight such doubts among member of the Committee and among States parties. Some Committee members pressed questions on relations with South Africa and asserted that CERD could not be denied the right to enquire into the way in which States parties discharged their obligations under Article 3;[164] others took the view that 'legal obligations were limited to territories under the jurisdiction of the States parties'.[165] In response, Belgium asserted that the question of its relations with South Africa 'was highly political in nature' and fell within the competence of the General Assembly, the Security

[157] A/8718, Chapter IX.B.
[158] Fourth paragraph (paragraphs are not numbered).
[159] A/10018, Chapter VII. A. The decision is entitled 'Relations with racist regimes'.
[160] *Ibid.*, para. 1.
[161] *Ibid.*, para. 2.
[162] A/40/18, Annex IV, para. 4.
[163] *International Action*, p. 127.
[164] A/34/18, para. 225.
[165] *Ibid.*

Council, etc.[166] Belgium also clarified that it had not ratified the Convention against Apartheid 'for juridical reasons'.[167]

It is still the case that some reports of States parties on Article 3 simply recall their opposition to the policies of apartheid South Africa, even as the political relations targeted by the early recommendations have become the material of history. GR 19 has not been an entirely successful corrective to these limited approaches. Even States which are 'latecomers' to the Convention are not immune to the attraction of simple historical recall. Thus, the first report of Turkey recalled that:

> [d]uring the *apartheid* regime, no official contact took place between Turkey and South Africa. Turkey has always been actively engaged in the efforts of the United Nations for the elimination of any kind of racism and racial discrimination. It strongly opposed the apartheid regime, and consistently voted for all relevant United Nations resolutions condemning it. This position lasted until it had become clear that apartheid was going to be abandoned and replaced by a democratic government based on majority rule.[168]

The report added that

> Turkey was an active member of the United Nations Council for Namibia and supported every international action against apartheid and colonialism. Turkey also contributed regularly to the United Nations Trust Fund for South Africa and the United Nations Fund for Namibia, of which it was one of the trustees.[169]

A short perusal of relatively recent State reports on Article 3 reveals others in similar vein. Thus, Cameroon 'condemned, at the time, the practice of apartheid in South Africa, which was officially ended when equal votes for all were introduced'.[170] Cuba linked its 'brotherly and internationalist assistance' to Angola with its desire to safeguard Angola from 'the expansionism of the racist apartheid regime of South Africa'.[171] India observed that it had been 'privileged to play a special role in support of the long and difficult struggle to end colonialism and discrimination symbolized by apartheid in Africa, especially South Africa'.[172] Article 3 reports including such information may also add references to the Durban World Conference against Racism and/or recall the adherence of the State party to the Convention against Apartheid and related instruments.[173] In some cases, the recall of apartheid is embedded in a longer discourse on Article 3,[174] whereas in others the reference is offered as a complete account of obligations under the article.

VI. Undertake to Prevent, Prohibit, Eradicate

The obligation to 'prevent, prohibit and eradicate' segregation and similar practices is wide ranging and includes action against both private and public segregation practices. In

[166] A/34/18, para. 231.
[167] *Ibid.*
[168] CERD/C/TUR/3, para. 89.
[169] *Ibid.*, para. 91.
[170] CERD/C/CMR/115-18, para. 116 (2009).
[171] CERD/C/CUB/14-18, para. 120 (2010).
[172] CERD/C/IND/19, para. 55 (2006).
[173] Cameroon, Cuba, and India as immediately above; examples also figure in the reports of Antigua and Barbuda, CERD/C/ATG/9, para. 37 (2006); Cambodia, CERD/C/KHM/18, para. 72 (2009); Democratic Republic of the Congo, CERD/C/COD/15, para. 59 (2006); El Salvador, CERD/C/SLV/14-15, para. 31 (2009); and Ethiopia, CERD/C/ETH/7-16, para. 49 (2009).
[174] The report of The Philippines is a good example, CERD/C/PHL/20, paras 102–15 (2008).

swathes of contemporary manifestations of discrimination and segregation, the emphasis has shifted decisively from public to private modes, from discrimination emanating from State bodies towards failures to regulate the activities of private persons adequately. In terms of the undertakings in Article 3, the obligations are as hard-edged as elsewhere in the Convention: prevention, prohibition, and eradication are obligations replicated, or assumed under alternative terminology, throughout the Convention, in light of the overall project to 'eliminate' all forms of racial discrimination. It is abundantly clear from the Committee's archive that segregation issues arise frequently in the private sector. Segregation implicating State bodies is also in evidence and does not necessarily take drastic forms such as administrative territorial zoning or explicit racial classification: State provision in the field of education has generated numerous expressions of concern. The fulfilment of obligations—'undertakings'—under Article 3 requires, as does Article 2 more generally, self-scrutiny of State or State-sponsored actions as well as scrutiny of private, including corporate, bodies. In view of the special opprobrium among the canons of discrimination that attaches to segregation and apartheid, the necessary scrutiny, appraisal, and remedial action for segregation situations amount to a particularly demanding portfolio of obligations.

VII. All Practices of this Nature

Article 3 of the Convention requires States parties to address 'all practices of this nature'; that is, of the 'nature' of segregation or in the nature of apartheid. The span of segregation practices identified in the work of CERD is already wide, and GR 19 has been crucial in extending the range of applicability of the article to manifold cases of private action. It is not clear from the work of the Committee what might amount to 'segregation-like' practices that is not already segregation. Similarly, the fundamental question to be answered in the current world order is what constitutes apartheid rather than what constitutes a practice in the nature of apartheid. The implications of what counts as apartheid have not been explored by CERD to the extent they have been for segregation. The potential to elaborate the former concept disjunctively has not been realized in view of its umbilical attachment to the ostensibly broader concept of segregation, neither concept being defined in the Convention.

Taking together, the definitions of apartheid in the Apartheid Convention and the Statute of the International Criminal Court (ICC), apartheid, wherever found, may be defined to involve domination of a racial group or groups by others, the commission of inhuman acts, linked to a systematic, institutionalized process of domination. Falk applies the prohibition of apartheid to racial practices where 'a dual structure of rights and duties are imposed by . . . law on a subordinated people'.[175] The requirement in the Apartheid Convention of systematic oppression over a range of dehumanizing actions, combined with the criteria in the ICC Statute of scale, knowledge, system, and intention, together set the bar high for the identification of apartheid regimes or addressing individual culpability. The characterization of a system as apartheid or apartheid-like appears in part comparative and historical in light of the reference in the Apartheid Convention to

[175] *Report of the Special Rapporteur on . . . Human Rights in the Palestinian Territories Occupied since 1967*, A/65/331, 30 August 2010, para. 5. See also A/HRC/14/17, Special Rapporteur Dugard, paras 58–62, recommending an advisory opinion from the ICJ on whether Israeli practices in the Occupied Territories amounted to apartheid or colonialism.

'similar policies and practices' to those of the former South Africa. However, among the listed instances of inhuman acts,[176] such practices as dividing the population along racial lines through the creation of reserves and ghettos, the prohibition of mixed marriages, and expropriation of landed property, appear, when integrated into an overall system of racial domination, closest to the heart of a regime appropriately described as apartheid.

While the practice of the Committee has shed little light on what constitutes an apartheid regime under current circumstances, attention has focused on the situation in Israel, particularly with regard to the Occupied Territories. Following its 2007 dialogue with Israel, CERD noted 'with deep concern that separate "sectors" are maintained for Jewish and Arab persons, in particular in the area of housing and education and that according to some information, such separation results in unequal treatment and funding';[177] the State party was invited to assess the extent to which the maintenance of such sectors may amount to racial discrimination.[178] An extensive rejection of the Committee's position was offered by Israel,[179] according to which 'the term "sector" ... is used solely for distinguishing between the different religion-related populations. The term does not bear any legal implications nor does it reflect any kind of unequal treatment in the form of separation.'[180] This was followed by extensive citations of Israeli case law, an account of the existence of mixed communities, and intercultural initiatives. Other forms of segregation attracting the attention of the Committee included potential exclusions from State-controlled land in Israel,[181] whilst a number of paragraphs on the Occupied Palestinian Territories state concerns in relation to the construction of the Wall and on restrictions on freedom of movement.[182]

Concluding observations in 2012 on the Occupied Territories draw attention to 'two entirely separate legal systems and sets of institutions for Jewish communities grouped in illegal settlements ... and Palestinian populations living in Palestinian towns and villages'; reference is also made to 'the hermetic character of the separation', all of which led to the Committee's conclusion regarding practices 'which violate ... Article 3 of the Convention'.[183] In response, Israel referred to the dialogue with the Committee and the challenge in the State party's opening statement to 'any spurious claim regarding apartheid or racial segregation in Israel'.[184] The Committee has made an unusually high number of references to Article 3 in concluding observations on the territories occupied by Israel,[185] employing the language of grave concern or deep concern and, more unusually, as a violation, though without individuating the elements of the article.[186] In a separate recommendation, the State party's concept of 'demographic balance' is also challenged

[176] The language of Article 2 of the Apartheid Convention suggests that the listed acts are illustrative and not exhaustive.

[177] CERD/C/ISR/CO/13, para. 22. This observation concerned the situation within Israel, not the Occupied Territories. See the discussion of territoriality issues in Chapter 8.

[178] *Ibid.*

[179] CERD/C/ISR/CO/13/Add.1.

[180] *Ibid.*, para. 19.

[181] CERD/C/ISR/CO/13, para. 23.

[182] *Ibid.*, paras 33 and 34.

[183] CERD/C/ISR/CO/14-16, para. 24.

[184] A/68/18, Annex VII, para. 12.

[185] CERD/C/ISR/CO/14-16, paras 24, 25, 26, and 27.

[186] CERD/C/ISR/CO/14-16, para. 24.

under, *inter alia*, Article 3.[187] In a vigorous response, Israel referred to its opening statement and reply 'which strongly challenged any spurious claim regarding apartheid or racial segregation in Israel. Use of these terms or descriptions is tenacious and inappropriate',[188] a statement supplemented with further detail and the claim that the State party's information and arguments were not properly addressed by the Committee.[189]

VIII. Territories Under their Jurisdiction

As noted in the present commentary on Article 2, whereas that article makes no reference to either territory or jurisdiction, Article 3 refers to both. It was also noted that the jurisdiction reach of ICERD has been interpreted broadly in practice, with an emphasis on the notion of its extension through effective control, a conception broadly endorsed by other international bodies.[190] In the case of the ICCPR, the Human Rights Committee reads the comparable obligation of a State party in Article 2(1) to respect and ensure Covenant rights to individuals 'within its territory and subject to its jurisdiction' in liberal fashion:[191]

> This means that a State party must respect and ensure the rights laid down in the Covenant to anyone within the power or effective control of that State party, even if not situated within the territory of the State party . . . This principle also applies to those within the power or effective control of the forces of a State party acting outside its territory, regardless of the circumstances in which such power or effective control was obtained.[192]

The provision is in effect read disjunctively, with 'territory' not being allowed to trump 'jurisdiction' taken broadly.

With regard to ICERD, Ruggie reports that:

> [t]he territorial limitation set out in Article 3 applies to specific types of racial discrimination, namely racial segregation and apartheid. The Convention is silent as to whether any territorial limitation exists in relation to other forms of racial discrimination. One could thus conclude that

[187] *Ibid.*, para. 25. Further paragraphs in the concluding observations (paras 26 and 27) invoke Article 3 along with other articles.

[188] A/68/18/Annex VII, Comments of States Parties on the Concluding Observations adopted by the Committee, Comment of Israel, para. 12. Opening statement of the delegation of Israel in CERD/C/SR.2131.

[189] In a wealth of literature on whether the situation in the Occupied Territories may be characterized as apartheid and not merely occupation, see J. Dugard and J. Reynolds, 'Apartheid, International Law and the Occupied Palestinian Territory', *EJIL* 24 (2013), 867–913. At the 2012 CERD dialogue with Israel, the case for a clear characterization by CERD of the situation in the Occupied Territories as one of apartheid was made in an oral briefing to the Committee: available at <http://tbinternet.ohchr.org/_layouts/treatybodyexternal/SessionDetails1.aspx?SessionID=397&Lang=en>. See also V. Tilley, *Beyond Occupation: Apartheid, Colonialism and International Law in the Occupied Palestinian Territories* (Pluto Press, 2012); some sixty-one pages, canvassing pro and contra opinions, are devoted to the apartheid analogy in <http://en.wikipedia.org/wiki/Israel_and_the_apartheid_analogy>.

[190] See Chapter 8.

[191] 'The text of Article 2(1) of the ICCPR seems expressly to exclude liability for a State party for acts that occur outside its territory. However the [Human Rights Committee] has taken a liberal approach to the jurisdictional extent of a State's ICCPR obligations': S. Joseph, J. Schultz, and M. Castan, *The International Covenant on Civil and Political Rights* (2nd edn, Oxford University Press, 2004), p. 88.

[192] Human Rights Committee, GC No. 31, *The Nature of the General Legal Obligation Imposed on States Parties to the Covenant* (2004), HRI/GEN/1Rev.9 (vol. I), pp. 242–47, para. 10. See also International Court of Justice, *Armed Activities on the Territory of the Congo (Democratic republic of Congo v Uganda)*, 19 December 2005, *Advisory Opinion on the Legal Consequences of the Construction of a Wall in the Occupied Palestinian Territory*, 9 July 2004, paras. 107–09.

the Convention does not preclude extra territorial jurisdiction. The Committee does not, however, provide any further guidance on either territorial limitations or extra territorial jurisdiction matters.[193]

The lack of guidance referred to by the Special Representative may refer to the absence of a general recommendation rather than an absence of practice with regard to extraterritorial application of the Convention: there is practice, even if not 'guidance' detailing the Committee's reading of principle. In any case, 'territories under their jurisdiction' is less ostensibly restrictive than the ICCPR's 'within its territory and subject to its jurisdiction'. Accordingly, practice under Article 3 merges into the broader CERD archive of applying the Convention extraterritorially, particularly in cases of occupation or control of territory, the 'spatial' extension of the Convention. The Committee's 2012 recommendations to Israel vis-à-vis activities in '[t]he Occupied Palestinian Territory, including East Jerusalem, and the Occupied Golan' furnishes a clear example of the extension of Article 3 to territories under the jurisdiction of a State party but beyond its internationally recognized borders.

D. Comment

The provisions of Article 3 deliver a short lesson in the history and ethics of the Convention, reaching back to its founding impulses in the rejection of the apartheid policy of South Africa, and the rejection of segregation as practised in the US; reflection on these cases is helpful in identifying the 'mischief' in segregation. South Africa had defended its policy of separate development, arguing, *inter alia*, the need for group differentiation in complex, multiracial communities, as a neutral, optimum strategy for achieving social progress.[194] The South African viewpoint was extensively deconstructed by Judge Tanaka in his dissenting opinion in *The South-West Africa cases, Second Phase* (1966),[195] which notably distinguished between imposed systems of separation on racial grounds, and the possibility for groups to cultivate their own religious, educational, or linguistic values as an aspect of their enjoyment of human rights and fundamental freedoms. In the latter category may be included the positive, permissive provisions of the minorities regime of the League of Nations and, for example, the standards for separate educational provision set out in the UNESCO Convention on Discrimination in Education, factored into the preamble to the ICERD. Judge Tanaka concluded that even if some differentiation in the apartheid system could be justifiable,[196] the overall motive was evil,[197] and the necessary logical and material link between difference and different treatment did not exist: apartheid was fundamentally unreasonable and unjust.

[193] *Mapping State obligations for corporate acts: An examination of the UN Human Rights Treaty System, Report No. 1*, prepared for the Special Representative of the Secretary-General on Human Rights and Transnational Corporations and other Business Enterprises (18 December 2006), para. 16.

[194] H.J. Richardson, 'Self-Determination, International Law and the South African Bantustan Policy', *Columbia Journal of Transnational Law* 17 (1978), 185–219.

[195] ICJ Reports 1966, 4, at 284–316. There is a fuller account of the Opinion in P. Thornberry, *International Law and the Rights of Minorities* (Clarendon Press, 1991), pp. 314–18.

[196] For example in the field of separate education and schooling that were equivalent to minority rights provisions; the same could not be said of, for example, the separate use of public facilities.

[197] Judge Tanaka described South African references to 'cultural population groups' as 'dissimulating the underlying racial intention'.

A similar trajectory was followed in the US through rejection in *Brown v the Board of Education*[198] of the doctrine of 'separate but equal' accepted in *Plessy v Ferguson* and subsequent cases.[199] McKean notes that the *Brown* court, unlike Judge Tanaka, did not embark on a lengthy disquisition on the concept of equality but asked whether the segregation of children in public schools solely on the basis of race deprived the children of equal educational opportunities,[200] answering the question in the affirmative. In finding that there was a breach of equality, *Brown* added the poignant note that 'to separate children for others of a similar age and qualifications solely because of their race generates a feeling of inferiority as to their status in the community that may affect their hearts and minds in a way unlikely ever to be undone'.[201] The *Brown* observations on 'status in the community' and 'inferiority' have particular resonance for ICERD, which sets out an uncompromising opposition to doctrines, ideas, and theories of racial or ethnic superiority. Even in the absence of an explicit 'doctrine' of superiority or inferiority, a policy of segregation strongly suggests the taint of group inferiority, attacking dignity through the implication that the group is not fit to belong in the society of others.[202] Comments such as those of the plaintiff in *Lacko* on the 'humiliation and degradation' associated with segregation shed further light on the psychological effects on victims of such a practice.[203]

In light of its emergence from a matrix of argument regarding equality and discrimination, segregation has essentially been regarded as a concentrated form of discrimination through exclusion and the implicit or explicit ranking of populations, the psychology of which may not be far removed from 'ethnic cleansing' though it does not generally take such a drastic form. Apartheid represents a further concentration of the segregation phenomenon, possessing additional characteristics in terms of domination, imposition of hierarchy, assignment of racial identity by fiat, all holistically integrated into a determinate public policy. As observed, neither segregation nor apartheid is defined in the Convention. Following the demise of official apartheid in Africa, clearer specification of the meaning of apartheid has hardly been forthcoming in CERD practice; analyses of the anti-segregation norm, on the other hand, have been delivered in abundance. The lack of definitive, specifying international practice regarding post-South Africa apartheid has not assisted the Committee in the identification of

[198] *Brown v the Board of Education for Topeka County* 347 US 483 (1954); see also *Sweatt v Painter*, 339 US 629 (1950).

[199] 163 US 537, 41 (1893). See the discussion in McKean, *Equality and Discrimination*, pp. 228–57. In relation to Article 1 of the Convention, Meron discusses whether the words 'on an equal footing' would legitimate the 'separate but equal' doctrine, responding that, in addition to the argument that separate facilities are never entirely equal, 'intangible considerations, such as the felling of inferiority or the stigma that attaches to separate facilities for minority groups, are sufficient to render separate and facilities and services unequal, or even inherently unequal'—*Brown v Board of Education* is footnoted—T. Meron, 'The Meaning and Reach of the International Convention on the Elimination of All Forms of Racial Discrimination', *AJIL* 79 (1985), 285–318, 290. See further discussion of the phrase 'on an equal footing' in Chapter 6.

[200] W.A. McKean, *Equality and Discrimination under International Law* (Clarendon Press, 1983), p. 232.

[201] *Ibid.*

[202] J. Waldron, *The Harm in Hate Speech* (Harvard University Press, 2012), esp. Chapters 4 and 5. Article 4(1) of the UNESCO Declaration on Race and Racial Prejudice also hints at the 'mischief' of segregation in providing that '[a]ny restriction on the complete self-fulfilment of human beings and free communication between them which is based on racial or ethnic considerations is contrary to the principle of equality in dignity and rights; it cannot be admitted.'

[203] For a concise and revealing account of the effects of discrimination, see T. Makkonen, *Equal in Law, Unequal in Fact* (Martinus Nijhoff, 2012), pp. 83–90.

contemporary 'apartheid' situations appropriate for condemnation. Further, the listing of apartheid in the infamous canon of crimes against humanity, as a violation of international customary law and of peremptory norms, may be additional factors militating against making overt comparisons between apartheid and the public policies of modern States. In recent practice, while the set of concluding observations regarding the conduct of Israel in the Occupied Territories resorted to Article 3 as part of its general characterization of the governance of the territories, the Committee did not 'split' the article into component parts or make an explicit 'charge' of apartheid against the State party. Any claims of apartheid or racial segregation in Israel were rejected by the State party in unequivocal terms.[204]

Because of its centrality to the historical siting of the Convention as part of an anti-colonial project, a significant number of States still have difficulty in turning Article 3 inwards to address national racial and ethnic issues, preferring instead to trace the external, diplomatic, and historical pathways of their opposition to apartheid and associated evils. While the number of States limiting Article 3 to a recall of policy against apartheid has diminished, the contents of periodic reports continue to suggest a lack of shared appreciation of its scope, as evidenced by the wide variations in the materials canvassed to illustrate the responses of States to the Convention. According to a CERD paper of 2004 related to the Durban process,

> [t]he implementation of States parties' obligations under Article 3 of the Convention has been hindered by the fact that many States parties interpret the scope of the Article as directed exclusively to apartheid in South Africa and fail to examine whether forms of de facto racial segregation are occurring on their own territory. Segregation, as defined in Article 3 of the Convention, still occurs in various forms in a number of States, in particular in housing and education, and its eradication should be considered a matter of priority by all States parties to the Convention.[205]

Many States refer to their legislation on genocide and crimes against humanity as examples of provisions relevant to Article 3; this is still, along with the apartheid-focused reports, the most common response to reporting requirements, an extensive version of which is manifested in reports of Cuba.[206] Programmes of teaching about the Holocaust have also been reported under Article 3.[207] As an alternative to the reports focusing on apartheid and/or crimes against humanity, some States deny any active role for Article 3 in claiming that the legal system excludes racial segregation and that it does not exist in practice within the State, and neither does apartheid,[208] and/or that it has not been necessary to adopt measures—legal, administrative, or judicial—on the basis of the article.[209] Other

[204] A/68/18, Annex VII, comments by Israel, para. 12, supra, n. 188.

[205] Views of the Committee on the Elimination of Racial Discrimination on the Implementation of the International Convention on the Elimination of All Forms of Racial Discrimination and its Effectiveness, E/CN.4/WG.21/10, 17 September 2004.

[206] CERD/C/CUB/14-18, paras 106–11; see also the detailed account of international humanitarian law, CERD/C/PER/118-21, paras 100–2.

[207] Estonia furnishes one such example: CERD/C/EST/8-9, paras 43–5.

[208] Periodic reports of Armenia, CERD/C/ARM/5-6, para. 72; Cambodia, CERD/C/KHM/18, para. 72; El Salvador, CERD/C/SLV/16-17, para. 35; Estonia, CERD/C/EST/10-11, para. 84; Japan, CERD/C/JPN/3-6, para. 36; Lithuania, CERD/C/LTU/4-5, para. 93; Panama, CERD/C/PAN/15-20, para. 23; USA, CERD/C/USA/7-9, para. 34; Uzbekistan, CERD/C/UZB/6-7, para. 330.

[209] Periodic report of Iceland, CERD/C/ISL/20, para. 75.

reports omit any reference to Article 3.[210] In these last cases the omission may be dictated by the structure of the report when, for example, it concentrates on responding to earlier recommendations of CERD; in others, the article is implicitly treated as inapplicable or irrelevant to the situation in the State party.

While a focus on past responses to apartheid, references to crimes against humanity, and denials of the relevance of Article 3 may represent easier routes for reporting States, a gently increasing number have reported on Article 3 in the context of self-critical accounts of their situation, though the specific meaning to be attributed to the article may not be abundantly clear. In the case of Bolivia, sundry events exacerbating racial discrimination and segregation were deemed to fall under Article 3 including the prohibition of indigenous dress, the humiliation of indigenous individuals, physical attacks on human rights defenders, and racist hate speech;[211] a generalized rubric of 'inciting racial segregation, violence, discrimination, and separatism throughout the country' is also utilized, implicating a number of articles in the Convention.[212] Others have endeavoured to find substance in the article by focusing on its implications for regional development,[213] on the importance of free, prior and informed consent for indigenous peoples,[214] and on the situation of migrant communities.[215] States parties have also focused on sectoral discrimination, including education, housing,[216] and the labour market.[217] Issues of integration are raised in a number of reports, and in the case of the UK there is an extensive account of programmes of 'community cohesion'.[218] Romania recalls the importance of CERD GR 19 in framing measures to combat segregation.[219]

Criticism from the Committee based on Article 3 can meet with strong reactions from States parties, even as no particular element in the article is identified as the mischief to be combated. Responding to remarks by CERD, the periodic report of the Dominican Republic referred in somewhat acerbic terms to the 'supposed [by the Committee?] segregation, mainly of the Haitian population confined in sugar mill work camps, is seen as the tropical manifestation of South African apartheid or, earlier, Nazi ghettos'.[220] The report added that the State party subscribed fully to Article 3, and this is why it did 'not possess any ghettos, slums, back alleys, housing estates, public and/or private sites,

[210] Examples include the Report of Nicaragua, CERD/C/NIC/14 (2007); and The Netherlands, CERD/C/NLD/18 (2008).

[211] CERD/C/BOL/17-20, paras 64–5.

[212] *Ibid.*, para. 65.

[213] Report of Iraq, CERD/C/IRQ/15-21, paras 54–5; Morocco, CERD/C/MAR/17-18, paras 93–100.

[214] Report of The Philippines, CERD/C/PHL/20, paras 102–15, citing a range of international instruments commencing with the UN Charter, the equal protection principles in the Constitution of The Philippines, and the manifestation of these obligations and principles in the Indigenous Peoples' Rights Act [IPRA] of 1997.

[215] Report of Ireland, CERD/C/IRL/3-4, paras 205–7.

[216] Report of Romania, CERD/C/ROU/16-19, paras 180–6; the USA, CERD/C/USA/7-9, paras 34–46.

[217] Report of Denmark, CERD/C/DEN/19-19, paras 36–7. Japan recalls the constitutional provision (Article 22(1)) that every person 'shall have freedom to choose and change . . . residence and to choose . . . occupation to the extent that it does not interfere with the public welfare', and the provision (Article 26(1)) that all people 'shall have the right to receive an equal education correspondent to, their ability, as provide by law': CERD/C/JPN/7-9, para. 82.

[218] CERD/C/GBR/18-20, paras 85–102; para. 85 recalls that in UK law (Section 1(2) of the Race Relations Act 1976) segregation on racial grounds is unlawful, adding that: '[n]evertheless, the Government recognises that in order to build a truly cohesive society other, non-legislative, measures are needed.'

[219] CERD/C/ROU/16-19, para. 179. The report of the US echoes the language of GR 19 in referring to 'proper monitoring of all trends that can give rise to racial discrimination': CERD/C/USA/7-9, para. 35.

[220] CERD/C/DOM/13-14, para. 228 (2012).

geographical zones or other kinds of rural or urban settlement designed or employed as a way of segregating people on the basis of their race and/or nationality'; no area was 'exclusively reserved to members of a particular group, to the deliberate exclusion of others'.[221] The segregation paradigm rejected in the statement is that of deliberate, planned exclusion along the lines of an apartheid system: the message of GR 19 regarding informal, private modes of segregation, appears to have been 'lost in translation'. The reaction of Israel to the categorization by the Committee of State policies in the Occupied Territories under Article 3 has already been noted; in that case, the Committee placed strong emphasis on deliberate planned policies and practices.[222]

Article 3 is expressed in condemnatory and prohibitory mode and does not outline a specific policy orientation to countermand racial segregation; GR 19 contents itself with a reference to working towards 'the eradication of any negative consequences' from trends towards such segregation.[223] CERD responses to the State reports on Article 3 frequently focus on promoting integration. While implementation of the Convention as a whole stands as the appropriate response to racial segregation, the Convention grammar and the CERD preference for 'integration' merits interrogation for its relationship to segregation as well as non-discrimination generally. The preamble's stated aversion to 'racial barriers' and the provisions of Article 2(1)(e) encouraging integrationist multiracial organizations and movements are among elements deepening the description of the Convention as an 'integrationist' instrument. As with social inclusion, the committee has not essayed a definition of integration, though its parameters may be approximated from practice in general. In some instances, the term is broadly rendered, hence the recommendation to Canada on the 'integration . . . of African Canadians into Canadian society by effectively ensuring the implementation of its non-discrimination legislation'.[224] More specific accounts of integration are also in evidence. Integration is the recommended strategy for sundry groups protected by the Convention. Recommendations for the integration of non-citizens, refugees, and asylum-seekers represent a constant in CERD practice, perhaps in light of the concept of integration—local integration—as one of the 'durable solutions' for refugees.[225] In light of the collective dimensions of ICERD as a whole, it is notable that the Committee uses the language of 'integration' to describe the integration of groups as well as that of individuals;[226] recommends dialogue with groups to facilitate integration,[227] and their participation in the design and implementation of integration policies.[228]

Integration-related concepts such as social inclusion increasingly surface in State reports. In the case of the Convention, the focus is on ethnic integration and on policies

[221] *Ibid.*, paras 61 and 62. The statements on segregation are backed up by statements in relation to sundry rights including, *ibid.*, para. 194, the right to housing

[222] CERD/C/ISR/CO/14-16, paras 24, 25, and 27; see also paras 11 and 15 regarding Israel's national territory.

[223] Para. 4.

[224] CERD/C/CAN/CO/19-20, para. 16.

[225] R. da Costa (consultant), *Rights of Refugees in the Context of Integration: Legal Standards and Recommendations* (UNHCR, June 2006, POLAS/2006/2)

[226] Concluding observations on Kazakhstan, CERD/C/KAZ/CO/4-5, para. 8; on The Netherlands, CERD/C/64/CO/7, para. 10.

[227] Concluding observations on Georgia, CERD/C/GEO/CO/4-5, para. 15.

[228] Concluding observations on Denmark, CERD/C/DEN/CO/17, para. 22; Greece, CERD/C/GRC/19, para. 16.

of ethnically related social inclusion in order to remedy social exclusion, bearing in mind that social exclusion—and remedial inclusion strategies—may be based on factors other than race/ethnicity.[229] States have accordingly been recommended to 'strengthen the race and cultural dimensions' of a social inclusion agenda.[230] Many recommendations to sustain, develop, or improve inclusion strategies and social development programmes have concentrated to a significant degree on European States parties, in particular regarding Roma inclusion. References to the Decade of Roma Inclusion,[231] and to EU-related policies and programmes, including national action plans for Roma inclusion, surface in CERD recommendations to participating States.[232] The CERD approach to social inclusion is, however, of general scope, implicating all regions and all ICERD-protected groups.[233] Social inclusion is not defined in Committee practice,[234] though it is assumed to be in conformity with such as CERD GR 27 on Discrimination against Roma, and is generally treated as a subset or application of policies of 'integration'. Cyprus was advised to ensure that its national strategy for Roma inclusion did not 'perpetuate the situation of de facto segregation of the Roma community, but rather secure[d] their integration and address[ed] the stigmatization, marginalization and racial discrimination they experience'.[235]

The approach of CERD to social inclusion policies mirrors its approach to development strategies and poverty alleviation programmes in that it stresses the importance of addressing the ethnic/racial dimensions of strategies and programmes, the links between poverty and racism,[236] recommending upgrading the participation of affected groups in programme design and implementation. Hence Italy was recommended, in view of its 'National Strategy for the inclusion of Roma, Sinti and Camminanti communities' to 'initiate consultations with these communities as well as organizations representing them for the implementation, monitoring and evaluation of this strategy'.[237] The Committee's approach in this last respect is informed by the concepts expressed in Article 5(e)(vi) of the Convention and Article 15 of the ICESCR, read against the background right of members of minorities, expressed in the United Nations Declaration on Minorities (UNDM) and

[229] M. Bell, *Racism and Equality in the European Union* (Oxford University Press, 2008), Chapter 6: 'Social Inclusion: Education, Health, and Housing'.

[230] Concluding observations on Australia, CERD/C/AUS/CO/15-17, para. 14.

[231] The Decade of Roma Inclusion is an initiative of twelve countries which have significant Roma minorities. Examples of CERD responses include concluding observations on Bosnia and Herzegovina, CERD/C/BIH/CO/7-8, para.12; Bulgaria, CERD/C/BGR/19, para. 15; and Slovakia, CERD/C/SVK/CO/9-10, para. 11.

[232] For example, concluding observations on Italy, CERD/C/ITA/CO/16-18, para. 19; Portugal, CERD/C/PRT/CO/12-14,para. 119, referring, *inter alia*, to European Union requirements.

[233] Concluding observations on Australia, *ibid.*; Mexico, CERD/C/MEX/CO/16-17, para. 18; Venezuela, CERD/C/VEN/CO/19-21, para. 10.

[234] For a general, ethnically unspecific definition taken from EU sources, see Bell, *Racism and Equality*, p. 117; also, *ibid.*, pp. 123–7 on 'Mainstreaming ethnic equality into social inclusion policy'.

[235] CERD/C/CYP/CO/17-22, para. 16; also concluding observations on Sweden, CERD/C/SWE/CO/19-21, para. 14.

[236] 'The Committee urges the State party to continue implementing social inclusion and identity-based development programmes that reduce inequalities and poverty . . . The Committee recommends that action be taken to break the link between poverty and racism': concluding observations on Honduras, CERD/C/HND/CO/11-5, para. 7; the paragraph focuses on the situation of indigenous peoples and Afro-Honduran communities.

[237] CERD/C/ITA/CO/16-18, para. 19. See also concluding observations on Estonia, CERD/C/EST/CO/8-9, para. 14.

elsewhere, to participate in cultural, religious, social, economic, and public life,[238] and in decisions affecting them.[239] A shorthand description for this policy preference is 'integration through participation'.

The descriptions of recommended integration programmes or policies are often information and sector-dependent,[240] and, where necessary, 'cultural' elements inform and limit the recommendations. Cultural elements lie behind the Committee's critique of the Estonian integration strategy, regarded as having an 'overemphasis' on language; *inter alia*, the State party was called upon to review legislation restricting 'the use of minority languages in public services only to counties where minorities make up half of the population'.[241] In the case of Namibia, CERD expressed concern that 'integration policies and programmes might be detrimental to the protection of ethnic and cultural diversity', and recalled that 'the principle of non-discrimination requires that the cultural characteristics of... groups be taken into consideration', finally urging the State party 'to ensure that its integration policies and programmes respect and protect the cultural identities of persons belonging to national or ethnic minorities'.[242] With regard to 'ghettoes', a paradigmatic term to describe a segregated community, the Committee stated that, while it appreciated Denmark's objective in its 'anti-ghettoization law' of preventing 'marginalized groupings' and not 'ethnic groupings', it recommended an assessment of the impact of the policy 'on the rights of various ethnic groups to practise their culture, and ensure that it does not have an assimilationist effect that leads to the loss of cultural identities by those affected'.[243]

While this may not always have been the case in CERD practice, it is clear that the Committee currently distinguishes integration from assimilation, and does not treat the Convention as an assimilationist instrument.[244] The parameters of minority and associated cultural rights have been too clearly drawn in recent decades, and incorporated into Committee practice in manifold ways, to permit laxity in the recognition and protection of the cultural rights of groups.[245] Diaconu places the matter in historical perspective:

> the text of the Convention reflects the period when it was concluded, when apartheid and segregation were the most serious forms of racial discrimination... subsequent practice showed, however, that such fears [assimilation of minorities, etc] were not justified: these provisions of the

[238] UNDM, Article 2(2).

[239] *Ibid.*, Article 2(3).

[240] For example, recommendations to Belgium on persons of foreign origin with regard to the labour market, CERD/C/BEL/CO/16-19, para. 15; a final sentence in the paragraph adds a reference to the facilitation of access to housing.

[241] CERD/C/EST/CO/8-9, para. 13.

[242] CERD/C/NAM/CO/12, para. 24.

[243] CERD/C/DNK/CO/18-19, para. 15. The policy is outlined in the report of Denmark, CERE/C/DNK/18-19, paras 131–5; for explanations, see CERD/C/SR.2035, paras 16 and 48, and comments by members of the committee, *ibid.*, paras 36 and 39 (Crickley).

[244] For reflection on early practice under the Convention, see Thornberry, *International Law and the Rights of Minorities*, pp. 276–80. Successive early Committees exhibited a pronounced division of views (or confusion) as to the policy and principles of the Convention with regard to minorities, and whether 'integration' meant the disappearance of minority ethnic identities, absorbed into the national mainstream; States parties also expressed divided views on these issues. As pointed out in various chapters of the present work, the emergence of bodies of human rights standards, notably those on indigenous peoples and ethnic and religious groups, parallel to those on racial discrimination, has influenced the Committee in its reading of the Convention as a 'living instrument'. The question is summarized in the concluding chapter of the present work.

[245] See, *inter alios*, F. Lenzerini, *The Culturalization of Human Rights Law* (Oxford University Press, 2014), esp. Chapter 3, pp. 116–212.

Convention were never used against . . . ethnic groups, against their preoccupations to have their identity respected and to be recognised as minorities.[246]

'Integration' is not a particularly helpful trope in the case of indigenous peoples, for whom the term has historically equalled assimilation or worse even when employed in international instruments drafted ostensibly for their benefit.[247] The term figures as a negative in the UNDRIP in the context of demanding protection against 'any form of forced assimilation or integration',[248] and is difficult to accommodate in a framework of rights that converges under the rubrics of self-determination, autonomy, and control. In sum, the concept of 'integration' requires careful structuring and cultural nuancing to function as the apposite riposte to 'segregation'. Indigenous groups may regard policies of integration as nothing more than assimilation in disguise.

Practice has not completely illuminated all aspects of Article 3, including whether and to what extent that anti-segregation occupies a distinct normative space in the Convention distinguishing it from discrimination more generally. Article 3 has been interpreted as reaching down into social practice, raising the question as to what extent segregation resulting from the activities of private persons is appropriately taken under the umbrella of ICERD, bearing in mind the relationship of Article 3 to the 'freedom' provisions in the Convention, including freedom of assembly and association, or freedom of residence.[249] The limitation of the Convention to discrimination 'in public life' is another contextual element for interpretation.

The relationship between the prohibitory aspect of the anti-segregation norm and the separating elements of minority or indigenous rights raises further questions, though the Committee has worked over decades to harmonize the concepts, drawing on developments in international human rights law to inform its opinions. In this sense, segregation has been partly 'culturalized' and integrated into acceptance of the validity of rights that are freely chosen by the ethnic groups or peoples concerned and not imposed.[250] As with other driving forces that propelled the Convention into existence, the anti-apartheid and anti-integration currents remain important to the ethics of the Convention even if they have lost some of their original charge, having merged into a broader conceptual stream.

[246] I. Diaconu, *Racial Discrimination* (Eleven International Publishing, 2011), p. 202.

[247] The operation of International Labour Organization (ILO) Convention 107 on Indigenous and Tribal Populations 1957 is a case in point; the instrument was (is—the Convention is still in force) regarded by indigenous peoples as highly assimilationist and dangerous to the survival and flourishing of their cultures, a position that was eventually accepted by the ILO in moving to Convention 169 on Indigenous and Tribal Peoples 1989: an ILO Committee of Experts in 1988 was 'unanimous in concluding that the integrationist language of Convention 107 is outdated, and . . . the application of this principle is destructive in the modern world', cited in P. Thornberry, *Indigenous Peoples and Human Rights* (Manchester University Press, 2002), p. 338. The integration–assimilation nexus is considered further in the concluding chapter of the present work.

[248] Article 8(2)(d).

[249] With regard to Denmark's 'anti-ghettoization' law, in addition to highlighting cultural aspects, the Committee asked how it impacted 'on the affected people's rights to freedom of residence': CERD/C/DNK/CO/18-19, para. 15.

[250] Lenzerini, *The Culturalization of Human Rights Law*, passim.

11. Article 4

Racist Hate Speech

States Parties condemn all propaganda and all organizations which are based on ideas or theories of superiority of one race or group of persons of one colour or ethnic origin, or which attempt to justify or promote racial hatred and discrimination in any form, and undertake to adopt immediate and positive measures designed to eradicate all incitement to, or acts of, such discrimination and, to this end, with due regard to the principles embodied in the Universal Declaration of Human Rights and the rights expressly set forth in Article 5 of this Convention, *inter alia*:

(a) Shall declare an offence punishable by law all dissemination of ideas based on racial superiority or hatred, incitement to racial discrimination, as well as all acts of violence or incitement to such acts against any race or group of persons of another colour or ethnic origin, and also the provision of any assistance to racist activities, including the financing thereof;

(b) Shall declare illegal and prohibit organizations, and also organized and all other propaganda activities, which promote and incite racial discrimination, and shall recognize participation in such organizations or activities as an offence punishable by law;

(c) Shall not permit public authorities or public institutions, national or local, to promote or incite racial discrimination.

A. Introduction

Article 4 is the principal focus in the Convention for addressing 'racist hate speech', through the use of penal provisions. The term 'hate speech' is not used in Article 4 or other articles of the Convention, though its use by the Committee has steadily advanced: building upon earlier usage, a thematic discussion on 'racist hate speech' was held in 2012, followed in 2013 by General Recommendation 35 (GR 35) on 'combating racist hate speech'.[1] The Committee on the Elimination of Racial Discrimination (CERD) understands racist hate

[1] 'Hate speech' is identified by the Committee of Ministers of the Council of Europe as a term 'covering all forms of expression which spread, incite, promote or justify racial hatred, xenophobia, anti-Semitism or other forms of hatred based on intolerance, including: intolerance expressed by aggressive nationalism and ethnocentrism, discrimination and hostility against minorities, migrants and people of immigrant origin': Appendix to Council of Europe Committee of Ministers Recommendation No. R (97) 20; the definition was referred to by the ECtHR in *Gündüz v Turkey*, App. No. 35071/97; ECHR 2003-XI [2003], paras 22 and 43. In a significant body of literature, the essays in I. Hare and J. Weinstein (eds), *Extreme Speech and Democracy* (Oxford University Press, 2009) offer a range of critical commentary [henceforth *Extreme Speech*]; see also J. Waldron, *The Harm in Hate Speech* (Harvard University Press, 2012) [henceforth *The Harm in Hate Speech*]. According to Post, to prohibit hate speech is 'to forbid expression of "extreme" intolerance or "extreme" dislike', the qualification 'extreme' is prerequisite 'because intolerance and dislike are necessary human emotions which no legal order could pretend to abolish': R. Post, 'Hate Speech' in Hare and Weinstein, *Extreme Speech*, pp. 123–38, p. 123. For many offences, on the other hand, the speech provocation may be expressed in mild language but intended to provoke 'extreme' hatred with its attendant consequences.

speech, as distinct from racially motivated 'hate crimes', as 'a form of other-directed speech which rejects the core human rights principles of human dignity and equality and seeks to degrade the standing of individuals and groups in the estimation of society'.[2] Beyond this generic statement, the approach of the Committee is to find the meaning of racist hate speech in the Convention itself, the provisions of which 'cumulatively enable the identification of expression that constitutes hate speech'.[3] GR 35 also makes it clear that the burden of combating racist hate speech does not fall on Article 4 alone, bearing in mind that 'effectively combating racist hate speech involves the mobilization of the full normative and procedural resources of the Convention'[4] that may be invoked by States in the pursuance of anti-hate speech policies. The recommendation gives pride of place among such 'resources' to Article 5 with particular reference to freedom of opinion and expression—5(d)(viii)—and to Article 7, whilst reiterating that Article 4 remains central to the struggle against racial discrimination.[5]

The track record of the Committee evidences significant continuity through volatile operating contexts in its approach to Article 4, though GR 35 strikes fresh notes in refining, revisiting, and elaborating CERD practice. While the proscription of 'racist' hate speech is supported in broad terms by all States, the 'overlapping consensus'[6] on the relationship between hate speech and basic freedoms, notably the freedoms of expression and assembly, is narrower. States and sundry non-governmental actors take divergent views on hate speech, self-presenting as occasion demands as warriors for freedom or zealots for proscription; the issue is rarely conducive to a benign neutrality. Philosophical, political, and cultural factors influence positioning on the freedom-proscription axis. In drafting the Convention, Western States struck agonistic poses in defence of freedom of expression, while others, notably the Communist States and the newly independent States, took a tougher stance on suppressing racist speech. All the 'freedom-protecting' reservations are from Western or Western-aligned States or States with an inheritance of colonial legislation, and Western States are still the most reluctant to assimilate the Committee's prescriptions in this area; it remains to be seen whether the emergence of GR 35 will encourage revaluations of the hitherto obdurate retention of reservations.

Issues related to Article 4 of the International Convention on the Elimination of All Forms of Racial Discrimination (ICERD) have produced a raft of international human rights provisions. Bearing in mind that the chapeau of Article 4 of ICERD makes specific reference to 'the principles embodied' in the Universal Declaration of Human Rights (UDHR), elements of particular relevance in the UDHR include Articles 19 and 20 on freedom of opinion and expression, and freedom of assembly, respectively, as well as Article 7, particularly its second sentence on equal protection against discrimination and against any incitement to such discrimination, and Article 12, referring *inter alia*, to 'attacks

[2] GR 35 (2013), para. 10. Waldron, *The Harm in Hate Speech*, argues that dignity 'is precisely what hate speech laws are designed to protect . . . dignity in the sense of a person's basic entitlement to be regarded as a member of society in good standing, as someone whose membership of a minority group does not disqualify . . . from ordinary social intercourse': p. 104.

[3] GR 35, para. 5.

[4] Para. 3.

[5] GR 35, para. 10, citing para. 1 of GR 15.

[6] J. Rawls, *Political Liberalism* (Columbia University Press, 1993 and 1996), Lecture IV.

upon . . . honour and reputation'; the general limitations on human rights provisions set out in Articles 29 and 30 are also prominent in the network of principles. Relevant statements in 'core' treaties emanating from the UDHR include Article 19 of the International Covenant on Civil and Political Rights (ICCPR) which incorporates a general statement according to which the exercise of the right to freedom of expression 'carries with it special duties and responsibilities' and may be subject to restrictions but only such 'as are provided by law and are necessary: (a) for respect of the rights or reputations of others; (b) for the protection of national security or of public order (*ordre public*), or of public health or morals'.[7] This 'freedom provision' in the ICCPR is directly followed by Article 20, which makes mandatory the prohibition by law of 'any propaganda for war',[8] and any advocacy 'of national, racial or religious hatred that constitutes incitement to discrimination, hostility or violence'.[9]

Besides the above, Article 13 of the International Convention on the Protection of the Rights of All Migrant Workers and members of their Families (CMW), Article 9.2 of the African Charter on Human and Peoples' Rights (ACHPR), Article IV of the American Declaration of the Rights and Duties of Man, Article 13 of the American Convention on Human Rights (ACHR), and Article 10 of the European Convention on Human Rights (ECHR) incorporate principles on freedom of expression. These expressions of principle usually incorporate limitations which are either specific to the right in question or are of a general kind applicable to all the rights in the instrument in question and/or interface with provisions on hate speech. Article 13 of the CMW is one example of a 'compound Article' that combines freedom of expression with a provision on hate speech.[10]

Article 4 of the Inter-American Convention against Racism, Racial Discrimination and Related Intolerance, under the rubric of duties of the State, refers to undertakings to 'prevent, eliminate, prohibit and punish' manifestations of racism, etc that include

> [p]ublication, circulation or dissemination, by any form and/or means of communication, including the internet, of any racist or racially discriminatory materials that: a. Advocate, promote, or incite hatred, discrimination, and intolerance. b. Condone, justify, or defend acts that constitute or have constituted genocide or crimes against humanity as defined in international law, or promote or incite the commitment of such acts.

[7] The right to freedom of opinion, on the other hand, is not expressed as subject to restrictions. Building on earlier GCs and a wealth of cases under the First Optional Protocol to the ICCR, the Human Rights Committee issued GC 34 on freedoms of opinion and expression on 2011. The specific reference to and citations of GC 34 by CERD GR 35 indicates that the approach taken by the Human Rights Committee has been influential on the formation of CERD opinion.

[8] GC 11 of the Human Rights Committee states, para. 2, that 'propaganda for war' does not prohibit advocacy for self-defence or the right of peoples to self-determination and independence in accordance with the UN Charter, nor, presumably, wars sanctioned by the UN Security Council under the terms of the UN Charter: HRI/GEN/1/Rev.9 (Vol. I), p. 182.

[9] Some fourteen States parties maintain reservations, declarations, etc, in relation to Article 20: <https://treaties.un.org/pages/viewdetails.aspx?chapter=4&src=treaty&mtdsg_no=iv-4&lang=en>.

[10] Note also para. 5 of Article 13 of the American Convention on Human Rights, which, following a lengthy account of freedom of expression, includes a paragraph 5 in the following terms: 'Any propaganda for war and any advocacy of national, racial, or religious hatred that constitute incitements to lawless violence or to any other similar action against any person or group of persons on any grounds including those of race, colour, religion, language, or national origin shall be considered as offences punishable by law.'

Additional accounts of freedom of expression and hate speech are included in a range of texts in the narrower context of instruments on minority rights.[11] Among the texts on indigenous peoples, the UN Declaration on the Rights of Indigenous Peoples (UNDRIP) notably combines freedom of expression with hate speech-related protections.[12] Strong hate speech provisions are also found in the field of international criminal law, including the Genocide Convention which lists 'direct and public incitement to commit genocide' among the prohibited acts.[13] Numerous exercises in domestic law proscribe denials of genocide and crimes against humanity,[14] as does Article 6 of the Additional Protocol to the Council of Europe's Convention on Cybercrime.[15]

As regards freedom of assembly and association, implicated in the prohibitions in Article 4(b), general standards are set out in a spectrum of instruments. As in Article 5 of ICERD, both freedoms appear in Article 20 of the UDHR, while they are split in the ICCPR into the rights of peaceful assembly (Article 21) and freedom of association, including trade union rights (Article 22).[16] Regional instruments also include the rights;[17] freedom of association is also implicated in the Declaration on Human Rights

[11] *National Minority Standards: A Compilation of OSCE and Council of Europe Texts* (Council of Europe Publishing, 2007), *passim*; see in particular Article 9 of the Council of Europe Framework Convention for the Protection of National Minorities.

[12] Preamble, para. 4, and Articles 8(e), 15.2 and 16.2.

[13] Article 3. The prohibition is elaborated in *Prosecutor v Nahimana, Barayagwiza and Ngeze*, Case No. ICTR-99-52-T (ICTR Trial Chamber, 2003), the 'Media Case'; the case was followed by a judgment of the Appeals Chamber of the same tribunal in 2007, *Nahimana et al. v The Prosecutor*, Case No. ICTR-99-52-A. The Appeals Chamber, with reference to the ICCPR and ICERD, elaborated, *ibid.*, para. 692, on the distinction between hate speech in general (or inciting discrimination and violence) and direct and public incitement to commit genocide... 'in most cases, direct and public incitement to commit genocide can be preceded or accompanied by hate speech, but only direct and public incitement to commit genocide is prohibited under... the Statute [of the Tribunal]'.

[14] R.A. Kahn, *Holocaust Denial and the Law: A Comparative Study* (Palgrave Macmillan, 2004); M. Whine, 'Expanding Holocaust Denial and Legislation Against It', in Hare and Weinstein, *Extreme Speech*, pp. 538–56, who observes that fourteen separate European States have criminalized Holocaust Denial; with regard to the support given by the European Commission and Court of Human Rights to proscriptions of Holocaust denial, see, *inter alia*, the Commission decisions in *X. v F.R.G.*, App. No. 9235/81 (1982); *Honsik v Austria*, App. No. 25062/94 (1995); *Marais v France*, App. No. 31159/96 (1996); *Garaudy v France*, App. No. 65831/01 ECtHR 2003, where the Court said that because the Holocaust was 'clearly established historical fact', it was removed from the protection of Article 10 on freedom of expression: compare the Statement in the Canadian case of *R. v Zundel* [1992] 2 SCR 731 where it was argued that falsehoods may still have a value as a form of expression. For a general review of the treatment of 'deniers' under the European Convention on Human Rights, see P. Lobba, 'Holocaust Denial before the European Court of Human Rights', *EJIL* (2015) 26, 237–53. Views of UN bodies are considered later in the present chapter.

[15] 2003, ETS No. 189. See also the European Council Framework Decision on Combating Certain Forms and Expressions of Racism and Xenophobia by Means of Criminal Law, 008/913/JHA (28 November 2008), which provides for the following to be treated as punishable acts: 'Publicly condoning, denying or grossly trivialising crimes of genocide, crimes against humanity and war crimes as defined in the Statute of the International Criminal Court (Articles 6, 7 and 8) directed against a group of persons or a member of such a group defined by reference to race, colour, religion, descent or national or ethnic origin, and crimes defined by the Tribunal of Nuremberg (Article 6 of the Charter of the International Military Tribunal, London Agreement of 1945) directed against a group of persons or a member of such a group defined by reference to race, colour, religion, descent or national or ethnic origin.... The reference to religion is intended to cover, at least, conduct which is a pretext for directing acts against a group of persons or a member of such a group defined by reference to race, colour, descent, or national or ethnic origin.'

[16] Trade union rights are expressed in greater detail in Article 8 of the ICESCR and in a raft of instruments under the auspices of the International Labour Organization (ILO) and the ILO Committee on Freedom of Association. See chapter 14.

[17] ACHR Article 16; ACHPR, Article 10; Arab Charter on Human Rights, Article 24; ECHR, Article 11.

Defenders.[18] In the ICCPR, the possibilities for restricting either right are narrowly drawn, though neither right is listed as non-derogable.

Incitement to discrimination and measures to eradicate it are flagged up in the Declaration on Racial Discrimination, Article 9 of which provides that:

1. All propaganda and organizations based on ideas or theories of the superiority of one race or group of persons of one colour or ethnic origin with a view to justifying or promoting racial discrimination in any form shall be severely condemned.
2. All incitement to or acts of violence, whether by individuals or organizations against any race or group of persons of another colour or ethnic origin shall be considered an offence against society and punishable under law.
3. In order to put into effect the purposes and principles of the present Declaration, all States shall take immediate and positive measures, including legislative and other measures, to prosecute and/or outlaw organizations which promote or incite to racial discrimination, or incite to or use violence for purposes of discrimination based on race, colour or ethnic origin.

While there are important differences between this text and the Convention, the Declaration's condemnations of propaganda and ideas and incitement to racial discrimination and violence served as starting points for the later instrument.

B. *Travaux Préparatoires*

The *travaux* of Article 4 are extensive, a measure of the strongly contested nature of the discussions from the outset, where the topic of racist speech brought forth a wide span of suggestions.[19] Texts incorporating provisions on incitement were submitted by Abram,[20] by Ivanov and Ketrzynski jointly,[21] Cuevas Cancino and Ingles jointly,[22] and Ketryznski.[23] The Abram draft commenced with a paragraph whereby incitement to racial hatred and discrimination was to be declared 'an offence against society and punishable under law',[24] a phrase culled from the Declaration. This was followed by paragraphs which included a provision whereby the State party would not permit 'its officials or any agency or organization supported... by government funds' to promote or incite racial hatred and discrimination; there was also a paragraph on establishing a national policy 'designed to eradicate all incitement to racial discrimination and hatred'. The Abram draft linked the provisions declaring incitement an offence with remedies: 'Each State party shall provide remedial relief for any individual who has suffered substantial harm as the result of racial violence, hatred or discrimination.' The Ivanov/Ketrzynski draft focused on 'racist, fascist and other organizations practising or inciting... racial discrimination' which States parties would undertake to 'prohibit and disband'.[25] This draconian provision was accompanied by another whereby the State undertook to

[18] General Assembly resolution 53/144, 8 March 1999.

[19] The heading for what became Article 4 of the Convention in the report of the Sub-Commission was '[t]he obligation of States to adopt positive measures to eradicate incitement to racial discrimination': report of the Sixteenth Session of the Sub-Commission, E/CN.4/873, p. 29.

[20] E/CN.4/Sub.2/L.308/Add.1/Rev.1/Corr.1.

[21] E/CN.4/Sub.2/L.314.

[22] E/CN.4/Sub.2/L.330.

[23] E/CN.4/Sub.2/L.331.

[24] E/CN.4/873, para. 74.

[25] *Ibid.*, para. 75.

consider participation in the activity of such organizations as well as incitement to violence or acts of violence against individuals or groups because of race, national, or ethnic origin as 'a criminal offence counter to the interest of society punishable under law, and to prosecute those guilty thereof'.[26] The draft also introduced a specific undertaking not to admit 'propaganda of any kind of the superiority of one race or national group over another' or propaganda with a view to justifying or promoting racial discrimination in any form.[27]

Cuevas Cancino and Ingles submitted a later text incorporating the propaganda point introduced by Ivanov/Ketrzynski, to the effect that States parties would 'severely condemn' propaganda justifying or promoting racial discrimination and undertake to initiate 'immediate and positive' measures to eradicate all incitement to such discrimination.[28] To this end, *inter alia*, measures included penalization of incitement to racial discrimination 'resulting in or likely to cause acts of violence',[29] the prohibition or outlawing of organizations promoting or inciting racial discrimination,[30] and a prohibition on government officials or State-supported organizations promoting or inciting racial discrimination; a 'remedial relief' provision similar to that in the Abram draft was also included. During discussion of this last text, Ketrzynski introduced a new text[31] which contained sub-paragraphs on taking appropriate measures to institute judicial proceedings against those inciting or committing acts of violence targeting 'a race or group of persons of a different colour or ethnic origin', against those implicated in propaganda aimed at inciting racial hatred, etc, and against organizations 'including fascist movements' which aim at inciting violence or racial discrimination.[32] This draft also referred to a national policy to 'eradicate all prejudices based on ideas of differentiation or inequality among races'. A revised text from Cuevas Cancino and Ingles produced further discussion and amendments and was adopted unanimously by the Sub-Commission.[33]

[26] *Ibid.*, para. 75.

[27] *Ibid.*

[28] E/CN.4/873, para. 77.

[29] *Ibid.*

[30] *Ibid.* Commenting on the text, Abram, in an observation which foreshadowed much of the discussion of Article 4, argued that 'it was not always necessary to suppress a racist organization in order to put an end to its activities . . . the prohibition of what was regarded as offensive might prove to be a double-edged weapon . . . it would be dangerous and useless to stipulate that States should prohibit organizations on the sole ground that they promoted racial discrimination': E/CN.4/Sub.2/SR.420, pp. 4–5. As an example he referred to the Ku Klux Klan, in relation to whose activities laws had been adopted in a number of states of the US requiring members to, *inter alia*, keep their faces uncovered during demonstrations. On the other hand, Ivanov emphasized the need for preventive measures, so that action 'should be taken before racist organizations poisoned the minds of young people by implanting in them hatred of certain races; otherwise the situation would soon be beyond the control of the authorities. That was what had happened in the case of the racist doctrine of hitlerism. If laws had been passed soon enough to prevent the dissemination of those harmful ideas, it would perhaps have been possible to avoid the catastrophe in which the modern world had been engulfed': E/CN.4/Sub.2/SR.420, p. 6.

[31] E/CN.4/Sub.2/L.331.

[32] E/CN.4/873, para. 79. Ketrzyinski had 'mentioned fascist movements because, although the term had given rise to several interpretations, no one could deny that all fascist movements were also racist': E/CN. 4/Sub.2/SR.420,p. 9. Capotorti, *ibid.*, p. 11, regarded the reference to fascist movements as inappropriate on the ground that 'some countries which, unlike Italy, did not possess very specific legislative and constitutional provisions on the subject might use that text as a reason for not acceding to the Convention'.

[33] E/CN.4/Sub.2/L.330/Rev.1; E/CN.4/873, para. 81.

Accordingly, the Commission had before it the following text of Article IV:

States parties condemn all propaganda and organizations which justify or promote racial hatred and discrimination and undertake to adopt immediate and positive measures designed to eradicate all incitement to such discrimination, and to this end, *inter alia*:

(a) Shall declare an offence punishable by law all incitement to racial discrimination resulting in or likely to cause acts of violence;[34]
(b) Shall declare illegal and prohibit organizations, and also organized propaganda activities, which promote and incite racial discrimination;
(c) Shall not permit public authorities or public institutions, national or local, to promote or incite racial discrimination.

Amendments to the Sub-Commission's text were proposed by the USSR,[35] the US,[36] Poland,[37] Costa Rica,[38] and Denmark,[39] in addition to oral amendments.[40] The USSR amendment to the chapeau proposing the addition of 'severely' after 'States parties' attracted comment to the effect that this would only weaken the condemnation of racial discrimination elsewhere in the draft convention by raising the issue of degrees of condemnation, whilst adding nothing to the legal strength of the article.[41] A more substantial USSR amendment that proposed to add 'based on ideas or theories of the superiority of one race or group of persons of one colour or ethnic origin' after 'organizations'[42] attracted significant comment. In support of the proposal, the text of Article 9.1 of the Declaration on Racial Discrimination was recalled and the contention was made that it was in keeping with the spirit of the Convention as a whole if organizations were to be condemned even if they did not put these 'ideas or theories' into practice. Against, it was claimed that in order to be condemned, the organizations would have to meet two qualifications instead of one,[43] limiting the applicability of the article. The representative of Ecuador added to the 'ideas or theories' discussion the observation that 'many racist acts had been based not on theories or systematized ideas, but rather on emotion, on hatred stemming from deep-seated prejudice'.[44] The debates also touched on the question of whether racial discrimination 'was necessarily founded on explicit or implicit concepts of racial superiority',[45] as claimed by the USSR but disputed by India.[46]

[34] The final Article 4 of the Convention does not link incitement with violence in the manner suggested in this draft.

[35] E/CN.4/L.681.

[36] E/CN.4/L.688.

[37] E/CN.4/L.699.

[38] E/CN.4/L.702.

[39] E/CN.4/L.704.

[40] Commission on Human Rights, Report on the Twentieth Session, February–March 1964, E/CN.4/874, paras 144–71.

[41] The amendment was rejected by 6 votes to 5, with 10 abstentions: E/CN.4/874, para. 173. Negative comments on the insertion of 'severely' were offered by a number of representatives, including the representative of The Philippines who claimed that 'the insertion of the word "severely" . . . might destroy the balance between the various Articles of the Convention', and Dahomey, for whom the insertion of the word 'would not only be superfluous, but would prejudge the nature of the penalty to be imposed by the competent organs of the State': E/CN.4/SR.791, pp. 7–8.

[42] As orally revised by India: E/CN.4/874, para. 147.

[43] E/CN.4/874, para. 158. See comment of Italy, E/CN.4/SR.792, p. 13.

[44] E/CN.4/SR.791, p. 10.

[45] E/CN.4/SR.792, p. 6.

[46] E/CN.4/SR.792, pp. 7–8. The representative used the homely example of a building concern, having built a group of houses, 'might find that the price of the dwellings tended to go down if they were offered to all

An Indian oral amendment replaced 'or likely to cause acts of violence' in the Sub-Commission's text by 'acts of violence as well as all acts of violence or incitement to such acts against any race or group of persons of another colour or ethnic origin'.[47]

On paragraph (b), an amendment by the US to add the words 'activities of' after 'organizations' raised once more the issue of banning racist organizations as such because, it was argued, under the law of many countries, organizations as such could not be prohibited while persons engaged in illegal activities could be prosecuted.[48] It was also claimed that attempts to outlaw 'speech' in the absence of 'acts' would be open to abuse, allowing the authorities to decide whether or not particular expressed opinions were punishable.[49] Other representatives made the subtle point that the formation of organizations constituted acts, and not merely thoughts, and if the organizations promoted discrimination, they must be banned.[50] Support was also expressed for the banning not only of dangerous organizations but also for the leaders of organizations and persons who provided assistance.[51] A Costa Rican amendment to soften the text by adding, after 'organizations', 'or the activities of organizations, as appropriate' attracted opposition on the basis that it would open the door to subjective choices by States parties.[52]

Two statements in particular give a flavour of the polarized debate on freedom of speech and organizations. In the view of the United States, 'pernicious ideas could not be eliminated by forcing them underground . . . the ideas of an organization operating in secrecy became subversive for the very reason they were not open to scrutiny'.[53] A colourful counter-analogy was offered by the representative of the USSR who recalled that

> there had been organizations which murdered for a fee; the notorious 'Murder incorporated' was an example. That organization had been set up for a definite object: the commission of crime. It would be curious logic to consider that it had the right to exist as long as it was not actually guilty of a murder, or that it was necessary to wait for a murder to be committed before prohibiting such an organization.[54]

Among other amendments, the proposal by the USSR to replace 'and' between 'promote' and 'incite' by the word 'or' also generated significant discussion. Recalling Article 9(3) of the Declaration on Racial Discrimination which used the expression 'promote or incite', it was asked whether both 'incitement' and 'promotion' of racial discrimination would be

buyers without distinction. To protect its interests, the concern might decide that only certain racial groups would be allowed to buy . . . It could hardly be said in that case that the concern was motivated by ideas of racial superiority; it simply wanted to make the largest possible profit.'

[47] E/CN.4/874, para. 149: the amendment was adopted unanimously: *ibid.*, para. 177.

[48] Comments of Canada, E/CN.4/SR.791,pp. 5–6; United Kingdom, *ibid.*, p. 9; Ecuador, *ibid.*, p. 10; France, E/CN.4/SR.792, pp. 11–12; Italy, *ibid.*, p. 14.

[49] United Kingdom, E/CN.4/SR.793, p. 5.

[50] Comment of the Ukrainian SSR, E/CN.4/SR.792, pp. 12–13.

[51] Observation by the USSR, E/CN.4/SR.794, pp. 6–7.

[52] E/CN.4/874, para. 169. The words 'as appropriate' were the subject of a separate roll-call vote on the request of the USSR, and were retained in the text by 15 votes to 3, with 3 abstentions, with Poland, the Ukrainian SSR and the USSR voted against: E/3873; E/CN.4/874, para. 180. The whole Costa Rican amendment was adopted on a roll-call vote by 15 votes to 4, with 2 abstentions: E/CN.4/874, para. 181. Again, the Soviet bloc, plus India, voted against.

[53] E/CN.4/SR.792, p. 10.

[54] E/CN.4/SR.794, p. 10. 'Murder incorporated' or 'Murder Inc.' was the name given by the press to an organized crime group in the US that carried out murders in the 1930s and 1940s. The title of the group was a journalistic invention.

necessary in order to tackle organizations and their activities when the obvious answer was that only one was needed. The report of the Commission summarizes this discussion:

> Several representatives objected to the amendment on the ground that while incitement was a conscious and motivated act, promotion presented a lower degree of motivation and might occur even without any real intention or endeavour to incite. Consequently, since the two words had different meanings . . . either the word 'and' should be retained, as there could not be incitement without promotion, or the word 'promote' should be deleted.[55]

The USSR also proposed to add the words 'as also the rendering of any assistance whatsoever to such organizations and their activities, including their financing' at the end of paragraph (b), recalling that the Nazis had been financed by industries and monopolies and that fascist organizations were springing up and securing financial support.[56] A Polish amendment to paragraph (b) to add 'and shall declare participation in such organizations or activities to be an offence punishable by law' attracted supporters and critics.[57] In favour, it was argued that the consequences of participating in organizations should be spelled out while others felt that it was going too far.[58] Paragraph (c) as submitted by the Sub-Commission was adopted unanimously as was Article IV as a whole.[59]

The Third Committee had before it the following text of Article IV:

> States parties condemn all propaganda and organizations which are based on ideas or theories of the superiority of one race or group of persons of one colour or ethnic origin, or which justify or promote racial hatred and discrimination in any form, and undertake to adopt immediate and positive measures designed to eradicate all incitement to such discrimination, and to this end, *inter alia*:
>
> (a) Shall declare an offence punishable by law all incitement to racial discrimination resulting in acts of violence, as well as all acts of violence or incitement to such acts against any race or group of persons of another colour or ethnic origin;
> (b) Shall declare illegal and prohibit organizations or the activities of organizations, as appropriate, and also organized propaganda activities, which promote and incite racial discrimination;
> (c) Shall not permit public authorities or public institutions, national or local, to promote or incite racial discrimination.

The substantive discussion of the article was prefaced by a robust intervention by the representative of the United Kingdom who stated that the article went to the very heart of the Convention, since freedom of speech

> was the foundation-stone on which many of the other human rights were built . . . [the United Kingdom] . . . was taking legal and practical steps to tackle the problem of racial discrimination, but . . . also defended the right of all organizations, even fascist and communist ones, to exist and to

[55] E/CN.4/874, para. 169. The amendment was rejected by 12 votes to 8, with 1 abstention: E/CN.4/874, para. 178; opposition came principally from Western states.

[56] *Ibid.*, para. 170. The amendment, as revised—E/CN.4/L.703, para. 1—was rejected by 9 votes to 5, with 7 abstentions: E/3873; E/CN.4/874, para. 183. Opposition came mainly from Western States.

[57] E/CN.4/L.699. The amendment was rejected by 10 votes to 4, with 7 abstentions: E/CN.4/874, para. 184.

[58] Thus, the Italian delegation 'could not accept the Polish amendment . . . under which a person could be punished simply because he belonged to an organization some of whose other members engaged in discrimination': E/CN.4/SR.792, p. 15.

[59] E/CN.4/874, paras 187 and 188.

make their views known ... The views of such organizations were tolerated with one provision – that their expression did not involve incitement to racial violence.[60]

A number of representatives reacted to the statement of the UK in equally strong terms. For Czechoslovakia, freedom of expression 'was not entirely unrestricted',[61] and 'it was no proof of democracy that movements directed towards hatred and discrimination were allowed to exist. Her delegation was passionately dedicated to freedom of speech, but not when it was misused in the service of hatred, war and death.'[62] For Poland, 'every freedom was subject to certain limitations'.[63] The representative of Ceylon drew a distinction between the use and the abuse of freedom of speech, stating that an individual 'could not be punished merely for speaking against a particular race'.[64]

At the 1316th meeting, Nigeria submitted a full text to replace the whole of Article IV:

States parties condemn all propaganda and organizations which are based on ideas or theories of superiority of one race of group of persons of one colour or ethnic origin, or which attempt to justify or promote racial hatred and discrimination in any form, and undertake to adopt immediate and positive measures designed to eradicate all incitement to, or acts of, such discrimination and, to this end, with due regard to the principles embodied in the Universal Declaration of Human Rights and the rights expressly set forth in Article 5 of this Convention, inter alia:

(a) Shall declare an offence punishable by law all dissemination of ideas based on racial superiority or hatred, incitement to racial discrimination, as well as all acts of violence or incitement to such acts against any race or group of persons of another colour or ethnic origin, and also the provision of any assistance to racist activities, including the financing thereof;
(b) Shall declare illegal and prohibit organizations, and also organized and all other propaganda activities, which promote and incite racial discrimination, and shall recognize participation in such organizations or activities as an offence punishable by law;
(c) Shall not permit public authorities or public institutions, national or local, to promote or incite racial discrimination.[65]

An attempt by Argentina to provide a further replacement text for paragraphs (a) and (b) was rejected.[66] The proposed text for paragraph (a) would have omitted reference to dissemination of racist ideas, confining itself to declaring as punishable offences 'all incitement to' and 'all promotion of racial discrimination' and 'all acts of' racist violence or incitement to such violence. However, the 'ideas' element re-surfaced in a proposed paragraph (b): 'Shall declare illegal, prohibit and declare an offence punishable by law all propaganda and organizations based on theories of the superiority of one race, or of a group of persons of one colour or national or ethnic origin, and having as their purpose the justification or promotion of racial discrimination in any of its forms.' While the

[60] A/C.3/SR.1315, para. 1. The representative added: '[s]peech should be free, but incitement to violence should be repressed': A/C.3/SR.1315, para. 2.

[61] A/C.3/SR.1315, para. 5. The representative cited, *inter alia*, Article 29 (2) of the Universal Declaration of Human Rights.

[62] A/C.3/SR.1315, para. 6.

[63] A/C.3/SR.1315, para. 16.

[64] A/C.3/SR.1315, para. 21. Reference to the distinction between use and abuse of freedoms was also made by the representative of France, arguing that the Commission's text had made that distinction sufficiently clear: A/C.3/SR.1315, para. 19.

[65] A/C.3/L.1250, A/6181, para. 72.

[66] A/C.3/L.1253, introduced by the representative in A/C.3/SR.1318, para. 7. For the voting, see A/6181, para. 74, sub-paragraphs (c) and (g).

proposals of Argentina attracted some support,[67] the proposal of Nigeria enjoyed greater support, despite recognition by some that it was not perfect.[68] Continuing doubts were expressed on the provisions regarding the dissemination of ideas:

> the application of penal law to the dissemination of ideas of racial superiority . . . was not the best way of combating such ideas, negative and harmful though they were. The best approach was through education. While his delegation could agree that States should be asked to prohibit racial discrimination, it doubted whether it was desirable to provide that ideas, however regrettable they might be, should be punished by law.[69]

Others, however, took the view that the Commission had taken too timid an approach to 'the very important question of the dissemination of racist ideas'.[70]

A separate vote was taken at the request of Ethiopia on the 'due regard' clause, which was adopted by 76 votes to 1 with 14 abstentions. Separate votes were also taken at the request of Colombia on the dissemination of ideas aspect of paragraph (a),[71] and at the request of Austria on the reference in that paragraph to assistance to racist activities, etc.[72] The voting favoured the Nigerian text as 'the clearest expression of the views of the majority',[73] and although the abstention count was high on specific issues, Article IV as a whole was adopted by 88 votes to none, with 5 abstentions.[74] In explanations of vote, a number of delegations took the view that the 'due regard' clause represented 'a reasonable accommodation between the requirement to create a new offence and the fundamental right to freedom of association'.[75] The US interpreted the Article on the understanding that it 'did not impose on a State party the obligation to take any action impairing the right to freedom of speech and freedom of association'.[76] A last chance attempt by Argentina, Colombia, Ecuador, Panama, and Peru in the plenary session of the General Assembly to amend the beginning of Article 4, paragraph (a) to read that States parties '(a) Shall declare an offence punishable by law all incitement to racial discrimination, particularly discrimination based on racial superiority or hatred', was defeated.[77] In the words of the representative of Argentina, the proposal was designed to secure the point that the 'mere expression of ideas is not in itself punishable if it is not accompanied by incitement to discrimination or racial hatred'.[78] In a lengthy explanation of vote, the representative of Colombia commented that 'to penalize ideas, whatever their nature, is to pave the way for tyranny, for the abuse of power . . . ideas are fought with ideas and reasons; theories are refuted with arguments and not by resort to the scaffold, prison, exile,

[67] See, for example, the remarks by the representative of Austria, A/C.3/SR.1318, para. 13.

[68] For example, remarks by the representative of Argentina, A/C.3/SR.1318, para. 7; and the representative of Italy, *ibid.*, para. 18.

[69] Remarks by the representative of Italy, A/C.3/SR.1318, para. 20.

[70] Representative of Senegal, A/C.3/SR.1318, para. 31.

[71] Adopted by 57 votes to none, with 35 abstentions.

[72] Adopted by 57 votes to 1, with 33 abstentions. The representative had argued that 'the reference to racist activities lacked the precision which was desirable in any penal law': A/C/3/SR.1318, para. 46.

[73] Remark by the representative of Syria, A/C.3/SR.1318, para. 58.

[74] A/6181, para. 74.

[75] Representative of Canada, A/C.3/SR.1318, para. 52. See remarks by the representatives of The Netherlands, Chile, the UK, Spain, France, Austria, US, and New Zealand, A/C.3/SR.1318, paras 47, 49, 51, 53, 54, 57, 59, 60, respectively.

[76] *Ibid.*, para. 59.

[77] A/L.480

[78] A/PV.1406, para. 49.

confiscation or fines'; accordingly, the supporters of the Article as it stood were voting 'without seriously pondering on the dangers involved in authorizing penalties under criminal law for ideological offences'.[79]

Comment on the Travaux

The *travaux* demonstrate that, broadly congruent with the strict approach taken in the Declaration, a majority of governments favoured the 'hard line' on hate speech restrictions. Both racial discrimination instruments adopt a rigorous stance against racist organizations. The condemnation of racist organizations in the Declaration is transmuted into a demand for their prohibition as such, a demand that is expressed as not depending on their pursuit of racist activities: it is enough simply to be 'Murder Incorporated'. The condemnation of 'propaganda', 'ideas', and 'theories' of racial superiority is sustained throughout the two texts, even though the opposition to the penalization of the expression of ideas was always significant. 'Dissemination' of racist ideas was added to the lexicon of prohibited acts in the course of discussion, so that incitement and violence are not the only forms of activity to be sanctioned. Incitement is to be addressed as such, and the case for its criminalization is not stated to depend on any consequences that follow from the act of incitement. The *travaux* also highlight the wide scope of the eventual Article in that, as in the Convention as a whole and excepting the mention of apartheid in Article 3, no particular 'isms'—Nazism, fascism—are identified as necessary for its engagement, only the ethnic/racial framework. They also help to make the point that punishment for the impugned activities is not simply an end in itself but has an underlying preventive justification. Arguments to the effect that education was at least equal to penal sanctions as a long-term preventive measure did not disturb the general direction of the text. On freedom of expression, the 'due regard' clause was a softened version of drafts that offered stronger protection to this freedom. The 'due regard' was understood by the majority to refer to the whole of the UDHR including but not limited to its principles on freedom of expression and association.

C. Practice

I. Reservations and Declarations

Reservations and declarations self-describe in varied terms:[80] that of Antigua and Barbuda is styled a 'declaration'; the interpretation by Fiji of Article 4 is part of its 'reservation and declarations' but is referred to specifically as its 'interpretation' of the Article; Ireland makes a 'reservation/interpretative declaration' on Article 4, and Italy a 'declaration'; Japan refers to its 'reservation', as do Monaco, Switzerland, Thailand, and Papua New Guinea; Tonga's reading of Article 4 is part of its 'declaration'; the UK sets out a 'reservation and interpretative statements'; the advice and consent of the US Senate is subject to 'reservations'. The preferred terminology of the UK was explained in discussions with the Committee

[79] A/PV.1406, paras 70 and 72; the representative regarded the Article as 'a retrograde measure': A/PV.1406, para. 74.

[80] <https://treaties.un.org/pages/ViewDetails.aspx?src=TREATY&mtdsg_no=IV-2&chapter=4&lang=en>.

[a]n interpretative statement was not a reservation but expressly recorded what the United Kingdom had always understood to be the correct legal interpretation of Article 4. His government recognised that . . . many members of the Committee took a different view . . . In practice, however, the positions were not so far apart. The United Kingdom did not assert that the right to freedom of expression was absolute.[81]

For Antigua and Barbuda and Thailand, legislation or measures under Article 4 would be enacted only where it is considered that 'the need arises' for such;[82] Australia declared that it was not at present in a position to treat as offences matters covered in Article 4(a) but would seek such legislation 'at the first suitable moment':[83] such reservations effectively subtract from the Article 4 requirement to adopt 'immediate and positive measures'. Most of the reserving States make reference to the principles of freedom of expression which were not to be jeopardized by Article 4, and repeatedly refer to the Universal Declaration of Human Rights, Articles 19 and 20,[84] Article 5 of the Convention, and Articles 19 and 21 of the ICCPR.[85] The essence of these reservations is that measures to implement Article 4 will only be adopted to the extent they are, in the view of the reserving States, compatible with principles of freedom of expression, assembly, and association. On the scope of the statements, whereas the majority cover the whole of Article 4, that of Australia addresses only Article 4(a), while those of Italy (ambiguously) and Japan relate to 4(a) and 4(b). Despite repeated requests by the Committee to withdraw or narrow reservations, some States parties have made it clear that they intend to maintain the reservation. Hence the statement of Japan in its consolidated third to sixth report that:

Article 4 may cover an extremely wide range of acts carried out in various situations and in various manners. Restricting all these acts with punitive laws that go beyond the existing legal system in Japan may conflict with what the Constitution guarantees, including the freedom of expression that strictly demands the necessity and rationale for its restrictions, and with the principle of legality of crime and punishment that requires concreteness and clarity in determining the punishable acts and penalties. It is on the basis of this judgment that the Japanese Government made its reservations . . . Japan was advised to retract the reservation it made about Article 4 (a) and (b) in the concluding observations of the Committee on the Elimination of Racial Discrimination . . . However, for the reasons given above, Japan does not intend to retract the said reservation.[86]

While some reservations may also have remained 'on the books' due to bureaucratic inertia, it remains to be seen whether, following GR 35, they will be withdrawn:

As part of its standard practice, the Committee recommends that States parties which have made reservations to the Convention withdraw them. In cases where a reservation affecting Convention provisions on racist speech is maintained, States parties are invited to provide information as to why

[81] CERD/C/SR.1589, paras 31 and 32.

[82] 'Ad hoc' legislation in the phrase of Malta; see also the statements of Nepal, Papua New Guinea, Tonga, *ibid.*, and the UK.

[83] Australia became a party to the Convention in 1975. Paragraph 26 of the 2009 report of Australia (CERD/C/AUS/15-17) makes the following statement: 'Australia made the reservation to Article 4(a) at the time of ratification because it was not in a position to treat all of the matters covered by Article 4 as offences. The RDA [Racial Discrimination Act] prohibits discrimination and vilification on the basis of race, and contains civil remedies. All states and territories have enacted legislation that prohibits discrimination and, in some cases, vilification.'

[84] Italy makes reference to Article 29 (2) of the UDHR.

[85] Belgium adds references to Articles 10 and 11 of the ECHR.

[86] CERD/C/JPN/3-6, para. 38.

such a reservation is considered necessary, the nature and scope of the reservation, its precise effects in terms of national law and policy, and any plans to limit or withdraw the reservation within a specified time frame.[87]

II. Guidelines

The CERD-specific guidelines do not greatly elaborate the language of Article 4 though there are nuances of difference between the Article and the guidelines, which also make some additions.[88] The chapeau condemnation of propaganda and organizations is transmuted into a request for information on measures to '*publicly* condemn' propaganda, etc.[89] In cases where no specific legislation has been enacted to implement Article 4, States parties should explain the reasons for its absence and their difficulties in implementing the Article, as well as inform the Committee on 'the manner and extent' to which the application of existing laws effectively fulfils their obligations. Finally, information on tribunal and other decisions relevant to 4(a) and 4(b) is requested, as well as statistical data (to be qualitatively assessed) on related complaints, prosecutions and sentences. The guidelines recall GR 7 and GR 15 and would benefit in due course from alignment with GR 35.

III. Character of the Article

Article 4 has been the subject of a series of general recommendations that cumulatively provide a sense of how the Committee envisages its character and functions. In GR 1 (1972), the Committee noted, on the basis of consideration of reports at its fifth session, that the legislation of a number of States parties did not include the provisions of Article 4(a) and 4(b) of the Convention 'the implementation of which . . . is obligatory under the Convention for all States parties'. Accordingly the Committee recommended that States parties should consider supplementing such 'deficient' legislation with provisions conforming to Article 4(a) and 4(b).[90] The Committee returned to the issue in GR 7 (1985),[91] which makes a point on 'the preventive aspects of the Article to deter racism and racial discrimination as well as activities aimed at their promotion or incitement',[92] recommending that, *inter alia*, necessary steps be taken with a view to 'satisfying the mandatory requirements of that Article'.[93]

GR 15 (1993) provides an analysis of the requirements of the Article, coupled with an explanatory justification. The recommendation reads the *travaux* of the Convention to the effect that the drafters regarded Article 4 as central to the struggle against racial discrimination in view of 'a widespread fear of the revival of authoritarian ideologies';[94] organized violence based on ethnic origin and the political exploitation of ethnic difference have only enhanced the relevance of Article 4.[95] The description of Article 4 as 'central' and 'crucial' in the struggle against racial discrimination was preferred to its description as the 'key Article', because this might give rise to misunderstanding concerning the force of

[87] GR 35, para. 23; the paragraph is adapted from the Committee's GR 32 on special measures, para. 38.
[88] CERD/C/2007/1, section C (CERD-Specific Guidelines).
[89] CERD-Specific Guidelines, Article 4, para. A, sub-para. 2 (present author's emphasis).
[90] A/8718, Chapter IX, section A.
[91] A/40/18, Chapter 7, section B.
[92] Final preambular paragraph of the recommendation.
[93] GR 7, para. 1.
[94] GR 15, para. 1.
[95] Para. 1.

other articles.[96] The 'mandatory character' of the article is recalled, and its implementation requires not only the enactment of appropriate legislation but the effective enforcement of such.[97] The latter point is made explicit in *Gelle v Denmark*: 'The Committee observes that it does not suffice, for purposes of Article 4 of the Convention, merely to declare acts of racial discrimination punishable on paper. Rather, criminal laws and other legal provisions prohibiting racial discrimination must also be effectively implemented by the competent national tribunals and other State institutions. This obligation is implicit in Article 4 . . . it is also reflected in other provisions of the Convention.'[98]

The Committee understands Article 4 as having a preventive function. Paragraph 2 of GR 15 notes that, because 'threats and acts of racial violence easily lead to other such acts and generate an atmosphere of hostility, only immediate intervention can meet the obligations of effective response'. Further, on Article 4(b), the recommendation rejects the claim by 'some States' that 'it is inappropriate to declare illegal an organization before its members have promoted or incited racial discrimination';[99] on the contrary, it is important to act against racist organizations at the earliest possible moment through banning them forthwith. Thus, States 'are bound to enact implementing legislation . . . even if they allege that racial discrimination is unknown or that there are no racist organizations in their respective jurisdictions'.[100] Situations of threat need to be defused 'when threats of racial violence are made, and especially when they are made in public and by a group, it is incumbent upon the State to investigate with due diligence and expedition'.[101]

The danger of racist discourse in stirring up hatred and the need to prevent it is also adverted to by the Committee in its indicators adopted in 2005 of 'patterns of systematic and massive racial discrimination'.[102] The indicators include 'systematic and widespread use and acceptance of speech or propaganda promoting hatred and/or inciting violence against minority groups, particularly in the media', and 'grave statements by political leaders/prominent people that express support for affirmation of superiority of a race or an ethnic group, dehumanize and demonize minorities, or condone or justify violence against a minority; the indicators also refer to 'extreme political groups based on a racist platform'. The concepts in these indicators are close to criteria developed by the Committee to engage its early warning and urgent action procedure.[103]

The above themes are taken up and expanded in GR 35. The point on the importance of Article 4 is reiterated in paragraph 10 of GR 35, followed by an expanded reading of its functions: 'Article 4 comprises elements relating to speech and the organizational context for the production of speech, serves the functions of prevention and deterrence, and provides for sanctions when deterrence fails. The Article also has an expressive function in

[96] Discussions of the draft in CERD/C/SR.980, paras 77–98. See also CERD/C/SR.981, para. 79 on the deletion of the term.

[97] GR 15, para. 1.

[98] *Gelle v Denmark*, CERD/C/68/D/34/2004 (2006), para. 7.3. The facts of the case are set out in Chapter 8.

[99] GR 15, para. 6.

[100] CERD 1986, para. 221.

[101] *L.K. v The Netherlands*, CERD/C/42/D/4/1991 (1993), para. 6.6.

[102] A/60/18, para. 20.

[103] Revised (2007) indicators on the early warning and urgent action procedure in A/62/18, Annex III.

underlining the international community's abhorrence of racist hate speech.'[104] The point made in *Gelle* is also given an expansive reading:

> The Committee reiterates that it is not enough to declare the forms of conduct in Article 4 as offences; the provisions of the Article must also be effectively implemented. Effective implementation is characteristically achieved through investigations of offences set out in the Convention and, where appropriate, the prosecution of offenders. The Committee recognizes the principle of expediency in the prosecution of alleged offenders, and observes that it must in each case be applied in the light of the guarantees laid down in the Convention and in other instruments of international law. In this and other respects under the Convention, the Committee recalls that it is not its function to review the interpretation of facts and national law made by domestic authorities, unless the decisions are manifestly absurd or unreasonable.[105]

The recommendation reinforces the point on prevention, explaining the provisions in Article 4 on dissemination of ideas as 'a forthright expression of the preventive function of the Convention', and 'an important complement' to the provisions on incitement.[106] Paragraph 10 of the recommendation adds the function of 'deterrence' to 'prevention' with respect to Article 4, and also finds 'an expressive function in underlining the international community's abhorrence of racist hate speech'.

CERD takes the view that Article 4 is non-self-executing,[107] a stance reiterated in GR 35 which reminds States parties that they are 'required the terms of Article 4 to adopt legislation to combat racist hate speech that falls with its scope';[108] the legislation should cover all elements of the Article.[109] GR 35 introduces 'contextual factors' to be taken into account in qualifying certain forms of conduct as criminal offences:[110] the chapeau to paragraph 15 of the recommendation notes that while Article 4 requires certain forms of conduct to be declared offences punishable by law it does not supply detailed guidance for the qualification of forms of conduct as criminal offences.

IV. Protected Groups and Persons

The chapeau of Article 4 condemns all propaganda and all organizations based on ideas or theories of the 'superiority of one race or group of persons of one colour or ethnic origin' over another. The Committee observes that the term 'based on' (in the chapeau and 4(a)) is understood in relation to Article 1 as equivalent to 'on the grounds of', and in principle holds the same meaning in Article 4.[111] The listing of race, colour, and ethnic origin omits 'descent' and 'national origin', both of which appear in Article 1. The *travaux* are not illuminating in this respect and should not be read to suggest that particular categories remain bereft of protection from hate speech. In *Gelle v Denmark*, speech against Somalis

[104] Para. 10.
[105] Para. 17.
[106] Para. 11.
[107] CERD Study on 'Positive measures designed to eradicate all incitement to, or acts of, racial discrimination' (United Nations, 1986), para. 216. [CERD 1986]. The study was prepared for the Second World Conference on Racism in 1983 as A/CONF.119/10.
[108] Para. 13.
[109] Paragraph 9 states that '[a]s a minimum requirement, and without prejudice to further measures, comprehensive legislation against racial discrimination, including civil and administrative law as well as criminal law, is indispensable to combating racist hate speech effectively'.
[110] Para. 15.
[111] GR 35, para. 11.

was understood as 'degrading or insulting to an entire group of people . . . on account of their *national or* ethnic origin'.[112] It is also clear from practice that descent-based groups are included: section 4 of GR 29 envisages States parties taking measures 'against any dissemination of ideas of caste superiority and inferiority or which attempt to justify violence, hatred or discrimination against descent-based communities', as well as 'strict measures against any incitement to discrimination or violence against the communities'.[113]

Regarding 'intersectionality',[114] practice treats Article 4 along the same lines as Article 1. Among victims of racist hate speech, paragraph 6 of GR 35 outlines a list of affected groups and singles out 'speech directed against women members of these and other vulnerable groups' as a specific subject of concern. In cases where there is a perception of an overlap between ethnicity and religion, as in discrimination against Jews and Sikhs,[115] or against Tatars, described as 'Muslim ethnic minorities'[116] etc, the Committee experiences little difficulty in applying the Convention. Thus, in *Jewish Community of Oslo v Norway*[117] the question of the reach of Article 4 to cover anti-Jewish hate speech by the 'Bootboys' did not trouble the Committee. In some areas of practice, there is a contrast between a relaxed approach taken in the concluding observations and a stricter approach in the context of Article 14 communications.

Thus, while the Committee has made reference in concluding observations to Islamophobia,[118] and to intolerance and hatred against 'Muslims' even without an apparent 'intersection' with ethnicity,[119] the case law exhibits greater caution. *P.S.N. v Denmark* concerned alleged violations of Articles 1(d), 4, and 6 of the Convention through statements published on a website by a Member of Parliament against immigration and Muslims, under the headline 'Articles no one dares to publish'.[120] The opinions expressed were reiterated in an interview given to a newspaper, and some had been previously published in a book. The petitioner filed complaints under the Danish Criminal Code, section 266b of which prohibits racial statements, on the grounds that the website statements targeted a specific group, Muslims, were degrading and propagandistic and were published to a large audience; analogous complaints related to the book and the interview. The State party argued against admissibility, stating that the case fell outside the scope of Article 1 of the Convention in referring to Muslims, while acknowledging that 'it is possible to argue to a certain extent that the statements refer to second-generation immigrants and set up a conflict between "the Danes" and them, thereby falling to some degree within the scope of the Convention'.[121] The petitioner contended that 'Islamophobia, just like attacks against Jews, has manifested itself as a form of racism in many

[112] *Gelle v Denmark*, para. 7.4 (emphasis added).

[113] A/57/18, Chapter XI F, paras (r) and (s).

[114] N. Ghanea, 'Intersectionality and the Spectrum of Racist Hate Speech: Proposals to the UN Committee on the Elimination of Racial Discrimination', *HRQ* (2013) 25, 935–54 [henceforth 'Intersectionality'].

[115] Concluding observations on the UK, A/58/18, para. 539.

[116] Concluding observations on Moldova, A/63/18, para. 267.

[117] *Jewish Community of Oslo and ors v Norway*, CERD/C/67/D/30/2003 (2005).

[118] CERD/C/63/CO/11, para. 21 (United Kingdom). Paragraphs 20 and 21 of the UK concluding observations are contextualized as relating to 'immigrant communities', an implicit ethnic connection.

[119] Examples include Australia, CERD/C/AUS/CO/14, para. 13; Canada, CERD/C/61/CO/3, para. 24; and Switzerland, CERD/C/60/CO/14, para. 9.

[120] *PSN v Denmark*, CERD/C/71/D/36/2006 (2007), para. 1.1.

[121] Para. 4.1. The State party also contended (*ibid.*, para. 4.12) that 'the right to freedom of expression is particularly imperative for an elected representative of the people'.

European countries'.[122] Hatred, it was claimed, had been stirred up against peoples of Arab and Muslim background, and 'culture and religion are connected in Islam'.[123]

In its admissibility decision, CERD observed that 'the impugned statements specifically refer to the Koran, to Islam and to Muslims in general', without any reference to the five grounds set out in Article 1 of the Convention.[124] Further, while the elements in the case file did not allow the Committee to ascertain the intention of the statements, 'it remains that no specific national or ethnic groups were directly targeted', and that 'Muslims currently living in the State party are of heterogeneous origin'.[125] The Committee recognized 'the importance of the interface between race and religion' and stated that 'it would be competent to consider a claim of "double" discrimination on the basis of religion and another ground specifically provided for in Article 1', which was not the case with the petition in question.[126] According to the Committee, the petition was based on religion alone, and 'Islam is not a religion practised solely by a particular group'.[127] The communication was therefore declared inadmissible. Reference to Islamophobia resurfaces in GR 35 in a partial list of communities targeted by hate speech which have engaged the attention of the Committee;[128] another paragraph refers to the use of indirect language to disguise the targets of speech.[129] It remains to be seen whether a greater awareness of 'racialized' communities will be factored into CERD practice.[130]

In the area of hate speech, citizenship is not a relevant factor in calibrating entitlement to protection under Article 4, though in line with practice deriving from Article 1, a general reference to 'foreigners' as targets of hate speech will not be enough to engage the Convention.[131] Paragraph 11 of CERD GR 30 refers to the taking of steps 'to address xenophobic attitudes and behaviour towards non-citizens, in particular hate speech and racial violence', and paragraph 12 recommends 'resolute action to counter any tendency to target, stigmatize, stereotype or profile, on the basis of race, colour, descent and national or ethnic origin, members of non-citizen population groups'.[132] In cases from

[122] Para. 5.3.

[123] Para. 5.3. The petitioner cited (para. 5.3.) the Committee's concluding observations of 2002 and 2006 on Denmark linking people of 'Arab and Muslim' background.

[124] Para. 6.2.

[125] Para. 6.2.

[126] Para. 6.3. The analysis of the possibility of grounding a 'double discrimination' claim will also apply to hate speech premised on the combination of, for example, race/ethnicity and gender.

[127] Para. 6.3. See also *A. W.R.A.P. v Denmark*, CERD/C/71/D/37/2006 (2007).

[128] GR 35, Para. 6.

[129] Para. 7.

[130] For a critique of CERD's position in the Danish hate speech cases, see S. Berry, 'Bringing Muslim Minorities within the ICERD—Square Peg in a Round Hole?' *Human Rights Law Review* 11.3 (2011), 423–50 [henceforth *Muslim Minorities*]; the discussion, 447–9, cites instances in national law where findings of indirect discrimination were made in circumstances not dissimilar to P.S.N. Ghanea, 'Intersectionality', 951, questions Berry's view that 'one can legitimately come to the general conclusion for a whole minority group in a particular region, regardless of the detailed facts, that "discrimination against Muslims constitutes indirect discrimination under ICERD"'. Whatever the merits of the critique and the response, the Committee evidently paid attention to facts and context in making its assessment, and, as noted, left the door open to future appraisals of 'double discrimination'. The resolution of the case links to the Committee's standard view that derogatory general references that do not identify targets of discrimination with adequate clarity are not caught by the Convention: *Quereshi, infra*, n. 131. Such cases are resolved in context, and it is difficult to draw general conclusions therefrom as to the degree of specificity required to engage the prohibitions of the Convention.

[131] *Quereshi v Denmark*, CERD/C/66/D/33/2003 (2005), discussed in Chapter 7.

[132] A/59/18, Chapter VIII.

Yilmaz-Dogan onwards, the nationality of hate speech victims has not been an issue.[133] Protection from xenophobic hate speech supports the overall project of the Convention in line with the corpus of international human rights standards including the forceful condemnation of xenophobic phenomena in the Durban process.[134] GR 35 summarizes the past practice of the Committee on intersectionality, citizenship, caste, etc, in a compendious paragraph which may be assumed to represent the current stance of CERD:

> Racist hate speech addressed in Committee practice has included all the specific speech forms referred to in Article 4 directed against groups recognized in Article 1 of the Convention—which forbids discrimination on grounds of race, colour, descent, or national or ethnic origin—such as indigenous peoples, descent-based groups, and immigrants or non-citizens, including migrant domestic workers, refugees and asylum seekers, as well as speech directed against women members of these and other vulnerable groups. In the light of the principle of intersectionality, and bearing in mind that 'criticism of religious leaders or commentary on religious doctrine or tenets of faith' should not be prohibited or punished,[135] the Committee's attention has also been engaged by hate speech targeting persons belonging to certain ethnic groups who profess or practice a religion different from the majority, including expressions of Islamophobia, anti-Semitism and other similar manifestations of hatred against ethno-religious groups, as well as extreme manifestations of hatred such as incitement to genocide and to terrorism. Stereotyping and stigmatization of members of protected groups has also been the subject of expressions of concern and recommendations adopted by the Committee.[136]

It is clear from the cited paragraph that any suggested limitation of hate speech offences to the three grounds of race, colour, and ethnic origin, is transcended in the view of the Committee through the description of the bulk of Article 4 offences as based on 'race, colour, descent or national or ethnic origin', a practice-based list that replicates the widest statement of grounds in Article 1 of the Convention.

V. Chapeau

In the chapeau, 'ideas or theories of superiority' are not, *ex facie*, condemned as such; the chapeau recites a condemnation of propaganda or organizations based on such ideas or theories.[137] The Convention as a whole suggests a wider 'condemnation' of ideas of racial superiority, bearing in mind the condemnation of superiority doctrine in the preamble, and the demand to punish 'all dissemination of ideas' based on racial superiority or hatred in 4(a); a phrase which does not necessarily imply an organizational context. The assault on racist propaganda includes attempts at 'justification' of racial hatred and discrimination, and not simply their promotion. In GR 35, justification of hatred, etc, makes the leap from the chapeau to the operational aspect of Article 4—offences to be punishable by law—but only when it amounts to incitement.[138] The re-assignment of 'justification' to the category of offences punishable by law also impacts on genocide and crimes against humanity: 'public denials or attempts to justify crimes of genocide and crimes against humanity, as defined by international law, should be

[133] *Yilmaz-Dogan v The Netherlands*, CERD/C/36/D/1/1984 (1988); *L.K. v The Netherlands*, CERD/C/42/D/4/1991 (1993). On non-nationals generally, see Chapter 7.

[134] Recall the title of the 2001 Durban World Conference against Racism, Xenophobia and Related Intolerance

[135] Human Rights Committee GC 34, para. 48.

[136] GR 35, para. 6.

[137] Author's emphasis.

[138] Paras 13 and 14 of GR 35.

declared as offences punishable by law, provided that they clearly constitute incitement to racial violence or hatred'. The Committee also underlines that '"the expression of opinions about historical facts" should not be prohibited or punished'.[139]

Condemnations of justification suggest that a distinction be made between justification of racial hatred and discrimination and explanations, including explanations of a 'scientific' nature. GR 35 alludes to the need to protect serious discussion of racial matters in a paragraph focused on Article 5 of the Convention:

> The Committee considers that the expression of ideas and opinions made in the context of academic debates, political engagement or similar activity, and without incitement to hatred, contempt, violence or discrimination, should be regarded as legitimate exercises of the right to freedom of expression, even when such ideas are controversial.[140]

The term 'propaganda' in the chapeau is carried through from the Declaration on Racial Discrimination and also appears in 4(b).[141] Although etymologically 'propaganda' is not a pejorative term, it has acquired a negative meaning in connection with its use in war and for political causes (isms).[142] In an assessment by one State party, 'propaganda' implies scale, systematic action, and extensive dissemination.[143] Propaganda[144] may be described as appealing to the emotions rather than reason and is intended to persuade to a point of view. Whilst propaganda has been described as 'epistemically defective',[145] the Committee commented in *Jewish Community* that 'the lack of logic of particular remarks is not relevant to the assessment of whether or not they violate Article 4';[146] ambiguity of utterance has, however, been treated as relevant to such an assessment.[147]

In observations, CERD has frequently linked the term 'propaganda' to the media and the Internet,[148] bearing in mind that the chapeau refers to '*all* propaganda' and 4(b) to 'organized and *all other propaganda* activities'.[149] CERD also recommends, where appropriate, ratification of the Additional Protocol to the Convention on Cybercrime. GR 35 widens the concern with hate speech to include, as well as the Internet, electronic media in

[139] Para. 14. The quotation marks in the paragraph refer to paragraph 49 of GC 34 of the Human Rights Committee.

[140] GR 35, para. 25.

[141] With regard to GC 11 of the Human Rights Committee on Article 20, authors comment that 'it is unfortunate that the HRC did not take the opportunity in its General Comment to define the meaning of 'propaganda' for war': S. Joseph and M. Castan, *The International Covenant on Civil and Political Rights* (3rd edn, Oxford University Press, 2014), p. 628. [henceforth *The International Covenant*].

[142] E.S. Herman and N. Chomsky, *Manufacturing Consent: the Political Economy of the Mass Media* (Pantheon Books, 1988).

[143] Statement in the thirteenth periodic report of Denmark, cited in *POEM and FASM v Denmark*, CERD/C/62/D/22/2002 (2003), para. 3.7.

[144] From the Latin gerund of '*propagare*', meaning to propagate.

[145] S.T. Ross, 'Understanding propaganda: the epistemic merit model and its application to art', *Journal of Aesthetic Education*, 3 No. 1 (2002), 16–30.

[146] *Jewish Community*, para. 10.4.

[147] Hence in a case involving a Danish politician's verbal reaction to an incident outside a nightclub, 'the *statement, despite its ambiguity, cannot necessarily be interpreted as claiming that persons of Somali origin* were responsible for the attack in question. Consequently . . . the Committee cannot conclude that her statement falls within the scope of. . . Article 4': *Jama v Denmark*, CERD/C/75/D/41/2008 (2009), para. 7.4.

[148] Examples include concluding observations on Canada, CERD/C/CAN/CO/18, 8; Finland, CERD/C/FIN/CO/19, para. 16; Germany, CERD/C/DEU/CO/18, para. 16; and the Russian Federation, CERD/C/RUS/CO/19, para. 16.

[149] Emphasis added.

general, and social networking sites.[150] In terms of the extent or reach of hate speech, dissemination on the Internet is listed among the contextual factors to be taken into account in qualifying speech as criminal,[151] while the potential contribution of the Internet to promoting a sense of responsibility in the dissemination of ideas is also underlined.[152]

VI. The 'Due Regard' Clause

The chapeau to Article 4 incorporates the famous 'due regard' clause contextualizing the forms of specific action that are, *inter alia*, envisaged in the following paragraphs to fulfil the objectives of the Article. The broadly penal nature of the measures in 4(a) and 4(b) does not necessarily exhaust the range of 'immediate and positive measures' referred to in the *chapeau*, leaving open the question of what further measures might be required in specific situations. The nature and significance of 'immediate and positive measures' is partly explained in GR 35:

> The chapeau of Article 4 incorporates the obligation to take 'immediate and positive measures' to eradicate incitement and discrimination, a stipulation that complements and reinforces obligations under other Articles of the Convention to dedicate the widest possible range of resources to the eradication of hate speech. In general recommendation No. 32 (2009) on the meaning and scope of special measures in the Convention, the Committee summarized 'measures' as comprising legislative, executive, administrative, budgetary and regulatory instruments . . . as well as plans, policies, programmes and . . . regimes.[153]

As is evident from the reservations to Article 4, the interpretation of the 'due regard' clause is an important issue since it contextualizes the measures to be adopted by States parties towards racist speech and organizations. Since the provisions of Article 4 against incitement and violence are legally commonplace, attention shifts to the relationship between dissemination and allied provisions in light of the principles of freedom of expression and association. With reference to the 'due regard' clause, the 1986 CERD study of Article 4 made the observation that:

> [a]nother factor hindering the full application of Article 4 . . . is the interpretation that implementation of the Article might impair or jeopardize freedom of opinion and expression and freedom of . . . assembly and association. This is the extreme position. Midway lies the proposition that a 'balance' has to be struck between Article 4(a) and freedom of speech, and between Article 4(b) and freedom of association. The weight of opinion inclines to the view that the rights of free speech and of free association are not absolute, but subject to limitations.[154]

The 'extreme position' in this reading is that which allows the least intrusion into freedom of expression, etc. Banton reads the study as defending the view that States 'may not invoke the protection of civil rights as a reason to avoid implementation of the Convention.'[155] An analysis by Partsch outlined three different views on the effect of the 'due regard' clause, the first being that States are not authorized to take action that would impair the 'freedoms',

[150] Para. 7.
[151] Para. 15.
[152] Para. 39. On the importance of the Internet to freedom of expression, see *Yildirim v Turkey*, EctHR, App. No. 3111/10 (2012), para. 54 (ECHR).
[153] *ibid.*, para. 10, drawing on GR 32, para. 13.
[154] *CERD Study*, para. 225.
[155] Banton, *International Action*, p. 203.

the second being that a balance must be struck between the freedoms and the duties under the Convention, and the third being the above-cited reading ascribed to the CERD study by Banton.[156] It is not entirely clear that the practice can be reduced to the emollient metaphor of 'balancing' rights and restrictions;[157] there is also the element of the Committee responding to situations under review through a form of situation or context-dependent interpretation, and interpretations that respect the differing responsibilities of States parties and the Committee.[158] In some cases, the statement of freedom of expression has been uppermost in the Committee's observations. Thus, the Committee has reminded a State party of the 'obligation to respect the right to freedom of opinion and expression when implementing Article 4',[159] and recommended another that it 'guarantee respect for the freedoms of expression and association in its implementation of Article 4 (a) and (b)'.[160] In other cases, CERD addressed the situation with a different emphasis, expressing concern at impending litigation challenging the prohibition of hate speech as a violation of freedom of expression.[161]

In the *Jewish Community* case, which concerned public anti-Jewish statements by a leader of the 'Bootboys', the Committee noted that 'the principle of freedom of speech has been afforded a lower level of protection in cases of racist and hate speech dealt with by other international bodies',[162] commenting that

> the 'due regard' clause relates generally to all principles embodied in the Universal Declaration of Human Rights, not only freedom of speech. Thus, to give the right to freedom of speech a more limited role in the context of Article 4 does not deprive the 'due regard' clause of significant meaning, all the more so since all international instruments that guarantee freedom of expression provide for the possibility, under certain circumstances, of limiting the exercise of this right.[163]

[156] *Ibid.*, citing K.J. Partsch, 'Racial speech and human rights: Article 4 of the Convention on the Elimination of All Forms of Racial Discrimination', in S. Coliver (ed.), *Striking a Balance: Hate Speech, Freedom of Expression and Non-Discrimination* (Article 19, 1992), pp. 21–28. Partsch favoured the 'balance' position between freedoms and State obligations.

[157] For an attempt to recast the debate as a conflict of liberties, based on the notion that protection from hate speech is a methodology to promote participation in public discussion and a liberty rather than a restriction, see O. Fiss, *The Irony of Free Speech* (Harvard University Press, 1996).

[158] See, for example, the remarks of Wolfrum in discussions on the eighth and ninth periodic reports of Denmark, CERD/C/SR.864, para. 64: 'Article 4 could not be invoked to assert that protection against racial discrimination took precedence over freedom of opinion. It emerged from that Article that it was for the State and not the Committee to determine whether respect for freedom of opinion and . . . information . . . should take precedence over the prohibition of incitement to racial discrimination.' Compare remarks of Aboul-Nasr, CERD/C/SR.865, para. 8, and Lamptey, *ibid.*, para. 9. The discussions are summarized in A/45/18, para. 56.

[159] Belarus, CERD/C/65/CO/2, para. 8.

[160] Mauritania, CERD/C/65/CO/5, para. 13.

[161] CERD/C/BEL/CO/15, para. 11.

[162] Para. 10.5.

[163] Para. 10.5. In the context of the European Convention on Human Rights, the 'abuse clause'—Article 17—has been utilized from time to time by the Strasbourg organs: 'Nothing in this Convention may be interpreted as implying for any State, group or person any right to engage in any activity or perform any act aimed at the destruction of the rights and freedoms set forth herein or at their limitation to a greater extent than is provided for in the Convention.' For applications, notably in the case of right-wing or Neo-Nazi movements, see ECommHR, *Glimmerveen and Hagenbeek v The Netherlands*, App. Nos 8348/78 and 8406/78 (1979); *Kühnen v Germany*, App. No. 112194/86 (1988); ECtHR *Norwood v The UK*, App. No. 23131/03 (2004); also *Garaudy v France*. Comment in D. Keane, 'Attacking Hate Speech under Article 17 of the European Convention on Human Rights', *Netherlands Quarterly of Human Rights* 25 (2007), 641–63; H. Cannie and D. Voorhoff, 'The Abuse Clause and Freedom of Expression in the European Human Rights Convention: An Added Value for Democracy and Human Rights Protection?' *Netherlands Quarterly of Human Rights* 29 (2011), 54–83.

The role of the freedoms was thus reduced in the racist context through an extrapolation from the texts of international law which restrict their exercise, including the text of the UDHR. While the Committee found meaning and utility in the 'due regard' clause, the invocation of the UDHR in its fullness and not only in relation to freedom of expression tilted the argument towards greater permissibility of restrictions on hate speech in the racist context. The statement on the 'due regard' clause in *Jewish Community* is counterpointed by GR 35:

> Article 4 requires that measures to eliminate incitement and discrimination must be made with due regard to the principles of the Universal Declaration of Human Rights and the rights expressly set forth in Article 5 of the Convention. The phrase 'due regard' implies that, in the creation and application of offences, as well as fulfilling the other requirements of Article 4, the principles of the Universal Declaration of Human Rights and the rights in Article 5 must be given appropriate weight in decision-making processes. The due regard clause has been interpreted by the Committee to apply to human rights and freedoms as a whole, and not simply to freedom of opinion and expression,which should, however, be borne in mind as the most pertinent reference principle when calibrating the legitimacy of speech restrictions.[164]

Although the invocation of the UDHR in Article 4 is explicit, it may be suggested that, as elsewhere in CERD practice, the extent of the restrictions to which the Convention obligates States parties may be gauged through accounting for the Convention text as a whole measured in light of wider international standards and practice. The interrelationship between the Convention and the wider span of principles on freedom of speech is strongly asserted for interpretative purposes in GR 35:

> By virtue of its work in implementing the Convention as a living instrument, the Committee engages with the wider human rights environment, awareness of which suffuses the Convention. In gauging the scope of freedom of expression, it should be recalled that the right is integrated into the Convention and is not simply articulated outside it: the principles of the Convention contribute to a fuller understanding of the parameters of the right in contemporary international human rights law. The Committee has integrated this right to freedom of expression into its work on combating hate speech, commenting where appropriate on its lack of effective implementation and, where necessary, drawing upon its elaboration in sister human rights bodies.[165]

Part of the difficulty with Article 4 has been that it appeared to be less 'permeable' than other Convention articles—'the text of Article 4 is abundantly clear'[166]—and perhaps harder to integrate with broader standards. The adoption by the Committee of GR 35 in 2013 represents a determined attempt at 'integration' of the text of Article 4 into the broader stream of human rights principles, throwing into relief some earlier stances of CERD on the persistently controversial issue of racist speech.

VII. Article 4(a)

In *Deutscher v Germany*, the Committee, apparently subsuming 'dissemination of ideas' under 'propaganda' stated that the list 'in Article 4, paragraph (a) . . . does not enumerate all conceivable discriminatory acts, but rather acts in which violence is used or where racist

164 Para. 19.
165 Para. 4.
166 I. Diaconu, *Racial Discrimination* (UNDP Romania, 2007), p. 192.

propaganda in the goal'.[167] A literal analysis of Article 4(a) reveals that States parties shall declare as offences punishable by law: dissemination of ideas based on racial superiority; dissemination of ideas based on racial hatred; incitement to racial discrimination; acts of violence against any race or group of persons of another colour or ethnic origin; incitement to such acts of violence; and provision of assistance to racist activities including their financing. This classification omits 'incitement to racial hatred',[168] introduced as a component of the paragraph by GR 15,[169] departing from the literal wording of 4(a) which does not refer to incitement to racial hatred but to incitement to racial discrimination.[170] Concluding observations are replete with references to incitement to racial hatred, welcoming greater stringency in addressing incitement to racial hatred, references to which have been supplemented by references to 'ethnic'[171] or 'tribal'[172] hatred. The Committee has also recommended extension of the crime of incitement to racial hatred to cover offences motivated by religious hatred against immigrant communities.[173] The Committee justifies its interpretation of Article 4 as including incitement to racial hatred by referring to the preventive aim of the Convention.[174]

GR 35 subsumes incitement to hatred into its classification of Article 4 offences and adds wider terminology on the basis of further Committee practice. Taking paragraphs of Article 4 together, the Committee recommends that States parties 'declare and effectively sanction as offences punishable by law':

(a) All dissemination of ideas based on racial or ethnic superiority or hatred, by whatever means;
(b) Incitement to hatred, contempt or discrimination against members of a group on grounds of their race, colour, descent, or national or ethnic origin;
(c) Threats or incitement to violence against persons or groups on the grounds in (b) above;
(d) Expression of insults, ridicule or slander of persons or groups or justification of hatred, contempt or discrimination on the grounds in (b) above, when it clearly amounts to incitement to hatred or discrimination;
(e) Participation in organizations and activities which promote and incite racial discrimination.[175]

The list of offences to be declared, incorporating terms such as 'insults', 'ridicule', 'slander', and 'contempt', which are not described as such in the article, grafts elements of subsequent practice and understandings on to the skeleton of the article. The result is to widen the scope of Article 4, unless the refreshed terminology is understood as derived from the text and is not simply innovative. In practice, any implicit widening of the scope

[167] *Zentralrat Deutscher Sinti und Roma (on behalf of Zentralrat Deutscher Sinti und Roma and ors) v Germany*, CERD/C/72/D/38/2006 (2009), para. 4.3.

[168] See also CERD GR 31, para. 4(a) of which includes reference to incitement to racial hatred: HRI/GEN/Rev.9 (Vol. II), p. 309.

[169] The first four are set out in paragraph 3 of the recommendation, the fifth (financing activities) is set out in paragraph 5.

[170] Incitement to discrimination is referred to in paragraph 4 of GR 15 with reference to Article 20 of the ICCPR, and in paragraph 6 in connection with Article 4(b) of ICERD.

[171] CERD/C/60/CO/4, para. 12 (Croatia).

[172] CERD/C/65/CO/4, para. 13 (Madagascar).

[173] CERD/C/63/CO/11, para. 21 (United Kingdom).

[174] Principle 12 of Article 19's *Camden Principles on Freedom of Expression and Equality* (2009) define 'hatred' and 'hostility' to refer to 'intense and irrational emotions of opprobrium, enmity and detestation towards the target group'. The reference to irrationality is appropriate in the context of incitement to racial hatred but in other contexts there may be perfectly rational justifications for hatred of those who commit great wrongs.

[175] Para. 13.

of the offences to be declared is likely to be countered by the more stringent requirements for the operation of law set out particularly in paragraphs 12, 14, 15, 16, 18, 20, and 25 of the recommendation.

Article 4 appears to represent a kind of apotheosis of the punitive approach to addressing racial discrimination through its references to 'an offence punishable by law'.[176] Despite the possible interpretation that 'offence punishable by law' could refer to, for example, the use of administrative or other sanctions, it has been observed that few Committee members 'have been persuaded that alternatives to criminal punishment are appropriate under 4(a)'.[177] CERD tended to adopt a strict, criminal law approach to the phrase: 'In saying that certain acts shall be punishable, the Convention requires sanctions under the criminal law. Actions prohibited under other Articles of the Convention can be dealt with under other branches of law: administrative law, constitutional law, civil law, labour law, and so on, but not those to which Articles 4(a) and 4(b) relate.'[178] While maintaining the centrality of criminal law in the application of Article 4 through references to 'criminalization', paragraph 12 of GR 35 introduces important nuances: 'the criminalization of forms of racist expression should be reserved for serious cases, to be proven beyond reasonable doubt, while less serious cases should be addressed by means other than criminal law, taking into account, *inter alia*, the nature and extent of the impact on targeted persons and groups';[179] adding that, as a 'minimum requirement, and without prejudice to further measures, comprehensive legislation against racial discrimination, including civil and administrative law as well as criminal law, is indispensable to combating racist hate speech effectively'.[180]

VIII. Dissemination and Incitement

The prohibition of the 'dissemination' of ideas based on racial superiority or hatred—from the Latin '*disseminare*' meaning to scatter, and defined simply as to 'spread widely',[181]—has been the subject of much urging by CERD. Statistics on cases brought, prosecutions launched, and penalties imposed under the dissemination rubric are requested in similar fashion to other data sought. The Committee has been critical of criminal provisions on 'dissemination' that confine the prohibition to dissemination among the public,[182] though the Committee has also commented on 'statements . . . made squarely in the public arena, which is the central focus of the . . . the Convention'.[183] On the dissemination of ideas, the provisions in GR 35 on denials of genocide and crimes against humanity should be

176 Article 4 of ICERD and Article 13(5) of the American Convention on Human Rights refer the offending speech as 'punishable by law', whereas Article 20(2) of the ICCPR requires that it be 'prohibited by law'. Paragraph 2 of the general comment of the Human Rights Committee on Article 20 (GC 11) refers to 'an appropriate sanction 'in case of violation rather than simply 'punishment': HRI/GEN/1/Rev.9 (Vol. I), p. 182.

177 D. Mahalic and J.G. Mahalic, 'The limitation of provisions of the International Convention on the Elimination of All Forms of Racial Discrimination', *HRQ* 9 (1987), 74–101, 94.

178 M. Banton, *International Action against Racial Discrimination* (Clarendon Press, 1996), p. 205, citing Wolfrum, another former member of the Committee.

179 GR 35, para. 12.

180 *Ibid.*, para. 9.

181 *Concise Oxford English Dictionary* (11th edn, Oxford University Press, 2004), p. 414.

182 A/58/18, para. 474 (Norway).

183 *Gelle v Denmark*, para. 6.5; also *Jama v Denmark*, para. 6.5. See further discussion of 'public' and 'private' in Chapters 6 and 8.

understood in light of previous practice .[184] The Committee has not criticized laws against Holocaust denial and took a step further in supporting the criminalization by France of 'attempts to deny war crimes and crimes against humanity as defined in the Statute of the International Criminal Court, and not only those committed during the Second World War',[185] as well as welcoming education on the Holocaust and on the 'causes of the genocide of Jews and Roma'.[186] GR 35 does not refer to the Statute of the International Criminal Court (ICC) but opts for a broader formulation. Statements based on racial superiority can in particular contexts be taken as incitement,[187] and 'Holocaust denial' can also function as a framework for incitement to discrimination; without specific reference to the Holocaust, GR 35 makes it clear that penalization of denials is permissible only when such denials constitute incitement.[188]

Incitement, or the stirring up of—usually—violent or unlawful behaviour, is a staple of systems of criminal law. Whereas the application of criminal law to incitement to racial discrimination and hatred and, *a fortiori*, to racial violence is unremarkable, its application to dissemination of ideas raises more questions. CERD has on occasions taken a strict line on the mental element supporting criminal liability for dissemination and incitement alike. The CERD study published by the United Nations in 1986 stated baldly that

> [t]wo things are prohibited to be disseminated under penalty of law... ideas based on racial superiority and ideas based on racial hatred. It is also clear that the mere act of dissemination is penalized, despite lack of intention to commit an offence and the consequences of the dissemination, whether they be grave or insignificant.[189]

Such a stance approaches the domain of strict or absolute liability, and such an absence of culpability elements beyond the act of dissemination would do violence to basic principles of criminal liability in many if not most jurisdictions.[190] Equally, on the definition of

[184] GR 35, para. 14.

[185] CERD/C/FRA/CO/16, para. 20.

[186] Concluding observations on Moldova, CERD/C/MDA/CO/15, para. 6.

[187] In *Jewish Community of Oslo v Norway*, para. 10.4, statements made by the leader of the 'Bootboys' 'contain ideas based on racial superiority or hatred; the deference to Hitler and his principles and "footsteps" must... be taken as incitement at least to racial discrimination, if not to violence'.

[188] Para. 14, which footnotes paragraph 49 of GC 34 of the Human Rights Committee, which states that laws 'that penalize the expression of opinions about historical facts are incompatible with the obligations that the Covenant imposes... The Covenant does not permit general prohibition of expressions of an erroneous opinion or an incorrect interpretation of past events... Restrictions on freedom of opinion should not go beyond. What is permitted in paragraph 3 [of Article 19] or required under Article 20.' The paragraph in GC 34 cites *Robert Faurisson v France*, CCPR/C/58/D/550/1993 (1996), where the author of the communication denied the existence of gas chambers for the extermination of Jews in concentration camps, and argued that the Gayssot Act of 1990 promoted the Nuremberg trial and judgment to the status of dogma by imposing criminal sanctions on those who challenged their findings and premises. The Human Rights Committee upheld the ban under Article 19(3)(a) of the ICCPR with regard to respect for the rights and reputation of others because (para. 9.6.) the restriction 'served the respect of the Jewish community to live free from fear of an atmosphere of anti-Semitism'. The Views on the Gayssot Act are tailored to the facts, while the comment in paragraph 49 of GC 34 'seems to indicate that laws prohibiting Holocaust denial, or indeed the denial of any particular historical facts, are incompatible with Article 19': Joseph and Castan, *The International Covenant*, p. 643. See also *Ross v Canada*, where the Human Rights Committee recalled Faurisson, adding that the restrictions upheld in the latter case 'also derive support from the principles reflected in Article 20 (2) of the Covenant': CCPR/C/70/D/736/1997 (2000), para. 11.5.

[189] CERD 1986 Study, para. 83.

[190] See T. Meron, 'The meaning and reach of the International Convention on the Elimination of All Forms of Racial Discrimination', *AJIL* 79 (1985), 283–318, Banton, *International Action*, pp. 202–9; S. Farrior,

incitement in Article 4(a), the same paper concluded that 'what is penalized . . . is the mere act of incitement, without reference to any intention on the part of the offender or the result of such incitement, if any'.[191]

Whatever comment might be made concerning a causal link between 'dissemination' of a racist tract and awareness of criminality,[192] the elements of striving to bring about a particular result or the creation of an imminent risk are commonly built into the notion of incitement, whether or not the results or consequences follow. It is not unreasonable to read the Convention to the effect that the local application of these provisions will be embedded in standard criminal law principles.[193] 'Hard-line' statements on behalf of the Committee rejecting the need for proof of *mens rea* for incitement and dissemination stand in stark contrast to GR 35, which in paragraph 16 rejects 'strict liability':

> Incitement characteristically seeks to influence others to engage in certain forms of conduct, including the commission of crime, through advocacy or threats. Incitement may be express or implied, through actions such as displays of racist symbols or distribution of materials as well as words. The notion of incitement as an inchoate crime does not require that the incitement has been acted upon, but in regulating the forms of incitement referred to in Article 4, States parties should take into account, as important elements in the incitement offences, in addition to the considerations outlined in paragraph 15 above, the intention of the speaker, and the imminent risk or likelihood that the conduct desired or intended by the speaker will result from the speech in question, considerations which also apply to the other offences listed in paragraph 13.

Paragraph 15 of GR 35 refers to a range of 'contextual factors' in the qualification of dissemination and incitement as offences punishable by law: the content and form of speech, the economic, social and political climate, the position or status of the speaker, the reach of the speech, and the objectives of the speech, each subdivided into subsets of factors. The combination of provisions in paragraphs 15 and 16 constricts freewheeling approaches to criminal prosecution for speech offences. Instances where the Committee urged a State party to consider relaxing the strict requirement of intent (wilful conduct) in incitement to racial discrimination,[194] and welcomed an amendment to the penal code so that it was no longer necessary that incitement to racial hatred be intentional in order to

'Moulding the matrix: the historical and theoretical foundations of international law concerning hate speech', *Berkeley Journal of International Law* 14 (1996), 1–98, for samples of Committee practice.

[191] *CERD 1986 Study*, para. 96. Re dissemination and incitement together, see, *ibid.*, para. 235: 'The legislation of some States parties subjects . . . [dissemination and incitement] . . . to certain conditions, for example that the dissemination or incitement must be intentional, or must have certain objectives such as "to stir up hatred", or that they be "threatening, abusive or insulting" . . . these conditions are restrictive and ignore the fact that Article 4(a) of the Convention declares punishable the mere act of dissemination or incitement, without any conditions.'

[192] 'Laws against incitement to racial discrimination or hatred are . . . necessary to protect public order and the rights of others. The majority of the Committee is convinced that the same applies without distinction to the dissemination of ideas based on racial superiority': CERD 1986, para. 231; this formulation indicates that even in 1983 when the report was prepared for the World Conference the Committee was not unanimous on this question.

[193] The *travaux* are not outstandingly clear on this question. Referring to the prohibition in Article 4(b), the report of the Commission on Human Rights summarized a discussion on the distinction between 'incite' and promote' in terms of incitement being 'a conscious and motivated act', while promotion might occur 'without any real intention or endeavour to incite': E/CN.4/874, para. 169. This suggests that the standard criminal law character of incitement was well understood.

[194] Ukraine, CERD/C/UKR/CO/18, para. 9.

be construed as an offence,[195] are not in accord with current practice as represented by GR 35. Concluding observations and communications that centre on intention to disseminate may be expected to respond to the reading of Article 4 set out in GR 35.

Racial and ethnic stereotyping and stigmatization have also been drawn into general discourse on Article 4. GR 35 refers to these forms of speech but does not list them as offences punishable by law, noting only that '[s]tereotyping and stigmatization of members of protected groups has also been the subject of expressions of concern and recommendations adopted by the Committee'.[196] The recommendation also asserts the power of free speech as such 'in the deconstruction of racial stereotypes',[197] and regards 'the avoidance of stereotyping' as a desideratum in media representations of ethnic, indigenous, and other groups.[198]

Assistance to racist activities is the last in the list of the 4(a) offences to be declared by law. GR 15 reminds States parties that Article 4(a) also penalizes the financing of racist activities, which the Committee takes to include all the offences to be declared under 4(a). The Committee has recommended the amendment or introduction of legislation to make such assistance a discrete criminal offence.[199] Whereas the 'provision of any assistance' may be consistent with general notions of assistance to crime, the financing aspect may also be associated with the organization-directed 4(b). Assistance to racist activities is not referred to explicitly in the list of offences in paragraph 13 of GR 35.

IX. Article 4(b)

The banning of organizations in Article 4(b) is a strongly contested provision of Article 4, along with 'dissemination' in 4(a). The requirement to ban racist organizations in line with Article 4(b) has produced many exchanges between the Committee and States parties. If the reluctance of some States to ban racist groups has not significantly abated, neither has the Committee's resolve to press for such action to be taken. Paragraph 4(b) requires that States parties declare illegal and prohibit organizations which promote and incite racial discrimination, organized propaganda activities which promote and incite racial discrimination, and all other propaganda activities which promote and incite racial discrimination. Additionally, participation in the above organizations shall be recognized as an offence punishable by law, as shall participation in all other (racist) propaganda activities. GR 15 is combative:

> Some States have maintained that in their legal order it is inappropriate to declare illegal an organization before its members have promoted or incited racial discrimination. The Committee is of the opinion that Article 4(b) places a greater burden upon such States to be vigilant in proceeding against such organizations at the earliest moment. These organizations, as well as organized and other propaganda activities, have to be declared illegal and prohibited. Participation in these organizations is, of itself, to be punished.[200]

[195] A/56/18, para. 262 (Cyprus).

[196] Para. 6.

[197] Para. 29.

[198] Para. 40.

[199] 'The Committee recommends that the State party establish provisions making each of the criminal acts referred to in the relevant paragraphs of Article 4 . . . a criminal offence, including assistance to and financing of racist activities': concluding observations on Togo, CERD/C/TGO/CO/17, para. 12.

[200] GR 15, para. 6.

CERD insists that the organization is to be banned on the basis of its character—its purposes, aims, and objectives—without any hiatus, before it attempts to engage in nefarious activities. GR 35 reiterates the basics of 4(b):

> The Committee underlines that Article 4 (b) requires that racist organizations which promote and incite racial discrimination be declared illegal and prohibited. The Committee understands that the reference to 'organized . . . propaganda activities' implicates improvised forms of organization or networks, and that 'all other propaganda activities' may be taken to refer to unorganized or spontaneous promotion and incitement of racial discrimination.[201]

Participation in every case is to be punished by law, a requirement that overlaps with the assistance/financing reference in 4(a). The emphasis in 4(b) is presumably on private actors, since 4(c) addresses the possibility of promotion or incitement of racial discrimination by the public authorities.

Accordingly, CERD expresses concern about the absence of legislation prohibiting racist organizations or situations in States where the law focuses on prohibition of activities conducted by racist organizations rather than on the prohibition of the organizations as such.[202] The Committee has, *inter alia*, insisted on 'specific',[203] 'explicit',[204] or 'specific and unambiguous'[205] criminal legislation banning racist organizations. It has not been receptive to arguments that a formal ban on organizations would not be useful because the groups involved were loose networks rather than formal organizations,[206] nor to arguments that banning organizations would have adverse effects.[207] The argument that banning organizations would merely 'drive them underground' comes to mind in such cases; an 'organization driven underground by repressive measures might be much more dangerous than one allowed to act openly'.[208]

X. Article 4(c)

The paragraph underscores the law and policy obligation in relation to public authorities as well as widening obligations beyond the application of criminal law. Lerner observes that 4(c) does not impose obligations regarding internal criminal law 'but only urges them to adjust their policies to principles in accordance with the Convention and to take care that public officers, on the national and local levels, do not depart from such policies. In that sense it complements Article 2, paragraph 1'.[209] Another author comments that 4(c) adds little to the other two paragraphs of Article 4 though it does 'serve to illustrate the particular evil of public officials and bodies engaging in racist activities'.[210] In more

[201] GR 35, para. 21.

[202] Concluding observations on Canada, CERD/C/61/CO/3, para. 21.

[203] Concluding observations on Jamaica, CERD/C/60/CO/6, para. 6.

[204] Concluding observations on Uganda, CERD/C/62/CO/11, para. 12.

[205] Concluding observations on Fiji, CERD/C/FJI/CO/17, para. 20.

[206] Concluding observations on Norway, CERD/C/63/CO/9, para. 13. The representative of Norway, CERD/C/SR.1603, para. 36, had observed that the government 'had not introduced a ban on racist organizations, since such a ban could have the indirect effect of making informal racist networks appear lawful'.

[207] Concluding observations on Trinidad and Tobago, A/56/18, para. 349.

[208] K. Boyle and A. Baldaccini, 'A Critical Evaluation of International Human Rights Approaches to Racism', in S. Fredman (ed.), *Discrimination and Human Rights: The Case of Racism* (Oxford University Press, 2001), Baldaccini, pp. 135–91, p. 162.

[209] *The UN Convention*, p. 51.

[210] T. Mendel, 'Equality and freedom of expression: an accommodative framework', Background Paper for 11 December 2008 Meeting for Promoting Equality within a Free Speech Framework.

general terms, racist expression by public figures or officials has been judged by CERD to be of particular concern in view of the influence or power they exercise. Hence in one case, the Committee was 'deeply concerned about reported instances of hate speech directed against national and ethnic minorities, including statements attributed to high-ranking government officials and public figures . . . reported to have a significant detrimental effect on the population'.[211] On public and private authorities/institutions, in *Deutscher v Germany*, the petitioners complained under, *inter alia*, Article 4(c), about a letter published in a professional police journal that contained disparaging remarks about Roma and Sinti. The State party submitted that the letter was published by the author as a private person and not in his official capacity, adding that the 'absence of public charges and of a conviction by public prosecutorial authorities cannot be considered to be a violation of this provision, as promotion and incitement requires significantly more than merely refraining from further criminal prosecution'.[212] The Committee did not elaborate on the term 'permit' but agreed with the contention that the professional association that published the letter was not a State organ and that the letter was written in a private capacity, declaring that part of the claim to be inadmissible.[213]

GR 35 makes only limited reference to this paragraph of Article 4, focusing on the individuals who staff public authorities and institutions:

> Under the terms of Article 4 (c) regarding public authorities or public institutions, racist expressions emanating from such authorities or institutions are regarded by the Committee as of particular concern, especially statements attributed to high-ranking officials. Without prejudice to the application of the offences in subparagraphs (a) and (b) of Article 4, which apply to public officials as well as to all others, the 'immediate and positive measures' referred to in the chapeau may additionally include measures of a disciplinary nature, such as removal from office, where appropriate, as well as effective remedies for victims.[214]

The special responsibility of public figures to provide anti-racist and pro-tolerance leadership is a recurring motif in CERD work.

D. Comment

The Committee considers it an obligation to 'ensure the coherence of the interpretation of the provisions of Article 4'.[215] The words and phrases and internal conceptual arrangement of the Article raise their own questions, as does its relationship to the Convention as a whole and to sibling provisions in human rights. Historically, CERD practice has tended towards literalism in downplaying the psychological, motivational elements in hate speech, and the circumstances and consequences of its production. Literalist tendencies were never complete in that practice includes the recognition of a wider span of victims of hate speech than strictly mandated by Article 4, augmenting the victim-oriented ethos of ICERD,[216] while the emphasis on State obligations in the Article has

211 Concluding observations on Turkmenistan, CERD/C/TKM/CO/5, para. 11.

212 Para. 4.6.

213 Para. 7.5.

214 GR 35, Para. 22.

215 *Jewish Community*, para. 10.3.

216 P. Thornberry, 'Bringing the victims to light under the International Convention on the Elimination of All Forms of Racial Discrimination', in M.A. Jovanović and I. Krstić (eds), *Human Rights Today—60 Years of the Universal Declaration* (Eleven International Publishing), pp. 145–70.

not ruled out its conceptualization as a right of individuals to be protected.[217] The perception of ICERD as a 'draconian' regulatory model that is less than generous to freedom of speech principles has nonetheless been widespread and is in some respects justified, particularly as regards the offence of dissemination of ideas based on superiority and hatred,[218] and the stern attitude to the banning of racist organizations where the 'Murder Incorporated' paradigm retains its lustre. The logic of the principled structure of the Convention is recalled in GR 35, when offences of dissemination and incitement are categorized as addressing the 'upstream' and 'downstream' manifestations of racist speech,[219] and the dissemination of ideas provisions are understood as 'a forthright expression of the preventive function of the Convention'.[220]

The emergence of GR 35 appears to mark an *aggiornamento* of the overall approach to Article 4 and racist hate speech in general.[221] As elsewhere in the operation of the Convention, and in light of its conceptualization as a 'living instrument', fresh currents of opinion have propelled the Committee towards a re-evaluation of the relationship between the proscription of hate speech and respect for freedom of expression,[222] standards which should 'be seen as complementary and not the expression of a zero sum game where the priority given to one necessitates the diminution of the other'.[223] Apart from replenishing the 'philosophy' and details of Article 4, the recommendation locates the article in the wider context of the 'resources of the Convention', an evocation that weakens the propensity 'to account for all appearances from as few principles as possible'.[224] Hence, the vision of Article 4 as the nucleus around which the other particles of the Convention circulate, has somewhat receded. The incorporation into the recommendation of Articles 5 and 7, which underline the potential of free speech and education to counter hate speech. Criminal law has a rightful place in the legal armoury against hate speech, and may be educative in itself, but also benefits through integration with a wider repertoire of law and policy: as noted, in GR 35, it is recommended that 'the criminalization of... racist expression should be reserved for serious cases... while less serious cases should be addressed by means other than criminal law'.[225] Taking a cue from the Human Rights Committee—and wider international understandings of freedom of

[217] '[T]he fact that Article 4 is couched in terms of States parties' responsibilities, rather than inherent rights of individuals, does not imply that they are matters to be left to the internal jurisdiction of States parties... If such were the case, the protection regime established by the Convention would be weakened significantly... the Convention's "rights" are not confined to Article 5': *Jewish Community*, para. 10.6. See further discussion in relation to Article 6 in Chapter 16.

[218] The dissemination ideas provision 'is unusual among human rights instruments in referring to the penalization of speech without an express link to the possibility that such speech will incite hatred or violence or discrimination': *TBB-Turkish Union in Berlin/Brandenburg v Germany*, CERD/C/82/D/48/2010 (2013), Vázquez dissent, para. 5.

[219] Para. 30.

[220] Para. 11.

[221] While 'hate speech' in Article 4 principally relates to crime, it is distinguishable from the broader question of 'hate crimes', that is, crimes in general aggravated by racist motivations: see commentary in Chapter 8 on Article 2 of the Convention.

[222] Footnotes to the recommendation accord prominence to GC 34 of the Human Rights Committee and The Rabat Plan of Action on the Prohibition of the Advocacy of National, Racial or Religious Hatred that Constitutes Incitement to Discrimination, Hostility or Violence.

[223] Para. 45.

[224] Smith, *The Theory of Moral Sentiments* (1790), VII.ii.2.14, cited in A. Sen, *The Idea of Justice* (Penguin Books, 2010), 394.

[225] Para. 12; also *TBB-Turkish Union*, Vázquez dissent, para. 13.

speech principles—the recommendation insists that the 'application of criminal sanctions should be governed by principles of legality,[226] proportionality and necessity'.[227] Further, in light of the 'due regard' clause, the 'chilling effects' on freedom of speech of vaguely drafted laws and over-zealous approaches to criminal prosecution should also be borne in mind.[228]

With regard to the details of Article 4, GR 35 subtly widens the list of offences while placing stronger freedom of speech safeguards around their implementation. For incitement, recommendations on the mental and consequential aspects of the definition of crime, expressed in terms of intention and imminence of risk, would place greater constraints upon prosecutions than before.[229] The definition of incitement appears to mark a departure from earlier pronouncements, though, as paragraph 15 of the recommendation also makes clear, the understanding of context in the definition and application of offences is always crucial. 'Context' points made by paragraph 15 recall, *inter alia*, that '[d]iscourses which in one context are innocuous may take on a dangerous significance in another': genocidal discourses represent only the most potent case in point.[230] The provision on genocide denial suggests careful crafting of laws against, for example, Holocaust denial, though the public speech of the deniers may well have the capacity to provoke and incite in specific circumstances.

The dissemination offence is also subject to the modifiers in the recommendation, with its notable provision to protect academic and political speech from suppressive action, provided it does not amount to incitement.[231] *A fortiori*, human rights defenders should also not be subject to speech suppression. Serious discussions of racial questions are not in principle caught in the net of Article 4; they would not, *ex facie*, equate with 'propaganda' or preaching unless we succumb, *mirabile dictu*, to that classic of Oliver Wendell Holmes: 'Every idea is an incitement . . . Eloquence may set fire to reason.'[232] In *Poem and Fasm v Denmark*, the State party took the view that Article 4 did not impugn 'scientific theories put forward on differences of race, nationality or ethnicity . . . [and] . . . probably also . . . statements that were not made in a scientific context proper, but otherwise as part of an objective debate'.[233] The distinction between 'scientific contexts' and 'objective debate' on the one hand, and racist manipulation of opinion on the other is not always easy to draw, and the Committee may not be overly impressed by the cultural or academic credentials of an author or a publication. In *TBB-Turkish Union*, the fact that the impugned interview with the author (Sarrazin), headed 'Class instead of Mass', was published in the German cultural journal *Lettre International* (and subsequently included in a book) did not save his non-prosecution from criticism by the Committee, despite the comment by the State party that the comments were made in the context of 'a critical

[226] The essence of being 'provided by law' is that laws should be formulated with sufficient precision so that conduct can be appropriately regulated in advance.

[227] GR 35, para. 12.

[228] *Ibid.*, para. 20.

[229] The list of offences in paragraph 13.

[230] GR 35, para. 15.

[231] *Ibid.*, para. 25.

[232] In *Gitlow v New York*, 268 U.S. (1925). Perhaps less well known is his statement that a 'new and valid idea is worth more than a regiment and fewer men can furnish the former than can command the latter', in H.C. Shriver (ed.), *Justice Oliver Wendell Holmes: His Book Notices and Uncollected Papers* (Central Book Co., 1936), p. 181.

[233] Para. 4.10.

discussion of economic and social problems' in Berlin.[234] The implied issue of genres of discourse was adverted to in the dissent of Committee member Vázquez, who argued that 'States parties should take account of the context and the genre of the discussion in which the statements were made . . . whether the statements were part of a vitriolic *ad hominem* attack or . . . were presented as a contribution, to reasoned debate on a matter of public concern, as the State party found'.[235] The history of race theory unfortunately shows that rabid views were regularly expressed through the best publishing vehicles for academic discussion. By contrast, the context of scientific research on a specific ethnic group saved the writers and the State in *Aksu v Turkey*, where a book and two dictionaries were alleged to have contained material offensive to Roma.[236] The 'academic' setting did not save Mr Sarrazin.[237]

Logic suggests that a line should be drawn between bringing racist arguments to light, in a sense 'disseminating' them, and endorsing such statements, though the distinction may be a fine one. The conviction by the Danish courts of a journalist (Jersild) for presenting a television programme containing racist statements from a group known as 'the greenjackets' is a case in point. The European Court of Human Rights (ECtHR) in *Jersild v Denmark*[238] took the view that the journalist had not intended to promote racism but to bring it to light, and the conviction had violated Jersild's right to freedom of expression under Article 10 of the ECHR. The case is instructive in that the relevant Danish law was passed to conform to its obligations under ICERD, while the European Court took the view that its own interpretation of Article 10 of the ECHR was also compatible with ICERD.[239]

What mode of superiority, if any, was being disseminated engaged the attention of the Committee in *TBB-Turkish Union*. The chapeau to Article 4 refers to 'theories of superiority of one race or group of persons of one colour or ethnic origin', while 4(a) refers curtly to 'ideas based on racial superiority or hatred'. For the majority, the ideas expressed by Sarrazin were ideas of 'racial superiority, denying respect as human beings and depicting generalized negative characteristics of the Turkish population'.[240] For dissenting member Vázquez, on the other hand, the issue was one of 'statements of superiority on the basis of nationality or ethnicity' and whether such were caught in the net of Article 4(a); whether or not such statements were to be declared as offences under

[234] *TBB-Turkish Union v Germany*, para. 4.4. In para. 8.1, the petitioner cites a 'scientific opinion' qualifying Sarrazin's interview statements as racist: there appears to have been, *vide* Swift, a 'battle of the books'.

[235] *TBB-Turkish Union v Germany*, Vázquez dissent, para. 14.

[236] EctHR, *Aksu v Turkey*, App. Nos 4149/04 and 41029/04 (2012). With regard to the book, the Court stated that it was 'consistent with the . . . case law to submit to careful scrutiny any restrictions on the freedom of academics to carry out research and publish their findings' (para. 71); it was also consistent 'to consider the impugned passages not in isolation but in the context of the book as a whole and to take into account the method of research' (para. 72). See also the concurring opinion of Evatt and Kretzmer, co-signed by Klein in *Faurisson v France*, para. 10 of which observed that while 'there is every reason to maintain protection of bona fide historical research against restriction, even when it challenges accepted historical truths . . . anti-Semitic allegations of the sort made by the author, which violate the rights of others . . . do not have the same protection . . . The restrictions placed on the author did not curb the core of his right to freedom of expression, nor . . . his freedom of research; they were intimately linked to . . . the right to be free from incitement to racism or anti-Semitism.'

[237] For an approach to a different branch of science, see the Inter-American Convention against Racism, Article 4 (xiii).

[238] ECtHR, App. No. 15890/89 (1994).

[239] *Jersild*, para. 30.

[240] *TBB-Turkish Union*, para. 12.6.

4(a), he did not find that Sarrazin had asserted 'the inferiority of Turkish culture or Turks as a nationality or ethnic group'.[241] The majority did not unpack the race/ethnicity nexus, leaving unanswered what degree or quality of superiority was being asserted. However, Article 4(a) uses 'racial superiority' and 'racial discrimination' in the same sentence, making it somewhat implausible to argue that 'racial superiority' is to be understood narrowly as only 'race', while 'racial discrimination' carries the usual expansive meaning set out in Article 1; further the identified targets of hate speech in 4(a) include not only race but also groups of persons 'of another colour or ethnic origin'. The majority may also have detected a hint of biological racism in summarizing the author's suggestion that Turks were 'neither able nor willing' to integrate, and exhibited 'a collective mentality that is aggressive and ancestral';[242] the additional references to the intelligence of a population were also not helpful; the positive appreciation of the intelligence of other populations may only have hardened, not softened, the impression of an aggressive, racist discourse. The majority also found elements of incitement in the impugned discourse, an important consideration in light of GR 35, which consolidates the forms of superiority into 'ideas based on racial or ethnic superiority or hatred',[243] folding elements in the chapeau into the offences to be declared by law.

Ideas and theories of 'superiority' should be distinguished from ethnocentric expression in general and *a fortiori* from defensive 'recognition' or 'identity' politics practised by groups seeking their place in society: 'superiority' does not simply equal 'difference'. While this may seem an obvious point to labour, the Convention should not be understood as a homogenizing force but as one supporting diversity and self-expression, hostile only to certain categories of discourse. The justification of reaction against racist ideas would lose force if extended from a critique of racist hate as asserting racial hierarchies, to a generalized critique of expressive nationalisms of various kinds.

This above reading of Article 4 may offer a perspective on claims that the Convention is an 'outlier' among international instruments in the area of free speech,[244] and whether, in particular, it is 'compatible' with Articles 19 and 20 of the ICCPR. According to its General Comment (GC) 11,[245] the Human Rights Committee regards the prohibition in Article 20 as compatible with freedom of expression.[246] Paragraph 50 of GC 34 maintains that 'Articles 19 and 20 are compatible with and complement each other'; paragraph 52

[241] *TBB-Turkish Union*, Vázquez dissent, para. 8.

[242] *TBB-Turkish Union*, para. 12.6.

[243] GR 35, para. 13(a).

[244] See, *inter alia*, T. McGonagle, 'The Council of Europe against online hate speech: Conundrums and Challenges: Expert Paper': <http://hub.coe.int/c/document_library/get_file?uuid=62fab806-724e-435a-b7a5-153ce2b57c18&groupId=10227>.

[245] 'Prohibition of propaganda for war and inciting national, racial or religious hatred', HRI/GEN/1/Rev.9 (Vol. I), p. 182.

[246] On the prohibitions in Article 20, para. 2 of the comment states: 'In the opinion of the Committee, these required prohibitions are fully compatible with the right of freedom of expression as contained in Article 19, the exercise of which carries with it special duties and responsibilities. The prohibition under paragraph 1 extends to all forms of propaganda threatening or resulting in an act of aggression or breach of the peace contrary to the Charter of the United Nations, while para. 2 is directed against any advocacy of national, racial or religious hatred that constitutes incitement to discrimination, hostility or violence, whether such propaganda or advocacy has aims which are internal or external to the State concerned . . . For Article 20 to become fully effective there ought to be a law making it clear that propaganda and advocacy as described therein are contrary to public policy and providing for an appropriate sanction in case of violation. The Committee, therefore, believes that States parties which have not yet done so should take the measures necessary to fulfil the obligations contained in Article 20, and should themselves refrain from any such propaganda or advocacy.'

adds that it is 'only with regard to the specific forms of expression indicated in Article 20 that states parties are obliged to have legal prohibitions. In every case in which the State restricts freedom of expression it is necessary to justify the prohibitions and their provisions in strict conformity with Article 19', a stipulation requiring that Article 20 be interpreted in line with Article 19(3), which limits the range of justifications for restriction of the right.[247] Elements of this restrictive scenario (rights and reputation of others, public order, etc.) accord with the criminal law provisions of Article 4 relating to incitement to discrimination and violence, especially as restrictively interpreted in GR 35, where, *inter alia*, the mens rea requirements are 'upgraded',[248] prosecution is envisaged as reserved for serious cases,[249] and the 'due regard' principle is more closely linked to freedom of expression than in previous practice.[250] As regards 'the rights of others' (ICCPR, Article 19(3)), GR 35 carries the message that the conceptual nexus of the ICERD is complex and not reducible to a simple choice between a prohibition and a freedom: the protection of persons from racist hate speech

> is not simply one of opposition between the right to freedom of expression and its restriction for the benefit of protected groups: the persons and groups entitled to the protection of the Convention also enjoy the right to freedom of expression and freedom from discrimination in the exercise of that right. Racist hate speech potentially silences the free speech of its victims.[251]

On the other hand, authors discern an element of dissonance between CERD and the Human Rights Committee with regard to denials of genocide, etc. Temperman argues that paragraph 14 of GR 35, (demanding that States declare denials of genocide, etc, as offences when they constitute incitement), despite 'importing' phrases from GC 34 of the Human Rights Committee ('the expression of opinions about historical facts should not be prohibited or punished'), 'fails to distract from the fact that CERD has embarked on a fundamentally different path [to] its UN colleague'.[252] As noted, GC 34 has taken a sternly recalcitrant stance on denials.[253]

'Convergence' between the ICCPR and the ICERD criminalization of 'dissemination of ideas' also raises difficult questions. The Article 4 provision is stricter than Article 20

[247] Aside from GC 11 and the reference in GC 34, the Human Rights Committee has left the content of Article 20 somewhat undeveloped in cases where the State party was alleged to have offered insufficient protection against racial vilification. In *Vassilari v Greece*, CCPR/C/95/D/1570/2007 (2009), Roma complainants were threatened with militant action if they failed to comply with a petition calling for their eviction. The case was declared inadmissible because the facts could not be adequately substantiated. In *Anderson v Denmark*, CCPR/C/99/D/1868/2009 (2010), the complainant's claim that a politician had compared Islamic headscarves with Nazi swastikas was deemed inadmissible because she had not been personally affected. In light of these jurisprudential limitations, Joseph and Castan raise the question of 'whether an Article 20(2) complaint can ever be admissible': *The International Covenant,* p. 629.

[248] GR 35, para. 16.

[249] Para. 12.

[250] Para. 19.

[251] GR 35, para. 28. See also *Sangathan v Union of India*, Indian Supreme Court, March 2014, where the court stated that 'hate speech seeks to delegitimise group members in the eyes of the majority, reducing their social standing and acceptance within society ... Hate speech ... impacts a protected group's ability to respond to the substantive ideas under debate, thereby placing a serious barrier to their full participation in ... democracy': cited in S. Benesch, 'Defining and Diminishing Hate Speech', in P. Grant (ed.), *State of the World's Minorities and Indigenous Peoples 2014* (Minority Rights Group, 2014), pp. 18–25, p. 21.

[252] J. Temperman, 'Laws against the Denial of Historical Atrocities: A Human Rights Analysis', *Religion and Human Rights* 9 (2014), 151–80, 162.

[253] Comment by Joseph and Castan, *The International Covenant.*

ICCPR which refers to 'advocacy... that constitutes incitement', which is to be 'prohibited by law' and not necessarily criminalized.[254] For dissemination of ideas as well as incitement crimes, the fresh reading of Article 4 takes the Convention closer to the ICCPR; context is equally insinuated into the qualification of the dissemination crime, as well as the 'risk or likelihood' of consequences resulting from speech.[255] Overall, it may be argued that GR 35 takes CERD practice nearer to 'libertarian' currents regarding the prosecution of hate speech crimes; the suggested criminal law requirement of the need for 'imminence' of the consequences of incitement may be more stringent than in many jurisdictions.[256]

With regard to Article 4(b), the principal Convention right against which it is to be calibrated is 'the right to freedom of peaceful assembly and association' in Article 5(d)(ix).[257] The freedom of association right, the essence of which is the freedom to join together in order to pursue common interests, implicates groups such as political parties, NGOs, trades unions, professional associations, corporations, etc. Regarding restrictions on association, much of the litigation before international bodies has revolved around the situation of political parties.[258] In *Vona v Hungary*,[259] a case involving the Hungarian Guard Movement, much of whose rhetoric centred around protection from 'Gypsy criminality', the ECtHR upheld the dissolution of the Movement in light of its race-based opposition of the Roma minority to the ethnic Hungarian majority that went beyond the peaceful articulation of political views.[260] In light of the frequently stressed preventive function of 4(b), it was also stated in Vona that the ECHR did not require that authorities to delay their intervention until anti-democratic action had been taken, or violence had erupted;[261] a concurring judgement made the point in even stronger terms.[262] As observed, Article 4(b) has been interpreted strictly, and the line does not appear to have moved following GR 35; explicit or implicit references to the position of associations are found in a number of paragraphs.[263]

In addition to the technicalities of textual interpretation, the issue of application to local circumstances adds a further dimension to complexity. Attention to locality includes the history of the country, the area and the groups implicated as oppressors and victims. Locality, as *Jewish Community* demonstrates, may also contribute to a finding of incitement

[254] The 'advocacy' provision in Article 20 includes 'religious hatred', which Article 4 of ICERD explicitly does not. Note however, para. 6 of GR 35.

[255] Paragraph 16 of GR 35, which would restrict criminalization to cases carrying a risk or likelihood of (negative) consequences resulting from speech that were 'desired or intended by the speaker'. While the syntax of the provision is better suited to incitement than to 'dissemination of ideas', the restrictive approach brings all the offences in Article 4 under a common rubric.

[256] On the wider 'integration' of Standards, see paragraph 4 of GR 35, discussed earlier in this chapter.

[257] See the commentary on Article 5 in the present work.

[258] See, *inter alia*, EctHR, *Refah Partisi and Others v Turkey* (2003), 37 EHRR 1; *United Communist Party of Turkey and Others v Turkey* (1998), 26 EHRR 121.

[259] EctHR, App. No. 35943 (2013).

[260] Para. 62, and paras 13 and 14.

[261] Paras 57 and 68. The Court cited Articles 1, 2, and 4 of ICERD as part of the legal framework in Hungarian domestic law.

[262] Judge Pinto de Albuquerque, following extensive citation of ICERD and other legal materials, stated that 'States parties to the Convention [the ECHR] have the duty to criminalize speech or any other form of dissemination of racism, xenophobia or ethnic intolerance, prohibit every assembly and dissolve every group, organisation, association or party that promotes them... Such an international positive obligation must be acknowledged... as a principle of customary international law, binding on all States, and a peremptory norm.'

[263] Paras 24, 39, 40, 41, 43, and 44.

and presumably its negation and penetrate the very construction of what counts as 'hate'. Locality is also culture, bearing in mind that different societies take different views on dignity and freedom, acceptable and unacceptable speech, and that all societies, even the most 'liberal', have their taboos. In this scenario, whilst the liberal defence of freedom of speech in relation to 'the marketplace of ideas' has intrinsic attraction, the stress laid on freedom of speech as permitting abuse, ridicule, statements that 'offend, shock or disturb', etc[264] may speak to certain kinds of society, the attributes of which may not be widely shared. As to whether the restatement of the relationship between freedom of speech and hate speech prohibitions in the recommendation speaks to hate speech phenomena across a wide cultural span, only time will tell.

Discourses of racial superiority, dehumanization, denigration, and contempt continue to direct themselves energetically to the categories of person recognized in Convention practice, and we may recognize freshly minted 'phobias' and 'isms' in the babble of sulphurous outpourings.[265] Half a century after the adoption of the Convention, it is depressingly evident that racist hate speech remains a significant social phenomenon, so that basic Convention framework for addressing it retains its *raison d'être*. The rationale of taking racist speech seriously can be understood by reflecting on the discourses of dehumanization that are characteristic elements of genocidal processes, or, less dramatically, on the climate of oppression that can flourish if unchecked against vulnerable minorities through normalization or banalization of discourses of racial inferiority and superiority. Targeted groups well appreciate that the walls between thought, public discourse, and oppressive action can be very thin.

I. On Defamation of Religions

Parallel with reflections within CERD on how discrimination on the ground of religion should be treated under the Convention, a series of UN resolutions dating back to 1999 addressed the question of 'defamation of religions';[266] Human Rights Council resolution 7/19 may be taken to exemplify the series.[267] No definition of 'defamation of religions' is attempted therein, but the facets of defamation include negative stereotyping of religions, their adherents, and sacred persons, the identification of Islam with terrorism, the profiling of Muslims after 11 September 2001, laws controlling and stigmatizing Muslim minorities, and attacks on businesses, cultural centres, and places of worship. The resolution urges State action to prohibit 'the dissemination . . . of racist and xenophobic ideas and material aimed at any religion or its followers that constitute incitement to racial and religious hatred, hostility and violence',[268] and provide protection against 'acts of hatred, discrimination, intimidation and coercion resulting from the defamation of any religion'.[269] On the relation between 'defamation of religions' and freedom of expression, the resolution is robust: 'respect of religions and protection from contempt is an essential

[264] EctHR, *Handyside v UK* (1976), 1 EHRR 737, para. 49.

[265] N. Ghanea, '"Phobias" and "Isms": Recognition of Difference or the Slippery Slope of Particularisms?' in N. Ghanea, A. Stephens, and R. Walden (eds), *Does God Believe in Human Rights?* (Martinus Nijhoff Publishers, 2007), pp. 211–32.

[266] E/CN.4/Res/1999/82.

[267] Adopted at the 40th meeting of the Council on 27 April 2008 by 21 votes to 10, with 14 abstentions; see also A/HRC/RES/4/9 (2007); A/HRC/RES/10/22 (2009), A/HRC/RES/13/16 (2010).

[268] Resolution 7/19, para. 8.

[269] *Ibid.*, para. 9.

element conducive for the exercise by all of the right to freedom of expression'.[270] 'Religion' is not defined: the emphasis is on religions in the plural. The issue intersected with discussions on possible amendments to ICERD.

As noted earlier, ICERD extends its protection to religious communities under defined circumstances, even if critics claim that extension to 'documented' religions that separate beliefs, theologies, and principles of right action from wider social practice, is beyond the Committee's mandate.[271] While *P.S.N.*[272] and *A. W.R.A.P.*[273] posit a boundary to speech directed at religious communities that are not coterminous with ethnic communities, GR 35 reaches out to 'Islamophobia' and 'ethno-religious groups' included by virtue of race/ religion intersectionality.[274]

For those seeking to combat 'defamation of religions', ICERD superficially offers an attractive model on account of its list of offences to be declared by law, its tough stance on dissemination of ideas, its continuing hostility to racist organizations, and the unremitting demands to make the provisions of the convention effective in practice. Part of the attraction has been the supposed clarity and impermeability of the Article, a position challenged by recent developments in CERD practice. The spectrum of hostile speech outlined in the defamation resolutions includes actions more aggressive than 'defamation' in the commonly understood sense of a civil law 'tort'.[275] It does, however, include elements familiar in CERD practice such as dissemination, incitement, stereotyping, profiling, and stigmatization. The CERD ethos of favouring education for tolerance, and promoting dialogue—inter- and intra-religious,[276] inter-cultural,[277] between governments and ethnic or indigenous groups,[278] and governments and religious groups,[279]—should equally not be forgotten in the contexts envisioned by the resolutions.

The scope of 'defamation' in the resolutions is broadly matched by the scope of Article 4, but one major area of mismatch is that of the subject of the respective protections.[280] While the resolutions refer to religions, followers of religions, persons of certain ethnic and religious backgrounds, minorities, adherents of religion, etc, the protection of 'religions' remains the principal focus. The distinction between addressing the community and

[270] *Ibid.*, para. 10.

[271] See comment by the Islamic Republic of Iran on the concluding observations of CERD regarding its sixteenth and seventeenth periodic report, A/58/18, Annex VII.

[272] *P.S.N. v Denmark*, CERD/C/711/D/36/2006 (2007).

[273] *A. W.R.A.P. v Denmark*, CERD/C/71/D/37/2006 (2007).

[274] GR 35, para. 6.

[275] Defamation may be treated as a crime in some jurisdictions; criminal libel, for example. For a 'map' of such jurisdictions see: <http://www.Article19.org/advocacy/defamationmap/map/>.

[276] Concluding observations on the Holy See, CERD/C/304/Add.89, para. 6.

[277] CERD/C/GUY/CO/14, para. 22.

[278] Including, for example, in New Zealand, CERD/C/DEC/NZL/1, para. 7; Canada, CERD/C/CAN/ CO/18, para. 6.

[279] In concluding observations on Belgium, the Committee welcomed the election of a body representing Muslim communities with a view to maintaining and developing dialogue with public authorities, CERD/C/ 60/CO/2, para. 9. In concluding observations on Germany, CERD/C/DEU/CO/18, para. 13, the Committee welcomed 'the establishment of the Islam Conference, as a forum in which representatives of... Muslim communities living in Germany meet with representatives of German authorities with the aim of establishing continuous dialogue to address Islamophobic tendencies and discuss relevant policy responses'.

[280] The most fundamental criticism of the defamation concept is that 'religions do not have any "right" as such to be protected from criticism': T. McGonagle, *Minority Rights, Freedom of Expression and of the Media: Dynamics and Dilemmas* (Intersentia, 2011), p. 365.

addressing community beliefs and practices can be a fine one.[281] ICERD centres on protection of persons and communities, empowering human beings to sustain the codes and beliefs they regard as integral to their identity. This is not equivalent to affirming the truth of the codes themselves which may be competitive and contradictory.[282] GR 35, citing GC 34 of the Human Rights Committee, invites its addressees to bear in mind that '"criticism of religious leaders or commentary on religious doctrine or tenets of faith" should not be prohibited or punished'.[283] While Human Rights Council resolution 16/18 shifts the emphasis from defamation of religions towards combating religious intolerance and discrimination, incitement to violence and violence against persons on account of their religious belief,[284] Lerner notes that 'the borderline between defamation and incitement is difficult to determine'.[285] His view is focused principally on Article 20 of the ICCPR; with regard to 'defamation of religions', the difficulties he refers to are compounded in the case of CERD because of its primary focus on race rather than religion.

[281] It may be interpreted as a racist attack on a community as such to claim or insinuate that it supports anti-human rights practices: *Gelle v Denmark*, para. 7.4.

[282] 'The civic dignity of the members of a group stands separately from the status of their beliefs': Waldron, *The Harm in Hate Speech*, p. 133.

[283] GR 35, para. 6. See also GC 34 of the Human Rights Committee, para. 48, where blasphemy laws are stated to be incompatible with freedom of expression. Compare *I.A. v Turkey* App. No. 2560/94/ (2002), paras 29 and 32, commentary in T. McGonagle, 'An Ode to Contextualization: I.A. v Turkey', *Irish Human Rights Law Review* 1 (2010), 237–51.

[284] Combating Intolerance, Negative Stereotyping and stigmatization of, and Discrimination, incitement to Violence and violence against, Persons Based on Religion or Belief, 12 April 2011, A/HRC/RES/16/18; S. Berry, 'Is Defamation of Religions Passé?', *George Washington International Law Review* 44 (2012), 431–539; L. B. Graham, 'Defamation of Religions: the End of Pluralism', *Emory Journal of International Law* 23 (2009), 69–84; L. Langer, 'The Rise (and Fall?) of Defamation of Religions', *Yale Journal of International Law* 35 (2010), 257–533; S. Parmar, 'Uprooting "Defamation of Religions" and Planting a New Approach to Freedom of Expression at the United Nations', in T. McGonagle and Y. Donders (eds), *The United Nations and Freedom of Expression and Information* (Cambridge University Press, 2015), pp. 373–427. For a wide review of issues including 'defamation of religions', see I. Cismas, *Religious Actors and International Law* (Oxford University Press, 2014).

[285] N. Lerner, 'Freedom of Expression and Advocacy of Group Hatred, Incitement to Hate Crimes and Religious Hatred', *Religion and Human Rights* 5 (2010), 137–45, 143.

12. Article 5

Introduction and Drafting

In compliance with the fundamental obligations laid down in article 2 of this Convention, States Parties undertake to prohibit and to eliminate racial discrimination in all its forms and to guarantee the right of everyone, without distinction as to race, colour, or national or ethnic origin, to equality before the law, notably in the enjoyment of the following rights:

(a) The right to equal treatment before the tribunals and all other organs administering justice;
(b) The right to security of person and protection by the State against violence or bodily harm, whether inflicted by government officials or by any individual, group or institution;
(c) Political rights, in particular the right to participate in elections—to vote and to stand for election—on the basis of universal and equal suffrage, to take part in the Government as well as in the conduct of public affairs at any level and to have equal access to public service;
(d) Other civil rights, in particular:
   (i) The right to freedom of movement and residence within the border of the State;
   (ii) The right to leave any country, including one's own, and to return to one's country;
   (iii) The right to nationality;
   (iv) The right to marriage and choice of spouse;
   (v) The right to own property alone as well as in association with others;
   (vi) The right to inherit;
   (vii) The right to freedom of thought, conscience and religion;
   (viii) The right to freedom of opinion and expression;
   (ix) The right to freedom of peaceful assembly and association;
(e) Economic, social and cultural rights, in particular:
   (i) The rights to work, to free choice of employment, to just and favourable conditions of work, to protection against unemployment, to equal pay for equal work, to just and favourable remuneration;
   (ii) The right to form and join trade unions;
   (iii) The right to housing;
   (iv) The right to public health, medical care, social security and social services;
   (v) The right to education and training;
   (vi) The right to equal participation in cultural activities;
(f) The right of access to any place or service intended for use by the general public, such as transport, hotels, restaurants, cafés, theatres and parks.

The Organization of the Commentary on Article 5

Because of the length and complexity of Article 5, the present and following chapters depart from the general style of presentation for individual articles of the Convention.

After the short introduction in the present chapter to the article, its *travaux*, and reservations thereto, and the general aspects of the reporting guidelines, Chapters 13 and 14 take the paragraphs and sub-paragraphs of the article sequentially. The discussion of each paragraph or sub-paragraph includes a brief, schematic account of relevant background international standards, followed by a modest selection of practice that highlights the principal concerns of the Committee in the application of the right in question. The chapters do not purport to delve deeply into background aspects of human rights practice outside the Convention. Chapter 15 reflects on the evidences of discrimination highlighted in Chapters 13 and 14, and comments critically on the interpretation of Article 5, taking its *travaux*, text, and the archive of CERD practice as the starting points.

A. Introduction

Article 5 is the workhorse article of the Convention, and the longest of the substantive articles. It incorporates a complex obligation to prohibit and eliminate all forms of racial discrimination, and to guarantee equality before the law on a non-discriminatory basis. The equality guarantee applies to the enjoyment of an extensive, unclosed list of rights—'notably in the enjoyment of the following rights'—so that other, unnamed rights are also subject to its protection. The explicit naming of rights in Article 5 is unique in the Convention. Whereas the preamble and other articles refer generically to human rights, rights, and freedoms, or human rights and fundamental freedoms, Article 5 draws out the implications of the reference to rights and freedoms in Article 1, and is expressly linked to Article 2. As *Jewish Community of Oslo v Norway* makes clear, Article 5 is not the only article in the International Convention on the Elimination of All Forms of Racial Discrimination (ICERD) to evoke the notion of rights, notwithstanding the characteristic ICERD framework of obligations and undertakings to eliminate racial discrimination, and their fulfilment through the languages of condemnation, assurance, and prohibition[1]—discussions in the present work elaborate on the ICERD rights framework as a whole, notably in connection with Articles 2, 4, 6, and 7.

Article 5 does not replicate the style of the Declaration on the Elimination of Racial Discrimination, which does not carry a stand-alone article on rights but spreads a limited portfolio of rights across a number of articles.[2] Equally, while following the contours and inspiration of the Universal Declaration of Human Rights (UDHR), Article 5 is not its carbon copy, and concentrates on positive statements of rights to be protected from discrimination, including, for example, the right to inherit, and the right of access to places open to the public, rights that are absent from the UDHR.[3] The last named right, stemming from the reaction against apartheid-era practices of segregated public facilities, has particular resonance for a convention crafted in the glare of international and domestic action against racial segregation; the emblematic prohibition of discrimination in the right to marriage similarly recalls a history of anti-miscegenation statutes.[4] The

[1] *Jewish Community of Oslo et al. v Norway*, CERD/C/67/D/30/2003 (2005), para. 10.6, discussed in chapter 11.

[2] N. Lerner, *Group Rights and Discrimination in International Law* (Martinus Nijhoff, 1991), pp. 55–56.

[3] Article 3(2) of the Declaration on Race provides that everyone shall have 'equal access to any place or facility intended for use by the general public' without distinction as to race, colour, or ethnic origin.

[4] See the discussion of Article 3 in Chapter 10.

elements of governmental systems dedicated to racially exclusive and exclusionary politics, and racially segregated housing and education, are alike made subject to the equality/non-discrimination critique of Article 5. The scope of the article exemplifies the UDHR principle of the interdependence and indivisibility of human rights through a darker lens, as discriminatory denials of disparate rights intersect and reinforce each other, creating downward spirals of deprivation.

The list of rights in Article 5 covers all the principal 'categories' of rights: civil, political, economic, social, and cultural, each presented in succinct form, without the further elaboration found in the UDHR itself, and in the Convention on the Elimination of All Forms of Discrimination against Women (CEDAW) and other human rights instruments. The rights set out in Article 5, formulated using economical and porous language, made it almost inevitable that its interpretation and application would be influenced by developments in the broader international canon of human rights to which it is organically connected. The rights are described rather than defined, without the detailed apparatus of limitation or restriction clauses and specifications of permissible and impermissible derogations found in most other human rights instruments. They are also open-ended, a feature that presents a continuing challenge to the monitoring body—CERD—as to which version of the rights is subjected to critical appraisal under the Convention.

Further interpretative complexity results from the looseness of textual boundaries within the confines of the article, and from overlaps and inconsistencies with other elements in the Convention. CERD opinions, decisions, and concluding observations frequently couple or conflate Article 5 with other articles so that even the strenuous individuation of practice on a paragraph or sub-paragraph basis may not be fully determinative of its range of meaning.

While CERD practice may not illuminate every corner of the rights listed or rights implied in Article 5, it serves to highlight areas of sharp human rights detriment to persons and communities through its metric of racial discrimination. A practice that identifies where discrimination bites serves to illuminate important dimensions of human rights in general, uncovering the face of racial discrimination and testifying to its malign influence on human affairs.

B. *Travaux Préparatoires*

The Abram text before the Sub-Commission focused on taking effective measures, necessary steps, etc, to secure equal access to 'any place or facility intended for use by the general public', and to prohibit racial discrimination therein; to prevent racial discrimination 'in the enjoyment of political and citizenship rights', including 'the right to participate in elections through universal and equal suffrage and to equal access to public service'; to 'assure everyone within its jurisdiction the right to equality before the law and equal justice under the law', as well as 'the right to security of person and protection by the State against violence or bodily harm, whether inflicted by government officials or by any individual, group or institution'.[5]

The Calvocoressi text focused on equality before the law, security of the person against bodily harm, equal access to public places, participation in elections, and eligibility for

[5] E/|CN.4/Sub.2/308, extracted in E/CN.4/873, para. 85.

public service.[6] The Ivanov and Ketrzynski text included a wide range of rights, subsuming the civil rights to political participation, equality before the law and access to public places in analogous fashion to Calvocoressi and Abram, adding provisions against discrimination in the right to marriage, in the 'granting and enjoyment of the right to form and join trade unions', and on admitting no racial discrimination in the field of 'economic rights'. The 'economic rights' included 'the right to employment and equal pay', education and training, housing, health, and social security.[7]

The Sub-Commission working group submitted a text in which can be glimpsed the eventual structure and content of Article 5 of the Convention,[8] the chapeau referring to the undertaking not to admit—and to eliminate[9]—racial discrimination 'notably in the enjoyment of the following rights'; a non-exhaustive list followed. Members of the Sub-Commission debated whether there should be a list of rights taken from the UDHR, or a general formula, with some members counselling that, if a list were adopted, the omission of a particular right could lead to misunderstanding.[10] However, in Ketryzinski's view, 'there was no reason to fear that the scope of the Convention might be reduced if all the rights... in the Universal Declaration of Human Rights were not listed... it was perfectly clear from the Preamble... that the provisions of the Convention applied to all the rights set out in the Universal Declaration of Human Rights'.[11] The working group's text combined the equality, security, and access provisions in the other drafts together with a range of civil rights including freedom of thought, conscience, and religion and freedom of opinion and expression, the right to nationality, and economic, social, and cultural rights, adding 'equal participation in cultural activities' to the Ivanov/Ketrzynski listing.[12] A far-reaching and innovative proposal by Ivanov to insert into the 'governance' elements of the working group text a reference to 'the right of racial, national and ethnic groups of the population to take part on a real footing of equality in the work of legislative and executive organs' was later withdrawn.[13] Sub-Commission member Ferguson objected to the proposal, arguing that inserting group rights might give rise to serious difficulties because 'the rights in question derived from membership of a group and not from the

[6] E/CN.4/Sub.2/L.309.

[7] E/CN.4/Sub.2/L.334. Krishnaswami—E/CN.4/Sub.2/L.310—submitted amendments to the Abram text, including the portmanteau: 'Each State shall prevent racial discrimination in the fields of civil rights, access to citizenship, education, religion, employment, occupation and housing.'

[8] E/CN.4/Sub.2/L/334.

[9] There was considerable discussion on the difference between not to 'permit' racial discrimination and not to 'admit' it. In the view of Capotorti, 'eliminate' covered both terms: E/CN.4/Sub.2/SR.423, p. 4.

[10] Ferguson (E/CN.4/Sub.2/SR.423, p. 4) considered that 'it would be dangerous to enumerate the rights, for fear of omitting some of them', preferring the formula of Capotorti who, for part of the draft article had suggested, *ibid.*, that it should refer to the elimination of racial discrimination 'in the enjoyment of civil, economic, social and cultural rights as set out in the Universal Declaration of Human Rights'.

[11] E/CN.4/Sub.2/SR.423, pp. 4–5.

[12] The working group draft referred to political rights as 'granted to any person in his own country'. The term 'granted' was proposed for deletion by Saario, a proposal supported by the Chairman (Santa Cruz), who declared that '"granted" was not satisfactory because it seemed to imply that rights which were in fact acquired rights had to be granted': E/CN/4/Sub.2/SR.424, p. 5. Mudawi, *ibid.*, suggested that the political rights paragraph under discussion 'would make it necessary to have a limiting clause specifying that aliens, in the host country, could not take advantage of the provisions in question'.

[13] E/CN.4/Sub.2/L.335. Among other objections, it was felt by Calvocoressi that 'by introducing the idea of the rights of groups [the] proposal might involve the Sub-Commission in a prolonged debate': E/CN.4/Sub.2/SR.423, p. 7. In withdrawing the proposal, Ivanov considered nonetheless that 'those groups had the right to take part in the work of legislative and executive organs': E/CN.4/Sub.2/SR.424, p. 6.

merits of the individual members', and thus 'the proposal departed from individual rights and might lead to discrimination in reverse'.[14]

Accordingly the Commission on Human Rights had before it the following text:

In compliance with the fundamental obligations laid down in article [2], States parties undertake to prohibit and to eliminate racial discrimination in all its forms notably in the enjoyment of the following rights:

(a) The rights to equality before the law and to equal justice under the law;
(b) The right to security of person and protection by the State against violence or bodily harm, whether inflicted by government officials or by any individual, group or institution;
(c) Political rights, in particular the rights to participate in elections through universal and equal suffrage, to take part in the Government as well as in the conduct of public affairs at any level and to have equal access to public service;
(d) Other civil rights, in particular:
  (i) the right to freedom of movement and residence within the border of the State;
  (ii) the right to leave any country including his own, and to return to his country;
  (iii) the right to nationality;
  (iv) the right to marriage;
  (v) the right to own property alone as well as in association with others;
  (vi) the right to freedom of thought, conscience and religion;
  (vii) the right to freedom of opinion and expression;
  (viii) the right to freedom of peaceful assembly and association;
(e) Economic, social and cultural rights, in particular:
  (i) the right to work, free choice of employment, just and favourable conditions of work, protection against unemployment, equal pay for equal work, just and favourable remuneration;
  (ii) the right to form and join trade unions;
  (iii) housing;
  (iv) public health, medical care and social security and social services;
  (v) education and training;
  (vi) equal participation in cultural activities;
(f) Access to any place or service intended for use by the general public such as transport, hotels, restaurants, cafés, theatres, parks.

The article was discussed at the 796th to the 800th meetings of the Commission. There was broad agreement in the Commission that the structure of the article was satisfactory,[15] though some representatives preferred a general formulation rather than a detailed list of rights.[16] The report of the Commission summarizes discussion to the effect that 'many of the rights proclaimed in the Universal Declaration had been left out but that the word "notably" preceding the list of rights implied that there had been a selection of rights to which special attention should be accorded. On the other hand, it was pointed out that

[14] E/CN.4/Sub.2/SR.423, p. 7.

[15] 'Although the list did not cover all the rights set forth in the Universal Declaration, article V none the less mentioned all the rights which most frequently suffered as a result of racism': observation of the representative of The Philippines, E/CN.4/SR.796, p. 9.

[16] The representative of Italy echoed the sentiments of a number of delegations, notably those of Denmark, France, and the United Kingdom, and 'would have preferred a shorter and more general text. The listing of a number of rights involved the double risk of omitting important rights and defining others badly': E/CN.4/SR.796, p. 12. The representative suggested, *ibid.*, that 'the Commission should ask itself whether there were any fields of social life, such as those mentioned in sub-para. (f) which were insufficiently protected against racial discrimination by existing international instruments, and should take special measures to protect them'.

the selection was so wide as to nullify this intention.'[17] The difficulties experienced by some delegations were adverted to by the representative of The Netherlands who suggested that they arose 'largely due to the fact that their national legislation did not enable them fully to guarantee the rights listed... But the purpose of the article was not to proclaim that the rights... enumerated must be fully respected, but merely to prohibit racial discrimination with regard to their enjoyment'.[18]

In the introductory paragraph, Poland (joined by France) proposed to insert after 'racial discrimination in all its forms' the words 'and to guarantee, without distinction as to race, colour or ethnic origin, the right of everyone to equality before the law'.[19] A principal argument in favour of the Polish text was that it was appropriate to include the right to equality before the law in the introductory paragraph because that right

> was a general principle which the others merely served to illustrate; what was important in the exercise of the rights embodied in the other sub-paragraphs was that there should be no inequality before the law. It would accordingly be better to state the general principle before those other rights, which were important examples but by no means exhaustively enumerated.[20]

In processing the Polish proposals, the word 'citizen' in the first version[21] was replaced by 'everyone'.[22] On paragraph (a), Poland proposed to redraft it as '[t]he right to equal justice under the law',[23] later replaced by a joint amendment of France, Italy, and Poland which was revised orally to read[24] '[t]he right to equal treatment before the tribunals and all other organs administering justice'[25]; the revised paragraph survived into the text of the Convention. The expression 'equal justice under the law' used in the Sub-Commission text and the Polish amendment was ultimately regarded as too vague. A proposal to refer to 'equal treatment before the courts' also gave rise to misgivings, and the final, accepted phrasing on 'tribunals and all other organs administering justice' was designed to widen the remit of the Convention to include justice before, for example, administrative bodies as well as courts.[26] A Polish amendment to add 'the right to inherit' to paragraph (d) was adopted by 19 votes to none, with 2 abstentions.[27]

[17] Commission on Human Rights, report on the twentieth session, E/CN.4/874, para. 200. The representative of the UK 'thought it unfortunate that there was so long a catalogue of rights... only ten of the rights proclaimed in the Universal Declaration of Human Rights have been left out. That was certainly not good drafting': E/CN.4/SR.797, p. 3.

[18] E/CN.4/SR.796, p. 15.

[19] E/CN.4/L.699, E/CN.4/L.699/Rev.1, E/CN.4/874, paras 192–95.

[20] The position of Poland is summarized in E/CN.4/SR.796, pp. 6–7.

[21] E/CN.4/L.699.

[22] 'If the Convention was to be effective, it must protect not only citizens, but also aliens and non-citizens against racial discrimination': observation of the representative of Lebanon, E/CN.4/SR.796, p. 9. On the other hand, Italy regarded the word 'citizen' as appropriate to sub-para. (c) which dealt with political rights: E/CN.4/SR.796, p. 11. The Convention's provisions on citizenship are discussed principally in Chapter 7.

[23] E/CN.4/L.699 and E/CN.4/699/Rev.1

[24] E/CN.4/L.708.

[25] E/CN.4/874, para. 198.

[26] *Ibid.*, para. 207. Paragraph (a) as amended was adopted unanimously. The French version of the text, which at one point included the phrase '*droit a une justice egale devant la loi*', was criticized by Italy 'because either justice was equal or it was not justice': E/CN.4/SR.798, p. 11. For further discussion of tribunals and national institutions, see Chapter 16 on Article 6.

[27] E/CN.4/874, paras 199 and 211. The UK abstained in the vote on the right to inherit because, according to its representative, it was undesirable to extend the list of rights further, and 'the inclusion of that right was unjustified since discrimination based on colour or race must be extremely rare in questions of inheritance': E/CN.4/SR.800, p. 4.

In explanations of vote, France voted in favour of Article 5 while considering that the list set out in the article 'did not necessarily relate to rights in the strict sense of the term. The representative stated that in sub-paragraph (e) for example, 'the term *droit au logement* (right to housing), which had no counterpart in French law, must obviously be interpreted with considerable latitude'.[28] Italy considered that in sub-paragraph (d), the use of the word 'other' before the words 'civil rights' was inappropriate after an enumeration of political rights; Italy also had difficulty accepting the right to nationality and suggested that it should be replaced 'by an expression such as "equality with regard to the conditions for obtaining citizenship"'.[29]

The Third Committee had before it the following text:

In compliance with the fundamental obligations laid down in Article [2] of this Convention, States parties undertake to prohibit and to eliminate racial discrimination in all its forms and to guarantee the right of everyone, without distinction as to race, colour or ethnic origin, to equality before the law, notably in the enjoyment of the following rights:

(a) The right to equal treatment before the tribunals and all other organs administering justice;
(b) The right to security of person and protection by the State against violence or bodily harm, whether inflicted by government officials or by any individual, group or institution;
(c) Political rights, in particular the rights to participate in elections through universal and equal suffrage, to take part in the Government as well as in the conduct of public affairs at any level and to have equal access to public service;
(d) Other civil rights, in particular:
    (i) The right to freedom of movement and residence within the border of the State;
    (ii) The right to leave any country including one's own, and to return to one's country;
    (iii) The right to nationality;
    (iv) The right to marriage;
    (v) The right to own property alone as well as in association with others;
    (vi) The right to inherit;
    (vii) The right to freedom of thought, conscience and religion;
    (viii) The right to freedom of opinion and expression;
    (ix) The right to freedom of assembly and association;
(e) Economic, social and cultural rights, in particular:
    (i) The right to work, to free choice of employment, to just and favourable conditions of work, to protection against unemployment, to equal pay for equal work, to just and favourable remuneration;
    (ii) The right to form and join trade unions
    (iii) The right to housing;
    (iv) The right to public health, medical care, social security and social services;
    (v) The right to education and training;
    (vi) The right to equal participation in cultural activities;
(f) The right of access to any place or service intended for use by the general public such as transport, hotels, restaurants, café, theatres and parks.[30]

Relatively few amendments to draft Article 5 were proposed in the Third Committee. The representative of Ghana made the observation that 'the Convention was intended to eliminate racial discrimination and not to grant rights which might not be recognized in

[28] E/CN.4/SR.800, p. 4. See Chapters 10 and 14 for discussion of housing rights.
[29] *Ibid.*
[30] A/6181, para. 76, 'café' appears in para. (f) instead of 'cafés'.

certain countries'.[31] An attempt to harmonize the wording of the chapeau of Article 5 with Article 1 was made by the representative of Czechoslovakia who orally proposed to insert the words 'descent, national' before 'or ethnic origin'.[32] A request 'not to insist on the inclusion of the word "descent" in the introductory paragraph'[33] was made by the representative of Austria and accepted by Czechoslovakia,[34] while 'national' was retained. The summary records do not shed light on the reasons for withdrawing the reference to 'descent'. The result of the omission is that the list of prohibited grounds of discrimination in Article 5 is shorter than for Article 1. While India had feared that the inclusion of 'everyone' in the chapeau 'might be regarded as including non-citizens as well as citizens', the representative's fears had been assuaged by 'the clause in Article 1 stating that the Convention would not apply to distinctions made by a State party between citizens and non-citizens'.[35] In the course of discussions, the right in paragraph (c) to participate in elections was elaborated on the suggestion of Bulgaria to include 'to vote and to stand for election',[36] and the right to marriage was clarified to include the right to choice of spouse.[37]

The right to equal participation in cultural activities in the Commission's text elicited a (rejected)[38] proposal by Mauritania, Nigeria, and Uganda to replace it by '[t]he equal right to organize cultural associations and to participate in all kinds of cultural activities'.[39] The proposal attracted comment to the effect that the reference to cultural associations 'omitted the right of each individual to take part in cultural activities other than through an organization',[40] and that it 'introduced a collective notion' whereas the existing wording referred to an individual right.[41] The representative of Bolivia added that care should be taken to ensure that a clause on cultural associations 'did not have the effect of limiting the right of the individual to participate in existing cultural activities'.[42] The representative of India observed that there was a genuine difference between the right to participate in cultural activities on an individual basis and the right to organize cultural associations, and that the views of the sponsors of the amendment should be accommodated.[43] In the event, the original Commission text on cultural participation was retained.

The text of Article 5 as a whole was adopted unanimously.[44] In view of the frequent reading of the article as not creating rights but only forbidding discrimination in their

[31] A/C3/SR.1306, para. 16.

[32] A/C.3/SR.1309, para. 3.

[33] *Ibid.*, para. 4.

[34] *Ibid.*., para. 5.

[35] A/C.3/SR.1309, para. 2. See discussion in Chapters 6 and 7.

[36] A/6181, para. 80, adopted by 86 votes to none, with 10 abstentions. The representative of France observed that 'the right to participate in elections and the right to elect were not identical and . . . it was possible to participate in elections without actually electing anyone': A/C.3/SR.1308, para. 61.

[37] A/6181, para. 82, adopted by 90 votes to none with 3 abstentions. The representative of Ghana explained that the reference to choice of spouse was to be supported because 'the law in some countries prohibited interracial marriage': A/C.3/SR.1306, para. 16. Restrictions on interracial marriage are referred to in Chapter 10 on Article 3.

[38] A/6181, para. 84, narrowly rejected by 37 votes to 33 with 24 abstentions.

[39] A/C.3/L.1225, A/6181, para. 83.

[40] A/C.3/SR.1309, para. 16 (Italy)

[41] *Ibid.*, para. 18 (Chile). The representative of Argentina (*ibid.*, para. 19) argued that, in any case, the right to freedom of association already covered the right to cultural associations. The representative of Liberia considered the amendment redundant since 'the notion of participation included organization', *ibid.*, para. 21.

[42] A/C.3/SR.1309, para. 24.

[43] A/C.3/SR.1309, para. 22.

[44] A/6181, para. 84.

enjoyment, the remark of the representative of Canada that the article 'attempted both to grant certain rights and to guarantee freedom from discrimination in the exercise of those rights' retains its interest.[45]

C. Practice

I. Reservations and Declarations

Article 5, despite its breadth of coverage, has attracted few reservations. The reservation by the US includes Article 5 along with other articles in its rejection of regulation of private conduct by the Convention 'except as mandated by the Constitution and laws of the United States'.[46] Yemen maintains a reservation regarding 5(c) and 5(d)(iv), (vi), and (vii) which has attracted numerous objections,[47] including a lengthy objection by Finland.[48] As with other reservations, CERD has invited States parties to consider removing them.[49]

II. General Part of the Reporting Guidelines

The reporting Guidelines for Article 5 are more detailed overall than those for the other substantive articles,[50] requesting information categorized (a) in relation to particular rights and also (b) information by groups of victims or potential victims.[51] Regarding the situation of women, States parties are requested to describe 'as far as possible in quantitative and qualitative terms, factors affecting and difficulties experienced in ensuring the equal enjoyment by women . . . of rights under the Convention'.[52] Accordingly they should pay attention also to 'complex forms of disadvantage in which racial discrimination is mixed with other causes of discrimination'—reference is made to discrimination based on age, sex, and gender, religion, disability, and low economic status.[53] The general elements of the Guidelines conclude with the recommendation that where 'no quantitative data relevant to the enjoyment of these rights is available, States parties should provide relevant information derived from social surveys, and report the opinions of representatives of disadvantaged groups'.[54] Further aspects of the Guidelines are outlined in the following two chapters in relation to specific rights.

[45] A/C.3/SR.1309, para. 6. The representative also regarded the phrase 'equality before the law' as limiting, recalling, *ibid.*, the reference in the Romanian amendment to the preamble—A/C.3/L.1219—to 'equal before the law and entitled to equal protection of the law'—the version of that appears in the final text of the Convention.

[46] A complex reservation by Fiji relating to elections and alienation of land was withdrawn in 2012; Tonga also withdrew reservations to Article 5.

[47] Reservations to the Convention, and objections thereto, etc, are set out in <https://treaties.un.org/Pages/ViewDetails.aspx?src=treaty&mtdsg_no=iv-2&chapter=4&lang=en>.

[48] See the commentary on reservations—Article 20—in Chapter 18.

[49] The reservation to Article 5 by Yemen had 'the effect of neglecting the core purposes and objectives' of the Convention: concluding observations of the Committee, CERD/C/YEM/CO/17-18, para. 13 (2011).

[50] CERD/C/2007/1, pp. 8–13.

[51] *Ibid.*, pp. 12–13. Reference is made, p. 12, para. A, to information on refugees and displaced persons; non-citizens, including immigrants, refugees, asylum-seekers and stateless persons; indigenous peoples; minorities including the Roma; descent-based communities; and on women—GR 25.

[52] *Ibid.*, p. 12, para. A.

[53] *Ibid.*, p. 13, para. B.

[54] *Ibid.*, p. 13, para. C.

13. Article 5

Civil and Political Rights

The first three sets of rights in Article 5 are not placed under the rubric of 'civil' or 'civil and political'; paragraph (d) however, in referring to 'other civil rights', suggests the appropriate nomenclature.

Chapeau: Prohibit and eliminate racial discrimination . . . guarantee the right of everyone, without distinction as to race, colour, or national or ethnic origin, to equality before the law

International standards on equality and non-discrimination are referred to throughout the present work. Commencing with the Universal Declaration of Human Rights (UDHR), specific provisions in the International Covenant on Economic, Social and Cultural Rights (ICESCR), the International Covenant on Civil and Political Rights (ICCPR), and the substantive articles of the Convention on the Elimination of All Forms of Discrimination Against Women (CEDAW), plus the preamble, make reference to equality; the notion of equality similarly infuses the Convention on the Rights of Persons with Disabilities (CRPD).[1] The standards are replicated and developed in regional instruments—including the African Charter on Human and Peoples' Rights (ACHPR), the American Convention on Human Rights (ACHR), the Arab Charter on Human Rights, and the European Convention on Human Rights (ECHR).[2] The account of equality in the Inter-American Convention against Racism and Racial Discrimination is among the more extensive in the international canon, and includes equality before the law as well as 'equal protection against racism, racial discrimination and related forms of intolerance',[3] together with the right to equal 'recognition, enjoyment, exercise, and protection' of human rights and fundamental freedoms 'at both the individual and collective levels'.[4] Specialized instruments regarding groups the subject of standard Committee on the Elimination of Racial Discrimination (CERD) concerns, such as International Labour Organization (ILO) Convention 169, the UNDRIP, the United Nations Declaration on Minorities (UNDM), and the Framework Convention for the Protection of National Minorities (FCNM), are also underpinned by notions of equality and non-discrimination, as may be expected in instruments dedicated to the promotion of the rights of self-identifying peoples and communities.

'Equality before the law' in the chapeau of Article 5 may be contrasted with phrases elsewhere in the Convention such as 'equal protection of the law' in the preamble, 'on an equal footing' in Article 1, 'full and equal enjoyment of human rights' in Article 2 as well

[1] See also Articles 2 and 28 of the CRC, plus some twelve provisions in the ICRMW. For a more detailed account of basic standards, see Chapter 6.

[2] See the list of instruments in Chapter 6.

[3] Article 2.

[4] Article 3. See also Article 10.

as other references, and might suggest a certain narrowing of conception. De Schutter comments that, while 'equality before the law' is 'addressed to law enforcement authorities',[5] whether executive or judiciary, 'equal protection of the law' is addressed to the lawmaker.[6] On the other hand, the scope of 'equality before the law', which was adopted in part to cover the alleged vagueness of 'equal justice before the law', was not discussed to any great extent and appears to have been accepted as a principle that was not to be interpreted narrowly.[7] In practice, 'equality before the law' does not appear to be highlighted by the Committee with any frequency and, in any case, represents only one aspect of the vision of equality in Article 5, which also accounts for 'equal treatment before the tribunals', 'equal suffrage', 'equal access to public service', 'equal pay for equal work', and 'equal participation in cultural activities'. On one reading, the deployment of multiple references to equality in Article 5 may express little more than an accumulation of tautologies; an alternative, more persuasive reading is that its message of equality implicates wider, more generous meanings than a simple focus on the institutions of justice.

Enough has been said elsewhere in the present work to underline the point that, in its work on Article 5 and other articles, the Committee deploys broad understandings of equality, with an overall focus on active, positive notions of equality that transcend formal statements of principle. Many variants on the equality theme have been referred to, including 'formal equality', 'de facto equality',[8] 'equality of rights',[9] 'equality in the enjoyment of rights' of various groups,[10] 'effective equality',[11] 'the values of equality and non-discrimination',[12] 'racial equality',[13] 'equality of women and girls',[14] 'substantive equality',[15] and so on.

Compared with Article 1, the list of 'grounds' in the chapeau of Article 5 is reduced from five to four with the omission of 'descent', an omission that has not inhibited the Committee from applying the framework of Article 5 to descent-based groups, nor to other groups on the basis of intersectionality. General Recommendation (GR) 29 on descent-based discrimination names a spectrum of civil, political, economic, social, and cultural rights drawn from this article that have special resonance for the groups in question.[16] As noted in Chapter 12, the drafting records of Article 5 do not illuminate the reasons for the elision of 'descent' from the list of grounds. Article 5 also uses

[5] O. De Schutter, *International Human Rights Law* (Cambridge University Press, 2012), p. 577; the phrase 'equal protection of the law' incorporates 'a general prohibition of discrimination on forbidden grounds... whenever it manifests itself in law': P. Thornberry, *International Law and the Rights of Minorities* (Clarendon Press, 1991), p. 285, and references therein. See also W. Vandenhole, *Non-Discrimination and Equality in the View of the UN Human Rights Treaty Bodies* (Intersentia, 2005), Chapter II [henceforth *Non-Discrimination and Equality*].

[6] *Ibid*., p. 596. Cf. Article 26 ICCPR.

[7] See discussion in Chapter 12.

[8] GR 32, para. 6. See Chapters 6, 7, and 9 for further discussion.

[9] Concluding observations on Bolivia, CERD/C/BOL/CO/17-20, para. 14; Guatemala, CERD/C/GTM/CO/12-13, para. 5.

[10] Concluding observations on Laos, CERD/C/LAO/CO/16-20, para.15 (gender equality); Portugal, CERD/C/PRT/CO/12-14, para.18 (gender equality); United Arab Emirates, CERD/C/ARE/CO/17, para. 11 (equality between citizens and non-citizens).

[11] Concluding observations on Serbia, CERD/C/SRB/CO/1, para. 16 (Roma, Ashkali, and Egyptians).

[12] Concluding observations on Moldova, CERD/C/MDA/CO/8-9, para. 17.

[13] Concluding observations on Uruguay, CERD/C/URU/CO/16-20, para. 16.

[14] Concluding observations on the Czech Republic, CERD/C/CZE/CO/8-9, para. 18.

[15] Concluding observations on Mauritius, CERD/C/MUS/CO/15-19, para. 14, special measures directed towards the achievement of substantive equality: see also GR 32, para. 6.

[16] See Chapter 6.

'distinction' rather than 'discrimination', whereas 'distinction' is only one member of the typology of discrimination in Article 1.[17] In practice, 'discrimination' and 'distinction' are treated as interchangeable: GR 20 on 'non-discriminatory implementation of rights and freedoms' refers simply to the obligation of States under Article 5 to guarantee the enjoyment of rights 'without racial discrimination'.[18]

5(a) Equal Treatment before Tribunals and all other Organs Administering Justice

The guidelines for 5(a) request information on measures taken to ensure that actions by States parties in the fight against terrorism do not involve racial discrimination and that individuals 'are not subjected to racial or ethnic profiling or stereotyping'.[19] The request footnotes the Committee's 2002 statement on racial discrimination and terrorism in which it was stated, *inter alia*, that the principle of non-discrimination is to be observed 'in particular in those [matters] concerning liberty, security and dignity of the person, equality before the courts and due process of law, as well as international cooperation in judicial and police matters' in these fields'.[20]

Background standards on fair trials include Articles 10 and 11 of the UDHR, Article 14 of the ICCPR, and many of the UN human rights treaties, including the Convention against Torture (CAT),[21] the Convention on the Rights of the Child (CRC),[22] the Convention on Migrant Workers (CMW),[23] and the Convention on the Rights of Persons with Disabilities (CRPD),[24] as well as the leading regional treaties.[25] The standards are amplified by such as General Comment (GC) 29 of the Human Rights Committee, and have been regarded as of *jus cogens* quality; in terms of derogability under the ICCPR, fair trial standards, even if not explicitly listed as non-derogable, 'create safeguards for those norms that are explicitly listed . . . such as the right to life and the prohibition against torture'.[26] On the equality aspect, Shah summarizes the analogous situation under the ICCPR in terms of derivation from Article 26, and implying equal access to courts, equality of arms, and the right to be treated without discrimination.[27]

The Committee has been greatly exercised in its lifetime by racial disparities in the justice system, including matters of prison sentencing,[28] the death penalty,[29] the treatment

[17] See Chapter 6.

[18] GR 20, para. 1.

[19] CERD/C/2007/1; the 5(a) guidelines also request States parties to ensure that claims of racial discrimination are investigated thoroughly, that claims against officials are subject to independent and effective scrutiny, and that GR 31 should be implemented.

[20] A/57/18, Chapter XI.C, para. 6.

[21] Article 15.

[22] Article 40.

[23] Article 18.

[24] Article 13.

[25] For a fuller list, see S. Shah, 'Detention and trial', in D. Moeckli, S. Shah, and S. Sivakumaran (eds), *International Human Rights Law* (2nd edn, Oxford University Press, 2014), pp. 259–85, pp. 270–1.

[26] *Ibid.*, p. 271.

[27] *Ibid.*, p. 273.

[28] Concluding observations on the US, CERD/C/USA/CO/6, paras 20 and 21, the latter with regard to disproportionate use of life sentences without parole against young offenders from racial, ethnic, and national minorities; also CERD/C/USA/CO/7-9, paras 20, 21, 22, and 23, on criminal justice issues more broadly.

[29] CERD/C/USA/CO/6, para. 23; CERD/C/USA/CO/7-9, para. 20.

of young offenders, the plight of indigent accused,[30] disproportionate numbers of minorities in the prison system as a result of structural discrimination, etc.[31] The problem of racialization of justice systems is not confined to criminal processes and extends to civil process and other areas of justice administration, though the Committee has devoted greater space to tribunals that judge criminal cases. The statement in GR 35 on the importance of independent, impartial, and informed judicial bodies in justice systems will be recalled;[32] this advice, promoted in the context of combating racist hate speech, is applicable across the spectrum of rights and institutions called upon to address issues of racial discrimination.

GR 31 on racial discrimination in the criminal justice system, adopted by the Committee in 2005, represents its broadest treatment of justice issues.[33] The recommendation implicates Article 5 but also Articles 1 and 6, as well as calling to mind other CERD general recommendations[34] and a swathe of human rights instruments.[35] In addition to advocating legislative and policy strategies to address racism in the justice system, the recommendation outlines a series of essential steps to be taken at all stages, from access to law and justice, reporting of racist incidents, initiation of judicial proceedings, arrest and detention, through to trial and judgment, sentencing and punishment.[36]

Issues arising from State responses to the threat of terrorism have been of concern, particularly since the events of 11 September 2001. The Committee has acknowledged the national security concerns of States but insists that human rights obligations condition the security responses. The treatment of non-citizens under anti-terrorism legislation has occasioned many comments. GR 30—the recommendations of which straddle various paragraphs of Article 5—recommends that States parties ensure 'that non-citizens detained or arrested in the fight against terrorism are properly protected by domestic law that complies with international human rights, refugee and humanitarian law'.[37] Stereotyping of certain groups as associated with terrorism has been the subject of criticism.[38] Practices such as identity, entry, and residence checks on foreigners, extradition,[39] and the spectre of *non-refoulement* have all engaged attention,[40] as well as legislation providing for the indefinite detention of non-nationals suspected of terrorism without charge or trial.[41] The application of loosely drafted anti-terrorism legislation

[30] *Ibid.*, para. 22.

[31] Concluding observations on Colombia, CERD/C/COL/CO/14, para. 21, Afro-Colombian and indigenous persons. See also concluding observations on Mexico, linking the high numbers of indigenous in prison with shortcomings in the justice system, particularly with regard to the shortage of interpreters and qualified bilingual justice officials: CERD/C/MEX/CO/16-17, para. 14.

[32] Para. 18, further discussed in Chapter 11.

[33] A/60/18, chapter IX; further discussion in Chapter 16.

[34] The three GRs (27, 29, and 30) regarding, respectively, the Roma, descent-based groups, and non-citizens.

[35] The reporting guidelines envisage the blanket implementation of GR 31.

[36] Sentencing practices where foreigners found guilty of crimes under Belgian law received more severe sentences than Belgians were highlighted by the Committee: CERD/C/BEL/CO/15, para. 14.

[37] A/59/18, ch. VIII, para. 20; see also Chapter 7.

[38] Concluding observations on Australia, CERD/C/AUS/CO/15-17, para. 12, concerning the collection of biometric data of applicants for Australian visas in certain countries.

[39] Concluding observations on Albania, CERD/C/ALB/CO/1, para. 25.

[40] Discussed, *infra*, in relation to Article 5(b).

[41] Concluding observations on the United Kingdom, CERD/C/63/CO/11, para. 17. The Committee has also recommended avoiding arbitrary detention: concluding observations on Australia, CERD/C/AUS/CO/15-17, para. 24; New Zealand, CERD/C/NZL/CO/18-20, para. 20; in the case of Israel, the Committee asserted a violation 'under international human rights law' with regard to practices of administrative detention, CERD/C/ISR/CO/14-16, para. 27.

against ethnic and indigenous groups has also been the subject of concern.[42] The insertion of specific anti-discrimination clauses into anti-terrorism legislation has been recommended by the Committee.[43] In welcoming the United Kingdom's new system to review control orders under counter-terrorism legislation, and in light of information regarding the targeting of Muslims, the Committee recommended that the State party ensure that the system 'includes safeguards against abuse and the targeting of certain ethnic and religious groups', and invited the UK to provide data on the impact of the system, disaggregated by religious belief and ethnic origin.[44]

Practices of racial profiling are raised with some regularity before the Committee, reaching beyond anti-terrorism contexts. GR 31 addresses the practice: States parties should take all necessary steps 'to prevent questioning, arrests and searches which are in reality based solely on the physical appearance of a person, that person's colour or features or membership of a racial or ethnic group, or any profiling which exposes him or her to greater suspicion'.[45] Racial or ethnic profiling is regarded as dangerous in that it promotes racial prejudice and stereotypes,[46] and it has been contested by the Committee in concluding observations in relation to a range of target groups including persons of African descent,[47] 'Arabs, Muslims and South Asians',[48] 'migrants, asylum-seekers and refugees',[49] Roma and Travellers,[50] 'foreigners or members of "visible minorities"',[51] and others.[52]

In line with CERD practice in general, guidelines also request States to ensure that claims of racial discrimination are thoroughly investigated and that claims of racist behaviour by officials are subject to 'independent and effective' scrutiny.[53] In *Narrainen v Norway*, the author of the communication, of Tamil origin, was arrested and jailed in connection with a drug-related offence. He alleged that racial bias on the part of two jurors affected the fairness of the trial process. While no specific provisions of the Convention were invoked by the author, the Committee took the view that the principal

[42] Concluding observations on Chile regarding the application of anti-terrorism legislation to members of the Mapuche community engaged in protests: CERD/C/CHL/CO/15-18, para. 15.

[43] Canada, CERD/C/CAN/CO/18, para. 14.

[44] CERD/C/GBR/CO/18-20, para. 21.

[45] GR 31, para. 20. Compare the definition by the European Commission against Racism and Intolerance (ECRI): 'The use by the police, with no objective and reasonable justification, of grounds such as race, colour, language, religion, nationality or national or ethnic origin in control, surveillance or investigation activities': CRI (2007) 39, General Policy Recommendation No. 11 on Combating Racism and Racial Discrimination in Policing, para. 1. The Explanatory Report on the recommendation observes (para. 27) that racial profiling 'constitutes a specific form of racial discrimination', adding in para. 29 that in order for the police 'to avoid racial profiling, control, surveillance or investigation activities should be strictly based on individual behaviour and /or accumulated intelligence.'

[46] Ireland, CERD/C/IRL/CO/3-4, para. 18.

[47] Panama, CERD/C/PAN/CO/15-20, para. 21.

[48] USA, CERD/C/USA/CO/6, para. 14.

[49] Canada, CERD/C/61/CO/3, para. 24.

[50] Denmark, CERD/C/DNK/CO/18-19, para. 10.

[51] Ukraine, CERD/C/UKR/CO/19-21, para. 10. The use of the term 'visible minorities' in this context is not without its ironies, since the Committee has repeatedly criticized its use by authorities in Canada: CERD/C/CAN/CO/18, para. 13; CERD/C/CAN/CO/19-20, para. 8.

[52] Canada, CERD/C/CAN/CO/19-20, para. 11 (African Canadians); Russian Federation, CERD/C/RUS/CO/20-22, para. 14 (Chechens and other persons originating from the Caucasus, Central Asia or Africa, as well as Roma); Sweden, CERD/C/SW/CO/19-21, para. 16 (minority communities); Thailand, CERD/C/THA/CO/1-3, para. 21 (special laws in southern border provinces affecting groups including Malayu Thais).

[53] CERD/C/2007/1, p. 12, section I, para. A.2.

issue was the right under 5(a) to equal treatment before the tribunals: '5(a) applies to all types of judicial proceedings, including trial by jury'.[54] In the event, the Committee took the view that the competent judicial bodies of Norway had examined the issue, that it was not for the Committee to interpret the relevant rules on disqualification of jurors, and it was not possible to conclude that a breach of the Convention had occurred.[55] The Committee nonetheless made the recommendation that 'every effort should be made to prevent any form of racial bias from entering into judicial proceedings' and that in criminal cases 'due attention be given to the impartiality of juries'.[56] The strictures logically extend to proceedings for war crimes, which should be 'effectively investigated and prosecuted, irrespective of the ethnicity of the victims and the perpetrators involved'.[57]

Access to justice also implicates legal aid and support for programmes of test cases to clarify the rights of minorities and other disadvantaged groups.[58] In individual sets of observations on justice issues, the Committee has expressed concern regarding the high standards of proof required of indigenous claimants in land rights litigation that inhibits their ability to secure the recognition of their rights.[59] Preference has been expressed in a number of cases for alternative dispute mechanisms and negotiation to achieve outcomes acceptable to indigenous groups and to States[60] and the Committee has criticized aggressive, overly adversarial litigation strategies pursued by States in such contexts.[61]

The development of cultural integrity norms has influenced justice mechanisms as much as other areas of action.[62] Traditional authorities and justice systems and customary law are subject to the non-discrimination critique: 'respect for customary law and practices should not be ensured through a general exception to the principle of non-discrimination, but should rather be implemented through positive recognition of cultural rights'.[63] The principle that customary and religious systems are required to respect the non-discrimination standard may have particular salience where systems run the risk of multiplying the forms of discrimination experienced by women. The Committee has insisted on a number of occasions that the principle of free choice of system must be applied in order, *inter alia*, to protect 'particularly marginalized and vulnerable persons such as women in traditional societies'.[64] The approach resonates with that adopted by the Human Rights Council's Expert Mechanism on the Rights of Indigenous Peoples (EMRIP) in a study pointing out that indigenous juridical systems are not static and

[54] CERD/C/44/D/3/1991 (1994), para. 9.2.

[55] *Ibid.*, para. 9.5.

[56] *Ibid.*, para. 10.

[57] Concluding observations on Croatia, CERD/C/HRV/CO/8, para. 15.

[58] CERD/C.CAN/CO/18, para. 26; CERD/C/CAN/CO/19-20, para. 21.

[59] CERD/C/AUS/CO/15-17, para. 18.

[60] CERD/C/CAN/CO/18, para. 22.

[61] CERD/C/CAN/CO/19-20, para. 20.

[62] 'Traditional' justice mechanisms pertaining to indigenous peoples and other groups are discussed in Chapter 16 on Article 6.

[63] Concluding observations on Zambia, CERD/C/ZMB/CO/16, para. 9.

[64] Concluding observations on Ethiopia, CERD/C/ETH/CO/7-16, para. 12. In the same paragraph, the Committee 'welcomed the... information that the application of religious and customary laws practised by some ethnic groups is subject to the consent of the concerned individuals or groups'. In the case of Namibia, it was recommended that the State party introduce 'a system which allows individuals a choice between customary law systems and the national law while ensuring that the discriminatory aspects of customary law are not applied': CERD/C/NAM/CO/12, para. 11.

unchanging but dynamic and capable of demonstrating respect 'for both the legal autonomy of indigenous peoples and international human rights law',[65] including the demand 'that women's dignity and physical integrity be respected'.[66]

5(b) The Right to Security of the Person and Protection by the State Against Violence or Bodily Harm, Whether Inflicted by Government Officials or by any Individual, Group, or Institution

Background standards regarding violence and bodily harm are many and various in international human rights law, stemming from Article 3 of the UDHR, which enshrines rights to life, liberty, and security of person, and Article 5 which provides that no-one 'shall be subjected to torture or to cruel, inhuman or degrading treatment or punishment. Core protections include the right to life and freedom from torture and ill-treatment, as well as protection from the violence associated with genocide and crimes against humanity, and war crimes. The right to life is protected by treaty and customary international law and implicates the issue of application of the death penalty. The prohibition of torture has generated a specific convention (the CAT) as well as a Sub-Committee on the Prevention of Torture, and is treated as a prohibition to be respected under customary international law as well as *jus cogens*.[67] Issues of violence are briefly addressed in the Inter-American Convention on Racism and Racial discrimination.[68] Among groups implicated in CERD recommendations, issues of 'life, liberty and security' are addressed in Article 7 of the UNDRIP, while 'force' is referred to in the context of prohibiting forced assimilation or population transfer, and forcible removal from lands;[69] ILO Convention 169 also supplies relevant standards.[70] Violence against women is also the subject of considerable current attention at the international level, particularly following the Declaration on the Elimination of Violence against Women, adopted by the General Assembly in 1993, and the establishment of the mandate of a Special Rapporteur on violence against women in 1994; the adoption by CEDAW of GR 19 also stands as a landmark development. Specific instruments also address the issue, including the 1994 Inter-American Convention on the Prevention, Punishment and Eradication of Violence against Women (Convention of Belém do Pará),[71] and the Council of Europe Convention on Preventing and Combating Violence against Women and Domestic Violence.[72]

The wide orbit of the paragraph covers sources of violence whether public or private; its purpose is, according to Lerner, 'to avoid any distinction in the protection of individuals

[65] *Study of Access to Justice in the Promotion and Protection of the Rights of Indigenous Peoples*, A/HRC/27/65, para. 23.

[66] *Ibid.*, citing R. Sieder and M.T. Sierra, 'Indigenous Women's Access to Justice in Latin America', Christian Michelsen Institute Working Paper No. 2010.2 (CMI, 2010).

[67] For a concise review of relevant international norms and standards see N. Rodley, 'Integrity of the Person', in Moeckli et al., *International Human Rights Law*, pp. 174–94; the chapter provides an extensive account of 'hard' and 'soft' legal provisions as well as a concise reading list and a list of relevant websites.

[68] In particular, Article 4.

[69] See in particular Articles 8 and 10.

[70] Especially Articles 9, 10, and 11. For minorities, see Article 6 of the FCNM.

[71] 33 ILM 1534 (1994).

[72] CETS No. 210 (2011).

against any violence, whoever inflicts it'.[73] Article 5 is complemented in this respect by Article 4, under which acts of violence are to be declared as offences.[74] The sweep of the protected right also recalls the references in Article 2 to discrimination by persons, groups, and organizations. Reporting guidelines for 5(b) request a wide spectrum of information, including on measures to prevent violence and to ensure no degree of impunity for perpetrators, to prevent illegal use of force by police, and encourage communication and dialogue between police and victims or potential victims of racial discrimination. The guidelines also refer to encouraging police recruitment of personnel from groups protected under the Convention and to ensuring that non-citizens 'are not returned to a country or territory where they are at risk of being subject to serious human rights abuses, including torture', etc.[75]

Searching the term 'security' in CERD practice throws up multiple references to national security concerns, notably in the context of measures against terrorism,[76] to social security,[77] and even to 'private security personnel'.[78] There is ample practice regarding security of persons, as might be expected in light of the everyday nature of discrimination against groups leading to violence, frustrating the aspiration voiced in the preamble to 'peace and security among peoples'. The need for 'security of person',[79] 'security and integrity',[80] 'legal security',[81] 'security and freedom',[82] have all been referred to by the Committee in many contexts, some of which stand outside the spectrum of violence.[83] Besides measures set out in the guidelines, measures to guarantee freedom of worship, legal documentation, and regularization of migration programmes, larger-scale restoration of peace and security, police force training, and resolute action to punish perpetrators of violence, are all standard CERD recommendations. The approach is holistic in that personal security may be threatened by a variety of discriminatory practices that require complex, multifaceted responses on the part of State authorities.

Allegations of killings and violence, including allegations of torture,[84] punctuate the Committee records, whether of members of particular ethnic groups through inter-ethnic violence or otherwise, and of human rights defenders.[85] Concerns expressed may

[73] N. Lerner, *The International Convention on the Elimination of All Forms of Racial Discrimination* (Sijthoff and Noordhoff, 1980), p. 57.

[74] See Chapter 11.

[75] CERD/C/2007/1, p. 9, section B.

[76] Discussion of Article 5(a) in the present chapter.

[77] Discussed below in relation to Article 5(e)(iv).

[78] Concluding observations on Nigeria, CERD/C/NGA/CO/18, para. 19.

[79] Concluding observations on Korea, CERD/C/63/CO/9, para. 10, with regard to migrant workers.

[80] Concluding observations on Italy, CERD/C/ITA/CO/16-18, para. 18, of non-citizens and Roma and Sinti.

[81] Concluding observations on Rwanda, CERD/C/RWA/CO/13-17, para. 14, predictability and legal security required of a criminal law, with respect to legislation on 'the ideology of genocide'.

[82] Concluding observations on Yemen, CERD/C/YEM/CO/17-18, para. 16, security and freedom of worship.

[83] Including the reference to 'nutritional security' in concluding observations on Guatemala, CERD/C/GTM/CO/12-13, para. 12.

[84] Concluding observations on Kyrgyzstan, CERD/C/KGZ/CO/5-7, para. 7.

[85] Sundry examples include concluding observations on Venezuela, CERD/C/VE/CO/19-21, para. 17, murder and killings of the Yupka people; Mexico, CERD/C/MEX/CO/16-17, para. 12, human rights defenders; Kenya, CERD/C/KEN/CO/1-4, para. 15, post-election violence; Australia, CERD/C/AUS/CO/15-17, para. 23, assaults on Indian students; Pakistan, CERD/C/PAK/CO/20, paras 16 and 17, against foreigners, and Baluchi and minority women; China, CERD/C/CHN/CO/13, para. 17, inter-ethnic violence.

be roughly categorized into concerns over State actors, non-State actors, and, in some classifications, deserving a separate space to itself, the treatment of asylum-seekers and irregular immigrants. In terms of violence, etc., on the part of State officials, common points of reference outlined in GR 31 include 'police and army personnel, customs authorities, and persons working in airports, penal institutions and social, medical and psychiatric services'.[86] The recommendation enjoins States parties to 'prevent and ... severely punish violence, acts of torture, cruel, inhuman or degrading treatment' perpetrated by State officials against members of groups covered by the Convention.[87] The recommendation further invokes the canon of supporting international standards regarding the conduct of State officials, including 'the general principle of proportionality and strict necessity in recourse to force'.[88] Allegations of police violence or misconduct directed against Roma,[89] asylum-seekers, and persons of African descent continue to trouble the Committee,[90] which criticizes the absence of independent monitoring mechanisms with powers to investigate complaints of police misconduct. The over-representation—or even 'the striking overrepresentation'[91]—of members of ethnic groups in prisons is another indicator for the Committee that racial discrimination may be at work in justice processes. The poignant issue of deaths in custody has also been the subject of questioning and comment by the Committee.[92]

As regards non-State actors, racist incidents involving groups such as 'skinheads', neo-Nazis,[93] and Cossacks,[94] 'settler violence',[95] and larger-scale inter-ethnic or analogous clashes,[96] may equally be drawn into the 5(b) framework. Racism in sporting events has also been a focus,[97] leading to the generalization in GR 35, encouraging States parties 'to work with sports associations to eradicate racism in all sporting disciplines'.[98]

Violence against all groups included within the purview of ICERD is a regrettable commonplace that colours the understanding of 'discrimination' taken as a global phenomenon.[99] In the spectrum of victims, violence against women members of ethnic groups has attained notable prominence; GR 25 devotes a paragraph to the issue:

[86] GR 31, para. 21.

[87] GR 31, para. 21.

[88] *Ibid.*, para. 22. The paragraph recalls the Basic Principles on the Use of Force and Firearms by Law Enforcement Officials adopted by the Eighth UN Congress on the Prevention of Crime and the Treatment of Offenders (1990).

[89] Comparable cases under the ECHR include *Angueluova v Bulgaria*, ECtHR, App. No. 38361/97 (2002); *Mižigárova v Slovakia*, App. No. 74832/01 (2010); *Velikova v Bulgaria*, App. No. 41488/98 (2000).

[90] Examples may be found in concluding observations regarding Italy, CERD/C/ITA/CO/15, para. 19; Romania, CERD/C/ROU/CO/16-19, para. 15; Russian Federation, CERD/C/RUS/CO/19, para. 13 (against Georgians); Slovakia, CERD/C/SVK/CO/6-8, para. 14; and Ukraine, CERD/C/UKR/CO/18, para. 12.

[91] Concluding observations on Australia, CERD/C/AUS/CO/14, para. 21; the observation strikes an intersectional note with the comment that 'indigenous women constitute the fastest-growing prison population.'

[92] *Ibid.*, see also the UK, CERD/C/63/CO/11, para. 18.

[93] Or even 'neo-nazi skinhead groups': concluding observations on Bulgaria, CERD/C/BGR/CO/19, para. 18; Slovakia, CERD/C/SVK/CO/6-8/Add.1, para. 12.

[94] Concluding observations on the Russian Federation, CERD/C/62/CO/7, para. 16; and CERD/C/RUS/CO/19, para.18.

[95] Concluding observations on Israel, CERD/C/ISR/CO/14-16, para. 28.

[96] Concluding observations on Kyrgyzstan, CERD/C/KGZ/CO/4, para. 10.

[97] Concluding observations on Romania, CERD/C/ROU/CO/16-19, para. 17, 'racism in sport, particularly football'; also Serbia, CERD/C/SRB/CO/1, para. 13.

[98] Para. 43.

[99] See remarks and discussion in Chapter 6 (on 'intersectionality) and Chapter 20.

Certain forms of racial discrimination may be directed towards women specifically because of their gender, such as sexual violence committed against women members of particular racial or ethnic groups in detention or during armed conflict; the coerced sterilization of indigenous women; abuse of women workers in the informal sector or domestic workers employed abroad by their employers. Racial discrimination may have consequences that affect primarily or only women, such as pregnancy resulting from racial bias-motivated rape; in some societies women victims of such rape may also be ostracized. Women may also be further hindered by a lack of access to remedies and complaint mechanisms for racial discrimination because of gender-related impediments, such as gender bias in the legal system and discrimination against women in private spheres of life.[100]

Domestic violence against women, including 'spousal violence',[101] has been the subject of strong recommendations in light of Article 5(b).[102] Other egregious forms of violence that have attracted attention include coerced sterilization and female genital mutilation (FGM) procedures on women belonging to certain ethnic groups. For the former, CERD has recommended full compensation packages for victims of the practice, promotion of awareness of international guidelines including those on informed consent, waiver of any statutes of limitation, and monitoring of relevant institutions.[103] In the case of Slovakia, CERD enlisted the support of three judgments of the European Court of Human Rights,[104] recommending that they be fully implemented, ensuring full reparation and compensation, as well as prosecution of offenders; the State party was also encouraged to adopt appropriate measures that included 'the organization of special training for all medical staff on how to obtain informed consent before carrying out sterilization [and] sensitization . . . on respecting diversity'.[105]

As regards FGM, the duty of the State is to eradicate the practice.[106] Specific points of reference include GR 25 against the background of developing international standards and concern.[107] In the case of Norway, CERD requested an evaluation of the action plan against FGM—as well as the plan to combat forced marriage—'and an assessment of how these also promote the rights of women and girls from certain minority groups without stigmatizing them'.[108] The last observation suggests that care should be taken in implementing policies that primarily relate to vulnerable groups in the

[100] Para. 2.

[101] Concluding observations on Japan, CERD/C/JPN/3-6, para. 17. Bearing in mind that, while not completely 'gendered', spousal violence is predominantly experienced by women.

[102] Concluding observations on Denmark, CERD/C/DNK/CO/18-19, para. 13; Japan, CERD/C/JPN/CO/3-6, para. 17; Pakistan, CERD/C/PAK/CO/20, para. 17, the recommendations are related to 'foreign women' (Denmark and Japan), and women, 'especially those of minority background' (Pakistan).

[103] Czech Republic, CERD/C/CZE/CO/8-9, para. 19; Slovakia, CERD/C/SVK/CO/6-8/Add.1, para. 19.

[104] ECtHR, *I.G. and others v Slovakia*, App. No. 15966/04 (2012); *V.C. v Slovakia*, App. No. 18968/07 (2011); *N.B. v Slovakia*, App. No. 29518/10 (2012).

[105] CERD/C/SVK/CO/9-10, para. 13.

[106] Concluding observations on Tanzania, CERD/C/TZA/CO/16, para. 13.

[107] See, *inter alia*, CEDAW GRs 14, 19, and 24; Human Rights Committee GC 28 (Equality of Men and Women); Commission on the Status of Women, *Ending FGM*, E/CN.6/2010/L.6, 10 March 2010; UN Declaration on the Elimination of Violence against Women, A/RES/48/104, 20 December 1993, Article 2; General Assembly resolution on *Intensifying Global Efforts for the Elimination of Female Genital Mutilations*, A/RES/67/146, 20 December 2012; reports of the Special Rapporteur on Violence against Women, inaugurated by Commission on Human Rights resolution 1994/40, 4 March 1994, confirmed by resolution 2003/45, 23 April 2003. In the regional context, see in particular the Protocol to the African Charter on Human and Peoples' Rights on the Rights of Women in Africa (2003), Articles 2, 4, and 5; African Charter on the Rights and Welfare of the Child (1990), Article 21; Inter-American Convention on the Prevention, Punishment and Eradication of Violence against Women (1994).

[108] CERD/C/NOR/CO/19-20, para. 15.

population, while remaining faithful to the principle of non-discrimination.[109] In cases where the practice is located in 'traditional communities', the Committee's recommendations have stressed, *inter alia*, 'sensitization programmes directed at promoting changes in attitudes towards this practice, in consultation with [the] communities'.[110]

Human trafficking presents itself, in many cases, as another example of 'intersectional' discrimination. Sometimes explicitly coupled with violence,[111] the phenomenon of trafficking has received considerable attention from the Committee.[112] The strong gender connotations of international trafficking may obscure the 'intersection' with racial discrimination:

> Trafficking is usually considered to be a gender issue and the result of discrimination based on sex. It is rarely analyzed from the perspective of race discrimination . . . However, when attention is paid to which women are most at risk of being trafficked, the link of this risk to their racial and social marginalization becomes clear. Moreover, race and racial discrimination may not only constitute a risk factor for trafficking, it may also determine the treatment that women experience in countries of destination. In addition, racist ideology and racial, ethnic and gender discrimination may create a demand in the region or country of destination which could contribute to trafficking in women and girls.[113]

States parties have been encouraged to ratify relevant instruments on trafficking in persons, especially women and children.[114] The racial dimension is adverted to by referring to trafficking practices that target non-citizens, ethnic minorities including Roma, migrant workers, etc.

As regards asylum-seekers, or simply under the rubric of 'non-citizens',[115] the principle of non-refoulement is frequently addressed,[116] sometimes linked to a specific citation of 5(b),[117] or to GR 30 on non-citizens,[118] paragraph 27 of which states that States parties are to 'ensure that non-citizens are not returned or removed to a country or territory where they are at risk of being subject to serious human rights abuses, including torture

[109] Reference was made, *ibid.*, to 'the perceived excessive focus' on these issues 'which may be seen as stigmatizing women and girls belonging to certain minority groups'.

[110] CERD/C/TZA/CO/16, para. 13.

[111] *Ibid.*, para. 16.

[112] A.T. Gallagher, *The International Law of Human Trafficking* (Cambridge University Press, 2010) provides an extensive commentary on the subject of trafficking. See also Office of the United Nations High Commissioner for Human Rights (OHCHR) (A.T. Gallagher, consultant), *Commentary on the Recommended Principles and Guidelines on Human Rights and Human Trafficking* (UN Publication: Sales No. E.10.XIV.1, 2010).

[113] *The Race Dimensions of Trafficking in Persons—Especially Women and Children*, background paper for the World Conference against Racism, Xenophobia and Related intolerance: <http://www.un.org/WCAR/e.kit/trafficking_e.pdf>.

[114] Concluding observations on the Maldives recommended ratification of the 2000 Protocol to Prevent, Suppress and Punish Trafficking in Persons, Especially Women and Children, supplementing the UN Convention against Transnational Organized Crime: CERD/C/MDV/CO/5-12, para. 12.

[115] Reporting guidelines, CERD/C/2007/1, p. 9, request information on measures taken to ensure 'that non-citizens are not returned or removed to a country or territory where they are at risk of being subject to serious human rights abuses, including torture and cruel, inhuman or degrading treatment'.

[116] Concluding observations on Australia, CERD/C/AUS/CO/15-17, para. 24; Cambodia, CERD/C/KHM/CO/8-13, para. 14; Italy, CERD/C/ITA/CO/16-18, para. 22; Korea, CERD/C/KOR/CO/15-16, para. 13; Morocco, CERD/C/MAR/CO/17-18, para. 14.

[117] Concluding observations on Australia, CERD/C/AUS/CO/15-17, para. 24.

[118] Paragraph 27 of GR 30 sets the general standard, exemplified in concluding observations in cases such as Azerbaijan, CERD/C/AZE/CO/4/Add.1, para. 13; Kyrgyzstan, CERD/C/KGZ/CO/4, para. 9. See also the comments on GR 22 in Chapter 7.

and cruel, inhuman and degrading treatment'. In some cases, recommendations of the Committee simply recycle the provisions of international refugee law, recommend ratification of relevant instruments and, where necessary, cooperation with the UN High Commissioner for Refugees. In many cases, recommendations in this field are directed to the protection of non-citizens in general from abuse and in support of their rights under refugee law; in other cases the emphasis is on discrimination among non-citizens. Discrimination, coupled with strictures regarding the use of force, is adverted to in recommendations to Japan, prompted by reports that, 'preferential standards apply to asylum-seekers from certain countries and that asylum-seekers with different origins and in need of international protection have been forcibly returned to situations of risk'.[119]

5(c) Political Rights: Elections, Government, Public Affairs, Public Service

Article 5(c) has attracted few reservations, one of which elicited the comment that 'a reservation to Article 5 has the effect of negating the core purposes' of the Convention, and should be withdrawn.[120] Reporting guidelines amplify the scope of the paragraph. In addition to requesting information from State parties on how political rights are guaranteed and enjoyed in practice, they ask whether 'members of indigenous peoples and persons of different ethnic or national origin exercise such rights to the same extent as the rest of the population', and if 'they are proportionately represented in all State public service and governance institutions'. Information is also requested on the extent to which groups are involved in policies and programmes affecting them, on measures to promote awareness 'of the importance of their active participation in public and political life'; States parties are requested to eliminate obstacles to such participation.[121]

Rights of political participation have a complex ancestry, stemming, in the era of the United Nations, from Article 21 of the UDHR, which addresses political representation, access to public service, and periodic elections 'by universal and equal suffrage', and provides that 'the will of the people shall be the basis of the authority of government'. The other key referent for Article 5(c) is Article 25 of the ICCPR, which appropriates the language of the UDHR and applies it as a right of 'every citizen'.[122] Closely analogous political participation rights are found in CEDAW (Article 7), the CRPD (Article 29), and, regionally, the ACHPR (Article 13), ACHR (Article 23), the Arab Charter on

[119] Concluding observations on Japan, CERD/C/JPN/CO/3-6, para. 23.

[120] Concluding observations on the Yemen, CERD/C/YEM/CO/17-18, para. 13; the withdrawal of a similar reservation by Fiji in 2012 was welcomed by the Committee: CERD/C/FJI/CO/18-20, para. 4.

[121] CERD/C/2007/1, pp. 9–10.

[122] In *Gillot v France*, the Human Rights Committee observed that 'the right to vote is not an absolute right and that restrictions may be imposed upon it provided that they are not discriminatory or unreasonable': *Gillot and ors v France*, CCPR/C/75/D/932/2000 (2002), para. 12.2. CERD has noted the disproportionate impact of disenfranchisement laws in the US, urging that 'denial of voting rights is used only with regard to persons convicted of the most serious crimes': CERD/C/USA/CO/6, para. 27; on barring convicted felons from voting, see US Supreme Court, *Richardson v Ramirez* 418 US 24 (1974). See also CERD/C/USA/CO/7-9, para. 11, regarding *Shelby v Holder*, 570 US _ 2013, understood by the Committee as invalidating certain procedural safeguards—'federal preclearance'—against potential discriminatory effects on voting regulations; the paragraph also adverted to the denial of voting rights to residents of the District of Columbia (DC) 'half of whom are African Americans'.

Human Rights (Article 24), and the ECHR (Article 3 of Protocol 1). The inter-American Convention against Racism and Racial Discrimination includes among undertakings by States parties that their legal and political systems 'appropriately reflect the diversity within their societies in order to meet the legitimate needs of all sectors of the population', in accordance with the scope of the Convention.[123] Important aspects of participation rights emerge from instruments on minorities and indigenous peoples, including the UNDM,[124] ILO Convention 169,[125] and the UNDRIP.[126]

Controversy over political rights is evident from the drafting of the Convention, where a proposed Article VIII was deleted following contestations regarding the political rights of non-nationals, and of distinct ethnic groups.[127] Article 5 distinguishes 'political' rights from 'other civil rights', the syntax suggesting that the 'political' rights are a subset of 'civil' rights. While 'civil' is not included in the fields to be protected from discrimination in Article 1, and 'political' rights are so included, in view of the connection made in Article 5 between 'civil' and 'political' rights—and sheer common sense—it may be assumed that the 'civil' field is included in the protection of Article 1 and the Convention as a whole.[128]

As elsewhere in Article 5, the areas of political activity set out in paragraph (c) are indicative and not exhaustive according to the formula 'political rights, in particular'; the paragraph opens up the widest prospectus of governance activity to be secured equally and without discrimination. There is a point to Diaconu's observation that many civil rights listed in Article 5 'are highly political and can hardly be separated from . . . participation in the conduct of public affairs'.[129] In consequence, it is often difficult to separate recommendations for narrowly 'political' participation from recommendations for participation in other areas.[130] Perhaps the attempt to separate should not be made, bearing in mind the wide currency and scope of the concept of participation in the contemporary human rights canon,[131] including, as noted, its presence in key texts on minorities and indigenous peoples.[132]

[123] Article 9.

[124] Article 2. In more general terms, see the Organization for Security and Co-operation in Europe (OSCE) *Lund Recommendations on the Effective Participation of National Minorities in Public Life*, and the *Commentary on the Effective Participation of Persons belonging to National minorities in Cultural, Social and Economic Life and in Public Affairs* by the Advisory Committee on the FCNM, Appendix I and II, respectively, to M. Weller (ed.), and K Nobbs (assistant ed.), *Political Participation of Minorities* (Oxford University Press, 2010).

[125] Articles 5, 6, and 7 in particular.

[126] See remarks below on consent, etc.

[127] Discussed in Chapter 7 with regard to non-citizens.

[128] The civil field is 'in no way' excluded from the definition in Article 1(1): I. Diaconu, *Racial Discrimination* (Eleven International Publishing, 2011), p. 38.

[129] *Ibid.*, p. 37.

[130] In any case, 'politics' has widened its definition from that which relates to citizens to one of 'achieving and exercising positions of governance or organized control over a community . . . politics is the study or practice of the distribution of power and resources within a given community . . . as well as the interrelationships between communities':<https://en.wikipedia.org/?title=Politics>.

[131] The SIM human rights database found 61 references to 'participation' in 'binding' human rights instruments, a figure that excludes 'soft law' texts.

[132] See the extensive collection of essays in Weller and Nobbs, *Political Participation of Minorities* (Oxford University Press, 2010), in particular the introduction by Weller, lvii to lxiii, and the essays by Machnyikova and Hollo, 'The Principles of Non-discrimination and Full and Effective Equality and Political Participation', pp. 95–149; and by Melansek, 'Universal and European Standards of Political Participation', pp. 345–62. The essays by Verstichel, 'Understanding Minority Participation and Representation and the Issue of Citizenship', pp. 72–94; Bird, 'Gendering Minority Participation in Public Life', pp. 150–73; and Rodríguez-Piñero Royo on 'Political Participation Systems Applicable to Indigenous Peoples, pp. 308–42, also discuss issues germane to the present commentary.

Comments on participation in the present section may therefore be taken to implicate Article 5(c) and, *mutatis mutandis*, Article 5 more widely.[133]

The emphasis on proportionate, or 'approximately proportionate',[134] representation in public affairs has been amplified in specific recommendations.[135] These references suggest that the Committee envisages numerically proportionate representation of groups as entailed by the principles of equality and non-discrimination. The inference is not fully compelling: references to proportionality may also be understood in the context of 'disproportion' signalling a potentially discriminatory situation that the Committee is obliged to query; the flexible understanding of equality in practice may also be recalled to argue against a purely statistical concept of representation. In other cases, the stress has been on securing 'due representation',[136] 'adequate representation',[137] 'fair and adequate' representation',[138] 'appropriate representation',[139] 'equitable ethnic representation'.[140] In these respects, CERD is close to the Inter-American Convention on Racism and Racial Discrimination, for which, as noted, political arrangements should 'appropriately reflect diversity'.[141] In the case of Cyprus, the Committee linked the right to self-identification with 'the free exercise of... political rights', in recommending that the State party define 'minority' and the rights of persons belonging to minorities: the situation results in part from the provisions of the 1960 Constitution of Cyprus whereby Armenians, Maronites, and Latins were compelled to identify with either the Greek Cypriot and Turkish Cypriot communities, and treated narrowly as 'religious communities' to the detriment of their right to political participation and associated rights.[142]

The immense diversity of political arrangements also militates against drawing expansive conclusions from particular cases. Thus, while guaranteed seats in legislative bodies and mandatory quotas have been suggested as a means of securing effective participation,[143] going beyond the cautious phrasing of GR 32 regarding preferential schemes, these may not be appropriate for generalization beyond situations of particular vulnerability.[144] Neither the Convention nor the ensemble of recommendations stemming from

[133] See discussion in Chapter 14 of the right to equal participation in cultural activities, Article 5(e)(vi).

[134] Concluding observations on Moldova, CERD/C/MDA/CO/7, para. 16, with regard to the Roma.

[135] Hence the recommendation to facilitate proportionate representation of Jordanians of all ethnic origin as well as non-national residents in its politics and decision-making: CERD/C/JOR/CO/13-17, para. 13; concluding observations on Kyrgyzstan, CERD/C/KGZ/CO/5-7, para. 9.

[136] Concluding observations on Armenia, CERD/C/ARM/CO/5-6, para. 13; Nepal, CERD/C/64/CO/5, para. 17.

[137] Concluding observations on Croatia, CERD/C/HRV/CO/8, para. 14; Mauritius, CERED/C/MUS/CO/15-19, para. 18.

[138] Concluding observations on China, CERD/C/CHN/10-13, para. 18.

[139] Concluding observations on Albania, CERD/C/ALB/5-8, para. 9.

[140] Concluding observations on Kenya, CERD/C/KEN/CO/1-4, para. 20.

[141] Article 9.

[142] CERD/C/CYP/CO/17-22, para. 14. Regarding a denial of the right to vote of an individual citizen, see European Court of Human Rights (ECtHR), *Aziz v Cyprus*, App. No. 69949/01 (2004), finding a violation of Article 3 of Protocol 1 in conjunction with Article 143, non discrimination.

[143] Concluding observations on the Russian Federation in relation to small indigenous peoples in the North, Siberia and the Russian Far East, in light of their lack of representation in the State Duma of the Federal Assembly, CERD/C/RUS/CO/19, para. 20.

[144] Where such schemes have been established, including reserved seats, the Committee will seek to ensure that the laws are applied without discrimination against particular groups. Concluding observations on India with respect to members of scheduled castes and scheduled tribes recommended that they enjoy the right 'to freely and safely vote and stand for election and to fully exercise their mandate if elected to... reserved seats', CERD/C/IND/CO/19, para. 17; see further Chapter 9.

it point towards specific forms of governance structures, provided that the equality and non-discrimination provisions are respected.[145] An excess of 'democratic' zeal can, it seems, give cause for concern, if not to the same degree as oppressive authoritarian structures. Hence, concern was expressed in one case about the xenophobic tone of 'popular initiatives' to curb immigration, expel foreign criminals, etc.[146] In another, proposals to enhance local decision-making generated the recommendation that groups vulnerable to racial discrimination be involved in the design, implementation, and monitoring of procedures to implement the 'localism' project.[147] Article 5(c) adds 'at any level' to the formulations on the UDHR and the ICCPR, extending the concept of democratic guarantee to regions and localities, echoing the locality contexts in Article 2(1)(a) and 2(1)(c).[148]

Overall, the dominant emphasis in Committee practice on participation and representation is on effective participation, with States being reminded that 'legal guarantees of equal right to be elected are not sufficient as regards political participation of minorities':[149] as elsewhere, legal guarantees must be made effective in order to secure non-discrimination objectives. On voting, the same principles apply, hence the call to France to ensure equal treatment with regard to the right to vote.[150] Securing better representation of ethnic groups in government service may necessitate a range of action to support such representation, including the removal of obstacles to recruitment and promotion such as lack of proficiency in a State language.[151] Special measures may be recommended to support the political participation of under-represented groups[152] to be implemented on the basis of active consultation frameworks.[153]

Recommendations for community participation may be further disaggregated to focus on the representation—usually, the under-representation—of women in politics and public life.[154] As regards the participation of non-citizens in the political process, GR 20 on Article 5 recalls that the rights to participate in elections, to vote, and to stand for elections, are the rights of citizens,[155] a reading of international standards that limits the application of Article 5(c) to non-citizens. As observed in Chapter 7, CERD GR 30 on non-citizens refines the position set out in GR 20, observing that while some rights 'such as the right to participate in elections, to vote and to stand for election, may be confined to citizens, human rights are, in principle, to be enjoyed by all persons', which leads to the 'obligation to guarantee equality in the enjoyment of these rights to the extent recognized

145 See comment in the present chapter on the views of the human rights Committee in *Mikmaq Tribal Society v Canada*, CCPR/C/43/D/205/1986, 4 November 1991.

146 Concluding observations on Switzerland, CERD/C/CHE/CO/7-9, para. 12.

147 Concluding observations on the United Kingdom, CERD/C/GBR/CO/18-20, para. 14.

148 With regard to political parties as such, the 2014 ECRI *Charter of European Political Parties for a Non-Racist Society* retains its interest: <http://www.coe.int/t/dghl/monitoring/ecri/activities/38-seminar_ankara_2011/Charter.asp>.

149 Concluding observations on Armenia, CERD/C/ARM/CO/5-6, para. 13.

150 CERD/C/FRA/CO/17-19, para. 16.

151 CERD/C/KGZ/CO/4, para. 11. Provisions conditioning voter participation on literacy standards have been regarded by the Committee as incompatible with 5(c): A/31/18 (1976), paras 78 and 80.

152 Including Roma, GR 27, para. 41; and caste/descent groups: GR 29, para. 6(aa).

153 See GR 32 on consultation and participation of communities, discussed in Chapter 9.

154 Concluding observations on China, CERD/C/CHN/CO/10-13, para. 18; Croatia, CERD/C/HRV/CO/8, para. 16; Mexico, CERD/C/MEX/CO/16-17, para. 16; Tajikistan, CERD/C/TJK/CO/6-8, para. 12. See also GR 23 of CEDAW on women in 'Political and Public Life'.

155 GR 20, para. 3.

under international law'.[156] The question of voting rights for non-citizens preoccupied the Committee over decades.[157] The Committee has recommended the facilitation of participation in local elections of non-citizens who are permanent residents,[158] and allowing non-citizens to participate in political parties,[159] aspects of non-citizen political participation that are broadly in line with international standards.[160]

On the broader front of peace agreements, the Committee has expressed impatience with some post-conflict ethnically based power-sharing arrangements, while recognizing that they may be justified under particular circumstances. In the case of Bosnia and Herzegovina, the Committee expressed its deep concern that existing legal structures exclude 'from the House of Peoples and the Presidency all persons who are referred to as "Others," that is persons belonging to national minorities or ethnic groups other than Bosniaks, Croats, or Serbs', adding that

> [a]lthough the tripartite structure of the State party's principal political institutions may have been justified, or even initially necessary to establish peace following the armed conflict within the territory of the State party, the Committee notes that legal distinctions that favour and grant special privileges and preferences to certain ethnic groups are not compatible with Articles 1 and 5 (c) of the Convention. The Committee further notes that this is especially true when the exigency for which the special privileges and preferences were undertaken has abated.[161]

In this instance, bearing in mind that the Committee advised remedial action in the combined first to sixth report submitted by the State party, speed of action to eliminate discrimination took precedence over the 'interim' maintenance of 'ethnic balance' in the

[156] GR 30, para. 3. Accordingly the recommendation does not elaborate a platform of appropriate political rights for non-citizens. Diaconu, *Racial Discrimination*, p. 147, distinguishes between non-citizens with a right to permanent residence on the territory of a State, who may enjoy some political rights, and non-citizen temporary residents, who are not so entitled. Compare Weissbrodt, *The Human Rights of Non-Citizens* (Oxford University Press, 2008), Chapter 3.

[157] K.J. Partsch, 'Elimination of Racial Discrimination in the Enjoyment of Civil and Political Rights', *Texas International Law Journal* 14 (1979), 191–250, 237–8.

[158] Concluding observations on Latvia, CERD/C/63/CO/7, para. 12.

[159] In concluding observations on Estonia, CERD/C/EST/CO/7, the Committee welcomed that fact that non-citizens had the right to participate in local elections (para. 6), and recommended (para. 14) in relation to non-citizens and political parties that, taking into account 'the high number of long-term residents of Estonia who are stateless', the State party give due consideration to the possibility of allowing non-citizens to participate in political parties.

[160] While the ICCPR refers to political rights only in the context of citizens, the Human Rights Committee has requested information on whether limited rights of political participation are conferred on non-citizens with regard to local elections and particular public service positions: GC 25, para. 3. See also the Council of Europe Convention on Participation of Foreigners in Public Life at Local Level, CETS 144 (1992).

[161] CERD/C/BIH/CO/6, para. 11. The Committee also observed, para. 4, that the Dayton structure 'may have been necessary, on an interim basis, to secure peace' but that the 'Constitution's . . . assignment of important rights based on ethnicity' may impede the full implementation of the Convention; see also para. 5 noting the recognition by the State party of the need to amend its constitution. The recommendation to address the situation is reiterated in CERD/C/BIH/CO/7-8, para. 7, reiterating the earlier recommendation. The Committee's views are allied with those of the European Court of Human Rights in *Sejdić and Finci v Bosnia and Herzegovina*, App. No. 27996/06, 34836/06 (2009). Both the Committee's opinion and the ECHR case have been developed against the background of the Bosnian Constitution, annexed to the Dayton Peace Agreement of 1995. Under the Dayton arrangements, the House of Peoples was open only to representatives of constituent peoples, Bosniak, Croats and Serbs, as was the presidency, thus excluding Sejdić and Finci, persons of Roma and Jewish origin, respectively, both of whom were involved in public affairs. The ECHR decided that the restriction was disproportionate and lacked objective and reasonable justification. The ECHR case was subject to a highly charged dissent from Judge Bonello who referred to the unravelling of Dayton by a human rights court that 'sows ideals and harvests massacre'.

State; in light of the Committee's initial conclusions, the Dayton arrangements are not referred to in the later concluding observations.

Consultation and Consent

Particularly in the field of territorial resource exploitation, background international standards on non-discrimination, self-determination, and participation have coalesced in the case of indigenous peoples—and Afro-descendants—into a principle that appears to have a life of its own, that of 'free, prior and informed consent' (FPIC), 'currently invoked by virtually all bodies dealing with indigenous peoples' rights'.[162] According to a UN source, 'free' implies that there is no coercion, intimidation, or manipulation; 'prior' that consent is to be sought sufficiently in advance of authorization or commencement of activities; 'informed' implies that a range of information is provided that covers a range of subjects; consultation and participation are envisaged as part of a 'consent' process.[163]

In general UN instruments on human rights, the Committee on Economic, Social and Cultural Rights has intimated that the FPIC standard applies as an aspect of the right of everyone to take part in cultural life.[164] Key case referents from the Human Rights Committee include *Ilmari Länsman et al. v Finland*,[165] and *Poma Poma v Peru*.[166] In finding no violation by Finland, the Human Rights Committee referred to the fact that consultations with Sámi reindeer herders over the impact of stone quarrying on their herding area had taken place, suggesting that a standard less than FPIC satisfied the requirements of the ICCPR, though as the amount of 'cultural damage' was limited, more serious interferences would arguably have necessitated something closer to a consent standard. In finding a violation of Article 27 of the ICCPR in *Poma Poma*, with reference to measures—diversion of groundwater—which substantially interfered with traditional subsistence farming of alpacas and llamas, regarded as 'culturally significant economic activities', the underlying concept of participation was deemed by the Human Rights Committee to require 'not mere consultation but the free, prior and informed consent of the community'.[167] The cases suggest a 'sliding scale' approach, demanding that the more

[162] M. Barelli, 'Free, Prior and Informed Consent in the Aftermath of the UN Declaration on the Rights of Indigenous Peoples: Developments and Challenges Ahead', *International Journal of Human Rights* 16.1. (2012), 1–24, 2. See also J. Gilbert and C. Doyle, 'A New Dawn over the Land: Shedding Light on Collective Ownership and Consent', in S. Allen and A. Xanthaki (eds), *Reflections on the UN Declaration on the Rights of Indigenous Peoples* (Hart Publishing, 2011), pp. 289–328.

[163] United Nations High Commissioner for Human Rights, *Free, Prior and Informed Consent of Indigenous Peoples*: <http://www.ohchr.org/Documents/Issues/IPeoples/FreePriorandInformedConsent.pdf>. The range of information necessary to satisfy FPIC criteria includes 'the nature, size, pace, reversibility and scope of any proposed project or activity; the purpose of the project as well as its duration; locality and areas affected; a preliminary assessment of the likely economic, social, cultural and environmental impact . . . This process may entail the option of withholding consent'. Barelli, *Free, Prior and Informed Consent*, summarizes part of the informational aspect as requiring that information 'should be accurate and in a form that is accessible, meaning that indigenous peoples should fully understand the language used'. See also Permanent Forum on Indigenous Issues, *Report of the International Workshop on Methodologies regarding Free, Prior and Informed Consent and Indigenous Peoples*, E/C.19/2005/3 (17 February 2005); Expert Mechanism Advice No. 2 (2011), *Indigenous Peoples and the Right to Participate in Decision-Making*, A/HCR/18/42, Annex, para. 25 [henceforth EMRIP Advice No. 2].

[164] E/C.12/GC/21, 21 December 2009, para. 37.

[165] CCPR/C/52/D/511/1992, 8 November 1994.

[166] CCPR/C/95/D/1457/2006, 27 March 2009.

[167] *Poma Poma v Peru*, para. 7.6.

serious the threatened harm to the community, the more pressing becomes the need for consent and not 'mere' consultation, an approach that is also reflected in the jurisprudence of the Inter-American and African human rights systems in the *Saramaka* and *Endorois* cases, respectively.[168]

As far as specific instruments on indigenous peoples are concerned, sources of FPIC may take as a starting point the participation principles in ILO Convention 169, which are, however, explicitly directed to consultation with indigenous peoples in general terms as well as in specific contexts such as exploration or exploitation of natural resources, while, with one exception (relocation) eschewing stronger notions of consent.[169] The UNDRIP is harder edged in light of its general endorsement of the principle of self-determination that inclines borderline cases towards demanding full consent. Article 32 of the UNDRIP refers to consultation and cooperation in good faith with the indigenous peoples 'in order to obtain their free and informed consent prior to the approval of any project affecting their lands or territories and other resources', a provision that substitutes an earlier, stronger requirement that States simply 'obtain' free and informed consent.[170] Any softening of consent requirements should be subject to the 'sliding scale' gloss placed on Article 32 by *Saramaka*, which specifically cited the UNDRIP as well as CERD's concluding observations on Ecuador.[171] In some instances, the UNDRIP signals that no softening of consent requirements is permissible.[172] As regards the establishment of a general principle, the Inter-American Court of Human Rights in *Sarayaku v Ecuador* treats the right to consult as a general principle of international law,[173] a position that is not incompatible with stronger assertions regarding the necessity of consent in appropriate cases.

Building on Article 5(c), the Committee has stressed obligations of consultation with representatives of indigenous peoples over a range of political, social environmental, and

[168] In *Saramaka People v Suriname*, IACtHR, Ser. C 172 (2007), the Inter-American Court stated, para. 134, that in the case of projects with a major impact on indigenous peoples, the duty to consult is transformed into a duty to obtain the free, prior and informed consent of the people concerned 'according to their customs and traditions'; a similar determination was made by the African Commission on Human and Peoples' Rights in *Centre for Minority Rights development (Kenya) v Kenya*, 276/2003 (2010) [henceforth *Endorois v Kenya*], with regard to the necessity for FPIC in relation to development or investment projects that have a major impact on territory: para. 291.

[169] The provisions on participation and consultation in ILO Convention 169 have been the subject of 'general observations' by the ILO Committee of Experts on the Application of Conventions and Recommendations [henceforth CEACR]. In a general observation of 2010, the CEACR observed that consultation of indigenous and tribal peoples is specifically required by Article 6, 15, 17, 27, and 28, whereas free and informed consent on the part of the peoples is required in cases of relocation of peoples from lands they occupy, is considered necessary as an exceptional measure, and participation is required under a raft of provisions: Articles 2, 5, 6, 7, 15, and 23. With regard to consultation as a principle underpinning the Convention, the Committee stressed that 'pro forma consultations or mere information would not meet the requirements of the Convention. At the same time, such consultations do not imply a right to veto, nor is the result of such consultations necessarily the reaching of agreement or consent': *CEACR General Observation*, Indigenous and Tribal Peoples, eighty-first Session, 2010, pp. 8–9.

[170] Barelli, *Free, Prior and Informed Consent*, p. 10.

[171] CERD/C/ECU/CO/19, para. 16.

[172] See in particular Article 10, no relocation without FPIC; Article 29, regarding storage of hazardous materials.

[173] *Kichwa indigenous Community of Sarayaku v Ecuador*, IACtHR, Ser. C No. 245, 27 June 2012, para. 164; see comment in L. Brunner and K. Quintana, 'The Duty to Consult in the Inter-American System: legal Standards after Sarayaku': <http://www.asil.org/insights/volume/16/issue/35/duty-consult-inter-american-system-legal-standards-after-sarayaku>.

land issues, raising the question of informed consent to projects affecting their rights and interests, including resource exploitation operations,[174] the construction of dams,[175] the creation of protected areas, or expulsions from territories to make way for game parks or similar operations.[176] Regarding the format of consultations, the Committee has stressed that States parties should take due account of relevant indigenous customary law.[177] As the reference to CERD in the Saramaka case suggests, the Committee's practice contributes to the general understanding of FPIC in international law, as well as being influenced by such developments, particularly since the emergence of the UNDRIP. In some instances, the appeal to international standards is explicit, as in the 2012 concluding observations on Canada where the Committee recommended the State to 'implement in good faith the right to consultation and to free, prior and informed consent of aboriginal peoples whenever their rights may be affected by projects carried out on their lands, as set forth in international standards'.[178] The approach has been challenged by Canada:

> in the Canadian context, free, prior and informed consent... [is]... a process of reconciliation through which the rights and interests of indigenous peoples... [are]... taken into account. The Special Rapporteur on Indigenous Peoples had noted in 2009 that such consent did not provide indigenous peoples with a 'veto power', but rather established the need to frame consultation procedures in such a way as to build consensus. Canada shared that perspective... indigenous peoples [do] not have the right to veto legitimate government decisions made in the public interest. The concept... should focus... on fostering partnerships to ensure that indigenous peoples were more fully involved, consulted and, where appropriate, accommodated in decision-making... that directly affected their rights and interests.[179]

Australia has argued in response to the Committee (before the adoption of the UNDRIP) that there is no international obligation to obtain 'informed consent' in relation to the exercise of executive or legislative power,[180] and that 'individuals and peoples do not have a right to participate in a State's political process in a specific way'.[181] Echoing Article 32 of UNDRIP, CERD has advocated the development of 'appropriate mechanisms' to address indigenous claims; such mechanisms would, paradigmatically, be expected to

[174] Citing Article 5 of ILO Convention 169, Panama was recommended to 'conduct consultations with communities potentially affected by development projects and the exploitation of natural resources so as to obtain their prior, informed and voluntary consent'; it was also recommended that the State party desist from delegating its responsibilities in this respect to private firms: CERD/C/PAN/CO/15-20, para. 14.

[175] CERD/C/IND/CO/19, para. 19, where India was recommended to seek 'the prior and informed consent' of communities affected; protection against encroachment on community territories was also advised.

[176] Ethiopia was requested to provide information on the 'effective participation of indigenous communities in the decisions directly relating to their rights and interests, including their informed consent to the establishment of national parks': CERD/C/ETH/CO/15, para. 22.

[177] Concluding observations on Namibia, CERD/C/NAM/CO/12, para. 18.

[178] CERD/C/CAN/CO/19-20, para. 20.

[179] CERD/C/SR.2142, para. 42.

[180] CERD/C/AUS/CO/14/Add. 1, para. 23.

[181] *Ibid.*, para. 19. The statement appears to echo the views of the Human Rights Committee in *Mikmaq Tribal Society v Canada*, to the effect that the Article 25 participation right does not mean that 'any directly affected group, large or small, has the unconditional right to choose the modality of participation in public affairs' (para. 5.5), a proposition that hardly applies to processes of consultation that are compatible with a variety of institutional architectures, nor to one that addresses the specifics of indigenous peoples as contrasted with an indeterminate 'group'. For a critique of Mikmaq, see M.E. Turpel, 'Indigenous Peoples' Rights of Political Participation and Self-Determination: Recent International Legal Developments and the Continuing Struggle for Recognition', *Cornell International Law Journal* 25 (1992), 579–602.

engage with traditional dispute settlement and representational mechanisms as a starting point.[182]

The use by the Committee of 'free, prior and informed consent' builds upon earlier CERD references to 'consent', with or without qualifiers. GR 23 called for the effective participation of indigenous peoples in public life and 'that no decisions directly relating to their rights and interests are taken without their informed consent', also envisaging return of lands and territories of which they have been deprived 'without their free and informed consent'. Recommendations have since made increasingly bold endorsements of 'free, prior and informed consent' in indigenous contexts in relation generally to 'decisions affecting them',[183] 'their permanent rights as a group',[184] and in sundry situations involving lands and resources including those 'owned or traditionally used'.[185] In some cases the 'free, prior and informed consent' formula is altered, in one case to free, prior, and informed 'consultations with a view to consent' with regard to investment projects that 'could negatively affect . . . health and livelihoods';[186] a State party has also been recommended to provide opportunities for ethnic groups 'to define development in their own terms'.[187] Usage has not always been consistent but has gradually moved towards standardization of FPIC within the interpretative frame of the Convention. In light of the endorsement by the Committee of the Inter-American Court's ruling in *Saramaka*,[188] the Committee's approach to FPIC extends to Afro-Descendant populations

Self-Determination

GR 21 of 1996 forges a link between Article 5(c) and the 'internal aspect' of the right of self-determination,[189] 'the right to every citizen to take part in the conduct of public affairs at any level, as referred to in article 5(c) of the . . . Convention'.[190] The anti-colonialist provenance of the Committee's version of self-determination is clear enough in that the language of the general recommendation echoes the 'Colonial Declaration' of 1960 and the 'Declaration on Friendly Relations' of 1970,[191] though only the latter is specifically evoked. The recommendation also evokes the Charter of the United Nations, the ICCPR, the ICESCR, and the UNDM. The distinction between internal and external

[182] Concluding observations on Fiji, CERD/C/FJI/CO/18-20, para. 14; New Zealand, CERD/C/NZL/CO/18-20, para. 18. See also Article 6 of ILO Convention 169; *Yatama v Nicaragua*, IACtHR, Ser. C No. 127 (2005); EMRIP Advice No. 2, paras 9, 30, and 32 on the role of women in traditional mechanisms.

[183] Concluding observations on Thailand, CERD/C/THA/CO/11-3, para. 16.

[184] Concluding observations on Fiji, CERD/C/FJI/CO/18-20, para. 14.

[185] Concluding observations on New Zealand, CERD/C/NZL/CO/18-20, para. 18.

[186] Concluding observations on Chile, CERD/C/CHL/CO/19-21, para. 13.

[187] Concluding observations on Laos, CERD/C/LAO/CO/16-18, para. 18.

[188] Concluding observations on Suriname, CERD/C/SUR/CO/12, para. 13; in para. 18, referring to *Saramaka People v Suriname*. Reference was also made to the *Moiwana Village* case as well as Saramaka with regard to delays in complying with the Court judgment, and included a recommendation for consultation 'with the indigenous and Maroon communities concerned': *Moiwana Community, Members of the Moiwana Village v Suriname*, IACtHR Ser. C No. 124 (2005).

[189] See the discussion in Chapter 5.

[190] Para. 4. The citation of 5(c) is approximate in that the paragraph does not explicitly refer to citizenship as a qualification on the enjoyment of rights. As observed above, the Committee has treated the political rights of non-citizens in a cautious manner in light of general limitations recognized by international law; GR 30 exemplifies the general approach, discussed in Chapter 7.

[191] Contained in General Assembly resolutions 1514(XV), and 2625(XXV), respectively.

self-determination is linked to the Committee's assertion that 'international law has not recognized a general right of peoples unilaterally to declare secession',[192] and the conclusion (drawing upon the UN Secretary-General's Agenda for Peace)[193] that 'a fragmentation of States may be detrimental to the protection of human rights as well as the preservation of peace and security',[194] hence the stress on 5(c) and participation in the life of the State.

The recommendation confirms that self-determination may apply within independent States as well as linking it to 'the rights of persons belonging to ethnic groups, particularly their right to lead lives of dignity, to preserve their culture, to share equitably in the fruits of national growth and to play their part in the government of the country of which they are citizens'. The connections made by the recommendation between Article 5(c), human rights more broadly, and the rights of 'ethnic groups' were ostensibly influenced by its calling into play of, *inter alia*, UNDM with its portfolio of rights including rights to existence and identity, and participation rights, rights which have been expanded and amplified in the case of indigenous peoples.

Especially considering its importance as a motor of decolonization processes at the time of drafting the Convention, self-determination is referred to infrequently by the Committee in current applications.[195] It may be endorsed indirectly through citations of the UN Declaration on the Rights of Indigenous Peoples (UNDRIP), the text of which is suffused by the concept of self-determination, explicitly mentioned in the preamble and in Articles 3 and 4.[196] Whilst Canada argues that it is 'a non-legally-binding document that did not reflect customary international law',[197] the Committee has interpreted it as part of the body of standards on which it draws, and uses it to 'flesh out' the requirements of the Convention as applied to indigenous peoples. Since its adoption by the UN General Assembly in 2007, the Declaration has been cited by the Committee with some regularity, support for its adoption has been commended, and failure to implement it is subject to criticism.[198] Concluding observations on the US go so far as to recommend using the Declaration 'as a guide to interpret the State party's obligations under the Convention relating to indigenous peoples',[199] and Canada was recommended to consider adopting a national plan of action to implement the Declaration.[200]

The self-determination and participation concepts in the UNDRIP take it beyond the limited formulations in GR 21. Lenzerini sums up the requirements of indigenous self-determination as:

> [n]on-discrimination and cultural integrity . . . right to conserve the possession of their traditional lands and natural resources; right to social welfare and development; right to self-government in the

[192] GR 21, para. 6. An exception is made for freely arrived at arrangements: discussion in Chapter 5, p. 85.

[193] *An Agenda for Peace, Preventive Diplomacy, Peacemaking and Peace-Keeping*, Report of the Secretary-General, A/47/277–S/24111, 17 June 1992.

[194] GR 21, para. 6.

[195] Concluding observations on Suriname, CERD/C/SUR/CO/12, para. 18.

[196] See H. Quane, 'The UN Declaration on the Rights of Indigenous Peoples: New Directions for Self-Determination and Participatory Rights?' in S. Allen and A. Xanthaki (eds), *Reflections on the UN Declaration on the Rights of Indigenous Peoples* (Hart Publishing, 2011), pp. 259–87.

[197] *Ibid.*, para. 39.

[198] CERD/C/JPN/CO/3-6, para. 20.

[199] CERD/C/USA/CO/6, para. 29.

[200] CERD/C/CAN/CO/19-20, para. 19.

twofold characterization of autonomy (i.e. the right to conserve their own institutions and traditional law) and participation in . . . decisions affecting them.[201]

The Committee has generally avoided making wide pronouncements on the right to self-determination, concentrating instead on practical applications, mostly with reference to indigenous peoples, including in the context of self-identification. In the case of Finland,[202] the State party was recommended to 'accord due weight to the rights of the Sámi people to self-determination concerning their status in Finland, to determine their own membership, and not to be subjected to forced assimilation'.[203] In connection with implementing the judgments of the Inter-American Court in *Saramaka* and the *Moiwana Village*, the Committee urged 'in particular, the recognition of the communal and self-determination rights of the Saramaka people'.[204] The Committee's approach to self-determination has, in line with changes in geopolitical systems that include the virtual ending of Western colonial systems, focused on applications within States—on the 'internality' of the principle—bearing in mind, *inter alia*, the potentially negative consequences for human rights of exercises in secession.

5(d) (Other) Civil Rights

5(d)(i) The Right to Freedom of Movement and Residence Within the Border of the State

Article 13(1) of the UDHR represents the *fons et origo* of the right to freedom of movement and residence 'within the borders of each State', replaced in 5(d)(i) of ICERD by 'within the border of the State'. Other background standards include Article 12 of the ICCPR, Article 39 of the CMW, and Article 18 of the CRPD. In the case of the ICCPR, the right includes freedom to move within the whole territory of the State, choice of residence,[205] and freedom to leave—treated separately in ICERD.[206] Regional human rights conventions also enshrine the right.[207] Article 15 of CEDAW provides that men and women shall have the same rights 'with regard to the law relating to the movement of persons and the freedom to choose their residence and domicile'.[208] Instruments on minorities and indigenous peoples incorporate adapted readings of freedom of movement in the light of its cultural implications. Thus, Article 14(1) of ILO 169 refers to paying

[201] F. Lenzerini, 'The Trail of Broken Dreams: The Status of Indigenous Peoples in International Law', in F. Lenzerini (ed.), *Reparations for Indigenous Peoples: International and Comparative Perspectives* (Oxford University Press, 2008), pp. 73–116, p. 101.

[202] Discussed in Chapter 9.

[203] CERD/C/FIN/CO/20-22 (2013), para. 12; see further discussion in Chapter 9.

[204] CERD/C/SUR/CO/12, para. 18.

[205] The individual right to reside as a matter of personal choice is restricted when (in addition to obvious cases of public or private right) for example, land is provided for an indigenous group: *Lovelace v Canada*, CCPR/C/13/D/24/1977 (1981), regarding the right to reside on a reserve. The case was decided in favour of the applicant on other grounds, Article 27 of the ICCPR.

[206] The right is elaborated in GC 27: HRI/GEN/1/Rev.9 (Vol. I), pp. 223–7; it applies to all 'lawfully within the territory of a State and may not be restricted (Article 12(3)) except as provided by law, on grounds of national security, public order, public health or morals, and the rights and freedoms of others, consistent with the other rights recognized in the Covenant'.

[207] Article 12 ACHPR; Article 22 ACHR; Article 26 of the Arab Charter; Article 2 of Protocol 4 to the ECHR.

[208] Article 15(4).

particular attention to the situation of 'nomadic peoples and shifting cultivators' in connection with land rights, and incorporates protection against removals and relocations; penalties are also envisaged for unauthorized intrusion into indigenous lands. A similar range of provisions is reflected in Articles 7, 8, and 10 of UNDRIP, supplemented by implications from other articles regarding cultural aspects of movement, and by the principle of self-determination.[209] An extension of the movement framework that constrains its containment within national borders may be inferred from statements of a right to cross-border contacts in cultural and related contexts in the UNDM, ILO 169, and UNDRIP.[210]

Reporting guidelines do not elaborate on this right, the violation of which was registered in the communication procedure under Article 14. In *Koptova v Slovakia*,[211] the Committee decided that in a case where municipal regulations forbade the author and other Roma from entering two municipalities, the right to freedom of movement and residence was violated. While the wording of regulations referred explicitly to Roma previously domiciled in the municipalities, and to issues regarding permanent residence rights, etc, it was clear that other Romas would equally have been prohibited from settling.[212] The author of the communication, of Roma ethnicity, was a 'victim' 'since she belonged to a group of the population directly targeted' by the resolutions.[213] The Committee recommended that necessary measures were taken to ensure that practices restricting the freedom of movement and residence of Roma under its jurisdiction were 'fully and promptly eliminated'.[214]

Concerns with regard to movement and residence have engaged attention on a number of fronts, implicating aspects of State practice such as language requirements restricting access to social housing and public lands,[215] or the use of planning and zoning laws to achieve 'demographic balance'.[216] Discrimination against certain ethnic groups—including but not confined to Roma—in residence registration or authorization systems has attracted comments and recommendations. This issue connects with circumstances in a variety of countries. A rough summary of the required response from States parties is

[209] Article 8 of UNDRIP echoes elements of the definition of genocide in Article II of the Genocide Convention in references to forced population transfer and 'destruction of their culture'.

[210] Articles 2(5), 32, and 36, respectively; see also the analogous Article 17 of the FCNM, the explanatory report to which suggests that the right to movement within the State was effectively covered by other articles in the Convention, making it too obvious to require a separate statement.

[211] CERD/C/57/D/13/1998 (2000). See commentaries in the present work on Articles 2 and 3. The paragraph has been at issue elsewhere—see, for example, *L.K. v The Netherlands*, CERD/C/42/D/4/1991 (1993)—even though the Committee's disposition of the case did not rely on a finding that this specific right had been violated. Impeding access to particular areas has been claimed by petitioners as amounting to a breach of Article 3: in *Dawas and Shawva v Denmark*, CERD/C/80/D/46/2009 (2012), the Committee decided that, although the Convention had been violated, the Article 3 claim had not been substantiated: para. 6.2.

[212] *Koptova v Slovakia*, para. 10.1. See discussion in Chapter 4 on 'victims'.

[213] *Ibid.*, para. 6.5.

[214] *Ibid.*, para. 10.3. See further discussion in Chapter 10.

[215] Concluding observations on Belgium, CERD/C/BEL/CO/15, para. 16.

[216] CERD/C/ISR/CO/14-16, para. 25. Numerous other issues, broadly implicating freedom of movement appear in sundry concluding observations regarding Israel, even without specific identification as such: see for example CERD/C/ISR/CO/14-16, paras 15, 18, 20, 24, 25 (demographic balance), and 29, where freedom of movement is identified; CERD/C/ISR/CO/13, paras 33 and 34, the latter is explicit in itemizing 'severe restrictions on freedom of movement in the Occupied Palestinian Territories, targeting a particular national or ethnic group, especially through the wall, checkpoints, restricted roads and permit system'. The recommendations indicate that despite the intraterritorial language of the right, it is subject to extraterritorial application; a similar approach has been taken by the Human Rights Committee: CCPR/C/ISR/CO/3 (2010).

articulated in concluding observations on the Russian Federation, recommended to 'monitor the implementation of its system of residence registration, sanction officials who deny registration on ethnically discriminatory grounds, and provide effective remedies to victims, with a view of eliminating the discriminatory impact of the registration system on ethnic minorities'.[217] The Committee observed that, in the instant case, while Federal legislation provided that registration should not constitute a precondition for the exercise of citizens' rights, in practice the enjoyment of many rights and benefits depended on it.[218] Calls have also been made to respect the rights of refugees and asylum-seekers to freedom of movement within the borders of the State; a recommendation that may be linked to the provision of identity documents. The treatment of internally displaced persons in the matter of residence is another concern, for which the Committee frequently recalls guiding principles on internal displacement,[219] suggesting that they be observed.[220] In the case of the Bedoun (stateless persons) of Kuwait, many of whom had lived in Kuwait for lengthy periods, the concluding observations expressed concern that, *inter alia*, they were 'not always able to return to Kuwait, in contravention of the right to freedom of movement'—Articles 2, 5, and 6 were cited in support of the recommendations overall, as well as GR 30.[221]

In relation to groups the culture of which is intimately bound up with movement—nomadic or semi-nomadic groups, Travellers, etc—recommendations characteristically link the question of movement to rights to land, housing, access to education, and participation in decisions affecting them.[222] In other cases, the primary stress is laid on freedom of movement itself. In the case of France, a recommendation on freedom of movement was made for the abolition of travel permits for Travellers 'to ensure equal treatment for all citizens of the State party'.[223] In the case of Tanzania, the State party was requested to provide detailed information on the situation of nomadic and semi-nomadic ethnic groups and special measures taken with view to ensuring enjoyment of rights under ICERD, notably freedom of movement and right to participate in decisions which affect them.[224]

The Committee has been critical of cases where relocation and similar State policies have been designed or applied, contrary to international standards, to 'sedentarize' populations such as hunter gatherer or other nomadic groups and effectively prevent them from handing on their culture to subsequent generations.[225] Forced sedentarization and allied expulsionist policies inevitably involve violation of a spectrum of undifferentiated and differentiated (group-specific) human rights, civil and political, economic,

[217] Concluding observations on the Russian Federation, CERD/C/RUS/CO/19, para. 22. See also para. 23, *ibid.*, for the question of access to residence registration for former Soviet citizens.

[218] *ibid.*, para. 22. See also CERD/C/RUS/CO/20-22, para. 16.

[219] UN Doc. E/CN.4/1998/53/Add.2.

[220] Concluding observations on Indonesia, CERD/C/IDN/CO/3, para. 18, and The Philippines, CERD/C/PHL/CO/20, para. 19.

[221] CERD/C/KWT/CO/15-20, para. 17.

[222] GR 27 recommends States parties to 'take the necessary measures, as appropriate, for offering Roma nomadic groups or Travellers camping places for their caravans, with all necessary facilities': para. 32.

[223] CERD/C/FRA/CO/17-19, para. 16 (2010).

[224] CERD/C/TZA/CO/16, para. 16. The groups referred to were the Barbaig, Maasai, and Haqdzabe.

[225] Concluding observations on Botswana, CERD/C/61/CO/2, para. 13; on Israel, CERD/C/ISR/CO/14-16, paras 20 and 25 (Bedouin). For a general view of sedenterization and allied policies, see J. Gilbert, *Nomadic Peoples and Human Rights* (Routledge, 2014).

social, and cultural, individual and collective. Recommendations have been directed towards achieving compliance with international standards on relocation, typically utilizing dimensions such as cultural impact, consultation, and consent as part of overall analysis of discrimination,[226] preceded or accompanied by calls to recognize the groups in accordance with international standards.[227]

5(d)(ii) The Right to Leave any Country, Including One's Own, and to Return to One's Country

The right to leave and to return draws upon Article 13(2) of the UDHR, and is found in other international instruments including Article 12 of the ICCPR, Article 8 of the CMW, and Article 10 of the CRC. The right is also recognized in regional instruments including Article 12 of the ACHPR, Article 22 of the ACHR, Article 27 of the Arab Charter, and Protocol 4 of the ECHR. The right is the subject (in part) of an extensive general comment by the Human Rights Committee, which explains that the right of a person 'to enter his or her own country recognizes the special relationship of a person to that country' and includes the right to remain and the right to return: the latter is regarded as 'of the utmost importance for refugees seeking voluntary repatriation'; the right also implies prohibition of enforced population transfers or mass expulsions to other countries.[228]

The right has not been extensively addressed by CERD. In light of the comments of the Human Rights Committee regarding refugees and asylum-seekers, GR 22 'on Article 5 and refugees' recalls GR 20 and applies the obligation to eliminate discrimination across the spectrum of human rights. Conditions and circumstances of repatriation have been raised in a number of instances, and concern that repatriation was not carried out on a voluntary basis.[229]

The spectre of collective expulsions with possible racial motivations has been addressed in concluding observations. In the case of France, the term 'collective repatriation' (of Roma), and not 'expulsion', was employed by the Committee.[230] Concerns were expressed that 'groups of Roma have been returned to their country of origin without the free, full and informed consent of all the individuals concerned'.[231] In the case of Italy, the Committee made explicit reference to 'breaches of international norms regarding protection of refugees or asylum-seekers',[232] as demonstrated by a case decided by the

[226] Concluding observations on Guatemala, CERD/C/GTM/CO/12-13, para. 11; Laos, CERD/C/LAO/CO/16-18, para. 18; Mexico, CERD/C/MEX/CO/16-17, para. 17; the very extensive recommendation concerning Guatemala recommended that the State party ensure the observance of Article 16(2) of ILO Convention 169 and Article 10 of the UNDRIP.

[227] See discussion in Chapter 6.

[228] GC No. 27, paras 19 and 20.

[229] Concluding observations on Cuba, CERD/C/CUB/CO/14-18, para. 20; on Laos, CERD/C/LAO/CO/16-18, para. 12 (regarding the Hmong people); on Moldova, CERD/C/MDA/CO/8-9, para. 13.

[230] The Committee noted reports that groups of Roma have been 'returned to their country of origin without the free, full and informed consent of all the individuals concerned' and recommended that, in particular, the State party avoid 'collective repatriations': CERD/C/FRA/CO/17-19, para. 14. Article 4 of Protocol No. 4 to the ECHR prohibits the collective expulsion of aliens: with regard to Roma, see *Čonka v Belgium*, ECtHR App. No. 51564/99 (2002).

[231] CERD/C/FRA/CO/17-19, para. 14.

[232] CERD/C/ITA/CO/16-18, para. 22.

European Court of Human Rights,[233] recalling that 'the State party has the obligation under . . . international human rights law to respect the principle of non-refoulement and to ensure that migrants are not subject to collective expulsion'. A more elaborate account of the required non-discriminatory framework in the field of deportation is found on recommendations to the Dominican Republic, where the Committee was concerned with information suggesting that migrants of Haitian origin were detained and subject to collective deportations without due process. The State party was recommended to ensure

> that laws concerning deportation or other forms of removal of non-citizens do not discriminate on the basis of race, etc.;
>
> that non-citizens are not subject to collective expulsion, 'in particular where there are insufficient guarantees that the personal circumstances of each of the persons concerned' have been taken into account;
>
> that expulsions be avoided that may result in a disproportionate interference with the right to family life; that non-citizens have equal access to effective remedies including the right to challenge expulsion orders;
>
> and that 'humane and internationally accepted' measures be adopted for dealing with undocumented migrants.[234]

5(d)(iii) The Right to Nationality

The CERD-specific reporting guidelines request information on measures to ensure that 'particular groups of non-citizens are not discriminated against with regard to access to citizenship or naturalization'.[235] Information is also requested on the specific situation of long-term or permanent residents and 'whether different standards of treatment for accessing citizenship are applied to non-citizen spouses (female and male) of citizens',[236] and on action taken to reduce statelessness.

International law from its inception concerned itself with the rights and interests of 'aliens' or non-nationals in light of the pragmatic case that ill-treatment of the nationals of another State will most likely provoke international repercussions;[237] the specific treaties and declarations on the protection of 'minorities' represented analogous exercises in pragmatism.[238] Nationality was defined in the *Nottebohm* case as 'a legal bond having as its basis a social fact of attachment, a genuine connection of existence, interests and sentiments, together with the existence of reciprocal rights and duties'.[239] The European Convention on Nationality, summarizing nationality as 'the legal bond between a person and a State', adds that nationality in this sense 'does not indicate the person's ethnic origin'.[240] While matters of nationality are generally considered as within the domestic

233 The unnamed case referred to is *Hirsi Jamaa and Others v Italy*, App. No. 27765/09 (2012), concerning the return of Somalian and Eritrean migrants to Libya following their interception at sea by Italian authorities. Violations were found of Article 4 of Protocol No. 4 on collective expulsion, as well as of other articles, including Article 3 on inhuman and degrading treatment. There was no concomitant finding of discrimination, racial or otherwise.

234 CERD/C/DOM/CO/12, para. 13.

235 See also Chapter 7 on non-citizens.

236 See Chapter 7.

237 For a succinct historical review with references, see R. Kolb, 'The Protection of the Individual in Times of War and Peace', in B. Fassbender and A. Peters (eds), *The Oxford Handbook of the History of International Law* (Oxford University Press, 2012), pp. 317–37.

238 P. Thornberry. *International Law and the Rights of Minorities* (Clarendon Press, 1991).

239 *Nottebohm (Liechtenstein v Guatemala)*, ICJ Reports 1955, p. 23.

240 ETS 166 (1997), Article 2.

jurisdiction of States,[241] the legal possibilities of restricting this freedom of States were presaged in generic terms by the 1930 Hague Convention on Certain Questions relating to the Conflict of Nationality Laws,[242] which provided that, while it is for each State to determine who are its nationals, the determination will be recognized 'in so far as it is consistent with international conventions, international custom and the principles of law generally recognized with regard to nationality'. In *Yean and Bosico v Dominican Republic*, the Inter-American Court of Human Rights stated that although 'the determination of who has a right to be a national continues to fall within a State's domestic jurisdiction . . . its discretional authority in this regard is gradually being restricted with the evolution of international law'.[243] The notion of a right to nationality, and the avoidance of racial discrimination in the conferment, denial, and deprivation of nationality, function as significant contemporary restrictions on the exercise of discretion by the State.

Background standards on nationality are scattered through human rights instruments.[244] Article 15 of the UDHR proclaims the right to a nationality in unequivocal terms and that no-one shall be arbitrarily deprived of nationality or the right to change nationality. Morsink contextualizes the drafting of the right in UDHR as part of the reaction to Nazi policy that stripped Jews of their citizenship, citing Conot for the claim that deprivation of citizenship was more important in sealing their fate than the Nuremberg laws.[245] The *lex imperfecta* aspect of the right in the UDHR—it does not identify the carrier of the obligation to grant citizenship—is remedied to some extent in later instruments, notably the ACHR (Article 20) which refers to a right to the nationality of the State in which a person was born, provided they do not have the right to any other nationality. Article 24(3) of the ICCPR affirms the right of every child to acquire a nationality, a provision developed further by Articles 7 and 8 of the CRC to include the right to an identity that includes nationality—the implementation of which is to be ensured, 'in particular where the child would otherwise be stateless'; and by Article 29 of the CMW. The CRPD (Article 18) also enshrines the right to nationality, while Article 9 of CEDAW is designed to ensure that the right to nationality is applied equally to men and to women. Regional provisions on the right to nationality include Article 20 of the ACHR, and Article 29 of the Arab Charter. It will be recalled that nationality provisions figured among the rights under the Minorities Treaties of the League of Nations,[246] though not in the UNDM of 1992; the UNDRIP is straightforward: 'Every indigenous individual has the right to a nationality.'[247]

Provisions in generic human rights texts are complemented by two major conventions on statelessness: the 1954 Convention Relating to the Status of Stateless Persons and the 1961 Convention on the Reduction of Statelessness, with the former focused on protection of stateless persons and the latter on reducing the phenomenon of statelessness. As

241 *Tunis and Morocco Nationality Decrees*, PCIJ Reports (1923), Series B, No. 4.

242 179 LNTS 80.

243 *Dilcia Yean and Violeta Bosico v Dominican Republic*, IACtHR, Ser. C, No. 130 (2005), para. 140.

244 D. Weissbrodt, *The Human Rights of Non-Citizens* (Oxford University Press, 2008), *passim*.

245 *The Universal Declaration*, p. 80, citing R.E. Conot, *Justice at Nuremburg* (Harper and Row, 1983). Morsink adds, in relation to statelessness, that to 'be without a nationality or not to be a citizen of any country at all is to stand naked in the world of international affairs. It is to be alone as a person, without protection against the aggression of States . . . As . . . Nazi practices show, the right to a nationality is not the luxury some people think it is.'

246 See Chapter 2.

247 Article 6; indigenous citizenship is addressed in Article 33.

noted in Chapter 7, nationality is a prohibited ground of discrimination in relatively few instruments[248] but may fall to be addressed under 'national origin' or 'other status'.[249] While it is not strictly accurate in the context of universal human rights to treat the right to nationality as 'the right to have rights',[250] nationality and citizenship are a gateway to the enjoyment of human rights in practice, with the right to nationality regarded by the Inter-American Commission as one of the most important human rights 'after the right to life itself'.[251] In the context of ICERD, the expression of the right to nationality in Article 5 counterpoints the provisions of Article 1(2) and 1(3).

Non-discrimination functions as a restriction on the freedom of States in matters of nationality, applicable to the acquisition of nationality, transmission or change of nationality, and deprivation of nationality; discrimination is also integral to 'arbitrary deprivation' of nationality. The provisions of ICERD are complemented by Article 3 of the 1954 Convention whereby the provisions of that convention are to be applied to stateless persons 'without discrimination as to race, religion or country of origin'; and Article 9 of the 1961 Convention, which provides that a contracting State 'may not deprive any person or group of persons of their nationality on racial, ethnic, religious or political grounds'.

GR 30 on discrimination against non-citizens includes a significant section (IV) on 'access to citizenship', which besides the issue of non-discriminatory 'access', addresses deprivation and denial of citizenship, the reduction of statelessness, and the regularization of the status of former citizens of predecessor States within the jurisdiction of the State party.[252] The provision on deprivation is canonical, recognizing that deprivation of citizenship on the basis of race, etc, 'is a breach of States parties' obligations to ensure non-discriminatory enjoyment of the right to nationality'.[253]

On the acquisition of nationality, the status of long-term residents in a State party and the need to normalize their situation has elicited reasoning that echoes general concepts of international law such as 'genuine and effective link'. In the case of Kuwait's *Bedoun*, the recommendation was to consider the naturalization of 'in particular, persons who have lived in Kuwait for a long time, who can prove a genuine and effective link to the State, or have served or serve in the police, army and other State institutions'.[254] Similar issues arise when access to citizenship of the state of residence is made difficult for particular groups on account of their national origin,[255] or in some cases their religion: in the case of the Maldives, concerns relating to 'national or ethnic origin' intersected with concern regarding religious affiliation.[256] The recommendations to ensure that naturalization procedures

[248] For example, Articles 1 and 7 of the CMW.

[249] Vandenhole, *Non-Discrimination and Equality*, Chapter III.

[250] Justice Warren in *Perez v Brownell* (1958) 356 US 44, 64, cited in Weissbrodt, *The Human Rights of Non-Citizens*, p. 81.

[251] *Inter-American Commission on Human Rights, Third Report on the Situation of Human Rights in Chile*, cited in *Written Comments on the Case of Dilcia Yean and Violeta Bosico v Dominican Republic*, Open Society Justice Initiative, April 2005, p. 20.

[252] GR 30, section IV; see Chapter 7 for further discussion.

[253] *Ibid.*, para. 14.

[254] CERD/C/KWT/CO/15-20, para. 17.

[255] Concluding observations on Italy, CERD/C/ITA/CO/116-18, para. 24, regarding Roma who arrived in Italy following the dissolution of Yugoslavia but had not been allowed access to citizenship.

[256] In a forthright observation, the Committee expressed particular concern about 'discriminatory provisions in the Constitution that all Maldivians should be Muslims... affecting mainly people of a different national or ethnic origin'. In its critical remarks, CERD referred specifically to GR 30 and to Article 5(d)(vii): CERD/C/MDV/CO/5-12, para. 10.

do not discriminate against 'particular groups of non-citizens' reflects standard practice, and echoes Article 1(3).[257]

Linguistic barriers to successful naturalization stand as one access concern; in most cases the recommendation is to lower the language standard in order to give real substance to the right.[258] Burdensome bureaucratic procedures for the acquisition of citizenship documentation that appear to apply predominantly to one group have also generated Committee criticism.[259] Pressures to change names in order to gain citizenship have attracted comment from the Committee, which has taken the opportunity to recall that 'the name of an individual is a fundamental aspect of cultural identity',[260] a proposition that opens out the Convention the right to a name in its ethnic/cultural context.[261] The issue of statelessness has been expressly linked to the enjoyment of rights,[262] including the recognition that stateless persons may, on account of their situation, be 'deprived of human rights and freedoms in practice'.[263]

Regarding gender intersectionality, Otto observes that GR 25 focuses predominantly on violence against women,[264] a critique that is accurate as far as the recommendation is concerned in that the examples of gender/race intersection in paragraph 2 concentrate on coerced sterilization, racial bias-motivated rape, etc. CERD's concern with nationality transmission adds another perspective to the critique in that the almost invariable context is that of restrictions on the right of women to pass on their nationality to spouses and children on an equal basis with men, hence the glut of recommendations to remove the restriction and equalize the situation in gender terms.[265]

5(d)(iv) The Right to Marriage and Choice of Spouse

The CERD-specific guidelines do not elaborate the right.

Background human rights instruments provide that marriage shall be entered into only with the free and full consent of the intending spouses;[266] the provision on choice of

[257] Concluding observations on Cyprus, CERD/C/CYP/CO/17-22, para. 18; Maldives, CERD/C/MDV/CO/5-12, para. 10.

[258] Concluding observations on Estonia, CERD/C/EST/CO/8-9, para. 13.

[259] Concluding observations on Cambodia, CERD/C/KHM/CO/8-13, para. 18, regarding the Khmer Krom.

[260] Concluding observations on Japan, CERD/C/JPN/CO/3-6, para. 16.

[261] On names generally, see the Article 24 ICCPR; Articles 7 and 8 CRC, and with specific regard to minorities, Article 11.1 of the FCNM. See also *Müller and Engelhard v Namibia*, CCPR/C/24/D/919/2000 (2002); *Coeriel and Aurik v The Netherlands*, CCPR/C/52/D/453/1991; *Stjerna v Finland*, ECtHR App. No. 18131/91 (1994).

[262] Concluding observations on Serbia, CERD/C/SRB/1, para. 19. Concluding observations on, *inter alios*, Estonia, Latvia, and Slovenia, have raised the issue of statelessness with reference to groups of persons who have been on the territory of the State party in question since independence.

[263] CERD/C/TKM/CO/6-7, para. 118.

[264] 'Women's Rights', in Moeckli *et al. International Human Rights Law*, pp. 316–32, at pp. 329–30; see also Chapter 6 on 'intersectionality'.

[265] For situations addressed see, for example, concluding observations on Jordan, CERD/C/JOR/CO/13-17, para. 11; Kuwait, CERD/C/KWT/CO/15-20, para. 18; Oman, CERD/C/OMN/CO/CO/1, para. 18; Qatar, CERD/C/QAT/CO/13-16, para. 16.

[266] Article 16 of the UDHR stands as the principal background inspiration of ICERD in providing that: (1) Men and women of full age, without any limitation due to race, nationality or religion, have the right to marry and to found a family. They are entitled to equal rights as to marriage, during marriage and at its dissolution. (2) Marriage shall be entered into only with the free and full consent of the intending spouses. (3) The family is the natural and fundamental group unit of society and is entitled to protection by society and the State. See also the extensive list of prescriptions in Article 16 of CEDAW regarding entry into marriage, choice of spouse, rights

spouse reappears in Article 16 of CEDAW. In light of the background inspiration for the Convention with regard to interracial marriage,[267] Schwelb asserts bluntly that: '[p]rohibitions against mixed marriages between persons of different races, so-called anti-miscegenation statutes . . . are incompatible with the Convention'.[268] Only one State maintains a specific reservation to 5(d)(iv).[269]

Formal legal prohibitions on racial miscegenation do not currently present themselves, although marriage laws and practices continue to command the attention of the Committee in connection with categories of persons and communities. Restrictions on the right to marry, such as a requirement of prior ministerial approval for marriages between nationals and non-nationals, have concerned the Committee, as well as failure to guarantee such marriages unless the non-nationals are nationals of a particular regional grouping of States.[270] Legislation to address the problem of sham or forced marriages has also attracted attention from the perspective of discrimination. While not challenging the positive human rights motivation of such legislation, the Committee has indicated that too much zeal in combating forced marriages—such as a 'special investigation' in cases where there are young foreign spouses[271]—may raise issues of discrimination against particular communities. In the case of Norway, while the Committee welcomed the State party's Action Plan against Forced Marriage, it expressed concern that excessive focus on the issue could be seen 'as stigmatizing women and girls belonging to certain minority groups'.[272] In the case of the UK, concern was expressed at the increase in the marriage visa age for purposes of family reunification in order to protect against forced marriages; the Committee expressed the opinion in unusually direct terms that the increase violated 'the rights of persons who satisfy the legal minimum age of marriage as it principally affects ethnic minorities' as well as other persons.[273]

and responsibilities during marriage and dissolution, etc, and GR 21 on *Equality in Marriage* (1994). See also, *inter alia*, Articles 6 and 7 of the Protocol to the African Charter on Human and Peoples' Rights on the Rights of Women in Africa (2003). Article 17 of the ACHR, Article 33 of the Arab Charter on Human Rights, and Article 12 of the ECHR also include provisions on marriage and family.

[267] See Chapter 10 on Article 3; also P. Pascoe, *What Comes Naturally: Miscegenation Laws and the Making of Race in America* (Oxford University Press, 2010). Anti-race miscegenation laws were prevalent in a significant number of countries: for a brief synopsis, see <http://en.wikipedia.org/wiki/Racial_segregation>, and discussion in Chapter 10.

[268] Page 1026. He exempts 'obstacles' to marriage between persons of different citizenship or religion, presumably because of the limiting provision in Article 1(2) and because 'religion' is not specifically listed in Article 1 or Article 5 as a prohibited ground of discrimination. Partsch, 'Elimination of Racial Discrimination in the Enjoyment of Civil and Political Rights', *Texas International Law Journal 14* (1979), 191–250, at 245, is also direct: the reference to choice of spouse was included 'in order to void the laws existing in some countries that prohibit interracial marriage'.

[269] Yemen.

[270] Concluding observations on Qatar, CERD/C/60/CO/11, paras 13 and 14. In the latter instance, the Committee regarded the distinction as one based on national origin.

[271] Concluding observations on Iceland, CERD/C/ISL/CO/20, para. 17; concluding observations on Denmark, CERD/C/DNK/CO/18-19, para. 14. In the latter case, Denmark was recommended to assess the racial impact of its family reunification legislation on the right to family life, marriage, and choice of spouse; the legislation required that for family reunification purposes, both spouses must have attained the age of 24 and that their ties with Denmark must have been stronger than those with any other country. The State party was invited to consider, *ibid.*, whether 'the limitation on the rights affected' outweighed 'the mischief it seeks to prevent, namely forced and early marriages'.

[272] CERD/C/NOR/CO/19-20, para. 15.

[273] CERD/C/GBR/CO/18-20, para. 26.

Social or cultural impediments to the freedom to marry have also raised issues. For descent-based groups, States parties are enjoined in GR 29 to take 'resolute measures to secure rights of marriage for members of... communities who wish to marry outside the community'.[274] Concluding observations on India express concern at 'the persistence of social norms of purity and pollution which de facto preclude marriages between Dalits and non-Dalits' as well as violence and social sanctions against inter-caste couples.[275] In the case of Japan, with regard to the Burakumin, the Committee recommended prohibiting the use of the family registration system for discriminatory purposes.[276] With regard to Canada, the Committee urged the State party to 'effectively address the discriminatory effects of the Indian Act on the rights of aboriginal women ... to marry, to choose one's spouse, to own property and to inherit', in consultation with First Nations organizations and communities, including Aboriginal Women's organizations.[277]

In addition to legal or social impediments generated by extra-community forces, recommendations have also addressed the claimed prevalence of early or child marriage among certain groups.[278] The general tendency of recommendations in this area is to suggest that the practice be resolutely addressed, in consultation with the communities concerned.[279] In the case of Croatia, the Committee noted with concern that Roma girls tend to be married at an early age in spite of legal provisions prohibiting such early marriages; the State party was recommended to 'ensure the effective implementation of its laws concerning the legal age of marriage in consultation with the communities affected and undertake awareness raising campaigns among the groups concerned regarding the illegality of such marriages'—attention was drawn to GR 25 and GR 27.[280] In another instance, a request was made for detailed information on the 'marriage rules and practices that apply in the indigenous and tribal communities' in order to ensure that 'the rights of women are respected, irrespective of the community they belong to'.[281] Expressions of concern that customary laws may disadvantage women in the fields of marriage and inheritance confirm the wide approach of applying Article 5 beyond the formalities of State legislation and State-supported action. Most of the issues raised in relation to marriage customs are thoroughly 'gendered'.[282]

Although 'family' is not referred to as such in the Convention, the Committee has referred compendiously to 'the right to family life, marriage and choice of spouse'[283] and

[274] GR 29, para. 6 (ff).

[275] CERD/C/IND/CO/19, para. 18.

[276] CERD/C/JPN/CO/3-6, para. 18.

[277] CERD/C/CAN/CO/18, para. 15. Compare the ICCPR case of *Lovelace v Canada*, A/36/40, 166 (1981).

[278] Concluding observations on Italy, CERD/C/ITA/CO/15, para. 20, concerning 'early marriage, in particular of Roma girls'.

[279] In the case of India, the recommendation was simply that the State party should 'effectively enforce the prohibition of child marriage', CERD/C/IND/CO/19, para. 18.

[280] Concluding observations on Croatia, CERD/C/HRV/CO/8, para. 18. See, *inter alia*, the 2015 resolution of the Human Rights Council, *Strengthening Efforts to Prevent and Eliminate Child, Early and Forced Marriage*, A/HRC/29/L.15 and the Joint General Recommendation 31 of CEDAW and GC 18 of the CRC on harmful practices.

[281] Concluding observations on Suriname, CERD/C/64/CO/9, para. 25.

[282] See the discussion of Article 5(d)(iii) on gendered rules concerning the transmission of nationality.

[283] Concluding observations on Denmark, CERD/C/DNK/CO/18-19, para. 14. For the human rights context, see, *inter alia*, in addition to the above-cited Article 16 UDHR: Article 23 ICCPR; Article 10 ICESCR; Article 16 CEDAW, Articles 5 and 10 CRC; Articles 44 and 50 CMW; Article 23 CRPD; further references to

has expressed concern regarding impediments to family reunification on numerous occasions, including in decisions.[284] Family situations may generate a variety of human rights concerns. Recommendations to the Czech Republic focusing on education rights and 'special schools' generated the further concern that disproportionate numbers of Roma children were being removed from their families and placed in State institutions, leading to the recommendation to ensure that the children were 'not deprived of their right to family life' as well as to education.[285]

5(d)(v) The Right to Own Property Alone or in Association with Others

One reservation (specifically styled as a 'reservation') stands against the provision, whereby Tonga reserves the right not to apply the Convention to the extent that any law 'which prohibits or restricts the alienation of land by the indigenous inhabitants' may not fulfil the obligations under 5(d)(v). No objections to the reservation are recorded.

CERD-specific guidelines do not elaborate the right.

The expression in Article 5 (d)(v) repeats (part of) the formula in Article 17(1) of the UDHR.[286] The right to property does not find a place in either the ICCPR or the ICESCR, but is referred to in CEDAW,[287] the CMW,[288] the CRPD[289] and regional human rights instruments,[290] as well as functioning as a prohibited ground of discrimination in UN 'core' human rights instruments and elsewhere.[291] In terms of groups within the practical scope of CERD, Articles 13 and 14 of the Convention on Refugees address various property categories, movable, immovable, and industrial.[292] The theme of property is also prominent in ILO 169, principally focused on collective ownership of

family are scattered within these instruments. On connections between family, culture, and ethnicity, see *Hopu and Bessert v France*, CCPR/C/60/D/549/1993 (1997).

[284] Decision 2 (65), A/59/18, para. 17, regarding the suspension by Israel, for a renewable one year period, of the possibility of family reunification between an Israeli citizen and a person residing in the West Bank, etc. For a later comment on the legislation, see CERD/C/ISR/CO/14-16, para. 18, where in light of the concern at the targeting of Palestinian citizens of Israel, the Committee urged the State party 'to revoke the Citizenship and Entry into Israel (Temporary Provision) and to facilitate family reunification of all citizens irrespective of their ethnicity or national or other origin'.

[285] CERD/C/CZE/CO/7, para. 17.

[286] ICERD omits any reference to deprivation of property: Article 17 of the UDHR provides that everyone 'has the right to own property alone as well as in association with others', and that no one 'shall be arbitrarily deprived of his property'. In principle the right applies to bother individual and collective forms of ownership: C. Krause and G. Alfredsson, 'Article 17', in G. Alfredsson and A. Eide (eds), *The Universal Declaration of Human Rights: A Common Standard of Achievement* (Martinus Nijhoff Publishers, 1999), pp. 359–78. The reference to the possibility of deprivation indicates that the right is not absolute. For a general review, see T.R.G. Van Banning, *The Human Right to Property* (Intersentia, 2002).

[287] Articles 15 and 16.

[288] Article 15.

[289] Articles 12 and 30.

[290] Articles 14 and 21 of the ACHPR, the latter referring to the individual and collective aspects of the right of peoples to free disposal of wealth and natural resources; Article 23 of the American Declaration on the Rights and Duties of Man; Article 21 of the ACHR; Article 31 of the Arab Charter on Human Rights; and Article 1 of Protocol 1 to the ECHR under the rubric of 'peaceful enjoyment of possessions', clarified by the Court as reflecting the right to property: ECtHR, *Marckx v Belgium*, App. No. 6833/74 (1979), para. 63.

[291] Article 2 of the UDHR, Article 2 of the ICESCR, Articles 2, 24, and 26 of the ICCPR; Article 2 of the CRC; and Articles 1 and 7 of the CMW.

[292] See also *Housing and Property Restitution in the Context of the Return of Refugees and Displaced Persons: Final Report of the Special Rapporteur* (The Pinheiro Principles), E/CN.3/Sub.2/2005/17, 28 June 2005, and Chapter 14.

lands and territories, the 'rights of ownership and possession of the peoples concerned over the lands which they traditionally occupy shall be recognized', etc.[293] The UNDRIP refers to varieties of property, 'cultural, intellectual, religious and spiritual',[294] pertaining to indigenous peoples, to which may be added the overall concern of that instrument with indigenous lands, territories, and resources.[295] In general human rights law, 'property' has been given a wide reading, consonant with the French expression '*biens*', to include moveable and immoveable property.

The Committee has emphasized equal treatment in attempts to repossess property following return after conflicts[296] or after deportations (for 'formerly deported' groups), as well as restitution and compensation, and called for respect for property rights irrespective of the ethnic or national origin of owners. Post-conflict standards are set out in GR 22, which addresses the aftermath of conflicts creating refugee flows and displacements on the basis of ethnic criteria. Paragraph 2(c) of the recommendation emphasizes that all such refugees and displaced persons 'have, after their return to their homes of origin, the right to have restored to them property of which they were deprived in the course of the conflict and to be compensated appropriately for any such property that cannot be restored to them'. The questions of restoration and compensation have been addressed in a number of cases, notably in States of the former Soviet Union and the former Yugoslavia.[297] In the case of Ukraine, restoration of political, social, and economic rights of Tatars was called for, 'in particular the restitution of property including land or . . . compensation for its loss'.[298] In similar vein, recommendations were made regarding Meshketian Turks in the case of Georgia.[299] The Committee has also essayed criticism of restrictions on purchase and ownership of property by migrant workers and foreign residents,[300] using GR 30 to reinforce the point.

The phrase 'alone or in association with others' suggests a right with collective dimensions. The phraseology of Article 5(d)(v) is structurally similar to the property right expressed in the UDHR and, *mutatis mutandis*, to Article 27 of the ICCPR: the right of persons belonging to minorities to be enjoyed 'in community with the other members of their group'. Minority rights are normally phrased as rights of individuals subject to collective exercise; for example, in the short text of the UNDM, the phrase 'persons belonging to minorities' is used twenty-five times. Such phraseology is not fully equated with 'hard' collective or group rights, which would allow for group action on the basis of rights against individuals comprising the group as well as defence against the external world. Rights of indigenous peoples are structured in both 'hard' and 'soft' group right senses, suggesting in many instances the prevalence of a communitarian conception of right, rather than individual aggregations thereof, subsumed in the case of the UNDRIP to an overarching right of self-determination.[301]

[293] Article 14; see also Article 4, and Articles 15–19.

[294] Articles 11 and 31.

[295] The African Commission on Human and Peoples Rights recognizes that land constitutes property under Article 14 of the ACHPR: *Malawi African Association and Ors v Mauritania*, ACHPR Comm. Nos. 54/91, 61/91, 98/93, 164/97, 196/97, 2110/98, para. 128; also *Endorois v Kenya*, para. 187.

[296] Concluding observations on Croatia, CERD/C/60/CO/4, paras 13 and 15.

[297] For the latter, see Decision 1(55), A/54/18, p. 10 (1999).

[298] CERD/C/UKR/CO/19-21, para. 17.

[299] CERD/C/GEO/CO/4-5, para. 18.

[300] CERD/C/QAT/CO/13-16, para. 18.

[301] See further discussion in Chapter 15.

While the communitarian, collective conception is most widely reflected in international instruments on the rights of indigenous peoples, a remarkable doctrinal expansion of collective conceptions of property rights has taken place in instruments that, like ICERD, do not make specific reference to indigenous peoples—notably the organs of the Inter-American system, centring in particular on Article 21 of the ACHR, which commences with the statement that '[e]veryone has the right to the use and enjoyment of his property'. A key referent is *Mayagna (Sumo) Awas Tingni Community v Nicaragua.*[302] In the absence of title deeds to lands claimed by the community,[303] the Inter-American Court interpreted the Inter-American Convention to embrace an autonomous meaning of property rights that differed from formal titling of land but was based in the case of indigenous peoples on 'a communitarian tradition regarding a communal form of collective property of the land, in the sense that ownership of the land is not centred on an individual but rather on the group', the right of the community to live on their land stemmed from 'the fact of their very existence'.[304] Further cases in the stream of jurisprudence recognizing the distinctive and autonomous nature of collective property rights include, besides *Saramaka v Suriname*, *Moiwana v Suriname*, and *Yakye Axa v Paraguay*,[305] *Sawhoyamaxa v Paraguay*,[306] and *Mary and Carrie Dann v the US.*[307] It may be noted that the interpretative processes employed by the Inter-American human rights bodies parallel the interpretative modalities employed by CERD, in that the relevant articles of the Inter-American are understood in the light of an evolutionary understanding of human rights in international law.[308] In turn, CERD has drawn upon developments in the inter-American and other regional systems in order to ground its own readings of the right to be protected from racial discrimination.[309]

Accordingly, communal holding of property, particularly by indigenous peoples and Afro-descendant communities, has brought forth a raft of recommendations and expressions of major concern under the system of periodic reports and the early warning and urgent action procedure. The sense of the Committee's view is to treat individual and collective title holding as entitled to equal respect under the Convention. Early markers were set by the Committee in reacting to proposed legislative modifications by Australia of the Native Title Act 1993 (NTA), which had been passed into law following the groundbreaking case of *Mabo v Queensland*, which had rejected the racially discriminatory doctrine of *terra nullius*.[310] Despite the fragility of native title compared to freehold, an

[302] IACtHR, Ser C No. 79 (2001).

[303] Compare, ECtHR, *Doĝan and Ors v Turkey*, App. No. 8803-11/02, 8813/02, 8815-19/02 (2004).

[304] Para. 149. Compare CERD Decision 2 (54) on Australia, A/54/18, pp. 5–7, para. 4: 'The Committee recognizes ... that the land rights of indigenous peoples are unique and encompass a traditional and cultural identification of the indigenous peoples with their land that has been generally recognized.'

[305] IACtHR Ser. C No. 125 (2005).

[306] Ser. C No. 146 (2006).

[307] IACommHR, Case No. 11.140 (2002).

[308] *Yakye Axa v Paraguay*, para. 125: 'human rights are live instruments, whose interpretation must go hand in hand with evolution of the times and of current living conditions'. See also Chapters 5 and 20.

[309] In Decision 1 (68) on the United States of America, with regard to the Western Shoshone, the Committee drew on the case of *Mary and Carrie Dann v United States*, in particular on the statement that the State party's position was made on the basis of processes 'which did not comply with contemporary international human rights norms, principles and standards, that govern determination of indigenous property interests'; the Committee recalled GR 23 on the rights of indigenous peoples 'in particular their right to own, develop, control and use their communal lands, territories and resources': A/61/18, pp. 7–10.

[310] See Chapter 2 of the present work.

imbalance capable of raising equality and non-discrimination issues,[311] the NTA was deemed acceptable by the Committee as a product of genuine negotiations with the indigenous population and their informed consent. The Native Title Amendment Act (NTAA) on the other hand prompted the country rapporteur to question whether the amendments 'had unsettled the compromise between the rights of native title-holders and non-native title-holders, giving greater weight to non-native title'.[312] Strong statements by the Committee reinforced the impression that whatever the defects of native title at common law and under the NTA, the NTAA had rolled back protective provisions in a manner that generated concerns under Articles 2 and 5, intimations challenged by the State party in terms of the justifiable and proportional nature of the changes. In forming its judgements on the compatibility of legislative changes with the Convention and the perceived reduction of rights, the Committee was influenced by concerns over effective participation by indigenous peoples and the importance of securing their informed consent.[313]

The CERD archive of recommendations relating to communal or collective ownership of indigenous peoples lands is extensive, drawing on a full spectrum of such peoples across the continents. The general injunction in GR 23 to 'recognise and protect the rights of indigenous peoples to own, develop, control and use their communal lands, territories and resources', backed up by recommendations regarding return, restitution and compensation, will be recalled.[314] In addition to references in GR 23 and GR 34, the nexus between land and culture in the case of indigenous and other groups has been explicitly recognized in Committee practice,[315] as well as the spiritual significance of land.[316] As basic requirements, States parties are called upon to recognize communal, customary ownership of ancestral lands through legal acknowledgement,[317] demarcate territories,[318] protect those who seek to exercise their rights to such lands,[319] and refrain from exploitation or 'development' of lands of indigenous peoples unless based on principles of consultation and informed consent, and ensure the participation of the peoples in the exploitation, management and conservation of the associated natural resources.[320] In light of frequent imbalances in resources between government and indigenous litigants, mediation may be suggested for the resolution of disputes as an alternative to litigation. Issues of burden of proof and evidence in land disputes have also arisen, with questions being asked of the State party regarding the extent to which deficiencies in documentary evidence on the indigenous part can be remedied, taking into account the oral tradition of such groups.[321]

[311] CERD/C/SR.1323, paras 26 and 33, CERD member and country rapporteur McDougall.

[312] CERD/C/SR.1323, para. 30.

[313] CERD/C/304/Add. 101, paras 9, 10, and 11; Decision 2(54) on Australia, para. 9, A/54/18, pp. 5–7.

[314] GR 23, para. 5.

[315] CERD/C/LAO/CO/16-18, para. 16, where the State party was called upon 'to review its land regime with a view to recognizing the cultural aspect of land as an integral part of the identity of some ethnic groups'.

[316] With regard to the Western Shoshone, see CERD/C/USA/DEC 1(2006), para. 7(b), with regard to 'destructive activities . . . conducted and/or planned on areas of spiritual and cultural significance to the Western Shoshone peoples'.

[317] Concluding observations on Cambodia, CERD/C/KHM/CO/8-13, para. 16; Suriname, CERD/C/SUR/CO/12, para. 12.

[318] Concluding observations on Argentina, CERD/C/65/CO/1, para. 16; Guyana, CERD/C/GUY/CO/14, para. 16; Nicaragua, CERD/C/NIC/C/14, para. 21; Venezuela, CERD/C/VEN/CO/19-21, para. 17.

[319] Concluding observations on Cambodia, CERD/C/KHM/CO/18-13, para. 17.

[320] Concluding observations on Laos, CERD/C/LAO/CO/16-18, para. 17.

[321] Concluding observations on Sweden, CERD/C/SWE/CO/18, para. 19.

As with the Inter-American jurisprudence on the Saramaka and other groups, CERD has assimilated aspects of the rights of Afro-descendant communities to those of indigenous peoples. GR 34 on Racial Discrimination against People of African Descent refers to the entitlement to exercise 'individually or in community with other members of their group, as appropriate' a range of rights including the right to property 'and to the use, conservation and protection of lands traditionally occupied by them and to natural resources where their ways of life and culture are linked to their utilization of lands and resources'.[322] Afro-descendant communities that utilize communal property conceptions in relation to lands and resources have been identified in a range of countries in the Americas, and issues pertaining to such communities and indigenous peoples are often linked together in a common recommendation. This is illustrated in the case of Colombia, where the State party—commended for its recognition of collective land ownership for Afro-Colombian and indigenous communities—was nonetheless requested to 'ensure that collective land ownership of Afro-Colombian communities and indigenous peoples is recognised, respected and can be exercised in practice'.[323]

Discussions on land rights issues with States parties regularly result in recommendations to ratify or support relevant international instruments. In cases where natural resources are stated to be the property of the nation as a whole for national development, a reminder that development must be exercised consistently with indigenous rights may follow. This last principle has been stated primarily with respect to indigenous groups but applies to other groups and to rights beyond property rights: the Committee has been resolute in stressing that 'economic development does not come at the expense of the rights of vulnerable persons and groups' covered by the Convention but must be exercised consistently with those rights.[324] In other words, the exigencies of 'development' or 'national development' do not provide a licence to discriminate. It may be noted here that 'development' is not a prerogative of States. Under the UN Declaration on the Right to Development, it is a right recognized in 'every human person and all peoples', and the human person 'is the central subject of development'.[325] Development is also, *inter alia*, a right of 'all peoples' under the African Charter on Human and Peoples' Rights,[326] a violation of which was found in *Endorois v Kenya* and other cases by the African Commission on Human and Peoples' Rights.[327]

5(d)(vi) The Right to Inherit

It will be recalled that reservations entered by Yemen include a reservation to this subparagraph, and that objections have been made to the reservation.[328] Reporting guidelines do not elaborate the right.

[322] Para. 4.

[323] CERD/C/COL/CO/14, para. 19. See also concluding observations on Paraguay, CERD/C/PRY/CO/1-3, para. 15.

[324] Concluding observations on Cambodia, CERD/C/KHM/CO/8-13, para. 16.

[325] *Declaration on the Right to Development*, Articles 1 and 2, A/RES/41/128, 4 December 1986.

[326] Article 22.

[327] *Centre for Minority Rights Development (Kenya) and Minority Rights Group International on behalf of the Endorois Welfare Council v Kenya*; see also *Sudan Human Rights Organization on Centre on Housing Rights and Evictions (COHRE) v Sudan*, Comm. Nos. 279/03-296/05 (2009).

[328] See also concluding observations, CERD/C/YEM/CO/17-18, paras 13, reiterating previous concluding observations on the issue.

The right to inherit is occasionally invoked by the Committee. Background standards commonly cited include international provisions on the right to property, notably Article 17 of the UDHR, as well as Article 16 of CEDAW,[329] and Article 21 of the Protocol to the ACHPR on Women in Africa, highlighting situations of gender-based inheritance discrimination. Discrimination against women and denial of inheritance rights is also linked to other rights including adequate standard of living, health, and development.

Current recommendations regarding this right are predominantly focused on its gender dimensions and may refer to inheritance, marriage, and property rights taken together. Examples of gender focus include Canada with regard to the rights of women belonging to First Nations, where the Committee urged adoption of legislation to remedy the situation regarding inheritance.[330] In the cases of Chad and Namibia, the gendered customary inheritance practices of some ethnic groups were identified as sources of discrimination. For Chad, the remedy proposed was twofold: take measures to eliminate the practice by raising awareness and educating the population concerned, and adopt a legal code on the Individual and the Family.[331] In a later concluding observation, the Committee recalled GR 25 on gender-based discrimination, and the rights of women, 'in particular the right to own or inherit land'.[332] In the case of Namibia, in addition to a review of laws, the State party was invited 'to consider introducing a system which allows individuals a choice between customary law systems and the national law while ensuring that the discriminatory aspects of customary laws' were not applied.[333]

Residual effects of older attitudes and laws produced the unusual case of Greenlandic people, considered to be '"legally fatherless" because they were born out of wedlock to Danish men . . . in the 1950s and 1960s. This status has an impact on matters of family law, land ownership and inheritance'; the State party was invited to address the problems faced by those holding this status.[334] In the wider, social sense of 'inheritance', reference has been made to the 'cultural heritage' of groups including Crimean Tatars, Karaites, and Roma,[335] to 'ethnic groups',[336] or to minorities in general.[337]

5(d)(vii) The Right to Freedom of Thought, Conscience, and Religion

The CERD reporting guidelines add little to the bare bones of 5(d)(vii) in recalling 'the possible intersectionality of racial and religious discrimination, including the effects of

[329] On which, see also GC 29 of CEDAW on *Economic Consequences of Marriage, Family Relations and their Dissolution*, 26 February 2013.

[330] Concluding observations on Canada, CERD/C/CAN/CO/19-20, para. 18.

[331] Concluding observations on Chad, CERD/C/TCD/CO/15, para. 17. The recommendations to the Lao People's Democratic republic, CERD/C/LAO/CO/16-18, para. 16, emphasised the need to address discriminatory customs, 'primarily through education and other culturally sensitive strategies'.

[332] CERD/C/TCD/CO/16-18, para. 13: the paragraph is headed 'harmful traditional practices concerning women', relating to 'some ethnic groups'.

[333] Concluding observations on Namibia, CERD/C/NAM/CO/12, para. 11. Article 21 of the Protocol to the African Charter on Human and Peoples Rights on the Rights of Women provides: '1. A widow/widower shall have the right to inherit each other's property. In the event of death, the surviving spouse has the right, whatever the matrimonial regime, to continue living in the matrimonial house. 2. Women and girls shall have the same rights as men and boys to inherit, in equal shares, their parents' properties.'

[334] Concluding observations on Denmark, CERD/C/DNK/CO/18-19, para. 17.

[335] Concluding observations on Ukraine, CERD/C/UKR/CO/18, para. 18.

[336] Concluding observations on Laos, CERD/C/LAO/CO/16-18, para. 21.

[337] Concluding observations on Georgia, CERD/C/GEO/CO/4-5, para. 16, with particular reference to Armenian and Azeri communities.

anti-terrorism measures, which may lead to discrimination on ethnic grounds against members of specific religious communities'.[338] A subsequent paragraph requests that particular attention should be paid by reporting States to 'complex forms of disadvantage in which racial discrimination is mixed with other causes of discrimination (such as... religion...)... and to refer to any available social indicators of forms of disadvantage that may be linked with racial discrimination'.[339] As previously noted, appraisals of racial discrimination require that the specific characteristics of ethnic, cultural, and religious groups be taken into consideration.[340]

Background human rights standards on religion are extensive, commencing in the era of the League of Nations with the minorities regime and its assurance of protection without any distinctions on the ground of, *inter alia*, religion, and provisions on the rights of 'racial, religious or linguistic minorities'.[341] In the modern era, the prohibition of distinctions based on 'race, sex, language, or religion' in the UN Charter has been followed through a range of human rights instruments, including the UDHR and the Covenants, and is recalled in the preamble to ICERD. Freedom of religion figures as a substantive right in a range of UN and regional instruments, following the standard set by Article 18 of the UDHR,[342] including notably Article 18 of the ICCPR, complemented by Article 27 on the rights of ethnic, religious, and linguistic minorities. The Human Rights Committee issued a general comment (22) on Article 18 which, *inter alia*, does not attempt to define religion in terms for example of historicity,[343] though it observes that the protection afforded by Article 18 'is not limited... to traditional religions' and includes non-majoritarian religions—religious minorities.[344] The Human Rights Committee intimates that 'worship' includes ritual and ceremonial acts, 'observance and practice' includes, *inter alia*, customs such as dietary regulations, distinctive clothing, and the use of a particular language customarily spoken by a group, while 'practice and teaching of religion' includes freedom to choose religious leadership, establish seminaries, and distribute religious texts of publications.[345] Among general regional instruments on human rights, Article 8 of the ACHPR guarantees freedom of conscience and the free practice of religion, as does Article 12 of the ACHR, and Article 9 of the ECHR, and Article 30 of the Arab Charter on Human Rights.

[338] CERD/C/2007/1, 5. I.D.

[339] *Ibid.*, 5 II. B.

[340] Discussed in Chapter 6.

[341] See Chapter 2.

[342] 'Everyone has the right to freedom of thought, conscience and religion; this right includes freedom to change his religion or belief and freedom, either alone or in community with others and in public or private, to manifest... religion or belief in teaching, practice, worship and observance.' Article 18(1) ICCPR adds 'practice and teaching' to worship, observance, introduces a paragraph forbidding coercion in the matter of religion (18(2)), and intimates the possibility of restricting the manifestation of religion on grounds of public, safety, order, health or morals or the rights and freedoms of others (18(3), and includes an undertaking to respect the liberty of parents and guardians in the religious and moral education of their children. Article 4(2) lists freedom of thought, conscience and religion among the articles in the Convention that cannot be derogated from.

[343] This has not inhibited the Committee from ruling out protection of 'religions' based on the care, cultivation, etc, of cannabis: *M.A.B., W.A.T., J.-A.Y.T. v Canada*, CCPR/C/50/D/570/1993 (1994); compare *Prince v South Africa*, CCPR/C/91/D/1474/2006 (2007).

[344] GC 22, *Freedom of Thought, Conscience and Religion*, HRI/GEN/1/Rev.9 (Vol. I), pp. 204–7, para. 2.

[345] GC 22, para. 4.

While a global convention on religious freedom, intolerance, or discrimination did not emerge following the 'split' in UN work on racial and religious questions,[346] the UN Declaration on the Elimination of All Forms of Intolerance and of Discrimination based on Religion or Belief is effectively a 'soft law' counterpart of ICERD,[347] and draws upon it in conceptualizing intolerance and discrimination.[348] The Declaration, besides elaborating principles of tolerance and non-discrimination, sets out the conceptual, institutional, educational, financial, and celebratory parameters of religious freedoms,[349] and states the conviction that religious freedom should contribute 'to the elimination of ideologies or practices of... racial discrimination'.[350]

The findings of CERD on discrimination in this field focus to a significant extent on the treatment of the beliefs and practices of minorities, indigenous peoples, and non-citizens, rather than on religion in general. In the field of minorities, the UNDM includes persons belonging to religious minorities in its compass, and the FCNM addresses sundry aspects of the religious identity of national minorities. ILO Convention 169 addresses the spiritual values and practices of the peoples at various points,[351] while concepts of spirituality—traditions, property, religious traditions, spiritual development, spiritual relationship with lands, territories, etc, the spiritual impact of development activities, etc—suffuse the UNDRIP.[352] While thought and conscience extend beyond religion, the Committee has not (yet) identified communities of atheists or agnostics, pacifists, vegans or vegetarians claiming to suffer discrimination on racial grounds.

In light of the drafting split between instruments on racial discrimination and instruments on religious intolerance, neither Article 1 nor Article 5 includes religion among the grounds of discrimination;[353] the discussion of the 'intersectionality' of religion with the explicit grounds in the Convention will be recalled.[354] On a strict interpretation of the Convention, the element of religion is to be addressed where freedom of religion is 'nullified or impaired' on the grounds in Articles 1 and 5: that is, where freedom of religion is denied on 'racial' grounds. Committee practice is characterized by linking freedom of religion to identities that relate to the types of community implied in the grounds of discrimination. Thus, the Committee, echoing the grounds of discrimination in Articles 1 and 5, described Shia in Bahrain as distinguished 'by virtue of tribal or national origin, descent, culture or language'.[355] In most cases where the Committee addresses discrimination against religious practice on ethnic/racial grounds, attention is drawn to the 'intersectionality' thesis to buttress the relevant recommendations.[356]

[346] Discussed in Chapter 3.
[347] Adopted by GA resolution 36/55, 25 November 1981.
[348] Para. 2(2).
[349] Notably in Article 6.
[350] Para. 6 of the preamble to the Declaration.
[351] Preamble, Articles 5, 7, and 13.
[352] Preamble, Articles 11, 12, 17, 25, 32, 34, and 36.
[353] Discussed in Chapter 3.
[354] Chapter 6.
[355] BHR/CO/7, para. 16.
[356] An interesting confirmation of the intersectionlity thesis appears in connection with the report of France, discussed in 2010, where the representative, while arguing that the wearing of the Burka did not come within the remit of the Committee and that discussing it would 'involve a dangerous equation of race and religion', nonetheless conceded that 'discriminatory acts could be motivated by different concomitant factors, such as race and religion, race and gender or race and disability': CERD/C/SR.2027, para. 36. See further ECtHR, *S.A.S. v France*, App. No. 43835/11 (2014); *Dogru v France*, App. No. 27058/05 (2008); *Kervanci v France*, App. No.

The Committee has been highly critical of treating religion as a *conditio sine qua non* for access to a bundle of rights. In the case of the Maldives, concern was expressed at 'discriminatory provisions in the Constitution that all Maldivians should be Muslims, thus excluding non-Muslims from obtaining citizenship or from accessing public positions',[357] a situation deemed to affect 'people of a different national origin'.[358] The Committee found the core of the discrimination to be the potential negative effect of the religious stipulation on non-citizens, recalling that GR 30 requests parties to ensure that particular groups of non-citizens are not discriminated against with regard to access to citizenship or naturalization.[359]

As regards more specific or localized expressions of discrimination, practices in registering religions or religious organizations have frequently engaged attention on the basis that registration may be used to frustrate the enjoyment of the freedom of religion of particular groups. In the case of Moldova, the State party was urged, in light of concerns regarding 'Muslim groups' in particular, to respect 'the rights of members of registered and unregistered religions to freely exercise their freedom of religion, review existing registration regulations and practices', and register 'religious groups who wish to be registered'.[360] In the case of Vietnam, concern was expressed at restrictions on religious practices, including issues of registration, affecting 'some Christian and Buddhist denominations among Khmer Krom, Degar (Montagnard) and Hmong', identifying this as 'a phenomenon of double discrimination faced by ethnic minorities belonging to unrecognized religious groups'.[361] While critiques of registration practices may be based on comparing the treatment of favoured religions with the treatment of others, and attacks on believers and property belonging to minority communities are treated as condemnable in themselves, the 'comparator element' cited in theses on discrimination may add little or nothing to the calculus of discrimination.

Reports of vandalism and despoliation of religious sites belonging to minorities,[362] or impeding access to them,[363] and attacks on religious personnel or property,[364] have all

31645/04 (2008); *Leyla Şahin v Turkey*, App. No. 44774/98 (2005); *Ahmet Arslan v Turkey*, App. No. 41135/98 (2010); Human Rights Committee, *Raihon Hudoybergarova v Uzbekistan*, CCPR/C/82/D/931/2000 (2004); *Singh Bhinder v Canada*, CCPR/C/37/D/208/1986 (1989); *Ranjit Singh v France*, CCPR/C/102/D/1876/2009 (2011).

[357] CERD/C/MDV/CO/5-12, para. 10 (2011). See further, M. Evans, *Manual on the Wearing of Religious Symbols in Public Areas* (Martinus Nijhoff, 2008).

[358] *Ibid.*

[359] *Ibid.* See also para. 9 of the concluding observations.

[360] CERD/C/MDA/CO/8-9, para. 14. The concluding observations cited, *inter alia*, resolution 2005/40 (2005) of the UN Commission on Human Rights which had expressed serious concern with 'the misuse of registration procedures as a means to limit the right to freedom of religion or belief of members of certain religious communities'.

[361] CERD/C/VNM/CO/10-14, para. 16; the litany of issues set out in the relevant paragraph also included 'violent attacks and threats' against religious groups and activities and the prohibition of religious activities deemed to violate national security and 'negatively affect the unity of the people or the nation's fine cultural traditions'; see also, *ibid.*, para. 17.

[362] Concluding observations on Ukraine, CERD/C/UKR/CO/18, para. 8.

[363] Concluding observations on Israel CERD/C/ISR/CO/13, para. 36.

[364] Concluding observations on Moldova, CERD/C/MDA/CO/8-9, para. 14. The compendious recommendation refers to issues of intimidation, registration impediments, sanctions applied to members of unregistered religious organizations, sanctions against religious activities in public places carried out without advance notification, identity checks on Muslims, and inadequate responses to anti-Semitic events and vandalism of religious sites.

generated recommendations. The potential for discrimination in the sphere of education is addressed in concluding observations on, for example, Ireland where the Committee, bearing in mind the situation of minorities and immigrant communities, expressed a preference for promoting non-denominational or inter-denominational schools.[365] The criticism of the Irish educational arrangements was amplified in later concluding observations: reference was made to the fact that there was an insufficient number of alternative, non-denominational schools in the national system, and that Catholic students were favoured for admission to Catholic schools in case of a shortage of places.[366] 'Intersectionality' of racial and religious discrimination is referred to in the later set of observations without reference to any particular communities affected by the legislation, although the earlier conclusions identifying relevant communities are explicitly cited therein.

The individuation of a 'religion' as a separate entity from cultural practices is not a feature of every society comprehended by the Convention. Discrimination against community cultural practices may effectively engage the right in 5(d)(vii) along with other rights even if a specific 'religion' is not identified. Hence, bundles of rights including property rights cluster around the spiritual relationship of indigenous peoples to their lands and territories and may implicate a spectrum of Article 5 provisions. In addition to reiterating its decision on the Western Shoshone,[367] CERD recommended that the USA 'take all appropriate measures, in consultation with indigenous peoples concerned... to ensure that activities carried out in areas of cultural and spiritual significance to Native Americans do not have a negative impact on the enjoyment of their rights under ICERD'.[368] In the case of Argentina, reference was made to the connection between ancestral lands and sacred sites,[369] while Indonesia was recommended to 'treat equally all religions and beliefs' and ensure the enjoyment of rights by ethnic minorities and indigenous peoples.[370] In the case of The Philippines, the Committee expressed concern regarding mining operations on Mount Canatuan, a sacred site of the Subanon people, undertaken without their prior consent,[371] an issue that had already been addressed under the early warning procedure.[372]

Religion, like culture, takes many forms. For many communities, including but not confined to indigenous peoples, clear lines between culture or tradition and 'religion' may not exist, and defining such lines may amount to an attempt to graft exogamous concepts and structures on to such communities and their life projects.[373] Many societies evoke religion and spirituality through a holistic narrative of self-understanding, rather than a series of cultural subsets with defined conceptual or physical boundaries. Indigenous and

[365] Concluding observations on Ireland, CERD/C/IRL/CO/2, para. 18.

[366] CERD/C/IRL/CO/3-4, para. 26. See comment in GC 22 of the Human Rights Committee, paras 6 and 9.

[367] Decision 1(68).

[368] CERD/C/USA/CO/6, para. 29.

[369] CERD/C/65/CO/1, para. 16.

[370] CERD/C/IDN/CO/3, para. 21. The concern expressed related to distinctions between 'recognized' and 'unrecognized' religions, the latter including religions of ethnic minorities and indigenous peoples outside the framework of 'Islam, Protestantism, Catholicism, Hinduism and Buddhism'. The Committee did not challenge the recognition category as such but was exercised by the possible 'adverse impact' of the distinction with regard to identity documents, marriage registration, and birth certification.

[371] CERD/C/PHL/CO/20, para. 25.

[372] A/63/18, para. 27.

[373] M. Blaser, H.A Feit, and G. McRae (eds), *In the Way of Development: Indigenous Peoples, Life Projects and Globalization* (Zed Books, 2004).

analogous forms of spirituality are fully entitled to the protection of 5(d)(vii) as well as all the forms of cultural protection enshrined in the Convention and wider international law, including protection against forced assimilation. The link between religion, spirituality, culture, and ethnicity is well-understood in general international law—including in such as the Convention against Genocide—even if appraisals in human rights terms may be appreciably narrower and framed in the language of 'traditional' and 'non-traditional' belief systems, or 'world religions'.

5(d)(viii) The Right to Freedom of Opinion and Expression

Reflecting the relationship between Articles 4 and 5, the reporting guidelines do not elaborate the right to freedom of opinion and expression, and footnote the 'compatibility thesis' of GR 15—the prohibition of the dissemination of ideas based on racial superiority or hatred is compatible with the right to freedom of opinion and expression.[374]

Key elements of the international human rights framework of freedom of opinion and expression are set out earlier in the commentary on Article 4 (notably Article 19 of the UDHR, 'freedom of opinion and expression'), and Article 19 of the ICCPR (freedom 'to hold opinions without interference' and 'freedom of expression'); further global and regional provisions are also accounted for.[375] It will also be recalled that the numerous reservations and interpretative declarations on Article 4 focus principally on the protection of the rights set out in Article 19 of the UDHR and the ICCPR in relation to the 'due regard' clause of Article 4.[376] The leading provisions also refer to potential restrictions on freedom of expression, but not freedom of opinion,[377] whether in terms of respect for the rights and reputation of others, or elements associated with public order, health, and morals;[378] restrictions should be prescribed by law, necessary in a democratic society and be for a legitimate and proportionate aim; the concept of 'duties and responsibilities' associated with freedom of expression also figures in the legal substratum. The degree of protection to be accorded to the many possible forms of expression is a variable, with political speech accorded a higher level of protection than, for example, commercial speech.[379] The freedoms are intrinsically linked to the concept of pluralist, participatory democracy.[380] Positive obligations to secure the right to freedom of expression have also been identified,[381] analogous to the undertaking in Article 5 to guarantee non-discriminatory enjoyment of rights.

[374] See Chapter 11.

[375] Article 19 (2) provides that freedom of expression 'shall include freedom to seek, receive and impart information and ideas of all kinds, regardless of frontiers, either orally, in writing or in print, if the form of art, or through any other media of... choice'. Further discussion in Chapter 11.

[376] See Chapters 11 and 18.

[377] Human Rights Committee, GC 34, paras 9 and 10; *Kang v Republic of Korea*, CCPR/C/78/D/878/1999 (2003).

[378] See, *inter alia*, Article19(3) of the ICCPR, Article 10(2) of the ECHR

[379] *Ballantyne, Davidson and McIntyre v Canada*, CCPR/C/47/D/359/1989 and 385/1989/Rev. 1 (1993).

[380] See, *inter alia*, ACHPR, *Media Rights Agenda and Constitutional Rights Project v Nigeria*, ACHPR, Comm. No. 105/93, 128/94, 130/94, 152/96, cited in G. Gilbert, 'Expression, Assembly, Association' in M. Weller (ed.), *Universal Minority Rights* (Oxford University Press, 2007), pp. 149–77, p. 160. [henceforth 'Expression, Assembly, Association']; also ECtHR cases of *Arslan v Turkey*, App. No. 23462/94 (1999), para. 44; *Handyside v the United Kingdom*, App. No. 5493/72 (1976), para. 48; also *Fressoz and Roire v France*, App. No. 29183/95 (1999; *Zana v Turkey*, App. No. 118954/91 (1997).

[381] *Dink v Tur*key, ECtHR App. No. 2668/07 (2010).

In addition to the general instruments individuating the rights, instruments on minorities and indigenous peoples incorporate rights to freedom of opinion and expression, if not always in explicit terms, through the use of complex provisions on cultural and linguistic expression, and standards on ownership or control of media.[382] The FCNM is exceptional in elaborating that the right to freedom of expression of persons belonging to national minorities 'includes freedom to hold opinions and to receive and impart information and ideas in the minority language', and that such persons 'are not discriminated against in their access to the media'.[383] In terms of practice there is also a considerable international archive of cases concerning restrictions on minorities in the area of speech freedoms, characteristically though not invariably associated with the use of minority languages and other expressions of identity,[384] as well as for example peaceful advocacy of a separate national entity.[385]

The concept of freedom of expression has been regarded, through the works of J.S. Mill and others,[386] as central to the 'Enlightenment' and to liberal democracy.[387] The tension between the freedom and its restriction is also in evidence historically,[388] intersecting with the tension between conceptions of the right as instrumental in the service of a greater ideology, whether nationalist,[389] religious, anti-colonial, or Marxist, and as a self-validating human right premised on subjective autonomy, dignity, and equality. As noted in connection with the drafting of Article 4,[390] a fundamental intellectual tension manifested itself in strongly worded and argued debates between representatives of States in the Soviet orbit, generally favouring speech restrictions, and of Western States, who characteristically accorded a higher value to the freedom, with others offering a spectrum

[382] With regard to ILO Convention 169, see Section VI on 'Education and Means of Communication'; for the UNDRIP, see in particular Articles 12, 13, 16, and 31.

[383] Article 9; see also Article 7, in addition to the wide range of linguistic rights, and Gilbert, *Expression, Assembly, Association*, *passim*.

[384] *Egítim ve Bilím Emekçileri Sendíkasi v Turkey*, ECtHR App. No. 20641/05 (2012), where a trade union promoted education in Kurdish, Article 10 of the ECHR was deemed (para. 71) to encompass 'the freedom to receive and impart information and ideas in any language which affords the opportunity to take part in the public exchange of cultural, social and political information and ideas of all kinds'; *Singer v Canada*, CCPR/C/51/D/455/1991 (1994).

[385] *Ozgür Gündem v Turkey*, ECtHR App. No. 23144/93 (2000), para. 70.

[386] J.S. Mill, *On Liberty* (Longman, Roberts and Green, 1869; Hackett Publishing, 1978). According to Mill, 'there ought to exist the fullest liberty of professing and discussing, as a matter of ethical conviction, any doctrine, however immoral it may be considered': Mill, *On Liberty* (1978), p. 15.

[387] Among many further reading possibilities, E.C. Baker, *Human Liberty and Freedom of Speech* (Oxford University Press, 1989); I. Hare and J. Weinstein (eds), *Extreme Speech and Democracy* (Oxford University Press, 2009); S. Hayman, *Free Speech and Human Dignity* (Yale University Press, 2008); J.D. Peters, Courting the Abyss: Free Speech and the Liberal Tradition (University of Chicago Press, 2010); see the general summary by D. van Mill, 'Freedom of Speech', in E.N. Zalta (ed.), *The Stanford Encyclopaedia of Philosophy* (Spring 2015): <http://plato.stanford.edu/cgi-bin/encyclopedia/archinfo.cgi?entry=freedom-speech>.

[388] 'All that makes existence valuable to anyone depends on the enforcement of restraints', J.S. Mill, *On Liberty* (Hackett Publishing,), p. 5. See also, *inter alia*, S. Fish, *There's No Such Thing as Free Speech, and It's a Good Thing Too* (Oxford University Press, 1994)

[389] Commenting on the case of Hrant Dink, killed by nationalist extremists for challenging the official version of the Armenian massacres, White comments that the process 'of ring-fencing official versions of history is both ludicrous and dangerous, raising the prospect of different States pursuing their own version of history by demanding that writers, journalists and . . . citizens keep to a script . . . approved by the government . . . subjugating . . . freedom of expression to nationalist agendas': A. White, 'A New Vision of Values, Accountability and Mission for Journalism', in T. McGonagle and Y. Donders (eds), *The United Nations and Freedom of Expression and Information* (Cambridge University Press, 2015), pp. 350–72, p. 364.

[390] See Chapter 11.

of opinions intermediate between the Soviet–West polarity. In the result, the Convention contains a detailed provision on speech restrictions in Article 4, and a lightly drafted reference to freedom of opinion and expression in Article 5. The more detailed and stringent 'hate speech' provisions of Article 4 have received greater attention from the Committee than freedom of opinion and expression in Article 5, a contrast that also applies between Article 4(b) on racist organizations and freedom of assembly and association in Article 5. In consequence, there is only limited elaboration by CERD of the parameters of Article 5(d)(viii) and (ix).

It is not therefore unreasonable to suggest the treatment of freedom of opinion and expression in CERD practice is better understood through a process of 'reverse engineering', in that the contours of the freedom in Article 5 have largely been shaped through practice on Article 4.[391] In other words, the emphasis in the Committee has been placed as much on the suppression of speech as its validation: the institutional culture of the Committee has largely been dominated by the strategy of combating hate speech, particularly through the application of criminal law. Hence, as with the guidelines, 'freedom of expression and opinion' in the Committee's archives is characteristically linked to the 'compatibility thesis'.[392] It remains to be seen whether the fuller but incomplete account of freedom of expression set out in GR 35 will have an appreciable effect on the tenor of the Committee's statements.

GR 35, in addition to presenting a framework for the application of Articles 4 and 7 in light of the Committee's evaluation of the roles of criminal prohibitions and education, respectively, in combating hate speech, also reflects on Article 5. The recommendation focuses principally on freedom of opinion and expression as a contribution to countering hate speech, drawing upon, in addition to the text of ICERD, concepts and language from instruments including GC 34 of the Human Rights Committee, and the Rabat Plan of Action.[393] On freedom of expression generally, paragraph 4 of the recommendation asserts that 'the principles of the Convention contribute to a fuller understanding of the parameters of this right in contemporary international human rights law'.[394]

The specific section in the recommendation on Article 5 is short, commencing with a recall of the structure of Article 5. The Committee affirms that ideas and opinions expressed in the context of 'academic debates, political engagement or similar activity' and 'without incitement to hatred, contempt, violence or discrimination' are legitimate exercises of the right to freedom of expression, 'even when such ideas are controversial'.[395] As observed earlier,[396] it may be difficult to draw lines in this area. While GR 35 addresses

[391] This is a true of the communications procedure under Article 14 as it is of reporting under Article 9. In *Hagan v Australia*, CERD/C/62/D/26/2002 (2003), Article 5(d)(viii) was included among the grounds of complaint, a claim roundly dismissed by the State party (para. 4.16) and not further considered by the Committee at the admissibility and merits stages.

[392] The bulk of searches of Universal Human Rights Index under 'freedom of expression' in the work of the Committee recall the compatibility thesis.

[393] *Rabat Plan of Action on the Prohibition of Advocacy of National, Racial or Religious Hatred that Constitutes Incitement to Discrimination, Hostility or Violence*, 5 Oct 2012: <http://www.ohchr.org/Documents/Issues/Opinion/SeminarRabat/Rabat_draft_outcome.pdf>.

[394] See Chapter 11 for the full text of the paragraph.

[395] Para. 25. See also paras 14, 15, 20, and 35. Compare para. 11 of the *Rabat Plan of Action*: 'The right to freedom of expression implies that it should be possible to scrutinize, openly debate and criticize belief systems, opinions and institutions, including religious ones.'

[396] See discussion in Chapter 11.

itself to general statements, distinctions between unacceptable forms of racist speech, and legitimate discussion of race, culture, and related matters, were sharply at issue in *TBB-Turkish Union v Germany*, where the Committee, with one dissenting voice, found that statements reviewed in the proceedings went beyond an academic or discursive remit and fell into the category of impugned speech under Article 4.[397]

The limited elaboration of the right to freedom of opinion and expression in GR 35[398] accentuates in standard fashion the 'duties and responsibilities' attached to the freedom and the possibility of restrictions, while stating that the latter are permissible 'only if they are provided by law and are necessary for the protection of the rights or reputations of others and for the protection of national security or public order, or of public health or morals'—a recall of Article 19(3) of the ICCPR.[399] A further cautious note is sounded in the statement that the freedom should not 'aim at the destruction of the rights and freedoms of others, including the right to equality and non-discrimination'.[400]

Building upon the Durban Declaration and Programme of Action which affirmed the positive role of freedom of opinion and expression in combating racial hatred,[401] the recommendation includes a strong statement of the compound virtues of freedom of expression in sustaining the rights of persons and groups protected by the Convention:

> Freedom of expression, indispensable for the articulation of human rights and the dissemination of knowledge regarding... civil, political, economic, social and cultural rights, assists vulnerable groups in redressing the balance of power among the components of society, promotes intercultural understanding and tolerance, assists in the deconstruction of racial stereotypes, facilitates the free exchange of ideas, and offers alternative views and counterpoints States parties should adopt policies empowering all groups within the purview of the Convention to exercise their right to freedom of expression.[402]

As discussed in relation to Article 4, another paragraph underlines this last point in observing that the right to freedom of opinion and expression of those within the protective umbrella of the Convention requires protection from the potentially silencing effects of racist speech.[403]

[397] The dissenting opinion of CERD member Vázquez doubted (para. 7) the Committee's characterization of the statements under review, suggesting that they were 'not outside the scope of reasoned discourse'.

[398] Article 19 of the UDHR refers to a compound 'right to freedom of opinion and expression', a pattern followed by ICERD; Article 19 of the ICCPR addresses rights to opinion and expression separately.

[399] Para. 26. GC 34 of the Human Rights Committee explains in para. 28, that 'the term "others" relates to other persons individually or as members of a community. Thus, it may, for instance, refer to individual members of a community defined by its religious faith or ethnicity.' In an 'ethnic' context, see *Ballantyne, Davidson and McIntyre v Canada*, CCPR/C/47/D/359/1989, 385/1989/Rev.1 (1993), where Canadian language legislation restricting commercial speech was deemed to contravene Article 19—the rights of others, the Francophone minority within Canada—were not jeopardized by commercial outdoor advertising in a language other than French.

[400] Para. 26. The preamble to the Camden Principles on Freedom of Expression and Equality includes the statement that, too often, 'the rights to freedom of expression and equality have been construed as being in opposition to one another, or as being in direct conflict, with attention focused on the potential for tension between them. The Principles assert the affirmative relationship between freedom of expression and equality, identifying the complementary and essential contribution they make to the securing and safeguarding of human dignity, and the fact that together they are key to the indivisibility and universality of human rights. Observed and upheld they enable and strengthen respect for human rights for all': <https://www.article19.org/data/files/pdfs/standards/the-camden-principles-on-freedom-of-expression-and-equality.pdf>.

[401] Durban Declaration, para. 90; Outcome Document of the Durban Review Conference, paras 54 and 58.

[402] Para. 29. See also para. 28, discussed in Chapter 11.

[403] Para. 28.

In consequence of the hitherto lapidary quality of the Committee's approach to Article 4, there has been only limited practical illumination of the scope and significance of 5(d)(viii). Cases where minorities were threatened through over-zealous approaches by State authorities to the prohibition of racist hate speech form the bulk of the examples, though the exercise of the freedom can also be threatened by the acts of private individuals. Accordingly in the case of Turkmenistan, the Committee expressed concern 'at the overly broad provisions of... the Criminal Code such as on "enmity" or "offending ethnic pride" which may lead to unnecessary or disproportionate interference with... freedom of expression' and recommended clearer definition of such offences. In so doing the Committee drew attention to GC 34 (2011) of the Human Rights Committee.[404] In the case of Rwanda, critical comments were made on the 'genocide ideology law' of 2008, in that the definition of this punishable offence was too broad and that intention was not one of the constituent elements of the crime.[405] While freedom of expression was not referred to in concluding observations that focused on legal certainty and predictability, they may be inferred therefrom.[406]

Boyle and Shah underline the foundational nature of freedom of expression as 'the touchstone of all rights. Not only is freedom of expression inseparable from freedom of thought, association, and assembly, it is essential for the enjoyment of all rights.'[407] With regard to the persons and communities recognized in CERD practice, rights in the field of language, culture, information, participation, education, health, freedom of thought, conscience, and religion, and freedom of assembly and association, all depend for their effective fulfilment on the non-discriminatory enjoyment of freedom of expression. While an equivalent claim could be made for principles of equality and non-discrimination as foundational to the human rights enterprise, and for others such as the right to education, the stress should preferably be placed on interdependence and indivisibility of rights rather than the construction of a competitive hierarchy. The effects of discrimination flow simultaneously or sequentially into disparate areas of life that are not easily segmented into neat packages of rights.

In the context of Article 5, the two principles of freedom of expression and equality theoretically coalesce, so that practice should ideally demonstrate their integration, especially in the pluralistic setting of communities protected by the Convention. In the context of such pluralism, and integrated with cultural and linguistic rights in general, the Committee has moved incrementally towards a more rounded appreciation of the virtues of freedom of expression as a protective device for communities, even if the right is not always defined, or named as such.

[404] CERD/C/TKM/CO/6-7, para. 16. See also para. 25, *ibid.*, regarding limitations on access to the Internet for human rights NGOs, 'mainly concerning minority groups', where the Committee advises the Sate party to avoid 'arbitrary impediments' to Internet access, 'and refrain from restricting the operation of websites, blogs or any other Internet-based information in violation of the freedom of expression as provided for by international law'.

[405] CERD/C/RWA/CO/13-17, para. 14.

[406] Among recent comments on the right, see concluding observations on Ukraine, CERD/C/UKR/CO/19-21, para. 13, on the need to ensure both freedom from discrimination and freedom of expression; Vietnam, CERD/C/VNM/CO/10-14, para. 17, regarding the practice of detention for activities 'that would, under international standards, constitute the peaceful exercise' of rights to freedom of expression and of peaceful assembly and association.

[407] K. Boyle and S. Shah, 'Thought, Expression, Association and Assembly', in Moeckli *et al.*, *International Human Rights Law*, pp. 217–37, p. 225.

5(d)(ix) The Right to Freedom of Peaceful Assembly and Association

Following the model of Article 20 of the UDHR, ICERD combines freedoms of peaceful assembly and association into one statement of rights,[408] whereas, as noted in Chapter 11, the ICCPR splits them into distinct articles on peaceful assembly and freedom of association; the ICCPR model is followed in other instruments.[409] Freedom of assembly has its roots in the trade union movement; the right to form and join trade unions is also part of Article 5, listed under 'economic, social and cultural rights', a further illustration of the interconnections among protected rights, transcending any limiting categorizations. Freedom of assembly is closely related to freedom of expression,[410] and, in specific circumstances, to identity rights.[411] All international instruments with the exception of the ACHR require that the right be exercised peacefully.[412] Logically, assemblies consist of more than one person.[413] Freedom of association is also historically linked to trade union rights, but is understood as broader and not confined to them.[414] Protection from discrimination with regard to the right to form and join trade unions is separately addressed under economic, social and cultural rights in Article 5(e)(ii) of ICERD. Freedom of association also implicitly figures in the notions of community adumbrated from the era of the League of Nations,[415] and has thus been 'seen as central from the outset to international minority group protection'.[416]

While the UDHR, the ICCPR, and ICERD do not specify any teleological basis for the right, Article 16 of the American Convention Human Rights refers to the right to establish associations for 'ideological, religious, political, economic, labour, social and cultural, sports, or other purposes'.[417] With regard to minorities and indigenous peoples, Article 27 of the ICCPR implies a right of association through the reference to rights being enjoyed 'individually or in community'; the UNDM specifies that '[p]ersons belonging to minorities have the right to establish and maintain their own associations',[418] while the UNDRIP is shot through with formulations of rights that presuppose and reach beyond freedom of association to implicate larger forms of political association, communities or nations, up to and including the right of self-determination. In the words of Boyle and Shah, the right of peaceful assembly 'protects non-violent, organized

[408] See also Article 11 ECHR.

[409] See Chapter 11. Other kinds of assembly intimated in the ICCPR include religious assemblies under Article 18 and family assemblies under Article 17.

[410] *Rassemblement Jurassien and Unité Jurassien v Switzerland*, 17 DR 93 (1979); peaceful assemblies in support of autonomy or secession should not therefore be prohibited: *Stankov United Macedonian Organization 'ILINDEN' v Bulgaria*, ECtHR, App. Nos. 29221 and 29225/95 (2001).

[411] Gilbert observes that 'the right of persons belonging to minorities to assemble together in private or in public is fundamental... protecting the existence and identity of the group': G. Gilbert, *Expression, Assembly, Association*, pp. 172–3, citing *Djavit An v Turkey*, ECtHR App. No. 20652/92 (2003), a case which also establishes (para. 57) a positive obligation to secure the effective enjoyment of the right, for which see also *Platform Ärtzte für das Leben v Austria*, Ser. A No. 139 (1991).

[412] Article 11 of the ACHPR, which commences with the simple statement that 'every individual shall have the right to freely assembly with others'.

[413] *Coleman v Australia*, CCPR/C/87/D/1157/2003 (2006).

[414] *United Communist Party of Turkey v Turkey*, ECtHR App. No. 19392/92 (1998).

[415] *Greco-Bulgarian Communities Case*, PCIJ Ser. B No. 17 (1930).

[416] Gilbert, *Expression, Assembly, Association*, p. 152.

[417] Boyle and Shah comment that freedom of association is 'of central importance to the activities of human rights defenders', citing the Declaration on Human Rights Defenders, GA resolution 53/144 (8 March 1999): Moeckli *et al. International Human Rights Law*, p. 232.

[418] Article 2.4.

gatherings in public and private', including protests and counter-protests, while assemblies encompassed include 'political, economic, artistic, and social' gatherings.[419] Freedom of association, a linked but distinct concept, protects the right 'to form associations for common purposes, free from government interference'.[420] The rights are not unlimited: restrictions may be imposed on assembly and association under Article 21(2) and 22(2) of the ICCPR. In the case of ICERD, the major line of restriction stems from Article 4(b), while common restrictions found in other international standards are implicitly accepted by the Committee provided they do not involve racial discrimination.

It will be recalled that the Committee takes the view that the freedom set out in Article 5(d)(ix) does not extend to racist organizations; a position further elaborated in paragraph 21 of GR 35. Protection of the right to freedom of assembly and association remains as an issue in reservations linked to Article 4, particularly 4(b) which requires States parties to prohibit racist organizations and punish participation in them.

Article 5(d)(ix) is not further explicated in the CERD cases under Article 14, and is rarely referred to.[421] Practice normally takes the twin aspects of 5(d)(ix) together; the implicit racial or ethnic connections to engage the provisions of the Convention concern, as with other rights, the full span of groups under its protection. On 'peaceful' exercise of the right, rare references in concluding observations include the appeal to indigenous protesters in a dispute over natural resources 'to make their demands and hold their demonstrations in a peaceful manner, respecting the human rights of others'.[422] On the other side of the equation, the Committee has recommended that counter-terrorism legislation should not be applied to peaceful protest and legitimate assertions of rights.[423] Threats from public or private sources to human rights defenders, including defenders working for the elimination of racial discrimination, are a frequent subject of concern.[424] In one case, the State party was called upon to 'consider releasing those in detention for activities that would, under international standards, constitute the peaceful exercise' of rights.[425]

The link between the enjoyment of cultural rights and freedom of association also attracts comment. In the case of Greece, concern was expressed regarding the obstacles encountered by some ethnic groups in exercising this right, noting information 'on the forced dissolution and refusal to register some associations including words such as "minority", "Turkish" or "Macedonian"',[426] as well as the explanation for such refusal.[427]

419 *International Human Rights Law*, p. 234.

420 *Ibid.*, p. 231.

421 *Hagan v Australia*, paras 1, 3.1, 4.16.

422 Concluding observations on Peru, CERD/C/PER/CO/14-17, para. 15, thus reflecting a common restriction on the enjoyment of rights, respect for the rights and freedoms of others.

423 Concluding observations on Chile, CERD/C/CHL/CO/19-21, para. 14.

424 Concluding observations on Belarus, CERD/C/BLR/CO/18-19, para. 10; Bolivia, CERD/C/BOL/CO/17-20, para.19; Guatemala, CERD/C/GTM/CO/12-13, para. 9; Mexico, CERD/C/MEX/CO/16-17, para. 15. In the case of Guatemala, serious attacks, including murder of social activists and human rights defenders elicited a request for specific legislation to protect defenders, 'taking into consideration the Declaration on the Rights and Responsibility of Individuals, Groups and Organs of Society to Promote and Protect Universally Recognized Human Rights and Fundamental Freedoms'.

425 Concluding observations on Vietnam, CERD/C/VNM/CO/10-14, para. 17.

426 CERD/C/GRC/CO/19, para. 15 (2009). Compare *Sidiropoulos and Ors v Greece*, ECtHR, App. No. 26695/95 (1998); *United Macedonian Organization ILINDEN v Bulgaria*.

427 The explanations by Greece may be found in CERD/C/SR.1944 and 1945. See also comments by Thornberry, CERD/C/SR.1944, para. 46, and Diaconu, *ibid.*, paras 55–58.

Measures were accordingly recommended for the effective enjoyment 'by persons belonging to every community or group of their right to freedom of association and of their cultural rights'.[428] A recommendation to Libya suggested enhancement of the right of association 'for the protection and promotion of Amazigh culture' as among remedies for the denial of their linguistic and cultural identity.[429] Freedom of association is also stressed in relation to the right to work, bearing in mind questions of collective bargaining and trades unions in the labour market, and the concerns generated by the treatment of migrant workers.

Equally, political parties are encouraged to open their membership to ethnic minorities, or broaden their appeal to the diverse communities of the State; diversified political parties would satisfy criteria for the integrationist multiracial organizations referred to in Article 2 (1)(e). While political parties are regarded as vital to democratic processes, valorization does not extend to racist parties: the Committee regards their prohibition as an obligation under Article 4(b) and sundry aspects of Article 2.

[428] *Ibid.*
[429] CERD/C/64/CO/4, para. 15 (2004).

14. Article 5

Economic, Social, and Cultural Rights

In addition to specifying the economic, social, and cultural rights tabulated in Article 5, the Committee also makes generic endorsements of such rights to States parties. The data requested from States by the concluding observations of the Committee typically focuses on the extent to which economic, social, and cultural rights are enjoyed by groups or categories in the population, and includes requests for socio-economic statistics and indicators.[1] Other generic questions on this category of rights focus on whether special measures have been adopted and implemented to facilitate the enjoyment of rights;[2] whether the requisite documentation is available to particular groups in order to avail of economic, social, and cultural rights in practice—*de facto* and not merely *de jure*;[3] and whether structural forms of discrimination, including language barriers, impact negatively on the enjoyment of such rights.[4] Ratification of the International Covenant on Economic, Social and Cultural Rights (ICESCR) as among instruments which have a direct bearing on the issue of racial discrimination has been advocated by the Committee, as well as of instruments emanating from the International Labour Organization (ILO).[5] The effects of austerity[6] and economic and financial crises on the enjoyment of (primarily but not exclusively) economic, social, and cultural rights have been the subject of questioning and recommendations, as well as situations of poverty or extreme poverty affecting marginalized groups,[7] and the requisite poverty-reduction strategies.[8] These and other recommendations stress the linkages between poverty and racial discrimination,[9] identified as an

[1] Cyprus, CERD/C/CYP/CO/17-22, para. 19; Monaco, CERD/C/MCO/CO/6, para. 6; Rwanda, CERD/C/RWA/CO/13-17, para. 10.

[2] Sweden, CERD/C/SWE/CO/19-21, para. 20, regarding the Roma.

[3] Albania, CERD/C/ALB/CO/5-8, para. 14; Bosnia and Herzegovina, CERD/C/BIH/CO/7-8, para. 12; both recommendations concern access by Roma to necessary personal documents.

[4] Mauritius, CERD/C/MUS/CO/15-19, para. 20. See also concluding observations on Japan, where the impeding 'structure' is the military base on Okinawa, CERD/C/JPN/CO/3-6, para. 21, where the Committee 'reiterated the analysis of the Special Rapporteur on Contemporary Forms of Racism' that the 'disproportionate concentration of military bases in Okinawa [had] a negative impact on the residents' enjoyment of economic, social and cultural rights'.

[5] Fiji, CERD/C/FJI/CO/18-20, para. 17.

[6] The UK, CERD/C/GBR/CO/18-20, para. 13.

[7] Mexico was urged to take steps to eliminate historical and structural discrimination by adopting social inclusion policies to reduce inequality 'and the levels of poverty and extreme poverty' and fully guarantee the rights of 'all Mexicans, especially indigenous ones, to education, health, social security, housing, basic services and food, while respecting their cultural origins and consulting with the peoples who might be affected by such initiatives': CERD/C/MEX/CO/16-17, para. 18. Among many similar expressions of concern, see concluding observations on Rwanda, CERD/C/RWA/CO/13-17, para. 14; Vietnam, CERD/C/VNM/CO/10-14, para. 13. See also para. 34 of GR 27, referring to the incidence of 'extreme poverty' among Roma.

[8] Ecuador, CERD/C/ECU/20-22, para. 20; Kenya, CERD/C/KEN/CO/1-4, para. 23.

[9] See also concluding observations on Portugal, CERD/C/PRT/CO/12-14, para. 20. The Sustainable Development Goals are notable for linking a range of economic, social and cultural targets, including equality and non-discrimination, into the 2030 Agenda for Sustainable Development: A/RES/70/1, 21 October 2015.

'intersection'.[10] Observations in the preceding chapter also stress the interrelationships between economic, social, and cultural rights, and all other rights protected by the Convention.

5(e)(i) The Rights to Work, to Free Choice of Employment, to Just and Favourable Conditions of Work, to Protection Against Unemployment, to Equal Pay for Equal Work, to Just and Favourable Remuneration

The complex statement of rights reassembles and edits the main elements of Article 23 of the Universal Declaration of Human Rights (UDHR), absenting its references to social protection.[11] The UDHR provisions regarding work are significantly elaborated in the ICESCR, Articles 6–8, while Article 8 of the International Covenant on Civil and Political Rights (ICCPR) includes the prohibition of forced labour. Article 11 of the Convention on the Elimination of All Forms of Discrimination (CEDAW) outlines obligations on the elimination of discrimination against women in employment; the Convention on the Rights of Persons with Disabilities (CRPD) addresses non-discrimination, participation, and equality of opportunity in the area of work and employment; *inter alia*, the principle of reasonable accommodation is applied to the situation of persons with disabilities in the workplace.[12] The area of labour migration, the effects of and the reaction to which are standard situations of great concern to the Committee on the Elimination of Racial Discrimination (CERD), is regulated to a large degree by the Convention on Migrant Workers (CMW), while the ILO has been setting labour standards since the era of the League of Nations and is a regular interlocutor of the Committee; it is standard practice of the Committee to recommend ratification of the CMW, and relevant ILO instruments, under the general rubric of instruments that have a direct bearing on racial discrimination. On the citation of ILO instruments, CERD frequently recalls ILO 169 in connection with indigenous rights generally, and it is also an instrument that includes a section on 'recruitment and conditions of employment' of indigenous and tribal peoples; ILO Conventions 111 and, latterly, Convention 189 on decent work for domestic workers,[13] are also prominent, as well as ILO labour standards in general. General Comment (GC) 18 of the Committee on Economic, Social and

[10] Concluding observations on St Vincent and the Grenadines, CERD/C/63/CO/10, para. 10. The term 'intersection' is used loosely in this instance. In the author's understanding, 'intersection' signifies the recognition that two strands of identity, such as race/ethnicity and gender, inhere in one person. Comments of the Holy See on 'intersectionality' are discussed in Chapter 20.

[11] ICERD treats the right to form and join trade unions separately; the reference in Article 23(3) of the UDHR to remuneration to ensure 'an existence worthy of human dignity' is also absent, though dignity considerations inform the preamble to ICERD and the work of the Committee: the use of 'dignity' by the Committee is addressed principally in Chapter 5.

[12] Article 27 CRPD; general principles and obligations are set out in Articles 3 and 4 of the Convention; equality and non-discrimination is addressed by Article 5. Regional standards on the right to work include Article 15 of the ACHPR, Articles 6 and 7 of the Additional Protocol to the ACHR on Economic, Social and Cultural Rights; Article 34 of the Arab Charter; and Articles 1, 2, and 3, of the European Social Charter (Revised), which contains sundry further measures with regard to rights of workers.

[13] Concluding observations on Cyprus, CERD/C/CYP/CO/17-22, para. 21; Jordan, CERD/C/JOR/CO/13-17, para. 14; Kuwait, CERD/C/KUW/CO/15-20, para. 16; Qatar, CERD/C/QAT/CO/13-16, para. 13; Russian Federation, CERD/C/RUS/CO/20-22, para. 22.

Cultural Rights (CESCR) elaborates the right to work under Article 6 of the ICESCR, interpreting it as both a collective and an individual right—'to decide freely to accept or choose work'—further specified as 'decent work';[14] the collective element is primarily related to the role of trade unions.[15] The CESCR identifies the 'core obligation' of Article 6 ICESCR as 'to ensure non-discrimination and equal protection of employment'.[16]

There is no reservation specific to this sub-paragraph, though more wide-ranging reservations regarding admission of non-citizens may have repercussions on the labour market. Guidelines suggest that reports should, for example, '(a) indicate whether persons belonging to groups protected under the Convention are over- or underrepresented in certain professions or activities, and in unemployment; and (b) describe governmental action to prevent racial discrimination in the enjoyment of the right to work'.[17] In order to follow the guidance regarding representation of groups in the labour market, the existence of adequate data is a significant consideration, and its absence will be subject to the critique that an effective anti-discrimination policy cannot be pursued without it. Data requirements apply across the board regarding employment and unemployment, including but not limited to the case of migrant workers.[18] Statistical profiles may suggest that discrimination functions as a structuring factor in the jobs market, the composition of workforces, and registers of the unemployed.

The CERD-specific reporting guidelines intimate the basic requirement that access to the labour market needs to be established in a non-discriminatory fashion: the right to work applies across the spectrum of groups under the protection of the Convention.[19] Labour codes should also reflect this obligation by adopting legislation that includes provisions to combat indirect as well as direct discrimination, and by amending legislation that did not offer protection to domestic—usually foreign—workers;[20] labour code provisions should also ensure that contracts of employment are provided in the languages of migrant workers.[21] Additional to improving the quality of legislation and recognizing and dismantling 'formal' legal barriers to participation in employment, holistic approaches have been recommended that include awareness-raising in order to tackle racial prejudices and stereotypes, and measures to promote a 'change of mindset among employers'.[22] A potential barrier to access to employment opportunities is referred to in General Recommendation (GR) 29 whereby the States parties are recommended to take measures 'against public bodies, private companies and other associations that investigate the descent background of applicants for employment'.[23]

Training and apprenticeship programmes to facilitate access to the labour market have also been recommended by the Committee, including but not limited to members of Roma and descent-based communities, for which special measures are called for by GR 27

[14] Paras 6 and 7.

[15] Paras 2, 51, and 54 in particular.

[16] Para. 31.

[17] CERD/C/2007/1, Article 5, I, E 1.

[18] Concluding observations on Qatar, CERD/C/QAT/CO/13-16, para. 9.

[19] Concluding observations on Korea make clear that the right equally applies to refugees and asylum-seekers: CERD/C/KOR/CO/15-16, para. 13.

[20] *Ibid.*

[21] *Ibid.*, para. 12; also concluding observations on Kuwait, CERD/C/KWT/CO/15-20, para. 16.

[22] Concluding observations on Denmark, CERD/C/DNK/CO/18-19, para. 11

[23] Para. (ll).

and GR 29 in relation to employment;[24] in this last respect, India was recommended to extend job reservation policies in order to enhance the access of Dalits to the labour market,[25] a recommendation that also relates to Articles 1(4) and 2(2) on special measures. The prohibition of racial discrimination applies at the various stages of the employment process, including the termination of employment as well as access to employment and conditions of employment. In *Yilmaz-Dogan v The Netherlands*, the failure of the authorities in The Netherlands to address the issue of racial discrimination adequately in a letter of an employer terminating a contract meant that the applicant's right to work under Article 5(e)(i) 'was not protected.[26] Other employment cases under Article 14 have not been as successful, either because of failure to substantiate racial discrimination,[27] or because of defects with regard to the procedural requirements of ICERD.[28]

In terms of specific employment-related practices, CERD has expressed concern regarding bonded labour and child labour,[29] including in the context of situations where 'very large numbers of Dalits' were forced to work 'as manual scavengers and child workers . . . subject to extremely unhealthy working conditions and exploitative labour arrangements, including debt bondage'.[30] Reports of other practices of forced labour have also raised concern. In the case of the indigenous communities of the Chaco in Paraguay, CERD recommended intensification of efforts 'to prevent, investigate and duly prosecute cases of forced labour and to guarantee that the communities concerned have access to justice'; a plan of action involving a raising of awareness and a labour inspectorate was also recommended.[31] In the case of the Guaraní people of Bolivia, sensitization of the general public to issues of forced labour and servitude was recommended in the context of a broader preference for a national development plan to address their needs.[32]

The situation of domestic workers in the context of migration has been extensively addressed in practice. Cyprus was recommended to amend standard contracts of employment in order, *inter alia*, 'to prevent forced labour', supporting in this and other respects the recommendations in the 2013 report of the Ombudsman.[33] In many such cases, double discrimination against female workers—gender and national origin combined—animates the recommendations, even if the connections are not explicitly made.[34] ILO

[24] Paras 29 and (jj), respectively.

[25] CERD/C/IND/CO/19, para. 23.

[26] CERD/C/36/D/1/1984 (1988), para. 9.3. See also *L.G. v Republic of Korea*, CERD/C/86/D/511/2012 (2015), discussed in detail in Chapter 7.

[27] *Z.U.B.S. v Australia*, CERD/C/55/D/6/1995 (1999), where domestic procedures had assessed the case and were applied 'in a thorough and equitable manner' (para. 9.3); *B.M.S. v Australia*, CERD/C/54/D/81996 (1999), no discrimination in light of the fact that all overseas trained doctors were subject to the same quota system.

[28] *D.S. v Sweden*, CERD/C/53/D/9/1997 (1998); *Barbaro v Australia*, CERD/C/57/D/121998 (2000), failure to exhaust domestic remedies.

[29] Concluding observations on Nepal, CERD/C/64/CO/5, para. 18; Pakistan, CERD/C/PAK/CO/20, para. 21, where the State party was urged to 'intensify its efforts to implement the laws and programmes adopted to put an end to bonded labour and discrimination against marginalized groups such as the scheduled castes', and *inter alia*, to continue cooperation with the ILO in combating this phenomenon.

[30] CERD/C/IND/CO/19, para. 23.

[31] CERD/C/PRY/CO/1-3, para. 16.

[32] CERD/C/BOL/CO/17-20, para. 18.

[33] CERD/C/CYP/CO/17-22, para. 21.

[34] Concluding observations on Qatar, CERD/C/QAT/CO/13-16, para. 14, make the gender dimensions of domestic work explicit, in recalling GR 25 and strongly urging the State party to 'put in place effective measures to address multiple discrimination against female domestic workers including in their place of work'.

standards and practice have been highly influential in framing the Committee's observations, up to the point of recommending cooperation or continued cooperation between the State party and the agency to address employment and labour problems. Issues of trafficking of persons may also be connected with labour issues, including forced labour.[35]

For many groups or categories, notably including migrant workers, caste groups, and Roma, recommendations have combined issues of discrimination in employment with discrimination in housing, health, and education, intimating the systemic nature of racial discrimination as it moves across an unconfined spectrum of human rights, deprivation in one area leading to deprivation in another.

5(e)(ii) The Right to Form and Join Trade Unions

Brief references are made in the preceding chapter to trade unions in the context of freedom of association, discussed in Chapter 13. Background standards on trade unions include Article 23 of the UDHR on rights to work and employment, which includes an independent right (23(4)) to form and join trade unions, as does Article 22 of the ICCPR in the context of freedom of association.[36] Article 8 of the ICESCR provides for 'the right of everyone to form trade unions' for the promotion of their social and economic interests, as well as the right of such unions to federate and to 'function freely subject to no limitations other than those prescribed by law and which are necessary in a democratic society in the interests of national security or public order or for the protection of the rights and freedoms of others';[37] the article also provides for the right to strike, 'provided that it is exercised in conformity with the laws of the particular country'.[38] More extensive protection of trade union rights is offered by instruments of the ILO.[39] Reporting guidelines suggest that information should be provided on two main issues: the opening of trade unions to non-citizens, and 'whether the right to form and join trade unions is restricted for specific professions or for specific types of contract'—situations where persons belonging to groups protected under the Convention may be over-represented.[40]

There is little Committee practice regarding trade unions. Concern was expressed over the poverty and social exclusion endured by the Maya Quiche indigenous people, which adversely affected the enjoyment of rights including the right to form and join trade

[35] See the discussion in the present work of Article 5(b).

[36] Article 22(1); para. 3 of the article provides that nothing therein shall authorize States parties to the ILO Convention on 1948 on Freedom of Association and Protection of the Right to Organize, 'to take legislative measures which would prejudice, or to apply the law in a manner such as to prejudice, the guarantees provided for in that Convention'.

[37] Article 8(1)(c). Regional standards include Article 8 of the Additional Protocol to the ACHR on Economic, Social and Cultural Rights, Article 35 of the Arab Charter, and Article 6 of the Revised European Social Charter (the right to bargain collectively).

[38] 8(1)(d). For the ICCPR, the Human Rights Committee held that the Convention does not include a right to strike: *J.B. et al. v Canada*, No. 118/82 (1986). See further, S. Joseph and M. Castan, *The International Covenant on Civil and Political Rights: Cases, Materials and Commentary* (3rd edn, Oxford University Press, 2013), pp. 657–61; the authors, p. 661, point out more recent critical observations by the Human Rights Committee on restrictions on the right to strike as evidence of a possible 'change of heart' by the Committee.

[39] Notably the Convention on The Right to Organize 1948 (No. 87), and The Right to Organize and Collective bargaining Convention 1949 (No. 98).

[40] CERD/C/2007/1, p. 11.

unions.[41] In the case of Denmark, 'employers and trade unions' were among those listed as appropriate addressees for the better dissemination of the Convention.[42] The most extensive comment regarding trade unions emanates from concluding observations on Korea, when concern was expressed about information that 'migrant workers, especially those who become undocumented, cannot enjoy their right to organize and join a labour union, and that some union executive members have been expelled'; the States party was urged 'to guarantee the right of all persons to form and join trade unions freely';[43] CERD declared that it fully shared the equivalent recommendations of the CESCR.[44]

5(e)(iii) The Right to Housing

The right to housing, or 'the right to adequate housing', broadly interpreted by the CESCR as 'the right to live somewhere in security, peace and dignity',[45] is widely cited in international instruments either as a stand-alone right or as connected to the right to an adequate standard of living—as in the UDHR and the ICESCR.[46] In general instruments, housing appears in CEDAW,[47] the CRC,[48] the CMW,[49] and the CRPD.[50] Other instruments to refer to the right include the UNDRIP, Articles 21 and 23. 'Adequacy' is defined by the CESCR in terms of seven factors: legal security of tenure, availability of services, affordability, habitability, accessibility, location, and cultural adequacy; housing construction, materials, and supporting policies 'must appropriately enable the expression of cultural identity'.[51]

[41] A/50/18, para. 310.

[42] CERD/C/304/Add. 93, para. 14.

[43] CERD/C/KOR/CO/15-16, para. 11.

[44] E/C.12/KOR/CO/3, para. 19 of which drew attention to constitutional restrictions on the rights of public officials to join trade unions, and that trade unions in private and public universities were prohibited by law. The CESCR in turn endorsed 2001 comments made in by the ILO Committee of Experts on the situation. The CESCR took the view that the restrictions were 'in direct contravention' of Article 8 ICESCR.

[45] CESCR GC 4, 'The Right to Adequate Housing' (1991), para.7. See also GC 7 (1997), on forced evictions. See the detailed discussion of the work of the CESCR in B. Saul, D. Kinley, and J. Mowbray, *The International Covenant on Economic, Social and Cultural Rights: Commentary, Cases, and Materials* (Oxford University Press, 2014), pp. 926–76, under 'The Right to an Adequate Standard of Living' [henceforth Saul *et al.*, *The International Covenant on Economic, Social and Cultural Rights*].

[46] Articles 25 and 11, respectively. Article 11 of the ICESCR, inter alia, recognizes 'the right of everyone to an adequate standard of living... including adequate food, clothing and housing, and to the continuous improvement of living conditions'. See also Article 38 of the Arab Charter on Human Rights.

[47] Article 14.

[48] Article 27.

[49] Article 43(1)(d).

[50] Articles 9 and 28. The major regional human rights instruments instruments protect the right to housing as deriving from other rights such as privacy and property; in *Social and Economic Rights Action Centre (SERAC) v Nigeria*, decided in 2001, the African Commisson on Human and Peoples' Rights read the rights to property, health, and family life together to 'forbid the wanton destruction of shelter': <http://www.chr.up.ac.za/index.php/browse-by-subject/410-nigeria-social-and-economic-rights-action-centre-serac-and-another-v-ni>. The Revised European Social Charter is exceptional in making explicit reference to the right in Article 31: see European Committee on Social Rights, *FEANTSA v France*, Complaint No. 39/2006 (2007). In 2000, the Commission on Human Rights set up the position of Special Rapporteur on Adequate Housing as a component of the Right to an Adequate Standard of Living: Commission on Human Rights resolution 2000/9, 17 April 2000; for the development of the mandate and the work of the Special Rapporteur, see: <http://www.ohchr.org/EN/Issues/Housing/Pages/HousingIndex.aspx>.

[51] GC 4, para. 8.

Reporting guidelines on Article 5 offer examples to assist in determining levels of implementation. States parties should '(a) indicate whether groups of victims or potential victims of racial discrimination are concentrated in particular sectors or tend to concentrate in particular localities; (b) describe governmental action to prevent racial discrimination by those who rent or sell houses or apartments; and (c) describe measures taken to implement the right to housing of nomadic or semi-nomadic people, with full respect for their cultural identity'.[52]

Some aspects of the right are discussed in the present work in relation to Article 3 on segregation.[53] The issue of segregation is addressed in GR 27 on the Roma. GR 29 on descent-based discrimination makes similar provision regarding the avoidance of segregation,[54] and on 'access to adequate housing'.[55] In GR 30, the basic stipulations are adapted to non-citizens.[56] Indigenous peoples strongly figure in recommendations on housing, and also people of African descent: GR 34 advocates the development and implementation of policies and projects aimed at avoiding the segregation of people of African descent in housing, and the involvement of 'communities of people of African descent as partners in housing project construction, rehabilitation and maintenance'.[57] The right intersects with a range of other rights that are necessary to sustain it in practice, including, among rights listed in Article 5, freedom of residence and of association, the rights to own property, to participate in decision-making, and to security of the person. The importance of the right to housing for the enjoyment of other rights has been underlined by the Committee.[58]

The Committee's opinion in *L.R. v Slovakia*[59] addressed and found a violation of 5(e)(iii) along with other articles. In the case, councillors in a municipality adopted a resolution approving a plan to construct low-cost housing which was later revoked by a second resolution following a petition by local inhabitants who objected that the plan would lead 'to an influx of inadaptable citizens of Gypsy origin'.[60] While the impugned resolutions did not on their face refer to Roma, the Committee found indirect discrimination in light of the context and circumstances of the resolutions.[61] In relation to Article 5, petitioners contended that the State party had failed to safeguard the right of the petitioners to adequate housing; reference is made in the opinion to Roma living in appalling conditions, 'with most dwellings comprising thatched huts or houses made of cardboard and without drinking water, toilets, or drainage or sewage systems'.[62] While much of the argument in the case related to the legal nature of the municipalities as public bodies, petitioners argued in relation to the disputed status of a 'right to housing' in

[52] CERD/C/2007/1, p. 11.
[53] See Chapter 10.
[54] GR 29, para. (o).
[55] *Ibid.*, para. (mm).
[56] GR 30, para. 32.
[57] Para. 60.
[58] With regard to the Roma, the Committee recommended that Slovakia 'strengthen its measures aimed at ameliorating the housing conditions of the Roma in view of the importance of such conditions for their enjoyment of other rights enshrined in the Convention': CERD/C/SVK/CO/6-8, para. 17.
[59] CERD/C/66/D/31/2003 (2005); see further discussion in Chapter 8.
[60] *L.R. v Slovakia*, para. 2.2. The State party challenged this construction of the nature of the original resolution, para. 7.6. See also para. 7.7, and 7.8.
[61] *Ibid.*, para. 10.4.
[62] *Ibid.*, para. 2.1.

Slovak law, that when a State party confers a benefit that it may not have had the obligation to confer, such a benefit cannot be conferred in a discriminatory fashion.[63] The State party argued on the other hand that the municipal council's resolution did not confer an enforceable right to housing but amounted to one step in a complex process of policy development in the field of housing. The implication of this argument was 'that the second resolution of the council, even if motivated by ethnic grounds . . . did not amount to a [discriminatory] measure'.[64] In rejecting the argument of the State party, the Committee treated the sequence of Council resolutions together, finding that a right to housing protected by Article 5 and by Article 11 of the ICESCR existed in Slovak law and that this right had been impaired.[65] The parameters of the right would presumably be illuminated by reference to Article 11 of the ICESCR in light of the severe conditions of deprivation described in the statement of facts by the petitioners.[66] The case suggests some of the problems stemming from policy initiatives to influence the composition of neighbourhoods. In the case of Germany, attempts to create socially stable residential structures and balanced housing estates by permitting landlords to refuse to rent apartments came under scrutiny for 'possible negative effects in terms of indirect discrimination'.[67] More widely, Khaliq and Churchill read *L.R. v Slovakia* to mean that that States parties 'must ensure that the implementation of a policy related to any substantive right must be adopted and implemented in a manner that does not discriminate on the grounds prohibited in Article 1'; further, the 'approach adopted by the . . . Committee has significant consequences for States parties, and the obligation, if taken seriously, should prove effective in seeking to ensure that discriminatory intent is removed in the context of economic and social rights'.[68]

Housing discrimination or potential discrimination against a broad spectrum of groups of victims represents a consistent concern, including against 'vulnerable groups, such as non-nationals, refugees and asylum-seekers'[69] and undocumented migrants.[70] In many instances, the condition of housing is only one element in situations characterized by poor living conditions overall: conditions in detention and reception centres for migrants and asylum-seekers have also been subject to critical evaluations.[71] Violations of the right to

[63] *Ibid.*, para. 5.5; the petitioners cited the *Belgian Linguistics* case before the ECHR as authority for this proposition, as well as the supplementary principle, *ibid.*, para. 8.4, that 'having decided to implement a certain measure—in this case to pursue the housing scheme—a State party cannot later decide not to implement it and base itself on discriminatory considerations'. See ECtHR, *Case relating to Certain Aspects of the Laws on the Use of Languages in Education in Belgium*, App. Nos. 1474/62, 1677/62, 1691/62, 1769/63, 1994/63, 2126/64 (1968).

[64] *L.R. v Slovakia*, para. 10.6.

[65] *Ibid.*, para. 10.7; the paragraph is more fully cited in Chapter 8.

[66] Paras. 2.1, 5.4, and 5,5. Information regarding the follow-up to the communication is set out in A/62/18, Annex VI (2007). The dialogue between the State party and the Committee was reported in 2008, A/63/18, Annex VII. In concluding observations in 2010, the Committee noted the delegation's assurances that the State party was committed to follow up the recommendations in *L.R. v Slovakia*: CERD/C/SVK/CO/6-8, para. 20.

[67] CERD/C/DEU/CO/18, para. 17.

[68] U. Khaliq and R. Churchill, 'The Protection of Economic and Social Rights: A Particular Challenge?' in H. Keller and G. Ulfstein (eds), *UN Human Rights Treaty Bodies: Law and Legitimacy* (Cambridge University Press, 2012), pp. 199–260, p. 240 [henceforth 'The Protection of Economic and Social Rights'].

[69] Potential discrimination on the part of housing agencies was highlighted against such groups in the case of Luxembourg: CERD/C/LUX/CO/13, para. 17.

[70] Concluding observations on Hungary, CERD/C/61/CO/6, para. 14.

[71] Concluding observations on Malta, CERD/C/MLT/CO/15-20, para. 13; Spain, CERD/C/ESP/CO/18-20, para. 13.

housing of Roma have been consistently highlighted in practice. Regarding the Roma and Travellers, GR 27 makes a series of statements on the exigencies of housing policy. In addition to expressing concern on segregation of communities,[72] firm action is recommended against a series of potential actions in the field of housing on the part of public and private authorities, including denial of residence and engaging in unlawful expulsions of Roma, or placing them in camps outside population areas which are without access to health care and other facilities.[73] Bearing in mind also that some Roma practise a travelling lifestyle, it is also recommended that camping places 'with all necessary facilities' should be provided.[74] In concluding observations on the United Kingdom with regard to evictions of the Gypsy and Traveller community at Dale Farm, the Committee recommended that 'alternative culturally appropriate accommodation' be provided to the community before any evictions were carried out.[75] The Committee has, *inter alia*, urged that the resettlement of Roma should not involve forced evictions, and that 'procedural protections which respect due process and human dignity be put in place';[76] considerations of 'dignity' were similarly invoked in relation to the Dale Farm expulsions in the UK.[77]

The problem of forced evictions figures prominently in the CERD archives. The practice of forced eviction is defined by the CESCR as 'the permanent or temporary removal against their will of individuals, families and/or communities from the homes and/or land which they occupy, without the provision of, and access to, appropriate forms of legal protection',[78] a protection that is, in the view of the CESCR, to be applied immediately and is not subject to 'progressive development'.[79] Categorizing practices as violations of 'the right to housing' may be adequate to capture the essence of some cases of dispossession;[80] other violations may be connected with policies as extreme as 'ethnic cleansing' for which the standard rights vocabulary may be necessary but hardly sufficient to reflect the scale of damage caused. Practices of large-scale dispossession and displacement, eviction and segregation are among factors to trigger the Committee's early warning/urgent action procedure[81] and are prominent in its 'indicators of patterns of systematic and massive racial discrimination'.[82] As will be gathered from references in

[72] GR 27, para. 30.

[73] *Ibid.*, para. 31.

[74] *Ibid.*, para. 32.

[75] CERD/C/GBR/CO/18-20, para. 28 (2011). Compare the concept of 'cultural adequacy' in relation to housing set out in CESCR General Comment No. 4, 'The Right to Adequate Housing', para. 8 (1991).

[76] Concluding observations on Serbia, CERD/C/SRB/CO/1, para. 14.

[77] CERD/C/GBR/CO/18-20, para. 28.

[78] CESCR General Comment No. 7: The Right to Adequate Housing (Article 11.1): Forced Evictions, para. 3 (1997).

[79] *Ibid.*, para. 8.

[80] As an example of a more serious construction placed on a violation of housing rights, see Committee against Torture, *Hajrizi Dzemajl v Serbia and Montenegro*, CAT/C/29/D/161/2000 (2002), a case arising from a mass attack on a Roma settlement, where the Committee found a violation of Article 16 of the CAT which deals with 'cruel, inhuman or degrading treatment'; individual opinions in the case construed the attack as amounting to torture. See also *Sesana et al v Attorney-General*, Botswana High Court 2006, where elements in the action taken against the Basarwa indigenous people were in violation of the constitutionally protected right to life: <http://www.chr.up.ac.za/index.php/browse-by-country/botswana/1118.html>; see also *Mosetlhanyana v Attorney General*: <https://www.escr-net.org/docs/i/1620112>, Botswana Court of Appeal at Lobatse (2011).

[81] A/62/18, Annex III (2007).

[82] CERD/C/67/1 (2005).

sundry CERD general recommendations, all the 'standard' victim groups under ICERD are represented in the melancholy catalogue of forced evictions and dispossessions.[83]

'Eviction' has been employed by the Committee in relation to housing/accommodation in the narrow sense but also to expulsion from lands and territories; in such cases, the primary legal reference point, when identified by the Committee, may be the right to property—Article 5(d)(v)—overlapping with 5(e)(iii). Many cases of large-scale dispossessions or relocations identified by the Committee have involved indigenous peoples. Background international standards—and decisions—on indigenous peoples assist the Committee to refine the categorization of relevant norms and procedures to be observed in eviction cases and may be specifically cited.[84] Guatemala was advised that, in exceptional cases in which the relocation of indigenous peoples is considered necessary, it must ensure the observance of Article 16(2) of ILO Convention 169 and Article 10 of the UNDRIP, 'which require free and informed consent and fair and equitable compensation' and provide relocation sites equipped with basic utilities.[85] Similar recommendations were made to Argentina in terms of appropriate mechanisms and procedures to be followed, including consultation with a view to obtaining consent, compensation, and adequately equipped relocation sites, as well as punishment for those who violate legal norms.[86] With regard to Israel, concern was expressed in relation to Bedouin communities 'particularly with regard to the policy of demolitions, notably of homes and other structures' as well as access to land, housing, education, and other rights on a basis of equality with Jewish inhabitants; the State party was recommended, *inter alia*, to withdraw a proposed law on Bedouin settlement in the Negev, 'which would legalize the ongoing policy of home demolitions and forced displacement of the indigenous Bedouin communities'.[87]

The follow-up to natural disasters has also prompted recommendations under the sub-paragraph. In the case of the US, concern was expressed regarding the disparate impact caused by Hurricane Katrina in 2005 on 'low-income African American residents' many of whom continued to be displaced two years after the event. The ensuing recommendation combines a number of CERD preoccupations: facilitation of the return of displaced persons to their homes, 'or to guarantee access to adequate and affordable housing, where possible in their place of habitual residence'. The State party was also called upon to make every effort 'to ensure genuine consultation and participation of persons displaced . . . in the design and implementation of all decisions affecting them'.[88]

[83] ECHR eviction cases involving Roma and Travellers include *Buckley v UK*, App. No. 20348/92 (1996); *Chapman v UK*, App. No. 27238/95 (2001); *Connors v UK*, App. No. 66746/01 (2004); *Yordanova v Bulgaria*, App. No. 25446/06 (2012); *Winterstein v France*, App. No. 27013/07 (2013).

[84] Thus, Kenya was urged to respond to the decisions of the African Commission on Human and Peoples Rights with respect to the forced evictions of the Endorois and Ogiek peoples from their lands 'and to ensure that all marginalized communities and peoples involved are provided with redress as ordered': CERD/C/KEN/CO/1-4, para. 17. See comment on the *Endorois v Kenya*, and *COHRE v Sudan* in Chapter 13; other cases cited there such as Indigenous Community of *Yakye Axa v Paraguay*, IACtHR Ser. C No. 125 (2005), and *Sawhoyamaxa v Paraguay*, IACtHR Ser. C No. 146 (2006) have clear implications in relation to the right under discussion.

[85] CERD/C/GTM/CO/12-13, para. 11, brought under Article 5(d) (v).

[86] CERD/C/ARG/CO/19-20, para. 26.

[87] CERD/C/ISR/CO/14-16, para. 20; the Committee did not identify a specific paragraph on which the conclusion is based.

[88] CERD/C/USA/CO/6, para. 31.

5(e)(iv) The Right to Public Health, Medical Care, Social Security, and Social Services

The statement of protected rights in this sub-paragraph conflates rights listed separately in Articles 22 and 25 of the UDHR (social security and health, respectively), and Articles 9 and 12 of the ICESCR (social security, health).[89] GCs on health (GC 14) and social security (GC 19) have been adopted by the CESCR.[90] As articulated by the CESCR, the right to 'the highest attainable standard of physical and mental health' is interpreted as a rights complex embracing a 'wide range of socio-economic factors that promote conditions in which people can lead a healthy life' including food, nutrition and sanitation, housing and work conditions and a healthy environment.[91] The right is also visualized as 'related to and dependent upon the realization' of a range of other human rights',[92] and is understood as 'a right to the enjoyment of a variety of facilities, goods, services and conditions necessary for the realization' of the highest attainable standard of health.[93] The right to social security, on the other hand, is understood as the right to maintain benefits in order to secure protection form such as a lack of work-related income on account of sickness, disability, etc, or because of unaffordable healthcare or insufficient family support.[94]

CERD reporting guidelines commence with the assertion that '[d]ifferent groups of victims or potential victims of racial discrimination within the population may have different needs for health and social services.' Accordingly, 'States parties should (a) describe any such differences and (b) describe governmental action to secure the equal provision of these services.'[95]

CERD has not fully elaborated its understanding of the rights in 5(e)(iv), though group-related general recommendations (GR 27 on gender, GR 29 on descent-based discrimination, and GR 34 on racial discrimination against People of African Descent) include references to health and social security: in the case of the Roma, and descent/caste-

[89] Also Article 10(2).

[90] On the right to social security, see also Articles 11(1)(e) and 14(2)(c) of CEDAW; Article 26 of the CRC; and Article 61 of the CMW. Among regional instruments, the American Declaration on the Rights and Duties of Man, Articles 16 and 35, make reference to social security, as does Article 9 of the Additional Protocol to the Inter-American Convention on Human Rights in the area of Economic, Social and Cultural Rights, and Article 12 of the European Social Charter (Revised). With regard to health, the SIM human rights database lists 100 references, a number of which are not articulations of the right to health but a restriction on rights on grounds of 'public health'. Leading references to the rights include Article 12 of CEDAW and Article 24 of the CRC (also Article 3); Articles 22, 25, and 26 of the CRPD, and a number of the Convention on Migrant Workers, notably Articles 43 and 45. The right is listed extensively among regional instruments that include the ACHPR, Articles 16 and 18, and its protocol on the rights of women in Africa (Article 1), and the African Charter on Rights and Welfare of the Child (Article 20), as well as the American Declaration on the Rights and Duties of Man (Article 11) and its Protocol on Economic, Social and Cultural Rights (Article 10); Article 11 of the Revised European Social Charter enshrines 'the right to protection of health'. The African Charter on the Rights and Welfare of the child is notable to including a health provision in Article 21 on protection from harmful social or cultural practices.

[91] General Comment No. 14, *The Right to the Highest Attainable Standard of Health*, E/C.12/2000/4, para. 4.

[92] *Ibid.*, para. 3.

[93] *Ibid.*, para. 9. The work of the CESCR and other bodies is complemented by the work of the Special Rapporteur on the Right of Everyone to the Enjoyment of the Highest Attainable Standard of Physical and Mental Health: <http://www.ohchr.org/EN/Issues/Health/Pages/SRRightHealthIndex.aspx>.

[94] General Comment No. 19, *The Right to Social Security*, E/C.12/GC/19 (2008), para. 2.

[95] CERD/C/2007/1, p. 11.

based communities, particular emphasis has been placed on equal access to the goods of healthcare and social security and the involvement of affected communities in the design and implementation of programmes and projects.[96] To this basic arrangement, GR 27 adds a recommendation with regard to Roma—'mainly women and children'—to focus on 'their disadvantaged situation due to extreme poverty and low level of education, as well as to cultural differences',[97] a concern taken forward to the assertion in guidelines regarding differences in needs.[98] In practice, all the groups within the purview of the Convention are brought within the remit of the sub-paragraph, including minorities, indigenous peoples, descent-based communities, sundry categories of non-citizens that include refugees, and internally displaced persons (IDPs); there is also a strong inter-sectional element in many recommendations that refer to the position of women. Cases involving women belonging to Roma communities and indigenous women have generated recommendations from the Committee with regard to practices of forced sterilization.[99]

Decisions under the communications procedure have rarely addressed the sub-paragraph: the issue of access to social security benefits raised in *D.F. v Australia* in connection with a claim of discrimination on the basis of national origin was not sustained by the Committee.[100] More substantially, despite the finding of inadmissibility, the case of *Kenneth Moylan v Australia*, based generally on Articles 2(2), 5, and 6, made use of 5(e)(iv).[101] The petitioner, an Aboriginal Australian man, claimed that, in light of the lower life expectancy for Aboriginal Australians, he should have been able to access an age pension under the Social Security Act at a lower age than that set for Australians generally, between 65 and 67 years of age.[102] Special measures, he argued, were mandated by the Convention in order to close the gap between indigenous Australians and others.[103] In response, the State Party offered a narrow interpretation of 5(e)(iv), arguing that the enjoyment of the age pension, 'as distinct from social security more generally', was not required to fulfil the obligations under the Convention, and that Australian social security law was not directly or indirectly discriminatory.[104] Further, given that 5(e)(iv) 'requires the equal and not universal enjoyment of social security', the State party was entitled to set criteria to determine when social security should be available' in order to target those most in need.[105]

[96] GR 27, paras 33 and 34; GR 29, (nn) and (oo); GR 34, paras 55 and 56.

[97] GR 27, para. 34: the syntax of the sentence suggests that Roma disadvantage, etc, is community-wide; see also GR 25 on gender-related dimensions of racial discrimination, para. 2.

[98] Later recommendations concerning health issues of Roma include those on Albania, CERD/C/ALB/CO/5-8, para. 11; Bosnia and Herzegovina, CERD/C/BIH/CO/7-8, para. 12; Slovenia, CERD/C/SVN/CO/6-7, para. 10; and the UK, CERD/C/GBR/CO/18-20, para. 27 (Gypsies and Travellers).

[99] Concluding observations on Mexico, CERD/C/MEX/CO/15, para. 17; on Slovakia, CERD/C/SVK/CO/9-10, para. 13; and Vietnam, CERD/C/304/Add.127, para. 10.

[100] CERD/C/72/D/39/2006 (2008).

[101] CERD/C/83/D/D/47/2010 (2013), discussed in relation to special measures, Chapter 9.

[102] *Inter alia*, the petitioner cited GC19 of the CESCR on the right to social security, 'where it is stated that differences in the average life expectancy of men and women can also lead directly or indirectly to discrimination in the provision of benefits': *Moylan*, para. 3.2.

[103] The State party and then petitioner made extensive references to CERD GR 32 on special measures.

[104] *Moylan*, para. 4.10.

[105] *Ibid.*, para. 4.11. The petitioner disputed most aspects of the interpretation by the State party, claiming, *inter alia*, that in light of the objectively different situation of Aboriginal Australians compared to the rest of the population, mere *de jure* equality was not enough, and steps taken to address indirect discrimination would provide for equal enjoyment of the rights in question: para. 5.9.

As previously noted, the case was declared inadmissible for failure to exhaust domestic remedies, 'without prejudice to the question . . . regarding the alleged structural discrimination related to pension entitlements'.[106] In terms of Article 5, the case raises questions of the latitude in interpreting 'social security', the range of rights protected by Article 5, and in particular whether the article points, through its guarantee of equality, to substantive obligations to secure basic rights. The Committee's cautious recall of the claim regarding structural discrimination may suggest that while it was perhaps too much to expect a wholesale revision of the pension system, there was a strong case for enhanced measures to address the perceived disparities in health and life expectancy.

Reference to the sub-paragraph is often generic, repeating its formulation without a separation into constituent elements. Where elements are individuated, recommendations in the area of social security are overwhelmingly directed to the question of access and the removal of obstacles thereto such as the non-availability of appropriate personal documents[107] or other administrative hurdles to enjoying the benefits of the system such as burdensome registration systems:[108] the burdens placed members of affected groups in this respect run across the span of economic, social, and cultural rights.

Inferior access to health services and the incidence of poor health and life expectancy among minorities and indigenous peoples are regrettably frequent subjects of situations brought to the attention of the Committee. Health issues are the most commonly individuated aspects of the compound right in 5(e)(iv), including reproductive and sexual health,[109] and HIV/AIDS, testing for which should 'not infringe the principle of non-discrimination'.[110] The Committee constantly presses for the reduction of health disparities through programmes of special measures where necessary.[111] The incidence of specific conditions such as malaria and cholera have been referred to, the former in the context of environmental pollution and mercury contamination linked to mining activities affecting indigenous peoples.[112]

Health issues may also be subsumed under generalized concerns regarding environmental degradation affecting the lives of indigenous peoples and others.[113] In the case of the Western Shoshone, the Committee, basing itself on information regarding the prospective opening of a nuclear waste repository, open-pit gold mining activities, and the alleged issuance of geothermal energy leases on areas of spiritual and cultural

[106] *Ibid.*, para. 6.6. See Chapter 9.

[107] Concluding observations on Albania, CERD/C/ALB/CO/5-8, para. 14.

[108] Concluding observations on China, CERD/C/CHN/CO/13, para. 14.

[109] Detailed recommendations on sexual and reproductive health have been made to, among others, the USA: CERD/C/CO/6/Add.1, para. 33; and India, CERD/C/IND/CO/19, para. 24.

[110] Concluding observations on Moldova, CERD/C/MDA/CO/8-9, para. 13: the concluding observations relate to the 'deep concern' of the Committee that non-citizens were subjected to mandatory HIV/AIDS testing and could not take up residence in the State party if the test proved positive. See also *L.G. v Korea*, discussed in Chapter 7, where the Committee found that HIV/AIDS testing for purposes of employment violated Articles 2(1)(c) and (d), 5(e)(i), and 6; the allegations of the petitioner relating to Article 5(e)(iv) were not examined separately: *ibid.*, paras 7.5 and 8.

[111] See comments in *Moylan*, and concluding observations on Australia, CERD/C/AUS/CO/14, para. 19.

[112] Regarding Suriname, Decision 3 (62) under the early warning procedure, A58/18, para. 18, and concluding observations, CERD/C/64/CO/9, para. 15; on Guyana, CERD/C/GUY/CO/14, para. 19.

[113] With regard to adverse environmental effects through large-scale exploitation of natural resources in the Delta Region and other States, particularly the Ogoni areas, the Committee forcefully urged the taking of measures to combat 'environmental racism' and degradation: concluding observations on Nigeria, CERD/C/NGA/CO/18, para. 19; cf. *SERAC v Nigeria*, African Commission on Human and Peoples' Rights (2002), with respect to contamination of soil, water an air, with long-term health impacts.

significance to the Shoshone, urged the United States to 'pay particular attention to the right to health and cultural rights of the Western Shoshone people, which may be infringed upon by activities threatening their environment and/or disregarding the spiritual and cultural significance they give to their ancestral lands'.[114] Potential dangers to the right to health and related rights have animated calls for environmental impact statements. As with other rights, the need for appropriate indicators may be suggested as indispensable to securing full implementation. Measures of redress may also be called for.[115] Health issues are also integrated with concerns regarding poverty and malnutrition impacting upon particular communities: in such respects, the Committee has extended the vocabulary of the Convention in referring to 'the right to food'.[116] As with housing, the recommendations on the 'living conditions' of groups regularly include observations on the right to health.

Concluding observations have also paid attention to the cultural dimensions of health policy, including linguistic aspects. In the case of indigenous peoples, a number of articles in the UNDRIP address the right to traditional medicines, health practices, flora and fauna, etc, as well as non-discriminatory access to social and health services.[117] The Committee has absorbed some of this regulation into its concluding observations, though the aspect of 'need' in the guidelines as including cultural needs was part of CERD practice before the Declaration emerged in 2007. Sundry dimensions of health issues are summed up in a compendious recommendation to Mexico to draw up,

> in close cooperation with the communities concerned, a comprehensive and culturally sensitive strategy to ensure that indigenous peoples receive quality health care. The implementation of the strategy should be guaranteed by an adequate allocation of resources, the collection of indicators and transparent monitoring of progress. Particular attention should be paid to improving access to health care for indigenous women and children. The Committee underlines the need for interpreters in this area... It is important that the health system recognize, coordinate, support and strengthen indigenous health systems and use them as the basis for achieving more effective and culturally sensitive coverage[118]

Important elements emerging from the recommendation include the stress on cultural sensitivity, the linguistic dimensions of the delivery of healthcare, coordination between indigenous health systems and national systems (implying mutual respect and acknowledgement), and an emphasis on 'close cooperation' between State authorities and indigenous peoples that strongly suggests community participation in the delivery of

[114] Decision 1 (68) A/61/18, ch. II A, para. 8. Health issues are also highlighted in subsequent concluding observations regarding the Shoshone: CERD/C/USA/CO/6, para. 29, where nuclear testing, toxic waste storage, mining, and logging, 'carried out or planned in areas of spiritual and cultural significance to Native Americans', raised concerns of negative impact on the rights to own property, to health, and to equal participation in cultural activities.

[115] Among later recommendations, see CERD/C/CHL/CO/19-21, para. 13, regarding ancestral lands; reiterating and expanding on earlier recommendations, CERD/C/CHL/CO/15-18, para. 21.

[116] See in particular the interrelated set of recommendations to Guatemala: CERD/C/GTM/CO/12-13, paras 11, 12, 13, and 14.

[117] In particular, Articles 21, 24, 29, and 31.

[118] CERD/C/MEX/CO/16-17, para. 19. See also concluding observations on Colombia, CERD/C/COL/CO/14, para. 21 (Afro-Colombian and indigenous persons); Ecuador, CERD/C/ECU/CO/20-22, para. 21, which offers a succinct version of the desiderata for the enjoyment of this right in recommending 'necessary steps to ensure access to appropriate basic services and institutional health care... that are adapted to the different linguistic and cultural characteristics of indigenous peoples'.

care services. The allocation of resources for 'intercultural health' units has also been the subject of recommendations.[119]

Social security and broader issues regarding social services have also engaged attention. Many questions regarding access to social security have concerned Roma claimants;[120] other groups have also been implicated.[121] With regard to social services more generally, there is a strong Committee emphasis on the cultural dimensions of their delivery. In the case of Finland, the Committee recommended that the State party 'effectively ensure social and health services in Sámi languages to Sámi people in their Homeland'.[122] In the case of Laos, following an expression of concern regarding unequal access to public services, in part because of language barriers, the Committee recommended delivery of and access to 'culturally adequate' public services, as well as information on steps taken 'to overcome the language obstacle'.[123] In the case of Mexico, the recommendation was to guarantee the rights of all Mexicans, especially indigenous ones, to 'education, health, social security, housing, basic services and food', while 'respecting their cultural origins and consulting with the peoples who might be affected by such State initiatives'.[124] As with other rights in Article 5, the thematics of participation and cultural appropriateness run through the recommendations on the right to health.

5(e)(v) The Right to Education and Training

Questions regarding the education of members of minority communities were prominent in the League of Nations minority regime; *Minority Schools in Albania* expanded the understanding of equality and discrimination in the field of education and more widely,[125] elaborating the distinction between formal or ostensible equality, and between equality in fact and equality in substance.[126] The attention devoted to the education rights in the League schema is testament to the importance of education to the continued existence of minority groups and the perpetuation of their culture, concerns that have not abated but intensified under the stresses of globalization. With respect to a span of groups under the protection of the Convention, education in its varied forms, the complex right to education, continues to play a crucial role in the intergenerational transmission of communal culture. In the words of the UN Forum on Minority Issues:

> [e]ducation is an inalienable human right, and is more than a mere commodity or . . . service . . . education is a human right that is crucial to the realization of a wide array of other human rights and an indispensable agency for the expansion of human capabilities and the enhancement of human

[119] Concluding observations on Ecuador, CERD/C/ECU/CO/19, para. 20; CERD/C/GTM/CO/12-13, para. 13.

[120] Later examples include concluding observations on Albania, CERD/C/ALB/CO/5-8, para. 11; Belarus, CERD/C/BLR/CO/18-19, para. 16; Bosnia and Herzegovina, CERD/C/BIH/CO/7-8, para. 12; Ukraine, CERD/C/UKR/CO/19-21, para.15.

[121] Concluding observations on Kuwait, CERD/C/KWT/CO/15-20 (Bedoun); Mexico, CERD/C/MEX/CO/16-17, para. 18 (indigenous peoples); Yemen (Al-Akhdam), CERD/C/YEM/CO/17-18, para. 15.

[122] Concluding observations on Finland, CERD/C/FIN/CO/20-22, para. 14.

[123] Concluding observations on Laos, CERD/C/LAO/CO/16-18, para. 19; the Committee also noted, *ibid.*, the political will of the State party 'to reduce poverty in rural areas and to improve ethnic groups' enjoyment of economic and social rights'.

[124] Concluding observations on Mexico, CERD/C/MEX/CO/16-17, para. 18.

[125] *Minority Schools in Albania*, Advisory Opinion, [1935] PCIJ, Ser. A/B No. 64.

[126] P. Thornberry, *International Law and the Rights of Minorities* (Clarendon Press, 1991), Chapter 3.

dignity. Education plays a formative role in socialization for democratic citizenship and represents an essential support for community identity.[127]

Similarly, for the CESCR, education is 'both a human right in itself and an indispensable means of realizing other human rights';[128] commentary also refers to interrelated 'instrumental' and 'primordial' aspects of education, the former relating to the necessity of education to achieve other goals, the latter tied to essential aspects of identity.[129]

The right to education is among the Convention rights borrowed from the UDHR Article 26;[130] this does not include 'training' as part of the right though it does refer to 'technical and professional education'.[131] Article 26 of the UDHR includes a provision on the aims of education: 'the promotion of understanding, tolerance and friendship among all nations, racial or religious groups', phrases subsumed, *mutatis mutandis*, by Article 7 of ICERD.[132] The UDHR right was translated into treaty form as Article 13 of the ICESCR and is the subject of an extensive general comment by the CESCR.[133] In relation to the principle of non-discrimination and equal treatment, the general comment draws upon ICERD, as well as CEDAW, the CRC, and ILO Convention 169 on Indigenous and Tribal Peoples,[134] and the UNESCO Convention against Discrimination in Education 1960, which describes discrimination as including deprivation of access to education or limiting education to an inferior standard.[135] Education is a key component in texts on minorities and indigenous peoples, and subject to elaboration by monitoring bodies. The United Nations Declaration on Minorities (UNDM) addresses education in the mother tongue, and with regard to promoting knowledge of the history and traditions, etc, of minorities.[136] ILO Convention 169 on Indigenous and Tribal Peoples devotes an extensive section to 'education and means of communication',[137] while the UNDRIP contains a wealth of provision on access to all forms of public education as well as 'the right to establish and control their own educational systems and institutions providing

[127] *Minorities and the Right to Education*, Recommendations of the First Session of the Forum on Minority Issues, para. 1, A/HRC/10/11/Add.1 (2009).

[128] GC 13, *The Right to Education*, E/C.12.1999/10, para. 1.

[129] Commentary on Education by the Advisory Committee on the FCNM, ACFC/25Doc(2006)002, section 1.3; the Commentary goes on to state that the distinction is to some extent artificial, hence a situation of additive bilingualism both strengthens cognitive and emotional capabilities and also develops a sense of linguistic identity.

[130] P. Thornberry, 'Education' in M. Weller (ed.), *Universal Minority Rights: A Commentary on the Jurisprudence of International Courts and Treaty Bodies* (Oxford University Press, 2007), pp. 325–62 [henceforth 'Education'].

[131] Article 26 of the UDHR.

[132] Discussed in Chapter 17.

[133] GC 13, HRI/GEN/1/Rev.9, pp. 63–77, para. 6. CERD issued a general recommendation in 1993 that addresses the training of law enforcement officials in the protection of human rights: GR 13.

[134] *Ibid.*, paras 31–37. Standards on education in regional instruments include Article 17 of the ACHPR, Article 13 of the Additional Protocol to the ACHR on Economic, Social and Cultural Rights, Article 30 of the Arab Charter on Human Rights, and Article 2 of the First Protocol to the ECHR.

[135] UNESCO Convention against Discrimination in Education 1960, 429 UNTS 93. On the other hand, separate systems set up 'for religious or linguistic reasons' are not discriminatory provided that attendance at such institutions is optional and that they conform to standards for comparable levels of education: UNESCO Convention, Article 2(b).

[136] Article 4.

[137] Articles 26–31: the provisions exemplify a multi-track and demanding approach to education, combining concepts of equality, participation, establishment of own (indigenous and tribal) institutions, cultural appropriateness, language development, and education of the general public regarding indigenous culture and traditions.

education in their own languages, in a manner appropriate to their cultural methods of teaching and learning',[138] points further developed in, *inter alia*, the first 'advice' of the UN Expert Mechanism on the Rights of Indigenous Peoples (EMRIP).[139]

CERD-specific Reporting Guidelines briefly suggest that States parties should '(a) indicate any variations in the level of education and training between members of groups protected under the Convention; (b) provide information on languages spoken and taught in schools; and (c) describe governmental action to prevent racial discrimination in the enjoyment of this right'.[140] In light of the overlap with the Article 7 obligations on 'teaching, education, culture and information', and the strictures in Article 3 on segregation, practice on the right to education is difficult to individuate on an article-by-article basis.[141] The question of education rarely surfaces in the communications procedure, though a specific violation of the right to education and training was found in *Murat Er v Denmark*.[142] State reports and Committee practice characteristically focus on the institutional access framework, and the anti-racist and pro-tolerance aspect of the educational experience; while the former primarily relates to Article 5 and the latter to Article 7, the complex and multi-layered right to education resists attempts to confine it within precise conceptual and analytical boundaries.

Practice is wider than the issues suggested in the guidelines. General recommendations, notably 27 (Roma), 29 (descent/caste), 34,[143] and 35 (combating racist hate speech) address aspects of the right, without necessarily distinguishing between Articles 5 and 7. Ten paragraphs of GR 27 on the Roma address issues of inclusion, segregation, harassment, education of nomadic groups, the situation of women and girls, teacher training, dialogue between the school and Roma parents and community, adult literacy, and the improvement of knowledge of the history and culture of the Roma in society at large. In GR 29 on descent-based discrimination, segregation appears as a separate issue, while the section on education again addresses inclusion and drop-out rates, harassment, education of the population as a whole, and the removal of stereotyped references and image of descent-based communities, to be replaced by materials 'which convey the message of the inherent dignity of all human beings'.[144] GR 35 addresses educational issues in the context of Article 7, though references to 'intercultural bilingual education', and to 'training' also fit the frame of Article 5.[145]

[138] Article 14; see also Articles 12, 13, and 15. The numerous references in the UNDRIP to autonomous and self-determining cultural development have implications for education processes, insinuating a holistic approach that integrates a complex of considerations.

[139] 'The right of indigenous peoples to education includes the right to provide and receive education through their own traditional methods of teaching and learning, and the right to integrate their own perspectives, cultures, beliefs, values and languages in mainstream education. The Right . . . is a holistic concept incorporating mental, physical, spiritual, cultural; and environmental dimensions': Expert Mechanism Advice No. 1 (2009) on *The Rights of Indigenous Peoples to Education*, annexed to the *Study on Lessons Learned and Challenges to Achieve the Implementation of the Right of Indigenous Peoples to Education*, A/HRC/12/33.

[140] CERD/C/2007/1, p. 11.

[141] Further discussion in Chapters 10 and 17.

[142] CERD/C/71/D/40/2007 (2007).

[143] Section XII of GR 34 includes elements related to Article 5 and Article 7; with regard to the former, the recommendation refers to dropout rates for students of African descent (para. 63), the guarantee of equitable access to education (para. 64), and general avoidance of discrimination in access to education (paras 62 and 64). See also GR 30 on non-citizens, section VII; GR 31 on the administration of justice, section 2B; and GR 32 on special measures.

[144] GR 29, para. vv.

[145] GR 35, para. 33.

States parties have been treated to compendium recommendations on minority education regarding resources, staffing, and curriculum content,[146] recommendations for which may be highly specific.[147] Many recommendations to ratify the UNESCO Convention on Discrimination in Education have been made by the Committee, which has also counselled States to follow the guidelines on education from the UN Forum on Minority Issues[148] and the Expert Mechanism on the Rights of Indigenous Peoples.[149] The stress in these instruments on effective participation of groups in the development of educational policies and strategies, a concept amply validated by international standards, is echoed in a raft of CERD recommendations to States parties.[150] Consistent attention has been paid to access to education for groups under the protective umbrella of the Convention, segregation,[151] and the cultural/linguistic component of educational practice.[152]

The Committee has been notably concerned with barriers to access, insisting, as it does throughout the normative spectrum of the Convention, on 'effective access'[153] to all levels of education, a proposition repeatedly referred to in the case of the Roma.[154] Barriers may arise from a variety of factors,[155] including poverty,[156] and States have been invited to address the educational consequences of such poverty through school subsidies or scholarships for poorer segments of the population or other means.[157] Illiteracy has also been identified as a barrier requiring strong measures to reduce or eliminate it.[158] Linked to the notion of access is that of educational segregation.[159] An active approach to desegregation

[146] Concluding observations on Kazakhstan, CERD/CKAZ/CO/4-5, para. 9: referring to ensuring the adequate quality of the minority schools, adequate funding and resources 'particularly for schools using languages of smaller ethnic groups', the provision of 'adequate professional staff and minority language textbooks', and improved access to university education for students of all ethnic groups without discrimination, including through the adoption of special measures'; the recommendation 'that school textbooks include appropriate consideration of the cultures, traditions and history of minorities and their contribution to Kazakh society', also flows from Article 7.

[147] Such as the recommendation to New Zealand to include references to the Treaty of Waitangi in the final version of the New Zealand Curriculum, CERD/C/NZL/CO/17, para. 20. A Waitangi chapter is included: <http://nzcurriculum.tki.org.nz/The-New-Zealand-Curriculum>.

[148] Concluding observations on Slovakia, CERD/C/SVK/CO/6-8, para. 16.

[149] Concluding observations on Paraguay, CERD/C/PRY/CO/1-3, para. 14.

[150] Sundry examples of consultation/participation recommendations include those for Argentina, CERD/C/65/CO/1, para. 19; Australia, CERD/C/AUS/CO/15-17, para. 21; Colombia, CERD/C/COL/CO/14, para. 22; Czech Republic, CERD/C/CZE/CO/8-9, para. 12; and Ukraine, CERD/C/UKR/CO/19-21, para. 14; the language of consultation with stakeholders may be used, and on the use of cultural mediators.

[151] See discussion of Article 3 in Chapter 10.

[152] The education of women and girls belonging to minorities, in light of phenomena of double discrimination, is a regular subject of recommendations: for example, concluding observations on Burkina Faso, CERD/C/BFA/CO/12-19, para. 9; Turkmenistan, CERD/C/CO/12-19, para. 20.

[153] Concluding observations on Albania, CERD/C/ALB/5-8, para. 16.

[154] Concluding observations on Belarus, CERD/C/BLR/CO/18-19, para. 16; concluding observations on the Russian Federation, CERD/C/RUS/CO/20-22, para. 17.

[155] The recommendations of the UN Forum on Minority Issues on education refer to three overlapping dimensions of access: discrimination, physical accessibility, and economic accessibility; the recommendations also refer to 'cultural, gender and linguistic barriers' that may have equivalent access-denying effects: A/HRC/10/11/Add.1, 5 March 2009, section IV, 'Equal Access to Quality Education for Minorities'. The Forum recommendations in this respect are adapted from GC 13 of CESCR.

[156] CERD/C/ZAF/CO/3, para. 20.

[157] Concluding observations on India, CERD/C/IND/CO/19, para. 25.

[158] Concluding observations on China, CERD/C/CHN/13, para. 23.

[159] Chapter 10 of the present work.

has been called for in some cases,[160] and policies of segregation, *de facto* or otherwise, roundly criticized as incompatible with equal access of all to quality education. As noted earlier,[161] the over-representation of Roma in specialized classes or schools is a problem to be vigorously addressed, replacing the segregation by integration into mainstream education.[162] The Committee has also issued anti-segregationist strictures on mono-ethnic schools in some contexts, or schools of two (ethnically-based) classes under one roof, physically separated and following different curricula.[163] The methods by which integration may be achieved have been placed in context with regard to travelling families of Roma and others: States parties have been recommended to 'find appropriate solutions' for integrating the children of travelling communities, 'taking into account the community's lifestyle', or more accurately, their culture;[164] the Committee also recognizes the importance of 'culturally sensitive education'.[165]

The limitation of the teaching medium to a particular language or languages may also create educational barriers.[166] With regard to special needs schools, the Committee was implicitly critical of the use of language as the criterion for assignment to such schools, supporting State initiatives to reject such a criterion and requesting information on its implementation.[167] The linguistic medium may also function to limit access to education in cases where pedagogical practice does not make adequate allowance for minority or indigenous languages, to the disadvantage of children or other learners from those communities. As the reporting guidelines suggest, concern with language in education is broader than the question of access. Recommendations have emanated from the Committee for bilingual and multilingual education, as well as multicultural and intercultural education.[168] The context is characteristically that of finding a way forward for minority or indigenous groups to preserve and sustain their own languages and cultures while accessing the language of the majority, often coterminous with the national or official language. In this light, bilingual education may be a mechanism for achieving a non-assimilationist objective, while its abolition, especially in the case of threatened languages, is treated as a matter of serious concern.[169]

As evidenced by the foregoing, education questions are prominent in the work of the Committee and its recommendations are copious and increasingly detailed. While

[160] Concluding observations on Namibia, CERD/C/NAM/CO/12, para. 13; USA, CERD/C/USA/CO/6, para. 17.

[161] Chapter 10 on Article 3, discussion of 'segregation'.

[162] Concluding observations on Slovakia, CERD/C/SVK/CO/9-10, para. 11. In addition to *D.H. v Czech Republic*, and *Oršuš v Croatia*, discussed in Chapter 10, analogous ECHR cases include *Horváth and Kiss v Hungary*, App. No. 11146/11 (2013); *Lavida and Ors v Greece*, App. No. 7923/10 (2013); *Sampanis and Ors v Greece*, App. No. 32526/05 (2008); *Sampani and Ors v Greece*, App. No. 59608/09 (2012).

[163] Concluding observations on Bosnia and Herzegovina, CERD/C/BIH/CO/6/Add.1, para. 23.

[164] Concluding observations on Norway, CERD/C/NOR/CO/19-20, para. 20.

[165] Concluding observations on Colombia, with regard to Afro-Colombian and indigenous children, CERD/C/COL/CO/14, para. 23.

[166] Concluding observations on Mauritius, CERD/C/MUS/CO/115-19, para. 20.

[167] Concluding observations on Austria, CERD/C/AUT/18-20, para. 17.

[168] See the brief discussion of terminology in Thornberry, 'Education', pp. 328–30.

[169] Concluding observations on Australia, CERD/C/AUS/CO/15-17, para. 21: in response to the abolition of bilingual education in the Northern Territory of Australia, the Committee recommended 'programmes to revitalize indigenous languages and bilingual and intercultural education for indigenous peoples, respecting cultural identity and history'. Cf. the recommendation for language revitalization to El Salvador, CERD/C/SLV/CO/14-15, para. 21.

practice is more coherent than a wilderness of single instances, the Committee has not issued a dedicated general recommendation to subsume the main issues into an integrated text.

5(e)(vi) The Right to Equal Participation in Cultural Activities

The cultural participation right in ICERD connects closely with Article 27 of the UDHR on 'participation in the cultural life of the community'. The UDHR standard on cultural participation is notably taken forward by Article 15 of the ICESCR, Article 13 of CEDAW, Article 31 of the CRC, and Articles 43 and 45 of the CMW, which open out participation from the 'life of the community' (singular) in the UDHR to 'cultural life'; ICERD is similarly broad in referring to 'cultural activities'. Regional provisions on culture and participation in culture include Articles 17 and 22 of the ACHPR, Article 14 of the Additional Protocol to the ACHR on Economic, Social and Cultural Rights, and Articles 25 and 42 of the Arab Charter on Human Rights. Key instruments recognizing the identity rights of particular groups are replete with cultural references in line with basic understandings of 'minority' and 'indigenous peoples'.[170]

As expressed in Article 5 of the Convention, the culture sub-paragraph overlaps significantly with Article 7 and with the immediately foregoing provision in Article 5 on education, as well as, *inter alia*, the 'civil rights', particularly participation, freedoms of thought, conscience, and religion, and freedom of opinion and expression. While CERD has not issued a general recommendation on participation in cultural activities, culture in a broad sense functions as part of the intellectual scaffolding of a Convention focused on ethnicity and allied concepts, and informs the body of general recommendations and concluding observations.[171]

Reporting guidelines for Article 5 request information on 'participation in cultural life, while at the same time respecting and protecting cultural diversity', and on measures to 'encourage creative activities' by persons belonging to protected groups, and measures to enable such persons 'to preserve and develop their culture'. Information is also requested on facilitating access to media and establishment of own media, measures to 'prevent racial hatred and prejudice in competitive sports', and 'on the status of minority, indigenous and

[170] The definition of 'minority by UN Special Rapporteur Capotorti, cited in Chapter 6, is one of many informal definitions in the international canon that focus on culture, traditions, religion and language'*: Study on the Rights of Persons belonging to Ethnic, Religious and Linguistic Minorities* (United Nations, 1991), para. 568; the culture reflex is built into Article 27 of the ICCPR, which includes for persons belonging to minorities 'the right . . . to enjoy their own culture', and to the UNDM, in addition to referring to the protection of identity in Article 1—essentially cultural identity—refers throughout to cultural elements to be recognized and enjoyed; the Council of Europe's FCNM is similarly suffused with cultural concerns throughout its length. Equally, indigenous rights are essentially about the survival of discrete and distinctive groups, whose rights as expressed in ILO Convention 169 or the UNDRIP are culturally based; the very concept of indigenousness is culturally bounded. Among a raft of publications, for basic accounts of the development of international standards with regard to minorities, see Thornberry, *International Law and the Rights of Minorities*; Weller (ed.), *Universal Minority Rights* (Oxford University Press, 2007); for indigenous peoples see, *inter alia*, S.J. Anaya, *Indigenous Peoples in International Law* (Oxford University Press, 1996), and P. Thornberry, *Indigenous Peoples and Human Rights* (Manchester University Press, 2002). Extensive further references appear in the bibliography to the present work.

[171] Among the general recommendations, see in particular Nos 5, 21, 27, 30, 32, 34, and 35. For a rare, explicit reference to the right, see *Hagan v Australia*, CERD/C/62/D/26/2002 (2002), paras 1, 4.16, and 5.7.

other languages in domestic law and in the media'.[172] The schedule of requested information pictures culture as a complex of creative activity, institutions, and ways of life pertaining to a plurality of communities, with language presented as a prominent marker of community identity.[173] Insofar as 'cultural activities' may suggest mere 'manifestations' of culture or cultural 'events', organized or otherwise, any such limitations have been subsumed by the Committee into the broader, organic metaphor of 'cultural life'.

The sub-paragraph has not been developed to any significant extent in the communications procedure under Article 14. According to the petitioner in *Hagan v Australia*, the presence of a racially offensive sign at a football ground carried the consequence of an inability on his and his family's part to attend the ground, thus impairing their right to equal participation in cultural activities;[174] the specific point was not commented upon by the Committee.

Whereas 'participation' in Article 5(c) is, *ex facie*, focused on political processes and public service (albeit interpreted more broadly),[175] 5(e)(vi) links with an undefined prospectus of 'cultural activities'. The understanding of 'participation' and 'taking part' set out in CESCR GC 21 implies activity and engagement through the use of phrases such as 'act freely', 'to choose', 'to identify or not' (with communities), 'to take part', 'to engage', 'to express oneself' (in the language of choice), to 'know and understand', 'to learn', 'to follow a way of life', 'to be involved', etc; issues of access and contribution to cultural life are also regarded as intrinsic to the concept.[176] In CESCR and ICERD, the envisaged active citizenship in political life is paralleled by choice, freedom, and opportunity in cultural life. 'Equal' participation must be assumed to carry its standard meaning in practice, requiring action on the part of the State to secure the effective enjoyment of the right. In particular contexts, participation may become a particularly demanding obligation on governments, intensified by the right to self-determination of indigenous peoples, and the right of persons belonging to minorities, recognized in a variety of instruments, to participation in decisions affecting them.[177] As is evident from the present and immediately preceding chapter, the theme of 'participation' runs though the spectrum of rights in Article 5 as a whole.

The influence of the work of the Committee on Economic, Social and Cultural Rights (CESCR) on the practice of CERD in this respect is notable. In the words of the former Committee, culture 'is a broad, inclusive concept encompassing all manifestations of human existence. The expression "cultural life" is an explicit reference to culture as a living process, historical, dynamic and evolving, with a past, a present and a future.'[178]

[172] CERD/C/2007/1, pp. 11–12.

[173] The reference to racial hatred in competitive sports is more closely attuned to Articles 4 and 7: CERD GR 35, para. 43.

[174] *Hagan v Australia*, para. 5.7; the case is discussed at greater length in Chapter 17. In response to the point on 5(e)(v), the State party observed, para. 4.16, that it was beyond the Committee's mandate to ensure that the right was established; the mandate was rather to monitor its implementation once granted on equal terms.

[175] See Chapter 13.

[176] CESCR GC 21, paras 14 and 15. See also Advisory Committee on the Framework Convention for the Protection of National Minorities, Commentary on the Effective Participation of Persons belonging to National Minorities in Cultural, Social and Economic Life and in Public Affairs, ACFC/31DOC(2008)001.

[177] Discussed in the preceding chapter.

[178] GC No. 21 on the Right of Everyone to Take Part in Cultural Life (Article 15(1)(a) of the International Covenant on Economic, Social and Cultural Rights), E/C.12/GC/21 (2009), para. 11. See also, *ibid.*, paras 12 and 13.

The preamble to the UNESCO Declaration on Cultural Diversity similarly treats culture as 'a set of distinctive material spiritual, material, intellectual and emotional features of a society or a social group ... [that] ... encompasses, in addition to art and literature, lifestyles, ways of living together, value systems, traditions and beliefs'.[179] The complex term 'culture' may be divided into a triad of (perhaps Western-centric) 'high' culture, mass or globalized culture, and culture as a way of life or culture in the anthropological sense.[180] The right in Article 5(e)(vi) of ICERD to participation in cultural activities is only one expression amidst a critical mass of references to 'culture' in the archive of the Committee. CERD broadly recognizes the extended sense of culture as that which animates the spirit of communities. Understandings have developed along a trajectory from a conception of culture as intellectual and moral improvement or artistic excellence to a broadly anthropological vision of culture as ways of life, with the proviso that the various meanings simultaneously coexist.[181]

The developmental and pervasive quality of 'culture' envisioned as a living process (CESCR), its encompassing nature, and doubts as to whether an activity can be classified as a cultural activity with certainty, can make it difficult to be precise about when or how a right-holder is being subjected to unequal or discriminatory treatment. Commentators on cultural rights have suggested that instead of basing human rights on such an amorphous idea, and applying something like a principle of subsidiarity, rights be broken down into discrete fragments such as education and language; that they are better understood and more suitable for practical realization than 'culture'.[182] Cultural elements are, as observed,

[179] UNESCO Universal Declaration on Cultural Diversity, 2 November 2001, available at: <http://portal.unesco.org/en/ev.php-URL_ID=13179&URL_DO=DO_TOPIC&URL_SECTION=201.html>.

[180] Compare the entry in R. Williams, *Keywords* (Fontana Press, 1988), pp. 87–93. Williams describes culture as 'one of the two or three most complicated words in the English language', to which may be added 'and other languages also'. In her first report to the Human Rights Council, A/HRC/14/36, June 2010, the Independent Expert in the Field of Cultural Rights, in the absence of a general definition of cultural rights, underlined that they 'relate to a broad range of issues, such as expression and creation ... information and communication; language; identity and belonging to multiple, diverse and changing communities of shared cultural values; development of specific world visions and the pursuit of specific ways of life; education and training; access, contribution and participation in cultural life; the conduct of cultural practices and access to tangible and intangible cultural heritage. Cultural rights protect the rights for each person ... as well as groups of people, to develop and express their humanity, their world view and the meanings they give to their existence and their development through, *inter alia*, values, beliefs, convictions, languages, knowledge and the arts, institutions and ways of life. They may also be considered as protecting access to cultural heritage and resources.'

[181] See J. Ringelheim, 'Cultural Rights', in D. Moeckli, S. Shah, and S. Sivakumaran (eds), and D. Harris (Consulting editor), *International Human Rights Law* (2nd edn, Oxford University Press, 2014), pp. 286–302.

[182] Specific rights to language, education, etc, are laid out *in extenso* in the relevant international instruments on minorities and indigenous peoples in particular, with the instruments on indigenous peoples explicitly extending the rights with cultural attributes to for example, as set out in the UNDRIP, protection to lands and territories, cultural understandings of group belonging, 'archaeological and historical sites, artefacts, designs, technologies, and visual and performing arts and literature' (Article 11), 'spiritual and religious traditions, customs and ceremonies' and ceremonial objects (Article 12), 'languages, oral traditions, writing systems and literatures' and 'names for communities, places and persons' (Article 13), etc. One author recalls arguments that 'the use of culture is usually misleading and that it would be better and more accurate to identify specific rights, for example, to expression, association, religion, specific minority rights, etc.': D. McGoldrick, 'Culture, Cultures and Human Rights', in M. Baderin and R. McCorquodale (eds), *Economic, Social and Cultural Rights in Action* (Oxford University Press, 2007), pp. 447–72, at pp. 450–1 [henceforth 'Culture, Cultures and Human Rights']; McGoldrick, *ibid.*, p. 451, cites T. Eriksson, 'Between Universalism and Relativism: A Critique of the UNESCO Concepts of Culture', in J. Cowan, M. Dembour, and R. Wilson (eds), *Culture and Rights: Anthropological Perspectives* (Cambridge University Press, 2001): instead of invoking culture, 'if one talks about ... local arts, one could simply say local arts; if one means language, ideology, patriarchy, children's

already widely distributed throughout the Convention, meeting the argument of the critics at least in part. The pervasiveness of 'cultural' elements in CERD practice makes its own contribution to broader claims regarding the cultural embedding of human rights.[183]

CERD has further deconstructed the right by focusing principally on individuated applications in overlapping institutional contexts such as the media, education, and official, national, and minority language regimes, while retaining the general concept of culture.[184] The 'cultural activities' have been further pluralized beyond the 'community' of Article 27 of the UDHR into the cultures of 'communities' under the protective umbrella of ICERD.[185] The pluralization of culture enables discussions of 'multiculturalism' and the reiterated use of the dialogic process term, 'intercultural', in educational and other contexts.[186]

Pluralization also facilitates the double concept of participation in cultural activities in 'one's own community' and participation in the larger community of nation and State. Hence the understanding of the sub-paragraph as demanding cultural support for minority, indigenous, and other self-defining communities, including support for the maintenance of cultural identity and distinctiveness,[187] the promotion of knowledge of mother-tongue in educational processes,[188] and community history,[189] and the right to buy into the national cultural context on the basis of equal access.[190] Recognition of a range of communities in States also militates against the Convention being used as a vehicle of assimilation;[191] on the contrary, the notion of pluralization leans heavily in

rights, food habits, ritual practices or local political structures, one could use those equivalent terms instead of covering them up in the deceptively cosy blanket of culture'.

[183] F. Lenzerini, *The Culturalization of Human Rights Law* (Oxford University Press, 2014); see in particular Chapter 20 of the present work.

[184] See commentary on Article 7 in the present work.

[185] Among a multitude of potential references see later references in concluding observations on Argentina, CERD/C/65/CO/1, para. 16, indigenous communities; Ecuador, CERD/C/ECU/CO/19, para. 13, indigenous peoples and Afro-Ecuadorians; Iran, CERD/C/IRN/CO/18-19, para. 17, Arab Azeri, Balochi, Kurdish, Baha'i and other communities; Former Yugoslav Republic of Macedonia, CERD/C/MKD/CO/7, para. 18, Roma communities; and Norway, CERD/C/NOR/CO/19-20, para. 18, cultural identity of Sámi communities.

[186] For a brief comment on the Committee's appreciation of 'multiculturalism' and discussions thereon, see P. Thornberry, 'Multiculturalism, Minority Rights, and the Committee on the Elimination of Racial Discrimination', in K. Thűrer and Z. Kędzia (eds), *Managing Diversity: Protection of Minorities in International Law* (Schulthess, 2009), pp. 79–94. The Committee held a general and inconclusive debate on multiculturalism in 2005, CERD/C/SR/1694, the transcription of which is on file with the Secretariat; see also CERD/C/SR.1724.

[187] Many recommendations simply refer to respect for the existence and cultural identity of all ethnic groups in the State party concerned: examples include concluding observations on Botswana, CERD/C/BWT/CO/16, para. 9; the Democratic Republic of Congo, CERD/C/COD/CO/15, para. 14; Vietnam, CERD/C/VNM/CO/10-14, para. 12. State parties may be counselled to take due account of ethnic diversity in the nation-building process: for example, the Committee expressed concern to Botswana, *ibid.*, that 'the State party's objective to build a nation based on the principle of equality for all has been implemented in a way detrimental to the protection of ethnic and cultural diversity'; similarly, the Committee noted that the Constitution of the Democratic Republic of the Congo envisages building a nation based on the principle of equality for all, with safeguards for ethnic and cultural diversity; the Committee contrasted this laudable aim with the State party's non-recognition of indigenous peoples on its territory.

[188] See comment in the present chapter on the right to education and training.

[189] See Chapter 17 on Article 7.

[190] In many instances, CERD has emphasized the contribution of minority cultures to a 'pluralized' national identity: examples include concluding observations on Botswana, CERD/C/61/CO/2, para. 14; Norway, CERD/C/NOR/CO/18, para. 17; Uruguay, CERD/C/URY/CO/16-20, para. 19.

[191] For comment on forced assimilation, see concluding observations on Finland, CERD/C/FIN/CO/20-222, para. 12; Turkmenistan, CERD/C/TKM/CO/5, para. 12; in the latter case, CERD recalled that 'policies of forced assimilation amount to racial discrimination and constitute grave violations of the convention'.

favour of support for cultural maintenance and flourishing for a variety of groups, including special measures where appropriate. As one author has commented: '[a] right to participate in a culture can only exist if there is a culture'.[192]

On the limits of cultural rights in general, and the corresponding 'cultural activities', debates may be phrased in the language of universalism and cultural relativism, or cultural rights and universality of human rights.[193] On the CERD approach to some traditional practices in light of demographic realities of ethnic and cultural diversity,[194] one dilemma was given succinct expression by CERD member de Gouttes in the Committee's 2005 debate on multiculturalism:

> Although the Committee was called upon to recognize the inherent value of each culture, it was nevertheless necessary to impose a limit on that recognition. That limit could be understood as the universality of human rights, which was the need to ensure universal respect for fundamental human rights, regardless of... culture, tradition, etc. What that meant was that the Committee should not go so far as to support cultures that engaged in practices or customs that ran counter to the core human rights, as defined by United Nations human rights treaties. He believed that all Committee members could agree on such a limit.[195]

Questions such as 'harmful customs', caste discrimination and caste-based prostitution, or analogous social discrimination against such groups as Burakumin, '*osu*', '*trokosi*', female genital mutilation, marriage customs, etc, have all exercised the Committee from time to time and will continue to do so. These questions often connect with rights of women although their scope is wider. Committee decision–making in the face of evidence of certain practices depends on two interconnected steps: (a) verifying the existence of a practice or questioning the practice in the light of human rights standards, and (b) deciding what to do about practices which the Committee regards as challenging basic principles of human rights. The step of deciding what is or is not a violation of human rights is essentially interpretative, bearing in mind also the flexibility of the principle of non-discrimination as set out above. In some cases, a particular determination that the principle has been violated will suggest itself; in other cases, the situation may be less clear. Difficulties do not cease after a determination by CERD or other human rights body that practice X violates human rights norm Y. It is not always clear what precisely is expected to result from observations recommending efforts by the State party to ensure that the rights of women are respected, irrespective of the community they belong to, especially where marriage is concerned, and calling for detailed information on the marriage rules and practices that apply in indigenous and tribal communities, when the Committee takes note at the same time of the State party's desire to respect the marriage customs of the various groups.[196]

Specific recommendations are usually context-driven. CERD has on occasions adopted the expedient of referring in general terms to GR 25[197] or other relevant general

[192] McGoldrick, 'Culture, Cultures and Human Rights', p. 454.

[193] For background standards, see, *inter alia*, para. 5 of the Vienna Declaration of the World Conference on Human Rights; Article 5(a) of CEDAW; Article 4 of the UNESCO Universal Declaration on Cultural Diversity; Article 2 of the UNESCO Convention on the Protection an Promotion of the Diversity of Cultural Expressions; and in the context of specific groups, Article 4(2) of the UNDM; Article 46 of the UNDRIP.

[194] See discussion in the present work of Article 1.

[195] CERD/C/SR.1724, para. 23.

[196] *Ibid*. For further reflections, see Chapter 20.

[197] Concluding observations on Ghana, A/58/18, para. 114.

recommendations.[198] In most cases, CERD indicates a general preference for non-coercive, educative strategies, in effect envisioning that the 'constructive dialogue' prized by the Committee should be carried on within States as well as between the Committee and the reporting State. Situations where the claims of culture are weakened—when there is evidence of mass defection and the notion of cultural 'belonging' is challenged—embolden the Committee into taking its strongest line against cultural practices that it recognizes as inconsistent with human rights.

5(f) Access to Public Places and Services

This right does not have a counterpart in the UDHR but raises issues of special sensitivity in the racial discrimination context on account of its association with segregation and apartheid. The right in the Convention is elaborated on the basis of examples: the list of places and services open to the public is prefaced by 'such as', so that analogous places or services will presumably be those *in pari materia* with the listed cases.[199] The Declaration on the Elimination of All Forms of Racial Discrimination proclaims the right in more general terms: that '[e]veryone shall have equal access to any place or facility intended for use by the general public'.[200] The question of access to public places features in a number of general recommendations, including GR 27 on the Roma, GR 29 on descent-based discrimination,[201] and GR 30 on non-citizens.[202]

The right set out in 5(f) has figured in a number of communications under Article 14.[203] In *B.J. v Denmark*,[204] the author of the communication was refused entry to a discotheque along with a colleague on the ground that they were 'foreigners'.[205] Whilst the case was dealt with by the Committee on Article 6 and no violation was found, CERD stated that violations of the right in 5(f) were particularly appropriate for compensation in addition to any fining of a perpetrator of racial discrimination:

> Being refused access to a place of service intended for the use of the general public solely on the ground of a person's national or ethnic background is a humiliating experience which . . . may merit economic compensation and cannot always be adequately repaired or satisfied by merely imposing a criminal sanction on the perpetrator.[206]

In *M.B. v Denmark*,[207] a case concerning public access to a restaurant, a specific point was made in connection with 5(f) concerning the duty of States parties to ensure, 'in particular

[198] Notably those concerning communities: indigenous peoples, Roma, Caste groups.

[199] Para. 35 of GR 27 on Discrimination against Roma offers a different listing of public access venues to include 'restaurants, hotels, theatres and music halls, discotheques and others'. While the listing of venues is subject to social and cultural changes over time, the underlying principle of spaces and facilities open to 'the public' without discrimination remains unchanged; the sub-paragraph repudiates the notion of racially separate public facilities.

[200] Article 3.2. Elements drawn from ICERD language appear in the CRPD, which is the most developed of the UN 'core' human rights instruments in the matter of access, including access on an equal basis with others 'to the physical environment, to transportation . . . and to other facilities and services open or provided to the public': Article 9.1.

[201] Section 3 (o).

[202] Para. 38.

[203] See discussions in the present work of cases under Article 3.

[204] CERD/C/56/D/17/1999 (2000).

[205] *Ibid.*, para. 2.1.

[206] *Ibid.*, para. 6.3.

[207] CERD/C/60/D/20/2000 (2002).

by prompt and effective police investigations of complaints, that the right . . . is enjoyed without discrimination by all persons, nationals or foreigners'.[208] Access issues concerning persons of Roma ethnicity were raised in *Lacko v Slovakia,*[209] and *Durmic v Serbia and Montenegro.*[210] The former concerned admission to a railway restaurant in Kosice, Slovakia. The petitioner and other Roma were told to leave in accordance with company policy not to serve Roma or to serve only 'polite' Roma. Counsel for the petitioner claimed that the State party's 'failure to provide any remedies and the absence of any legal norm expressly prohibiting discrimination in access to public accommodations constitute failure to comply with Article 3'.[211] Counsel also referred to the 'humiliation and degradation' suffered by the petitioner in consequence of the events in question,[212] suggesting that psychological consequences are relevant to the conceptualization of segregation. In its decision, CERD did not pronounce on Article 3, referring only to Article 5(f).[213] In *Durmic*, a human rights centre carried out a series of 'tests' across Serbia to check if Roma individuals were being discriminated against while attempting to access clubs, discotheques, restaurants, etc.[214] In the course of this campaign, two Roma persons including the petitioner were refused entry to a discotheque on the basis that it was a private party that required an invitation, whereas their non-Roma companions were admitted without any such invitation. The petitioner invoked a number of Convention articles including Article 3, which placed an obligation on the State party to 'prevent, prohibit and eradicate all practices of this nature'.[215] The Committee did not pursue the point on Article 3, preferring instead to ground its finding of a violation on Articles 5(f) and 6.

Regarding Article 5(f), in *Lacko*,[216] the State party was requested to complete its legislation in order to guarantee the right of access to public places and to sanction refusals of access; in *Durmic*, the State party failed to investigate the claim under 5(f) thoroughly so that, in consequence, Article 6 was violated.[217] In *L.A. v Slovakia*,[218] another discotheque access 'testing' case, claims of violations of Articles 2 and 5 were concentrated into an argument on Article 6, which was found not to have been violated. It is open to argument whether access to public spaces may be regarded as inhibited or impaired on racial grounds by demeaning or insulting language publicly displayed. The point was adverted to by the petitioner in *Hagan v Australia*,[219] but did not elicit comment from the Committee.

Despite the passing of time since State-sponsored segregation in public facilities featured in the legislation and public policy of States such as apartheid-era South Africa,

[208] *Ibid.*, para. 10.
[209] CERD/C/59/D/11/1998 (2001).
[210] CERD/C/68/D/29/2003 (2006).
[211] *Lacko v Slovakia*, para. 3.4.
[212] *Ibid.*, para. 3.6.
[213] *Ibid.*, para. 11. No violation was found in light of sanctions imposed against the manager of the restaurant.
[214] *Durmic v Serbia and Montenegro*, para. 2.1. See further discussion in Chapters 4, 9, and 16.
[215] *Ibid.*, para. 3.10.
[216] *Lacko v Slovakia*, para. 11.
[217] *Durmic v Serbia and Montenegro*, para. 10.
[218] CERD/C/85/D/49/2011 (2014).
[219] *Hagan v Australia*, para. 5.7; according to the petitioner, the inability of the petitioner and his family to attend a sports ground because it was known by a racially offensive epithet 'impaired their rights under Article 5, including the right to equal participation in cultural activities'; see also para. 3.1.

invocations of Article 5(f) are not uncommon in concluding observations. Actions of private individuals, not adequately disciplined by the State authorities, characterize current situations. In the case of Japan, concern was expressed about 'cases of race and nationality-based refusals' of access to places open to the public 'such as restaurants, family public bathhouses, stores and hotels':[220] the Committee accordingly recommended a programme of education and 'a national law making illegal the refusal of entry to places open to the public'.[221] Concerns have been expressed over denials of access to public places in relation to Dalits,[222] Roma,[223] non-citizens or persons of migrant background,[224] and persons of African descent.[225]

Coda

In a stimulating article published in 2002, Felice wrote that a 'review of the CERD Committee's concluding observations for the past five years reveals a glaring meekness in their approach to the economic and social rights of minority racial groups. Economic and social rights clearly have not been a priority for the Committee.'[226] Part of the critique—the 'meekness' aspect—related to expressions of 'concern' or calls for 'monitoring' on the part of the Committee, when, in the view of the author, stronger and more forceful language was called for in view of the plight of communities identified. Following a lengthy list of country examples of recommendations 'void of any content', the author concluded that the Committee was 'adept at identifying the issues confronting racial minorities within the States party to the CERD, but... not very resourceful in identifying the actions that these nations needed to take to address these issues'.[227] The overall preference of the author is for the Committee to recommend specific policies to end racial discrimination in areas such as health and education.[228]

In response, and bearing in mind the wealth of recommendations outlined in the present chapter, it would appear that CERD practice in the present century has undergone a

[220] For comments regarding a ban on sleeping in public places, see remarks of CERD members Kut and Vázquez in relation to the periodic report of Norway, CERD/C/SR.2373, paras 19 and 29, and SR.2374, para. 53.

[221] CERD/C/JPN/CO/3-6, para. 24, reiterated in substance in CERD/C/JPN/CO/7-9, para. 15.

[222] Concluding observations on India, CERD/C/IND/CO/19, para. 13.

[223] Concluding observations on Albania, CERD/C/ALB/CO/5-8, para. 11; Belarus, CERD/C/BLR/CO/18-19, para 16; Norway, CERD/C/NOR/CO/19-20, para. 20; Romania, CERD/C/ROU/CO/16-19, para. 14.

[224] Concluding observations on Austria, CERD/C/AUT/CO/18-20, para. 14, referring to 'arbitrary denial of access to public places by persons of migration background based on their appearance'.

[225] Concluding observations on the Dominican Republic, CERD/C/DOM/CO/13-14, para. 15: discrimination based on colour or national origin, with reference to 'dark-skinned people of African descent'.

[226] W.F. Felice, 'The UN Committee on the Elimination of All Forms of Racial Discrimination: Race, and Economic, Social and Cultural Rights', *HRQ* 24 (2002), 205–36, 217.

[227] *Ibid.*, 224. The author added that the criticisms of the work of CERD were 'directed at the complacency of the State parties... and not the expert members of the Committee', a point that is difficult to understand, bearing in mind that the impugned recommendations were formulated by the Committee and not by the States parties. The author develops a wider critique of human rights implementation, directed particularly at reporting mechanisms, so that critical remarks subsume CERD practice but are not confined to it; his remedy is for CERD to adopt the 'capabilities approach' developed by Amartya Sen, which the author translates, 229 ff, into a series of steps to be taken by CERD, including the development of accurate social indicators, investments in health care, education, etc, presumably to be incorporated into CERD recommendations.

[228] *Ibid.*, 236.

significant expansion in relation to economic, social, and cultural rights, as it has in other areas of work. While expressions of concern and requests for information remain embedded in the Committee's lexicon, they are supplemented by more specific, direct suggestions in a constantly expanding canvas of recommendations. The amount of attention devoted to areas such as work, housing, health and education belies any charge of neglect on the part of the Committee. Khaliq and Churchill distinguish their position from that of Felice in finding that the current attitude of CERD 'represents a progressive and committed attitude towards economic and social rights'.[229] They add that CERD work has contributed to the notion of the justiciability of economic and social rights, though it has not spelled out what this means in any detail. What is also striking in current practice is the intersecting nature of human rights issues afflicted by racial discrimination. In CERD practice, there is no relegation of one particular category of rights to subaltern status.

While the ICESCR incorporates rights subject to progressive implementation, the CESCR treats the obligation not to discriminate as one of immediate effect: as 'an immediate and cross-cutting obligation in the Covenant'. Commentators have distinguished between the 'immediate' obligation to eliminate de jure discrimination and the obligation to eliminate *de facto* discrimination 'as speedily as possible'.[230] The obligation in Article 5 is 'to eliminate racial discrimination' and to 'guarantee . . . equality before the law', to which may be added the peremptory demands in the chapeau of Article 2 to 'pursue a policy of eliminating racial discrimination 'without delay', and in Article 2(1)(d) to bring discrimination 'to an end'. The requirements cover racial discrimination 'in all its forms'. The progressive implementation argument has been raised in communications, without comment from the Committee.

[229] Khaliq and Churchill, 'The Protection of Economic and Social Rights', p. 241; they add, pp. 242–3, that it 'is clear that the CERD Committee has not treated economic and social rights as inferior to or in any way different from civil and political rights . . . economic and social rights are important to the CERD Committee's mandate and are an aspect to which it has shown . . . a clear and strong commitment'.

[230] Saul *et al.*, *The International Covenant on Economic, Social and Cultural Rights*, pp. 203–5, p. 204.

15. Article 5

Comment and Conclusions

The chapeau to Article 5 makes an explicit link with obligations under Article 2 of the Convention and goes on to repeat the undertaking to eliminate racial discrimination—an unnecessary repetition according to some views.[1] Commentators have observed that there is a lack of 'fit' between Article 5 and Article 1,[2] including the reference to 'civil rights' in Article 5 but not in Article 1, and, further, that as noted, the 'grounds' of prohibited discrimination in Article 5 omit 'descent'. The lack of limitation regarding non-citizens in Article 5 has proved serviceable in facilitating more generous interpretations of the scope of the Convention vis-à-vis Article 1(2). In *D.R. v Australia*, the Committee took into account General Recommendation (GR) 30 'and in particular the necessity to interpret Article 1, paragraph 2 of the Convention in the light of article 5', rejecting the State party's claim that the communication was inadmissible.[3]

On interpretation of Article 5, three interrelated issues in particular have generated discussion: (1) whether rights are 'established' by the Convention or merely acknowledged where they appear in the legal system of the State and require protection from discrimination; (2) the question of which rights does Article 5 protect from discrimination, bearing in mind that the list of rights is not closed; and (3) the requirements flowing from the chapeau statements on discrimination and equality. A preliminary excursus by the Committee in 1973 registered a variety of views but without a consensus on the interpretation of an article described therein as obscure on more than one point.[4] The views expressed were summarized by Partsch according to three perspectives,[5] the first of which, 'the extremely wide concept',[6] was that Article 5 established the listed rights as legal obligations so that failure to comply with them would violate the Convention; the second, 'the extremely narrow concept',[7] held that the list of rights established the field of application of the principle of non-discrimination; a third, 'the intermediate concept',[8] expressed the position that Article 5 prohibited discrimination and guaranteed the right to equality before the law.[9] Meron notes a wide acknowledgement that

[1] N. Lerner, *The U.N. Convention on the Elimination of All Forms of Racial Discrimination* (Sijthoff and Noordhoff, 1980), p. 55.

[2] Schwelb, p. 1004.

[3] Para. 6.3.

[4] A/9018, Chapter V, paras 55 and 61.

[5] K.J. Partsch, Elimination of Racial Discrimination in the Enjoyment of Civil and Political Rights, *Texas International Law Journal* 14 (1979), 191–250.

[6] *Ibid.*, 215; according to Partsch, the concept 'was formulated by the rapporteur [Sayegh] in order to show it was unacceptable'.

[7] *Ibid.*, 216.

[8] *Ibid.*, 216.

[9] According to Committee member Haastrup, A/9018, para. 53, 'the essential element of article 5 was the right of everyone to equality before the law.' Aboul-Nasr on the other hand, argued, *ibid.*, para. 53, that the article was concerned only with discrimination in respect of the rights enumerated therein. See also the introduction to the debate by Sayegh, *ibid.*, paras 40–44, and comments in by Committee members Calovski, Macdonald, Ortiz-Martin, Partsch, Soler, and Tomko. Sayegh observed, *ibid.*, para. 42, that it should not be pretended that

the catalogue of human rights in article 5 does not create those rights but merely obligates a State to prevent racial discrimination in the exercise of those which it has recognised. Article 5 could have been drafted in a manner that clearly defined this limitation. But a more explicit formulation would have emphasised the liberty of States to deny some of the rights listed, which would possibly have weakened the authority of... [the UDHR]... and undermined the status of some rights as customary law.[10]

The ambiguities adverted to by Meron were spotted in the drafting of the Convention: the remarks of the representative of Canada who read Article 5 as granting rights as well as guaranteeing non-discrimination in their exercise will be recalled.[11]

The interpretative issues were further addressed by the Committee in GR 20 of 1996 which commences with the statement that 'the rights and freedoms mentioned in Article 5 do not constitute an exhaustive list',[12] recalling the UN Charter and the Universal Declaration of Human Rights (UDHR) 'at the head of these rights and freedoms' as well as the elaboration of rights in the international covenants. The recommendation observes that States parties are 'obliged to acknowledge and protect the enjoyment of human rights', while 'the manner in which the obligations are translated into the legal order of States parties may differ'.[13] Paragraph 1 makes a general position statement:

Article 5 of the Convention, apart from requiring a guarantee that the exercise of human rights shall be free from racial discrimination, does not of itself create civil, political, economic, social or cultural rights, but assumes the existence and recognition of such rights. The Convention obliges States to prohibit and eliminate discrimination in the enjoyment of such human rights.

The statement that Article 5 'assumes' the existence and recognition of rights is not unambiguous in that such an 'assumption' may carry a certain normative force, facilitating Article 5 critiques of the absence of certain rights in the constitutions or laws of States parties. Vandenhole recalls a more extensive interpretation by the Committee in concluding observations on Malawi: the State party was reminded that Article 5 implied the existence of civil, political, economic, social, and cultural rights, and that 'full respect for human rights is the necessary framework for the efficiency of measures adopted to combat racial discrimination'.[14] While the explicit recommendations by the Committee for States parties to broaden their range of human rights commitments suggest that Article 5 does not 'establish' such commitments, the rights listed in Article 5, together with rights that may be implicit in or derived from them, increasingly appear to be treated as standard, canonical requirements. The Committee does not restrict the range of its examination of reports on being informed that this or that human right is not guaranteed in the domestic or international portfolio of the State party concerned; on the contrary, the State party will be invited to remedy its absence as well as securing its enjoyment without discrimination.

article 5 amounted to a convention on civil, political, economic, social, cultural and other rights... the only human right given obligatory force by article 5 was the right of everyone to be protected from racial discrimination and to benefit from equality before the law in the enjoyment of fundamental human rights'.

[10] T. Meron, 'The Meaning and Reach of the International Convention on the Elimination of All Forms of Racial Discrimination', *American Journal of International Law* 79 (1985), 283–318, 294.

[11] Ch. 12.

[12] Para. 1.

[13] Para. 1.

[14] CERD/C/63/CO/13, para. 7, cited in W. Vandenhole, *Non-Discrimination and Equality in the View of the UN Human Rights Treaty Bodies* (Intersentia, 2005), p. 10.

Arguments on 'granting' or 'recognition' of rights intersect with interpretations of the range of protected rights. The final paragraph of GR 20 asserts, in light of 'notably' in the chapeau to Article 5, that the rights and freedoms referred to in 'and any similar rights' shall be protected. With regard to the *travaux* of Article 5, Lerner comments that '"notably" was used in order to avoid a restrictive interpretation of the rights enumerated... some delegations would have preferred a more general and less detailed wording, with a view to preventing such an interpretation'.[15] The recommendation's reference to 'similar rights' opens out to unlisted human rights displaying similar characteristics to those listed. Commentators go further. O'Flaherty suggests that the Convention addresses all rights regardless of source,[16] while Diaconu argues that Article 5 'extends to all rights', and if 'a certain right is granted, whether in an international [instrument] or through internal legislation, no discrimination is allowed with regard to its exercise'; he makes an analogy between Article 5 and Protocol 12 to the European Convention on Human Rights (ECHR), which forbids discrimination in relation to rights 'established by law'.[17] The Inter-American Convention on Racism, etc, with the advantage of much later adoption (2013) than the International Convention on the Elimination of All Forms of Racial Discrimination (ICERD), defines racial discrimination in its Article 1 as nullifying or curtailing the enjoyment of the 'human rights and fundamental freedoms enshrined in the international instruments applicable to the States parties', while Article 3 extends the anti-discrimination portfolio to 'all human rights and fundamental freedoms enshrined in... domestic law and in international law applicable to the States parties'.

If the range of protected rights subject to the equality/discrimination critique is understood expansively, the analytical point on whether Article 5 'establishes' or 'assumes' the rights becomes less important, though not without practical consequences in States that specifically recognize only a limited portfolio of rights. The bulk of commentary on ICERD aligns itself with wider views on the range of rights subject to undertakings under Article 5, which may thereby be described as setting out a floor of rights, not a ceiling, a description that resonates with the promise of the Convention to address all forms of racial discrimination. CERD practice suggests that the relevant international law applicable to States parties and treated as furnishing background standards of rights to be protected from discrimination extends beyond treaty law into rights presumptively generated through the operation of customary international law. Hence, for example, the regular endorsements by the Committee of the UNDRIP, treated as representing the best contemporary standard of indigenous rights, and particularly of its concept of indigenous self-determination.

Rights unspecified in Article 5 but alluded to in the practice outlined in Chapters 13 and 14 of this work include language rights; the right to a name and identity rights writ large; participation rights widened beyond the 'political' sphere; reproductive rights; the right to family life; the right to food; a battery of rights associated with refugees and asylum-seekers including non-refoulement, the right to asylum, and the right to appeal against denials of refugee status; economic, social, and cultural rights including the right

[15] N. Lerner, *The U.N. Convention on the Elimination of All Forms of Racial Discrimination* (Sijthoff and Noordhoff, 1980), p. 56.

[16] M. O'Flaherty, 'Substantive Provisions of the International Convention on the Elimination of All Forms of Racial Discrimination', in S. Pritchard (ed.), *Indigenous Peoples, the United Nations and Human Rights* (Zed Books and the Federation Press, 1998), pp. 162–83, p. 179.

[17] I. Diaconu, *Racial Discrimination* (Eleven International Publishing, 2011), pp. 217–19, at p. 218.

to an adequate standard of living, the right to water, and the right to register the births of children. The rights are derived from contemporary international practice as developed in universal (undifferentiated by category) and group-specific instruments, as well as customary law. Processes of discrimination can affect a number of rights simultaneously. The internal categories—civil rights, economic, social, and cultural rights—are interrelated and indivisible, so that violations of one right almost inevitably violate others. Racial discrimination characteristically targets or affects individuals and communities not in respect of rights punctiliously marked out but across the span of personal and communal rights and interests swept up in its wake.

As noted in Chapter 12, the rights in Article 5 are not 'fleshed out' through inclusion in a complex of a core rights statement subject to permissible limitations and derogations. In practice, Article 5 is treated as covering the various unstated facets of the expression of rights and limitations thereon. With regard to restrictions on the enjoyment of rights, GR 20 states that:

> [w]henever a State imposes a restriction upon one of the rights listed in Article 5 of the Convention which applies ostensibly to all within its jurisdiction, it must ensure that neither in purpose or effect is the restriction incompatible with Article 1 of the Convention as an integral part of international human rights standards. To ascertain whether this is the case, the Committee is obliged to inquire further to make sure that any such restriction does not entail racial discrimination.[18]

The admonition in *L.R. v Slovakia* regarding the inadmissibility of shielding stages in the implementation of a human right from scrutiny for racial discrimination may also be borne in mind.[19] The approximate, cursory statements of rights in Article 5, coupled with endorsement of rights from multiple sources have, nonetheless, the potential to generate indeterminacy in subjecting the rights protected by Article 5 to a standard discrimination analysis. Statements of rights subjected to discrimination analysis by the Committee are derived from their content as expressed in international law glimpsed through CERD lenses. CERD displays a tendency to optimize both the range and the standard of the rights to be protected from discrimination, in effect developing its own vision of them as a holistic construct emerging from a synthesis of multiple sources that includes their elaboration in the Convention.

Pertinent to the rights to be protected under Article 5 of ICERD, some general comments of the CESCR follow the '4A scheme', which translates rights into discrete but interconnected elements in order to clarify obligations deriving from them, facilitate their analysis, and measure the extent of their implementation. One such '4A' articulation appears in General Comment (GC) 13 on the *Right to Education*,[20] which measures the right in terms of its availability, accessibility, acceptability, and adaptability.[21] For education, *availability* refers to the existence of functioning educational institutions in the State party including the right of private parties to establish schools; *accessibility* focuses on discriminatory barriers to enjoyment of the rights; *acceptability* requires the

[18] Para. 2.

[19] *L.R. v Slovakia*, CERD/C/66/D/31/2003 (2005), para. 10.7. See further discussion in Chapter 8.

[20] E/C.12/1999/10.

[21] Footnote 2 of the GC states that the approach 'corresponds with the Committee's analytical framework adopted in relation to the rights to adequate housing and food, as well as the work of the United Nations Special Rapporteur on the right to education'; the note also refers to GC No. 4 (right to adequate housing) and GC 12 (right to adequate food).

provision of curricula that are relevant, culturally appropriate and of good quality, including a safe and healthy school environment; *adaptability* signifies flexibility and responsiveness to the needs of students in diverse cultural settings. With nuances of difference, the '4A' formula has been repeated in later general comments, and is represented as '5A' in the later General Comment on *The Right to Take Part in Cultural Life* with the addition of *appropriateness*,[22] which ratchets up the cultural dimension of rights in referring to 'the realization of a specific human right in a way that is pertinent and suitable to a given modality or context, that is, respectful of the culture and cultural rights of individuals and communities, including minorities and individuals'.[23]

While, as noted in Chapter 8, CERD has not explicitly adopted the '4A' or '5A' formulae of the CESCR, practice under Article 5 largely follows these contours. The principal focal points of practice are those of the provision of rights, linked to the argument as to the 'establishment' of rights by Article 5, or their 'availability' in the 4A formula, access to rights, and cultural appropriateness.[24] The listed rights, those derived from them, and background international law standards, are expected to be 'available', following the GR 20 vocabulary of 'assuming' the existence of rights. In terms of access to the enjoyment of rights, examples of racial, ethnic, and caste barriers to such enjoyment run through practice under Article 5, the need to address racial 'barriers' links with the statement in the preamble of their repugnancy to the ideals of any human society. 'Cultural' elements go beyond the category of economic, social, and cultural rights, and invest the understanding of rights in general.[25] The application of civil and political rights to, for example, justice and security areas is as likely to be as culturally influenced as rights to education or housing or the concept of participation in cultural activities itself. The stress on the limits of 'culture' from a human rights perspective, discussed elsewhere in the present work,[26] does not detract from its pervasiveness in providing templates for the interpretation and application of rights in a multiplicity of local contexts.

In particular, Committee practice has endorsed notions of culturally influenced collective rights associated with particular communities, notably indigenous peoples but also including Afro-descendant communities and others,[27] that present communal visions of human rights. Including but not confined to indigenous rights, international—and domestic—human rights standards have also embraced collective as well as individual rights.[28] While the collective rights addressed in practice move beyond the list in Article 5, the Committee treats their recognition as governed by principles of equality and non-discrimination. The work of other human rights bodies has been drawn upon in this area, notably the Inter-American Commission and Court of Human Rights, which has developed an understanding of the corpus of collective rights from constituent instruments on the rights of persons, applying their limited textual standards to the realities of communal

[22] E/C.12/GC/21 (2009).

[23] Paragraph 16 (e), which adds: The Committee wishes to stress . . . the need to take into account . . . cultural values attached to, inter alia, food and food consumption, the use of water, the way health and education services are provided and the way housing is designed and constructed'.

[24] On 'availability' and necessary infrastructures of rights, see Chapters 8 and 16 in particular.

[25] See further Chapter 20.

[26] In particular Chapters 6, 14, and 20.

[27] See among other judgments cited in Chapter 13, *Saramaka People v Suriname*, IACtHR Ser. C No. 172 (2007); also CERD GR 34; see further Chapter 20.

[28] G. Pentassuglia, *Minority Groups and Judicial Discourse in International Law* (Martinus Nijhoff Publishers, 2009).

particularities and cultural diversity.[29] Article 5 of ICERD protects the rights of 'everyone'. In its interpretation of the right of 'everyone', CERD practice is in line with the position on cultural rights in GC 21 of the Committee on Economic, Social and Cultural Rights, which states that the word may denote 'the individual or the collective . . . In other words, cultural rights may be exercised by a person (a) as an individual, (b) in association with others, or (c) in a community or group, as such'.[30] This flexibility, shared by CERD, contributes to the understanding that human rights, if they are to pursue a 'universal' vocation, cannot be inexorably tied to fundamentalist Liberal conceptions of rights as applying only paradigmatically or uniquely to 'individuals'.

The emphasis on the effect on CERD practice of developments in collective human rights under general international law should not detract from collective elements intrinsic to the Convention which, according to a member of the Committee in 1982,[31] represented 'a unique case in the international instruments on human rights'. The judgement of uniqueness is longer accurate but the comment on the intrinsic quality of the Convention retains its validity. Whatever the original drafting intentions behind the Convention, the reference to General Assembly resolution 1514 (XV) (the Colonial Declaration) in the preamble to the Convention serves to undermine any argument that ICERD is unfamiliar with collective rights, even in the 'hard' sense of rights inhering in a community as such. The outreach to collective concepts of rights has functional instrumentality in light of paradigmatic discriminatory practices that target groups, or target individuals on account of real or imagined appurtenance to racial/ethnic groups, of their actual or perceived membership thereof. The text of the Convention as a whole is not relentlessly 'individualistic' in its descriptions,[32] and should not be treated as a culturally assimilationist instrument, though it has been understood as such in (some) past practice.[33] Appraisals of discrimination against groups, taken holistically, and not simply of discrimination against individuals are an outstanding feature of the CERD repertoire. The raised profile of identity standards, particularly since the 1980s and 1990s, has further contoured the applications of equality and non-discrimination principles, directing attention towards gross collective harms.[34]

The practice generated by Article 5 presents a complex profile of racial discrimination, illustrating multiple forms and contexts of discrimination and denials of equality, their

[29] Concluding observations on Nicaragua, CERD/C/NIC/CO/14, para. 21, refer to the judgement of the Inter-American Court of Human Rights in the *Awas Tingni case*, IACtHR Ser. C No. 79 (2001); observations on Paraguay, CERD/C/PRY/CO/11-3, para. 17, refer to the judgments of the Inter-American Court of Human Rights in *Yakye Axa v Paraguay*, IACtHR Ser C No. 125 (2005); *Sawhoyamaxa v Paraguay*, IACtHR Ser. C No. 146 (2006); and *Xákmok Kásek v Paraguay*, IACtHR (2010). Decision 1 (68) on the Western Shoshone, A/61/18, Chapter II, applied aspects of the case of *Mary and Carrie Dann v United States* before the Inter-American Commission on Human Rights: Case 11.140, 27 December 2002. Note also the Committee's support for the decisions of the African Commission on Human and Peoples' Rights in the Endorois, Comm. 276/2003, *Centre for Minority Rights Development (Kenya) and Minority Rights Group international on behalf of the Endorois Welfare Council v Kenya* (2010); and *Ogiek* cases, now a judgement of the African Court of Human Rights, App. No. 006/2012, 15.03.2013, CERD/C/KEN/CO/1-4, para. 17.

[30] Para. 9.

[31] Devetak, A/37/18, para. 468.

[32] *Inter alia*, the right in 5(d)(v), referring to owning property 'alone as well as in association with others', may be recalled.

[33] P. Thornberry, *International Law and the Rights of Minorities* (Clarendon Press, 1991), Chapter 30, especially with reference to then situation of Turkish communities in Bulgaria.

[34] Discussed in Chapter 20.

institutional settings, and contemporary targets. The abstract grounds of discrimination on Article 1, in practice undiminished in scope under Article 5 despite the omission of 'descent', metamorphose into human form in the complex, interlocking narratives that characterize global practice in the vindication and denial of rights. Ethnic minorities—notably including Roma in many States and not simply in Europe—indigenous peoples, Afro-descendants, caste groups, multiple categories of non-citizens, groups and persons identified through intersectionalities, particularly women and religious groups, bear the brunt of discrimination, as shown in the melancholy record of 'concerns' over rights and their violations that populate the archives of Article 5.

Large-scale human vulnerabilities are also exposed to view, whether the result of historical exclusion and dispossession, the operation of prejudices and antipathies, residues of hierarchical classification including the racial (perhaps transmuted into denigration of cultures),[35] or choice or compulsion to leave countries of nationality. The identification of potential victims of discrimination in the universalist framework of the Convention has resolved itself into micro-identifications of categories of persons under threat, a process facilitated and constructed through utilizing legal classifications and statements of rights from the human rights canon writ large, including the categories of minorities and non-citizens that were largely put aside in the drafting process. While the utilization of such categories by CERD tends to be approximate, and their descriptions overlapping, they serve the purposes of pinpointing where discrimination operates and of facilitating judgements of compatibility with legal standards. The enjoyment and exercise of civil, political, economic, social, and cultural rights in their various aspects are all potentially subject to diminution by racially discriminatory practices on the part of States, individuals, communities, and corporations.

[35] See Chapter 6.

16. Article 6

Remedies for Racial Discrimination

States parties shall assure to everyone within their jurisdiction effective protection and remedies, through the competent national tribunals and other State institutions, against any acts of racial discrimination which violate his human rights and fundamental freedoms contrary to this Convention, as well as the right to seek from such tribunals just and adequate reparation or satisfaction for any damage suffered as a result of such discrimination.

A. Introduction

In general international law, 'breach of an engagement involves an obligation to make reparation in an adequate form':[1] reparations are owed for every breach of an international obligation.[2] The traditional rules of international law regarding reparations apply to interstate claims, and while they may have 'limited utility when the claimant is an individual, group or organization,' they are without prejudice to rights 'accruing directly to a person or entity other than a State',[3] leaving it to primary rules to define such rights.[4] The corpus of international human rights law contains an abundance of such 'primary rules' including those in Article 6 of the International Convention on the Elimination of All Forms of Racial Discrimination (ICERD). The function of a system of remedies in international human rights law is eloquently expressed in the Vienna Declaration of the World Conference on Human Rights:

[1] *Chorzów Factory*, Claim for Indemnity, Jurisdiction (*Germany v Poland*) [1927] PCIJ, Ser. A, No. 9, p. 21, reaffirmed in *Reparations for Injuries Suffered in the Service of the United Nations*, Advisory Opinion, ICJ rep 1949, para. 184.

[2] Such 'reparation must, as far as possible, wipe out all the consequences of the illegal act and re-establish the situation that would, in all probability have existed if that act had not been committed': *Chorzów Factory*, Merits [1928] PCIJ, Ser. A, No. 17, p. 47. See also the International Law Commission's *Draft Articles on the Responsibility of States for Internationally Wrongful Acts*, 2001, commended to States by the UN General Assembly in resolution 56/83, December 12, 2001, Articles 30 (Cessation and Non-repetition); 31 (Reparation); 34, full reparation for the injury caused by the internationally wrongful act 'shall take the form of restitution, compensation and satisfaction'; Article 35 (Restitution); Article 36 (Compensation), while Article 37 defines satisfaction as consisting in 'an acknowledgement of the breach, an expression of regret, a formal apology or another appropriate modality', adding 'insofar as it cannot be made good by restitution or compensation'.

[3] D. Shelton, 'Reparations for Indigenous Peoples: the Present Value of Past Wrongs', in F. Lenzerini (ed.), *Reparations for Indigenous Peoples: International and Comparative Perspectives* (Oxford University Press, 2008), 47–72 at 59.

[4] Nonetheless, in Antkowiak's reading, human rights instruments 'do not offer specific guidance as to how States should repair violations. Without many explicit parameters, the international bodies formulating remedies for victims of human rights abuse initially turned to principles of State responsibility': T.M. Antkowiak, 'A Dark Side of Virtue: The Inter-American Court and Reparations for Indigenous Peoples', *Duke Journal of Comparative and International Law* 25 (2014), 1–80, 6 [henceforth 'The Inter-American Court and Reparations'].

Every State should provide an effective framework of remedies to redress human rights grievances or violations. The administration of justice, including law enforcement and prosecutorial agencies and, especially, an independent judiciary and legal profession in full conformity with applicable standards contained in international human rights instruments, are essential to the full and non-discriminatory realization of human rights and indispensable to the processes of democracy and sustainable development.[5]

The right to a remedy is a key aspect of international human rights law[6] and is reflected in a wide variety of global and regional instruments, as well as in instruments of humanitarian law and international criminal law.[7] 'Remedial' provisions may be included in general statements or with regard to specific rights. The Universal Declaration of Human Rights (UDHR) provides that '[e]veryone has the right to an effective remedy by the competent national tribunals for acts violating the fundamental rights granted him by the constitution or by law'.[8] Among the UN 'core' treaties, the International Covenant on Civil and Political Rights (ICCPR) contains a general clause on remedies and specific clauses in connection with arrest, detention and conviction,[9] while the Convention on the Elimination of All Forms of Discrimination against Women (CEDAW) includes general language on remedies,[10] as does the Convention on Migrant Workers (CMW).[11] Redress and compensation for torture victims are referred to in the Convention against Torture (CAT).[12] Protection against attacks on privacy, family, home, etc, and on honour and reputation, is envisaged in a number of treaties.[13] The International Convention for the Protection of All Persons from Enforced Disappearance (CPED) includes a number of provisions regarding remedies, notably the comprehensive Article 24, where the 'right to reparation' is deemed to cover 'material and moral damages and, where appropriate, other forms of reparation such as: (a) restitution; (b) rehabilitation; (c) satisfaction, including restoration of dignity and reputation; (d) guarantees of non-repetition'. Article 24 of the Convention on the Rights of Persons with Disabilities (CRPD) calls for measures to

[5] Vienna Declaration and Programme of Action, adopted by the World Conference on Human Rights, Vienna, 25 June 1993, Article 27; text available at: <http://www.ohchr.org/EN/ProfessionalInterest/Pages/Vienna.aspx>.

[6] D. Shelton, *Remedies in International Human Rights Law* (2nd edn, Oxford University Press, 2005). Other general treatments include M. Evans and S. Konstadinides (eds), *Remedies in International Law: The Institutional Dilemma* (Hart Publishing, 1998); C. Gray, *Judicial Remedies in International Law* (Clarendon Press, 1987).

[7] See, *inter alia*, Article 75 of the Statute of the International Criminal Court, requiring the Court to 'establish principles relating to reparations . . . including restitution, compensation and rehabilitation'. Issues are discussed broadly in E-C. Gillard, 'Reparation for Violations of International Humanitarian Law', *International Review of the Red Cross* 85 (2003), 529–53; L. Zegveld, Remedies for Victims of Violations of International Humanitarian Law', *ibid.*, 497–526.

[8] Article 8.

[9] Articles 2(3), 9(5), and 14(6). See Human Rights Committee, General Comment No. 31, *The Nature of the General Legal Obligation Imposed on States Parties to the Covenant* (2004), paras 15–16; in para. 16 the Committee notes that 'where appropriate, reparation can involve restitution, rehabilitation and measures of satisfaction, such as public apologies, public memorials, guarantees of non-repetition and changes in relevant laws and practices, as well as bringing to justice the perpetrators of human rights violations'.

[10] Article 2(c).

[11] Article 83.

[12] Article 14.

[13] Including Article 12 of the UDHR; ICCPR, Article 17; CRC, Article 16.

promote 'the physical, cognitive and psychological recovery, rehabilitation and social integration of persons with disabilities'; habilitation and rehabilitation are elaborated in Article 26. Key regional instruments incorporating principles on reparation include the African Charter on Human and Peoples' Rights (ACHPR),[14] the American Convention on Human Rights (ACHR),[15] the Arab Charter on Human Rights,[16] and the European Convention on Human Rights (ECHR).[17]

In the field of racism and related intolerance, the Declaration against Racial Discrimination provides that everyone 'shall have the right to an effective remedy and protection against any discrimination he may suffer on the ground of race, colour or ethnic origin with respect to his fundamental rights and freedoms through independent national tribunals competent to deal with such matters'.[18] The Inter-American Convention against Racism, etc, includes the undertaking to ensure 'that victims of racism, racial discrimination, and related forms of intolerance receive equitable and non-discriminatory treatment, equal access to the justice system, expeditious and effective proceedings, and fair compensation in the civil or criminal sphere'.[19]

The section of the Durban Declaration on remedies, etc, sets out a prospectus that addresses issues of historical memory, the importance of knowing the truth about abuses deriving from racism, honouring the victims of racist practices—including victims of the transatlantic slave trade—and apologies and reparation for race-related massive violations of human rights.[20] The Declaration takes note of the fact that some members of the international community have apologized or expressed regret and remorse for 'those dark chapters in history' and calls on others 'who have not yet contributed to restoring the dignity of the victims to find appropriate ways to do so'.[21] If many paragraphs in the section on remedies focus on past evils, the Durban Declaration also orients itself to the present day and incorporates elements of Article 6 of ICERD in affirming as a pressing requirement of justice,

> that victims of human rights violations resulting from racism [etc], especially in light of their vulnerable situation socially, culturally and economically, should be assured of having access to justice, including legal assistance where appropriate, and effective and appropriate protection and remedies, including the right to seek just and adequate reparation or satisfaction for any damage suffered as a result of such discrimination, as enshrined in numerous international and regional human rights instruments.[22]

[14] Articles 7, 21, and 26; Article 21 envisages the remedy of 'lawful recovery of its property' as well as 'adequate compensation' for a dispossessed people in case of spoliation.

[15] Articles 8, 10, and 25.

[16] Article 12.

[17] Article 13.

[18] Article 7(2).

[19] Article 10.

[20] 24 March was proclaimed by the General Assembly as the International Day for the Right to Truth Concerning Gross Human Rights Violations and for the Dignity of Victims: A/RES/65/196, 21 December 2010; see also the proclamation by the Human Rights Council, A/HRC/RES/14/7, 23 June 2010; *Study on the Right to Truth*, Report of the Office of the United Nations High Commissioner for Human Rights, E/CN.4/2006/91, 8 February 2006. 24 March commemorates the assassination of Archbishop Oscar Romero of El Salvador, who had denounced violations of the human rights of vulnerable populations including indigenous peoples. The UN has instituted a Special Rapporteur on Truth, Justice, Reparation and Guarantees of Non-Recurrence; for the mandate see: <http://www.ohchr.org/EN/Issues/TruthJusticeReparation/Pages/Mandate.aspx>.

[21] Para. 101.

[22] Para. 104.

The broad and narrower prescriptions in the Durban Declaration are followed up in the Programme of Action which recommends that national legislative frameworks should, *inter alia*, 'provide effective judicial and other remedies of redress, including through the designation of national, independent, specialized bodies',[23] and that access to such remedies 'should be widely available, on a non-discriminatory and equal basis'.[24] Within the overall redress framework the Programme of Action underlines the importance of access to the law and to the courts for complaints of racism and racial discrimination and draws attention to 'the need for judicial and other remedies to be made widely known, easily accessible, expeditious and not unduly complicated'.[25] The paragraph following adds to the tabulation of remedies a reference to designing 'effective measures to prevent the repetition of... acts' of racial discrimination.[26]

Reparation principles have been specifically elaborated for the benefit of particular constituencies such as indigenous peoples.[27] International Labour Organization (ILO) Convention 169 addresses the right of indigenous peoples to return to their lands and territories after relocation,[28] as well as sundry issues of compensation.[29] The UN Declaration on the Rights of Indigenous Peoples is replete with provisions regarding reparation, redress, restitution, compensation, and repatriation of ceremonial objects and human remains.[30] The broadest prescription is contained in Article 28:

1. Indigenous peoples have the right to redress, by means that can include restitution or, when this is not possible, just, fair and equitable compensation, for the lands, territories and resources which they have traditionally owned or otherwise occupied or used, and which have been confiscated, taken, occupied, used or damaged without their free, prior and informed consent.
2. Unless otherwise freely agreed upon by the peoples concerned, compensation shall take the form of lands, territories and resources equal in quality, size and legal status or of monetary compensation or other appropriate redress.[31]

A body of substantive human rights provisions on reparations was synthesized into a set of *Basic Principles and Guidelines on the Right to a Remedy and Reparation for Victims of Gross Violations of Human Rights*, adopted by the UN General Assembly in 2005,[32] the

[23] Para. 163.
[24] Para. 164.
[25] Para. 165.
[26] Para. 166.
[27] See the extensive set of essays in F. Lenzerini (ed.), *Reparations for Indigenous Peoples: International and Comparative Perspectives* (Oxford University Press, 2008). Group-oriented discussions of reparations drawing on more than one academic stream are included in R.L. Brooks, *Atonement and Forgiveness: A New Model for Black Reparation* (University of California Press, 2004); M. du Plessis, 'Historical Justice and International Law: An Exploratory Discussion of Reparation for Slavery', *HRQ* 25 (2003), 624–59; R.E. Howard-Hassmann and A. P. Lombardo, *Reparations to Africa* (University of Pennsylvania Press, 2008); J. Miller and R. Kumar (eds), *Reparations: Interdisciplinary Perspectives* (Oxford University Press, 2007).
[28] Article 16(3).
[29] Articles 15(2), and 16(4), 16(5).
[30] Articles 8, 10, 11, 12, 20, 27, 28, 32, and 40, deal with various aspects of remedial processes.
[31] For broader comment, see International Law Association, The Hague Conference (2010), Rights of Indigenous Peoples, pp. 39–43: <http://www.ila-hq.org/ ... cfm/ ... /9E2AEDE9-BB41-42BA-9999F0359E79F62D>.
[32] *Basic Principles and Guidelines on the Right to a Remedy and Reparation for Victims of Gross Violations of International Human Rights Law and Serious Violations of International Humanitarian Law*, adopted and proclaimed by GA resolution 60/147 of 16 December 2005 [henceforth *Basic Principles and Guidelines*]. See also Special Rapporteur on Rights of Victims of Gross Violations of Human Rights and Fundamental Freedoms, M. Cherif Bassiouni, *The Right to Restitution, Compensation and Rehabilitation for Victims of Gross Violations of Human Rights and Fundamental Freedoms, Final Report*, E/CN.4/2000/62 (18 January, 2000). For

preamble to which recites the recognition that, 'in honouring the victims' right to benefit from remedies and reparation, the international community keeps faith with the plight of victims, survivors and future human generations and reaffirms the international legal principles of accountability, justice and the rule of law'. The *Basic Principles and Guidelines* elaborate the basic obligation to respect human rights law, etc, in terms of appropriate measures to prevent violations, prompt investigation of violations, taking action against those responsible for violations, access to justice and effective remedies.[33] Victims are deemed to have a right to equal and effective access to justice, adequate, effective, and prompt reparation for harm suffered, as well as access to information on violations and reparation mechanisms.[34]

The concepts are elaborated in a manner that echoes the inter-State principles of State responsibility set out in the Draft Articles of the International Law Commission (ILC).[35] Reparation is understood as intended to promote justice, and should be proportional to the gravity of the violations and harms suffered.[36] Reparation is sub-divided into restitution (designed to restore victims to the original pre-violation situation),[37] compensation (related to economically assessable damage that includes mental, physical, and moral harm as well as material losses),[38] and satisfaction (including measures aimed at cessation of violations, verification of the facts, apologies, sanctions, commemorations, and tributes to victims).[39] The *Basic Principles and Guidelines* also elaborate on such matters as rehabilitation of victims,[40] and on guarantees of non-repetition, a concept that involves a complex 'structural' prospectus that includes strengthening the independence of the judiciary and human rights education.[41] The focus on gross violations of human rights does not rule out adaptation to smaller scale violations. What counts as a gross violation has exercised the Committee on the Elimination of Racial Discrimination (CERD), particularly in connection with the criteria for taking action under its urgent procedure.[42] The emphasis on the gravity and scale of violations appropriate to trigger the procedure does not rule out its application to smaller populations where the impact of violations may be disproportionately large.[43]

In addition to the provisions cited in the present chapter laying out the duties of States to provide protection and remedies, in the terms of Article 6 'to everyone within their jurisdiction', it may be noted that some international conventions devolve significant

the development of the *Basic Principles*, including the seminal work by T. van Boven, *Study Concerning the Right to Restitution, Compensation and Rehabilitation for Victims of Gross Violations of Human Rights and Fundamental Freedoms*, E/CN.4/Sub.2/1993/8, 2 July 1993, see the collection of essays in K. de Feyter, S. Parmentier, M. Bossuyt, and P. Lemmens (eds), *Out of the Ashes: Reparation for Victims of Gross and Systematic Human Rights Violations* (Intersentia, 2006).

33 *Basic Principles and Guidelines*, para. 3.
34 *Ibid.*, para. 11.
35 Draft Articles on the Responsibility of States for Internationally Wrongful Acts, *supra*, n. 2.
36 *Basic Principles and Guidelines*, para. 15.
37 Para. 19.
38 Para. 20.
39 Para. 22.
40 Para. 21.
41 Para. 23.
42 Discussed in Chapter 4.
43 The point is referred to in Chapter 4.

remedial powers to their monitoring bodies in the context of binding court judgments.[44] Hence, regarding the jurisdiction and functions of the Inter-American Court of Human Rights, Article 63(1) of the Inter-American Convention on Human Rights provides that the Court may order in appropriate cases that the consequences of a breach of rights or freedoms protected by the Convention be remedied and compensation paid. The Inter-American Court in particular has been highly creative in extending the jurisprudential lexicon of remedies,[45] and its prescriptions have been influential in the work of other bodies, including CERD.[46]

B. *Travaux Préparatoires*

In the Sub-Commission, the Abram text proposed that each State party 'shall assure to everyone within its jurisdiction' a right to an effective remedy for racial discrimination 'through independent national tribunals competent to deal with such matters', and also 'remedial relief for any individual who has suffered substantial harm as a result of racial violence, hatred or discrimination'.[47] The Calvocoressi,[48] and the later joint Abram, Calvocoressi, and Capotorti text also referred to effective remedies.[49] In discussions, Capotorti referred to the draft article as designed 'to ensure that the party responsible for causing injury as a result of racial discrimination, whether it was the State itself or a

[44] Article 41 of the ECHR, under the heading of 'Just Satisfaction', provides that if the Court 'finds that there has been a violation of the Convention or the protocols thereto, and if the internal law of the High Contracting Party allows only partial reparation to be made, the Court shall, if necessary, afford just satisfaction to the injured party'.

[45] 'For its part, the Inter-American Court of Human Rights stands as the only international tribunal with binding jurisdiction that has ordered all . . . remedies. The depth and breadth of its reparations jurisprudence are unparalleled. Often in potent combinations, the Court has ordered wide-ranging measures such as monetary compensation, restitution, cessation, medical and psychological rehabilitation, apologies, memorials, legislative reform, and training programmes for State officials . . . This approach sharply contrasts with . . . the European Court of Human Rights. The European Court has historically favoured only monetary compensation and declaratory relief, although exceptions . . . have appeared during recent years': Antkowiak, *The Inter-American Court and Reparations*, 10. See also J. Pasqualucci, 'The Americas', in D. Moeckli, S. Shah, and S. Sivakumaran (eds), *International Human Rights Law* (2nd edn, Oxford University Press, 2014), 398–415, 408–10, who observes, 408, in the context of the Court's 'enhancement of the concept of reparations' that 'the Court has ordered victim-centred reparations as well as reparations that . . . benefit specific communities or society as a whole'. Examples of the latter include return of ancestral lands, *Yakye Axa v Paraguay*, IACtHR Ser. C No. 125 (2005); a campaign to educate on the work of environmental activists, *Kawas Fernándes v Honduras*, IACtHR Ser. C No. 196 (2009); to reopen a school and a medical clinic, *Aloeboetoe v Suriname*, IACtHR Ser. C No. 15 (1993); to invest in collective service for the benefit of the community, *Awas Tingni v Nicaragua*, IACtHR Ser. C No. 79 (2001); and to develop programmes in the areas of health, housing, and education, *Moiwana Village v Suriname*, IACtHR Ser. C No. 125 (2005). Aspects of these cases are discussed in the present work, principally in connection with Article 5.

[46] References to the organs of the Inter-American system are found in, *inter alia*, concluding observations on Ecuador, CERD/C/ECU/CO/20-22, para. 8, welcoming the commitment to comply with the Court's ruling in the *Sarayaku* case (*Kichwa Indigenous People of Sarayaku v Ecuador*, IACtHR (27 June 2012)); Paraguay, CERD/C/PRY/CO/1-3, para. 17, re the Yakye Axa, Sawhoyamaxa, and Xamok Kasek indigenous communities; Suriname, CERD/C/SUR/CO/12, para. 18, implement the Court's judgments in *Moiwana* and *Saramaka (Saramaka People v Suriname)*, IACtHR Ser. C No. 185 (2008) cases, and para. 19, respond to the analysis by the inter-American organs regarding deficiencies in providing adequate remedies for collective rights. See also Chapter 13.

[47] E/CN.4/Sub.2/L.308.

[48] E/CN.4/Sub.2/L.309.

[49] E/CN.4/Sub.2/L.339.

private individual or organization, should provide effective remedy to the victim'.[50] A reference to remedial relief, 'including payment of damages' was incorporated into the text prepared by Cuevas Cancino and Ingles.[51] The reference to 'payment of damages' did not survive into the text presented to the Commission:

States parties shall assure to everyone within their jurisdiction effective remedies and protection through independent tribunals against any racial discrimination and the right to obtain from such tribunals reparation for any damage suffered as a result of racial discrimination.[52]

A number of amendments to the Sub-Commission's text were submitted, notably that of the United Kingdom to add 'contrary to the present Convention' after 'racial discrimination'[53] and that of Austria to replace 'reparation' by 'just satisfaction'.[54] The USSR proposed the insertion of 'competent to consider such cases' after 'independent tribunals'.[55] An amendment by Lebanon proposed that the Sub-Commission's text be redrafted as follows:

States parties shall assure to everyone within their jurisdiction effective remedies and protection through independent tribunals, competent to consider such cases, against any acts of racial discrimination which, contrary to this Convention, violate his human rights and fundamental freedoms, and the right to obtain from such tribunals remedial decisions for reparation of any damage suffered as a result of such discrimination.

It was pointed out that the reference to 'national' tribunals was important and that this qualification on the nature of the tribunal had been inadvertently omitted from the Sub-Commission's text.[56] The amendment proposed by the USSR on the tribunals issue suggested to some that only specially convened tribunals could deal with racial discrimination cases,[57] though 'competent' could also mean simply competent under national legislation.[58] The suggested addition of 'impartial' to the qualifications of tribunals did not find favour: insisting on impartiality in the text could, according to one representative,

[50] E/CN.4/Sub.2/SR.425, pp. 3–4.

[51] E/CN.4/Sub.2/L.330.

[52] Commission on Human Rights, Report on the Twentieth Session, E/CN.4/874, para. 213.

[53] E/CN.4/L.700.

[54] E/CN.4/L.711. The amendment was later withdrawn in favour of an amendment by Costa Rica to the revised proposal of Lebanon (E/CN.4/874, para. 220) to add 'or satisfaction' after 'reparation': E/CN.4/874, para. 221. This was accepted by 19 votes to none, with 2 abstentions: E/CN.4/874, para. 228.

[55] E/CN.4/L.681.

[56] Representative of the USSR, E/CN.4/SR.800, pp. 10–11, who noted that 'national' tribunals had also been referred to in the Abram text (E/CN.4/Sub.2/L.308) before the Sub-Commission. The Calvocoressi text (E/CN.4/Sub.2/L.309) had also referred to 'a national authority or tribunal'.

[57] Representative of Ecuador, E/CN.4/SR.800, p. 14, to which the reply of the USSR (*ibid.*) was that the purpose of the USSR amendment 'was not to set up new tribunals but to ensure that use was made of the competent national tribunals that already existed.' A number of representatives accepted the notion of 'competent national tribunals' provided 'its use did not in any way prejudice the right of victims of racial discrimination to turn to international bodies' for help: representative of Austria, E/CN.4/SR.801, p. 5; see also the representative of Italy, E/CN.4/SR.801, p. 8.

[58] According to the representative of the United Kingdom, 'The word "competent"... was necessary to indicate that the tribunals concerned were those which would naturally handle the types of cases in question': E/CN.4/SR.801, p. 7. At the request of the Representative of Austria, a separate vote was taken on the word 'competent'; the term was adopted by 20 votes to none, with 1 abstention: E/CN.4/874, para. 230. Cf. Article 8 of the UDHR where the phrase 'competent national tribunals' is employed, whereas the phrase 'independent and impartial tribunal' appears in its Article 10.

be seen as casting a slur on the administration of justice in certain countries.[59] A UK amendment was designed, according to its representative, to make clear that the tribunals would be competent to deal with discrimination the subject of obligations under other articles of the Convention;[60] against this, it was argued that the impression should not be given that the scope of the Convention was narrow and remedies outside it were not possible.[61] Suggestions to refer to 'acts of racial discrimination' rather than discrimination in general, and to 'acts' violating human rights and fundamental freedoms were eventually included: according to one representative, 'a remedy was not against abstract principles but against specific acts'.[62]

On reparations generally, representatives questioned whether the Sub-Commission text was correct to refer to a right to obtain reparation, since what was to be assured was the right to approach tribunals which would then decide on the merits of the case;[63] it would be better, therefore, to refer to the 'right to seek' reparations.[64] The Austrian suggestion to add 'just satisfaction' was understood by some discussants to meet the case where pecuniary damages were insufficient, thereby bringing into play the idea of equitable reparation.[65] Discussions produced additional terminology to the Austrian proposal so that the phrase became 'just and adequate reparation or satisfaction', despite doubts as to whether this would unduly burden tribunals and whether such remedies could be found in all cases of racial discrimination.[66] The expanded terminology was accepted.[67] It was observed that the right to obtain reparations should be stated broadly since it concerned not only reparation for financial damage, but also the restoration of the rights of victims.[68]

The term 'protection' was not much discussed in the Commission. The representative of Liberia made the substantive point that it should be retained, because 'even if a person

[59] Representative of Lebanon, E/CN.4/SR.800, p. 8; and according to the representative of Italy, the draft convention, 'like any other United Nations convention, should take for granted the independence and impartiality of the courts' of member States: E/CN.4/SR.801, p. 8.

[60] 'Although the expression "racial discrimination" was already defined in Article I, his delegation thought it would be useful to make even clearer that the obligations assumed by the State parties under this article [VI] related to the obligations they had assumed under articles II, III, IV and V': comment of the representative of the UK, E/CN.4/SR.800, p. 5.

[61] See in particular the remarks by the representative of The Philippines, E/CN.4/SR.800, pp. 5–6; and the USSR, *ibid*., p. 11: the UK amendment 'might give the impression that effective remedies and protection would be available only in the event of discriminatory acts in violation of [the] convention, as if its scope was narrow and outside it no remedies were possible. That restriction . . . was inconceivable. Racial discrimination had been declared illegal in principle.'

[62] Representative of France, E/CN.4/SR.800, p. 12.

[63] Representative of the United Kingdom, E/CN.4/SR.801, p. 7.

[64] E/CN.4/SR.801, p. 6, representative of Costa Rica. France initially suggested referring to the 'possibility' to obtain reparations in preference to the 'right' to do so: E/CN.4/SR.800, p. 12.

[65] E/CN.4/SR.801, p. 5. The *travaux* reveal divergent views regarding the meaning of 'reparation', with a number of representatives assuming that it related to monetary compensation whilst others argued for a wider meaning; see, for example, comments by Poland, Austria, and Lebanon, E/CN.4/SR.801, pp. 4–5.

[66] For example remarks of the United Kingdom, E/CN.4/SR.801, pp. 6–7.

[67] At the request of the United Kingdom, a separate vote was taken on the words 'and adequate' in the Lebanese amendment; the term was retained by 13 votes to 4, with 4 abstentions: E/CN.4/874, para. 229.

[68] Remarks of the representative of Poland, E/CN.4/SR.800, p. 9. The representative of Italy, E/CN.4/SR.801, p. 8, observed that 'satisfaction' 'was primarily concerned with non-monetary compensation, whereas "reparation", which was a very broad term, covered both non-monetary and monetary damage . . . "adequate" should be inserted to indicate that the amount of the reparation must reflect the seriousness of the injury suffered.' In similar vein, the representative of Lebanon, *ibid*., 'understood that the word "reparation" included not only monetary reparation but also all forms of remedy'.

was offered a remedy in the event of a violation or denial of his rights under the Convention, before attempting to obtain reparation from a tribunal, he must have the assurance that the latter would protect him'.[69] On the other hand, Italy argued that 'protection' was redundant because to be effective a remedy had to assure protection.[70]

The Third Committee examined the following text:

> States parties shall assure to everyone within their jurisdiction effective protection and remedies, through the competent national tribunals, against any acts of racial discrimination which violate his human rights and fundamental freedoms contrary to this Convention, as well as the right to seek from such tribunals just and adequate reparation or satisfaction for any damage suffered as a result of such discrimination.[71]

A first amendment that proposed adding 'and other State institutions' between 'tribunals' and 'against'[72] was adopted by an overwhelming majority.[73] A second amendment sought to insert 'where appropriate' after 'adequate reparation' but was subsequently withdrawn:[74] the sponsor of the amendment explained that 'there might be cases in which monetary compensation would not be adequate or appropriate, for instance the case of a person refused hotel accommodation because of his race. The words "where appropriate" would indicate that in such circumstances other forms of redress were necessary.'[75] On 'reparation' the representative of the UK added that 'for her delegation, "reparation" meant simply money, and no court in her country could put a price on an act of discrimination. It was difficult enough to set a price in cases of divorce or loss of limb; in the case of racial discrimination there could be no price',[76] to which it was pointed out that the draft article referred to 'reparation or satisfaction'.[77]

C. Practice

I. Reservations and Declarations

Six States parties maintain declarations and interpretations on Article 6: France, Italy, Malta, Nepal, Tonga, and the UK,[78] most of which are couched in uniform terms: the government of Malta states that it 'interprets the requirement in article 6 concerning "reparation or satisfaction" as being fulfilled if one or other of these forms of redress is made available and interprets "satisfaction" as including any form of redress effective to bring the discriminatory conduct to an end'; the same formula is employed by Nepal, Tonga, and the UK. The statement by France is brief: 'France declares that the question of remedy through tribunals is, as far as France is concerned, governed by the rules of ordinary law'; while Italy adds that claims for damage suffered must be brought against the persons responsible for malicious or criminal acts which caused the damage.

[69] E/CN.4/SR.802, p. 4.
[70] E/CN.4/SR.801, p. 7.
[71] A/6181, para. 86.
[72] Amendment by Bulgaria, A/C.3/L.1218, A/6181, para. 87.
[73] *Ibid.*, para. 89: the voting was 88 to 1 with 9 abstentions.
[74] By Mauritania, Nigeria, and Uganda, A/C.3/L.1225. A/6181, para. 88.
[75] Representative of Nigeria, A/C.3/SR.1309, para. 34.
[76] A/C.3/SR.1309, para. 40.
[77] *Ibid.*, para. 41; remark by the representative of Mexico as Chairman.
[78] <https://treaties.un.org/Pages/ViewDetails.aspx?src=treaty&mtdsg_no=iv-2&chapter=4&lang=en>.

II. Guidelines

Guidelines for the Common Core Document request that States provide information on the machinery for the protection of human rights. This includes information on the 'remedies . . . available to an individual who claims that any of his or her rights have been violated, and whether any systems of reparation, compensation and rehabilitation exist for victims'.[79] This is supplemented by a paragraph requesting 'general information . . . on the nature and scope of remedies provided in . . . domestic legislation against violations of human rights and whether victims have effective access to these remedies'.[80]

The CERD-specific guidelines request information on the 'legislative, judicial, administrative or other measures' giving effect to Article 6,[81] and on the practice and decisions of courts and other judicial and administrative organs relating to 'cases of racial discrimination'. The guidelines also summarize important considerations associated with 'effective protection and remedies'. Paragraph 2 requests information on measures taken 'to ensure (a) that victims have adequate information concerning their rights; (b) that they do not fear social censure or reprisals; (c) that victims with limited resources do not fear the cost and complexity of the judicial process; (d) that there is no lack of trust in the police and judicial authorities; and (e) that the authorities are sufficiently alert to, or aware of, offences with racial motives'. The institutional contexts for the handling of complaints of racial discrimination are referred to in paragraph 3 in relation to 'national human rights institutions and ombudspersons and other similar institutions', while paragraphs 4 and 5 request information on 'types of reparation and satisfaction' considered adequate in domestic law, and the burden of proof in civil proceedings for racial discrimination; footnotes in the guidelines refer to General Recommendations (GRs) 23, 26, 30, and 31. The guidelines conclude by referring to the communications procedure under Article 14, suggesting that States should indicate whether they intend to accede to the procedure, and in the case of those which have opted in to the procedure, whether they have designated a body competent to receive petitions from individuals and groups claiming to be victims of racial discrimination.[82]

III. Everyone Within their Jurisdiction/Effective Protection and Remedies

The effective protection and remedies referred to must be assured to everyone within the jurisdiction: Article 6 is the second substantive article to refer to jurisdiction, the other being Article 3.[83] The open texture of Article 2 with regard to extraterritorial jurisdiction and the acceptance of extended jurisdiction under Article 3, discussed in previous chapters, suggest that similar principles may be applied, *mutatis mutandis*, to Article 6, which omits mention of territory or territories. In the case of the Occupied Palestinian Territory, the Committee commented in relation to violence by Jewish settlers that the State party 'should ensure that such incidents are investigated in a prompt, transparent and independent manner, the perpetrators are prosecuted and sentenced, and that

[79] HRI/GEN/2/Rev.5, p. 11, para. 42(e).

[80] *Ibid.*, para. 59.

[81] CERD/C/2007/1, p. 13.

[82] *Ibid.*, pp. 13–14. See discussion in Chapter 4.

[83] Article 6 has a certain unity that makes difficult the detachment of sections to illustrate the practice; observations below address issues that interrelate and overlap. Article 6 is the only substantive article in the Convention to use gendered language.

avenues of redress are offered to the victims'.[84] The Committee has expressed concerns regarding practices of administrative detention, the competence of military tribunals to try Palestinian children, and 'the monetary and physical obstacles faced by Palestinians seeking compensation before Israeli tribunals for loss suffered'.[85] In consequence, citing, *inter alia*, Article 6, CERD recommended that 'the State party ensure equal access to justice for all persons residing in territories under the State party's effective control', and urged the ending of the current practice of administrative detention 'which is discriminatory and constitutes arbitrary detention under international human rights law'.[86]

Article 6 is expressed in mandatory terms—the use of 'shall assure' governs the whole of the article. As with Article 5, the universalist language of 'everyone' is treated as compatible with adaptation to the circumstances of a plurality of groups, including non-citizens.[87] While Article 6 contains an independent obligation, opinions under the communications procedure frequently read it together with other articles, as the basis of the decision.[88]

The requests for information in the Guidelines suggest some of the content of the demands of 'effectiveness' placed upon States parties. If the system of remedies in the State party is to function effectively, the public must be aware of it and have confidence in its workings. The absence of complaints of racial discrimination in a particular jurisdiction is not generally regarded as a positive sign or an accurate measure of the incidence of racial discrimination: a standardized version of this caution, recycled through numerous recommendations to States parties, is presented in GR 31 on the administration of criminal justice:

> The absence or small number of complaints, prosecutions and convictions relating to acts of racial discrimination... should not be viewed as necessarily positive... It may... reveal either that victims have inadequate information concerning their rights, or that they fear social censure or reprisals, or that victims with limited resources fear the cost and complexity of the judicial process, or that there is a lack of trust in the police and judicial authorities, or that the authorities are insufficiently alert to or aware of offences involving racism.[89]

Concerns regarding the small numbers of national cases on racial discrimination have been recycled through successive concluding observations; the concerns regarding low numbers of complaints reflect the Committee's sceptical approach to the (occasional) claims as to the absence or low incidence of racial discrimination in the States parties.[90] Concern has also been expressed about high numbers of discontinued cases,[91] including

[84] CERD/C/ISR/CO/13, para. 37; an earlier paragraph (35) recommended that, although different legal regimes may apply to Israeli citizens in the Occupied Territories and Palestinians, 'the State party should ensure that the same crime is judged equally, not taking into consideration the citizenship of the perpetrator'.

[85] CERD/C/ISR/CO/14-16, para. 27.

[86] *Ibid.*

[87] See Chapter 7 on non-citizens; it will be recalled that many communications under Article 14 have concerned non-citizens.

[88] As in, for example, *L.R. v Slovakia*, CERD/C/66/D/31/2003 (2005); *Gelle v Denmark*, CERD/C/68/D/34/2004 (2006); *Murat Er v Denmark*, CERD/C/71/D/40/2007 (2007).

[89] Para. 1(b).

[90] The point is made in broad terms in GR 31 among the 'factual indicators' of racial discrimination. Scepticism might appropriately be extended to the low numbers and national distribution of cases brought to the attention of CERD under Article 14, most of which emerge from a small coterie of States among the more than 50 acceptances of the procedure.

[91] Concluding observations on Belgium, CERD/C/BEL/CO/15, para. 13.

where police officers or public figures are involved, and cases of impunity.[92] Basic principles were recalled by the Committee in the case of Bolivia with regard to conflicts and acts of racist violence and campesino peoples and nations, some of which resulted in deaths, and the climate of impunity surrounding the events, in relation to which the Committee reaffirmed 'the duty of the State party to put an end to impunity for these acted' and, urging it 'to expedite the administration of justice, the investigation of the complaints ... the identification and prosecution of the perpetrators and ... guarantee victims and their family members an effective remedy'.[93] The training of the judiciary to discern and address issues of racial discrimination has also been suggested as correlated with the low numbers of cases.[94] As GR 31 suggests, the low profile of racial discrimination complaints may be linked with fear of reprisals on the part of human rights defenders, or lack of civil space for non-governmental organizations (NGOs) and others to take up cases involving 'racial' elements.[95] While the Committee requests data in order to inform its dialogues with States parties, the data on the profile of complaints to tribunals and other bodies, as with other data requested, are treated as essential to designing effective national anti-discrimination policies.

Bearing in mind the references in the *travaux* to the relationship between the competence and the independence of tribunals, the presence of an independent judiciary in the State party is as crucial to achieving the objectives of Article 6 as it is to other aspects of the Convention. GR 35 observes that:

> [i]ndependent, impartial and informed judicial bodies are crucial to ensuring that the facts and legal qualifications of individual cases are assessed consistently with international standards of human rights. Judicial infrastructures should be complemented in this respect by national human rights institutions in accordance with the principles relating to the status of national institutions for the promotion and protection of human rights (Paris Principles).[96]

IV. Duty of Effective Investigation

The practical working through of an institutional infrastructure providing effective protection and remedies is taken to imply that cases concerning racial discrimination must be properly investigated; a great many decisions under the Article 14 procedure revolve around this fundamental point. In *L.K. v The Netherlands*, the point of contention was whether police and judicial authorities had properly addressed the complaint of the author following an anti-foreigner petition by residents of a municipal housing development and threats of violence. The Committee found the response by police and judicial authorities incomplete and inadequate and a denial of effective protection, adding the observation that '[w]hen threats of racial violence are made, and especially when they are made in public and by a group, it is incumbent upon the State to investigate with due diligence and expedition'.[97]

[92] Concluding observations on Bolivia, CERD/C/BOL/CO/17-20, para. 17; Denmark, CERD/C/DNK/CO/18-19, para. 9; Serbia, CERD/C/SRB/1, para. 22; see also the Committee's Declaration on the Prevention of Genocide, A/60/18, ch. VIII, para. 11.

[93] CERD/C/BOL/CO/17-20, para. 17.

[94] GR 31, paras 4 and 5.

[95] Para. 1.

[96] GR 35, para. 18.

[97] CERD/C/42/D/4/1991 (1993), para. 6.6.

In *Kashif Ahmad v Denmark*, the claim was that racial insults against the applicant, family members, and friends who were waiting outside a school examination room had not been properly investigated by the police. In light of the discontinuation of proceedings, and the block on further prosecution by the Public Prosecutor, the author was 'denied any opportunity' to establish whether his rights under the Convention had been violated, from which it followed that he had been 'denied effective protection against racial discrimination and remedies attendant thereupon' by the State party.[98] *Habassi v Denmark* follows the same pattern: the State party should have investigated 'the real reasons' behind a bank's policy on refusing loans to foreigners to see if racial discrimination was involved.[99] Lack of effective investigation was also part of the motivation for decisions in *Durmic v Serbia and Montenegro*,[100] *Gelle v Denmark*,[101] *Adan v Denmark*,[102] *TBB-Turkish Union in Berlin/Brandenburg v Germany*,[103] and *Dawas and Shawva v Denmark*.[104] In the last-named case, which concerned an attack by a group of youths on the house of the petitioners, both of whom are Iraqi citizens recognized as refugees, the Committee found, *inter alia*, a failure to investigate the racist character of the attack, observing that

> [i]n circumstances as serious as those in this case, where the petitioners were subjected, in their own house, to a violent assault by 35 offenders, some of them armed, enough elements warranted a thorough investigation by public authorities of the possible racist nature of the attack against the family. Instead, the possibility was set aside at the level of the criminal investigation, thereby preventing the issue from even being adjudicated at the criminal trial. The Committee considers that the onus was on the State party to initiate an effective criminal investigation, instead of giving the petitioners the burden of proof in civil proceedings. The Committee recalls its jurisprudence, according to which when threats of violence are made, it is incumbent upon the State party to investigate with due diligence and expedition. The obligation is a fortiori applicable in the present case, where 35 individuals actually participated in an assault on the family.[105]

The State party dissented on fact and law from the Committee's conclusions, arguing, *inter alia*, that the evidence necessary to prove racist motivation was not available, that the number of thirty-five was disputed by witnesses, and that the petitioners had not referred to any racial motivation in their original statements. Further, on the Committee's conclusion that the investigation into the incident was incomplete, the State party wondered what further investigative steps could have been taken to shed light on the incident, bearing in mind that all identified witnesses had been interviewed.[106] The

[98] CERD/C/56/D/16/1999 (2000), para. 6.4; see also para. 9.
[99] CERD/C/54/D/10/1997 (1999), para. 9.3.
[100] CERD/C/68/D/29/2003 (2006), para. 10.
[101] *Gelle v Denmark*, para. 7.6.
[102] CERD/C/77/D/43/2008 (2010), para. 7.7.
[103] CERD/C/82/D/48/2010 (2013), paras 12.8 and 12.9.
[104] CERD/C/80/D/46/2009 (2012), para. 7.5.
[105] *Ibid.*, para. 7.4. In regard to remedies, the Committee recommended, *ibid.*, paras 9 and 10, that the State party grant the petitioners adequate compensation for the material and moral injury they had suffered and review policy and procedures in the matter of prosecution in cases of alleged racial discrimination or violence.
[106] A/67/18, Annex IV, 160–5. At a meeting with a representative of the State party, the Rapporteur on communications conveyed the Committee's position that the opinion was not subject to reconsideration in light of the absence of any such provision in the rules of procedure; the dialogue was stated to be ongoing. On the absence of reconsideration by the Committee, information was later conveyed by the State party reiterating the view that the Committee's opinion was based on misunderstandings and that the recommendation to pay compensation would not be applied, while the recommendation to review policy and procedures had generated

investigations carried out by national authorities have been regarded as satisfactory in other cases, leading to findings of no violation.[107] A State party has pointed out that the Convention 'does not specify which authority should decide to initiate prosecution or at what level of the hierarchy the decision should be taken',[108] to which the answer is presumably the authority in the best position to address the issues in light of the principle of effectiveness.

The mantra of 'effective investigation' also runs through the concluding observations on State reports. The Committee has called for the effective investigation of racially motivated offences,[109] and violations of the rights of ethnic and racial groups, as well as for 'the investigation of investigations' in order to be sure that an investigative methodology for such offences such as terrorism is not itself 'racialized' and that due process and the rule of law are effectively applied.[110] In addition to general statements, including those regarding racist political discourse,[111] the various groups protected by the Convention have been the subject of recommendations to investigate allegations of offences against them, including ethnic minorities,[112] indigenous peoples and Afro-descendants,[113] migrant workers and 'foreigners',[114] caste groups,[115] and specific, named nationalities and ethnicities.[116]

V. The Expediency Principle

With regard to prosecutions following on from investigations, the Committee has referred to the expediency principle: the discretion/freedom to prosecute criminal offences or not to prosecute.[117] In *Yilmaz-Dogan v The Netherlands*, it was stated that

> the freedom to prosecute criminal offences—commonly known as the expediency principle—is governed by considerations of public policy . . . the Convention cannot be interpreted as challenging the *raison d'ètre* of that principle. Notwithstanding, it should be applied in each case of alleged racial discrimination in the light of the guarantees laid down in the Convention.[118]

developments in Danish law and practice. The Committee treated the State party's response as partly satisfactory and discontinued the follow-up procedure: A/70/18, Annex II, 26–7.

[107] For example, *Quereshi v Denmark*, CERD/C/63/D/27/2002 (2003), para. 7.4; *Jama v Denmark*, CERD/C/75/D/41/2008 (2009), para. 7.4.

[108] *POEM and FASM v Denmark*, CERD/C/62/D/22/2002 (2003), para. 4.6.

[109] Concluding observations on Vietnam, CERD/C/VNM/CO/10-14, para. 10.

[110] The Committee recommended that that State party 'ensure that the new system of terrorism prevention and investigation include includes safeguards against abuse and the deliberate targeting of certain ethnic and religious groups': Concluding observations on the UK, CERD/C/GBR/CO/18-20, para. 21; see also para. 9, investigation and prosecution of riot-related cases.

[111] Concluding observations on Slovenia, CERD/C/SVN/CO/6-7, para. 11.

[112] *Ibid.*

[113] Concluding observations on Paraguay, CERD/C/PRY/CO/1-3, paras 15 and 16.

[114] Concluding observations on Kazakhstan, CERD/C/KAZ/CO/4-5, para. 16; Mauritius, CERD/C/MUS/CO/15-19, para. 22.

[115] Concluding observations on India, CERD//IND/CO/19, para. 26.

[116] Concluding observations on Russian Federation, CERD/C/RUS/CO/19, paras 12 and 13, Chechens, Roma, Africans, and Georgian nationals and ethnic Georgians; Slovakia, CERD/C/SV/CO/6-8, paras 15 and 16; Roma, Jews, Hungarians; Venezuela, CERD/C/VEV/CO/19-21, paras 16 and 17, Yanomami and Yupka peoples.

[117] *L.K. v The Netherlands*, CERD/C/42/D/41991 (1993), para. 3.3.

[118] CERD/C/36/D/1/1984 (1988), para. 9.4.

TBB-Turkish Union raised issues including Committee review, effective investigation, and the expediency principle.[119] The Committee has frequently recalled that it is not its function to review the interpretation of facts and national law made by domestic authorities, unless the decisions are manifestly absurd or unreasonable.[120] In this instance, the Committee recalled its standard position on review, along with the observations of the State party that the contested statements of Sarrazin against the Turkish population had been appraised as not capable of disturbing the peace and that there was no increased risk for the petitioner or its members becoming victims of future criminal acts. Nonetheless, with reference to the elements of Article 4(a) (incitement, dissemination of ideas), the Committee found that by concentrating on the fact that the statements 'did not amount to incitement to racial hatred and were not capable of disturbing the public peace', the State party 'had failed in its duty to carry out an effective investigation into whether or not Mr Sarrazin's statements amounted to dissemination of ideas based on racial superiority or hatred'.[121] In other words, the State party's appraisal of the impugned statements had, on this view, been narrowly focused on incitement, absenting the 'dissemination of ideas' limb of Article 4 from effective scrutiny. The absence of an effective investigation amounted to a violation of Articles 6, 2(1)(d), and 4.

The opinion in *TBB-Turkish Union* was the subject of a vigorous and wide-ranging dissent on, *inter alia*, the application of the expediency principle, by Committee member Vázquez, who asserted that the Convention 'does not require the criminal prosecution of every expression of ideas of racial superiority or every statement inciting to racial discrimination, but leaves States parties with discretion to determine which prosecutions best serve the goals of the Convention'.[122] In his view, even if statements were not protected by freedom of expression, it did not follow that prosecution posed no risks, bearing in mind that criminal punishment is the most severe form of punishment that States can impose; criminal prosecution may cause greater harm to the goals of the Convention than other forms of response to offending statements. Further, the Convention 'does not preclude States from adopting a policy of prosecuting only the most serious cases . . . such a policy would appear to be required by the principle that any restriction on the right of free expression must conform to the . . . tests of necessity and proportionality'.[123] The Committee's concern with the State party's focus on disturbance of the peace was also stated to be misplaced in that it was only one element in the decision not to prosecute, and, in any case, considerations of public order are not irrelevant to the application of Article 4.[124]

TBB-Turkish Union was decided before the adoption of GR 35, and elements of both the majority and dissenting opinions surface in the later text. The standard formula on the expediency principle is restated in the recommendation as applicable in light of the guarantees laid down in the Convention 'and in other instruments of international law'. The additional phrase is innovative and situates the application of the principle in a wider normative field; the principle of respect for the domestic interpretation of law and facts 'unless the decisions are manifestly absurd or unreasonable', is also recalled.[125] Points

[119] For a further review of the 'hate speech' aspects of the opinion, see Chapter 11.
[120] *Murat Er v Denmark*, para. 7.2; *TBB-Turkish Union in Berlin/Brandenburg v Germany*, para. 12.5.
[121] *TBB-Turkish Union*, para. 12.8.
[122] *TBB-Turkish Union*, Appendix, para. 10.
[123] *Ibid.*, para. 13.
[124] *Ibid.*, para. 15.
[125] GR 35, para. 17.

close to the Vázquez dissent appear from the statement that 'the criminalization of forms of racist expression should be reserved for serious cases . . . while less serious cases should be addressed by means other than criminal law'.[126] That the emphasis on criminalization in this paragraph may be adapted to the issue of prosecution is suggested by the sentence in the same paragraph that '[t]he application of criminal sanctions should be governed by principles of legality, proportionality and necessity'. Further, while paragraph 15 of the recommendation refers somewhat ambiguously to the 'qualification' of forms of conduct as criminal offences on the basis of a range of contextual factors, the factors are transposable to the question of whether or not to prosecute.

VI. On Civil and Criminal Law

It is clear that from the above that besides the provision of civil remedies, the required infrastructure to deliver 'effective protection and remedies' necessarily includes the institutions of criminal justice. Views thereon are elaborated in GR 31 on 'the prevention of racial discrimination in the administration and functioning of the criminal justice system'.[127] The lengthy preamble includes references to Articles 1, 5, and 6, as well as GR 27 (Roma), GR 29 (descent), and GR 30 (non-citizens), Article 16 of the Convention on Refugees, and paragraph 25 of the Durban Declaration, which expressed its profound repudiation of the racism, racial discrimination, xenophobia, and related intolerance that persist in some States in the functioning of the penal system and in the application of the law, as well as the actions and attitudes of institutions and individuals responsible for law enforcement, especially where this has contributed to certain groups being over-represented among persons under detention or imprisoned. The recommendation characterizes racial discrimination in the administration of justice as a particularly serious violation of the principles of the Convention and equality principles generally.

Factual indicators of a malfunctioning system, besides the low number of cases referred to earlier, include numbers and percentages of persons belonging to Article 1 groups who are victims of aggression, especially aggression by police and State officials; attribution of high crime rates to such groups, their insufficient representation in the ranks of the justice system, and percentages held in detention.[128] The recommendation ranges widely over linked issues of information on the functioning of the justice system, human rights and tolerance training strategies, plans of action to eliminate structural discrimination which should include, *inter alia* and in the context of structural discrimination, 'guidelines for prevention, recording, investigation and prosecution of racist or xenophobic incidents, assessment of the level of satisfaction among all communities concerning their relations with the police and the system of justice'.[129] Sections on access to justice, reporting, and legal proceedings follow the general considerations in the opening sections of the recommendation, which concludes with recommendations on trials, sentencing, and punishment that include observations on remedying prejudice and corruption, and promoting racial/cultural sensitivity at all processual stages. In post-conflict situations, where legal institutions have been weakened or destroyed, the recommendation refers to setting up of reconstruction plans and to States parties availing themselves of international technical

[126] *Ibid.*, para. 12. See further discussion in Chapter 11.
[127] A/60/18, Chapter IX.
[128] GR 31, paras 1, 2, and 3.
[129] *Ibid.*, para. 5(i).

assistance.[130] Extensive use is made in the recommendation of norms of hard and soft law emanating from treaty bodies and other sources.[131]

Civil remedies have been regarded as inadequate where the complaint alleges a criminal offence. In *Lacko v Slovakia*,[132] the petitioner, a person of Roma ethnicity, was required to leave a restaurant because of its policy not to serve Roma. A subsequent investigation found that no criminal offence had been committed. The State party argued that sundry administrative and civil avenues of complaint had not been exhausted by the petitioner and that the matter before CERD should be dismissed because of non-exhaustion of domestic remedies. In declaring the communication admissible, the Committee intimated that for some types of conduct, only criminal remedies are adequate, observing that

> [t]he State party failed to demonstrate that a petition for review, which would be a remedy against the legality of the decision, could in the present case lead to a new examination of the complaint. Furthermore, the Committee finds that the facts of the claim were of such a nature that only criminal remedies could constitute an adequate avenue of redress. The objectives pursued through a criminal investigation could not be achieved by means of civil or administrative remedies of the kind proposed by the State party. Therefore, the Committee found that no other effective remedies were available to the petitioner.[133]

In some instances, alternative forms of legal redress—prosecutions instigated by those claiming as victims, and civil procedure—are available as remedies. In *Sadic v Denmark*, an altercation between the petitioner and his employer resulted in a stream of racist abuse on the part of the latter. The specific provision of the penal code, subject to prosecution *ex officio*, was not pursued because of lack of evidence as to whether the altercation was sufficiently public to engage the legislation. An alternative form of prosecution for defamatory statements (not specific to racial discrimination) was available to the petitioner, as well as civil proceedings. In this case, the Committee accepted that the defamation proceedings were capable of constituting an effective remedy.[134] *Sadic* was distinguished in *Gelle v Denmark*, a case that concerned an insulting letter written by a politician regarding Somalis, where the 'defamation route' to prosecution was deemed not to be an effective remedy. The Committee in *Gelle* read *Sadic* as being related to a personal dispute that was 'essentially private',[135] whereas in *Gelle*, 'the statements were made squarely in the public arena, which is the central focus of the Convention' and the relevant Danish legislation.[136] Civil proceedings were also regarded as not effective in *Gelle* insofar as the petitioner sought a full criminal investigation of the politician's statements.[137]

Article 6 does not, in the view of the Committee, 'impose upon States parties the duty to institute a mechanism of sequential remedies, up to and including the Supreme Court

[130] *Ibid*, para. 5(h).

[131] Extra-Convention guidelines and principles are referred to in paras 14, 22, 33, and 38.

[132] CERD/C/59/D/11/1998 (2001).

[133] Para. 6.3. In the event, the situation regarding prosecution was reviewed by the Slovak authorities, resulting in a conviction. The Committee, despite the delay of over three years in convicting and sanctioning the manager of the restaurant, found no violation of the Convention.

[134] CERD/C/62/D/25/2002 (2003), paras 6.3, 6.4.

[135] Para. 6.5. In *Quereshi v Denmark*, the *Sadic* situation was further distinguished as concerning 'comments . . . essentially private or . . . made within a very limited circle': CERD/C/66/D/33/2003 (2005), para. 6.3.

[136] *Gelle v Denmark*, para. 6.5.

[137] *Ibid.*, para. 6.6. Also *Jama v Denmark*, para. 6.5; *Adan v Denmark*, para. 6.3.

level, in cases of alleged racial discrimination'.[138] The limitation was given a nuanced reading in *Quereshi v Denmark*, where the Committee, citing *Yilmaz-Dogan*, reflected that while Article 6 'might be interpreted to require the possibility of judicial review of a decision not to bring a criminal prosecution in a particular case alleging racial discrimination', noted the statement by the State party that it was open under national law to judicially challenge a prosecutor's decision.[139]

VII. Traditional Mechanisms of Justice

Additional to points on necessary access to the institutional apparatus of justice in the States, the recognition of traditional justice mechanisms, especially those of indigenous peoples, is a notable feature of CERD's oeuvre.[140] Background standards on indigenous justice mechanisms include ILO Convention 169, Articles 8–12, and the UN Declaration on the Rights of Indigenous Peoples, notably Article 34. While GR 31 focuses principally on 'formal' national systems of justice, it also recommends 'respect for, and recognition of the traditional systems of justice of indigenous peoples, in conformity with international human rights law'.[141] Examples include Mexico, where the State party was urged 'to respect the traditional systems of justice of indigenous peoples, in accordance with international human rights standards, including by establishing special indigenous courts'.[142] GR 31 was invoked in the case of Australia, encouraged to adopt a justice reinvestment strategy 'continuing and increasing the use of indigenous courts and conciliation mechanisms, diversionary and prevention programmes and restorative justice strategies'.[143] In terms of formal State justice tribunals, training of judges and prosecutors regarding indigenous rights has also been the subject of recommendations.[144]

Issues of coordination between justice systems have also engaged the Committee.[145] The knock-on effects on justice for indigenous peoples of failure to recognise the indigenous system is another aspect. Thus, in the case of Guatemala, concerns were raised regarding 'the problems experienced by indigenous peoples in gaining access to the justice system . . . because the indigenous legal system is not recognised and applied'.[146] Recommendations to strengthen indigenous tribunals have also been issued, with critical comments made on the non-binding nature of their decisions in State law and recom-

[138] *Yilmaz-Dogan v The Netherlands*, para. 9.4.

[139] CERD/C/63/D/27/2002 (2003), para. 7.5.

[140] See the discussion in the 'Comment' section of Chapter 8. For elaborations of key points regarding such systems, see Expert Mechanism Advice No. 6 (2014): *Restorative Justice, Indigenous Juridical Systems and Access to Justice for Indigenous Women, Children and Youth, and Persons with Disabilities*, A/HRC/EMRIP/2014/3/Rev.1, included in the same document as the background study on the same [henceforth EMRIP Advice No. 6; EMRIP Study on Restorative Justice].

[141] GR 31, para. 5(e).

[142] CERD/C/MEX/CO/16-17, para. 12; see also concluding observations on Nicaragua, CERD/C/NIC/CO/14, para. 18; Venezuela, CERD/C/VEN/CO/19-21, para. 18.

[143] CERD/C/AUS/CO/15-17, para. 20.

[144] Concluding observations on India, CERD/C/IND/CO/19, para. 12.

[145] In the case of Venezuela, CERD/C/VEN/CO/19-21, para. 18, the Committee recommended ensuring that the main objective of a draft bill would be 'to regulate and harmonize the functions, powers and responsibilities of indigenous peoples' system of justice and the national system'.

[146] Concluding observations on Guatemala, CERD/C/GTM/CO/11, para. 15; on Ecuador, CERD/C/ECU/CO/19, para. 12, and CERD/C/ECU/CO/20-22, para. 19.

mendations for entrenchment.[147] References to international human rights standards in recommendations also address the concern that traditional justice mechanisms should not fall below human rights standards in their conception or implementation.[148] Additional to the element of recognition as such to the institutions of indigenous peoples, recommendations in this area have also pointed to the limits of State institutions for particular groups in terms of access to justice, an issue not confined to the case of indigenous peoples.[149]

VIII. 'Acts' of Discrimination

The reference to protection and remedies against 'acts of discrimination' appears to introduce an ambiguity in suggesting that an act of racial discrimination would have to be legally established before protection became available. The Declaration on Racial Discrimination deflects such an interpretation in providing that 'everyone shall have the right to an effective remedy and protection against *any discrimination* he may suffer on the ground of race, colour or ethnic origin with respect to his fundamental rights and freedoms through independent national tribunals competent to deal with such matters'.[150] In *L.R. v Slovakia*, the Committee observed that:

> [w]ith respect to the claim under article 6, the Committee observes that, at a minimum, the obligation requires the State party's legal system to afford a remedy in case where an act of racial discrimination . . . has been made out, whether before the national courts or, in this case, the Committee. The Committee having established the existence of an act of racial discrimination, it must follow that the failure of the State party's courts to provide an effective remedy discloses a consequential violation of article 6 of the Convention.[151]

The restrictive construction of Article 6 was qualified in *Durmic v Serbia and Montenegro*:

> Although on a literal reading of the provision it would appear that an act of racial discrimination would have to be established before a petitioner would be entitled to protection and a remedy, the Committee notes that the State party must provide for the determination of this right through the national tribunals and other institutions, a guarantee that would be void were it unavailable in circumstances where a violation had not yet been established. While a State party cannot be reasonably required to provide for the determination of rights under the Convention no matter

[147] Concluding observations on New Zealand, CERD/C/NZL/CO/17, para. 18; CERD/C/NZL/CO/18-20, para. 7.

[148] Article 34 of the UNDRIP states that promotion, etc, of indigenous juridical systems must be done 'in accordance with international human rights standards'. Treaty bodies have expressed concerns regarding the position of indigenous women within their societies: CEDAW/C/MEX/CO/7-8, para. 34; the Human Rights Committee has expressed concern regarding the case of corporal punishment in the community justice system in Bolivia: CCPR/C/BOL/CO/3, para. 16. CERD has referred to the treatment of women in traditional societies, often adopting the unspecific terminology of 'multiple, intersectional discrimination' which may not necessarily specify the precise sources of discrimination. EMRIP Advice No. 6, para. 16, states that indigenous juridical systems 'should ensure that indigenous women, children and youth, and persons with disabilities are free from all forms of discrimination. The participation of indigenous women, children and youth, and persons with disabilities in indigenous justice systems should be respected and promoted. Accessibility should bee ensured for indigenous persons with disabilities.' See also Chapter 13.

[149] CERD/C/UKR/CO/19-21, para. 15, concerning the issuance of identification documents to Roma in order to facilitate their access to the courts.

[150] Article 7.2 (present author's emphasis).

[151] CERD/C/66/D/31/2003 (2005), para. 10.10.

how unmeritorious the claims may be, article 6 provides protection to alleged victims if their claims are arguable under the Convention.[152]

IX. Compensation: Must Be Considered

The second element in Article 6 is a more sharply focused 'reactive' provision on remedies that employs the traditional international law language of reparation and satisfaction for damage suffered as a result of discrimination. The use of 'satisfaction' in Article 6 alongside 'reparation' sits oddly with the *Basic Principles and Guidelines* where 'satisfaction' is an aspect of 'reparation'. Article 6 is not a model of clarity and this has necessitated considerable reflection on its details; the collective dimension of rights has induced further complexities in its application. In GR 26 on Article 6,[153] the Committee took the view that the degree to which racial discrimination and racial insults 'damage the injured party's perception of his/her own worth and reputation is often underestimated'.[154] Accordingly, the Committee notified States parties that:

> the right to seek just and adequate reparation or satisfaction for any damage suffered as a result of such discrimination . . . is not necessarily secured solely by the punishment of the perpetrator of the discrimination; at the same time, the courts and other competent authorities should consider awarding financial compensation for damage, material or moral, suffered by a victim whenever appropriate.[155]

In *B.J. v Denmark*,[156] the author of the communication, a Danish national of Iranian origin, was refused entry to a discotheque by a doorman who was subsequently fined. The case was brought under Article 6 and other articles of the Convention[157] in connection with the alleged failure of the State authorities to provide effective satisfaction and reparation in that the author's claim for pecuniary compensation was rejected by a court because it was not of such grave or humiliating character as to justify the granting of pecuniary compensation. While satisfied that no violation of the Convention had taken place, CERD considered that:

> the conviction and punishment of the perpetrator of a criminal act and the order to pay economic compensation to the victim are legal sanctions with different functions and purposes. The victim is not necessarily entitled to compensation in addition to the criminal sanction. However, in accordance with Article 6 of the Convention, the victim's claim for compensation has to be considered in every case, including those cases where no bodily harm has been inflicted but

[152] Para. 9.6. The drafting proposal by the representative of France in the Commission on Human Rights (E/CN.4/SR.800) referred to effective protection and remedies 'against any act of racial discrimination which . . . *would* violate his fundamental rights and freedoms' (present author's emphasis), lessening the ambiguity in the final version of Article 6. On arguable claims under Article 13 of the ECHR, see ECtHR, *Klass v Germany*, App. No. 5029/71 (1978); *Boyle and Rice v the UK*, App. Nos 9659/82 and 9658/82 (1988); *Powell and Rayner v the UK*, App. No. 9310/81 (1990).

[153] A/55/18, p. 153.

[154] For a short reflection on the damage caused by racial discrimination in terms of its negative social and economic impact, consequences for the sense of personal and group identity and moral worth, and psychological and health effects, see T. Makkonen, *Equal in Law, Unequal in Fact: Racial and Ethnic Discrimination and the Legal Response Thereto in Europe* (Martinus Nijhoff, 2012), pp 83–90; with regard to 'hate speech' see J. Waldron, *The Harm in Hate Speech* (Harvard University Press, 2012).

[155] Para. 2.

[156] CERD/C/56/D/17/1999 (2000).

[157] Article 2.1 (a), (b), and (d), of which (d) appears to have been the most relevant to the case which concerned discrimination by private persons; Article 5 (f), right of access to public places.

where the victim has suffered humiliation, defamation or other attack against his/her reputation and self-esteem.[158]

This reference to considering the compensation aspect 'in every case' is a stronger formulation of the duty of States than the notification in GR 26 that the authorities 'should consider' compensation 'whenever appropriate'.

In *Adan v Denmark*, the Committee recommended the provision of adequate compensation for moral injury caused to the petitioner by speech implicating Somalis in the practice of female genital mutilation.[159] In follow-up proceedings, the State party declared its willingness to compensate for pecuniary damage (there was none) but not for non-pecuniary damage because the impugned political speech did not target the petitioner directly,[160] recalling a similar refusal in *Gelle* which the Committee had found satisfactory. The State argued that it nonetheless found it reasonable to pay the costs of legal assistance, an approach rejected by the Committee because it 'considered that legal aid cannot be considered as a payment of compensation'. In some cases, legislative change to ensure closer conformity with the Convention has been recommended as a remedy, as well as more effective and less prolonged investigative processes,[161] and publicity for the Committee's opinion.[162]

Combined criminal and civil remedial elements are envisaged in GR 29 on descent-based discrimination, which, *inter alia*, enjoins States to ensure 'the prosecution of persons who commit crimes against members of descent-based communities and the provision of adequate compensation for victims of such crimes'.[163] Measures against perpetrators of discriminatory practice are also envisaged, including 'against public bodies, private companies and other associations that investigate the descent background of applicants for employment'.[164]

X. Reparation and Satisfaction: Article 14

The forms of 'reparation or satisfaction' accounted for in CERD practice are many and various and echo the complexities evident from statements of international law principles and international human rights law.[165] The concluding observations of CERD on State reports are expansive, whereas the range of remedies recommended under the Article 14 procedure is less so, a situation largely determined by the provenance of the applications and the nature of the injuries prompting the communications.[166] The practice under Article 14 should therefore be understood as without prejudice to the additional reparatory concepts recommended in concluding observations under Article 9 for indigenous peoples and other groups, particularly in relation to the element of 'satisfaction', which is,

[158] *B.J. v Denmark*, CERD/C/56/D/17/1999 (2000), para. 6.2.

[159] CERD/C/77/D/43/2008 (2010), para. 9.

[160] A/68/18, Annex IV; the dialogue between the Committee and Denmark was stated to be ongoing.

[161] *Lacko v Slovakia*, para. 11: a criminal penalty had already been applied for the offending conduct, refusing access to a restaurant because of Roma origin.

[162] *Murat Er v Denmark*, para. 9.

[163] GR 29, para. (w).

[164] *Ibid.*, para. (ll); concluding observations on Japan provide a point of reference for this provision: CERD/C/JPN/CO/3-6, para. 19.

[165] See, *inter alia*, the ICJ Declaration on Access to Justice and Right to a Remedy in International Human Rights Systems, Geneva 2012: <http://icj.wpengine.netdna-cdn.com/wp-content/uploads/2012/12/Congress-Declaration-adoptedFINAL.pdf>.

[166] See Chapter 4.

however, accounted for under Article 14 in relation to, for example, recommendations for the cessation of violations.

Article 14 recommendations have been made to use good offices to secure alternative employment for the complainant,[167] pay due attention to the impartiality of juries,[168] to review policy,[169] provide relief commensurate with moral damage,[170] simplify national procedures for dealing with racial discrimination,[171] take measures to counteract racial discrimination in the national loan market,[172] complete legislation to guarantee access to public spaces,[173] reconsider legislation,[174] take necessary measures to secure freedom of movement,[175] remove a racially offensive sign,[176] ensure that rights are not violated in future,[177] conduct thorough investigations into allegations of racial discrimination,[178] give publicity to the Committee's opinions,[179] take effective measures to ensure that housing agencies refrain from discriminatory practices,[180] remind States of previous concluding observations,[181] etc. The lengthiest list of such recommendations is set out in *L.G. v Korea*, where 'adequate compensation' is (unusually) stated to include lost wages of the complainant.[182] While the recommendations are situation-specific, the Committee, in keeping with its limited powers, has not engaged in practices of precise quantification. The findings and recommendations under Article 4 are subject to a follow-up procedure which maintains the overall dialogic relationship between the Committee and State parties; recommendations may also be integrated with the reporting procedure under Article 9.

While references to remedies such as forms of redress such as restitution or apology tend to surface primarily in the reporting procedures,[183] reparations terminology, including apology, was extensively considered in *L.A. et al. v Slovakia*.[184] According to the facts as submitted by the petitioners (Roma of Slovak origin), they had been refused entry into a discotheque on the ground that it was a private club, and were then followed by a group of non-Roma human rights activists who were admitted to the discotheque without being required to display club membership.[185] Criminal proceedings ensured against the staff

[167] *Yilmaz-Dogan v The Netherlands*, para. 10.

[168] *Narrainen v Norway*, CERD/C/44/D/3/1991 (1993).

[169] *L.K v The Netherlands*, para. 6.8.

[170] *Ibid.*, para. 6.9; or reparation or satisfaction commensurate with any damage suffered: *Habassi v Denmark*, para. 11.2; reparation or satisfaction, including economic compensation, where the discrimination has not resulted in physical damage but in humiliation or similar suffering: *B.J. v Denmark*, CERD/C/56/D/17/1999 (2000), para. 7.

[171] *Z.U.B.S. v Australia*, CERD/C55/D/16/1999, para. 11.

[172] *Habassi v Denmark*, para. 11.1.

[173] *Lacko v Slovakia*, para. 11.

[174] *Sadic v Denmark*, para. 6.8.

[175] *Koptova v Slovakia*, CERD/C/57/D/13/1998 (2000), para. 10.3.

[176] *Hagan v Australia*, para. 8.

[177] *L.R. v Slovakia*, para. 12.

[178] *Jama v Denmark*, para. 9.

[179] *Murat Er v Denmark*, para. 9; *TBB-Turkish Union v Germany*, CERD/C/82/D/48/2010 (2013), para. 14.

[180] *F.A. v Norway*, CERD/C/58/D/18/2000 (2001), para. 8.

[181] *P.S.N. v Denmark*, para. 6.5.

[182] CERD/C/86/D/512012, para. 9.

[183] For instances where petitioners sought an apology from State authorities, see *Kashif Ahmad v Denmark*, para. 3.1, and *Hagan v Australia*, para. 3.5. Restitution is adverted to in GR 23 on indigenous peoples.

[184] CERD/C/85/D/49/2011 (2014).

[185] According to the facts as submitted by the petitioners, there was no indication of the private nature of the club at its entrance; *L.A. v Slovakia*, para. 2.1.

member who refused the group, but were discontinued on the ground that no offence had occurred. A written apology and financial compensation was requested from the company that owned the premises but only an apology was ordered by the District Court, a decision that was upheld on appeal. At the level of the appeal, compensation was refused on the ground that the petitioners had not suffered 'a real and grave diminution of their human dignity'.[186] In relation to Article 6, the petitioners complained that the State party had not provided them with effective protection and remedy, and that, *inter alia*, the civil courts had:

> failed to recognize that racial discrimination impairs human dignity and constitutes prima facie damage . . . which is perceived subjectively by the injured person psychologically or emotionally [but] cannot necessarily be objectified as damage that can be proved or measured.[187]

The State party, on the other hand, argued that the petitioners had not proved 'a considerable diminishment of their dignity, social status or social functioning and that there had been no proven intent of the defendant to deeply discredit them';[188] the strict criteria for financial compensation for moral damage had accordingly not been met; further, the individual letters of apology ordered by the Court refuted the claim that State authorities had failed to ensure the elimination of discrimination in general.[189]

In the event, the Committee found that the decisions of the courts had been reasoned and based on legislation.[190] As to whether letters of apology constituted an effective remedy under Article 6, the Committee recalled United Nations *Basic Principles and Guidelines* including the principle that 'reparation should be proportional to the gravity of the violations and the harm suffered', deciding that it was not its role to decide what remedy should be awarded but 'to assess whether this remedy can be seen as an effective remedy in accordance with international principles and that it is not manifestly arbitrary or . . . a denial of justice'.[191] Accordingly, Article 6 was not violated, though the Committee regretted that the law in question did not provide sanctions to be imposed which could have had a preventive or deterrent effect.[192] In the circumstances, the five years of judicial procedure to determine the case did not amount to an undue delay in light of the complexities of jurisdiction and the fact that the decisions were mostly made in response to appeals by the petitioners.[193]

XI. Individual and Collective Dimensions

Recommended programmes of reparations have included individual and group victims, and in some cases respond to attributions of collective rights. For the Roma in general, GR 27[194] advocates a range of remedial measures for protection against racial discrimination and violence, addressing such matters as prompt action by police and judiciary to investigate and punish racist violence, rejection of impunity for perpetrators of racist acts,

186 *Ibid.*, para. 2.5.
187 *Ibid.*, para. 3.3. See discussions in Chapter 5 of the concept of 'dignity'.
188 *Ibid.*, para. 4.4.
189 *Ibid.*, para. 4.5.
190 *Ibid.*, para. 7.2.
191 *Ibid.*, para. 7.4.
192 *Ibid.*, para. 7.4.
193 *Ibid.*, para. 7.5.
194 A/55/18, Annex V.C.

acknowledgement of historical wrongs done to the Roma, and consideration of ways to compensate therefore, the taking of firm action against discriminatory practices in the field of housing, and punishment for discrimination against Roma in access to places and services for the use of the general public. In the case of individual Romani women victims of forced sterilization, a State party was recommended to:

> facilitate full reparation and compensation . . . give consideration to *ex gratia* compensation procedures, generate awareness among patients, doctors and the public on the Guidelines of the International Federation of Gynaecology and Obstetrics and put in place safeguards to avoid similar incidents . . . The Committee recommends that the State party consider legislating for a permanent waiver to limitation on all cases relating to compensation due to illegal sterilization.[195]

A general platform of remedial measures was recommended to address the situation of 'the erased' in Slovenia, including the granting of 'full reparation, including restitution, satisfaction, compensation, rehabilitation and guarantees of non-repetition, to all affected by the "erasure"'.[196] Restitution,[197] rescue and rehabilitation,[198] apology,[199] non-repetition, and other remedial modes have all at various times been commended to States parties. The introduction of specific remedies such as Amparo and Habeas Corpus is evaluated positively by the Committee.[200] The reconciliatory role of truth commissions has also been recognised,[201] and failure to act on their recommendations criticized.[202]

The most extensive account of modalities of reparations in their collective aspects emerges from Committee practice with regard to indigenous peoples,[203] practice that adapts the forms of reparation to accommodate their characteristic claims and rights.[204] GR 23 affirms that 'discrimination against indigenous peoples falls under the scope of the Convention', and includes principles on rights and reparations. Paragraph 3 states that the Committee is conscious of past and present discrimination against the peoples, and that 'in particular . . . they have lost their land and resources to colonists, commercial companies and state enterprises'; consequently, the preservation of their culture and their historical identity 'has been and still is' jeopardized. In paragraph 4, States parties are

[195] Concluding observations on the Czech Republic, CERD/C/CZE/CO/8-9, para. 19.

[196] CERD/C/SVN/CO/7, para. 13.

[197] Recommendations for restitution are not confined to indigenous peoples but include them: see, for example, concluding observations on Estonia, CERD/C/EST/CO/8-9, para. 18; Greece, CERD/C/GRC/CO/16-19, para.10; Serbia, CERD/C/SRB/CO/1, para 18, all dealing with general remedies for acts of racial discrimination. For restitution specific to indigenous peoples—restitution of their ancestral lands—see concluding observations on Chile, CERD/C/CHL/CO/19-21, para. 13; Colombia, CERD/C/COL/CO/14, para. 19; and Paraguay, CERD/C/PRY/CO/1-3, para. 15.

[198] Concluding observations on Senegal with regard to the problem of child beggars, CERD/C/SEN/16-18, para. 14; rehabilitation in the sphere of housing rights of Roma, CERD/C/SVK/CO/9-10, para. 12.

[199] Concluding observations on Slovakia, CERD/C/65/CO/7, para. 12, recommendation to ensure effective remedies 'including compensation and apology' are granted to victims (Roma women) of forced sterilization.

[200] For Amparo, see concluding observations on the Dominican Republic, CERD/C/DOM/CO/13-14, para. 4(a); Mexico, CERD/C/MEX/CO/16-17, para. 4; for Habeas Corpus, Uzbekistan, CERD/C/UZB/CO/6-7, para. 4.

[201] Concluding observations on Kenya, CERD/C/KEN/CO/1-4, para. 14

[202] Concluding observations on Paraguay, CERD/C/PRY/CO/1-3, para. 12.

[203] See the collection of essays in F. Lenzerini (ed.), *Reparations for Indigenous Peoples: International and Comparative Perspectives* (Oxford University Press, 2008); F. MacKay, 'Indigenous Peoples' Rights and the UN Committee on the Elimination of Racial Discrimination', in S. Dersso (ed.), *Perspectives on the Rights of Minorities and Indigenous Peoples in Africa* (Pretoria University Law Press, 2010), pp. 155–204.

[204] Elements of the critique in this section apply also to certain peoples of African descent, see CERD GR 34 on Racial Discrimination against People of African Descent, section VIII (Administration of Justice).

called upon to take a range of measures including recognition and respect for distinct indigenous culture and history; ensuring freedom from discrimination and the provision of conditions allowing for sustainable development 'compatible with their cultural characteristics'; ensuring equal rights in respect of effective participation in public life; and to ensure that 'rights to practise and revitalize' cultural traditions and customs 'and to practise . . . languages' can be exercised. Reparations language becomes more explicit in paragraph 5 with reference to deprivation of lands without the 'free and informed consent' of the peoples, where States parties are called upon:

> to take steps to return those lands and territories. Only when this is for factual reasons not possible, the right to restitution should be substituted by the right to just, fair and prompt compensation. Such compensation should as far as possible take the form of lands and territories.

The formulation of the paragraph is closely related to ILO Convention 169,[205] which was in force when the recommendation was adopted (1997), and the UNDRIP,[206] preliminary drafts of which were available to the Committee.[207] With regard to applications of the second limb of Article 6, a report by the International Law Association observes that reparation for indigenous peoples attains a particularly high degree of complexity 'in light of the holistic vision of life of these peoples', a paramount element to be considered in programmes of reparations, where it is essential to go beyond the classical Western-shaped language that conceives reparation as individual and not collective, and where monetary compensation is the leading goal. In the event of dispossession of indigenous lands, the form of reparation to be pursued is *restitutio in integrum*, except where it is objectively unfeasible, making return of lands and territories the only means to provide redress:

> In other situations . . . due to the specific circumstances of the case, even *restitutio in integrum* may not represent the best practicable means of reparation, or can even be inadequate when the relevant human rights breaches take place in an environmental context characterized by social inequality or other structural situations incompatible with the individual and collective dignity of indigenous peoples. In such situations . . . *restitutio in integrum* . . . would simply recreate the pre-existing unacceptable social structure . . . Rectification of the pre-existing situation—aimed at removing the social and cultural roots favouring perpetration of human rights abuses—is therefore essential.[208]

Thus, in the context of the Convention, the 'remedy' is the full implementation of the programme of the Convention, interpreted and applied in the light of the best practices of international law with regard to indigenous rights.[209]

The reparation concepts in Article 6 and GR 23, in tandem with broader expressions associated with the 'satisfaction' pole of reparations law, have been recycled through multiple concluding observations and decisions of the Committee. Situations where effective remedies available to individuals were unavailable to indigenous peoples to vindicate their collective rights have been subjected to criticism by the Committee; in such instances, recognition of the collective existence and forms of land tenure of the

[205] Discussion above.
[206] Discussion above.
[207] For the early drafts of the UNDRIP, see P. Thornberry, *Indigenous Peoples and Human Rights* (Manchester University Press, 2002), Chapter 15.
[208] Interim Report of ILA Conference on Indigenous Peoples (2010), pp. 39–40.
[209] See comment by van Boven, *infra*.

peoples may have a further distinctive salience in the context of reparation.[210] In the case of Suriname, CERD observed that judicial remedies under the draft mining Act were not available to indigenous peoples who were compelled to depend instead on appeals to the Executive:[211] their traditional (communal) rights could not be vindicated before the courts because of lack of juridical recognition of indigenous peoples. The message conveyed is that differences in treatment between communal and individual claims may amount to discrimination: communal land tenure is in principle entitled to a level of protection equivalent to that enjoyed by individual tenure.[212]

Bearing in mind CERD's understanding that the ethnic and cultural distinctiveness of groups is to be taken into account in gauging discrimination, lack of recognition of the distinctiveness of indigenous peoples, and their subjection to processes identical to other rights claimants may amount to discrimination. Instances in a number of countries with regard to difficulties in establishing aboriginal title represent a case in point—recommendations to Canada reiterated the need to facilitate proof of aboriginal title and criticized the 'strongly adversarial positions' taken by the federal and provincial governments in this respect;[213] similar comments have been made to Australia[214] and New Zealand.[215] The Committee's critiques reflect underlying concerns that requirements for proof of title or related legal procedures in the general laws of States may not sufficiently accommodate indigenous traditions and thus potentially amount to discrimination in effect. Critiques also hint at the presence of inbuilt 'structural' or 'institutional' discrimination in laws and legal processes that negatively affect groups that historically have played little or no part in institutional developments.

XII. Rights

In *Jewish Community v Norway*, the Committee stated that the notion of rights in the Convention is not confined to Article 5. Thus, Article 14 states that the Committee may receive complaints relating to 'any of the rights set forth in this Convention': the fact that Article 4 is couched in terms of State obligations rather than inherent rights of individuals:

[210] S.J. Anaya, 'Reparations for Neglect of Indigenous Land Rights at the Intersection of International and Domestic Law: the Maya Cases in the Supreme Court of Belize', in Lenzerini, *Reparations for Indigenous Peoples*, pp. 567–603, at p. 567.

[211] CERD/C/64/CO/9, para. 14.

[212] See, *inter alia*, Decision 1(66), on the New Zealand Foreshore and Seabed Act 2004, where the Committee found 'discriminatory aspects' in legislation 'in particular in its extinguishment of the possibility of establishing Maori customary titles over the foreshore and seabed and its failure to provide a guaranteed right of redress, notwithstanding the State party's obligations under Article 5 and 6 of the Convention': A/60/18, ch. II. Further discussion in C. Charters and A. Erueti (eds), *Māori Property Rights and the Foreshore and Seabed: The Last Frontier* (Victoria University Press, 2007).

[213] CERD/C/CAN/CO/18, para. 22: 'The Committee is . . . concerned that the claims of aboriginal land rights are being settled primarily through litigation, at a disproportionate cost for the Aboriginal communities concerned due to the strongly adversarial positions' taken by the federal and provincial governments'; see also para. 26.

[214] CERD/C/AUS/CO/15-17, para. 18, where the Committee regretted 'the persisting high standards of proof required for recognition of the relationship between indigenous peoples and their traditional lands, and the fact that despite a large investment of time and resources by indigenous peoples, many are unable to obtain recognition of their relationship to land'; see also para. 19. On the earlier, heated debates between the Committee and Australia over amendments to Australia's Native Title Act, see the discussion in P. Thornberry, *Indigenous Peoples and Human Rights* (Manchester University Press, 2002), pp. 218–23.

[215] CERD/C/NZL/CO/18-20, para. 13.

> does not imply that they are matters to be left to the internal jurisdiction of States parties, and as such immune from review under article 14 . . . The Committee's conclusion is reinforced by the wording of article 6 . . . by which States pledge to assure . . . effective protection and a right of recourse against any acts of racial discrimination which violate their "human rights" under the Convention . . . this confirms that the Convention's "rights" are not confined to article 5.[216]

The assertion that Article 6 extends the portfolio of rights in the Convention is not inherently surprising. Article 6 makes two references to rights: human rights and fundamental freedoms that are violated by racial discrimination, and 'the right to seek just and adequate reparation or satisfaction'. The assertion may have a clarifying function in the context of a convention largely given over to statements of obligation. In a number of cases, the Committee has found violations of Article 6 without finding a violation of any of the substantive articles.[217] In *Hagan v Australia*, the State party claimed that Article 6 is an accessory right and can only be found to have been violated 'once a separate violation of the specific rights in the Convention has been established (under articles 2, 4, 5 and 7)';[218] earlier in the case it had, inconsistently, made the qualified claim that Article 2 is also an 'accessory right'.[219] In *Kenneth Moylan v Australia*, the proposition as to the accessory nature of Article 6 was again advanced: 'where no substantive right is violated, there can be no claim under Article 6',[220] and specifically rejected by the Committee.[221] In light of the text of Article 6 and the Opinions and recommendations of the Committee, it is appropriate in the ICERD context to conclude that the article elaborates 'a right to a remedy'.

D. Comment

Article 6 and the other international instruments cited above refer to the obligations of national authorities to provide remedies at the level of domestic law to 'everyone within their jurisdiction'. The engagement of the Committee is essentially subsidiary to the protection of rights nationally. In theory, the greater the effectiveness of the national recourse mechanisms, the less pressing is the need to engage international bodies. The range of defects in national mechanisms identified by the Committee over the decades of its operation reveals significant gaps in the general justice infrastructures of States parties and inefficiencies in their operation, as well as a lack of focus and adaptation to issues of racial discrimination. It is not without significance that Article 6 is the most litigated article under the Article 14 procedure, and that many cases turn on its application, alone or in conjunction with other articles.

The drafting of Article 6 reveals a complex trajectory towards the provisions in their present form, with amendments oscillating between more and less demanding approaches to the achievement of justice. The stronger notion of a right to reparation was replaced by one to 'seek' reparation, a phrase that nonetheless emphasizes the importance of dismantling racial barriers for those who attempt to access remedies; and explicit provisions on the

[216] *Jewish Community of Oslo v Norway*, para. 10.6. See also Chapter 11.
[217] *Habassi v Denmark; Ahmad v Denmark.*
[218] CERD/C/62/D/262002 (2003), para. 4.18.
[219] *Ibid.*, para. 4.4.
[220] CERD/C/83/D/47/2010 (2013), para. 4.16.
[221] *Ibid.*, para. 6.2, citing *Habassi*, *Ahmad*, and *Durmic*.

payment of damages were not adopted. The discussions on the impartiality and independence of tribunals, and their 'competence', in the *travaux* reveal sensitivities regarding opening up national systems to scrutiny, which did not, however, prevent the emergence of tolerably clear provisions on the necessary infrastructures of justice systems. Weakening amendments such as replacing 'reparation' by 'satisfaction' only, and conditioning remedies by 'where appropriate' were rejected, as was, implicitly, the reduction of 'reparation' to monetary compensation—the 'monetarization' of the remedial spectrum. It would appear from the *travaux* that the inclusion of the ambiguous 'acts of racial discrimination' was intended not to narrow the article but make it more precise on the basis that racial discrimination is constituted by acts, not abstractions. Notable statements emphasized that claimants were not barred by Article 6 from approaching international tribunals for the vindication of their claims. In the result, the article echoes the complex classifications of international law, though phrasing the principles as 'reparation or satisfaction' does not faithfully reflect the international template. In this, the pattern of reservations may be recalled: a few States regard either reparation *or* satisfaction as satisfying the Convention standard.[222] In applying the article, the Committee has treated reparations together with satisfaction as comprising the broad range of internationally recommended possibilities.

Shelton outlines the meaning of 'remedies' as containing 'two separate concepts, one procedural and one substantive. In the first sense, remedies are the processes by which arguable claims of human rights violations are heard, whether by courts, administrative agencies, or other competent bodies. The second notion refers to the outcome of the proceedings, the relief afforded the successful claimant'.[223] Shelton elaborates that the:

> obligation to afford remedies for violations of human rights requires in the first place the existence of remedial institutions and procedures to which victims may have access. Refusal of access to the tribunals of a country is considered a primary manifestation of the concept of denial of justice... Access to justice implies that the procedures are effective, i.e. capable of redressing the harm that was inflicted.[224]

The institutional/substantive pairing also assists in characterizing Article 6, a helpful summary of which was provided by Denmark in connection with one of the numerous Article 14 cases in which it has been involved: the first part, on 'effective protection and remedies', 'imposes on the States parties a positive obligation to introduce remedies that are available, adequate and effective', that protect against racial discrimination, make it possible to establish whether persons have been subject to racial discrimination, and make it possible for the acts of discrimination to be brought to an end.[225] '[A]dequate reparation or satisfaction' on the other hand, means that the racial discrimination is brought to an end and 'the consequences for the victim are remedied in such a manner that the State of affairs prior to the violation is restored to the greatest extent possible'.[226]

The essence of reparation in the context of the Convention is the restoration to a former state of those who have been damaged by racial discrimination. Remedies, as Shelton states, 'aim to place an aggrieved party in the same position as he or she would

[222] Present author's emphasis.
[223] Shelton, *Remedies in International Human Rights Law*, p. 7.
[224] *Ibid.*, pp. 8–9.
[225] *Mostafa v Denmark*, CERD/C/59/D/19/2000 (2001), para. 4.5.
[226] *Ibid.*, para. 4.6.

have been had no injury occurred',[227] to which might be added the collective 'they' in the context of ICERD in order to recall the collective aspects of reparations appropriate to indigenous peoples and other groups.[228] Van Boven observes that 'when collective rights are involved, redress and reparational action through the lodging of individual claims appear of limited avail. Adequate provisions should be made to honour collective claims and to obtain collective reparation'; he adds that in this context special measures may be better at affording opportunities for development and self-advancement—they 'are intended to have remedial effects and may serve the purpose of effective protection and remedies in a broader structural sense'.[229] In this sense, Article 6 is integrated into the project of the Convention as a whole, notably in the field of combating structural discrimination through programmes of special measures and analogous means.

Van Boven also makes the point that CERD seeks to tailor remedies to the particular needs and circumstances of disadvantaged groups, whereas the Article 14 procedure is mainly for aggrieved individuals; the observation remains highly pertinent. Reporting procedures and communications procedures are not alternatives in the rehabilitation of individuals and communities. Both procedures have a role to play in their respective spheres. It is possible that the individual communications procedure will, in time, 'open out' to embrace other reparations modes, a development that depends to a large extent on making greater use of the facility for 'groups of individuals' was well as 'individuals' to engage Article 14.[230]

The first limb of Article 6 requires that effective protection and remedies are to be 'assured', a term that suggests they must be guaranteed through structures capable of delivering remedial justice. As is evident from repeated Convention practice, the mere enactment of laws will not be enough to satisfy its demands: laws must also be effectively implemented through an infrastructure of mechanisms appropriate to the task. The justice infrastructure requirements of Articles 2 and 5—notably 5(a)—are complemented by the specific requirements of Article 6.[231] The general part of Article 6 looks to the provision of effective protection and remedies for racial discrimination through the State apparatus, not limited to the judicial branch.[232] In contemporary societies, this will, *de minimis*, include institutions such as National Human Rights Institutions, national and regional Ombudsmen,[233] including specialized equality ombudsmen,[234] and community defenders.[235]

[227] *Ibid.*, p. 10.

[228] The Committee's endorsements of collective claims to rights and remedies are not confined to indigenous peoples, hence the recommendation that States parties take 'all necessary steps to secure equal access to the justice system for all people of African descent including by providing legal aid, facilitating individual *or group claims*, and encouraging non-governmental organizations to defend their rights': GR 34 on Racial Discrimination against People of African Descent, para. 35 (present author's emphasis).

[229] T. van Boven, 'Common Problems linked to all Remedies available to Victims of Racial Discrimination', background paper for the Expert seminar on Remedies in preparation for the World conference against Racism, HR/GVA/WCR/SEM.1/2000/BP.5, p. 11; special measures are discussed in Chapter 9.

[230] See Chapter 4.

[231] See Chapters 8 and 13.

[232] The basic requirement is summarized in *Jewish Community of Oslo v Norway*, CERD/C/67/D/30/2003 (2005), para. 10.6, as 'effective protection and a right of recourse against any acts of racial discrimination'.

[233] Concluding observations on the Russian Federation, CERD/C/RUS/CO/20-22, para. 10.

[234] Concluding observations on Sweden, CERD/C/SWE/CO/19-21, para. 9; on Chile, CERD/C/CHL/CO/19-21, para. 7.

[235] Concluding observations on Colombia, CERD/C/COL/CO/14, para. 15.

Further, the extensive practice of the Committee with regard to indigenous groups demonstrates a concern with informal as well as formal systems of justice, and consideration of the role of customary law. In light of the concern of Article 6 with 'national tribunals and other State institutions', it will be recalled that the drafts went through various permutations of language, from 'independent national tribunals', 'independent tribunals', 'competent national tribunals', and the final addition of 'other State institutions'. In light of the underdevelopment of indigenous rights at the time of drafting, and the focus on undivided nations emerging from decolonization processes rather than sub-State ethnicity, the summary records do not reveal that the drafters contemplated a role for traditional justice mechanisms; on the other hand, 'other State institutions' should not be interpreted narrowly, and suggests a concern with multiple forms of governance apt to include traditional, customary institutions which are recognized in many States and, from a non-discrimination perspective, ought to be recognized.[236] The Expert Mechanism on the Rights of Indigenous Peoples (EMRIP) Study on Restorative Justice observes that the traditional justice systems of indigenous peoples:

> have largely been ignored, diminished or denied through colonial laws and policies of subordination to the formal justice systems of States. However, law is a complex notion arising in explicit and implicit ideas and practices. It is grounded in a people's worldview and the lands they inhabit, and is inextricably linked to culture and tradition . . . a narrow view of justice that excludes the traditions and customs of indigenous peoples violates the cultural base of all legal systems. Without the application and understanding of traditional indigenous conceptions of justice, a form of injustice emerges that . . . is based on unacceptable assumptions.[237]

The criterion of effectiveness runs through the Convention, surfacing explicitly in Articles 2, 6, and 7 and implied in the Convention project as a whole. In this, the principle of effectiveness in the interpretation of treaties is extended to their application in practice, and 'effectiveness' correlates with obligations to rectify *de facto* as well as *de jure* discrimination—towards substantive and not merely formal equality. The concept of 'just and adequate' reparation or satisfaction is implicated in the effectiveness standard to the same extent as that of 'effective' protection and remedies, while the right to 'seek' remedies, although less demanding than the right to 'obtain', implies the existence of genuine possibilities of accessing, and benefiting from, the institutions of justice. Evaluation of the effectiveness of a remedy essentially relates to criteria such as the independence of the body to which the victim appeals; the accessibility of the authority, and the flexibility—adaptability—of the procedure.

The criteria for effective remedies parallel the '4A' scheme for the enjoyment of human rights piloted by the Committee on Economic, Social and Cultural Rights (CESCR) and followed by others.[238] In light of the criterion of adaptability, the measurement of

[236] For comment on varieties and levels of governance and State obligations, see Chapter 8; for comments on legal pluralism and recognition of indigenous justice systems and customary law in many States, see EMRIP Study on Restorative Justice, paras 14–19; for a broad-based account of custom more generally, see B. Tobin, *Indigenous Peoples, Customary Law and Human Rights: Why Living Law Matters* (Routledge, 2014).

[237] A/HRC/EMRIP/2014/3/Rev.1, para. 8, the footnote cites J. Borrows, *Canada's Indigenous Constitution* (Toronto University Press, 2010), pp. 6–9. EMRIP Advice No. 6, para. 4, provides that, in accordance with the UNDRIP, 'States must recognize indigenous peoples' right to maintain, develop and strengthen their own juridical systems, and . . . value the contribution that these systems can make to facilitating indigenous peoples' access to justice.'

[238] See Chapters 14 and 15.

effectiveness is inevitably contextual, raising the general problematique of anti-discrimination legal regimes: that they should not simply mimic bureaucratic impulses to homogenize solutions to practical problems but relate to the circumstances of the persons and groups caught up in the situations under review. The integrated nature of the effectiveness/context relationship implicates all the parameters of Article 6. For remedies, as with anti-discrimination laws in general, they are required to function in the real world of those who suffer racial discrimination, and not merely within the Elysium of elegantly drafted abstract legal prescriptions. The concept of a remedy is as nuanced as the concept of discrimination itself.

Article 6 is an essential component of the Convention, integral to its overall conception and to the prospects of making a difference. The article insinuates that remedial justice processes have a vital role to play in buttressing and securing the human rights of threatened individuals and groups, a role that is complementary to but distinct from legislation that directly confronts racial discrimination. Justice processes also have educational and expressive functions in demonstrating the commitment of States to treating racial discrimination as a reprehensible, socially disruptive phenomenon, fully deserving of condemnation. In cases where the justice infrastructure fails to deter and protect from racial discrimination, the reparatory aspect of Article 6 is important in symbolizing dedication to the 'repair' of individuals and communities damaged by racial discrimination, the recognition of their dignity, and the restatement of their entitlement to the effective enjoyment of human rights.

THORNBERRY

17. Article 7

The Role of Education in Combating Racial Discrimination

> States parties undertake to adopt immediate and effective measures, particularly in the fields of teaching, education, culture and information, with a view to combating prejudices which lead to racial discrimination and to promoting understanding, tolerance and friendship among nations and racial or ethnical groups, as well as to propagating the purposes and principles of the Charter of the United Nations, the Universal Declaration of Human Rights, the United Nations Declaration on the Elimination of All Forms of Racial Discrimination, and this Convention.

A. Introduction

While Article 7 specifically implicates the educational cultural and informational fields, the use of 'particularly' to highlight their prominence as means to achieve the objectives of the article, does not rule out measures in other fields; in this, the structure of Article 7, on the fields where measures are to be taken, is similar to Article 5 with its use of 'notably' to indicate an essentially uncircumscribed portfolio of protected rights. The sources of the right to education in international law are many and varied, and include provisions from instruments referred to in the preamble to the Convention, notably the UN Declaration of Human Rights (UDHR), the UNESCO Convention against Discrimination in Education, and the Declaration on the Elimination of All Forms of Racial Discrimination.[1] Rights in regard to culture also have a complex background in terms of sources[2] and are prominent in Article 5,[3] while information as a right has, *inter alia*, been associated in international instruments with freedom of opinion and expression. Through its various modalities, Article 7 essentially specifies an obligation to engage in a process of teleologically oriented public education in a broad sense, suggesting at the same time a disaggregated concept of the 'public' to include the groups that comprise the society in question.

Specifications of the right to education in international instruments characteristically highlight its role as a vector in the furtherance of human rights, tolerance, and social peace, desiderata that take inspiration from Article 26(2) of the UDHR:

[1] The legal bases of education rights in human rights instruments are summarized in Chapter 14. Additionally, the reference in the UN Charter (Article 13) to the work of the General Assembly in 'promoting international cooperation in the economic, social, cultural, educational, and health fields' is another point of reference, as is the further elaboration of educational programmes and objectives linked to other UN bodies in Articles 55, 57, 62, 73, 76, and 83; the reference to 'educational preparedness' in para. 2 of the Colonial Declaration (lack of which should not serve as a pretext for delaying independence) may also be borne in mind.

[2] See Chapters 13 and 14; useful appraisals of the right to information as a right in international human rights include: M. McDonagh, 'The Right to Information in International Human Rights Law', *HRLR* 13 (2013), 25–55; H Darbishire, 'Ten Challenges for the Right to Information in the Age of Mega-Leaks', in T. McGonagle and Y. Donders (eds), *The United Nations and Freedom of Expression and Information: Critical Perspectives* (Cambridge University Press, 2015), pp. 271–303 [henceforth *The UN and Freedom of Expression*].

[3] Discussed in Chapter 14.

> Education shall be directed to the full development of the human personality and to the strengthening of respect for human rights and fundamental freedoms. It shall promote understanding, tolerance and friendship among all nations, racial or religious groups, and shall further the activities of the United Nations for the maintenance of peace.[4]

Traces of the language of the UDHR are found in the conventions developing its principles. Article 13 of the International Covenant on Economic, Social and Cultural Rights (ICESCR) recites that education shall, *inter alia*, 'promote understanding, tolerance and friendship among all nations and all racial, ethnic or religious groups'.[5] The aims and objectives of education, including education in human rights in general, the principles of particular conventions, and education for tolerance, are all referred to in UN core human rights conventions including, in addition to the International Convention on the Elimination of All Forms of Racial Discrimination (ICERD), the Convention on the Elimination of Discrimination against Women (CEDAW),[6] the Convention on the Rights of the Child (CRC),[7] the Convention against Torture,[8] the Convention on Migrant Workers (CMW),[9] the Convention on Persons with Disabilities (CRPD),[10] and the Convention against Disappearances (CPED).[11] The UNESCO Convention against Discrimination in Education includes a provision similar to Article 7 of ICERD, to the effect that education

> should be directed to the full development of the human personality and to the strengthening of respect for human rights and fundamental freedoms; it shall promote understanding, tolerance and friendship among all nations, racial or religious groups, and shall further the activities of the United Nations for the maintenance of peace.[12]

With regard to the role of information in the context of Article 7, the right thereto is often conceived as part of universal rights of freedom of expression, a connection developed by, *inter alia*, Article 19 of the UDHR and the International Covenant on Civil and Political Rights (ICCPR),[13] the latter further elaborated and developed by GC 34 of the Human

[4] In the drafting process of the UDHR, there was a notable shift from a position of directing education to combat 'the spirit of intolerance and hatred against other nations or racial or religious groups' (proposal of the World Jewish Congress, E/CN.4/SR.8, p. 4), towards more positive statements of education as the promoter of values; in the process, references to 'peoples' were replaced by references to nations, and racial and religious groups, on which Morsink comments that the 'more expansive phrase brought the need to combat intolerance and hatred for nations and peoples that are different from one's own into the text in an indirect way': J. Morsink, *The Universal Declaration of Human Rights: Origins, Drafting and Intent* (University of Pennsylvania Press, 1999), p. 217; also Morsink, *ibid.*, pp. 212–17. The point made by the representative of the World Jewish Congress was that it was not enough to envisage a technical framework for the development of educational policies; the spirit in which education was conducted was crucial, neglect of which in Germany had been the cause of catastrophic wars.

[5] Elaborated in General Comment 13 of the CESCR, E/C.12/1999/10, para. 4.

[6] Article 10.

[7] Article 29.

[8] Article 10.

[9] Article 33.

[10] Articles 4, 8, and 24; Article 8 is specifically directed to 'awareness-raising'.

[11] Article 23.

[12] Article 5(1)(a).

[13] The right to freedom of opinion and expression in Article 19 of the UDHR includes 'freedom . . . to seek, receive and impart information and ideas through any media and regardless of frontiers'; Article 19(2) of the ICCPR adds ideas 'of all kinds . . . either orally, in writing or in print, in the form of art, or through any other media of his choice'. See also Articles 13 and 17 of the CRC; Article 9(1) of the ACHPR; Article 13(1) of the ACHR; Article 32(1) of the Arab Charter on Human Rights; Article 10(1) of the ECHR. With regard to Article 13 of the American Convention on Human Rights, see *Claude Reyes and Ors v Chile*, IACtHR, Ser. C No. 151 (2006), para. 77.

Rights Committee on Freedoms of Opinion and Expression.[14] Additionally, it may be observed that most if not all human rights, and the ability to react against violations thereof, depend upon 'information', so that, in addition to its specification as a human right, information is an essential requirement for the enjoyment of other rights, which would be undermined by its absence. The notion of a right to information is explicit in, for example, the concept of 'free, prior and informed consent', a prominent feature of the landscape of indigenous rights,[15] as well as in the contested parameters of consent in areas such as racially segregated schooling, and forced sterilization.[16]

Additional to universalist prescriptions and provisions in international human rights law, instruments on the rights of particular groups under the Committee on the Elimination of Racial Discrimination's (CERD) umbrella apply and refine the message of Article 7: to combat prejudices and encourage mutuality of respect and appreciation through education and analogous means. The International Labour Organization (ILO) Convention 169 on Indigenous and Tribal Peoples resonates with Article 7 of ICERD in requiring that:

> [e]ducational measures shall be taken among all sections of the national community, and particularly among those that are in most direct contact with the peoples concerned, with the object of eliminating prejudices that they may harbour in respect of these peoples. To this end, efforts shall be made to ensure that history textbooks and other educational materials provide a fair, accurate and informative portrayal of the societies and cultures of these peoples.[17]

The UN Declaration on the Rights of Indigenous Peoples (UNDRIP) provides that the diversity of cultures, traditions, histories, and aspirations of indigenous peoples shall be 'appropriately reflected' in education and public information, and that effective measures shall be taken 'in consultation and cooperation' with the indigenous peoples concerned, 'to combat prejudice and eliminate discrimination and to promote tolerance, understanding and good relations among indigenous peoples and all other segments of society'.[18] In the field of information, media are enjoined to reflect indigenous cultural diversity, in mandatory terms in the case of the State-owned media.[19]

On minorities, the United Nations Declaration on Minorities (UNDM) takes an explicit reciprocity approach: States 'should, where appropriate, take measures in the field of education, in order to encourage knowledge of the history, traditions, language and culture of the minorities existing within their territory. Persons belonging to minorities should have adequate opportunities to gain knowledge of the society as a whole.'[20]

[14] See in particular paras 11, 12, 13–16, 18–19. See further, M. O'Flaherty, 'Freedom of Expression: Article 19 of the International Covenant on Civil and Political Rights and the Human Rights Committee's General Comment No. 34', *HRLR* 12 (2012), 627–54; M. O'Flaherty, 'International Covenant on Civil and Political Rights: Interpreting Freedom of Expression and Information Standards for the Present and the Future', in McGonagle and Donders, *The UN and Freedom of Expression*, pp. 55–88.

[15] In the context of the ICCPR, see *Poma Poma v Peru*, CCPR/C/95/D/1457/2006 (2009), especially paras 7.6 and 7.7. See discussion of Article 5 (c) in Chapter 13.

[16] See Chapters 10, 13, and 14.

[17] Article 31. Compare Article 4(4) of the UN Declaration on the Rights of Persons belonging to Minorities. See further Article 6(1) of the Council of Europe's Framework Convention on the Protection of National Minorities, and paras 48 and 49 of its Explanatory Report.

[18] Article 15.

[19] Article 16.

[20] Article 3(4): see *Commentary on the United Nations Declaration on the Rights of Persons belonging to National or Ethnic, Religious and Linguistic Minorities*, E/CN.4/AC.5/2001/2; P. Thornberry, 'Education', in

The Council of Europe's Framework Convention on National Minorities employs similar terms: States parties 'shall, where appropriate take measures in the field of education and research to foster knowledge of the culture, history, language and religion of their national minorities and of the majority'.[21] In relation to media, the Framework Convention enjoins adequate measures to 'facilitate access to the media for persons belonging to national minorities and in order to promote tolerance and permit cultural pluralism'.[22] The recommendations on education of the First UN Forum on Minorities summarize the objectives of Article 7 of ICERD in key respects in recommending that education 'should work actively towards the elimination of prejudices among population groups and the promotion of mutual respect, understanding and tolerance among all persons residing in the State, whatever their ethnic, religious or cultural background or sex';[23] human rights education for all 'should be made an integral part of the national educational experience'.[24]

General statements regarding the importance of human right education also appear in landmark texts emanating from world conferences on human rights[25] and against racism;[26] a generality of concerns is expressed in paragraph 136 of the Durban programme of Action, which calls upon States to

> ensure that education and training, especially teacher training, promote respect for human rights and the fight against racism, racial discrimination, xenophobia and related intolerance and that educational institutions implement policies and programmes . . . on equal opportunities, anti-racism, gender equality, and cultural, religious and other diversity, with the participation of teachers, parents and students . . . It further urges all educators, including teachers at all levels of education, religious communities and the print and electronic media, to play an effective role in human rights education, including as a means to combat racism, racial discrimination, xenophobia and related intolerance.

Building on the United Nations Decade for Human Rights Education, the UN General Assembly inaugurated the World Programme for Human Rights Education.[27] The first phase of the programme concentrated on human rights education in schools, whereas the second phase, according to the UN High Commissioner for Human Rights, 'focuses on human rights education for teachers and educators, civil servants, law enforcement officials and military personnel'.[28] In the programme, the content of human rights

M. Weller (ed.), *Universal Minority Rights: A Commentary on the Jurisprudence of International Courts and Treaty Bodies* (Oxford University Press, 2007), pp. 325–62.

[21] Article 12(1): see P. Thornberry, 'Article 12', in M. Weller (ed.), *The Rights of Minorities in Europe: A Commentary on the European Framework Convention for the Protection of National Minorities* (Oxford University Press, 2005), pp. 365–93.

[22] Article 9: commentary on Article 9 by J. Packer and S. Holt in M. Weller (ed.), *The Rights of Minorities in Europe*, pp. 263–300.

[23] A/HRC/10/11/Add.1 (2009), para. 43; also, *ibid.*, paras 13, 57, 64, 66, and 67. Paragraph 6.1 of the Council of Europe's Framework Convention for the Protection of National Minorities is another point of reference: commentary by G. Gilbert, in M. Weller (ed.), *The Rights of Minorities in Europe*, pp. 177–91.

[24] Para. 44.

[25] Vienna Declaration and Programme of Action, Part I, paras 33–34; Part II, paras 78–82.

[26] Durban Declaration, paras 95–97, and Programme of Action, paras 129–39; Durban Review Conference, paras 22 and 107.

[27] General Assembly resolution 59/113, 10 December 2004.

[28] <http://www2.ohchr.org/english/issues/education/training/programme.htm>. See also *World Programme of Human Rights Education, Plan of Action, Second Phase* (UNHCHR and UNESCO, 2012) [henceforth *World Programme Plan of Action*] available at: <http://www.ohchr.org/Documents/Publications/WPHRE_Phase_2_en.pdf>.

education is provided by key international human rights instruments including ICERD; human rights education is defined as 'any learning, education, training and information efforts aimed at building a universal culture of human rights', including, inter alia, 'the promotion of understanding, tolerance, gender equality and friendship among all nations, indigenous peoples and minorities'.[29] In 2011, the General Assembly adopted the United Nations Declaration on Human Rights Education and Training,[30] which recites, *inter alia*, that 'States are duty-bound . . . to ensure that education is aimed at strengthening respect for human rights and fundamental freedoms'.[31] According to this instrument, human rights education and training encompasses education about human rights, education through human rights, 'which includes learning and teaching in a way that respects the rights of both educators and learners', and education for human rights, which includes 'empowering persons to enjoy and exercise their rights and to respect and uphold the rights of others'.[32] The United Nations overall has invested heavily in human rights training and education, providing information on, *inter alia*, human rights treaty bodies such as CERD.[33] Relevant educational texts and principles drawn from the archive of UNESCO are referred to at various points in the present chapter.

B. *Travaux Préparatoires*

The *travaux* of Article 7 are sketchy, though questions regarding the role of education as opposed to more coercive methods of combating racial discrimination illuminate the drafting archives as a whole.[34] Education to combat racial discrimination figured in some Sub-Commission texts, with ideas following on from Article 8 of the Declaration on the Elimination of Racial Discrimination:

> All effective steps shall be taken immediately in the fields of teaching, education and information, with a view to eliminating racial discrimination and prejudice and promoting understanding, tolerance and friendship among nations and racial groups, as well as to propagating the purposes and principles of the Charter of the United Nations, of the Universal Declaration of Human Rights, and of the Declaration on the Granting of Independence to Colonial Countries and Peoples.

The Abram text referred to taking immediate steps, through educational or other means, 'to promote or encourage the elimination of racial discrimination in any form and to promote understanding, tolerance, and friendship among all nations and peoples'.[35] A proposed amendment by Krishnaswami suggested the addition of references to the Charter of the United Nations, the Universal Declaration of Human Rights and the Colonial Declaration.[36] The Sub-Commission's unanimously adopted text,[37] proposed

[29] *World Programme Plan of Action*, pp. 12–13.

[30] A/RES/66/137, 19 December 2011, Annex [UN Declaration on Human Rights Education]

[31] UN Declaration on Human Rights Education, preambular para. 4.

[32] *Ibid.*, Article 2.

[33] *The Committee on the Elimination of Racial Discrimination*, Human Rights Fact Sheet No. 12 (United Nations, 1991).

[34] See, *inter alia*, the discussion in Chapter 11 of the *travaux* of Article 4.

[35] E/CN.4/Sub.2/L.308.

[36] E/CN.4/Sub.2/L.310. See also the very brief text submitted by Calvocoressi and Capotorti, E/CN.4/Sub.2/L.339: 'States parties shall take immediate steps through education to promote and encourage the elimination of racial discrimination in any form.'

[37] E/CN.4/Sub.2/SR.425.

by the Chairman, retained the listing of human rights instruments, substituting the reference to the Colonial Declaration with a reference to the UN Declaration on Racial Discrimination:

> States parties undertake to adopt immediate and effective measures, particularly in the fields of teaching, education and information, with a view to promoting understanding, tolerance and friendship among nations and racial or ethnic groups, as well as to propagating the purposes and principles of the Charter of the United Nations, the Universal Declaration of Human Rights, and the United Nations Declaration on the Elimination of All Forms of Racial Discrimination.[38]

The draft was considered by the Commission at its 802nd meeting. An amendment by the UK, orally revised by Lebanon, proposed for the first part of the article that: 'States parties undertake to adopt immediate and effective measures, particularly in the fields of teaching, education and information with a view to combating prejudices which lead to racial discrimination and promoting' understanding, etc.[39] The representative of the UK explained that the Sub-Commission's text, while referring to understanding and toleration, 'did not give sufficient attention to racial discrimination itself';[40] there was also a need to make explicit reference to racial prejudices, which were at the root of many forms of discrimination.[41] Responding to a question on why there was a divergence between the language of Article 4 which referred to 'racial hatred', and the proposal for Article 7 that referred to 'racial discrimination', the representative of the UK replied that racial discrimination was the subject of the draft convention and that Article 4 was the only place where the term 'racial hatred' had been employed.[42] The amendment was adopted unanimously.[43]

In the Third Committee only two amendments were proposed: the first to add a fourth term 'culture' to 'teaching, education and information';[44] the second to add 'and of this Convention' at the end of the article.[45] Both amendments were adopted.[46] The summary records do not shed light on the reasoning behind the amendments, which widen the field of action expected from States and underline the educational functions of the principles expressed in the Convention as a whole.

I. Reservations and Declarations

No reservations subsist with regard to Article 7.

[38] The adopting resolution altered 'ethnic' in the above to 'ethnical'.

[39] E/CN.4/L.700, as revised: E/CN.4/874, paras 235 and 236.

[40] E/CN.4/SR.802, p. 6.

[41] *Ibid.* The representative of the Lebanon added, E/CN.4/SR.802, p. 8, that the article in question dealt with 'mental attitudes and cultural relations—areas in which prejudices made themselves felt'.

[42] E/CN.4/SR.802, pp. 7–8.

[43] E/CN.4/874, para. 240.

[44] Submitted by Bulgaria, A/C.3/L.1218.

[45] Submitted by Czechoslovakia, A/C.3/L.1220.

[46] A/6181, para. 94; A/C.3/SR.1309, para. 41.

C. Practice

I. Guidelines

The Guidelines for the Common Core Document for UN human rights reporting request a range of information on the dissemination of human rights principles and promotion of human rights awareness through education that touches directly on Article 7:

> States should set out the efforts made to promote respect for all human rights in the State. Such promotion may encompass actions by government officials, legislatures, local assemblies, national human rights institutions, etc., together with the role played by the relevant actors in civil society. States may offer information on measures such as dissemination of information, education and training, publicity, and allocation of budgetary resources... attention should be paid to the accessibility of promotional materials and human rights instruments, including their availability in all relevant national, local, minority or indigenous languages.[47]

The Guidelines include detailed references to raising human rights awareness among public officials and other professionals,[48] an extensive list comprising 'government officials, police, immigration officers, prosecutors, judges, lawyers, prison officers, members of the armed forces, border guards, as well as teachers, medical doctors, health workers and social workers';[49] they also refer to promotion of human rights awareness through educational programmes and government-sponsored public information,[50] and through the mass media.[51]

The CERD-specific reporting guidelines restate the language of Article 7 and add guidance on key elements, recommending that State party reports should group the requisite information under the separate headings of (a) education and teaching, (b) culture, and (c) information.[52] The data provided should further sub-divide into (i) measures to combat prejudices which lead to racial discrimination, and (ii) measures to promote tolerance and understanding, etc. The guidelines provide a significant level of detail suggesting the nature of the actions required and their ideal institutional context for their furtherance, concluding with a reference to the importance of 'building an inclusive society while respecting the human rights and cultural identity' of all groups, a statement that captures the ideals of the Convention as interpreted in CERD practice; the Guidelines also envisage an educational process that conveys 'the message of the inherent dignity of all human beings and their equality in the enjoyment of human rights'.[53]

II. General

Aspects of Article 7 have been addressed in three broad-based recommendations: General Recommendation (GR) 5, GR 13, and GR 35; for particular groups and categories,

[47] HRI/GEN/2/Rev.5, chapeau to para. 43.
[48] HRI/GEN/2/Rev.5, para. 43(d).
[49] *Ibid.*
[50] Para. 43(e).
[51] Para. 43(f).
[52] CERD/C/2007/1, pp. 14–15.
[53] *Ibid.*, p. 14.

aspects of education figure in GR 27,[54] GR 29,[55] GR 30,[56] and GR 34.[57] GR 5[58] is drafted along the lines of a resolution with a preamble and an operative part, and makes specific reference to Article 7 along with Article 9 on the related reporting requirements. The preamble underlines the relevance of the prescriptions in the article as 'important and effective means of eliminating racial discrimination', and criticizes States parties for reporting on the article in a 'general and perfunctory' manner; States parties are reminded that the obligations under Article 7 are binding on all States, and must be fulfilled by them, 'including States which declare that racial discrimination is not practised on the territories under their jurisdiction', a form of negation by States parties that has diminished appreciably over the life of the Committee. The operative part requests information on Article 7—if necessary through a special report distinct from that required by Article 9—on the 'immediate and effective measures' which give effect to its provisions, and supplies a cursory breakdown of Article 7 into its components for the purpose of organizing the necessary information. It may be noted that, in contradistinction to the reference in GR5 to 'in territories under their jurisdiction', the guidelines refer to the provision in educational materials of information regarding groups 'living on the State's territory'.[59]

GR 13 'on the training of law enforcement officials in the protection of human rights'[60] underlines the importance of such training in the fulfilment of obligations under Article 2(1) of the Convention: fulfilment 'very much depends upon national law enforcement officials who exercise police powers, especially the powers of detention and arrest, and upon whether they are properly informed about the obligations their State has entered into under the Convention'.[61] To implement Article 7, States parties are called upon 'to review and improve' the training of the officials.[62] The principles outlined in GR 13 are further elaborated in GR 31 on the prevention of discrimination in the criminal justice system, which, besides anti-discrimination training programmes, encourages 'sensitization to intercultural relations [of] law enforcement officials: police personnel, persons working

[54] Paras 17–26.

[55] Section 8, which includes recommendations 'to educate the population as a whole in a spirit of non-discrimination and respect for the communities subject to descent-based discrimination', and to review language in textbooks 'which conveys stereotyped or demeaning images, references, names or opinions concerning descent-based commmunities and replace it by images, references, names and opinions which convey the message of the inherent dignity of all human beings and their equality of human rights'.

[56] Paras 29, 30, and 31.

[57] Paras 61–66. Para. 61 reprises the GR 29 theme of reviewing derogatory language in text books; para. 66 recommends, *inter alia*, the inclusion in textbooks of 'chapters about the history and cultures of peoples of African descent and preserve this knowledge in museums and other forums for future generations'.

[58] A/32/18, ch. IV.C.

[59] CERD/C/2007/1, p. 14. With respect to extraterritorial jurisdiction, see discussion in Chapters 8 and 10.

[60] A/48/18, ch. VIII. B.

[61] GR 13, para. 2, which also envisages 'intensive training' for law enforcement officials 'to ensure that in the performance of their duties they respect as well as protect human dignity and maintain and uphold the human rights of all persons' without distinction as to race, colour, or national or ethnic origin; it is not clear why the ground of 'descent' is omitted

[62] *Ibid.*, para. 3. The recommendation provoked brief discussion centring on whether the text should refer to 'powers of detention or arrest', or 'powers of detention and arrest'; the latter was chosen to make it clear that officials were forbidden to engage in practices of racial discrimination in both cases: CERD/C/SR.979, especially para. 77 (Committee member Wolfrum): 'If the Committee deleted the reference to the power of detention, the text might be interpreted as implying that law enforcement officials were free to engage in practices of racial discrimination against individuals under detention, although not with respect to those under arrest.'

in the system of justice, prison institution, psychiatric establishments, social and medical services, etc'.[63] The recommendation also refers to fostering of dialogue and cooperation on the part of police and judiciary with representatives of the groups expressly or impliedly protected by Article 1. The strategies recommended in paragraph 5 of the Recommendation approximate to holistic approaches in that the training element is envisaged as working together with, *inter alia*, better representation of persons belonging to racial and ethnic groups in the police and judiciary, and attention to issues of structural discrimination.

GR 35 on combating racist hate speech addresses general and specific aspects of Article 7, the basic undertakings of which are highlighted in paragraph 31:

> Under article 7, States parties undertake to adopt immediate and effective measures, particularly in the fields of teaching, education, culture and information, with a view to combating prejudices which lead to racial discrimination and to promoting understanding, tolerance and friendship among nations and racial or ethnic groups, as well as to propagating universal human rights principles, including those of the Convention. Article 7 is phrased in the same mandatory language as other articles in the Convention, and the fields of activity—'teaching, education, culture and information'—are not expressed as exhaustive of the undertakings required.

Article 7 does not figure to any great extent in the Article 14 procedure; *E.I.F. v The Netherlands*[64] and *Hagan v Australia*[65] raise relevant issues. In *E.I.F.*, the author, a Dutch citizen of Surinamese origin cited a battery of racist statements alleged to have been made by staff as evidence that he was dismissed from The Netherlands Police Academy on racial grounds. In the case, the Article 7 element is tagged on to a list of articles alleged to have been violated—Articles 2, 5, 6, and 7. The Committee, in finding no violation of the Convention,[66] considered that while some of the allegations submitted by the author had racial connotations of a serious nature, there was no evidence that the decision to dismiss the author from the Academy was taken on racial grounds.[67] The case does not elaborate the specific Article 7 ground which appears to centre on the government's failure to combat the claimed (by the author of the communication) institutional racism within the police service.[68]

Hagan concerned a racially offensive sign in a sporting ground in Queensland to which the author, an Australian citizen of Aboriginal background, strongly objected. Several articles of the Convention were invoked in the complaint. With respect to Article 7, the petitioner alleged that the lawfulness in Australia of such racist language ran 'counter to the objectives of article 7, which indicates that States parties undertake to combat prejudices leading to racial discrimination'.[69] Responding specifically to the Article 7 element of the claim, the State party recalled that a wide range of measures had been adopted over the years 'to combat effectively racial prejudice and promote racial harmony'.[70] Further, 'the fact that the petitioner had been unsuccessful in pursuing his claim before the Australian courts did 'not detract from the immediacy or effectiveness of

[63] GR 31, para. 5(b); the 'etc.' is in the original.
[64] CERD/C/58/D/15/1999 (2001).
[65] CERD/C/62/D/26/2002 (2003). See also *Murat Er v Denmark*, CERD/C/71/D/40/2007 (2007).
[66] *E.I.F. v The Netherlands*, para. 7.
[67] *Ibid.*, para. 6.2.
[68] *Ibid.*, para. 4.15. The allegation was rejected by the State party.
[69] *Hagan v Australia*, para. 3.3.
[70] *Ibid.*, para. 4.19.

measures taken by the State party's governments to combat racial prejudice and to promote racial harmony'.[71] Without finding a violation, the Committee recommended, *inter alia*, that the State party secure the removal of the offending sign.

III. Immediate and Effective Measures

The principle of the Convention that laws and other measures are to be quickly and effectively implemented is carried through to Article 7 in its reference to immediacy, the references in the preamble to speedy elimination of racial discrimination; in Article 2 to pursuing a policy of eliminating discrimination 'without delay'; and in Article 4 to adopting 'immediate and positive measures' to eradicate discrimination and incitement thereto, will be recalled.[72] There is no reason to suppose that the concept of immediacy or of 'measures' in respect of Article 7 differs from its elaboration elsewhere in the Convention.

The text of Article 7 refers to immediate and effective measures in four named areas of action—teaching, education, culture, and information—which are treated only as illustrative. The scale of the task of promoting greater mutuality of respect among groups in society suggests a multiplicity of modes of action, up to the maximal set of possibilities under the Convention. In spite of the divergences in the drafting of the Convention on the respective merits of 'education' and 'law' as means of eliminating discrimination, too sharp a distinction between 'law' and 'education' should not be drawn.[73] In light of the overall emphasis of Article 7, legal measures are implicated as part of the 'educational' process, and implementation methodologies characteristically demand a grounding in law. The educational function of law as conveying the approval or disapproval of forms of conduct—its expressive function—should not be neglected in the construction of an educational or informational strategy to fulfil the demands of the Convention;[74] the point is reinforced by Article 2(1)(d).

As with the requirement of immediacy, 'measures' should be treated as consistent with 'measures' elsewhere in the Convention, summarized in GR 32 and reiterated in GR 35 as comprising 'legislative, executive, administrative, budgetary and regulatory instruments... as well as plans, policies, programmes and ... regimes'.[75] Measures related to the objectives of Article 7 have included the entire list in GR 32. In some instances the recommended implementation measures have been general and unspecific; in most cases goals are to be achieved through instituting programmes targeting key sectors of society and of the State apparatus, such as the police and judiciary, the media, education professionals, the political classes, and in sport. Awareness-raising campaigns,[76] codes of conduct, intercultural

[71] *Ibid.*, para. 4.19. The reference to 'governments' implicated administrations at the Federal, State, and territory levels. The author, *Ibid.*, para. 5.7, disputed this element in the arguments of the State party, claiming that it had failed to identify any measure of 'teaching, education, culture and information' directed against discriminatory conduct by the Trustees of the sports facility or at promoting reconciliation; the case report erroneously includes this aspect of the claim under Article 5.

[72] Discussed in Chapters 5, 8, and 11; see also Chapter 15.

[73] Well illustrated by the *travaux* of Article 2. See also Chapters 11 and 20.

[74] The expressive function of legislation in line with Article 4 of the Convention is underlined in GR 35, para. 10.

[75] GR 32, para. 13, recalled in para. 10 of GR 35; see discussion in Chapters 8, 9, and 11.

[76] A search of the Universal Human Rights Index (UHI) brought up seventy-five CERD entries under 'awareness raising': <http://uhri.ohchr.org/search/results>.

dialogue between communities,[77] dissemination of knowledge of the cultural heritage of groups,[78] multicultural education,[79] etc, have all at various times been recommended for adoption by States parties. The envisaged ensemble of activities and methodologies in support of interethnic understanding and tolerance implicates the whole of the Convention, so that prescriptions grouped under Article 7 are integral to the programme of ICERD as a whole.

IV. Education and Teaching

The guidelines on education and teaching under Article 7 request,[80] in addition to information on general legislative and administrative measures, information on school curricula, teacher training, and training of other professionals, towards the objectives of Article 7. As with the other fields indicated in Article 7, States are mandated to provide pro-tolerance and anti-racist education in the school system.[81] GR 35 frames the general issue:

> The School systems in States parties represent an important focus for the dissemination of human rights information and perspectives. School curricula, textbooks and teaching materials should be informed by and address human rights themes and seek to promote mutual respect and tolerance among nations and racial and ethnic groups.[82]

A series of interconnected paragraphs buttresses the case for anti-racist and pro-tolerance education:

> Measures should be adopted in the field of education aimed at encouraging knowledge of the history, culture and traditions of 'racial and ethnical' groups present in the State party, including indigenous peoples and persons of African descent. Educational materials should, in the interests of promoting mutual respect and understanding, endeavour to highlight the contribution of all groups to the social, economic and cultural enrichment of the national identity and to national, economic and social progress.[83]
>
> Appropriate educational strategies in line with the requirements of Article 7 include intercultural education, including intercultural bilingual education, based on equality of respect and esteem and genuine mutuality, supported by adequate human and financial resources. Programmes of intercultural education should represent a genuine balance of interests and should not function in intention or effect as vehicles of cultural assimilation.[84]

The Committee places considerable emphasis on intercultural education as a means of combating intolerance and prejudice. While references to such education are legion, no general account of principles of intercultural education—beyond their invocation in specific situations—has been elaborated by the Committee. Amongst an abundance of

[77] Ten CERD UHI entries are filed under 'intercultural dialogue', mostly concentrated in later years.

[78] Concluding observations on Georgia, CERD/C/GEO/CO/4-5, para. 16; LAO PDR, CERD/C/LAO/CO/16-18, para. 21.

[79] Concluding observations on Malta, CERD/C/MLT/CO/15-20, para. 17; Norway, CERD/C/NOR/CO/19-20, para. 9; Serbia, CERD/C/SRB/CO/1, para. 21.

[80] Guideline for Article 7, section A.

[81] See remarks of CERD member Vázquez on the promotion of tolerance through educating pupils from different groups together: CERD/C/SR.2368, para. 51.

[82] Para. 32.

[83] GR 35, para. 34.

[84] GR 35, para. 33.

available definitions, UNESCO has elaborated basic principles of intercultural education that should (1) respect the identity of the learner, (2) provide learners with the knowledge and skills necessary to participate fully in society, and (3) provide learners with the knowledge and skills, etc, 'that enable them to contribute to respect, understanding and solidarity among individuals, ethnic, social, cultural and religious groups and nations'.[85] Through group engagement and participation, genuine intercultural education has the capacity to challenge 'structural' discrimination.

While concern for intercultural education has been expressed by CERD across a wide spectrum of societies, there is a focus in practice on indigenous peoples, as well as immigrant groups and Roma.[86] In the case of indigenous peoples, the simple reference to 'intercultural education' may be expanded by recommendations for 'intercultural bilingual education', 'bilingual and intercultural education', or variants thereof.[87] The intercultural metaphor is extended in practice to include promotion of intercultural dialogue,[88] intercultural coexistence,[89] 'interculturalism', and 'intercultural mediators'.[90] In some cases, the intercultural 'balance' appears to favour the participation in society component (UNESCO Principle 2), in others the cultural specifics of the learning group are more prominent. 'Multicultural' is used most often as a descriptor of State and society, and intercultural education has sometimes been understood as advancing general policies of building a multicultural State.[91] CERD practice does little to distinguish intercultural from multicultural education—recommendations tend to take their colour from usage in the State concerned. As with other policy elements throughout ICERD, intercultural education and related policies must be backed up by resources and put into practice effectively.

In the absence of a general recommendation on education and racial discrimination with an elaboration of key terms, CERD has nonetheless provided guidance to States parties on the fulfilment of obligations. The depth of guidance has increased over recent years, even if it does not approach the detail of micro-management of outcomes. Some concluding observations elaborate the necessary components of principle and strategy

[85] *UNESCO Guidelines on Intercultural Education* (UNESCO, 2006). Further detailed specification of the UNESCO Principles, *ibid.*, pp. 33–38, suggests, *inter alia*, building on the cultural heritage of learners through culturally appropriate teaching and language strategies including the promotion of learning environments that respect cultural diversity (Principle 1); guaranteeing equal and equitable opportunities in education by eliminating discrimination in education and promoting mutual knowledge among minority and majority groups (Principle 2); developing critical awareness of the struggle against racism and racial discrimination and the value of cultural diversity, understanding, and respect for all peoples, and 'awareness not only of rights but also of duties incumbent upon individuals, social groups and nations towards each other' (Principle 3).

[86] Re immigrant groups, see concluding observations on Iceland, CERD/C/ISL/CO/19-20; and Malta, CERD/C/MLT/CO/15-20, para. 17; regarding Roma, concluding observations on Italy, CERD/C/ITA/CO/16-18, para. 20 (Roma and Sinti); and recommendations for intercultural dialogue, Slovakia, CERD/C/SVK/CO/9-10, para. 12.

[87] Concluding observations on Argentina, CERD/C/ARG/CO/19-20, para. 19; Australia, CERD/C/AUS/CO/15-17, para. 21; Ecuador, CERD/C/ECU/CO/19, para. 20, CERD/C/ECU/CO/20-22, para. 22.

[88] Concluding observations on Bolivia, CERD/C/BOL/CO/17-20, para.11; Bosnia and Herzegovina, CERD/C/BIH/CO/7-8, para. 13; Malta, CERD/C/MLT/CO/15-20, para. 17; Slovakia, CERD/C/SVK/CO/9-10, para. 12.

[89] Concluding observations on Guatemala, CERD/C/GTM/CO/11, para. 12.

[90] In concluding observations on Luxembourg, the Committee welcomed the provision of school curricula promoting interculturalism: CERD/C/LUX/CO/13, para. 11; concluding observations on Guatemala, CERD/C/GTM/CO/12-13, para. 3, a similarly positive appreciation.

[91] Concluding observations on Argentina, CERD/C/ARG/CO/19-20, para. 19.

more fully than others; for the rest, an inductive approach taking practice within States as a basic datum has assisted context-specific elaborations of standards. In the case of Australia, recommendations were made to provide adequate resources to preserve indigenous languages, hold a national enquiry into bilingual education for indigenous peoples in consultation with them, and 'adopt all necessary measures to preserve native languages and develop and carry out programmes to revitalize indigenous languages and bilingual and intercultural education for indigenous peoples, respecting cultural identity and history'.[92] Bosnia and Herzegovina was recommended to continue fostering intercultural dialogue, tolerance, and understanding 'paying due attention to the culture and history of different ethnic groups' within the State party.[93] Recognition of the truth of history and reparations to victim populations are envisaged as part of intercultural processes.[94] It is evident from the frequent coupling of 'intercultural' with 'bilingual' canvassed above that the linguistic component of intercultural education is often envisaged as taking that form, while intercultural education 'in mother tongue' has also been recommended.[95]

Further, while the conditions of indigenous, minority and other groups in the States parties are the trigger for the concerns expressed, intercultural education is envisaged by CERD as appropriate for all components of society: phrases such as intercultural understanding or dialogue, etc, 'between all ethnic groups' are better understood as implicating society as a whole. Genuine mutuality is the key, otherwise so-called interculturalism could be little more than a synonym for assimilation through education. In this context, concluding observations stress group participation in educational initiatives.[96]

Taking up themes expressed in general recommendations, the CERD-specific guidelines request information on steps taken 'to review all language in textbooks which conveys stereotyped or demeaning images, references, names or opinions' concerning groups protected by the Convention'.[97] Textbooks should include chapters on the history and culture of protected groups 'living on the State's territory' as well as books, TV and radio programmes about their history and culture 'including in languages spoken by them'.[98] Intensive training for law enforcement officials to respect and protect human dignity and uphold human rights without discrimination is also recommended.[99] The history theme is reprised by GR 35:

> In order to promote inter-ethnic understanding, balanced and objective representations of history are essential, and, where atrocities have been committed against groups of the population, days of remembrance and other public events should be held, where appropriate in context, to recall such human tragedies, as well as celebrations of successful resolution of conflicts. Truth and reconciliation commissions can also play a vital role in countering the persistence of racial hatred and facilitating the development of a climate of inter-ethnic tolerance.[100]

[92] CERD/C/AUS/CO/15-17, para. 21.
[93] CERD/C/BIH/CO/7-8, para. 13.
[94] Concluding observations on Australia, CERD/C/AUS/CO/15-17, para. 21. See also Chapter 16.
[95] Concluding observations on Nicaragua, CERD/C/NIC/CO/14, para. 8.
[96] See also para. 33 of GR 35.
[97] *Ibid.*, section A.3.
[98] *Ibid.*, section A.4.
[99] *Ibid.*, section A.5.
[100] GR 35, para. 35.

The point was made in the recommendation in relation to Article 7 and also resonates with Article 6. A number of countries have reported on memorializing the Holocaust, in some cases including the Roma holocaust as well as the Holocaust of the Jewish people.[101] Acknowledgement of the deleterious effects and wrongs of the transatlantic slave trade and colonialism on peoples of African descent in the past, and their continuing effects, figures among the recommendations in GR 34.[102] With regard to the social consequences of the transatlantic slave trade, the Dominican Republic was invited, in a compendious recommendation that made specific reference to Article 7, to institute a commission

> to analyse the implications of the transatlantic traffic in persons and slavery so as to determine their historical significance in the building of national identity, the persistence of their consequences... including the expressions of racism, racial discrimination, xenophobia and other related forms of intolerance, in particular towards the darker-skinned population of African descent from the Dominican Republic or Haiti, and identify the barriers that limit the equitable development of those populations.[103]

The specific post-conflict relevance of Article 7 has been emphasized in concluding observations to Kyrgyzstan, where it was expressed that, following a recent conflict,

> a climate of discriminatory attitudes, racial stereotypes, suspicion between the majority ethnic group and the minorities, widespread nationalistic discourse and exclusion continue to exist... The Committee recommends that the State party strengthen its efforts, including through education, culture, awareness-raising campaigns, to combat racial stereotypes, discriminatory attitudes, nationalistic discourse, including in media, with a view to promoting reconciliation, tolerance and understanding, and to build a peaceful and inclusive society.[104]

In the case of Georgia, amid post-conflict concerns that, *inter alia*, members of some minorities had been depicted as 'enemies', the Committee recommended that,

> in addition to legal and policy levels, the State party make every effort to build mutual confidence and reconciliation between the majority and minority populations and promote a peaceful and tolerant coexistence in inter-ethnic relations through political discourse, awareness-raising campaigns and by removing derogatory or insulting references to minorities in school textbooks.[105]

In the case of Kenya, the State party was called upon to 'step up educational efforts to promote national cohesion and reconciliation, including by ensuring that they effectively address ethnic prejudices and stereotypes as well as the history of inter-ethnic violence, utilizing media that reach all segments of the population'.[106] With regard to ongoing

[101] Recent references to the Roma holocaust, under 'positive aspects', are made in concluding observations on the Czech Republic, CERD/C/CZE/CO/8-9, para. 3; Moldova, CERD/C/MDA/CO/7, para. 6; Romania, CERD/C/ROU/CO/16-19, para. 4; and Ukraine, CERD/C/UKR/CO/19-21, para. 3: in the case of Moldova, CERD noted with appreciation 'that the State party has included education on the Holocaust and the causes of the genocide of the Jews and Roma between 1941 and 1944 in school curricula, and that modern history textbooks contain chapters on the Holocaust and genocide of Jews and Roma'.

[102] GR 34, para. 17. See also the extensive recommendation to the Dominican Republic, CERD/C/DOM/CO/13-14, para. 9.

[103] CERD/C/DOM/CO/13-14, para. 9; the paragraph recites that it was built upon a set of previous recommendations in CERD/C/DOM/CO/12.

[104] CERD/C/KGJ/CO/5-7, para. 14.

[105] CERD/C/GEO/CO/4-5, para. 14.

[106] CERD/C/KEN/CO/1-4, para. 24.

conflict, in a paragraph not linked to a specific article of the Convention, Cyprus was requested to provide information on intercommunal initiatives 'to restore mutual confidence and improve relations between ethnic and/or religious communities as well as raise awareness through the impartial teaching of the history of Cyprus in schools and other State institutions'.[107]

V. Culture and Information

The CERD guidelines on 'culture' request information on the role of institutions or associations 'working to develop national culture and traditions, to combat racial prejudices and to promote intra-national and intra-cultural understanding, tolerance and friendship among all groups';[108] the support provided by the States parties to such institutions and associations, and more generally, action taken to ensure the respect and promotion of cultural diversity, for example in the area of artistic creation; 'the linguistic policies adopted and implemented by the State party'.[109]

The paragraphs on 'information' read as a counterpoint to the characteristic concerns of Article 4 with legal prohibitions of hate speech, particularly with regard to the role of the media.[110] The requested data suggest that the media should play a positive role in disseminating the ideals of the Convention in light of its 'particular responsibility' not to encourage prejudice; responsibilities include, *inter alia*, the responsibility 'to avoid reporting incidents involving individual members of groups . . . in a way which blames such groups as a whole', while self-monitoring of media institutions is also referred to. In the context of racist hate speech, reaching out to Article 7, CERD GR 35 recommends that:

> [i]nformation campaigns and educational policies calling attention to the harms produced by racist hate speech should engage the general public; civil society, including religious and community associations; parliamentarians and other politicians; educational professionals; public administration personnel; police and other bodies dealing with public order; and legal personnel, including the judiciary. The Committee draws the attention of States parties to general recommendation No. 13 (1993) on the training of law enforcement officials in the protection of human rights[111] and to general recommendation No. 31 (2005) on the prevention of racial discrimination in the administration and functioning of the criminal justice system. In these and other cases, familiarization with international norms protecting freedom of opinion and expression and norms protecting against racist hate speech is essential.[112]

107 CERD/C/CYP/CO/17-22, para. 7.

108 On participation in culture generally, see Chapter 14.

109 With regard to the role of institutions and associations see, for example, concluding observations on Israel, CERD/C/ISR/CO/13, para. 27, recommending that 'laws and programmes be equally devoted to the promotion of cultural institutions and the protection of holy sites of both Jewish and other religious communities'; Serbia, CERD/C/SRB/1, para. 13: a recommendation to '[e]ncourage and support non-governmental organizations and institutions that combat racial discrimination and promote a culture of tolerance and cultural and ethnic diversity.'

110 The United Nations Declaration on Human Rights Education, Article 1(1), provides that '[e]veryone has the right to know, seek and receive information about all human rights and fundamental freedoms and should have access to human rights education and training.'

111 *Official Records of the General Assembly, Sixtieth Session, Supplement No. 18* (A/60/18), ch. VIII, sect. B.

112 Para. 36.

Other paragraphs of GR 35 referring to Article 7 are similarly not confined to hate speech phenomena:

Informed, ethical and objective media, including social media and the Internet, have an essential role in promoting responsibility in the dissemination of ideas and opinions. In addition to putting in place appropriate legislation for the media in line with international standards, States parties should encourage the public and private media to adopt codes of professional ethics and press codes that incorporate respect for the principles of the Convention and other fundamental human rights standards.[113]

Developing its endorsement of diversified media, the recommendation observes that:

[t]he principles of the Convention are served by encouraging media pluralism, including facilitation of access to and ownership of media by minority, indigenous and other groups in the purview of the Convention, including media in their own languages. Local empowerment through media pluralism facilitates the emergence of speech capable of countering racist hate speech.[114]

VI. Combating Prejudice

Instruments in the genre of Article 7 make frequent reference to prejudice or prejudices, the combating of which is deemed essential to addressing discrimination. Makkonen summarizes that prejudice 'refers to unfairly or unreasonable formed negative opinions, assumptions and/or feelings towards a group of people' and, utilizing social research, breaks the concept down into (a) negative stereotypes (Cognitive component); (b) negative feelings (affective component); and behavioural patterns (behavioural component)'.[115] He observes that while individual personality dynamics have a significant role to play,[116] 'it is social norms rather than these personality dynamics that determine the overall levels of prejudice in particular groups and societies',[117] adding that 'prejudices tend to generate discrimination'—a sentiment specifically endorsed by Article 7.[118]

Notifications of a social climate of prejudice against groups protected by the Convention have accordingly generated a stream of country-specific recommendations, most of which are linked to Article 4 but which also implicate Article 7. Much of the comment by

[113] Para. 39.

[114] GR 35, para. 41. Compare Article 9 of the FCNM, providing, in addition to provisions on access to media as a contribution to the promotion of tolerance and cultural pluralism, that 'persons belonging to minorities are granted the possibility of using their own media': comment by J. Packer and S. Holt, 'Article 9', in M. Weller (ed.), *The Rights of Minorities in Europe*, pp. 263–300. With regard to indigenous peoples, see Article 16 of the UNDIP: 'Indigenous peoples have the right to establish their own media in their own languages and to have access to all forms of non-indigenous media without discrimination . . . States shall take effective measures to ensure that State-owned media duly reflect indigenous cultural diversity. States . . . should encourage privately owned media to adequately reflect indigenous cultural diversity.' The *Rabat Plan of Action on the Prohibition of Advocacy of National, Racial or Religious Hatred that Constitutes Incitement to Discrimination, Hostility or Violence* includes the provision (para. 26) that States have the responsibility 'to ensure space for minorities to enjoy their fundamental rights and freedoms, for instance by facilitating registration and functioning of minority media organizations. States should strengthen the capacities of communities to access and express a range of views and information and embrace the healthy dialogue and debate that it can encompass': <http://www.ohchr.org/Documents/Issues/Opinion/SeminarRabat/Rabat_draft_outcome.pdf>.

[115] T. Makkonen, *Equal in Law, Unequal in Fact: Racial Discrimination and the Legal Response Thereto in Europe* (Martinus Nijhoff Publishers, 2012), pp. 72–4 [henceforth *Equal in Law, Unequal in Fact*].

[116] A significant reference in this respect is to T.W. Adorno *et al.*, *The Authoritarian Personality* (Norton, 1982), *Equal in Law, Unequal in Fact*, p. 74.

[117] *Ibid.*, p. 75.

[118] *Ibid.*, p. 77.

the Committee on prejudiced expressions concerns the media. In addition to the above-cited paragraphs, the fomenting of prejudice is referred to in GR 35:

> Media representations of ethnic, indigenous and other groups within the purview of Article 1 of the Convention should be based on principles of respect, fairness and the avoidance of stereotyping. Media should avoid referring unnecessarily to race, ethnicity, religion and other group characteristics in a manner that may promote intolerance.[119]

As a partial remedy for intolerant expression, the Committee encourages 'self-regulation and compliance with codes of ethics by Internet service providers, as underlined in the Durban Declaration and Programme of Action'.[120]

Broad-based general recommendations regarding the condition of the media have been offered to a wide range of States. In the case of the United Kingdom, the Committee commented in 2003 on 'the increasing racial prejudice against ethnic minorities, asylum-seekers and immigrants reflected in the media' and the reported lack of effectiveness of the Press Complaints Commission in addressing the situation.[121] In 2011, the UK was reminded about 'continuing virulent statements in the media that may adversely affect racial harmony and increase racial discrimination'; the recommendation in this latter case was linked to Article 4.[122] The media prejudice drawn to the attention of the Committee may concern a range of groups, amounting—or almost amounting—to a generalized anti-minority or xenophobic perspective alleged to exist among the population at large, or it may be directed more intensely against certain groups. In line with the broad constellation of victims of racial prejudice and discrimination identified in the present work, ethnic minorities, indigenous peoples, migrants, and persons of African origin figure in the archive as frequent targets of negative media attention, as do the Roma. Recommendations regarding the media regularly refer to 'public and private' media in general,[123] or 'mainstream media' and 'established publishing houses',[124] and include the Internet.

In the case of the Roma, GR 27 refers to the responsibility of the media not to disseminate prejudices, and 'avoid reporting incidents involving individual members of Roma communities in a way which blames such communities as a whole'.[125] The provision has been backed up by numerous country-specific recommendations.[126] GR 29 on descent-based discrimination was the first of the general recommendations to refer to the role of the Internet, followed up in GR 30 on non-citizens and many subsequent recommendations. GR 34 advises States parties to take measures 'to raise awareness among media professionals of the nature and incidence of discrimination against people of African descent, including the media's responsibility not to perpetuate prejudices';[127]

[119] GR 35, para. 40; see commentary in the present work on Article 1.

[120] GR 35, para. 42.

[121] A/58/18, para. 532.

[122] A/66/18, p. 115, para. 11.

[123] Examples include concluding observations on Ecuador, CERD/C/ECU/CO/19, para. 22, reiterated in CERD/C/ECU/CO/20-22, para. 16; Mexico, CERD/C/MEX/CO/15, para. 18; Serbia, CERD/C/SRB/CO/1, para. 13.

[124] Concluding observations on the Russian Federation, CERD/C/RUS/CO/19, para. 16.

[125] GR 27, para. 37: see also paras 36, 38, 39, and 40.

[126] Later examples include concluding observations on Italy, CERD/C/ITA/CO/16-18, para. 17, where GR 27 was recalled on reporting of incidents involving individuals that stigmatizes communities as a whole; Serbia, with regard to Roma, Ashkali, and Egyptians, CERD/C/SRB/1, para. 16; Sweden CERD/C/SWE/CO/19-21, para. 20.

[127] Para. 30.

for such persons, States parties have been advised, *inter alia*, to 'adopt measures that focus on the social role of the media... to combat the racial prejudice that can lead to racial discrimination':[128] the paragraph is explicitly linked to Article 7, as well as 4(a). The focus on the media as generators of prejudiced attitudes is displaced or in some cases enlarged by expressions of concern with the role of the political classes, including specific political parties: most such recommendations are linked in the first place to Article 4.[129]

Whereas in the context of Article 4 of the Convention, criminal and other sanctions may be intimated for outpourings of racist hate speech, reports of generalized media prejudice have also led to urgent suggestions to develop media or journalistic codes of ethics. In the case of Ecuador, the recommendation was for a media code 'which commits the media to show respect for the identity and culture of the indigenous peoples and Afro-Ecuadorian communities'.[130] The respect and fairness agenda of the Committee is also reflected in the demand for 'adequate media representation of issues concerning... ethnic and religious minorities, with a view to achieving true social cohesion among all ethnic groups, castes and tribes' (of Pakistan).[131] In the case of the Internet, unspecific measures or increased efforts to prevent the dissemination of racist speech have been recommended, as well as monitoring the medium, removal of discriminatory or racist material therefrom, and where appropriate, ratification of the Additional Protocol to the Council of Europe's Convention on Cybercrime.[132]

VII. Promoting Understanding, Tolerance, and Friendship

The calls to promote understanding, tolerance, and friendship complement provisions in the preamble and the chapeau of Article 2. Conjoined with combating prejudice, the tropes of promoting understanding and tolerance recur with considerable regularity in CERD practice. The concept of 'tolerance' employed by the Committee reaches beyond passive acceptance of the presence of groups on the territory of States parties towards active engagement with their organizations, rights, and interests. The goals of the pro-tolerance enterprise are variously described, minimally as promoting greater understanding among groups, more forcefully as implicating social cohesion or solidarity,[133] peaceful coexistence,[134] and respect for diversity, and promoting these values. Respect for diverse identities and cultures figures strongly in the matrix, and, in line with general Committee practice, recognition of the multi-ethnic nature of State populations as an aspect of

[128] Concluding observations on Ecuador, CERD/C/ECU/CO/20-22, para. 16.

[129] See, for example, concluding observations on Belgium, CERD/C/BEL/CO/15, para. 11; Japan, CERD/C/JPN/CO/3-6, para, 14, CERD/C/JPN/CO/7-9, para. 11.

[130] CERD/C/ECU/CO/19, para. 22.

[131] CERD/C/PAK/CO/20, para. 24. Other concluding observations that include recommendations for media or journalistic codes of ethics include those to Bolivia, CERD/C/BOL/CO/17-20, para. 15; Guatemala, CERD/C/GTM/CO/12-13, para. 17; Iran, CERD/C/IRN/CO/18-19, para.10; and Serbia, CERD/C/SRB/1, para. 13.

[132] The Protocol is dedicated to criminalization of racist and xenophobic acts and in the present work is discussed principally in relation to Article 4.

[133] Concluding observations on Fiji, CERD/C/FJI/CO/118-20, para. 16; India, CERD/C/IND/CO/19, para. 27; Serbia, CERD/C/SRB/CO/1, para. 16; Tajikistan, CERD/C/TJK/CO/6-8, para. 13: the recommendations for Serbia and Tajikistan encourage campaigns to promote solidarity with the Roma.

[134] Concluding observations on Bosnia and Herzegovina, CERD/C/BIH/CO/7-8, para. 10; Cameroon, CERD/C/CMR/CO/15-18, para. 20, the recommendation envisages a role for traditional leaders in building peace; Georgia, CERD/C/GEO/CO/4-5, para. 14.

contemporary reality. Recommendations to promote tolerance extend to the creation and development of a culture of tolerance.

The potential beneficiaries of positive measures (nations, racial or ethnical groups in Article 7) are also variously described—'persons of different ethnic origins',[135] 'ethnic groups', 'racial groups in the State party', 'individuals and groups of different ethnic origins or religious beliefs', 'ethnic groups, castes and tribes',[136] 'minority groups', particular groups such as Roma, immigrants, or indigenous peoples and Afro-descendant groups, caste groups, or even 'the public at large'.[137] Describing the beneficiaries of Article 7 as 'nations' is less common. The use of 'nations' in relation to indigenous peoples as 'first nations' recurs over various ICERD articles in relation to Canada and Australia; the phrase 'campesino peoples and nations' has also been employed in the case of Bolivia.[138] The practicalities of promoting 'understanding, tolerance and friendship' suggest that calls for such virtues focus primarily on respect for indigenous 'nations' by majority populations, bearing in mind the pressures to which many of the former are subjected.

VIII. Human Rights Purposes and Principles

Additional to recommendations on human rights education and training in general terms and with regard to specific groups,[139] CERD regularly requests States parties to disseminate the Convention and the concluding observations addressed to them. There has been some variation in the format of requests regarding the Convention and the concluding observations. One major issue is that of language, bearing in mind the enormous variation in the linguistic complexity of States and the different circumstances of ethnic and other groups therein—the question of 'vernacularization' referred to earlier.[140] Formulations have been applied according to the States concerned, and include requests to disseminate in official or national languages, minority languages, languages of indigenous peoples, and immigrants and other ethnic groups. In some instances, specific languages are named as particularly appropriate to receive the translations.[141] The standard (though not invariable) formula implicates the reports of the State party and the concluding observations thereon: the recommendation is that

> the State party's reports be made readily accessible to the public at the time of their submission, and that the observations of the Committee with respect to these reports be similarly publicized in the official and other commonly used languages, as appropriate.[142]

[135] Concluding observations on Austria, CERD/C/AUT/CO/18-20, para. 11; Greece, CERD/C/CO/16-19, para. 11.

[136] Concluding observations on Pakistan, CERD/C/PAK/CO/20, para. 24.

[137] Concluding observations on Croatia, CERD/C/HRV/CO/8, para. 21; Montenegro, CERD/C/MNE/CO/1, para. 20.

[138] Concluding observations on Bolivia, CERD/C/BOL/CO/17-20, para. 13.

[139] See remarks of CERD member Diaconu to the effect that human rights education is an obligation placed on States parties, and not a question for decision by individual schools and teachers: CERD/C/SR.2368, para. 68; see also the recall in the UN Declaration on Human Rights Education that States are duty-bound to ensure that education is human rights-oriented, *supra*, n. 31.

[140] See Chapter 8.

[141] Concluding observations on Ukraine, A/61/18, para. 432, have referred to Russian as well as Ukrainian, while those on Turkmenistan, A/60/18, para. 332, advocate translation into, besides Turkmen, the main minority languages, in particular Russian.

[142] Concluding observations on Iceland, A65/18, p. 67, para. 24. The UN Declaration on Human Rights Education, Article 3(3), makes the general point that human rights education and training 'should use languages and methods suited to target groups, taking into account their specific needs and conditions'.

Less precise formulations such as 'appropriate languages'[143] may, however, surface in particular cases, while in others the scope is reduced to 'official and national languages',[144] an inherently unsatisfactory formula unless there is confidence that the bulk of the population, especially ethnic and other minorities, are capable of understanding these languages. Specific references to minorities, or 'main minority languages' may also be added,[145] as can references to 'international languages' that may play a role in the dissemination of information within the State.[146] GR 35 makes an elaborate recommendation regarding publicity for the work of the Committee:

> With particular reference to the Convention, States parties should disseminate knowledge of its standards and procedures, and provide associated training, particularly for those concerned with its implementation, including civil servants, the judiciary and law enforcement officials. The concluding observations of the Committee should be made widely available in the official and other commonly used languages at the conclusion of the examination of the report of the State party; opinions of the Committee under the article 14 communications procedure should similarly be made available.[147]

The Committee has insisted that, in programmes of human rights training, adequate attention should be paid to the Convention as such; hence in the case of Belarus, it was recommended that 'in addition to general human rights training, law enforcement and judicial officials receive training specifically on the provisions of the Convention, and that mechanisms be established to evaluate the effectiveness of such training'.[148] In the case of Kyrgyzstan, it was recommended that 'the State party redouble its efforts to ensure that law enforcement officers receive training in human rights and in particular with regard to the provisions of the convention. The State party should also include human rights education in school curricula and conduct awareness-raising campaigns on human rights, including on racial discrimination'.[149]

D. Comment

While the drafting of Article 7 was a brief and relatively uncontentious process, vivid arguments on the relative merits of 'law' and 'education' in combating racial discrimination animated the drafting sessions on a number of articles. The 'pro-law' camp emphasized speed and severity of response, law was quicker, education slower and less judgmental, while criminal law in particular sent out a stark, unequivocal message of condemnation. 'Pro-education' speakers emphasized profundity and endurance of response; combating racial discrimination necessitated changes of mentalities and attitudes to achieve inter-ethnic harmony in the longer term, criminal law was not enough. The rival camps were bracketed by their politics and world views, and there were evident suspicions of *mala fides* and political manoeuvring on both sides, with Western powers to

[143] South Africa 2006.
[144] Pakistan, A/64/18, pp. 73–4, para. 29.
[145] Concluding observations on Togo, A/63/18, para. 467.
[146] Concluding observations on Ethiopia, A/62/18, para. 158.
[147] GR 35, para. 44.
[148] CERD/C/BLR/CO/18-19, para. 18.
[149] CERD/C/KGZ/CO/54-7, para. 20; see also concluding observations on the Dominican Republic, CERD/C/DOM/CO/12, para. 21.

some degree taking a defensive posture. On the politics of the Convention, the dropping of the explicit reference in Article 7 to the Colonial Declaration is significant in turning the Convention away from an uncomplicated anti-colonial, one united nation stance in the mode of the 1960s, towards recognition and acceptance of intra-State communal complexities, which have been better understood as the following decades progressed. In the event, the Convention stresses both law and education, intertwining their respective roles. In the life of the Committee, the dominance of the law—or criminal law—paradigm has to some extent abated, even in the context of Article 4.[150]

Compared with the attention given to (particularly) Article 4, the contents of country reports on the 'educational' Article 7 were initially sketchy; this deficiency is the specific motivation triggering GR 5, which laments that 'few States parties' had included reporting information on Article 7. In spite of its obligatory nature, Article 7 has also appeared, according to some authorities, to have suffered neglect by the Committee.[151] This assessment—by Boyle and Baldaccini—suggesting that Article 7 'deserves deeper attention both from governments and CERD',[152] appears in a publication of 2001. By that time, CERD had approved a study of Article 7 for presentation to the Second World Conference to Combat Racism and Racial Discrimination in 1983,[153] and had adopted two general recommendations with respect to the article—GR 5 and GR 13. Both recommendations are, however, narrowly constructed: the first does little more than regret the perfunctory nature of references to the article in State reports and invite the States to do better; the second focuses on the training of law enforcement officials.

Where perfunctory references to Article 7 in State reports occur under present conditions, a wide-ranging recommendation from the Committee is likely to follow.[154] GR 35 on combating racist hate speech includes an extensive section that reflects on the potential contribution of Article 7. Observations on the marginalization of Article 7 are thus open to reassessment: in remarks that include and go beyond the hate speech context, the recommendation asserts that:

> [t]he importance of article 7 has not diminished over time: its broadly educational approach to eliminating racial discrimination is an indispensable complement to other approaches to combating racial discrimination. Because racism can be the product of, *inter alia*, indoctrination or inadequate education, especially effective antidotes to racist hate speech include education for tolerance, and counter-speech.[155]

[150] See discussion of Article 4 in Chapter 11; as noted therein, GR 35 attempts to rebalance the respective contributions of penal law regimes and broadly educational regimes to realizing the objectives of the Convention.

[151] K. Boyle and A. Baldaccini, 'A Critical Evaluation of International Human Rights Approaches to Racism', in S. Fredman (ed.), *Discrimination and Human Rights: the Case of Racism* (Oxford University Press, 2001), pp. 135–91, at pp. 164–65 [henceforth *Discrimination and Human Rights*].

[152] *Ibid.*, p. 165.

[153] *Teaching, Education, Culture and Information as Means of Eliminating Racial Discrimination*, study prepared by Special Rapporteur G. Ténékidès, CERD/3, UN Publication Sales No. E.85.XIV.3 (United Nations, 1985) [henceforth Ténékidès Study].

[154] In the case of Jordan, the Committee urged the making of 'a systematic and inter-agency assessment of... existing measures to combat racial prejudice and discrimination', and that 'the results of such an assessment be used to guide... the State party's policies and programmes to address discrimination in education, culture, media, as well as to facilitate further increase in knowledge of the Convention': CERD/C/JOR/CO/13-17, para. 17.

[155] GR 35, para. 30.

Even if its boundaries are fuzzy, Article 7 serves to specify and highlight that any prospects of achieving the high objectives of the Convention require attention to 'root causes' of discrimination, that it is not adequate to focus on suppression and sanction without more, however attractive the processes of criminal law appear, even allowing for their supplementary 'educational' functions. The matter is well expressed by Boyle and Baldaccini:

> The duties it [Article 7] requires of States reflect the thesis that racist ideas are not innate, but are transmitted to the young through others: parents, peers, teachers, politicians, and other opinion leaders. Unless such ideas are tackled at their source, they will continue to be handed down from generation to generation. The importance of full implementation of these provisions for the long-term success of the goals of ICERD and the right to equality cannot be underestimated.[156]

The Committee presents the same thought in the context of racist hate speech:

> Whereas the provisions of article 4 on dissemination of ideas attempt to discourage the flow of racist ideas upstream, and the provisions on incitement address their downstream effects, article 7 addresses the root causes of hate speech, and represents a further illustration of the "appropriate means" to eliminate racial discrimination envisaged in article 2, paragraph 1(d).[157]

The primary focus of Article 7 is on the aims and objectives to be pursued by 'teaching, education, culture and information', and the modalities for achieving them. In terms of the structure of ICERD, whereas the protection from discrimination in Article 5 encompasses 'the right to education and training'[158] and 'the right to equal participation in cultural activities',[159] reflecting broad-based rights recognized throughout a range of international human rights instruments, the obligations in Article 7 have a distinctive focus. The highlighted fields of activity and other relevant but unnamed 'fields' must be directed to combat prejudices which lead to racial discrimination, promoting understanding and tolerance, and propagating human rights, including the Convention. In this light, Article 7 makes its own contribution to world programmes for human rights education and similar initiatives.

The triple objectives of the article—'understanding, tolerance and friendship'—are interrelated and mutually reinforcing. The prospects of achieving 'understanding' are related in the first place to the availability of knowledge and information; 'understanding' in Article 7 looks less an intellectual construct and closer to empathy, an affective response to other groups that is more likely to be associated with non-discriminatory behaviour. Standing alone, tolerance has limited appeal as an ideal. Armstrong observes that tolerance 'involves acceptance, sometimes grudging, of beliefs, values, and practices with which one disagrees or of which one disapproves, and that may understandably be felt as something less than the full recognition and equal treatment that dignity and respect require'.[160] In the words of E.M. Forster,

[156] Boyle and Baldaccini, *Discrimination and Human Rights*, p. 165.

[157] GR 35, para. 30.

[158] Article 5(e)(v).

[159] Article 5(e)(vi).

[160] P.B. Armstrong, 'Two Cheers for Tolerance: E.M. Forster's Ironic Liberalism and the Indirections of Style', *Modernism/Modernity* 14 (2009), 281–99, from 'excerpt of the content'.

[t]olerance is a very dull virtue. It is boring. Unlike love, it has always had a bad press. It is negative. It merely means putting up with people, being able to stand things. No one has ever written an ode to tolerance, or raised a statue to her.[161]

Forster nonetheless supported tolerance as an appropriate virtue, taking into account the impossibility of grounding public affairs in the virtues of respect and solidarity, especially in light of the conditions of his time (post-Second World War reconstruction). Despite Forster's less than glowing report, tolerance is treated as an important political and social tenet, especially under conditions of ethnic, religious, and ideological pluralism that increasingly characterize contemporary societies. In CERD practice, tolerance exhibits group as well as individual dimensions, is associated with interethnic dialogue, is treated as conducive to integration rather than assimilation, and does not merely serve to maintain the status quo. Taken together with 'understanding' and 'friendship' in the terms of Article 7, the combined aims are of a more ambitious, optimistic, and active cast than 'mere' toleration, especially in the context of the whole Convention with its commitment to dignity and equality, individual and collective.

The UNESCO Declaration on Principles of Tolerance (1995) throws further light on the Article 7 goal of 'tolerance', introduced as 'respect, acceptance and appreciation of the rich diversity of our world's cultures, our forms of expression and ways of being human... Tolerance, the virtue that makes peace possible, contributes to the replacement of the culture of war by a culture of peace';[162] the notion of 'harmony in difference' is implicated in the explanation, which also treats tolerance as a moral duty. The Declaration goes on to explain that tolerance can be exercised by 'individuals, groups and States', affirms the standards set out in human rights instruments and that tolerance does not mean toleration of social injustice, that it accepts 'the fact that human beings, naturally diverse in their appearance, situation, speech, behaviour and values, have the right to peace and to be as they are'.[163] At the level of the State, tolerance requires, *inter alia*, 'just and impartial legislation, law enforcement and judicial and administrative process'. The Declaration develops the theme of Article 7, describing education as 'the most effective means of preventing intolerance. The first step in tolerance education is to teach people what their shared rights and freedoms are... and to promote the will to protect those of others';[164] educational strategies include devoting special attention to teacher training and educational curricula 'with a view to educating caring and responsible citizens open to other cultures'.[165] The group dimension of the Declaration—that tolerance can be exercised by individuals and groups—is close to the endorsements in Article 7 that apply to nations and racial or 'ethnical' groups.

[161] E.M. Forster, 'The Unsung Virtue of Tolerance: It is Very Easy to see Fanaticism in Other People', BBC Radio, July, 1941 *Vital Speeches of the Day*, Vol. VIII, pp. 12–14.

[162] Article 1(1): <http://www.unesco.org/webworld/peace_library/UNESCO/HRIGHTS/124-129.HTM>.

[163] Article 1(3), 1(4). The Declaration (Article 2(4)) cites Article 1(20 of the UNESCO Declaration on Race and Racial Prejudice: 'All individuals and groups have the right to be different'. One commentator describes the explanation of tolerance in Article 1 of the Declaration as 'rather disjointed' and as failing 'to elucidate the nature of tolerance': T. McGonagle, *Minority Rights, Freedom of Expression and of the Media: Dynamics and Dilemmas* (Intersentia, 2011), pp. 238–55, p. 242. Nonetheless, the author, *ibid.*, p. 244 affirms the usefulness of the Declaration 'in its exploration of the different ramifications of tolerance and pluralism in a way that is hardly feasible within the strictures of legally binding instruments. By tracing various strands of tolerance and pluralism, the Declaration contributes to their elucidation.'

[164] Article 4(1).

[165] Article 4(4).

On the third element in the triumvirate, the ideal of promoting friendship has been little individuated in practice. Philosophical discourses on friendship often find their moorings in Aristotle,[166] while Vattel is among the legal luminaries who have meditated on the significance of friendship for relations among nations.[167] The contemporary legal discourses on friendly relations, stemming from the UN Charter,[168] and treaties of friendship have refined the concept at the level of inter-State relations, which also encompass the concept of 'unfriendly acts'.[169] The friendship referred to in Article 7 is a high ideal, and concerns mutuality and respect for difference as well as sameness. In the work of the Committee, variations on the theme of friendship include friendship 'among all racial, ethnic and national groups',[170] among 'peoples, civilizations and religions',[171] 'between individuals irrespective of their origins',[172] or simply 'interethnic' friendship and solidarity.[173] The Convention envisages a legal and normative order that generates expectations of tolerant and mutually respectful behaviour, and is inherently 'intolerant' of injustice and discrimination.

Absent a full statement by CERD on the implications of Article 7, the Convention as a whole provides pointers to the interpretation of the requirements of the article. The terms of the preamble elaborating the basic aspiration to eliminate racial discrimination (the *raison d'être* of the Convention), the statement of the repugnancy of racial barriers and vision of harmony of peoples, and its resolution to prevent and combat racist doctrines and practices 'in order to promote understanding between races', may all be recalled as complementary to Article 7; the inclusion in the preamble of the UNESCO Convention against Discrimination in Education, is another obvious reference point. The fundamental obligation set out in the chapeau to Article 2(1) to pursue 'by all appropriate means and without delay' a policy of eliminating racial discrimination 'and promoting understanding among all races' is yet another marker, as is the encouragement in 2(1)(e) of integrationist multiracial organizations and movements, and the general exhortations to take effective measures towards achieving the aims of the Convention. In effect, as a CERD study observed, the guidelines to be

166 *Nicomachean Ethics*, Book VIII, translation by W.D. Ross available at: <http://classics.mit.edu/Aristotle/nicomachaen.8.viii.html>. See further, *Stanford Encyclopaedia of Philosophy*, available at: <http://stanford.edu/entries/friendship>, discussing friendship in terms of mutual caring, intimacy and shared activity—for the last of which the background intuition is 'never to share activity with someone . . . is not to have the kind of relationship . . . that could be called friendship . . . Friends engage in joint pursuits, in part motivated by the friendship itself.' The emphasis in Article 7 on mutuality, reciprocity and intercultural learning resonates with the intuitions regarding 'shared activity'.

167 'Every nation is obliged to cultivate the friendship of other nations, and carefully avoid whatever might kindle their enmity against her', in B. Kapossy and R. Whitmore (eds), Emer de Vattel, *The Law of Nations, Or, Principles of the Law of Nature, Applied to the Conduct and Affairs of Nations* and *Sovereigns*, Book II, Chapter I, para. 12 (Liberty Fund, 2008): <http://oll.libertyfund.org/titles/2246>. See also S. Koschut and A. Oelsner (eds), *Friendship and International Relations* (Palgrave Macmillan, 2014).

168 Notably in the context of self-determination; Articles 1(2) and 55, as well as the overall commitment of the Charter to securing international peace.

169 D. Richter, 'Unfriendly Act', *Max Planck Encyclopedia of Public International Law*, available at: <http://opil.ouplaw.com/view/10.1093/law:epil/9780199231690/law-9780199231690-e423>.

170 Concluding observations on Korea, CERD/C/KOR/CO/14, para. 12.

171 Concluding observations on Tunisia, CERD/C/TUN/CO/19, para. 7; the State party was commended for its efforts in this respect.

172 Concluding observations on Israel, CERD/C/ISR/CO/14-16, para. 23.

173 Concluding observations on Fiji, CERD/C/FJI/CO/18-20, para. 16. Elements of the basic desiderata set out in Article 7 are reflected in the UN Declaration on Human Rights Education, Article 5(3) of which provides that such education and training 'should embrace and enrich, as well as draw inspiration from, the diversity of civilizations, religions, cultures and traditions of different countries'.

followed 'in accordance with article 7, by teachers, educators and persons responsible for the mass media are to be found in the basic principles enunciated in the Convention as a whole'.[174] This approach does not reduce the importance of analysing the specific contribution to the Convention made by Article 7, which, embedded in the larger context of human rights education, is 'couched in the same obligatory language' as other articles in the Convention, with no less mandatory force.[175]

Intersecting lines of: education for tolerance, work to eliminate prejudice and discrimination, and human rights education generally, characterize the background standards and similarly characterize Article 7. The potential for pluralization of educational standards and endeavours is also strongly in evidence in both cases. Article 7 makes a legally binding statement of principle that strengthens the body of international obligations.

Article 7 is now regularly accounted for in State reports—the lack of reporting adverted to by GR 5—has largely been remedied. Reports and concluding observations do not always sharply distinguish Article 7 from the overlapping paragraphs on education and culture in Article 5. A sample of 2014–15 State reports reveals variation in the entries for Article 7, which range over:

strategies for ethnic recruitment into public service and social studies education;[176]

education in the values of the Republic and secularism, awareness-raising and Holocaust memorialization;[177]

the fight against right-wing extremism and education to prevent racist thinking, civic education and education to respect human dignity and avoid stereotypes, education on the history and culture of groups protected by the Convention, the fight against racism on the Internet;[178]

strengthening of indigenous languages and promotion of indigenous rights and culture, accreditation of spiritual guides, safeguarding of access to sacred places, media campaigns to disseminate knowledge of indigenous rights;[179]

integration plans, introduction of human rights principles through media;[180]

mainstreaming of human rights, interculturalism and gender equality, organization of travel for young persons to 'build intercultural citizens';[181]

community centres for cultural development and removal of demeaning language from textbooks, translation of UN and other human rights documents into indigenous languages, promotion of traditional crafts, expansion of dialogue with civil society;[182]

outreach to State, tribal and human rights organizations; outreach to domestic protections that implement ICERD obligations.[183]

[174] Ténékidès Study, para. 26.

[175] J. Bengoa, I. Garvalov, M. Mehedi, and S. Sadiq Ali, *Joint Working Paper on Article 7 of the International Convention on the Elimination of All Forms of Racial Discrimination*, E/CN.4/Sub.2/1998/4, para. 7; the authors' assessment of the mandatory nature of Article 7 is reiterated in para. 31 of GR 35 on combating racist hate speech: 'Article 7 is phrased in the same mandatory language as other articles in the Convention, and the fields of activity—"teaching, education, culture and information"—are not expressed as exhaustive of the undertakings required.'

[176] CERD/C/DNK/20-21, paras 195–206.

[177] CERD/C/FRA/20-21, paras 256–308.

[178] CERD/C/DEU/19-22, paras 152–66.

[179] CERD/C/GTM/14-15, paras 271–300.

[180] CERD/C/EST/10-11, paras 314–30.

[181] CERD/C/PER/18-21, paras 241–6.

[182] CERD/C/SLV/16-17, paras 174–206.

[183] CERD/C/USA/7-9, paras 210–16.

The sample suggests that the provisions are open to divergent practice, and widely divergent interpretations, and that local context is important in the application of the standards. Despite the relatively open character of the required undertakings, the Committee has been in a position to critique the insufficiency or otherwise of State responses, including in the fields of language and culture, contribution to integration or assimilation, educational curricula, the training of personnel, the performance of the media, and the dissemination of international standards. The verbs 'promote', 'combat', and 'propagate' are drawn upon by the Committee in order to judge whether States parties have complied with their obligations.

As with the concept of 'tolerance' and the direction of the interpretation of the Convention over time, the application by CERD of Article 7 has been thoroughly 'pluralized' in a manner that also seeks to respect mutuality and commonality of concerns between minorities and majorities.[184] Concepts such as intercultural and bilingual education have been adapted and applied to the Convention, and are understood as being applicable for all students, not simply those belonging to minorities. Cleansing textbooks of derogatory references to ethnicities is regarded as a key educational manoeuvre. The memorialization of history concerns the nation as a whole but, equally, its component parts, whose contribution to the life of the nation should be recognized. The active contribution of minorities and indigenous peoples to education and media is regularly stressed, as is the need to respect the dignity and equality of groups, and reciprocity of respect on their part towards others in society. The application of 'immediate and effective measures' is disaggregated according to the standard groupings suggested by Article 1 of the Convention—for all relevant groups, not only the 'racial or ethnical' groups adverted to by Article 7. Sundry inter-ethnic dialogic processes are regular focal points of recommendations.

In sum, the application of Article 7—as elsewhere in the Convention—has been subject to normative influences from developments in international human rights law that recognize multiple categories of victims and claimants. All of this suggests that the teaching of human rights principles including 'the principles of the Convention', should also be adjusted to the realities of normative and institutional change. Pluralization and mutuality effectively furnish basic starting points for initiatives in the field of education, culture, and information. Projects of culture, education, and information that fail to recognise multicultural complexity do not furnish an adequate response to the demands of the article. The Convention thus ranges itself against monolithic, assimilationist approaches to education, and recognizes *locus standi* in the groups protected by the Convention towards the determination of their own futures.

[184] Without explicit naming of particular communities or groupings, the UN Declaration on Human Rights Education, Article 5(4), includes the stipulation that human rights education 'should take into account different economic, social and cultural circumstances, while promoting local initiatives in order to encourage ownership of the common goal of the fulfilment of all human rights'.

18. Article 20

Reservations

1. The Secretary-General of the United Nations shall receive and circulate to all States which are or may become Parties to this Convention reservations made by States at the time of ratification or accession. Any State which objects to the reservation shall, within a period of ninety days from the date of the said communication, notify the Secretary-General that it does not accept it.
2. A reservation incompatible with the object and purpose of this Convention shall not be permitted, nor shall a reservation the effect of which would inhibit the operation of any of the bodies established by this Convention be allowed. A reservation shall be considered incompatible or inhibitive if at least two thirds of the States Parties to this Convention object to it.
3. Reservations may be withdrawn at any time by notification to this effect addressed to the Secretary-General. Such notification shall take effect on the date on which it is received.

A. Introduction

The making of reservations is a power that derives from the sovereign prerogative of States to refuse to give their consent to particular provisions in a treaty. A reservation is defined in general terms under the Vienna Convention on the Law of Treaties (VCLT) as a 'unilateral statement, however phrased or named, when signing, ratifying, accepting, approving, or acceding to a treaty, whereby it purports to exclude or modify the legal effect of certain provisions of the treaty in their application to that State'.[1] Reservations should be distinguished from interpretative declarations and understandings which do not purport to exclude or modify the legal provisions of a treaty: terminology is not conclusive in that a statement described as an 'interpretation' or similar may constitute a reservation if it excludes or modifies provisions of the Convention.[2] The International Law Commission (ILC) *Guide to Practice* states that the character of a statement as a reservation or an interpretative declaration is determined by 'the legal effect that its author purports to produce, and that to determine the nature of a statement, it should be 'interpreted in good faith in accordance with the ordinary meaning to be given to its terms, with a view to identifying . . . the intention of its author'.[3] States also make unilateral statements that do not fall into the category of reservations or unilateral declarations, including statements

[1] 1969, UNTS 1155, p. 331, Article 2(1)(d); the VCLT was opened for signature 23 May 1969, in force 27 January 1980.

[2] Interpretative declarations are not addressed by the VCLT. The ILC *Guide to Practice on Reservations to Treaties* [henceforth *Guide to Practice*] para. 1. 2, defines an interpretative declaration as 'a unilateral statement, however phrased or named, made by a State or an international organization, whereby that State or that organization purports to specify or clarify the meaning or scope of a treaty or of certain of its provisions': <http://legal.un.org/ilc/texts/instruments/english/draft%20articles/1_8_2011.pdf>. Para. 1(4) of the *Guide to Practice* labels as a reservation a 'conditional interpretative declaration' that ties a State's consent to be bound by a treaty to a specific interpretation thereof.

[3] 1.3 and 1.3.1.

that are essentially of political intent—in the case of the International Convention on the Elimination of All Forms of Racial Discrimination (ICERD), a number of States have declared that their accession to the Convention does not imply recognition of Israel or entry into relationship with Israel in matters covered by the Convention.[4]

The general 'contractual' rule of international law was that a reservation required the consent of all other parties to a treaty; if such was not obtained, the options available to a State purporting to make a reservation were to become a party to the treaty in its pristine purity, or not become a party at all. The Advisory Opinion of the ICJ *Reservations to the Convention on the Prevention and Punishment of Genocide* signalled a move away from the 'consent of all' approach in holding that a State making a reservation that has been objected to by some parties but not by others can still be regarded as a party provided that the reservation is compatible with 'the object and purpose' of the Convention.[5] While the Reservations Opinion took the special character of the Genocide Convention into account in formulating its position, the object and purpose concept was adopted as a 'default approach for all treaties'[6] by the VCLT, Article 19 of which provides that States may formulate reservations unless prohibited by the treaty or incompatible with its object and purpose.[7] In terms of acceptance and legal effects of reservations, the VCLT profiles an interactive regime, providing, *inter alia*, that unless a contrary intention is definitely expressed by an objecting State, an objection to a reservation does not preclude the entry into force of the treaty between reserving and objecting States.[8] Modifications of the legal relationships between objecting and reserving States on account of a reservation do not affect the position of other parties *inter se*.

On the implications of the Vienna scheme, some schools of thought privilege the regime of objections to reservations by other States parties as the primary mode of determination of legal effect, while others take the question of 'whether a reservation is contrary to the treaty's object and purpose becomes a question lexically prior to whether States can object to a State party's statement'.[9] The ILC *Guide to Practice* reads Article 19 VCLT as laying down objective criteria for permissibility, treating a reservation contrary to object and purpose as devoid of legal effect.[10] The ILC stance signals a move from a consensual (acceptance or rejection) to an 'axiological' (valid or not valid) approach to

[4] Bahrain, Iraq, Kuwait, Libya, Syria, United Arab Emirates, Syria, and Yemen: <https://treaties.un.org/pages/ViewDetails.aspx?src=TREATY&mtdsg_no=IV-2&chapter=4&lang=en>.

[5] *Reservations to the Convention on the Prevention and Punishment of the Crime of Genocide* (Advisory Opinion) [1951] ICJ Rep 15, 23.

[6] E.T. Swaine, 'Treaty Reservations' in D.B. Hollis (ed.), *The Oxford Guide to Treaties* (Oxford University Press, 2014), pp. 277–301, p. 297 [henceforth 'Treaty Reservations'].

[7] A special rule requiring acceptance by all parties is retained by Article 20(2) for cases where a 'limited number of... negotiating States and the object and purpose of the treaty' make application in its entirety an essential condition of consent to be bound.

[8] Article 20(4).

[9] B. Çali, 'Specialized Rules of Interpretation: Human Rights, *Oxford Guide to Treaties*, pp. 525–48, pp. 534–7, p. 535.

[10] *Guide to Practice* 4.5.1. 'Acceptance of an impermissible reservation by a contracting State or... organization shall not affect the impermissibility of the reservation': *Guide to Practice* 3.3.3. The nullity of an invalid reservation does not depend on... objection or... acceptance by a contracting State or... organization': *Guide to Practice* 4.5.2. Commenting on the *Guide to Practice*, Milanovic and Sicilianos write that 'Articles 20–23 VCLT only deal with reservations which are objectively valid under Article 19; they do not pertain to reservations which are in fact invalid... while States may object to reservations that they consider invalid, this is merely persuasive evidence of invalidity': <http://www.ejiltalk.org/the-ilcs-clever-compromise-on-the-validity-of-reservations-to-treaties/>.

reservations that applies to treaties generally, and is not specific to treaties on human rights.[11]

The Genocide Convention/VCLT regimes raise, *inter alia*, questions as to the meaning of object and purpose as a determinant of validity, and on the bodies or institutions possessing the authority to determine legal effects. For the appraisal of reservations, the VCLT does not provide an interpretation of the 'object and purpose' of a treaty. Citing a range of authorities, including those sceptical of the object and purpose test, Swaine comments that the 'inscrutability of the object and purpose test is widely acknowledged'.[12] The ILC *Guide to Practice* offers an abstract determination: a reservation is incompatible with object and purpose if it affects an essential element of the treaty that 'is necessary to its general tenor, in such a way that the reservation impairs the *raison d'être* of the treaty'.[13] The *Guide to Practice* links this with the general VCLT approach to the interpretation of treaties in suggesting that object and purpose is to be determined by taking into account the terms of the treaty in their context, in particular the title and the preamble; recourse may also be had to 'the preparatory work of the treaty and the circumstances of its conclusion, and, where appropriate, the subsequent practice of the parties'.[14] As regards authority to determine the effects of reservation, the VCLT does not address the role of treaty monitoring bodies, many of which, in the field of human rights, post-date its coming into force in 1980. The *Guide to Practice* outlines a role for monitoring bodies in assessing reservations while observing that the assessment made by such a body in the exercise of this competence has no greater legal effect than that of the act which contains it:[15] in other words, it does not empower bodies to do more than they are permitted to do by their constituent instruments.

Although the object and purpose principle extolled by the Vienna regime applies in principle across the body of international treaty law, the growth of human rights instruments and their attendant treaty bodies has generated controversy as to whether reservations to human rights conventions are governed by the general VCLT regime or represent a special case that departs from it. Contractual approaches to treaty reservations have severely limited attractions for large multiparty treaties on account of the fragmentation and legal confusion they are capable of producing; the problem is intensified in the case of human rights treaties, the hollowing out of which does not merely affect the interests of States but directly touches the lives of human beings. For the UN human rights framework, General Comment (GC) 24 of the Human Rights Committee stands as a *locus classicus* on the interlinked questions in the human rights context of object and purpose, authority to determine the effects of reservations, and legal consequences.[16] Unlike ICERD, the International Covenant on Civil and Political Rights (ICCPR)

[11] F. Mégret, 'Nature of Obligations', in D. Moeckli, S. Shah, and S. Sivakumaran (eds), *International Human Rights Law* (2nd edn, Oxford University Press, 2014), pp. 96–108, p. 118.

[12] 'Treaty Reservations', p. 286, n. 43.

[13] *Guide to Practice*, 3.1.5. See Articles 31 and 32 of the VCLT, discussed in the concluding chapter of the present work.

[14] *Ibid.*, 3.1.5.1. Cf, Article 31 of the VCLT (ordinary meaning, object and purpose, context, subsequent practice), and 32 (supplementary means, including the travaux). For a succinct review, see R. Gardiner, 'The Vienna Convention Rules on Treaty Interpretation', *Oxford Guide to Treaties*, pp. 475–506; R. Gardiner, *Treaty Interpretation* (Oxford University Press, 2008); U. Linderfalk, *On the Interpretation of Treaties: The Modern International Law as Expressed in the 1969 Vienna Convention on the Law of Treaties* (Springer, 2007).

[15] Section 3.2.1.

[16] HRI/GEN/1/Rev.9 (Vol. I), pp. 210–17.

neither prohibits reservations nor mentions any type of permitted reservation, so that the question of reservations under the Covenant and its First Optional Protocol is governed by international law.

Article 19(3) of the VCLT is recalled by the Human Rights Committee as a provider of 'relevant guidance',[17] and the object and purpose test, 'governs the matter of interpretation and acceptability of reservations'.[18] The object and purpose of the Covenant is broadly defined in the comment as the creation of 'legally binding standards for human rights by defining certain civil and political rights and placing them in a framework of obligations... and to provide for an efficacious supervisory machinery'.[19] Carrying through the implications of this approach, reservations to peremptory norms and to customary international law, the right to self-determination, the obligation to respect and ensure rights on a non-discriminatory basis, and to non-derogable provisions of the Convention,[20] are all regarded as impermissible.[21] In a series of paragraphs, GC 24 turns to the question of authority to determine the permissibility of reservations, asserting that the Vienna scheme is too limiting to address the problem of reservations to human rights treaties 'which are not a web of inter-State exchanges of mutual obligations', but 'concern the endowment of the individual with rights'.[22] The general comment points to the uncertain results of the 'interactive' Vienna approach, concluding that it 'necessarily falls to the Committee to determine whether a specific reservation is compatible with the object and purpose of the Covenant', established 'objectively, by reference to legal principles'. Further, inadmissible reservations 'will generally be severable, in the sense that the Convention will be operative for the reserving party without benefit of the reservation'.[23]

Although the general practice of the Human Rights Committee has been cautious,[24] the views expressed in GC 24 evoked strong objections from a number of States,[25] the paradigm of a 'legal struggle' adverted to in the Committee on the Elimination of Racial Discrimination (CERD) reflections on the reservations debate (see following) as a consequence to be avoided.[26] With regard to *jus cogens*, the US commented that, while it is clear that a State cannot exempt itself from a peremptory norm of international law by

[17] GC 24, para. 6, the reference is to Article 19 (c) of the VCLT.

[18] GC 24, para. 6; paras 13 and 14 state the object and purpose principles with regard to the First Optional Protocol; *ibid.*, para. 5 for comment on the reservation provision for the Second Optional Protocol.

[19] GC 24, para. 7. Hence (para. 11), 'a reservation that rejects the Committee's competence to interpret the requirements of any provisions of the Covenant would... be contrary to the object and purpose of the treaty'.

[20] Adding, *ibid.*, para. 10, that while there is 'no automatic correlation between reservations to non-derogable provisions, and reservations which offend against the object and purpose of the Covenant, a State has a heavy onus to justify such a reservation'.

[21] Paras 8, 9, and 10. Para. 11 states the impermissible nature of reservations to the supporting infrastructure of the Covenant, the institutional framework to secure the rights.

[22] Para. 17.

[23] Para. 18. On severability of reservations, the Human Rights Committee affirmed the views expressed in GC 24 in *Kennedy v Trinidad and Tobago*, CCPR/C/74/D/845/1998 (2002); Human Rights Committee members Ando, Bhagwati, Klein, and Kretzmer issued a dissenting opinion, arguing (para. 16) that the severability approach was only 'generally' applicable and cannot apply when it was 'abundantly clear' that the reserving State's agreement to being a party was 'dependent on the acceptability of the reservation'. Under the European Convention on Human Rights, see *Belilos v Switzerland*, ECtHR, App. No. 10328/83 (1988); *Loizidou v Turkey* [Preliminary Objections] ECtHR 20 EHRR 99 (1995).

[24] Relevant practice of the Human Rights Committee involving indigenous groups includes *T.K. v France*, CCPR/C/37/D/220/1987 (1989); *Hopu and Bessert v France*, CCPR/C/60/D/549/1993/Rev.1 (1997).

[25] See observations by France, A/51/40,104–6; by the USA, A/A/50/40/Annex VI, 126–9; by the UK, A/50/40, Annex VI, 1130–4.

[26] Discussed in the present chapter.

making a reservation, '[i]t is not at all clear that a State cannot choose to exclude one means of enforcement of particular norms by reserving against inclusion of those norms in its Covenant obligations'; with regard to reservations and customary international law, the views of the Human Rights Committee were 'wholly unsupported by and in fact contrary to international law'; 'an object and purpose analysis by its nature requires consideration of the particular treaty, right, and reservation in question'. The UK did not agree that customary international law may not be reserved against but accepted the view that reservations thereto are permitted provided that the right was not deprived of its basic purpose.[27] France argued that the duty to observe customary international law should not be confused with agreement to be bound by the expression of principle in a treaty, did not agree that the VCLT regime was inappropriate, and opposed the idea of severability. The US also asked if the Committee really intended to say that any reservation was impermissible or only those that wholly vitiated the right in question. On severability, the US disagreed with the Human Rights Committee, arguing that its reservations were 'integral parts of its consent to be bound'.[28]

The arguments precipitated claims of a dichotomy between the approaches of international law 'generalists', and those engaging in *droits-de-l'hommisme*.[29] The *Guide to Practice* effects what Milanovic and Sicilianos describe as a 'clever compromise' between the generalists and the specialists,[30] through interpreting the general treaty regime as capable of accommodating the concerns of human rights lawyers, proposing objective criteria for the validity of reservations, and supporting the competence of monitoring bodies to assess permissibility.[31]

B. *Travaux Préparatoires*

In the working paper on alternative final clauses,[32] the Secretary-General proposed three alternative texts on reservations,[33] 'the most 'extreme' of which excluded the possibilities of reservations to the Convention'.[34] The officers of the Third Committee suggested a

[27] Para. 7. *The Guide to Practice* (3.1.5.3) states that '[t]he fact that a treaty provision reflects a rule of customary international law does not in itself constitute an obstacle to . . . a reservation to that provision'.

[28] Swaine notes cases where States, principally Nordic States have 'asserted a right to objections with "super maximum effect"—effectively severing the reservation and asserting a binding relationship between the States under the entire treaty, including provisions to which the reservations pertain': *Treaty Formation*, p. 294; and *ibid*, pp. 294–6, particularly footnotes 85–7.

[29] Comment by Pellet, the ILC rapporteur on reservations, *Droits-de-L'Hommisme at Droit International*, <http://www.droits-fondamentaux.org/IMG/pdf/df1peldhd.pdf>; the characterization of human rights lawyers as a homogeneous group asking for special treatment for human rights conventions is described as misleading by Elíbol and Çali: <http://www.ejiltalk.org/the-ilcs-clever-compromise-on-the-validity-of-reservations-to-treaties-a-rejoinder-to-marko-milanovic-and-linos-alexandre-sicilianos/#more-10610>.

[30] <http://www.ejiltalk.org/the-ilcs-clever-compromise-on-the-validity-of-reservations-to-treaties/>; the authors describe the ILC approach as 'Vienna plus'.

[31] Para. 3.2.1 of the *Guide to Practice* provides that a treaty body may assess the permissibility of reservations but that the assessment 'has no greater effect than that of the act which contains it'—in other words, it does not purport to invest the treaty body with new powers. Further, para. 3.2.4 provides that the competence of a treaty body 'is without prejudice to the competence of the contracting States . . . to assess the permissibility of reservations'. A short, helpfully referenced critique of the ILC's approach is offered by Swaine, 'Treaty Reservations', pp. 298–301.

[32] E/CN.4/L.679.

[33] *Ibid.*, pp. 12–13.

[34] N. Lerner, *The International Convention on the Elimination of All Forms of Racial Discrimination* (Sijthoff and Noordhoff, 1980), p. 95.

text on reservations applying to all the articles in the Convention, paragraph 1 of which read: 'At the time of signature, ratification or accession, any State may make reservations to any article of the Convention'.[35] In the Committee, Canada proposed the deletion of the entire reservations clause, bearing in mind the length and the controversial nature of the Convention, and the need to 'obtain the greatest possible number of signatures and ratifications or accessions'.[36] Deletion was opposed by Ghana whose representative argued that, without a reservations clause, 'the way would be open for some State parties to make reservations that would eventually destroy the Convention'.[37] The Canadian amendment was adopted by 25 votes to 19, with a large number of abstentions—34.[38] Uruguay criticized the deletion of the reservations clause, arguing that the result 'was a considerable weakening of the Convention'.[39]

At the plenary session of the General Assembly, a thirty-three-power amendment reversed the decision of the Third Committee and re-inserted a reservations clause,[40] which was introduced and defended by the representative of Ghana in dramatic terms: 'the absence of a reservations clause from the draft Convention is a major flaw that could conceivably nullify the effect of the Convention *ab initio*. That the reservations clause was deleted in the Third Committee... was itself a tragic circumstance'.[41] Introducing the two-thirds rule—reservations are incompatible with the Convention when at least two-thirds of States parties object—the representative remarked that while this is a departure from the traditional concept of unanimity, it 'is no innovation but is a clause which this Assembly as master of its house can adopt to save the Convention from destruction and a great number of law suits over interpretation'.[42] Further, any

> suggestion that the International Court of Justice replace the States in this matter is untenable, for it is the States that have negotiated and will adopt this Convention. It is their intent which is vital to any judicial construction as to interpretation and it is they who must have the primary responsibility of guaranteeing the integrity of the Convention. Their actions, even if political, will be based on their understanding of the consensus achieved in adopting the Convention and as to the purpose and object they mutually had in mind when inserting the various articles.[43]

The representative went on to underline still further the responsibility of States parties to ensure the integrity of the Convention, described without postmodern irony as 'the result of a remarkable compromise between gentlemen'.[44] In opposing the two-thirds rule in Article 20, the representative of Argentina recalled that 'even if there is no reservation

[35] A/C.3/L.1237.

[36] A/C.3/SR.1368, paras 81 and 90 (Canada); also *ibid.*, para. 82 (Greece).

[37] A/C.3/SR.1368, para. 83; Hungary, *ibid.*, para. 84.

[38] A/C.3/SR.1368, para. 92. Poland argued in line with its rejected proposal that, in the absence of a specific clause, the provisions of international law would apply, and 'no reservation could be made with respect to the substance of the articles which had been accepted': *ibid.*, para. 94.

[39] A/C.3/SR.1368, para. 93.

[40] Contained in A/L.479.

[41] A/PV.1406, para. 7.

[42] A/PV.1406, para. 37. It may be noted that, in 'alternative drafts' of the VCLT by Sir Hersch Lauterpacht in his first report on the law of treaties in 1953, a system was envisaged of collegial control of the validity of reservations by two thirds of the States concerned: *YBILC* 1953, Vol. II, A/CN.4/63, pp. 124–33.

[43] A/PV.1406, para. 38.

[44] 'We cannot therefore conceive of a State wishing to frustrate its object and purpose, an object and purpose that is already bound by the Charter... But if a State wishes to do this, then other like-minded States... are duty bound to ensure the integrity of the Convention and prevent it becoming a variety of conventions': *ibid.*, para. 40.

clause, reservations must not inhibit the aims and purposes of the Convention',[45] while foreshadowing a role for the Committee 'entering into negotiations with the State or States concerned with a view to inducing them to reconsider their attitude . . . and even with a view to making suggestions to the General Assembly. This way might be less spectacular than requiring sanction by a two-thirds majority, but it might also be more effective in practice.'[46]

The reservations article as a whole was overwhelmingly adopted.[47]

C. Practice

Reservations and declarations specific to articles of the Convention are set out in the relevant chapters of the present work. Fewer than one-third of States parties have entered reservations and declarations, and many statements have been withdrawn; objections to reservations are currently lodged by twenty-four States.[48] The range of the reservations and declarations is limited in that most statements relate to Articles 4 and 22, and Articles 17 and 18; a smaller group relates to Articles 2 and 5. Reservations of a broader nature have been made by Saudi Arabia, Thailand, Turkey, the United States, and Yemen; objections have largely focused on the reservations/declarations of Saudi Arabia, Thailand, and Yemen. Saudi Arabia declares its willingness to implement the provisions of the Convention provided they do not 'conflict with the precepts of the Islamic Shariah'; Thailand interprets the Convention as not imposing obligations beyond its Constitution and laws; Yemen acceded to the Convention in 1989 with reservations relating to various rights under Article 5.[49] Many reservations have remained 'on the books' for considerable periods, though States coming afresh to ratify ICERD—such as Turkey, Thailand, and the US—have sought to clarify their position on points of principle by entering reservations, declarations, and interpretations. While the number and scope of reservations to ICERD has not generated concerns comparable to those expressed regarding reservations to the other leading anti-discrimination instrument—the Convention on the Elimination of All Forms of Discrimination against Women (CEDAW)[50]—there have been frequent calls for their withdrawal, including those emanating from the 2001 Durban World Conference against Racism and the 2009 Durban Review Conference.[51]

On the powers of the Committee with regard to reservations, in 1976 CERD called for a memorandum on the legal effect of a unanimous decision by the Committee that a

[45] A/PV.1406, para. 46.

[46] *Ibid.* In an explanation of vote, the representative of Greece stated that it would have been preferable to have the matter of reservations decided by 'a juridical body, such as the Legal Section of the United Nations Secretariat': A/PV.1406, para. 129.

[47] By 82 votes to 4, with 21 abstentions: A/PV.1406, paras 55–7.

[48] <https://treaties.un.org/pages/ViewDetails.aspx?src=TREATY&mtdsg_no=IV-2&chapter=4&lang=en>. For a review of the spectrum of reservations, early withdrawals, etc, see E. Lijnzaad, *Reservations to UN Human Rights Treaties: Ratify and Ruin?* (Martinus Nijhoff, 1995) [henceforth *Reservations to UN Human Rights Treaties*]. For statements relating to Article 14 and other international bodies for the settlement of disputes, see Chapter 4.

[49] See Chapter 12.

[50] See *inter alia*, Statements by the CEDAW Committee on Reservations to the Convention on the Elimination of All Forms of Discrimination against Women, A/53/38,Rev.1 (1998), pp. 47–50.

[51] Paras 68 and 77 of the Durban programme of Action; Durban Review Conference, para. 39; see also CERD GR 28 on Follow-Up to the WCAR, para. 4.

reservation was incompatible with the object and purpose of the Convention, when such a reservation had already been accepted, and the effect of such under Article 20(2). The legal opinion from the Secretariat stated that even a unanimous decision of the Committee on the unacceptability of the reservation could not have legal effect.[52] In a general discussion by the Committee on the question of reservations in 1978, members agreed that the Committee must take into account reservations, but agreed with the Secretariat opinion that even a unanimous decision by the Committee that a reservation was impermissible had no legal effect. On the other hand, declarations had no effect on the obligations of the declaring State, as otherwise they would have to be considered as reservations.[53]

At its sixty-second session in 2003, members of the Committee prepared an Opinion 'on the issue of reservations to treaties on human rights'.[54] Although the document was not formally adopted as a decision of the Committee, it may be taken as generally cohering with practice, and has not been supplemented by a later general statement.[55] The Opinion recalls that reservations to human rights treaties are a fact of life,[56] and that many States parties would not have ratified the Convention if reservations had not been permitted—a comment that echoes discussions in the drafting process. In principle, it is stated that the Convention parallels the Vienna (VCLT) regime, maintaining its 'object and purpose' clause as the standard for evaluating the admissibility of a reservation,[57] while adding the criterion of whether a reservation inhibits the operation of the bodies established by the Convention.[58] The two-thirds 'collegiate' procedure in Article 20 is stated as representing a special rule—perhaps a '*lex specialis*'[59]—that departs from the Vienna regime in terms of the procedure to determine compatibility. The Opinion observes that the collegiate procedure has not worked, and that all reserving States 'are considered parties to the Convention'. Comments are offered on the nature of the reservations, including the difficult issue of States privileging their domestic law in self-evaluations of conformity to the Convention. The criticism that such states are in effect refusing to accept international obligations is rejected in relation to the Convention 'because their legislation may already respond to . . . its provisions, at least partially'.[60] The Opinion expresses doubt as to what remains of the reservations in light of their age and the development of State legislation over the years, adding that

> [i]t seems that the reservations remain more the limit of . . . State to State relationships and commitments, than the limit of what States undertake as measures to implement the Convention. As is well known, no State has initiated a procedure according to article 11, or a dispute before the

[52] United Nations Juridical Yearbook 1976, pp. 219–21.

[53] A/33/18, chapter VI, paras 370–77.

[54] CERD/C/62/Misc.20/rev.3, 13 March 2003. The authors of the opinion were CERD members Diaconu, Rechetov, and Sicilianos; an earlier opinion by Diaconu and Rechetov (CERD/C/53/Misc.23), is referred to in A/54/18, notes following para. 575.

[55] The working paper is referred to and partly summarised in the Committee's annual report for 2004: A/59/18, para. 11.

[56] '*Le mal necessaire*', *ibid.*, para. 1.

[57] The incorporation of the 'object and purpose' criterion in ICERD (1965) pre-dates the VCLT (1969).

[58] Para. 1.

[59] *Ibid.* The opinion does not use this term, referring to 'a special rule' 'to be applied instead of the procedure described in the Vienna Convention'.

[60] *Ibid.* Compare the response of the Human Rights Committee to US reservations, recalled in O De Schutter, *International Human Rights Law* (Cambridge University Press, 2010), p. 118.

International Court of Justice according to article 22,[61] in order to consider the admissibility of a reservation by another State party and the effects of such a reservation on the implementation of the Convention.[62]

Paragraph 2 of the Opinion advances two complementary propositions:

> It is true that human rights treaties are not a web of inter-State exchange of mutual obligations and that they concern the endowment of individuals with rights:[63] the implementation of ICERD . . . is not a matter of reciprocity. But at the same time, they [the human rights treaties] remain treaties, with all the consequences resulting from the law of treaties and general international law . . . It is the expression of the will of a State to be committed by a treaty which lies at the origin of individual rights enshrined in the treaty, and the reservation is an integral part of the consent of the State to become party to a treaty.[64]

The Opinion states that CERD can take a critical view on the compatibility of reservations with the object and purpose of the Convention and recommend changing or withdrawing reservations, an approach which is 'more profitable than opening a legal struggle with all the reserving States and insisting that some . . . reservations have no legal effect, that . . . in spite of their will when ratifying the Convention, they are bound by its integral text'.[65] The preferred way forward for the Committee is one of 'fruitful dialogue' rather than 'legal struggle'.

The Committee has returned to the subject of reservations on occasions since 2003. A brief discussion in August 2006 elicited sundry views of members, including a robust assertion that 'the Committee had no authority to pronounce on the validity of a State party's reservation'.[66] In light of the general practice of the Committee and its admitted limitations, the last statement regarding 'authority' may be interpreted to signify that, while the Committee may and has 'pronounced' on reservations, its pronouncements are not, according to the letter of Article 20, determinative of legal effects.

The question of reservations to ICERD was addressed by the International Court of Justice, in *Armed Activities on the Territory of the Congo (New application: 2002) (Democratic Republic of the Congo v Rwanda)*.[67] The Democratic Republic of the Congo (DRC) sought to invoke the jurisdiction of the Court on the basis, *inter alia*, of Article 22 of ICERD. Rwanda argued that its reservation to Article 22 precluded this jurisdiction, pointing out that the DRC had not raised any objection to that reservation or to any similar reservations made by other States.[68] The DRC on the other hand, regarded Rwanda's reservation as unacceptable 'on the ground of its incompatibility with the object and purpose of the treaty'; additionally, the prohibition of racial discrimination

[61] Article 22 has since been invoked before the ICJ in *Georgia v Russian Federation*, see Chapter 19.

[62] *Opinion*, para. 1. See below on the Armed Activities case before the International Court of Justice.

[63] The language recalls para. 17 of GC 24 of the Human Rights Committee. See also *Reservations to the Convention on the Prevention and Punishment of the Crime of Genocide*, Advisory Opinion, ICJ Rep 1951 15, 23–24; European Commission on Human Rights, *Austria v Italy*, App. No. 788/60 European Convention on Human Rights Yearbook, 4 (1961), 116, 140; Inter-American Court of Human Rights, *The Effect of Reservations on the Entry into Force of the . . . Convention*, Advisory Opinion OC-2/82 (1982).

[64] The present author has edited English language aspects of this citation and the paper as a whole but not the substance.

[65] *Opinion*, para. 4.

[66] Aboul-Nasr, CERD/C/SR.1785, para. 6.

[67] Jurisdiction and Admissibility, Judgment, ICJ reports 2006, p. 6. For a short summary of the case with regard to reservations, see HRI/MC/2005/5/Add.1, paras 2–5.

[68] *Armed Activities*, para. 72.

was a peremptory norm and, in keeping with the spirit of Article 53 of the VCLT,[69] the reservation should be considered 'as contrary to *jus cogens* and without effect'—hence the lack of objection 'was of no consequence'.[70] The DRC advanced the further contention that the reservation 'had lapsed or fallen into desuetude' on account of Rwanda's undertaking, enshrined in its Fundamental Law, to withdraw reservations to human rights treaties[71]—on which point the Court noted the provisions for withdrawal of reservations in Article 20(3) of the Convention, which had not been engaged by Rwanda.[72] In concluding that it had no jurisdiction in the dispute, the Court, recalling Article 20(2), noted that the reservation had not been objected to by at least two-thirds of States parties to the Convention, concluding that it 'could not therefore be regarded as incompatible with the Convention's object and purpose'; the Court also recalled that the DRC had raised no objection to the reservation.[73] With regard to the DRC's argument on the *jus cogens* quality of the Convention, the Court stated:

> The fact that a dispute concerns non-compliance with a peremptory norm of general international law cannot suffice to found the Court's jurisdiction to entertain such a dispute, and there exists no peremptory norm requiring States to consent to such jurisdiction in order to settle disputes relating to the Convention on Racial Discrimination.[74]

A joint separate opinion by five judges[75] noted developments since the 1951 Advisory Opinion of the Court on reservations to the Genocide Convention, including whether, in particular, 'a role as regards assessment of compatibility with object and purpose is to be assigned to monitoring bodies established under United Nations multilateral human rights treaties'.[76] The Joint Opinion added that the practice of such bodies is 'not to be viewed as "making an exception" to the law as determined in 1951 . . . we take the view that it is rather a development to cover what the Court was never asked at the time, and to address new issues that have arisen subsequently'.[77] Further, in a developmental perspective:

> [h]uman rights courts and tribunals have not regarded themselves as precluded by this Court's 1951 Advisory Opinion from doing other than noting whether a particular State has objected to a reservation. This development does not create a 'schism' between general international law as represented by the . . . 1951 . . . Opinion, a 'deviation' therefrom by these various courts and tribunals. Rather, it is to be regarded as developing the law to meet contemporary realities, nothing in the specific findings of the Court in 1951 prohibiting this. Indeed, it is clear that the practice of

[69] 'A treaty is void if, at the time of its conclusion, it conflicts with a peremptory norm of general international law . . . a peremptory norm . . . is a norm accepted and recognized by the international community of States as a whole from which no derogation is permitted'.

[70] *Armed Activities*, para. 73.

[71] *Ibid.*, para. 73.

[72] *Armed Activities*, para. 75.

[73] *Ibid.*, para. 77.

[74] *Ibid.*, para. 78. In another context—the relationship between immunity claims and *jus cogens*—Klabbers comments that rigid distinctions between substantive law and procedural rules (the fact that States concerned could not be sued) does not detract from their possible guilt and the fundamental nature (jus cogens) of the rules breached 'seems too clever by half': J. Klabbers, 'The Validity and Invalidity of Treaties', *Oxford Guide to Treaties*, pp. 551–75, p. 572.

[75] Judges Higgins, Elaraby, Kooijmans, Owada, and Simma.

[76] *Armed Activities*, Joint Separate Opinion, para. 12.

[77] *Ibid.*, para. 16.

the International Court itself reflects this trend for tribunals and courts . . . to pronounce on compatibility with the object and purpose, when the need arises.[78]

With regard to the compatibility or incompatibility of reservations with the 'object and purpose' of Conventions, the Joint Opinion states that

> [m]uch will depend upon the particular convention . . . and the particular reservation. In some treaties not all reservations to specific substantive clauses will necessarily be contrary to the object and purpose of the treaty . . . Conversely, a reservation to a specific 'procedural' provision . . . could be contrary to the treaty's object and purpose. For example, the treaty bodies set up under certain United Nations conventions may well be central to the whole efficacy of those instruments. As the Human Rights Committee pointed out . . . the periodic submission of reports by States parties . . . and . . . examination thereof, are at the heart of the Covenant system. If a State purported to accept the substantive obligations . . . but refused to report on them or to participate in the examination of States reports, that could be contrary to the object and purpose of the Covenant. The same might well be true of other monitoring bodies in instruments whose whole efficacy turns upon the State reporting system.[79]

D. Comment

As noted, the incorporation in the Convention of any form of reservations clause was the subject of controversy and contradictory stances by the drafting bodies, centring on the effects of a clause with the potential to discourage ratification of the instrument, and the integrity of the Convention as a whole. Proponents of the clause visualized it as saving the Convention from destruction through reservations that might cut into its substance; opponents argued the case for deleting the clause and encouraging the greatest number of ratifications of a 'controversial' Convention, leaving the matter of reservations to be addressed under general international law. The two-thirds 'collegiate' rule emerged as a kind of *deus ex machina*, a guillotine to dampen future controversies over the interpretation and application of the Convention, and keep reservations under the overall control of States. It also seems clear that in drafting the Convention, the States did not intend to grant determining powers over reservations to the Committee. In the event, the Convention, unlike CEDAW and the Convention on the Rights of the Child (CRC), has not had substance bleached out of it by reservations to any great extent; neither is it apparent that the incorporation of the reservations clause has had appreciable effects on encouraging or discouraging the adherence of States parties to the Convention.

Within its self-regulating sphere, Article 20 of ICERD is only semi-detached from wider international standards on reservations, and represents, *inter alia*, an early inclusion in a multilateral treaty of the 'object and purpose' test for the validity of reservations, drawing upon the criterion developed by the International Court of Justice in the case of *Reservations to the Genocide Convention*.[80] The criterion, subsequently incorporated in the VCLT, is widely assumed to represent customary international law. Broader discussions of reservations thus remain relevant to the application of Article 20, as the above-cited

[78] *Ibid.*, paras 22 and 23.

[79] *Ibid.*, para. 21.

[80] Advisory Opinion ICJ Rep. 1951, 15. Thus, 'the same criterion of substance' (object and purpose) is common to both the VCLT and the Convention: I Diaconu, *Racial Discrimination* (Eleven International Publishing, 2011), p. 259.

Opinion recognizes. Characterization of Article 20 as a special rule should not obscure the interconnections between ICERD and the VCLT.

The object and purpose criterion appears to govern only one aspect of Article 20(2); the provision on inhibiting the bodies established under the Convention is treated separately, *ex facie* suggesting that the inhibition criterion is not governed by 'object and purpose'—a situation somewhat at a tangent to the approach of the Human Rights Committee.[81] In light of the possibility that objection to a supervisory procedure could frustrate the effective implementation of the Convention, it is unclear whether the dichotomy between 'object and purpose', and inhibition of ICERD bodies, represents a matter of principle. As noted by Lijnzaad, at first glance, Article 20 appears to provide a transparent system, but on a second glance, all is not necessarily clear.[82] The inhibition criterion presumably relates to CERD itself, and to the Ad Hoc Conciliation Commission envisaged in Article 12, and possibly to any of the bodies established in Part II of the Convention.[83] The International Court of Justice, referred to in Article 22, owes its 'establishment' to procedures independent of the Convention, and is not established by the Convention. 'Bodies established by the Convention' would presumably include bodies set up by the Committee using its powers of delegation to improve its performance as a whole, inasmuch as any such bodies work under the overall authority of the Committee, which is itself 'established by the Convention'.

With regard to the two-thirds rule, in the 'collegiate' approach to determining the acceptability of reservations, deemed in the Committee's Opinion not to have worked, the envisaged 'determination' of incompatibility or inhibitory effect continues to move further away from reality as the number of States parties increases.[84] In light of the current figure of 177 States parties to the Convention, it is unlikely that any reservation will be determined as incompatible under the procedural formalities of Article 20(2). The ICJ's view in *Armed Activities* that a reservation 'could not be regarded as incompatible' with the Convention if not declared to be such by the 'college' of States parties, should not be taken to suggest that any and every reservation is in substance compatible with ICERD. There is a difference between the power of determination, granted to the 'college', and assessments of compatibility regularly made in CERD practice, even if hard legal effects do not follow the latter. Further, on a literal reading of Article 20(2), while the two-thirds rule is highlighted as determining compatibility and incompatibility, the provision does not expressly rule out other possible 'determinants'. The asserted uniqueness of the method of determining the legal quality of reservations depends on reading the provision as an expression of the rule *expressio unius, exclusio alterius*, coupled with a restrictive reading of the *travaux* that rules out alternative possibilities.

Reservations chatter continues to be heard at both inter-State and Committee levels. Objections to the statement of Saudi Arabia refer to the object and purpose of the Convention and the lack of specification of which articles are affected by the reservation, the combination of which contributes to the undermining of international treaty law;

81 Human Rights Committee, GC 24, para. 11.

82 *Reservations to UN Human Rights Treaties*, p. 133.

83 In the drafting process, Ghana, Mauritania, and The Philippines envisaged prohibiting reservations to Articles 8–14, the supervisory system: A/C.3/L.1314; A/6181, para. 192; comment in Lijnzaad, *Reservations to UN Human Rights Treaties*, p. 137. Reservations subsist with regard to Article 15, regarded by some States parties—Tonga and the UK—as instituting a discriminatory procedure; see Chapter 4.

84 Lijnzaad, *Reservations to UN Human Rights Treaties*, p. 136.

hence the objection of Austria to the 'general and unspecified' nature of the reservation as creating doubts as to the commitment to obligations under the Convention 'essential for the fulfilment of its object and purpose'.[85] Objections to the statements by Thailand point to their vagueness of effect, with a number of objectors declaring that the interpretative declaration is in fact a reservation—hence, the statement by France that with 'a reservation of such a general and indeterminate scope . . . it is not possible to ascertain which changes to obligations . . . it is intended to introduce'.[86] A raft of objections subsist with regard to reservations made by Yemen. Remarks by Canada state that Yemen's reservations are incompatible with the object and purpose of the Convention, while hinting also at customary law, under which 'the principle of non-discrimination is generally accepted and recognized in international law and therefore is binding on all States'. For Finland, the reservations by Yemen 'concern matters which are of fundamental importance in the Convention . . . provisions prohibiting racial discrimination in the granting of such fundamental political rights and civil liberties as the right to participate in public life, to marry and choose a spouse, to inherit and to enjoy freedom of thought, conscience and religion are central in a convention against racial discrimination'. For Mexico, the reservation 'would result in discrimination to the detriment of a certain sector of the population, and . . . would violate Articles 2, 16 and 18' of the Universal Declaration of Human Rights.

In most instances, the objection concludes with a variant of the proposition that it 'shall not preclude', or does not constitute an obstacle to the entry into force of the Convention between the reserving and objecting States. In a minority of cases, the objecting State takes a more forceful approach. Recalling Swaine's characterization of the 'super maximum effect' of objections to reservations associated with some Nordic States,[87] Austria objects to the reservation by Saudi Arabia, asserting that the Convention shall apply 'in its entirety' between Austria and Saudi Arabia, without benefit of the reservation. Addressing the Turkish statement that it will implement the Convention only in relation to States with which it has diplomatic relations, Sweden asserts in forceful terms that the Convention 'enters into force in its entirety between the two States, without Turkey benefiting from the reservation'.

State-Committee reservations dialogues, conceived by some participants in the drafting process as alternative to the State collegiate procedure, continue to function on a regular basis. The issue of reservations regularly circulates in discussions of periodic reports, if rarely in the communications procedure.[88] CERD takes a critical line regarding reservations, recommending their removal, questioning their necessity, and recommending legislation to conform to the Convention.[89] In some cases, the Committee has stated bluntly that the reservation in question is inconsistent with the obligations of the State

[85] Information gathered from UN pages on reservations to the Convention: <https://treaties.un.org/Pages/ViewDetails.aspx?src=treaty&mtdsg_no=iv-2&chapter=4&lang=en>.

[86] Cf. Article 57.1 of the ECHR: 'Reservations of a general character shall not be permitted'.

[87] Supra, n. 30.

[88] Australia invoked its reservation to Article 4 in *Stephen Hagan v Australia*, Communication No. 26/2003, A/58/18, Annex III A, para. 4.7. In its analysis of the merits of the issue, the Committee made no reference to this question, though the petitioner commented, *ibid.*, para. 5.5, that 'the reservation is "probably invalid" as incompatible with the object and purpose of the Convention. Even if valid . . . the reservation is temporally limited . . . given that the State party contends that [legislation] implements its obligations under the article, the reservation must now have lapsed.'

[89] A/48/18, chapter VIII. B.

party.[90] In comments on Yemen, the Committee expressed the belief that the reservation to Article 5 had 'the effect of negating the core purposes and objectives of the Convention'.[91] With regard to Thailand, concern was expressed that 'the interpretative declaration . . . made by the State party, according to which it does not recognize any obligation beyond the confines of its Constitution and law, is incompatible with the obligation of the State party . . . to use all means . . . to prohibit and bring racial discrimination to an end'.[92] To Saudi Arabia, the Committee commented that the 'broad and imprecise nature of the State party's general reservation' raised concerns 'as to its compatibility with the object and purpose of the Convention'.[93] Jamaica was recommended to 're-examine its broad and vague reservation to the Convention, and consider withdrawing it to ensure that the provisions of the Convention are fully applicable in the State party'.[94] In the case of reservations on special measures but applicable more generally, GR 32 offers a challenging invitation to States parties to provide information 'as to why such a reservation is considered necessary, the nature and scope of the reservation, its precise effects in terms of national law and policy, and any plans to withdraw the reservation within a specified time frame'.[95] In line with its overall dialogic approach to engagement with States parties, the Committee speaks out when confronted by reservations that appear to challenge the depth of the State party's commitment to the principles of the Convention. The absence of an explicit determinative role for the Committee in Article 20 has not cajoled it into a normative silence.

The reservations and objections, coupled with the frequent comments by the Committee on reservations, raise the issue of which reservations may be appropriately regarded as contrary to the object and purpose of the Convention. As elsewhere in the human rights field, the contours of the 'object and purpose' rule are a matter of contention. Bearing in mind that the Human Rights Committee has treated reservations to customary international law as impermissible, and that the prohibition of racial discrimination is commonly understood as representing such a principle, what is to be made of the reservations to the Convention that embodies this fundamental principle? The Convention formally admits reservations, and the double aspect of customary and treaty law has not inhibited States from making reservations thereto. The assertions hitherto made by States parties and the Committee regarding the object and purpose rule do not greatly clarify its import. The purpose of the Convention is to eliminate racial discrimination; its method is to

[90] The Committee's concluding observations of 2001 on Japan, CERD/C/304/Add.114, para. 11, expressed concern that Japan's interpretation of Article 4 (styled a 'reservation' by the Committee) was 'in conflict with the State party's obligations'. A snapshot of CERD approaches to reservations by a variety of States is set out in HRI/MC/2005/Annex 1.

[91] Concluding observations on Yemen, CERD/C/YEM/CO/17-18, para. 13.

[92] Concluding observations on Thailand, CERD/C/THA/CO/1-3, para. 8; see also, *ibid.*, para. 8 regarding the State party's approach to Article 4. The ILC *Guide to Practice* (3.1.5.5) states that a reservation re internal law may be formulated 'only insofar as it does not affect an essential element of the treaty nor its general tenor', the approach is more generous than the Committee to the reserving State party.

[93] Concluding observation on Saudi Arabia, CERD/C/62/CO/8, para. 9.

[94] CERD/C/JAM/CO/16-20, para. 6, the reservation states that 'ratification of the Convention by Jamaica does not imply the acceptance of obligations going beyond the constitutional limits nor the acceptance of any obligation to introduce judicial processes beyond those prescribed under the Constitution'.

[95] Para. 38. The approach is reiterated, *mutatis mutandis*, by para. 23 of GR 35.

combine specification of norms with a supervisory machinery. Hence, the object and purpose criterion potentially concerns both normative and institutional (procedural) dimensions, despite the dichotomous treatment in Article 20 of object and purpose and inhibition of the bodies established by the Convention. The reservations by Yemen are deemed by the objecting States to infringe object and purpose by depriving populations of a raft of basic protections. The vague, unspecific nature of some reservations, rendering opaque the level of commitment to the Convention, suggests a further normative dimension to the object and purpose rule. On the other hand, the fundamental reservations by the US have passed unscathed by formal comment from other States parties, though the Committee has taken a resolute, critical stance in relation to them.

In the context of a focused, short, and normatively interconnected convention such as ICERD, refining in wholly abstract terms which reservations would infringe the object and purpose test based on criteria such as integrity, essential elements, raison d'être, core purposes of the text, relationship of the non-discrimination principle to customary international law, etc, may lead to suggestive but inconclusive outcomes, bearing in mind that, *in abstracto*, 'object and purpose' is not a test of great precision.[96] On the other hand, moving from abstractions to specifics, the complex preamble to the Convention and the operative text intimate what should be regarded as impermissible in terms of reservations. As the objections suggest, reservations purporting to freeze out particular groups from the protection of the Convention through discrimination in purpose or effect, or through exclusionary, segregationist structures and rejection of group participation in the life of the State and nation, would represent violations of principle, a consideration that runs through the raft of protections incorporated in the Convention. The object and purpose criterion is also not static, especially in light of the development of identity categories through the life of the Convention, so that reservations dedicated to negation of group identity, group assimilation, or worse, especially on a large scale, would infringe Article 20. The 'living history' of the Convention with its attendant changes in Committee practice impacts on the understanding of the criteria for the permissibility of reservations as it has done on understanding the normative fundamentals of discrimination.

It is too soon to conclude that Article 20 has not worked. Reservations have not troubled the Committee to the same extent as reservations to other core UN human rights conventions have troubled their monitoring bodies. Compared to the situation with regard to comparable human rights conventions, the mix of reservations, declarations, interpretations, and statements of political principle has engaged Committee practice to only a minor extent. The consensus supporting the Convention's goal to eliminate racial discrimination has generated comparatively little principled dissent from the Convention or the Committee's methodology. It is also the case that, in some respects, the Convention does not engage as deeply with processes of social transformation as comparable instruments in the field of human rights. The Committee has been mindful of State

[96] *The ILC Practice Guide*, 3.1.5.6, states with regard to reservations to treaties with interdependent rights and obligations that, in assessing object and purpose, 'account shall be taken of that interdependence as well as the importance that the provision has within the general tenor of the treaty and the extent of the impact that the reservation has on the treaty'.

sovereignty, group self-determination, and local practices, while also intimating their limits, increasingly so in more critical later practice. Challenges to the Committee's interpretation and application of the Convention have tended to come through the medium of dialogue and comment available to States parties under the 'regular' procedures, rather than through the medium of reservations.

THORNBERRY

19. Article 22

Role of the International Court of Justice

Any dispute between two or more States Parties with respect to the interpretation or application of this Convention, which is not settled by negotiation or by the procedures expressly provided for in this Convention, shall, at the request of any of the parties to the dispute, be referred to the International Court of Justice for decision, unless the disputants agree to another mode of settlement.

A. Introduction

A number of core UN human rights treaties envisage recourse to the International Court of Justice for the settlement of disputes regarding the interpretation or application of the Convention in question; they include the Convention on Enforced Disappearances (CPED),[1] the Convention on the Elimination of All Forms of Discrimination against Women (CEDAW),[2] the Convention against Torture (CAT),[3] and the Convention on Migrant Workers (CMW).[4] The Convention against Trafficking,[5] the 1951 Refugee Convention,[6] and the Convention against Genocide,[7] also contain such a provision. While the International Convention on the Elimination of All Forms of Racial Discrimination (ICERD) refers to negotiation or the procedures expressly provided under the Convention as alternative means of solving disputes,[8] later instruments are closer to the pattern of CEDAW:

> Any dispute between two or more States parties concerning the interpretation or application of the present Convention which is not settled by negotiation shall, at the request of one of them, be submitted to arbitration. If within six months from the date of the request for arbitration the parties are unable to agree on the organization of the arbitration, any one of those parties may refer the dispute to the International Court of Justice by request in conformity with the Statute of the Court.[9]

The equivalent reference in Article 30 of the CAT—the parties are 'unable to agree to the organization of the arbitration'—was used by the International Court of Justice in finding jurisdiction in *Questions Relating to the Obligation to Prosecute or Extradite* (*Belgium v Senegal*).[10]

[1] Article 42.
[2] Article 29.
[3] Article 30.
[4] Article 92.
[5] Article 15.
[6] Article 38.
[7] Article IX.
[8] See discussion below on whether these must be employed prior to seising the ICJ.
[9] Article 29(1); the second paragraph of the article makes provision for a declaration by a State party that it 'does not consider itself bound by paragraph 1'. For examples of dispute settlement clauses, including settlement by the ICJ, see D.B. Hollis (ed.), *The Oxford Guide to Treaties* (Oxford University Press, 2012), pp. 734–40.
[10] Judgment of 20 July 2012, <http://www.icj-cij.org/docket/index.php?p1=3&p2=3&case=144>; Article 30 CAT. See also *Armed Activities on the Territory of the Congo (DRC v Rwanda), Jurisdiction and Admissibility*, ICJ Rep. 2006, p. 6.

B. *Travaux Préparatoires*

Regarding the role of the International Court of Justice (ICJ), a range of model clauses on settlement of disputes offered in the working paper of the Secretary-General,[11] and considered by the Officers of the Third Committee. A provision closely related to Article IX of the Convention on the Political Rights of Women was put to the Third Committee:

> Any dispute between two or more States parties with respect to the interpretation or application of the Convention, which is not settled by negotiation, shall at the request of any of the parties to the dispute, be referred to the International Court of Justice for decision, unless the disputants agree to another mode of settlement.

Poland proposed to change 'any' to 'all' (States parties to the dispute), an amendment that was supported by some,[12] vigorously challenged by others,[13] and eventually voted down.[14] The principal issue was the appropriateness of consent to the jurisdiction of the ICJ being agreed in advance through a provision in the Convention: according to one representative, the Committee had to decide what was 'in accord with the spirit of the Convention and would ensure the most satisfactory settlement of disputes'.[15] The addition of 'or by the procedures expressly provided for in this Convention' to the negotiation option for dispute settlement was the result of an amendment by Ghana, Mauritania, and The Philippines.[16] The amendment did not provoke significant discussion and was adopted unanimously.[17]

In a comment relied upon by the International Court of Justice in *Georgia v Russian Federation* (Preliminary Objections),[18] the representative of Ghana stated to the Third Committee that, in Article 22, provision 'had been made in the draft Convention for machinery which should be used in the settlement of disputes before recourse was had to the International Court of Justice'.[19] The statement was interpreted by the ICJ to confirm its conclusion that recourse to this machinery constituted a pre-condition to seisin by the Court. The representative of Canada regarded the clause as allowing considerable latitude in that no time limit was imposed for resort to negotiation or other modes of settlement: 'A controversy could thus be protracted almost indefinitely before recourse was had to the Court.'[20] The

[11] E/CN.4/L.679, pp. 15–16.

[12] Remarks of the representative of the Ukrainian SSR, A/C.3/SR.1367, para. 27; USSR, *ibid.*, paras 33–5; Tanzania, *ibid.*, paras 36–7.

[13] Canada argued that 'if all parties to a dispute had to consent to its submission to the International Court of Justice, there was no need for a special provision on the subject, since any inter-State dispute could be brought before the Court with the common consent of the parties': A/C.3/SR.1367, para. 24. The representative of the US, *ibid.*, para. 32, recalled that while it was true that the jurisdiction of the ICJ depended on consent, the 'optional clause' in Article 36 of the Statute of the Court was not the only way of indicating consent, which in the Statute included consent stemming from matters especially provided for in treaties and conventions in force. See also remarks of Colombia, *ibid.*, para. 31; France, *ibid.*, para. 38; Trinidad and Tobago, *ibid.*, para. 41.

[14] The amendment was defeated by 37 votes to 26, with 26 abstentions: A/6181, para. 200.

[15] Remarks of the representative of Italy, A/C.3/SR.1367, para. 39.

[16] A/C.3/L.1313.

[17] A/6181, para. 200.

[18] See discussion in the present chapter.

[19] Remarks of the representative of Ghana, A/C.3/SR.1367, para. 29.

[20] A/C.3/SR.1367, para. 25.

representative of Belgium interpreted the clause as 'offering ample opportunity for agreement before the Court was resorted to'.[21]

C. Reservations and Declarations

Article 22 is the subject of a significant number of reservations,[22] a situation presaged by comments made during the drafting process. The reservations are generally to the effect that the express consent of all parties to the dispute is required before submission to the ICJ. The reservation by Cuba diverges from the standard formula in expressly asserting that the disputes envisaged in Article 22 'should be settled exclusively by the procedures expressly provided for in the Convention through the diplomatic channel', while Israel states tersely that it 'does not consider itself bound by the provisions of Article 22 of the... Convention'. As noted, the inter-State procedure involving the Committee on the Elimination of Racial Discrimination (CERD) has not been formally activated.[23] Article 22 does not allocate a role to the Committee in engaging the International Court of Justice: CERD procedures are simply referred to in Article 22 along with 'negotiation'. The Committee was not involved in *Georgia v Russian Federation*, though aspects of its practice were adverted to by the ICJ.

D. Practice

Reservations and Declarations

Article 22 has been cited as a basis for ICJ jurisdiction in key cases before the Court. As noted earlier,[24] in *Armed Activities, Democratic Republic of the Congo v Rwanda*, the Democratic Republic of the Congo (DRC) alleged that Rwanda had engaged in massive violations of human rights and humanitarian law on the territory of the Congo, citing ICERD as among the conventions violated. Rwanda referred to its reservation to Article 22, which had not been objected to by any State including the DRC, as precluding jurisdiction.[25] Bearing in mind also that the reservation had not been objected to by the 'college' of two-thirds of States parties, the ICJ was unable to find jurisdiction on the basis of Article 22.

The refusal to entertain jurisdiction in *Armed Activities* meant that Article 22 was not subjected to further analysis by the ICJ until *Georgia v Russian Federation*.[26] The case

[21] *Ibid.*, para. 40.

[22] Reservations subsist for Afghanistan, Bahrain, China, Cuba, Egypt, Equatorial Guinea, India, Indonesia, Iraq, Israel, Kuwait, Lebanon, Libya, Madagascar, Morocco, Mozambique, Nepal, Saudi Arabia, Syrian Arab Republic, Thailand, Turkey, the US, and Yemen. No objections are lodged against the reservations: <https://treaties.un.org/pages/ViewDetails.aspx?src=TREATY&mtdsg_no=IV-2&chapter=4&lang=en 0>.

[23] See Chapter 4.

[24] See Chapter 18.

[25] *Case Concerning Armed Activities on the Territory of the Congo (New Application: 2002) (Democratic Republic of the Congo v Rwanda), Jurisdiction of the Court and Admissibility*, Judgment of 3 February 2006, paras 71–9.

[26] *Application of the International Convention on the Elimination of All Forms of Racial Discrimination (Georgia v Russian Federation)*, Provisional Measures, Order of 15 October 2008, ICJ Rep. 2008, p. 353; Preliminary Objections, 1 April 2011, ICJ Rep. 2011, p. 70. For comment on the Provisional Measures case, see P. Okowa, 'The Georgia v Russia Case: A Commentary', available at: <http://www.haguejusticeportal.net/

stemmed from an armed conflict in South Ossetia and Abkhazia in August 2008. Georgia almost immediately commenced proceedings against the Russian Federation,[27] alleging Russian sponsorship of racial discrimination up to and including mass expulsion of ethnic Georgians, in violation of the Convention; Georgia sought to found the jurisdiction of the Court on the basis of Article 22,[28] requesting the Court to indicate provisional measures on the basis of an 'extremely urgent threat of irreparable harm'.[29] The parties disagreed on the territorial scope of ICERD, Georgia claiming that ICERD does not include any territorial limitation,[30] while Russia disputed this, arguing, *inter alia*, that Article 2 and 5 of ICERD cannot govern the conduct of a State outside its own borders.[31] In the event, the Court found no restriction of a general nature in ICERD relating to territorial application, nor was there a specific territorial limitation in Articles 2 or 5.[32] In light of the disagreement on the scope of the Convention, and on whether the issue was related to the Convention, as contended by Georgia,[33] or related to the use of force, non-intervention, self-determination, and humanitarian law, as contended by Russia,[34] the Court found that a dispute existed as to the interpretation and application of ICERD within the terms of Article 22.[35] In the Court's view, the acts alleged by Georgia appeared to be capable of contravening rights under ICERD, 'even if certain of these acts might also be covered by other rules of international law, including humanitarian law'.[36]

As to the procedural conditions laid down in Article 22, Georgia contended that the reference to a dispute not settled by negotiation or recourse to the procedures expressly provided by the Convention did not imply that negotiation or recourse constituted preconditions for the seisin of the Court;[37] Russia argued that Article 22 did set out preconditions.[38] The Court sided with Georgia, interpreting Article 22 'in its plain meaning' as suggesting that formal negotiations in the framework of the Convention did not constitute a precondition for seising the Court; on the other hand, some attempt should have been made by the claimant party to initiate discussions on issues that fell under ICERD, noting that such had been raised in bilateral contacts, and had manifestly not been resolved.[39] The fact that ICERD has not been specifically mentioned in a

Docs/Commentaries%20PDF/Okowa_Georgia_ICJ_EN.pdf>; on the Preliminary Objections case, P. Okowa, 'The International Court of Justice and the Georgia/Russia Dispute', *HRLR* 11/4 (2011), 739–57 [henceforth 'Georgia/Russia Dispute']; N. Lucak, 'Georgia v Russian Federation: A Question of the Jurisdiction of the International Court of Justice', *Maryland Journal of International Law* 27 (2012), 323–54. Disputes between Georgia and the Russian Federation have also generated litigation before the European Court of Human Rights: see for example *Georgia v Russia* (I), App. No. 13255/07(2014); *Georgia v Russia* (II), App. No. 38263/08; *Georgia v Russia* (III), App. No. 61186/09.

[27] 12 August 2008.

[28] Georgia acceded to the Convention in 1999 without any reservations; the reservation to Article 22 made by the USSR in 1969 was withdrawn in 1989—the Russian Federation continued the legal personality of the USSR.

[29] 14 August 2008.

[30] *Provisional Measures*, paras 92 and 108. See the discussion of extraterritorial effects of the Convention in Chapters 8 and 10.

[31] *Ibid.*, paras 72, 100, 108.

[32] *Provisional Measures*, para. 109.

[33] *Ibid.*, para. 20, citing Articles 2, 3, 4, 5, and 6 of ICERD.

[34] *Provisional Measures*, para. 83.

[35] *Ibid.*, para. 112.

[36] *Provisional Measures*, para. 112.

[37] *Ibid.*, paras 88, 94, 113.

[38] *Provisional Measures*, paras 83, 101, 102, 113.

[39] *Ibid.*, para. 114.

bilateral or multilateral context was not an obstacle to seisin on the basis of Article 22. In ordering provisional measures, the Court observed that it was not called upon to judge breaches of ICERD but whether the rights in question, in particular Article 5(b) and (d)(i) of ICERD,[40] were of such a nature that prejudice to them would be irreparable.[41] In light of the vulnerable situation of ethnic groups in the population, including ethnic Ossetians and Abkhazians as well as ethnic Georgians, and the ongoing instability and tensions, the Court concluded that there was an imminent risk that the rights at issue might suffer irreparable prejudice.[42]

A joint dissenting opinion by seven judges considered that the acts attributed by Georgia to the Russian Federation were unlikely to fall within the provisions of the Convention.[43] The Joint Opinion reasoned narrowly that the armed activities could not constitute acts of racial discrimination within Article 1 of the Convention unless it was proven that they 'were aimed at establishing a "distinction, exclusion, restriction or preference based on race, colour, descent, or national or ethnic origin"'[44]—a narrower view of discrimination than that taken in CERD practice.[45] The Joint Opinion summarized the issues as (1) whether there was a dispute as to the interpretation or application of the Convention, and (2) whether the precondition that the dispute had not been settled by negotiation or under the procedures expressly provided for in the Convention had been met.[46] The dissenting judges argued that the Court had assumed the existence of a dispute simply because parties had manifested disagreement over the applicability of Articles 2 and 5 of the Convention,[47] and that 'the very substance of CERD was never debated between the Parties before the filing of a claim before the Court'.[48] Thus, it was not sufficient that 'there have been contacts between the parties'; such contacts 'must have been regarding the subject of the dispute, either the interpretation or application of the Convention'.[49] As to preconditions, the dissenters asserted that the majority view confirmed neither the ordinary meaning of Article 22, nor its object and purpose, which was to encourage the maximum number of States to submit to the jurisdiction of the Court, with the assurance that the procedures provided for in the Convention will first be exhausted.[50] The dissenting group also argued that the Order by the Court failed to demonstrate the likelihood of irreparable harm or the existence of an urgent situation.[51]

[40] Article 5(b) addresses security of person and protection against violence, while d (i) refers to freedom of movement and residence, discussion in Chapter 13.

[41] Article 5(b) refers to security of the person and protection against violence; (d)(i) addresses freedom of movement and residence within the border of the State.

[42] *Provisional Measures*, paras 142–6, 149.

[43] Vice-President Al-Khasawneh, and Judges Ranjeva, Shi, Koroma, Tomka, Bennouna, and Skotnikov.

[44] *Provisional Measures*, Joint Dissenting Opinion, para. 9.

[45] See Chapter 6 for discussion of the concept of discrimination in Article 1.

[46] *Provisional Measures*, Joint Dissenting Opinion, para. 6.

[47] *Ibid.*, para. 10; thus, 'an argument expounded during oral proceedings has mutated into evidence of the existence of a dispute'.

[48] *Provisional Measures*, Joint Dissenting Opinion, para. 12.

[49] *Ibid.*, para. 15.

[50] *Provisional Measures*, Joint Dissenting Opinion, para. 18. In an interesting addition (para. 18), the Opinion stated that the Court could have considered that the seriousness of the situation did not allow recourse to the procedures provided for in Article 22, 'but this would set little store by the procedure for urgency and rapid alert established by the Committee on the Elimination of Racial Discrimination in 1993'.

[51] *Ibid.*, paras 21 and 22.

In its judgment of 2011, the preliminary objections of Russia that there was no dispute on the interpretation or application of ICERD when Georgia filed its application, and that the Article 22 'preconditions' had not been met, were addressed. The result was a *volte-face* by the Court in its overall reading of Article 22. Drawing on the proliferation of terms in the Convention—'matter', 'complaints', and 'disputes'—Russia argued that 'dispute' had a special meaning that is narrower than in public international law generally and more difficult to satisfy,[52] a contention that was rejected by Georgia.[53] The assertion that a special, narrower meaning should be applied to 'dispute' in Article 22 was also rejected by the Court; it was not clear in any case what form this narrower interpretation might take. Recalling its established case law,[54] the Court stated its understanding of 'dispute' as

> [a] disagreement on a point of law or fact, a conflict of legal views or of interests . . . Whether there is a dispute in a given case is a matter for 'objective determination' by the Court . . . It must be shown that the claim of one party is positively opposed by the other . . . The Court's determination must turn on an examination of the facts. The matter is one of substance, not of form . . . while the existence of a dispute and the undertaking of negotiations are distinct as a matter of principle, the negotiations may help to demonstrate the existence of the dispute and delineate the subject-matter. This dispute must in principle exist at the time the Application is submitted to the Court . . . In terms of the subject-matter . . . [under] . . . the terms of Article 22 . . . the dispute must be with respect to the interpretation or application of the [the] Convention.[55]

Reviewing the evidence for the existence of a dispute, it was noted that Georgia had become a party to the Convention in 1999 and claimed the existence of a dispute reaching back beyond the point when it became a party to the Convention.[56] Elements in the documentation presented by Georgia, however, suggested to the Court that the main issue at the time was the status of Abkhazia—references to IDPs and return of refugees were incidental elements in a larger claim and in any case, such elements could not have been based on the interpretation or application of the Convention, the only kind of dispute relevant to the proceedings before the Court.[57] Following the entry into force of the Convention as between the parties, the Court noted that reports to CERD operated in a process of dialogue between the State party and the Committee that was not designed to involve other States;[58] other documentation regarding the ongoing tensions between Georgia and Russia addressed to the Secretary-General and the Security Council did not focus on CERD or human rights generally.[59]

[52] *Preliminary Objections*, paras 23, 26, 27.

[53] *Ibid.*, paras 24 and 28.

[54] 'A dispute is a disagreement on a point of law or fact, a conflict of legal views or of interests between two persons': *Mavromattis Palestine Concessions*, [1924] PCIJ, Ser. A, No. 2, p. 11; and is a matter for objective determination by the Court; *Interpretation of Peace Treaties with Bulgaria, Hungary and Romania*, First Phase, Advisory Opinion, ICJ Rep. 1950, p. 65; 'It must be shown that the claim of one party is positively opposed by the other': South *West Africa (Ethiopia v South Africa; Liberia v South Africa), Preliminary Objections*, ICJ Rep. 1962, p. 328; *Armed Activities*, Jurisdiction and Admissibility, p. 40, para. 90; the existence of a dispute is a question of substance, not of form: *Land and Maritime Boundary between Cameroon and Nigeria (Cameroon v Nigeria)*, Judgment, ICJ Rep. 1998, p. 275, para. 89.

[55] *Preliminary Objections*, para. 30, parentheses omitted.

[56] *Preliminary Objections*, paras 34 and 50.

[57] *Ibid.*, paras 63, 64.

[58] *Ibid.*, para. 69.

[59] *Preliminary Objections*, paras 73, 74, 76, 81, 91, 92, 93, 95, 96, 99, 103, 104.

The Court found that before 2008 there was insufficient evidence of a dispute between the parties related to ICERD, and that conduct had been attributed to separatist forces in the above territories; the Court construed the conduct of Russia in this period as a peacekeeper.[60] The position changed in 2008 when there was a dispute between the parties regarding the subject matter of the Convention. Allegations of ethnic cleansing of Georgians by Russian forces, and of ethnic cleansing of Abkhazians and Ossetians by the Georgian leadership, brought the matter into the domain of ICERD, with Georgia making direct allegations against Russia. The Court concluded that by 12 August, the date of the application by Georgia, a dispute between the two parties existed.[61] Accordingly, Russia's first preliminary objection—that there had been no dispute between Georgia and Russia at the date of the application—was dismissed.[62]

The understanding of dispute in the majority judgement is narrowly focused, with deliberate emphasis on the need for the dispute to relate to the interpretation or application of the Convention. Some judges in the minority took a broader view of the existence of a dispute, even in the absence of a specific starting date for a dispute.[63] Judge Owada pointed out that the Court's approach was too stringent, bearing in mind that Georgia had time and time again made its concerns over ethnic cleansing and return of refugees abundantly clear.[64] Judge Simma found that the relevant dispute had been under way long before armed hostilities in 2008;[65] Judge Abraham took a similar view in light of the earlier jurisprudence of the Court, finding that the judgment had adopted a formalistic approach instead of treating the identification of a dispute as a realistic and practical task.[66] Judge Cançado Trindade, in the course of a lengthy peroration that ranged over the ethics and processes of interpretation of human rights treaties, found that the Court had laboured through a process of formalistic reasoning to find that a dispute had crystallized only after the outbreak of an open and declared war between Georgia and Russia.[67] Judge Donoghue criticized the suggestion in the Court's understanding of a dispute that the claim of one party be positively opposed by another—this should only be seen as part of the Court's overall determination of the existence of a dispute.[68] In contrast, Judge Koroma emphasized the condition that the dispute must be about the interpretation and application of ICERD; disputes on such matter as territorial integrity, armed conflict, etc, do not fall within CERD's compromissory clause.[69] Judge Skotnikov took a similar line, arguing that the exchange of accusations during an armed conflict are not sufficient to determine the existence of a dispute with respect to the application or interpretation of ICERD.[70]

[60] Para. 103.

[61] *Preliminary Objections*, para. 113.

[62] *Ibid.*, para. 103. In favour: President Owada, Judges Al-Khasawneh, Simma, Abraham, Keith, Sepúlveda-Amor, Bennouna, Cançado Trindade, Yusuf, Greenwood, Donoghue, Judge ad hoc Gaja; against: Vice-President Tomka, Judges Koroma, Skotnikov, Xue.

[63] Joint Dissenting Opinion of President Owada, Judges Simma, Abraham, Donoghue and Judge ad hoc Gaja; separate opinions of Judges Owada, Tomka, Koroma, Simma, Abraham, Skotnikov, Cançado Trindade, Greenwood, and Donoghue.

[64] *Preliminary Objections*, Owada Opinion, paras 10–14. Judge Tomka on the other hand regarded references by Georgia to ethnic cleansing as merely a feature of wartime rhetoric.

[65] *Preliminary Objections*, Simma Opinion, paras 23–57.

[66] *Preliminary Obj*ections, Abraham Opinion, paras 14, 22, 24, 25.

[67] *Preliminary Objections*, Cançado Trindade Opinion, paras 88–118.

[68] *Preliminary Objections*, Donoghue Opinion, paras 7–12; 18–20.

[69] *Preliminary Objections*, Koroma Opinion, para. 7.

[70] *Preliminary Objections*, Skotnikov Opinion, paras 10 and 12.

To the second preliminary objection by Russia, that Georgia had failed to satisfy procedural preconditions—negotiation or recourse to the procedures in the Convention—Georgia responded that the two modalities did not amount to preconditions, there being neither an obligation to negotiate or utilize the CERD procedures; in the view of Georgia, Article 22 simply referred to the existence of a dispute as a matter of fact, not as a triggering qualification for seisin of the Court.[71] Applying the test of 'ordinary meaning', including the principle that the words of Article 22 must be given effect, the Court decided that the references to negotiation and CERD procedures constituted preconditions; the references to two modes of settlement suggested an affirmative duty to resort to them prior to the seisin of the Court.[72] This conclusion was reinforced by comparing the use of the simple present in English with the use of the future perfect in French—'*[t]out différend . . . qui n'aura pas été réglé par voie de négociation ou au moyen des procédures expressément prévues par la convention*'—which suggested that a previous action must have taken place before another action (referral to the Court) could be pursued.[73]

The ordinary meaning interpretation was further supported by recourse to the *travaux préparatoires* which, according to the Court, were elaborated at a time when the idea of compulsory settlement of disputes by the ICJ was not readily acceptable to a number of States; it was therefore reasonable to assume that preconditions would apply in order to facilitate wider acceptance of the Convention.[74] The above-cited statement of the representative of Ghana during the drafting of the Convention—that provision had been made in the draft Convention 'for machinery which should be used in the settlement of disputes before recourse was had to the International Court of Justice'[75]—was cited in the judgement in order to confirm the Court's conclusion that the terms of Article 22 'establish preconditions to be fulfilled before the seisin of the Court'.[76] The majority judgment of the Court observed that although 'no firm inferences can be drawn from the drafting history' as to whether negotiations or Convention procedures were preconditions, 'the *travaux préparatoires* do not suggest a different conclusion from that at which the Court has already arrived through the main method of ordinary meaning interpretation'.[77] The Court left aside the question of whether the preconditions were alternative or cumulative.

As to whether the preconditions were complied with, it was noted that Georgia had made no attempt to engage the procedures provided by the Convention. The Court also understood that 'negotiations' were distinct from protests or disputes, requiring, *de minimis*, a genuine attempt by one of the disputing parties to engage in discussions with the other with a view to resolving the dispute;[78] where negotiations have been attempted or commenced, the precondition is only satisfied when there has been a failure of negotiations, or they have become futile or deadlocked.[79] Further, the subject-matter of

[71] *Preliminary Objections*, Judgement, para. 126.
[72] *Ibid.*, para. 141.
[73] *Ibid.*, para. 135. The other authentic texts—Chinese, Spanish, and Russian—were deemed not to contradict this interpretation.
[74] *Preliminary Objections*, Judgment, para. 147.
[75] A/C.3/SR.1367, para. 29.
[76] *Preliminary Objections*, Judgment, para. 141.
[77] *Ibid.*, para. 147.
[78] Para. 157.
[79] *Preliminary Objections*, para. 159.

the negotiations must relate to the subject-matter of the dispute which in turn must concern the substantive obligations in the treaty in question.[80] The Court averred that it had become less formalistic in its understanding of what constituted negotiations.[81] In this case, the Court turned to the question of whether Georgia had genuinely attempted negotiations that implicated the provisions of ICERD.

Because of the finding that the dispute had arisen only in the period immediately before the filing of Georgia's application, it was only necessary to examine a short span of time to assess whether negotiations took place. The Court concluded that, while claim and counter claims regarding ethnic cleansing and 'extermination' attested to the existence of a dispute regarding ICERD matters, they did not demonstrate an attempt to negotiate these matters; Georgia and Russia did not engage in negotiations with regard to Russia's obligations under ICERD.[82] Accordingly, neither precondition in Article 22 had been satisfied and the Court decided, by ten votes to six,[83] that it did not have jurisdiction over the merits of the case.

A joint dissent by five judges[84] read the phrase 'which is not settled' as a statement of fact simply that a dispute had not been settled rather than a precondition, and that the majority had taken a formalistic, not a realistic approach to negotiation in light of Russia's intransigence.[85] Further, even if Article 22 established preconditions, they were alternative, not cumulative.[86] The joint dissent criticizes the use by the Court of the principle of effectiveness, to the detriment of concentrating on the literal meaning of the text which, *ex facie*, neither requires nor suggests an attempt at settlement prior to the seisin of the Court, though the Opinion also regards the text of Article 22 as ambiguous.[87] In sum, the Joint Opinion addresses the interpretative issues in stark terms:

80 *Ibid.*, para. 161.

81 *Preliminary Objections*, para. 160.

82 *Ibid.*, paras 180–2.

83 In favour: Vice-President Tomka, Judges Koroma, Al-Khasawneh, Keith, Sepúlveda-Amor, Bennouna, Skotnikov, Yusuf, Greenwood, and Xue; against: President Owada, Judges Simma, Abraham, Cançado Trindade, Judge ad hoc Gaja.

84 President Owada, Judges Simma, Abraham, Donoghue, and Judge Ad Hoc Gaja. Additionally, separate and dissenting opinions were offered by President Owada (separate opinion), Vice-President Tomka (declaration), judges Koroma (separate opinion), Skotnikov (declaration), Simma (separate opinion), Abraham (separate opinion), Cançado Trindade (dissenting opinion), Greenwood (separate opinion), and Donoghue (separate opinion).

85 Paras 83 and 84.

86 *Preliminary Objections, Joint Dissenting Opinion*, para. 12. In favour of treating the modalities referred to in Article 22 (negotiation or CERD procedures) as alternatives rather than cumulative, the Joint Opinion, para. 43, examples the case 'where a State has already tried, without success, to negotiate directly with another State against which it has grievances', in which case 'it would be senseless to require it to follow the special procedures in Part II . . . It would make even less sense to require a State which has unsuccessfully pursued the intricate procedure under Part II to undertake direct negotiations destined to fail before seising the Court.' Paragraphs 45–7 of the Joint Opinion also cite the move in the *travaux* to add 'the procedures expressly provided for in this Convention' to the earlier draft that referred only to 'negotiation', as evidence that the addition was adopted, 'not as a change in the text to make it more restrictive but as a natural . . . clarification', cementing the view that the procedural modalities referred to in Article 22 are alternative and not cumulative.

87 The general rule of interpretation—ordinary meaning in the light of object and purpose—'is applied in the Judgment in a way that amounts to nothing more than applying the principle of "effectiveness"'; *Joint Dissenting Opinion*, para. 21; the Opinion adds, *ibid.*, that, in relation to the Court's reflection on different tenses employed in English (present indicative) and in French (future perfect), the conclusion 'is hardly a solid one, since the problem of interpretation remains whatever the tense employed'; further, the authors of the Opinion assert (para. 22) that the principle of effectiveness 'is never as all-determinative as the Court would appear to treat it in the present case; it does not suffice by itself', and (para. 23) that the literal meaning of 'any

Thus, there is no unassailable argument supporting the interpretation of Article 22 upheld by the Court... namely, that the clause establishes 'preconditions'... Neither textual analysis of the language, which is ambiguous, nor the prior jurisprudence, which appears to have fluctuated, nor an examination of the *travaux préparatoires*, which are inconclusive, necessarily leads to the position the Court has decided to adopt in this case—at variance with the position it took on a prima facie basis three years ago in the same case.[88]

Regarding negotiations, the Joint Opinion argues that the assessment must be made on a case-by-case basis, not in formal or procedural terms but as a matter of substance,[89] and that Georgia had satisfied the negotiation criterion.[90] Various aspects in the Joint Opinion are elaborated, nuanced, and to some extent recycled in the nine separate opinions appended to the judgment. Most of the opinions offer further comment on the meaning of terms intrinsic to Article 22—'dispute',[91] 'negotiation', 'with respect to the interpretation or application of this Convention', in the light of evidence presented to the Court by the parties. While the opinions seek to lend greater precision to the article in contention, they focus as much on consistency and inconsistency in the jurisprudential archive of the International Court of Justice as on the text and drafting of the Convention.

E. Comment

The case is the first case before the International Court of Justice to focus exclusively on the interpretation of the Convention. If the point of contention concerns a procedural and not a substantive provision of the Convention, the Court and the separate opinions nonetheless intimate points of significance for substance as well as procedure.

On the textual puzzle of Article 22, differences over the concept of a 'dispute'—taking into account the history of this concept in the life of the ICJ and its predecessor—did not generate the same level of dissent as the second preliminary objection by the Russian Federation, whether the article implied preconditions of negotiations or utilization of CERD procedures before seising the ICJ.[92] It is evident that a literal reading of the text of Article 22 does not resolve the options of 'preconditions' as opposed to the 'simple statement of fact' that the matter under dispute had not been settled by negotiation or CERD procedures.[93] Inevitably, the conditions and implications of the drafting process and environment were called into play by the Court and the dissenters in order to incline the argument one way or another. The Court's ultimate judgment that Article 22 set out

dispute which is not settled by' 'neither suggests nor requires that an attempt at settlement must necessarily have been made before reference to the Court... the CERD drafters chose, deliberately or not, the wording least capable of being interpreted literally as laying down a "precondition" requiring a prior attempt to negotiate a settlement'.

88 *Preliminary Objections*, *Joint Opinion*, para. 34.

89 *Ibid.*, para. 57.

90 *Ibid.*, para. 38.

91 Discussed above.

92 The Joint Opinion views the Court's stance on this as being out of step with its more recent jurisprudence, citing the 2008 case regarding *Croatia v Serbia*, which allowed a condition not met at the time the proceedings were instituted to be met later, but before the Court ruled on jurisdiction: *Application of the Convention on the Prevention and Punishment of the Crime of Genocide, (Croatia v Serbia), Preliminary Objections*, Judgment, ICJ Rep. 2008, p. 441, para. 85, cited in *Joint Opinion*, para. 35.

93 Compare the reading by the Court of the travaux of ICERD with their reading in the *Joint Opinion*, paras 45–7.

preconditions sets a strict standard, bearing in mind that 'negotiation' was also treated strictly (formalistically, according to the dissenting opinions) by the Court, potentially reducing any future flow of cases. On the other hand, the fact that the Court left open the question of whether the conditions were alternative or cumulative somewhat broadens the possibilities of seising the Court; in this case, the views elaborated at some length by the Joint Dissenting Opinion and individual judges may have significant persuasive effect for future cases.

On the relationship of the Convention to other bodies of law—on what precisely is an ICERD issue and how such can be individuated—it is instructive that the allegations by Georgia of 'ethnic cleansing' were influential in allowing the Court to conclude that there was a dispute with respect to the interpretation or application of the Convention. As discussed in Chapter 8 of the present work, CERD practice suggests that the Convention and the rules of humanitarian law may be simultaneously applicable; the views of the Court (above) are to similar effect. The degree of prominence accorded to 'ethnic' issues in any theatre of conflict is a strong indicator of whether ICERD norms are implicated. Extending this appreciation to disputes as to interpretation or application of the Convention, Judge Skotnikov argued that the Court must satisfy itself that the alleged dispute related to distinctions, etc, on the grounds in Article 1 of the Convention, and distinguished between wartime propaganda on the one hand and statements which point to the emergence and crystallization of a dispute under ICERD on the other. The focus on Article 1 is instructive, though the condemnation of racist propaganda in Article 4 should also be borne in mind. It is also not clear in such situations whether characterization as 'an ICERD question' always depends on deliberate acts. Whilst Okowa doubts whether the elements of conflict between Russia and Georgia presented to the Court were really 'about' the Convention and were really 'about' other areas of international law such as the use of force;[94] characterizations as one or the other are not mutually exclusive. If Convention-based arguments may be invoked instrumentally by contending parties,[95] this does not negate the utility of employing the principle of racial discrimination to ground legal and moral assessments of conduct, up to and including ethnic cleansing and genocide. The Court and the dissenters did not offer characterizations of the case that would have marginalized the relevance of the Convention.[96]

The interrogation by the Court of the meaning to be attributed to Article 22 in *Georgia v Russian Federation* is notable for its array of interpretative approaches towards international instruments, including human rights instruments, and the varied canons of interpretation invoked by majorities and minorities, often to contradictory effect. The broadest approach, subsuming and transcending the Vienna Convention on the Law of Treaties (VCLT), is taken by Judge Cançado Trindade, who integrates his specific

[94] 'It is inconceivable that there were any international lawyers who would have characterized the dispute as one that was principally concerned with violations of the provisions under CERD . . . the issue of racial discrimination was only a marginal aspect of a much larger dispute in another area of international law . . . carefully re-characterized for the purpose of giving the Court jurisdiction.' Okowa, *Georgia/Russia Dispute*, 755.

[95] In expressing reservations regarding the conduct of the parties in the case, Okowa argues, *ibid.*, 756, that 'even where the provisions invoked on the face of it provide the Court with jurisdiction, it should be prepared to decline an application by appealing to considerations of propriety'.

[96] Okowa, *Georgia/Russia Dispute*, 757, is critical of this stance, observing that the Court and the dissenters 'were not prepared to address the key issue that the centrality of this dispute had very little to do with racial discrimination: it was an incidental question'.

comments into larger perspectives on the interpretation of human rights instruments, and on the nature and significance of the structures of international law. On this approach, the key question is the realization of justice under the historically important Convention on the Elimination of All Forms of Racial Discrimination through accounting for its intrinsic nature. From this perspective, the interpretation of the Convention is necessarily victim-oriented, a dimension he finds absent from the Court's reasoning. In the language of the VCLT, the key interpretative move is therefore the instrumentalization of the object and purpose of the Convention, a consideration that applies to procedure as well as substance. The strictness of the Court with regard to access did not in his view take sufficient account of the Convention in its context as a living human rights instrument.

The approach adumbrated by Judge Trindade has significant commonalities with the overall practice of CERD. With exceptions principally related to Article 4, the Committee's concluding observations on State reports, in the interests of furthering the objectives of the Convention, generally transcend a narrow textual literalism—the nature of the instrument determines the hermeneutic approach, and the plight of oppressed populations is the preponderant concern. The concept of the 'living instrument' is another point of convergence between Judge Trindade and the Committee. If *Georgia v Russian Federation* demonstrates anything regarding the meaning of the Convention, it is that text and *travaux* signpost interpretative directions that are unlikely to be fully determinative, especially in a text assembled rapidly under the discipline of structured negotiation and of time. The teleology of the instrument—its goals, objectives, raison d'être, and placement in the pantheon of human rights—assists further in filling out the interpretative frame, even if the task is always unfinished. Whether by the ICJ or the Committee, meaning is ultimately assigned through decisions by the bodies mandated to take them, the validity of which are constantly tested for their logic, coherence, consistency, professionalism, and by diplomatic reaction. Faithfulness to the spirit of the text also makes its own primordial claims.

THORNBERRY

20. The Convention on the Elimination of All Forms of Racial Discrimination

A Summary Reflection

A. General

On 26 November 2015, the Committee on the Elimination of Racial Discrimination hosted a commemoration of the fiftieth anniversary of the Convention, one of many such events likely to mark the passage of time.[1] Sessions were held on lessons learned and good practices, and on current challenges and ways forward. Invited panellists made their presentations, and engaged in summary dialogue with States parties and other stakeholders. Participants signalled their support for the principles of the Convention and the work of the Committee. The event, as the session titles suggest, looked back on the history of the Convention—and at the forty-five years of the operation of the Committee—attempting also to understand the challenges emanating from the early twenty-first-century environment as the principal guide to future developments. The Convention transmits and further defines the humanitarian message of the UN Charter and the UN Declaration of Human Rights (UDHR) and stands secure in the firmament of UN human rights instruments. The principles of the Convention are widely accepted as representing conduct prohibited by customary international law and even, at least in gross or systematic forms, *jus cogens*.[2]

[1] See 'Celebrating the 50th Anniversary of CERD': <http://www2.ohchr.org/english/> (November/December 2015).

[2] See Opinion of Judge Tanaka, *South-West Africa cases*, ICJ Rep 1966, pp. 3, 293: 'the norm of non-discrimination or non-separation on the basis of race has become a rule of customary international law'. The treatment of racial discrimination throughout the canon of human rights in the age of the UN Charter and the UDHR, including Article 55 and 56 of the Charter, Articles 2 and 7 of the UDHR, and the placement of the prohibition in the Covenants on Human Rights is treated as cementing the claim. According to the Restatement of Foreign Relations Law of the United States, a State violates international law when 'as a matter of policy, it practices, encourages, or condones any of the following . . . (f) systematic racial discrimination': *I Restatement*, para. 702 (1987). For academic support for the claim that racial discrimination—and not only systematic racial discrimination—is prohibited under customary international law, see W.A. McKean, *Equality and Discrimination under International Law* (Clarendon Press, 1983), Chapters XIV and XV; for Meron, 'respect for and observance of human rights and fundamental freedoms for all, without distinction as to race' is 'by now accepted into the corpus of customary international law': T. Meron, 'The Meaning and Reach of the International Convention on the Elimination of All Forms of Racial Discrimination', *AJIL* 79 (1985), 283–318, 283; E. Schwelb, 'The International Court of Justice and the Human Rights Clauses of the Charter', *AJIL* 66 (1971), 337–51, 351; P. Thornberry, *International Law and the Rights of Minorities* (Clarendon Press, 1991), Chapters 35–7 [henceforth *Rights of Minorities*]. With regard to *jus cogens*—peremptory norms of general international law under Articles 53 and 64 of the VCLT—the International Law Commission lists the prohibition of racial discrimination and apartheid as among the most frequently cited candidates for *jus cogens* status: *ILC Report of the Study group on the Fragmentation of International Law*, A/CN.4/L.682 (2006), para. 374; Brownlie argues that the 'least controversial examples' of *jus cogens* were provided by the prohibition on genocide, and discrimination based on race, religion, and sex: I. Brownlie, *Principles of Public International Law* (4th edn, Oxford University Press, 1990), p. 513; see also McKean, *Equality and Non-Discrimination*, p. 283, for a critique, see Thornberry, *Rights of Minorities*, pp. 326–8. In the estimation of the Committee on the Elimination of Racial Discrimination, the prohibition of racial discrimination 'is a peremptory norm of international law from which no derogation is permitted': Statement on Racial Discrimination and Measures

Beyond the general statements condemning racial discrimination and supporting the work of the Committee on the Elimination of Racial Discrimination (CERD), the Convention was described by more than one participant as a living instrument,[3] an appreciation endorsed in the practice of the Committee. The biological tenor of 'living instrument' suggests an organism making responsive adaptations to changes in the ecosystem in which it operates and contributing to such changes. As has been intimated at many points in the present study, the environment of the 1960s differs in key respects from the present, while the Convention remains as it was, unamended.[4] The result has been an evolution in the interpretation and application of the text by the Committee through taking positions that have, for the most part, have not elicited reactions from States parties. 'Convergence' between the opinions of the Committee and States parties is not, however, a given, but rather, in light of the limited 'powers' of the Committee, a desideratum achievable only through ongoing, persistent, and patient dialogue.[5] The content and form of the State-Committee dialogues have moved through a series of phases, not sharply defined, the results of which are analysed in earlier chapters and summarily recalled here.

B. The Adoption of the Convention

Following the adoption of the Convention, the air was filled with talk of landmarks and resounding victories, of 'hymns of reconciliation',[6] but also with cautious assessments. The stirring remarks of Verret, the representative of Haiti, quoted in Chapter 2, included a less stirring reference to the fledgling Convention as only 'reasonably reassuring'.[7] Delivering a peroration that ranged from Magna Carta through the human rights documents of the French and American revolutions to the Universal Declaration of

to Combat Terrorism, A/57/18, pp. 106–7, para. 4. See also *Barcelona Traction, Light and Power Company (Belgium v Spain)* ICJ Rep 1970, 3, which referred to obligations *erga omnes* in contemporary international law, including protection from slavery and racial discrimination'. For a general treatment, see E. de Wet, 'Jus Cogens and Obligations Erga Omnes', in D. Shelton (ed.), *The Oxford Handbook of International Human Rights Law* (Oxford University Press, 2015), pp. 541–61; A. Bianchi, 'Human Rights and the Magic of Jus Cogens', *EJIL* 19 (2008), 491–508.

[3] *Hagan v Australia*, CERD/C/62/D/26/2002 (2003), para. 7.3; for further comment, see Chapter 5; also G. Letsas, 'The ECHR as a Living Instrument: Its Meaning and its Legitimacy': <http://papers.ssrn.com/sol3/papers.cfm?abstract_id=2021836> (2012).

[4] See in particular, Chapters 3, 5, and 10. The Ad Hoc Committee on the Elaboration of Complementary Standards was established in 2006 to advance the implementation of the Durban Declaration and Programme of Action, with a mandate to 'elaborate, as a matter of priority and necessity, complementary standards in the form of either a convention or additional protocol(s) to the Convention on the Elimination of All Forms of Racial Discrimination': Human Rights Council decision 3/103, 8 December 2006. No additional protocols or other comparable texts have emerged, despite a wealth of discussion on issues regarding race, religion, xenophobia, etc, see A/HRC/AC.1/2/2, 26 August 2009, prepared by the Chairperson-Rapporteur of the Ad Hoc Committee, for a summary of submissions received; a succinct account of the work referred to here is included in S. Berry, 'Bringing Muslim Minorities within the International Convention on the Elimination of All Forms of Racial Discrimination—Square Peg in a Round Hole?', *Human Rights Law Review* 11 (2011), 433–50, 436–9.

[5] For challenges from States parties with regard to, eg, the Committee's interpretation of the criterion of 'descent', see Chapter 6; the maintenance of reservations to key norms of the Convention—such as Article 4—is a further example of 'non-convergence', see Chapter 18; the Committee constantly urges narrowing or withdrawal of such reservations.

[6] Verret, the representative of Haiti: A/PV/1406, paras 79–87.

[7] Verret, *ibid.*

Human Rights, Lamptey, the representative of Ghana, expressed a mixture of disillusion and satisfaction with the emergence of the Convention, stating that many delegates had hoped for better 'but realism dictated that we take an infant step', adding that it 'was Santayana who remarked that he who does not know the past is doomed to repeat it. In taking this first step in providing the nations of the world with a multilateral treaty... capable of enforcement, we have demonstrated our capacity not to forget.'[8] That delegates should express a great variety of sentiments, with some hesitating to confine themselves to merely optimistic conclusions regarding the instrument adopted and its future prospects, is not altogether surprising. The Convention emerged in the midst of a conflicted process of decolonization. Sensitivities about newly won sovereignties were at their sharpest, while peoples were still struggling to gain their freedom. By the mid-1960s, the full effects of General Assembly resolution1514 (XV) had still not become fully apparent,[9] and apartheid appeared solid and embedded. The Convention was treated by some delegates as a protraction of decolonization and anti-apartheid struggles, by others as a protraction of the Cold War.[10]

The anti-colonial stance of many drafting contributions is notable, becoming more pronounced as the drafting moved from the body of experts in the Sub-Commission on Prevention of Discrimination and Protection of Minorities to the political bodies of the United Nations—the Human Rights Commission and (principally) the Third Committee of the General Assembly, as well as the Plenary of the Assembly. The anti-colonial positions centred on the principle of self-determination, the unity of newly independent States and colonial territories, and the intrinsic connection between racial discrimination, colonialism, and apartheid.[11] The disconnect between the focus on 'externalities' such as the principle of self-determination,[12] and the development of 'introvert' norms on the treatment of ethnic and racial groups, was resolved for many delegates by imagining that racial discrimination occurred only or primarily in (Western) colonial systems, and under apartheid.[13]

Any such 'resolution' of tensions sits uneasily with the language of the Convention. The definition of discrimination in Article 1 and the import of the substantive articles of the

[8] *ibid.*, paras 93 and 94.

[9] The United Nations had 122 members in 1965, compared to its current (2015) membership of 193; for a chronology of the growth of membership and the 'surges' occasioned by the decolonization of Western Empires, the ending of the USSR and Yugoslavia, see the listing at: <http://www.un.org/en/members/growth.shtml>; see also, *inter alia*, General Assembly resolution 2105 (XX) of 20 December, 1965, *The Implementation of the Declaration on the Granting of Independence to Colonial Countries and Peoples*, adopted on the day before the adoption of the Convention on the Elimination of All Forms of Racial Discrimination.

[10] See Chapters 3, 5, and 11 in particular.

[11] See Chapter 5 on the Convention's Title and Preamble.

[12] The paradigm case of self-determination in the mid-1960s was the achievement of independence from the yoke of the colonial powers, as expressed the 'Colonial Declaration', General Assembly 1514 (XV) of 1960: see discussions in Chapters 5 and 13. For a classic treatment, see A. Cassese, *Self-Determination of Peoples: A Legal Reappraisal* (Cambridge University Press, 1995); also N. Ghanea and A. Xanthaki (eds), *Minorities, Peoples and Self-Determination: Essays in Honour of Patrick Thornberry* (Martinus Nijhoff, 2005); C. Tomuschat (ed.), *Modern Law of Self-Determination* (Martinus Nijhoff, 1993). Concepts of 'internal' self-determination were at most *in statu nascendi*; self-determination of indigenous peoples was a very distant prospect: ILO Convention 107 of 1957 on the Protection and Integration of Indigenous and Other Tribal and Semi-Tribal Populations in Independent Countries did not envisage self-determination for such 'populations', nor it may be added, does the later Convention 169 on Indigenous and Tribal Peoples, which does not address the matter, but leaves it to the wider UN framework. For CERD's stance on self-determination, see Chapters 5 and 13 in particular.

[13] Or on account of segregation practices in the US.

Convention present an unrestricted prospectus in political terms. The rhetoric of some of those who participated in drafting the Convention, suggesting political or geographical limitations on its scope, did not match the reality of what they had agreed. The confident assertions of limitations did not lead to the eclipse of alternative drafting inputs that emphasized the potential ubiquity of racial discrimination, while the inclusion of a specific reference to apartheid and the exclusion of an equivalent on anti-Semitism did not prospectively confine the Convention to a unidirectional anti-colonial path. The drafting of an article on apartheid—then a contemporary State policy—was much to be expected, while anti-Semitism is clearly within the boundaries of racial discrimination, of which it remains a paradigmatic example,[14] a 'light sleeper', easily awoken and aroused into action.[15]

C. External Developments

Any purported identification of racial discrimination with specific political systems did not survive serious examination by the Committee, and fractured over the life of the Convention, which has, in the succeeding half-century, been witness to geopolitical changes and game-changing mutations in the framework of human rights. Developments in the overall rights matrix include the emergence of the Covenants on Human Rights, of a sister instrument to the International Convention on the Elimination of All Forms of Racial Discrimination (ICERD) in the Convention on the Elimination of All Forms of Discrimination against Women (CEDAW), and a raft of UN 'core' treaties, along with key regional human rights developments, notably those in Africa, the Americas, the Arab world—the Americas and Europe having paved the way earlier with the American Declaration on the Rights and Duties of Man, and the European Convention on Human Rights (ECHR). The holding of world conferences on human rights and on racial discrimination and related forms of intolerance has also affected the work of the Committee, with current concluding observations of CERD consistently rehearsing the mantra of the indivisibility and interdependence of human rights, and recommending States parties to give effect to the Durban Declaration and Programme of Action of 2001 and the outcome document of the Durban Review Conference in 2009.[16] The work of

[14] Concluding observations of the Committee continue to evoke the spectre of anti-Semitism: on Belgium, CERD/C/BEL/CO/16-19, para. 10; Moldova, CERD/C/MDA/CO/8-9, para. 10; Monaco, CERD/C/MCO/CO/6, para.10; Poland, CERD/C/POL/CO/19, para 7, and CERD/C/POL/CO/20-21, para. 14. The last observation, which recalled 'the tragic experience of the Jewish community in Poland' and 'its virtual extermination' in the period of the Second World War was the subject of a vigorous rebuttal by Poland, underlining that this 'was neither orchestrated nor executed by the Polish authorities', that 'between 1939 and 1945 Poland was occupied by the foreign powers, namely Nazi Germany and Soviet Union': A/69/18, Annex VII B. See also concluding observations on Slovakia, CERD/C/SVK/CO/6-8, para 12; Yemen, CERD/VC/YEM/CO/17-18, para. 16; see also GR 35, para. 6, includes hate speech of an anti-semitic and Islamophobic nature under the rubric of racist hate speech.

[15] *A Very Light Sleeper: The Persistence and Dangers of Anti-Semitism* (Runnymede Trust, 1994), available at: <http://www.runnymedetrust.org/uploads/publications/pdfs/AVeryLightSleeper-1994.PDF>; the phrase 'a light sleeper' appears in C.C. O'Brien, *The Siege: The Saga of Israel and Anti-Semitism* (Faber and Faber, 1986).

[16] The Committee's endorsement of the Durban process, recalled through many concluding observations and the inclusion of a chapter on Durban and Durban Review 'follow-up' in annual reports to the General Assembly, finds initial expression in GR 28 on the Follow-up to the World Conference against Racism, Racial Discrimination, Xenophobia and Related Intolerance, A/57/18, ch. XI, E; see also GR 33, *Follow-up to the Durban Review Conference*, A/64/18, Annex VIII; *Statement on the Commemoration of the Tenth Anniversary of the Adoption of the Durban Declaration and Programme of Action*, A/66/18, ch. X.

the Committee is increasingly integrated with UN and regional human rights mechanisms and procedures. In the reporting and early warning procedures in particular, members of the Committee are systematically informed of developments in related human rights bodies and mechanisms, including the universal periodic review (UPR), which shed light on the reports of States parties.[17]

The decolonization phase gradually petered out with the collapse of the Western empires. Apartheid took longer to dismantle, and eventually South Africa became a 'normal' member of the family of the United Nations and a State party to the Convention—its first report was examined by the Committee in 2006.[18] The ending of the Soviet Union and the dissolution of Yugoslavia were further key 'external' events associated with the inauguration of a phase of 'identity politics', associated with the emergence of group-based instruments or individual provisions therein, validating the rights of minorities and indigenous peoples, including Article 27 of the International Covenant on Civil and Political Rights (ICCPR) and Article 30 of the Convention on the Rights of the Child (CRC), International Labour Organization (ILO) Convention 169 of 1989, the United Nations Declaration on Minorities (UNDM) 1992, the UNDRIP 2007, as well as the Council of Europe's Framework Convention for the Protection of National Minorities (FCNM) in 1995, are among instruments the principles of which have helped to shape the application of the Convention.[19] The application of the Convention has also responded to developments in the field of migration through a multiplicity of concluding observations and general recommendations on non-citizens and refugees; the Committee is increasingly aware of human rights issues stemming from migration.

The passage of geopolitical events and the growth of complementary human rights standards continue to influence the application of the Convention. That events and standards impact on the interpretation of human rights conventions is not a truth confined to CERD. Human rights bodies characteristically borrow concepts that did not originate with their constituent instruments and build the insights they derive from the reception activity into their normative frame; bodies also export concepts into the broader stream of human rights. On the other hand, as noted particularly in Chapter 15, ICERD is a relatively porous instrument in its delineation of protected rights that does not, with a few exceptions, define its terms with great precision.[20] The structure of Article 5 best demonstrates the ICERD characteristic of being open-textured in that many of the rights it explicitly seeks to protect are normative sketches derived largely from the UDHR, compounded together without expressions of limits or provision for derogation and in practice receptive to the importation of unlisted rights. The construction of ICERD raises difficult questions regarding the employment of interpretative techniques and the assignment of boundaries to a human rights instrument conceived as a discrete entity; the development of 'intersectionalities' has the capacity to stretch the boundaries farther.

[17] See Chapter 6.

[18] CERD/C/461/Add.3; referred to in Chapter 10.

[19] See in particular, Chapters 6, 13, 14, and 15.

[20] The provisions of Articles 2 and 4 constitute something of an exception, and it may also be argued that the definition of racial discrimination in Article 1 is also relatively precise. The 'porosity' attaches principally to the listing of rights in Article 5, and the general provisions of Articles 6 and 7.

D. Emblematic Developments in the Life of the Convention

I. Approach to Interpretation

As Sinclair noted, there 'are few topics in international law which have given rise to such extensive doctrinal dispute as the topic of treaty interpretation',[21] a caution that applies equally or *a fortiori* to the interpretation of human rights treaties,[22] which 'presents itself to many as an insoluble Gordian knot'.[23] The basic scheme of interpretation of treaties in the Vienna Convention on the Law of Treaties (VCLT) is well known. Articles 31–33 of the VCLT combine analytical literalism, intention of the parties, and teleology in a synthesis that is commonly taken to represent customary international law.[24] The basic rule in Article 31(1) states that a treaty should be interpreted 'in good faith in accordance with the ordinary meaning to be given to their terms of the treaty in their context and in the light of its object and purpose'. 'Context' includes, *inter alia*, the preamble and annexes,[25] and the role of subsequent practice is also accounted for;[26] the *travaux* are deemed to have a supplementary role where other routes to a conclusion deliver only ambiguities or manifestly absurd or unreasonable conclusions.[27] There is also a significant body of opinion that stresses the special qualities of human rights interpretation in light of their protective, vertical, and sovereignty-challenging nature, and their moral dimension.[28] The wide use of abstract terms is another feature of human rights conventions. To these general qualities of human rights may be added the complex growth of 'categories' of rights, the increased gravity and pervasiveness of human rights discourse,[29] its strands integrated into networks of interdependence and indivisibility, capable of reaching down to the capillaries of society.[30] All of which reflections on the character, substance, and context in which human rights treaties operate, suggests that a one-size-fits-all approach to their interpretation is unlikely to assist the process of divining results or explaining them retrospectively.

[21] I. Sinclair, *The Vienna Convention on the Law of Treaties* (Manchester University Press, 1973), p. 69, who also, *ibid.*, quotes Julius Stone for the suggestion that interpretation is an exercise in ex post facto rationalization of a conclusion reached on other grounds or as a cover for judicial creativity: 'Fictional Elements in Treaty Interpretation', *Sydney Law Review* 1 (1955), 344–68.

[22] On interpretation of human rights treaties, see G. Letsas, *A Theory of Interpretation of the European Convention on Human Rights* (Oxford University Press, 2007); B. Schlütter, 'Aspects of Human Rights Interpretation by Treaty Bodies' [henceforth 'Aspects of Human Rights Interpretation'], in H. Keller and G. Ulfstein (eds), *UN Human Rights Treaty Bodies: Law and Legitimacy* (Cambridge University Press, 2012), pp. 261–319; J. Tobin, 'Seeking to Persuade: A Constructive Approach to Human Rights Treaty Interpretation', *Harvard Human Rights Journal* 23 (2010), 1–50.

[23] Schlütter, 'Aspects of Human Rights Interpretation', p. 263.

[24] See the brief summary of the principles of interpretation in general international law in M. Shaw, *International Law* (6th edn, Cambridge University Press, 2008), pp. 932–8.

[25] Article 31(2).

[26] Article 31(3) provides: 'There shall be taken into account, together with the context (a) any subsequent agreement between the parties regarding the interpretation of the treaty or the application of its provisions; (b) any subsequent practice in the application of the treaty which establishes the agreement of the parties regarding its interpretation; (c) any relevant rules of international law applicable in the relations between the parties.'

[27] Article 32.

[28] Schlütter, 'Aspects of Human Rights Interpretation', pp. 263–6.

[29] See in general S. Moyn, *The Last Utopia: Human Rights in History* (Harvard University Press, 2010).

[30] In the case of ICERD, generating concern with 'everyday discrimination': T. Makkonen, *Equal in Law, Unequal in Fact: Racial and Ethnic Discrimination and the Response Thereto in Europe* (Martinus Nijhoff Publishers, 2012) Chapter 8.

With regard to ICERD, while interpretation that takes the text at face value represents the first principle of interpretation, it may not carry the interpreter very far. ICERD was drafted swiftly, in part on the basis of political and diplomatic compromises in addition to expert input, and does not consistently exhibit the virtues of coherence and consistency throughout its text.[31] In order to read the convention in contemporary contexts, the whole 'race' vocabulary stands to be interrogated, explained, and put to work, together with broad signifiers such as 'discrimination', 'segregation', 'dignity', 'equality', 'public', and a lexicon of qualifiers such as 'nullify or impair', 'appropriate', 'effective',' adequate', etc. Analysis of a technical nature—etymology, syntax, parsing of terms, juxtaposing articles, paragraphs and sub-paragraphs—is undeniably important and necessary, even if it may not supply immediate answers to all questions: reason has short wings.[32] The Committee's approach was expressed in concise form in response to Israel's contention that its duties under the Convention did not extend to the Occupied Territories: 'The Committee recommends that the State party review its approach and interpret its obligations under the Convention in good faith, in accordance with the ordinary meaning to be given to its terms in their context, and in the light of its object and purpose.'[33] The broadest characterization of the interpretative approach employed by the Committee appears from General Recommendation (GR) 32 on special measures:

> The Convention . . . is a living instrument that must be interpreted and applied taking into account the circumstances of contemporary society. This approach makes it imperative to read its text in a context-sensitive manner. The context . . . includes, in addition to the full text of the Convention including its title, preamble and operative articles, the range of universal human rights standards . . . Context-sensitive interpretation also includes taking into account the particular circumstances of States parties without prejudice to the universal quality of the norms of the Convention. The nature of the Convention and the broad scope of the Convention's provisions imply that, while the conscientious application of Convention principles will produce variations in outcome among States parties, such variations must be fully justified in the light of the principles of the Convention.[34]

In terms of interpretative techniques, and so as not 'to elevate formalism over substance',[35] the Committee has arrived at distinctive stances weighted towards the aims and objectives of the Convention, utilizing the principle of effectiveness in the interpretation of treaties and an emphasis on evolving practice, together with markedly less emphasis on the *travaux préparatoires*,[36] a positional contrast with the importance given to the *travaux* by the ICJ in *Georgia v Russian Federation* to the interpretation of Article 22.[37]

ICERD stands as a key articulation of the meaning of human rights in the UN Charter, takes its place among the core international human rights conventions, and is a prime mover in the human rights system. Interpretative practice should not be understood as a

[31] See Chapters 5, 6, 13, and 16 in particular.

[32] From Dante, *Paradiso*, Canto II: 'poi dietro ai sensi, vedi che la ragione ha corte l'ali'; English translation by H.W. Longfellow, available online at: <https://en.wikisource.org/wiki/The_Divine_Comedy/Paradiso/Canto_II>.

[33] CERD/C/ISR/CO/13, para. 32.

[34] GR 32, para. 5.

[35] *L.R. v Slovakia*, CERD/C/66/D/31/2003 (2005), para. 10.7.

[36] References to the travaux make occasional appearances nonetheless: for example in GR 32 on special measures, para. 24; *P.S.N. v Denmark*, CERD/C/71/D/36/2006 (2007), para. 6.3, discussed in the present work under Article 4.

[37] Discussed in Chapter 19.

matter only of importation of concepts from 'outside', as if the Convention were simply parasitic on systemic developments elsewhere or a straight derivation therefrom. In light of the principle of the indivisibility and interdependence of human rights, practice under the Convention enlarges the understanding of the human rights addressed in its remit.[38]

II. Procedures

The developments in the procedures of the Committee, discussed principally in Chapter 4, have resulted in a remarkable broadening in the scope of its work. As noted, the ebb and flow of its procedures parallels changes in the external context of the Convention. While the decolonization procedure under Article 15 has for some time been treated as largely formulaic, and the inter-State procedure inoperative or dormant, the procedures under Article 9 have developed significantly to become the mainstay of the Convention, including the early warning and urgent action procedure. The last-named procedure also shows the influence of identity politics in that, over decades, the focus has shifted significantly towards the protection of specific groups of peoples in Convention practice, though events on the grand scale affecting whole nations continue to be addressed. Massive ethnic conflicts in Africa and the former Yugoslavia have provoked responses by the Committee through, *inter alia*, the issuance of statements and recommendations,[39] and the adoption of a declaration on the prevention of genocide.[40] Article 9 procedures enjoy a constantly increasing level of input from civil society, to which the Committee has steadily become more receptive since the caution of the Cold War era.

The optional communications procedure under Article 14, on the other hand, has not made the impact that might have been expected in terms of the number of States parties 'opting in', despite constant urging by the Committee. Residues of the reluctance shown in the drafting stages towards a supranational monitoring body with sharp edges may still inhibit the acceptance of the communications procedure. Perhaps especially for States in the vanguard of the decolonization movement, the fact that the procedure may lead to findings of violations of the Convention as opposed to the more dialogic approaches and expressions of concern under Article 9 is another possible factor in controlling its uptake, as is the existence of alternative 'judicialized' complaints procedures, both global and regional.[41] It remains to be seen whether the Article 14 procedure will gain greater momentum.[42]

[38] See Chapter 15.

[39] Examples include the 1999 Statement on Africa that subsumed earlier statements on Burundi, the DRC, Rwanda, and Sudan: A/54/18, ch. II; the report was notable for a raft of statements on crises including Decisions 1(54) on Yugoslavia; 3(54) on Rwanda; 4(54) and 3(55) on the DRC; 5(54) on Sudan, and 1(55) on Kosovo. Among other examples see Decision 1(62) on Côte D'Ivoire, A58/18, ch. II; Decision 2(66) on Darfur, A/60/18, ch. II; Decision 1(76) on Nigeria, A/65/18, ch. II, and 1(77) on Kyrgyzstan, *ibid.* See also Decision 1(85) on Iraq, A/70/18, ch. II.

[40] A/60/18, ch. XI.

[41] See S.M. García and B. Çali (eds), *The Legalization of International Law: Multidisciplinary Perspectives on Human Rights and Human Rights Law* (Routledge, 2006), R. Hirschl, 'The Judicialization of Mega-Politics and the Rise of Political Courts': <http://papers.ssrn.com/sol3/papers.cfm?abstract_id=1138008>; P. Sands, 'Developments in Geopolitics—The End(s) of Judicialization': <http://www.jus.uio.no/pluricourts/english/news-and-events/events/2015/esil-2015-en/video-and-streaming/final-lecture.html>.

[42] T. van Boven, 'CERD and Article 14: The Unfulfilled Promise', in G. Alfredsson, J. Grimheden, B. Ramcharan, and A. De Zayas, *International Human Rights Monitoring Mechanisms: Essays in Honour of Jakob Th. Möller* (Martinus Nijhoff Publishers, 2001), pp. 153–66.

III. Discrimination

As regards the concept of racial discrimination, the fundamental definitional statement in Article 1 of the Convention has undergone a distinctive practical evolution. The application of the non-discrimination standard has moved outwards from anti-colonial paradigms, from claims of 'no discrimination here' and approaches to negative equality, towards an understanding of the range of human rights to be protected from discrimination that accepts and recognizes the multi-ethnic and multicultural character of States.[43] The expansion of the modalities of discrimination—from the intention/effect coupling in Article 1 of the Convention, towards direct and indirect discrimination, and structural or institutional discrimination, etc—is a notable development.[44] Allied with the treatment of the Convention as an instrument that expresses 'positive' obligations not confined to 'special measures', the expansion of the modalities of anti-discrimination policy places heavy legislative and policy burdens on States parties, obligated to move in an increasingly interventionist direction. Critics have also pointed to the temptations of 'conceptual inflation' whereby differences in, for example, educational or employment attainments or outcomes are characteristically attributed to discrimination[45] (though not necessarily unfairly),[46] a temptation that may converge particularly on indirect and structural discrimination, where the facts of discrimination are disconnected from motivation.

On the other hand, the expanding palette of discrimination encourages the growth of proactive approaches by States parties to tackle racial discrimination with renewed vigour. The Committee's explorations and complex recommendations on the many modalities of discrimination motivate mindful reflection on the negative possibilities flowing from legal and institutional practices that were crafted with limited awareness of their discriminatory potential. As may be gathered from the analyses in Chapter 6, the Committee has not fully elaborated its understanding of the discrimination terminology currently employed, nor exhaustively refined the scope and limits of discrimination. Concepts of discrimination and equality have nonetheless been stretched and amplified in Committee practice, with the elimination of *de facto* discrimination and *de facto* equality in the enjoyment of human rights granted pride of place among the elevating goals of the Convention.

Discussions of discrimination characteristically focus on the use of comparators to measure advantage and disadvantage. Equally, analyses of discrimination by the Committee may function in the context of comparators applied or insinuated in practical contexts, notably through the communications procedure under Article 14. However, taking the Convention as a whole—the range of its procedures and the breadth of the substantive norms—the Committee is generally less concerned with comparative treatment of groups than with group oppression as such. When ethnic and other groups within the purview of the Convention groups are targeted, neglected, forcibly segregated, have

[43] See particularly Chapters 13 and 14. For a short commentary on the Committee's stance on multiculturalism, see P. Thornberry, 'Multiculturalism, Minority Rights, and the Committee on the Elimination of Racial Discrimination (CERD)', in D. Thurer and Z. Kędzia (eds), *Managing Diversity, Protection of Minorities in International Law* (Schulthess, 2009), pp. 79–94.

[44] See Chapter 6.

[45] M. Bell, *Racism and Equality in the European Union* (Oxford University Press, 2008), p. 12, citing R. Miles and M. Brown, *Racism* (2nd edn, Routledge, 2003), p. 58.

[46] Lack of proportional representation of ethnic groups in government, or the police, or employment, may be a sign that something is wrong and needs investigating: S. Fredman, *Discrimination Law* (2nd edn, Oxford University Press, 2011), p. 181.

their languages and cultures suppressed, their economies marginalized, their defenders imprisoned or killed, their lands and waters despoiled, their place in the nation 'erased' to the point of physical displacement or even elimination, the notion of comparison adds little or nothing to the analysis of their plight: equality concerns equality in the enjoyment of rights, not equality in deprivation. Much of Convention practice is about 'discrimination' in this profound, larger sense. This is discrimination as group-directed oppression or violence, which takes cases over and beyond filigreed distinctions between one individual or group and another.[47] While even 'racial discrimination' may be an inadequate term to capture the grosser violations of human rights, the targeting of groups noted in CERD practice is properly brought under the rubric of racial discrimination as a necessary baseline description. Stripping away racial contexts and reading oppressive conduct as a violation of human rights *simpliciter* is to misread the character of the activity and misread the necessary remedies.[48] Racial discrimination in the Convention is directed at individuals on account of their actual or purported membership of ethnic and other groups and is also directed at groups as such; it encompasses both large-scale oppression and smaller scale disadvantage, and all the gradations in between.

IV. Grounds of Discrimination

Regarding the grounds of discrimination, it is notable that the concept of 'race', broadly accepted by many among the drafters of the Convention and deeply embedded in the Convention as a whole, is under challenge from (some) States parties, while the Committee's application of the ground of 'descent' is resisted strongly by other States,[49] particularly India and Japan. The ground of 'national origin', on the other hand, heavily contested in the drafting, is more generally accepted as a partner concept to ethnic origin. The listing of national and ethnic origin among the grounds has, despite the ambiguities attaching to 'national', facilitated the shift in focus from race and colour to ethnicity and ethnic minorities—Vandenhole observes that CERD treats discrimination against minorities as a specific theme, 'regardless of which prohibited grounds are involved'.[50] The substantive Convention basis for this ethnicization of discrimination is extensive: 'ethnic origin' is referred to in the preamble and Articles 1, 4, and 5, while Article 7 refers to 'ethnical groups', to which it may be recalled that the dominant application of 'national origin' in the Convention relates to ethnicity rather than citizenship. In light of the practical emphasis on self-identification, the focus on ethnicity need not imply a reification of cultures and works against cultural determinism—where persons are assigned to

[47] 'The oppression of violence consists not only in direct victimization, but in the daily knowledge shared by all members of oppressed groups that they are liable to violation, solely on account of their group identity': I.M. Young, *Justice and the Politics of Difference* (Princeton University Press, 1990), Chapter 2 'Five Faces of Oppression', p. 62.

[48] The European Court of Human Rights (ECHR) has sometimes shown reluctance to engage the issue of discrimination through invoking Article 14 of the ECHR, preferring to base its judgments on individual substantive norms: for a short critique, see J. Goldston, 'The Struggle for Roma Rights: Arguments that have Worked', *Human Rights Quarterly* 32/2 (2010), 311–25, at 321–5. The analysis in the present chapter is not designed to endorse such an approach, but merely to highlight that race-based 'discrimination' functions up to the level of gross violations of human rights, even if other legal terminology also contributes to shaping the legal categorization of discriminatory conduct.

[49] See discussion in Chapter 6.

[50] W. Vandenhole, *Non-Discrimination and Equality in the View of the UN Human Rights Treaty Bodies* (Intersentia, 2005), p. 95.

membership of an ethnic group irrespective of their consent.[51] As noted earlier,[52] translated into the vocabulary of racism, ICERD is significantly and even predominantly concerned with what may be termed 'cultural' or 'difference' racism: 'racial discrimination' subsumes and transcends discrimination based on 'race'.[53]

The serious engagement by the Committee with the grounds of discrimination argues against treating the Convention into a straightforward equality instrument, that is, if the conceptual difference between the two ideal types is taken to mean that, while an anti-discrimination paradigm implies that what is not prohibited is allowed, an equality text mandates equality subject to exceptions. The continuing attention paid to the grounds of discrimination weighs against describing ICERD simply as an equality-based text, even as the grounds lose some of their purchase in cases of indirect, structural, or institutional discrimination, when group-based discrimination is alluded to without specification of any ground, and the scope of the equality norms expressed in the Convention is constantly expanded. On the other hand, any assumption that non-discrimination is associated with formal equality and an equality text with positive action do not work well in the case of ICERD: the demand for positive action runs through the text as a whole and is expressed in the settled practice of the Committee.

V. Intersectionality Challenged

As observed in earlier chapters, the understanding of the grounds of discrimination has been enlarged through the use of the conceptual device of 'intersectionality'.[54] The concept is forcefully expressed in relation to gender, less so in regard to religion, while other potential identity 'intersections' have been observed but hardly developed. In the case of religion, apart from questioning the appropriateness of the intersection metaphor in cases where 'religion' and 'ethnicity' are largely coterminous,[55] the 'split' at the United

[51] In this last respect, CERD aligns the Convention with the principle of non-compulsion expressed in Article 3(2) of the UNDM: 'No disadvantage shall result for any person belonging to a minority as the consequence of the exercise or non-exercise of the rights set forth in the present Declaration', commentary by P. Thornberry, 'The UN Declaration on the Rights of Persons Belonging to National or Ethnic, Religious and Linguistic Minorities: Background, Analysis, Observations, and an Update', in A. Rosas and A. Phillips (eds), *Universal Minority Rights* (Abo Akademi, 1995), pp. 13–76; and the Council of Europe's Framework Convention on the Protection of National Minorities: 'Every person belonging to a national minority shall have the right freely to choose to be treated or not to be treated as such and no disadvantage shall result from this choice or from the exercise of the rights which are connected to that choice', commentary by H.-J. Heintze, in M. Weller (ed.), *The Rights of Minorities in Europe, A Commentary on the European Framework Convention for the Protection of National Minorities* (Oxford University Press, 2005), pp. 107–37.

[52] Chapter 5.

[53] 'While biological racism in the antipathy, exclusion and unequal treatment of people on the basis of their physical appearance or other imputed physical differences . . . cultural racism builds on biological racism a further discourse which evokes cultural differences from and alleged . . . "civilized" norm to vilify, maginalize or demand cultural assimilation': T. Modood, '"Difference": Cultural Racism and Anti-Racism', in B. Boxill (ed.), *Race and Racism* (Oxford University Press, 2001), pp. 238–56, p. 239. Also E. Balibar, 'Is there a Neo-Racism?', in E. Balibar and I. Wallerstein, *Race, Nation, Class: Ambiguous Identities* (Verso, 1991), 17–28; J. Blaut, 'The Theory of Cultural Racism', *Antipode* 23 (1992), 289–99; R. Miles and M. Brown, Racism; A. Giddens and P. Sutton, *Sociology* (7th edn, Polity Press, 2013), Chapter 16, 'Race, Ethnicity and Migration'. Bell comments that one of 'the limitations in the culturalist vision of racism is its emphasis on individual prejudice as a cause of racism . . . a behavioural aberration which should fade away with the passage of time': Bell, *Racism and Equality in the European Union*, pp. 10–11. This is not the meaning intended here, bearing in mind the attention paid by CERD to 'structural' and other manifestations of racism and racial discrimination: see Chapter 6; see also Chapter 5.

[54] See particularly Chapters 6 and 13.

[55] See Chapter 13.

Nations between work on religious discrimination and work on race remains influential.[56] While there is evidence of more liberal CERD practice in course of development through the recognition of hybrid terms such as 'ethno-religious' in GR 35 and elsewhere, practice on the race/religion intersection reflects caution with regard to the boundaries of the Convention and the mandate of the Committee. With regard to intersectionality, a fundamental challenge to the *modus operandi* of the Committee with respect to intersectionality emerges from comment by the Holy See. In unequivocal terms, the Holy See reported its views on treaty interpretation to the Committee in an 'originalist' spirit, concentrating on understandings of the Convention at the time of drafting, signalling that

> Committee proposals that add new terminology or create new obligations depart from the original spirit of the CERD and would constitute an unforeseen and fundamental change of circumstances, which in turn, would have the effect of 'radically' transforming the extent of the Holy See's obligations still to be performed under the treaty within the meaning of Article 62 (1)(b), VCLT... the Holy See would, as a result, be permitted to invoke such a fundamental change of circumstances as a ground for 'terminating or withdrawing' from the treaty or... 'suspending the operation of the same'.[57]

At first glance, the interpretation of the Convention by the Holy See appears to depart fundamentally from the evolutionary approach taken by the Committee, devoted to making the Convention an effective presence in light of the ambitious goals that characterize the title and preamble. Where the State party sees 'radical change of circumstances', the Committee sees necessary adaptation in response to situations that did not present themselves to the drafters.[58] The import of the statement by the Holy See is,

[56] See Chapter 3 for the divergence in UN work, see, among other commentaries, N. Lerner, 'Freedom of Expression and Advocacy of Group Hatred: Incitement to Hate Crimes and Religious Hatred', *Religion and Human Rights* 5 (2010), 137–45.

[57] CERD/C/VAT/16-23, para. 3. Article 62(1) of the VCLT provides that 'a fundamental change of circumstances which has occurred with regard to those existing at the time of the conclusion of a treaty, and which was not foreseen by the parties, may not be invoked as a ground for terminating or withdrawing from the treaty unless: (a) the existence of those circumstances constituted an essential basis of the consent of the parties to be bound by the treaty . . . and (b) the effect of the change is radically to transform the extent of obligations still to be performed'. The ICJ stated that for change of circumstances to be invoked, it should 'have resulted in a radical transformation of the extent of the obligations to be performed' [and] 'must have increased the burden of the obligations to be executed to the extent of rendering the performance essentially different from that originally undertaken': *Fisheries Jurisdiction* (United Kingdom v Iceland), ICJ Rep 4 [1973], para. 43. Article 65 VCLT sets out procedural requirements for the application of the doctrine. Commenting on Article 65, Fitzmaurice observes that it signals a shift from 'subjective auto-interpretation to the possibility of a more objective legal ruling': M. Fitzmaurice, 'Exceptional Circumstances and Treaty Commitments', in D. Hollis (ed.), *The Oxford Guide to Treaties* (Oxford University Press, 2012), pp. 605–33, p. 623.

[58] In the sphere of human rights, the most outstanding example of the use of 'radical change of circumstances' was applied to the post-First World War engagements on the treatment of minorities by the *Study of the Legal Validity of the Undertakings Concerning Minorities*, UN Doc E/CN.4/367, undertaken by the UN Secretariat in 1950, which concluded that between 1939 and 1947 circumstances as a whole changed to such an extent that, generally speaking, the system should be considered as having ceased to exist; the view was based not on ordinary causes of extinction such as implicit abrogation or population transfers and movements, but in effect on the *clausula rebus sic stantibus*: fundamental change of circumstances. For comment on the Study, see P. Thornberry, *International Law and the Rights of Minorities* (Clarendon Press, 1991) Chapters 4 and 9; N. Feinberg, 'The Legal Validity of the Undertakings regarding Minorities and the *Clausula Rebus Sic Stantibus*, *Studies in Law, Scripta Hierosolymitana* 5 (1958), 95–131; S. Rosenne, '*Rebus Sic Stantibus* and the Minority Treaties: An Afterword', *Israel Yearbook of Human Rights* 12 (1982), 330–3. Even in the face of the momentous changes indicated in the study, the use of the concept of *Rebus Sic Stantibus* by the UN Secretariat was strongly criticized by the authors cited above. In the present case, the position of the Holy See is difficult to reconcile with the fact that CERD issues 'proposals of a non-binding nature' under Article 9(2), 'which could not create new obligations': remarks by CERD member Vázquez, CERD/C/SR.2394, para. 10; also comments

however, perhaps narrower in that it relates primarily to the insertion of gender intersectionality into the discourse of the Committee, rather than 'intersectionality' in general;[59] this appears to be the only 'innovation' specifically at issue, a position that somewhat undercuts the generality of the objections. The Holy See has not attached a reservation to ICERD.[60]

The contemporary stress on intersectionality also prompts questions on the limits of the individual human rights instruments in addressing the complexities of personal and group identity. The application of the grounds of discrimination tends, on one perspective, towards a fragmentation of identity into 'essentialized' categories. International human rights law, however, places considerable stress on self-definition to mitigate an assumed 'essentialization' and avoid cultural determinism. While access to categories of rights may assist in the 'construction' of specific identifications, the categories have also served to empower oppressed and neglected groups by focusing attention on their particular grievances through culture-sensitive perspectives. In the case of CERD and other human rights bodies, the characteristics alluded to in the list of grounds have been transmuted in practice into a spectrum of identifiable groups, uncovering the human faces of abstract 'victims';[61] thus the 'universal' becomes particularized.

VI. The Non-Citizen 'Gap'

Integrated into the general understanding of discrimination in the Convention, the ungenerous Article 1(2) on citizens and non-citizens has, on the basis of assertive interpretation by the Committee, been largely deprived of a determining role in limiting the enjoyment of equality and freedom from discrimination to the citizenry of States parties. Constitutions and other legal provisions that sharply distinguish the human rights of citizens from those of non-citizens in any but the narrowest political spheres are treated as matters of concern by the Committee, and rectification of the legal situation under scrutiny will inevitably be recommended.[62] While the need expressed during the drafting of the Convention by the representatives of new sovereignties to build up loyal, citizen-based bureaucratic structures may have abated over time,[63] citizen/non-citizen distinctions in public service continue to resonate in State practice, notably along with distinctions in the fields of citizenship and employment—two areas which have significant gender dimensions. The citizen/non-citizen gap in human rights protection has been appreciably narrowed but

by members Bossuyt, Kemal, and Diaconu, *ibid.*, paras 34, 37, and 40; the points are adverted to in the concluding observations of the Committee, CERD/C/VAT/CO/16-23, paras 6 and 7.

[59] CERD/C/VAT/16-23, para. 5(a). In discussions with the Committee, the Holy See explained that it 'was less concerned about the idea of intersectionality per se than it was about the possibility that an admission of that concept could pave the way for . . . other concepts that it would find unacceptable': CERD/C/SR/2395, para. 5. With regard to intersectionality between race and religion, the view of the Holy See was that this 'should probably be addressed on a case-by-case basis so that religion would become a force for . . . equality': CERD/C/SR.2395, para. 40.

[60] The Holy See 'was concerned that enlarging the scope of the Convention could interfere with . . . work under other international human rights instruments or entail the addition of substantive obligations . . . that had not been accepted by States parties': CERD/C/SR.2395, para. 5. The delegation placed considerable emphasis on one 'intersection': that between racism and poverty.

[61] See Chapter 15.

[62] See particularly Chapters 7 and 13.

[63] See Chapters 3, 6, 7, and 13.

not closed. If current migration crises are taken as a guide to likely future developments, Committee concern with migration and non-citizens appears destined to increase in the foreseeable future.[64]

VII. On Legal Infrastructures

The Committee's insistence on the potential ubiquity of racial discrimination has meant that all reporting States are, without exception, expected to have the necessary legislation and policy structures in place. The Committee has recalled the need for legislation against racial discrimination to be as specific and comprehensive as possible throughout the branches of law, criminal, civil, and administrative law, with the burden of proof in civil cases adjusted to advance the possibility of taking claims to a successful conclusion.[65] As noted principally in connection with Articles 2 and 6, the Committee sets forth requirements on the necessary infrastructures to support the application of the primary rules, including rules on 'reparation or satisfaction', in the various legislative branches.[66]

Further, the absence of cases on racial discrimination is not treated as evidence of an enviable situation in the State party concerned but rather as evidence of a defective implementation of the necessary rules, whether because of lack of confidence in the judiciary, or inadequate publicity accorded to the cases, or limited public awareness of discrimination and how to counter it. Adjustments to legislation are persistently called for by the Committee, and in this respect, it would appear that intentional or direct discriminatory legislation on the part of the State is much rarer than at the time of drafting.[67] The focus of discriminatory activity across the span of States is therefore as likely to concern responsibility for the acts of individuals as that for the actions of organs of State. In the case of applications of Article 2, the concentration on private bodies is a notable feature of practice, including private bodies acting extraterritorially.[68] The most dramatic change of focus from public to private (the 'privatization' of racial discrimination) relates to Article 3, for which, as GR 19 makes clear, State-sponsored segregation is treated as less of a contemporary challenge than segregation resulting from the acts of private bodies.[69] At the same time, allegations of 'apartheid'—the most egregious form of State-directed segregation—are treated with reserve by the Committee.[70]

VIII. On Criminal Law

In the legislative and judicial structures promoted by the Committee, it occasionally appears as if the treatment of racial discrimination as a matter of criminal law represented a *summum bonum* in the normative legal spectrum. The preference for the use of criminal law as the ideal correctional instrument in the field of racial discrimination reached a kind

[64] Committee on the Elimination of Racial Discrimination, *Statement on Current Migrant Crises*, A/70/18, Chapter II.

[65] See Chapters 8 and 16.

[66] Chapter 16.

[67] A change doubtless stimulated by the continual pressing of States parties by the Committee on the basic question of anti-discrimination legislation, as well as the efforts of the raft of human rights bodies addressing 'race' as a ground of discrimination within their constituent instruments.

[68] Chapters 8 and 10.

[69] Discussed in Chapter 10; see also Chapter 5.

[70] See Chapter 10.

of apogee in the Committee's treatment of Article 4, as represented in GR 15.[71] The declaration of offences 'punishable by law' required by the article has been interpreted almost exclusively as signifying the declaration (creation) of criminal offences, to be effectively applied in practice. Addressing hate speech though the medium of criminal law in relation to serious matters of incitement or violence is of course entirely appropriate; however, to elevate the model of Article 4 to the status of paragon in addressing the gamut of racial discrimination is to exaggerate. It is characteristic of the fresh thinking in GR 35 that, while the criminal mode is firmly anchored in the normative arsenal of the Convention, and is elaborated with appropriate precision, counter-speech and education are also allotted prominent roles in the methodological repertoire for combating racist hate speech, and the use of criminal law advocated for only the more serious cases. As with hate speech, so also with the application of the Convention as a whole, witnessing a gradual movement towards recognizing a stronger role for education on the Convention and human rights, and on the need for inter-ethnic understanding, tolerance, and friendship, in anti-discrimination strategies. As indicated in Chapter 17, the full potential of Article 7 beyond its role in combating hate speech has still to be explored.

IX. Culture and Collective Rights

As noted particularly in Chapters 14 and 15, the understanding of rights in Committee practice has become increasingly embedded in cultural understandings, a feature of human rights law that leads one author to write of the 'culturalization' of human rights, signifying, *inter alia*, that the practice is not confined to CERD but reaches out to the full spectrum of human rights bodies, as well as other bodies, including those concerned with the application of humanitarian, environmental, and trade law.[72]

Sensitivity in CERD practice to culture extends to multiple aspects of its work, commencing with the definition of racial discrimination, understood as open to cultural contexts and the notion of human dignity; in cultural understandings of special measures; in the concepts of segregation and separation; in justice process and reparations; in cultural and other contexts in the matter of racist hate speech; in the interpretation and application of civil and political, economic, social, and cultural rights; in the field of self-determination; and in the basic notions of human rights education and disseminating the message of the Convention under the inspiration of Article 7. The cultural vision in the application of rights represents a distance travelled from the period of drafting the Convention and the distance understood by many delegates between the protection of minorities and the prevention of discrimination.[73] The Committee has been receptive to currents deriving from parallel instruments devised for the protection of identifiable groups as well as a notable contributor to the 'culturalist' stream of discourse. Its cultural applications of the Convention include but are not confined to concerns with indigenous peoples, but extend to its treatment of the rights of ethnic and other minorities, Afro-descendant peoples, and non-citizens, in principle to any group that potentially comes under the protective embrace of the Convention.

[71] Discussed in Chapter 11.

[72] F. Lenzerini, *The Culturalization of Human Rights Law* (Oxford University Press, 2008); see also Chapter 5.

[73] Se in particular Chapters 2, 3, 5, and 6.

Although the cultural interpretation of Convention principles is not exclusively concerned with questions of collective and individual rights, issues regarding the relationship between these evocations of human rights have surfaced in practice. Parallel with its exploration of cultural nuances in the rights and obligations under the Convention, CERD has made its own contribution to the widening of the vision of the Convention concerning collective rights.[74] The term 'collective rights' is ambiguous in that it conceals a distinction between rights invested in individuals to be exercised collectively, such as language, religion, and 'culture', and rights invested in the community as such. In addition to calls through a series of concluding observations to respect and protect the collective rights of indigenous peoples,[75] GR 23 is clear in its affirmation that the provisions of the Convention apply to the peoples,[76] including their rights to 'control, use, etc, their communal lands, territories, and resources.[77] The language of the recommendation differentiates individual rights—rights of members—from the collective rights of indigenous peoples; both are to be respected. Elsewhere the Committee has referred to 'communal ownership' or the rights of a named people, including 'Saami rights'.[78] In general, it may be said that in addition to the question of inter-individual equality, a characteristic concern of the Convention is with what MacNaughton terms 'bloc' equality'[79] or bloc discrimination, in the sense that the invocation of discrimination and equality is not simply inter-individual but is strongly linked to particular groups.

Rights conflicts in the context of ICERD and elsewhere are not necessarily confined to tensions between individual and collective rights—recall the strained relationship in the Convention between proscribed 'hate speech' (Article 4) and the validation of freedom of opinion and expression (Article 5).[80] However, as with the claims of 'culture' more generally, the endorsement of collective rights, particularly in the 'harder' sense of the group as the primary holder of rights, has clear potential to raise challenges regarding the protection of individual rights. In the case of Fiji, the State party was invited to explain how the enjoyment of indigenous rights affected the enjoyment of rights by others in the State, bearing in mind the dominant position enjoyed by the indigenous majority. Referring to ILO Convention 169, on which the questions of some CERD Committee members were based, the representative of Fiji expressed awareness that the term 'peoples' under that Convention was not to be interpreted in a manner that would undermine the rights of individuals.[81] Endorsement of the UNDRIP raises its own questions on the

[74] From a vast literature, see P. Jones, 'Human Rights, Group Rights, and Peoples' Rights', *HRQ* 21 (1999), 80–107; M. Jovanović, *Collective Rights: A Legal Theory* (Cambridge University Press, 2012), and 'Recognizing Minority Identities Through Collective Rights', *HRQ* 27 (2005), 625–51; W. Kymlicka, Multicultural Citizenship: A Liberal Theory of Minority Rights (Clarendon Press, 1995), Chapter 3; W. Kymlicka (ed.), *The Rights of Minority Cultures* (Oxford University Press, 2005); C. Tavani, *Collective Rights and the Cultural Identity of the Roma: A Case Study of Italy* (Martinus Nijhoff Publishers, 2012, esp. Chapter 4 'Individual v Collective Rights'; P. Thornberry, *Indigenous Peoples and Human Rights* (Manchester University Press, 2002).

[75] See particularly Chapters 13 and 14.

[76] GR 23, paras 1 and 2.

[77] *Ibid.*, para. 5.

[78] P. Thornberry, 'Integrating the UN Declaration on the Rights of Indigenous Peoples into CERD Practice', in S. Allen and A. Xanthaki (eds), *Reflections on the UN Declaration on the Rights of Indigenous Peoples* (Hart Publishing, 2011), pp. 61–91, p. 88 [henceforth *Indigenous Peoples in CERD Practice*].

[79] G. MacNaughton, 'Untangling Equality and Non-Discrimination to Promote the Right to Health Care for All', *Health and Human Rights* 11.2. (2009), 47–63.

[80] See Chapters 11 and 13.

[81] CERD/C/SR/1850, para. 3.

individual/collective rights relationship, including that stemming from Article 35, according to which 'indigenous peoples have the right to determine the responsibilities of individuals to their communities'; this and other puzzles supplement larger questions regarding the relationship between self-determination, collective rights, and individual rights.[82]

X. Cultural Practices

Addo writes regarding CERD that an apparent bias in the Committee towards upholding rather than challenging minority cultural practices may lead to cases where 'opportunities to address harms within minority culture can easily be overlooked or missed'.[83] On the other hand, over-concentration on intra-group, 'internal' discrimination has a downside in that highlighting negative practices in minority communities may go in tandem with neglecting similar practices in the population at large, as well as potentially contributing to the denigration of groups under the protection of the Convention. Challenges to cultural practices are part of the standard Committee repertoire and characteristically attempt to tread a line between rejection of the harm while avoiding the stigmatization of whole communities.[84] In this respect, the dialogic, educational approach of the Committee under Article 9 may serve purposes of accommodation or reconciliation rather better than the 'quasi-judicial' approach under Article 14. In one example, practices 'within some ethnic groups, particularly regarding inheritance and early marriage', elicited a recommendation to take account in public policies 'of the need to address discriminatory customs, primarily through education and other culturally sensitive strategies'.[85]

In normative terms, the oft-cited participation and community self-determination rights should also play a role in attempting to resolve contradictions of principle. In order to meet the challenge of potential tensions stemming from its simultaneous endorsements of individual and collective rights, CERD may need to sharpen its conceptual tools through the elaboration of a general recommendation or by other means.[86] In particular, the raft of CERD practice on the rights of women, in tandem with the practice of sister bodies such as CEDAW, can materially assist in developing such a recommendation, though the issues involved are wider and go to the heart of the human rights enterprise.[87]

[82] Discussion by Thornberry, *Indigenous Peoples in CERD Practice*, pp. 86–8.

[83] M. Addo, 'Practice of United Nations Human Rights Treaty Bodies in the Reconciliation of Cultural Diversity with Universal Respect for Human Rights', *Human Rights Quarterly* 32 (2010), 601–64; at 654, 658.

[84] Conceptual tools suggested to distinguishing the limits of cultural interventions include that between external and internal protections of ethnic groups: that groups require external protections from oppression from the outside world but individuals in such groups require internal protections, W. Kymlicka, *Multicultural Citizenship: A Liberal Theory of Minority Rights* (Clarendon Press, 1995); that human rights interventions should protect the 'core values' of communities and not attempt to export 'complete ways of life or conceptions of the good': A Hurrell, 'Power, Principles and Prudence: Protecting Human Rights in a Deeply Divided World', in T. Dunne and N.J. Wheeler (eds), *Human Rights in Global Politics* (Cambridge University Press, 1999), pp. 277–302, pp. 281–2; that rights have been presented to many communities 'according to a cultural scheme extraneous to that of the communities concerned, which were therefore unable to perceive them properly and translate them into practice', resulting in 'the artificial imposition of rules which could not find concrete application within many human societies' hence the need for rights to be 'culturally adjustable in light of the different needs of diverse human communities': Lenzerini, *The Culturalization of Human Rights Law*, pp. 245–6; see also P. Thornberry, *Indigenous Peoples* and Human Rights, Chapter 17.

[85] Concluding observations on the Lao People's Democratic Republic, CERD/C/LAO/CO/16-18, para. 15.

[86] Thornberry, *Indigenous Peoples in CERD Practice*, p. 85.

[87] See discussion in Chapter 14 of the Committee's approach to customs particularly as they affect women.

The text of the Convention is compatible with the endorsement of both particularism and universalism, of collective and individual visions of rights. Oscillation between endorsement of individual rights and endorsement of collective rights is not unique to CERD. A universal vision of rights is necessarily plural, open to a variety of cultural contributions. In this sense the principle of non-discrimination may serve as an anti-fragmentation device that treats communities within the States parties as equal in dignity, without hierarchy or condescension. The task of the Committee and the States parties should be to seek a productive synthesis between the two polarities, guided by the text and teleology of the Convention.

E. Coda

The adoption of the Convention in 1965 represented the outcome of a series of interconnected developments since the UN Charter that gave explicit legal grounding to norms of a humanitarian character and to expediting the disappearance of colonialism along with its integral racial manifestations. The text, carrying to fruition the ethic of the Declaration on Racial Discrimination by means of a legally binding instrument, provided a fresh normative and institutional synthesis that combined universal human rights with the rejection of theories of racial superiority, but not entirely of the infrastructure of racial differentiation—the work of UNESCO in 'deconstructing' race was subjected to divergent interpretations by delegates.[88] The Declaration and the Convention stood, and continue to stand, as Janus-faced statements looking backwards at the hopeful demise of an era of racial discrimination, and projecting forward to concerted international action against it.[89] Through the Convention, the United Nations reinvigorated its human rights mission. ICERD was the first of the UN 'core' human rights treaties, and inaugurated an international monitoring body—the Committee on the Elimination of Racial Discrimination—designed to move the instrument from complacent 'virtue signalling' towards its practical application in the service of humanity.[90]

The present and previous chapters have endeavoured to appraise the principal conceptual and practical developments in the life of the Convention over the half-century. The primary focus has been on the work of the Committee on the Elimination of Racial Discrimination, the body charged by the international community with the task of monitoring its progress, though critical observations by States parties are also accounted for, including resistances to Committee stances, and obdurate refusals to 'converge' with its views. The present work is not as such a history of the Convention, and while transitions in the understanding and application of the Convention are accounted for, heavy emphasis is placed on more recent developments as the principal guide to the form and content of future State–Committee dialogues. The distinctive rights culture developed by the Committee over the course of time has inspired many, and made an enormous contribution to the solidification of principle that brands racial discrimination as unacceptable State practice. Racial discrimination by design is now regarded as

[88] See discussion in Chapter 3.

[89] Janus-faced, not as hypocritical or deceitful, but in the image of a god (Janus) that looks both ways, to the future and the past, to beginning, passages, and endings.

[90] Virtue signalling refers to activities intended to indicate a person's virtuousness to an audience: <http://www.collinsdictionary.com/submission/16361/virtue%20signalling>, a concept that can be extended appropriately to States and governments.

indefensible, while discrimination through accident or negligence is treated as culpable. A finding of racial discrimination merits the full weight of moral opprobrium from the international community. The work of the Committee, in conjunction with other human rights organizations, and with States and civil society, has profiled the relevant legal and moral baselines with an impressive clarity of principle, even if the finer details are open to contestation and reconstruction.

The chapters have also outlined a broad range of conceptual and practical challenges in the field of racial discrimination on the basis of an article by article analysis of the principal strands of ICERD. The tasks mandated by the Convention to the States parties are immense. Despite the switch in emphasis in current crises away from ethnicity to the clashes of civilizations and religious intolerance and worse,[91] the archive of practice distilled in the chapters of the present work should sufficiently demonstrate the continuing force of ethnic identification, inter-ethnic rivalry, competition, and hostility in human affairs, and oppression on the basis of ethnic affiliation. In this sense the Convention appears to pit Gramscian optimism of the will against pessimism of the intellect,[92] as to which Banton's characterization of the promise of the Convention to eliminate racial discrimination as a noble lie may be recalled.[93] However, history also demonstrates possibilities of living together on the basis of tolerance and friendship, of mutuality of respect and inter-ethnic harmony. Embedding the prohibition of racial discrimination in State constitutions, laws, plans, and policies makes a further contribution to peaceful possibilities, even if law and planning, etc, are first steps, if more than the 'infant step' glimpsed by Lamptey on the adoption of ICERD.

The World is Everything that is the Case

If racial discrimination is unlikely to be eliminated for all, it can be eliminated for some; its prohibition can make a difference in reaching down to the capillaries of human existence, recognizing and restoring dignity, helping to repair damaged human beings.[94] Prohibition of reprehensible forms of conduct is important but not enough, nor is anti-discrimination a complete policy, however far-reaching. Besides the effective implementation of normative promises accounted for in the present work, anti-discrimination is only one strategy, and one in largely negative mode—a *via negativa*—that constructs a binary of victim and perpetrator, and even in some instances an unhelpful culture of blame. In an ideal theatre of human rights, the rights would be sustained for all and enjoyed on an equal basis without the need for victims and a spectrum of oppressors. Anti-discrimination in this sense is a beginning, a methodological step towards an egalitarian future of multicultural self-assurance that seeks to remove impediments to the full enjoyment of rights. While the anti-discrimination ethic is in itself less than salvation, it nonetheless addresses the truth of what is the case, and traces an upward path towards a better, more dignified ordering of human affairs.

[91] S.P. Huntington, *The Clash of Civilizations and the Remaking of World Order* (Simon and Schuster, 1996); P. Thornberry, 'Minority and Indigenous Rights at "the End of History"', *Ethnicities* 2 (2002), 515–37.

[92] A. Gramsci, *Letter from Prison*, 19 December 1929: see 'W.J. Morgan, 'The Pedagogical Politics of Antonio Gramsci—"Pessimism of the Intellect, Optimism of the Will"', *International Journal of Lifelong Education* 6 (2006), 295–308.

[93] M. Banton, *International Action against Racial Discrimination* (Clarendon Press, 1996), pp. 50 and 305.

[94] Derek Mahon, 'Tractatus', *New Collected Poems* (The Gallery Press, 2012), after Wittgenstein.

APPENDIX

International Convention on the Elimination of All Forms of Racial Discrimination

Adopted and opened for signature and ratification by General Assembly resolution 2106 (XX) of 21 December 1965 entry into force 4 January 1969, in accordance with Article 19

The States Parties to this Convention,

Considering that the Charter of the United Nations is based on the principles of the dignity and equality inherent in all human beings, and that all Member States have pledged themselves to take joint and separate action, in co-operation with the Organization, for the achievement of one of the purposes of the United Nations which is to promote and encourage universal respect for and observance of human rights and fundamental freedoms for all, without distinction as to race, sex, language or religion, Considering that the Universal Declaration of Human Rights proclaims that all human beings are born free and equal in dignity and rights and that everyone is entitled to all the rights and freedoms set out therein, without distinction of any kind, in particular as to race, colour or national origin,

Considering that all human beings are equal before the law and are entitled to equal protection of the law against any discrimination and against any incitement to discrimination,

Considering that the United Nations has condemned colonialism and all practices of segregation and discrimination associated therewith, in whatever form and wherever they exist, and that the Declaration on the Granting of Independence to Colonial Countries and Peoples of 14 December 1960 (General Assembly resolution 1514 (XV)) has affirmed and solemnly proclaimed the necessity of bringing them to a speedy and unconditional end, Considering that the United Nations Declaration on the Elimination of All Forms of Racial Discrimination of 20 November 1963 (General Assembly resolution 1904 (XVIII)) solemnly affirms the necessity of speedily eliminating racial discrimination throughout the world in all its forms and manifestations and of securing understanding of and respect for the dignity of the human person,

Convinced that any doctrine of superiority based on racial differentiation is scientifically false, morally condemnable, socially unjust and dangerous, and that there is no justification for racial discrimination, in theory or in practice, anywhere,

Reaffirming that discrimination between human beings on the grounds of race, colour or ethnic origin is an obstacle to friendly and peaceful relations among nations and is capable of disturbing peace and security among peoples and the harmony of persons living side by side even within one and the same State,

Convinced that the existence of racial barriers is repugnant to the ideals of any human society,

Alarmed by manifestations of racial discrimination still in evidence in some areas of the world and by governmental policies based on racial superiority or hatred, such as policies of apartheid, segregation or separation,

Resolved to adopt all necessary measures for speedily eliminating racial discrimination in all its forms and manifestations, and to prevent and combat racist doctrines and practices in order to promote understanding between races and to build an international community free from all forms of racial segregation and racial discrimination,

Bearing in mind the Convention concerning Discrimination in respect of Employment and Occupation adopted by the International Labour Organisation in 1958, and the Convention against Discrimination in Education adopted by the United Nations Educational, Scientific and Cultural Organization in 1960,

Desiring to implement the principles embodied in the United Nations Declaration on the Elimination of All Forms of Racial Discrimination and to secure the earliest adoption of practical measures to that end, Have agreed as follows:

Part I

Article 1

1. In this Convention, the term "racial discrimination" shall mean any distinction, exclusion, restriction or preference based on race, colour, descent, or national or ethnic origin which has the purpose or effect of nullifying or impairing the recognition, enjoyment or exercise, on an equal footing, of human rights and fundamental freedoms in the political, economic, social, cultural or any other field of public life.
2. This Convention shall not apply to distinctions, exclusions, restrictions or preferences made by a State Party to this Convention between citizens and non-citizens.
3. Nothing in this Convention may be interpreted as affecting in any way the legal provisions of States Parties concerning nationality, citizenship or naturalization, provided that such provisions do not discriminate against any particular nationality.
4. Special measures taken for the sole purpose of securing adequate advancement of certain racial or ethnic groups or individuals requiring such protection as may be necessary in order to ensure such groups or individuals equal enjoyment or exercise of human rights and fundamental freedoms shall not be deemed racial discrimination, provided, however, that such measures do not, as a consequence, lead to the maintenance of separate rights for different racial groups and that they shall not be continued after the objectives for which they were taken have been achieved.

Article 2

1. States Parties condemn racial discrimination and undertake to pursue by all appropriate means and without delay a policy of eliminating racial discrimination in all its forms and promoting understanding among all races, and, to this end:
   (a) Each State Party undertakes to engage in no act or practice of racial discrimination against persons, groups of persons or institutions and to ensure that all public authorities and public institutions, national and local, shall act in conformity with this obligation;
   (b) Each State Party undertakes not to sponsor, defend or support racial discrimination by any persons or organizations;
   (c) Each State Party shall take effective measures to review governmental, national and local policies, and to amend, rescind or nullify any laws and regulations which have the effect of creating or perpetuating racial discrimination wherever it exists;
   (d) Each State Party shall prohibit and bring to an end, by all appropriate means, including legislation as required by circumstances, racial discrimination by any persons, group or organization;
   (e) Each State Party undertakes to encourage, where appropriate, integrationist multiracial organizations and movements and other means of eliminating barriers between races, and to discourage anything which tends to strengthen racial division.
2. States Parties shall, when the circumstances so warrant, take, in the social, economic, cultural and other fields, special and concrete measures to ensure the adequate development and protection of certain racial groups or individuals belonging to them, for the purpose of guaranteeing them the full and equal enjoyment of human rights and fundamental freedoms. These measures shall in no

case entail as a consequence the maintenance of unequal or separate rights for different racial groups after the objectives for which they were taken have been achieved.

Article 3

States Parties particularly condemn racial segregation and apartheid and undertake to prevent, prohibit and eradicate all practices of this nature in territories under their jurisdiction.

Article 4

States Parties condemn all propaganda and all organizations which are based on ideas or theories of superiority of one race or group of persons of one colour or ethnic origin, or which attempt to justify or promote racial hatred and discrimination in any form, and undertake to adopt immediate and positive measures designed to eradicate all incitement to, or acts of, such discrimination and, to this end, with due regard to the principles embodied in the Universal Declaration of Human Rights and the rights expressly set forth in article 5 of this Convention, inter alia:

(a) Shall declare an offence punishable by law all dissemination of ideas based on racial superiority or hatred, incitement to racial discrimination, as well as all acts of violence or incitement to such acts against any race or group of persons of another colour or ethnic origin, and also the provision of any assistance to racist activities, including the financing thereof;
(b) Shall declare illegal and prohibit organizations, and also organized and all other propaganda activities, which promote and incite racial discrimination, and shall recognize participation in such organizations or activities as an offence punishable by law;
(c) Shall not permit public authorities or public institutions, national or local, to promote or incite racial discrimination.

Article 5

In compliance with the fundamental obligations laid down in article 2 of this Convention, States Parties undertake to prohibit and to eliminate racial discrimination in all its forms and to guarantee the right of everyone, without distinction as to race, colour, or national or ethnic origin, to equality before the law, notably in the enjoyment of the following rights:

(a) The right to equal treatment before the tribunals and all other organs administering justice;
(b) The right to security of person and protection by the State against violence or bodily harm, whether inflicted by government officials or by any individual group or institution;
(c) Political rights, in particular the right to participate in elections-to vote and to stand for election-on the basis of universal and equal suffrage, to take part in the Government as well as in the conduct of public affairs at any level and to have equal access to public service;
(d) Other civil rights, in particular:
    (i) The right to freedom of movement and residence within the border of the State;
    (ii) The right to leave any country, including one's own, and to return to one's country;
    (iii) The right to nationality;
    (iv) The right to marriage and choice of spouse;
    (v) The right to own property alone as well as in association with others;
    (vi) The right to inherit;
    (vii) The right to freedom of thought, conscience and religion;
    (viii) The right to freedom of opinion and expression;
    (ix) The right to freedom of peaceful assembly and association;
(e) Economic, social and cultural rights, in particular:
    (i) The rights to work, to free choice of employment, to just and favourable conditions of work, to protection against unemployment, to equal pay for equal work, to just and favourable remuneration;
    (ii) The right to form and join trade unions;

(iii) The right to housing;
(iv) The right to public health, medical care, social security and social services;
(v) The right to education and training;
(vi) The right to equal participation in cultural activities;

(f) The right of access to any place or service intended for use by the general public, such as transport hotels, restaurants, cafes, theatres and parks.

Article 6

States Parties shall assure to everyone within their jurisdiction effective protection and remedies, through the competent national tribunals and other State institutions, against any acts of racial discrimination which violate his human rights and fundamental freedoms contrary to this Convention, as well as the right to seek from such tribunals just and adequate reparation or satisfaction for any damage suffered as a result of such discrimination.

Article 7

States Parties undertake to adopt immediate and effective measures, particularly in the fields of teaching, education, culture and information, with a view to combating prejudices which lead to racial discrimination and to promoting understanding, tolerance and friendship among nations and racial or ethnical groups, as well as to propagating the purposes and principles of the Charter of the United Nations, the Universal Declaration of Human Rights, the United Nations Declaration on the Elimination of All Forms of Racial Discrimination, and this Convention.

PART II

Article 8

1. There shall be established a Committee on the Elimination of Racial Discrimination (hereinafter referred to as the Committee) consisting of eighteen experts of high moral standing and acknowledged impartiality elected by States Parties from among their nationals, who shall serve in their personal capacity, consideration being given to equitable geographical distribution and to the representation of the different forms of civilization as well as of the principal legal systems.
2. The members of the Committee shall be elected by secret ballot from a list of persons nominated by the States Parties. Each State Party may nominate one person from among its own nationals.
3. The initial election shall be held six months after the date of the entry into force of this Convention. At least three months before the date of each election the Secretary-General of the United Nations shall address a letter to the States Parties inviting them to submit their nominations within two months. The Secretary-General shall prepare a list in alphabetical order of all persons thus nominated, indicating the States Parties which have nominated them, and shall submit it to the States Parties.
4. Elections of the members of the Committee shall be held at a meeting of States Parties convened by the Secretary-General at United Nations Headquarters. At that meeting, for which two thirds of the States Parties shall constitute a quorum, the persons elected to the Committee shall be nominees who obtain the largest number of votes and an absolute majority of the votes of the representatives of States Parties present and voting.
5. (a) The members of the Committee shall be elected for a term of four years. However, the terms of nine of the members elected at the first election shall expire at the end of two years; immediately after the first election the names of these nine members shall be chosen by lot by the Chairman of the Committee;
   (b) For the filling of casual vacancies, the State Party whose expert has ceased to function as a member of the Committee shall appoint another expert from among its nationals, subject to the approval of the Committee.

6. States Parties shall be responsible for the expenses of the members of the Committee while they are in performance of Committee duties.

Article 9

1. States Parties undertake to submit to the Secretary-General of the United Nations, for consideration by the Committee, a report on the legislative, judicial, administrative or other measures which they have adopted and which give effect to the provisions of this Convention:
   (a) within one year after the entry into force of the Convention for the State concerned; and
   (b) thereafter every two years and whenever the Committee so requests. The Committee may request further information from the States Parties.
2. The Committee shall report annually, through the Secretary General, to the General Assembly of the United Nations on its activities and may make suggestions and general recommendations based on the examination of the reports and information received from the States Parties. Such suggestions and general recommendations shall be reported to the General Assembly together with comments, if any, from States Parties.

Article 10

1. The Committee shall adopt its own rules of procedure.
2. The Committee shall elect its officers for a term of two years.
3. The secretariat of the Committee shall be provided by the Secretary General of the United Nations.
4. The meetings of the Committee shall normally be held at United Nations Headquarters.

Article 11

1. If a State Party considers that another State Party is not giving effect to the provisions of this Convention, it may bring the matter to the attention of the Committee. The Committee shall then transmit the communication to the State Party concerned. Within three months, the receiving State shall submit to the Committee written explanations or statements clarifying the matter and the remedy, if any, that may have been taken by that State.
2. If the matter is not adjusted to the satisfaction of both parties, either by bilateral negotiations or by any other procedure open to them, within six months after the receipt by the receiving State of the initial communication, either State shall have the right to refer the matter again to the Committee by notifying the Committee and also the other State.
3. The Committee shall deal with a matter referred to it in accordance with paragraph 2 of this article after it has ascertained that all available domestic remedies have been invoked and exhausted in the case, in conformity with the generally recognized principles of international law. This shall not be the rule where the application of the remedies is unreasonably prolonged.
4. In any matter referred to it, the Committee may call upon the States Parties concerned to supply any other relevant information.
5. When any matter arising out of this article is being considered by the Committee, the States Parties concerned shall be entitled to send a representative to take part in the proceedings of the Committee, without voting rights, while the matter is under consideration.

Article 12

1. (a) After the Committee has obtained and collated all the information it deems necessary, the Chairman shall appoint an ad hoc Conciliation Commission (hereinafter referred to as the Commission) comprising five persons who may or may not be members of the Committee. The members of the Commission shall be appointed with the unanimous consent of the parties to the dispute, and its good offices shall be made available to the States concerned with a view to an amicable solution of the matter on the basis of respect for this Convention; (b) If the States parties to the dispute fail to reach agreement within three months on all or part of the composition of the Commission, the members of the Commission not agreed upon by

the States parties to the dispute shall be elected by secret ballot by a two-thirds majority vote of the Committee from among its own members.

2. The members of the Commission shall serve in their personal capacity. They shall not be nationals of the States parties to the dispute or of a State not Party to this Convention.
3. The Commission shall elect its own Chairman and adopt its own rules of procedure.
4. The meetings of the Commission shall normally be held at United Nations Headquarters or at any other convenient place as determined by the Commission.
5. The secretariat provided in accordance with article 10, paragraph 3, of this Convention shall also service the Commission whenever a dispute among States Parties brings the Commission into being.
6. The States parties to the dispute shall share equally all the expenses of the members of the Commission in accordance with estimates to be provided by the Secretary-General of the United Nations.
7. The Secretary-General shall be empowered to pay the expenses of the members of the Commission, if necessary, before reimbursement by the States parties to the dispute in accordance with paragraph 6 of this article.
8. The information obtained and collated by the Committee shall be made available to the Commission, and the Commission may call upon the States concerned to supply any other relevant information.

Article 13

1. When the Commission has fully considered the matter, it shall prepare and submit to the Chairman of the Committee a report embodying its findings on all questions of fact relevant to the issue between the parties and containing such recommendations as it may think proper for the amicable solution of the dispute.
2. The Chairman of the Committee shall communicate the report of the Commission to each of the States parties to the dispute. These States shall, within three months, inform the Chairman of the Committee whether or not they accept the recommendations contained in the report of the Commission.
3. After the period provided for in paragraph 2 of this article, the Chairman of the Committee shall communicate the report of the Commission and the declarations of the States Parties concerned to the other States Parties to this Convention.

Article 14

1. A State Party may at any time declare that it recognizes the competence of the Committee to receive and consider communications from individuals or groups of individuals within its jurisdiction claiming to be victims of a violation by that State Party of any of the rights set forth in this Convention. No communication shall be received by the Committee if it concerns a State Party which has not made such a declaration.
2. Any State Party which makes a declaration as provided for in paragraph 1 of this article may establish or indicate a body within its national legal order which shall be competent to receive and consider petitions from individuals and groups of individuals within its jurisdiction who claim to be victims of a violation of any of the rights set forth in this Convention and who have exhausted other available local remedies.
3. A declaration made in accordance with paragraph 1 of this article and the name of any body established or indicated in accordance with paragraph 2 of this article shall be deposited by the State Party concerned with the Secretary-General of the United Nations, who shall transmit copies thereof to the other States Parties. A declaration may be withdrawn at any time by notification to the Secretary-General, but such a withdrawal shall not affect communications pending before the Committee.
4. A register of petitions shall be kept by the body established or indicated in accordance with paragraph 2 of this article, and certified copies of the register shall be filed annually through

appropriate channels with the Secretary-General on the understanding that the contents shall not be publicly disclosed.

5. In the event of failure to obtain satisfaction from the body established or indicated in accordance with paragraph 2 of this article, the petitioner shall have the right to communicate the matter to the Committee within six months.
6. (a) The Committee shall confidentially bring any communication referred to it to the attention of the State Party alleged to be violating any provision of this Convention, but the identity of the individual or groups of individuals concerned shall not be revealed without his or their express consent. The Committee shall not receive anonymous communications;
   (b) Within three months, the receiving State shall submit to the Committee written explanations or statements clarifying the matter and the remedy, if any, that may have been taken by that State.
7. (a) The Committee shall consider communications in the light of all information made available to it by the State Party concerned and by the petitioner. The Committee shall not consider any communication from a petitioner unless it has ascertained that the petitioner has exhausted all available domestic remedies. However, this shall not be the rule where the application of the remedies is unreasonably prolonged;
   (b) The Committee shall forward its suggestions and recommendations, if any, to the State Party concerned and to the petitioner.
8. The Committee shall include in its annual report a summary of such communications and, where appropriate, a summary of the explanations and statements of the States Parties concerned and of its own suggestions and recommendations.
9. The Committee shall be competent to exercise the functions provided for in this article only when at least ten States Parties to this Convention are bound by declarations in accordance with paragraph 1 of this article.

Article 15

1. Pending the achievement of the objectives of the Declaration on the Granting of Independence to Colonial Countries and Peoples, contained in General Assembly resolution 1514 (XV) of 14 December 1960, the provisions of this Convention shall in no way limit the right of petition granted to these peoples by other international instruments or by the United Nations and its specialized agencies.
2. (a) The Committee established under article 8, paragraph 1, of this Convention shall receive copies of the petitions from, and submit expressions of opinion and recommendations on these petitions to, the bodies of the United Nations which deal with matters directly related to the principles and objectives of this Convention in their consideration of petitions from the inhabitants of Trust and Non-Self-Governing Territories and all other territories to which General Assembly resolution 1514 (XV) applies, relating to matters covered by this Convention which are before these bodies;
   (b) The Committee shall receive from the competent bodies of the United Nations copies of the reports concerning the legislative, judicial, administrative or other measures directly related to the principles and objectives of this Convention applied by the administering Powers within the Territories mentioned in subparagraph (a) of this paragraph, and shall express opinions and make recommendations to these bodies.
3. The Committee shall include in its report to the General Assembly a summary of the petitions and reports it has received from United Nations bodies, and the expressions of opinion and recommendations of the Committee relating to the said petitions and reports.
4. The Committee shall request from the Secretary-General of the United Nations all information relevant to the objectives of this Convention and available to him regarding the Territories mentioned in paragraph 2 (a) of this article.

Article 16

The provisions of this Convention concerning the settlement of disputes or complaints shall be applied without prejudice to other procedures for settling disputes or complaints in the field of discrimination laid down in the constituent instruments of, or conventions adopted by, the United Nations and its specialized agencies, and shall not prevent the States Parties from having recourse to other procedures for settling a dispute in accordance with general or special international agreements in force between them.

Part III

Article 17

1. This Convention is open for signature by any State Member of the United Nations or member of any of its specialized agencies, by any State Party to the Statute of the International Court of Justice, and by any other State which has been invited by the General Assembly of the United Nations to become a Party to this Convention.
2. This Convention is subject to ratification. Instruments of ratification shall be deposited with the Secretary-General of the United Nations.

Article 18

1. This Convention shall be open to accession by any State referred to in article 17, paragraph 1, of the Convention.
2. Accession shall be effected by the deposit of an instrument of accession with the Secretary-General of the United Nations.

Article 19

1. This Convention shall enter into force on the thirtieth day after the date of the deposit with the Secretary-General of the United Nations of the twenty-seventh instrument of ratification or instrument of accession.
2. For each State ratifying this Convention or acceding to it after the deposit of the twenty-seventh instrument of ratification or instrument of accession, the Convention shall enter into force on the thirtieth day after the date of the deposit of its own instrument of ratification or instrument of accession.

Article 20

1. The Secretary-General of the United Nations shall receive and circulate to all States which are or may become Parties to this Convention reservations made by States at the time of ratification or accession. Any State which objects to the reservation shall, within a period of ninety days from the date of the said communication, notify the Secretary-General that it does not accept it.
2. A reservation incompatible with the object and purpose of this Convention shall not be permitted, nor shall a reservation the effect of which would inhibit the operation of any of the bodies established by this Convention be allowed. A reservation shall be considered incompatible or inhibitive if at least two thirds of the States Parties to this Convention object to it.
3. Reservations may be withdrawn at any time by notification to this effect addressed to the Secretary- General. Such notification shall take effect on the date on which it is received.

Article 21

A State Party may denounce this Convention by written notification to the Secretary-General of the United Nations. Denunciation shall take effect one year after the date of receipt of the notification by the Secretary General.

Article 22

Any dispute between two or more States Parties with respect to the interpretation or application of this Convention, which is not settled by negotiation or by the procedures expressly provided for in this Convention, shall, at the request of any of the parties to the dispute, be referred to the International Court of Justice for decision, unless the disputants agree to another mode of settlement.

Article 23

1. A request for the revision of this Convention may be made at any time by any State Party by means of a notification in writing addressed to the Secretary-General of the United Nations.
2. The General Assembly of the United Nations shall decide upon the steps, if any, to be taken in respect of such a request.

Article 24

The Secretary-General of the United Nations shall inform all States referred to in article 17, paragraph 1, of this Convention of the following particulars:

(a) Signatures, ratifications and accessions under articles 17 and 18;
(b) The date of entry into force of this Convention under article 19;
(c) Communications and declarations received under articles 14, 20 and 23;
(d) Denunciations under article 21.

Article 25

1. This Convention, of which the Chinese, English, French, Russian and Spanish texts are equally authentic, shall be deposited in the archives of the United Nations.
2. The Secretary-General of the United Nations shall transmit certified copies of this Convention to all States belonging to any of the categories mentioned in article 17, paragraph 1, of the Convention.

Select Bibliography

Addo, Michael, 'Practice of United Nations Human Rights Treaty Bodies in the Reconciliation of Cultural Diversity with Universal Respect for Human Rights', *Human Rights Quarterly* 32.3 (2010), 601–64.

Alfredsson, Gudmundur and Eide, Asbjørn (eds), *The Universal Declaration of Human Rights: A Common Standard of Achievement* (Martinus Nijhoff Publishers, 1999).

Allen, Stephen, *The Chagos Islanders and International Law* (Hart Publishing, 2014).

Allen, Stephen and Xanthaki, Alexandra, *Reflections on the UN Declaration on the Rights of Indigenous Peoples* (Hart Publishing, 2011).

Alston, Philip and Crawford, James, *The Future of UN Human Rights Treaty Monitoring* (Cambridge University Press, 2000).

Anghie, Antony, *Imperialism, Sovereignty and the Making of International Law* (Cambridge University Press, 2004).

Anghie, Antony, 'The Evolution of International Law: Colonial and Postcolonial Realities', *Third World Quarterly* 27.5 (2006), 739–53.

Angst, Doris, 'La Convention Internationale sur L'Elimination de Toutes les Formes de Discrimination Raciale', in Randall, Maya and Hottelier, Michel (eds), *Introduction aux Droits de L'Homme* (Schulthess, 2014), pp. 268–80.

Antkowiak, Thomas, 'A Dark Side of Virtue: The Inter-American Court and Reparations for Indigenous Peoples', *Duke Journal of Comparative and International Law* 25.1. (2014), 1–80.

Appiah, Kwame, *The Ethics of Identity* (Princeton University Press, 2005).

Armstrong, David, 'Law, Justice and the Idea of a World Society', *International Affairs* 75.3 (1999), 547–61; Article 19, *The Camden Principles on Freedom of Expression and Equality* (London: Article 19, 2009), available at: <https://www.article19.org/data/files/pdfs/standards/the-camden-principles-on-freedom-of-expression-and-equality.pdf>.

Assefa, Getachew, 'Human and Group Rights Issues in Ethiopia: a Reply to Kjetil Tronvoll', *International Journal on Minority and Group Rights* 16.2 (2009), 245–59.

Augenstein, Daniel and Kinley, David, 'When Human Rights "Responsibilities" become "Duties": the Extra-Territorial Obligations of States that Bind Corporations', *University of Sydney Law School, Legal Studies Research Paper* (September 2012), available at: <http://ssrn.com/abstract=2149921 1>.

Aust, Anthony, *Handbook of International Law* (2nd edn, Cambridge University Press, 2010).

Baderin, Mashood and McCorquodale, Robert (eds), *Economic, Social and Cultural Rights in Action* (Oxford University Press, 2007).

Balibar, Etienne and Wallerstein, Immanuel, *Race, Nation, Class: Ambiguous Identities* (Verso, 1991).

Bamforth, Nicholas, Malik, Maleiha, and O'Cinneide, Colm, *Discrimination Law: Theory and Context* (Sweet and Maxwell, 2008).

Banton, Michael, *Racial Theories* (Cambridge University Press, 1987).

Banton, Michael, *Discrimination* (Open University Press, 1994).

Banton, Michael, *International Action against Racial Discrimination* (Clarendon Press, 1996).

Banton, Michael, *The International Politics of Race* (Polity Press, 2002).

Banton, Michael, 'States and Civil Society in the Campaign against Racial Discrimination', *Nationalism and Ethnic Politics* 18 (2012), 385–405.
Barelli, Mauro, 'Free, Prior and Informed Consent in the Aftermath of the UN Declaration on the Rights of Indigenous Peoples: Developments and Challenges Ahead', *International Journal of Human Rights* 16.1 (2012), 1–24.
Barkan, Elazar, *The Retreat of Scientific Racism* (Cambridge University Press, 1992).
Bashford, Alison and Levine, Philippa (eds), *The Oxford Handbook of the History of Eugenics* (Oxford University Press, 2010).
Bayefsky, Anne, *The UN Human Rights Treaty System: Universality at the Crossroads* (Kluwer Law International, 2001).
Bell, Mark, *Racism and Equality in the European Union* (Oxford University Press, 2008).
Bell, Mark, *Anti-Discrimination Law and the European Union* (Oxford University Press, 2002).
Benedict, Ruth, *Race, Science and Politics* (Viking Press, 1940).
Berry, Stephanie, 'Bringing Muslim Minorities within the International Convention on the Elimination of All Forms of Racial Discrimination—Square Peg in a Round Hole?', *Human Rights Law Review* 11.3 (2011), 433–50.
Bianchi, Andrea, 'Human Rights and the Magic of Jus Cogens', *European Journal of International Law* 19.3 (2008), 491–508.
Bidault, Mylène, *La Protection Internationale des Droits Culturels* (Bruylant, 2009).
Bjorge, Eirik, *The Evolutionary Interpretation of Treaties* (Oxford University Press, 2014).
Boas, Franz, *Race, Language and Culture* (University of Chicago Press, 1940).
Boas, Franz, *Race and Democratic Society* (J.J. Augustin, 1945).
Bob, Clifford, '"Dalit Rights are Human Rights": Caste Discrimination, International Activism, and the Construction of a New Human Rights Issue', *Human Rights Quarterly* 29.1 (2007), 167–93.
Boxill, Bernard (ed.), *Race and Racism* (Oxford University Press, 2001).
Brown, Chris, World Society and the English School: an "International Society" Perspective on World Society', London: LSE Research online, available at: <http://eprints.lse.ac.uk/archive/00000743>.
Buergenthal, Thomas, 'Implementing the UN Racial Convention', *Texas International Law Journal* 12 (1977), 187–2221.
Buys, Cindy, 'Application of the International Convention on the Elimination of All Forms of Racial Discrimination', *American Journal of International Law* 103 (2009), 294–99.
Cassese, Antonio, *Self-Determination of Peoples* (Cambridge University Press, 1995).
Charters, Claire and Erueti, Andrew (eds), *Maori Property Rights and the Foreshore and Seabed: The Last Frontier* (Victoria University Press, 2007).
Castellino, Joshua, 'The Protection of Minorities and Indigenous Peoples in International Law: A Comparative Temporal Analysis', *International Journal on Minority and Group Rights* 17.3 (2010), 393–422.
Claeys, Gregory, '"The Survival of the Fittest" and the Origins of Social Darwinism', *Journal of the History of Ideas* 61.2 (2000), 223–40.
Cismas, Ioana, *Religious Actors and International Law* (Oxford University Press, 2014).
Coliver, Sandra (ed.), *Striking a Balance: Hate Speech, Freedom of Expression and Non-Discrimination* (Article 19, 1992).
Committee on the Elimination of Racial Discrimination, *Positive Measures Designed to Eradicate All Incitement to, or Acts of, Racial Discrimination: Implementation of the International Convention on the Elimination of All Forms of Racial Discrimination, Article 4* (United Nations, 1986).
Connelly, John, 'Nazis and Slavs: From Race Theory to Racist Practice', *Central European History* 32.1 (1999), 1–33.

Connor, Walker, 'A Nation is a Nation, is a State, is an Ethnic Group, is a ...', in Hutchinson, John and Smith, Anthony (eds), *Nationalism* (Oxford University Press, 1994), pp. 36–46.

Crenshaw, Kimberlé, 'Gender-related aspects of race discrimination', background paper for the Expert Meeting on Gender and racial Discrimination, 21–24 November 2000, Zagreb, Croatia, EM/GRD/2000/W.P.1.

Crenshaw, Kimberlé, Gotanda, Neil, Peller, Gary, and Kendall, Thomas (eds), *Critical Race Theory: The Key Writings that Formed the Movement* (New Press, 1995).

Cruft, Rowan, Liao, Matthew, and Renzo, Massimo (eds), *Philosophical Foundations of Human Rights* (Oxford University Press, 2015).

De Feyter, Koen, Parmentier, Stephan, Bossuyt, Marc, and Lemmens, Paul (eds), *Out of the Ashes: Reparation for Victims of Gross and Systematic Human Rights Violations* (Intersentia, 2006).

De Schutter, Olivier, *International Human Rights Law* (Cambridge University Press, 2010).

De Schutter, Olivier, Eide, Asbjørn, Khalfan, Ashfaq, Orellana, Marcos, Salomon, Margot, and Seiderman, Ian, 'Commentary to the Maastricht Principles on Extraterritorial Obligations of States in the Area of Economic, Social and Cultural Rights', *Human Rights Quarterly* 34.4 (2012), 1084–1169.

Diaconu, Ion, *The definitions of racial discrimination*, background paper for the World Conference against Racism, E/CN.4/1999/WG.1/BP.10 (1999).

Diaconu, Ion, *Racial Discrimination* (Eleven International Publishing, 2011).

Diaconu, Ion, *Speaking Different, Living Together: Linguistic Rights* (Editions Offre Joie, 2015).

Du Plessis, Max, 'Historical Justice and International Law: An Exploratory Discussion of reparation for Slavery', *Human Rights Quarterly* 25.3 (2003), 624–59.

Egan, Suzanne, *The UN Human Rights Treaty System: Law and Procedure* (Bloomsbury, 2011).

Egan, Suzanne, 'Strengthening the United Nations Human Rights Treaty Body System', *Human Rights Law Review* 13.2 (2013), 209–43.

Evans, Malcolm, *Manual on the Wearing of Religious Symbols in Public Areas* (Martinus Nijhoff, 2008).

Farrior, Stephanie, *Equality and Non-Discrimination under International Law*, Vol. II (Ashgate, 2015).

Fassbender, Bardo and Peters, Anne, *The Oxford Handbook of the History of International Law* (Oxford University Press, 2012).

Feinberg, Nathan, 'The Legal Validity of the Undertakings regarding Minorities and the *Clausula Rebus Sic Stantibus*', *Studies in Law, Scripta Hierosolymitana* 5 (1958), 95–131.

Felice, William, 'The UN Committee on the Elimination of All Forms of Racial Discrimination: Race, and Economic and Social Human Rights', *Human Rights Quarterly* 24.1 (2002), 205–36.

Fish, Stanley, *There's No Such Thing as Free Speech, and It's a Good Thing Too* (Oxford University Press, 1994).

Fiss, Owen, *The Irony of Free Speech* (Harvard University Press, 1996).

Fitzmaurice, Malgosia and Sarooshi, Dad (eds), *Issues of State Responsibility before International Judicial Institutions* (Hart Publishing, 2004).

Fredman, Sandra, *Discrimination Law* (2nd edn, Oxford University Press, 2011).

Frostell, Katarina, 'Gender Difference and the Non-Discrimination Principle in the CCPR and the CEDAW', in Hannikainen, Lauri and Nykänen, Eeva (eds), *New Trends in Discrimination Law; International Perspectives* (Turku Law School, 1999), pp. 29–57.

Gallagher, Anne, *The International Law of Human Trafficking* (Cambridge University Press, 2010).

Gardiner, Richard, *Treaty Interpretation* (Oxford University Press, 2008).

Gearty, Conor and Mantouvalou, Virginia, *Debating Social Rights* (Hart Publishing, 2011).

Ghanea, Nazila, 'Are Religious Minorities really Minorities?' *Oxford Journal of Law and Religion* 1.1 (2012), 57–79.

Ghanea, Nazila and Xanthaki, Alexandra (eds), *Minorities, Peoples and Self-Determination: Essays in Honour of Patrick Thornberry* (Martinus Nijhoff Publishers, 2005).

Ghanea, Nazila, '"Phobias" and "Isms": Recognition of Difference or the Slippery Slope of Particularisms?', in Ghanea, Nazila, Stephens, Alan, and Walden, Raphael (eds), *Does God Believe in Human Rights?* (Martinus Nijhoff Publishers, 2007), pp. 211–32.

Gibney, Mark, Howard-Hassmann, Rhoda, Coicaud, Jean-Marc, and Steiner, Niklaus, *The Age of Apology: Facing up to the Past* (University of Pennsylvania Press, 2008).

Gutmann, Amy (ed.), *Multiculturalism: Examining the Politics of Recognition* (Princeton University Press, 1994).

Hakimi, Monica, 'State Bystander Responsibility', *European Journal of International Law* 21.2 (2010), 341–85.

Hannikainen, Lauri and Nykänen, Eva (eds), *New Trends in Discrimination Law—International Perspectives* (Turku Law School, 1999).

Hare, Ivan and Weinstein, James (eds), *Extreme Speech and Democracy* (Oxford University Press, 2009).

Hennebel, Ludovic and Hochmann, Thomas, *Genocide Denials and the Law* (Oxford University Press, 2011).

Henrard, Kristen, 'Non-Discrimination and Full and Effective Equality', in M. Weller (ed.), *Universal Minority Rights: A Commentary on the Jurisprudence of International Courts and Treaty Bodies* (Oxford University Press, 2007), pp. 75–147.

Henrard, Kristin, 'The Protection of Minorities through the Equality Provisions in the UN Human Rights Treaties: The UN Treaty Bodies', *International Journal on Minority and Group Rights* 14.2–3 (2007), 141–80.

Heyns, Christoph and Viljoen, Frans, *The Impact of the United Nations Human Rights Treaties at the Domestic Level* (Kluwer Law International, 2002).

Hollis, Duncan (ed.), *The Oxford Guide to Treaties* (Oxford University Press, 2012).

Holmström, Leif (ed.), *Concluding Observations of the UN Committee on the Elimination of Racial Discrimination* (Kluwer Law International, 2002), pp. 171–7.

Jones, Peter, 'Human Rights, Group Rights, and Peoples' Rights', *Human Rights Quarterly* 21.1 (1999), 80–107.

Jørgensen, Rikke and Slavensky, Klaus (eds), *Implementing Human Rights—Essays in Honour of Morten Kjaerum* (Danish Institute for Human Rights, 2007).

Joseph, Sarah, 'The Right to Housing, Discrimination, and the Roma in Slovakia', *Human Rights Law* Review 5.2. (2005), 347–9.

Joseph, Sarah, Schultz, Jenny, and Castan, Melissa, *The International Covenant on Civil and Political Rights: Cases, Materials and Commentary* (2nd edn, Oxford University Press, 2011).

Joseph, Sarah and Castan, Melissa, *The International Covenant on Civil and Political Rights: Cases, Materials and Commentary* (3rd edn, Oxford University Press, 2013).

Jovanović, Miodrag, 'Recognizing Minority Identities Through Collective Rights', *Human Rights Quarterly* 27.2 (2005), 625–51.

Jovanović, Miodrag, *Collective Rights: A Legal Theory* (Cambridge University Press, 2012).

Kambel, Ellen-Rose and MacKay, Fergus, *The Rights of Indigenous Peoples and Maroons in Suriname* (IWGIA, 1999).

Kastanas, Elias, 'The Preventive Dimension of the Activities of United Nations Treaty Bodies', in Sicilianos, Linos-Alexandre (ed.) and Bourloyannis-Vrailas, Christiane (associate ed.), *The Prevention of Human Rights Violations* (Sakkoulas Publishers, Martinus Nijhoff Publishers, 2001), pp. 57–66.

Kateb, George, *Human Dignity* (Harvard University Press, 2011).

Keane, David, *Caste-based Discrimination in International Human Rights Law* (Ashgate, 2007).

Keane, David, 'Attacking Hate Speech under Article 17 of the European Convention on Human Rights', *Netherlands Quarterly of Human Rights* 25.4 (2007), 641–63.

Keane, David and Waughray, Annapurna (eds.), *Fifty Years of the International Convention on the Elimination of All Forms of Racial Discrimination: A Living Instrument* (Manchester University Press, 2017).

Kędzia, Zdzislaw and Thűrer, Daniel (eds), *Managing Diversity: Protection of Minorities in International Law* (Schulthess, 2009).

King, Hugh, 'The Extraterritorial Human Rights Obligations of States', *Human Rights Law Review* 9.4. (2009), 521–56.

Keller, Helen and Ulfstein, Geir, *UN Human Rights Treaty Bodies: Law and Legitimacy* (Cambridge University Press, 2012).

Khaitan, Tarunabh, *A Theory of Discrimination Law* (Oxford University Press, 2015).

Knop, Karen, *Diversity and Self-Determination in International Law* (Cambridge University Press, 2002).

Kowner, Rotem and Demel, Walter (eds), *Race and Racism in Modern East Asia: Western and Eastern Constructions* (Brill, 2012), p. 68.

Kramnick, Isaac, *The Portable Enlightenment Reader* (Penguin Books, 1995).

Kruckenberg, Lena, *The UNreal World of Human Rights: An Ethnography of the UN Committee on the Elimination of Racial Discrimination* (Nomos Verlagsgesellschaft, 2012).

Kühl, Stefan, *For the Betterment of the Race: The Rise and Fall of the International Movement for Eugenics and Racial Hygiene* (Palgrave Macmillan, 2013).

Kymlicka, Will, *Multicultural Citizenship: A Liberal Theory of Minority Rights* (Clarendon Press, 1995).

Kymlicka, Will (ed.), *The Rights of Minority Cultures* (Oxford University Press, 2005).

Lauren, Paul, 'Human Rights in History: Diplomacy and Racial Equality at the Paris Peace Conference', *Diplomatic History* 2.3 (1978), 257–78.

Lauren, Paul, 'First Principles of Racial Equality: History and Politics and Diplomacy of Human Rights Provisions in the United Nations Charter', *Human Rights Quarterly* 5.1 (1983), 1–26.

Leary, Virginia, *International Labour Conventions and National Law* (Martinus Nijhoff Publishers, 1982).

Le Melle, Tilden, 'Race in International Relations', *International Studies Perspectives* 10.1 (2009), 77–83.

Lempert, David, 'Why We Need a Cultural Red Book for Endangered Cultures NOW: How Social Scientists and Lawyers Need to Join Forces', *International Journal on Minority and Group Rights* 17.4 (2010), 511–50.

Lenzerini, Federico, *The Culturalization of Human Rights* Law (Oxford University Press, 2014).

Lenzerini, Federico (ed.), *Reparations for Indigenous Peoples: International and Comparative Perspectives* (Oxford University Press, 2008).

Lerner, Natan, *The U.N. Convention on the Elimination of All Forms of Racial Discrimination* (Sijthoff and Noordhoff, 1980).

Lerner, Natan, *Group Rights and Discrimination in International Law* (Martinus Nijhoff, 1991).

Lerner, Natan, 'Freedom of Expression and Advocacy of Group Hatred: Incitement to Hate Crimes and Religious Hatred', *Religion and Human Rights* 5.2–3 (2010), 137–45.

Lerner, Natan, *The UN Convention on the Elimination of All Forms of Discrimination* (Brill/Nijhoff, reprint revised by Natan Lerner, 2015).

Letsas, George, *A Theory of Interpretation of the European Convention on Human Rights* (Oxford University Press, 2009).

Levitt, Peggy and Merry, Sally, 'Vernacularization on the Ground: Local Uses of Global Women's Rights in Peru, China, India and the United States', *Global Networks* 9 (2009), 441–61.

Lijnzaad, Liesbeth, *Reservations to UN Human Rights Treaties: Ratify and Ruin?* (Martinus Nijhoff Publishers, 1995).

Linderfalk, Ulf, *On the Interpretation of Treaties: The Modern International Law as Expressed in the 1969 Vienna Convention on the Law of Treaties* (Springer, 2007).

Lindley, Mark, *The Acquisition and Government of Backward Territory in International Law* (Negro Universities Press, reprinted from 1926).

Lindsay, Lisa, *Captives as Commodities: The Transatlantic Slave Trade* (Prentice Hall, 2008); Italian translation by Falcioni, Rinaldo, *Il Commercio degli Schiavi* (Mulino, 2011).

Lobba, Paolo, 'Holocaust Denial before the European Court of Human Rights', *European Journal of International Law* 26.1 (2015), 237–53.

Lubell, Noam, *Extraterritorial Use of Force against Non-State Actors* (Oxford University Press, 2010).

Lurie, Edward, 'Louis Agassiz and the Races of Man', *Isis* 45.3 (1954), 227–42.

McColgan, Aileen, *Discrimination Law: Text, Cases and Materials* (2nd edn, Hart Publishing, 2005).

McColgan, Aileen, *Discrimination, Equality and the Law* (Hart Publishing, 2014).

McCorquodale, Robert and Simons, Penelope, 'State Responsibility for Extraterritorial Violations by Corporations of International Human Rights Law', *Modern Law Review* 704 (2007), 598–625.

McCrudden, Christopher, 'Human Dignity and Judicial Interpretation of Human Rights', *European Journal of International Law* 19.4 (2008), 655–724.

McDonagh, Maeve, 'The Right to Information in International Human Rights Law', *Human Rights Law Review* 13.1 (2013), 25–55.

McGoldrick, Dominic, 'The Limits of Freedom of Expression on Facebook and Social Networking Sites', *Human Rights Law Review* 13.1 (2013), 125–51.

McGonagle, Tarlach, *Minority Rights, Freedom of Expression and of the Media: Dynamics and Dilemmas* (Intersentia, 2011).

McGonagle, Tarlach and Donders, Yvonne (eds), *The United Nations and Freedom of Expression and Information: Critical Perspectives* (Cambridge University Press, 2015).

McGonagle, Tarlach, 'The Council of Europe against online hate speech: Conundrums and Challenges: Expert Paper', available at: <http://hub.coe.int/c/document_library/get_file?uuid=62fab806-724e-435a-b7a5-153ce2b57c18&groupId=10227>.

MacKay, Fergus, 'Indigenous Peoples' Rights and the UN Committee on the Elimination of Racial Discrimination', in Dersso, Solomon (ed.), *Perspectives on the Rights of Minorities and Peoples in Africa* (Pretoria University Law Press, 2010), pp. 155–204.

McKean, Warwick, *Equality and Discrimination under International Law* (Clarendon Press, 1983).

MacNaughton, Gillian, 'Untangling Equality and Non-Discrimination to Promote the Right to Health Care for All', *Health and Human Rights* 11.2 (2009), 47–63.

Mahalic, Drew and Mahalic, Joan, 'The Limitation Provisions of the International Convention on the Elimination of All Forms of Racial Discrimination', *Human Rights Quarterly* 9.1 (1987), 74–101.

Makkonen, Timo, *Equal in Law, Unequal in Fact: Racial and Ethnic Discrimination and the Response Thereto in Europe* (Martinus Nijhoff Publishers, 2012).

Malloy, Tove, 'The Title and the Preamble', in Weller, Marc (ed.), *The Rights of Minorities in Europe* (Oxford University Press, 2005), pp. 49–72, at p. 56.

Martinez, Jenny, *The Slave Trade and the Origins of International Human Rights Law* (Oxford University Press, 2012).

Mechlem, Kerstin, 'Treaty Bodies and the Interpretation of Human Rights', *Vanderbilt Journal of Transnational Law* 42 (2009), 905–47.

Meron, T., 'The Meaning and Reach of the International Convention on the Elimination of All Forms of Racial Discrimination', *American Journal of International Law* 79.2 (1985), 283–318.

Merry, Sally, 'Transnational Human Rights and Local Activism: Mapping the Middle', *American Anthropologist* 108 (2006), 38–51.

Miller, Jon and Kumar, Rahul (eds), *Reparations: Interdisciplinary Perspectives* (Oxford University Press, 2007).

Minette, Sophie (ed.), 'Special Issue: Global, and Local Religious Hatred: International Law and Interdisciplinary Perspectives', *Religion and Human Rights* 9.2–3 (2014), 101–225.

Minority Rights Group, *State of the World's Minorities and Indigenous Peoples* (Minority Rights Group International, annual publication).

Moeckli, Daniel, Shah, Sangeeta, and Sivakumaran, Sandesh (eds), Harris, David (Consultant editor) *International Human Rights* (2nd edn, Oxford University Press, 2014).

Moyn, Samuel, *The Last Utopia: Human Rights in His*tory (Belknap Press of Harvard University Press, 2010).

Nakano, Jenji, Yutzis, Mario, and Onoyama (eds), *Descent-Based Discrimination* (International Movement against All Forms of Discrimination and Racism, 2004).

Ndahinda, Felix (ed.), 'Special Issue: Contrasted Perspectives on Recognition and Implementation of Indigenous Rights', *International Journal on Minority and Group Rights*, 18.4 (2011), essays at 413–540.

O'Flaherty, Michael, 'Freedom of Expression: Article 19 of the International Covenant on Civil and Political Rights and the Human Rights Committee's General Comment No. 34', *Human Rights Law R*eview 12.4 (2012), 627–54.

Okowa, Phoebe, 'The International Court of Justice and the Georgia/Russia Dispute', *Human Rights Law Review* 11.4 (2011), 739–57.

Orakhelashvili, Alexander, 'The Idea of European International Law', *European Journal of International Law* 17.2 (2006), 315–47.

Pagden, Anthony, 'Dispossessing the Barbarian: the Language of Spanish Thomism and the Debate over the Property Rights of the American Indians', in Pagden, Anthony (ed.), *The Languages of Political Theory in Early Modern Europe* (Cambridge University Press, 1990), pp. 79–98.

Partsch, Karl Josef, 'Elimination of Racial Discrimination in the Enjoyment of Civil and Political Rights', *Texas Journal of International Law* 14 (1979), 191–250.

Pentassuglia, Gaetano (ed.), 'Special Issue: Reforming the UN Human Rights Machinery: What does the Future Hold for the Protection of Minorities and Indigenous Peoples?' *International Journal on Minority and Group Rights* 14.2–3 (2007), 127–397.

Pentassuglia, Gaetano, *Minority Groups and Judicial Discourse in International Law: A Comparative Perspective* (Martinus Nijhoff, 2009).

Pritchard, Sarah (ed.), *Indigenous Peoples, the United Nations and Human Rights* (Zed Books and the Federation Press, 1998).

Prouvez, Nathalie, 'Committee on the Elimination of Racial Discrimination: Confronting Racial Discrimination and Inequality in the Enjoyment of Economic, Social and Cultural Rights', in Langford, Malcolm (ed.), *Social Rights Jurisprudence: Emerging Trends in International and Comparative Law* (Cambridge University Press, 2009), pp. 517–39.

Pulitano, Elvira (ed.), *Indigenous Rights in the Age of the UN Declaration* (Cambridge University Press, 2012).

Rattansi, Ali, *Racism: A Very Short Introduction* (Oxford University Press, 2007).

Rex, John, *Race and Ethnicity* (Open University Press, 1986).

Rodríguez-Piñero, Luis, *Indigenous Peoples, Postcolonialism, and International Law: The ILO Regime (1919–1989)* (Oxford University Press, 2005).

Rosen, Michael, *Dignity: its History and Meaning* (Harvard University Press, 2012).

Ruggie, John, 'Business and Human Rights: The Evolving International Agenda', *American Journal of International Law* 101.4 (2007), 819–40.

Runnymede Trust, *A Very Light Sleeper: The Persistence and Dangers of Anti-Semitism* (Runnymede Trust, 1994), available at: <http://www.runnymedetrust.org/uploads/publications/pdfs/AVeryLightSleeper-1994.PDF>.

Saul, Ben, Kinley, David, and Mowbray, Jacqueline, *The International Covenant on Economic, Social and Cultural Rights: Commentary, Cases, and Materials* (Oxford University Press, 2014).

Scales-Trent, Judy, 'Racial Purity Laws in the United States and Nazi Germany: The Targeting Process', *Human Rights Quarterly* 23.2 (2001), 260–307.

Scheinin, Martin and Toivanen, Reetta (eds), *Rethinking Non-Discrimination and Minority Rights* (Åbo Akademi University, 2004).

Schwelb, Egon, The International Convention on the Elimination of All Forms of Racial Discrimination', *International and Comparative Law Quarterly* 15/4 (1966), 996–1068.

Shahabuddin, Mohammad, '"Ethnicity" in the International Law of Minority Protection: the Post-Cold War Context in Perspective', *Leiden Journal of International Law* 25.4 (2012), 885–907.

Shaw, Malcolm, *International Law* (6th edn, Cambridge University Press, 2008).

Shelton, Dinah, *Remedies in International Human Rights Law* (2nd edn, Oxford University Press, 2005).

Shelton, Dinah (ed.), *The Oxford Handbook of International Human Rights Law* (Oxford University Press, 2013).

Shirane, Daisuke, *ICERD and CERD: A Guide for Civil Society Actors* (International Movement against All Forms of Discrimination and Racism (IMADR), 2011).

Shue, Henry, *Basic Rights, Subsistence, Affluence and U.S. Foreign Policy* (2nd edn, Princeton University Press, 1996).

Sicilianos, Linos-Alexandre, 'L'actualités et les Potentialités de la Convention sur L'Elimination de la Discrimination Raciale', *Revue Trimestrielle des Droits de L'Homme* 16 (2005), 869–921.

Stamatopoulou, Elsa, *Cultural Rights in International Law* (Martinus Nijhoff, 2007).

Sweet, James, 'The Iberian Roots of American Racist Thought', *William and Mary Quarterly* 54.1 (1977), 143–66.

Szewczyk, Bart, 'Application of the International Convention on the Elimination of All Forms of Racial Discrimination (Georgia v Russian Federation, Preliminary Objections)', *AJIL* 105.4 (2011), 747–54.

Takezawa, Yasuko (ed.), *Racial Representations in Asia* (Kyoto University Press and Trans Pacific Press, 2011).

Tanaka, Atsuko and Nagamine, Yoshinobu, *The International Convention on the Elimination of All Forms of Racial Discrimination: A Guide for NGOs* (Minority Rights Group International and International Movement against All Forms of Discrimination and Racism (IMADR), 2001).

Tavani, Claudia, *Collective Rights and the Cultural Identity of the Roma: A Case Study of Italy* (Martinus Nijhoff Publishers, 2012).

Temperman, Jeroen, 'Laws against the Denial of Historical Atrocities: A Human Rights Analysis', *Religion and Human Rights* 9.2–3 (2014), 151–80.

Thornberry, Francesca and Viljoen, Frans, *Overview Study on the Rights of Indigenous Peoples in Africa* (ILO and African Commission on Human and Peoples' Rights, 2009).

Thornberry, Francesca, Les Droits Fonciers des Peuples Autochtones dans le Bassin du Congo—Pour un Meilleur Cadre Legal', in Bellier, Irène (ed.), *Terres, Territoires, Ressources: Politiques, Pratiques et Droits des Peuples Autochtones* (Paris: Projet SOGIP, Ecole des Hautes Etudes en Sciences Sociales, 2015), pp. 141–56.

Thornberry, Patrick, *International Law and the Rights of Minorities* (Clarendon Press, 1991).

Thornberry, Patrick, 'Minority and Indigenous Rights at "The End of History"', *Ethnicities* 2.4 (2002), 515–37.

Thornberry, Patrick, *Indigenous Peoples and Human Rights* (Manchester University Press, 2002).

Thornberry, Patrick, 'Confronting Racial Discrimination: A CERD Perspective, *Human Rights Law Review* 5.2 (2005), 239–69.

Thornberry, Patrick, 'Bringing the victims to light under the International Convention on the Elimination of All Forms of Racial Discrimination', Jovanović, M.A. and Krstić, I. (eds), *Human Rights Today—60 Years of the Universal Declaration* (Eleven International Publishing, 2010), 145–70.

Thornberry, Patrick, 'Forms of Hate Speech and the Convention on the Elimination of All Forms of Racial Discrimination (ICERD)', *Religion and Human Rights* 5.2–3 (2010), 97–117.

Thornberry, Patrick and Martín Estébanez, María, *Minority Rights in Europe* (Council of Europe Publishing, 2004).

Thűrer, Daniel and Zdzislaw, Kędzia (eds), *Managing Diversity: Protection of Minorities in International Law* (Schulthess, 2009).

Tierney, Brian, The Idea of Natural Rights: Studies on Natural Rights, Natural Law, and Church Law, 1150–625, (Eerdmans, 2001).

Tobin, Brendan, *Indigenous Peoples, Customary Law and Human Rights: Why Living Law Matters* (Routledge, 2014).

Tobin, John, 'Seeking to Persuade: A Constructive Approach to Human Rights Treaty Interpretation', *Harvard Human Rights Journal* 23 (2010), 1–50.

Todorov, Tzvetan, *The Conquest of America: The Question of the Other* (Harper and Row, 1992).

Tomuschat, Christian, *Human Rights: Between Idealism and Realism* (Oxford University Press, 2008).

Tronvoll, Kjetil, 'Human Rights Violations in Federal Ethiopia: When Ethnic Identity is a Political Stigma', *International Journal on Minority and Group Rights* 15.1 (2008), 49–79.

Truscan, I., *The Independence of UN Human Rights Treaty Body Members* (Geneva Academy, 2012).

UNESCO, *Four Statements on the Race Question* (UNESCO, 1969).

UNESCO Guidelines on Intercultural Education (UNESCO, 2006).

United Nations, *Protection of Minorities: Special Protective Measures of an International Character for Ethnic, Religious or Linguistic Groups* (United Nations, 1967).

United Nations, *The Effects of Racism and Racial Discrimination on the Social and Economic Relations between Indigenous Peoples and States: Report of a Seminar* (United Nations, 1989).

United Nations, *The First Twenty Years, Progress Report of the Committee on the Elimination of Racial Discrimination* (United Nations, 1991).

United Nations: *Report of the Seminar on the Political, Historical, Economic, Social and Cultural Factors Contributing to Racism, Racial Discrimination and Apartheid* (United Nations, 1991).

United Nations, *National Human Rights Institutions: History, Principles, Roles and Responsibilities* (United Nations, 2010).

United Nations, *Human Rights Indicators: A Guide to Measurement and Implementation* (Office of the High Commissioner for Human Rights, 2012).

United Nations, *Selected Decisions of the Committee on the Elimination of Racial Discrimination*, Vol. I (United Nations, 2012).
United Nations, *Handbook for Human Rights Treaty Body Members* (United Nations, 2015)
Valencia Rodriguez, Luis, 'The International Convention on the Elimination of All Forms of Racial Discrimination', in *Manual on Human Rights Reporting* (United Nations, 1997), p. 299.
Van Banning, Theo, *The Human Right to Property* (Intersentia, 2002).
Van Boven, Theo, 'Discrimination and Human Rights Law; Combating Racism', in Fredman, S. (ed.), *Discrimination and Human Rights: The Case of Racism* (Oxford University Press, 2001), pp. 112–33 at p. 113.
Van Boven, Theo, 'CERD and Article 14: The Unfulfilled Promise', in Alfredsson, Gudmundur, Grimheden, Jonas, Ramcharan, Bertrand, and De Zayas, Alfred, *International Human Rights Monitoring Mechanisms: Essays in Honour of Jakob Th. Möller* (Martinus Nijhoff Publishers, 2001), pp. 153–66.
Vandenhole, Wouter, *Non-Discrimination and Equality in the View of the UN Human Rights Treaty Bodies* (Intersentia, 2005).
Waibel, Michael, 'Demystifying the Art of Interpretation', *European Journal of International Law* 22 .2 (2011), 571–88.
Waldron, Jeremy, *The Harm in Hate Speech* (Harvard University Press, 2012).
Waughray, Annapurna, 'Caste Discrimination and Minority Rights: the Case of India's Dalits', *International Journal on Minority and Group Rights* 17.2 (2010), 327–53.
Waughray, Annapurna, 'Capturing Caste in Law: Caste Discrimination and the Equality Act 2010', *Human Rights Law Review* 14.2 (2014), 359–79.
Weissbrodt, David, *The Human Rights of Non-Citizens* (Oxford University Press, 2008).
Weissbrodt, David, 'The Approach of the Committee on the Elimination of Racial Discrimination to Interpreting and Applying International Humanitarian Law', *Minnesota Journal of International Law* 19.2 (2010), 327–61.
Weller, Marc (ed.), *The Rights of Minorities in Europe: A Commentary on the European Framework Convention for the Protection of National Minorities* (Oxford University Press, 2005).
Weller, Marc (ed.), *Universal Minority Rights: A Commentary on the Jurisprudence of International Courts and Treaty Bodies* (Oxford University Press, 2007).
Weller, Marc (ed.) and Nobbs, Katherine (assistant ed.), *Political Participation of Minorities* (Oxford University Press, 2010).
Wilde, Ralph, 'Triggering State Obligations Extraterritorially: The Spatial Test in Certain Human Rights Treaties', *Israel Law Review* 40.2 (2007), 503–26.
Williams, Raymond, *Keywords* (Fontana Press, 1988).
Wolfrum, Rüdiger, 'Discrimination, Xenophobia and Racism', in Symonides, Janusz (ed.), *Human Rights: New Dimensions and Challenges* (Ashgate, 1998), pp. 181–97.
Wolfrum, Rüdiger, 'The Committee on the Elimination of Racial Discrimination', in von Bogdandy, Armin, and Wolfrum, Rüdiger (eds), *Max Planck Yearbook of United Nations Law* (Martinus Nijhoff Publishers, 1999), pp. 489–519.
Young, Iris, *Justice and the Politics of Difference* (Princeton University Press, 1990).

Index of Names

Subject Index

The manufacturer's authorised representative in the EU for product safety is Oxford University Press España S.A. of el Parque Empresarial San Fernando de Henares, Avenida de Castilla, 2 – 28830 Madrid (www.oup.es/en or product.safety@oup.com). OUP España S.A. also acts as importer into Spain of products made by the manufacturer.

www.ingramcontent.com/pod-product-compliance
Lightning Source LLC
LaVergne TN
LVHW082016200926
848481LV00010B/2868
9780198827405